Music of the
Fourth of July

Also by James R. Heintze

The Fourth of July Encyclopedia
(McFarland, 2007)

Music of the Fourth of July

A Year-by-Year Chronicle of Performances and Works Composed for the Occasion, 1777–2008

JAMES R. HEINTZE

McFarland & Company, Inc., Publishers
Jefferson, North Carolina, and London

LIBRARY OF CONGRESS CATALOGUING-IN-PUBLICATION DATA

Heintze, James R.
Music of the Fourth of July : a year-by-year chronicle of performances
and works composed for the occasion, 1777–2008 / James R. Heintze.
p.   cm.
Includes bibliographical references and index.

ISBN 978-0-7864-3979-9
softcover : 50# alkaline paper ∞

1. Fourth of July — Songs and music — Chronology.   2. Fourth of
July — Songs and music — Bibliography.   3. Patriotic music — United
States — History and criticism.   4. Fourth of July celebrations —
Chronology.   I. Title.
ML3561.F68H45   2009   781.5′990973 — dc22   2009010115

British Library cataloguing data are available

Cover photograph ©2009 Comstock

Manufactured in the United States of America

*McFarland & Company, Inc., Publishers
Box 611, Jefferson, North Carolina 28640
www.mcfarlandpub.com*

Acknowledgments

Special thanks to Dennis R. Burian, Head, Marine Band Branch, Division of Public Affairs, U.S. Marine Corps, MGySgt Michael Ressler, Chief Librarian, Sergeant Kira M. Wharton, and GySgt Jane Cross of the U.S. Marine Band Library for providing access to their archives and for permissions, materials, and photographs; thanks to Philip Koslow, executive director, and Keith Neel, director of operations/special events of the Las Vegas Philharmonic for a tour of their executive office and copies of photographs and concert programs; to Donald Hester, euphonium player in the City of Fairfax Band, for his information on the band; to Earl R. Kreder for information on the St. Charles Municipal Band; to George Arnold, reference librarian, American University, Washington, D.C., for his photographs and information on the George Washington monument in Paris, France; to David and Ginger Hildebrand for information on their Fourth of July concerts; John Slader, superintendent, and Susan Juza, researcher, of Fort Atkinson State Historical Park for information and photographs; to Cecelia and Christopher Jaquez for information and photographs of the Richmond Concert Band and to Mark W. Poland, band director; Lawrence Robinson for a tour of the carillon in the World War I memorial in Richmond, Virginia; Jeff Stockton for information and photograph of the Excelsior Cornet Band; Bridget P. Carr, archivist, Boston Symphony Orchestra, for information and programs of the BSO; Gail H. Tyler, Northern Mariposa County History Center, Coulterville, California, for a photograph of the Coulterville Band; thanks to John Bisharat, who provided a compact disc of his piece *I Am St. Joseph*; to Debra Adleman, Hilary Caws-Elwitt and Betty Smith of the Susquehanna County Historical Society and Free Library Association for photographs and information regarding the soldier's monument in Montrose, Pennsylvania; to Rebecca Bayreuther Donohue for information on celebrations in Mystic, Connecticut, in 1876 and 2008; to Kim Campbell, executive director, Becky Geddes, operations manager, and Courtney Dodson, past operations manager, of the Dallas Wind Symphony for information and photographs; to Eileen O'Donnell, vice president, Westfield Community Band, for information on the band's performances; Bob Sandeen of the Nicollet County Historical Society for a photograph of the Redman Band; Dave Haight, president of the Palatine Concert Band, for information on the band's performances; to SFC Sarah Anderson for concert programs of the U.S. Army Field Band and Soldiers' Chorus; to G. Thomas Cherrix, conductor of the Greenbelt (Maryland) Concert Band for helpful information; to Scott Dettra and Christopher Jacobson, organists at Washington National Cathedral for concert programs; to Douglas A. Beck, organist at St. Paul's Episcopal Church in Alexandria, Virginia, for a concert program; to David T. Kehler, association conductor of the Dallas Wind Symphony for information on his concerts; thanks to Piotr Gajewski, conductor of the National Philharmonic Orchestra at Strathmore near Washington, D.C., for an illustration of a score by Andreas Makris; to Liz Barrett, founder/director, All Children's Chorus of Annapolis, for a photograph and information; to Olivia Gentile and Donna Trent of The Cathedral Shrine of the Diocese of Virginia for information on the annual Bishop's Bluegrass Festival; to Dianne S.P. Cermak, public relations officer, North American Guild of Change Ringers, and Geoffrey Davies, professor, Department of Chemistry & Chemical Biology, Northeastern University, for information regarding bell ringing at The Church of the Advent in Boston; to Pam Picard, producer, Boston 4 Celebrations, for information on the performance of the 1812 Overture in Boston; to Jonathan Silberman, American University Library, for scanning a photograph; to my son Terry Heintze for photographs of the Lafayette monument in Paris; to my wife, Yolanda Heintze, for her encouragement and for assisting me in selecting photographs for this volume; to the following composers who provided helpful information about their compositions: James A. Beckel, Jr., Phillip Bimstein, Nolan Gasser, Bruce Craig Roter, David Schiff, James Stephenson, and Barbara White.

Table of Contents

Preface

This is the first comprehensive reference work on music and the Fourth of July, the most important holiday in the United States. The chronology provides examples of musical performances that took place over the course of the nation's history and musical compositions composed especially for Independence Day. The information highlights the importance of patriotic music on the Fourth and points to musicians whose contributions to the heritage and traditions deserve attention, as well as the locations of those events. Although extensive, this study is not exhaustive. It is intended, however, to demonstrate the trends and changes in the myriad ways music has been used to express patriotism and how performances served to reflect the expressions and sentiments that individuals felt about the founders of this country, those who served in the Revolutionary War, the many Americans who were called into public service and the freedoms we all enjoy.

The significance of music on the Fourth of July over its history has been remarkable. Bands and orchestras, vocal groups, small ensembles, and soloists performed popular tunes and patriotic songs on Independence Day for audiences that frequently numbered in the thousands. An invitation to perform for a parade or ceremony was considered an honor and musicians were held in high esteem by their respective communities. Some of the favorite orchestras, bands, and vocal ensembles that had wide-spread prominence included: Boston Brigade Band; Dodworth's Band, Nyer's Twelfth Regiment Band, Gilmore's Band; Seventh Regiment Band; Goldman Band; Schreiner's Orchestra; Fort McHenry Band; Dudley Buck Glee Club; Tammany Glee Club; Kaltenborn Symphony Orchestra; Naval Academy Band; New York Philharmonic; Seidl Orchestra; Hugo Riesenfeld's symphonic orchestra; Chautauqua Symphony Orchestra; Vermont Symphony Orchestra; Nashville Symphony; Pittsburgh Symphony Orchestra; St. Louis Symphony; Atlanta Symphony; and the National Symphony Orchestra; "The President's Own" United States Marine Band; United States Navy Band, Sea Chanters, and Commodores; United States Air Force Concert Band and Singing Sergeants; United States Army Field Band and Chorus; U.S. Coast Guard Band; Boston Pops; Las Vegas Philharmonic; and many others.

During the nineteenth and early twentieth centuries, many ensembles representing the working classes performed on the Fourth, including: New York Banks Glee Club; Brooklyn Letter Carriers' Band; Escondido Merchants' Associations Band; First Hose Fife, Drum and Bugle Corps (Hagerstown, Maryland); Ogden Business Men's Band; U.S. Engineer Band; Naval Gun Factory Band; and Manhattan Concert Band of the Works Progress Administration. Ensembles of minorities and ethnic groups included: Native American bands of upper New York state; African-American Band of Boston; American Ladies Orchestra; Female Brass Band of Chippewa Falls, Wisconsin; Ladies' Symphony Orchestra; Italian Bersaglieri Band; Worcester French and Irish Bands; United German

Societies; Mozart Maennerchor; Swedish Brass Band; Washington Federation of Colored Church Choirs; and New York Mainzer Carnaval Verein.

Among the many composers who wrote music for the Fourth were Leroy Anderson, George Antheil, Robert Russell Bennett, William Billings, Dudley Buck, Carl Busch, George F. Bristow, Arthur Farwell, Arthur Foote, George Geib, Rubin Goldmark, Morton Gould, Ferde Grofé, Anthony Philip Heinrich, James Hewitt, Uri K. Hill, Alan Hovhaness, Charles Ives, George K. Jackson, Edwin Jocelyn, Edwin Markham, Lowell Mason, Robert George Paige, Victor Pelissier, William H. Santelmann, William Schuman, William Selby, Oliver Shaw, John Philip Sousa, Max Spicker, Igor Stravinsky, Rayner Taylor, and John Williams. In recent years, there has been a surge of new music written for the Fourth, some for specific orchestras, such as Andreas Makris, *Fourth of July March* (1982), for the National Symphony Orchestra, and Richard McGee, *Las Vegas Rhapsody* (2005) for the Las Vegas Philharmonic. Other composers received grants under the auspices of the Contential Harmony Project (2000–2008) for composing music that reflected regional areas of the country with many works premiered on the Fourth of July.

Some vocal and instrumental soloists active on the Fourth included: William Dempster, Louise Natlie, Conrad Behrens, Crystal Waters, Eddie Cantor, Ethel Ennis, Rosemary Clooney, Johnny Cash, Willie Nelson, Gloria Estefan, Vic Damone, Lena Horne, Pearl Bailey, and Maureen McGovern, vocalists; Edward Reményi, violinist; Jules Levy, Walter Emerson, Waino Kauppi, and Adam Seifert, cornetists; Bruce Hall and Doc Severinsen, trumpet players. In the nineteenth century, ensembles consisted of trios, quartets, brass, cornet, and reed bands, and in the early twentieth century full orchestras, as well as jazz bands. After 1950 rock groups were added to the mix.

Throughout the nation's history music performed included both sacred and popular genres, as well as ceremonial music used to heighten the merrymaking in parades, public dinners, and other entertainments. Although in the nineteenth century such songs as "Hail Columbia," "The Star-Spangled Banner," "America" ("My country, 'tis of thee") and "America the Beautiful" achieved national anthem status on the Fourth, there were other tunes that also gained similar patriotic popularity, such as "The Flag Without a Stain," "Columbia, the Gem of the Ocean," "Flag of the Free," "American Hymn," and "Sword of Bunker Hill." Music to honor presidents and other politicians was also performed on the Fourth. Favorites were "President's March," "Washington's March," "Hail to the Chief," "Jefferson's March," "Madison's March," "Monroe's March," "Jackson's March," "Van Buren's Grand March," and "Clay's March."

This compilation lists numerous songs that were premiered on the Fourth of July with the greatest activity during the 1790s to the 1840s. Lyrics were often printed in newspapers, which provided dissemination over wide geographical areas. Some of the outstanding nineteenth-century poets and lyricists represented in this volume include, among others: Thomas Dawes, Francis Hopkinson, Samuel Low, Daniel George, Della Crusca, Robert Treat Paine, Jr., James Flint, Hannah Flagg Gould, Alexander Wilson, Edward C. Holland, Anne C. Lynch, Margaretta V. Faugeres, William B. Tappan, A.M. Wells, William Pitt Smith, Jonathan Mitchell Sewall, Walter Townsend, Nathaniel H. Wright, Francis Scott Key, Samuel Woodworth, Samuel Francis Smith, Lydia Huntley Sigourney, Henry Mellen, Joseph W. Brackett, B.B. French, William Cullen Bryant, Willis Gaylord Clark, John Greenleaf Whittier, Julia Ward Howe, Ralph Waldo Emerson, Sidney Lanier, Bayard Taylor, Oliver Wendell Holmes, Harriet Prescott Spofford, and Katharine Lee Bates.

Music was directly connected to a number of different traditions on the Fourth. For example, the practice of accompanying fireworks displays with instrumental music began in the early nineteenth century. On July 4,

1804, in Hudson, New York, "a beautiful and excellent display of fireworks, consisting of rockets, wheels, bee-hives, shells, serpents, &c." was "accompanied by music from the band." Another early instance of this "pleasing effect" occurred in Newburyport, Massachusetts, on July 4, 1806, when the Newbury Band played from a church steeple as 2000 persons gazed in merriment at the fireworks. Another instance occurred in New York on July 4, 1822, when musical interludes were provided during a fireworks spectacle. On that same day in Boston, fireworks on the Common were "accompanied by national airs from a full band."[1] The Fourth of July also gave rise to the use of multiple choirs and bands performing in tandem, sometimes referred to as "monster concerts." Beginning in the latter half of the nineteenth century, German singing societies staged gigantic instrumental and choral performances and introduced music by European composers, such as Beethoven, Schumann, and Wagner, to American audiences. In Newark, New Jersey, on July 4, 1891, 5,000 Saengerbunders accompanied by an orchestra of 200 instrumentalists programmed an aria from Wagner's *Tannhauser* in tandem with the "Star-Spangled Banner" and other patriotic music. In the same city on July 4, 1906, the Northeastern Saengerbund of America, Carl Lenz, bund president, staged another festive event with 100,000 persons attending. On July 4, 1902, 600 members of United German Societies of Allegheny (Pennsylvania) sang "The Star-Spangled Banner" in Schenley Park, Pittsburgh, for President Theodore Roosevelt. Other spectacular events included 3,000 voices that sang "My Old Kentucky Home" in honor of Stephen Foster, in Bardstown, Kentucky, on July 4, 1933.

Popular also were musical plays, pageants, ballets, and other patriotic productions performed on the Fourth: *The Fourth of July, or the Sailors Festival* (1788); *Fourth of July or, Temple of American Independence* (1799); *The Feast of Terpsichore, in the Temple of Independence* (1800); *Federal Oath; or, the Independence of 1776* (1802); *The Glory of Columbia:*

Her Yeomanry (1803, 1804, and 1820); *Point of Honor, or, A School for Soldiers* (1803, 1815, 1820, 1821, and 1826); *Poor Soldier* (1797, 1805, 1815); *He Would Be a Soldier* (1806, 1821); *Independence of Columbia* (1809); *The Rival Soldiers* (1810); *Fourth of July, Or, Huzza for Independence!!* (1811); *American Naval Pillar, or, A Tribute of Respect to the Tars of Columbia* (1812); *The Prize* (1813); *The Launch of the Independence* (1814); *Soldier Daughter* (1814); *Hero of the North; or, The Deliverer of His Country* (1815); *The Purse, or The American Tar* (1817); *Battle of New-Orleans, or, The Glorious 8th of January* (1818); *Tars from Tripoli, or the Heroes of Columbia* (1819); *She Would be a Soldier, or the Plains of Chippewa* (1819 and 1821); *The Launch, or, the Pride of America, Her Navy* (1820); *Capture of Major Andre* (1824); *Patriotic Volunteer* (1824); *Jubilee, or the Triumph of Freedom* (1826); *The Dragon's Flight! Or The Pearl Diver* (1847); *Fourth of July in the Morning* (1862); *National Guard* (1862); *At Freedom's Gate* (1902); *Girl of the Golden West* (1910); *The Spirit of Preparedness* (1916); *The Call of the Allies* (1917); *The Continental Congress* (1917); *"Fighting for Freedom": Independence Day Pageant* (1918); *Our Own United States* (1924); *The Story of America* (1926); *The Spirit of the Snohomish* (1928); *Pageant of the Years* (1929); *Never-the-less Old Glory* (1930); *Gettysburg* (1938); *Three Cheers* (1941); *Minstrels of the Masses* (1944); *1776* (1969); *Forge of Freedom* (1976).

Noteworthy occasions and topics in this compilation include music at the White House and the presidents, music by immigrant and ethnic groups, musical associations active on the Fourth, cornerstone ceremonies, dedications of statues and monuments, artillery salutes, construction of railroads, canals and other civic projects, social movements; military bands, municipal bands and orchestras; symphony and philharmonic orchestras; significant occasions representing milestones of the nation's progress, including the Centennial (1876) and Sesquicentennial Exposition (1926) in Philadelphia, World's Columbian Exposition (1893), The Trans-Mississippi and International Exposition in Omaha, Nebraska (1898), Chicago World's Fair (1934), New York World's Fair (1939), and Bicentennial (1976). Also included are events in other countries, musicians' strikes on the Fourth, music that accompanied balloon ascensions, music in prisons, circuses, and music played on steamboats and other vessels, amusement parks such as those on Coney Island, New York, and at Glen Echo, Maryland; music at the Capitol, Independence Hall, Faneuil Hall, Mount Vernon, and other patriotic landmarks, educational institutions, and naturalization ceremonies.

Celebratory Music to the Civil War

A precedent for American patriotic music and verse was in place prior to declaring independence and was carried over into community life after the Revolutionary War. John Dickinson's "Liberty Song" (1768), for example, was written to protest the British Stamp Act of 1765 and became a rallying cry for independence. Other songs gained popularity and helped to foster a tradition of heralding the struggles and similar heroic efforts of the patriots. Some songs represented local areas while others were topical, such as those that described specific battles. "Siege of Savannah" expressed how Americans were held off the coast of Georgia by the British and "On Christmas day in seventy-six" (first line), described the battle of Trenton.[2] One of the favorite tunes of the period was "Chester" composed by William Billings and published in 1770 in his tunebook *The New-England Psalm-Singer*. The tunebook's second edition (1778) included the tune with the popular lyrics "Let tyrants shake their iron rod." Notable performances of "Chester" on the Fourth included Marblehead, Massachusetts (1801), and Boston (1806 and 1808). In the twentieth century William Schuman used the Billings tune in the third movement ("Chester") in a three-part orchestral work titled *New England*

Triptych (1956). Schuman's version was one of the most popular classical works played on the Fourth of July beginning with its first identified performance on July 4, 1958, by the United States Marine Band at the dedication of Theodore Roosevelt Island in the Potomac River in Washington, D.C.

Following the Revolutionary War, numerous songs and tunes were written for and performed on the Fourth of July to commemorate not only the battles waged, but also the Americans who had fought gallantly on behalf of their new country. Subsequent wars such as the War of 1812 and Civil War provided additional opportunities for composing new music for Independence Day.

Another important aspect of the Revolutionary War era that greatly influenced the years that followed were the formation of militia bands and fife and drums corps whose purpose it was to provide music for military, social, and ceremonial events. These bands were typically described as "martial music" in newspaper reports to distinguish them from other bands and they often led Independence Day parades of military regiments, citizens, and town officials that marched usually in the morning from designated points of assembly, such as taverns, hotels, and court houses, to the meeting houses, churches, and other sites where the official exercises or ceremonies were held. Early bands were modeled according to "customs borrowed from the British army" in pre–Revolutionary America. Instruments included clarinets, oboes, French horns, and bassoons.[3] Fife and drums, usually associated with field music in wartime, were performed on the Fourth in ceremonies, such as flag raisings, and at dawn to signal the arrival of the holiday.

Other parade bands consisted of both amateur and professional musicians who either volunteered to perform for the day or were paid for their services. The marching order of the bands in the parades, the "order of exercises" and music for the ceremonies, and the locations and times of the events, were typically arranged well in advance by committees selected for that purpose and the information was often published in local newspapers on or before the day of celebration.

One of the most important bands in the history of celebratory music was the United States Marine Band ("The President's Own"), established by act of Congress in 1798, making it the oldest professional musical organization in the country. The band played its first Independence Day events in Philadelphia in 1800 and at the White House in 1801. Its skilled musicians and extensive repertoire quickly elevated the ensemble's status as the single most important military band that performed on the Fourth of July during the nineteenth century.

By the 1840s, brass bands were common with such notable ensembles as Flagg's Brass Band (Boston), Dodworth's Band (New York), Brooklyn Brass Band, and Salem Brass Band, followed by cornet bands in the 1850s, such as Bond's Boston Cornet Band, Lowell Cornet Band, Mahawie Cornet Band, and Hodge's Cornet Band of North Adams, Massachusetts.

Newspapers provided descriptions about the music and performers. For example, vocal groups sang popular songs as they marched in parades on Independence Day. Vocalists also marched in tandem with local bands (Mendham, New Jersey, 1799, and Shoreham, Vermont, 1802) each performing alternately as the groups progressed through city streets (Bloomfield, New Jersey, 1815; Lebanon, New Hampshire, 1819; and Scituate, Massachusetts, 1820).[4] In Deerfield, Massachusetts (1813), singers in the choir marched in pairs. The music sung and played in processions was mostly secular and included favorite marches and patriotic tunes. Some new works were written specifically for these parades. For example, Philadelphia composer Alexander Reinagle wrote a "Grand March" for his city's parade in 1788. Other parades featured the popular standard tunes of the day. In Killingworth, Connecticut (1802), citizens marched to the tune "Jefferson's March," and in Southhold, New York (1809), spectators heard the strains of "Yankee Doodle" performed by its local band. Some of the parades had multiple

bands, such as in Salem, Massachusetts (1802), and Castleton, Vermont (1809). The revelry provided by these parades was lively and pleased spectators, such as the event in Patterson Landing, New Jersey (1814), where a band of "martial musick" and 186 ladies "all dressed in white, and heads trimmed with ribbon, singing Columbia at every interval of the martial music" paraded. Some towns had multiple celebrations, each with its own music, such as Ballston Spa, New York (1816), and Salem, Massachusetts (1834). When parades reached their destinations, musicians continued to play as persons entered the churches and meeting houses (Worcester, Massachusetts, 1798, and Bloomfield, New Jersey, 1815).

Exercises frequently began with a musical selection and followed a pattern similar to a typical Protestant church service in which the usual scripture readings and sermons alternating with the singing of hymns and psalms were replaced with readings of the Declaration of Independence, orations, alternating with patriotic or other festive music. Some exercises included both instrumental and vocal music. Organ voluntaries were popular. Psalms, hymns, anthems, and oratorios were sung, and numerous odes were composed and set to both previously written and newly composed tunes. Female, mixed, and juvenile choirs were common. The number of choristers were occasionally mentioned in the sources studied. A Scotch Plains, New Jersey (1811), report describes "forty young ladies all dressed in uniform" who sang several odes that day. Sometimes the reports described the seating arrangements for the musicians. For example, musicians at the New Dutch Church in New York (1791) and the choir members at the Second Baptist Meeting House in Newport, Rhode Island (1811), and the church in Hackensack, New Jersey (1817), sat in the front galleries.

Another important facet of Fourth of July celebrations were the drinking of patriotic toasts, usually a ritual for males only. Toasting was accompanied by secular music, huzzahs, and the firing of artillery or muskets.

There were "regular" and "volunteer" toasts, the regulars written by or submitted to a committee for approval in advance of the celebration while the volunteers were offered on the spot by visitors, guests, and others who were not part of the official program.[5] Frequently the lists of toasts with names of presenters and the music performed were printed in local newspapers following the event and were circulated widely throughout the states. Reading these newspapers was one way for musicians to learn more about the repertoire performed elsewhere.[6] Sets of regular toasts numbered either thirteen, symbolizing the original number of states, or the number of states in the union in the year of the event. The number of voluntary toasts varied. Cheers were offered in sets of 3, 6, and 9. The tremendous noise created by artillery blasts heightened the effect of the music.[7]

The order of presentation and subjects for toasts were carefully considered. Many were presented to honor important persons, such as the country's founders, notable political figures, clergymen, Revolutionary War heroes, and military leaders, while other toasts were topical, some touting the country's advances in agriculture, manufactures, commerce, and arts and sciences.

Usually, someone on the organizing committee was requested to arrange for the music that was to accompany the toasts and to assist the musicians if needed in choosing pieces that connected to the specific sentiments and themes presented. For example, in Newburgh, New York, on July 4, 1806, the tune "Liberty Tree" was sung or played to accompany a toast to "The Rising Generation," and in Washington, D.C., on July 4, 1811, the song "How Sweet through the Woodlands" was performed after a toast to "roads and canals." Whereas raising glasses to Revolutionary War heroes resulted in much cheering and general revelry, toasts to George Washington were often presented standing and in silence in remembrance of his death. Usually a solemn dirge such as "Death March," "Pleyel's Hymn" or "Roslin Castle" was played in the background by a small band. When a more upbeat effect was desired, "Washington's March" was played. By tradition, the last regular toast was offered in honor of women. Frequently designated "The American Fair," females were toasted for their physical beauty and stewardship of freedom and patriotism; for example, the toast "May they set up the love of country as the standard of fashion, and we shall all become patriots" was followed by the tune of "Rural Felicity" in Scituate, Massachusetts, on July 4, 1814. Other tunes frequently sung or played on behalf of the women included "Come Haste to the Wedding," "Barney Leave the Girls Alone," "Lass of Richmond Hill," and "Columbia's Fair."

Other tunes accompanied these specific topical toasts: "The President's March" and "Hail to the Chief," for politicians; "Speed the Plough" for agricultural interests; "Ode to Science" for science. Some tunes were selected to accompany derogatory sentiments. For example, "Rogue's March" was played to deride or mock specific individuals for their political views or their handling of issues in their official duties as in Baltimore (1803) and Hudson, New York (1806). Another derisive tune was "Go to the Devil and Shake Yourself," played in Perrysburg, Ohio (1813), to ridicule "enemies" of the country and in Granby, Connecticut (1805), after a toast that mocked the Constitution of Connecticut. The popular ditty "Oh! Dear What Can the Matter Be" was sometimes sung or played to highlight misgivings about persons in political leadership positions. For example, a band performed the tune in 1811 in New York at a meeting of the Hamilton Society after this toast to "present rulers" was offered: "Like idiots gazing on a brook, they leap at stars — and fasten in the mud." Another tune used to encourage scornful laughter following certain toasts was William Billings' unusual and dissonant tune "Jargon," performed in Roxbury, Massachusetts (1813), Hanover, New Hampshire (1814), and Boston (1815, 1819, and 1820).

The rise of social movements such as abolition, education, temperance, and suffrage saw the introduction of new music and lyrics for the Fourth of July that advocated nationalism, the importance of extending equality to all, good citizenship for youth, immigrants, and the general population, as well as the abstinence of alcohol. "My country, 'tis of thee," premiered by a juvenile choir led by noted music educator Lowell Mason on July 4, 1831, in Boston, inspired a sense of nationalism. Anti-slavery and temperance movements were influenced by such songs performed on the Fourth as "Freedom's Jubilee" (1830), "Shall Afric's children be forgot" (1832), and "Soon Afric's long enslaved sons" (1835), "Daughter of Temperance, arise from thy mourning" (1836), and "The Life Boat: A Cold Water Song" (1837).

Music was introduced in Fourth of July celebrations on the frontier in the 1790s with the arrival of settlers and their musical traditions. One of the earliest Independence Day celebrations that included music west of the Alleghany Mountains occurred in 1788 in Lexington, Kentucky, and took place at an entertainment held at Captain Thomas Young's tavern. A festive ode written especially for the event celebrated "Kentucke, the land most favour'd of the earth" and was sung to the tune "Rule Britannia" by the ladies and gentlemen assembled there.[8] On the Tennessee frontier at Nashville on July 4, 1800, a fife and drum ensemble played "Washington's March," Roslin Castle," "Hail Columbia," and "Yankee Doodle" at a liberty pole raising ceremony.[9] Musical traditions were also carried west by military units, for example, the 6th U.S. Army Regiment Band, first active in Plattsburgh, New York, ca. 1817–19, and later on the Fourth of July at Fort Atkinson (now Nebraska) in 1824. Their repertoire consisted of no less than twenty-four works, some performed both in Plattsburgh and Fort Atkinson. Another military unit was the Independence Volunteers Band of Ohio and Kentucky at Fort Meigs (1813) with a repertoire of 16 works, in present-day Perrysburg, Ohio. By the early 1850s, annual musical events for Fourth of July celebrations in Salt Lake City, Utah, had been established.

The secession of six southern states in 1860 signaled the end of Fourth of July celebrations in the South while northern states continued to celebrate throughout the war years with parades, fireworks, and celebratory ceremonies that included the singing and playing of Union songs and military marches. Traditional tunes and lyrics that all Americans sung each year on the Fourth were reprinted in small songsters that Union soldiers carried with them on the battlefield. On July 4, 1862, General George B. McClellan encouraged his bands to perform patriotic music for the Army of the Potomac camped along the James River in Virginia, an event that suggests how important it was to continue the Fourth of July musical traditions in wartime. Brass and cornet bands, as well as larger military bands often predominated musically at Fourth events in northern cities and towns. Some of the more outstanding bands included the Grafulla and Gilmore bands, as well as the performances of the Seventh Regiment Band (New York), New Boston Cornet Band (New Hampshire), and the Union Cornet Band (Buffalo, New York). Popular minstrel groups performed on the Fourth, such as Christy's Minstrels (Brooklyn, New York), Rainford's Empire Minstrels (Cincinnati), and Sharpley's Minstrels (Chicago), and helped ease the tensions from the war, if only temporarily.

A surge of new music was composed during the war years that served as inspiration and hope for millions of Americans as they waited eagerly for news from the front. New songs focused on flags and other similar American icons. New battle hymns were penned, with the most endearing example, "Mine eyes have seen the glory of the coming of the Lord," lyrics by Julia Ward Howe to a tune by William Steffe, first performed on July 4, 1862, in Newton, Massachusetts, at a Grand National Union Concert presented by Sabbath and public school children. Many in the North continued to believe strongly in the abolition of slavery as witnessed by the performance of new anti-slavery songs during early years of the war. After Lincoln issued the

Emanicipation Proclamation on January 1, 1863, the anti-slavery song movement was replaced with civil rights causes. In 1865, some Fourth of July celebrations featured public readings of the proclamation and most cities favored festive music by bands and choirs on the Fourth that reflected the end of the war.

Celebratory Music after the Civil War

During the 1860s and '70s important musical organizations gave concerts on the Fourth including the Theodore Thomas Orchestra (New York), Blanchard-Fitzgerald Band (Los Angeles), Worcester National Band, Mayer's 47th Regiment Band, and Hall's First Regimental Band. Cornet and brass band concerts continued to be popular events. The Centennial celebration in 1876 (see discussion, 1876) was a catalyst for spectacular concerts across the nation as well as inspiration for new music composed especially for the occasion.

That year also marked the formation of the Music Teachers National Association (MTNA) in Delaware, Ohio, by Theodore Presser and a group of teachers. The association's mission was directed to "mutual improvement by interchange of ideas, to broaden the culture of music, and to cultivate fraternal feeling," as well as to foster the performance of American music. Some of their meetings were held on the Fourth of July, including Cleveland (1884); Indianapolis (July 5, 1887) which featured the first MTNA concert whose program consisted entirely of American compositions; Chicago (1888); Philadelphia (1889); Detroit (1890); Chicago, a World's Fair musical congress including the MTNA, Women's Musical Congress, College of American Musicians, and Illinois Music Teachers' Association (1893); Saratoga Springs, New York (1894); Put-in Bay, Ohio (1902).[10]

Following the Centennial, new musical trends emerged. First, women vocalists were encouraged to participate as soloists on Independence Day, and especially in the singing of the national anthem, a tradition that continues today. Some of the "Star-Spangled Banner" performances included Clara Louisa Kellogg in Hartford, Connecticut (1876); Miss Anna L. Fuller in Philadelphia (1880); Miss Agnes B. Huntington in London (1882); Miss Lida Clinch in Sacramento, California (1885); Mrs. Mamie Perry Davis in Los Angeles (1886), Miss Mollie Phelan in Ogden City, Utah (1888), Miss Josie Welden in Downey, California (1890), Miss Sadie Marsh in Asbury Park, New Jersey (1894), Mrs. Celia Fisher in Los Angeles (1895), Mattie Wade and Mrs. Thomas C. Noyes in Washington, D.C. (1898 and 1906, respectively), Hannah Larsen in Castledale, Utah (1901), and Luella Guymon of Huntington, Utah (1905). Second, a new sense of nationalism was reflected in Independence Day ceremonies and events, especially in immigrant communities. German Männerchor and Sängerbunders, for example, hosted large Independence Day musical events in Chicago, New York, Washington, D.C., and cities in New Jersey, Ohio, and Pennsylvania. Some of these events were massive in scope. An Irish parade in New York on July 4, 1921, featured 50 bands totaling 922 musicians.

A significant musician during this period was Charles Ives (1874–1954) who was the first American composer recognized for his combining unique compositional techniques with distinctive American themes. His work *Variations on "America"* for organ, which he played in concert in February 1892,[11] became a favorite piece in its orchestral arrangement (1964) by William Schuman with numerous performances on the Fourth beginning in 1974. Another work, *Holidays* (1909–13), includes the boisterous "Fourth of July" movement in which Ives was the first composer to have orchestral instruments depict the raucous sights and sounds — cannons, multiple bands marching in parades, and fireworks — of the typical Independence Day celebration he experienced growing up in his hometown of Danbury, Connecticut. Ives commented on his Independence Day experience in a series of essays he wrote:

His festivities start in the quiet of the midnight before, and grow raucous with the sun. Everybody knows what it's like — if everybody doesn't — Cannon on the Green, Village Band on Main Street, firecrackers, shanks mixed on cornets, strings around big toes, torpedoes, Church bells, lost finger, fifes, clam-chowder, a prize-fight, drum-corps, burnt shins, parades (in and out of step), saloons all closed (more drunks than usual), baseball game (Danbury All-Stars vs Beaver Brook Boys), pistols, mobbed umpire, Red, White and Blue, runaway horse, — and the day ends with the sky-rocket over the Church-steeple, just after the annual explosion sets the Town-Hall on fire. All this is not in the music, — not now.[12]

By the 1920s large symphony orchestras, military service bands, and other new bands had been established and provided exciting patriotic musical programs on the Fourth. John Philip Sousa rose to unprecedented fame as a band leader and composer of such popular marches as *The Stars and Stripes Forever* and *The Liberty Bell March* and was among the first to introduce American patriotic music to European audiences. Classical composers saw the holiday as an opportune time to have new works heard. *The Fourth of July* (1909) and *A Chant from the Great Plains* (1920) by Carl Busch had holiday premieres. *Concerto Grosso for Small Dance Band and Symphony Orchestra* by Robert Russell Bennett and *Circus Day* by Deems Taylor had their New York premieres at Lewisohn Stadium on July 4, 1934. Other premieres included *This Is Our Time* and *Prayer 1943* by William Schuman at Lewisohn Stadium and the Watergate in Washington, D.C., on July 4, 1940, and July 4, 1943, respectively; *Lincoln Portrait* (Washington, D.C. premiere) by Aaron Copland on July 4, 1942; *Hudson River Suite* by Ferde Grofé at Lewisohn Stadium on July 4, 1955.

Another important aspect that influenced future musical events on the Fourth were the creation of outdoor amphitheaters that provided for enjoyable concerts under the stars. Notable examples include the Sylvan Theater (1917), the first government-owned and -funded outdoor amphitheater located on the grounds of the Washington Monument, the Hollywood Bowl (1922) in Los Angeles, and the Hatch Shell (original structure, 1928) at the Charles River Esplanade in Boston. The first Independence Day concert given by Arthur Fiedler and the Boston Symphony Orchestra at the Esplanade in 1929 and subsequent concerts by later directors after the permanent Hatch Shell was built also drew huge crowds and influenced other cities to build outdoor theaters.

During this period, jazz and swing band music was performed on the Fourth, and new songs that expressed sentiments about World War I and II were typically included on ceremonial programs. An important American patriotic song introduced and still a favorite today was "God Bless America," composed by Irving Berlin and first sung by the popular vocalist Kate Smith on Armistice Day, November 11, 1938. The song was quickly catapulted to American heritage status with numerous historic performances, two of which occurred on July 4, 1940: one rendition sung at the New York World's Fair by 100 children and another sung at the presentation ceremony of Hyde Park Library to the federal government by President Franklin D. Roosevelt.[13]

Beginning in the 1920s, musical performances broadcast by radio and later TV, reached mass audiences across wide areas of the country. Some of these included the "Parade of States" broadcast over KFI on July 4, 1932; the dedication of Morristown National Historical Park, with the U.S. Marine Band over WEAF, on July 4, 1933; and *The Stars and Stripes Show*, hosted by TV personality Ed McMahon, and broadcast over NBC-TV on July 4, 1972.

The Bicentennial celebration (see discussion, 1976) was the largest Fourth of July occasion in the twentieth century. At least twelve new musical works were written for the two hundredth anniversary of the founding of the country. The 1980s are noted for the performance of well-known movie themes on the Fourth of July. John Williams, who was named conductor of the Boston Pops in 1980 and gave his first Independence Day concert at the Esplanade that year, greatly influenced this trend, due largely to the numerous popular movie scores he wrote, many of which had excerpts subsequently performed on the Fourth by bands and orchestras across the country. Some of his scores programmed included *Jaws*, *Star Wars*, *Return of the Jedi*, *Superman*, *Raiders of the Lost Ark*, *E.T. the Extra-Terrestrial*, *Born on the Fourth of July*, *Jurassic Park*, and *Schindler's List*. Williams also composed some noteworthy patriotic pieces performed on the Fourth, including *Liberty Fanfare* for the rededication ceremony for the Statue of Liberty on July 4, 1986, and *Celebrate Discovery* for the five hundredth anniversary of the 1492 discovery voyages on July 4, 1990, in Boston. Also popular during this period were the mega-entertainments that featured popular headliners, such as Boston Pops events, "Sunoco Welcome America" celebrations in Philadelphia, "Capitol Fourth" annual events in Washington, D.C., "Fair St. Louis," and New York's "Macy's Fourth of July" fireworks shows.

Performers that emerged as post–1950s American icons included the Beach Boys, Statler Brothers, and singers Willie Nelson and Don McLean. The Beach Boys[14] became closely identified with Independence Day, due largely to the popularity of the American themes in their California-inspired music such as "Surfin' U.S.A." and "California Girls" and the furor from their fans that resulted from being banned from performing on the Mall in Washington on the Fourth of July in 1983 by order of James Watt, secretary of the interior. Watts wanted to dissuade "the wrong element"—youths that consume alcohol and drugs—from attending the celebration. Undaunted, the group gave a free Independence Day concert that year in Atlantic City, New Jersey. In 1984 the Beach Boys were invited back to the Mall on July 4 and performed to a crowd of 200,000. The Statler Brothers were one of the top country music groups for nearly forty years. From 1970 to 1994, they gave an annual "Happy Birthday U.S.A." concert for charities in their hometown of Staunton, Virginia, drawing tens of thousands of music fans.[15] Willie Nelson started a series of Fourth

of July picnics, the first in 1973 in Dripping Springs, Texas, where non-mainstream country artists such as Waylon Jennings, Charlie Rich, and Kris Kristofferson were featured, with the 2008 show in Houston, Texas. Don McLean has had numerous Fourth of July concerts over the years.[16] He released his top-hit single "American Pie" in 1971 and the song became a significant popular work in America's vocal literature. Recently the song has served as an American theme at recent Independence Day celebrations, such as "American Pie with Don McLean: A 4th of July Celebration," in Irvine, California in 2008 and on July 3–5 of that year at the Freemont Street Experience in Las Vegas where a Viva Vision light and sound show titled "Don McLean's American Pie," based on the story behind the album, was premiered.[17] During this period, retrospective musical tributes to Leroy Anderson, Harold Arlen, Louis Armstrong, the Beatles, Irving Berlin, Nat "King" Cole, Stephen Foster, John Philip Sousa, George Gershwin, George M. Cohan, Glenn Miller, Richard Rodgers, Elvis Presley, Frank Sinatra, and Bruce Springsteen continued to be popular.

In 1984 Lee Greenwood released an outstanding patriotic song, "God Bless the U.S.A." With its passionate lyrics and powerful tune, it created a sensation after the beginning of Operation Desert Storm in 1991 and has had innumerable performances on the Fourth of July since then. "This Land Is Your Land," written in 1940 by Woody Guthrie[18] and popular as a folk anthem in the 1960s, was once again revitalized with new performances on the Fourth beginning in the mid–1980s. Similarly "This Is My Country," a song composed in 1940 by Al Jacobs, had numerous performances on the Fourth beginning in 1949 in Washington, D.C.

An important orchestral composition performed annually on the Fourth was the 1812 Overture by the Russian composer Pyotr Ilyich Tchaikovsky. First performed in Moscow in 1882, Tchaikovsky's score called for both live carillon (pealing bells) and live cannon shots. The first identified American pa-

This site and grouping of permanent metal chairs in Staunton, Virginia, was dedicated to the Statler Brothers ("A tribute Don Reid, Harold Reid, Phil Balsley, Jimmy Fortune & Lew DeWitt") who from 1970 to 1994 presented Fourth of July concerts in this their hometown and with all proceeds going to local charities. A plaque reads: "A tribute to Staunton's own The Statler Brothers. The most awarded group in country music history. Dedicated July 5, 2004 with pride, appreciation and affection by the people of Staunton" (author's photograph).

triotic performance for Independence Day occurred at the Century Theatre in New York in 1911 by an orchestra conducted by Elliott Schenck.[19] Other early performances with the added sounds included two in Chicago by the Chicago Symphony Orchestra, the first with live gunfire, given on July 4, 1935, at Grant Park with Eric DeLamarter, conductor,[20] and another "with bells and cannon crackers" on July 4, 1942, at Ravinia Park with Dimitri Mitropoulos, conductor.[21]

On July 6, 1950,[22] the National Symphony Orchestra under the baton of Howard Mitchell, performed the 1812 Overture accompanied by the sound of four 75mm live Howitzer cannons. The cannons were paired off and placed in different locations. Musicians Fritz Maile, a violinist in the orchestra, and Emerson Meyers, a Washington, D.C., pianist and composer, stood next to the artillery and signaled the appropriate moment to fire the guns.[23] Another milestone in the performance of the work occurred on July 4, 1974, when Arthur Fiedler and the Boston Pops utilized live cannons, church bells, and fireworks in tandem with orchestral instruments (see also 1974). Since then, each year the bells are rung live at The Church of the Advent on Beacon Hill and amplified electronically onsite at the Esplanade through the technical facilities of Boston 4 Celebrations.[24] By the 1990s, the Richmond (Virginia) Concert Band had the distinction of performing the 1812 Overture in Richmond's Dogwood Dell with live artillery, live bells from the World War I Memorial Carillon in Byrd Park located adjacent to the concert site, and added fireworks.[25]

In the 1980s and 1990s, orchestral performances on the Fourth increased annually, including those by important symphonies representing the cities of Akron, Austin, Bismarck-Mandan, Carmel, Chautauqua, Corpus Christi, Houston, Indianapolis, Johnstown, Lancaster, Longmont, Nashville, New Bedford, San Diego, San Francisco, Santa Rosa, South Bend, St. Joseph, Syracuse, and Vallejo. Notably, the first two major symphony orchestras ever to give their debut performances on Independence Day were the Hollywood Bowl Orchestra (re-established) on July 2–4, 1991, and the Las Vegas Philharmonic on July 4, 1998. The community volunteer band and chorus movement also gained considerable momentum during this period. Popular classical works that were programmed with regularity included: *Lincoln Portrait* and *Fanfare for the Common Man* by Aaron Copland; Overture to *Candide* and selections from *West Side Story* by Leonard Bernstein; and *American Salute* by Morton Gould. At least two works were written in memory of September 11, 2001, and both premiered on July 4, 2002: *Singing in the Dark* for jazz alto saxophone and string quartet by David Schiff in Portland, Oregon, and *Tribute for Orchestra* by James Grant in Gadsden, Alabama.[26]

Research Methodology

Two publications were helpful in confirming the identification of many early American works cited in this volume: Oscar Sonneck's *Early Concert-Life in America: 1731–1800* (1907) and *A Bibliography of Early Secular American Music* (1945). His studies had considerable impact in establishing widespread recognition of the significance of American music and helped to encourage further research. Richard J. Wolfe's *Secular Music in America: 1801–1825* (1964) provided a guide to important sources, composers, and performers of music in the period studied.

Several online databases were consulted, including: *American Periodical Series Online* (1740–1900; Proquest); *An American Time Capsule: Three Centuries of Broadsides and Other Printed Ephemera* (Library of Congress); *California Sheet Music Project* (Museum Informatics Project, University of California, Berkeley); *Chronicling America: Historic American Newspapers* (Library of Congress); *Colorado's Historic Newspaper Collection* (Colorado State Library, Colorado Historical Society, and the Collaborative Digitization Program); *Early American Imprints, Series 1: Evans, 1639–1800* (Readex); *Early American Newspapers, Series 1, 1690–1876* (Readex); *Eighteenth Century Collections Online* (Gale); *Historic Missouri Newspaper Project*; *Historical Newspapers of Washington*; *Illinois Digital Newspaper Collection*; *Kentuckiana Digital Library*; *Maryland Early State Records Online*; *19th-Century American Sheet Music Digitization Project* (University of North Carolina); *Northern New York Historical Newspapers* (Northern New York Library Network); *Pennsylvania Civil War Newspapers*; *Utah Digital Newspapers* (University of Utah); *Broadsides Collection* (Center for Popular Music, Middle Tennessee State University); *Winona Newspaper Project* (Winona State University, Minnesota); and *LexisNexis Academic*.

Stand-alone digital and other online newspapers examined included: *Atlanta Constitution* (1868–1929), *Brooklyn Daily Eagle*, *Chicago Tribune* (1849–1985), *The Columbia Spy* (1830–89), *Lancaster Journal* (1816–36), *Los Angeles Times* (1881–1985), *New York Times* (1851–2003), *Pennsylvania Gazette* (1728–1800), *Quincy Daily Herald* (Illinois, 1835–1919), and *Washington Post* (1877–1996). Research was supplemented by examining relevant print and microfilm copies of newspapers held at the Library of Congress and the University of Maryland at College Park.

Collections examined individually include musical programs of the Boston Symphony and Pops in the archives of the Boston Symphony Orchestra, and collections held in the United States Marine Band Library, Washington, D.C. Information on performances of the "The President's Own" U.S. Marine Band, the oldest musical organization in the country, are based on "Leader (beginning in 1916)" and "Library Logs" of the band, as well as individual program information held in vertical files; all hereafter cited in this volume as "Program Records."

Information in book is arranged chronologically by year and divided by **Publications**, listed alphabetically, and **Performances**, alphabetically arranged by state and city. Sources are cited in chronological order and variant spellings of musical works are cited as identified in the sources, particularly in the period up to the Civil War. Wherever first lines for poetry and songs are cited, full lyrics are found in the sources provided. Most of the performances included in this compilation occurred on July 4, but if that date fell on Sunday, secular performances were frequently postponed until the following day. The years that July 4 fell on a Sunday include 1779, 1784, 1790, 1802, 1813, 1819, 1824, 1830, 1841, 1847, 1852, 1858, 1869, 1875, 1880, 1886, 1897, 1909, 1915, 1920, 1926, 1937, 1943, 1948, 1954, 1965, 1971, 1976, 1982, 1993, 1999, 2004. Some programs are cited in full to provide readers a better understanding of the order in which musical works were performed. Primary materials are generally cited in their respective entries, with the addition of notes for additional primary and secondary sources or further interesting and noteworthy information, or both. A handy reference work that can be used in tandem with this work is the author's *The Fourth of July Encyclopedia* (McFarland, 2007) which includes general articles on the history of the Fourth of July, complemented with information regarding some musical performances on Independence Day.

The book includes a number of facsimile pages from relevant scores, songsters, and other primary material, as well as examples of buildings and churches where Independence Day events occurred. A bibliography, index of first lines of poetry, and general index complete this volume.

THE CHRONOLOGY

1777

Performances

Massachusetts

Boston: At the General Court, "the following Hymn from Dr. [Isaac] Watts's collection, somewhat altered, was sung upon the occasion." First line: "Nature with all her pow'rs shall sing."[27] (*The Separation of the Jewish Tribes, after the Death of Solomon, accounted for, and applied to the Present Day in a Sermon Preached before the General Court, on Friday, July the 4th, 1777 being the Anniversary of the Declaration of Independency*. By William Gordon[28] (Boston: Printed by J. Gill, 1777, 37).

Pennsylvania

Philadelphia: The Hessian Band of music "taken in Trenton the 26th of December last, attended and heightened the festivity with some fine performances suited to the joyous occasion" at a dinner prepared for Congress in Philadelphia.[29] Toasts were accompanied by "a suitable piece of music by the Hessian Band" (*Independent Chronicle and the Universal Advertiser*, 24 July 1777, 2; *Providence Gazette*, 2 August 1777, 4; *Virginia Gazette*, 18 July 1777, 2–3).

1778

Performances

Pennsylvania

Philadelphia: Newspaper reported a "Band of Musick"[30] provided celebration music at the City Tavern in Philadelphia. William Ellery[31] writing in his diary provided an excellent description:

> The glorious fourth of July I celebrated in the City Tavern with Brother Delegates of Congress and a number of other gentlemen, amounting [sic] in the whole to about 80.... The entertainment was elegant and well conducted. At the end of the Room opposite the upper Table, was erected an Orchestra.... As soon as Dinner began, the Musick consisting of Clarinets, Hautboys, French horns, Violins and Bass Viols, opened and continued, making proper pause, until it was finish.[32]

1779

Massachusetts

Boston: At Concert Hall, Boston, "This day being the 5th July, 1779, will be a concert[33] of vocal and instrumental music, to celebrate the independency of America — at which time will be performed an Ode suitable to the occasion — Tickets to be had at Mr. Gill's, Printing-Office, and at Messr. Drapes and Folson's, at 25 dollars each. Note: no tickets to be delivered, or money taken at the hall-doors" (*Independent Ledger*, and the *American Advertiser*, 5 July 1779, 4). The concert was postponed to July 9.

Pennsylvania

Philadelphia: On Sunday, July 4, members of Congress attended "divine worship" in Christ Church. Then they assembled at the Catholic chapel by "invitation from the honorable the Minister of France" where there heard a "Te Deum solemnly sung by a number of very good voices, accompanied by the organ and other kinds of music." On July 5, Congress, in turn, provided an entertainment for the French minister that included music, toasts and "thirteen vollies" (*Independent Ledger*, 26 July 1779, 2).

1780

Publications

"God Bless the Thirteen States,"[34] to be sung on the 4th of July. "Made by a Dutch gentleman at Amsterdam." According to the *Providence Gazette*, this and another song, "God Save the Thirteen States!" were written at the Hague "for the Americans at Am-

A "faithful reconstruction" of City Tavern, established in 1773, on its original site in Philadelphia. This was the location for numerous musical occasions and concerts on the Fourth beginning in 1778, when a "band of musick" serenaded members of Congress at a Fourth of July dinner. The U.S. Marine Band gave its first Independence Day performance here in 1800 (author's photograph).

sterdam" at the July 4, 1779, celebration (*Pennsylvania Packet*, 1 January 1780, 4; *Providence Gazette*, 1 January 1780).

1781

Performances

Pennsylvania

Philadelphia: Congress, military officers, citizens, and others celebrated in the hall of the university where commencement exercises were held that day. "An excellent band of musick striking up," as Congress entered the hall "and playing until his excellency the president and the hon. Board of Trustees and faculty of the university were seated, ushered in the exercises of the day, and by interludes, between the several performances [speeches] of the young gentlemen, heightened the pleasure of the entertainment" (*Massachusetts Spy*, 2 August 1781, 4).

1782

"A Song. Composed and sung on the anniversary of American independence."[35] first line: "To hail the day that annual rolls" (*Virginia Gazette, and Weekly Advertiser*, 27 July 1782, 4).

1783

Performances

Massachusetts

Boston: William Billings' anthem: "Independence" ("The States, O Lord, with songs of praise"),[36] performed at the Brattle Square Church (J.I. Young, "The Pioneer of American Church Music," *Potter's American Monthly* [October 1876]: 255–56).

New York

Poughkeepsie: A dinner celebration included the singing of a song, with the first line: "Columbia, Columbia, to glory arise" (*New York Packet*, 17 July 1783).

North Carolina

Salem: Governor Alexander Martin of North Carolina issued the first state order on 18 June for celebrating the Fourth which in turn prompted the Moravian community of Salem to create a special service and musical "Lovefeast" on the 4th of July. Music included, in part, a Te Deum "sung to trombone accompaniment," "a musical psalm of thanksgiving," and "in the evening, after the hymn of praise: Praise be to Thee, that dwells above the Cherubim, is sung in the Gemeinsaal, there will be a procession with music and song through the town which will be illuminated."[37]

South Carolina

Charleston: After a city parade, members of the militia, the Governor and his "Privy Council," and other dignitaries enjoyed a collation at the governor's residence. Toasts were offered accompanied by the following music performed by a band: God Save the Thirteen States — Jove in His Chair — King of France Guard March — The Hero Comes — Dirge[38] (*South Carolina Gazette and General Advertiser*, 5 July 1783, 4; *Pennsylvania Gazette*, 30 July 1783).

1784

Publications

"The following was sung at the celebration of the anniversary of American Independence, at Portsmouth in New Hampshire." First line: "Thus the sons of Columbia, retired from arms" (*Independent Journal*, 24 July 1784, 2; *Massachusetts Spy; or, Worcester Gazette*, 29 July 1784, 3; *Political Intelligencer and New-Jersey Advertiser*, 3 August 1784, 4; *Vermont Journal*, 25 August 1784, 4).

"Song for the Fourth of July. Tune, 'Gaho Dobbin.'" First line: "When America's sons were fast bound in a chain." Song begins with a "Recitative," (*Pennsylvania Packet, and General Advertiser*, 13 July 1784, 3).

1785

Publications

"Ode for the Anniversary of American Independence, July 4, 1785. Tune, 'That Power Who Form'd the Unmeasur'd Seas.'" First line: "Sons of Columbia all attend"[39] ("Poetry for the *Columbian Herald*," *Columbian Herald*, 15 July 1785, 4).

Performances

Massachusetts

Boston: "At twelve o'clock the trains of artillery, belonging to this town and Roxbury, commanded by Majors Davis and Spooner, with the Band of Musick, escorted His Excellency the governour, his Honour the Lieutenant Governour, the Hon. The Council, Senate and House of Representatives to the Stone Chapel" (*Massachusetts Centinel*, 6 July 1785, 3).

Pennsylvania

Philadelphia: "Citizens were agreeably entertained in the Hall of the University, by a display of music and oratory ... before as large an audience as ever convened there on any occasion.... Both the English and German music, which heightened exceedingly the festive celebration, did much honor to the courtesy and abilities of the performers" (*Independent Gazetteer*, 9 July 1785, 3; *Maryland Journal*, 12 July 1785, 2).

1786

Publications

"Anniversary Ode, for the Fourth of July, in Commemoration of American Independence." "Written by a gentleman at New-York." First line: "As time rolls ceaseless round the sphere" (*Daily Advertiser; Political, Historical, and Commercial*, 4 July 1786, 2; "Cabinet of Apollo: Original Poetry," *Massachusetts Centinel*, 12 July 1786, 4; *Essex Journal*, 19 July 1786, 4; *Worcester Magazine*, 22 July 1786, 204; *Massachusetts Spy; or, Worcester Gazette*, 27 July 1786, 204; *Cumberland Gazette*, 24 August 1786, 4).

"'Columbia.' A Cantata for the Fourth of July, 1786." First line (recitative): "Where Alleghany rears her lofty brow." Includes three airs (*Pennsylvania Packet, and Daily Advertiser*, 21 July 1786, 3; *Worcester Magazine*, 8 August 1786, 228).

"Song, for the New-York Society of the Cincinnati, July Fourth, 1786 (Tune — 'The Dushy Night'). " First line: "This happy day renews our joy" ("Poets' Corner," *Independent Ledger and the American Advertiser*, 24 July 1786, 4; *New-Hampshire Mercury and the General Advertiser*, 2 August 1786, 4).

"'A Song,' on the Anniversary of American Independence. Tune — 'Rule Britannia.' July Fourth, 1786." First line: "Th' auspicious morn again is come" (*New-York Journal, or the Weekly Register*, 6 July 1786, 3).

Performances

Boston: At the "Chapel-Church," after an oration given by Jonathan L. Austin, "an anthem [was] performed on the organ, and vocally, entitled Independence" (*American Recorder and the Charlestown Advertiser*, 7 July 1786, 3).

1787

Publications

"A New Song. Sung on the Fourth of July, 1787." First line: "In a chariot of light, from the regions above."[40] "From the *Petersburg* (Virginia) *Intelligencer*," and printed in *Worcester Magazine*, 23 August 1787, 275; *Providence Gazette and Country Journal*, 1 September 1787, 4).

"Ode on the Anniversary of American Independence." First line: "Still does reluctant peace refuse" (*Massachusetts Centinel*, 1 August 1787, 156).

"Song, composed and sung on the celebration of American Independence. Tune, "Vain Britons boast no longer." First line: "Come, come, fill up your glasses" ("Miscellany, from the (New York) *Daily Advertiser*," as published in *Massachusetts Centinel*, 18 July 1787, 139; *New Hampshire Spy*, 21 July 1787, 312).

Performances

Connecticut

New Haven: At the brick meeting house the exercises attended by town officials, president and "scholars of the university," clergy, and "gentlemen of the town seated themselves and "a federal salute was fired. The 18th Psalm set to music adapted to the occasion was then sung by a number of Gentlemen and Ladies, who had been pleased to prepare themselves for the performance of this very entertaining part of the exercises of the day." After a prayer, "another Psalm was then sung, after which David Daggert Esq favoured the audience with an Oration, the sentiment, style and delivery of which did him great honour as a man of genius.... A most pleasing Anthem closed the exercises" (*New Haven Chronicle*, 10 July 1787, 3; *New-Haven Gazette, and the Connecticut Magazine*, 12 July 1787, 166).

Massachusetts

Boston: An "Ode to Independence,"[41] by Thomas Dawes and "set to musick by Mr. [William] Selby was admirably performed ("solo parts by Mr. Deverell")" at the Stone Chapel, "the solo parts by a select company of singers" (first line: "All hail! Sublime she moves along."). John Quincy Adams was in the audience. (*Massachusetts Centinel*, 4 and 7 July 1787; *Massachusetts Gazette*, 6 July 1787, 3; *American Herald*, 9 July 1787, 2; *Boston Gazette*, 9 July 1787, 3; *Salem Mercury*, 10 July 1787, 3; *Essex Journal*, 11 July 1787, 3; *Worcester Magazine*, 12 July 1787, 194; *Pennsylvania Packet, and Daily Advertiser*, 13 July 1787, 3; *Independent Gazetteer*, 17 July 1787, 2; Adams 2: 249; McKay, 621); a number of military units and the State Society of Cincinnati "marched in procession, with accompaniments of music from martial instruments, and ringing of bells, to the new German Lutheran Church, in Race Street" where services were held (*Independent Gazetteer*, 6 July 1787, 3).

Virginia

Petersburg: "A number of citizens of this town" gathered at the establishment of Robert Armistead to celebrate. In addition to the firing of artillery, "a song composed on the occasion, was sung" (*Maryland Chronicle, or the Universal Advertiser*, 19 July 1787, 3).

1788

This was an important year for the Fourth of July as the country continued its deliberations for the ratification by all states of the Constitution of 1787. Philadelphia mounted a spectacular parade along city streets designed to garner unity and additional support for the Constitution. Referred to as the "Grand Federal Procession," the event was organized largely by Francis Hopkinson, a musician, poet, and signer of the Declaration of Independence. Perhaps as many as 5,000 persons, many in costumes representing the city trades, marched with their banners in the parade, and others attended a collation feast that followed the procession. For the amusement of spectators, the journeymen, tradesmen, musicians, and others busily demonstrated their crafts and skills as they marched. The parade included a band (see **Performances** below) and a float drawn by four horses with a nine-foot-stage with a fully operating printing press issuing copies of the ode "Oh for a muse of fire!" composed for the occasion by Hopkinson (see **Publications** below). Hopkinson's "The Raising: A Song for Federal Mechanics" (first line: "Come muster, my lads, your mechanical tools"[42] was also written for this Independence Day celebration, as were a number of other songs.

Publications

"Anniversary Ode for July 4th, 1788." First line: "Fair freedom, the glory of man in all stations." ("Poetry," *New Jersey Journal*, 9 July 1788, 4; *New-Hampshire Spy*, 22 July 1788, 104; *Fairfield Gazette; or, The Independent Intelligencer*, 23 July 1788, 4.)

"Anniversary Ode on American Independence, for the Fourth of July, 1788. Tune, 'In a Mouldering Cave,' &c."[43] First line: "In the regions of bliss, where the Majesty reigns." (*An Oration Delivered at Portsmouth, New-Hampshire, on the Fourth of July, 1788, being the Anniversary of American Independence.* By one of the inhabitants [Jonathan Mitchell Sewall (1748–1808]. (Portsmouth: Printed by George Jerry Osborne, 1788, 21–23; *Vermont Gazette or Freemen's Depository*, 29 September 1788, 4.)

"Cantata for the Fourth of July, 1788." Consists of airs, a duet and trio. First line: "Rise, America! Rise!" ("Pegasus of Apollo!," *Worcester Magazine*, 24 July 1788, 4.)

"A Federal Song. Composed for the 4th of July, 1788." First line: "Of their tutelar saints let the nations be vain." ("Poetry," *Massachusetts Gazette*, 15 July 1788, 4; *City Gazette and Daily Advertiser*, 26 July 1788, 4; *United States Chronicle*, 31 July 1788, 4; *Connecticut Gazette and the Universal Intelligencer*, 1 August 1788, 4).

"Ode for the Federal Procession, upon the Adoption of the New Government. Composed by Mr. [Samuel] L[ow]." First line: "Emerging from old ocean's bed." Broadside, New York?: 1788?; *Daily Advertiser*, 25 July 1788, 2; *New-York Packet*, 25 July 1788, 2; *Independent Journal*, 26 July 1788, 3.

"An Ode for the 4th of July" (Phil: printed by M. Carey, 1788).[44] By Francis Hopkinson. First Line: "Oh for a muse of fire! to mount the skies." ("The following Ode, composed by Francis Hopkinson, Esq. was printed at the Federal Press, during the Grand Procession in Philadelphia, on the 4th ult. and distributed among the people.") (*Pennsylvania Mercury*, 5 July 1788, 4; *New-York Packet*, 11 July 1788, 3; "Poets Corner," *Carlisle Gazette and the Western Repository of Knowledge*, 23 July 1788, 4; *City Gazette and Daily Advertiser*, 24 July 1788, 4; *Albany Journal*, 4 August 1788, 3; reprinted, "Poet's Corner," *New-York Journal and Patriotic Register*, 6 July 1790, 4. Facsimile in Library of Congress, *An American Time Capsule: Three Centuries of Broadsides and Other Printed Ephemera*.

"On the Anniversary of American Independence. Tune — 'Rule Britannia.' 'July Fourth.'" First line: "Th' auspicious morn again is come." ("Heliconian Fount," *New-Hampshire Spy*, 26 July 1788, 108.)

"A Song for the anniversary of American independence, on the supposed ratification of the Federal Constitution. To the tune of 'Rule Britannia.'" ["From the Gazette of the State of Georgia."] First line: "Ye friends to this auspicious day!" ("Poetry," *Columbian Herald or the Independent Courier of North-America*, 4 August 1788, 4.)

Performances

Connecticut

Hartford: The Society of the Cincinnati met at the Council Chamber and then marched to the North Meeting House for the exercises. "In the intervals, several select pieces of vocal and instrument music, were performed by the gentlemen and ladies of the town; a numerous and respectable collection of people from this and the neighboring towns graced the assembly. To add to the splendour of the day, there arrived, at the moment of concluding divine service, a letter to the President [of the Society], announcing the ratification of the new Constitution by the State of Virginia; upon the communication of which every face brightened and every hand clapped for joy, ad the same instant the Music performing a pleasing symphony, closed the joyful scene" (*Connecticut Courant*, 7 July 1788, 2).

New Haven: After a "grand procession through the city streets to the "brick" meeting house, "the literary exhibitions were begun, under the superintendence of the Rev. Dr. Stiles, by the reading of the monumental act of independence, by Josiah Meigs, Esq. After which was sung the 67th hymn" ("Barlow's version" according to another newspaper). After a prayer and oration, "the exhibitions at the meeting-house were closed by singing a federal hymn, composed for the occasion by Mr. Barna [sic] Bidwell, one of the tutors of Yale College." ("Litchfield, July 14," *Weekly Monitor*, 14 July 1788, 3; *Massachusetts Gazette*, 18 July 1788, 4; *Boston Gazette, and the Country Journal*, 21 July 1788, 2; *United States Chronicle*, 24 July 1788, 2).

Delaware

Dover: In the morning after an artillery salute, "the friends of freedom paraded the square with their artillery under flying colours and music" and then processed outside of town near the Dover River where the exercises were held (*Independent Gazetteer*, 11 July 1788, 2).

New Hampshire

Portsmouth: At the close of the town's entertainment, "several songs (sung by Major Flagg, in his usual stile of excellence) accompanied by a band of musick" were performed. Another newspaper reported: "Several federal songs were sung, in a masterly style, by Major Flagg, J.M. Sewall, Esq. and other gentlemen, accompanied by a band of musick" ("Anniversary of American Independence," *New-Hampshire Spy*, 5 July 1788, 83; *New-Hampshire Gazette*, 10 July 1788, 2).

Pennsylvania

Philadelphia: The "Grand Federal Procession," the largest parade on the Fourth of July in the 18th century, included a band of musicians performing "a grand March" composed for this event by Philadelphia composer Alexander Reinagle. At the Opera House at Southwark, "a concert; between the parts will be delivered (gratis) a comic lecture, in five parts, on the 'Disadvantage of Improper Education.' . . to which will be added, an opera, in one act *The Fourth of July, or the Sailors Festival*" (*Pennsylvania Packet and Daily Advertiser*, 4 July 1788, 3; *Independent Gazetteer*, 4 July 1788, 3).

Rhode Island

Providence: The town celebrated "in commemoration of the adoption of the Federal Constitution by nine states" and the exercises at the Baptist Meeting House, "some select pieces of music were interspersed, and well performed, instrumentally as well as vocally, in the latter of which some female voices added inimitable grace" (*United States Chronicle: Political, Commercial and Historical*, 10 July 1788, 3).

1789

Publications

"Anniversary Ode, for July 4th, 1789. Tune — 'Columbia.'" First line: "Let laureates endeavor their monarchs to praise." *Christian's, Scholar's, and Farmer's Magazine*, 1/4 (October/November 1789): 518–19; *New-York Packet*, 1 August 1789, 2.

"*Faederal march as performed in the grand procession in Philadelphia, the 4th of July 1788.*[45] Composed and adapted for the piano forte, violin, or German flute by Alexander Reinagle" [Philadelphia?: s.n., 1789?].

"The following ode was sung at Boston, on the day of independence. Ode." First line: "Once more we hail the happy day" ("Independence," *American Herald and the Worcester Recorder*, 16 July 1789, 4).

"Ode for American Independence (July 4, 1789).[46] Words by Daniel George, music by Horatio Garnet." First line: "'Tis done! The edict past, by heav'n decreed." Boston: Isaiah Thomas & Company, 1789. *The Massachusetts Magazine* 1/7 (July 1789): 453; *Gazette of the United States*, 1 July 1789, 91; *Pennsylvania Packet*, 4 July 1789, 2; *New York Journal and Weekly Register*, 16 July 1789, 4; *Worcester Magazine*, 16 July 1789, 4.

"A Federal Song, composed at New York for the Fourth of July, 1789." First line "Ye friends to this auspicious day!" Tune: "Rule Britannia." (*Gazette of the United States*, 20 June 1789, 79; *Federal Gazette and Philadelphia Evening Post*, 23 June 1789, 3; *Herald of Freedom and the Federal Advertiser*, 30 June 1789, 124; *American Herald and the Worcester Recorder*, 16 July 1789, 4; *American Herald and the Worcester Recorder*, 16 July 1789, 4; *Worcester Magazine*, 16 July 1789, 4).

Performances

Connecticut

New Haven: "On Thursday, the 9th instant, was celebrated in this city, the Anniversary of American Independence, by the Society of Cincinnati of the State of Connecticut." They first met at the State House and marched to the brick meeting house where a prayer, sermon, and oration by Col. David Humphreys was presented. "The music performed by a splendid collection of gentlemen and ladies added greatly to the beauty and harmony of the day" (*Daily Advertiser*, 25 July 1789, 2).

Massachusetts

Boston: At the municipal celebration, a "Concert of instrumental and vocal music," and "the ceremony at the Chapel concluded with an Ode, sung by Mr. Eaton, accompanied by Mr. Selby on the Organ; the chorus by a select choir of singers" (*Boston Gazette*, 6 July 1789, 3; *Herald of Freedom*, 7 July 1787, 131; *Salem Mercury*, 7 July 1789, 3; *Worcester Magazine*, 9 July

1789, 3; *Pennsylvania Packet and Daily Advertiser*, 16 July 1789, 2). See **Publications** above.

Raynham: A procession to the meeting house included "thirteen young ladies, belonging to the Musical Choir-eleven of whom were dressed in white."[47] At the meeting house,

> the troops opened, and paid the salute, while the gentlemen and ladies walked in, and took the seats previously assigned them; the troops then marched in, while the fifes, violins, and bass-viol, were tuned in symphonious accord to the martial step. When seated, a select choir of musicians, under the direction of Capt. Hall, their instruments introduced the exercises by singing the tune called "Amity," set to the following words, viz.

> > How pleasant 'tis to see,
> > Kindred and Friends agree,
> > Each in their proper station move,
> > And each fulfil their part,
> > With sympathizing heart, &c.

While several speakers addressed the assemblage, "at proper intervals, eleven pieces of music, both vocal and instrumental, were excellently performed; all conspiring to heighten those joyous sensations, the natural result of the occasion" ("Celebration of Independence at Raynham," *Independent Chronicle and the Universal Advertiser*, 23 July 1789, 4.)

New Hampshire

Portsmouth[48]: "Mr. [Horatio] Garnet[49] intends performing a concert of vocal and instrumental music on Monday Evening the 6th inst. At the Assembly Room — Consisting of some new federal songs, choruses, etc which he hopes will give satisfaction to those who shall honour him with their attendance. The concert will begin precisely at half past six o'clock, P.M. and at eight will be opened a ball...." (*Osborne's New Hampshire Spy*, 30 June 1789, 73); on July 4, after a parade by the militia, at the Globe Tavern, "a number of patriotic toasts were drank and several excellent songs were sung, accompanied with instrumental musick" (*Osborne's New-Hampshire Spy*, 23 June 1789; *New-Hampshire Gazette*, 9 July 1789, 3).

Pennsylvania

Philadelphia: A parade of the Society of the Cincinnati and milita from the State House to the Second Presbyterian Church included "martial music" (*New-York Daily Gazette*, 13 July 1789, 674).

1790

Publications

"A new song. For the Fourth of July. Tune — 'The Dauphin.'" First line: "Behold an empire's day." (*City Gazette and Daily Advertiser*, 16 August 1790, 4.)

"Ode on the Fourth of July, 1790." First line: "In the

regions of bliss where the majesty reigns." *Gazette of the United States*, 24 November 1790, 652.

Performances

Connecticut

Hartford: The Society of the Cincinnati processed from the State House to the North Church. "The joy of the day [was] enlivened by music" (*Connecticut Journal*, 14 July 1790, 3).

Pennsylvania

Philadelphia: At Christ Church, on Sunday, July 4, the Reverend Blagrove from Virginia presented a sermon in the afternoon and "sang an anthem,[50] which had a most enchanting effect. His voice is admirably fine, clear, and melodious, and he displayed great taste and judgment in the management of it. We do not recollect ever to have been so delighted with church music" (*New York Daily Gazette*, 9 July 1790, 650); At Gray's Gardens, on July 5, a "Duet" (first line: "Peace and Science! heav'nly maids!") and an ode (first line: "Amidst the joys of this auspicious day") were part of a concert presented (*Pennsylvania Packet, and Daily Advertiser*, 2 July 1790, 1; *Universal Asylum and Columbian Magazine* 5/1 (July 1790): 57; *Federal Gazette*, 10 August 1790, 1; at Gray's Ferry, a group of participants in costume, at the "Federal Temple, performed the ode on Federal Liberty; towards evening they sang in a grove the federal love-song — the shepherds with full music began 'The man of independent soul,' and continued the two first verses: the shepherdesses then replied, 'yet feels the sway of sacred love,' and performed the latter verses in a different, very pathetic, tune, supported only by the violins; then the last verse was repeated by the whole band vocal and instrumental, to wit:

'His country and his virtuous fair,
Close to his heart united lie,
They are his joy, his darling care,
For them he lives, for them will die.'

In the evening an ode, in honor of France, was performed with vocal and instrumental music, at the place where the arms of the United States, and of France were entwined by liberty. Is this: 'Amidst the joys of this auspicious day.'" (*Federal Gazette and Philadelphia Evening Post*, 12 July 1790, 2.)

1791

This year marks the 15th Anniversary of the signing of the Declaration of Independence. The editor of a New York City newspaper printed the following:

Monday next, the 4th July, will complete fifteen years since the glorious declaration of American Independence, by the Congress of the United States, John Hancock, president — The importance of this then astonishing event hourly increases, and the augmentation of the political duties of the Sons of America is witnessed by every diurnal revolution of yon great orb of light — May it be the pride of Americans to acquire such knowledge as is requisite to the preservasion of the "Rights of Man"— and may they glory in transmitting to latest posterity those principles of freedom and good government, which now inspire them to celebrate this memorable day.[51]

A musical highlight on this day was the first Independence Day performance on the new Tannenberg organ in Zion Church in Philadelphia.

Publications

"'A Favorite Song.' Sung on the Fourth of July, by a number of the true Sons of Columbia. Tune, 'God Save Great Washington.'" First line: "All hail auspicious day"[52] (*Mail; or, ClayPoole's Daily Advertiser*, 8 July 1791, 2).

"An Ode, composed for the occasion, at the request of the Society. By Dr. William Pitt Smith." First line: "Now elevate your hymns of joy." (*The Blessings of America: a Sermon Preached in the Middle Dutch Church, on the Fourth July, 1791, being the Anniversary of the Independence of America; at the Request of the Tammany Society, or Columbian Order*. By William Linn, D.D.")

"Ode for July 4, 1791. Composed by Mr. Lathrop of Boston." First line: "Fill! Fill to Washington" (*New-Hampshire Gazette and General Advertiser*, 7 July 1791, 3).

"Ode, for the 4th of July, 1791." First line: "While changeful seasons shall on earth appear" ("From the *New-York Magazine* as published in *New-York Journal and Patriotic Register*, 2 July 1791, 207).

"Ode for the Fourth July, 1791." First line: "Hail smiling cherub, child of light"[53] (*Gazette of the United States*, 9 July 1791, 83).

Performances

Massachusetts

Worcester: At the town's exercises, "previously to the delivery of the Oration, the following Ode, composed for the occasion, was performed by the Musicians of this town, vocally and instrumentally. 'An Ode for July 4th, 1791.' (Tune — 'God save the King.')"[54] First line: "Hail blest America!" The ode was composed by O. Fiske. (*An Oration, Delivered at Worcester, on the Fourth of July, 1791. Being the Anniversary of the Independence of the United States*. By Edward Bangs,[55] Esq. Worcester, MA: Isaiah Thomas, [1791]; *Worcester Magazine*, 7 July 1791, 3; *The Mail, or, ClayPoole's Daily Advertiser*, 13 July 1791, 2).

New Hampshire

Dover: "The procession formed and moved on to the meeting-house, where, after an introductory ode, an animated, learned and elegant oration was delivered by William Atkinson, esquire, after which the duties of the day were closed by an ode composed by Henry Mellen [1757–1809],[56] esquire, and set to music" (*Mail, or, ClayPoole's Daily Advertiser*, 22 July 1791, 3).

New York

New York: The Tammany Society's services were held at the New Dutch Church. Musicians sat in the front gallery. Music was performed while the audience took their seats (*Daily Advertiser*, 2 July 1791, 2).

Pennsylvania

Elizabethtown: A "divine service" was held "which was accompanied with the enchanting music of Mr. Spicer and his brilliant choir of scholars" (*Mail, or, Claypoole's Daily Advertiser*, 19 July 1791, 1).

Philadelphia: "Grays' Gardens. A concert of vocal and instrumental musick will begin on Monday, the glorious Fourth of July at 6 o'clock in the morning, and conclude at ten at night, should the day be fair, to celebrate American Independence. Songs, with harmony and martial musick, in honor of the day, will be performed" (*Pennsylvania Gazette*, 29 June 1791; *Mail, or, ClayPoole's Daily Advertiser*, 1 July 1791, 4; *Pennsylvania Mercury and Universal Advertiser*, 2 July 1791, 1; *General Advertiser and Political, Commercial, Agricultural and Literary Journal*, 4 July 1791, 3); at Zion Church, the Society of the Cincinnati, militia, and citizens assembled for the exercises. "The excellent organ[57] of Zion Church accompanied with fine vocal music added much to the pleasures of the day" (*Federal Gazette, and Philadelphia Evening Post*, 5 July 1791, 2).

1792

Publications

"Independence, an Ode." Includes a recitative, airs, and choruses. First line: "Bowing, immortal Liberty, to you" (*Mail; or, Claypoole's Daily Advertiser*, 17 July 1792, 2).

"An ode, performed at Taunton, July 4th, 1792 — at the celebration of American independence. Tune — 'Great George.' By Mr. Stoddard." First line: "Come all ye sons of song" ("Poet's Corner," *United States Chronicle: Political, Commercial, and Historical*, 23 August 1792, 4).

Performances

Massachusetts

Taunton: At the town's exercises, "an ode, composed by the orator [A. Stoddard] of the day, was performed with much applause" ("Sixteenth Anniversary of American Independence," *Mail; or, Claypoole's*

Daily Advertiser, 17 July 1792, 2). See **Publications** above.

New Hampshire

Hanover: At the college chapel of Dartmouth College, the senior class convened for a ceremony that included "a piece of musick, performed almost inimitably by the Musical Society" (*Connecticut Courant*, 30 July 1792, 3; *Norwich Packet*, 2 August 1792, 3).

Pennsylvania

Carlisle: "Citizens of this borough and its vicinity" met at Mr. Robert Gibson's Farm. The group "formed a large circle" and "toasts were drank, accompanied with three cheers and instrumental music." After the toasts "the celebrated song, viz. O'er the vine cover'd hills and gay regions of France, &c. was sung by a number of excellent voices, accompanied by instrumental music" (*Carlisle Gazette, and the Western Repository of Knowledge*, 18 July 1792, 3).

Virginia

Norfolk: The cornerstone laying ceremony for Bignall's Norfolk Theatre took place and included a procession and "band of music" (*Mail; or, Claypoole's Daily Advertiser*, 17 July 1792, 2).

1793

Publications

"Columbia; Ode for the Fourth of July. First lines, respectively: "Columbia, Columbia, to glory arise" and "Come, let us join the cheerful song." Broadside, Boston (?), 1793 (?). Place and date of publication suggested by description of ceremony below. Copy in Brown University.

"The Declaration of Independence: a Poem, Accompanied by Odes, Songs, &c. Adapted to the Day. By a Citizen of Boston [George Richards (1755?–1814)]."[58] Boston: [Isaiah Thomas & E. T. Andrews,] 1793. Copy in Library of Congress. A reprint (Tarrytown, NY: W. Abbatt, 1929) contains an "anthem composed for Thursday morning, July 4, 1793," pp. 51–52.

"The following ode was composed by a young gentleman in this town [Portsmouth], for the 4th of July, 1793 and sung at one of the parties assembled to celebrate the anniversary of that day." First line: "Full sev'teen years their round have run" (*Oracle of the Day*, 6 July 1793, 3).

"A Hymn on Peace." First line: "Behold, array'd in light." Attributed to Abraham Wood. Sung at a "Tammany, or Columbian Order" celebration. Broadside ([New York]: J. Harrisson, printer [1793]). Copy in New York Historical Society.

"Mr. Brown, the following was composed for a select company, and intended to be sung on the Fourth of July; if you think a corner of your paper would not be improperly filled therewith, it is very much at your service." First line: "While loud Bellona's thunder roars" (*Federal Gazette, and Philadelphia Evening Post,* 12 July 1793, 2; *Salem Gazette,* 30 July 1793, 4).

"New York. The following 'Song' was sung on the 4th inst. at the house lately called Belvedere Club House, but now known by the name of Liberty Hall. Air — 'Indian Chief.'" First line: "When a nation's obsorb'd under tyranny's chain" (*New Jersey Journal,* 10 July 1793, 4).

"Ode for Independence, 1793. Composed and set to music by Dr. Willard." First line: "Behold! the glorious day appears!" (*A Sermon, Delivered in Stafford, on the Anniversary of American Independence, July 4th, A.D. 1793.* By Nathan Williams, A.M. Pastor of the Church of Christ in Tolland. Hartford: Printed by Hudson and Goodwin, 1793.)

"'Song' — to follow the Prayer. Tune — 'Rule Britannia,' &c." First line: "When exil'd Freedom, forc'd to roam." "To conclude the Service. To the tune of 'Dorchester's March.'" First line: "At length War's sanguine scenes are o'er." (*An Oration, Delivered at Elizabeth-Town, New-Jersey, Agreeably to a Resolution of the State Society of Cincinnati, on the Fourth of July, M.DCC.XCIII. Being the Seventeenth Anniversary of the Independence of America.* By Elias Boudinot, L. L. D. Elizabeth-Town: Printed by Shepard Kollock, at His Printing-Office and Book-Store, 1793; *New Jersey Journal,* 10 July 1793, 3; *Dunlap's American Daily Advertiser,* 16 July 1793, 3; *Oracle of the Day,* 27 July 1793, 4).

Performances

Maine

Portland: Citizens and members of the Artillery Company marched from the Assembly Room to the Rev. Deane's Meeting House where the exercises were begun with an oration. "After the oration, a piece of music was performed by a choir of singers composed of young ladies and gentlemen from the several societies in this town, and accompanied by bass viols — words from Dr. Belknap's Centenary Discourse[59]: [first line]'When guided by the Almighty Hand.'" Later at Mr. Motley's New Tavern, a "Song, God Save Columbia's Son! &c" by N. Fosdick, Esq."[60] was sung. Another "Song-in celebration of the day" was sung by Col. May ("Fourth of July," *Eastern Herald,* 6 July 1793, 3).

Maryland

Baltimore: A band of music played "through the streets" on the eve of the Fourth. Also, "a large and respectable company also partook of an elegant entertainment at Mr. Gray's at Chatsworth where "the harmony of a well chosen band of music had a most pleasing effect" ("Celebration of the Fourth of July in Baltimore," *Daily Advertiser,* 12 July 1793, 2); at the Theatre the Maryland Company had the following

production on July 5, *America's Independence; or, Fourth of July* with the performance concluding with "Hail Columbia"[61] (2 July 1793, *Maryland Journal*[62]).

Chestertown: The citizens marched to the church, "where divine service was performed by the Rev. Citizen Walker, closed by a patriotic Hymn." At a dinner, "a number of French citizens joined in our festive joys, and the patriotic Song of 'Ca Ira,' was sung with very happy effect" (*Chestertown Gazette,* 9 July 1793, 2).

Massachusetts

Boston: At the Universal Meeting House, Mr. [George] Richards recited a poem titled "The Declaration of Independence," in which "every patriot, from New Hampshire to Georgia" who signed the original document is included. Below are the instructions for including music in the recitation:

A celebrated band of singers, eminently distinguished for their accurate knowledge in the science of vocal harmony, have generously offered their assistance, on the present occasion. A much admired Ode to Independence[63] will open the performance. A momentary pause at the 120th line of the Poem, will be succeeded by an Ode to Freedom, generally supposed to have been composed by Della Crusca,[64] and allowed to be unrivalled in the compass of language. A second momentary rest will be made at the 234th line, and afford room for the introduction of "Columbia, Columbia, to Glory Arise,"[65] written by the animated and animating Dr. Dwight.[66] At the conclusion of the 360th line, an original Anthem, of the high Hallelujah metre, and never before published, will be sung, accompanied by Instruments.

"Concluding Anthem composed for Thursday morning, July 4, 1793."[67] First line: "Hail! the first, the greatest blessing." (*Columbian Centinel,* 3 July 1793, 3; *Federal Gazette,* 29 July 1793, 3.) See **Publications** above.

New Hampshire

Portsmouth, see **Publications** above.

Rhode Island

Providence: After a large military parade, exercises at the Baptist Meeting House included the performance of "an Ode suited to the occasion, accompanied with vocal and instrumental music, especially adapted to it.... After the oration another Ode was performed, attended with vocal and instrumental music" (*Providence Gazette and Country Journal,* 6 July 1793, 2; *United States Chronicle: Political, Commercial, and Historical,* 11 July 1793, 2).

1794

Publications

"Ode for Independence.[68] Composed and set to music by Dr. Willard." First line: "Behold! the glorious day appears!" (*Dunlap's American Daily Advertiser*, 7 August 1794, 3.)

"An ode for the eighteenth anniversary of American independence. To the tune of Columbia." First line: "America's birth-day bids freemen arise." A note preceding the ode states: "The following Ode was sung in the Presbyterian Meeting-House in Newark, on Friday the 4th instant" (*Philadelphia Gazette*, 12 July 1794, 3).

"Ode for the Fourth of July." First line: "Hail lovely maid! hail power devine!" (*Weekly Museum*, 5 July 1794, 2).

"Ode on the Fourth of July, 1794. Tune—'A Dauphin's Born,' &c." First line: "Eventful point of time!" (*Weekly Museum*, 5 July 1794, 2).

"'On Liberty.' The following elegant Hymn was sung at Hartford, at the anniversary meeting of the Cincinnati, on the Fourth of July." First line: "Behold a glorious theme." ("Apollo's Museum," *Norwich Packet*, 28 August 1794, 4; *Oracle of the Day*, 4 October 1794, 4.)

"The following Song,[69] composed for the occasion, upon request, by a citizen of Lancaster, was sung to the tune of the Marseilles Hymn,[70] by the different companies on the 4th of July." First line: "Hail! Sons of Freedom! Hail the day." (*Dunlap's American Daily Advertiser*, 2 August 1794, 3.)

"The two following Songs were composed for the occasion, and sung at the celebration of American Independence, at New-Port, Rhode Island, July 4, 1794. (By a young gentleman. 'Columbia Relieved.'[71] Tune—'The Death of General Wolfe.'" First line: "To a mouldering cavern, the mansion of woe." "God Save Great Washington." First line "To Heaven's empyreal height." One newspaper reported the songs were sung with instrumental accompaniment at the Baptist Meeting House (*Daily Advertiser*, 21 July 1794, supplement 2; *American Apollo*, 24 July 1794, 4).

"Song—for the Fourth of July, 1794. And sung at Windsor Hall. Tune—'Jack, the brisk young drummer; The Vicar of Bray; or, Yankee Doodle.'" First line: "When freedom's sons, at heav'ns command."[72] (*Independent Gazetteer*, 9 July 1794, 3.)

"'A Song' for the Fourth of July 1794. Tune of Great Washington." First line: "Hail thou auspicious day." (*New Jersey Journal*, 9 July 1794, 1.)

Performances

Maine

Portland: At a local tavern, N.F. Fosdick sang "God Save Columbia's Son" after a toast to George Washing-

ton and the firing of "15 guns" (*Eastern Herald*, 5 July 1794, 3).

Maryland

Baltimore: The 5th and 27th Maryland regiments marched, "music playing," to the grand parade of military units. Throughout the day "many toasts and songs were given on the occasion" (*Baltimore Daily Intelligencer*, 7 July 1794, 3).

New Jersey

Newark: At the Presbyterian Church, citizens, militia, and 260 students assembled for the exercises. "In the intervals between the prayer, the reading the Declaration of Independence and the oration, and at the close, Mr. Kimbal's singing school bore their part in the celebration of the day, by singing several hymns and anthems calculated for the occasion. The young ladies of the school were dressed in white—the elegance of their persons and melody of their voices, merits a distinguishing rank in the honors of the day." Later 160 citizens had dinner and after that toasts were drunk, "in the intervals of which, a number of patriotic songs were sung, which, while they exhilarated the spirits, animated the mind with flowing sentiments of liberty. The French citizens performed the Carmagnole and the Marsellois Hymn and although the language was their own and but little understood, yet the animation which accompanied their song, made a sensible impression on the minds of every hearer" (*Philadelphia Gazette*, 15 July 1794, 3). See **Publications** above.

New York

New York: At the Tammany Society meeting, "toasts were drank, and interspersed with a number of songs sacred to the cause of liberty" (*Columbian Gazetteer*, 7 July 1794, 3; *Diary or London's Register*, 8 July 1794, 3).

Pennsylvania

Philadelphia: "On Friday next, the 4th of July, the 18th year of American Independence, there will be held at Harrowgate a Concert of Vocal and Instrumental Music, to begin at ten o'clock in the morning precisely, and conclude in the evening, should the weather prove fail.... Tickets to be had at the front of the house, at one quarter of a dollar each, by the public's most obedient and very humble servant, George Esterly" (*Dunlap's American Daily Advertiser*, 2 July 1794, 2); at a "civic feast" held at Gen. Brewster's by a number of men from the university and others, an "Ode to Independence" composed and set to music by Mr. Abner Cheny, and happily adapted to the joyful occasion, was inimitably performed, with instruments and voices, on a stage erected for that purpose, over the 'civic' table, amidst a respectable crowd of spectators, who crowned the exhibition with applause" ("Fourth of July," *General Advertiser*, 15 July 1794, 2; *Dunlap's American Daily Advertiser*, 2 July 1794, 2).

West Chester: "At 11 o'clock agreeably to notice, they all [Republicans] met at the court house; and after Washington's March had been played by Major Frazer on the flute, and Mr. P. Derrick on the Forte Piano, Mr. Jos. Hemphill delivered an excellent oration, suited to the glorious occasion of the meeting." The group then marched to Liberty Grove to the accompaniment of "martial music." After a dinner the "procession returned to the court house where "the company being seated in the court, Messrs. P. Derrick, Frazer, [Major. John] Shippen and Hemphill sang a patriotic ode, composed for the day by Mr. P. Derrick, to the tune of 'Rule Britannia,' chorus by numbers. After the song, three cheers were unanimously given in compliment to the author. The whole company then dispersed with due order and decorum" (*Dunlap's American Daily Advertiser*, 16 July 1794, 4).

Rhode Island

Providence: A military parade included "excellent martial music belonging to the Troop of Horse." The exercises were held at the Baptist Meeting House and begun with "an Ode, performed with music vocal and instrumental, a second Ode performed after a prayer, and an anthem." "The Odes were elegant, poetical and ingenious — the composition of a young gentleman of this town, whose abilities in this way had already honourably distinguished him" (*Providence Gazette and Country Journal*, 5 July 1794, 3). See **Publications** above.

Virginia

Alexandria: The militia and citizens met at the Presbyterian Meeting House. Included in the exercises, "an anthem, prepared for the occasion, with other pieces, were sung, accompanied with instrumental music" (*Dunlap's Daily American Advertiser*, 15 July 1794, 3).

The Old Presbyterian Meeting House in Alexandria, Virginia, constructed in 1775 but rebuilt (shown here) after an 1835 fire, was one of numerous meeting houses along the Eastern Seaboard that served as venues for musical performances on the Fourth of July. This meeting house hosted an Independence Day ceremony in 1794 when an anthem and other works, accompanied by musical instruments, were sung (author's photograph).

1795

Publications

"Anthem for the Fourth of July." First line: "With songs of honour chanting high" ("Court of Apollo," *Weekly Museum*, 4 July 1795, 4).

"Hymn, composed by Barnabus Bidwell, and sung at a celebration at Richmond [Massachusetts], in 1795." First line: "Once more on freedom's holiday." The text of this hymn was presented to the chief marshall of the celebration of Independence Day in Pittsfield, Massachusetts, on July 4, 1855 ("The Celebration of the Fourth," *Pittsfield Sun*, 12 July 1855, 2).

"From the *Dartmouth Eagle*. An Ode composed and set to music, for the celebration of the Anniversary of American Independence." First line: "Columbians join in the festival lay" ("Parnassian Blossoms," *Amherst Journal and the New-Hampshire Advertiser*, 14 August 1795, 4).

"A Song, for the Fourth of July, 1795. Sung at the General Society of Mechanics and Tradesmen, at the celebration of the independence of America, July 4. Tune — Indian Chief." First line: "Ye sons of Columbia, come forth and rejoice" ("Poet's Corner," *Greenleaf's New York Journal and Patriotic Register*, 11 July 1795, 4).

Performances

Maine

Portland: The town's procession moved from the Columbian Tavern to "Rev. Dr. Deane's meeting house" where "the service of the day commenced with musick." After an oration, "a Symphony composed by Mr. Boullay"[73] was performed. "The following Ode, composed by a citizen for the occasion, and set to musick by Mr. Herrick,[74] was intended to have been performed, but omitted: 'Ode to Independence.' [first line] 'Strike, strike, with joy, the festive lyre.' ... As the procession entered the house, the French Marseillois Hymn was performed; and Washington's March as they retired....A number of jovial and patriotic songs were sung among which was the following composed for the day and sung by N. Fosdick, Esq.": "Ode for the Fourth of July, 1795. By Mr. D.G."[75] First line: "Hail! Hail! auspicious day" ("American Independence," *Eastern Herald*, 6 July 1795, 3).

Massachusetts

Stockbridge: "On Friday last a very considerable number of Gentlemen from various parts of the County, assembled in this town to commemorate the era of American Independence. About noon, the company moved in procession from Mr. Seymour's to the meeting house, where, after an excellent prayer by the Rev. Doct. West, an Ode, composed for the occasion, was sung by a select choir of singers — after which an elegant and animated Oration was delivered by Barnabas Bidwell, Esq. to a large, respectable and approving audience." The Ode was set to the tune of "Denmark"; first line: "Behold once more the glorious day" ("Celebration of Independence," *Western Star*, 7 July 1795, 3; *An Oration, Delivered at the Celebration of American Independence, in Stockbridge, July, 1795*. By Barnabas Bidwell, Esquire. Published at the request of the committee. Stockbridge, [MA], Loring Andrews, 1795).

Worcester: A dinner at Free Mason's Hall for the men included the singing of "a song — Hail, America, Hail, &c." (*Massachusetts Spy*, 8 July 1795, 3).

New York

New York: "The joint societies, viz. the Democratic, Tammany, Mechanic, and the Military" assembled at the Battery at 11 A.M. and marched to the Presbyterian Church, where the exercises where held. The included the performance of "a piece of solemn vocal music." The end of the ceremony concluded with "chanting the following Ode to Freedom, composed by Mr. S.A. Law, upon the occasion": first line, "Behold a glorious theme." The societies dined at various locations. For example, the democrats at Hunter's Hotel where "toasts were given, interspersed with patriotic songs, amid bursts of applause" ("American Independence," *Greenleaf's New York Journal and Patriotic Register*, 8 July 1795, 1). See **Publications** above.

Rhode Island

Newport: "At 11 o'clock, A. M., a procession" consisting of citizens and military units marched to the Baptist Church where, among the exercises, "the vocal music, previously prepared for the occasion, gave pleasure to the audience, and did honour to the ladies and gentlemen who performed" ("Fourth of July," *Newport Mercury*, 7 July 1795, 3; "Fourth of July," *Philadelphia Gazette & Universal Daily Advertiser*, 17 July 1795, 2).

1796

Publications

"'Hymn to Liberty.' For the Fourth of July, 1796. Tune, 'Rule Britannia.' Sung at the celebration of the Independence at Maumouth, on the 4th inst." First line: "When Exil'd Freedom, forc'd to roam" (*Greenleaf's New York Journal and Patriotic Register*, 12 July 1796, 2).

"An Ode composed by B. Bidwell, Esq. for the celebration of independence, at Richmond [Massachusetts], July 4th, 1796." First line: "Once more, on freedom's holiday" (*Western Star*, 26 July 1796, 4; *Gazette of the United States*, 3 August 1796, 3; *Columbian Herald*, 22 August 1796, 4).

"Ode to be sung at Christ-Church ['New York'], next Monday, being the Fourth of July." First line:

"Nations rejoice, Jehovah reigns." ("For the Weekly Museum," *Weekly Museum*, 2 July 1796, 4; *The Argus, or Greenleaf's New Daily Advertiser*, 5 July 1796, 3; *Spooners Vermont Journal*, 29 July 1796, 4; *Rural Magazine; or, Vermont Repository* 2/8 [August 1796]: 415.) One newspaper reported that an anthem was also sung at Christ Church.

"Ode. Written on the Fourth of July." First line: "Hail, independence! Freedom, hail" ("Court of Apollo," *Weekly Museum*, 16 July 1796).

"'Ode,' written on the 4th of July, 1796. From the *Pennsylvania Herald*, printed at York." First line: "'Tis true I'm proud to greet the day." ("Tongue of Apollo," *Rural Repository*, 4 August 1796, 4.)

"Odes for the Fourth of July, 1796." First line: "Dread Goddess on this happy day." First line: "Symphonious numbers loud and clear." Broadside. [Providence, RI:, 1796]. *Early American Imprints, Series I: Evans.*

"'A Song,' for the Fourth of July, 1796, Composed at Patterson [NJ]. Tune — 'Nature's Holiday.'" Messrs. Editors, by inserting the following, you will much oblige a constant reader." First line: "Well met, ye Sons of Liberty" ("Poet's Corner," *Centinel of Freedom*, 9 September 1796, 4).

Performances

Massachusetts

Boston: The Boston Artillery's dinner event held at Faneuil Hall had the following music provided by the Artillery musicians after each successive toast: Yankee Doodle — Washington's March — Warren's March — Governor's March — Lieutenant Governor's March — He Comes, the Hero Comes — La Carmignole — Rural Felicity — Wayne's March[76] — Massachusetts March ("Boston, July 6," *Gazette of the United States*, 12 July 1796, 2).

New Hampshire

New Ipswich: A parade started at 2 P.M. and ended at the meeting house. "After the audience was seated a piece of music was performed by voices and instruments. The notes being part of Handel's Oratorio of Saul and David: Recitative [first line] 'Already see the daughters of the land.'"

After singing of the Recitative, a procession of ladies dressed in white walked up the broad ile [sic]. An oration was then pronounced, by Samuel Worcester, A.B. Then were sung the following Songs — To the tune of the Wanderer [first line] 'Here let joy and mirth abound.' After singing of the two last lines, Ceres was represented by a young lady, attended by two young misses, strewing flowers &c. — to tune of British Here, and 2d verse of the same. — 'Prepare, prepare, your songs prepare.' To the tune of Vicar of Bray [first line] 'Our yoke is broken, we are free' [*Rising Sun*, 2 August 1796, 3].

New Jersey

Middletown Point: "At 12 o'clock, being announced by the discharge of a field piece, an oration was delivered to a respectable assemblage of ladies and gentlemen, by the Rev. William Hobrow. A hymn to liberty, composed by the same gentleman, was then sung, accompanied by the audience, with all that animation which the subject must ever inspire in the breasts of Americans" (*Claypoole's American Daily Advertiser*, 16 July 1796, 3).

North Carolina

Halifax: At Mr. Hopkin's Tavern, "toasts were drank, each accompanied by a patriotic song." Later, "the evening closed with a ball at the Long-Room, at which were present a brilliant assemblage of ladies" ("Halifax, July 11," *North Carolina Journal*, 11 July 1796, 3).

Pennsylvania

Philadelphia: According to George Esterly, plans were made for "an elegant concert of music at Harrowgate, the gardens ... in complete order and considerably improved since the last season" ("Concert at Harrowgate, July 4, 1796," *Claypoole's American Daily Advertiser*, 1 July 1796, 3).

Virginia

Alexandria: "The Fourth of July; or, American Glory,"[77] performed on July 4.

1797

Publications

"Anthems sung on the occasion [Newark, NJ]": first lines, "With songs of honor chanting high"; "Hail! the first, the greatest blessing." "Hymn on War": first line, "While sounds of war are heard around." (*An Oration Delivered in the Presbyterian Church at Newark, on the Fourth of July, 1797, at the Request of the Citizens of Newark it being the Twenty-First Anniversary of American Independence*. By Isaac Watts Crane, A. M. Newark: Printed by John Woods, 1797, 22–24; *Centinel of Freedom*, 12 July 1797, 4).

"Cantata, for the celebration of American Independence." Includes recitatives, airs, and choruses and was sung in New York (*The Diary or Loudon's Register*, 4 July 1797, 3).

"'Hymn to Liberty.' For the Fourth of July. Tune — Rule Britannia." First line: "When exil'd Freedom, forc'd to roam." ("Poet's Corner," *Centinel of Freedom*, 4 July 1797, 4.)

"An Ode for the Fourth of July, 1797. Tune — 'God Save America.'" First line: "Let acclamations roll" (*The Herald; a Gazette for the Country*, 8 July 1797, 3).

"Ode (composed for the occasion, by P. Freneau)[78]

the musick performed by the Uranian Society." First line: "Once more our annual debt to pay." In *Means for the Preservation of Public Liberty: An Oration Delivered in the New Dutch Church on the Fourth of July, 1797.* By G.J. Warner.[79] (New York: Printed at the Argus Office for Thomas Greenleaf and Naphtali Judah, 1797); *Diary of Loudon's Register*, 5 July 1797, 3; *Greenleaf's New York Journal and Patriotic Register*, 5 July 1797, 3; *Time Piece; and Literary Companion*, 10 July 1797, 208.

"A Song, composed, and sung by Capt. Hamilton, at the anniversary of American independence, in this town, July 4th, 1797." First line: "Let all Americans combine." ("Pegasus of Apollo," *Massachusetts Spy, or, the Worcester Gazette*, 12 July 1797, 4.)

Performances

Connecticut

Guilford: "At 4 o'clock in the morning the day was ushered in by a discharge of canon, ringing of bells, & martial music." At noon a procession of 600 citizens and others marched to the meeting house where "three Odes composed for the occasion, were also handsomely sung, accompanied by instrumental music" (*Connecticut Journal*, 19 July 1797, 3).

Massachusetts

Boston: "The commander in chief was escorted to Boston, by a brilliant military band" (*City Gazette and Daily Advertiser*, 3 August, 1797, 2).

Salem: A comic opera titled *The Mountaineers* and "the celebrated musical entertainment called *The Poor Soldier* were performed at Washington Hall (*Salem Gazette*, 4 July 1797, 3).

New Jersey

Caldwell:

Sixteen young Ladies uniformed in white, with garlands in their hats, conducting another in their centre bearing the Cap of Liberty, enwreathed with laurel and all singing Columbia in concert with the German flute.... The Declaration of Independence was then read, with an animated descriptive introduction by Dr. Cyrus Pierson. Immediately after which Independence was happily performed in a Chorus of Vocal and Instrumental music [*Centinel of Freedom*, 7 July 1797].[80]

Newark: At the service, "several hymns and anthems are to be sung in church, and some instrumental music given by a number of gentlemen of the town. It is likewise expected, that a concert will be given under the Bower on the Common, when they young lads and lasses may 'Dance on the Green'" ("American Independence," *Centinel of Freedom*, 4 July 1797, 3). See **Publications** above.

New York

New York: After a procession by several societies, including the New-York Coopers' Society, the Democratic Society, General Society of Mechanics and Tradesmen, and the Tammany Society, to the New Dutch Church, the exercises included "Billings' Anthem of Independence, sung by the Uranian Society, and accompanied by the organ." After an oration, "an Ode composed for the occasion, [see **Publications** above] was sung by the Uranian Society, accompanied by the organ, with great applause" (*Claypoole's American Daily Advertiser*, 8 July 1797, 1; "The Fourth of July," *Weekly Museum*, 8 July 1797, 3); "Vauxhall Garden, Broadway, no. 112, will be decorated and illuminated in a beautiful manner, and the ever memorable day will be celebrated with music and singing; the whole will call to mind the American heroes who have contributed to its independence.... A concert of vocal and instrumental music — as follows":

Act I.
Grand Overture, Haydn
Song, "Little Sally,"[81] Miss Moller
Quartetto, for the French Horn, Violin, Tenor and Bass, Messrs. Dupois, Hewit, Gilfert and Dezeze
Song, "Three Sweethearts I Boast," Miss Moller
Glee, "Lightly Tread This Hollow Ground"
Battle Overture, in commemoration of the 4th of July, Hewitt[82]
Act II.
Concerto flute, Mr. Saliment
Song, "Tantivy Hark Forward," Miss Moller
Sonata, Piano forte, Mr. Moller
Song, "I Am in Haste," Miss Moller
Glee, "Here in Cool Grot"[83]
Finale, Pleyel

("Fourth of July," *Minerva & Mercantile Evening Advertiser*, 4 July 1797. 3); "Peter Thorin, respectfully informs his friends and the public in general, that he has fitted up New Vauxhall Garden, no. 5 Pearl Street, near the Battery, in as elegant a manner as the place would admit for the reception of ladies and gentlemen on the 4th July, when he will have a regular band of music and fire works to entertain the company. The music to commence precisely at 7 o'clock. Admittance as usual" (*Daily Advertiser*, 4 July 1797, 3).

1798

Publications

"Anthem for the Fourth of July." First line: "With songs of honor chanting high." (*Weekly Museum*, 30 June 1798, 2.)

"The following Patriotic Song, wrote by a citizen of Philadelphia, and sung at the Theatre with great applause, is intended to be sung on the 4th of July next, in this town [Elizabethtown, NJ], accompanied with instrumental music. Tune — The President's March." First line: "Hail Columbia! happy land" (*New-Jersey Journal*, 3 July 1798, 4).

"To-Morrow will be published, and for sale at

S. Sower's printing-office, no. 67, Market-street, at his book-store in Fayette-street, and at Thomas, Andrews and Butler's book-store (Price, eleven-pence) *The Patriotic Songster*, for July 4th, 1798. (Addressed to the Volunteers of Baltimore.) Containing all the later Patriotic Songs that have been published. Also, a Song for the 4th of July, tune 'Hail Columbia,' and many others that have never before appeared in print. June 29" (*Federal Gazette & Baltimore Daily Advertiser*, 3 July 1798, 1).

"Columbia, Columbia, to Glory Arise," in *American Musical Miscellany: a Collection of the Newest and Most Approved Songs Set to Music*, by Andrew Wright.[84] Northampton, Mass, 1798; reprint, Da Capo, 1972.

"The Farmer's Patriotic Ode. By P. Pencil. Tune — Vicar of Bray." First line: "From th' soil our fathers dearly bo't." At end of poem: "N.W. corner of Mess. Colon & Spendee's shop, July 4, '98. [Walpole, NH?]" ("Native Poetry," *Farmer's Weekly Museum*, 31 July 1798, 4).

"The Genius of Columbia. A Song." First line: "Awake from delusion, ye sons of the brave" ("The Fount," *Columbian Centinel*, 4 July 1798, 4).

"An Ode for the Fourth of July"[85]: first line, "Come all ye sons of song"; "an Ode for the Fourth of July. By Daniel George — set to music by Horatio Garnet": first line, "'Tis done! the edict past." (*American Musical Miscellany* (1798), 130–32 and 142–47, respectively.)

"An Ode, for the Celebration of Independence." First line: "Columbian voices tune the lay." Broadside. [Sag Harbor, NY: Printed by David Frothingham, 1798.] Copy in the American Antiquarian Society.

"Ode for the 4th of July, 1798."[86] *A Collection of Songs selected from the Works of Mr. Dibdin to which are added, the newest and most favourite American patriotic songs*. Philadelphia: J. Bioren for H & P Rice, 1799, 323–25. First line: "There's Ichabod has come to town."

"An Ode or Song, for the Fourth of July, 1798. To the tune of 'God Save the King.'" First line: "Columbian Patriots! rise! (*A Poem, on the Fourth of July, 1798. Being the Anniversary of the Independence of the United States of America*. By John Miller Russell, A.M. Boston: Printed by Manning & Loring, 1798.)

"Ode sung at Mendham the Fourth of July." First line: "Columbia, Columbia, thy glory decays" ("Selected Poetry," *Carey's United States' Recorder*, 21 July 1798, 4).

"An Ode. Sung at the celebration of the Fourth of July, in this town [Newark, NJ]. To the tune of— 'Unity.'" First line: "Hail, ever-memorable day!" (*The Centinel of Freedom*, 10 July 1798, 4).

"Ode to Liberty." First line: "Hail, liberty! thou goddess bright." Signed "Sylvia" (*Weekly Museum*, 30 June 1798, 2).

"A Patriotic Song, for July Fourth, 1798. Tune — 'Dauphine.' Written by Mr. Dunham, of Hanover, N.H. and sung there in the last anniversary." First line: "Hail independence, hail." Also, "A Parody, of the 'Marseilles Hymn,' as sung at the late celebration at Hanover." First line: "Ye Sons of Freedom, wake to glory!"[87] (*Oration, for the Fourth of July, 1798; Delivered in the Meeting-House, in the Vicinity of Dartmouth College, at Hanover, in New Hampshire... By Josiah Dunham*. 2nd ed. Hanover: Benjamin True, [1798], 14–15; "Independence," *Massachusetts Mercury*, 10 July 1798, 2; *Courier of New Hampshire*, 17 July 1798, 4; *Connecticut Gazette*, 18 July 1798, 4; *Green Mountain Patriot*, 20 July 1798, 4; *Massachusetts Spy*, 1 August 1798, 4; *The Companion and Commercial Centinel*, 4 August 1798.)

The Patriotic Songster for July 4th, 1798. (Addressed to the volunteers of Baltimore.) Containing all the late patriotic songs that have been published.[88] Baltimore: printed and sold at S. Sower's printing office, no. 67, Market Street, at his book-store in Fayette Street, and at Thomas, Andrews and Butler's bookstore, 1798.

"A Song for the Fourth of July." First line: "Freedom, blest offspring of the skies." (*Western Star*, 3 July 1798, 4.)

"Song for the Fourth of July." Tune — "The Mason's Daughter." First line: "Come hail the day, ye sons of mirth" (*Massachusetts Spy: or, the Worcester Gazette*, 11 July 1798, 3).

"Song, sung at a public dinner, in the City of Richmond, on the Fourth of July." First line: "Hail Patriots all! This day combine"[89] ("Pegasus of Apollo," *Massachusetts Spy, or, the Worcester Gazette*, 8 August 1798, 4; *The Companion, and Commercial Centinel*, 11 August 1798, 3; *Courier*, 18 October 1798, 6).

"A Song sung [on] the 4th of July. To the tune, "There's no luck about the house." First line: "Hail Independence, happy morn" (*New-Hampshire Gazette*, 31 July 1798, 4).

"Song. Tune — 'God Save Great Washington.'" First line: "Columbians all unite" (*Alexandria Advertiser*, 4 July 1798, 2).

Performances

Connecticut

Brooklyn: A procession from Capt. Murdock's Inn to the meeting house was "accompanied with music." The exercises were "interspersed with three pieces of vocal and instrumental music" (*Windham Herald*, 19 July 1798, 3).

Norwich: A parade to the meeting house included "a band of music." The exercises included a prayer and oration. "The ceremony [was] interspersed with two pieces of vocal music" (*The Courier*, 5 July 1798, 3).

Maine

Freeport: "The artillery company in uniform paraded; an oration was pronounced by the Rev. Mr. Johnson, and after dinner the usual number of Federal toasts were given, with firings, cheers, and patriotic songs," including a "Song. Composed and sung by Mr. Burrill." First line: "Guardians of our nation, stand firm in your station" (*Gazette* [Portland], 9 July 1798, 2).

Wiscasset: At a "sumptuous entertainment given by Gen. Abiel Wood ... several patriotic songs were sung, among which 'Adams and Liberty' was not forgotten, but echoed responsively from every heart that glowed with the radiating fire of federalism" ("From Wiscasset," *The Gazette*, 16 July 1798, 2).

Massachusetts

Boston: At the exercises "Thomas Edwards, Esq. then announced the orator of the day, and informed the audience that, in addition to the usual exhibition of the anniversary, Mr. Paine's[90] two patriotic Songs, of 'Rise Columbia,'[91] and 'Adams and Liberty,'[92] would be performed by a select choir — This annunciation was received with the greatest applause — The Oration by Josiah Quincy, Esq. followed." According to the *Massachusetts Mercury*, Mr. Rea[93] sang "Rise Columbia." "At three o'clock, the officers of the Boston Regiment, in complete uniform ... marched to Julien's Hotel, accompanied with a band of music (*Russell's Gazette*, 5 July 1798, 3; "American Independence," *Massachusetts Mercury*, 6 July 1798, 2; see also, *Massachusetts Mercury*, 3 July 1798, 2).

Newburyport: Procession "formed in State-street, with a respectable band of music at their head, under Mr. S. Holyoke"[94] (*Salem Gazette*, 10 July 1798, 3).

Salem: At the town's celebration, "Hail Columbia, and many other Patriotic Songs were sung, among which was the following, composed on that day, for the occasion, by Mr. Honeywood." First line: "Veterans brave, in battle tried!" (*Northern Centinel*, 9 July 1798, 3).

Worcester:

At 11 o'clock, a number of Gentlemen, from various parts of the County, all wearing the national cockade, and among them a number of the Clergy, assembled at Masons' Hall; there formed a procession, and walked to the South Meeting House, headed by the High Sheriff of the County, and escorted by the Worcester Company of Artillery. Music, on various instruments, performed by a number of young Gentlemen, saluted the Procession as it entered the Church. A Prayer well adapted to the occasion, was addressed to the throne of Grace, by the Rev. Mr. Sumner, of Shrewsbury. Music again resounded. The Rev. Mr. Austin, of this town, delivered, with an animated eloquence, suited to the day, a sensible, interesting and patriotic Oration, Which was received with the warm plaudits of a gratified audience. The celebrated song, 'Adams and Liberty' — uninfluenced by any, and dictated to by none.

At the dinner that followed at another hall the song "Adams and Liberty" was sung after a toast to John Adams and again after a toast to the President. Also sung was a "New Song, to the tune 'Yankee Doodle.'" (First line: "Sing Yankee Doodle, that fine tune"

("Worcester, July 11" and "Pegasus of Apollo," *Massachusetts Spy*, 11 and 18 July 1798, 3 and 4, respectively).

New Hampshire

Portsmouth: After a military parade, soldiers and others gathered at Capt. Whidden's Assembly Room where they "partook of as elegant an entertainment as could be provided." Toasts were drank "and many capital songs sung. And among the most celebrated performances of the day, we record with pleasure the following classical effusion from the harmonious pen of a gentleman of Portsmouth [likely Jonathan Mitchell Sewall], which may justly be denominated the Portsmouth Federal Song; and claims literary kindred with the animated pencilings of the Boston Bard [likely Paine]": "The Song. Tune — 'God Save the King.'" First line: "All hail auspicious day" ("Celebration of Independence at Portsmouth, and the Vicinity," *Oracle of the Day*, 7 July 1798, 3).

Walpole: At the meeting house, "a sacred ode preceded an appropriate, forcible and happily conceived prayer, by the Rev. Mr. Fessenden, succeeded by the 'Adams and Liberty' of Mr. Paine, sung agreeably, and with interest, by a sprightly choir" (*Farmer's Weekly Museum: New Hampshire and Vermont Journal*, 10 July 1798, 3).

New Jersey

Newark: After a procession by town citizens from the Episcopal Church to the Presbyterian Church, exercises were held and "in the interval" of two orations, "several tunes were sung, suitable to the occasion" ("Anniversary Celebration," *Centinel of Freedom*, 10 July 1798, 2).

Princeton: In the Princeton College Hall, exercises were held in which "a band of the students, with different instruments, introduced the orations by playing the President's March.[95] In the orchestra, in which they were placed, was inscribed in large characters 'let independence be our boast.' The orations were concluded by some piece of musick, and the ladies and gentlemen below joining with their voices, the whole produced a very fine and animating effect." Later, dinner was provided for 40 men at Mr. Ferguson's. As toasts were presented, "in the intervals several patriotic songs were sung by the gentlemen" (*Gazette of the United States*, 11 July 1798, 2).

New York

Kinderhook: "The day was ushered in by a federal salute and a display of the national standard from the cupola of the academy. At 10 o'clock A.M., divine service was performed in the church." After a discourse by the Rev. Isaac Labagh, "the celebrated ode 'The American Hero,' was sung to the tune of 'Bunker-Hill,' by a select choir in the gallery" ("Celebration of the Fourth of July at Kinderhook," *Albany Centinel*, 10 July 1798, 3).

New York: "The several Societies having assembled

on the Battery, proceeded from thence through Beaver, Broad, Pearl and Beckman streets to the Brick Church in the following order:

Citizens,
Tammany Society.
Coopers Society
Band of Music
Democratic Society.
General Society of Mechanics and Tradesmen —
   and a number of civil and military officers.

Mr. M.L. Davis then read the Declaration of Independence, and Mr. George Clinton, Jun. delivered an Oration, which abounded with many noble and patriotic sentiments, and was received with unbounded applause. An elegant Ode, written for the occasion by Margaretta V. Faugeres, was then sung by a select company" (First line: "Welcome morn, whose genial ray.") ("Fourth of July: New-York Celebration," *Weekly Museum*, 7 July 1798, 3, and 14 July 1798; *An Oration, Delivered on the Fourth of July, 1798, before the General Society of Mechanics and Tradesmen, the Democratic Society, the Tammany Society or Columbia Order, the New York Cooper's Society, and a Numerous Concourse of Other Citizens. By Geo. Clinton, Jun. New York: Printed by M. L. & W.A. Davis, 1798*); "Columbia Garden, Grand Concert, and Transparent Paintings, on the Fourth of July. The Band conducted by Mr. Henri:

Part I.
Song, Adams and Liberty, Mr. Hodgkinson
Song, As Sure as a Gun, Miss H. Westray
Song, The Bird When Summers Charm No More,
   Mrs. Hodgkinson
Song, Mr. Tyler
Song, Jane of Aberdeen, Miss Brett
Duo, Time has not thinn'd my flowing hair, Mr.
   and Mrs. Hodgkinson
Part II.
Song, Mr. Tyler
Song, The Silver Moon, Miss E. Westray
Song, Tantivy, Miss Brett
Song, Jen e vois entend pas, monsieur, Mr.
   Hodgkinson
Ladies New Patriotic Song, Washington's March,
   Mrs. Hodgkinson[96]

("Fourth of July," *Daily Advertiser*, 4 July 1798, 3); "Ranelagh Garden, near the Battery, lately known by Vauxhall, this evening, Wednesday, July 4 a grand concert of vocal and instrumental music. B. Isherwood respectfully informs the ladies and gentlemen, that he has taken the adjoining lot for their accommodation, which will afford a pleasant, airy and extensive walk.

Ye Sons of Dull Sloth, Mrs. Seymour[97]
   Knowing Joe, or Plowman Turned Actor, Mr. Jefferson
   How Can I Forge the Fond Hour, Miss Broadhurst
   In Honour of the Day, the boron

Patriotic Song, Adams and Liberty, Mr.
   Williamson
Where is the Harm of That, Mrs. Seymour
Dickey Gossip, Mr. Jefferson
Duett Hey Dane: to the Fiddle and Tabor, Mrs.
   Seymour and Mr. Jefferson
Bonny Charley, Miss Broadhurst
The New-York Federal Song, Washington and the
   Constitution, Mr. Williamson
The Little Farthing Rush-Light, Mr. Jefferson
And, Hail Columbia, Mr. Williamson

"The Garden will be brilliantly with variegated coloured lamps. The concert to begin at 8 o'clock. Tickers 4s. to entitle each the bearer to a glass of ice cream, punch, lemonade, &c. (*Daily Advertiser*, 4 July 1798, 3).[98]

Pennsylvania

Easton: Several hundred citizens and militia assembled in the church for the exercises. "A German translation of 'Hail Columbia' was sung accompanied by the organ." After a reading of the Declaration of Independence, performed were "vocal and instrumental music by a band from Bethlehem and Nazareth." Additional music was performed after an oration in German. Another oration was presented, this one in English, after which was sung "'Hail Columbia' in English accompanied by the band" (*Gazette of the United States*, 11 July 1798, 2).

Philadelphia: At a celebration of the Philadelphia Volunteer Company of grenadiers, "the following song, composed and sung by a member of the corps, was received with loud applause." First line: "Come all grenadiers let us join hand in hand" (*Daily Advertiser*, 9 July 1798, 2).

Rhode Island

Newport: "The Artillery Company partook of a splendid entertainment in the State House, after which the following toasts were drank, accompanied with Patriotic Songs, Martial Music, &c" (*Companion, and Commercial Centinel*, 7 July 1798, 3).

Vermont

Brandon: The exercises were held on the common near the meeting house. The following piece was sung: "Let the poets of Europe write odes on their kings" (first line) ("Communication," *Rutland Herald*, 23 July 1798, 3).

Rutland: An "ode, composed and set to music for the occasion by Mr. Fessenden,[99] was inimitably performed by a numerous and brilliant choir of singers, under the tuition of Mr. Thom. H. Atwell."[100] The *Massachusetts Mercury* and *Newburyport Herald* titled this ode "The Stockbridge Federal Ode." First line: "Ye sons of Columbia, unite in the cause" (*Rutland Herald*, 9 July 1798, 2; *Massachusetts Mercury*, 3 August 1798, 4; *Newburyport Herald*, 7 August 1798, 224; *Federal Gazette and Baltimore Daily Advertiser*, 13 August 1798, 2; *Alexandria Advertiser*, 17 August 1798,

2; *Maryland Herald and Elizabeth-Town Advertiser*, 23 August 1798, 4; *Green Mountain Patriot*, 24 August 1798, 4; *Farmer's Weekly Museum*, 27 August 1798, 4). See also **Publications** above.

1799

Publications

"Convivial Song. Sung at Windsor (Vermont) on the Fourth of July. Composed for the occasion by Royal Tyler, Esq.[101] Tune 'Here's to Our Noble Selves, Boys.'" First line: "Come fill each brimming glass, boys" (Broadside, Windsor, VT: Printed by Alden Spooner, 1799; *Spooners Vermont Journal*, 16 July 1799, 3; *Windham Herald*, 15 August 1799, 4; *The Federal Songster Being a Collection of the Most Celebrated Patriotic Songs, Hitherto Published, with a Variety of Others, Sentimental and Convivial* (New-London: James Springer, 1800).

"For the Fourth of July. Tune — 'President's March.'" First line: "Arise ye bards and tune the lyre" (*Centinel of Freedom*, 2 July 1799, 4).

"Fourth of July — an Ode." By Philip Morin. First line: 'Tis past-another anniversive day." Philadelphia: Printed for the author. From the press of D. Hogan — and sold at his store, no. 222 South Third-Street, and at the office of the *Aurora*, December 30, 1799; *Centinel of Freedom*, 16 July 1799, 4.

"'The Genius of Columbia: An Ode' for the Fourth of July, 1799.[102] Written by the honorable Timothy Todd."[103] First line: "As down a dark valley with shadows surrounded." (*Oration, Delivered at Rutland, in the State of Vermont, on the Anniversary of American Independence, July 4th, 1799*. By Nathan Osgood, Esq. Rutland: S. Williams, 1799).

"A New Song." First line: "America, thou glorious nation" (*Centinel of Freedom*, 16 July 1799, 4).

"A new song, calculated to be sung the Fourth of July. Tune — 'Howe's Invitation.'" First line: "Hail, ye sons of freedom's cause" (*Centinel of Freedom*, 2 July 1799, 4).

"A New Song, for the Fourth of July. Tune 'Alknomack.'"[104] First line: "Let Columbia enraptur'd rejoice on the day" ("Poets Corner," *Herald of Liberty*, 1 July 1799, 4).

"Ode for Independence." First line: "Shades of heroes, chiefs and sages" (*City Gazette and Daily Advertiser*, 4 July 1799, 2).

"Ode for the Fourth of July, 1799. The anniversary of American independence." First line: "Long sunk beneath disgraceful chains." Signed "G.T." ("Miscellany," *Connecticut Gazette*, 10 July 1799, 4).

"Song composed for and sung on the 4th July, 1799. Tune — 'Rural Felicity.'" First line: "Hail freedom's birth-day, hail, thou fam'd Fourth of July" ("Miscellany," *Connecticut Gazette*, 24 July 1799, 4).

"An Ode, composed for the occasion, at the Re-

quest of the Society. By Dr. William Pitt Smith... Set to music by Mr. Van Hagen."[105] First line: "Now elevate your hymns of joy." *The Blessings of America. A Sermon Preached in the Middle Dutch Church, on the Fourth July, 1791, being the Anniversary of the Independence of America: At the Request of the Tammany Society, or Columbian Order*. By William Linn, D.D. (New York: Printed by Thomas Greenleaf, 1791), 37–39.

"Song for the Celebration of the 4th July, 1799.[106] (By J.M. Sewall, Esq. of Portsmouth.) Tune — 'In a mouldering Cave — or the Gods of the Greeks.'" First line: "Late Jove and blue Neptune in conference met"; another song by Sewall, to the tune "President's March": first line, "Heav'n and the fates this day decreed" (*Oracle of the Day*, 6 July 1799, 3; *New Hampshire-Gazette*, 9 July 1799, 3; "The Blossoms of Parnassus," *Massachusetts Spy, or Worcester Gazette*, 24 July 1799, 4).

"To Arms Columbia. A new patriotic Song.[107] Written by Thos. Paine & sung with great applause by Mr. Barrett at the Theatre on the 4th of July, 1799." New York: Printed & Sold at J. Hewitts Musical Repository, no. 23 Maiden Lane. Sold also by B. Carr, Philadelphia & J. Carr, Galtimore. In *A Collection of New & Favorite Songs* (Philadelphia, ca. 1800), 176–77.

"Walpole Ode: written by Mr. Alexander Thomas,[108] and sung at the late celebration of American independence. Tune — 'President's March,'" First line: Fa'rite land of freedom, hail!" (*New Hampshire Sentinel*, 13 July 1799, 4; *The Federal Songster Being a Collection of the Most Celebrated Patriotic Songs, Hitherto Published, with a Variety of Others, Sentimental and Convivial* [New-London: James Springer, 1800]).

"Westminster Ode, for the 4th of July 1799. To the tune of — 'Come now all ye social powers.'" First line: "Join to hail this festive morn" (*Farmers' Museum, or Lay Preacher's Gazette*, 22 July 1799, 4).

"Windsor Ode, composed by R. Tyler, and sung at the Celebration of the 4th of July." First line: "The blushing east displays the dawn" ("Parnassian Rivulet," *Green Mountain Patriot*, 15 August 1799, 4; "Poets' Corner," *Vergennes Gazette and Vermont and New-York Advertiser*, 22 August 1799, 4).

Performances

Connecticut

Hartford: After a procession of city officials, the governor, military and citizens, from the State House to the North Meeting House, "the exercises at the church were introduced by an Anthem, performed by the choir of the society, led by Mr. Benjamin, and accompanied by several instruments. To this succeeded a pertinent, elegant, and fervent Address to the Deity, by the Rev. Mr. Flint, an Anthem, an Oration, by William Brown, Esq. and a Hymn composed for the occasion. It would be doing feeble justice to the performances, to say that they were executed in a highly satisfactory manner" (*Claypoole's American Daily Ad-*

vertiser, 15 July 1799, 2; *Litchfield Monitor*, 17 July 1799, 1).

Lebanon: A town procession was "led by a group of singers, a band of instrumental music, and four military companies." The exercises "were closed by the patriotic song of Adams and Liberty" (*Norwich Packet*, 18 July 1799, 3).

Litchfield: In the morning, "Ranney's company of Regular Troops, Capt. Phelps's Light Infantry, and the uniformed companies of Captains Goodwin and Kilbeurn paraded, with a double complement of music and a band." After a parade to the meeting house, "the solemnities were opened by Church music" (*American Mercury*, 11 July 1799, 3).

Warren: A procession "preceded by the militia and music" moved to the meeting house where the exercises included "music (an Ode for the 4th of July)." An oration was "succeeded by music (Dr. Dwight's celebrated Columbia)" (*Litchfield Monitor*, 17 July 1799, 1).

Maine

Kennebunk: A procession to the meeting house included a band of music (*Jenks's Portland Gazette*, 8 July 1799, 2).

Portland: After exercises at the meeting house, the assemblage marched to the "New Assembly Hall" where dinner and toasts were accompanied by "several patriotic songs [that] were sung with spirit, and received with applause" (*Jenks's Portland Gazette*, 8 July 1799, 2).

Maryland

Baltimore: Four militia regiments paraded and each was read the Declaration of Independence followed by the performance of "The President's March" and "Yankee Doodle" played by two bands (*Daily Advertiser*, 10 July 1799, 2).

Massachusetts

Belchertown: At the meeting house, an anthem was sung "by the lovers of musick"(*Political Repository*, 16 July 1799, 3).

Boston: At the Old Brick Meeting House, after a prayer, "'Rise Columbia,' an Ode, [was] sung by Mr. Rea. The whole audience joined in the thrilling chorus: 'Rise Columbia, brave and free/Poise the glove, and bound the sea!'" "Adams and Liberty" was also sung ("National Puberty," *Political Repository*, 23 July 1799, 3).

Lancaster: Some eighty male citizens and "two companies of militia" celebrated with a dinner and toasts "accompanied with repeated huzza's, patriotic songs, instrumental music" ("Celebration at Lancaster," *Massachusetts Spy*, 17 July 1799, 2).

Petersham: The "inhabitants of this town ... proceeded from Mr. Ripley's Inn, with music to the Meeting House, where the solemnities of the day commenced with music.... Several select pieces of music were performed, vocal and instrumental" during the exercises ("Celebration at Petersham," *Massachusetts Spy*, 17 July 1799, 2).

Worcester: After a procession from Major Mower's Hall to the South Meeting House, "a select Band performed a number of appropriate pieces of Music." Back at the Hall, a "handsome entertainment" was provided including toasts "under the discharge of cannon" and the following pieces of music: Song — 'American Independence,' by Mr. William Charles White[109] — tune, Adams & Liberty. First line: "Let patriot ardor distinguish the day." This work was sung both at Worcester and Rutland, Vermont ("American Independence," *Massachusetts Spy; or, The Worcester Gazette*, 10 July 1799, 2, 4). See also, Rutland, Vermont, below.

New Hampshire

Alstead: The exercises included an oration by Samuel Mead, "after which, 'To thine Almighty arm we owe, the triumphs of the day,' &c was chaunted by a brilliant choir of ladies and gentlemen, succeeded by a flourish of martial music" (*Farmer's Weekly Museum*, 15 July 1799, 3).

Claremont: A parade of militia and residents was "preceded by Martial music" and marched to the meeting house. At the end of the exercises, "a tuneful choir chaunted, with spirit, the fashionable 'Adams and Liberty'" (*Farmers' Museum*, 22 July 1799, 3).

Hopkinton: A parade that began at the "town house" included the Musical Society and "a select corps of Light Infantry, preceded by martial music." The exercises took place at the meeting house where the attendees "were highly entertained by a well chosen piece of music" (*Courier of New Hampshire*, 6 July 1799, 3).

Keene: A procession of "Federal citizens" and the Company of Infantry from the "Meeting House common" marched through city streets back to the meeting house, where the services included prayer and oration was presented. "When the orator had closed, several pieces of music were performed by the Society in this town and the Federal songs of 'Hail Columbia' and 'Adams & Liberty,' sung with spirit and effect. The assembly then retired from the meeting house, and having dined, at three o'clock, P.M. assembled on the common, and in concert with the companies, of militia, drank the following toasts, with military and musical honors" ("Fourth of July, *New-Hampshire Sentinel*, 6 July 1799, 3).

Meredith: At the meeting house, "the attention of a large assembly was given to a federal song, by Simon F. Williams, and Richard Boynton, Jr.— a short comedy was then acted by the same — after which an Oration was delivered by Simon F. Williams, and the exhibition closed by singing the noted and celebrated song called 'Lady Washington'"[110] ("The Ever Memorable 4th of July," *New Hampshire Gazette*, 16 July 1799, 3).

Portsmouth: The Light Infantry Company and citizens assembled at Capt. Whidden's Assembly Room for dinner, toasts and music. "Among the songs that received the best applauses, was a most excellent and spirited performance inserted in the *Oracle* of the 22d ult ["Song for the 4th of July, 1799. To the tune of the 'Vicar of Bray.'" First line: "While Holland gag'd and fetter'd sprawls!"].[111] The author (a gentleman in one of our country towns) is requested to receive the thanks of the company for the pleasure which he has thus afforded them. Two original compositions by J.M. Sewall,[112] Esq. were received with high plaudits. And Paine's Adams & Liberty echoed through the vaulted dome" ("Poetical Repository" and "Independence!" *Oracle of the Day*, 22 June and 6 July, 1799, 3 and 3, respectively; *Claypoole's American Daily Advertiser*, 18 July 1799, 3). See **Publications** above.

Rochester: At the meeting house, included in the exercises were "two Odes also, by the same hand in which the poet and the patriot seemed equal competitors for the muse, were set to music and performed by the singing band to the most lively satisfaction of the assembly." The dinner included the singing of "a variety of humorous, American, Anti-Gallican songs illustrated with some ingenious drawings by a citizen of this town" (*New Hampshire Gazette*, 16 July 1799, 3).

Walpole: "A procession composed of soldiers and citizens, and cheered by an excellent band of music, proceeded at 11, to the Meeting House.... At intervals several favorite marches were played, and the 'pleasing sorcery' of music produced all its enchantment on the mind. An Ode, composed by 'certain of our own poets,' was performed to the popular tune of 'Hail Columbia,' to which was added, 'When first the sun o'er ocean glow'd,"[113] a well known production of Mr. [R.] T. Paine.... In the evening, a large and brilliant party danced away the merry hours at the inn of Mr. S. Grant" ("Fourth of July," *Farmers' Museum or Lay Preacher's Gazette*, 8 July 1799, 3; *Claypoole's American Daily Advertiser*, 17 July 1799, 3; *Maryland Herald and Elizabeth-Town Advertiser*, 25 July 1799, 2; "Fourth of July," *Columbian Museum and Savannah Advertiser*, 6 August 1799, 2). See **Publications** above.

New Jersey

Mendham: "The morning was introduced by discharging of cannon, beating of drum, sounding of trumpet, ringing of the bell, and displaying the American flag." Five hundred individuals marched to the sound of martial and vocal music from Mr. M'Carter's to the church. The exercises consisted of

1. Prayer by the Rev. Mr. Armstrong.
2. Psalm sung — Tune, "Montgomery."[114]
3. Declaration of Independence read by Mr. Henry Axtell, jun.
4. An Ode sung — Tune, "Joy Inspiring Born."
5. An Oration, delivered to a very attentive audience, by Mr. Noah Crane.
6. An Ode sung — Tune, "Anacreon."[115]
7. Select passages of the United States' Constitution, read by Mr. Henry Axtell, jun.

8. An Ode sung — Tune, "Columbia."
["Fourth of July," *Centinel of Freedom*, 16 July 1799, 2].

Newark: The ceremonies in the Presbyterian Church included the performance of one anthem, one hymn, and two odes ("Fourth of July," *Centinel of Freedom*, 2 July 1799, 3).

Trenton: Nearly 100 ladies "with an equal number of gentlemen" hosted a tea party at the State House. "After tea, dancing commenced, which concluded with the song 'Hail Columbia' by the ladies" (*Claypoole's American Daily Advertiser*, 13 July 1799, 2).

New York

New York: A procession of "Uniformed Military Corps" from the Battery to St. Paul's Church included a band of music, third in line. At the Garden of Joseph Delacroix, the sixteen summer house were decorated and the sixteen colors of each was carried to the sound of music to the Grand Temple of Independence (*New-York Gazette and General Advertiser*, 5 July 1799, 2); "Columbia Garden. Grand concert of vocal and instrumental music, and transparent paintings." The order of the concert will be expressed in the bills of the day" ("Fourth of July," *Daily Advertiser*, 4 July 1799, 3); a "splendid, allegorical musical drama," The *Fourth of July or, Temple of American Independence*, with music by Pelesier[116] at the Park Theatre (*Daily Advertiser*, 4 July 1799, 3; *New-York Gazette and General Advertiser*, 5 July 1799, 2).

Northampton: "The following toasts were drank at Northampton the 4th of July": Song, Adam and Liberty — A Plaintive Song — A Song — A Song (*Spectator*, 17 July 1799, 3).

Pennsylvania

Philadelphia: At the Centre House Tavern, proprietor John Mearns presented a Fourth of July "full concert ... presented to the public gratis." Mearns had recently acquired a "grand organ of the first power and tone" ("Elegant Organ," *Claypoole's American Daily Advertiser*, 3 July 1799, 2).

Rhode Island

Providence: A company of comedians presented a play at the theater titled *Isabella or the Fatal Marriage*, followed "by a collection of patriotic songs" (*Newport Mercury*, 9 July 1799, 2).

South Carolina

Charleston: "Ode. The following ode, by Mr. Heresford, for the Fourth of July, 1799, being the twenty-third anniversary of the sovereignty and independence of the United States of America, was performed in St. Michael's Church, Charleston, before the Cincinnati and Revolution Societies." First line: "Lo! the cloud of battle scowls." Also, "Ode on the anniversary of American Independence. This ode was written for last Thursday's Gazette, but did not come to hand in time." First line: "Hail, thou ever grateful day!" Signed "Agricola." (*City Gazette and Daily Advertiser*, 8 July 1799, 3); "Toasts, of the 2d troop, 1st squadron, 8th regiment of cavalry, annexed to the 7th brigade South Carolina militia, on the Fourth of July" included various trumpet calls and music (*City Gazette and Daily Advertiser*, 9 July 1799, 3).

Vermont

Rutland: A parade from Kelley's Tavern to the meeting house was "accompanied with martial music. The pleasing solemnities of the day were introduced by the very pertinent and patriotic song of 'Hail Columbia.'" Following a prayer and oration, "the exercises were closed by an agreeable union of vocal and instrumental music, in a new patriotic, and highly poetical Ode, written by Mr. [William Charles?] White of Worcester." Later a dinner included toasts "announced by a discharge of cannon and a flourish of martial music" including these pieces: Song, Hail Columbia (sung following toasts 1 and 2)— Song, Adams & Liberty — Song, Hail Godlike Washington — Song, The Farmer's Patriot Ode — Song, The Farmer — Song, Queen Bess — Hunting Song (*Massachusetts Spy, or Worcester Gazette*, 10 July 1799, 3).

Westminster: A parade was led "by a band of martial music." At the meeting house a reading of the Declaration of Independence, "was followed by a piece of solemn music which prepared their minds for a fervent, solemn, and patriotic prayer." After an oration there "was chaunted, by a select choir, an Ode, composed for the day, to the tune of 'Come Now All Ye Social Powers,' the chorus of which was joined and aided by the harmonious voices of the village fair; to which succeeded Mr. Hopkinson's 'Hail Columbia'" (Celebration of Independence," *Farmer's Weekly Museum*, 15 July 1799, 3).

Windsor: See **Publications** above.

1800

"The day has been celebrated with lively ardour in every part of the country from which we have heard. Its importance in the annals of the world has been fully felt. May it ever continue to be realized in the hearts of Americans!"[117] The highlight of this year is the first Fourth of July performance by the United States Marine Band ("The President's Own") in Philadelphia. This band is the oldest professional musical organization in the country and has served every president since John Adams. It was established by Act of Congress on July 11, 1798.

Publications

"Columbia Relieved." First line: To a mouldering cave, the mansion of woe" ("Court of Apollo," *Constitutional Telegraph*, 3 September 1800).

"Fourth of July, or an Ode to Independence. By Thomas Pike Lathy, author of 'Reparation,' 'New-England Captive,' &c. in the press and will be ready in a few days. The author trusts, that no American patriot will think his possession of such a pamphlet dear at 9d. To be had at all the printing offices and bookstores. June 21, 1800." Boston. (*Columbian Centinel*, 28 June 1800, 4.)

"Freeman's Holiday. Tune — 'Nature's Holiday'" First line: "Well met ye sons of liberty" (*Kline's Carlisle Weekly Gazette*, 9 July 1800, 2).

"Independence — For the 4th of July." First line: "For ages on ages by tyranny bound." Printed in *The Nightingale; or Rural Songster* (Dedham [MA]: Printed by H. Mann, 1800).

"A New Song. For the Fourth of July. Tune — 'Rule Brittannia.'" First line: "When God from his celestial throne" (*The Federal Songster Being a Collection of the Most Celebrated Patriotic Songs, Hitherto Published, with a Variety of Others, Sentimental and Convivial* (New-London: James Springer, 1800).

"An Ode composed for the celebration of American independence." First line: "Lo! from her star throne, plum'd with rays supernal" (*Russell's Gazette*, 31 July 1800, 4; *Newburyport Herald*, 5 August 1800, 4).

"Ode for Independence." First line: "Behold! the glorious day appears!" (*Courier*, 9 July 1800, 3).

"Ode for the Fourth of July, 1800. By Samuel Low. Sung after the delivery of the preceding Oration" (*Oration, Delivered in St. Paul's Church on the Fourth of July, 1800; Being the Twenty-Fourth Anniversary of Our Independence, before the General Society of Mechanics & Tradesmen, Tammany Society or Columbian Order, and Other Associations and Citizens.* By M[atthew] L[ivingston] Davis, of the General Society of Mechanics & Tradesmen. New York: Printed by W.A. Davis, Greenwich-Street, 1800); "Ode for the 4th of July, 1800. Composed by Mr. Low." First line: "Again the signal day." Broadside, New York: W.A. Davis, Greenwich-Street, 1800. Listed in Heard, 182; printed in Samuel Low, *Poems* (New York: T. & J. Swords, 1800) II: 113.

"Ode for the Fourth of July 1800." First line: "Swift strike the lyre and sweep the sounding string" (*Baltimore Weekly Magazine*, 5 July 1800, 88).

"Union Forever! & the Birth-Day of Freedom!: or, the Fourth of July: a Patriotic Song Written as an Expression of Respect and Good Will for His Adopted Country." By William Goodwin. New Haven, CT: W. Goodwin [18 —].

Performances

Connecticut

New London: "The observance of the day commenced with the discharge of cannon at Fort Trumbull; at 12 o'clock, a federal salute was fired, when a procession consisting of three companies of militia, a band of music, the corporation of the city and civil authority of the town, the orator of the day, committee of arrangement, with a long train of private gentlemen, advanced from the parade to the meeting-house" (*Connecticut Gazette*, 9 July 1800, 3).

Norwich: At 11:30 A.M. a procession that had assembled at the hotel, marched, "preceded by martial music and the flag of the United States" to the Rev. Mr. King's Meeting House. The exercises were "interspersed with two pieces of vocal music" (*Courier*, 9 July 1800, 3).

Massachusetts

Boxford: A procession led by a "band of music." At the meeting house, "after the musicians had performed a short Ode, the solemnity was opened with prayer by the Rev. Peter Eaton, and an Oration, delivered by Samuel Holyoke, A.M. well adapted to the occasion.—After performing an Ode, composed and set to music by Mr. Holyoke, the procession formed and marched a small distance (the musicians playing the 'President's March')."[118] ("Celebration of the 4th of July, 1800," *Newburyport Herald*, 15 July 1800, 3).

Worcester: "At 12 o'clock a respectable procession was formed at Maj. Mower's Tavern, composed of the citizens of the town and vicinity under the escort of the company of Artillery commanded by Capt. Healey, which proceeded to the North Meetinghouse, where they were received with instrumental music." After the exercises, "the procession returned to the Hall of Major Mower, and dined." Music accompanied the toasts: Song—Dirge (*Massachusetts Spy, or Worcester Gazette*, 9 July 1800, 3).

New Hampshire

Marlborough: A parade of citizens, clergy, and military "preceded by martial music" to the meeting house where the exercises were introduced with music, followed by a prayer. "When our ears had again received the harmonious sounds of the united efforts of the voice and flute, in chanting a Federal Ode," an oration followed. "Mr. Paine's 'Rise Columbia' was then handsomely performed which concluded the ceremonies" ("From Marlborough," *New-Hampshire Sentinel*, 12 July 1800, 3).

New Jersey

Newark: The order of exercises at the Presbyterian Church:

Anthem.
Prayer.
Ode.
Declaration.
Hymn.
Oration.
Ode.
Prayer.
["Fourth of July," Centinel of Freedom, 2 July 1799, 3].

Woodbridge: "at 10 o'clock A.M. the republican citizens met at the house of Mr. John Manning; at 1, a song well adapted to the occasion was sung; at 2, agreeably to the order of the day, the Declaration of Independence was read by Col. Manning, and at half after 2, they sat down to a very elegant dinner prepared for the occasion" (*Centinel of Freedom*, 15 July 1800, 3).

New York

New York: A "one night only" presentation at the Theatre included a performance of *The Feast of Terpsichore, in the Temple of Independence*, consisting of music—recitation—song and dance" ("Theatre," *Commercial Advertiser*, 3 July 1800, 3).

Richmond County (Staten Island): A procession of military companies, "accompanied by a band of music, the clergy, civil officers of the County, the Farmers Society, distinguished by ears of wheat in their hats, citizens and strangers" and "100 lovely girls and boys" marched to "a plain near the Moravian Meeting House." After dinner toasts were drank and one offered to George Washington was accompanied by "drums muffled, beat the Presidents March. Soon after, Miss Journey, daughter of Mr. Wm. Journey, accompanied by several young Ladies, was introduced, and by particular request, sung the much admired song Hail Columbia, &c. After which she delivered, with peculiar grace and propriety, an Oration in Poetry, most happily adapted to the day, and calculated to inspire her audience with Patriotic enthusiasm, and the highest idea of her sentiments and talents" (*Commercial Advertiser*, 8 July 1800, 3).

Pennsylvania

Philadelphia: The U.S. Marine Band,[119] overseen by Col. Burrows, provided music for the Society of the Cincinnati celebration held at the City Tavern and is the first performance by this band on the Fourth of July. The "animating notes of martial music by the band" accompanied the toasts presented (*Aurora General Advertiser*, 7 July 1800, 2; *Universal Gazette*, 10 July 1800, 1); the Republican Greens met "at the middle Ferry, Schuylkill" and during the toasts "a volunteer song" with the "subject the tr[?] dhery of Arnold" was sung (*Universal Gazette*, 10 July 1800, 1).

Rhode Island

Warren: "The inhabitants of this town, inspired with the spirit of '76, assembled at the Spread Eagle Tavern, where they participated in a rich repast ... drank a federal round of toasts, and sung a number of patriotic songs, under the shadow of the American flag" (*Providence Journal, and Town and Country Advertiser*, 9 July 1800, 3).

South Carolina

Charleston: A gathering of the Society of the Cincinnati and the Revolution Society at St. Philip's Church heard "several elegant pieces of music performed on the organ" ("Fourth of July," *City Gazette and Daily Advertiser*, 7 July 1800, 3).

Virginia

Norfolk: At Borough Tavern, citizens and military officers gathered and heard "a variety of toasts and songs well suited to the occasion" (*New Hampshire Gazette*, 22 July 1800, 3).

1801

This year marks the first Fourth of July musical performance at the White House. This occasion quickly established a tradition that was to continue through several presidencies. In a letter Margaret Bayard Smith wrote in July 1801, regarding the Fourth of July in Washington and at the Executive Mansion, "the city was thronged with visitors from George Town, Alexandria and the surrounding country. They were national festivals, on which the doors of the Presidential mansion were thrown open for persons of all classes, where abundance of refreshments were provided for their entertainment." When the mayor of Washington approached Jefferson regarding celebrating the president's birthday "with proper respect," Smith wrote that Jefferson said, "'The only birthday I ever commemorate,' replied he, 'is that of our Independence, the Fourth of July.' During his administration it was in truth a gala-day in our city. The well uniformed and well appointed militia of the district, the Marine-Corps and often other military companies, paraded through the avenues and formed on the open space in front of the President's House, their gay appearance and martial musick, enlivening the scene, exhilarating the spirits of the throngs of people who poured in from the country and adjacent towns."[120]

Publications

"Columbia. Composed for the 4th of July. The words by a member of the Washington Literary Society. The music by Mr. U.K. Hill."[121] "First line: "Columbians raise your cheerful songs." For 4 voices. *The American Musical Magazine* (Northampton, 1801), 40–41.

"The following Song, was composed by a gentleman of Great Barrington, in Massachusetts, and sung on the Anniversary of Independence, July 4th. 'The Ship *Constitution*.' Tune, 'Bill Bobstay.'"[122] First line: "Up anchor-clear decks, boys, and each to his station" (*Courier*, 19 August 1801, 4).

The 4th of July. A Grand Military Sonata for the Piano Forte. Composed in Commemoration of that Gorious Day and Dedicated to Mdlle Sansay.[123] By James Hewitt. New York: J. Hewitt's Musical Repository, [1801].

"Lines intended to be sung on the ensuing anniversary: composed for the occasion — by a citizen of Orange." First line: "Freedom hail! fair child of Heaven!" ("Poetic Recess," *Centinel of Freedom*, 30 June 1801, 4).

"The Newport Republican Hymn, for July 4th, 1801." First line: "Hark! notes melodious fill the skies" (*Guardian of Liberty*, 11 July 1801, 4).

"Ode addressed to the Society of Cincinnati; sung at Trinity-Church, Newport, 4th July, 1801. Tune — 'God Save Great Washington!'" First line: "Hark! Freedom's silver horn" (*Newport Mercury*, 7 July 1801, 4; *Columbian Centinel*, 11 July 1801, 4).

"Ode for the Fourth of July. Tune, 'Rule Britannia.'" First line: "Shades of Columbia's patr'ot band" (*Columbian Courier*, 19 June 1801, 4).

"Ode, written on the Fourth of July." First line: "Muse of Freedom snatch thy lyre." ("Selected Poetry," *Constitutional Telegraphe*, 18 July 1801, 4.)

"The Rush Light. Sung at a meeting of Irish aliens on the 4th July." First line: "When Britain's tame degenerate sons" ("For the *American Citizen*," *American Citizen and General Advertiser*, 16 July 1801, 3).

"Song for the Fourth of July." First line: "While fierce Bellons rages wild" (*Weekly Museum*, 4 July 1801).

"A Song for the Fourth of July." First line: "Ye sons of sensibility" (*Political Repository*, 7 July 1801, 4).

"'Song for the Fourth of July.' From the *Wilmington Mirror*. Tune — 'Jefferson and Liberty.'"[124] "By Dr. Moses Younglove, of Lebanon Springs." First line: "Fair Independence wakes the song (*American Citizen and General Advertiser*, 1 July 1801, 2; *Constitutional Telegraphe*, 4 July 1801, 4; *Vermont Gazette*, 6 July 1801, 4; "Divertisement," *Bee*, 12 August 1801, 4).

Performances

Connecticut

Killingworth: Citizens celebrated on July 6 with a parade from the residence of Col. George Morgan to the meeting house "escorted by the artillery company under the command of Capt. Noah Lester, with a band of music." The exercises included vocal and instrumental music, with performances of "Jefferson and Liberty" and "Washington's March" (*The Bee*, 15 July 1801, 2).

Norwich: "The rising sun was saluted with the ringing of bells, and the music of the fife and drum" (*Courier*, 8 July 1801, 3).

Stafford: At Hyde's Inn, citizens celebrated the Fourth on August 13, in order to "provide for his own house" and "not being at leisure on the 4th of July." The song "Jefferson and Liberty" was sung at the event ("Better Late than Never," *American Mercury*, 27 August 1801, 3).

District of Columbia

A "Song" (first line: "Hail Columbia! happy land")[125] sung by "Capt. Tingey"[126] and "composed for the occasion by Mr. Law," after a toast to "The Day, and those who value it," at a dinner celebration for heads of departments, military officers, and foreign officials (*National Intelligencer*, 6 July 1801, 2; *Columbian Centinel*, 18 July 1801, 4; *Oracle of Dauphin and Harrisburgh Advertiser*, 27 July 1801, 4; *Norwich Courier*, 29 July 1801, 1; *New Hampshire Gazette*, 11 August 1801, 4); U.S. Marine Band[127] gave first performance at the Executive Mansion in Washington, D.C. for Thomas Jefferson and guests at a reception there. "The band of music played with great precision and with aspiring animation the Presidents March. ... The band at intervals during the morning, played martial and patriotic airs.... During the dinner, and until the company separated, a full band of music ... played patriotic and festive airs" (*National Intelligencer*, 6 July 1801, 2; *Poulson's American Daily Advertiser*, 10 July 1801, 2; *New-Hampshire Sentinel*, 25 July 1801, 2).

Maine

Gorham: "A number of gentlemen met at Mr. Staple's Tavern, and formed a procession to the Meeting-House where an oration was delivered by Mr. John P. Little, adapted to the occasion — the same being accompanied by vocal and instrumental music, consisting of an Ode on Independence, Adams and Liberty, &c." ("Celebration of Independence at Gorham," *Jenks' Portland Gazette*, 13 July 1801, 3).

Massachusetts

Dighton: At the meeting house, included among the exercises: "a choir of vocal and instrumental music, consisting of gentlemen and ladies belonging to the town and vicinity, added very much to the harmony of the day" ("At Dighton," *Independent Chronicle and the Universal Advertiser*, 6 July 1801, 1).

Marblehead: Billings' "Chester" was sung "in Billing's own verses" according to the Rev. William Bentley. "This was as appropriate as the Marseilles Hymn or the French Ca Ira," he wrote (*The Diary of William Bentley* ... 5 July 1801, II:378).[128]

New York

New York: The Mechanic, Cooper's and Tammany societies assembled on Broadway, marched to the Battery and then "through the principal streets in the city, to the brick meeting house, where the following Ode, composed by Mr. Low, was sung, accompanied with appropriate instrumental music." First line: "O'er the corn-cover'd fields, and each forest-crown'd height." One newspaper reported the location as the "New Brick Presbyterian Church" (*New-York Gazette*, 2 July 1801, 3; "Celebration," *American Citizen and General Advertiser*, 6 July 1801, 2; *Weekly Museum*, 18 July 1801); the Franklin Typographical Association met at the house of Philip Becanon where the exercises and an "elegant entertainment" included toasts "interspersed with convivial and patriotic songs" (*Gazette of the United States*, 9 July 1801, 2; *Salem Gazette*, 14 July 1801, 2); a set of toasts presented in New York with the following music was printed in a newspaper in Newburyport, MA: Yankee Doodle — Hail Columbia — The Death of the Mammoth — Paddy Whack — Britains Strike Home! — Jefferson's March —

Great A___Little A___ron [sic] — Rogue's March (*American Intelligencer and General Advertiser*, 16 July 1801, 3).

Pennsylvania

Philadelphia: Stoney Point[129] — America, Commerce and Freedom[130] — Ca-Ira — Carmagnole — Handel's Pastoral Symphony — Hymn to Peace — Jefferson's March[131] (played twice) — Marseilles Hymn — Ou Puet [sic] on etre Mieux, qu' au Sein de sa Famille[132] — The People's March[133] — Social Power — Soft Music by Mr. Carr — Washington's Solemn Dirge — Yankee Doodle,[134] performed by a "band of music" at Francis's Hotel with Governor Thomas McKean present (*National Intelligencer*, 10 July 1801, 4).

York: Reported in a Portsmouth, New Hampshire, newspaper: "The following appropriate toasts were given some time past in York, Pennsylvania, at a meeting of the Mechanic Society, and followed respectively by Yankee Doodle, Stony-Point, Washington's March, and other American tunes. In so interior a part of our country, 'Carmagnole, Marsailloise, Ca Ira, Go to the Devil, and Shake Yourself,' are not known. The mechanics of York, it seems, are not Frenchmen, but Americans, without French hotels, French cooks, French airs, or any thing a la Francoise" (*New Hampshire Gazette*, 21 July 1801, 3).

North Carolina

Hillsborough: "The morning was ushered in by the firing of cannon at day break. At 12 o'clock another salute being fired as a signal, the men of the town collected together at the market house, and thence walked in procession, accompanied with the drum and fife, round one of the squares to the court house, where a handsome oration suited to the day, was pronounced by Mr. A.D. Murphy, before a numerous audience of both sexes" (*City Gazette and Daily Advertiser*, 24 July 1801, 3).

French Guiana

Cayenne: In addition to federal salutes and flag raisings, there was a dinner for Americans at the Government House replete with toasts and music: air, Veillons au salut de l'empire — air La victoire ên chantant — Sol mi Music — Celebrons le hon ménage — Le Vengeur — Valeureun Francais-Lodoisha (*New-York Gazette and General Advertiser*, 11 August 1801, 3; *Constitutional Telegraphe*, 22 August 1801, 4; *Vermont Gazette*, 24 August 1801, 3).

1802

Publications

"The following song from the pen of Mitchell Sewall, Esq. of poetic fame, was lately sung at Portsmouth. Washington Hall. An Ode for the celebration of the 4th of July, 1802. Tune—Adams and Liberty." First line: "Ye vot'ries of freedom! dire anarchy's foes!" Several newspapers cite the author as Jonathan M. Sewall (*United States Oracle and Portsmouth Advertiser*, 10 July 1802, 3; *New-York Evening Post*, 13 July 1802, 2; *New-York Her*ald, 17 July 1802, 4; *Republican, or Anti-Democrat*, 19 July 1802, 4; *Newport Mercury*, 20 July 1802, 4; *New Hampshire Sentinel*, 24 July 1802, 4; *Edes' Kennebec Gazette*, 30 July 1802, 4).

"A national song in commemoration of American Independence. Tune—Rise Cynthia."[135] Signed "Americus." First line: "Rise Columbians Rise" ("Poetry," *Merrimack Intelligencer*, 2 July 1802, 4).

"New Jefferson and Liberty. Tune—'Anacreon in Heaven." First line: "Brave sons of Columbia! salute the blest day" (*American Mercury*, 5 August 1802, 4).

"A New Ode.[136] Sung by Mr. Eaton at the Celebration of the Anniversary of American Independence, Boston, July 4th 1802. Written for the occasion by Amyntas." [First line: "See the bright-hair'd golden sun lead Columbia's birthday on."] Printed with the consent of the Author by Mallet & Graupner, Conservatorio. [1802]. Copies in Harvard and Brown Universities. This ode was "sung at the Old-South Meeting House on Monday last" and is printed in "Native Poetry," *New-England Palladium*, 9 July 1802, 1; "National Birth-Day," *Independent Chronicle*, 12 July 1802, 2.

"An Ode for the Fourth of July, 1802, sung at Kennebunk [Maine]." First line: "In ages long past when Columbia's plains" (*United States Oracle and Portsmouth Advertiser*, 17 July 1802, 3; "The Muses' Apartment," *Kennebec Gazette*, 20 August 1802, 4).

Ode for the twenty-seventh anniversary of American independence, July 4th, 1802. Sung in Caldwell Church, New Jersey." First line: "We hail once more the annual morn" (*American Citizen and General Advertiser*, 27 July 1802, 2).

"Odes, Composed to be Sung on the Anniversary of American Independence, at Plympton [Mass.], July 5, 1802." Providence: Printed by J. Carter, [1802]. Ode I: "To Independence" (first line: "Hail independence, hail!"); Ode II: "The Triumph of Liberty" (first line: "When ign'rance, wild, with lust and pride."

"Song Sung on the 4th of July.[137] Tune—'Jefferson & Liberty.'" First line: "Fair Independence wakes the song" (*American Mercury*, 22 July 1802, 2; *American Citizen and General Advertiser*, 28 July 1802, 2).

Performances

Connecticut

Bristol: The celebration occurred on July 5 and began with a procession to the meeting house. The exercises included an "ode intitled the Death of Washington, and rise of Jefferson, set to music" that was sung. Later at a dinner prepared by Mrs. Newell, toasts were drank "accompanied by appropriate music by the band" ("Anniversary of American Independence," *American Mercury*, 22 July 1802, 3).

Granby: Men and women from Suffield, Windsor, and Simsbury, and military totaling some 400 persons paraded with a band of music to the meeting house. "Odes appropriate were sung" and later at the green in front of Capt. Joel Clark's house, "several pleasing airs were performed on the band—and odes suitable to the occasion were sung under the tree of liberty, by a select choir" (*American Mercury*, 29 July 1802, 3).

Hartford: Denmark—Felton's Gavot[138]—Guardian Angels—Hail Columbia—Jefferson's March—Lass of Richmond Hill—New York Fusileers—Orn's March—Rural Felicity—Smith's Minuet—Soldier's Joy—Washington's March—Yankee Doodle, by a band at City Hall with 300 persons present (*American Mercury*, 8 July 1802, 3).

Killingworth: Citizens celebration on July 6 began at the house of Mrs. Mehitable Crane, where a procession was formed and marched to the meeting house, "with the tune of 'Jefferson's March' played by a respectable band of musicians." The public exercises began with singing and after "the message of our illustrious president Thomas Jefferson, at the commencement of the last session of Congress" was read, "the tune of 'Jefferson and Liberty' was then played by the band." There was additional singing and the exercises closed with a performance of "Washington's March." Afterwards, "the precession then formed in the same order as before, and marched with the tune of 'Jefferson and Liberty'" to the Academy where dinner and toasts took place. The following pieces of music were performed: Columbus—Jefferson's March—Jefferson and Liberty—Mount Vernon[139]—Washington's Farewel [l]—Liberty—St. John's—Roslin Castle—Orphan Boy[140]—Yankee Doodle—Matross—Mol o' the Wad—Green's March—St. Albans—Lass of Richmond Hill[141]—Washington's March (*American Mercury*, 22 July 1802, 3).

District of Columbia

At a dinner celebration, attended by members of Congress, the President's cabinet, and other distinguished individuals, toasts were given with a "discharge of from 1 to 16 guns, and by a patriotic air, played by Col. Burrow's Band [U.S. Marine Band], interspersed with songs" at the Navy Yard (*National Intelligencer*, 7 July 1802, 3; *Aurora General Adevertiser*, 10 July 1802, 3; "National Birth Day," *The Independent Chronicle*, 15 July 1802, 2).

Maryland

Baltimore: At Stewart's Inn at Fell's Point, a "respectable meeting of republicans and others assembled" and drank toasts accompanied by the following music: Hail Columbia—Washington's March—Dead March—Jefferson's March—White Cockade—Stony Point—Yankee Doodle—Billy's Undone by the War—America, Commerce and Freedom—Money in Every Pocket—Jack's Morning Blush—New Convention—New Congress—Erin Go Bragh (*Democ-*

ratic Republican and Commercial Daily Advertiser, 6 July 1802, 3).

Massachusetts

Boston: On July 5 the exercises included the singing of an Ode "on the occasion, written at Cambridge, and sung by Mr. Eaton, was peculiarly appropriate, and expressive of the harmony of the day" ("Independence," *Boston Gazette*, 8 July 1802, 2). See **Publications** above.

Marblehead: At the meeting house of the second parish, "excellent music there filled the soul with rapture." A repast for 170 guests at the town hall "was abundantly exhibited in numerous toasts and songs, patriotic and convivial" (*Salem Register*, 8 July 1802, 2).

Salem: The Salem Artillery and Salem Cadets paraded through the streets. The officers "were escorted by the non-commissioned officers, accompanied by the regimental music" to Frye's Tavern to dine. "The Trojan Band[142] also honored the day, by marching thro' the streets, conducted by their preceptor" ("Birth Day of the United States," *Salem Register*, 8 July 1802, 2).

Mississippi

Natchez: "On Monday, the 5th instant, the inhabitants of Natchez and its vicinity, assembled at the house of Mr. James Moore, where an oration was delivered by William Murray, Esquire, to a crouded [sic] audience of gentlemen and ladies. After which, the following song, composed by the orator, and accompanied with music was sung: Tune, 'President's March.'" First line: "Behold! again, Heav'n's glorious ray" (*South-Carolina State Gazette and Timothy's Daily Adviser*, 15 September 1802, 2).

New Hampshire

Portsmouth: "On Monday the 5th instant a large company of Gentlemen dined at Jefferson Hall. ... the following Song, composed for the occasion, by John Wentworth, Esq (late Attorney General for his Britannic majesty, for Prince Edward County, Nova-Scotia) was sung and repeated": first line, "All hail to the day that bids us display"; "a number of respectable citizens dined at Jefferson Hall — after a few toasts, the company demanded a song — John Wentworth, Esq. being distinguished, by a call — he sang derry down, down, hey derry, down 'one and all'" (*United States Oracle and Portsmouth Advertiser*[143], 10 July 1802, 3; "The Muses' Apartment," *Edes' Kennebec Gazette*, 30 July 1802, 4); at Piscataqua Bridge, Federalists assembled for an entertainment with toasts. "Adams and Liberty, Hail Columbia, and a number of other patriotic songs were sung, after the song of the day" ("Independence," *The Olio*, 29 July 1802, 35).

New York

Cooperstown: The celebration of toasts at William Stevens' House included "a volley of small arms, a

song, music, and cheers, to each toast": President's March, song Hail Columbia — music, How Imperfect is Expression[144] — music, Adams and Liberty — music German Air — music, French King's March — music, Success to the Farmer — music, How Imperfect is Expression — music, York Fusilier — music, Cold Stream March — music, Rule America — music, Washington's March — music, Duke of Holstein's March — music, Greene's March[145] — music, Rural Felicity — How Imperfect is Expression ("Independence," *Otsego Herald*, 8 July 1802, 2).

New York: "The Officers of the Brigade of Military and Regiment of Artillery, met at the City Hotel to celebrate" with a dinner and toasts with the following music: Music, Yankee Doodle, Music, Roslin Castle,[146] Music, Presidents March — Music — Music, the General — Music, Hail Columbia — Music, Yankee Doodle — Music — Music — Music, Marsellois Hymn — Music — Music, Dirge — Music, God of Love (*Daily Advertiser*, 7 July 1802, 3); on July 5 at Vauxhall Garden, a ceremony honoring the heroes of the American Revolution included performances of "Washington's March" and "Hail Columbia" ("Anniversary of American Independence," *New York Gazette and General Advertiser*, 1 July 1802, 3).

Rockland County: "On the 3d instant (the 4th falling on Sunday) a very numerous and respectable company met at the house of Mr. Smith, at New City, in Clark's Town." The assemblage marched to the Court House for the exercises. "The exercises of the morning were interspersed and enlivened by vocal music, and concluded with a patriotic Ode composed for the day by a lady of Rockland County, and sung by the scholars of Mr. Cole" ("Communication," *American Citizen and General Advertiser*, 10 July 1802, 2).

Pennsylvania

Philadelphia: On July 5, a "Pantomimical Sketch" titled *Federal Oath; or, the Independence of 1776*[147] is premiered, preceded by a performance of *Jefferson's March* by Alexander Reinagle, and ending with *A National Invocation and Chorus*, music by "Mr. [Benjamin] Carr" (*Philadelphia Gazette & Daily Advertiser*, 3 July 1802, 2; *Aurora General Advertiser*, 5 July 1802, 3).

Vermont

Middlebury: Citizens of the town, including fifty students of Middlebury College, attended the exercises at the Court House where "the audience were highly entertained with some excellent pieces of music, previously selected. The song Adams and Liberty, particularly, was received with much applause." Later at a "green bower," the group enjoyed dinner with toasts "accompanied with discharges of musketry, and with martial music" ("Celebration of American Independence," *Middlebury Mercury*, 7 July 1802, 3).

Shoreham: A procession of military companies and citizens included "martial music" and a group of marching singers made their way to the meeting house where the exercises began with "sacred music" and "appropriate music" after the oration ("Celebration at Shoreham," *Middlebury Mercury*, 11 August 1802, 2).

Windsor: Republicans met at Mr. Smeed's Inn and paraded to the meeting house "on entering which, the following lines were sung by a choir of singers who had previously assembled for that purpose" (first line: "The morning sun shines from the east"). "Divine service commenced by singing one of Watt's psalms.... Previous to leaving the meeting house the following sentimental song was sung by the singers" (first line: "Ye vot'ries of freedom, who firmly oppos'd"). (*Spooners Vermont Journal*, 6 July 1802, 3.)

1803

Publications

"Fourth of July.[148] Tune — Derry-Down." First line: "America's birth-day bids freemen arise" (*Hornet*, 5 July 1803, 3).

The Glory of Columbia: Her Yeomanry, a Play in Five Acts: the Songs, Duets, and Chorusses, Intended for the Celebration of the Fourth of July at the New-York Theatre. By William Dunlap. New York: Printed and published by D. Longworth at the Shakespeare-Gallery, 1803.

"A hymn for the Fourth of July, 1803, by Jacob Fisher"[149] and "An ode for the Fourth of July, 1803, by S. Sewall" in Samuel Emerson, *An Oration on the Independence of America: Pronounced at Kennebunk, July 4th, 1803* (Kennebunk, Maine: Printed by S. Sewall, 1803), 11–13.

"An ode for the Fourth of July 1803." First line: "Hail thou auspicious day" (*Newburyport Herald*, 5 July 1803, 3).

"Ode. Sung at the Republican Festival in Boston, on the 4th of July 1803. First. Tune — 'President's March.'" First line "Not two ages yet have fled." Second. Tune — 'He Comes! He comes!' First line: "Behold! Behold! with generous hand" (*Gazetteer*, 6 July 1803, 3; "Poetry," *Providence Phoenix*, 30 July 1803, 4; William McCarty, *The New National Song Book, Containing Songs, Odes, and Other Poems, on National Subjects. Compiled from Various Sources* [NY: Leavitt and Allen, 184–?]).

"Ode to Jefferson. Paraphrased from'The Dauphin.' For the 4th of July, 1803." First line: "Ye free-born Whigs attend" (From the *Bee*, as published in *Merrimack Gazette*, 2 July 1803, 3; *Hornet*, 5 July 1803, 3).

"(The following Odes, composed for, and sung at Lee, (Mass.) on the late anniversary of our Independence, are inserted by request.). Ode I." First line: "Welcome once more the era bright." "Ode II." First line: "Wake to song the cheerful air." "Ode III. (Tune Newburgh.)." First line "Ye sons of freedom join" ("The Wreath," *Balance, and Columbian Repository*, 19 July 1803, 232).

"New Song sung at the celebration of the 4th of July, at Saratoga and Waterford, N.Y. By William Foster."[150] First line: "Brave sons of Columbia, your triumph behold" (*The American Republican Harmonist: or, a Collection of Songs and Odes* (Philadelphia: William Duane, 1803, 4).

"Ode for the Fourth of July." First line: "Americans! welcome, and hail the blest day" (*Weekly Museum*, 2 July 1803; *Independent Chronicle*, 11 July 1803, 4).

"Ode to the Fourth of July, 1803 by Walter Townsend ; set to music by Dr. Jackson."[151] First line: "Once more has the morn op'd the portals of light." Broadside. [New York]: John C. Totten, [1803].

"Ode to the Fourth of July (written by a young gentleman of Castleton)." First line: "All hail, glad day, July the Fourth" (*Vermont Mercury*, 4 July 1803, 3).

"Odes prepared and sung at Newark on the Fourth of July, 1803." First lines: "We hail once more the annual morn"; "In Britain's Isle, when freedom's name" ("Poetic Recess," *Centinel of Freedom*, 6 July 1803, 4).

"Song for the Fourth of July." First line: "All hail Columbia's natal day!" ("For the Morning Chronicle," *Morning Chronicle*, 4 July 1803, 3).

"Song, for the Fourth of July, 1803: Blessings of Fredon, (U.S.)." First line: "Come, celebrate your happy state." Broadside. [New York]: G & R. Waite, 1803. Copy in Brown University.

"Song [for the Fourth of July, 1803]."[152] First line: "In years which are past, when America fought" (*The American Republican Harmonist: or, a Collection of Songs and Odes* (Philadelphia: William Duane, 1803, 105).

Performances

Connecticut

Berlin: A procession to the meeting house included a band of music. Later at Mr. Loveland's Assembly Room where a dinner was prepared, "toasts were drank to accompanied by music and a discharge of cannon" ("Anniversary of American Independence," *American Mercury*, 11 August 1803, 2).

Granby: At noon "430 ladies and gentlemen" formed a procession, "preceded by a band and martial music" and local militia and marched to the meeting house where among the exercises, "odes were sung appropriate to the occasion." Later at "an elegant bower situated on a beautiful green fronting the house of Capt. Joel Clark" the assemblage heard an address and "the most harmonious vocal music, attuned to the patriotic song of 'Jefferson and Liberty' shot forth a scene so gay and brilliant that caused every heart to beat high with a sense of national independence" ("Anniversary of American Independence," *American Mercury*, 28 July 1803, 2).

New London: At a Republicans' dinner held at Fox's Tavern, the following music was interspersed with the toasts: Music, Boston March — Yankee Doodle — Hail Columbia — Song, Well Met Fellow

Freemen[153]— Jefferson's March — Dead March — West Point — Rural Felicity — Dauphin, a Song (*American Mercury*, 21 July 1803, 2; *American Citizen*, 26 July 1803, 3; "Newburgh, July 13," *Republican Watch-Tower*, 27 July 1803, 1).

Suffield: The "Republican citizens" celebrated with a procession, "preceded by a band and other martial music," from Col. Kent's to the East Meeting House where the exercises were held ("Anniversary of American Independence," *American Mercury*, 4 August 1803, 3).

District of Columbia

At Stelle's Hotel, U.S. Marine Band accompanied the toasts presented with the following music: Jefferson's March — Washington's March — Roslin Castle — Yankee Doodle. Also, sung at Stelle's was an "Impromtu" by "Mr. Minifir": "This Day We Find Munroe's Success,"[154] to the tune "Yankee Doodle": first line, "This day we find Munroe's success" — Washington's March (*National Intelligencer*, 6 July 1803; *Republican Star or General Advertiser*, 12 July 1803, 3); a "Neopolitan" band[155] of music performed for Thomas Jefferson at the Executive Mansion (*National Intelligencer*, 6 and 15 July 1803, 3 and 3, respectively).

Maine

Kennebunk: At a celebration held by 100 Republican citizens at Mr. Barnard's Hall, the exercises included "an appropriate hymn." Dinner, toasts, with the following music followed: Air Washington's March — Hail Columbia — Jove in His Chair — Jefferson's March — God Save Great Jefferson — Roslin Castle — Hymn — Madison's March — New Administration — Rural Felicity — Count Rochambeau's March — Caira — Governor Strong's March — New Pump-Room[156] — President Jefferson — Mason's Favorite (*The Gazetteer*, 23 July 1803, 3). See **Publications** above.

Readfield: Following a procession, "preceded by music, under the direction of Lieut. Simmons, martial for the day," the exercises at the Methodist Meeting House "began with music prepared for the occasion ... and the ceremonies at the Meeting House closed with instrumental and vocal music" ("Celebration of the Anniversary of American Independence at Readfield, on the 4th Inst.," *Kennebec Gazette*, 21 July 1803, 1).

Waterville: At Capt. Bacon's Hotel, an "elegant entertainment" included: Hail Columbia — President's March — Farmer's Song — Yankee Doodle — How Beauteous Are Their Feet — The Mason's Daughter ("Fourth of July, from Waterville," *Kennebec Gazette*, 14 July 1803, 2 and 4).

Maryland

Baltimore: At Fells Point, "a large company, composed principally of gentlemen of Fells' Point, dined at Peck's Hotel." The toasts included the following

music: America, Commerce and Freedom — Stoney Point — President's March — Rogue's March[157]— Union of Parties — Roslin Castle — Yankee Doodle[158]— Hail Columbia — Washington's March — White Cockade[159]— Heave the Lead (*Baltimore Patriot*, 12 July 1803, 3; *Hornet*, 19 July 1803, 2).

Massachusetts

Boston: At the Theatre on Federal Street, "the popular play of the *Point of Honor, or, A School for Soldiers*" (*Independent Chronicle*, 4 July 1803, 3).

Newburyport: At a Republican celebration at "Mr. Moses Davenport's ... toasts (interspersed with a number of excellent songs) were drank." Another newspaper reported that "the day was puffed with great conviviality, & a glow of rapture expressed at the chorus of each song, that echoed the name of him, who is, his country's boast and pride, the friend of science, and advocate of man" ("American Independence," *Merrimack Gazette*, 9 July 1803, 3; "July Fourth," *Salem Register*, 11 July 1803, 2); the Newburyport Regiment and Washington Light Infantry marched to the hill above High Street for "a sumptuous dinner," with toasts and music: Tune, President's March — Tune, Washington's March — Tune, Yankee Doodle — Solemn Dirge (*Newburyport Herald*, 5 July 1803, 3).

Pittsfield: "At 12 o'clock at noon, a numerous and respectable procession was formed, which, preceded by a band of music, and escorted by the Cavalry, Artillery, and Infantry Companies moved to the Meeting House" ("National Jubilee," *Sun*, 11 July 1803, 3).

New Hampshire

Greenfield: After the raising of a liberty pole and a procession to the meeting house, the exercises included "appropriate" music ("Celebration of the 4th July at Greenfield," *Farmer's Cabinet*, 21 July 1803, 3).

Nashua: After the exercises, "the assembly moved in procession under a military escort, preceded by a band of music, to behold the novel sight of a launch from the banks of the Nashua, a little above its confluence with the Merrimac. This was a fine flat bottomed vessel of forty tons" and represented "the first attempt at navigation on this stream. She is appropriately called *The Nashua.*" About 100 individuals, including a band of music, were invited aboard and all were "gratified with a sail down the river" ("Independence," *Farmer's Cabinet*, 7 July 1803, 4).

New Jersey

Chester: "About seven hundred citizens of this vicinity met at this place" and paraded to the church where the exercises took place. After the oration was presented, "several hymns were sung" (*The Centinel of Freedom*, 26 July 1803, 2).

Elizabethtown: The Society of the Cincinnati and others marched to the Presbyterian Church for the following exercises:

1. A hymn of praise to God for our national deliverance.
2. Prayer.
3. Ode for the day.
4. Reading the Declaration of Independence by General Cummings.
5. Oration by Dr. Ebenezer Elmer.
6. Ode to the memory of Gen. Washington.
7. Oration by Mr. George Williamson.
8. Ode for the day.

["Fourth of July," *New Jersey Journal*, 12 July 1803, 3].

Lansingburgh: Capt. Lansing's military company "joined a general procession" to the brick church taking a circuitous rout [sic] through the principal streets in this village." The exercises began with "a hymn, selected for the occasion," and another "appropriate hymn" after a reading of the Declaration of Independence (*Farmers' Register*, 12 July 1803, 2).

Newton: "A number of Republicans convened at the house of Mr. Isaac Basset, for the purpose of taking a social dinner and paying a suitable respect to the day which gave birth to our beloved Country." Following dinner, "toasts were drank interspersed with a variety of patriot songs" ("Republican Festivity," *Centinel of Freedom*, 26 July 1803, 2).

Scotch Plains: A procession from Col. Swan's to the meeting house included choristers and martial music. At the flagstaff, "there the drum & fife gave place to the vocal harmony of an ode suited to the occasion." At the church, three odes were sung, including these two: "Begin the grateful song" (first line) to the tune "Scotch Plains"; "To-day let every heart rejoice" under the title "Liberty" to the tune "Lavonia" ("Scotch Plains, July 5, 1803" and "Poetic Recess," *Centinel of Freedom*, 12 and 19 July 1803, 3 and 4, respectively; *New Jersey Journal*, 12 July 1803, 2).

New York

New York: A "Band of Instrumental Music" in the procession that was nearly a mile long and marched through the city streets to the New Dutch Church. The exercises there included an "Anthem, under the direction of Capt. Christopher Prince, by a select number of volunteer vocal performers; words by Washington McKnight[160] — set to music by S. Freeman," a "voluntary by the band" as a collection was taken; an "Ode, composed by Mrs. Jackson — Set to music by Dr. G.K. Jackson,[161] by Volunteer Vocal and Instrumental performers, under the direction of an Amateur"; another "Ode, composed by Walter Townsend — set to Music by Dr. Jackson, by Volunteer Vocal and instrumental performers, also under the direction of an Amateur (first line: "Once more has the morn op'd the portals of light"); "Stanzas — by Mrs. Jackson (set to music by Dr. Jackson)" (first line: "When generous Freedom leaves her downy bed").[162] Another newspaper reported that "the vocal and instrumental performances were of the most exquisite kind. The audience, which was a most crowded one,

were highly gratified" ("Fourth of July," *Evening Post*, 2 July 1803, 3. see **Publications** above; *American Citizen*, 6 July 1803, 2; *New York Herald*, 6 July 1803, 2; *National Intelligencer*, 15 July 1803, 3;); at the Theatre,

in commemoration of the glorious day, which gave existence to our country as a nation, will be performed (for the first time) a play in five acts, written for the occasion, interspersed with songs, duets and choruses, called *The Glory of Columbia, Her Yeomanry*. Music by M. Pellisier[163].... After the play, will be sung by Mr. Shapter, and others of the company, an Ode, composed for the day, by Mrs. Jackson, of this city. The music composed by Dr. G.K. Jackson.

See **Publications** above (*Morning Chronicle*, 29 June 1803, 2; *Daily Advertiser*, 2 July 1803, 2); at the Mount Vernon Theatre, in honor of the day:

The entertainments to commence with "A Monody" in memory for those illustrious chiefs who have fallen in the service of America, including "An Eulogium on the Character of Washington," by Mr. Hallam. A favorite song, "Jemmy of the Glen,"[164] Mrs. Seymour. A new song — "True Courage," Mr. Turnbull. "A Comic Mirror," in which will be delineated the following characters: the Cit, John Trott, the Surly Squire, the Jolly Toper, the Honest Peasant, the Wandering Tar, and the War-Worn Soldier, to conclude with "An Eulogium on Women," by Mrs. Hallam. In the course of the evening, Mr. Hallam will recite the humorous story of *Hippesley's Drunken Man*. The song of "The Bonny Bold Soldier,"[165] Mrs. Seymour. A new patriotic song, called "The Health of Our Sachem, and Long May He Live,"[166] by Mr. Turnbul."

The evening concluded with fireworks. (*Daily Advertiser*, 4 July 1803, 3.); Republican Greens had an entertainment at the Union Hotel that included toasts with the accompanying music: Hail Columbia — Washington's March — Dead March — Farewell to Ireland — President's March — Yankee Doodle — music, Peace and Plenty — Grand music — Steddiford's March — Green's Quick Step — Independent Quick Step — Rogues March — Erin go Bragh — Haste to the Wedding (*Republican Watch-Tower*, 9 July 1803, 2).

Newburgh: The Youths of Newburgh met at Mr. Case's Hotel and drank toasts "accompanied with patriotic songs" (*Republican Watch-Tower*, 27 July 1803, 1).

Salem: This town, located in Washington County, had a procession and after exercises at the Presbyterian Meeting House, the "citizens of Salem and the towns in its vicinity" had dinner at the house of Mr. Pennel where "toasts were drank with an appropriate number of cheers and interspersed with animating and patriotic songs" (*Farmers' Register*, 12 July 1803, 2).

Pennsylvania

Philadelphia: At a dinner celebration held by the Light Infantry Company at Lombardy Gardens: America, Commerce and Freedom — Jefferson's March — Yankee Doodle (*National Intelligencer*, 13 July 1803, 3); a dinner celebration by the Philadelphia Rifle Rangers "in the gardens back of the Pennsylvania Hospital" included the singing of the following "Song" to the tune "How Blest a Life a Sailor Leads"[167]: first line, "Of all the changing scenes of life" (*American Citizen*, 14 July 1803, 3).

Rhode Island

Dighton: "The inhabitants of the whole county of Bristol, agreed by a general committee, to solemnize this civic feast together." A procession, "preceeded by a concert of instrumental music and Capt. Andrews's Company of Horse, with other military gentlemen in uniform, moved from Mr. Deane's tavern to the Meeting House." During the exercises, "several well selected Psalms were sung, to give variety and solemnity to the services of the Day." After the dinner which took place "in a neighboring field ... the musicians in concert with instruments sung with spirit and festivity 'Jefferson's Hymn' a parody from the Dauphin — 'Ye Freeborn Whigs Attend,'[168] &c. They then drank to the following toasts which were accompanied with discharges of cannon and appropriate music": Hail Columbia — Jefferson & Liberty ("American Independence: Republican Celebration at Dighton," *Providence Phoenix*, 30 July 1803, 1–2).

1804

Publications

"'Independence.' Tune 'Liberty Tree.'[169] By A.H." First line: "Independence! a word of amazing import" (*Vermont Gazette*, 17 July 1804, 4).

"Ode for the Fourth of July." First line: "Oh, for a muse of fire — whose active soul" (from the *Charleston Courier*, as printed in *Spectator*, 25 July 1804, 1).

"Ode for the Fourth of July, 1804. By J. Woodcock. (Set to music by W. Pirsson." First line: "Dark dismal night declines." Includes, recitative, air, duet, semi-chorus, and full chorus (*American Citizen*, 6 July 1804, 2; *Republican Watch-Tower*, 7 July 1804, 2).

"Ode for the Fourth of July, 1804. By a brother of Tammany Society. Tune — 'President's March.' Accompaniments & choruses by W. Pirsson." First line: "Welcome bright auspicious morn" (*Republican Watch-Tower*, 7 July 1804, 2).

"An ode for the 28th anniversary of American independence, in imitating 'Victor's celebrated ode.'" First line: "For joy and mirth, ye sons prepare" ("Poetry," *Independent Chronicle*, 25 June 1804, 4; *Political Calendar*, 28 June 1804, 4).

"Ode to Independence. Written by William Bigelow, A.M. and Sung by Mrs. Jones'[170] at St. Peter's Church, in Salem, on Wednesday last." First line: "When Britain gigantic, by justice unaw'd." (*Salem Gazette*, 6 July 1804, 2–3; "Poesy," *Boston Gazette*, 9 July 1804, 4; *Massachusetts Spy*, 18 July 1804, 4; *Kennebec Gazette*, 2 August 1804, 4).

"An ode to the anniversary of American independence." First line: "All hail! thou ever glorious morn!" (*Maryland Herald and Hager's-Town Weekly Advertiser*, 4 July 1804, 3).

"An ode, written by Doctor R. Clark, and sung on the 4th of July, at Whiting, Vermont. Tune — 'To Anacreon in Heaven.'" First line: "Hail! Sons of Columbia! the day which our sires" (*Salem Register*, 6 August, 1804, 3; "Poetry," *Kennebec Gazette*, 16 August 1804, 4).

"Patriotic Ode, composed and sung at Portsmouth, 4th July. By John Wentworth,[171] Esq." First line: "Sound, sound thy trump, eternal fame" ("Poetry," *Weekly Wanderer*, 6 August 1804, 4); "Patriotic odes composed by John Wentworth, Esq. and sung at Jefferson Hall [Portsmouth]." First lines: "Sound, sound the trump, eternal fame"; "How joyful and grateful our praises." Another untitled ode likely sung that day was printed the following week: first line, "Hail the bright day, and let nature rejoice" (*Political Star*, 12 and 19 July 1804, 3 and 3, respectively). A broadside was published that included both odes: "Sound, sound thy trump, eternal fame" to the tune "Let There Be Light." Copy in American Antiquarian Society.

"A patriotic ode, for July 4, 1804. Tune, Bunker's Hill." First line: "Sound the loud clarion to our country's glory" ("Miscellany," *Suffolk Gazette*, 2 July 1804, 4).

"Song — Composed for the Anniversary of American Independence, July 4th, 1804. Tune, 'Tom Bowling.'" First line: "This was the day — the Fourth of July" (*Maryland Herald and Hager's-Town Weekly Advertiser*, 4 July 1804, 4).

"Song Composed for the Anniversary of Our Independence, and Sung on the Fourth Instant, at Salem [Massachusetts]." First line: "While round the full board independent and free." Sung in Concert Hall. (*Salem Gazette*, 6 July 1804, 3; *Repertory* 1/103 (10 July, 1804). Copy in Brown University.

"Song, for the Fourth of July. Tune — 'Anacreon in Heaven.'" First line: "All hail to the day, when assembled, as one"[172] ("Original Poetry," *Salem Register*, 21 June 1804, 4; "Poetry," *Political Calendar*, 25 June 1804, 4; "Poetry," *Independent Chronicle*, 2 July 1804, 4; *Republican Spy*, 3 July 1804, 4; *Eastern Argus*, 5 July 1804, 4).

See **Publications**, 1812

Performances

Connecticut

New London: The exercises at the Court House included an "Ode suitable to the day." Later a dinner was prepared for the assemblage at Frink's Coffee House.

Toasts were drank "interspersed with sentimental, patriotic songs and music": Tune, Jefferson and Liberty — Tune, President's March — Tune, Roslin Castle — Tune, War Worn Soldier — Tune, Yankee Doodle — Tune, Rural Felicity — Tune, Liberty Hall — Tune, White Cockade (*Suffolk Gazette*, 16 July 1804, 2).

Norwich: "Martial music" in the procession and at the exercises at "Mr. Strong's meeting house," various music including an anthem, "Bless the Lord, O My Soul" ("Norwich, July 11th, 1804," *The Courier*, 11 July 1804, 3); the "Federal Republicans" celebrated with an "uncommonly long" procession "which after moving in proper order around the Square, preceded by the Matross Company handsomely equipped, with music, &c. they proceeded to the Meeting House." Included in the exercises was "vocal music, captivatingly performed" ("Fourth of July," *Connecticut Centinel*, 10 July 1804, 3).

Saybrook: At 10 A.M. a group of Republicans gathered at the meeting house for a procession, "preceded by a Company of Artillery and a Band of Music." After the exercises dinner was followed by toasts and select pieces of music including: Tune, Liberty — Dirge — Jefferson & Liberty — St. John — Yankee Doodle — Rural Felicity ("Anniversary of American Independence," *American Mercury*, 16 August 1804, 3).

Simsbury: At 11 A.M. a procession was "accompanied by enlivening music." At the meeting house, after the Declaration of Independence was read, a "Hymn to Peace" was sung and "the 21st psalm, entitled national blessings acknowledged, sung." Also, "the 58th Psalm entitled a warning to magistrates, [was] sung. The first verse and the first pause of the 104th psalm, entitled the glory of god in creation and providence [was] sung." Later at a grove near the meeting house, there were toasts "accompanied by discharges of cannon, and appropriate music from the band" ("Anniversary of American Independence," *American Mercury*, 2 August 1804, 3).

District of Columbia

Many dignitaries and military units attended the reception at the Executive Mansion. "The pleasure of the company was considerably promoted by patriotic and popular airs, played at intervals by the Italian band." Later at Stelle's Hotel, the assemblage enjoyed dinner and heard "appropriate vocal and instrumental music" (*Eastern Argus*, 19 July 1804, 1).

Massachusetts

Boston: The governor and other dignitaries, militia, citizens, and others paraded from the State House to Old South Church where after the oration by Thomas Danforth, there was performed "an original Ode, sung by the choir of singers, who politely attended on this occasion." Another newspaper reported that "the military were called out by the warlike drum and shrill fife." At Faneuil Hall, two dirges were

played (*The Democrat*, 7 July 1804, 2; "Celebration of the Fourth of July at Boston," *Portsmouth Oracle*, 7 July 1804, 3).

Ludlow: "A procession of 400 persons was formed" at Mr. Sikes Tavern "and marched to the Meeting House, accompanied by a Band of Music from South-Hadley" ("Celebration at Ludlow," *Republican Spy*, 17 July 1804, 2).

Salem: A procession that marched from Court Street to the East Meeting House was "accompanied with an excellent band of musick." The exercises included "several pieces of vocal and instrumental musick ... performed with much taste and judgement. Among others, was an excellent Ode written for the occasion. This is a meritorious production, and gave universal satisfaction." Another report noted that the exercises occurred at St. Peter's Church and that "an Ode, written by Mr. Biglow, was sung by Mrs. Jones, accompanied by the band, in that style of excellence which has rendered herself her only competitor in the art." Later at the Concert Hall, following dinner, toasts were accompanied by the following pieces of music: Tune, Yankee Doodle — Dead March — Adams and Liberty — Galley Slave ("Fourth of July," *Salem Gazette*, 6 July 1804, 2; "The Glorious Fourth of July," *Salem Register*, 9 July 1804, 3). See **Publications** above.

Warwick: "A procession was formed at Mr. Wilson's Hall and escorted to the meeting house, attended with instrumental musick" ("Celebration of the 4th of July at Warwick, (Mass.)," *Political Observatory*, 28 July 1804, 3).

West Springfield: Citizens of this town and others from Northampton and Springfield assembled for a procession that gathered at Mr. Solomon Stebbins' at 11 A.M., "escorted by a band of music and detachment of artillery, proceeded to the New Meeting House. The exercises were introduced by singing" and "closed with the tune of Jefferson and Liberty." Later at a dinner prepared at Stebbins' place, toasts were accompanied "with music from the band, and patriotic songs": Anacreon in Heaven — Jefferson and Liberty — Hail Columbia — Music — Washington's March (*Republican Spy*, 10 July 1804, 3).

New Hampshire

Langdon: Farmers of Langdon assembled "with their ladies about four o'clock P.M. at a place called Liberty corner.... The following lines (being composed on said day, for the occasion) were sung": "Independence." first line: "Hail! Victo'rous! Columbia's sons!" ("Celebration of the 4th of July, at Langdon, Newhampshire," *Political Observatory*, 14 July 1804, 3).

Portsmouth: A parade by The Governor Gilman's Blues, commanded by Capt. Larkin was later followed by dinner at Washington Hall. "The enjoyments of the day were greatly heightened by an excellent song from the pen of the celebrated author of 'War and Washington,' — it combined the first classic elegance with the pure spirit of Washingtonian principles, and was sung amidst the bursts of reiterated applause by Capt. Larkin[173] with a judgment and taste that, at once, did justice to the poet[174] and honor to himself and the company." After dinner, toasts were accompanied with the following music: Hail Columbia — Yankee Doodle — Knox's March — Rise Columbia — Washington's March [performed twice] — Speed the Plough — Hobbies — Yo Heave Ho — Boston March — Roslin Castle — Rogue's March. Also sung as this celebration was a song "by J.M. Sewall, Esq. Tune, Hail Columbia." First line: "Hail the day when from the yoke" (*Portsmouth Oracle*, 7 July 1804, 3; *Political Star*, 12 July 1804, 2). See **Publications** above.

Walpole: A parade from Mr. Southard's Hall to the meeting house included "a band of music." The exercises opened with "an air by the band." There were three odes "adapted to the occasion." Back at Southard's, food was served and toasts drunk "under the discharge of cannon, and interspersed with a variety of pleasing and animating songs" ("Walpole," *Political Observatory*, 7 July 1804, 2).

New York

Claverack: Federalists celebrated at the Columbian Hotel. Dinner and toasts and the following music: Song, Bunker Hill, tune, God Save &c. — New Song, tune, Mason's Farewell, see Balance of last week[175] — Song, New Yankee Doodle, see this day's Bal.[176] — Song, The Drum[177] — The Genuine Song, tune Black Slovin [sic], see Balance, no. 16[178] — Encore, New Yankee Doodle — Song, Tom Teugh ("Independence," *The Balance, and Columbian Repository*, 10 July 1804, 222).

Hudson: A procession included a band of music that marched to the Presbyterian Church where the exercises included "appropriate music." Later at Nichols's Hotel, toasts were offered accompanied by the following music: Fourth of July March — Washington's and Dead March — Hail Columbia — Jefferson & Liberty — Vice-President's March — Yankee Doodle — Rule Columbia — New York Fusileers — Boston March — Liberty Tree — Rural Felicity — Bennington March — Banks of Kentucke.[179] That evening "a beautiful and excellent display of fireworks" was accompanied by music from the band (*The Bee*, 10 July 1804, 3).

New York: The day began with a civil and military procession from the Park to the Brick Presbyterian Church where the exercises were in this order:

1. Voluntary by the band.
2. Then Declaration of Independence read by Hopkins Robinson, from the Society of Taylors.
3. Ode composed for the occasion, the music by a select company, under the direction of W. Pirsson.[180] See **Publications** above.
4. The Oration by Major John W. Mulligan, from the military.
5. A voluntary by the band, during which a collec-

tion will be made to defray the necessary expences of the day.
6. Ode 2d, with original music by W. Pirsson[181]; the performance by a select company.

(*American Citizen*, 3 July 1804, 2; *Republican Watch-Tower*, 4 July 1804, 4; *The Spectator*, 4 July 1804, 3.). See **Publications** above; "The anniversary of American independence was celebrated on Wednesday the 4th inst. by the New-York Mercantile Society, at Mr. Tuttles in Nassau Street, by whom a handsome entertainment was provided. After dinner the following toasts were drank, interspersed with convivial and patriotic songs" ("Communication," *Morning Chronicle*, 7 July 1804, 2); at Vauxhall Garden, "a band of music will perform patriotic airs during the evening" beginning at 6 P.M. (*American Citizen*, 3 July 1804, 2; *Morning Chronicle*, 3 July 1804, 3; *Daily Advertiser*, 4 July 1804, 3); at the Theatre, *The Glory of Columbia, Her Yeomanry*, "music by Mr. Pellisier" was performed (*Daily Advertiser*, 2 July 1804, 3).

Newburgh: Music interspersed between toasts at the dinner celebration: Washington's March — Hail Columbia — Yankee Doodle — Rogues March[182] — Belle-Isle March — Liberty — Roslin Castle — Hearts of Oak (*American Citizen*, 16 July 1804, 2; "Toasts Drank at Newburgh," *Republican Watch-Tower*, 18 July 1804, 1).

Pennsylvania

Philadelphia: Rayner Taylor's "celebrated patriotic songs" at Lombardy Gardens. (*Aurora General Advertiser*, 4 July 1804).[183]

Rhode Island

Raynham: "A numerous and respectable audience heard an oration and then "partook of a plentiful repast" after which "toasts were drank accompanied by a discharge of Artillery" and the following pieces of music: Yankey Doodle — President's March — Massachusetts March — Old Hundred[184] — Dirge — Rural Felicity — Col Ornes March — March in "The God of Love" (*Independent Chronicle*, 16 July 1804, 4).

Vermont

Shaftsbury: Citizens of Bennington, Pownal, Shaftsbury "and a number of gentlemen from the neighboring towns" met at Major Burnham's and paraded to the meeting house.

The exercises of the day were introduced by solemn music, followed by a well adapted prayer, by the Rev. Mr. Blood. After prayer the choir entertained the audience by striking on a new song, to the tune of 'Hail Columbia,' thro' three verses of which they had progressed, when a number of amiable little masters and misses, catched the strain at the door of the meeting house (the choir ceased their melody) and the infantile procession, with easy mien and lively voices keeping exact step to their own music, proceeded up to the head of the middle aisle, where the foremost of the band displayed to the right and left, and the two couple from the rear, bearing the declaration of independence, advanced and presented it with peculiar grace, to the Hon. Judge Tyler, who had previously been appointed to read it.

After the reading of the Declaration, "the ode to independence was then sung by the choir, with engaging regularity, and captivating melody." After the oration, "the poem, Genius of Columbia, a vision, was performed by the choir, and the procession then returned to Major Burnham's and from thence to a table, elegantly spread in the orchard adjacent" where toasts were "accompanied by appropriate songs." The "New Song" mentioned above was "by A.H.," with first line: "When the sound of war was loud" (*Vermont Gazette*, 10 July 1804, 3).

Westminster: After a procession of "patriotic citizens" from the Wales Hotel to the meeting house, the exercises included "an ode composed for the purpose by Mr. N.R. Smith" ("Celebration of the Fourth of July at Westminster, Vermont," *Political Observatory*, 7 July 1804, 3).

Virginia

Halifax: "Upwards of seventy gentlemen sat down to dinner at one time at the Bell Tavern occupied by Mr. Rawlins." Toasts were drank, each followed by appropriate music and "discharge of muskets": Music, Yanke [sic] Doodle — Music, Hail Columbia — Music, Washington's March — Music, Roslin Castle — Music, White Cockade — Music, Liberty for Ever — Music, Jefferson's March — Music, The Mulberry-tree — Music, The Spinning Wheel[185] — Music, Let Us Join Hearts and Hands — Music, Come Each Jolly Fellow &c. — Music, The Medley — Music, Come Ye Lads Who Wish to Shine — Music, The Tempest — Music, The Galley Slave[186] — Song, Says Plato Why Should Man be Vain[187] — Music, Lovely Woman, Pride of Nature. "The festival was concluded by a ball at Mr. Toot's Tavern in the evening, at which a very large and brilliant assembly of ladies & gentlemen attended, vieing with each other mirth in and good humor" ("Anniversary of American Independence," *Enquirer*, 21 July 1804, 4).

1805

Publications

"The Birth-Day of Freedom, an Ode. Sung on the Fourth of July, at the Celebration of American Independence, by the Young Federal Republicans of Boston. (Written by one of the Company.) Tune — Hail Columbia." First line: "Sons of Freedom! hail the day" (*Commercial Advertiser*, 12 July 1805, 2; *United States Gazette*, 12 July 1805; *New-York Spectator*, 13 July 1805, 3).

"The following Ode, written for the occasion, was sung at the festival of the Young Federal Republicans, the 4th inst. 'Ode for the Young Federal Republicans of Boston, July 4, 1805.' Tune — 'Adams and Liberty.'" First line: "Arise! Sons of Boston! of Freedom and Truth!" (*Repertory*, 9 July 1805, 1; *Newport Mercury*, 13 July 1805, 4; *Alexandria Daily Advertiser*, 20 July 1805, 3.)

"The following Odes were composed for the young Democratic Republicans, who celebrated our Nation's Birth Day; and sung with great skill and effect at the Universal Church:"

Ode 1st. Written by Mr. C.P. Sumner.[188] [First Line: 'Mid tears which Freedom loves to shed.']
Ode 2d. Written by Mr. Benjamin Gleason.[189] [First line: 'While the heralds of war front the annals of fame.']. "Sung by W.W. Bass — Tune, 'Anacreon in Heaven.'" Cited as "Ode 3d" in *Democrat*.
Ode 3d. Written by Mr. Nathaniel H. Wright.[190] [First line: Hail this happy, glorious day'].

(*Democrat*, 6 July 1805, 4; "Poetry," *Independent Chronicle*, 8 July 1805, 4; "Repository of the Muses," *Republican Spy*, 16 July 1805, 4; *National Aegis*, 17 July 1805, 4; "The Rivulet," *Sun*, 20 July 1805, 4.)

"A New Song for the Fourth of July. By a brother Democrat." First line: "Come ye Democrats join, let us hail the bright day" (*Evening Post*, 10 July 1805, 2).

"An Ode." First line: "Hail, glorious morn! Hail, glorious morn!" (*Albany Centinel*, 23 July 1805, 4).

"An Ode, for the anniversary of American independence — composed for the Fourth of July, 1805, and sung at the celebration of that day in Nottingham [New Hampshire]. Tune, Jefferson & Liberty." First line: "Columbia, rise, inspire your lay" (*New-Hampshire Gazette*, 16 July 1805, 4).

"Ode for the Fourth of July, 1805. Tune — 'Rule Britannia.'" First line: "You who have known oppression's galling chain" (*Newburyport Herald*, 5 July 1805, 3).

"Ode inscribed to the Fourth of July, 1805." By D.A. Leonard. First line: "Hence, laureat flattery's lambent strain" (*Independence Chronicle*, 15 July 1805, 1–2; *Kennebec Gazette*, 24 July 1805, 4; *Providence Phoenix*, 3 August 1805, 4).

"An Ode on the 4th of July. By J. Newhall." First line: "Rejoice sons of freedom on this glorious day." Words and music, voice and two instruments (From the *Republican Spy*, as printed in *Norfolk Repository*, 3 September 1805, 136).

"Original. An Ode, composed for the celebration of the 4th of July, 1805." First line: "Come heav'nly Muse, and strike the lyre" ("Poetry," *Sentinel of Freedom*, 25 June 1805, 4).

"Patriotic song, composed for, and sung at the Republican Festival in Portsmouth, July 4, 1805, after his excellency the governor retired." First line: "With shouts of joy and loud acclaim" (*New-Hampshire Gazette*, 16 July 1805, 4).

"A Song, for the Anniversary of Independence, July 4, 1805 — By S.M. Sewall, Portsmouth." First line: "All hail the glorious day. Tune, 'God Save the King.'" ("The union of genius and patriotism is rare and valuable, and deserves to be greeted with particular applause. For this reason the following very excellent Song merits a place in every paper in the Union, not only as a compliment to the author, but in justice to the nation.") ("Poetry," *Haverhill Museum*, 23 July 1805, 4; "Cabinet Pieces of Poesy: Patriotism and Poetry," *Post-Boy, and Vermont & New-Hampshire Federal Courier*, 23 July 1805, 240; *Weekly Wanderer*, 29 July 1805, 4; *Green Mountain Patriot*, 27 August 1805, 4).

"A Song, sung at the celebration of independence, in Turner, (Maine) 1804 [sic]." First line: "Americans, lift up your voice." *Eastern Argus*, 28 June 1805, 3.

Performances

Connecticut

Granby: A parade of 500 persons and militia included a band of music. The exercises at the church included singing, following by dinner at a bower. The toasts presented included the following music: Yankee Doodle — Washington's March — Jefferson's March — Honest is the Best Policy — Money in Both Pockets — Devil upon Two Sticks — Britons Strike Home — Rogues March[191] — Revellee — White Joke — The Scales Are Even — How Are the Mighty Fallen — Oh I am Lost — Hail Columbia — Centaur — Jefferson & Liberty — Come Haste to the Wedding (*American Mercury*, 25 July 1805, 2.)

Hartford: A large assemblage of Republicans sat down to a dinner served by Elijah Boardman. "After dinner the following toasts were drank to, under the discharge of cannon. A band of music, which attended at the entertainment, played, at the intervals between the toasts, those appropriate tunes annexed to them, with universal applause": Tune, Hail Columbia — Yankey Doodle — Jefferson and Liberty — New-York Fusiliers — Washington's March — Roslin Castle — Tune, Adams at [sic] Liberty — Tune, New-Haven Convention — New-England Aristocracy — Rural Felicity — No Song, No Supper — Money in Both Pockets — Truxton's Victory — Matross March — Grenadier's March — Soldier's Joy — Republican March (*American Mercury*, 11 July 1805, 3).

New London: The day began with a band of music performing music "from the top of Mason's Hall." A parade included "a detachment of militia, preceded by a band of music, under command of Capt. P. Beebe" that marched to the Court House for the exercises that included "singing under the conduct of Maj. J.P. Trott." Later at the hall, a dinner was provided that included toasting with these pieces of music performed by the band: Hail Columbia — Jefferson & Liberty — Liberty Hall — President's March — War Worn Soldier — Roslin Castle — Yankee Doodle — Rural Felicity — Hearts of Oak — White Cockade (*American Mercury*, 25 July 1805, 2).

District of Columbia

Stelle's Hotel, U.S. Marine Band played: Come Then All Ye Social Powers — Yankee Doodle — Washington's March — Jefferson's March — Roslin Castle — 104th Psalm — Independence — No. Fifty Four — Col. Wharton's March — The Battle — Rural Felicity — Come Let Us Prepare — How Sweet thro' the Woodland — Wilkinson's March[192] — Genl. Jackson's March — General Dearborn's March (bass drum and other drums) — Yankee Doodle (*National Intelligencer*, 8 July 1805, 2); at the Executive Mansion, "a powerful band of music [played] patriotic airs at short intervals" (*Ibid*).

Maine

Bangor: Federalists of Bangor and Orington celebrate at Greenleaf's Hall, "the music given in a fine style, and the cheers came from the heart": Hail Columbia — Adams and Liberty — Truxton's Victory[193] — Washington's March — In Clouds when Storms Obscure the Sky — Green Mountain Farmer — Ode to Science — Ca Ira — Vicar of Bray — Hail American — From the East Breaks the Morn ("Independence," *The Gazette*, 23 July 1805, 2); Republicans paraded to Dr. Dean's Meeting House "where several pieces of select music were performed by the members of a respectable musical society, who attended the procession." Later, dinner for "near two hundred citizens, besides about seventy citizen soldiers" heard toasts offered "accompanied with music from the band" ("The Day that Made Us Free," *Eastern Argus*, 5 July 1805, 3); "Federal Republicans" had exercises at the Rev. Mr. Kellogg's Meeting House. "The music given by a number of patriotic gentlemen, was select and appropriate — it raised the feelings of patriotism, and charmed the ear of the amateur" (*Portland Gazette*, 9 July 1805, 2).

Maryland

Baltimore: at Mr. Leaman's Columbia Garden, "a grand concert of vocal and instrumental music," with various performers, including Mr. Durang, orchestra conducted by Mr. Hupichle (?), principal violinists, and Mr. Wolf, principal clarionet, and vocal selections by Miss McMullin (*American and Commercial Daily Advertiser*, 4 July 1805, 2); at the Pantheon, "at least fifty commenced with a psalm of praise to Deity ... and the assembly by uniting in singing the 100th psalm" (*American and Commercial Daily Advertiser*, 6 July 1805, 3).

Massachusetts

Charlestown: After a procession of Republicans from the town hall to the Baptist Meeting House, "the services of the day were introduced by select pieces of musick by the band." After a reading of the Declaration, "a sacred ode then followed." After a prayer, another "ode composed for the day" was performed (first line: "Hail, glorious morn! Hail, glorious morn!"). The services "concluded by an ode, also composed for the occasion." A local newspaper reported that "the music was executed in a style of superior excellence" and another reported that the original Ode was "composed by a citizen of Charlestown." Later a dinner was served at Massachusetts Hall for 200 persons and "toasts were drank, accompanied with appropriate music" (*Independent Chronicle*, 8 July 1805, 2; *New-York Spectator*, 13 July 1805, 2).

Lenox: The exercises were held at the court house. "The solemnity of the occasion was closed with the favorite song of 'Hail Columbia'" (*The Sun*, 13 July 1805, 3).

Northampton: The "order of the procession" had 473 Republicans and included "music, consisting of the South-Hadley, Springfield, and part of the Hatfield Bands." At the exercises held at the church, included was "music played at suitable intervals" ("American Independence — Twenty-Ninth Anniversary," *Republican Spy*, 9 July 1805, 2).

Pembroke: A procession to the meeting house included a band of music. "The ceremonies were introduced by music" ("Celebration at Pembroke," *Democrat*, 10 July 1805, 2).

Pittsfield: A parade to the meeting house included the Pittsfield Republican Band of Music "under the command of Major Stocking. The exercises of the day were commenced with vocal and instrumental music." The ceremony was ended with music (*Pittsfield Sun*, 6 July 1805, 4).

Plymouth: Due to inconvenience on 4 July, this town celebrated the Fourth on 22 July. A procession included a band of music and at the meeting house, "an ode was sung" after the reading of the Declaration of Independence. "The voices of a full choir of singers, chaunting [sic] the blessings of liberty and independence" delighted the audience (*Witness*, 28 August 1805, 3).

Salem: At an "elegant entertainment" at the Lion, "appropriate toasts were announced, and accepted in the greatest harmony, enriched with such songs as were adapted to the principles of liberty, and the exalted reputation of Mr. Jefferson and of his administration...." ("Fourth of July," *Kennebunk Gazette*, 17 July 1805, 1).

New Hampshire

Portsmouth: A celebration of "federalists" included a "public dinner." "The following Song (from the elegant and ingenious pen of J.M. Sewall, Esq.) was sung by Capt. Larkin, and repeated with enthusiasm": "The Hobbies Parodied." First line: "That each has his hobby, we're not now to learn" (*Boston Gazette*, 11 July 1805, 2; *Commercial Advertiser*, 16 July 1805, 2; *New-York Spectator*, 20 July 1805, 1); at St. John's Church the exercises were begun with a "performance of several pieces of well adapted music by the Circean Musical Society." Later at Jefferson Hall "toasts and sentiments were drank, accompanied with songs" ("Fourth of July," *New Hampshire Gazette*, 9 July 1805, 3).

Westmoreland: "The citizens met at Capt. Butterfield's Hall, where they partook of a sumptuous entertainment. At two o'clock a procession was formed" and the assemblage moved to the Meeting House, where the exercises began with "appropriate music" ("Celebration at Westmoreland, [N.H.]," *Political Observatory*, 13 July 1805, 2).

New Jersey

Chatham: "At ten o'clock the citizens, military corps, and ladies, assembled and formed a brilliant procession" that included "martial music." They marched through the "east part of the town" and from there to the church where the exercises included "vocal music, led by Mr. Foster" (*Centinel of Freedom*, 16 July 1805, 2).

New York

New York: At a dinner celebration "given by the officers of the first Brigade Artillery" included: "Song. Parodied for the occasion, by T.G. Fessenden" (first line: "When cannons roar, when bullets fly"); "Song. Varied for the occasion by an officer of the Brigade" (first line: "Every man take his glass in his hand") (*Morning Chronicle*, 12 July 1805, 3); at the "new Vauxhall Garden in the Bowery":

After the duties of the field were closed, the officers of the first Brigade of Artillery sat down to an entertainment provided for them at the Mechanick Hall, honoured by the company of His Excellencey the Commander in Chief (Gov. Lewis) and his suit, the Lieutenant Governour, and Capt. Wylie, commandant of Fort Jay, &c. &c. During the entertainment the band of the Second Regiment performed a number of martial airs. After dinner a number of patriotick songs were sung by gentlemen of the company. The following written for the occasion the day before by T[homas] G. Fessenden, on request, was sung by Captain Smith, Assistant Major of Brigade. The reader will perceive it is a professed parody on the beautiful Sailors Song of "Lash'd to the Helm." ["Celebration of the Fourth of July," *Repertory*, 12 July 1805, 2].

The orchestra will be elegantly illuminated, and a select band of music engaged for the evening. At 6 o'clock precisely, Mr. Barrett, from the Theatre, Charleston, and formerly of N. York, for this night only, will sing "The Hobbies," in which will be pourtrayed the Scold's Hobby — the Beau's Hobby — Sailor's Hobby — Soldier's Hobby — Lady's Hobby — and the American Hobby.... At half past eight will commence a grand patriotic olio consisting of songs and recitations. Song — "Hail America, Huzza! Huzza!" by Mr. Shapter. The patriotic song, "Hail Columbia," or the days of independence. Mr. Barrett. Song — "Battle of Monmouth," — Mr. Shapter. ... Song — "Death of General Warren," — Mr. Shapter. Patriotic song written by R.T. Payne, Esq., "For ne'er shall the sons of Columbia be slaves" by Mr. Barrett. The orchestra will perform select patriotic airs between each of the songs and recitations. [*Commercial Advertiser*, 1 July 1805, 3].

Pennsylvania

Philadelphia: "Democratic association of the Friends of the People" met at Sheridan's, at the Upper Ferry for dinner. "The principal tables were kept in a constant course of hilarity, and enlivened by many excellent songs, some of which, written for the occasion, we hope to have the pleasure of publishing." Meanwhile, military units assembled at a camp on "the heights near the Upper Ferry, where tents for the two battalions of the legion, for the cavalry, artillery and rifle corps were pitched.... The different intervals were occupied by martial airs, the old Yankee Doodle, by the band of instrumental music formed by the members of the Republican Greens" ("Anniversary of American Independence," *Republican Watch-Tower*, 13 July 1805, 3).

Vermont

Bennington: Republican residents of "Bennington and its vicinity assembled at the Court House" and marched to the Meeting House, where

an appropriate psalm having been sung by the choir, the Rev. Mr. Marsh pathetically expressed the gratitude of the assembly in a solemn and impressive address to the Throne of Grace. An ode on Independence was then begun by the choir, and completed by a beautiful procession of young Masters and Misses, who entered the house in a regular, graceful, and dignified manner, introducing a young lady, decorated as the Genius of Liberty, attended by two young men bearing her spear and cap, with the Olive of Peace, and preceding a little boy, gracefully bearing the Declaration of Independence, and delivering it to Mr. Anthony Haswell, who after addressing the audience in a few words, read the invaluable Instrument, the product of wisdom, the purchase of the toil and blood of American Heroes. On the approach of Liberty to her place, it was found, that the crown of royalty, and the mitre of priestcraft had daringly usurped her seat; with peculiar dignity, the beauteous Nymph removed the incumbrances, and placing them at her feet, calmly seated herself, to preside over the exercises of the day. The elegant production, called "The Genius of Columbia, a Vision," written by Andrew Selden,[194] Esq. was then sung, and an Oration pronounced by Mr. Timothy Merrill....

The dinner held at the Court House included an array of toasts, "under the discharge of cannon, and accompanied with instrumental music and sentimental songs, producing a degree of hilarity, and a flow of dignified sentiment, suited to the occasion, and evincive of republican genius and equality": Song, Liberty Tree Revisited — Song, Columbia Comforted — Song, Independence — Song, Tribute to Merit — Song, The Tribute — Song, A View of Past

Scenes — Song, Federalism ("National Festival," *Vermont Gazette*, 8 July 1805, 3).

Poultney: After a procession of citizens and military, there were exercises at the meeting house. After a reading of the Declaration of Independence, "an ode was sung, composed for the occasion, followed by a suitable prayer; after which the choir sung the tune called Jefferson" ("Communication," *Vermont Gazette*, 22 July 1805, 3).

Westminster: "A large collection of respectable inhabitants assembled, and formed in procession in front of Mr. Edgell's house — from thence proceeded to the Meeting house, where the exercise of the day began, with appropriate music" ("Celebration at Westminster," *Political Observatory*, 3 August 1805, 1).

Virginia

Alexandria:

Fourth of July!! Minor theatre, (Spring Garden) will be presented a grand medley of entertainments in honor of the day. The evenings amusements will open with an Ode to Freedom: after which a new song on the Death of Washington. Collin's celebrated Ode on the Passions: Comic Song of Four and Twenty Fiddlers, in character, by Mr. Maginnis. After which by the ingenious Group of Artificial Commedians, will be presented, the full opera of the Poor Soldier.[195] The whole to conclude with a Grand Representation of the Bombarding of Tripoli: being in honor of the brave Columbian tars who fell in that glorious action.... [*Alexandria Daily Advertiser*, 2 July 1805, 3].

1806

Publications

"Among the songs sung on the 4th of July in Boston,[196] was the following written by Robert T. Paine, Esq. — Sung by Dr. Park. 'Song for July 4, 1806.'" "Tune — 'Whilst happy in my native land.'" First line: "Wide o'er the wilderness of waves" (*New-York Gazette & General Advertiser*, 11 July 1806, 2; "Poetry," *Reporter*, 19 July 1806, 4; *Polyanthos* [July 1806]:275).

"Another Song for the 4th of July, by Mitchell Susall, Esq," First line: "What terrible bustle the Democrats made!" (*New-York Herald*, 23 July 1806, 3).

"The Feast of the States. Sung at Bristol, R.I. on the 4th of July, 1806. Song — Written by D.A. Leonard, Esq. describing the staple commodity of each particular State. At the conclusion of each verse, one cannon. '[The traits of genius displayed in the following Song, notwithstanding the severity of some of its political allusions, richly entitle it to preservation on our files. Although some of the sarcastic allusions we do not fully understand, and some we think unjust, yet the candid reader will accept the good, and cast the exceptionable away, and laugh with us at the ingenuous humor of the author.] — Ed.'" First line: "The States were invited, at Jubilee's call." (*Independent Chronicle*, 28 July 1806, 1; "Poetry," *Freeman's Friend*, 6 August 1806, 4; *Salem Register*, 14 August 1806, 1; *Vermont Gazette*, 25 August 1806, 4).

"The following song, composed by William Ellison,[197] Esq. was sung at Camden (S.C.) on the last anniversary of the Fourth of July. Song, tune — 'Anacreon.'" First line: "To Jove in Olympus, while seated in state" ("Poetry," *National Aegis*, 24 September 1806, 4; *Providence Phoenix*, 4 October 1806, 4).

"Hail Liberty, " a "song ... for the Fourth of July" to the tune "Hail Liberty." First line: "Glorious, see the glorious sun" (*Aurora General Advertiser*, 4 July 1806, 2).

"Independence. Tune — Mason's Daughter." First line: "Columbians, to remotest time." Note: "The subsequent song was sung on the 4th of July last [1805], at an entertainment of our brave seamen, at Syracuse in Sicily. It was written by Wm. Ray, a Marine, and late prisoner in Triopli" ("The Museum," *Eastern Argus*, 3 July 1806, 4).

"Well Met, Fellow Freemen"[198] (first line) to the tune "To Anacreon in Heaven," sung at Stelle's Hotel [in Washington City] by "Mr. Cutting" (*National Intelligencer*, 7 July 1806, 3; *American Citizen*, 11 July 1806, 3).

"National Song. Tune, 'Rise Columbia.' Accompanying note in *New-York Spectator*: "The following Ode, written for the occasion, by Samuel Woodworth, was introduced and sung by Mr. King, in a style which did him honor." First line: "When from our shores Bellona's Car." (*New-York Spectator*, 12 July 1806, 2; *Hampshire Federalist*, 15 July 1806, 4; "Poetry," *Reporter*, 26 July 1806, 4.)

"'New Yankee Doodle.' Composed for, and sung on the late anniversary of American Independence, at Redhook [N.Y.]." First line: "Here's yankee doodle, strike the tune" ("Wreath," *Balance, and Columbian Repository*, 22 July 1806, 232).

"Ode for the Fourth of July, 1806: the anniversary of American independence. Tune — Anacreon in Heaven." Signed "Aldrigenus." First line: "Descendants of heroes, whose toils have secur'd" (*Massachusetts Spy*, 2 July 1806, 3).

"Ode on the Military Celebration at Salem of the Fourth of July, 1806. By S[tephen] C[leveland] Blyth.[199] Broadside, Salem, MA, 1806.

"Song composed for the anniversary of American Independence, July 4, 1806. Intended to be sung by a select company of 'Old Continentals' & other Federal Republicans assembled at Lefavour's Hotel, in Lynnfield [MA]. Tune 'White Cockade.'" First line: "In the warfare of life where temptations invade" (*Salem Gazette*, 4 July 1806, 2).

"Song, for the Celebration of American Independence, 1806." By. J.M. Sewall, Esq. of Portsmouth. First line: "Hail Independence! happy day" (*The Balance, and Columbia Repository*, 29 July 1806, 240).

"A Song for the Fourth of July, 1806." Also, titled 'New Yankee Doodle,' composed for, and sung on the late anniversary of American Independence, at Salem, Ms." "Its easy wit and humor, sported in the merry old tune of 'Yankee Doodle,' cannot fail to swell the mirth of the festive board, at the same time that they entitle it to a more extensive circulation than what its author destined it for." First line: "Yankee Doodle is the tune"[200] (*Salem Gazette*, 4 July 1806, 2; *New-England Palladium*, 11 July 1806, 4; "Poetry," *Newburyport Herald*, 25 July 1806, 4; *Republican Spy*, 30 July 1806, 4; *Otsego Herald*, 31 July 1806, 4; *Connecticut Herald*, 5 August 1806, 4; "Poetical Repository," *Farmers' Cabinet*, 5 August 1806, 4; *Salem Gazette*; *Port-Folio*, 30 August 1806, 121).

"Song" by Charles Prentiss.[201] Note: "Perhaps it would be difficult to mention a similar composition that for biting sarcasm, and keen irony, excels the following song." First line: "Round the festive board gather'd, let's honour the day" (*United States Gazette*, 12 August 1806, 3; *Hampshire Federalist*, 19 August 1806, 4; *Post-Boy*, 9 September 1806, 288).

Performances

Connecticut

Litchfield: "Martial music" was performed until sunrise, with more music at 8 A.M. Two hours later additional music was the "signal for the procession to form." At the Meeting House, "where, in the presence of a crowded audience," the music included "Psalm 95th, Tune, New-Hartford," an "Original Ode" (first line: "But hush ye sorrows of the soul"), "Song, composed for the occasion: Air — 'Jefferson and Liberty; or Gaudio" (first line: "Hail-hail the ever glorious day"). At the dinner held at "a large quadrangular bower," the toasts were "accompanied by a discharge of artillery" and "an air from the band, selected by an amateur" ("National Festival," *National Intelligencer and Washington Advertiser*, 27 August 1806, 1, from the *Litchfield Witness*; "Selected Poetry," *Salem Register*, 28 August 1806, 4; *Bee*, 2 September 1806, 2; *Eastern Argus*, 4 September 1806, 1).

New London: "At 10 o'clock A.M. the citizens assembled at Mason's Hall, when a procession was formed and proceeded to the Court House, escorted by a band of music and a large detachment of the independent and the other two Military Companies of the town, under the command of Capt. Peter Beebe. The exercises were commenced by singing." Later back at the Hall, dinner was served followed by toasts "under the discharge of cannon from Fort Trumbull, interspersed with sentimental and patriotic songs, and appropriate music from the band": Music, Hail Columbia — Jefferson & Liberty — Liberty Hall — President's March — War-Worn Soldier — Roslin Castle — Yankee Doodle — Rural Felicity — Hearts of Oak — White Cockade ("Celebration at New London," *American Mercury*, 24 July 1806, 2).

Simsbury: At the Meeting House, "exercises were

opened by singing" and concluded "by singing and prayer" ("Anniversary of American Independence," *American Mercury*, 17 July 1806, 2).

Thompson: Some 200 citizens, "escorted by a band of music and the Infantry Company, marched from Jonathan Converse's Inn to the Baptist Meeting House. "After the ceremonies the Band proclaimed the native invincible spirit of our forefathers in the strain of 'Yankee Doodle.'" A dinner hosted by Converse included toasts with the following music performed: Music, March by Burbank — Jefferson's March — March — Jefferson and Liberty — German Hymn — Washington's March — Mr. Lyon's Favorite — Music — Ode on Science[202] — Roslin Castle — March in Blue Beard — Gen. Orn's March — Scotch Alamand — Money Musk — Italian Serenade — Burbank's Lamentation[203] — White Cockade ("Anniversary of American Independence," *American Mercury*, 24 July 1806, 2).

Windham: "The procession, accompanied by a band of music, marched to the Meeting House," where "the performance of a piece of music" occurred ("Celebration at Windham," *American Mercury*, 24 July 1806, 2).

Maine

Monmouth: "Yesterday, the citizens of Monmouth, and many from Green, Lewiston, Leeds, Wayne, Winthrop, Readfield, Hallowell, Wales and Litchfield, celebrated our independence." After a procession from Prescott's Hall to the Centre Meeting House, "the per-

formances were interspersed by appropriate music" (*Eastern Argus*, 10 July 1806, 2).

Nobleborough: A celebration at Capt. Sleepers' included a procession of 100 Republicans "accompanied with suitable music" to "a shady green" for dinner, toasts, and the following music: Tune, White Cockade — Hail Columbia — Jefferson's March — Boston March — Union — Washington's Ode and March — Jefferson and Liberty — Roslyn Castle — On the Road to Boston — Yankee Doodle — God Save America — Old Hundred — Ode on Science — Gen. Green's March — Belisle March — Come, Haste to the Wedding (*Eastern Argus*, 17 July 1806, 2).

Maryland

Baltimore: The celebration of the Democratic Republicans that met at Major Stoddert's land, east side of Harris' Creek, included "an excellent band of musical amateurs, whose services" were provided throughout the day. Music interspersed between toasts included: Yankee Doodle — Hail Columbia — Washington's March — Jefferson's March — A Triumphant March — Solemn Dirge — St. Patrick's Day — Galley Slave — America, Commerce and Freedom — Plough Boy — Life Let Us Cherish[204] — Hail Wedded Love. "While the company was collecting [to leave], the gentlemen of the band placed themselves on the declivity of a hill and accompanied several excellent patriotic songs given by different citizens, in the choruses of which the people joined with enthusiasm." Concerning one song, sung to the tune "Anacreon in

"German Hymn," by Austrian composer Ignace Pleyel (1757–1831), a student of Joseph Haydn, had performances at toasting ceremonies on the Fourth (1806–21) in Thompson, Connecticut (1806); Newburyport (1807) and Scituate (1820), Massachusetts; Fishkill and Matteawan, New York (1820); Alexandria, Virginia (1820); and Baltimore (1821). Shown here is a printing of the music in *Wyeth's Repository of Sacred Music, Part Second* (Harrisburgh: John Wyeth, 1820) (author's collection).

Heaven," the newspaper reported that "the foregoing song was sung at an entertainment in London, to celebrate the anniversary of the instalment of Thomas Jefferson, as president of the U.S."[205] ("4th July," *American and Commercial Daily Advertiser*, 7 July 1806, 2–3); at Fells Point Academy, "three Odes, appropriate to the day, will be sung by the young ladies and gentlemen of the Academy" (*American and Commercial Daily Advertiser*, 3 July 1806, 3).

Massachusetts

Boston: At the Second Baptist Church, the exercises included:

Hymn (first line: "Let tyrants shake their iron rod")[206]
Ode on Science (first line: "The morning sun shines from the east")
Ode (first line: "When Boston rear'd its triple hills"), written by Benjamin Gleason
Ode-Independence (Billings)

("Order of Performance of the Young Democratic Republicans: at the Second Baptist Church in Boston, on the Fourth of July, 1806." Broadside. Boston: [s.n.], 1806, copy in Brown University; *Independent Chronicle*, 3 July 1806, 2).

Charlestown: At the Baptist Meeting House, "the odes for the day were appropriate and the music delightful" (*Independent Chronicle*, 10 July 1806, 2).

Lanesborough: "The day was ushered in with the firing of cannon, ringing of bells, and melodious strains from instruments of music. More than three hundred citizens of this and adjoining towns" paraded to the meeting house "preceded by a company of artillery and a band of music" (*Sun*, 12 July 1806, 3).

Newburyport: 2000 persons witnessed the fireworks. "Music from the Newburyport Band, who were stationed in a neighboring steeple during the display of fire-works, had a very pleasing effect" (*Newburyport Herald*, 8 July 1806, 3).

Salem: The Salem Independent Cadets had exercises at the Branch Meeting House, where there was a "performance of church music." Later at Crombie's Tavern, dinner and toasts were "accompanied with music by their excellent Band"[207] (*Salem Register*, 7 July 1806, 3). See also, **Publications**, 1812.

Springfield: "The dawn of our National Festival was ushered in by martial music, the ringing of bells, and the firing of cannon." A procession to the Meeting House included a band of music. After the exercises, "an excellent dinner was furnished under a pleasant bower erected for the purpose." Toasts were accompanied by "appropriate musick from the band" (*Hampshire Federalist*, 8 July 1806, 3; "Republican Celebration at Springfield," *National Aegis*, 23 July 1806, 2).

New Hampshire

Portsmouth: "The following song by J.M. Sewell, Esq. was one of those sung at the festive board." First line: "What a terrible bustle the democrats made!" "Two excellent songs composed by J.M. Sewall, Esq., added greatly to the enjoyment of the day" (*Newburyport Herald*, 8 July 1806, 2). See also **Publications** above; another song reportedly sung at Portsmouth was "When Albion dared attempt" (first line) ("Poetry," *Providence Gazette*, 26 July 1806, 4).

Westmoreland: Residents of this town and others from Keene and Putney processed to the Meeting House "where the exercises were performed in the following order:

Appropriate music
A devout and impressive prayer.
A Federal Republican, Republican Federal Oration was delivered by the Rev. C. Brown.
An ode selected for the occasion
["Celebration at Westmoreland, N.H.," *Political Observatory*, 11 July 1806, 3].

New York

Hudson: At a celebration following a derisive toast to Gov. Morgan Lewis by city democrats, the band was ordered to play the "Rogue's March," but "to their honor, absolutely refused." The incident created a scandal and was reported in numerous newspapers. The editor of Hudson's newspaper, *The Balance, and Columbia Repository*, printed: "Whatever opinion may be held with respect to the administration of Gov. Lewis, we think that the chief magistrate of a great and respectable state, should be treated with some sort of respect, even by his enemies. At any rate, if he does no criminal act, we can see no propriety in treating him as a rogue" (*The Balance, and Columbian Repository*, 8 July 1806, 211, and "Editor's Closet: The Rogue's March," 9 September 1806, 286; *Hampshire Federalist*, 22 July 1806, 3; *Litchfield Monitor*, 30 July 1806, 3).

New York: "The societies assembled in the Park precisely at 9 o'clock.... Tammany, as the national society led the van" in the process through city streets. A newspaper noted that "a full band of animating music gave additional éclat to the grand tout ensemble, the approach of which was occasionally announced to the public by a preceding trumpet." After the exercises at the New Dutch Church were completed, the assemblage returned to the Park, "where they were drawn up in a circle, several pieces of music performed, three cheers given, and dismissed each society retiring in their private order to the place of their respective meetings" ("Communication," *American Citizen*, 17 July 1806, 2); the "young Federalists" met at Association Hall. Following at a dinner, "the following sentiments were pledged in flowing bumpers, accompanied with appropriate odes and songs" (*New-York Commercial Advertiser*, 10 July 1806, 2).

Newburgh: At "Mr. June's where an excellent Dinner was provided," interspersed with toasts were "music and appropriate songs under the discharge of cannon": Marseilles Hymn — The Health of Our Sachem — Hail Columbia — Yankee Doodle — Liberty Tree — Erin Go Bragh ("Newburgh," *Republican Watch-Tower*, 18 July 1806, 3).

Pennsylvania

Philadelphia: At the New Theatre "on Friday evening, July 4, ... the celebrated comedy of *He Would Be a Soldier* ... End of the Play, 'Jefferson's March,' composed by Mr. Reinagle, after which, an 'Eulogium on The American Worthies,' will be recited by Mrs. Melmoth. Song — Mrs. Poe. Comic song, 'The Yorkshire Irishman; or, the Adventures of a Potatoe Merchant' — Mr. Bray. Song — 'The Soldier Tir'd of Wars Alarms' — Mrs. Seymour. Recitation — 'The Blackbirds' — Mrs. Melmoth. Comic song — 'Giles Scroggin's Ghost' — Mr. Jefferson. Song — 'He Stole My Heart Away' — Mrs. Poe. The Grand Panorama, of The Battle of Tripoli, will be exhibited — painted by Mr. Holland. Song — 'A Soldier is the Noblest Name' — Mr. Robbins. A characteristic dance ... (*Poulson's American Daily Advertiser*, 1 July 1806, 3); The Southwark Light Infantry Band and Republican Greens Band perform on Broad Street (*Universal Gazette*, 17 July 1806, 3).

Vermont

Bennington: After a march from the Court House to the Meeting House, an assemblage of hundreds of citizens heard the exercises which "were opened by vocal music performed by the choir with their usual harmony and precision." ... After the oration, the procession returned to the State-Arms Tavern where the toasts were accompanied with the following tunes: Song, tune, Anacreon — Song, tune President's March — Song, tune Yankee Doodle — Song, tune Liberty Tree — Song, tune Boyne Water — Song, tune Malbrough — Song, tune Shepherd's Complaint ("National Festival," *Vermont Gazette*, 7 July 1806, 3; *American Citizen*, 14 July 1806, 2).

Burlington: a choir performed at the opening exercises (*Aurora General Advertiser*, 16 July 1806, 2).

Montpelier: The citizens of this and adjacent towns assembled to celebrate the day. "At twelve o'clock the procession, escorted by a company of militia in perfect uniform, commanded by Maj. Lamb (Marshal of the day) with appropriate music, moved from Hutchins' Inn, to the State House ground, where, after hearing the Declaration of Independence, an able prayer and a psalm of praise," listened to an oration by Samuel Prentice, Jun. Dinner was provided at the Inn and the toasts included the following music: Yankedoodle [sic] — President's March — Jefferson's March — Scotch Luck — Yankedoodle — Col. Orn's March — Rogues March — Mrs. Cotilleon — Farmer's March — Green's March — Turk's March — Yankedoodle — Hamilton's March — Miss Morella — Duke of Holstein's March ("Fourth of July, 1806," *Green Mountain Patriot*, 22 July 1806, 3).

Woodstock: The services were held at the town's meeting house where vocal and instrumental music formed a part of the exercises of the day. A dinner was prepared at a bower and "toasts were drank, accompanied by discharges of cannon, and the cheers of martial music" (*Political Observatory*, 18 July 1806, 3).

1807

The unjust attack of the British warship *Leopard* on the USS *Chesapeake* off the coast of Norfolk on June 22, 1807, resulting in loss of American lives, caused great indignation among Americans and the nation's protesting of this event was reflected in newspaper articles, speeches, and ceremonies on the Fourth of July. Music was used in solidarity to support the sentiments of Americans. In New Haven, Connecticut, several pieces of "protest" music were performed, including the "Rogue's March" that followed a toast to "the British Leopard — a disgrace to the lion and unicorn."[208] In Charleston, South Carolina, at a meeting of the Military Club of the 28th regiment, a song written specifically to raise the emotions of the audience there included these lyrics:

> The despot of Britain shall sure rue the day/When the Leopard sprung basely on innocent prey/Till blood be aton'd, all concession we'll spurn/And the haughty proud Lion, shall bleed in his turn.[209]

Publications

"'American Independence.' By E. Ruston — of Liverpool. Tune — 'Liberty Tree.'" First line: "Ye men of Columbia! hail! hail the great day."[210] Accompanying note in *Suffolk Gazette*: "The following animated production is from the pen of Edward Rushton, the author of the stanzas on blindness (in our last) Mary le More, and a number of other elegant and pathetic pieces. It was written last year, and is in the strain of poetic excellence and patriotic fervor with his 'O'er the vine-cover'd hills and gay regions of France'" ("Poetry," *Democrat*, 2 September 1807, 1; *Suffolk Gazette*, 7 September 1807, 4; *Eastern Argus*, 1 October 1807, 4).

"American Independence."[211] First line: "Hail ever memorable Day!" (*New Jersey Journal*, 14 July 1807, 4).

"Anniversary Ode." First line: "While the slaves of a tyrant his birth-day revere" (*Eastern Argus*, 30 July 1807, 4).

"Billings Anthem for independence designed to be performed in this town [Dedham, MA], on Saturday the 4th July next, is this day published, by H. Mann, for the occasion, and for sale at his Printing Office. Price single 25 cents, $2 per dozen" (*Norfolk Repository*, 30 June 1807, 366).

"Columbia, Hail! We Celebrate that Day" (first line) sung by "Mr. Cutting" at Stelle's Hotel in Washington. "Originally sung on 4th of July, 1794, in London by a party of Americans" to celebrate the anniversary (*National Intelligencer*, 8 July 1807, 1).

"The Feast of the States." First line: "The States were invited, at Jubilee's call." Note: "From repeated solicitation, we have provided in the *Eagle*, a place for the following cantata, sung in this town [Bristol, RI], at the celebration of the 4th of July 1806" (*Mount Hope Eagle*, 3 July 1807, 3). See **Publications**, 1806.

"The following song, written for the occasion, by a gentleman of this city [Charleston], was sung on the 4th inst. by an Officer, at a meeting of the Military Club, of the 28th Regiment." First line: "When Britain, puff'd up conceiv'd the weak plan" ("From the *Charleston Times*," *American Mercury*, 6 August 1807, 1).

"Messrs. Printers, The following was written on the 4th ult. As appropriate to our 'Freedom's Natal Day;' if you think it not yet 'out of season,' you will confer a favor by inserting it in the valuable paper. Selim. 'Independence.' Tune-Adams and Liberty." First line: "The genius of Freedom, escap'd from the flood." ("Poetry," *Connecticut Herald*, 4 August 1807, 4.)

"Ode for Independence." First line: "Raise high your glad voices ye children of fame" ("Court of Apollo," *New-York Weekly Museum*, 18 July 1807, 4).

"An Ode for Independence. By Micam Bradley." First line: "Come brothers and make known your joy" (from the *Dartmouth Gazette* as printed in *Suffolk Gazette*, 24 August 1807, 4).

"Ode for the Fourth of July." First line: "Hark, hark! the Angel Trumpeters proclaim" ("Poetry," *Independent Chronicle*, 2 July 1807, 4).

"An ode for the Fourth of July." First line: "Columbia, Columbia! with songs and with mirth" (from the *Political Observatory* as printed in "The Museum," *Eastern Argus*, 16 July 1807, 4).

"Ode for the Fourth of July, tune — 'Rise Columbia.'" First line: "When from our shores Bellona's car" [by Samuel Woodworth] ("Court of Apollo," *New-York Spy*, 30 June 1807, 4). Another newspaper reported that this ode was also sung on July 4 at the meeting of the Philanthropic Literary Society held at its lodge or at the City Tavern,[212] Elizabethtown, N.J. (*New Jersey Journal*, 7 and 14 July 1807, 4 and 4, respectively).

"Ode, for the Fourth of July. By Leonard Jarvis, M.D. As sung at the Republican Festival, in Claremont, N.H." First line: "Columbia rise, 'tis heaven's decree" ("The Museum," *Eastern Argus*, 27 August 1807, 4).

"Ode for the Fourth of July 1807. Sung by the choir at the Republican celebration in this city, at the Baptist Meeting House." First line: "Freedom's glorious era hail!" ("Poetry," *True Republican*, 8 July 1807, 4.)

"Ode, sung at the celebration of American Independence, in this town [Elizabethtown, NJ], July 4, 1807." First line: "Say, should we search the globe around"; "another" [ode]: first line, "Welcome morn, whose genial ray"; "another" [ode]: "When exil'd Freedom, forc'd to roam" ("Poetry," *New Jersey Journal*, 7 July 1807, 4.)

"'Ode to Liberty.' Inscribed to the 4th of July, 1807." First line: "Oh Liberty, thou Goddess bright"

("Waters of Helicon," *Mount Hope Eagle*, 3 July 1807, 4).

"Odes for the 4th of July —1807." Contains three untitled songs. Broadside. Copy in American Antiquarian Society.

"Original Ode, written for the 4th July, 1807." First line: "Strike, strike the notes of lostleft joy" (*Enquirer*, 21 July 1807, 4).

"Patriotic Song." First line: "Hail patriots all this day combine" (from the *Virginia Argus* as published in *American Mercury*, 23 July 1807, 1). See also **Publications**, 1798.

"Song for July 4th, 1807. Tune — 'Jefferson and Liberty.'" First line: "The day arrives so dear to man" (*Newburyport Gazette*, 20 July 1807, 4).

"Song, sung at Salem on the 4th July, 1807, by the Washington Fire Club." First line: "In Anno Domini seventy five" (*New-York Commercial Advertiser*, 13 July 1807, 3; *New York Spectator*, 15 July 1807, 2).

"Songs for the 4th of July and 16th of August." First lines: "The fourteenth day's declining" (by A. Haswell); "Let's charge the smiling glass now" (by A. Selden); "Ye sons of Columbia who brave[ly have] fought" (by [R.] T. Paine; "Well met fellow freemen at Liberty's shrine" (by A. Haswell); "When Britain try'd with haughty pride" (by A. Haswell); "Och! if a song you would have me to sing" (by Dr. Burne); "Remember the glories of Patriots brave"; "When Britons, Tories, Indians" (by A. Haswell); "The sun had risen o'er the sea" (by A. Haswell); "The genius of Columbia" (by A. Selden); "When the horrors of war, sounding loud from each quarter" (by A. Haswell); "Around the urns where sleep our troubled sires" (by A. Selden). Broadside. Ca. 1807. Copy in Brown University.

Songs sung at the celebration in Bennington, VT: "'A Slight View of the World [by Anthony Haswell].' Taken July 4th, 1807. Tune 'Black Sloven.'" First line: "Attention my friends, and I'll sing you a song"; "'Liberty Universal.'[213] Tune — 'Liberty Tree.'" First line: "The clarion of Liberty sounds thro' the world"; "A Review of Past Scenes." First line: "When Britain dar'd in former times"; "Independence." First line: "Come freemen all in chorus join" (*Epitome of the World*, 13 July 1807, 4).

Performances

Connecticut

Chelsea: "At 12 o'clock, the procession in East Chelsea, formed at Kinney's Hotel, and marched preceded by a band of music to meet their brethren in procession under martial music from a spacious bower erected for the occasion on the heights of West Chelsea" (*True Republican*, 15 July 1807, 1).

Hartford: At a dinner celebration, "Yankee Doodle, the well known national song was then performed by the band" as was Hail Columbia — Duane's March — Freedom in His Native Land — Jefferson's March — America, Commerce and Freedom — The Farmer — Yankee Doodle — Roslin Castle — Tag-rag, and no more — Oh! Dear What Can the Matter Be — Washington's Resignation — Washington's March — The Rights of Man — Jefferson's March — Song, Tag-Rag, Exile of Erin — Independent Volunteers — Americans Strike Home ("Independence," *American Mercury*, 9 July 1807, 3).

New Haven: At the "Brick Meeting House ... the audience were favored with a patriotic song, by a number of gentlemen, whose performance was received with repeated acclamations" (first line: "Hail independence, hail!"). At "a very handsome entertainment, provided by Mr. Morgan," a band performed these works interspersed after a selection of toasts: Hail Columbia — Jefferson's March — Dead March in Saul — Roslin Castle — Ye Sons of Columbia Unite in the Cause — Columbia's Bald Eagle Displays in His Claws[214] — March in the Battle of Prague — Rogue's March — Capt. Kidd — Our Country is Our Ship d'ye See[215] — To the Standard Repair — Washington's March — Rural Felicity — Felton's Gavot — Whilst Happy in My Native Land — Yankey Doodle — Hail Patriots All, This Day Combine ("New Haven, July 7," *Connecticut Herald*, 7 July 1807, 3).

New London: "At 11 o'clock a procession was formed at the Hall, and accompanied by the military, and martial and band music, proceeded to the Baptist meeting-house. The exercises commenced with singing by the choir under the direction of Mr. L. Peck,[216] and an appropriate prayer by Mr. P. Griffing. An ode, prepared for the occasion, was then sung." Afterwards the assemblage returned to Masons' Hall for a "plentiful dinner" with toasts "accompanied by discharges of cannon from Fort Trumbull, and music from the band": Tune, Liberty Hall — Yankey Doodle — Hail Columbia — President's March — War Worn Soldier — Triumph of Liberty — Jefferson and Liberty — Funeral Thought — Roslin Castle — White Cockade — Peace and Plenty — Bunker Hill — Every Man to His Calling[217] — Friendship ("American Independence," *True Republican*, 8 July 1807, 3).

Windsor: At the Meeting House, "sacred music" was performed. Later at an adjacent grove, "nearly 200 ladies and gentlemen sat down to an entertainment" and heard the following pieces of instrumental music accompanying the toasts: President's March — Washington's March — Free and Easy — American Hero — Jefferson's March — Yankee Doodle — O What Can the Matter Be — How Imperfect is Expression — Trio Quick Step — Rogues March — Gen. Green's March — American March — Hail Columbia — Rights of Man — Stranger in His Native Land — The Rights of Man — Rural Felicity ("Celebration at Windsor," *Political Observatory*, 10 July 1807, 3; *American Mercury*, 30 July 1807, 3).

District of Columbia

U.S. Marine Band at the Executive Mansion and played "patriotic airs" at "regular intervals" (*National Intelligencer*, 8 July 1807, 1; *Pittsfield Sun*, 27 July 1807, 1); at a celebration of the Washington Light Infantry —

America, Commerce and Freedom — America's Birth Day — Around the Hugh Oak[218] — The Galley Slave — Hail Columbia — Jefferson's March — Logan Water — Oh Listen to the Voice of Love — The Ploughboy — Rogues March — Roslin Castle — The Spinning Wheel — Washington's March — Yankee Doodle (*National Intelligencer*, 20 July 1807, 2).

Maine

Brunswick: A procession, "preceded by a band of music" marched to the meeting house where "several pieces of Music [were] performed, [and] judiciously selected by the band for the occasion" ("Republican Celebration at Brunswick (Me)," *Eastern Argus*, 23 July 1807, 3).

Freeport: At Kendall's Equality Hall, "in the course of the entertainment a Patriotic Song composed by Mr. Kendall,[219] was sung with merited applause" ("National Birth-Day," *Eastern Argus*, 23 July 1807, 3).

North Yarmouth: After a procession of "a respectable number of Federal Republicans" from Capt. A. Richardson's to the Baptist Meeting House, the exercises there "were interspersed with pieces of music, executed with skill and animation" ("National Jubilee," *Portland Gazette and Maine Advertiser*, 20 July 1807, 3).

Portland: At the Rev. Kellogg's Meeting House military officers, "young federal republicans," and others gathered for the exercises which included "the performance of appropriate music," the group enjoyed a dinner at Washington Hall where the toasts included "a song, composed for the occasion" ("American Independence," *Portland Gazette and Maine Advertiser*, 6 July 1807, 2).

Maryland

Baltimore: At Fells Point, at the "mechanics" celebration held at Colegate's Creek, music interspersed between toasts included: President's March — Silence, Dead March — Hail Columbia — America, Commerce and Freedom — The Sons of Alkpornack (*American and Commercial Daily Advertiser*, 10 July 1807, 2).

Massachusetts

Boston: At the "meeting-house in Brattle Street," included in the exercises were "a psalm, by the choir" and "a hymn, composed for the occasion" ("National Birth-Day," *Independent Chronicle*, 6 July 1807, 2); at the Old South Meeting House, "several odes performed by a select choir" were reported as scheduled to be sung (*The Repertory*, 3 July 1807, 2); at a celebration by "Republican young men" at Richardson's Hall on Elm Street, "an original ode written for the occasion" was scheduled to be sung; another report notes that the Republican Young Men of Boston met at Liberty Hall on Elm Street and that "an ode composed for the occasion, by Mr. Samuel Parker, of Roxbury, was sung by Mr. Washburn" (*Democrat*, 4 July 1807, 3;

Independent Chronicle, 9 July 1807, 2); another celebration of Republicans took place at the Boston Coffee House and after a reading of the Declaration of Independence, the following pieces of music were performed as accompaniments to toasts: Hail Columbia — Jefferson's March — Yankee Doodle — Massachusetts March — Yankee Doodle — Washington's March — Massa. [sic] March — Wash. Inf. March — Yankee Doodle — Dirge [played twice] — Yankee Doodle ("Republican Dinner," *Democrat*, 8 July 1807, 1); at a celebration of "young Federal Republicans" at Washington Hall on Bromfield's Lane, the following music was presented with the toasts: Musick, Washington's March — Dead March in Saul — America, Commerce and Freedom — Hail Columbia — Boston March — Strong's March — Yankee Doodle — Adams and Liberty — Massachusetts March — Ode on Science — Orne's March — Hail Liberty — Jefferson's Hobby — Rise Columbia ("Fourth of July," *Repertory*, 10 July 1807, 1).

Groton: The town's Republicans met at the meeting house. "The services were graced by appropriate and well selected music." At the common a dinner was served and toasts were offered, accompanied by artillery salutes and the following music: Yankee Doodle — Jefferson and Liberty — Mass. March — Gen Green's March (*Democrat*, 22 July 1807, 3).

Hingham: Military companies, citizens, and town officials marched to "the Rev. Mr. Richardson's Meeting House" where "the auditory were saluted by a most animating performance of a numerous musical choir, which being graced with the presence of the fair, who charmingly mingled their voices, awakened the exquisitely fine feelings of the soul." After a prayer, "an Ode to Independence was sung with the spirit and with the understanding also." After a reading of the Declaration, "another appropriate piece of music was performed" after which the group marched to the house of Hawkes Fearing for dinner. The toasts drank were accompanied with the following pieces of music: Jefferson's March — Hail Columbia — Washington's March — Rural Felicity — Grand March in Blue-Beard ("Celebration of Independence at Hingham," *Independent Chronicle*, 9 July 1807, 3).

Lenox: In a procession to meeting-house in Lenox, the assemblage was "attended by a band of musick" ("National Birth-Day," *Pittsfield Sun*, 18 July 1807, 1).

Newburyport: "Federal Republican citizens assembled at the Court House and accompanied by a military escort and a band of music," marched to Mr. Coburn's Sun Hotel where the dinner included toasts and the following music: Tune, Washington's March — President's March — Downfal of Paris — Blue Beard March — Reed's March — Massachusetts March — Yankey Doodle — Green's March — Music — Pleyel's German Hymn[220] — Slow March in the Battle of Prague — Yankee Doodle — No Luck About the House — On the Road to Boston — Fisher's Hornpipe — Fare Well ye Green Fields. "Among the songs,

was the following written for the occasion": first line, "When dire oppression's iron hand" ("31st Anniversary of American Independence," *Newburyport Herald*, 7 July 1807, 3; *The Repertory*, 10 July 1807, 3); "Democratic toasts" were presented at Union Hall and were accompanied by the following pieces: Yankee Doodle — Jefferson's March — Boston March — Dirge — Tune, Woodcutters ("Celebration," *Newburyport Herald*, 10 July 1807, 2).

Watertown: A band from Waltham participated in a procession from Harrington's Tavern to the meeting house where the exercises were held. "An ode adapted to the occasion was sung by Mr. Babcock,[221] and a variety of music performed by the band with great accuracy and taste, between the several exercises." Later at Harrington's 200 citizens enjoyed dinner and toasts accompanied by "appropriate music" (*Democrat*, 8 July 1807, 2).

Worthington: A parade to the meeting house was "attended by a band of music." The exercises "were interspersed with pieces of music, vocal and instrumental, which were well performed" (*Republican Spy*, 14 July 1807, 3).

New Hampshire

Boscawen: Citizens of Boscawen, Concord, and Canterbury assembled at Carlton's Tavern and marched to the Meeting House where the exercises included "appropriate music performed by an excellent choir of singers" ("4th of July at Boscawen," *Concord Gazette*, 7 July 1807, 3).

Epsom: A procession of the 18th regiment and citizens, including "persons of distinction from the neighboring towns paraded "accompanied by martial music" to the meeting house for the exercises. "Occasional vocal and instrumental music was interspersed" (*New Hampshire Gazette*, 14 July 1807, 3).

New Castle: After exercises at the church, a dinner was served at Mr. Bell's Tavern. "Toasts were drank with appropriate music, under a discharge of Artillery": Hail Columbia — Washington's March — Jefferson's March — Yankee Doodle — Life Let Us Cherish — Bunker's Hill — Roslyn Castle — A Dirge — Yankee Doodle — Jefferson & Liberty — Battle of Prague — On the Way to Boston — Banks of Ohio — Rogue's March — Air ("Celebration at New-Castle," *New Hampshire Gazette*, 14 July 1807, 3).

Londonderry: At the Meeting House, the exercises began with an "Anthem." Later at "a spacious tent," appropriate toasts were drank, accompanied by music and the discharge of cannon ("Celebration at Londonderry," *Portsmouth Oracle*, 18 July 1807, 3).

New York

Hudson: "In the morning, the usual firing, ringing, music, &c, took place." A morning procession included a band of music. A dinner celebration of Republicans took place at Mason's Lodge; "toasts were drank, and proper music, with appropriate songs, exhilarated the enjoyment": Song, Hail Independence —

Yankee Doodle — Dead March — Jefferson and Liberty — New-York Fusileers — True Courage — The Drum[222] — Quick Step — Lexington March ("The Fourth of July," *Albany Register*, 10 July 1807, 3).

New York: Various trade societies and military officers proceeded from the Park to the "Brick Church opposite the Park." After the exercises, "a few select pieces" were "sung by a select company of singers under the direction of Joseph Kimbal. The business in church being over, the societies will return in the same order to the Park, when the Grand Marshal will form them into a circle; in the centre of which will be placed the grand Standard of the United States, and the music, encircled by all the different stands and banners. The music will perform a few appropriate pieces" ("Celebration of American Independence," *People's Friend & Daily Advertiser*, 3 July 1807, 3); at Vauxhall Garden, "at 6 P.M. a select and numerous Band of Music will commence and continue for the evening, a variety of patriotic airs, military pieces, &c. &c." ("Fourth of July: Vauxhall Garden," *People's Friend & Daily Advertiser*, 2 July 1807, 3).

Richmond, Staten Island: Citizens and soldiers alike marched to the Court House where among the exercises "a patriotic ode [was] sung after which the music played Yankee Doodle, and the procession returned in the same order to the Hotel [Peter Perine's]" for dinner and toasts, "accompanied with discharges of cannon and appropriate music" (*American Citizen*, 9 July 1807, 3; "Celebration of the Thirty-First Anniversary...," *Republican Watch-Tower*, 10 July 1807, 4).

White Plains: The celebration took place with "at least 400 respectable citizens from different parts of the county, accompanied with a very handsome collection of ladies." At Noon the procession assembled and marched in the following order:

1st. Capt. Odle's troop dismounted, with swords drawn.
2d. Band of Music.
3d. Citizens.
4th. Ladies.
5th Orators of the day.
6th Committee of Arrangement.

At the Court House, the Declaration of Independence was read by Ezra Lockwood, "and an Ode, applicable to the occasion, sung, accompanied by a Band of Music." After the principal address was given, "the procession retaining the same order of march, returned to Citizen Baldwin's Republican Hotel, where they sat down to an elegant repast prepared by him. Under a Booth, after dinner, the following toasts, interspersed with songs, &c. accompanied with a discharge from a brass three pounder": The Soldier's Return — Washington's March — Rogue's March — Roslin Castle — Jefferson and Liberty — New Convention — Hail Columbia — Yankee Doodle — Jolly Tar — Come Haste to the Wedding (*Public Advertiser*, 9 July 1807, 2).

South Carolina

Pineville: Music sung after toasts at the celebration: Tune, Yankee Doodle — Washington's March — The President's March — Road to Boston — Congress March — Light Infantry's March — The Rakes of Medlo — Solemn Dirge — Logan Water — Roslin Castle — Stoney Point — God Save the United States — Jefferson's March — Yankee Doodle — The Girl I Left Behind Me — Plough Boy — Light Infantry's March — The Fair American (*City Gazette and Daily Advertiser*, 8 July 1807, 2).

Vermont

Bennington: "The day was ushered in by the discharge of cannon." At 11 A.M. "nearly four hundred gentlemen" assembled at the Court House" and were "enlivened by the harmony of the Bennington Band, and respectfully escorted by Captain Hicks' troop of cavalry, marched under the discharge of cannon to the Meeting-house. The exercises were opened with vocal music by the choir." After the exercises, the assemblage returned to the Court House and "about 500 people partook of a rich repast at the Inns of Messrs. Cushman and Fassett." In the Court Chamber, toasts were read" and drank to the accompaniment of these works: Song, [A Slight] View of the World (first line: "Attention my friends, and I'll sing you a song") — Song, Liberty Universal — Song, Declaration of Independence — Song, Triumph of Principle — Song, Review of Past Scenes — Song, Independence. [See **Publications** above]. A local newspaper reported that "the several appropriate and excellent songs, written and prepared for the occasion by citizen Haswell, added greatly to the hilarity of the scene, and did honor to the head and heart of their patriotic author. They will be published as room shall offer hereafter" ("National Festival," *Epitome of the World*, 6 July 1807, 3; broadside, [Bennington, VT: A. Haswell?, 1807]. Copy in Brown University).

1808

Fisher Ames, a congressional representative from Massachusetts and president of Harvard College died on July 4. In 1811 he was toasted with musical accompaniment at the Hamilton Society Independence Day celebration in New York. A "funeral dirge" was played following this toast, "Fisher Ames — Thy country wept, when on her natal day, Heaven claimed its own and beckoned thee away."[223]

Publications

"'The Embargo.'[224] A Song composed by Henry Mellen, Esq, of Dover (N.H.) and sung there at the celebration of the 4th July. Tune — 'Come let us prepare.'" First line: "Dear Sirs, it is wrong."[225] (*Portsmouth Oracle*, 9 July 1808, 3; "Poetry," *Connecti-*

cut *Herald*, 26 July 1808, 4). Broadside, Dover Landing [N.H.]: Remich, 1808?

"Freedom and Peace, or The Voice of America."[226] First line: "While Europe's mad powers o'er creation are raging." Words by Alexander Wilson, music by Rayner Taylor. (*The Democrat*, 9 July 1808, 1; *Essex Register*, 13 July 1808, 4; *Washington Expositor*, 23 July 1808, 190; *The World*, 25 July 1808, 4; *National Aegis*, 3 August 1808, 4; *Otsego Herald*, 24 September 1808, 4; *Eastern Argus*, 20 October 1808, 4; *Columbian Phenix*, 12 November 1808, 4; *National Martial Music and Songs*[227] [Philadelphia: McCulloch, 1809]; William McCarty, *The New National Song Book, Containing Songs, Odes, and Other Poems, on National Subjects. Compiled from Various Sources* [NY: Leavitt and Allen, 184–?]).

"The heralds proclaim'd on Olympia's fam'd plains"(first line), in *The World*, 25 July 1808, 4.

"The Matter Recited, and the Cause Advocated in a series of airs, Composed for the Performance of the Band of Music, and a Choir of Singers in Bennington, in Celebrating the Thirty Second Anniversary of American Independence." By A. Haswell. [Bennington, VT]: Printed by Halwell & Smead, 1808. Without music. Broadside. Copy in New York State Library.

"Ode, Written for the Celebrarion [i.e., celebration] of the Republican Young Men, July 4, 1808" by Nathaniel H. Wright. Broadside. Boston?, 1808.

"An ode, written on the morning of the 4th of July, 1808, by a youth of Portland [Maine]." First line: "Rejoice, Columbia's sons and pay" ("The Museum," *Eastern Argus*, 14 July 1808, 4).

"Song ... first published in the Boston *Democrat* and copied into the *Register* from that paper." The song's author, John D. Wolfe, Jr. complained that his work was "handed to a friend who after mutilating it in such a manner as to render it perfectly ridiculous, sent it to your paper." First line: "The youthful sailor mounts the bark." ("Selected Poetry," *Essex Register*, 6 August 1808, 1; *Pittsfield Sun*, 13 August 1808, 4; *Political Observatory*, 15 August 1808, 4). The song, which according to one newspaper "bears the stamp of true genius," was later reprinted and titled "The Impressed Sailor," in *American Advocate and Kennebec Advertiser*, 7 October 1815, 4.

"Song. For the 4th of July." First line: "When proud Rome of old her dread eagle unfurl'd (*The World*, 25 July 1808, 4).

"Song for the 4th July, 1808. Composed for the occasion, and sung by Mr. Thomas." First line: "Sons of freedom awake! rend the veil from your eyes" ("Poetry," *Newburyport Herald*, 8 July 1808, 4).

"Song — Tune, 'Anacreon in Heaven.'" First line: "When our sky was illumin'd by Freedom's bright dawn" ("Poetry," *National Aegis*, 29 June 1808, 4).

Performances

Connecticut

Hartford: Republicans from this town and "many respectable gentlemen from the neighboring towns" marched from City Hall to the South Meeting House where the exercises included "an Ode" and "Hail Columbia" (*American Mercury*, 7 July 1808, 3); "The following beautiful piece of composition, was sung in this city, at the celebration of the 4th of July. Its origin is unknown; its excellence it carries with it. It was written for the 4th of March, the 2d era of American liberty — some slight alterations were made to accommodate it to the 1st era, the occasion on which we speak its having been improved." First line: "Brave sons of Columbia! salute, this blest day" ("Poetry," *American Mercury*, 15 September 1808, 4).

New London: "At 11 o'clock A. M. the citizens assembled at the Merchant's Coffee-house, formed a numerous and respectable procession, and proceeded to the Baptist Meeting House, escorted by a detachment from the Independent and Infantry Companies." The exercises included "appropriate singing, consisting of an 'Ode to Science,' &c. conducted by Maj. I.P. Trott." Later, a dinner was served at the Coffee House and toasts were offered "interspersed with sentimental and patriotic songs" ("American Independence Celebration at N. London," *American Mercury*, 14 July 1808, 2).

District of Columbia

Members of the U.S. Marine Band perform in Georgetown at Mr. Semmes's Tavern (*Universal Gazette*, 14 July 1808, 1).

Maine

Bath: Republican citizens of Bath and adjacent towns paraded from Richardson's Hall to the Fourth Meeting House where, after a prayer, "an original, pure and patriotic Ode, prepared on the occasion by Mr. Joseph Wingate, was then sung." Back at the Hall, toasts and the following music were heard: Yankee Doodle — Jefferson's March — Hail Liberty — Roslyn Castle — Washington's March — Ye Patriot Sons — Death or Victory — Rise Columbia — Rogue's March — Dirge — Come Haste to the Wedding ("At Bath," *Eastern Argus*, 14 July 1808, 2).

Gardiner: At the church, "several pieces of appropriate vocal and instrumental music were performed in a handsome manner" ("At Gardiner," *Eastern Argus*, 14 July 1808, 2).

Falmouth: At the meeting house, after a prayer, "an anthem by a select choir" was sung. The exercises "closed by an appropriate ode (in the performance of which, the powers of music, vocal and instrumental, were happily exerted & sensibly felt by a numerous audience of both sexes)." At a dinner, toasts were "enlivened with music & appropriate songs" ("At Falmouth (Me)," *Eastern Argus*, 14 July 1808, 2).

Gorham: "At 11 o'clock, a procession was formed

from Mr. Josiah Shaw's hall, and escorted to the meeting-house by the infantry company, commanded by Capt. James Irish, jun. where appropriate vocal and instrumental music was performed" ("Independence," *Portland Gazette and Maine Advertizer*, 18 July 1808, 2).

Wiscasset: Music at the meeting house was "performed with skill and spirit by the amateurs of the art." "An ode, written for and sung at the Republican Celebration" at Wiscasset: first line, "Sons of freedom arise! The day is return'd" ("At Wiscasset," *Eastern Argus*, 14 July 1808, 2).

Maryland

Annapolis: At a meeting of the Annapolis Ugly Club held at Mr. Coolidge's, "So G — for the Ugly Club" (first line: "Tho' the Mason's Declare"), written by a member of the club and set to the tune "Mason's March," was performed (*L'Oracle and Daily Advertiser*, 13 July 1808, 3; *Maryland Gazette*, 7 July 1808, 3; *Mercantile Advertiser*, 13 July 1808, 2; *Lady's Weekly Miscellany* 8/11 (7 January 1809): 167–68).

Baltimore: At Fells-Point, a celebration of the Columbia Blues included the following music that accompanied toasts: Stoney Point — Roslin Castle — President's March (*Enquirer*, 12 July 1808, 2–3).

Massachusetts

Belleville: At 11 A.M., citizens of the town and vicinity marched from Mr. G. Connor's Hotel to the new Meeting House, where after a prayer and oration, "an Ode on Science was sung, accompanied with instrumental music in a very superior style" (*Newburyport Herald*, 8 July 1808, 2).

Boston: At Bunker Hill Association dinner, Hail Columbia — Jefferson's March — Washington's March — In Freedom We're Born — Guardian Angels[228] — Yankee Doodle — Let Fame Sound Her Trumpet[229] — Long Life and Success to the Farmer — The Hero Comes — Pleyel's Hymn — Roslin Castle — Ere Round the Huge Oak — Tune, Dead March in Saul — Then Guard Your Rights — Are You Sure the News is True — Massachusetts March ("Boston, July 7," *City Gazette and Daily Advertiser*, 27 July 1808, 2); at Boston's New Baptist Meeting House, citizens and the Independent Fusileers attended the following program:

75th Psalm,[230] read by the Rev. Dr. Baldwin, who introduced it with a short appropriate address
Prayer by the Rev. Mr. Blood
Declaration of Independence, by Mr. Benjamin Homans
Hymn. Tune — "Chester" (first line: "Let tyrants shake their iron rod")

("Celebration at Boston," *Essex Register*, 9 July 1808, 3; *Albany Register*, 15 July 1808, 2; *Columbian Phenix*, 16 July 1808, 1; *Pittsfield Sun; or, Republican Monitor*, 16 July 1808, 3.)

Douglas: Procession, "accompanied by an excellent band of music." At the meeting house, "the exercises began with instrumental music" and later closed by a choir of excellent singers, accompanied by the band in performing several select pieces of music, to the great acceptance of the assembly" ("Celebration at Douglas," *Massachusetts Spy*, 13 July 1808, 3).

Groton: A town parade ended at the meeting house where "several excellent pieces of music were performed." Later there were toasts presented with the following musical works: Hail Columbia — Washington's March — Dirge — Soldiers Joy — Crazy Jane — Hear a Sheer Hath — Speed the Plough — Federal March — Kick the Beam — I'll Set Me Down and Cry — Gen. Green's March — Adams and Liberty ("Fourth of July Celebrations," *Columbian Centinel*, 13 July 1808, 1).

Ipswich: The town's Republicans marched from Mr. Treadwell's Inn to the Independent Society's Meeting House where the exercises were begun "by singing part of the 118th Psalm." The exercises were also closed with vocal music ("Republican Celebration of Independence at Ipswich," *Essex Register*, 13 July 1808, 3).

Newburyport: After a procession of 400 Republicans to the Rev. Mr. Giles' Meeting House, the exercises begun with "a hymn adapted to the occasion." Later at Union Hall, where 120 individuals enjoyed "an elegant dinner," toasts were drank accompanied with cheers and the following pieces of music: God Save America — Jefferson's March — Dirge — Rise Columbia — President's March — Rogue's March — Washington's March — Go [to] the Devil and Shake Yourself — Massachusetts March — All the Way to Boston — Jefferson and Liberty — Embargo — Humours of the Priest House — Yankee Doodle — O Dear, What Can the Matter Be[231] — Humours of Boston ("Celebration at Newburyport," *Essex Register*, 9 July 1808, 2); at another celebration clergy, militia and citizens assembled at the Mall and marched, "preceded by an excellent band of music," to the Meeting House on Pleasant Street "where after appropriate music by a select choir, and an address to the Throne of Grace by the Revd. Jon Andrews, Ebenezer Mosely, Esq. delivered the anniversary oration" (*Newburyport Herald*, 8 July 1808, 2).

Pittsfield: "The exercises of the day consisted of appropriate vocal and instrumental music" ("American Independence," *Pittsfield Sun*, 9 July 1808, 3).

Roxbury: A procession of citizens marched to "the Rev. Dr. Porter's Meeting House. The performances there were an appropriate prayer, by the Rev. Dr. Porter — Hymn to Freedom, composed by Mr. Samuel Parker[232] — Tune old hundred [first line: "Freedom, around thy glorious shrine"] — The Declaration of Independence was read by Mr. Abraham Fox — Oration by Mr. Nathaniel Smith — Ode for the Fourth of July, composed by Mr. Samuel Parker — tune 'Rise Columbia'" [first line: "When Britain proud and vengeful grown"] (*Independent Chronicle*, 7 July 1808, 2; *Democrat*, 9 July 1808, 3; *Essex Register*, 9 July 1808, 1; "Celebration at Roxbury," *Repub-*

lican Spy, 20 July 1808, 2; *An Oration Pronounced July 4, 1808, before the Citizens of the Town of Roxbury, in Commemoration of the Anniversary of American Independence*. By N. Ruggles Smith. Boston: Adams and Rhoades, 1808).

Wrentham: At the Meeting House a reading of the Declaration of Independence was followed by vocal and instrumental music ("Celebration at Wrentham," *Independent Chronicle*, 14 July 1808, 2).

New Hampshire

Dover: After a procession from Mr. Ela's Tavern to the Meeting House, "the exercises of the day were introduced by an appropriate Ode composed for the occasion by Moses L. Neil [ne Neal],[233] Esq. and performed by a band of singers, accompanied by instrumental music, in a manner at once lively and affecting." Neal then presented the oration which focused on the "causes which led to American Independence" ("Republican Celebration at Dover, N.H. on the 4th July, 1808," *New Hampshire Gazette*, 12 July 1808, 2); Federalists numbering "sixty gentlemen" paraded, "Preceded by a number of gentlemen musicians of this town," to the meeting house. "The publick exercises commenced with an appropriate Ode composed for the occasion by Henry Mellen, Esq. which was sung and played by a select band of musicians in a stile [sic] of superiour excellence." At the dinner, Mellen's song "Embargo" was sung, along with the following additional pieces: Washington's March — Grand March — Roslin Castle — Black Joke — Echo — Massachusetts March — French March — President's March — There Is No Luck About the House — Funeral Thought — Galley Slave — The Down Hill of Life — Bunker Hill — The Shipwreck — Yankee Doodle (*Portsmouth Oracle*, 9 July 1808, 3). See **Publications** above.

Portsmouth: The "Federal Republicans" celebrated at the Assembly Room. "The musick-loft was ornamented by a large handsome Ensign hung in festoons, military trophies and emblems of the Arts and Sciences" and after the dinner, "toasts were given accompanied with music and a variety of patriotic and entertaining songs, firing of cannon and cheerful acclamations, suited to the occasion": Yankee Doodle — Washington's March — Hail Columbia — Gen. Reed's March — Langdon's March [John Langdon] — O Dear What Can the Matter Be — Adams and Liberty — Are You Sure the News is True — God Save America — Randolph's Reel — Strong's March — Crane's March — Herrick's Air[234] — The Shade of Washington — Kean's March — Pickney's March. "The company are under obligation to the Gentlemen of the Portsmouth band of music for their polite attendance on the occasion; their performance did honour to the Company and themselves." ("The Anniversary," *Portsmouth Oracle*, 9 July 1808, 3; *New-England Palladium*, 15 July 1808, 1).

New Jersey

Allentown: A procession to the Presbyterian Church included music ("Celebration at Allentown," *Trenton Federalist*, 11 July 1808, 3).

Bridge Town: At a dinner prepared by Benajah Parvin, toasts were "accompanied with a discharge of cannon and appropriate music" ("Celebration at Bridge Town," *Trenton Federalist*, 11 July 1808, 3).

New York

Fairfield: The Alexandrian Society and an assemblage of additional men and women celebrated at the Fairfield Academy. The ceremony convened with singing. The day included "martial music," a "cold collation," and toasts with the following music: Hail Columbia — Speed the Plough — Yankee Doodle — Washington's March — Ode on Science — Jefferson and Liberty — Adams and Liberty — Death of Washington ("Communication. Fourth of July, 1808," *Herkimer Herald*, 26 July 1808, 3).

Hudson: During the town's procession, as a miniature merchant ship representing the embargo was towed along the streets and the American flag was raised, a band played "Washington's March," and as an embargo flag was raised on the ship, in derision the band played "Yankee Doodle." Later at an "entertainment provided by Mr. Stocking," the following pieces were played as toasts were presented: Tune, Yankee Doodle — Tune, Washington's March — Tune, Washington's Favorite — Song, Wife, Children and Friends[235] — Hail Columbia — Tune, Truxton's Victory — Tune, Hush Rude Boreas, Blustering Railer — Tune, Adams and Liberty — Tune, Charleroy — Tune, Roslin Castle — Tune, A Trip to Pluckenny — Tune, O, Dear! What Can the Matter Be! — Tune, I was a'ye See, a Water-Man — Tune, 10th Regiment — Tune, Columbia, Columbia, to Glory Arise — Tune, The Hobbies — Tune, Come Haste to the Wedding ("Independence Day," *The Balance*, 12 July 1808, 109).

New Lebanon: "The Republican citizens of this and the neighboring towns" formed a procession at 11:30 A.M. to the sound of "one gun and music." Two bands marched among other groups to the Meeting House where the exercises included vocal and instrumental music. At a dinner under a bower, "toasts were drank, each accompanied by a discharge of artillery and music from the band": Yankee Doodle — Federal March — American March — Jefferson's March — Roslin Castle — Entered Apprentice — The Drum (*Pittsfield Sun; or, Republican Monitor*, 23 July 1808, 1).

New York: "Stanton Island, held at Richmond": at the Court House, "a number of patriotic songs sung" (*American Citizen*, 8 July 1808, 2).

Utica: A procession "from the hotel to the Presbyterian Church was accompanied by martial music." The exercises began with a prayer, "then followed vocal music, in the words 'Before Jehovah's awful throne,' &c. The Declaration of Independence was then read by F.A. Bloodgood, Esq. succeeded by vocal music in words appropriate to the day." After an oration by Thomas Skinner, the following ode was sung: first line, "The Morning sun shines from the east" (From the *Utica Gazette* as published in *Republican Watch-Tower*, 15 July 1808, 3).

Rhode Island

Providence: A procession marched to the First Congregational Meeting House where "the exercises commenced with the singing an ode peculiarly adapted to the occasion": first line: "Come, let us join the cheerful song." After a prayer, an "ode published in our last was sung": "Martyrd Patriots," first line: "August the sacred day that gave." "The ode inserted in this day's paper concluded the proceedings at the meeting house": "An ode for the Fourth of July, 1808, written by Paul Allen,[236] Esq."; first line: "Fair Freedom once an eagle found" ("Glorious Anniversary," *Columbian Phenix*, 2 and 9 July 1808, 1 and 3–4, respectively).

Vermont

Fairfield: After a procession to the Town House, the exercises consisted of:

1. Sacred music.
2. A prayer, by the Rev. Benjamin Wooster.
3. Sacred music
4. An oration....
5. An Ode, selected for the occasion.
6. A prayer, by the Rev. P.V. Boge.
[*St. Albans Adviser*, 14 July 1808, 1].

Virginia

Alexandria:

The public are respectfully informed that the Alexandria Theatre will open on Monday, July 4, 1808, being the anniversary of American Independence, with the celebrated tragedy of Gustavus Vasa,[237] the deliverer of his country. Written by Henry Brooke, esq. author ... after which an Interlude (in honor of the day) called The Spirit of Independence; or Effusions of Patriotism. Consisting of singing, dancing, and recitation. Song, "The Standard of Freedom" the words by Mr. Mills, of the Philadelphia Theatre — the music by Mr. J. Cole of Baltimore, [sung by] Mr. Jacobs. Recitation, "Ode to Freedom," [sung by] Mr. Wood. Dance, A Hornpipe. [danced by] Miss Hunt. Song, "Fragrant Chaplets for the Soldiers bio Prepare,"[238] [sung by] Mrs. Seymour.... After which will be presented the admired musical entertainment of the Review; or, The Man of All Trades.... [*Alexandria Daily Advertiser*, 1 July 1808, 3.]

1809

Publications

"The following Ode, sung at the celebration of American Independence in Taunton, [Massachusetts]

was composed for the occasion, by Mr. James L. Hodges."[239] First line: "Columbia's sons appear" (*Old Colony Gazette*, 7 July 1809, 3).

"The following Ode, written by Mr. Ellison, was sung at the Festival given by the Federalists of Charlestown, on Independent day, by Mr. Stebbins,[240] in his usual style of excellence." First line: "Strike! strike the sounding lyre" ("Poetry," *Boston Mirror*, 8 July 1809, 4).

"The following Ode, written for the occasion, was sung in this town [Dedham, Massachusetts], at the celebration of independence, on Tuesday last, by the Union and Harmony Company." First line: "While sounding arms on Europe's shore" ("Poetry," *Norfolk Repository*, 6 July 1809, 4).

"Live Triumphant or Contending Die."[241] By J.W. Brackett. Set to music by James Hewitt. First line: "Auspicious day, the annual rite we bring." New York: J. Hewitt's Musical Respository & Library, [1809]. Copies in Center for Popular Music, Middle Tennessee State Universiry, and Levy Collection of Sheet Music. See New York below.

"Music for 4th of July. For sale by Cushing and Appleton (price half a dollar). The Occasional Companion no. 4, containing Avington; Independence, an anthem; Freedom, a national ode for the 4th of July; and a National anthem" (*Salem Gazette*, 4 July 1809, 3).

"Song, written for the 4th of July, and sung by the Republicans of Troy [Pennsylvania]." First line: "In the volume of fate, as the book was unfolded." (*Pennsylvania Herald, and Easton Intelligencer*, 9 August 1809, 4.)

"Song, written for the Fourth of July 1809. By James H. Price, Esq."[242] First line: "In the volume of fate, as the book was unfolded." ("The following elegant and patriotic effusion sours so much beyond the ordinary style of metrical composition, and the lame and vapid odes of the day, that we assign it a conspicuous place in our columns with no reluctant hand. It breathes the energy of feeling, and while it pleases the fancy it warms the heart. Intended by its author to be sung at the celebration of our national anniversary, in this village only, we have succeeded in obtaining a copy of it from Mr. Price, and are happy to be able, through the medium of the *Farmer's Register*, to give it a range proportionate to its merits.") ("National Birth-Day," *Farmers' Cabinet*, 25 July 1809, 4; *Weekly Wanderer*, 28 July 1809, IX/35: 4.)

Performances

Connecticut

New London: After a procession from Mr. D. Frink's to the Baptist Meeting House, the exercises included "an Ode by the choir of singers, conducted by Mr. L. Peck — prayer by Mr. P. Griffing — Ode — Declaration of American Independence, read by Mr. L. Fosdick — oration by Mr. B. Hempstead — Ode — concluding with prayer." Later at the dinner hosted by

Mr. Frink, toasts were drank "interspersed with various sentimental and patriotic songs" ("Republican Celebration," *American Mercury*, 20 July 1809, 2).

District of Columbia

At the Centre Market the U.S. Marine Band performed and a band of music from Captain Davidson's Company of Light Infantry performed "appropriate airs"at the church on F Street ("Fourth of July," *National Intelligencer*, 7 July 1809, 2); at the National Theatre, a musical entertainment titled *Independence of Columbia* was performed (*National Intelligencer*, 3 July 1809, 2).

Maine

North Yarmouth: The exercises at the Baptist Meeting House were begun with "music adapted to the occasion" ("Celebrations of Independence: At North-Yarmouth," *Freeman's Friend*, 15 July 1809, 3).

Portland: At Union Hall, the Republicans enjoyed toasts after dinner "accompanied with appropriate marches" ("National Festival!" *Independent Chronicle*, 20 July 1809, 1).

Maryland

Baltimore: In the "Grand Procession, the band led by Mr. Wolff, whose appropriate music during the procession, and after drinking the toasts, greatly added to the pleasures of the company, and the public." The dinner hosted two bands ("Grand Celebration, at Baltimore," *Enquirer*, 14 July 1809, 4; *Old Colony Gazette*, 28 July 1809, 4; "Grand National Jubilee," *Pittsfield Sun, or Republican Monitor*, 29 July 1809, 1–2; *National Aegis*, 9 August 1809, 4).

Massachusetts

Boston: Along with all the "Military Corps in Uniform" in the procession was "a new and full band of Black Musicians in a superb Moorish dress. Their appearance was novel and rich" ("National Birth Day," *New-England Palladium*, 7 July 1809, 2); the Bunker Hill Association celebrated with exercises at the Methodist Chapel that included:

I. Ode on Science.
II. Prayer, by the Rev. Mr. Sabim (?)
III. 75th Psalm.
IV. Introductory address. By David Everett, esq.
V. Hymn.
VI. Oration, by Wm. Chs. White, esq.
VII. Independence, an anthem. By the choir.

"The choir of singers of the Third Baptist Society, who gave their assistance on this joyful occasion, were harmonious beyond description" ("National Jubilee!" *Independent Chronicle*, 6 July 1809, 2).

Ipswich: Federalists of this town celebrated with a dinner at Major Swasey's Hall. "Toasts were given, accompanied with songs, discharge of cannon, &c" ("Celebration at Ipswich," *Salem Gazette*, 21 July 1809, 3).

Leominster: Republican citizens representing "the N. district in the county of Worcester" marched from Hale's Inn to the Meeting House where the exercises were held before "a crowded and brilliant audience. Most excellent and appropriate music, from a select band, enlivened the varying scenes." A dinner was held under an arbor back at the Inn and toasts were drank accompanied by the following pieces of music: Rise Columbia — Republican March — Ma Chere Amie[243] — Madison's March[244] — Gen. Green's March — Washington's March — Paris March — Swiss Guard March — The Farmer — Rural Felicity — Adams and Liberty — The Galley Slave — Massachusetts March — Movement in the Castle Spectre[245] — Duke of York's March — Yankee Doodle — Lord Barnett's March — Hail Columbia ("Fourth of July Celebration at Leominster," *Boston Patriot*, 12 July 1809, 2).

Newburyport: The event included a procession, exercises at the Meeting House on Federal Street, and "a collation, on the green near the State House." Toasts were announced, accompanied by music and the discharge of cannon: Yankee Doodle — Music, Pleyel's Hymn — Music, Washington's March — Music, Roslin Castle ("Fourth of July," *Newburyport Herald*, 7 July 1809, 3; "At Newburyport," *Freeman's Friend*, 15 July 1809, 3).

Pittsfield: "At 12 o'clock a numerous procession was formed, consisting of the Republican citizens of this and many other towns in this County, and a number of our friends from Hampshire County, which, preceded by a Band of Music, moved to the Meeting House, where the exercises were as follows: Music on the Organ, and a Psalm by the choir" followed by a reading of the Declaration of Independence and oration. "The exercises were closed by vocal and instrumental music" and later "Mr. Clarke's where an elegant dinner was provided, of which a large number partook, the usual number of toasts were drank, accompanied with music by the band, and the discharge of cannon." At "the celebration in this town, on the 4th inst. with the music accompanying them [the toasts], by the band": Yankee Doodle — American March — American Favorite — York Fuzileers — Felton's Gavot — Jefferson's March — A March — Greene's March — Handel's Clarionet — Cold Stream — Washington's March — 40th Regiment — Duke of Holstein — Trio — Fresh and Strong — Short Troop — Handel's Duett ("Grand National Jubilee," *Pittsfield Sun, or, Republican Monitor*, 8 and 15 July 1809, 3 and 2, respectively).

Rochester: At a meeting of Republicans of this and neighboring towns, the audience heard an "Ode to Liberty" that began the ceremony and an "Ode to Peace" that ended the event ("National Anniversary," *Old Colony Gazette*, 21 July 1809, 3).

Salem: At the North Meeting House, "music on the organ was performed at proper intervals" ("Fourth of July," *Salem Gazette*, 7 July 1809, 3).

New Hampshire

Danbury: A parade with "an excellent band of music from Salisbury" marched to a green for the ceremony which included a performance by the band of "Ode to Science" ("At Danbury," *New-Hampshire Patriot*, 18 July 1809, 4).

Deerfield: "A respectable number of citizens and strangers (of both sects)" gathered for a procession, escorted by Capt. Batchelder's Company of Cavalry and Capt. Haynes' of Artillery, together with a select band of excellent music [and] thence proceeded to the Congregational Meeting House" where the exercises were held ("Celebration at Deerfield," *New-Hampshire Patriot*, 18 July 1809, 4).

Pembroke: At the meeting house, during the exercises "an Ode was performed by a band of Instrumental Music." Following at "the green in front of Mr. Fisks, where an elegant entertainment was provided for the occasion," the toasts following dinner were "accompanied by Martial and Instrumental Music" ("Celebration of American Independence, at Pembroke," *Concord Gazette*, 11 July 1809, 3; "At Pembroke," *New-Hampshire Patriot*, 18 July 1809, 4).

Portsmouth: A large procession that included citizens from surrounding towns met at Jefferson Hall and, "attended by the Portsmouth Band of music," marched to the Meeting House where the exercises "were commenced with an Ode by the band and an excellent choir of singers." After a prayer, "an original Ode composed for the occasion" was presented. Following the exercises, the procession marched to Mechanic Hall for an "elegant and plenteous dinner" that included toasts "accompanied with music, and interspersed with songs": Music, Rise Columbia — Adams and Liberty — Madison's March — Let Fame Sound Her Trump — Soldier's Joy — Guardian Angels — Dead March in Saul — Bunker Hill — God Save America — Plough Boy — Yankee Doodle — Lamentation of Jeremiah — O Dear What Can the Matter Be — Old Hundred — A Parcel of Rogues in a Nation — Then Guard Your Rights — Virtus Triumphant ("Fourth of July," *New-Hampshire Gazette*, 11 July 1809. 3); a parade of Federal Republicans escorted by Gilman's Blues and "accompanied by the Exeter Band" proceeded to the South Meeting House, where "several Odes were sung appropriate to the occasion, by a select Choir accompanied by the Band, who did themselves infinite honour, and greatly gratified one of the most numerous, respectable and brilliant audiences, we ever remember to have witnessed in this place on a like occasion." Later at Capt. Whidden's Hall, 140 persons had dinner and heard "several original patriotick songs, interspersed with musick from the Band": Yankee Doodle — Hail Columbia — Shade of Washington — President's March — Gilman's March — Adams and Liberty — Oh Dear What Can the Matter Be — Molly Put the Kettle On — Plymouth Ode[246] — Mellen's Embargo — Speed the Plough — Herrick's Air — How Sweet's the Love That Meets Return. "The Exeter Band acquitted themselves in a most masterly manner very much to their honor and the gratification of the company" ("4th July, 1809," *Portsmouth Oracle*, 8 July 1809, 3).

Temple: Citizens from New Ipwich, Peterborough, Wilton, and adjacent towns paraded to the meeting house where the exercises included "select pieces of music." A dinner, with toasts, included: tune, Yankee Doodle — tune, Jefferson's March — tune, Adams & Liberty — tune, Major Minor — tune, Ipwich Master — Washington's March — Dead March — No Luck About the House — Devil's Dream — Battle of Prague — Downfall of Paris — Vicar of Bray — Green's March — Swiss Guards — Free Mason's March — Grand March — Oh! How I Long to be Married ("Fourth of July Celebrations," *Farmers' Cabinet*, 25 July 1809, 1).

Wilton: The exercises at the meeting house "were opened by instrumental music" and "closed with vocal and instrumental music, judiciously selected and well performed" (*Farmers' Cabinet*, 25 July 1809, 1).

New Jersey

Freehold: "A large and respectable number of Federal Republicans of the county assembled about two o'clock at the Inn of Thomas Thompson ... partook of an elegant entertainment prepared for the occasion." Toasts were "attended with martial musick and the discharge of cannon." After a toast to "the memory of Washington, ever dear to all true Americans," a "Song, 'Shade of Washington,' composed for the occasion [was sung] by W. Lloyd, Esq." Other works sung were a "Song, Federal Yankee-Doodle" and "Song, 'New Hail Columbia.'"[247] (*Trenton Federalist*, 10 July 1809, 3).

New York

Babylon: This town held the exercises at the meeting house where, after an opening prayer, "a psalm [was] sung by the choristers under the direction of Mr. Smith Muncy." The ceremony ended with vocal music ("Patriotic Celebration of the 4th July, 1809, at Babylon, Suffolk County, Long Island," *Republican Watch-Tower*, 18 July 1809, 4).

Cambridge: Located in Washington County, this town had a flag presentation and a parade with a band of music that marched to the meeting house. "Three patriotic odes, adapted to the occasion, were sung." Later the infantry and a band led the ladies to a separate dinner celebration. The men processed to a dinner held at a bower where the following music was performed: Tune, Hail Columbia — Tune, Handel's Water Piece — Tune, Greene's March — Tune, Washington's March — Tune, Short Troop — Tune, Holstein's March — Tune, President's March — Tune, Scotch Luck — Tune, Felton's Covert — Tune, Bag Pipes — Tune, Yankee Doodle — Tune, Governor Strong's March — Tune, 40th Regiment — Tune, Favorite Air — Tune, Federal March — Tune, Handel's Clarinett ("For the Balance," *The Balance and New-York State Journal*, 14 July 1809, 2–3).

New Lebanon: "The Republican citizens of the town of Canaan" were "joined by a large number of their political friends from different towns in the Counties of Columbia Rensselaer and Berkshire" with the residents of New Lebanon in a flag-raising ceremony "for an elegant flag staff erected for the purpose, more than one hundred feet in heighth." At the Meeting House, there were exercises followed by "a plentiful and elegant entertainment" at Maj. Doubleday's. "Toasts were drank, accompanied by a discharge of cannon and music from the band": Yankee Doodle — Hail Columbia — Bradent's March — American March — Jefferson's March — Death of Washington — Roslin Castle — Jefferson and Liberty — New-York Fusileers — Washington's March — Federal March — Entered Apprentice — Handel's Clarionet — Green's March — The Drum — Adams and Liberty ("Grand National Jubilee," *Pittsfield Sun, or Republican Monitor*, 22 July 1809, 3).

New York: The Washington Benevolent Society and its 2000 members dined together after laying a cornerstone for its new building, Washington Hall. A procession from the College Green to the site included two bands, the second followed by "gentlemen selected to sing the Ode." The cornerstone was laid "under a salute of thirteen guns and music from the bands." A local newspaper reported that "on forming the line the Washington Standard [was] received, the music playing 'Washington's March.'" The "Original Ode" was written by Joseph W. Brackett, Esq., "set to music by Mr. [James] Hewitt" and "sung before the Society with rapturous applause, is selected from among numberless other effusions of genius and patriotism, as meriting pre-eminent notice for its pure and spotless splendor." As noted on the score, as well as reported by one newspaper, the work was sung by "Mr. Caulfield"[248] at the North Church ("Patriotic Song." First line: "Auspicious day, the annual rite we bring" ("Glorious Anniversary," *Mercantile Advertiser*, 4 July 1809, 2; *Evening Post*, 5 July 1809, 2; *New-York Commercial Advertiser*, 5 July 1809, 3; *New-York Spectator*, 8 July 1809, 1; *New-Jersey Telescope*, 11 July 1809, 3; *Alexandria Gazette*, 12 July 1809, 3; "Poetry: Washington & Liberty," *Connecticut Herald*, 18 July 1809, 4; *Farmer's Cabinet*, 18 July 1809, 4; *Northern Whig*, 18 July 1809, 2). See **Publications** above.

Oxford: "About 300 Republican citizens" gathered at the Eagle Tavern for a procession, "preceded by music." Later at a dinner toasts were drank "accompanied by music, and vollies of musketry" ("Celebration of Independence at Oxford," *Olive-Branch*, 7 August 1809, 3).

Sag-Harbor: "Agreeably to previous public notice, a very large and respectable concourse of people assembled at Corey's Coffee House. At half past eleven, a procession marched to the meeting house, escorted by a volunteer detachment of artillerists, accompanied by a band of music.... The exercises were opened by vocal music." Later the "procession returned in the

same order to the Coffee House" where after dinner, "toasts were drank, accompanied with discharges of cannon and interspersed with patriotic songs and lively airs by the Band" ("A National Festival," *Suffolk Gazette*, 8 July 1809, 3).

Southold: Citizens and military of this town and Riverhead assembled at Mr. Moore's Inn and marched to the Meeting House, "the music playing the truly national tune of yankey doodle. The exercises commenced by singing." Following an oration and prayer "and singing Doctor Dwights version of 18th Psalm, the company returned to Mr. Moore's in the same order they had marched to the meeting-house (the music playing 'Union of All Parties')." ("Communication: The Fourth of July," *Suffolk Gazette*, 15 July 1809, 3.)

Westchester: "A band of music" at the Court House, followed by music at the dinner held at William Baldwin's Republican Hotel: Hail Columbia — Washington's March — O Lord, What Can the Matter Be — Governor's March — Yankee Doodle — Jefferson and Liberty — Hail Columbia — Roslin Castle — Why Soldiers Why — The Rogue's March — Liberty Tree[249] — Yankee Doodle — Jefferson's March — Lexington's March — Soldier's Return — Hail America — Come, Haste to the Wedding ("Fourth of July, Westchester Celebration," *Public Advertiser*, 13 July 1809, 2).

Pennsylvania

Easton: After a parade of the Light Infantry Company at the Court House and through the city streets, the company met at the house of Mr. Thomas Sebring for dinner. After a reading of the Declaration of Independence, toasts were "drank interspersed with appropriate songs and music": Song, Hail Columbia — Music, Yankee Doodle — Music, President's March — Song — Music, Roslin Castle — Yankee Doodle — Song, The Gods of the Greeks — Dead March — Song — Grenadiers March — America, Commerce & Freedom — Jefferson's March — Song, Here's a Health to All Good Lasses[250] ("Fourth of July," *Pennsylvania Herald, and Easton Intelligencer*, 12 July 1809, 2).

Philadelphia: At a dinner celebration by the American Republican Society, 500 persons heard the dinner call sounded at 3 pm by a "charge of cannon followed by 'Hail Columbia' from the band." After dinner the toasts were accompanied by the following pieces: Tune, Hail Liberty, Supreme Delight[251] — Tune, Hail Columbia — Tune, Madison's March — Tune, Roslin Castle — Tune, Yankee Doodle — Tune, Dead March in Saul — Tune, Life Let Us Cherish — Tune, Washington's March — Tune, America, Commerce and Freedom — Tune, Solemn Dirge — Tune, Stony Point — Tune, Ma Chere Amie (*Poulson's American Daily Advertiser*, 7 July 1809, 2; *Federal Republican*, 10 July 1809, 2; *Independent American and Columbian Advertiser*, 11 July 1809, 3; "American Republican Society," *Alexandria Daily Gazette, Commercial & Political*, 17 July 1809, 2).

Rhode Island

Newport: At the Second Baptist Meeting House, "the public exercises were intermingled with excellent and appropriate music." At the "elegant dinner" event held at Mr. Townsend's Coffee House, "toasts were drank, accompanied by a number of popular and patriotic songs": Hail Columbia — Washington's March — President's March — Rhode-Island March — Adams and Liberty — Hob Nob — Plough Boy — A March — Roslin Castle — Rise Columbia — A Spanish March — Boston March — March in the God of Love — The New Rigged Ship — Lenox — Rural Felicity ("Newport," *Newport Mercury*, 8 July 1809, 2–3).

Warren: After a procession to the Baptist Meeting House, "the services were introduced by singing and solemn prayer." After an oration, "the 'Ode on Science,' from the choir, concluded the exercises" ("Fourth of July!" *Bristol County Register*, 8 July 1809, 3).

Vermont

Bennington: In the parade "to the academy of the village, ... the Bennington Band of Music played for the march of the procession, and occasionally during the exercises" ("Bennington-Independence Celebration," *Green-Mountain Farmer*, 10 July 1809, 2).

Castleton: "Between 11 and 12 o'clock, a democratic procession was formed, and went to the meeting house — and though attended by two bands of music, and every exertion was used, yet much the greatest number of citizens remained behind, exclusive of the military" (*Vermont Courier*, 15 July 1809, 3).

Danby: At "a scaffold erected for the purpose where the exercises of the day commenced, ... an Ode purposely prepared was sung & the exercise closed by prayer" ("Celebration at Danby," *Rutland Herald*, 5 August 1809, 4).

Middlebury: "The day was ushered in by discharge of cannon and appropriate martial music." A parade consisting of "the inhabitants of Middlebury and of the adjacent towns," some of whom were Revolutionary War patriots moved through the town streets to the Meeting House where the exercises were held. "An appropriate and very devotional prayer" was "followed by sacred music, performed by ninety-five singers, and accompanied by instrumental music. The Declaration of Independence, read by Col. Seth Storrs, followed by an 'Ode on Independence,' and sung by the same choir." After the oration and reading of Washington's Farewell Address, the affair "closed by singing another Ode adapted to the occasion." A reported noted, "The choir of singers, under the direction of Mr. Bebee, merited and received uncommon applause." At the dinner "prepared by Mr. Nixon, on the common in front of his house, toasts were drank, accompanied by the discharge of artillery, cheers, "and appropriate

songs": Song, Hail Columbia — Song, Go Patter to Lubbers — Song, James Madison, My Joe Jem[252] — Song, Liberty — Song, Rise Columbia — Song, The Drum ("Celebration of the 4th of July, 1809," *Middlebury Mercury*, 12 July 1809, 3; "Celebration at Middlebury," *Rutland Herald*, 15 July 1809, 2).

Randolph: A parade was led by a "handsome band of elegant music, under the direction of Mr. Wm. W. Copp, composed of gentlemen who also volunteered on the occasion." At a dinner prepared by Maj. Williams, toasts were offered and the following selections performed: Madison's March — Washington's March — March to Boston — Duke of Holstein's March. "The festival was closed by the Ode to Science, sung by Mr. Copp" ("By Request, Fourth of July," *Weekly Wanderer*, 14 July 1809, 3).

1810

Publications

"The following elegant Ode, written by The Maid of the Grove, was sung at the late celebration by the Tammany Society [at Providence, RI]. 'Ode' for the Anniversary of American Independence, 1810.' Tune — 'Indian Chief.'" First line: "In a chariot ethereal from regions of light" ("Poetical Department," *Columbian Phenix*, 14 July 1810, 4); "Tammany Society, or Columbian Order, no. 1. Order of Exercises at the Town/House in Providence, on the Fourth of July, 1810." Includes, first line: "Great Lord of all, thy matchless power."/tune "Washington"; first line: "In a chariot ethereal from regions of light"/tune "Indian Chief." Broadside. [Providence: Printed by Jones & Wheeler, 1810]. Copy in Brown University.

"The following was sung at the Theatre, in New York, on the 4th July: 'The Freedom of the Seas.'[253] A new patriotic song written by W. Dunlap, Esq." First line: "Ye sons of free Columbia, whose fathers dar'd the waves" ("Poetry," *Newburyport Herald*, 17 July 1810, 4; *Concord Gazette*, 14 August 1810, 4).

"The Fourth of July." To the tune "Rule Britannia." By Thomas Paine. First line: "Hail great Republic of the world!" (*Lady's Weekly Miscellany*, 24 February 1819, 288).

"Liberty. A patriotic song, for the anniversary of American independence, July 4th, 1810. By John A. Schaeffer." First line: "Let Britain of her champions boast" (*American Citizen*, 7 July 1810, 2).

"An Ode, Composed for and Sung at the Celebration in Leominster, July 4, 1810." First line: "With patriotic zeal inspired." Broadside. Leominster, [MA], 1810. Copy in Brown university.

"Ode, for Independence, 1810.[254] By R.T. Paine, Jun. Esq. and sung in Faneuil Hall, Boston." First line: "Hail! hail ye patriot spirits!" (*New-York Spectator*, 11 July 1810, 1; *Berkshire Reporter*, 18 July 1810, 2; "Poetry," *Vermont Centinel*, 20 July 1810, 4; *Reporter*

(Brattleboro, VT), 21 July 1810, 4; *Washingtonian*, 24 July 1810, 2; *Hampshire Federalist*, 26 July 1810, 1).

"Ode for the Fourth of July, 1810. Tune – 'Rule Britannia.'" Broadside. Copy in Library of Congress.

"An Ode, sung at the celebration of American independence, July 4th, 1810, at the Third Baptist Meeting-House, Boston." First line: "Kind Heaven returns the glorious morn" ("Poetry," *Old Colony Gazette*, 13 July 1810, 4).

"Odes, Songs, &c. composed for the celebration for the 4th of July. The following Song was written for the Bunker Hill Association, and sung, after the 2d toast, by Capt. Bowman": first line: "When Freedom came down to the shores of the west"; "Ode, by Dr. Nathn'l Noyes – Tune, 'Chester'": first line: "Kind Heaven returns the glorious morn."; "Ode composed for the Young Republicans of Boston, by Mr. W. Parmenter, and sung at their celebration, after the 1st Toast. Tune, 'Adams and Liberty'": first line: Columbians arise! let the cannon resound!"[255]; "The author of the following Song, is Mr. Edward D. Bangs,[256] of Worcester. The measure is harmonious, the figures are beautiful and impressive, and the sentiments are pure and patriotic. It reflects high credit on the author, and will give rich pleasure to his brethren in principle. Tune – 'Adams and Liberty'": first line: "Of the victory won over tyranny's power."[257] In the *National Aegis*, accompanying this song was the following editorial note: "The following Song, for the purposes of this great national day, really seems to us to possess uncommon merit. The measure is harmonious, the figures are beautiful and impressive, and the sentiments are pure and patriotic. It reflects high credit on the author, and will give rich pleasure to his brethren in principle. We are indebted to Mr. Edward D. Bangs, of this town, for this beautiful production" (*National Aegis*, 4 July 1810, 2; *Boston Patriot*, 11 July 1810, 1; "Poetry," *Independent Chronicle*, 16 July 1810, 4; *American Advocate*, 19 July 1810, 2).

"A Song for the Fourth of July." First line: "How sweet the remembrance of that happy day." "Very hastily composed on that day" by Edgar Patterson, editor of the *Independent American*, for a celebration held at Mr. Crawford's Hotel in Georgetown (*Independent American*, 7 July 1810, 2).

"The Spirit of Seventy-Five. An Ode. Composed for and sung at the celebration in Leominster, July 4, 1810. Tune, Adams and Liberty." First line: "American patriots, whose deeds are enroll'd" (*Massachusetts Spy, or Worcester Gazette*, 15 August 1810, 4).

Performances

Connecticut

Cheshire: The students of the Episcopal Academy marched to the house of the Principal, "attended by a band of music," and then proceeded to the Academy for the exercises. Later at a "splendid dinner" at Mr. William L. Foot's, the band provided music after the toasts: Tune, Hail Columbia – Green's March – The March of the People – Federal March – Washington's March – Washington's Farewell – Rural Festivity – Molly Put the Kettle On – Ode to Science – Ancient Philosopher – Virtue Rewarded – The Illumination – The Students Delight – Too Many Cooks – Yankey Doodle – The Graces ("Celebration of Independence," *American Mercury*, 19 July 1810, 3).

Hartford: In a procession to the South Meeting House was "a very excellent Band of Musick" and at an "entertainment" at "Mr. Griswold's ... appropriate musick was played by the Band": Tune, Independence – Yankee Doodle – President's March – York Fusiliers – Washington's March – Jefferson and Liberty – Roslin Castle – Retaliation[258] – Friendship to Every Freeborn Man – Hail Columbia – Armstrong's Delight – Rogue's March – America, Commerce and Freedom – Governor's March – Rural Felicity – Jove in His Chair – Come Haste to the Wedding (*American Mercury*, 12 July 1810, 3).

Norwich: Republican members of Dartmouth and others celebrate with a dinner, "accompanied with music and the discharge of cannon" ("Celebration at Norwich, VT," *New Hampshire Patriot*, 17 July 1810, 2).

District of Columbia

In Georgetown, a public dinner and ball were held at Crawford's Hotel. "After each toast an appropriate air by a band of music" was performed (*Independent American*, 7 July 1810, 2). See **Publications** above; at the Washington Theatre, "an entertainment, called Columbia's Independence[259] or, The Temple of Liberty" was presented. Included was a "new song, 'Little Jane of the Mill,'" sung by Mrs. Wilmot (*National Intelligencer*, 4 July 1810, 3).

Maine

Augusta: "The Republican citizens of Augusta, Hallowell, Gardiner, and the neighbouring towns" celebrated at "the spacious and elegant house of Joshua Gage, Esq." A parade began at Noon "in front of the Court House, escorted by a detachmnet of Capt. Eastman's troop of cavalry.... At half past twelve, the procession consisting of about three hundred republican gentlemen, preceded by music arrived at Mr. Gage's." The exercises began with a prayer followed by "the performance of appropriate music," the reading of the Declaration of Independence and an oration. At the dinner "toasts were then given, accompanied with appropriate music, and reiterated shouts of applause" ("Thirty-Fourth National Anniversary," *American Advocate*, 12 July 1810, 2); at the courthouse, "Ode to Independence, sung by a choir of singers," "a national song, set to some music," and "a national song, set to some lofty strains of vocal and instrumental music" (*Herald of Liberty*, 10 July 1810, 3).[260]

Bath: After the ringing of the bells and firing of artillery, a procession "consisting of Revolutionary officers & soldiers, and officers in commission" formed at 10 A.M. and "preceded by the 'Lincoln Band of music' marched" through city streets and met up with "three hundred Republican citizens" and proceeded to "the Rev. Mr. Jenk's Meeting House, where, in the presence of a brilliant, respectable and crowded audience, the performances commenced with an excellent piece of music from the Band." The exercises were ended with music. Later the assemblage processed to a green arbor "near the house of Peleg Tallman, Esq. where between two and three hundred persons partook of an excellent dinner" after which "toasts were drank accompanied with the discharge of cannon and appropriate music": Yankee Doodle — Washington's March — President's March — March in the God of Love — Jefferson's March — Roslin Castle — A March — Bennetts March — St. John's March — Massachusetts March — Go to the Devil and Shake Yourselves[261] — O Dear What Can the Matter Be — Green's March — Handel Clarionett — Quick Step — Come Haste to the Wedding ("Celebration at Bath," *Eastern Argus*, 12 July 1810, 2).

Buck Old: "The inhabitants of Backfield, Hartford and Sumner, with a number of their fellow citizens from the adjoining towns, met at Mr. Benjamin Spaulding's, and at 11 o'clock formed a procession and proceeded to the Hill on the Common, where they had previously planted the Tree of Liberty for the occasion." They marched "preceded by very excellent martial music" ("Celebration at Buck Old (Me.)," *Eastern Argus*, 12 July 1810, 2).

Fairfield: The celebrations included members of the Somerset Halcyonic and Logical Societies and citizens and soldiers. A procession from Mr. Lawrence's Inn to the South Meeting House, included a musical ensemble ("Celebration at Fairfield," *American Advocate*, 12 July 1810, 2).

Jay: On the occasion of the installation of a liberty pole, "136 feet in the air," at a bower, the exercises included "an appropriate Hymn, sung by a select choir.... The exercises were closed by music in its highest style of excellence." Later "toasts were drank, succeeded by discharges of platoon firing from a beautiful Volunteer Company, commanded by Captain Lamkin, together with repeated plaudits and music from the Martial Band" ("Independence," *Eastern Argus*, 16 August 1810, 2).

Limington: A procession of the town's Republican citizens and military offices, led by "martial music," marched to a grove where the principal oration was given ("Celebration at Limington," *Eastern Argus*, 12 July 1810, 2).

Minot: Both Federalists and Republican citizens assembled at the house of Cyrus Clark where they marched, "accompanied by a military escort and martial music," to Jonathan Scott's Meeting House "where the exercises commenced by excellent vocal and instrumental music." Later at a dinner held at Clark's house, toasts were presented "accompanied with platoon firings and martial music" ("Celebration of the 4th of July," *Portland Gazette and Maine Advertizer*, 16 July 1810, 2).

New Gloucester: The "Federalists of this and a number of the adjoining towns met ... at Capt. Johnson's Hall, whence it proceeded to the meeting house, preceded by martial music. The exercises of the day were opened by singing an appropriate Psalm." After an oration, "the whole closed by performing that charming piece of music, the 'Ode on Science'" (*Portland Gazette, and Maine Advertizer*, 16 July 1810, 1).

Portland: Republican citizens "and their friends from the neighboring towns assembled at Union Hall" and paraded to "the Rev. Dr. Dean's meeting house," where "the exercises commenced with excellent music by the Portland Band." Later back at the Hall a dinner included toasts that were "accompanied with discharges of cannon and airs from an elegant band of music, whose performances were such as to confer upon them the greatest honor" (*Public Advertiser*, 13 July 1810, 3).

Thomaston: Members of the Social Library Society and others "together with a large singing company" at the North Meeting House, "musick of the best vocal kind, exhilarated the auditors, both before and after the Oration, and added to their joyous sensations on the recollection of the day. The several Military Companies, then took under their escort, the Society aforesaid, and other respectable citizens, and attended by a choir of musicians unusual in number, many of whom were under the age of twelve years, and completely versed in melodious martial (trains) proceeded to Mr. John Gleason's hotel" ("Celebration of Independence at Thomaston, 1810," *Portland Gazette, and Maine Advertizer*, 30 July 1810, 1).

Turner: A parade of citizens began at the house of Mr. Seth Staples and ended at the meeting house. After an oration, "an excellent Ode on Science" was sung "and other well adapted pieces of music, conducted by Maj. Cary" ("Celebration at Turner," *Eastern Argus*, 19 July 1810, 2).

Waldoborough: "At 10 o'clock, a newly raised company of light infantry, in an elegant uniform dress, under the command of Capt. Isaac G. Reed, paraded and escorted a group of citizens to the Meeting House, where the exercises there included 'an appropriate anthem and prayer.'" Capt. Reed's infantry provided the music. "Four of the musicians, whose skill was surprising, were under the age of twelve years" ("Federal Celebration of the 4th of July in Waldoborough," *Portland Gazette and Maine Advertizer*, 16 July 1810, 2).

Wiscasset: After "divine service" at the Meeting House, "the Federal Republicans moved in procession, attended by martial music, from Mr. Tinkham's Hotel to Washington Hall, where they partook of a sumptuous collation, provided with much taste and elegance" ("Celebration of Independence at Wiscasset," *Portland Gazette, and Maine Advertizer*, 16 July 1810, 2).

Yorke: "At twelve o'clock a grand procession, consisting of ecclesiastical, civil and military characters, and citizens, was formed, and being preceded by the celebrated Exeter Band, marched to the Meeting

House, where after instrumental music, and an appropriate hymn, read by that venerable Republican, the Rev. Mr. Litchfield, and sung by a select choir, the throne of grace was addressed by the Rev. Mr. Messinger, in a very excellent and uncommonly pertinent prayer." After an oration, "the exercises were closed by music in its highest style of excellence, and the procession being again formed, proceeded to the Hall of the Court House, which was handsomely decorated, and where an elegant entertainment was prepared." Toasts were drank, "succeeded by discharges from Capt. Howard's Artillery, repeated plaudits, and music by the band": The Day that Made Us Free — Grand Sonata, or Democratic March — Huzza for the Constitution — Madison's March — Pleyel's Hymn — Adams & Liberty — Jefferson's March — The Empire of the Laws — Massachusetts March — Washington's March — Yankee Doodle — The Loom and the Distaff — New-England Patriotism — Quick March — Village Curate — Love in a Village — National Character ("Celebration of the Fourth of July, at Yorke, Me," *Boston Patriot*, 14 July 1810, 1; "County Celebration at York," *Eastern Argus*, 19 July 1810, 2).

Maryland

Baltimore: The public exercises occurred at the circus, Chevalier Granpre, with the doors opening after 11 A.M. As more than 1000 persons, including members of the Washington Society, entered "the noise and confusion were drowned by the lively music of the band, composed principally of members. "'Washington's March' was struck up by the band, and was received with great applause from the area, and by manifestations of pleasure in some of the visitors." Meanwhile a group of "Democrats and Liberty men" forced their way into the circus and fights ensued.

A Requiem, composed for the occasion by Mr. John Cole,[262] a member of the Society, was then sung. The effect produced upon the audience is the best eulogium upon the musical taste and talents of Mr. Cole. The music issuing from behind the cannon which supported the platform, containing the military trophies, the bust of Washington, wreaths and crown of laurel, and other emblems, was tenfold more sweet and melodious, appearing to be at a distance, and being concealed from view.

("The Fourth of July," *Poulson's American Daily Advertiser*, 11 July 1810, 3; *Public Advertiser*, 17 July 1810, 2; *The Repertory*, 17 July 1810, 2.)
Williamsport: This town enjoyed "martial music" on the Fourth and at a dinner in the long room of the Columbian Inn, songs were sung (*Hagers-Town Gazette*, 10 July 1810, 3).

Massachusetts

Abington: At the Meeting House "a very numerous and respectable audience, composed of the Republican inhabitants of that and several of the adjoining towns" gathered. The local newspaper reported: "The music composed for the occasion by Mr. David Pool, of this town, was performed by the band and others, in a style of very great excellence." Later the dinner toasts "were drank, accompanied with music by the band, and firing by Capt. Smith's Artillery" ("National Festival," *Independent Chronicle*, 12 July 1810, 1); the exercises at the "Meeting House of the Second Congregational Society ... concluded with the performance of a patriotic Ode." At the dinner held at Dyer & Perry's Hall, "toasts were drank, accompanied with the enlivening song" ("Celebration at Abington," *Boston Patriot*, 11 July 1810, 2).

Becket: Militia and residents marched to the meeting house, "attended by a band of music." The exercises included the singing of "an ode composed for the occasion" ("Fourth of July," *Berkshire Reporter*, 18 July 1810, 3).

Boston: At the Old South Meeting House, "where religious exercises were performed by the Rev. Mr. Channing, and an Oration delivered (agreeably to the ancient institution of the town) by Alexander Townsend, Esq. The following original Ode was also sung." First line: "Again we hail the festal morn." According to the *Trenton Federalist*, the "stanzas [were] written by Hon. Thomas Dawes." Two hymns were also sung: "The mighty God is our defence" (first line) and "Shine, Lord, on this thy people shine" (first line) (*New-York Spectator*, 11 July 1810, 1; "Independence," *Trenton Federalist*, 16 July 1810, 2; "Order of Exercises at the Municipal Celebration of the Thirty Fourth Anniversary of American Independence, July 4, 1810," broadside [Boston: J. Eliot, 1810]); at the exercises held by the Bunker Hill Association and "joined by the Young Republicans," the assemblage heard the "149th Hymn, 2d book, from Dr. Watts — Tune 'Mear'" (first line: "Eternal Sovereign of the sky") and an "Ode composed for the occasion, by Dr. Nathl. Noyes — Tune 'Chester'" (first line: "Kind Heaven returns the glorious morn"). Later members and guests marched to the Exchange Coffee House where "after the removal of the cloth, toasts were drank, accompanied by the plaudits of the company, the firing of cannon, and appropriate and animating music" ("Celebration of American Independence at Boston," *Farmers' Cabinet*, 10 July 1810, 2; *Columbian Phenix*, 14 July 1810, 1; *An Oration Pronounced at Boston on the Fourth Day of July, 1810, before the "Bunker-Hill Association."* ... By Daniel Waldo Lincoln [Boston: Printed for Isaac Munroe, 1810], 19–20); at the Third Baptist Meeting House with the Governor present, the services included "hymns, an anthem, and an ode, composed for the occasion" and "sung by a select choir" ("Executive Celebration," *Public Advertiser*, 13 July 1810, 2; *Columbian Phenix*, 14 July 1810, 1; "Executive Celebration," *Bunker Hill*, 26 July 1810, 2). See **Publications** above.

Dedham: The Democratic Republicans gathered at 1 P.M. at Mr. Marsh's Tavern and "escorted by Capt. Eaton's Company of Light Infantry, and a band of musick, it proceeded to the Rev. Mr. Bates's Meeting

House. The exercise was begun by musick by the band." Back at the Court House Hall dinner was served by Marsh and "appropriate toasts were drank, accompanied with discharges of cannon, and musick by the band" ("Celebration at Dedham," *Boston Patriot,* 11 July 1810, 1).

New Bedford: A procession included "citizens from various parts of Bristol & Plymouth Counties, which moved to the sound of martial music, to the meeting house" where the exercises included two psalms and "an original Ode, performed with great taste, to the air of 'Ode on Science'" ("Celebration of Independence," *Old Colony Gazette,* 6 July 1810, 3).

Pittsfield: A parade included "martial music, and the Pittsfield Band, under the direction of Messrs. Root, Perry and Butler who acted as marshals of the day." Exercises at the meeting house included "music by the choir and on the organ." Later at the dining hall of the hotel, a band of music performed tunes ("Great National Jubilee," *Pittsfield Sun,* 11 July 1810, 2).

Salem: A procession included "a numerous band of inimitable performers on various instruments, composed of gentlemen from Greenwich, who politely volunteered their services in honor of the memorable occasion; and it is but scanty justice to them to declare that their performance was indescribably delightful. They wore a handsome uniform, which greatly added to the splendor of the arrangement and were followed by two gentlemen, each bearing a stand of superb colours." Also performing that day was the Granville Band. After the exercises at the court house, the men assembled at the hotel for dinner and toasts accompanied by the following music: Tune, Hail Columbia — Tune, Yankey Doodle — Tune, Bellisarius — Tune, Strong's March — Tune, Federal March — Tune, Washington's March — Tune, Gen. Green's March — Holstein's March — Tune, The Apprentice Boy — Tune, Baron Steuben's March — Tune, Henry IV's March — Tune, Bonaparte's Favorite — Tune, Belles of New-York — Tune, Duke of York's March — Tune, Massachusetts March — Tune, Columbia's Sons Awake — Tune, Short Troop (*Northern Post,* 12 July 1810, 2); the Independent Cadet Company had dinner at Mr. Grant's Hall. "toasts were drank, accompanied by excellent music by the band, belonging to the corps." "Let tyrants shake their iron rod,"[263] to the tune "Chester" was "composed by a member of the company for the occasion" and "sung after the toasts were drank" (*Essex Register,* 7 July 1810, 2).

New Hampshire

Amherst: Several hundred Republican citizens marched "escorted by Capt. Patterson's Company of Artillery" and celebrated at the meeting house and later at a bower where "Herrick's Dirge" was performed (*New-Hampshire Patriot,* 10 July 1810, 2).

Portsmouth: A procession to the "minister's meeting house" included a band of music. The exercises included "odes written for the occasion" and "sung by

a full choir of ladies and gentlemen who are entitled to our warmest praises for their excellent performance." The odes are "Ode for the Fourth July, 1810, by S. Sewall" (first line: "Ye patriot sons, begin the lay"; "Ode, for Independence, 1810, by Joseph Bartlett, Esq." (first line: "When darknes [sic] roll'd on boundless space"). The exercises closed "with appropriate music" ("Celebration of American Independence," *Portsmouth Oracle,* 7 July 1810, 3, and 14 July 1810, 1; "American Independence," *New-Hampshire Gazette,* 10 July 1810, 3).

New Jersey

Allentown: After the ringing of bells and an artillery salute, a procession from Mrs. Forman's house to the Presbyterian Church included a music ensemble. The exercises at the church included "sacred music," "an Ode," and a performance of "Hail Columbia with alterations." Later Mrs. Forman provided "an elegant entertainment" replete with toasts "amidst discharges of musketry and the resound of martial music" ("Allentown Celebration," *Trenton Federalist,* 16 July 1810, 3).

Newark: The Musical Society was scheduled to march in the town parade and the exercises were to include three vocal works (*Sentinel of Freedom,* 26 June 1810, 3).

New York

Mamaroneck: The Republican citizens celebrated at the house of Mr. Benjamin Kirby. Toasts were drank "and some appropriate songs were sung to suit the occasion" ("Celebration at Mamaroneck," *Public Advertiser,* 12 July 1810, 2).

New York: Two bands of music participated in the parade of the Washington Benevolent Society and the Hamilton Society down Broadway and other streets to the Circus.

When the van had arrived at the Circus, the lines opened right and left, and marched from

> the rear through the line. As the officers of the Washington Society passed the different bands, they were saluted and as they entered the Circus, the Hamilton band stationed in the boxes over the pit door played Washington's March and continued the same tune until the whole were seated. After the members of the two societies were seated, a piece of Martial Music was performed by the military band. The Declaration of Independence was read by Major Vanhook. A piece of Solemn Music was performed by Mr. King's band.... The oration was followed by a piece of soft music, by the band of the Hamilton Society; during which a collection was taken up for the relief of indigent members. After the whole was concluded, the procession was formed in reversed order and proceeded down Broadway, and through Robinson street to the College Green, where after a grand final by the three bands, they were dismissed.

("National Festival," *Federal Republican & Commercial Gazette,* 12 July 1810, 2); The New York Typographical Society holds its inaugural meeting at Harmony Hall to hear an oration and later "at the house of Mr. Randolph in Fair-street, where a dinner" was served. Thereafter, "toasts, odes, and songs" were presented (*Mercantile Advertiser*, 30 June 1810, 2); the Hibernian Provident Society met in a park and later returned to the Union Hotel where dinner and toasts "were drank, interspersed with original and patriotic songs": Song, Let tyrants sing their birthday odes — Song, Hail Americans — Song, Hail Columbia — Song, Death of Warren — Song, Give us the men whose dauntless souls[264] — Song, The Honest Man — Song, No Syncophantic Babler — Song, Long life and success to the farmer — Song, Conscience never stings and knaves — Song, Come, then my jolly boys — It long has been said, but I'm sure it's a lie, that England ought our mistress to be — Song, Inconsistency's plan for there guide, they soon will confound one another — Song, Peter, Martin, and John, they together all met — Song, The sweet little girl of my heart ("Celebration of the Fourth of July, by the Hibernian Provident Society," *Public Advertiser*, 7 July 1810, 2).

Yonkers: "At 12 o'clock the procession was formed, and marched through the village as far as Mr. Howland's house, passing through his lawn in the following order —

1st A squadron of Captain Merrit's troop dismounted, under the command of Lieut Peter Underhill, with swords drawn, preceded by the president of the day, and commanding officers.
2d Band of music under the direction of Capt. Demerest.
3d Civil authority, headed by lieut. Rich, bearing a superb standard, executed in the village by Mr. Aaron Varick.
4th Grown male citizens, one hundred and thirty file.
5th Boys walking hand in hand, twenty pair.
6th Ladies, arm and arm, from sixty to seventy pair.
7th The orator of the day.

In the church yard, there were "three cheers from the citizens, and the appropriate tune of Hail Columbia by the band…. At the dinner "prepared by citizen Gilbert Fuion, under a booth, one hundred and thirty ladies graced the table with their presence." Following dinner, toasts were presented "accompanied with the discharge of the artillery, and appropriate music by Capt. Demarest's band," including: Yankee Doodle — Jefferson's March — Hail Columbia — Hail America — Solemn Dirge — Yankee Doodle — Rogue's March — The Loom and the Shuttle — Come Haste to the Wedding — Death of Warren — Jefferson and Liberty ("Celebration at Yonkers," *Columbian*, 12 July 1810, 2).

North Carolina

Swift Creek: "A numerous assembly of the respectable inhabitants of Swift and Fisten Creeks" gathered "at Mrs. Digg's Hotel" and "in solemn procession advanced to Shilow Church, (Preceded by music performed by Messrs. A. Bartlett, T. Polk, and R. Bracey) where an appropriate Psalm and Prayer were addressed to Almighty God by the Rev. Davis Collins; then the following Oration was delivered by Richard S. Moore, and closed with 'Columbia, Columbia, to glory arise!' sung by A. Bartlett and a select choir of singers" ("Communication," *Carolina Gazette*, 10 August 1810, 4).

Pennsylvania

Easton: Following a parade of militia through city streets, the Light Infantry Company sat down to a dinner, with toasts accompanied by the following music: Hail Liberty — Washington's March — President's March — Dead March — Yankee Doodle — To Arms, to Arms ye Brave — Hail Columbia — Here's a Health to All Good Lasses ("The Fourth of July," *Pennsylvania Herald, and Easton Intelligencer*, 18 July 1810, 2).

Nazareth: At a dinner celebration held at "Capt. Henry Jarrets," music following the toasts included: Hail Liberty — Hail Columbia — Roslin Castle — Anacreon — The Farmer — Washington's March — How Sleeps the Brave — Jefferson's March — Madison's March — Snyders March[265] — The Constitution — The Soldiers Return — Alknomook — Yankee Doodle — And Ne'er Shall the Sons of Columbia — The Lovely Bride ("Communication," *Pennsylvania Herald and Easton Intelligencer*, 18 July 1810, 2).

Philadelphia: At a celebration of the American Republican Society, "a large saloon, 265 feet long by 56 wide, was erected on a field near the banks of the Schuylkill, between Mr. Evan's tavern and Beck's shot tower … an orchestra was raised in the centre of the salon, where a full band of music attended." Some 700 persons heard the following pieces that accompanied the toasts: Yankee Doodle — Hail Columbia — Dead March — Roslin Castle — Wayne's March — President's March — Stoney Point — America, Commerce and Freedom — Battle of Prague — Hail Liberty ("Philadelphia, July 6," *Federal Republican & Commercial Gazette*, 9 July 1810, 2; "Philadelphia Celebration," *Trenton Federalist*, 16 July 1810, 3); at "Old Oak Place," a private residence, songs were sung and tunes played on the piano: Catch, 'Old Thomas Day, Dead and Turned to Clay' — Song by myself, 'Unfold Father Time' — 'Air' on the piano by my aunt Dina, Go to the Devil and Shake Yourself — Song by myself, 'In the Garb of Old Gaul' — Song by myself (assisted), Moderation. Tune 'Old Hundred' — Duet, my grandmother and aunt, Two Maidens sat Complaining — Here my grandmother favored us with the song of the 'Poor Old Woman of Eighty,'[266] 'till we shook ("Old Oak Place," *Tickler*, 18 July 1810, 3).

Rhode Island

Newport: Following a procession, the exercises at the Second Baptist Meeting-House, "several excellent odes were sung by a select choir in a manner that could not fail to warm the heart and elevate the mind" ("Fourth of July," *Rhode-Island American and General Advertiser*, 10 July 1810, 2); members of the Tammany Society and Republican residents marched through city street to the Methodist Chapel where the exercises were held. "A choir of excellent singers performed several pieces of musick in a skillful and appropriate manner. The gentlemen who composed the band, volunteered their services, and contributed greatly to the enjoyments of the day. Much credit is also due the vocal performers, particularly the ladies, whose judgment and skill added much to the pleasure and satisfactions, which a crowded audience universally felt" ("American Independence," *Rhode-Island Republican*, 11 July 1810, 2; *Columbian Phenix*, 14 July 1810, 2).

Providence: A Republican celebration by the Tammany Society began with a procession from the State House to the Town House. In the middle of the line "was placed the Band of Music, in full uniform." The services at the Town House began "with sacred music by an excellent choir of singers." After a prayer, there followed "the singing of an Original Ode, [to be published in our next] the execution of which by the female singers (assisted by the male in repeating the two last lines of each verse) was novel and elegant." The Declaration was then read by Levi Wheaton "and after a Voluntary by the Band" was performed. The oration followed that and "another voluntary by the band" after which the group then processed to Mr. Carey's Hotel for dinner. The toasts presented included the following pieces: Tune, Rise Columbia — Adams and Liberty — Jefferson's March — Grand March — Bunker-Hill — Washington's Counsel — O Dear What Can the Matter Be — Brave Montgomery — Hail Columbia — Yankee Doodle — Spinning-Wheel — Light in the East — Majesty — Rural Felicity — Indian Chief[267] — Rhode-Island March ("Republican Celebration," *Columbian Phenix*, 7 July 1810, 3); another celebration with exercises and militia participating took place at the First Congregational Meeting House followed by a dinner at Washington Hall. Performed there were the following "well adapted tunes by the band of music": Hail Columbia — Roslin Castle — President's March — Rhode Island March — Pleyel's Hymn[268] — General Green's March — Washington's March — Old Hundred — Hamilton's March — Oscar's Ghost[269] — How Sweet through the Woodland — Bunker's Hill — Cease Rude Boreas — Yankee Doodle — When storms and clouds obscure the sky — Pickering's March[270] — How imperfect is expression ("Independence," *Poulson's American Daily Advertiser*, 13 July 1810, 3); at the Providence Theatre, "the favorite dramatick piece, in four acts, called *The Child of Nature* was performed. At the end of the comedy, a celebrated Song, called 'Hail Liberty,' [was sung] by Mr. Darley."[271] Also performed was "the very popular comick opera, of *The Rival Soldiers*, the whole to conclude with an afterpiece, called *Preparations for a Cruise; or, Naval Gratitude*, ... with

appropriate characteristick [sic]songs and scenery adapted to the occasion" (*Rhode-Island American, and General Advertiser*, 3 July 1810, 3). See **Publications** above.

South Carolina

Charleston: After an early morning military parade, "at half past eleven o'clock, the '76 Association, preceded by a band of music, walked in procession to St. Philip's church," where the exercises of the day took place ("Fourth of July," *City Gazette and Daily Advertiser*, 6 July 1810, 3).

Vermont

Royalton: "A large concourse of citizens" celebrated the Fourth and "the public exercises were introduced, and regularly intersperced [sic] with animated and devotional musick" ("Celebration," *Spooners Vermont Journal*, 16 July 1810, 3).

Rutland: "A numerous procession" was led by "martial music" to the Meeting House where the exercises began and ended with "vocal music." The assemblage returned to Mr. Gordon's "where a green bowry was erected and an excellent dinner served up; about three hundred citizens, ladies and gentlemen, joined the festive board." After dinner toasts "accompanied by discharges of artillery and the cheers of martial music" were presented ("National Festival," *Rutland Herald*, 11 July 1810, 2).

1811

Publications

"A Federal Hymn, composed for a Tory mock celebration of July 4th, 1811." First line: "To thee, dear George, our sovereign king" ("Poetry," *Old Colony Gazette*, 28 June 1811, 4).

"The following beautiful ode, composed for the 4th July, 1811, by the Hon. Joseph Story,[272]was sung at the republican celebration in Salem." First line: "Welcome! Welcome the day, when assembled in one"[273] ("Native Poetry," *Columbian*, 19 July 1811, 3; *Green-Mountain Farmer*, 5 August 1811, 4; *New Jersey Journal,* 13 August 1811, 4).

"For the Fourth of July. Tune — 'General Wolfe.'" First line: "A council was held in the chambers of Jove" (*The Shamrock, or Hibernian Chronicle*, 29 June 1811, 3; "Poetry," *Independent Chronicle*, 4 July 1811, 4).

"The following pieces were sung on the Fourth of July, at the Second Baptist Meeting-House, for the Tammany Society [Newport, RI]. Ode for Independence: (first line: "We hail Columbia's natal day"); Psalm XXXIII (first line: "Blest is the nation, where the Lord"); Original Ode (first line: "To Heav'n let grateful paens rise") ("Poetry," *Rhode-Island Republican*, 10 July 1811, 4).

"Ode, for the 4th July, 1811." By John Phelps. First

line: "Hail, hail the day of Freedom's birth!/Ode, addressed to the revolutionary patriots of 1776. First line: "Sires of freedom, famed in history." Broadside, [Brattleboro, VT?], 1811. Copy in Brown University.

"Ode for the Fourth of July, 1811. By Doct. Peter Bryant.[274] Tune — 'Rise Columbia.'" First line: "Pour in deep tones the solemn strain." Note: "The following Ode was sung at the patriotic celebration of the 4th of July, in Hampshire County, Massachusetts. It is worthy of the county and the celebrators" (*Columbian Centinel*, 13 July 1811, 4; *Connecticut Herald*, 5 August 1811, 4; *Historical Magazine and Notes and Queries Concerning the Antiquities* [June 1873]:334).

"Ode — for the Fourth of July. By Samuel Brazer, Jr.[275] Tune — 'Heaving the Lead.'" First line: "Say, shall in Freedom's lov'd abode" (*National Aegis*, 3 July 1811, 2–3; *Old Colony Gazette*, 26 July 1811, 1; William McCarty, *The New National Song Book, Containing Songs, Odes, and Other Poems, on National Subjects. Compiled from Various Sources* [NY: Leavitt and Allen, 184–?]).

"Ode for the Fourth of July, 1811. By R.T. Paine, Jun. Esq. Tune — 'Battle of the Nile.'"[276] First line: "Let patriot pride our patriot triumph wake!"[277] The ode was sung at Faneuil Hall in Boston and published under the title "National Ode, Arouse! Arouse! Columbia's Sons Arouse! As sung by Mr. McFarland[278] at the concerts in Boston with Universal Applause" [Boston: G. Graupner, 1811].[279] The *Boston Gazette* noted that the song "was received with repeated applause. From the powerful simplicity of its poetical style, the admirable adaptation of the words to an impressive national tune, and the strong plain sense of its political principles, we have no doubt it will become the favourite popular song of the day" ("National Ode," *Boston Gazette*, 8 July 1811, 1; *New-England Palladium* 9 July 1811, 1; *New-York Commercial Advertiser*, 12 July 1811, 3; *Poulson's American Daily Advertiser*, 16 July 1811, 3; *Old Colony Gazette*, 19 July 1811, 1; *Merrimack's Intelligencer*, 20 July 1811, 4; "Wreath," *Balance, and State Journal*, 23 July 1811, 240; *Connecticut Herald*, 23 July 1811, 4; *Rhode-Island Republican*, 24 July 1811, 4; "Poetry," *Columbian Phenix; or, Providence Patriot*, 27 July 1811, 4; *Columbian*, 31 July 1811, 2; *Columbian Centinel*, 3 August 1811, 3; *Independent American*, 6 August 1811, 4).

"An Ode composed for the Fourth of July, 1811." First line: "Let mimic thunder shake the skies" (*Sentinel of Freedom*, 23 July 1811, 4).

"An ode for the Washington Benevolent Society. By Uri K. Hill. Sung at the National Jubilee — New York, Fourth of July, 1811." First line: "Ye patriots, rejoice, while ye hail this glad morning" ("Poetry," *Rhode-Island American*, 12 July 1811, 1; *Berkshire Reporter*, 13 July 1811, 4).

"Ode, written for the 35th anniversary of American independence in Faneuil Hall, by Lucius M. Sargent, Esq[280]; musick by Mr. Hewitt." Broadside, [Boston, 1811].

"Song for the 4th July 1811." By James Newhall.

First line: "Of Liberty once could Columbia boast." Broadside. [n.p., 1811]. Copy in Brown University.

"Song ["Printers' Ode"], written by Mr. Samuel Woodworth[281] of New York, and sung by Mr. D.H. Reins[282] on the celebration of the 4th of July, before the Typographical Society of that city. Tune — 'Anacreon in Heaven.'" First line: "From the crystalline courts of the temple of light."; "Ode on the Art of Printing" (first line: "When wrapp'd in folds of papal gloom,"[283] tune: "Rise Columbia." (George Ashbridge, *An Oration, delivered before the New York Typographical Society, at their second anniversary, on the Fourth of July* [New York: C.S. Van Winkle, 1811]; *Columbian*, 9 July 1811, 2; *New-England Palladium*, 16 July 1811, 4; *American Watchman*, 20 July 1811, 1; *Chenago Weekly Advertiser*, 26 July 1811, 4; *Columbian Phenix*, 27 July 1811, 1; *Otsego Herald*, 27 July 1811, 1; *New-Hampshire Patriot*, 30 July 1811, 4; *National Aegis*, 31 July 1811, 4; *The Bee*, 2 August 1811, 2; *New Jersey Journal*, 6 August 1811, 4.)

"The Star of the West." "The following song was composed by William Harper, and sung at the celebration of the anniversary of independence, the 4th July." First line: "All hail to the day! when a nation arose" (from the *Columbian Gazette* as printed in *The Columbian*, 8 August 1811, 3; "Poetry," *Independent Chronicle*, 9 December 1811, 4).

See **Publications**, 1812.

Performances

District of Columbia

President Madison was escorted by military troops to the "Church in F Street" where the day's exercises were performed including "a number of appropriate airs from an elegant band of music." At "a plentiful dinner" on the banks of the Tiber River, with 200–300 citizens in attendance, the U.S. Marine Band performed: America, Commerce and Freedom — District March — Hail Columbia — How Sweet through the Woodlands — Jefferson's March — Madison's March — Roslin Castle — Yankee Doodle. One reporter noted that "an original song to the tune of 'Hail Columbia' from the pen of J.J. Moore" was played as well as "A Grand March" (*National Intelligencer*, 6 July 1811, 2; *Enquirer*, 12 July 1811, 2).

Maine

Fairfield: At the Meeting House, music by a choir with "an appropriate hymn" (*American Advocate*, 17 July 1811, 2).

New Sharon: After a parade "to the booths prepared to keep them [Republicans] from the scorching sun," the exercises were held which included the reading of a psalm "which was sung with delightful harmony and devotion" ("Fourth of July Celebration at New-Sharon," *American Advocate*, 28 August 1811, 3).

Maryland

Baltimore: The Washington Society of Maryland "convened at the School Room, and proceeded in a body to the Theatre, headed by the President. The exercises commenced with Washington's March, by a full band of music, consisting chiefly of members seated behind the decorated platform. The sweetness and melody of the music were heightened by issuing from a retired and concealed part of the stage. Its effect is the best eulogium upon the musical talents and taste of Mr. John Cole."

After the Declaration of Independence was read,

"Hail Columbia" was struck up by the band. Next, the Farewell Address of Washington was read by Mr. Solomon Ward. His introductory remarks were eloquent and pathetic, and were delivered with great sensibility. When the reading closed, a requiem, composed by Mr. Cole, was sung by several gentlemen. It was solemn and affecting, disposing all hearts to feelings of grief, gratitude and charity. The feelings of all being wound up to the highest pitch of sensibility, were let down by an enlivening Ode. [*Salem Gazette*, 12 July 1811, 2.]

Massachusetts

Boston: The Bunker Hill Association and distinguished guests met at a bower "on the heights of Bunker Hill." Their dinner included toasts, "mid the discharge of artillery, music from an excellent band, and the plaudits of the company": Tune, Hail Columbia — Pres. March — Col. Orne's March — Massachusetts March — In Freedom We're Born, &c — Hail Patriot Band! — Ode, Hark the Goddess of Fame — Jefferson's March — Pleyel's Hymn — Yankee Doodle — The Mariner — Long Life and Success to the Farmer — America, Commerce and Freedom — Boston March — Old Hundred — Rural Felicity ("National Jubilee!" *Independent Chronicle*, 8 July 1811, 2); the Washington Society met at the Exchange Coffee House at 2 P.M. for "a splendid and sumptuous entertainment." After a reading of the Declaration, "an elegant and patriotic Ode, composed for the occasion, was sung in full chorus by the company." The toasts were "accompanied with repeated and unanimous cheers, and appropriate music by the African Band, in full uniform" ("The Washington Society," *Independent Chronicle*, 4 and 8 July 1811, 3 and 2, respectively); at 3 P.M. a "Federal procession" marched from Boylston Hall to Faneuil Hall for an entertainment that included toasts with the following music: Washington's March — Pleyel's Hymn — March — Knox's March — Bonaparte's March — Yankee Doodle ("Municipal Celebration," *Columbian Centinel*, 6 July 1811, 2).

Pittsfield: Following a procession to the Meeting House, "the choir of singers was numerous, and their performances admirable. As were also those of the instrumental music." At the dinner at the Hall in the hotel, toasts were drank "accompanied by the discharge of cannon and music from the band" ("National Birth-Day," *Pittsfield Sun, or, Republican Monitor*, 6 July 1811, 3).

Salem: "A fine band of music" in the procession to the Republican celebration at "the Rev. Mr. Spaulding's Meeting House": "Hymn on Independence, tune 'Old Hundred,' sung by an excellent Choir of singers, assisted by the band" — "Hymn, 'A Contrast between Europe and America'" — an "excellent Ode composed by the Hon. Joseph Story[284] was sung by a Choir of Females, with a melody and manner truly captivating, and the exercises were concluded with a march by the Band." (see **Publications** above.) At the dinner that followed, in the "lower hall of the Court House" were performed: Washington's March — Hail Columbia — Yankee Doodle — Anacreon in Heaven — America, Commerce & Freedom — Yankee Doodle — President's March — Jefferson's March — Tekeli[285] — Salem Cadet March ("Celebration of American Independence," *Essex Register*, 6 July 1811, 2); the Federalists of Salem, including soldiers and citizens marched to Dr. Barnard's Meeting House where "the exercises were interspersed by excellent and appropriate music." A dinner was then provided in Washington Hall where "toasts were given, interspersed with music from the band, and appropriate songs": Music, Yankee Doodle — Crazy Jane[286] — Dirge — Pickering's March[287] — O Dear, What Can the Matter Be — Jove in His Chair — Song, Let Rebels and Traitors All Hang in a String — Money in Both Pockets — Dirge — Wilkinson's March[288] — Old Hundred — Song, In a Shop of My Own, &c. — Brave Lads and Bonnie Lasses — Columbia's Sons! Awake to Glory &c. — Boston March — Col. Orne's March — New Song, Jim Madison, My Joe, Jim &c. — Rogue's March — Molly, Hang the Kettle On[289] — Tally Ho! — Gen. Derby's March[290] ("Fourth of July," *Salem Gazette*, 6 July 1811, 3).

New Hampshire

Amherst: A celebration at Converse's Hall resulted in "correct sentiment in flowing glasses passed around, with mirth and song" (*Farmer's Cabinet*, 9 July 1811, 3).

Concord: The day began with a procession that included music by two bands. At the Meeting House, "several Anthems selected for the occasion were very ably performed with vocal and instrumental music, which greatly enhanced the pleasures and solemnity of the day. The following verses, among others composed for the occasion, were sung to the tune of 'Machias.'" First line: "How pleasant 'tis to see" ("Celebration of American Independence," *New-Hampshire Patriot*, 9 July 1811, 3).

Henniker: The celebration at Henniker included "the citizens of the neighboring towns.... A procession was formed at 11 o'clock, escorted by Capt. Barns' Company of Cavalry, Capt. M'Neils Company of Grenadiers, Capt. Chases, and Capt. Ames' Companies of Artillery, preceeded by an excellent band of music, which moved from the north meeting-house to the Common by the fourth meeting-house, where all persons were served with suitable refreshment." Following, the exercises took place at the North Meeting House and the dinner on the Common. Toasts were presented accompanied by the following pieces: Lord Bayonet's March — Massa March — Washington's March — Read's March — President's March — Paris' March — Bonaparte's March — Capt. Miller's March- Oxford Camp — Litchfield March — Maj. Minot's March — Handel's Clarionet — St. John's March — Irish Wash-Woman — Jefferson and Liberty — Crane's March — Lady Bruce's Reel ("National Jubilee," *Farmers' Cabinet*, 9 July 1811, 3).

Portsmouth: Federalists paraded, "accompanied by a band of music," to the meeting house. "An appropriate Ode by Mr. S. Sewall" was presented. The exercises ended "by an original Ode from the pen of Joseph Bartlett, Esq.": "Song for the 4th July, 1811. Tune — Vicar of Bray," First line: "Time was, when this blest morn arose" ("Celebration of Independence," *Portsmouth Oracle*, 6 July 1811, 3).

New Jersey

Scotch Plains: A parade that began at Col. Swan's included "martial music" and "forty young ladies all dressed in uniform, with sprigs of laurel in their hands, chanting an appropriate ode on the occasion." At the Baptist Meeting House, the exercises included three odes "by the choristers." Later a dinner included "suitable music" (*New Jersey Journal*, 16 July 1811, 2).

Fancy Hill: At Col. Joshua Ladd Howell's residence, "an excellent band of music": Hail Liberty — Hail Columbia — Madison's March — Roslin Castle — Washington's March — the Songs of Harmony — Dead March in Saul — New Washington's March — New March — Spanish Patriotic Waltz — Yankee Doodle — Hamilton's Funeral Dirge — America, Commerce and Freedom — Learning and Leather — Brother Soldiers, All Hail — Yankee Doodle — Mon Cher Amie ("National Anniversary," *American Daily Advertiser*, 12 July 1811, 3).

New York

Chatham: The "Chatham Band of martial musick" accompanied a procession "to a stage which had been erected in field about the distance of a quarter of a mile" where the exercises began with an address and a reading of the Declaration of Independence "succeeded by 'Hail Columbia,' by the band." After an oration, "the band struck up 'Yankee Doodle.'" Later "Martial musick" was provided at the dinner ("At Chatham," *The Bee*, 12 July 1811, 2).

East Chester: "This day a select number of republicans of this town, and vicinity met at the house of Mr. James Armstrong, to enjoy the anniversary of our national jubilee...." Following dinner the toasts that were drank were "interspersed at proper intervals with appropriate songs" ("Communication," *Public Advertiser*, 10 July 1811, 2).

Hillsdale: "At 11 o'clock, the procession was formed at the house of Mr. Daniel Pierson, in the village of Greenriver [Green River], and, accompanied by the Hillsdale band of music, proceeded to the meeting-house." After the exercises which included a reading of Washington's Farewell Address, "the performances closed with vocal and instrumental music." An entertainment at Mr. Pierson's included toasts, artillery salutes, and music: President's March — Duke of Holstein's March — Death of Washington — Yankee Doodle — Handel's duet — [Rural] Felicity ("At Hillsdale," *Bee*, 12 July 1811, 3).

Hudson: Citizens from this and surrounding towns assembled on Parade Hill at noon and marched, "preceded by the excellent Republican Band of Musick and the Hudson Juvenile Society" to the court house for the exercises there. Later at Bement's Hotel, dinner was provided and the following two tunes were reported to have been performed: Tune, Bunker Hill — The Western District March (*The Bee*, 12 July 1811, 2).

New York: Hamilton Society at the Eagle Hotel, a "full band": Hail Columbia — Grand March in the Battle of Prague — America, Commerce and Freedom — The Union Patriots — Rural Felicity — Truxton's Victory — Solemn Music — Hamilton's Dirge[291]— Lexington March — Funeral Dirge[292]— Washington's March — Oh! Dear what can the matter be — Washington Hall — Patriotic Air — Go to the Devil and Shake Yourself— Come Haste to the Wedding (*New-York Commercial Advertiser*, 5 July 1811, 3); at the celebration of the Typographical Society at Coleman's, no. 10 Fair Street, toasts were drank and "original Odes, as well as patriotic and enlivening songs" performed (*Public Advertiser*, 4 July 1811, 3); several patriotic societies, including the Tammany Society, "accompanied by a grand band of music" marched through city streets to the Presbyterian Church where the exercises were begun with a prayer "succeeded by an appropriate piece of music." After a reading of the Declaration and oration, there followed "an anthem, music, and an ode composed for the occasion" ("Celebration of the Fourth of July," *Public Advertiser*, 3 and 6 July 1811, 2 and 2, respectively); the "Republican Greens, under the command of Major M'Clure" participated in a dinner and drank toasts, "accompanied by music, and some excellent songs": Music, Hail Columbia — Jefferson's March — Soldier's Joy — Strew the Hero's Grave with Flowers — New York Grand March — Vive La — Republican Green's Quick Step — Song, What Ship is that?—'Tis Liberty, Sweet Liberty — Washington's March — Yankee Doodle — Huzza My Brave Americans — The Spinning Wheel — The Tars of Tripoli — Ma Chere Amie (*Public Advertiser*, 6 July 1811, 2).

Pennsylvania

Allentown: Near the banks of the "Manaquecy" (Monocacy), on the farm of Captain Joseph Seigfreidt, ladies and gentlemen, including Revolutionary War soldiers, heard the following pieces of music as toasts were presented: Hail Columbia — Alknomack — Life

Let Us Cherish — How Sleep the Brave — Jefferson's March — Washington's March — Madison's March — Yankee Doodle — Anacreon — And Ne'er Shall the Sons of Columbia be Slaves — Long Life and Success to the Farmer — Hail Liberty — Rogues March — Soldier's Return — The Night Before Larry was Stretched[293] — The Constitution — Here's a Health to All Good Lasses ("Northampton County, Pa., Fourth of July 1811," *Kline's Weekly Carlisle Gazette*, 26 July 1811, 3).

Rhode Island

Newport: The events in this town included a procession and exercises at Trinity Church. "The ceremonies of the day were introduced and interspersed by vocal and instrumental music, selected with great taste and judgment, and performed in a style of excellence which has seldom been equaled. Great praise is due to Mr. Thomas Handy[294] for conducting, also to Messrs. Stebbins and Auchmuty, and to the ladies and gentlemen who assisted in the performances." That afternoon, at the dinner held at Mr. Townsend's Coffee House, "toasts were drank, accompanied by a number of popular and patriotic songs" ("National Birth-Day," *Newport Mercury*, 6 July 1811, 3); the Tammany Society of Newport paraded in their regalia to the Second Baptist Meeting House. "The performances were interspersed with patriotic musick, by a large choir of excellent singers, under the direction of Brother Moses Norman, which was executed in a style that reflected the highest credit on the ladies and gentlemen composing the choir." The choir sat in the front gallery of the church. Later at a dinner held at Eldred's Hotel, toasts were presented accompanied by the following music: Tune, Liberty — Tune, President's March — Tune, Clinton's March — Tune, America, Commerce and Freedom — Tune, Jefferson and Liberty — Tune, Rhode-Island Quick Step — Tune, Hearts of Oak — Tune, Dead March in Saul — Tune, Indian Chief — Tune, 'Twas Post Meridian — Tune, Go to the Devil — Tune, Hail Columbia — Tune, Rural Felicity ("Tammanial Celebration" and "The Tammany Society," *Rhode-Island Republican*, 3 and 10 July 1811, 3 and 3, respectively). See **Publications** above.

Providence: "A procession consisting of nearly 1000 Republican citizens of Rehoboth, Providence, and the vicinity, was formed under the auspices of the Columbian Order, in Tammanial style, and marched round the Green to the Baptist meeting-house, accompanied by the Tammanial Band of Music attached to Beaver Tribe, No. 1." After the oration, "the Tammanial Ode and sacred music skillfully performed by a choir of singers and the band" were performed. The "Order of Exercises" was as follows:

1. Sacred Music.
2. Prayer, by Elder Daniel Hix.
3. Original Ode-Tune, "Indian Chief."
4. Declaration of Independence, read by Br. J.L. Hodges.
5. Music-"Washington's March."
6. Oration by Ephraim Raymond, Esq.
7. Music.

("Independence" and "Republican Celebration," *Columbian Phenix; or, Providence Patriot*, 29 June and 6 July 1811, 2 and 3, respectively); another celebration took place at the Benevolent Congregational Meeting House. Music at some of the celebration dinners included: Hail to the Morning — President's March — Roslin Castle — Rhode-Island March — Arise, Arise! Columbia's Sons Arise — Washington's March — Moulines — Royal Quick Step — Swiss Guard's March — Abercrombie's March[295] — Yankee Doodle — General Bates's March[296] — March in the God of Love (*Providence Gazette*, 6 July 1811, 2); at the Providence Theatre, on July 4,

> in honour of American Independence ... the popular play in five acts, called the *Honey-Moon* ... to which will be added, a patriotick effusion, in one act, written by an American citizen, called the *Fourth of July, Or, Huzza for Independence!!*

Also performed was a

> patriotick song, "Hail Liberty," by Mr. Darley, after which, "The Standard of Liberty" will be recited by Mr. Powell, addressed to the Armies of the United States. To which will be added a new song, called "Fight, Conquer and be Free," by Mrs. Mills. And a *Pas Suel* and *Fancy Dance*, by Miss Drake. The whole to conclude with the patriotick song and chorus, called "God Save the United States," by Messrs. Darley, Dickinson, Drake, Entwisle, Robertson, Vaughan, &c. &c. [*Rhode-Island American, and General Advertiser*, 2 July 1811, 3].

Warren: Citizens of Warren at the Baptist Meeting House, "the exercises were interspersed with excellent music, performed by a full choir of singers" ("Celebration of American Independence at Warren," *Columbian Phenix: or, Providence Patriot*, 13 July 1811, 1).

1812

Publications

"The following elegant and patriotic Ode, is from the pen of Mr. Wm. C. Bryant, son of Doctor [Peter] Bryant of Cummington. An Ode. For the Fourth of July 1812. Tune 'Ye Gentlemen of England, &c.'" First line: "The Birth day of our nation" (*Poulson's American Daily Advertiser*, 22 July 1812, 2; "Poetry," *Newburyport Herald*, 28 July 1812, 4; *Bennington News-Letter*, 5 August 1812, 4).

"The following Ode was sung at Sanford [Maine], on the 4th of July 1812." First line: "All hail this glorious day" ("The Museum," *Eastern Argus*, 6 August 1812, 1).

"The following Song, was composed for the celebration of the 4th July at Edgefield [SC}, and sung by William Ellison, Esq." First line: "On a rock which frowns high o'er the neighboring heights" (*City Gazette and Daily Advertiser*, 15 July 1812, 3).

"The following Song, written for the occasion, was sung at the late celebration of Independence in this town. Tune 'Adams & Liberty.'" First line: "Tho' round our horizon the gloomy clouds rise" ("Poetry," *Newburyport Herald*, 10 July 1812, 4).

"The following song, written for the purpose, was sung at the celebration of American independence, in Philadelphia, on the 4th July last": first line: "Hail, sole republic of the world" ("Political Department," *The War* (Philadelphia), 22 August 1812, 40).

"March.[297] As performed by the Philadelphia military [sic] bands and also at the Olympic Theatre on the 4th of July, 1812. With variations for the piano forte." In *Pelissier's Columbian Melodies....* Composed by Victor Pelissier of Philadelphia. (Philadelphia: G. Willig, 1812), number 10, 93–94.

"March to Canada.[298] As performed by the Philadelphia military organizations & also at the Olympic Theatre on the Fourth of July, 1812. Inscribed to the army of the United States by Victor Pelissier" (Philadelphia, C. Taws's music store, 1813?).

"Ode, composed for the celebration of the 4th of July by the 'Associated Disciples of Washington.' Written by a member." First line: "What hero led to fight our sires?" ("Poetry," *Newburyport Herald*, 7 July 1812, 4).

"An Ode, composed for the thirty-sixth anniversary of American Independence, and sung at the Republican celebration in Fairhaven [Massachusetts] on the 4th inst." First line: "Blest be the land which kindly gave" ("The Rivulet," *New-Bedford Gazette*, 10 July 1812, 4).

"An Ode for the Brave." First line: "Hark! the drum — the bugle sounds!" ("Patriotic Poetry," *The War*, 4 July 1812, 8; "Poetry," *New Jersey Journal*, 11 August 1812, 4).

"Ode. For the 4th July, 1812. Written by Thomas G. Fessenden,[299] Esq. and performed by the choir, accompanied by the organ, at Walpole, N. H. Tune — 'Archdale.'" First line: "Columbia's sons, with loud acclaim" ("Poetry," *Constitutionalist and Weekly Magazine*, 11 August, 1812, 4).

"An Ode for the Fourth of July, tune — 'To Anacreon in Heaven.' By William C. Foster."[300] First line: "Hail, auspicious day! to Americans dear" (*Shamrock, or Hibernian Chronicle*, 11 July 1812, 4).

"Ode for the Fourth of July. Tune — 'Battle of the Nile.'" First line: "Let patriot pride our patriot triumph wake!" (*Columbian*, 26 June 1812, 3).

"Ode for the Fourth of July, 1812. Tune — Greenwich Pensioner." First line: "Natal morn of liberty" ("Poetry," *Constitutionalist and Weekly Magazine*, 23 June 1812, 4).

"Ode for the Fourth of July, 1812. Written by Thomas Sturtevant, jun. of the U.S. Army." First line:

"When first by heaven's supreme behest" ("Poetry," *American Advocate*, 30 July 1812, 4).

"An Ode for the Washington Benevolent Society.[301] Written, adapted to music and sung at New York July 4th 1812 by Mr. [Uri K.] Hill." First line: "Ye patriots rejoice while ye hail the glad morning." For voice, pianoforte and violin. N.p., 1812?. Text of ode printed in *An Oration Delivered before the Washington Benevolent Society and the Hamilton Society in the City of New York, on the Fourth of July, 1812.* By John Anthon. New York: Washington Benevolent Society, 1812; *New-York Spectator*, 8 July 1812, 2; *Bennington News-Letter*, 22 July 1812, 4; *Alexandria Gazette*, 23 July 1812, 3.

"Ode — Tune, 'Hail Columbia.'" First line: "Hail! sacred independence, hail!"[302] (*National Aegis*, 8 July 1812, 2; from the *National Aegis*, as published in *Green-Mountain Farmer*, 22 July 1812, 4).

"Original Song for toast table" sung at Blooming Grove, NY, "on the 4th instant." First line: "Old Johnny[303] now has got the gout" (*Orange County Patriot*, 21 July 1812, 3).

The Patriotic Vocalist, or Fourth of July Pocket Companion. A Selection of approved songs, on national subjects, for the use of public assemblies, celebrating the anniversaries of American independence, and Washington's birth day.[304] Salem: Cushing & Appleton, 1812.

Includes: "Rise Columbia! Written by R.T. Paine." First line: "When first the Sun o'er Ocean glow'd"; "Adams and Liberty. By R.T. Paine — 1799." First line: "Ye sons of Columbia, who bravely have fought"; "Song, for a select company of 'Old Continentals.' Tune — White Cockade." First line: "In the warfare of life where temptations invade"; "Ode for the military celebration at Salem of the Fourth of July, 1806 — by S.C. Blyth. Tune — Anacreon in Heaven." First line: "Ere the fiat of Heaven's almighty decree"; "Yankey Song, sung in Salem at a military celebration of the Fourth of July, 1806." First line: "Yankey Doodle is the tune"; "Ode, by Mr. Biglow — 1804." First line: "When Britain gigantic, by justice unaw'd"; "Song, by Mr. Biglow — 1804." First line: "While round the full board, independent and free"; "Columbia." First line: "Columbia! Columbia! to glory arise"; "Union of the Gods." First line: "To Columbia, who, gladly reclin'd at her ease"; "Ode by R.T. Paine — 1811. Tune — Battle of the Nile." First line: "Let patriot pride our patriot triumph wake!"; "The American Star." First line: "Come, strike the bold anthem, the war-dogs are howling"; "Song on the Non-Importation Act (Charlest. Pap.) — 1806." First line: "The motley band of demagogues, who rule our potent nation"; "Ode to Washington." First line: "The morning dawns with joyful ray"; "Washington's Birth Day. By a Lady." First line: "Hail, fairest Columbia! thy bold, rock shore." Advertised as "just published" in *Salem Gazette*, 3 July 1812, 3. Copy in Brown University and Library Congress.

"A Song for the Fourth of July. By a gentleman of this city [Elizabeth-Town, NJ]. From the *Baltimore Sun*." First line: "The Chief who fights in Freedom's cause." Signed "J.H.P." ("Poetry," *New Jersey Journal*, 7 July 1812, 4).

"'The Spirit of Freedom.' (An original Fourth of July ode.)" First line: "Bright Genius of Liberty, rise and rejoice!" (*Sentinel of Freedom*, 7 July 1812, 4).

"'The Times.' An Ode for the Fourth of July, 1812. Written by A. Davis. Tune — Vive la." First line: "Columbia's sons, your sires address you" (From the *Aurora* as printed in *New Jersey Journal*, 7 July 1812, 4). Two newspapers, *Independent Chronicle*, 16 July 1812, 1, and *Pittsfield Sun*, 25 July 1812, 4, cite the first line as "Times, alas! are most distressing."

See also, **Publications**, 1840.

Performances

District of Columbia

The U.S. Marine Band performed in the Hall of the House of Representatives at the Capitol with President James Madison in attendance (*National Intelligencer*, 8 July 1812, 2).

Maine

Georgetown: "At the fort, situated on a point on the Western side of the entrance of Kennebec River," the exercise included the singing of Psalm 101 "by a select choir of singers in the tune of Paris" and music was provided also in the procession ("Independence: Celebration at Georgetown," *Eastern Argus*, 23 July 1812, 2).

Hallowell: "At eleven o'clock the procession formed at the house of Maj. Robinson, under the escort of the Hallowell Light Infantry, commanded by Lieut. Coolidge, and proceeded with martial music, thro' the principal streets in Augusta to the Court House." After the exercises, the dinner was held at Maj. Robinson's Hall and the entertainment included "patriotic toasts, accompanied with music and a discharge of cannon" ("Independence — 4th July, 1812," *American Advocate*, 9 July 1812, 2).

Saco: At the Republican celebration, "several Odes and Hymns were sung which enlivened the scene" and music also at the dinner ("Independence: Celebration at Saco," *Eastern Argus*, 9 July 1812, 2).

Turner: After a procession from Staple's Hall to the Meeting House, the service included a prayer, a reading of "the President's Message, an oration, all "interspersed by several appropriate and well performed pieces of music, conducted by Daniel Cary, Esq. ("Independence: Celebration at Turner," *Eastern Argus*, 30 July 1812, 2).

Massachusetts

Boston: The Washington Society "assembled in the Court Room of the United States and at 3 proceeded in procession, preceded by the (late Castle) band, to the Hall of the Exchange Coffee House" for their ceremony. Among the guests was Robert T. Paine, signer of the Declaration of Independence ("National Birth-Day," *Independent Chronicle*, 9 July 1812, 2).

Fairhaven: The "Republican citizens of Fairhaven, and the neighbouring towns" assembled at Amos Pratt's Tavern and paraded to the Congregational Meeting House, "accompanied by an excellent band of music." The ceremony included "an Ode, composed for the occasion, by Lieut. Henry Whiting of the U.S. Army (for which see last page) was performed by a select choir with great taste." In addition, "several elegant pieces of music were performed by the band." Dinner at Pratt's Inn included the following music: Music, Hail Columbia — President's March — Pleyel's Hymn — Washington's March — Jefferson's March — Anacreon in Heaven — Yankee Doodle — Battle of Prague — Rodgers and Victory[305] — Rise Columbia — America, Commerce and Freedom — Speed the Plough — Over the Waters to Johnny[306] — United States March — Massachusetts March — Bunker-Hill March — Pickering's March — Come Haste to the Wedding ("4th of July," *New Bedford Gazette*, 3 and 10 July 1812, 3 and 2 respectively). See **Publications** above.

Marblehead: After a parade from the Town House to the New Meeting House, the order of exercises included:

1. Ode on Science.
2. 20th Psalm, omitting 3d verse, by the Rev. James Bowers.
3. Prayer by the Rev. Samuel Dana.
4. Ode — "All hail to Freedom's natal day."
5. Oration, by Jacob Willard, Esq.
6. Anthem on Independence.
7. Prayer, by the Rev. Ferdinand Ellis.
8. Ode — "God Save America."
["Marblehead," *Essex Register*, 8 July 1812, 2.]

Salem: The "Order of Performance" at the meeting house where the Republicans, military officers, and "citizens and gentlemen from neighbouring towns" assembled was:

1. Hymn.
2. Prayer.
3. Ode.
4. Declaration of Independence, Manifesto and Declaration of War.
5. Select Music by the Band.
6. Oration.
7. Select Music by Band.

("Celebration of National Independence," *Essex Register*, 4 July 1812, 3.); the *Salem Gazette* reported that a "voluntary on the organ" was to be performed by Mr. Dolliver[307] at the meeting house ("American Independence," *Salem Gazette*, 3 July 1812, 3).

New Hampshire

Gilmanton: "Excellent martial and instrumental music" in the procession of "the Republican citizens of Gilmanton and the neighboring towns" to the "Town House" ("National Jubilee," *New Hampshire Patriot*, 28 July 1812, 1).

Loudon: The Washington Republicans marched "with instrumental music" to the meeting house ("National Festival," *Concord Gazette*, 7 July 1812, 3).

Salisbury: "The Republican citizens of Salisbury and the adjacent towns" celebrated with a procession to the Meeting House "escorted by three companies of infantry and a junior company of artillery." The exercises included "the performance of several excellent pieces of music by a numerous vocal and instrumental choir." Later a procession assembled "on the Green in front of the Meeting House," where, after dinner, "toasts were drank, accompanied with appropriate music, and the discharge of cannon and musketry" ("Celebration at Salisbury," *New Hampshire Patriot*, 14 July 1812, 3).

New Jersey

Bloomfield: A parade included a choir of "vocal music" and "young ladies in uniform — singers included." At a bower, the exercises included 3 odes: "the vocal music, on account of its appropriate quality, and the skill with which it was performed, under the direction of Mr. Thomas Collins, Kitchell and Rutan, excited the admiration of all present" (*Centinel of Freedom*, 28 July and 11 August 1812, 1 and 2, respectively).

Newark: At the 1st Presbyterian Church, "after the singing of an ode, the exercises in the church were opened by a well adapted prayer by the Rev. James Richards. After singing another ode, the Declaration of Independence was read preceded by a few introductory observations. An ode followed, when an oration was pronounced by Mr. Philip Melaneton Whelpley," followed by another ode (*Newark Centinel*, 7 July 1812, 3).

Trenton: "The celebration of the day was opened with the firing of cannon — the ringing of bells, military music, and the decorations of the dwellings of the citizens on the principal streets." A procession marched from Warren Street to the Presbyterian Church. "In addition to the military music usual on the occasion, a select band of amateurs attended the procession, and afforded a pleasing variety to this interesting part of the scene." Included in the exercises were "the psalms selected for the occasion, well adapted, and sung with peculiar grace and propriety" (*Trenton Federalist*, 6 July 1812, 3; "Fourth of July," *Alexandria Daily Gazette, Commercial & Political*, 15 July 1812, 2).

New York

Brookhaven: The Washington Benevolent Society of this town, located in Suffolk County, paraded "attended by an excellent band of music, which added much to the respectability of the procession." The ceremony was held on the green and later a dinner was served at Capt Hartt's where the following pieces of music were heard: Music, Yankee Doodle — Music, Rosline Castle — Dirge — Music, Hamilton's Dirge — Music, America, Commerce and Freedom — Music,

The Ode to the Washington Society — Music, Yankee Doodle — Music, Heart of Oak — Music, All the Way to Boston — Music, Hail Columbia — Music, Washington's March — Music, Adams and Liberty — Music, Banks of Invarunay, Music, Rural Felicity — Music, Washington's March — Music, Yankee Doodle — Music, The Fair American ("American Independence," *New York Herald*, 18 July 1812, 4).

Hudson: "The Young Mechanics of both parties" assembled at Oliver Whitaker's Inn and, "preceded by martial music, under the command of Wm. Ray" marched through city streets to Parade Hill and then to the Court House for the exercises ("National Jubilee," *Bee*, 14 July 1812, 3).

New York: At the Debtor's Prison, 78 inmates and a number of guests heard the following music interspersed with the toasts: Music, Hail Columbia — Music, Madison's March — Music, Roslin Castle — Yankee Doodle — Washington's March — We'll Die or Be Free — Music, Tripoli — Battle of Prague — United We Stand, Divided We Fall — Galley Slave — O Dear What Can the Matter Be — Rogues March ("Debtors Prison," *Public Advertiser*, 9 July 1812, 2); "At a meeting of the Delegates of the General Committee of Arrangements" of the Tammany Society, the group resolved "that the thanks of this committee, in behalf of Tammany" be extended to the various individuals and groups that made the Fourth of July celebration successful. One acknowledgment was extended to "Messrs. Duren and Seymour, and the Choir of Singers in the [Baptist] Church under their direction." The exercises as the church included the performance of an anthem and ode and other works. (*Mercantile Advertiser*, 2 July 1812, 2; *Columbian*, 16 July 1812, 3.); the Hamilton Society and Washington Benevolent Society celebrated in tandem at Washington Hall and later a dinner at the Hamilton Hotel. "After dinner the following toasts were drank, accompanied with appropriate music": Hail Columbia — Rise Columbia — Washington's March — America, Commerce and Freedom — Roslin Castle — Hamilton's March — Hamilton's Dirge — Lexington March — Sons of Freedom Awake — The Union of Patriots — The Cheat — Anacreon — Yankee Doodle — President's March — The Handle of a Jug — Tid rei — Rural Felicity ("Hamilton Society," *New-York Spectator*, 8 July 1812, 2). See **Publications** above.

Pennsylvania

Philadelphia: At the Olympic Theater, *American Naval Pillar, or, A Tribute of Respect to the Tars of Columbia*, "a new musical entertainment, in two acts," was presented.[308] See also, **Publications** above.

Rhode Island

Newport: The procession that formed at the State House at 9 A.M. included "music and standards" ("The Fourth of July," *Newport Mercury*, 4 July 1812, 3).

Providence: "A number of the Republicans of this town assembled at Mr. Pedge's Hall" where the Declaration of Independence was read "and the company partook of a sumptuous dinner." Accompanying the toasts were cheers and "patriotic songs, and national music from the Columbian Band" ("Columbia's Birth Day," *Columbian Phenix, or Providence Patriot*, 11 July 1812, 2).

South Carolina

Charleston: At 11 A.M. eighty members of the Republican Military School of Fishing Creek paraded before a group of citizens while a band performed "Roslin Castle" and "Yankee Doodle." At the dinner that following a song, "which was written by Capt. Dunham" (of the U.S. Army) "some years ago, and has been frequently published since, was sung" ("Patriotic Celebration," *City Gazette and Daily Advertiser*, 31 July 1812, 3).

Virginia

Alexandria: The Washington Society and elements of the military heard the following music upon presentation of toasts "after partaking of an excellent dinner" provided for them at the Spring Gardens: Music, Hail Columbia — Music, Yankee Doodle — Music, Washington's March — Music, Come to the Bower — Music, Oh, for a Union of Parties — Music, Roslin Castle — Music, America, Commerce & Freedom — Music, Volunteer's March ("The Fourth of July," *Alexandria Herald*, 8 July 1812, 3); an "excellent band of music attached to captain Mcknight's Company" (*Alexandria Gazette*, 3 and 6 July 1812; *Alexandria Herald*, 8 July 1812, 3).

1813

Publications

At a meeting of Friends of the Revolution at Bell Tavern, "the following extempore Verses from the pen of Wm. Manford, Esq. were sung [in Virginia] with great glee to the music of 'On Chrismas [sic] Day in '76'": first line, "The month was June — the year 'Thirteen'" ("Fourth of July," *Enquirer*, 9 July 1813, 3).

"Dirge, on the death of Captain Lawrence: sung upon the Fourth of July." First line: "Hark from the main the voice of glory" ("Dirge," *Juvenile Port-Folio, and Literary Miscellany*, 17 July 1813, 160).

"The following Odes and Hymns, composed by gentlemen of this town [Salem, MA] for the occasion, were sung at the late Republican celebration of the anniversary of American independence": "Ode. Tune 'Anacreon in Heaven.'" First line: "Sound the trumpet of joy, the return of the morn"; "Ode. Tune 'Rise Columbia.'" First line: "All hail to freedom's natal day"; "Hymn. Tune 'Sicilian Mariner's Hymn.'" First line: "Now to the great and only king" (*Essex Register*, 7 July 1813, 1); "Elegant Song. The late anniversary of

American Independence, like most of the preceding, has presented us with a number of National Songs. The following, which was composed by a gentleman of Salem, Mass. and sung at the celebration in that town, is of the first order, for poetic as well as patriotic excellent. *T. True Amer.* Tune — Anacreon in Heaven." First line: "Sound the trumpet of joy — the return of this morn" ("Poetry," *Chronicle or Harrisburgh Vistor*, 2 August 1813, 4).

"The following song, written for that purpose, was sung at the celebration of American Independence, in Philadelphia, on the 4th July last.[in 1812]" First line: "Hail, sole republic of the world!" ("Selected Poetry," *Native American*, 21 April 1813, 4).

"For the Fourth of July. Tune, 'Wary Gods.'" First line: "Columbia's sons, ye patriots hail"; "Ode for the Fourth of July." First line: "Welcome! welcome the day, when assembled as [sic] one"; "Song for the Fourth of July. Tune–'Hail Columbia.'" First line: "Welcome great auspicious day"; "Ode for the Fourth of July." First line: "Ye patriots, rejoice, while ye hail this glad morning" (*Spirit of the Press*, 1 July 1813, 1–2.)

"An Ode, composed for the anniversary of American independence — Air, Arethusa." First line: "Join every Nymph, in sportive lay" ("Poetry," *New Jersey Journal*, 13 July 1813, 4; *Chronicle or Harrisburgh Vistor*, 19 July 1813, 4).

"Ode for the Fourth of July." To the tune "Hail Columbia."[309] Written "by a member of the [Washington] Society" ([Boston]: True & Rowe printers, State-Street [1813].

"Ode for the Fourth of July." First line: "Welcome! Welcome the day, when assembled as one" (*Spirit of the Press*, 1 July 1813, 2).

"Order of performance, for the 4th of July, 1813, at Tiverton [RI]." Contains Ode to the Revolution (first line, "Here liberty was doomed to rest"); Ode on Liberty, original (first line: "Hail liberty! celestial guest"). Broadside, Rhode Island, 1813. Copy in Brown University.

"Patriotic, July the 4th, 1813 — by P.M." First line: "Columbia's sons salute the morn" ("Poetry," *Chronicle of Harrisburgh Visitor*, 6 September 1813, 4).

"Song for Volunteers. On the Fourth of July. (The following song was intended for the Fourth of July last, but came to hand too late. It is perhaps not less appropriate at this moment, just when the brethren of the District [of Columbia] have returned to their homes, than it would have been at that time). Tune — 'Hail Columbia.'" First line: "Soldiers!— join a heart-warm lay" (*National Intelligencer*, 2 August 1813, 2).

"A Song written on the Fourth of July." First line: "Now Europe's convuls'd with the discord of war" (*The American Patriotic Song-Book, a Collection of Political, Descriptive, and Humourous Songs, of National Character, and the Production of American Poets Only. Interspersed with a Number Set to Music* [Philadelphia: W. M'Culloch, 1813]).

Performances

Connecticut

Hartford: Republication celebration "marched to a delightful grove on the margin of Connecticut river, led by a band of excellent music; composed of as many of his Excellency's Band, as could dispence with playing 'God Save the King!'" ("American Independence," *American Mercury*, 13 July 1813, 3).

Salem: A parade of Republicans included "an excellent band of music." A dinner that day at Lynn Mineral Spring Hotel, included toasts with the following music: Hail Columbia — President's March — Massachusetts March — Tune, God Save the King — Rise Columbia — Hail Columbia — Dead March in Saul — Dirge — Washington's March — Jefferson's March — Adams & Liberty — Yankee Doodle — Gen. Warren's March — The Lads of the Ocean — America, Commerce and Freedom — Gen Green's March (*Essex Register*, 7 July 1813, 3).

Delaware

New Castle County: "Near the Trap," a celebration consisting of "a respectable number of citizens from the neighboring county" featured "an excellent repast," a reading of the Declaration of Independence, and toasts "attended by the discharge of artillery and the plaudits of the company." Some of the toasts were accompanied by music: Music, Hail Columbia — Solemn Music — Yankee Doodle — Soldiers Return — Solemn Music — Hail Columbia — The Soldiers Return (*American Watchman*, 10 July 1813, 3).

Maine

Portland: Celebration of Republicans at "the Rev. Doct. Dean's meeting house," with "an excellent band of music"[310]: Washington's March — United States March — President's March — Swiss Guard March — Massachusetts March — Yankee Doodle — March in Abeilino — Hull's Guerriere — Circus March — Columbia in Glory — Rural Felicity — Decatur's Victory — Pleyal's Hymn — Augusta March — Rogues' March[311] — Azure — Battle of Prague — Go to the Devil and Shake Yourself[312] — Colonel Learned's March (*Eastern Argus*, 8 July 1813, 3).

Massachusetts

Boston: The Washington Republican Society celebrated at the Hall of the Exchange Coffee House, where after "an excellent dinner. ... sentiments were given, accompanied by appropriate music, and the plaudits of the company": Hail Columbia (After this toast an excellent Ode was sung, which is on our first page) [First line: "While clouds of darkness fill'd the west" to the tune "Hail Columbia"] — Rise Columbia — President's March — Gerry's March — Washington's March — Yankee Doodle — Capt. Hull's March — Dirge — Jefferson's March — Roslin Castle — Pleyel's Hymn (After this toast an appropriate Dirge was sung, which is on our first page) [First line:

"Lawrence! Valour's gen'rous lion!" to the tune "Pleyel's Hymn"] — God Save the Commonwealth — Dirge — Begone, Dull Care — America, Commerce and Freedom — March to Boston — Rural Felicity ("National Jubilee!" *Independent Chronicle*, 8 July 1813, 1–2).

Brookfield: "Members of the several Washington Benevolent Societies, and citizens" as well as a military company "accompanied by a band of musick" marched to the Meeting House where at the exercises it was reported "the musick was excellent — the exercises closed by an admirable song from Mr. Hamilton, of Worcester" (*Massachusetts Spy, or Worcester Gazette*, 14 July 1813, 3).

Charlestown: At the Universal Meeting House "the exercises were interspersed with suitable musick, by the choir of singers" ("Charlestown Celebration," *Independent Chronicle*, 8 July 1813, 2).

Deerfield: In the procession on "Tuesday the 6th, ... choir of singers in pairs," and music by the choir at the exercises (*Franklin Herald*, 22 June 1813, 3).

Lancaster: Citizens of this town and Sterling, as well as members of the Washington Benevolent Society celebrated together. "After the delivery of the oration a patriotick ode was sung by Mr. Newell, in a style and manner which proved him adept in musick, and an enthusiast in feeling" (*Massachusetts Spy, or Worcester Gazette*, 7 July 1813, 3).

Roxbury: Exercises were held at the "Town House" and the following music was performed at the dinner: Adams and Liberty — Yankee Doodle — President's March — Gerry's March — Jefferson's March — Liberty Tree — Washington's March — Hail Columbia — Dirge — Massachusetts' March — Captain Kidd — O Tempore, O micres[?] — Billings' Jargon (*Independent Chronicle*, 8 July 1813, 2).

Salem: At the Universal Meeting House, "performance of several patriotic odes written for the occasion, and the excellent music prepared for the day," (*Essex Register*, 7 July 1813, 2–3). See **Publications** above.

Sutton: This town celebrated a month early with a procession that included music. At the Meeting House, interspersed in the exercises were "pieces of instrumental music" by a band "with taste and skilful accuracy" ("Celebration of Our National Independence at Sutton," *National Aegis*, 7 July 1813, 3).

New Hampshire

Candia: Members of the Washington Benevolent Society and others "marched to the meeting house, stewards bearing the Constitution of the United States, and Washington's Farewell Address, preceeded by a choir of singers, and some excellent instrumental music, playing Washington's March, accompanied by a large concourse of people of both sexes. After being seated, the exercises of the day" were begun with "an excellent piece of music (Denmark) was performed by the singers, accompanied by instruments." After the Declaration was read, "a Hymn adapted to the occasion was then sung. (By field.)." Following the oration, the ceremony closed "with a piece of music. (Ode on Science.)" At the dinner, toasts were "accompanied by appropriate music" ("Celebration of Independence at Candia," *Concord Gazette*, 10 August 1813, 3).

Chesterfield: The celebration on the "3d inst. By the Philesian Society of Chesterfield" included "a procession formed by the students, singers, members of the Society, and Trustees, preceded by music" that marched from the Academy Hall to the meeting house where the "exhibition" was begun with "instrumental music." Included in the ceremony were "an Ode written for the occasion by L. Lyons" and another "Ode, written for the occasion by J.C. Smith." The local newspaper reported that "the Odes were sung by a respectable choir of singers, and the exercises written by the performers were exhibited to the approbation of the audience, and the honor of this juvenile fraternity" (*New-Hampshire Sentinel*, 17 July 1813, 3; *Reporter*, 24 July 1813, 3).

Hopkinton: The Washington Benevolent Society of this town and members representing towns of Concord and Dunbarton met at the court house for a procession, preceded by a band, to the meeting house. "Sacred Musick, aided in raising the affections of a numerous and respectable audience to the God of our fathers.... Of this we say no more than that the music ought to have been good — but the performers had probably seen Billings's Jargon"[313] ("Celebration of the Anniversary of American Independence at Hopkinton, July 5th," *New-Hampshire Patriot*, 27 July 1813, 1).

Keene: On July 5 the members of the Washington Benevolent Societies "and numerous other citizens ... consisting of nearly 400 persons were formed at Fish's tavern" and marched with a "full band of music" to the Meeting House "where the exercises commenced by sacred music." After an additional piece of sacred music, a reading of the Declaration of Independence and oration, "an original Song of Praise [to the tune, "Old Hundred"] composed by Mr. C. ... concluded the performances": first line, "Praise waits in Zion, Lord for Thee." Later at a "bower in front of the Court House," a dinner was served with toasts accompanied by music and a discharge of artillery ("Independence," *New-Hampshire Sentinel*, 10 July 1813, 3–4).

Portsmouth: The Washington Benevolent Society of New Hampshire and other "distinguished strangers and persons belonging to other similar institutions" celebrated on July 5. They assembled at the Insurance Office at 10 A.M. and marched to the Meeting House where the exercises included a reading of Washington's Farewell Address and "music, consisting of an original Hymn and an Ode selected for the occasion ... performed by a select choir in a superior style" ("Independence," *Portsmouth Oracle*, 10 July 1813, 3).

Washington: On Monday, July 5, the militia marched to the meeting house "escorted by military music. An appropriate hymn was sung" (Celebration at Washington, N.H.," *New Hampshire Patriot*, 20 July 1813, 1).

New Jersey

Jefferson Village: At a meeting for arrangements for celebrating the Fourth (possibly at Springfield), Watts Reeve and "Doctor Brown" were assigned the conductors of the music. Reeve also served as clerk of the celebration committee (*Centinel of Freedom*, 29 June 1813, 3).

New York

Deer Park: The celebration was scheduled to occur on July 5 at the house of John Kerr and a procession to include music, and exercises to include "a patriotic song" and a "musical play called 'The Prize'" ("Celebration of the Thirty-Seventh Anniversary of American Independence, in the Town of Deer Park," *Orange County Patriot*, 22 June 1813, 1).

Harpersfield: Some two thousand persons paraded accompanied by music to the Presbyterian Meeting House. A choir was present for the day's exercises (*Albany Argus*, 20 July 1813, 2).

New York: The Typographical Society met on July 5 at Mr. A. Ely's School Room for the exercises followed by dinner at the Bank Coffee House. "The following Ode, written by a member for the occasion, was sung after the last toast." First line: "Oh! ye votaries of Faust, and of Freedom combin'd" (from the *Columbian* as printed in "Typographical Society," *Albany Register*, 13 July 1813, 2; *The Yankee*, 16 July 1813, 4; *National Aegis*, 18 August 1813, 4).

Pine Plains: "A band of music" at "Mr. Trowbridge's Hotel": Washington's March — Tune, 4th of July — President's March — Tune, March to Boston — Jefferson and Liberty — Roslin Castle — King of Prussia's March — 17th Regt. — Funlem's March — Rogues' March — Battle of Prague — Galley Slave — Caledonia — Hail Columbia — Amoret — Yankee Doodle ("Celebration of Independence," *Columbian* 20 July 1813, 2).

Ohio

Perrysburg: At "Camp Meigs" for a Fourth of July celebration[314] that included an artillery salute, the Independent Volunteers Band of Ohio and Kentucky provided music following toasts with over 100 officers and soldiers present: Yankee Doodle — Go to the Devil and Shake Yourself— Hail Liberty — Rogue's March — Roslin Castle — Columbia, Columbia to Glory Arise — Washington's March — Stoney Point — Ere Around the Hugh Oak — Jefferson's March — Madison's March — Turks March — Harrison's March — The Soldier's Return — America, Commerce and Freedom — My Heart from My Bosom Would Fly ("Fourth of July in Camp," *National Intelligencer*, 28 July 1813, 1).

Rhode Island

Newport: The procession assembled at the State House "on Monday the 5th of July (the 4th being Sunday)" and marched to Trinity Church where the exercises included "vocal and instrumental music."

The musicians sat in the front gallery ("Anniversary of American Independence, *Newport Mercury*, 3 July 1813, 3).

Seekonk: At the Republican celebration, "the procession to the sanctuary was large, and a numerous company partook at the festive board. After the repast, the usual number of well seasoned sentiments were given, accompanied by discharges of cannon and music from the band" ("Independence," *Columbian Phenix, or Providence Patriot*, 10 July 1813, 2).

Vermont

Brattleboro: The Fourth was celebrated on July 6. A procession from the Academy Hall to the Meeting House included a band. "The exercises were introduced by singing, and an excellent well adapted prayer, by the Rev. Mr. Nye." After an oration, "an ode written for the occasion by Thomas G. Fessenden, esq. of Bellows Falls" was sung ("Celebration," *Reporter*, 10 July 1813, 3).

Fairhaven: Members of the Washington Benevolent Society "and a large concourse of other citizens from the vicinity" celebrated on July 5. The procession to the church consisted of more than two thousand people, escorted by a company of cavalry. A choir of singers preceded, and a band of music followed the "societies, accompanied by a group of young lads in the sailor dress, bearing an armed ship full rigged — also seventeen misses dressed in white, bearing olive branches. After singing a hymn composed for the occasion, the throne of grace was addressed by the Rev. Mr. Bigelow, of Middleton, in a most devost, solemn and impressive manner." Works performed included: "An Ode. For July 4th, 1813": first line, "On broad Potomack's margin lies"; "Independence Hymn": first line, "O God of Hosts, by thine own arm" ("Fairhaven Celebration," *Vermont Mirror*, 28 July 1813, 2; "Fairhaven (Vt.) Celebration," *Boston Daily Advertiser*, 6 August 1813, 2).

Ira: In the procession "on Saturday the 3d inst." were "700 citizens ... accompanied by martial and instrumental music, under command of Capt. Tower" ("American Independence: Celebration at Ira," *Rutland Vermont Herald*, 14 July 1813, 3).

Middlebury: "The 4th of July falling on the Sabbath, the anniversary of the declaration of our independence was celebrated by the Washington Benevolent Society of Addison County in this place, on Friday the 2d inst." After a procession from Mr. Bell's House to the Meeting House, "the following exercises were performed":

1. Sacred Music.
2. Prayer by the Rev. Mr. Merrill
3. Sacred Music.
4. Oration by B. Parks Esq.
5. Prayer by the Rev. Professor Hough
6. Sacred Music.

After the exercises "a numerous collection of citizens repaired to Mr. Mattocks's new hall, where they partook of an elegant dinner prepared by Mr. Bell and drank the following toasts, accompanied by the discharge of cannon and appropriate music by the Middlebury Band": Tune, Fourth of July — Washington's March — Gen. Green's March — Phyel's [sic] Hymn — Democratic Rage — Washington Dirge — God Save America[315] — Hail Columbia — Vermont March — Swiss Guard — Massachusetts March — Lord Dorchester's March — Turkish March — Boston Independent Cadets' March — Russian March — Air Rejoicing — Battle of Prague — Monro's March. "We cannot however omit to say, that the band of music belonging to this village, who performed on this occasion, distinguished themselves by their correct and elegant performance. Such an acquisition to this village is a subject of congratulation to every citizen and especially to the lovers of music" ("Celebration," *Vermont Mirror*, 14 July 1813, 1).

Poultney: Two pieces of sacred music were performed at the meeting house (*Rutland Vermont Herald*, 21 July 1813, 1–2).

1814

Publications

The American Star: being a choice collection of the Most approved patriotic and other songs, together with many original ones never before published[316] (Richmond [Va.]: Peter Cottom, 1814).

"'The Birth-Day of Freedom.' A National Song. Tune —'Anacreon in Heaven.'" First line: "All hail to the birth of the happiest land." By Henry C. Knight.[317] (*Port-Folio* 4/1, July 1814, 118–21).

"The Fourth of July. Tune, Rural Felicity." First line: "What heart but throbs high with sincerest devotion" (*New Hampshire Patriot*, 12 July 1814, 4).

"The Genius of Columbia. An Ode." First line: "Bright from the tumult of battle advancing" ("The Museum," *New-Hampshire Patriot*, 19 July 1814, 4).

"The Impressment of an American Sailor Boy: Sung on Board the British Prison Ship Crown Prince, the Fourth of July, 1814 by a Number of the American Prisoners." First line: "The youthful sailor mounts the bark." Broadside, 1814. Copy in the New York Historical Society.

"Hail Independence.[318] Tune — The Dauphin." First line: "Hail, Independence, hail!" (*New Hampshire Patriot*, 12 July 1814, 4; "Seat of the Muses," *Otsego Herald*, 21 July 1814, 4).

"Independence. Ode for the Fourth of July, 1814, by Nathan Guilford" (first line, "Again the glorious day returns"; "Ode, by Edward D. Bangs" (first line, "O'er the oak-cover'd hills and rich fields of the West." Broadside, [Worcester, MA, 1814].[319]

"Ode, for the celebration of American Independence, July 4, 1814 — By Henry Small." First line: "While the morn of blest liberty dawns in the east"

("Poetry," *Newburyport Herald*, 12 July 1814, 4; *Evening Post*, 19 July 1814, 2; *An Oration, Pronounced before the Federal Republicans of Charlestown, Massachusetts, July 4, 1814, being the Anniversary of American Independence.* By Joseph Tufts, Jun. Esq. Charlestown: Samuel Etheridge, Jun., 1814).

"Ode, for the 4th of July, 1814. By W.C. Bryant." First line: "Amidst the storms that shake the land" ("Poetry," *New Bedford Mercury*, 29 July 1814, 4).

"Odes to be sung at Acquacknonk [Acquack-anonck, NJ], July 4th, 1814." Contains three untitled songs. Broadside. Copy in American Antiquarian Society.

"Original Hymn and Ode, for July 4, 1814. Sung at the North Meeting House" in Portsmouth, NH. Hymn, first line: "Eternal God! thy children now." Ode, tune — "Rise Columbia," first line: "God of the sires, defend the sons." Note: "The musical performances added much to the pleasures of the audience. The original ode sung by Mr. Stanwood had a very fine effect" ("Poetry," *Portsmouth Oracle*, 9 July 1814, 4).

"Song. Tune — Rural Felicity." First line: "All Hail Happy Day, for Americans Glory." This work was introduced at the Union Guards celebration in New Castle, Delaware, at the "Hermitage." "Several patriotic songs were sung. The following was composed and sung by Mr. Evan Thomas, a member of the Union Guards" (*Delaware Gazette and Peninsula Advertiser*, 11 July 1814, 2).

Performances

Connecticut

New Haven: "A large and respectable audience assembled at the White-Haven Meeting House," and it was reported that in addition to a prayer and an address by David Daggett, "the whole was attended with appropriate Music, by a numerous choir of singers" ("Fourth of July," *Connecticut Journal*, 11 July 1814, 3).

Union: The Washington Benevolent Society and citizens of Warren, Waldboro, and Thomaston assembled for the exercises. "Two Hymns and an Ode were prepared for the occasion. They do great honor to their authors. The music has rarely been excelled on any similar occasion." "Ode for the Fourth of July, 1814 — sung at table. Tune — 'Adams and Liberty'" (first line: "Our fathers, impell'd by the zeal of reform"); "Hymn, sung in the meeting house. Tune — 'Old Hundred'" (first line: "Creator Go! the first, the last") ("Celebration of National Independence and of the Deliverance of Europe — at Union," *Weekly Messenger*, 15 July 1814, 3).

District of Columbia

At M'Keowen's Hotel "public officers, citizens, and strangers" that included members of Congress, "Heads of Departments" and military officers. At the dinner "Nathaniel Cutting, Esq. recited an appropriate ode, written by himself for the occasion" and the following pieces of music were performed following the toasts:

Washington's March — Hail Columbia — In Freedom We're Born — President's March — Hail Parriot [patriot?] Band — Pleyel's Hymn — Jefferson's March — Hark the Trump of Fame — Yankee Doodle — The Reveille — The Watery God — Hearts of Oak — America, Commerce and Freedom — Battle of Prague — White Cockade — Around the Hugh Oak — Rural Felicity ("Fourth July, 1814," *National Intelligencer*, 6 July 1814, 3; "National Birth-Day Celebrations," *Independent Chronicle*, 14 July 1814, 1).

In Georgetown on the grounds "of Mr. Parrott, adjoining his rope-walk," citizens and military (about 400 persons) assembled for an entertainment. "A number of gentlemen of Washington and Georgetown, composing a very fine band of musicians, volunteered their services for the day." Toasts were offered with the following music: Hail Columbia — Soldiers [Return?] — Washington's March — Madison's March — Jefferson's March — Yankee Doodle — By Jove We'll Be Free — Come All Ye Social Powers — Come Thou Lovely Peace — Stoney Point — The Tars of Columbia[320] — When War's Alarms — Way-Worn Traveler[321] — Mary's Dream[322] — Trip to Canada — The Top-Sail Shivers in the Wind[323] — America, Commerce and Freedom — Lads and Lasses ("Georgetown Celebration," *National Intelligencer*, 8 July 1814, 2).

Maine

Saco: The celebration included "a respectable number of citizens of that place and its vicinity, who cheerfully partook of a well served dinner prepared by Colonel Wm. Moody. On which occasion the Hon. John Holmes presided, & read in an impressive manner, the Declaration of our Independence, after which were drank the following toasts, accompanied by music and discharges of cannon" ("Independence: Celebration at Saco," *Eastern Argus*, 21 July 1814, 2).

Waterville: Republicans of Waterville and adjacent towns assembled at the West Meeting House after marching with a musical escort. The exercises began with "singing an appropriate hymn" ("National Anniversary," *American Advocate*, 16 July 1814, 2).

Maryland

Elkton: At the Court House, "'Ode to Science' was played by an elegant band of music, composed of the gentlemen of the town" ("Fourth of July," *Baltimore Patriot & Evening Advertiser*, 12 July 1814, 3).

Massachusetts

Boston: At the Old South Meeting House, "the musical services consisted of a symphony, under the direction of Mr. [Francesco?] Masi,[324] an anthem, and a hymn" ("Fourth of July," *Weekly Messenger*, 8 July 1814, 3).

Charlestown: A procession of Federalists marched from Washington Hall to the Rev. Dr. Morse's Meeting House where the "public services of the day were opened by an Anthem from the choir. The Rev. Mr. Green of Malden then led the devotions of the congregation in prayer. A Hymn and an Ode composed for the occasion by Mr. [Henry] Small, was sung with happy effect." "The music, vocal and instrumental, was such as to add to the general gratification" ("American Independence," *Newburyport Herald*, 12 July 1814, 1, 4). See **Publications** above.

Lexington: Up to 5000 persons assembled along with Vice President Elbridge Gerry and marched around the Lexington Monument (erected in 1794) to the Meeting House. After the exercises "the procession moved from the Meeting House with martial music, and entered the plain, where a sumptuous table was spread." The toasts were accompanied with the following music: Yankee Doodle — President's March — Gov. Gerry's March[325] — Green's March — Dirge — Adams and Liberty — Jefferson's March — Gen. Eaton's March[326] — Rise Columbia — Gov. Strong's March[327] — Yankee Doodle — Washington's March — Hail Columbia — Old Hundred — Rural Felicity ("Great National Jubilee at Lexington," *Yankee*, 8 July 1814, 2; "Great National Festival," *Essex Register*, 9 July 1814, 1).

Newburyport: At the "church in Federal Street ... the exercises were opened by an anthem." Throughout the event, "the music was judiciously selected and admirably performed by a select choir"; at a dinner celebration at Washington Hall, the following works were performed: Rise Columbia — Massachusetts March — March in Forty Thieves[328] — Dead March in Saul — Caravan's March — Duke of York's March — Yankee Doodle — Moll in the Wod — Here We Go Up, Up, Up, and Here We Go Down, Down, Downy — March in God of Love — Frog and Mouse — March in Blue Beard — Bona's March to Elba ("Anniversary Celebration" and "Public Dinner," *Newburyport Herald*, 8 July 1814, 2).

Pittsfield: "The Republican citizens of Berkshire" celebrated with a procession that formed at the Hotel "and proceeded to the Meeting House, accompanied with music from the band, where the customary exercises were performed" and which included "music from the choir" ("Our National Birth-Day" and "National Jubilee," *Pittsfield Sun*, 30 June and 7 July 1814, 3 and 3, respectively).

Salem: "A large concourse of people moved in procession from the Court House to the North Meeting House" where included in the exercises, "the music (particularly the sublime Hallelujah Chorus) led by Dr. Peabody, was performed with great effect." Mr. Dolliver performed a voluntary on the organ and Psalm 9 to the tune "Old Hundred" was sung. Later "a large party of gentlemen partook of a sumptuous dinner at the new Hall of the Essex Coffee House" where the toasts were presented with the following musical works: White cockade — Song — "In the down-hill of life, In my snug elbow chair, &c. — Massachusetts March — Strong's March — Dead March in Saul — Hail Columbia, Happy Land! — Lady Berkley's Whim — Hearts of Oak — Dirge — Yankee Doodle — Quebec March — There is No Luck

about the House[329] — Go to the Devil and Shake Yourself — Alas! Poor Robinson Crusoe! — Catch — Men in Buckram ("American Independence" and "Fourth of July," *Salem Gazette*, 4 and 8 July 1814, 1 and 3, respectively).

Scituate: After a procession and exercises at the Meeting House, the Republicans of Scituate and surrounding towns celebrated with a dinner that included toasts, "accompanied with music and the discharge of cannon": Hail Columbia — Adams and Liberty — President's March — Yankee Doodle — Jefferson's March — Old Hundred — Dead March in Saul — Go to the Devil and Shake Yourself — Rural Felicity ("Celebration of American Independence at Scituate," *Boston Patriot*, 9 July 1814, 2).

New Hampshire

Hanover: A parade of Washington Benevolent Societies of Hanover, Lebanon, Lime, and Norwich, citizens and students of Dartmouth was "preceded by a band of instrumental music" to the meeting house. "The ceremonies were commenced by the following hymn (marked no. 1), composed for the occasion by Mr. N.C. Betton, which was performed by a select choir." After a prayer, "the following hymn (marked no. 2) composed by Mr. George Kent, was sung by the choir. After an oration, "the following Ode, composed by Mr. Kent (marked no. 3) was sung by Col. Brewster, in a masterly style. Te Deum was performed by the choir": "Hymn" (no. 1) [tune] Old Hundred (first line: "Great Sovereign! of the wolds [sic] above"; "Hymn (no. 2) [tune] Denmark" (first line: "Eternal God! thy name we praise"); "Ode (no. 3) Tune — Anacreon in Heaven" (first line: "Rise, sons of Columbia! and hail the glad day"). Later at a bower, dinner was served with toasts "accompanied by airs played by the band": Swiss Guard's March — U.S. March — Reed's March — Favorite March Blue-Beard — Battle of the Nile — O Dear what Can the Matter Be — There is No Luck about the House — Washington's March — Massachusetts March — Jargon[330] — Knox's March — Pleyel's Hymn — Blue Bells of Scotland — Downfall of Paris — Old Hundred — Battle of Prague — Go to the Devil and Shake Yourself (*Concord Gazette*, 12 July 1814, 3).

Lyman: "At the place appointed for the exercises of the day," there were at least two pieces of music performed. The program was listed as follows

1. Music.
2. Prayer.
3. Music.
4. A Discourse by the Rev. Isaac Scarritt, from Ex. Xii. 14.
5. An Oration, by Caleb Emert, Esq.
6. Prayer.

["Celebration at Lyman," *Concord Gazette*, 19 July 1814, 3].

Manchester: The day "was celebrated by the Republican citizens of Manchester, Goffstown, and Bedford, and their vicinity" with a procession that began at 11:30 A.M. to the Meeting House. "After performance of church music by a band that roused the 'various movements of the breast,' the throne of Grace was addressed by the Rev. D. I. Morrill of Goffstown" ("Celebration at Manchester," *New-Hampshire Patriot*, 19 July 1814, 2).

New Jersey

Newark: In the procession and at the First Presbyterian Church, "Mr. Richmond and his choir of singers" ("Fourth of July Arrangements at Newark," *Centinel of Freedom*, 21 June 1814, 3); at a "sumptuous dinner" event by the Newark Independent Artillery at Moses Roff's, the following music was played as the toasts were presented: Bunker Hill — Liberty Tree — Hail Columbia — President's March — Patriot's Song — Firm United — Jersey Blue[331] — music Yankee Doodle — America, Commerce and Freedom — Roslin Castle — Dead March — Soldiers Return — Maid of the Mill — Rural Felicity — Freedom and Peace — Women and Wine — Soldiers Farewell — Tune, a Sailors Life at Sea — Victory or Death — The Volunteer — The Patriots Prayer[332] — To Arms — The Drum — The Votive Wreath (*The Centinel of Freedom*, 12 July 1814, 3).

Patterson Landing: A parade included a band of "martial musick" and 186 ladies "all dressed in white, and heads trimmed with ribbon, singing Columbia at every interval of the martial music." At the church, the exercises included singing three odes and one psalm (*Centinel of Freedom*, 26 July 1814, 2).

Springfield: Plans for the forthcoming celebration named Watts Reeve as leader of the "music, vocal and instrumental" contribution to the event at the church ("At Springfield," *Centinel of Freedom*, 21 June 1814, 3).

New York

Florida: The citizens of Goshen and Florida formed a procession that included the Middletown Band. The group marched to the church where the exercises were performed ("Fourth of July, 1814," *Orange County Patriot; or, the Spirit of 'Seventy-Six,'* 28 June 1814, 2).

New York: An interlude of songs and choruses performed titled *The Launch of the Independence* at the Theatre (*New-York Evening Post*, 2 July 1814, 2–3); "Ode (altered from R.T. Payne, Jun. Esq.). Adapted to the celebration of the 4th of July, 1814, by the Washington Benevolent Society. (Set to music and sung by Uri K. Hill)." First line: "Hail! hail ye patriot spirits!" (*New-York Commercial Advertiser*, 5 July 1814, 2; *New York Evening Post*, 2 July 1814, 2–3; *Poulson's American Daily Advertiser*, 8 July 1814, 2).

Pennsylvania

Carlisle: The Carlisle mechanics met "at Holmes's Spring, where an elegant dinner was prepared for the occasion. The time was occupied in rural sport, enlivened occasionally by an agreeable band of music."

After dinner toasts were offered accompanied by the following music: Tune — Washington's March — Yankee Doodle — Hail Liberty — Hail Columbia — Union — Yankee Doodle — The Wedding — Buckskins' March — Girl I Left Behind Me — Liberty Tree — Life Let Us Cherish — Rural Felicity ("The Fourth of July," *Kline's Weekly Carlisle Gazette*, 8 July 1814, 3).

Philadelphia: The Washington Guards and the Washington Benevolent Society celebrated at the Theatre, followed by dinner in the afternoon. Toasts were offered accompanied by the following music: Yankee Doodle — Roslin Castle — Tars of Columbia — Hail Columbia — Dead March in Saul — Life Let Us Cherish — Washington's March — See the Conquering Hero Comes — Grand Cossac March — The Rogue's March —'Twas on the 21st of June (*Poulson's American Daily Advertiser*, 7 July 1814, 3).

Rhode Island

Providence: At the Providence Theatre, which "opened for the season on Monday, July 4, 1814," the five-act comedy *Soldier Daughter* was presented and at the "end of the comedy, a new song, called 'Sandy and Jenny'" was sung by Mr. Garner and "a favourite song" sung by Mrs. Wheatley. A second play, *Fortune's Frolick, or, the True Use of Riches!* was presented, after which "a patriotick song by Mr. Garner" was sung (*Rhode-Island American, and General Advertiser*, 1 July 1814, 3).

Vermont

Middlebury: After a procession of Republicans "from the College green to the Court House," food and drink were provided back at the college. After the first toast to "the Fourth of July," an "Ode, composed for the occasion, by N.H. Wright, was sung in excellent style, by Mr. Thomas Hagar. Tune —'Hail Columbia.'" First line: "Sons of Freedom! hail the day" ("Fourth of July," *Columbian Patriot*, 6 July 1814, 3).

Poultney: Washington Benevolent Societies from several towns marched in the parade. "As the procession entered the meeting house, a choir of young ladies dressed in white, melodiously sung the Federal song, 'Hail Columbia happy land. Hail ye heroes heaven born band.'" The exercises opened with singing and "a national ode closed the exercises" ("Poultney Celebration," *Vermont Mirror*, 27 July 1814, 1).

1815

Publications

"American Independence. An Ode. For the Fourth of July 1798 (never before published)."[333] First line: "While savage war with ruthless hand" ("For the Evening Post," *New-York Herald*, 2 December 1815, 2;

"Pauperrimus," *Albany Advertiser,* 9 December 1815, 3; *Federal Republican,* 12 December 1815, 4).

"Columbia's Independence. Tune — 'Reels of Tullochgorum.'" First line: "Come crowd around the festive board" (*The Columbian,* 3 July 1815, 2).

"The following 'Ode,' for the 4th of July, is the production of Mr. Wm. C. Bryant, a young gentleman to whom we have been repeatedly indebted for his elegant and poetic effusions." First line: "This festive day when last we kept" (*New Bedford Mercury,* 21 July 1815, 4; *Connecticut Journal,* 24 July 1815, 2; "Patriotic Ode, Not in Bryant's Volumes," *Ballou's Monthly Magazine,* [February 1882]:162).

"Independence, a Song for the Fourth of July. Tune — Anacreon in Heaven." Signed "Bob Short." First line: "'Tis the birthday of freedom, Columbians rejoice" (*Mechanics' Gazette,* 3 July 1815, 2).

"National Song, for the 4th of July, 1815, the Birth-Day of American independence. '[Written by Mrs. Rowson,[334] and sung by Mr. Rowson, at the celebration in Lexington.]'" First line: "Strike! strike! the chord, raise! raise! the strain." Music by Samuel Arnold (1740–1802). ("Poetry," *Northern Post,* 3 August 1815, 4; *National Song for the 4th of July the Birth Day of American Independence.* Boston: Published and sold by G. Graupner at his music store, [1815]. Copy in Newberry Library); *National Intelligencer,* 14 July 1815, 3).

"New Song Composed for the 4th of July, 1815." First line: "It is not the latitude, climate or spot" (*National Intelligencer,* 25 July 1815).

"'No More the Loud Tones of the Trumpet Resound.' Written for the 4th July, 1815." To the tune "To Anacreon in Heaven." This work was sung in Petersburgh, VA. Text printed in John M'Creery, *A Selection from the Ancient Music of Ireland* (Petersburg, VA: Yancy & Burton, 1824), 204–05, and *Western American,* 30 September 1815, 1.[335]

"Ode for the Fourth of July, 1815."[336] First line: "In the east, full of light, darts the sun his bright ray" (*American Watchman,* 2 August 1815, 1).

"Ode, for the occasion, written by a lady." Note: "The following Ode was written by a young lady of this town for the Republican Celebration at Lexington, on the 4th of July, and was sung in the Meetinghouse by Mr. Rawson. It is an elegant and tasteful composition, and deserves the praise of combining noble sentiments with harmonious poetry." First line: "Hail! to the birth of America's glory" (From the *Boston Chronicle,* as published in "Poetry," *Union,* 25 August 1815, 4).

"An Ode ["Typographical Ode"].[337] Written by Mr. Samuel Woodworth, and sung before the New-York Typographical Society on the 4th of July, 1815. Tune — 'Let Fame Sound the Trumpet.'" First line: "Awake the loud trumpet, 'tis freedom invites" (*National Advocate,* 8 July 1815, 2; "Poetry," *Ulster Plebeian,* 29 August 1815, 4; Woodworth, *Melodies, Duets, Trios, Songs, and Ballads,* 136).

"Odes in celebration of independence, July 4th, 1815." By J. Fellowes.[338] Broadside, [Exeter, NH, 1815].

"Song for the Fourth of July." From the *Virginia Herald.* First line: "The yell of death is hush'd" (*Centinel of Freedom,* 11 July 1815, 4; *True American,* 13 July 1815, 2).

Performances

District of Columbia

At the Washington Theatre, "on Tuesday Evening, July 4, 1815, will be presented a celebrated play, in three acts interspersed with songs, called the *Hero of the North; or, The Deliverer of His Country.*" At the end of the play a "national scene" was displayed and included "the celebrated song of the 'Star-Spangled Banner,'[339] (written by F.S. Key, Esq. during the bombardment of Fort M'Henry) by Mr. Steward," and a "comic song, 'My Deary,' by Mr. Entwisle," followed by the presentation of the "comic opera of *The Poor Soldier*" ("Anniversary of American Independence," *National Intelligencer,* 3 July 1815, 3).

Maine

Hallowell: After exercises held at Social Hall, the participants returned to Palmer's Hotel "and partook of an elegant entertainment provided for the occasion." Toasts "were drank, accompanied by discharge of cannon and appropriate music" ("National Jubilee," *American Advocate and Kennebec Advertiser,* 8 July 1815, 2).

Maryland

Chaptico: "A considerable number of gentlemen" celebrated with dinner and toasts, "interspersed with a variety of patriotic songs" (*National Intelligencer,* 18 August 1815, 3).

Massachusetts

Boston: "The Washington Society celebrated the glorious anniversary of American independence in this town, at the Columbian Coffee House, by a public festival." An address by William Gale was presented and a dinner included toasts accompanied by the following pieces: Tune, a National Ode — U.S. March — President's March — Dirge — America, Commerce and Freedom — Dirge — Adams & Liberty — Jefferson and Liberty — Washington's March — Yankee Doodle — Around the Huge Oak — Rise Columbia — Dirge composed for the occasion. Tune, Pleyel's Hymn (first line: "Sweet remembrance of the brave!") — Go to the Devil and Shake Yourself — Billings Favor — Yid re I — O! Dear What Can the Matter Be — Come Haste to the Wedding (*Independent Chronicle,* 6 July 1815, 2; *Yankee,* 7 July 1815, 3); another newspaper reported this list of tunes sung with toasts that day: Dirge — Jefferson and Liberty — Yankee Doodle — Around the Hugh Oak — Rise Columbia — Dirge composed for the occasion. Tune, Pleyel's Hymn (first line: "Sweet remembrance of the brave") — Go to the Devil and Shake Yourself[340] — Billings' Jargon[341] — Tid-Re-I — O! Dear what Can

Francis Scott Key's original hand written copy of "The Star-Spangled Banner," September 14, 1814. Facsimile printed by the Potomac Edison Company, Hagerstown, Maryland (author's collection).

to increase patriotism and harmony among the American family on the principles of '76." The group later processed to "a bower near the North Meeting House" for dinner. Toasts were drank accompanied by the following pieces of music: Tune, Hail Columbia — Washington's March — Pres't March — Pleyel's Hymn — Dead March in Saul — America, Commerce and freedom — Go to the Devil and Shake Yourself — Yankee Doodle — Rule Britannia — Gen. Eaten's March — Jefferson's March — Roslin Castle — Rise Columbia — Adams & Liberty — Tompkin's March ("Celebration of Independence at Dorchester" and "Dorchester Celebration," *Independent Chronicle*, 29 June and 6 July 1815, 2 and 2, respectively).

Leominster: The Leominster Band provided music for toasts that followed "an agreeable collation" ("Celebration at Leominster," *National Aegis*, 12 July 1815, 2).

Lexington: "At the meeting house, appropriate music was performed by the band and the choir" and an ode was sung by Mr. Rowson. A band played two dirges at the dinner provided by Capt. Parker ("Fourth of July Celebration at Lexington," *The Yankee*, 7 July 1815, 3; *Essex Register*, 8 July 1815, 3). See **Publications** above.

Pittsfield: "The Republican citizens of Berkshire, and many from the neighboring counties" assembled "at an early hour, at the Pittsfield Hotel, and at 12 o'clock a large and respectable procession was formed" and "escorted by Capt. Chappell's company of Berkshire Blues, animated and enlivened by the excellent band of martial music from the Cantonment (many of whom assisted in animating our gallant heroes at the battles of Chippewa and Erie) and the Pittsfield Band" and marched to the Meeting House, where "the exercises were admirably performed....The odes sung by the choir, under the direction of Mr. Morgan, do him

the Matter Be — Go to the Devil and Shake Yourself (*American Watchman*, 15 July 1815, 1).

Braintree: After exercises at Mr. Storrs' Meeting House, a procession, "attended by Musick," marched to a bower for dinner and toasts with accompanying music ("Celebration of Independence, at Braintree," *New-England Palladium & Commercial Advertiser*, 7 July 1815, 2).

Dorchester: "The Fourth of July was celebrated at Dorchester by the Roxbury, Dorchester and Milton Association of Republicans" who marched to "Reverend John Codman's Meeting House" where the exercises were held. "The whole exercises were interspersed with select music by a choir of singers, and occasional performances on the organ, and calculated and his associates great credit for their skillful and happy performances, and gave a zest to the occasion, which will long be remembered." Back at the Pittsfield Hotel, "a sumptuous dinner was provided by Capt. Sabin" and "toasts were drank, accompanied with music from the bands, and a discharge of cannon" ("Great National Jubilee," *Pittsfield Sun*, 6 July 1815, 3).

Worcester: A morning procession of Republicans and militia ended at the South Meeting House. "The publick exercises were opened by vocal musick from an excellent choir of singers led by Mr. John Coolidge,"[342] and ended "by an appropriate anthem." Later at a dinner, "toasts were drunk, received with loud cheers and answered by the discharge of cannon. At proper intervals, patriotick songs were given, and echoed by the company" (*National Aegis*, 12 July 1815, 2).

New Hampshire

Londonderry: This town's celebration included the Washington Benevolent Societies of Londonderry, Hampstead, and Bedford and included a parade and exercises at the meeting house. "The performance of a number of pieces of music, by the Musical Society in Londonderry,[343] and the band from Haverhill, in a style of improved taste, tended much to increase the pleasure which a numerous assemblage manifestly derived from the other exercises of the day"[344] (*Farmers' Cabinet*, 22 July 1815, 1).

Meredith: "The anniversary of American Independence was celebrated at Meredith, by a respectable number of the Friends of Union of that, and the adjacent towns." At the dinner, "toasts were drank accompanied with music and guns": Yankee Doodle — Hail Columbia — Washington's March — Jefferson and Liberty — Jefferson's March — Blue Beard — Separation — Reed's March — Roslin Castle — Rural Felicity — There Is No Luck about the House — Danty Davy — Moll Brook — The Retreat — Miller's March — Major Minor — Knox's March — Gen. Green's March ("Celebration at Meredith," *New-Hampshire Patriot*, 25 July 1815, 3).

New Jersey

Bloomfield: A parade had 13 sections, including one for "martial music," one for "instrumental band" and another for "vocal music." The procession marched around the green, "while the vocal, instrumental, and martial music alternately aroused the attention of the assembly to the harmony of sound." In the church, "the vocal and instrumental band introduced the procession till being seated." Interspersed in the ceremony, "odes were sung by Mr. T. Collins' band, concluding with appropriate tune from the instrumental band." Later at a dinner, toasts were accompanied with: Tune, Hail Columbia — Vive la Constitution — President's March — Washington's March — Yankee Doodle — Soldier's Return — Jersey Blue — Restoration March — Roslin Castle — Rural Felicity — Madison and Liberty — Bellisle March —

Rogues March — Bonaparte's March to Elba — Downfall of Paris — Anacreon in Heaven — Rose Tree (*Centinel of Freedom*, 18 July 1815, 3).

Plainfield:

> The inhabitants of the township of Westfield and the surrounding neighborhood, met at Samuel Manning's tavern, at Plainfield, to celebrate the anniversary of independence. Between 11 and 12 o'clock the procession was formed — in which were about 60 of the venerable actors in the perilous days of '76 — the company was likewise gratified, and the procession adorned by the presence of about 400 ladies — 60 of the young ladies dressed in white, under the charge of Mr. Wm. Lever, music master, by whom they had been duly prepared to unite in singing, the odes selected for the day.

The group marched to the Academy where the exercises were held with 1200 persons attending. "In the intervals of the exercises three appropriate odes were sung — an ode was also sung as the procession moved to the academy, and another on its return" (*Centinel of Freedom*, 11 July 1815, 3; "Fourth of July," *New Jersey Journal*, 18 July 1815, 3).

Springfield: At a meeting for celebration arrangements, Watts Reeve was named "conductor of the music" and the musicians were assigned position no. 2 in the procession from the "house of Luther Bonuel to the church," where at the latter three odes were to be performed (*Centinel of Freedom*, 20 June 1815, 3).

New York

New York: The New York Typographical Society assembled at "the Rev. Mr. Mitchell's Church in Pearl St. at one o'clock to commence the celebrations of the day." After an "introductory prayer," a reading of the Declaration of Independence by "Mr. S. Woodworth" and an oration "by Mr. I. Hoit," was presented as well as "an Ode, written for the occasion, by Mr. [Samuel] Woodworth, and sung by Mr. Pritchard."[345] Later at the Exchange Tavern, the group dined and exchanged toasts "interspersed with a variety of patriotic and other songs, several of which were sung by Mr. Pritchard, in his usual style of excellence" (*Columbian*, 8 July 1815, 2; *Alexandria Herald*, 17 July 1815, 1; *National Advocate*, 8 July 1815, 2). See **Publications** above.

Troy: At the Presbyterian Meeting House,

> the exercises included the 'Ode to Science' (a very appropriate one for the occasion) was sung by an excellent and numerous choir, under the direction of Capt. George Allen, one of the staunch whigs who nobly took his stand in the first ranks in those perilous periods of the revolution which emphatically 'tried men's souls' — then an appropriate Psalm — which was followed by reading the Declaration of Independence.... After the oration, an Ode (prepared for the occasion) was sung, and the exercises were closed by an appropriate prayer, by the Rev. Mr. Wayland, and a hymn.

At the dinner that followed, toasts were drank accompanied by the following music: Hail Columbia — President's March — Long Way Off at Sea[346] — New-York Quick March — Tompkins' March — Yankee Doodle — Hearts of Oak — Washington's March — Jefferson & Liberty — Roslin Castle ("Independence," *Farmers' Register*, 11 July 1815, 2).

North Carolina

Salem: The Moravians presented a trombone concert in the orchard of the Brothers House.[347]

Rhode Island

Providence: On July 4, the "much admired play in 3 acts, called the *Point of Honor, or A School for Soldiers*" was presented at the Providence Theatre followed by an interlude that included the premiere of a song titled the "Proclamation and Ratification of Peace and Plenty," sung by Mr. Bray, followed by the song "Columbia, Land of Liberty" sung by Mr. Jones (*Providence Patriot & Columbian Phenix*, 1 July 1815, 3).

Vermont

Bennington: The Sons of Liberty assembled at the State Arms Tavern and with others, "preceded by an elegant band of music," marched to the Meeting House where the exercises were "accompanied at suitable intervals by solemn tunes, judiciously performed by the band." A dinner was held at the Tavern where the following songs were sung: "'Song for July 4th, 1815.' Tune, 'Bouyne Water.'" First line: "July the fourth effulgent springs."; "'National Independence.' Tune, 'Derry Down.'" First line: "'Tis the fourth of July that enlivens the strain."; "'A New Liberty Tree,' to its old proper tune." First line: "Well met fellow freemen at Liberty's shrine."; "'Song' written during the entertainment. Tune, 'Yankee Doodle.'" First line: "The diamond genius of the land" (*Green-Mountain Farmer*, 10 July 1815, 1).

Fairfield: Among the exercises of the day, "an Ode was sung adapted to the occasion" (*Burlington Gazette*, 28 July 1815, 3).

Hinesburgh: A parade of 1000 persons to the meeting house included Governor Martin Chittenden and other digitaries, as well as a band of music. "Appropriate music from the band" accompanied the toasts at the dinner: Tune, Massachusetts March — Washington's March — Jefferson's March — Hail Columbia — Lord Barnett's March — Paris March — Vermont Quick Step — Bugle Horn Quick Step — March in Forty Thieves — American Favorite[348] — Handel's Clarionet — March in the Battle of Prague — General Muster — Lesson by Morilli — Turkish March — Orn's March — Gen. Greene's March — Serenade ("Hinesburgh Celebration," *Columbian Patriot*, 19 July 1815, 3).

Poultney: "The procession was animated by a band of music, from Mr. Loomis's to an adjacent grove of sugar maple." The exercises included "select appro-priate vocal music." The toasts were accompanied by the following music: Bunkers Hill — Presidents March — The Wounded Hussar — Soldiers Return — Allens March Revillie — Strike your tents and march away — Rule Britannia — Jacksons March — O dear what can the matter be! — On the road to Washington — Hail Columbia Happy Land ("At Poultney," *Rutland Herald*, 26 July 1815, 3).

Rutland: "Federal Republican citizens," members of the Washington Benevolent Societies of this and surrounding towns, a "band of martial musick," and a "choir of singers" marched in a procession from Gould's to the meeting house. The service included singing of a "national ode" ("Communication," *Rutland Herald*, 12 July 1815, 3).

Sudbury: The day was celebrated "by a large and respectable concourse of the citizens of Sudbury and the adjacent towns, with suitable demonstrations of joy." At 11 A.M. a procession to the Meeting House was led by "martial music." The exercises included a reading of the Declaration of Independence "after which an Ode adapted to the occasion was sung." After the oration, "the service was closed by an excellent Ode, written by James O. Walker, Esq." ("Celebration at Sudbury," *Rutland Herald*, 26 July 1815, 3).

West Haven: At the new Meeting House, "services were introduced by sacred vocal music." "Martial Music" followed the reading of the Declaration of Independence. After the oration, "an Ode adapted to the occasion was performed by a select choir." Later "300 ladies and gentlemen partook of an excellent dinner" at a specially erected bower. The following "appropriate music" accompanied the toasts: Hail Columbia — Washington's March — Mountaineers — Jefferson's March — Speed the Plough — Yankee Doodle — Song, Freedom of the Seas — Steuben's March — Gen. Green's March — See the Conquering Hero Comes — Dirge, Logan Water — Bugle Quick Step — Caledonian Ladie.B — Song, Hotham's Victory, or Five to One[349] ("Celebration of Independence at West Haven," *Rutland Herald*, 2 August 1815, 3).

Virginia

Petersburg: A procession "accompanied by a fine band of music marched to the Presbyterian Church." After a reading of the Declaration of Independence, the band played "Hail Columbia" (*Richmond Enquirer*, 8 July 1815, 2).

1816

Publications

"The following Songs were composed by Maj. J[ames]. N. Barker, of Philadelphia, and sung by him at the Spring Garden on the Fourth of July." From the *Democratic Press*. "The Day": first line, "Since a toast you demand, and I can't say you nay";[350] "The Exile's Welcome"[351]: first line, "Hail to the Exile, whose crime was devotion"; "The Way to Be Happy": first line, "Some think it a hardship to work for their bread" (*Essex Register*, 20 July 1816, 4; *Rhode-Island Republican*, 24 July 1816, 4; *Washington Whig*, 29 July 1816, 3; *Shamrock*, 3 August 1816, 360; "Poetry," *Western American*, 17 August 1816, 4).

"An irregular Ode, commemorative of the naval and military glory of America; composed in honor of July 4, 1816, by J. Lathrop, esq." First line: "When, Heaven appeas'd, the ruin'd world" (*National Intelligencer*, 6 July 1816, 2).

"Ode, composed by Samuel Webber, A.B. and sung at the celebration of independence, in Hallowell, (Maine), July 4th, 1816." First line: "All hail to the morn, which again brightly beaming" ("Selected Poetry," *Dedham Gazette*, 19 July 1816, 4).

"Ode, for the celebration by the Washington Society, of the anniversary of American independence, Fourth July 1816. By a member of the Society. Tune — 'Adams and Liberty.'" First line: "Again we assemble, to honour the day" ("Poetry," *Independent Chronicle*, 11 July 1816, 4).

"Ode, for the Fourth of July." First line: "All hail to the day when fair Freedom arose" (*National Intelligencer*, 4 July 1816, 3; "Poetry," *Reporter*, 24 July 1816, 4).

"Odes sung at the celebration in Elizabeth-Town, July 4th, 1816." First lines: "To thee, who reign'st supreme above"; "To the great King of kings we raise" ("Poetry," *New Jersey Journal*, 9 July 1816, 4).

"Odes to be sung at Camptown, July 4th, 1816." Ode 1: first line, "Freemen all hail the glorious day"; Ode 2: first line, "Ye freeborn sons of freedom's soil"; Ode 3: first line, "When the merciless legions of Britain came o'er." Broadside, 1816.

"A Song written on the Fourth of July." First line: "Now Europe's convuls'd with the discord of war" (*The American Patriotic Song-Book, a Collection of Political, Descriptive, and Humourous Songs of National Character, and the Production of American Poets Only* [Philadelphia: John Bioren, 1816]).

The Star-Spangled Banner: Being a Collection of the Best Naval, Martial, Patriotic Songs, &c. (Wilmington, DE: J. Wilson, 1816). Contains among other songs: Hail Columbia — Merseilles Hymn — Meeting of the Waters — New Yankee Doodle — Ode by M.L. Sargent — Ode by J. Story — Ode by R.T. Paine — Star-Spangled Banner — Typographical Ode — Roslin Castle. Advertised for sale in *American Watchman*, 7 December 1816, 4.

Performances

Connecticut

Riverhead: Republicans of Lyme and Waterford, "at a sumptuous repast," enjoyed hearing these works: Hail Columbia — Green's March — Money in Both Pockets — Hölstein's March[352] — Jefferson's March — Rural Felicity — Fresh and Strong — Dead March — Go to the Devil and Shake Yourself — Yankee Doo-

dle — Soldier's Return[353] — Mason's Holiday — White Cockade — Banks of Kentucky — Fancy Cotillion — Lass of Richmond Hill (*The Columbian*, 16 July 1816, 2; "Communicated," *American Mercury*, 23 July 1816, 3).

Maine

Bath: "During the morning a large and respectable number of people from this and the neighboring towns, without distinction of party, assembled at the Hotel, and a little before noon, moved in procession thence to the South Meeting House, escorted by the Bath Light Infantry, accompanied by the Brigade Band of music, while a federal salute was discharged from the Artillery" ("Anniversary of the Declaration of Independence at Bath," *Portland Gazette and Maine Advertiser*, 16 July 1816, 1).

Maryland

Annapolis: Gaetano Carusi and his "superb" Italian band[354] presented an anniversary concert accompanying toasts presented for "Republican citizens" at the Assembly Room: Hail Columbia — Jackson's March — Madison's March — Washington's March — Yankee Doodle — Come Haste to the Wedding — Pleyel's Hymn (*Maryland Republican*, 6 July 1816).

Massachusetts

Boston: At the Old South Meeting House with John Adams in attendance, "several excellent pieces of music were sung by the Old South Choir; the audience joining in the stanza": "With grateful hearts, with joyful tongues" (*Commercial Advertiser*, 9 July 1816, 2).

Pittsfield: At the meeting house, after a reading of the Declaration of Independence, "appropriate music by the choir" was performed ... the exercises were closed by singing an ode" ("Our National Anniversary," *Pittsfield Sun*, 11 July 1816, 3).

Richmond: "A band of music" in the procession and at the dinner held at Mr. Peirson's ... toasts were drank, attended with discharges of a field piece, and music from an excellent Band" ("National Birth Day," *The Pittsfield Sun*, 11 July 1816, 3).

Worcester: Various military companies and citizens marched from Hathaway's Hall to the South Meeting House, "accompanied by a band of musick ... at the close of the publick services, the following 'Ode' written for the occasion, was sung, with taste and spirit, by Lt. Hamilton." First line: "Again fair Freedom's sons appear" ("National Festival," *Massachusetts Spy, or Worcester Gazette*, 10 July 1816, 2).

New Hampshire

Wilton: A town procession "was escorted to the meeting-house by a band of excellent music" (*Farmers' Cabinet*, 13 July 1816, 2; "Celebration of Independence at Wilton," *New-Hampshire Patriot*, 23 July 1816, 3).

Annapolis' "Assembly Rooms," built before the Revolutionary War and now home for City Hall and the mayor's office, was a favorite place for public entertainments and rebuilt by 1868 after a fire. George Washington was one of the favorite visitors. One of the notable Fourth of July events there took place on July 4, 1816, when the Italian Gaetano Carusi and his band played patriotic tunes for a celebration of "Republican citizens" (author's photograph).

New Jersey

Bloomfield: "Instrumental Band" and singers in procession to the church where "the vocal and instrumental music charmed the ear during the intervals." Later, "after dinner the citizens again met on the Green" and drank toasts interspersed with the following music: tune Hail Columbia — Tune, Yankee Doodle — Tune, vive La — Tune, Departed Heroes — Tune, Thunder Storm — Roslin Castle — Tune, Madison's March — Tune, Thurot's Defeat — Tune, Jersey Blue — Tune, Sailors Rights — Tune Freedom and Peace — Tune, Commerce and Freedom — Tune, March in Pizzaro — Tune, Come Haste to the Wedding — Tune, Tid re i — Tune, Soldiers Adieu — Tune, Lovely Fair — Tune, Happy Day ("Celebration of Independence at Bloomfield," *Centinel of Freedom*, 23 July 1816, 3).

Millville: After a noon-time dinner, citizens paraded to the Union school house for the exercises which began with a prayer. "A psalm from Davis's American version, entitled Independence, was then sung, after which a patriotic and eloquent oration was deliverd by Mr. William Curll" ("Fourth of July, at Millville," *Washington Whig*, 15 July 1816, 3).

Scotch Plains: A parade included "martial music" and the music at the Baptist Meeting House was under the direction of Aaron Ball.[355] Three odes were sung. Later the dinner included toasts accompanied by music (*New Jersey Journal*, 16 July 1816, 2).

Springfield: The procession included "military music" and "the choir of vocal and instrumental music conducted by Mr. Watts Reeve." After the exercises, "an Ode composed for the occasion, accompanied by Messrs Durands on the clarionet [sic] and flute, tune 'Liberty' ... Second Ode, tune 'Dauphin' — Third Ode, tune 'Independence.'" At the dinner, "a number of patriotic songs were sung by Mr. Reeve and others, accompanied by Mr. Durand on the clarionet" ("Celebration of the 4th of July at Springfield," *The Centinel of Freedom*, 16 July 1816, 3).

New York

Ballston Spa: The "order of procession" for the parade included the Saratoga Band of music and the exercises at the Baptist Meeting House included the performance of two odes; the Mechanical Association planned for its procession which was "escorted by the Band of Music" (*Independent American*, 26 June 1816, 3).

New York: At the Tammany celebration, the following pieces of music were performed between the toasts at the "dinner provided by brothers Martling and Cozzens: Hail Columbia — Columbia to Glory

Arise — Solemn Dirge — Washington's March — We Have Broke the Vassal Yoke — Madison's March — Governor Tompkins' March[356] — Hail! Great Republic of the World! — America, Commerce and Freedom — Hull's Victory[357] — Jefferson's March — Bolivar's March — Ere Around the Huge Oak — The Son of Alknomak — American Independence — The Spinning Wheel — The Sons of Tammany — Machere Amie ("Tammany Society," *The Shamrock*, 13 July 1816, 333).

Rhode Island

Foster: A military procession marched "with martial music to the Baptist Meeting-House, near the centre of the town" ("Celebration of Independence at Foster," *Providence Gazette*, 27 July 1816, 2).

Providence: "The people of this town and its vicinity" marched "through the principal streets to the Beneficent Congregational Church" where the exercises included prayers and an oration. "We should be neglectful, should we fail to mention that the well-adapted Psalms, which were so admirably sung, added much to the interest and solemnity of the scene" ("National Jubilee," *Rhode-Island American and General Advertiser*, 5 July 1816, 3).

South Carolina

Charleston: "The Indian Land Library Society, together with a large number of ladies and gentlemen of the first respectability, met at the house of Benjamin Person, Esq. York District, S.C. to celebrate the fortieth Anniversary of American Independence." At the dinner, the following pieces of music were played or sung as the toasts were presented: Yankee Doodle — Hail Columbia — Hail Liberty — America, Commerce and Freedom — Jefferson and Liberty — Life Let Us Cherish — Volunteers New Dead March — Traitors Go Home — Yankee Doodle — Tars of Columbia — Jackson's March — Na [sic] Luck about the House — Rights of Man — Baltimore — Rose Tree — Shillinaguira[358] — Sea Flower — Soldiers' Joy — Handels' Clarionet ("Celebration of the 4th of July," *City Gazette and Daily Advertiser*, 31 July 1816, 2).

Vermont

Bridport: a procession that included citizens and officials was led by the "Bridport band of music" and parade ended at the Meeting House where the exercises were as follows:

Ode sung by the choir.
Prayer by the Rev. Increase Graves.
Music from the Band.
Declaration of Independence read by the Rev. A. Stone.
Oration by the Hon. Charles Rich.
Music from the Band.
Prayer by Elder Henry Chamberlain.
Ode by the choir.

The band also provided music at the celebration of toasts that followed ("Union Celebration at Bridport," *National Standard*, 17 July 1816, 3).

Middlebury: "Agreeably to previous arrangement, a procession was formed on the College Green, at 10 o'clock A.M...." Included in the procession were the "Volunteer Music — Middlebury Band" and a "choir of singers and young ladies." At the meeting house were the following "Order of Exercises":

1. Sacred Music.
2. Prayer, by the Rev. Mr. Merrill.
3. Sermon, by the Rev. Mr. [Daniel O.] Morton.
4. Sacred music.
5. Oration, by Mr. Cha. G. Haines.
6. Ode, written by Mr. N. Hill Wright, and sung by the choir. [First line: "Let the loud clarion's notes resound"].
7. Concluding prayer, by the Rev. Mr. Kendrick.

At the dinner held at Mr. Campbell's Hotel, only the men attended and after "toasts were drank, accompanied by a discharge of cannon, and the music of the Band": Music, Valenciennes March — Hail Columbia — Vermont Quick Step — Gen. Greene's March — Serenade — Gen. Orne's March — Handel's Water-Piece — Monroe's March — Rise Columbia — Dorchester's March — Hail Liberty — First Lesson — Solemn Dirge — Washington's March — Battle of Prague — Waltz — Boston Cadets — Pleyel's Hymn — March in the God of Love ("Union Celebration of the 4th of July at Middlebury," *Vermont Mirror*, 26 June and 10 July 1816, 3 and 3, respectively; "Independence!" *National Standard*, 10 July 1816, 3).

1817

Publications

"The following Ode was sung at the celebration of independence by the Washington Society, in Boston on the 4th inst. It is from the pen of Mr. N.H. Wright. Air — 'Wreaths for the Chieftain.'" First line: "Wreaths for the heroes who gain'd independence" (*Essex Register*, 16 July 1817, 4; *National Aegis*, 16 July 1817, 4). The poem was printed under the title "American Independence" and cited as composed by "N. Hillwright" in *American Star*, 30 October 1817, 3.

"Ode, for the anniversary of American Independence, July 4th, 1817. Tune — 'Hail Columbia! happy land!'" By Edward D. Bangs. First line: "Hail the glad, the glorious day!" (*Massachusetts Spy, or Worcester Gazette*, 9 July 1817, 3; "Poetry," *Ulster Plebeian*, 26 July 1817, 4.); broadside (Worcester, MA, 1817). Copy in Brown University.

"Ode for the 4th July, 1817." Note: "The following ode, written for the occasion by a member of the Washington Society, was sung at their late celebration in this town [Boston]. Tune — 'Columbia Land of Liberty.'" First line: "Let grateful notes this day arise" ("Poetry," *Independent Chronicle*, 12 July 1817, 4).

"Ode for the 41st anniversary of American independence." First line: "All hail to the day that gave

Liberty birth!" (*Alexandria Gazette and Daily Advertiser*, 4 July 1817, 2).

"Ode for the Fourth of July, 1817. By Thomas Stuntevant, esq." First line: "Hail! independence blest!" (from the *Albany Argus*, as published in "Poetry," *Independent Chronicle*, 4 July 1817, 2).

"Ode on the 4th July, 1817." First line: "All hail! to the day, when from anarchy free" (*National Advocate*, 4 July 1817, 2).

"Ode, Sung on the 4th of July, 1817." Air: "The Hermit." First line: "'Remember the day,' cries the voice of the brave." Broadside. [Hanover, N.H.], 1817. Copy in Brown University.

"Patriotic Song, Commemorative of Opening the Union Hotel, in the City of Richmond Virga. On the Fourth of July, 1817." By Leroy Anderson, Esqr. Music by Miss S. Sully.[359] (New York; J.A. & W. Geib, [1817–21?] "Air —'Banish Sorrow, Grief's a Folly.'" First line: "Down the stream of time have glided" (*American Beacon and Commercial Diary*, 10–11 July 1817, 2 and 4, respectively; from the Richmond *Compiler*, printed in "Poetry," *Providence Patriot & Columbian Phenix*, 2 August 1817, 1).

"The Zone of Freedom." Sung at Dartmouth College, Hanover, NH. Published in Thomas Cogswell Upham, *The Home in the West: A Poem Delivered at Dartmouth College, July 4, 1817* (Hanover, NH: David Watson, Jun. printer, 1817).

Performances

Connecticut

Hartford: Celebration by "the Harmony Society, no. 2 and a number of citizens." A parade to the Baptist Meeting House included "an excellent band of Musick." Exercises included: "Ode, for the occasion, sung by the choir under the direction of Mr. George Bolles," a second "Ode," and third "Ode, composed by a brother for the occasion. The performance of the choir was admirable, and reflected much credit on its members and their ingenius and assiduous instructor." At the dinner held at the hall: Yankee Doodle — Hail Columbia — Washington's March — Adams and Liberty — Roslin Castle ("Independence," *The Times*, 8 July 1817, 3); another newspaper reported the second ode was "set to Handel's 148th" and that the exercises were closed with the ode together with a performance "by the band of a national air" (*Columbian Register*, 12 July 1817, 2).

New Haven: Members of the Harmony Society celebrated "together with a respectable audience of ladies and gentlemen" at Doolittle's Long Room. After an opening prayer, "an Ode, composed for the occasion, was then sung; the Declaration of Independence was then read, and succeeded by the patriotic ode of 'Adams and Liberty.' ... The choir of music was led by Mr. Allen Brown, and performed in a manner highly creditable to the talents of that gentleman. We take the liberty of inserting the Ode, which was composed by a member. It will not suffer by a compari-

son with any similar production that has appeared in the United States for the last ten years." "'Sapphic Ode.' Tune 'Bunker-Hill.'" First line: "When first Britannia, to enslave our country." ("Celebration of the Fourth of July, by Harmony Society, No. I (at New-Haven)," *Columbian Register*, 12 July 1817, 2).

Massachusetts

Amesbury: "The two parties of this and other adjoining towns united in commemorating" the day. After a procession to the Meeting House, the services "were opened by an Anthem from the choir." After a prayer, "two hymns were sung; & also an Ode, composed for the occasion" ("Independence," *Essex Patriot*, 12 July 1817, 3).

Boston: The Washington Society met at the Commercial Coffee House "where they partook of a splendid and sumptuous entertainment" and heard an address by Henry Orne. Toasts were presented "accompanied by military music, a number of national songs, and an ode, written for the occasion by a member of the Society" ("Washington Society," *Independent Chronicle & Boston Patriot*, 9 July 1817, 1).

Northampton: After the exercises at the church, and dinner "at the public house of Levi Lyman," the men attended a "ladies Tea Party, where as the mind and appetite had enjoined their feast, there was every thing selected and tastefully arranged, to please the eye and the fancy, heightened by the charms of music and the 'merry belles,' to delight the ear and the heart. The whole was succeeded by a ball, in the evening, from the gentlemen, which, by the courtesy of the ladies, was said to be, no unpleasant termination of the amusements of the day" ("Independence," *Boston Intelligencer, and Morning & Evening Advertiser*, 12 July 1817, 2).

Williamstown: "An excellent band of music" joined with "Capt. Harrison's company of infantry" and "marched east to the colleges and thence to the Meeting-House." After the exercises, at "the tables prepared for the ... excellent repast" there was "music from the band" ("National Birth-Day," *Pittsfield Sun*, 16 July 1817, 3).

Worcester: At the South Meeting House, "the exercises were commenced with an appropriate hymn from a select choir of singers ... An Ode, (which is inserted below), composed for the occasion by Edward D. Bangs,[360] Esq. was sung by Capt. S. Hamilton.... Several appropriate songs gave a high zest to the concluding part of the festivity" (*Massachusetts Spy, or Worcester Gazette*, 9 July 1817, 2–3). See **Publications** above.

New Hampshire

Meredith Bridge: Citizens of this and "adjoining towns assembled and proceeded to the Meeting House "where the Declaration of Independence was read in an interesting and solemn manner" and an "impressive discourse was delivered by H.H. Orne, preceded and followed by instrumental and vocal music." Toasts delivered included the following pieces: Handel's Clarionet — Rogue's March — Durham March — Jefferson's March — Funeral Dirge — Yankee Doodle — Katy's Rambles — Soldiers' Joy ("Celebration at Meredith Bridge," *New Hampshire Patriot*, 15 July 1817, 1).

New Jersey

Elizabethtown: The "Order of Procession" was assembled at the City Tavern at 9:30 A.M. and marched to the Presbyterian Church with "Martial Music" in the lead ("Amor Patria," *New Jersey Journal*, 24 June 1817, 3).

Hackensack: "At 11 o'clock, the large concourse of citizens who had assembled, together with the Military, the latter composing seven uniformed Companies, the Civil Officers, Bands of Musick, male and female schools, &c. were arranged in order of procession.... The Procession having moved a short distance, to the sprightly sound of national and patriotic airs from the Band, crossed the Green and halted at the Church." In the church, "the front seats of the Gallery being occupied by the Choristers and Music — and the residue by the Schools and Citizens." The exercises in the Church, were conducted in the following order:

1. Grace, by the Rev. Mr. Romeyn.
2. A patriotic Ode, with vocal and instrumental music.
3. The Declaration of Independence read by Mr. Archibald Campbell.
4. Ode — with music.
5. A well composed and patriotic Oration, delivered by Mr. Thomas M. Gahagan.
6. Ode — with music.
7. The Farewell Address of Washington read by Mr. James Romeyn.
8. Ode to Freedom — with music.
9. Conclusion with Prayer.

Later at the dinner held at the "Long Room of Jone's Hotel, ... toasts were drank, accompanied by music from the Band, and a discharge of Cannon" ("Celebration of the 41st Anniversary of American Independence, at Hackensack, N.J.," *Centinel of Freedom*, 29 July 1817, 2).

Newark: After a procession to the First Presbyterian Church, the exercises included "vocal music lead by Mr. E. Beach" and "the singing of an Ode." A reporter noted that "the music (with scarce any preparation) was pleasing and satisfactory" ("Fourth of July," *Centinel of Freedom*, 8 July 1817, 3).

New York

New York: Several societies of the city, including Tammany Society, Hibernian Provident Society, and Columbian Society, marched through city streets to Spring Street Church where the exercises were begun with a prayer, "succeeded by an 'Ode on Science,' by a choir of professors and amateurs." After parts of Washington's Farewell Address were read, an "Independence Anthem" was "sung with great spirit and taste by the ladies and gentlemen composing the choir." The services ended with "music from the band, and a prayer," as well as a "'Thanksgiving Anthem,' by the choir" ("National Anniversary Arrangements," *Commercial Advertiser*, 3 July 1817, 3; *New-York Columbian*, 3 July 1817, 3; "Fourth of July," *National Advocate*, 7 July 1817, 2); at Vauxhall Gardens, the proprietor provided a

> Musical entertainment of songs and recitations, to be performed by persons of known talents, in the elegant new orchestra, which will be richly illuminated with coloured lamps ... and a full orchestra of music [to] accompany the songs and other entertainments.... that the entertainments may not extend to a longer period than usual, the Concert will begin at an early hour, and is calculated to continue till the commencement of the fire-works. Military music during the afternoon.

The Concert will open with President Monroe's March, composed by Mr. Gilles,[361] sen. Dedicated and presented to the President on his late visit to this city, and accepted by his Excellency as his adopted march — arranged expressly for this occasion, with accompaniments for a completely full Military Band, in the style of the Imperial Music of France — by the author. After which, Mr. Betterton, from the Theatre Royal, Covent Garden, will deliver an appropriate address.

Military Song, "The Host that Fights for Liberty,"[362] written by the late J. Henry Mills, and to be sung by Mrs. Mills
Military Symphony, Full Orchestra
Song, "The Pillar of Glory," Mr. Green
Comic Recitation, "Grecian Fabulist," Mr. Betterton
Song, "Love and Valor," from Champions Freedom — music by an amateur, Mrs. Mills
Full Band, Hail Columbia

Tickets were 4 shillings and could be obtained from Mr. Paff's Music Store, Wall Street and Mr. Riley's Music Store, Chatham Street, and other venues (*New-York Columbian*, 1 July 1817, 3; *New York Evening Post*, 2 July 1817; *Commercial Advertiser*, 3 July 1817, 3; "Celebration of Independence at New York," *Independent Chronicle & Boston Patriot*, 9 July 1817, 2); at the Theatre, ... this evening, July 4, will be presented, the musical entertainment of *The Purse, or The American Tar*. Will Steady, Mr. Hilson. After which will be performed (for the 1st time in America, the Musical Drama of the *Slave, or the Triumph of Generosity*.... In the course of the evening, Mr. Baldwin, will sing the comic song of Arthur O'Bradley's Wedding. Hard Times or the Year 1762, by Mr. Barnes. The evening's entertainments, to conclude with the Farce of the *Tooth Ache, or, The Mistakes of a Morning*. Barogo, Mr. Hilson (*New-York Daily Advertiser*, 4 July 1817, 3).

Plattsburgh: At the U.S. Cantonment, near Platts-burgh, the officers of the 6th U.S. Regiment and "a few friends" dined in the Regimental Mess Room. Toasts were drunk with the following music performed by the Regimental Band: Hail Columbia— Tune, Pleyel's Hymn — The President's March — March in the Battle of Prague — Green's March — Tune, The Merry Diggers — Brown's March — Cossack Dance — Grenadier's March — the Volunteer — Soldier's Joy — March in Pizarro — Washington's March — Portuguese Hymn — Perry's Quick Step — Vision of Columbus — Copenhagen Waltz — She Lives in the Valley Below[363] ("Celebration of the 4th of July, 1817," *Plattsburgh Republican*, 2 August 1817, 2).

Sag Harbor: "The day was ushered in by the discharge of cannon, ringing of bells and music from an excellent martial band" ("Fourth of July," *Suffolk County Recorder*, 5 July 1817, 3).

West Point: Cadets of the Military Academy marched "to military music"[364] to the "arbor erected for the purpose" of sitting down to "an excellent dinner, prepared by the steward, under the management of a committee of cadets." Toasts were drank accompanied by cheers, artillery salutes, and the following pieces of music: Hail Columbia — President's March — Waltz — Pleyel's Hymn — Monroe's March — Yankee Doodle — Overture to Artaxerxes — Cadet's Grand March — Wounded Hussar[365] — Quick Step — Fort Erie March — Soldier's Return — Erin Go Bragh — Downfall of Paris — Portuguese Hymn — Trumpet March — Overture to St. Jean — Capt. Partridge's Quick Step Nightingale. "A ball was given in the evening, and the enjoyment of the dance terminated the celebration" (*Evening Post*, 12 July 1817, 2; *National Advocate*, 12 July 1817, 2; "Anniversary at West Point," *National Intelligencer*, 15 July 1817, 3; *New-York Herald*, 16 July 1817, 1).

Pennsylvania

Bethlehem: Citizens "assembled at 2 o'clock, P.M. on the Island, caused by the junction of that beautiful stream Monocasy with the river Lehigh." After an oration, toasts were presented with the following music: Hail Columbia — Dead March — Monroe's March — Bunker's Hill — Lexington March — Governor Strong's March — Marshal's March[366] — Washington's March — Yankee Doodle — Franklin's March — Battle of Prague, Slow March — Turkish Music — Pennsylvania Song — Pennsylvania March — Alexander's March — Decatur's Victory — President's March — Country Song ("Communicated," *Lancaster Journal*, 9 July 1817, 3).

Rhode Island

Providence: At the Beneficent Congregational Meeting-House, "a number of appropriate hymns had been sung" as part of the exercises attended "by a large number of strangers and citizens" ("National Jubilee," *Providence Gazette*, 5 July 1817, 2).

South Carolina

Charleston: The '76 Association paraded "preceded by a band of music" to St. Philip's Church. The Society of the Cincinnati and the American Revolution Society, "in conjunction, also preceded by a band of music, moved in procession to St. Michael's Church" (*City Gazette and Daily Advertiser*, 7 July 1817, 2).

Vermont

Windsor: Proposed "musical oratorio, to be performed by the amateurs of the vicinity. The pieces selected for the occasion are principally from Handel. The performance is to commence at 10 o'clock in the morning, and is to be resumed in the afternoon" and "we doubt not but that the public generally, and particularly the lovers of 'sacred song,' will find in the exercises, an intellectual treat worthy of the day designated for its enjoyment" ("Oratorio on the Fourth of July," *Vermont Intelligencer and Bellows' Falls Advertiser*, 23 June 1817, 3; *The Repertory*, 24 June 1817, 4).

Virginia

Petersburg: At a dinner celebration at Poplar Spring, the following pieces were performed as the toasts were given: Hail Columbia — Yankee Doodle — Star-Spangled Banner[367] — America, Commerce and Freedom — Hail Columbia — Jefferson's March — Madison's March — Jackson's March — President's March — Perry's Victory — Rural Felicity — Hail Columbia — Yankee Doodle — Jefferson and Lib.[erty] — Hail to the Chief[368] — Russian Dance ("Fourth of July," *American Star*, 7 July 1817, 3).

1818

Publications

"The following Ode, composed by Bellamy Storer,[369] esq. late of this town [Portland, ME], was sung at Cincinnati, at the celebration of the anniversary of independence." First line: "O, hallow the day, when from regions of light" (*Eastern Argus*, 4 August 1818, 3).

"Liberty's Birth Day"[370] (first line: "Hallow'd the birth-day"); "Fourth of July" (first line: "On the files of old time"); "July Fourth" (first line: "When Columbia arose"); "Fourth of July" ("Hail freedom's Aurora") "Weekly Song-Book," 7 books (Philadelphia" H.C. Lewis, 1818, books 5–7. Advertised with songs listed in *Ladys and Gentlemans Weekly Museum and Philadelphia Reporter* (1818): 32.

"Ode, for the anniversary of American Independence, A.D. 1818." First line: "Hail! to the glorious jubilee" ("Poetry," *Newport Mercury*, 4 July 1818, 4).

"Ode for the Fourth of July, 1818. Written for and sung at the late anniversary of the Washington Society, by a member. Tune — 'Rise Columbia.'" First line:

"When Freedom's fire first burst in flame" (*Independent Chronicle & Boston Patriot*, 18 July 1818, 4; "Poetry," *American Advocate and Kennebec Advertiser*, 25 July 1818, 4).

"Ode to Columbian Independence. By G.J. Hunt." First line: "Wake, Columbia! wake thy lyre" (from the *Republican Chronicle* as published in "Political Department," *Centinel of Freedom*, 21 July 1818, 4).

"Ode to Independence." First line: "The sun had risen' o'er the sea" (*Boston Patriot and Daily Chronicle*, 20 July 1818, 2; *Pittsfield Sun*, 5 August 1818, 1).

"Ode to Liberty. For the Anniversary of American Independence. (4th July, 1818)." The following lines are from the pen of a young gentleman of this city...." First line: "O liberty! whose parent sway" (*National Intelligencer*, 4 July 1818, 3).

"Song for the Fourth of July." First line: "Behold, from the brow of the mountain advancing" ("The Parterre," *Village Record, or Chester and Delaware Federalist*, 1 July 1818, 4).

"Sung in Boston, on the Fourth of July, 1794." First line: "Old Time looking over his wonderful page" (*The Idiot, or, Invisible Rambler*, 20 June 1818, 4).

Performances

Connecticut

New Haven: General Society of Mechanics at the meeting house, "an Ode, composed for the occasion, by a full choir of singers" and "the exercises will close by appropriate music by the choir" ("Fourth of July, *Connecticut Journal*, 30 June 1818, 3); the Harmonic Society organized an event held at the Old Church. The day began with a procession that included a band of music. The exercises at the church included:

1st. Music — An Ode by a choir of singers accompanied by a band.
2d. Introductory prayer by the Rev. Mr. Taylor.
3d. The Declaration of Independence, to be read by brother Henry C. Flagg.
4th. Music — an Ode composed for the occasion.
5th. An oration, by brother S.R. Crane.
6th. Prayer by the Rev. Mr. Croswell.
7th. Music — An Ode.
["Fourth of July," *Columbian Register and True Republican*, 30 June and 4 July 1818, 3 and 2, respectively].

District of Columbia

"The militia of this district, under the command of Capt. William Mckee" paraded and later "sat down to a handsome entertainment provided for the occasion." The utmost harmony, unanimity and hilarity prevailed — a few good songs contributed not a little to enliven the day." The following music accompanied a selection of toasts: Hail Columbia — President's March — Jefferson's March — Dead March — Erin Go Bragh — Yankee Doodle — Hail Columbia — Song, Hull, Decatur and Jones (*National Intelligencer*, 12 July 1818, 3).

Georgia

Milledgeville: After the exercises held at the State House, " a large company sat down to an excellent dinner" replete with toasts "interspersed with patriotic songs": Music, Yankee Doodle — President's March — Life Let Us Cherish[371] — Hail Columbia — Logan Water — Roslin Castle — Jefferson's March — Rural Felicity — Yankee Doodle — Hollow Drum — Jefferson and Liberty — White Cockade — Roslin Castle — Hail Columbia — Hail Columbia — Jefferson and Liberty — Hail Columbia — Washington's March — [Come] Haste to the Wedding ("Fourth of July," *Reflector*, 7 July 1818, 3).

Massachusetts

Boston: The Washington Society celebrated at the Exchange Coffee House, where they heard the following music performed: Rise Columbia — America, Commerce and Freedom — President's March — Battle of New-Orleans — Turn ye, turn ye, why will ye die? — Pleyel's Hymn — Adams and Liberty — Hail Columbia — Yankee Doodle — Siege of Tripoli — Washington's March — Rural Felicity ("Independence," *Independent Chronicle*, 8 July 1818, 1).

Pittsfield: At the "old" meeting house, "the music from the choir, interspersed as usual with the performances was happily performed, and gave delight to the auditory, and a rest to the animating occasion." Later in the hall of the hotel, toasts were given accompanied by martial music ("Celebration," *Pittsfield Sun*, 8 July 1818, 3).

Wrentham: In the meeting house, "some fine music [was] performed, led by Mr. Allen" ("National Jubilee," *Columbian Centinel*, 11 July 1818, 2).

New Jersey

Bergen: A large parade was "accompanied by an elegant band of music." At the church the exercises included "sacred music from the choir, and national airs from the band [which] added uncommon interests to the scene" ("Original Communications," *Centinel of Freedom*, 14 July 1818, 2).

Bridgeton: "Hail Columbia" was performed by the Harmonic Society at the Presbyterian Church (*Washington Whig*, 6 July 1818, 3).

Elizabethtown: The procession included "martial music" (*New Jersey Journal*, 30 June 1818, 4).

Newark: Arrangements for the Fourth designated "a full band of music will play several national airs from the 1st banister of the 1st Presbyterian Church." A procession included a "full band under the direction of Dr. B.W. Budd" and "on being seated in the church the band will play a national air." The exercises included three odes. "The evening amusements will be concluded with fireworks, and a national air from the band" ("Arrangements for the Ensuing Fourth of July," *Centinel of Freedom*, 30 June and 7 July, 1818, 3 and 3, respectively; *Commercial Advertiser*, 9 July 1818, 2).

Paterson: At the church, "in the different intervals" of the ceremony, "suitable Odes were sung, and the service of the church ended with prayer (*New York Columbian*, 14 July 1818, 2).

New York

Cooperstown: A parade to the Presbyterian Church included a "martial band." The exercises "were opened by singing the 144th psalm, and a prayer, after which an ode, suited to the occasion, was sung." Dinner was accompanied with "appropriate music" ("Independence," *Otsego Herald*, 6 July 1818, 2).

New York: At J. Scudder's American Museum, a Museum Band performed background music as spectators viewed a "Grand Cosmorama ... a superb view (never before exhibited in this city) of the whole city of Constantinople — a most splendid view of the emperor of China investing Tohao Hoci with the command of his army" and "a great variety of wax figures." Some of the musical pieces performed included:

1. Washington's Grand March
2. Grand Overture of Henry 4th
3. Gen. Jackson's Grand March
4. Robin Adair, with variations, Kent Bugle, arranged by Eley

("Museum. American Independence, July 4, 1776," *New-York Columbian*, 3 July 1818, 2); at a dinner celebration of the Typographical Society, the following pieces of music accompanied the toasts: Song, Hail to the Day Which Arises in Splendor — Ode, The Art of Printing[372] — Song, Honest Bill Bobstay[373] — Song, The Drum — Song, Ne'er Shall the Sons of Columbia be Slaves — Song, Victory No. 5 — Song, My Sweet Girl, My Friend and Pitcher ("The Typographical Society," *New-York Columbian*, 9 July 1818, 2; *National Advocate*, 10 July 1818, 2; *City of Washington Gazette*, 13 July 1818, 2; *American Beacon*, 17 July 1818, 2).

Plattsburgh: Citizens and military officers assembled at Green's Hotel. After dinner toasts were offered with music performed by the band of the 6th Regiment[374]: Hail Columbia — Yankee Doodle — Washington's March — Col. Jessup's March — Corolan's Concert[375] — Speed the Plough — President Monroe's March — N.Y. Volunteer Quick Step[376] — Gen. Swifts' March — Fort Erie Grand March — Com. Perry's March — Pleyel's Hymn — Col. Atkinson's March — Col. Snelling's March — Pioneer's March — Go to the Devil & Shake, &c. — Hail Columbia — Roberdeau's Waltz (*Plattsburgh Republican*, 11 July 1818, 3).

Pennsylvania

Delaware County, near West Chester: The Union Troop of Chester and Delaware met at the Spread Eagle Tavern for military drills parade and later had dinner with the following music in "an adjoining grove": Hail Columbia — Jefferson's March — Yankee Doodle — President's March — Roslin Castle — Dead March in Saul — Wayne's March — Duette, All's Well — Bluebeard's March — Yankee Doodle — Decatur's Victory — Ye Tars of Columbia — Quick Step — Washington's March — Life Let Us Cherish —

Oh! Welcome Once More to the Land of Thy Birth[377] — Song, Paddy Carey[378] — Roslin Castle — 'Round the Flag of Freedom, Rally — Is There a Heart That Never Loved — Free Mason's March — Hail Columbia — Yankee Doodle — Song, Eveleen's Bower (*Village Record, or Chester and Delaware Federalist*, 15 July 1818, 3).

Pittsburgh: The Pittsburgh Harmonic Society took a Barge trip on the Allegheny River, from Davis's Ferry to Foster's Ferry. The trip was "enlivened by the music of amateurs."[379]

South Carolina

Bradford Springs: At Mount Pisgah Church, "an appropriate hymn was sung." Following the oration, "a national air was afterwards sung, and the company retired to an abundant and excellent repast" ("Communicated," *Camden Gazette*, 18 July 1818, 3).

Charleston: "Between 10 and 11 o'clock, the '76 Association met at Jones', and after transacting the necessary business, walked in procession to St. Michael's Church, accompanied by a band of music" (*City Gazette and Daily Advertiser*, 7 July 1818, 2); "Extracts from Toasts Drank at Charleston, S.C." included the following music: Solemn Dirge and Washington's March — Jefferson's March — Adams and Liberty — Madison's March — South-Carolina Hymn[380] — Tune, Oil of Hickory — Huzza for the Constitution[381] — Solemn Dirge ("Fourth of July," *National Messenger*, 20 July 1818, 2).

Vermont

Middlebury:

I take the liberty to remind the public through the medium of your paper that the Handel Society and Middlebury College Singing Society hold their anniversary celebration tomorrow at 2 o'clock P.M. I should extremely regret to see the exertions of individuals, or the particular efforts of these Societies, to gratify the public with an exhibition of Sacred Music neglected. Music of this nature is not merely calculated to delight the ear, it is designed to warm the hearts, enliven the affections, and animate the devotions of Christians. It ever has and will continue to form a most interesting and important part of public worship; and therefore every laudable though feeble attempt to improve the style and elevate the character of Psalmody, ought to receive the countenance and support of all lovers of harmony and particularly of Christians. I hope that every individual who is delighted with the praises of Jehovah, will interest himself in the anticipated formation of a County Society, for the purpose of correcting the taste and improving the style of Church music. P.M.S. July 3, 1818. ["Communicated," *Christian Messenger*, 8 July 1818, 3.]

Virginia

Norfolk: At the Wig Wam Gardens, military companies assembled to enjoyed a dinner "provided by a committee from each of the corps" and heard toasts "accompanied by discharges of cannon and patriotic songs" ("National Festival," *American Beacon and Commercial Diary*," 7 July 1818, 3); at the Theatre, "this evening, Saturday 'July 4th,' 1818, will be performed (for the first time here) the Operatic Drama of *Brother & Sister*. The music by Mr. Besnor of London.... At the end of the drama, the following entertainments:

> Song — "The Star-Spangled Banner." By Mr.
>   Nichols.
> Prime! Bang up! By Mr. Spiller.
> A Hornpipe, by Miss Clarke.
> The National Song, written by Edwin C. Holland,[382] Esq called the "Pillar of Glory,"[383] by Mr. Page.

To which will be added (for the first time here) a new National Drama called the *Battle of New-Orleans, or, The Glorious 8th of January* written by William Spiller, Esq and performed in New-York and Charleston, with unbounded applause.... The whole to conclude with the grand chorus of 'God Save the United States,' by the characters." (*American Beacon and Commercial Diary*, 4 July 1818, 3).

Petersburg: At the Presbyterian Church "had assembled one of the most numerous audiences we have ever seen in Petersburg.... It is supposed the Church contained about a thousand persons; yet many, very many were there, who pressed in vain for admittance. Three discharges of cannon were the signal for the proceedings at the Church which were commenced by the singing the following Anthem of praise to the Deity. Anthem (Hundredth Psalm)." First line: "To God who rolls the orbs of light." After a reading of the Declaration of Independence, "the favorite national tune 'Hail Columbia' was given in elegant style by the Band of Amateurs." The oration by James S. Gilliam followed and "the proceedings at the Church were concluded by singing a new patriotic Ode, composed for the occasion by Mr. John M'Creery."[384] Later "there were several dining parties. The largest one assembled at Bath Springs" and the following tunes were sung or played following the presentation of the toasts: Hail Col. — Yankee Doodle — Marseilles Hymn — Wash. March — Dirge — How Sleep the Brave — Ere around the Huge Oak — Reveille — March — Liberty Walked, &c. — Madison's March — ? — Scots wha ha[385] — Hull's Victory — Though in the Dark Dungien — Liberty Boys — America, Commerce and Freedom — Ca Ira — Rural Felicity — Come Haste to the Wedding ("Fourth of July," *Richmond Enquirer*, 10 July 1818, 2); "Ode Sung at Petersburg on the 4th Day of July, (composed by Mr. John M'Creery, tune 'Anacreon')." First line: "When Brennus led down his fierce conquering hosts." (*Richmond Enquirer*, 10 July 1818, 4). Words printed in John M'Creery, *A Selection from the Ancient Music of Ireland* (Petersburg, VA: Yancy & Burton, 1824), 202.

1819

Publications

"Anniversary Ode. The Following Ode, written for the occasion, by a member,[386] was sung with great spirit and effect at the celebration, by the Washington Society in Boston, of the forty third Anniversary of Independence. Tune — 'Wreaths for the Chieftain.'" First line: "Sons of the heroes who nobly contended" ("Selected Poetry," *American Advocate, and Kennebec Advertiser*, 17 July 1819, 4).

"The following original Ode was sung by the Franklin Association, of this town, on the 5th ult. — written by a member). Tune — 'Scots who have with Wallace bled.'" First line: "Hail Columbia's natal day" ("Poetry," *Salem Gazette*, 13 July 1819, 4).

"The Fourth of July. A Hymn." ["The following lines were found among the papers of the Rev. William Ormond, who died on Greensville circuit, Virginia, October 30th, 1803"]. First line: "Almighty Sovereign deign to hear" ("Poetry," *Methodist Magazine* [July 1819]:2).

"Fourth of July. Tune — 'Anacreon in Heaven.'" First line: "'Tis night at noon-day, lo the angel of storm." "This political and national festival annually elicits some poetical offering to patriotism. The following, sung at Baltimore [by the Seventy-Six Society], is the best we have seen among the productions of the present year" (*New-England Galaxy & Masonic Magazine*, 16 July 1819, 160; *Essex Register*, 24 July 1819, 4; *Vermont Intelligencer and Bellows' Falls Advertiser*, 26 July 1819, 4).

"The Fourth of July, 1819. Tune — Anacreon in Heaven." First line: "Were the wrongs that our fathers endur'd" (*National Messenger* (District of Columbia), 14 July 1819, 2).

"Freedom's Jubilee. Tune — Scots wha ha' wi' Wallace bled." First line: "Freedom's jubilee again." Note: "The following beautiful Ode, composed by Samuel Woodworth, esq. printer, of New-York, was sung with excellent effect by Mr. Pomroy, at the North Meeting House, on Monday, 5th inst." ("Poetry," *Alexandria Herald*, 21 July 1819, 4).

"The Fourth of July. A National Jubilee" Signed "1.P."Intended to be sung in Georgetown, but reached the committee of arrangements too late. (*National Messenger*, 14 July 1819, 3).

"The Fourth of July, 1819" to the tune "Anacreon in Heaven." Verses partially illegible (*National Messenger*, 14 July 1819, 3).

"Hymn for the 4th of July." First line: "O God, once on the stormy deep" (*Concord Observer*, 5 July 1819, 3.)

"Ode for the Fourth of July, 1819." ["From the *New-York Columbian*."] "S of New Jersey." First line: "With wand'ring glance and laurell'd head." Note: "The following ode, though it lacks neither imagery nor sentiment, is nevertheless, throughout so tame in expression and long winded, that it tires one out to get at the author's point or to even catch his meaning: still there is a simplicity and smoothness in the versification, which added to the laudable intentions of the writer, demands some weight in recommending his seasonable and well meant effusion; patriotism and poetry, however, generally keep at as respectful a distance from each other, as poverty and riches"("From the *New-York Columbian*," *City of Washington Gazette*, 25 June 1819, 3).

"Ode, written by Lieut. N.G. Dana,[387] of the U.S. Army, and sung at the raising of the new flag, at Fort Constitution,[388] on the morning of the 4th of July last [1818]. Tune — 'Hail to the Chief.'" First line: "Hail to the day when from slumber of ages" (*Genius of Liberty*, 12 January 1819, 4; *Alexandria Herald*, 9 August 1819, 4).

"Song for the anniversary of American independence, 1819. Tune, 'Ye Mariners of England.'" First line: "All hail, blest independence." Broadside, Newburyport [MA]: E.W. Allen, 1819.

"Song-Fourth of July. By Thomas Paine. Tune — 'Rule Britannia.'" First line: "Hail! Great republic of the world" (*Palladium of Liberty*, 16 July 1819, 4).

Performances

Connecticut

Windsor: The Republican residents celebrated on Monday, July 5, with a procession that assembled at Drake's Hotel, and preceded by a band of martial music moved to the meeting house under the direction of the marshals of the day. The exercises were

1. Singing.
2. Prayer by the Rev. Henry A. Bowland.
3. Declaration of Independence by Joseph H. Russell, Esq.
4. A very appropriate oration by the Rev. Augustus Bolles.
5. Singing.
6. Prayer by the Rev. Coles Carpenter.
7. Singing, conducted by Mr. Chandler, which was performed in a very handsome style.

Later at a dinner were 130 persons gathered under a bower, toasts were drank "accompanied by appropriate music from an excellent band" ("Windsor Celebration," *Times*, 20 July 1819, 3).

District of Columbia

The U.S. Marine Band performed in the Hall of the House of Representatives at the Capitol and later that day at a dinner celebration held in the Congress Hall Hotel (*National Intelligencer*, 7 July 1819, 3); numerous citizens, militia and others marched "with a band of musick" to Christ Church for the exercises held there (*National Messenger*, 14 July 1819, 2). See **Publications** above.

Maine

New Castle: At Capt. Chase's, a "sumptuous entertainment" included "odes, songs, &c. appropriate to the occasion" (*Boston Patriot & Daily Mercantile Advertiser*, 28 July 1819, 2).

Massachusetts

Amesbury: A celebration "by the citizens of Amesbury, Salisbury and vicinity.... At 11 o'clock A. M. a respectable procession was formed at the Academy, with a good band of music, & proceeded to the meeting-house." After the exercises, "the procession again formed and moved to Mr. Valentine Bagley's Inn, where about 60 Gentlemen partook of a public dinner, served in a very handsome style.... Sentiments were given, accompanied with the Band of Music and regular discharge of Cannon" ("Communications," *Newburyport Herald*, 9 July 1819, 3).

Boston: At the dinner celebration of the Washington Society at "Forster's Coffee House in Court Street," the "music of an excellent band, and the singing of various patriotic and humorous songs, gave additional zest to the hilarity of the occasion." The music interspersed between the toasts included: Anniversary Ode — President's March — Dirge — America, Commerce and Freedom — Massachusetts' March — Yankee Doodle — Hull's Victory — Wreaths for the Chieftain — Gov. Wolcott's March — Boston Quick Step — Adams and Liberty — Billings' Jargon[389] — Come, Haste to the Wedding ("National Jubilee," *Boston Patriot & Daily Mercantile Advertiser*, 7 July 1819, 2; *Independent Chronicle* 7 July 1819, 2; *Baltimore Patriot*, 13 July 1819, 2); in the new meeting house "in School Street," the Republicans of Boston met for their exercises that included "a number of appropriate pieces of music [that] were performed by the choir in a scientific and masterly style." Later at Faneuil Hall, the group enjoyed a "Republican collation" and the following music was provided between the toasts at the dinner: Yankee Doodle — Adams and Liberty — Hail Columbia — President's March — Jefferson's March — Massachusetts March — Yankee Doodle — Dirge — Dirge — Victory is Ours — Friendship — Bunker Hill — The Wedding Day[390] ("Independence! *Independent Chronicle & Boston Patriot*, 7 July 1819; "National Jubilee," *The Yankee*, 8 July 1819, 2–3); a group of dignitaries and citizens had ceremonies at the Old South Meeting House. "The musical performances were by the choir of the Old South Society, and the effect of an ode, sung by Mr. Bailey, their leader, was electrical, particularly the following stanza:"

Long and bloody was the fray,
Ere Columbia gain'd the day;
Lowly many a hero lay,
Dying to be free.
But immortal Washington,
Led Columbia's patriots on,
Till the glorious prize was won,
Peace and liberty.

("Festival of Independence," *Columbian Centinel*, 7 July 1819, 2; *Independent Chronicle & Boston Patriot*, 10 July 1819, 1; *Connecticut Gazette*, 14 July 1819, 2).

Charlton: A large crowd met "in the centre" of the town, and "preceded by a band of music" marched to the meeting house where the exercises were begun with "an appropriate hymn." Later at the dinner the toasts "were drank with more than usual hilarity, accompanied by the discharge of cannon and interspersed with appropriate musick by the band" ("National Festival," *Massachusetts Spy, or Worcester Gazette*, 7 July 1819, 3; *National Aegis*, 14 July 1819, 3).

Salem: Citizens and members of the Association of the Essex Reading Room, Franklin Association, Mechanic Association, and Mechanic Light Infantry assembled at the "meeting house of the Rev. Mr. Abbott.... The religious services at the church were fervent and patriotic, and the music such as to give high satisfaction." Dinner at Pickering Hall included toasts accompanied by the following music: Hail Columbia—Carovan March—Washington's March—Massachusetts March—Monroe's March—Gov. Brook's March—Coronation March—Wreaths for the Chieftains—Mozart's Waltz—Queen of Prussia's Waltz ("Celebration in Salem," *Independent Chronicle & Boston Patriot*, 10 July 1819, 1).

Springfield: "At half past 10 o'clock, A.M. a procession, composed of a large number of citizens, of both political parties, was formed on the public ground, and moved with martial music, to the U.S. Chapel, where, after sacred music, and a solemn and fervent prayer, by the Rev. Mr. Dorchester, the Declaration of Independence was read by Edmund Bliss, Esq." After an oration, "the exercises at the Chapel closed with sacred music" ("Independence," *Hampden Federalist & Public Journal*, 7 July 1819, 3).

New Hampshire

Hopkinton: The town celebration on July 5. "At 12 o'clock, a procession was formed at the Court House, which proceeded from thence to the Meeting House, where an appropriate piece of music was performed by a select choir in a superior style." Later at the dinner held at the court house, the following music accompanied the toasts: Song, J(?) of Freedom — Hail Columbia — President's March — Roslin Castle — Rural Felicity — song, Yankee Thunders[391] — song, Adams and Liberty ("Celebration at Hopkinton," *New-Hampshire Patriot & State Gazette*, 13 July 1819, 3).

Lebanon: Citizens from this and adjacent towns paraded with "a band of martial and instrumental music, each playing alternately." Both vocal and instrumental music were performed at the ceremonies ("Celebration at Lebanon," *New-Hampshire Patriot & State Gazette*, 13 July 1819, 3).

Portsmouth: Troops from Fort Constitution paraded, "accompanied by an elegant band." Later at the Portsmouth Hotel, 13 toasts were drunk "enlivened by some excellent songs and musick" (*Portsmouth Oracle*, 10 July 1819, 3).

New Jersey

Belleville: The day began with "firing a national salute," ringing bells, and a flag presentation. A parade to the Dutch Reformed Church included a band attached to Capt. Dow's Company of Washington Volunteers. The services in the church included the performance of three odes ("Anniversary Celebration," *Centinel of Freedom*, 20 July 1819, 2).

Elizabethtown: An ode "composed for the occasion" to the tune "Miriam's Song" was performed, as well as "100th Psalm: tune, Denmark" and an anthem by Handel (*Washington Whig* [Bridgeton], 19 July 1819, 2).

South Orange: A procession from the house of Capt. Isaac Combs to the Academy included instrumental and vocal music. The exercises included the singing of three odes (*Centinel of Freedom*, 13 July 1819, 3).

Springfield: At a meeting for celebration arrangments of the inhabitants of the town, it was decided that the holiday would occur on July 5 and that Watts Reeve would "conduct the singing" (*Centinel of Freedom*, 15 June 1819, 3).

New York

Cherry Valley: "About 3 miles from the village," a number of men and women celebrated on Mount Independence with a "cold collation" after which they sang "the national song of 'Hail Columbia'" ("Anniversary of Our Independence," *Cherry-Valley Gazette*, 6 July 1819, 3; *Otsego Herald*, 12 July 1819, 3).

New York: "At a dinner given by the Company under the command of Captain Thomas Cooper, of the 11th Regiment of New-York State Artillery" held at the "Hotel of J.E. Hyde," the following pieces of music were sung as accompaniment to selected toasts: Song, Yankee Chronology — Song, When Vulcan forged the bolts of Jove — Song, Pillar of Glory — Song, I knew by the smoke that so gracefully curl'd[392] — Song, May we ne'er want a friend nor a bottle to give him (*National Advocate*, 9 July 1819, 2); at the Theatre, on July 5 the "historical drama, in 3 acts, interspersed with songs, of *She Would Be A Soldier, or the Battle of Chippewa*, written by M.M. Noah of this city." In addition the "musical entertainment of the *Tars from Tripoli, or, The Heroes of Columbia*. In the course of the entertainment the following Songs will be sung: 'The Origin of Gunpowder,' by Mr. Howard; 'The Bundle of Truths,' by Mr. Baldwin; the duet of 'All's Well,' (from the Opera of the English Fleet) by Messrs. Howard and Moreland; 'Barney Leave the Girls Alone,' by Mr. Barnes; and the patriotic ode of 'Rise, Columbia, Brave and Free'" (*Mercantile Advertiser*, 5 July 1819, 2; *New-York Daily Advertiser*, 5 July 1819, 2).

Sing Sing: Arrangements for the Fourth included services at the Presbyterian Church where "several pieces of sacred music will be sung by Mr. J.W. Purdy, and the young ladies and gentlemen of this village and

Tarrytown, under his tuition." After a reading of the Declaration of Independence and an oration, "the services in the church will conclude with several national airs by an excellent band of music, under the command of Mr. Little, from Greensburgh[Greensburg]" (*Westchester Herald*, 29 June 1819, 2).

West Point: On Monday, July 5, the cadets and "families resident at the post, and visitors" celebrated with a parade, ceremony at the chapel, and dinner, complete with toasts, cheers, artillery salutes, and music provided by the "military band of the academy." The following pieces accompanied the toasts: Hail Columbia — Dirge — Jefferson's March — Monroe's March — To Liberty's enraptured sight — Tompkins' Waltze — Jackson's March — Fort Erie March — Yankee Doodle — Spanish Patriots — Meeting of the waters[393] — Dead March — Star-Spangled Banner — Beautiful Maid (*National Advocate*, 17 July 1819, 2).

North Carolina

Raleigh: "After a sermon on the Day, the reading of the Declaration of Independence, and a Public Dinner, in the evening a concert of vocal and instrumental music was given by the musical amateurs in the Statehouse grove, which was tastefully ornamented and illuminated for the occasion, and the evening being very calm and pleasant, there was a very large assembly of ladies and gentlemen present, 'and this entertainment,' says the *Register*, 'proved a most agreeable conclusion to the festivities of the day.' No doubt of it — and we should be glad to see the example instated, wherever it can be, on future like occasions" ("Fourth of July," *National Intelligencer*, 14 July 1819, 3).

Pennsylvania

Philadelphia: At the Vauxhall Pavillion Theatre, "Mr. Hewitt" gave a grand concert in honor of the Fourth and "Mr. Lamb" of Boston premiered a new song, "Washington; or, when Freedom on the Hostile Main" (*Aurora General Advertiser*, 3 July 1819, 3).

Westchester: The Washington Society celebrated on July 5 with a parade, "accompanied by the excellent band of music attached to the Society," that ended at the Court House, "where the exercises opened by sacred music." Later at the Washington Inn, the Society had dinner, followed with toasts, "accompanied by songs, the band in the mean time playing patriotic airs": Dead March — Hail Columbia — President's March — Money in Both Pockets — America, Commerce and Freedom — Galley Slave — Life Let Us Cherish — Guardian Angels Protect Me, &c. — Tars of Columbia — Jackson's Victory — Roslin Castle ("Independence," *Village Record, or Chester and Delaware Federalist*, 14 July 1819, 3).

Rhode Island

Providence: On Monday, July 5, at the Second Baptist Meeting-House, there was a "performance of appropriate music by the Harmonic Society" that began the exercises. Another newspaper reported the audience included the governor and that the Harmonick Society was "directed by Mr. Chester Pratt,[394] their president" (*Rhode-Island American and General Advertiser*, 2 and 3 July 1819, 2 and 2, respectively; "National Birth-Day," *Providence Gazette*, 10 July 1819, 2).

1820

Publications

"The Fourth of July (A Volunteer song),"[395] words by William B. Tappan,[396] to the tune "Air, Auld Lang Syne." Sung on the 44th Anniversary of American Independence, at the dinner of the First Company Washington Guards of Philadelphia. In *Songs of Judah and Other Melodies* (p.163), words by William B. Tappan. (Philadelphia: S. Potter & Co., 1820).

"The 4th of July. Grand Chorus: Dedicated to the Choristers of the Churches in the United States." New York: Firth & Hall (Franklin Square), [1820s?].[397] First line: "Exalted day! Exalted day! We greet with music thy return." Copy in Johns Hopkins University.

"Independence." First line: "Freemen! arise, and salute the glad morning." Note: "We cannot better usher in the natal day of our nation, than with the following stanzas from a new Ode to 'Independence,' published in the last *Ladies Literary Cabinet*" (*Columbian Centinel*, 4 July 1820, 2).

"Ode for Independence." First line: "The death-shot of tyrants had sprinkled with gore" (*Newburyport Herald*, 4 July 1820, 3).

"An Ode for the 4th of July. To be sung in the tune of 'Bay of Biscay O.'"[398] First line: "The brazen note of battle is hush'd along the tide." (*Boston Patriot & Daily Mercantile Advertiser*, 4 July 1820, 2; *American Beacon and Norfolk & Portsmouth Daily Advertiser*, 1 August 1820, 2.)

"Ode, Sung at the Celebration of American Independence, 4th July, 1820." First line: "Sound-sound the trumpets, strike the bells." Broadside. [Boston]: True & Weston, printers, [1820]. Copy in New York Historical Society.

"Ode written by a member and sung at the celebration of American Independence, in Boston, by the Washington Society, July 4, 1820. Tune — Scots wha hae wi' Wallace bled." First line: "Hark! Again her clarion rings" (*Hillsboro' Telegraph*, 15 July 1820, 4; *City of Washington Gazette*, 18 July 1820, 3; *American Beacon and Norfolk & Portsmouth Daily Advertiser*, 20 July 1820, 2).

Performances

Arkansas

Arkansas Post: After a reading of the Declaration of Independence and "an excellent dinner prepared by Col. James Scull," toasts "were drank, during which many patriotic songs were sung, which added much to the conviviality of the occasion" ("Anniversary of American Independence," *Arkansas Gazette*, 8 July 1820, 3).

Connecticut

Hartford: At a dinner at the City Hotel: American Eagle — Go to the Devil and Shake Yourself— Governor's March — Grand March — Hail Columbia — Jefferson and Liberty — March to Glory — Nothing True but Heaven[399]— President's March — See the Conquering Hero Come[400]— Washington's March — Yankee Doodle ("Fourth of July," *The Times and Weekly Advertiser*, 11 July 1820, 3).

District of Columbia

On the banks of the Eastern Branch, "many officers of the Marine Corps and Navy" and citizens had a dinner celebration afterwhich the following music accompanied the toasts: tune, President's March — tune, Yankee Doodle — tune, Rights of Man — tune, Rural Felicity — tune, Jefferson's March — tune, America, Commerce and Freedom — tune, The Battle — tune, Jefferson and Liberty — tune, Dead March — tune, Jackson's March — tune, Academic Bowers — tune, Star-Spangled Banner — tune, Lassie with the lint white locks ("Eastern Branch Dinner," *City of Washington Gazette*, 7 July 1820, 3).

Georgetown: The Georgetown Harmonic Society "assembled at daybreak and saluted with several national airs the U.S. Flag raised in the town, and then adjourned to the appointed place of rendezvous." The Declaration was read by William Thompson, Jr., President of the Society and oration by Henry Ould. Music was provided for the toasts: Song, Freedom's Jubilee[401]— Washington's March — Hail Columbia — Yankee Doodle — America, Commerce and Freedom — Unblemished We'll Remain — Equal Liberty — Come Haste to the Wedding — Overture to Lodioiska — Major Stull's March and Rondo — Blue Eyed Mary[402]— Life Let Us Cherish — Liberty Tree — Societies Chorus — Overture Henry the 4th — Funeral dirge — Why What's That to You — Down Below — Union March — Hail to the Chief— Societies March and Quick Step (*Metropolitan*, 6 July 1820, 2).

Louisiana

Alexandria: Following a ceremony held at the Court House, "an elegant dinner at the Alexandria Coffee House" included toasts "interspersed with appropriate songs and cheers" ("4th of July," *Louisiana Herald*, 8 July 1820, 3).

Maine

Belfast: At 11 A.M. a procession marched to the Meeting House for the exercises. "The musical performances were excellent, an Ode was written by Dr. Hermon Abbott, and sung on the occasion" ("The Fourth of July, 1820," *Hancock Gazette*, 6 July 1820, 2).

Portland:

Union Hall. Celebration of Independence. The publc are respectfully informed that there will be a concert of vocal & instrumental music, this evening, 4th of July. When will be performed (gratis) a celebrated play, in three acts, (between the parts of the concert) called the Point of Honor, or School for Soldiers. After which will be exhibited, in honor of the day, two grand transparent columns, on the right and left of the Hall — The one supporting the emblems of agriculture, arts and sciences — The other, commerce, honor and glory. To conclude with Shakespeare's admired farce, in three acts, (gratis) called Catharine & Petruchio, or Taming the Shrew.... Tickets to the concert-box. 75, pit. 50 cents to be had of Mrs. Cutter, at the Hall.... [*Eastern Argus*, 4 July 1820, 3].

Maryland

Baltimore: At a "patriotic festivity" at Howard's Park, "the performances were commenced with national music from the Bands," including two "national airs" and were conducted in the presence of Charles Carroll, signer of the Declaration of Independence. Some 20,000 persons were present ("Baltimore Celebration," *National Messenger*, 3 July 1820, 3; "Independence," *American Beacon and Norfolk & Portsmouth Daily Advertiser*, 8 July 1820, 2; "Fourth of July at Baltimore," *National Intelligencer*, 8 July 1820, 3; *Observer*, 18 July 1820, 3; *Pittsfield Sun*, 19 July 1820, 2); at Mr. Coleman's Pavilion Garden, on the evening of July 4, "a divertissement, in three parts, called *Laugh When You Can*, consisting of comic and serious songs, tales, &c" was presented."

Part I.
A prelude from Raising the Wind,403 called How to Live Cheap.
    Diddler, Mr. Willis; Sam, Mr. Crampton; Fainwood, Mrs. Anness; Miss Plainway, Mrs. Anness; Miss Durable, Mrs. Crampton; Scots Song, "Tuilochgorum," Mr. Crampton; Comic song, "Giles Scroggins Ghost,"[404] Mr. Willis.
Part II.
    Recitation, "Somebody against Nobody," Mr. Anness; Comic song, "Barney leave the girls alone," by Mr. Willis; Irish Song, "Billy O Rourk," by Mr. Crampton; Comic Song, "London Fashions," Mr. Annes.
Part III
    Comic Tale, "Poach'd Eggs, or the Winter's Mistake," Mr. Willis; Irish Song, "Larry O'Gaff," Mr. Crampton; The Origin of Gunpowder, Mr. Willis.

Howard's Park (now known as Mount Vernon Place), the site for the cornerstone laying ceremony for the Washington Monument (shown) on July 4, 1815. The park was named after Col. John Eager Howard, a Revolutionary War hero from Baltimore and was one of the popular locations for musical perform- ances. One of the earliest was a Patriotic Festivity on July 4, 1820, when 20,000 spectators, including Charles Carroll, signer of the Declaration of Independence, heard a number of bands perform patri- otic music (author's photograph).

To conclude with a petite piece from "Review," called The Rival Servants.

Deputy Bull, Mr. Annes; John Lump, Mr. Willis; Looney M'Twolter (with the song of "Patrick's day in the morning"), Mr. Crampton; Grace Gaylove, Mrs. Crampton; Lucy, Mrs. Annes.

Tickets 50 cents each, to be had at the bar. The doors will be open at 7 o'clock, and the curtain rise at 8 [*Baltimore Patriot*, 1 July 1820, 3].

Massachusetts

Boston: The governor, citizens, dignitaries and oth- ers celebrated at the Old South Meeting House. "The sublime ode [by John Pierpont], written for the day, and given in the last *Centinel*, and an Anthem, were sung by a select choir, in a style of unusual excel- lence." First line of the ode: "Day of Glory! welcome day!"[405] Later, at Faneuil Hall, "a band from Fort In- dependence" played "martial and other airs." After the ceremonies and afternoon celebrations, an eve-

ning concert was presented at the amphitheatre at Washington Gardens ("Celebration of Indepedence [sic]," *Boston Daily Advertiser*, 4 July 1820, 2; *Columbian Centinel*, 4 and 8 July, 2 and 2, respec- tively). See also, **Publications** above; the Washing- ton Society celebrated "by a public dinner at the Marl- borough Hotel," and was presided by Elbridge Gerry. "After the removal of the cloth, the following senti- ments were announced, which were accompanied by the music of an excellent band, and by several patri- otic and humerous songs": Ode, Freedom's Jubilee — President's March — Washington's March — Waltz — Gov. Brooks' March — Fusiliers' March — Hull's Victory — Pleyel's Hymn — Adams and Liberty — America, Commerce and Freedom — O Dear What Can the Matter Be[406] — Billing's Jargon ("From the *Boston Patriot*," *Baltimore Patriot*, 12 July 1820, 2).

Bradford: A "band and choir of singers" provided an "excellent performance" at the Meeting House whose audience included "a large procession of citizens, without distinction of party" ("Celebration of Independence at Bradford," *New-England Palladium*, 21 July 1820, 2).

Brimfield: A procession assembled and marched to the Meeting House, where "the services commenced with a national song selected by Mr. Benjamin Salisbury, Jr. which together with the rest of the music prepared by him for the occasion was performed in his usual style of good singing" ("Fourth of July," *Hampden Federalist & Public Journal*, 12 July 1820, 111).

Leicester: At the meeting house, military companies and "citizens of that and the neighbouring towns" assembled. After the "eloquent and impressive prayer by the Rev. John Nelson, and the 100th Psalm was sung with powerful effect in the favourite tune of Old Hundred." Later at a "spacious bower ... nearly two hundred" enjoyed dinner and heard the toasts "accompanied by the discharge of cannon, and interspersed with appropriate musick by the band" ("National Festival," *Massachusetts Spy, or Worcester Gazette*, 12 July 1820, 3).

Milford: Exercises at "the Rev. Mr. Long's meeting house" included an oration. "Several select pieces of musick were performed under the direction of Col. Newhall,[407] in a style of correctness and excellence that reflected much credit upon him and the able choir of the Rev. Mr. Long's society." A dinner provided by Capt. D. Hemenway was accompanied by "musick and some national songs" ("Celebration at Milford," *Massachusetts Spy*, 12 July 1820, 3).

Scituate: The Hanover Artillery Band "and a band of music from Weymouth" marched with other military units and citizens to the Meeting House. In the exercises, "the Weymouth band, and an excellent choir of singers, alternately performed to the satisfaction of a crowded assembly." Afterwards there was an "elegant entertainment prepared under a pavilion, decorated with flags and evergreens, where about two hundred gentlemen" ate, drank wine, and listened to toasts "followed with cheers, guns, and airs from the band": German Hymn — President's March — Gov. Breck's March[408] — Breed's March — Massachusetts March — Freemason's March — Washington's March — Handel's Clarinet — Pleyel's Hymn — Dirge — Ipswich Muster — Soldier's Joy ("Scituate Celebration," *Boston Patriot & Daily Mercantile Advertiser*, 14 July 1820, 2; *Independent Chronicle*, 15 July 1820, 1; "Celebration of Independence," *New-England Palladium*, 18 July 1820, 1).

Stockbridge: "An excellent band of martial music" participated in the procession. At the meeting house, "the performance of the choir of singers, we believe, gave universal satisfaction — we hardly recollect to have heard a more delightful performance than the singing of Payne's beautiful Ode — the deep toned chorus of which was absolutely electrifying" ("Celebration of Independence," *Berkshire Star*, 13 July 1820, 3).

Waltham: "The performances in the meeting-house were commenced by singing the Chorus Anthem ... after which a psalm was sung to the tune of Old Hundred ... an Ode was then sung." At the dinner held at Russell Smith's Hotel, the following tunes were performed: Hail Columbia — Green's March — Monroe's March — Gov. Brook's March — Dead March in Saul — Ye Sons of Columbia — Washington's March — Rise Columbia — Forget and Forgive — Adams and liberty — Speed the Plough — Yankee Doodle — Gen. Brown's March — Hull's Victory — Russian Dance (Celebration of Independence in Waltham," *Boston Patriot and Daily Mercantile Advertiser*, 8 July 1820, 2; *Independent Chronicle and Boston Patriot*, 8 July 1820, 2).

Worcester: At the South Meeting House, "an appropriate Ode, selected for the occasion, was then sung by Capt. [John] Coolidge,[409] assisted by Maj. Samuel Graves and Capt. Marshall Flagg" (*National Aegis*, 12 July 1820, 2; *Pittsfield Sun*, 19 July 1820, 2).

New Hampshire

Mason: "At 10 o'clock a procession was formed at Warren's Tavern, and proceeded to the Meeting-House, escorted by four Uniform Companies, and one Company of Infantry, together with an excellent band of Music." Later "nearly seven hundred persons partook of a sumptuous entertainment" and heard the toasts "with the discharges of Artillery and appropriate Music" ("National Festival," *Hillsboro' Telegraph*, 15 July 1820, 3).

Warren: At noon a procession marched, "preceded by instrumental music," to the Meeting House where, after the seating of a "large and respectable audience which attended, a select piece of music was performed by the singers." Later, after a prayer there was a "performance of a select piece of sacred music" ("Celebration of National Independence at Warren," *New Hampshire Patriot & State Gazette*, 25 July 1820, 3).

New Jersey

Bergen: Various pieces of music and an ode were performed at the ceremony held at the church. At the dinner at Capt. A. Coulter's, toasts were drank, "accompanied by discharges of cannon and appropriate airs from the band" (*Centinel of Freedom*, 18 July 1820, 1).

Bridgeton: The exercises were scheduled to include a parade to the Presbyterian Church with the following program:

1. Invocation
2. Music, 133d Psalm
3. Prayer
4. Music-Columbia, an ode
5. Declaration of Independence
6. Music-Hail columbia
7. Oration
8. Music-Ode on Science
9. Benediction

Another report notes the performances by the Bridgeton Harmonic Society, "and the company had the satisfaction of hearing our appropriate national odes sung in a style suited to the occasion.... In the afternoon and evening the young ladies and gentlemen amused themselves with a delightful sailing party, accompanied with music, and closed the festivities of the day at an early hour" ("Fourth of July, 1820" and "Anniversary Celebration," *Washington Whig*, 3 and 10 July 1820, 3 and 2, respectively).

Fairfield: The residents assembled in the Presbyterian Meeting House at 3 P.M. "when the following order of exercises took place: introductory observations by the Rev. Mr. Osborn; singing from Dr. Watts; Prayer by Mr. Osborn; singing from Watts; reading the Constitution of the United States, by Dr. D.C. Pierson; an address suited to the occasion, by Dr. James B. Parvin; singing a national ode; singing Dismission. Mr. Moses Burt being appointed to lead the music, performed that service, as did the other persons designated to special duty, to entire satisfaction" ("Fourth of July in Fairfield," *Washington Whig*, 17 July 1820, 3).

Newark: "The day was ushered in as usual by the ringing of bells, a national salute, and some national airs by a Band from the steeple of the 1st Presbyterian Church." At that church, the exercises included "an Ode being then sung" and after the Declaration of Independence was read, "another Ode, and a national air from the band" were performed. After the presentation of the oration, "another Ode was then sung to a beautiful tune, composed by Mr. Moses Lyon of this town" ("Newark Centinel," *The Centinel of Freedom*, 11 July 1820, 3).

Paterson Landing: A procession from the Academy to the Reformed Dutch Church included various military units, clergy, citizens, and "Mr. Bogart, leader of the vocal music" followed by a "band of music." The ceremony at the church included three odes and the "Ode on Science" ("Fourth of July Celebrations," *Centinel of Freedom*, 18 July 1820, 1).

Roadstown: "At day-break one gun was fired and the reveille beaten." The exercises at the Baptist Church included "sacred music" and a dinner at a bower included toasts "interspersed with patriotic songs" ("Celebration of the Anniversary of American Independence, at Roadstown," *Washington Whig*, 10 July 1820, 2).

New York

Matteawan: After a procession to the church, the exercises included "an appropriate Ode," "appropriate music, by the band," a rendering of the "Ode on Science," and "Song of Liberty." Following a dinner, toasts were "interspersed with songs and music": Music, Hail Columbia — Music, German Hymn — Music, Yankee Doodle — Music, President's March — Music, Tompkins' March — Music, Clinton's March — Music, The Star-Spangled Banner — Music, Speed the Plough — Music, Spindle and Loom — Music, America, Commerce, and Freedom — Music, Washington's March — Music, Jefferson's March — Music Robin Adair. It was reported in a local newspaper that

In returning from church, the procession in the same order as before, proceeded to Matteawan, where an elegant Bower had been erected, covered with evergreens, ornamented on the top with the national standard, and three white flags, on which was handsomely painted, Agriculture, Manufactures, Commerce. The Bower (under which the table was spread) was festooned with a variety of fabrics from the Matteawan Factory — the columns were entwined with flags — from the centre were suspended two elegant scrolls, containing the Declaration of Independence, and the facsimiles of the hand writing of its authors [*American*, 14 July 1820, 3].

Mount Pleasant: The exercises at the church were "conducted in the following order":

1. Prayer by the Rev. G. Bourne.
2. A Hymn.
3. The reading of the Declaration of Independence by Mr. S. Marshall.
4. Ode on Science.
5. Oration by A. Ward, Esq.
6. An address by the Rev. G. Bourne.
7. Prayer by the Rev. J. Brouner.
8. An Anthem.

["Fourth of July," *Westchester Herald*, 27 June 1820, 3].

New York: "The General Committee of Arrangements for the celebration of the 44th Anniversary of American Independence, partook of their annual supper, at St. John's Hall, on the evening of the 12th instant.... Toasts and sentiments were drunk, accompanied by a well selected band of music, and the most unrestrained harmony, conviviality, and patriotic effusion": Liberty Tree — Hail Columbia — Washington's March — Solemn Dirge — Hail Liberty — President's March — Patriotic Air — Dulce Domum — Anacreon in Heaven[411] — Pleyel's Hymn — Patriotic Air — Washington's March — Yankee Doodle — Paddy Carey — Copenhagen Waltz (*The American*, 14 July 1820, 2); at the "Tammany Society or Columbian Order" celebration, the following pieces of music accompanied the toasts: Hail Columbia — Patriotic Song — Patriotic Song — Patriotic Song — War Song — Star-Spangled Banner — President's March — Tompkin's March — Yankee Doodle — Washington's March — Et-hah Song — Song — Music — Song (*National Advocate*, 7 July 1820, 2); at Vauxhall Garden, proprietor Joseph Delacroix presented a "concert of vocal and instrumental music. The Grand Military Band of the 9th Regiment, in full uniform, under the direction of Mr. Meline,[412] will entertain the company from 5 in the afternoon. Mr. Lamb and Mr. Banks will, with proper accompaniments sing the following songs:"

Act I.
Military Overture, Full Band
Song, "Scots wha ha Wallace bled," Mr. Lamb
Col. Muier's quick step, Meline
Comic Song, "Captain Mulligan," Banks

Mr. Laus from Europe, will perform a Fantasie on the pedal harp

The Star-Spangled Banner, Lamb

Song, "The Green Little Man," Banks

Variations on the harp, Laus

Song, "The Hunters' Horn,"[413] Lamb

Finale, First Act, Grand March, full band

Act II.

Military Overture, Mr. Meline

Tyrolese Song of Liberty, with accompaniment on the harp, by Mr. Laus, Lamb

Song, "And has she then fail'd in her truth,"[414] Lamb

Comic song, "High Down Derry," Banks

Military Rondo, Meline

Freedom's Jubilee, Lamb

Finale, Orchestra.

"In addition, Mr. Laus, in the afternoon and evening will perform on the pedal harp. The Concert will be in two acts — the first will be in the afternoon — the second after lighting the Gardens, and the only interval before the fire works" (*New-York Columbian*, 30 June 1820, 3; *New-York Evening Post*, 30 June 1820, 2; *Mercantile Advertiser*, 1 July 1820, 3); at the American Museum,

Mr. Scudder has engaged Mr. Plimpton,[415] with his celebrated apollino (a rare specimen of self taught American genius) to perform on the 4th. He will be accompanied by Mrs. and Miss Plimpton. The performance on the apollino, in the evening, will be as follows, viz.

Part I.

1. Grand Sonata, Perry's Victory on Lake Erie, composed by Mr. Plimpton, in which the apollino will be accompanied with the violin.
2. Song, The Tars of Columbia, by Mr. Plimpton, composed by Mr. Plimpton.
3. Solo on the bagpipes of the apollino.
4. Ode for the Fourth of July, Hail, America! Hail! by Mr. and Mrs. Plimpton, composed by Mr. Plimpton.
5. Washington's March, full band of the apollino.
6. The Bonny Bold Soldier, by Mrs. Plimpton.

Part II.

1. Song, The Drum, by Mr. Plimpton, accompanied with the drum, fife, trumpet, &c. of the apollino.
2. Hail Columbia and Yankee Doodle, full band apollino.
3. Song, Robin Adair, by Mr. Plimpton, accompanied with octavo flute of the apollino.
4. Song and Chorus, Hail, Liberty,[416] by Mr. and Mrs. Plimpton, accompanied with the apollino.
5. Catharine M'Cree, full band of the apollino and snare drum.
6. Comic song, by Mr. Plimpton.

(*The American*, 29 Jun 1820, 3; "Celebration of the 44th Year of American Independence," *National Advocate*, 1 July 1820, 3; *New-York Evening Post*, 1 July

1820, 3); at Chatham Garden, a "grand instrumental concert" took place at 2 P.M. that included "popular and patriotic airs." At 9 P.M. "a grand vocal concert" was featured with Mr. Lamb and Mr. Banks, vocalists, accompanied by Mr. Wilson "at the piano forte." The program consisted of

Part 1.

Grand Overture, Piano Forte — Mr. Wilson.

Son, Heigh Down Derry — Mr. Banks.

Song of Liberty — Mr. Lamb.

Waltz, Piano Forte — Mr. Wilson.

Duet, the Minute Gun at Sea — Lamb & Banks.

Song, The Origin of Gunpowder — Mr. Lamb.

Part 2.

Overture, Piano Forte — Mr. Wilson.

Song, Captain Mulligan — Mr. Banks.

Song, the Star-Spangled Banner — Mr. Lamb.

Song, Paddy Cary's Fortune — Mr. Banks.

Song, Freedom's Jubilee — Mr. Lamb.

Duet, All is Well — Lamb & Banks.

("Chatham Garden," *National Advocate*, 4 July 1820, 3); at the Theatre on Anthony Street," "the play of the *Glory of Columbia — Her Yeomanry or, What We Have Done We Can Do* was presented. Included were the songs "A Yankee Boy is Tall and Thin," "In Ireland so Frisky," and "I was the Boy for Bewitching Them," followed by an interlude titled *The Launch; or, The Pride of America — Her Navy*, that included "songs of 'The Army and Navy for Ever' and 'the Yankee Girls'" (*National Advocate*, 4 July 1820, 3).

Poughkeepsie: "At 12 o'clock the procession was formed at Mr. Leonard B. Van Kleeck's Inn, preceded by the Band of Music and the National and State Colors." Citizens and military companies marched to the Dutch Reformed Church for the exercises followed by dinner back at the Inn. The toasts "were drank, each of which was saluted by the discharge of cannon, and appropriate airs from the Band of Music" ("Republican Celebration," *National Advocate*, 27 July 1820, 2; *New-York Evening Post*, 3 July 1820, 3).

Salina: Opening of the Great Western Canal, amidst "the discharge of cannon, with strains of music, and the cheering shouts of thousands," boats entered the basin while "8 to 10 thousand people cheered" and "music was heard from the different boats" to the delight of Governor De Witt Clinton who "had been expressly invited to visit the Great Western Canal on this occasion, and had accordingly proceeded from Utica to Salina in the new and beautiful bark called the *Oneida Chief* " (*Observer*, 18 July 1820, 3).

Pennsylvania

Liverpool: "The citizens of Liverpool, Perry County, and its vicinity convened under a beautiful shade, on the bank of the Susquehanna River, adjacent to the town," and heard the following pieces as the toasts were presented: Tune, Hail Columbia — Washington's March — Logan Water — Hail to the Chief — Liberty Tree — President's March — Roslin Castle — Yankee Doodle — Brown's March — Speed the Plough — Pennsylvania March[417] — Washer Woman — Rogue's March — The Girl I Left Behind Me — Perry's Victory ("Liverpool, 4th July, 1820," *The Carlisle Republican*, 18 July 1820, 146).

Philadelphia: "About 800 [school children] with their teachers and directors" gathered at the Ebenezer Methodist Meeting House in Southwark "where a hymn prepared by Peter M'Gowing, one of the teachers, was sung in a complete and interesting manner." To close the exercises, an anthem, "composed by the Rev. Dr. Ely, was sung" ("44th Anniversary of American Independence," *National Advocate*, 10 July 1820, 2).

Rhode Island

Providence: Residents of the town marched to the First Baptist Meeting-House where the exercises began with "an appropriate ode and anthem ... in fine taste, by the choir" ("Independence," *Rhode-Island American and General Advertiser*, 7 July 1820, 2).

South Carolina

Charleston: "The Charleston Riflemen celebrated their 14th Anniversary, and the 45th of American Independence on the 4th July, on which occasion the following toasts were drank, accompanied by appropriate music from the elegant band attached to the Corps": Hail Columbia — Pleyel's Hymn — Marseilles Hymn — Adams and Liberty — Solemn Dirge — Yankee Doodle — The Star-Spangled Banner — Monroe's March — South Carolina March — Geddes's March — Hearts of Oak — Tyrolese Song of Liberty — True Courage — Pillar of Glory — Washington's March — Plough Boy — Erin Go Bragh — The Lucky Escape — The Centinel — The Light-House — Knight Errant ("Celebration of the 4th July," *City Gazette and Daily Advertiser*, 13 July 1820, 2).

Virginia

Alexandria: A procession of two companies of infantry marched through the streets of Alexandria "enlivened by appropriate and delightful music." Another newspaper reported that "an elegant band of music, led by Sig. Massi" accompanied "the most martial legion that has graced our streets for several years." Later the officers and "gentlemen composing the band, and a number of citizens, retired to the locust grove on the south side of Hunting Creek" to enjoy dinner and have toasts "interspersed with songs and appropriate music": Yankee Doodle — Hail Columbia — Washington's March — President's March — Gen. Lynn's March — Paddy Carey — Tars of Columbia — Col Hipkins' March — Marseilles Hymn — Congress March — Quick Step — Monroe's March — The Meeting of the Waters[418] — Pleyel's German Hymn — Roslin Castle — Col. Minor's March[419] — Bolivar's March — Waltz — Gen Lynn's Quick Step — Massachusetts March — Columbian March — Robin Adair — Jackson's March — Col. Minor's Quick Step — Jefferson's March — Yankee Doodle — Spanish Muleteers'

March — Cadet's March — Perry's Victory — Trumpet March[420] (*Alexandria Gazette*, 10 July 1820, 2; "Fourth of July Celebrations at Alexandria, DC," *City of Washington Gazette*, 10 July 1820, 2).

Norfolk: The exercises at the Presbyterian Church attended by 1,000 persons, included music by a band "attached to the Republican Blues." Later toasts were offered with the following music: Music, Yankee Doodle — Music, Roslin Castle — Washington's March — Marseilles Hymn — Music, Vive la Constitution. — President's March — Song, Missouri Question (new music)[421] — The Star-Spangled Banner — Song, The Battle of New-Orleans — Song, I knew by the smoke, etc. — Song, Hail Columbia ("Freedom's Jubilee" and "Toasts Drank by the Citizens," *American Beacon and Norfolk & Portsmouth Daily Advertiser*, 17 July 1820, 2).

Petersburg: "At the Theatre, the citizens, strangers, and their families had been collecting from 7 o'clock in the morning. Every seat, every avenue of the front part was completely occupied, and crowded to excess. The Ladies constituted much the larger portion of the assemblage, and the appearance was brilliant in the extreme. We think there could not have been present less than 1500." Both the reader of the Declaration of Independence and orator were announced by the sound of a cannon. Then "Mr. Caldwell of the Theatre, at the request of the General Committee, recited the following patriotic 'Ode,' composed for the occasion by John McCreery, Esq"; first line: "Oh! that I could with genius strong." Following that, a "Song, 'Jubilee of Freedom,' by Mr. Keene[422] of the Theatre" was sung. That afternoon at Bath Springs about 200 sat down to a dinner with toasts "accompanied by songs, music and cheers": Tune, Ca Ira — Tune, Rise Columbia, Brave and Free[423] — Tune, Yankee Doodle — Tune, The Pillar of Glory — Tune, Washington's March — Tune, Yankee Doodle and Dead March — Tune, Monroe's March — Tune, Jefferson's March — Tune, Madison's March — Tune, Go Where Glory Waits Thee[424] — Tune, Let Fame Sound the Trumpet — Tune, John Bull Caught a Tartar — Tune, Our Rights We Will Cherish — Tune Marseilles Hymn — Tune, Spanish Patriots — Tune, Empire of Freedom — Tune, How Sleep the Brave — Tune, Speed the Plough — Tune, America, Commerce and Freedom — Tune, Row the Keel — Tune, Rogue's March — Tune, Old Virginia — Tune, Love's Garland.[425] "The Dining Party left Bath Springs about 7 o'clock, P.M. in the greatest glee and good humor with each other" ("44th Anniversary of Independence," *American Beacon and Norfolk & Portsmouth Daily Advertiser*, 11 July 1820, 2).

Portsmouth: "Jubilee of Freemen" celebration held at Mr. Portlock's Hotel by the Independents and Junior Volunteers and Calvary, the following music was played or sung: Hail Columbia — Washington's Dirge — Washington's March — Yankee Doodle — Eveteen's Bower — Star-Spangled Banner — Battle of Trenton — Yankee Doodle — Waltz — Duke of York's March — Marseilles Hymn — Columbus — Sprig of

Shilolah (*American Beacon and Norfolk & Portsmouth Daily Advertiser*, 6 July 1820, 3).

1821

Publications

"'The Birth-Day of Freedom.' A National Song. By Henry C. Knight. Tune —'Anacreon in Heaven.'" First line: "All hail to the birth of the happiest land" (*Newburyport Herald*, 3 July 1821, 2).

"A Favorite Ode on Celebration of the Fourth of July. For the voice and piano forte.[426] Composed by Dr. G.K. Jackson. Words by Mrs. Jackson." Boston: E. W. Jackson, [1821–23]. Voice, piano, and violin accompaniment.

"The following pieces were sung at the celebration of Independence in this town [Newport], on Wednesday last": "Ode" (first line: "Returns again the hallow'd morn"); "Hymn"[427] (first line: "How vast thy gifts, Almighty King"); "Hymn" (first line: "Come, let us join the cheerful song") ("Poetry," *Rhode-Island Republican*, 11 July 1821, 4).

"Fourth of July Odes, Original and Selected. For the *Essex Register*. 'The Sons of the West.' A Song for July 4th. Tune —'Perry's Victory' —'O'er the Bosom of Erie,' &c." First line: "When the mandate of heaven was heard from afar."; "'Independence' by S. Woodworth." First line: "Freemen! arise, and salute the glad morning."; "Fourth of July." First line: "If the Dead from their dark-rolling halls in the sky" (*Essex Register*, 4 July 1821, 4).

"An Ode, for the celebration by the Washington Society, of the anniversary of American independence, July 4, 1821. By a member of the society." First line: "Genius of Freedom despondingly stood." To the tune "Adams and Liberty." Broadside, [Boston, 1821]. Copy in Brown University.

"A Hymn, for the Fourth of July." First line: "To thee, Most High, we humbly bow" (*Carolina Centinel*, 7 July 1821, 3).

"Mr. Editor — The following Ode was written for the 4th of July. You will confer a favor by inserting it in the Patriot. Z.X." Tune — "Wreaths for the Chieftain." First line: "Sons of our heroes who nobly contended" (*Essex Patriot*, 30 June 1821, 3).

"Ode for July 4, 1821. The following Ode, written for the occasion, by Timothy Paige, Jr. Esq. was sung at Southbridge, Worcester County, by a large choir of singers on the late Anniversary." First line: "Let hymns of triumph rise around" (*Columbian Centinel*, 18 July 1821, 3; *Pittsfield Sun*, 1 August 1821, 1; *An Oration, Pronounced July 4, 1821, in the Baptist Meeting House, in Southbridge, Mass. It Being the Forty-fifth Anniversary of American Independence. ... Subjoined to which is an Account of the Arrangements, with the Ode, Toasts and Proceedings of the Day*. Worcester [MA], Printed by Henry Rogers, 1821).

"Ode. Written by R.T. Paine, Esq. and sung at the Anniversary of American Independence, July 4, 1811, in Faneuil Hall, Boston. Tune 'Battle of the Nile.'" First line: "Let patriotic pride our patriot triumph wake!" (*Salem Gazette*, 3 July 1821, 4). See **Publications**, 1811.

"Odes to be sung at Pequannock [NJ?], July 4th, 1821. Written by S. Graham." Ode 1: first line, "Illustrious on the rolls of fame"; Ode 2:, first line: "Gone are the pangs of Freedoms birth"; Ode 3: first line, "The wheel of time rolls swiftly on." Broadside, 1821. Copy in Brown University.

"Order of Exercises for July 4th, 1821. "1. Voluntary. 2. 47th Psalm — Belknap's collection. 3. Prayer. 4. 100th Psalm — Belknap's Collection. 5. Oration by Mr. C. Cushing, A.M. 6. The following ode written for the occasion.... 7. Benediction." Broadside. [Newburyport, Mass.: s.n., 1821]. Copy in the New York Historical Society.

"The Song of Gratitude. Composed for the Mechanic Association, and to be sung at the Town-Hall, July 4, 1821. Air —'Soldier's Gratitude.'" First line: "The day that gave to freedom birth" (*Essex Register*, 4 July 1821, 2).

Performances

Connecticut

Hartford: At Bennett's Hotel, a dinner for the "republican citizens of this and the neighboring towns" was highlighted by toasts, "following with appropriate pieces of music from a band, and the discharge of cannon" ("Celebration of Independence," *American Mercury*, 10 July 1821, 3).

District of Columbia

Capitol, Hall of House of Representatives, "in the south wing,... "the Marine band played some patriotic airs, as Hail Columbia, &c when Mr. [John Quincy] Adams rose, and pronounced an oration of great compass." At the dinner celebration held for the party at Strother's Hotel, "a number of patriotic toasts were drank, accompanied by music from the Marine Band, and announced by the discharge of three guns each" ("National Celebration," *Boston Commercial Gazette*, 12 July 1821, 2); the "Club of Liberales" celebrated "at the house of Mr. Clephane in F Street, where Mr. Solomon Drew provided a sumptuous dinner." Many of the toasts were accompanied by music: Song, Scots wha hae wi Wallace bled — Song, The Independent Man — Original song by W.E. (tune — Fye let us a' to the Bridal; First line: "Come let us rejoice on the day, sire, so dear to American Freemen")[428] — Song, Common Sense One Night — Song, I've Oft Been Asked by Prosing Souls[429] — Song, Surely That Cannot Be Wrong Which Gives to Each His Liking — Song, If Gold Could Lengthen Life, I Swear — Fragment of an Ode by Mr. C — e (First line: "Proud day we would hail thee! Of time the most splendid") — Song, The Star-Spangled Banner — Song, Come Hoist Ev'ry Sail to the Breeze — Song, America, Commerce, and Freedom — Song, A Hunting We Will Go — Song, Away with Melancholy — Song, Believe Me If All Those Endearing Young Charms ("Independence Celebration," *Washington Gazette*, 6 July 1821, 2; "The Dinner at Strother's," *Pittsfield Sun*, 18 July 1821, 2).

Maryland

Baltimore: "An association of young gentlemen" met. "After the reading of the Declaration of Independence, the following Song, composed for the occasion by one of the company, was sung, accompanied by music": "Tune — Anacreon in Heaven." First line: "When the Goddess of Liberty, shrouded in night." Additional music included pieces that accompanied the toasts: Hail Columbia — Should Auld Acquaintance — Yankee Doodle — German Hymn — In the Downhill of Life[430] — Is There a Heart — Scots Wha Hae Wi' Wallace Bled ("The Fourth of July," *Baltimore Patriot*, 13 July 1821, 2); members of the Ciceronian Debating Society met at the Maryland Tavern, "four miles from town," for dinner. The following music accompanied the toasts: Columbia's Tars — The Star-Spangled Banner — Washington's March — Hail to the Chief — Hail Columbia — Dead March [repeated three times] — Columbia's Fair[431] ("The Fourth of July," *Baltimore Patriot*, 13 July 1821, 2).

Manchester: The Manchester Blues and citizens of the town met at 11 A.M. and "marched in procession, accompanied with elegant music, to Capt. Showers' Spring" and "partook of an elegant cold collation" ("Celebration at Manchester," *Baltimore Patriot*, 11 July 1821, 2).

Williamsport: "Citizens and farmers" heard the Declaration of Independence read and toasts were "accompanied at intervals with songs and music" ("Fourth of July," *Baltimore Patriot*, 11 July 1821, 2).

Massachusetts

Boston: The Washington Society celebrated by hosting a public dinner at the Marlboro Hotel. "A band of music was placed in the orchestra early in the day for the amusement of the numerous ladies and gentlemen who visited the hall.... After the cloth was removed, an able and eloquent address was pronounced by Andrew Dunlap, Esq. after which the following sentiments were given accompanied with music. The anniversary ode [see **Publications** above] by a member, and occasional songs were sung, which gave a very lively effect to the scene": Anniversary Ode, Adams & Liberty — Hail Columbia — President's March — Pleyel's Hymn — The Knight Errant — Ode on Science — Quick March — O Dear What Can the Matter Be — The Frog He Would a Woing Go[432] — Freedom's Jubilee — No luck about the House — Go to the Devil and Shake Yourself — Rural Felicity ("Washington Society," *Independent Chronicle and Boston Patriot*, 7 July 1821, 1; at the Amphitheater (or Washington Garden Theatre) at 7 P.M., "the celebrated military comedy, called the *Point of Honor; or — A School for Soldiers*" was performed by the Amateur Company. Included were "a number of patriotic songs by members of the Company" that included "Awake Ye Dull Mortals" (Mrs. Mills); "'Freedom's Jubilee Afterwards' (music composed expressly for the occasion, by Mr. F.C. Schaffer); an Air on the French Horn (Mr. Campbell), 'The Host That Fights for Liberty' (written by the late John H. Mills [sung by] Mrs. Mills; Song (Master Ayling); Air on the Royal Kent Bugle (Mr. Campbell)." "A grand display of fireworks" took place on the Common. The rockets, wheels, windmills, showers, fountains and other pyrotechnics were accompanied by the following music performed by a "full and select band": President's March — Masonic March — Waltz — Slow March — March in Don Quixote — Cadets March — Quick March — Governor's March — Marseilles March — Peruvian March — March in Tekeli — Masonic March — Yankee Doodle — Hail Columbia ("Grand National Jubilee," *Boston Commercial Gazette*, 2 July 1821, 3; *Columbian Centinel*, 4 July 1821, 3); at Faneuil Hall a dinner was served, followed by toasts and the following music: Hail Columbia — President's March — Brooks March[433] — Adams and Liberty — Speed the Plough — Perry's Victory — Marseilles Hymn — Gen. Jackson's March — Wreaths to the Chieftain — Dirge — Washington's March — Yankee Doodle — Jesse of Dunblane (*Pittsfield Sun*, 18 July 1821, 3).

Charlestown: A parade, ceremony, and dinner for 300 persons at the town hall, where the participants heard the following music: Hail Columbia — Adams and Liberty — Jefferson's March — President's March — Brooks' March — Massachusetts March — Yankee Doodle — Air — Washington's March — Caravan March[434] — Grand March in Battle of Prague — Grand March in Blue Beard — Rural Felicity ("Celebration at Charlestown," *Pittsfield Sun*, 25 July 1821, 1).

Dedham: "At 12 o'clock a large procession was formed at Gay's hotel" and included "the Dedham Light Infantry, commanded by Capt. Samuel Lewis, with a fine band of music," as well as participants in the exercises that took place at the Rev. Mr. Lamson's Meeting House. The services included:

1. A voluntary on the organ, by Mr. Taylor.[435]
2. A well adapted Prayer, by the Rev. A. Lamson.
3. Anthem, by the choir and organ.
4. The Declaration of American Independence, preceded by a pertinent introductory Address, by Mr. H. Mann (in the place of Dr. Ames, who was indisposed....
5. Anthem.
6. A most appropriate, spirited and eloquent Oration, by Jonathan H. Cobb, Esq....
7. Billings' Anthem for Independence. Benediction.

["Celebration of Independence," *Village Register and Norfolk County Advertiser*, 6 July 1821, 3.]

Haverhill: After a parade, the exercises began at 12:30 P.M. at Mr. Dodge's Meeting House. During the services, "three anthems were sung and we should be wanting in gratitude, did we not acknowledge the pleasure we received in listening to the correctness and melody with which they were executed" ("The Fourth of July," *Essex Patriot*, 7 July 1821, 3).

Hingham: Citizens and militia enjoyed a parade to the meeting house. "The performances commenced with singing." Later on the grounds of Mr. Wilder's, there was a dinner for 250 persons, including toasts with the following music: Swiss Guards — Old Hundred, sung by the company standing — Washington's March — Hail Columbia — No luck about the house — Yankee Doodle — Green's March — Serenade — President's March — Brooks' March — Lessons by Morelli — Volunteer — O dear what can the matter be — Volunteer by the Band (*Independent Chronicle and Boston Patriot*, 14 July 1821, 2).

New Bedford: "At eleven o'clock, agreeably to previous arrangements, a procession was formed at Col. Nelson's Hotel, under the direction of Eli Haskell, Esq. Marshal of the day, which was escorted by the Independent Company of Artillery, Capt. Harrison, and Capt. Swift's Company of Volunteers (accompanied by the excellent Band of Music from Taunton) to the 2d Congregational Meeting-house, where Prayers were offered in a very impressive manner by the Rev. Mr. Whitaker." After a reading of the Declaration of Independence and oration, "an Ode, selected for the occasion, was skillfully performed by a numerous choir accompanied by the Band." Among the toasts presented at the dinner held at Col. Nelson's Hotel, "several appropriate songs were sung, and received with applause" ("Celebration of Independence," *New Bedford Mercury*, 6 July 1821, 2).

Newburyport: After a procession of citizens, escorted by military companies, to the church[436] on "Pleasant Street, where a numerous audience of taste and beauty was already assembled," the exercises began with "a Voluntary on the organ[437] and a Hymn." After the prayer, another hymn was sung. Also, "the following Ode, written for the occasion, was then sung by a full choir of gentlemen and ladies": "God Bless the Day." First line: "Ye, whose fathers, on this day." Later, at the dinner held at the hotel on State Street, the following works were performed: Adams and Liberty — Washington's March — Hail Columbia — Rogues' March — Marseilles Hymn — Rise Columbia — Marseilles Hymn — President's March — Massachusetts March — Gov. Brooks' March — Hull's Victory — Yankee Doodle ("Celebration of the 45th Anniversary of the Independence of the United States," *Newburyport Herald*, 3 and 6 July 1821, 2 and 3, respectively). See **Publications** above.

Salem: A procession of the Salem Charitable Mechanic Association through city streets to the North Meeting House included "a fine band," with a bugle and drum. While the group entered the Meeting House, "Mr. Cooper[438] performed a voluntary upon the noble Organ of that House, in his best style, after which an original Ode, composed for the occasion, was sung by Mr. Hubon, with spirit and effect." After a reading of the Declaration of Independence, "the 100th Psalm was sung by the Choir in the noble tune of Old Hundred.... After the oration, the appropriate and beautiful Anthem, 'Sound the Loud Timbrel,'[439] was sung." The dinner was held at the town hall. Toasts were presented, "accompanied by discharges of artillery, and interspersed with songs and music by the band": Song, The Day that Gave to Freedom Birth, &c. — Music, Dirge — Dead March in Saul — Wreaths for the Chieftains — Washington's March — Roslyn Castle — Hail Columbia — Monroe's March — Gov. Brooks' March — Song, Columbia, Land of Liberty — Marseilles March — America, Commerce and Freedom — Waltz. One report noted that members of the orchestra included both women and men ("Fourth of July" and "National Anniversary," *Essex Register*, 6 and 7 July 1821, 3 and 2, respectively; *Salem Gazette*, 3 and 6 July 1821, 3 and 3, respectively).

South Deerfield: At the exercises held at B. Jenness' Hall, there was "music selected for the occasion" ("The Great Festival," *New-Hampshire Patriot & State Gazette*, 6 July 1821, 3).

New Hampshire

Effingham: "At two o'clock, P.M., a numerous procession formed at the academy, under the direction of Capt. J. Lord, chief marshal, and Lieut. T.P. Drake, assistant marshal, and proceeded from thence to the meeting-house, escorted by the Effingham Artillery Company, and bands of instrumental and martial music, each playing alternately. When the audience was seated and called to order, a piece of music was performed.... The exercises closed with music" (*New-Hampshire Patriot & State Gazette*, 16 July 1821, 3).

New Jersey

Newark: "Multitudes of people of both sexes flocked in from the adjacent towns and villages" to watch a procession that marched from the military common to the 1st Presbyterian Church. Included among the military units parading was a "Cadet Band and Martial Music." The music at the church was apparently well received: "The 'Harmonic Society' are entitled to much credit for the delightful airs which they performed between the other exercises. Their vocal and instrumental music contributed much to the gratification of an overflowing audience" ("Anniversary Celebration," *North Star*, 26 July 1821, 1).[439]

New York

New York: At Vauxhall Garden, the grounds were "brilliantly illuminated with upwards of 4000 lamps, and ornamented with several elegant transparent paintings analogous to the occasion; and to heighten the pleasure of the visitors, a concert [was] given in the evening ... at six o'clock," in three parts:

Part 1st.

Overturn [sic] Lodoiska, orchestra

Song, Freedom's Jubilee (from the Southern Theater, his first appearance this season), Mr. Lamb

Let Patriot Pride your Patriot triumph wake, Singleton

Savoyard Boy, Mrs. Stell

Yanke Land of Freedom, Mr. Morris

Auld Lang Syne, Mr. Lamb

On this Cold Flinty Rock, Mr. Singleton

Lovers, Mother, I have None,[440] Mrs. Stell

The Jew Pedlar, Mr. Mores

Rondo, Haydn, Orchestre.

Part 2d

Minuetto, Pleyel, Orchestre.

A favorite air, with variations on the Violin, by master Halloway, only nine years old

Song, Has She then Failed in Her Truth, Mr. Lamb

Let Fame Sound the Trumpet, Mr. Singleton

Oh What is the Matter, Mrs. Stell.

Recitation, in which is introduced the song of Richard and Betty at Hickleten Fair, Mr. Morris

Song, Home, Love, and Liberty, Mr. Lamb

Love Has eyes, Mr. Singleton

The Love Letter, Mrs. Stell

Dashing Tom in Search of a Wife, Mr. Morris

Allegro, Orchestre.

Part 3d.

The Sweet Air of Lulloby arranged for the violin, master Halloway

Song, Hit at the Fashions, Mr. Lamb

Love and Glory, Mr. Singleton

The Young Son of Chivalry, Mrs. Stell

Peter Zigzag and Dolly Nignag, Mr. Morris.

The Tyrolese Song of Liberty, Mr. Singleton

I Have a Heart, Mrs. Stell

Manchester, Cries, Mr. Morris

Finale, Orchestra.

[*New York Evening Post*, 29 June and 3 July 1821, 3 and 3, respectively].

North Carolina

Newbern: The Newbern Guards paraded, "amid the discharge of artillery, musketry and the ringing of bells. During this time, Hail Columbia and other patriotic airs were played by the band attached to the Company." Following the exercises at the Baptist Church, the group assembled and "proceeded, with music, to Mrs. Emery's, where a dinner had been provided for the occasion." Toasts were drank and an "Ode for the Day, written at the request of the Newbern Guards, sung by Mr. Nash. Air—'Pillar of Glory'" (first line: "Hail to the Day! when Columbia's glory"). Another "Song, written for the occasion," was also "sung by Mr. Nash" to the "Air—'Scots wha hae'" (first line: "Sons of those, who bravely fought"). (*Carolina Centinel*, 7 July 1821, 3.) See also **Publications** above.

Ohio

Cincinnati: Haydn Society performed with the Cincinnati Band at the First Presbyterian Church.[441]

A newspaper reported "some appropriate odes and anthems sung ... in a manner highly gratifying."

Pennsylvania

Columbia: At the farm of Mr. John Hinkle, "near the borough," a large number of citizens heard a performance of the "Dead March" (*Lancaster Journal*, 13 July 1821, 2).

New Holland: Citizens and militia marched to a grove "south west to the village," where food was served and the following music performed: Yankee Doodle—Hail Columbia—Washington's March—Dead March—Jefferson & Liberty—Pennsylvania Grand March—Dead March—What a Beau My Granny Was—Yankee Tars[442]—Rogue's March—Roslin Castle—Speed the Plough—Rashes O! (*Lancaster Journal*, 13 July 1821, 2–3).

Rhode Island

Bristol: At the Congregational Meeting House, "Sound the Loud Timbrel" was sung and following at the dinner event at Horton's Hotel, "several patriotic songs" were also sung ("Celebration at Bristol," *Providence Gazette*, 11 July 1821, 1).

Newport: Preceded by a procession to the Methodist Chapel, the exercises there included "performances ... interspersed with excellent music" ("Independence," *Rhode-Island Republican*, 11 July 1821, 2).

Providence: At the First Baptist Church, the exercises were begun "after the performance of sacred musick." Before "a crowded and splendid audience ... the services at the church were closed with 'Sound the Loud Timbrel,' which was sung by the choir in a very chaste and correct style." In the afternoon the Independent Cadets enjoyed "a sumptuous dinner at Mr. Blake's Hotel" and the toasts given were "interspersed with patriotick songs, and instrumental musick" ("National Jubilee," *The American*, 6 July 1821, 2; "Fourth of July," *Providence Gazette*, 7 July 1821, 2).

South Kingstown: At Little Rest, at the Congregational Meeting House, there was "singing of several very appropriate hymns" ("National Jubilee," *Rhode Island American, and General Advertiser*, 17 July 1821, 3).

Tennessee

Nashville: "Theatre. In Honor of the Day. This Evening, July 4. Will be presented, an Historical drama, in 3 acts, written by M.M. Noah, Esq. of New-York, called *She Would be a Soldier, or the Plains of Chippewa*. Between the Play and Farce, an omnium Gatherum, consisting of Songs, Recitations, &c. The whole to conclude with an admired Farce, called '*Tis All a Farce* (for particulars see bills.)" (*Nashville Whig*, 4 July 1821).[443]

Virginia

Petersburg: At a dinner held by "Messrs. Fenn & Cheves," hundreds of citizens enjoyed the toasts "accompanied by appropriate music, the firing of cannon, songs, and the cheers of the whole party" ("National Festival," *Richmond Enquirer*, 10 July 1821, 2).

Prince Edward County: At a spring near Miller's Tavern, toasts at a dinner included the following music: Hail Columbia — Dead March — Washington's March — Jefferson and Liberty — Life Let Us Cherish — Separation — Wounded Hussar — Yankee Doodle — Sailor Boy — Yankee Doodle — The Troop — Dead March — Rugue's March — Retreat — Our Chief is Dead — Hail Columbia — Ca Ira — Washington's Grand March (*Richmond Enquirer*, 20 July 1821, 3).

Richmond: "In the celebration of the late anniversary of independence at Richmond, Va. a Poetical Version of the Declaration of Independence was delivered at the City Hall & some songs in honor of the day were written and sung by Mr. Leroy Anderson" (*Hampden Patriot and Liberal Recorder*, 25 July 1821, 3).

1822

Publications

"The following pieces were sung at the Second Baptist Meeting House, on the 4th of July, 1822": "Ode, Tune — 'Westbury Leigh'" (first line: "Begin my soul, th' exalted lay"); "Ode — Tune 'Cranbrook'" (first line: "Behold enray'd in light"); Ode, Tune — 'Bringeton'" (first line: "Hark, freedom's silver horn"); "Ode on Science" (first line: "The morning sun shines from the east") ("Poetry," *Rhode-Island Republican*, 10 July 1822, 4).

"'National Song.' Sung on the Fourth of July, 1822, at a public dinner, given in Natchez. Written by a citizen of Natchez. Tune — 'Kate of Colerain.'" First line: "The Day Star of Liberty faintly was springing" (*Baltimore Patriot*, 17 August, 1822, 1).

"The following beautiful ode, written by O.W.B. Peabody, Esq.[444] of Exeter, was sung by Mr. S.T. Gilman, at the late celebration in that town. 'Ode for the Fourth of July.' Tune — 'Ye Mariners [of England],' &c." First line: "Ye freemen of New-England." The exercises were held at the Rev. Rowland's meeting house where the "Ode, composed for the occasion was sung in a style to which we can pay no higher compliment than to say that it was worthy of the ode" (*New-Hampshire Patriot & State Gazette*, 13 and 22 July 1822, 3 and 4, respectively).

"'Hail, glorious day, blest Freedom smiles.'[445] The following words were sung (to the above tune) at the celebration of Independence at Charlestown, Mass." To be sung to the tune of "Rise, Cynthia." *The Musical Cabinet* (Charlestown, 1822–[1823]).

"An Hymn for Independence. Tune — Blue-Bird." First line: "Hail fair Columbia! hail ye sons of freedom" (*Pittsfield Sun*, 3 July 1822, 3).

"An Hymn for Independence. Tune — Greenwich."

First line: "Hail fair Columbia, hail! all hail!" (*Pittsfield Sun*, 26 June 1822, 3).

"National Ode, to be sung at this place [Litchfield, CT] on the Fourth of July." First line: "Ye sons of Columbia, who bravely have fought" (*Litchfield Republican*, 3 July 1822, 3).

"Ode for the Fourth of July, 1822. Tune — Hail to the Chief." First line: "Bright glows the sun in his firmament splendor" ("The Fount," *American Federalist Columbian Centinel*, 17 July 1822, 4, from the *Baltimore Morning Chronicle*).

"Ode to Freedom, for the Fourth of July. By J. Frieze." First line: "Freedom hail! celestial goddess" (*Universalist Magazine*, 12 October 1822, 64).

"Ode, written for the occasion and sung at the celebration of independence by the Washington Society. By a member of the Society. Tune — 'Wreaths to the Chieftain.'"[446] First line: "Honor the statesmen a nation who founded" ("The Recess," *Independent Chronicle & Boston Patriot*, 10 July 1822, 4).

"Song, sung at the celebration of Independence, at Topsfield, in Massachusetts. Tune — Auld lang syne." First line: "Should gallant heroes be forgot" ("The Olio," *Alexandria Herald*, 17 July 1822, 4).

Performances

Connecticut

Norwich: "The celebration of our National Independence was observed in this city, in a manner highly gratifying to the patriotic, and commendable to our citizens. The dawn of the anniversary of that glorious day, which gave independence to millions of the human species, was announced by the discharge of ordnance from the Wharf-Bridge, and the beat of the reveilee [sic] by an excellent band of martial music." After the exercises that were held at the Presbyterian Meeting House whose "services commenced and concluded with sacred music," and a dinner "where about one hundred and thirty gentlemen partook of an excellent collation," the day's events concluded at "a bower previously erected for the purpose," where "the pleasures of the company were not a little enhanced by the civility of some of the ladies who executed several excellent tunes on the pianoforte" ("Independence," *Courier*, 10 July 1822, 3).

Maine

Bristol: A "regimental band" marched in a parade of citizens and military units to the meeting house where "the performances were accompanied by select and appropriate music, which did much credit to the performers" ("Celebration at Bristol," *Lincoln Intelligencer*, 18 July 1822, 3).

Maryland

Annapolis: In the Senate Room, "a hymn written for the occasion by John Brewer, Esq.[447] conspicuous for patriotic sentiments and poetical merit was sung." Also, "a national air was then played by a military band." The exercises concluded with "an appropriate hymn" ("Annapolis," *Baltimore Patriot*, 10 July 1822, 2).

Baltimore: "After the dismissal of the troops from the parade, the Baltimore Independent Blues attached to the First Regiment of Artillery, marched to Mr. John A. Mozer's Hotel one and a half miles from Baltimore, on the York road, where they partook of an elegant dinner prepared by him." Toasts were drank and included the following performances: Tune, Hail Columbia, full band; Pleyel's Hymn, full band — Auild Lang Syne, full band — Fayette's March, full band — Yankee Doodle, full band — Temple of Liberty, full band — Washington's March, full band — March 5th Infantry, full band — Tune, Neptune's Pride, full band — Capt. Wilson's Quick Step, full band — The Star-Spangled Banner, full band — Glee, Here's a Health to All Good Lasses. Additional volunteer toasts were drank "succeeded by songs, glees, &c. accompanied by the Band of the Baltimore Independent Blues" ("Fourth of July," *Baltimore Patriot*, 8 July 1822, 2).

Massachusetts

Boston: At the Old South Meeting House, there was a "performance of several pieces of music, executed by a select choir led by Mr. Bayley" ("National Birth Day," *American Federalist Columbian Centinel*, 6 July 1822, 2; *Salem Gazette*, 9 July 1822, 2); at the City Theatre, "in commemoration of the Fourth of July, a variety of entertainments" consisted of songs and dances, including "Comic Song of the Smokers' Club," by Mr. Roberts and Mr. Duff singing "for the second time, the new Patriotic Song, written by a gentleman of this city, called 'Sons of Freedom, Generous Land.'" Also, "'Barney Leave the Girls Alone,' by Mr. Roberts." (*Boston Commercial Gazette*, 4 July 1822, 3.); at Faneuil Hall, "the Republican and other citizens of Boston" celebrated and two odes were performed. "The following neat and appropriate Odes, written for the occasion, were sung at the celebration of independence by the Republicans and others at Faneuil Hall" — [First ode] first line, "Why did the nations rage?" "Second Ode"[448]: first line, "Like the bow in Eastern sky" (*Independent Chronicle & Boston Patriot*, 3 and 10 July 1822, 3 and 4, respectively; *American Federalist Columbian Centinel*, 6 July 1822, 2). See also **Publications** above.

Fall River: After a flag presentation ceremony and parade, the exercises were held at the meeting house where "the music was performed with taste and skill, and a highly patriotic and appropriate Ode, composed by Miss Eliza Dewey, was sung on the occasion" (*Rhode-Island Republican*, 17 July 1822, 2; "Celebration at Fall-River, Mass.," *Providence Patriot*, 24 July 1822, 2).

Newburyport: A large number of citizens escorted by the Light Infantry Company marched "to the church in Pleasant Street where several pieces of suitable music were performed with great skill and effect" ("Fourth of July," *Salem Gazette*, 12 July 1822, 2).

Mississippi

Natchez: "National Song. Tune — Kate of Colerain" sung at a public dinner in Natchez [Mississippi?]. "Written by a citizen of Natchez" (*Baltimore Patriot*, 17 August 1822, 1).

Missouri

St. Louis: At a dinner and toasts presented at "a beautiful arbour near the residence of Col. O'Fallon": Columbia, to Glory Arise — Federal March — Fort Erie — Fourth of March — Gen. Atkinson's March — Go to the Dead and Shake Yourself — Hail Columbia — Jefferson and Liberty — Madison's March — March in Blue Beard — Perry's Victory — Scot's oer the Border — Soldier's Joy — Star-Spangled Banner — Vive la Constitution — Volunteer's March — Washington's March — Western Waters — Wayne's March — Yankee Doodle (*St. Louis Enquirer*, 8 July 1822, 2).

New Hampshire

Chester: "The procession formed at the tavern of General Henry Sweetser ... proceeded to the Meeting House under escort of the Chester Light Infantry, accompanied by an excellent band of music." "Several pieces of music were performed by the choir with taste and correctness." The dinner hosted by Sweetser included toasts "accompanied by music and firing" ("Celebration at Chester," *New-Hampshire Patriot & State Gazette*, 15 July 1822, 2).

Portsmouth: A procession from Hassard's Inn to the "new meeting house," where the exercises began with "vocal music, of which Mr. Gideon Barker took the lead" (*Rhode-Island Republican*, 10 July 1822, 2).

New York

Ithaca: The "order of the day" consisted of a procession that assembled in front of the hotel and included a music ensemble. After a march to the Presbyterian Church, the exercises there included a prayer, psalm, reading of the Declaration, an "Ode on Science," oration, followed by music. One newspaper reported that "the intervals of these exercises were filled by select and appropriate music from a volunteer choir, whose performance had a pleasing and solemn effect, and entitled them to the thanks of the audience." Later at the dinner, the toasts were "accompanied by appropriate music and the discharge of cannon" ("National Anniversary," *Republican Chronicle*, 3 July 1822, 2; *American Journal*, 10 July 1822, 2).

New York: At Chatham Garden: "'Huzza! Here's Columbia for Ever' performed by Clifton,[449] of Baltimore," *Grand Symphony*, "composed by Haydn" (*New-York Advertiser*, 6 July 1822, 3); "God Save America," composed "by Mr. G. Geib,[450] and dedicated to the People of the United States." Performed at the City Theatre by "Mr. Lamb." Also performed was a "Grand Military Overture" by a "full band" (*New-York Advertiser*, 6 July 1822, 3; *New York American*, 2 July 1822, 3.)

Ohio

Cincinnati: The Haydn Society sang several odes, "accompanied by the Cincinnati Band," conducted by Josiah Warren.[451]

Vermont

Shaftsbury: "A respectable number of citizens of Shaftsbury and the adjacent towns, assembled at the Inn of Jonathan Draper.... Between the hours of 11 and 12, a procession was formed and marched under the direction of Col. Henry Robinson, marshal of the day, to the place appointed for the performance of the solemnities suited to the occasion. The Bennington band of music, with martial music, and Capt. Waters' company of matross, were the advance of the procession." Later after the exercises, the assemblage drank toasts "interspersed with songs of liberty, and enlivened by the usual demonstrations of hilarity and gratitude" (*Vermont Gazette*, 16 July 1822, 2).

1823

Publications

"Anniversary Song. Sung by its author at the democratic celebration in Philadelphia, on the 4th of July, 1823. Our Forefathers. By Alderman Barker.[452] Air — 'Hearts of Oak.'" First line: "When our forefathers dared the wild ocean to roam" ("Poetry," *Watch-Tower*, 4 August 1823, 4).

"Dithyrambic Ode, for the Fourth [of] July, 1823." Signed "J.H." First line: "Hark! to the floating strain" (*Carolina Centinel*, 5 July 1823, 3).

"The following Odes were sung at the Second Baptist Meeting House, in Newport [RI], at the celebration of the 4th July, 1823": "O praise the Lord, in that blest place"; "Wide o'er the boundless waves"; "Columbia! twice an hundred years"; "Today we sing the glorious toil" (*Rhode-Island Republican*, 9 July 1823, 4).

"The following Odes were sung at the Union Meeting House, in Portsmouth (R.I.) at the celebration of the forty-seventh anniversary of American independence": "Returns again the hallow'd morn"; "Hark, the sounds of joy are swelling" (*Rhode-Island Republican*, 9 July 1823, 4).

"Hymn for the 4th of July — 1823." First line: "Hail independence, hail." Note: "The following Ode was sung at the celebration of 4th inst. at Ipswich [Massachusetts]" ("Miscellany," *Salem Gazette,* 8 July 1823, 1).

"Ode for the Fourth of July. Tune — Scots Wha Hae Wi' Wallace Bled." First line: "Jackson, on this glorious day" (*Salem Gazette*, 15 July 1823, 2).

"Ode sung at a celebration in Salem, on the Fourth of July, 1811; composed by Hon. Joseph Story." First line: "Welcome! Welcolme the day, when assembled as one" ("Miscellany," Salem Gazette, 4 July 1823, 1).

"Ode to Independence." First line: "O hallow the day, when from regions of light" ("Selected Poetry," *Essex Register*, 3 July 1823, 4).

"Song for the Fourth of July. By Caerlayon." First line: "Unfurd [sic] your banners high" ("Poet's Corner," *Universalist Magazine*, 12 July 1823, 12).

"Song for the Fourth of July. Tune — 'Scots wha hae,' &c." First line: "Hark! the joyous bells proclaim" (*National Advocate, for the Country* [New York], 25 July 1823).

Performances

District of Columbia

The U.S. Marine Band[453] provided music on the steamboat *Washington* that carried excursionists from Alexandria, Virginia, to Mount Vernon. "When the boat arrived in sight of that sacred spot, the band struck up the plaintive air of Roslin Castle." Upon landing a procession was formed led by the band and the assemblage marched to the "pavilion near the sepulcre of Washington." After appropriate services, "the band were saluting Mrs. [Bushrod] Washington in the piazza of the mansion. The procession formed again; and, opening to the right and left, encircled the tomb. A solemn silence now pervaded the company, which was broken only by the beat of the muffled drum, at the door of the vault, and the sympathizing music of Pleyel's Hymn poured out by the full band." The company later returned to Alexandria for an "elegant dinner" where toasts were drunk and a brief address was given by Vice President Daniel D. Tompkins. "The following Ode, composed for the occasion by John L. Gow, Esq. was then sung": "The Birth Day of Freedom" (first line: "Shall the genius that dawn'd upon tyranny's night.") (*National Intelligencer*, 8 July 1823, 3; *Providence Patriot*, 19 July 1823, 1; "Celebration of Independence at Mount Vernon," *Richmond Enquirer*, 15 July 1823, 2).

Kentucky

Frankfort: Performed at a dinner celebration with the Governor present: Bruce's March — Clay's March — Jefferson's March — Madison's March — President's March — Shelby's March — Washington's March (*Argus of Western America*, 9 July 1823, 2).

Maine

Portland: "The day was ushered in, as usual, with ringing of bells, firing of guns, strains of music, and shouts of joy." At the exercises, "music suitable for the occasion was well performed by the Beethoven Society." The order of the services was as follows:

1. Music.
2. Prayer.
3. Hymn.
4. Oration.
5. Music.
6. Benediction.

["Celebration of Independence," *Eastern Argus*, 8 July 1823, 2].

Maryland

Baltimore: "The company, attached to the Fifth Regiment" marched to Washington Square for the exercises after which "the company, accompanied by the Fort Band, whose services had been politely tendered by Major Belton, of Fort McHenry, marched on board the steam boat Maryland, Captain Vickers, which conveyed them to Curtis' Creek." Later they returned to the city to have dinner, that included the following pieces of music to accompany the toasts: Yankee Doodle — Monroe's March — Decatur's Victory — United States March — Jackson's March — The Legacy — North Point — Vive la Bagatelle — Washington's March — Auld Lang Syne — Hail Columbia — Stoney Point — I Have Loved Thee[454] — Gen. McDonal's March — Gen Stricker's March — Gen Heath's March[455] — Huzza, Here's Columbia Forever — Star-Spangled Banner — Gen Sterrett's March[456] — Jefferson's March. One song was composed for the occasion and "sung by the author." (Tune — "Auld Lang Syne"). First line: "My fellow soldiers, right and left" ("Fourth of July," *Baltimore Patriot*, 9 July 1823, 2; *Richmond Enquirer*, 11 July 1823, 2); the First Baltimore Sharp Shooters had dinner at Carroll's Woods, with Capt. Deems's Band providing the following music to accompany the toasts: Hail Columbia — Yankee Doodle — Decatur's Victory — Star-Spangled Banner — Ye Sons of Columbia — Washington's March — President's March — Let Fame Sound the Trumpet — America, Commerce and Freedom — The Liberty-Tree — Pleyel's Hymn — Scots Wha Hae Wi' Wallace — Come Haste to the Wedding ("National Anniversary," *American & Commercial Daily Advertiser*, 8 July 1823, 2); the First Battalion Maryland Riflemen had a celebration dinner at Carroll's Spring. A band provided the following music for the toasts: Hail Columbia — Star-Spangled Banner — Hail to the Chief[457] — Morgan Volunteer's March — Monroe's March — Pleyel's Hymn — Washington's March — Spanish Double Quick March — Scots Wah Hae — How Sleep the Brave-Standing and Silent — Round the Flag of Freedom Rally — There's Nae Luck About the House — Dear Creatures, We Can't Do Without Them ("National Anniversary," *American & Commercial Daily Advertiser*, 8 July 1823, 2).

Massachusetts

Boston: At "the Rev. Dean's Meeting House, the new and beautiful Church in Bulfinch Street," the exercises included a Voluntary (first line: "O praise the Lord with one consent"), an Ode to the "Air — 'Ye Mariners of England'" (first line: "Rise sun of Freedom, glorious!"), another Ode (first line: "Let grateful millions join to raise"), an Anthem (first line, duet: "Come ever smiling liberty come" and first line, chorus: "Glory be to God on high"). "The Odes and Anthems were sung in an excellent manner and gave the greatest satisfaction to a large and brilliant audience." At Faneuil Hall, the dinner and toasts were accompanied by the following music: Tune, Yankee Doodle — Tune, Rise Columbia — Dirge — President's March — Adams and Liberty — Gov. Eustis' March[458] — To Liberty's Enraptur'd Sight[459] — Dirge — Massachusetts March — Hail Columbia — The Muses — Scots Wa Ha Wa Wallace Bled — Triumph of Reason (*American Federalist Columbian Centinel*, 4 July 1823, 2; "National Anniversary," *Independent Chronicle & Boston Patriot*, 9 July 1823, 4; "Miscellany," *Providence Patriot*, 12 July 1823, 1; *Pittsfield Sun*, 17 July 1823, 1; *An Oration, Delivered before the Republicans of Boston, on the Fourth of July, 1823*. By Russell Jarvis. Boston: True & Greene, 1823); the order of services at the Old South Meeting House:

1. Voluntary — a military movement adapted to the occasion, and performed by Mr. A.P. Heinrich[460]
2. Recitative and chorus — Haydn — "The host of Midian prevailed," &c.
3. Prayer
4. Duet — Handel — "Come ever smiling liberty," &c
5. Oration by Charles P. Curtis
6. Chorus — Handel — "Let their celestial concerts all unite"

("Boston, 4th of July, 1823," *American Federalist Columbian Centinel*, 4 July 1823, 2); the Washington Society met at Marlboro' Hall for a public dinner. "The following National Ode, written by a member of the society, was sung after the first sentiment [toast][461] with great effect by Mr. Benjamin Brigham": "Ode, Air — 'To Liberty's Enraptur'd Sight.'" First line: "When first with ray divinely bright" ("Washington Society," *Independent Chronicle & Boston Patriot*, 9 July 1823, 4; "Miscellany," *Providence Patriot*, 26 July 1823, 1). See also **Publications**, 1824.

Danvers: A parade from Benjamin Goodridge's Hall to the Rev. Mr. Walker's Meeting House was "accompanied by an excellent band" and the exercises included "singing by the choir of the society, assisted by the band, under the direction of Capt. Joseph W. Carey." Later a dinner was served to 170 persons at George Southwick's Hall where "patriotic sentiments interspersed with excellent songs seemed to raise the whole scene to the highest state of festive enjoyment" ("Celebration at Danvers," *Salem Gazette*, 8 July 1823, 2).

Marblehead: The Republicans and military units of this town paraded to the new meeting house where the exercises were held. "The music, directed by Mr. William Haskel, was excellent; and an Ode, written for the day, was sung by the whole choir in a style seldom surpassed" ("Celebration at Marblehead," *Independent Chronicle & Boston Patriot*, 9 July 1823, 4).

Newburyport: "In this town the day was ushered in by the ringing of bells, and the discharge of cannon. At 11 o'clock a procession was formed in the mall, which proceeded, under escort of the Washington Light Infantry Company, to the church in Pleasant street, which had been neatly and tastefully decorated for the occasion. The religious exercises were performed in a devout and impressive manner by the Rev. Mr. Williams, and the songs of praise & thanksgiving ascended from the united choirs of the several religious societies in town.... After the oration was sung a beautiful and patriotic Ode, written by R. Cross." The program for the exercises was published on the day of the celebration:

1. Voluntary on the Organ.
2. Anthem — "Blessed Be Thou," &c.
3. Prayer, by the Rev. Mr. Williams.
4. Psalm, from Dwight's Col.
5. Declaration of Independence.
6. Psalm, from Dwight's Col.
7. Oration.
8. Ode, written for the occasion.
9 Benediction.

"The following Ode, written for the celebration this day, will be performed immediately after the delivery of the Oration. Tune — 'Strike the Cymbals.'" First line: "Hush! Contention!" ("National Anniversary" and "Celebration," *Newburyport Herald*, 4 and 8 July 1823, 1–2 and 2, respectively).

Salem: A procession of militia, "distinguished citizens, and the Mechanic Association, marched to the North Meeting House "where we were first greated by a fine display of Mr. T. Cooper's talent upon the organ." After a prayer, "an appropriate Hymn was then sung by a large choir of singers who had volunteered their services on the occasion." After the Declaration of Independence was read, " a beautiful Ode [first line: "Again the glorious morn returns"], composed for the occasion, was next sung with thrilling effect, by Mr. Sharpe, of Boston." The Ode was written by Joseph G. Waters.[462] After an oration, "a Psalm was then sung in the appropriate tune of 'Old Hundred.'" Dinner at the Essex Coffee House followed, with the following music that accompanied the toasts: Tune, Adams & Liberty — Hail Columbia — Washington's March — Mass. Quick Step — President's March — Gov. Eustis' March — Gov. Brooks' March — Yankee Doodle — Wreaths to the Chieftain — Scots wha ha,' &c — Marseilles Hymn — German Waltz — My Love Is Like the Red Rose (*Salem Gazette*, 4 and 8 July 1823, 2 and 2, respectively; "Fourth of July," *Essex Register*, 7 July 1823, 2).

Springfield: "The Republican celebration in this town, on Friday last, was undoubtedly more splendid than has heretofore been witnessed on a similar occasion, in the old County of Hampshire." The day began with an artillery salute, "accompanied by peals on all the bells, and at 11 o'clock an unusually numerous procession moved from Chapman's Hotel to the Rev. Mr. Osgood's meeting-house" where "more than sixteen hundred persons were assembled." After an opening prayer, "the Declaration of Independance was read by Mr. Wm. F. Wolcott, in a manner suited to the

solemnity of that venerable and interesting state paper. The oration by Edward D. Bangs, Esq. fully justified the high expectation which had been raised by the reputation of the orator. In noticing the exercises and ceremonies of this occasion, we cannot pass in silence the distinguished liberality of Col. Warriner, and his choir of singers, in the able and judicious selection and performance of several pieces of music, to the great delight and admiration of the crowded auditory." Following there was a procession, "with escort and music to the ordnance yard, on the hill (whilst a federal salute was firing) where more than three hundred citizens partook of an excellent dinner." Later toasts were presented, "accompanied by discharge of cannon, and interludes of instrumental music" (*Pittsfield Sun*, 17 July 1823, 2).

Stoneham: At a celebration of "the Republican citizens of Stoneham" held at the meeting house, the event was "accompanied with appropriate music by a select choir of vocal and instrumental musicians." At the dinner that followed, the toasts were "accompanied with music" ("Republican Celebration in Stoneham," *Independent Chronicle & Boston Patriot*, 12 July 1823, 1).

Missouri

Franklin: After a parade by the Franklin Guards and exercises held on the banks of the Missouri River, the assemblage proceeded to a "dining arbour contiguous to the residence of Mrs. Peels." Thirteen toasts were offered accompanied by the following music: Hail Columbia — A Solemn Dirge — Yankee Doodle — Bunker Hill — President's March — the Harp of Freedom — America, Commerce & Freedom — Friendship, Love & Truth — Scots who ha' wi' Wallace bled — Moore's Martial Hymn — Come Haste to the Wedding ("National Anniversary," *Missouri Intelligencer*, 8 July 1823, 2).

New Hampshire

Hanover: The Handel Society[463] of Dartmouth College performed several pieces at the celebration held in the meeting house: Old Hundred — The Lord Sitteth Above the Flood Waters — Strike the Cymbals — Holy Lord God — Intercession[464] — Handel's Grand Hallelujah ("Dartmouth College Celebration," *New-Hampshire Patriot & State Gazette*, 14 July 1823, 2).

New Jersey

New Germantown (now Oldwick): A procession of "a large and respectable assemblage of citizens and strangers" as well as military companies, including a "band of music" made their way to the church. "National airs were played by the band, and several appropriate Odes sung by the choir with great taste and feeling." After the exercises, the procession reassembled and marched to the Bowery "where about 400 took dinner." The toasts that followed were "accom-

THE HALLELUJAH CHORUS. Finale.   241

George Frideric Handel's "Hallelujah Chorus" from the oratorio *Messiah* was a popular work sung on the Fourth of July in Salem, Massachusetts (1814), Hanover, New Hampshire (1823), Hartford, Connecticut (1826), Newburyport, Massachusetts (1854), New York (1876), and Washington, D.C. (1918 and 1951). Shown are the opening measures of an edition in L.O. Emerson and J.H. Morey, *The Sabbath Guest: A Collection of Anthems, Sentences, Chants and Choruses* (Boston: Oliver Ditson & Co., 1870) (author's collection).

panied by a discharge of cannon and musquetry and by appropriate airs by the band" (*Trenton Federalist*, 21 July 1823, 2).

Trenton: The exercises were held in the Presbyterian Church. Military companies were instructed to enter the church without music.

Invocation.
Music.
Prayer.
Music.
Declaration of Independence.
Music.
Oration.
Music.
Benediction.

"The music in the Church will be conducted by the Trenton Musical Association" ("Fourth of July, 1823," *Trenton Federalist*, 30 June 1823, 3).

New York

Union Village: At this town in Washington County, a procession began at 10 am "preceded by

musick moved through the principal streets to the Baptist Church." The exercises included "an ode prepared for the occasion by J.K. Horton" that was sung by a choir and another ode composed by Solomon Cobb ("Independence," *Saratoga Sentinel*, 15 July 1823, 2; *Vermont Gazette*, 22 July 1823, 3).

Virginia

Norfolk:

The dawn was announced by some lively and patriotic airs, performed by a band which had been organized for the occasion. At a little before 10 o'clock, a large portion of the 54th Regiment, with their new arms, appeared on the parade ground, were formed into a Battalion by Major Albert Allmand, and marched to the Market Square, preceded by the band. Here they displayed into line, and after the band had performed a number of patriotic and martial airs, in handsome style, the Battalion moved to Christ's Church, followed by a large concourse of citizens. A very appropriate hymn being sung, the Rev'd Mr. Wicks addressed the throne of grace in a fervent and impressive prayer, acknowledging the bounties of Providence to, and imploring a continued blessing on our favoured land.

Following was a reading of the Declaration of Independence and address ("Fourth of July," *Richmond Enquirer*, 8 July 1823, 2).

Petersburg: The exercises at the theatre included "Mr. Dunn [who], at the request of the general committee, delivered, in his most happy and forcible manner, the ode, composed for the occasion, by our townsman [John] M'Creery,[465] whose effusions, possessing the genuine spirit of poetry, never fail to produce the most happy effect." Printed under the title: "Ode for the Fourth of July, 1823": first line, "Man in Egyptian darkness lay" ("Fourth of July," *Richmond Enquirer*, 11 July 1823, 3–4).

1824

Publications

"The following neat and appropriate Hymn, written by a gentleman of this city [Boston?], was sung at the past celebration of American Independence in the Second Universalist Meeting-house." First line: "O Thou, who from Oppression's shore." (*Independent Chronicle and Boston Patriot*, 14 July 1824, 4).

"The following Ode, written by a member of the Washington Society, in Boston, was sung at the last year's celebration of independence, by Mr. Benj. Brigham. Ode, air — 'To Liberty's enraptur'd sight.'" First line: "When first with ray divinely bright" (*Essex Register*, 5 July 1824, 1).

"Ode for Independence." First line: "Aurora's blushes gild the orient sky" (*Essex Register*, 5 July 1824, 1).

"Ode for the Fourth of July. Air — 'Hail to the Chief.'" First line: "Hallow'd the day from the eastward advancing" ("Independence!" *Essex Register*, 1 July 1824, 3; *Portsmouth Journal of Literature and Politics*, 3 July 1824, 2; from the *Baltimore Morning Chronicle* as published in *Providence Gazette*, 7 July 1824, 1; *Lancaster Journal*, 16 July 1824).

"An Ode for the Fourth of July. By Daniel Bryan, Esq." First line: "While destruction's dark angel sweeps over the world" (*American Monthly Magazine* [August 1824]:168).

"Ode for the Fourth of July. By the Rev. Hosea Ballou." First line: "In Freedom's song let millions join" (*Universalist Magazine*, 10 July 1824, 12; "Sacred Lyre," *Christian Intelligence*, 17 July 1824, 20).

"Ode for the Fourth of July, 1824. Tune — 'Cranbrook.'" First line: "Hail glorious jubilee." Broadside. Copy in Brown University.

"Ode for the Fourth of July. Written by Mr. J[acob] B. Moore,[466] and sung as above. Tune 'Ye Mariners,' &c." First line: "Far o'er the gloomy waters" (*New-Hampshire Patriot & State Gazette*, 12 July 1824, 4;

Portsmouth Journal of Literature and Politics, 17 July 1824, 3).

"Ode." First line: "Like the bow in Eastern sky" (*Essex Register*, 1 July 1824, 3).

"Ode to Free America." First line: "Oh! happiest land beneath the sun" (*Essex Register*, 1 July 1824, 3).

"Ode. The following Ode was written by Lt. Gov. [Charles] Collins, and sung at the celebration of independence in this town [Newport] on Monday. Music composed by Mr. Searle." First line: "Hail, glorious jubilee!" ("Poetry," *Rhode-Island Republican*, 8 July 1824, 4).

"Ode, written for the National Republican Celebration of American Independence, at the Marlboro' Hotel, July 5, 1824." First line: "When first Columbia sprang to arms!"; "The following Ode, written by Mrs. Ware (wife of one of the warrant officers attached to the Navy Yard in Charlestown) was sung at the celebration of the late Anniversary of Independence at the Marlboro' Hotel, by Col. Newhall. We copy it with pleasure, and do not hesitate to pronounce it one of the best productions of the day; and equally honorable to the poetic talents and patriotism of the fair authoress. The last stanza would have done honor to the music of 'Philenia'" (*Columbian Centinel American Federalist*, 10 July 1824, 4; *Newburyport Herald*, 13 July 1824, 1; *Village Register*, 15 July 1824, 1; *Haverhill Gazette*, 17 July 1824, 4; *Pittsfield Sun*, 29 July 1824, 1).

"Song for Independence written by George Kent, Esq. and sung at Concord by Maj. J.D. Abbot." First line: "Hail to our country, in triumph advancing" (*New-Hampshire Patriot & State Gazette*, 12 July 1824, 4).

"A Song, written by one of the company for the celebration of the 4th of July at Milton [NH] and sung on that occasion by Maj. P.P. Furber." First line: "The Light hath broke o'er us, we hail its return" (*Portsmouth Journal of Literature and Politics*, 17 July 1824, 3).

Performances

District of Columbia

An "original ode" by S.R. Kramer titled "Blest Be the Day" was sung to the tune "Hail to the Chief" at the Columbia Typographical Society celebration (*National Intelligencer*, 7 July 1824, 3); a city parade included "the fine band of the Marine Corps playing patriotic airs, and was followed by the Marine Corps itself, in its beautiful uniform, which we have always admired, as uniting elegance and simplicity" (*Pittsfield Sun*, 5 August 1824, 1).

Maryland

Baltimore: "The performances at Monument Square, as well as the general arrangements of the committee, were chaste and highly appropriate to the occasion, and reflected great credit upon their taste, judgment, and talents." The exercises included a "fervent prayer," reading of the Declaration of Independence and an oration. "At intervals, the occasion was enlivened with national airs from an excellent band of music from Fort McHenry" ("The Celebration," *Baltimore Patriot*, 6 July 1824, 2); "The Regiment of 'National Guards,' accompanied by a number of invited guests, partook of a very excellent dinner on Monday, 5th July, ist. at Captain Smith's, on the Washington Road." Toasts drank were accompanied by the following music: Tune, Wreath the Bowl — Tune, Bright Be Their Dreems [sic] — Tune, Hail Columbia — Tune, The President's March — Tune, Star-Spangled Banner — Tune, United We Stand, Divided We Fall — Tune, White Cockade — Tune, Stephen's March[467] — Tune, March to the Battle Field — Tune, Hail to the Chief — Tune, To Ladies, Eyes Around Boys ("National Guards," *Baltimore Patriot*, 13 July 1824, 2); The First Baltimore Sharp Shooters "celebrated on the 5th inst. in the woods adjoining the residence of James Carroll, esq." Dinner included toasts "enlivened by the excellent music of the band attached to the Union Yagers, under the command of Capt. Deems, who politely volunteered their services on the occasion": Hail Columbia — Yankee Doodle — Ye Sons of Columbia — Washington's March — Hail to the Chief — Scots Wha Hae Wi Wallace Bled — Pleyel's Hymn — The Liberty Tree — O Breath Not His Name — Go Where Glory Waits Thee — Dirge to Gen. Wolfe — Let Fame Sound the Trumpet — Believe Me If All Those Endearing Young Charms.[468] "The following Song was written for the occasion, and sung by one of the company": First line: "Again the clarion trump of Fame" (Fourth of July: First Baltimore Sharp Shooters," *Baltimore Patriot*, 9 July 1824, 2).

Massachusetts

Boston: A procession was formed at Faneuil Hall and marched to the Second Universalist Meeting House where the "following order of exercises took place":

1st Music.
2d Hymn.
3d Prayer.
4th Ode.
5th Oration.
6th Ode.
7th Benediction.

A local newspaper reported "the performances by the choir were in their usual style of excellence." The dinner was held at Faneuil Hall and the following pieces of music accompanied the toasts: Yankee Doodle — Dirge — Hail Columbia — President's March — Adams & Liberty — Gov. Eustis' March[469] — Dirge — Wreaths to the Chieftain — To Liberty's Enraptured Sight — Peace and Plenty — The Muses — Triumph of reason — Go to the Devil and Shake Yourself ("Independence," *Independent Chronicle and Boston Patriot*, 7 July 1824, 2).

Natick: After a procession, at the meeting house ceremony "the choir of singers under the direction of Capt. Brett performed several pieces of music well adapted to the occasion, in a style of excellence seldom heard in the country" (*Village Register*, 8 July 1824, 2).

Newburyport: At a celebration the exercises included a "voluntary on the organ," "vocal music by the choir," and two original odes: "Forget not the valiant, who have honored our story" (first line), to the air "The Coronach" and "Oh! sublime was the warning America gave" (first line), by Caleb Cushing, to the air "Perry's Victory" (Broadside. "Order of exercises for the Celebration of the Forty-Eighth Anniversary of American Independence, July — 1824" in *An American Time Capsule: Three Centuries of Broadsides and Other Printed Ephemera*).

Northampton: "O Thou, Who from Oppression's Shore," a hymn sung at the Second Universalist Meeting House (*Boston Evening Gazette*, 10 July 1824, 2).

Pittsfield: At the Athenaeum of the Pittsfield Academy, "on the 5th instant ... the choir, under the direction of Mr. Warriner, performed in their more than usual stile of elegance" ("Literary Celebration," *Pittsfield Sun*, 15 July 1824, 3).

Quincy: At the meeting house, "services of the day were commenced with music by a band and a select choir of singers under the superintendance of Mr. Graupner[470] and Mr. Shaw."[471] At the dinner held at the town hall, "sentimental songs were sung by amateurs, assisted by a band of scientific musicians" ("Celebration of Independence at Quincy," *Independent Chronicle and Boston Patriot*, 14 July 1824, 2).

Salem: "The following will be the order of performances at the North Meeting House:

I.   Chant of Psalm 98.
II. Psalm 98. C. Metre.
III. Prayer.
IV. Declaration of Independence.
V.   Original ode (Composed for the occasion by Mr. Edwin Jocelyn.)[472] Tune. Columbia, Land of Liberty. First line: Hail! welcome morn, with rapture fraught!
VI. Oration.
VII. Hymn. C.M. Tune, Bowe.
VII. Benediction.

(*Essex Register*, 5 July 1824, 2; "Independence," *Salem Gazette*, 6 July 1824, 3); "The ancient and patriotic Corps, will celebrate the Day by a public parade, Dinner, &c. A considerable number of their fellow citizens will unite with them in the celebration. They will dine at the Salem Hotel, where an Address will be delivered, and the Declaration of Independence read.... We have been favored with a copy of the following excellent original Ode to be sung at this celebration: Ode, composed by a member of the corps of Independent Cadets, to be sung at the celebration of our National Independence, July 5, 1824. Tune — 'Adams and Liberty.'" First line: "Assembled to-day —

let us join heart and hand" ("Independent Cadets," *Essex Register*, 5 July 1824, 2).

Nebraska

Fort Atkinson: Near present-day Fort Calhoun, the 6th Army regiment and its band was stationed here and "the festivities of this gala day at the fort, were general, and conducted by all grades with the same decorum that is observed in less limited circles of the Union. After a reading of the Declaration of Independence and dinner, the following music accompanied the toasts: Hail Columbia — Yankee Doodle — Washington's March — Vive La Constitution — Scots who ha' vi' Wallace bled — Auld Lang Syne — Tyrolese Song of Liberty — Patriotic Diggers[473] — President's March — Tompkin's March — Pillar of Glory — Adams and Liberty — Liberty Tree — Soldiers Joy — America, Commerce & Freedom, Star-Spangled Banner — Cadet's March — Hail to the Chief— Hearts of Oak — American Star — Death of the Brave[474] — Hail Liberty, Supreme Delight — Speed the Plough — Love's Young Dream[475] (*Missouri Intelligencer*, 7 August 1824, 3).

New Hampshire

Amherst: "The hymns of praise and thanksgiving were appropriate, and were sang with animation" at "the proceedings in this town." The exercises were held at the Meeting House (*Farmers' Cabinet*, 10 and 17 July 1824, 2 and 2, respectively).

Concord: "The exercises at the meeting house [on July 5] were commenced by the Rev. Dr. M'Farland, by reading a select hymn, adapted to the occasion, which was performed by the Choir." "After dinner, the following sentiments, announced by Richard Bartlett, Esq. were drank, accompanied by the discharge of cannon, and the music of the band, interspersed with several songs, original and selected, spiritedly and well sung by Maj. J.D. Abbot." Songs sung included: Hail to the Country — Welcome Fayette[476] — by Maj. Abbot — Far o'er the Gloomy Waters ("Celebration at Concord," *New Hampshire Patriot & State Gazette*, 5 and 12 July 1824, 2 and 2, respectively). See **Publications** above.

Salisbury: At noon, a procession "proceeded under a military escort to the meeting house" where the exercises included a prayer, reading of the Declaration and an oration. "Several odes, hymns and psalms adapted to the occasion were sung by the Musical Society" ("Celebration at Salisbury, N. Hampshire," *New-Hampshire Patriot & State Gazette*, 12 July 1824, 2).

Sandbornton: A celebration on July 5 included a parade from Mason's Hall to the meeting house where "several pieces of select music [were] admirably performed." A dinner was accompanied "with the discharge of artillery and music from the instrumental band." Toasts were accompanied by the following music: Washington's March — United States' March — Soldier's Joy — President's March — Gen. Green's March — Massachusetts' March — Scotch Air ("Celebration at Sandbornton," *New Hampshire Patriot & State Gazette*, 12 July 1824, 2).

New Jersey

Flemington: "At 11 o'clock the procession formed in front of the Flemington Inn, whence it proceeded under an escort of Light Infantry and the band of martial music attached to Capt. M'Kinstry's volunteer corps, of New Germantown, to the Presbyterian Church, which had been handsomely decorated for the occasion." The exercises included no less than four pieces of music. "The band of martial music, conducted by Mr. Hyler, deserve much credit for their tasteful selection of tunes, and excellent performances." A dinner at the Flemington Inn included toasting, "accompanied by firing of cannon and musquetry, with appropriate music from the band" ("Flemington Celebration," *Trenton Federalist*, 2 August 1824, 2).

New York

Ballston Spa: At Sans Souci Hotel, "music from the band" as the toasts were presented: Tune, Yankee Doodle — Hail Columbia — Roslin Castle — Washington's March — Marseilles Hymn — Dead March in Saul — E'er Around the Huge Oak — United States Grand March — Speed the Plough — The Drum — Brave Yankee Boys [Truxton's Victory] — Soldier's Joy — New-York March — President's March — Governor's March — All Hail to the Morn[477] — Rural Felicity — Anacreon in Heaven — Hail Columbia — Money in Both Pockets — Scots Who Hae Wi Wallace Bled — Rogue's March — Pioneers March — Molly Hang the Kettle On (*Ballston Spa Gazette*, 13 July 1824, 2; *Saratoga Sentinel*, 20 July 1824, 2).

Ithaca: A procession gathered at the hotel and marched to the Presbyterian Meeting House for the day's exercises. Back at the hotel a dinner included toasts with the following music: Yankee Doodle — Hail Columbia — Portuguese Hymn — President's March — Star-Spangled Banner — Russian Dance — Yates' March[478] — Clinton's Grand Canal March[479] — Go to the Devil &c. — Hail to the Chief[480] — Chippewa — See, the Conquering Hero Comes! — Barney Leave the Girls Alone ("National Anniversary," *Ithaca Journal*, 7 July 1824, 2).

Mount Upton: Citizens of this town assembled at the church where after the presentation of the oration, "the 'Ode on Science'[481] was sung" ("Celebration at Mount Upton," *Watch-Tower*, 12 July 1824, 3).

New York: At Chatham Garden, a ballet titled the *Patriotic Volunteer* was performed at the new theater at Chatham Garden (*New York Daily Advertiser*, 5 July 1824, 2).

Saratoga Springs: At 11 A.M. a procession that included the Philadelphia Band of Musick gathered at the United States Hotel and marched through city streets to the Presbyterian Church where the exercises were as follows:

Musick from the Band.
Ode by the Choir, accompanied by the Band.

Reading of the Declaration of Independence.
Oration by W.L.F. Warren.
Benediction.

Later a dinner was held back at the Hotel for about 250 persons. Toasts were presented, "accompanied by music from the band and discharges of cannon": Hail Columbia — Yankee Doodle — Washington's Grand March — President's March — Gate's Victory — Knight Errant ("Fourth of July" and "American Independence," *Saratoga Sentinel*, 29 June and 6 July 1824, 3 and 3, respectively).

Pennsylvania

Columbia: At Cold Spring on Krentz Creek at an "elegant dinner," the event included a ceremony, toasts and the following music: tune, Hail Columbia — tune, Washington's March — tune, Auld Lang Syne — tune, Star-Spangled Banner — tune, Prime Bang Up — Tune, America, Commerce & Freedom — tune, Ode on Science — tune, Yankee Doodle — tune, Lady's Delight ("Celebration at Columbia," *Lancaster Journal*, 16 July 1824).

Rhode Island

Newport: A procession was scheduled in the morning and the exercises included "select music, by a choir, under direction of Mr. Benjamin Marsh, Jun." The choir's seating was in the front gallery of the meeting house (*Newport Mercury*, 3 July 1824, 3). See **Publications** above.

Providence:

In consequence of the 4th of July falling on Sunday, the Anniversary of American Independence will be celebrated at the Theatre on Monday, 5th inst. on which occasion, the interior will be handsomely and emblematically decorated. Round the Boxes will be displayed a number of transparencies, with the names of the most celebrated Naval and Military Heroes, with the five Presidents of the United States. On Monday evening, July 5, will be performed the extravaganza burletto of fun, frolic, flash and fashion, called *Tom and Jerry; or, Life in London*. To which will be added, for the only time, a national sketch, in 2 acts, called the *Capture of Major Andre*, and the preservation of West Point by the Yeomanry of America, taken from Dunlap's celebrated play of the *Glory of Columbus*, in course of which, a variety of national songs, airs, dances, &c. The piece concludes with a brilliantly illuminated temple, a "Dance with American Flags," by Mrs. Bray and Miss Clarke; and the curtain falls to the grand chorus of "Hail Columbia!" by the Company. ["Theatre," *Providence Gazette*, 3 July 1824, 3].

Vermont

Shaftsbury: The town celebrated on July 3 with a procession and exercises that included "a hymn well chosen for the occasion.... The choir of singers performed in a manner which deserves great applause,

and merits the thanks of the audience. The band of music discharged their part of the duties of the day with great credit to themselves, and the gratification of the assemblage" ("Our National Birth-Day," *Vermont Gazette*, 13 July 1824, 3).

West Virginia

Wheeling: At the Episcopal Church, "several national airs were sung by a select choir, accompanied by the church organ" ("Celebration of American Independence," *Wheeling Gazette*, 10 July 1824, 3).

1825

Publications

"'Independence and Adams. An Historical Ode.' For the forty-ninth anniversary of American independence. Tune — 'Anacreon in Heaven.'" First line: "All hail to the day when our nation was born" (*American Mercury*, 12 July 1825, 3).

"A National Song, for the Fourth of July, 1825. Tune — 'Hail to the Chief.'" First line: "Hail to the morning, so brilliantly beaming." Signed "N.B." ("The Rivulet," *Pittsfield Sun*, 21 July 1825, 1, from the *National Intelligencer*).

"Ode for the Fourth of July. Springfield, Mass. ["From the *Rockingham Gazette*."] First line: "Is there now a stranger" ("Poetry," *Middlesex Gazette*, 13 July 1825, 1).

"'Ode.' Written by John Everett, Esq. and sung at the Washington Society 4th of July Celebration in Boston." First line: "Hail to the day! When indignant a nation" ("Poetry," *New Hampshire Patriot & State Gazette*, 11 July 1825, 4).

Performances

District of Columbia

The U.S. Marine Band performed at the White House (*Virginia Herald*, 9 July 1825, 2).

Maine

Gorham: As a result of the loss of Dr. Dudley Folsom's house due to fire, the citizens came together to construct a new house for him on Independence Day. "At half past 7 o'clock, at the ringing and telling of the bell, a large concourse of men, women and children, was collected on the spot of the ruins, and having listened to the order of the day and a short address, united singing and prayer. The workmen then proceeded in their labour" ("Celebration of the Fourth of July," *Connecticut Courant*, 19 July 1825, 2).

Lincolnville: A procession that began "at the house of John Brooks, Esq." and marched to the Meeting House were

escorted by a company of infantry, under the command of Lieut. John P. Whitney, accompanied by a band of music.... The exercises there commenced with a hymn sung by a select choir, and a fervent and appropriate prayer by the Rev. Thos. M'Kinney; afterwards select music by the choir; then the Declaration of Independence was read by the Hon. Jonas Wheeler, and was succeeded by the old favorite song of "Ye sons of Columbia, who bravely have fought," sung by the choir in fine style, with a full chorus. An Oration replete with republican sentiments, and written in a neat and classical style, was then delivered by William J. Farley, Esq. and the exercises closed by the band's striking up the American Tune Yankee Doodle, "the oldest and gayest death song to despotism."

At the dinner "provided for at the House of Mr. Books," toasts "were drank, succeeded by the discharge of cannon and appropriate music by the band" ("Celebration," *Eastern Argus*, 14 July 1825, 2).

New Gloucester: "Democratic Republicans" of New Gloucester and adjoining towns, "preceded by an excellent band of music, marched to the Rev. Moseley's Meeting House. After a prayer, a hymn, "selected for the occasion," was sung. After a reading of the Declaration of Independence, another musical work was performed, "with great spirit and animation." After the oration, there was another "piece of music, performed in a manner, which did much credit to the judgment and taste of the Philo-Harmonic Society" ("Celebration of the Fourth of July at New-Gloucester," *Eastern Argus*, 12 July 1825, 2).

Maryland

Frederick: The "melody of sweet sounds" was heard at the dawn of day from two amateur bands of the town, who alternately played patriotic airs (*Frederick-Town Herald*, 9 July 1825, 3).

Massachusetts

Boston: John Everett's ode, "Hail to the Day," to the tune "Wreaths to the Chieftain" was performed at a meeting of the Washington Society (*Boston Courier*, 6 July 1825, 2). See **Publications** above; at the "Order of Services" held at the Old South Church, the music included a "voluntary on the organ" by S.P. Taylor and various choral works, the program ending with one by Haydn ("Independence," *Columbian Centinel*, 6 July 1825, 2; see also 2 July 1825); "A solo and chorus is to be sung this day at the Old South Church in Boston, in the following beautiful and appropriate lines (music by Stephenson)": first line, "Go forth to the mount — bring the olive branch home" (*Essex Register*, 4 July 1825, 2).

Danvers: The exercises were held in the South Meeting House and the dinner in Liberty Hall. "The following original ode is to be sung at the Danvers celebration. Tune — Adams & Liberty." First line: "All hail to the day when our forefathers met" (*Essex Register*, 4 July 1825, 2).

Dedham: At a cornerstone laying ceremony for the town's proposed new court house, music for the serv-ice at "Mr. Burgess' Meeting House" was provided by the Dedham Choir. The following were works scheduled for performance: "Hymn for 4th July. Tune, 'Lyons,' by Haydn. By J.B. Derby, Esq"[482] (first line: "Oh praise ye the Lord, prepare a new song"); "Hymn for Fourth of July, 1825. Tune,'Old Hundred' by Herman Mann"[483] (first line: "When on us pressed the tyrant's hand"); "Anthem [by] Dr. J. Clarke" (first line: "O give thanks unto the Lord"; "Ode on Science" (*Village Register*, 7 July 1825, 2–3).

Lanesborough: Union Society and local citizens met at the meeting house where "the singing, under the direction of Mr. G.R. Rockwell, was happy and satisfactory" ("Celebration at Lanesborough," *Pittsfield Sun*, 14 July 1825, 2).

Pittsfield: A "procession for the literary celebration of the young men of Pittsfield Academy" to the meeting house included an escort by the Berkshire Greys and the Brigade Band. Later at Merrick's Coffee House, a dinner, with toasts, discharges of cannon "and appropriate airs from the band" were provided to the assemblage (*Pittsfield Sun*, 7 July 1825, 2).

Salem: At the Salem Charitable Mechanic Association event, "a band of music" proceeded to the North Meeting House, where Mr. Pratt[484]opened the exercises by a "Voluntary on the Organ" and "the performance on the Organ, by Mr. Pratt, were creditable to his taste and skill; the anthem and hymns were sung by a powerful and well selected choir, with an effect seldom equaled; and the original Ode, composed by Mr. E.C. Jocelyn, adapted to the noble tune of Bruce's address to his army, and judiciously arranged for two voices alternately, with a chorus, was sung with admirable taste and execution by Messrs. Oliver and Kimball.[485] We never witnessed a more powerful sensation produced by a musical performance." At the dinner, held at the town hall, "the toasts were interspersed with appropriate music by the band, and many excellent songs, among which were two original Odes, composed for the occasion, one of which was published in our last — the other follows: 'Ode' tune — 'Bonny Boat.'" (first line: "Let ev'ry heart, with grateful zest"). The other "original ode" was sung to the "tune — 'Scots wha hae.'" (first line: "Sacred home of freedom still!"); "The following Song, composed for the occasion by a gentleman of this town, is to be sung at the Town Hall this day. Tune — 'Wreaths for the Chieftains'"; first line: "Welcome the day, when our Fathers, undaunted" (*Salem Gazette*, 28 June 1825, 2; "Celebration in Salem" and "Fourth of July," *Essex Register*, 4 and 7 July 1825, 2 and 2, respectively).

New Hampshire

Deering: "The day was ushered in by the firing of cannon. Three military companies voluntarily turned out on the occasion, attended with a band of music from Deering and Hillsborough." After a procession from the house of Russell Tubbs to the Meeting House, the exercises included "pieces of music well performed" ("Celebration at Deering," *New-Hamp-shire Patriot & State Gazette*, 18 July 1825, 2).

New York

Ballston Spa: After a procession by "a large collection of citizens and strangers" to the meeting house, "the exercises in the church, were very interesting. We were particularly gratified with the performance of the choir, under the direction of Mr. John Smith, of this village, who, in his usual happy style, performed the 'Pastoral Glee' to the admiration of all present." Later at the dinner held at the Sans Souci Hotel, "where about 200 of our citizens, and a number of visitants of the Spa drew around a sumptuous table ... toasts were drank under the discharge of artillery" and the following musical works: Yankee Doodle — Hail Columbia — President's March — Governor's March — Washington's March — Logan Waters — Grand Canal March — Genius of Liberty — Anacreon in Heaven — Back Side Albany — All Hail to the Morn — Speed the Plough — Giles Scroggin's Ghost (*Ballston Spa Gazette*, 12 July 1825, 2).

Ithaca: "Between eleven and twelve o'clock, the procession formed at the Hotel, in the order prescribed by the Committee of Arrangements, and preceded by an excellent band of music and escorted by the Ithaca Guards and Capt. Vickery's Company of Artillery, under the direction of Adjt. W.R. Gregory as Marshal, and Capt. S.B. Munn, Jr. Deputy Marshal, marched to the Presbyterian Meeting-house," where "the whole exercises were interspersed with appropriate odes, and select Psalms, sung in a most excellent and impressive style by a choir under the direction of Mr. Rollo, aided by the powerful voices of Mrs. and Miss Rollo"[486] ("National Anniversary," *Ithaca Journal*, 6 July 1825, 2).

Rhode Island

Newport: A procession gathered at the State House and among those marching was the Columbian Band. The exercises at the Second Baptist Meeting House included "select music by a choir [that sat in the front gallery] under the direction of Messrs. Benjamin Marsh, Jun[487]. and James Coggeshall" ("National Anniversary," *Newport Mercury*, 2 July 1825, 3).

1826

The anniversary of the signing of the Declaration of Independence was celebrated as a grand festival for the nation's first 50 years and as an expression of optimism for the future. Composers, poets, and writers utilized their artistic skills to produce new works that brought honor to this jubilee of freedom. Large crowds filled churches, meeting houses and theaters to observe the holiday and to share in the joyful ceremonies. In New York, "a new patriot piece" titled *Jubilee, or the Triumph of Freedom* was performed at the

city theater. In Providence, Rhode Island, the popular play *The Point of Honor, Or, A School for Soldiers* was presented with additional patriotic songs to highlight the Fourth. Baltimore composers Christopher Meineke and H.N. Gilles and Norfolk's C.A. Dacosia wrote new patriotic instrumental works. Poets in other cities wrote new lyrics for odes, hymns, and songs that were premiered. Stephen Foster, an icon of American song writers, was born on this day. Numerous events and naming opportunities were later staged on the Fourth in his honor.

Publications

"Adams and Liberty." First line: "Ye sons of Columbia, who bravely have fought." *Boston Commercial Gazette*, 3 July 1826, 2.[488]

"The following beautiful Hymn, written by a lady, and set to music by Mr. T.B. White, was sung at Newburyport, at the jubilee celebration." First line: "Who, when darkness gather'd o'er us" (*Essex Register*, 13 July 1826, 1).

"The following beautiful Ode and Hymn, written for the occasion, by a lady[489] of this city, will be sung at the celebration this day. 'Ode for the Fourth of July, 1826.' Adapted to the music of 'Scots, wha hae wi' Wallace bled.'" First line: "Clime! Beneath whose genial sun." "'Hymn,' on the fiftieth Anniversary of American Independence." First line: "Break forth — break forth in raptur'd song" (*American Mercury*, 4 July 1826, 3; *Connecticut Courant*, 10 July 1826, 3).

"The following Ode was composed by Mr. Samuel Woodworth, of New-York, a member of the N.Y. Typographical Society,[490] and sung before the Society at their late celebration on the 4th inst. Ode ['Printers' Jubilee']. Air — 'Hail to the Chief.'" First line: "Hark! 'twas the trumpet of Freedom that sounded" (*Boston Commercial Gazette*, 10 July 1826, 2; *Essex Register*, 13 July 1826, 1; *Richmond Enquirer*, 14 July 1826, 4; *Middlesex Gazette*, 19 July 1826, 1; *Republican Star and General Advertiser*, 21 November 1826, 4; Woodward, *Melodies, Duets, Trios, Songs and Ballads*, 140–41).

"The following Song written by a native of our town [Portland ME], of whom we are all proud, now resident at a distance, was sung with good effect by Major [J.F.] Deering. Tune — Auld lang syne." First line: "There was a land of Yankees true" (*Eastern Argus*, 7 July 1826, 2).

The Fourth of July. A Grand Parade March[491] (Baltimore: John Cole, 1826). Composed for a full military band and arranged for the piano forte by H.N. Gilles.

"Fourth of July, 1826. Tune ... Scots Wha' hae.'" First line: "Hail! glorious day! when freemen stand" ("Poetry," *Norwich Courier*, 28 June 1826, 4).

"Hymn for Fourth July —1826." First line: "Thee, we approach, Almighty King." By the Rev. Samuel Willard (1776–1859). Broadside. Copy in Memorial Hall Museum, Pocumtuck Valley Memorial Association, Deerfield, MA.

"Hymn for the Fourth of July." First line: "Arise, and hail the jubilee" (*Universalist Magazine*, 8 July 1826, 12).

"'Hymn to Liberty.' In commemoration of the half century celebration of American Independence. Written by Mrs. K.A. Ware,[492] and sung at the Lechmere Point [Massachusetts] celebration.— Tune, 'Rise Columbia.'" First line: "When o'er the somber face of night" ("Anniversary Exercises," *Boston Commercial Gazette*, 6 July 1826, 2; "Poetry," *Essex Register*, 10 July 1826, 1).

"Hymn, written by Mrs. H.L. Sigourney, of Hartford, and recommended to be sung in churches where collections were taken up in aid of the American Colonization Society, on the late jubilee." First line: "Stretch forth thine hand, thou lov'd of heaven" ("Poetry," *Essex Register*, 10 July 1826, 1).

"Hymn, written by the Rev. Dr. Holmes, and sung at the Cambridge celebration." First line: "With thankful heart and holy song." (*Boston Commercial Gazette*, 10 July 1826, 4.)

The Jubilee March, and Quick Step. Composed for the celebration of the Fourth of July, 1826, by C. Meineke. Baltimore: John Cole, 1826.

"[The following Ode, written for the occasion, by J.G. Percival,[493] was sung at the celebration in Berlin, on the 4th inst.] Ode for the Fourth of July, 1826." First line: "Bright day! when first the song." [Berlin, CT] (*American Mercury*, 11 July 1826, 3; *New-Hampshire Patriot & State Gazette*, 24 July 1826, 4).

"Ode for the Fourth of July, 1826. By a lady of Hartford, (Conn.)." First line: "Clime! beneath whose genial sun" (*Village Register*, 13 July 1826, 1).

"Ode for the Fourth of July. The following ode is from the gifted pen of Hon. Caleb Cushing, one of the senators from this county.[494] It merits a distinguished place among our national odes. We re-publish it from the *Newburyport Herald* of 1822." First line: "Hail, freemen of America" ("Selected Poetry," *Essex Register*, 3 July 1826, 1).

"Ode, in commemoration of the half-century of American independence, written by Thomas Wells." Broadside, [Boston, 1826].

"Ode— written for the Jubilee Celebration, and sung at the Exchange Coffee House. 'Fifty Years Ago!'" First line: "Fifty years have rolled away" (*Boston Commercial Gazette*, 10 July 1826, 4; *Essex Register*, 13 July 1826, 1).

"Odes to be Sung at Springfield at the Celebration of American Independence, July 4th, 1826." Ode (first line: "All hail, Columbia's sons, all hail!"; Ode (first line: "High tow'ring through the skies." Broadside, Springfield, NH, 1826. Copy in Brown University.

"Patriotic ode, written by himself, for the 4th of July, 1826, being the fiftieth or 'jubilee' anniversary of the Declaration of our National Independence.[495] By Samuel B. Beach. Tune 'Bruce's Address.'" First line: "Joyfully we wake the lay" (*National Intelligencer*, 9 July 1858, 2).

"Song— Fourth of July 1826. Tune—'Exile of Erin.'" First line: "When the champions of freedom first o'er the rude billow" (*Daily National Journal*, 4 July 1826).

Performances

Connecticut

Berlin: After a procession at 11 A.M. from Mr. Wilcox's Inn to the Meeting House, "the singing of the 18th Psalm by the united choirs of the town, and an appropriate Prayer by the Rev. Mr. Goodrich, opened the services of the day." Included also was "an Ode, composed for the occasion, by Dr. Percival" ("Celebration at Berlin," *Connecticut Courant*, 17 July 1826, 3; *American Mercury*, 18 July 1826, 3).

Hartford: At the Central Church, the exercises included a song titled "Sound an Alarm" (first line: "Sound an alarm, your silver trumpets sound"), an Ode and Hymn (see **Publications** above), and the "Grand Hallelujah Chorus" (Handel). (*Connecticut Courant*, 10 July 1826, 3.); the *American Mercury* reported that "the following song was composed for the occasion by a gentleman of this city": "Qui Transtulit Sustinet" (first line: "The warriour may twine round his temples the leaves"); the *Essex Register* identified the author as "Mr. Brainard, editor of the *Connecticut Mirror*") ("National Jubilee," *American Mercury*, 11 July 1826, 3; *Essex Register*, 13 July 1826, 1; "In Hartford," *Richmond Enquirer*, 21 July 1826, 2).

Lebanon: "A large procession, civil and military" included "a band of music which proceeded to the brick meeting house" where the ceremony was held. "The singing, led by Mr. Chandler of East Hartford, was in a superior style of excellence" (*Norwich Courier*, 12 July 1826, 2).

Lisbon: "At 10'clock P.M. a very large and respectable party of ladies and gentlemen assembled at the house of John Brown, and under the direction of Elijah Rose as marshal, proceeded to Mr. Nelson's meeting-house. The choir having raised their voices in a song of praise, the Rev. minister of the parish addressed the author of life, love, and liberty in an appropriate prayer." After an oration, an anthem was performed and music from a band ended the exercises. Later at a dinner held at the Assembly Room, "the melody of instruments" accompanied the toasts ("July Fourth at Lisbon," *Norwich Courier*, 12 July 1826, 3).

Norfolk: At the exercises held at the Meeting House, "sacred music was performed by the choir.... To the directors of the music and those engaged in its performance, the attentive regard of a gratified audience, must afford the most satisfactory commendation" ("Celebration at Norfolk," *Connecticut Courant*, 24 July 1826, 3).

Windham: A procession of "citizens, without distinction of party, and a number from the adjacent towns," gathered at the Bildad Curtiss Inn and marched "under an escort of martial music to the Meeting House" where the exercises were held. Later back at the inn a dinner was served and "toasts were drank and the company regaled with appropriate music": Tune, Hail Columbia — Serenade — Washington's Grand March — Alps March — The New Rigged Ship — Fresh and Strong — Civean March — Yankee Doodle — No Luck — Virginia Reel — Auld Lang Syne — American Eagle — Patty Carey ("National Jubilee," *Norwich Courier*, 12 July 1826, 2); "The fiftieth anniversary of American independence was celebrated in Scotland, Second Society, in Windham, by gentlemen and ladies." At 9 A.M. 400 persons gathered at the bower and marched

> escorted to the church by Capt. Hez. M. Baker's Company of Infantry, completely equipped in uniform, with good martial music, and while the procession was passing into the church, music by the band.

Included in the services was

> an Oratorio given by Mr. E. Tucker's School: 1st Tune, "O Come Let Us Sing Unto the Lord." 2d, Old Hundred. 3d, Walworth. 4th Braintree, 5th, to conclude, "Strike the Cymbal."[496] Then the procession was formed to march from the church to the table, as follows: Infantry, Gentlemen, Mr. Tucker's School, Ladies, President and Vice Presidents, Clergy, Band of Music. When opposite of the table, the procession opened to the right and left, and the band then played them to the table, where upwards of 400 partook of a sumptuous dinner, provided by Mr. R. Webb. ["Fourth of July, 1826," *Norwich Courier*, 12 July 1826, 3].

District of Columbia

The U.S. Marine Band performed in the U.S. Capitol ceremony, standing on the "interior spiral staircase" in the "Eastern Gallery" (*National Intelligencer*, 4 July 1826, 3).

Maine

Freeport: A parade proceeded to the Congregational Meeting House where the exercises took place. "An Ode composed by R [obert] R. Kendall,[497] Esq. for the occasion, and adapted to the tune of 'Auld Lang Syne,' was sung by the Freeport Musical Society,' whose performances would stand in competition with those of vastly superior advantages" ("Celebration at Freeport," *Eastern Argus*, 11 July 1826, 2).

Portland: After a parade, the exercises scheduled at "Mr. Jenkins' Meeting House in Congress Street" included the performance of two anthems and a hymn (*Eastern Argus*, 30 June 1826, 2).

Maryland

Baltimore: "The fiftieth anniversary of American independence was celebrated by a large number of the citizens of Pennsylvania ... at the Washington Hotel in Gay Street.... They partook of an excellent dinner [and] toasts were drunk, accompanied by an excellent band of music": Tune, Hail Columbia — Air, Star-Spangled Banner — Yankee Doodle — Washington's March — Jefferson's March — Auld Lang Syne — President's March — Governor's March — Jackson's March — Hail to the Chief — Hearts of Oak — [America] Commerce and Freedom — Come Haste to the Wedding ("Pennsylvania Celebration in the City of Baltimore," *Baltimore Patriot*, 6 July 1826, 2).

Massachusetts

Adams: A procession to the meeting house was accompanied by "martial music under the direction of Col. Isaac Howland and Capt. Daniel Jenks, marshals of the day." "During the performances in the church, several anthems were sung with great credit to the chorister, Mr. Wells, and all those that participated in the science of music — the performance was never surpassed in this town, and perhaps was equal to any similar performance in this country" ("Celebration at Adams," *Pittsfield Sun*, 20 July 1826, 2).

Boston: The "grand jubilee celebration" held by the Republican citizens at the Central Universalist Church where "several original odes and hymns, prepared for the occasion [were] sung by the choir of the church." One of the odes was written by Mrs. K.A. Ware and set to the tune "Anacreon in Heaven" (first line: "When through the dark clouds of political night") and a hymn was written by Mrs. A.M. Wells[498] and set to the tune "Old Hundred" (first line: "When, spurning Power's despotic yoke"). The Brigade Band provided music for the day (*Boston Commercial Gazette*, 29 June and 6 July 1826, 2 and 2, respectively; *Salem Gazette*, 7 July 1826, 2; *Essex Register*, 10 July 1826, 1.); at Faneuil Hall, toasts were drunk "interspersed with patriotic songs": Music, Sound the loud timbrel — Dirge — Auld Lang Syne ("Celebration at Boston," *Richmond Enquirer*, 21 July 1826, 2); at the Old South Meeting House, the exercises included "several pieces of music from a large and select choir of amateurs" (*Boston Commercial Gazette*, 3 July 1826, 2). See **Publications** above.

Franklin: The Franklin Artillery and the Franklin Cadets, "together with a large concourse of citizens of that and the neighboring towns" attended the exercises which included a "choir of singers, under the direction of Mr. William Metcalf" ("National Jubilee," *Village Register*, 6 July 1826, 3).

Manchester: After a collation at the town hall at 10 A.M., the town citizens marched, accompanied by military units and "a handsome band of music to the meeting house." During the exercises, "several select pieces of choice music were performed under the direction of Mr. J[ohn] C. Long, in a style which would have done credit to any choir in one of our populous towns." Later at the dinner a toast was offered by Long, who was also a member of the committee of arrangements, to Gov. Troup[499] ("Celebration at Manchester," *Essex Register*, 10 July 1826, 3).

Newburyport: "A hymn and ode, both original, were sung" at a dinner with 500 persons present ("In Newburyport," *Richmond Enquirer*, 21 July 1826, 2).

Pittsfield: A procession that included "surviving

patriots of the revolution" marched to the church, where "the singing, led by Mr. Lyman Warriner, was in a style of unusual excellence" ("National Jubilee!" *Pittsfield Sun*, 13 July 1826, 2).

Quincy: After a parade and flag presentation, the exercises at the meeting house "were opened by the Jubilee Anthem." The following "Ode" by George Washington Adams,[500] set to the tune "Adams and Liberty" was sung "with great point" and "closed the interesting services": first line, "Long ages of darkness man's soul had opprest" (*Columbian Sentinel*, 22 July 1826, 1; *Essex Register*, 24 July 1826, 2;); "Lord Byron's Hebrew Melody" (anthem): first line, "Go forth to the Mount, bring the olive-branch home."

Salem: A procession of military companies, "distinguished public characters," citizens, and veterans of the Revolution assembled at Washington Square and "a rich band of music gave a charm to the scene." At the Meeting House,

the services commenced by music on the Organ, performed in a superior style by Mr. Wilson. An animated anthem was then performed by the Mozart Society,[501] in the following words:

Lead on! Lead on! Judah disdains
The galling load of hostile chains.[502]

A fervent and impressive Prayer was offered by the Rev. Dr. [James] Flint, after which another Anthem, by Haydn, was performed, as follow:

Sing his praises, th' Almighty Conqueror's praises,
He the tyrant foe overthrew,
Eternal praises are his due.

The Hon. John Pickering then read the Declaration of Independence, accompanying it by an Address of considerable length. The following excellent Ode, written for the occasion by the Rev. Dr. Flint, was then sung by two gentlemen of the Mozart Society, accompanied by the whole choir in the chorus. [First line]: "When God his image stamp'd divine."

The Oration, by the Rev. Henry Colman, followed. A beautiful solo and chorus, by Stevenson, was then performed, in the following words. [First line]: "Go forth to the Mount, bring the olive-branch home."[503]

The local newspaper also commented "the music was appropriate, and executed in a style of superior excellence. The ode was sung admirably, and the bass solos in the closing anthem were given with entire effect." The dinner at Washington Square was attended by 700 persons and included toasts "accompanied by discharges of artillery, appropriate music, and cheerings." The music performed included: Sweet Home — Hail Columbia — President Adams's March — Massachusetts Quick Step — Trirolian Dirge — Lafayette's March[504] — Wreaths for the Chieftain — Yankee Doodle — Speed the Plough — Bonny Boat — Shuttle Hornpipe — Canal March — Here's a health to All Good Lasses. That evening, during the exhibition [of the fireworks], the excellent band

enlivened the hours with many appropriate pieces of music" ("National Jubilee" and "Town Celebration," *Essex Register*, 26 June and 3 and 6 July 1826, 1, 2 and 2, respectively; *Salem Gazette*, 7 July 1826, 2); a "Religious Celebration" was held at the Tabernacle Church with the following "order of exercises" that began at 4 o'clock:

I. Prayer, and reading of scriptures, by the Rev. Dr. Bolles.
II. Anthem.
III. Prayer, by the Rev. Brown Emerson.
IV. Hymn.
V. Address, by the Rev. S.P. Williams, of Newburyport.
VI. Collection, to aid the funds of the American Colonization Society.
VII. Anthem.
VIII. Concluding prayer.
IX. Doxology.
X. Benediction.
[*Essex Register*, 3 July 1826, 2].

Worcester: The Harmonic Society under the direction of Mr. Perry performed an anthem and several other works at the South Meeting House (*Massachusetts Yeoman*, 8 July 1826, 2).

Worthington: At the meeting house, "a national Ode and other appropriate music was sung by the choir" ("Celebration at Worthington," *Pittsfield Sun*, 27 July 1826, 2).

New Hampshire

Andover: A procession through city streets included "a band of music who voluntarily turned out on the occasion." At the meeting house, among the exercises were "several pieces of music [that] were performed by the choir." After the oration, "the exercises were closed by an appropriate Anthem by the choir whose performances merited the applause of the audience." At the dinner, toasts were accompanied "with excellent musick" ("Celebration at Andover," *New-Hampshire Patriot & State Gazette*, 24 July 1826, 2).

Boscawen: At "a house of divine worship," the ceremony ended with the following song, "composed for the occasion, by J.C. jun.": "A Song of Deliverance. For the Fourth of July. Tune —'Emmanuel.'" First line: "When first in Columb'a our fathers did land" ("Birth Day of Freedom," *New-Hampshire Patriot & State Gazette*, 24 July 1826, 3).

Hinsdale: The exercises included "sacred music by the Hinsdale Choir" (*New-Hampshire Sentinel*, 4 August 1826, 4).

Keene: At the Meeting House, the exercises began with a "Voluntary by the Musical Society, led by Mr. E. Briggs, Jr.,[505] 'Sing, O Heavens, and Be Joyful O Earth,' &c," a Hymn, "music, 'Sound the Loud Timbrel.'" The dinner at a bower included "music by the band" ("Celebration of Independence," *New-Hampshire Sentinel*, 7 July 1826, 3).

New Ipswich: At a flag presentation at the meeting house, "the exercises were accompanied with appropriate music, which was indeed of a high order" ("Fourth of July," *Farmer's Cabinet*, 22 July 1826, 3).

Portsmouth: At the meeting house, "some appropriate odes were sung" and "other music." Some music that day was provided by "Mr. Papanti[506] on the French Horn, and to the exquisite singing of his wife ... Mr. P. played on the Horn with surpassing skill, drawing forth every note of which that difficult instrument is capable with the utmost sweetness and delicacy. Of the exquisite singing of Mrs. Papanti we express the universal opinion of her audience that, in this town, nothing to compare with it has ever been heard. Her voice unites uncommon power with unrivalled sweetness, to these rare qualifications she adds a high degree of science, and these high powers are put forth with an unconsciousness and entire simplicity which give an admirable effect to her performances." According to another report, at the meeting house, "several suitable Odes were sung at intervals by a full choir, accompanied by the new organ, under the direction of Mr. Elliot." Yet another newspaper reported that "the music at the meeting house will be under the direction of Mr. Lewis Elliot"[507] ("National Jubilee 50th Anniversary of American Independence" and "The Jubilee Celebration," *Portsmouth Journal of Literature & Politics*, 1 and 8 July 1826, 2–3, and 3, respectively; "National Jubilee," *New-Hampshire Gazette*, 11 July 1826, 2).

Weare: A reporter wrote that at the ceremony held at the East Meeting House, "the closing scene was finished as began with some of the sweetest tones from the female tongue, accompanied by the band, that the writer has ever heard." Following the exercises, the residents marched accompanied by music to the place where a collation was served ("Celebration at Weare," *New Hampshire Patriot*, 24 July 1826, 2).

New York

Cooperstown: The procession formed on Main Street and included various military companies, music, and "citizens and strangers." The group then marched to the Presbyterian Meeting House where the exercises included music, an "original ode" and "national air" ("Freedom's Jubilee," *Watch-Tower*, 3 July 1826, 2).

Fishkill: A parade "headed by a body of cavalry" marched through town, ending at the Old Dutch Church. The assemblage entered the church. "A band of music occupied the whole front of the gallery, playing "Hail to the Chief."[508]

Lisbon: At "Mr. Nelson's Meeting House ... the choir ... raised their voices in a song of praise ... followed by an anthem, and closed by music from the band" ("July Fourth at Lisbon," *Norwich Courier*, 12 July 1826, 3, from the *New York Journal*).

Pennsylvania

Carlisle: "In front of the meeting house a handsome arch in honor of the day had been constructed by our ingenious mechanics, and was tastefully dec-

orated with laurel and flowers, over which waived the flag of the United States, and that of Pennsylvania." A band processed under the arch playing "Hail Columbia" (*Democratic Republican and Agricultural Register*, 5 July 1826, 2–3).

Philadelphia: "Is There a Heart" performed by a band at a dinner celebration by "friends of Andrew Jackson" held in the Masonic Hall (*Richmond Enquirer*, 14 July 1826, 4).

Pittsburgh: The Democratic Republicans celebrated at Elliot's Spring and toasts accompanied by music were drank after the dinner: Tune, Yankee Doodle — Hail Columbia — Washington's March — All the Way to Boston — Star-Spangled Banner — Hail to the Chief — Auld Lang Syne — Bruce's Address — Penn, March — The Tempest — Duncan Davy — Jesse the Flower of Dunblane; another group of Democratic Republicans celebrated at Foster's Grove about two miles outside of Pittsburgh. After dinner toasts were drank "accompanied by appropriate music"; the Pittsburgh Light Artillery celebrated "on the west side of the Allegheny River, opposite the city." At the dinner that was served by E.G. Nelson "in his garden in very handsome style," the following music was performed: Tune, Hail Columbia — Washington's March — Vive La Convention — Yankee Doodle — President's March — Governor's March — Auld Lang Syne — The Star-Spangled Banner — Columbia, Land of Liberty — Scots Wha' hae wi' Wallace Bled — Rejoice Columbia — Haste to the Wedding — Remember Thee! yes while There's Life in This Heart — Decator's Victory — Life Let Us Cherish — Thou of an Independent Mind — Hail to the Chief — Forget Not the Field Where They Perished — Sublime Was the Warning which Liberty Spoke — Wae to My Heart — Paddy Was Up to the Gauger — Dundlady of France — The Dead March in Saul ("The Jubilee" and "The Fourth of July," *Pittsburgh Mercury*, 12 July 1826).

Rhode Island

Newport: A procession from the Parade took place to the State House "which on this occasion was brilliantly decorated." Included in the exercises was a reading of the Declaration of Independence by Major John Handy, "who read the same Declaration, on that identical spot 50 years before, previous to again reading it.... Immediately after Major H. had concluded, an excellent Ode, composed by G. Wanton, Esq. was sung to the tune of 'Old Hundred,' in a masterly style, to a concourse of some thousands." A newspaper reported that "the odes were sung in the first style of excellence. The Columbian Band performed in their best manner.... In the evening, the State House was illuminated in a most brilliant manner, and the music by the Newport Band, was superior to any we have heard in this town, for years." Another report stated that the "select music by the choir [was] under the direction of B. Marsh, Jr. and J.B. Newton." That evening the "State House [was] brilliant illuminated, and the Columbian Band [performed] on the occasion, a new and appropriate selection of music. Yet another report stated that "two Odes, by Geo. W. Patten,[509] [were] finely executed by the choir, under the superintendence of Mr. Benj. Marsh, Jr." ("National Jubilee," *Rhode Island Republican*, 29 June 1826, 2; "Fiftieth Anniversary," *Newport Mercury*, 8 July 1826, 2; *Providence Patriot & Columbian Phenix*, 15 July 1826, 2).

Providence: At the Theatre, "a pathetic play, called *The Point of Honor, Or, A School for Soldiers*" to include "the celebrated 'Gun Hornpipe,' by Mrs. Spooner; a patriotic recitation, called 'The Standard of Liberty, by Miss Powell'; a patriotic song, called 'Columbia's Glory,' by Mr. Williamson; a 'National Hornpipe,' in character of a young American midshipman, by Miss C. McBride. To conclude with a laughable farce, called *The Spoil'd Child*" (*Providence Patriot & Columbian Phenix*, 4 July 1826, 3); militia, town citizens, and residents from Pawtucket paraded[510] to the meeting house that was "filled to excess." The Psallonian Society, with Mr. [Oliver] Shaw's accompaniment on the organ sang an ode (first line: "When Freedom moved to war") written by Joseph L. Tillinghast and set to an "original tune" by Shaw. The piece was reported as performed "in a very spirited manner." The Psallonian Society closed the exercises with singing an Ode (first line: "Joy, joy! for free millions now welcome the morn") by Albert G. Greene[511] and sung to the tune "Song of Miriam" (*Providence Patriot & Columbian Phenix*, 8 July 1826, 1–2; "Poetry," *Essex Register*, 10 July 1826, 1).

Tennessee

Knoxville: A song "All hail to the day when a people indignant" (first line), composed for the occasion, was sung (*Knoxville Register*, 12 July 1826, 2).

Virginia

Hampden Sydney College: The students met in the College Chapel for the exercises followed by "a dinner richly prepared by Col. Burwell, the College Steward." Toasts were offered accompanied by the following music: Music, Hail Columbia — Hail to the Chief[512] — Music, Stamp the Devil's Eyes Out (*Richmond Enquirer*, 18 July 1826, 2).

Norfolk: After a procession of the Independent Volunteers and other military companies, as well as participants in the ensuing ceremonies, the group entered Christ Church for the exercises. "The Mozart Band performed a soft and beautiful air," followed by a prayer by the Rev. Bishop Moore. "After the prayer, the 'thrilling thunders of the organ resounded through the aisles'; a grand military overture, composed for the occasion, by Mr. C.A. Dacosia, organist of the church, was performed by him in his best style, and gave full effect to the various powers of that fine instrument" (*Richmond Enquirer*, 14 July 1826, 1).

Petersburg: At the Petersburg Theatre after the Declaration was read and oration presented, "appro-

priate music from an excellent band, added a zest to the literary feast at the theatre." "At half past three o'clock, about two hundred citizens sat down to a plentiful and excellent dinner at Poplar Spring." The following pieces of music accompanied the toasts: tune, Hail Columbia — Yankee Doodle — Marseilles Hymn — Reville du Peuple — Ca Ira — Wash. March — Jefferson's March — Hail to the Chief— Dirge — Star-Spangled Banner — Hull's Victory — America, Commerce and Freedom — Madison's March — The Watchful Centinel — Scots wha hae — Tyrolese Song of Liberty — March in Bluebeard — Pillar of Glory — Come Haste to the Wedding ("The Jubilee," *Richmond Enquirer*, 11 July 1826, 1).

Staunton: At a dinner held at the Eagle Tavern, toasts were drank "amid the sweet breathings of appropriate music, and repeated discharges from a piece of artillery" ("Celebration at Staunton," *Richmond Enquirer*, 18 July 1826, 4).

Winchester: The early hours in Winchester had crowded streets and the sounds of "exhilarating fife and martial drum" music. At the Lutheran Church, "the services were opened by a select choir, who sung the Jubilee hymn with fine effect." Later at a dinner, "Jefferson and Liberty" was performed (*Richmond Enquirer*, 18 July 1826, 4).

West Virginia

Martinsburg: A group of "from eighty to an hundred individuals, of all parties, partook in harmony of the festivities" at a "pleasant grove on the farm of Capt. Matthew Ranson." After the dinner "toasts were drank, and discharges of Musquetry and soul-stirring music" (*Richmond Enquirer*, 18 July 1826, 4).

1827

The notable event this year was the emancipation of slaves in the state of New York that went into effect on July 4. Musical celebrations took place in New York City, New Haven, Connecticut, and likely other towns whose celebrations were not reported.

Publications

"Fourth of July" to the tune "Scots wha hae wi' Wallace bled." First line: "Day, by freemen hardly won" (From the *National Journal* as printed in *New-Hampshire Patriot & State Gazette*, 16 July 1827, 4).

"Hymn.[513] The following was sung at a meeting of colored people, on the 4th of July last, in New York." First line: "Afric's sons, awake, rejoice!"

"Independence Ode[514] sung at the celebration of our national independence, in Danville, Kentucky." By "Velasco." Tune, "Ode to Science." First line: "When Freedom, in the Eastern world."

"Ode." First line: "This day is freedom's jubilee" (*Essex Register*, 4 July 1827, 1).

"Ode." By R.S. Coffin. First line: "When freedom midst the battle storm" (*Essex Register*, 4 July 1827, 1).

"Ode for the Fourth of July, 1827. Sung at the Boston Exchange Coffee House on Wednesday last." First line: "To the sages who spoke — to the Heroes who bled"[515] (*Essex Register*, 9 July 1827, 1).

"Ode, written for the late national anniversary, and sung at Morristown, N.J. The Starry Banner. By Wm. P.M. Wood." First line: "Oh! loudly raise your grateful strains" (*Essex Register*, 12 July 1827, 1).

"Odes, sung at the celebration in this town [Newport, RI] on the 4th of July. 'Ode'— by G. Wanton, tune —'Charing.'" (First line: "Stand in unconquer'd might."); "'Ode'— by G.W. Patten, air —'Auld Lang Syne.'" (First line: "What sound is that, that wildly swells."); "'Ode'— by Alvan Barnaby, air —'Knight Errant.'" (First line: "When o'er the sable cloud of War."); "'Anthem — Strike the Cymbal.' Suited to the occasion, by G. Wanton." (First line: "Strike the cymbal") (*Rhode Island Republican*, 12 July 1827, 4.)

"The 'Roll of the Brave.' Tune —'Fie, let us a' to the Bridal,' &c. Washington, July 5, 1825. Gentlemen-Enclosed are a few lines intended as an Essay towards making a National Song. It was composed and sung some time since at a celebration of the national festival in this city. By giving it a place, in fair legible type, (such as Revolutionary officers can read) among your other articles of national intelligence, you will much oblige your old friend. Lycurgus the Younger." First line: "Come let us rejoice on this day, sirs" ("From the *National Intelligencer*," and republished in "Poetry," *New-Hampshire Patriot & State Gazette*, 16 July 1827, 4).

Performances

Connecticut

New Haven: "The African population of this city celebrated the 5th inst. in concordance with their brethren of New York on account of the abolition of slavery in that State." At the African Church, the exercises including "the singing of hymns." Following that the assemblage marched "to well-timed music" to "the foot of East Rock" for a repast (*Essex Gazette*, 14 July 1827, 3).

Norwich Falls: At daybreak reveille was played "by a band of martial music under Major Manning." At Morse's Hotel, a procession with "an excellent band of martial music" proceeded through city streets to the "3d District School House where they were joined by about 30 scholars, under their teacher, Miss Rodgers, and also a large choir of female singers, who were richly dressed in white." They marched to the Methodist Chapel where "the public services then commenced with an hymn sung by the choir, which was followed by singing another, given out by the Rev. Mr. Arnold." Later "after the exercises had been closed by the singing of some set pieces by the choir under the direction of Mr. C. Sharpe, the procession was formed as before, and after escorting to the school-house, Miss R., her juvenile scholars, and the fair female choir of singers, the procession returned to Mr. Otis Morse's Hotel" where a band played the following pieces of music in accompaniment to the toasts: Tune, Hail Columbia — Tune, Yankee Doodle — Tune, The March of Mind — Tune, Washington's Grand March — Tune, Who Would Fill a Coward's Grave — Tune, Jefferson and Liberty — Tune, Stoney Point — Tune, President's March — Tune, Perry's Victory — Tune, Rogue's March — Tune, Liberty Tree — Tune, I'll Try — Tune, American Eagle ("Celebration at Norwich Falls," *Norwich Courier*, 11 July 1827, 3).

District of Columbia

An amateur choir conducted by "Mr. McDuell" sang for President John Quincy Adams at "the church of Dr. Laurie" and "excellent music" was provided by the Marine Band (*National Intelligencer*, 6 July 1827, 3; *Republican Star and General Advertiser*, 17 July 1827, 2).

Maine

Hallowell: Old Hundred sung (*Hallowell Gazette*, 11 July 1827).[516]

New Gloucester: The Second Social Library celebrated with a procession to the Meeting House "of the 1st parish," where the exercises began with an anthem that was "sung in superior style by the Philharmonic Society." Also performed was an Ode by Andrew R. Giddinge. First line: "Sons of Freedom now assembled" ("Fourth of July," *Eastern Argus Semi-Weekly*, 13 and 17 July 1827, 2 and 1, respectively).

Portland: A procession was formed at 11:30 A.M. in front of the town hall and marched to the "Church of the Second Parish." The exercises there included an "appropriate Ode, composed for the occasion by Mr. Frederick Mellen," and "sung with great éclat: Air 'Ye Mariners of England.'" (First line: "Spirits of our Forefathers."). Afterwards the assemblage enjoyed dinner at Phoenix Hall to the sounds of the following musical works: Air, Hail Columbia — Home, Sweet Home[517] — John Q. Adams March — Let Patriot Pride — Perry's Victory — Governor Lincoln's March[518] — O Here No Fellers Cramp the Mind — When Sailing oe'r the Midnight Deep — Old Hundred — Speed the Plough — Cease Rude Boress — Columbia, Land of Liberty — Oh! Those Were Moments Dear and Height — O What a Rose, What a Rumpus, What a Rioting — Auld Lang Syne — I That Once Was a Plough Boy — Tyriolese Song of Liberty — Grecian Air — Song of the Spanish Patriots — O When I Left thy Shores O Naxos — Marseilles Hymn — Yankee Doodle — How Sleep the Brave — Ye White Cliffs of Dover. "The music was truly excellent and commanded the listening attention of the audience and showed our amateurs to be equal in talent and taste to any of our age" ("Fifty-First Anniversary of American Independence," *Eastern Argus*, 10 July 1827, 1).

Maryland

Easton: Officers and soldiers of the Forsyth Volunteers of Baltimore[519] joined the citizens of Easton at the Court House for the celebration. Toasts presented included "airs from a fine band of music attached to the Volunteers": air, Hail Columbia — air, Yankee Doodle — Sweet Home — air, Washington's March — air, Star-Spangled Banner — air, Lafayette's Welcome — air, Hail to the Chief— air, Soldier's Glory — air, Lafayette's March — air, Yankee Doodle — air, Auld Lang Syne — air, The Jubilee — air, O' 'Tis Love ("Celebration of the Fourth of July," *Republican Star and General Advertiser*, 10 July 1827, 3).

Baltimore: About 200 persons and military units celebrated at a dinner served by Mr. Christian Duncan followed by toasts accompanied with these musical works: Jefferson's March — Hail Columbia — Hail to the Chief— The Star-Spangled Banner — Baltimore Quick Step — Washington's March — Sweet Home — President's March — Lafayette's March — Yankee Doodle — Auld Lang Syne — Ladies Eye — Yankee Doodle — Pulaski's March ("Fifty-First Anniversary of American Independence," *American & Commercial Daily Advertiser*, 7 July 1827, 2).

Massachusetts

Haverhill: At the meeting house, "the singing by the choirs in this town, assisted by several individuals from towns in the vicinity, was performed with taste and spirit, and much to the gratification of the audience." Later at the Golden Ball Hotel, the dinner had "appropriate music and salutes" provided (*Essex Gazette*, 7 July 1827, 2).

Salem: Billed as a "Religious Celebration of American Independence," the following is the "order of exercises at the First Presbyterian Church (Branch Street)":

   I. Prayer and reading of scriptures, by the Rev. Brown Emerson.
  II. Anthem. [First line]: "Go forth to the mount, bring the olive branch home."
 III. Prayer, by the Rev. Charles W. Upham.
 IV. Hymn. [First line]: "How rich thy gifts, Almighty King!"[520]
  V. Address by the Rev. Rufus Babcock, Jun.
 VI. Collection to aid the funds of the American Colonization Society.
VII. Anthem. [First line]: "Oh praise God in his holiness."
VIII. Concluding Prayer, by the Rev. Geo. Leonard.
 IX. Doxology.
  X. Benediction.
[*Essex Register*, 2 July 1827, 3; *Salem Gazette*, 3 July 1827, 2].

New Hampshire

Portsmouth: The Democratic Republicans gathered at the Court House for a march, "accompanied by a band," through city streets to the Universalist Meeting House where the exercises consisted of:

  1st Instrumental music
  2d Prayer by the venerable Revolutionary patriot, Joseph Litchfield, of Kettery, Me.
  3d. Hymn by the choir.
  4th Declaration of Independence, read by Daniel P. Drown, Esq.
  5th Prayer by the Rev. Hosea Ballou, of Boston.
  6th Hymn.
  7th. Oration by Honorable Levi Woodbury.
  8th Anthem, "O Praise God in His Holiness."
  9th Benediction.

(*New-Hampshire Gazette*, 3 July 1827, 3; "Democratic Celebration of National Independence, July 4, 1827," *New-Hampshire Patriot & State Gazette*, 16 July 1827, 2); a procession from the Athenaeum to Franklin Hall included military, clergy, members of the state legislature and others. The program advertised was: music — prayer — ode — Declaration of Independence — ode — oration — ode — Benediction. Music accompanying toasts included Adams & Liberty — President's March — Yankee Doodle — Come Haste to the Wedding. "The following original song we sung after the delivery of the 6th regular toast[521]: Song — Brave Old Soldiers. Tune Auld Lang Syne." First line: "Shall brave old soldiers be forgot" (*Portsmouth Journal of Literature & Politics*, 30 June and 7 July 1827, 1 and 3, respectively).

New York

New York: Emancipation of African-Americans in New York State occurred on this day and at the Zion Church, orations were delivered by William Hamilton and John Mitchell before "the various societies of colored persons, in their uniform dresses and various badges." A parade through the public streets included "music [that] was unusually good; there were four or five bands, comprising a great variety of instruments, played with much skill, as will readily be believed, from the acknowledged talent for music of the African race." "A violent shower" forced the participants to end the parade. (*Salem Gazette*, 13 July 1827, 2). See also **Publications** above.

North Carolina

Raleigh: Odes were sung in the Methodist Church where exercises were held and later at a dinner at Goneke's Concert Room, with Governor Hutchins Gordon Burton present, toasts were offered "interspersed with a number of patriotic and convivial songs." That evening at the State House Grove, "a concert was given to the ladies, which concluded with a dance" (*Raleigh Register and North Carolina Gazette*, 6 July 1827, 3).

Pennsylvania

Pittsburgh: In a locust grove at the south end of the First Presbyterian Church, the Pittsburgh Sabbath School Union met. Three hymns were sung, one of which was written by W.B. Tappan: first line, "Our fathers rose in peril's day" ("The Fourth of July," *American Sunday School Magazine* 64 (September 1827): 276.

Rhode Island

Newport: After a parade through city streets, the exercises at Trinity Church "were commenced by vocal and instrumental music from a select choir, under the direction of Mr. Wm. R. Atkinson,[522] accompanied by the sweet and harmonious tones of the organ, delicately and inspiringly touched by the skilful hand of Miss Eliza Davis, the organist of that church" ("Fourth of July," *Rhode Island Republican*, 12 July 1827, 2). See also **Publications** above.

Providence: A procession made up of military units, veterans of the Revolutionary War, the governor of Rhode Island, and others marched from the bridge to the Universalist Chapel. "The Rev. Mr. Pickering introduced the services by a fervent prayer, and two pieces of musick, one an original ode for the occasion by Mr. Shaw, were executed with fine effect." Another newspaper reported that the pieces were "two original patriotic odes performed by the choir of the chapel." Further, regarding Oliver Shaw, "It was what might have been expected from his well known talents, as a composer, both in this country and in Europe" ("Fourth of July," *Rhode-Island American and Providence Gazette*, 6 July 1827, 2; *Providence Patriot*, 7 July 1827, 2).

Vermont

Sandgate: A town parade was "preceeded by a part of Capt. Harry Hurd's band of music," and escorted by a detachment from Capt. Smith's company of militia (*Vermont Gazette*, 17 July 1827, 3).

Virginia

Fleet's Springs: Performed following a toast at a dinner: America, Commerce, and Freedom — Come Haste to the Wedding — The Devil Awa' Wi the Excisemen — Ere Around the Hugh Oak — Hail Columbia — Hail to the Chief — Scots Wha Hae — Should Auld Acquaintance Be Forgot [Auld Lang Syne] — Tyrolese Song of Liberty — Washington's March — Yankee Doodle (*Richmond Enquirer*, 10 July 1827, 2).

Petersburg: Performed at a dinner celebration held at Bath Spring: Around the Hugh Oak — Auld Lang Syne — The Cambells [sp?] are Coming — Jefferson's March — Madison's March — Marseilles Hymn — Pillar of Glory — Scots Wha Ha — Tyrolese Air — Washington's March (*Richmond Enquirer*, 10 July 1827, 2).

1828

Publications

"Fourth of July. Tune, 'Scots wha hae.'" First line:

"Now, we view the joyful day!" (*Portsmouth Journal and Rockingham Gazette*, 5 July 1828, 4).

The Carrollton March[523] (Baltimore: John Cole, 1828), "performed at the ceremony of commencing the Baltimore & Ohio Railroad on the Fourth of July 1828." "Musick, Carrollton March, by a full band" ("Orders of the Grand Marshal to be Observed on the Fourth, 1828," *Baltimore Patriot*, 3 July 1828, 2).

"The following Ode was sung at the North Meeting House [in Portsmouth]." First line: "Hail, thou bright returning day" (*Portsmouth Journal and Rockingham Gazette*, 5 July 1828, 3).

"Fourth of July Ode, by James G. Brooks, Esq. of New York." First line: "Up with our star flag — let it stream in the wind" (*Portsmouth Journal and Rockingham Gazette*, 19 July 1828, 3).

"Morn of the Fourth of July." Written by R.S. Coffin. Composed by C. Meineke. Piano and voice. First line: "Behold from the brow of the mountain advancing." Baltimore: T. Carr's Music Store, n.d.

"Ode, prepared by the Chief Marshal for the celebration of the 4th July at the Factory Village in Wilton, N.H." First line: "When our great sires this land explored"[524] ("Poetry, *New-Hampshire Patriot & State Gazette*, 11 August 1828, 4).

"Odes. To be sung at New-Providence, N.J. July 4th, 1828." First line: "To God, our never-failing strength"; first line: "Say, should we search the globe around." Broadside. Copy in Brown University.

Rail Road March for the Fourth of July. Composed & arranged for the piano forte by C. Meineke. Dedicated to the Directors of the Baltimore & Ohio Rail Road. Baltimore: Geo. Willig, 1828.

"'Song'[525] — for the 4th of July, 1828. Tune — 'Auld Lang Syne.'" First line: "Though Adams now misrules the land." ["From the *Lancaster Journal.*"] ("Poetry," *New-Hampshire Patriot & State Gazette*, 7 July 1828, 4.)

Performances

Connecticut

Norwich: "Agreeable to arrangements made by the Mechanics' Society, a procession, consisting of that body, the City Authorities, Officers of the Town and State, and a large number of Citizens, formed at half past 10 o'clock, and proceeded, amid firing and the ringing of bells and the more harmonious music of the Chelsea Band,[526] to the Congregational meetinghouse." After a reading of the Declaration of Independence, "prayers and singing gave solemnity and interest to the exercises of the morning." The order of the exercises were as follows:

   I. Hymn.
  II. Prayer
 III. Hymn.
  IV. Declaration of Independence.
   V. Oration
  VI. Prayer

VII. Hymn
VIII. Benediction.

That evening "invited a dance, and never was there a merrier set than assembled to enjoy that exhilarating exercise" ("Order of Exercises" and "Fourth of July," *Norwich Courier*, 7 and 9 July 1828, 3 and 3, respectively).

District of Columbia

At a celebration for printers, music by "an excellent Band of Music" at a dinner celebration of the various printing offices of Washington: America, Commerce, and Freedom — Auld Lang Syne — Dead March in Saul — The Drum — Hail Columbia — Hail to the Chief — Lafayette's March — Let Us Haste to Kelvin Grove — Liberty's Birth-Day — Oh! Tis Love — President's March — Roslin Castle — Rural Felicity — Soldier's Glory — Star-Spangled Banner — Welcome Lafayette — Yankee Doodle (*National Intelligencer*, 7 July 1828, 3).

Maryland

Baltimore: On the occasion of "the ceremony of laying the first stone of the Baltimore and Ohio Railroad," the Association of Blacksmiths gathered at the Vauxhall Gardens for dinner and toasts accompanied by the following music: President's March — Carrollton March — Washington's March — Auld Lang Syne — Lafayette's March — Music by the Band — Music by the Band — Music, full band — Hail Columbia — Yankee Doodle — Music, full band — Music ("Celebration of the Fourth of July, by the Association of Blacksmiths," *Baltimore Patriot*, 16 July 1828, 2). See **Publications** above.

Massachusetts

Boston: At Faneuil Hall, accompanying the dinner was the following music: Gen. Greene's March — God Save the King — Hail Columbia — Jefferson's March — Oh Come to the Bower — Oh Dear What Can the Matter Be — The Retreat — The Trumpet Sounds — U.S. March — Washington's March — Yankee Doodle (*Boston Statesman*, 8 July 1828).

Newburyport: The "order of exercises at the Federal-Street Church" (First Presbyterian Church) began with an anthem, and later included an original hymn to the tune "Old Hundred," an original ode to the tune "Pillar of Glory," and voluntary by the band. Broadside, [Newburyport, MA]: Printed at the Herald office, [1828].

Salem: "Religious Celebration. At the Tabernacle Church, July 4, 1828. Order of Exercises":

   I. Prayer and Reading of the Scriptures, by the Rev. T.W. Coit.
   II. Original Hymn.
   III. Prayer by the Rev. A. Drinkwater.
   IV. Original Hymn.
   V. Address — by the Rev. J. P. Cleaveland.
   VI. Collection to aid the fund of the American Colonization Society.

   VII. Anthem.
   VIII. Concluding Prayer — By the Rev. Brown Emerson.
   IX. Doxology.
   X. Benediction.

(*Salem Gazette*, 1 July 1828, 2.); exercises at the North Church consisted of a "Voluntary on the organ by Miss Mallet,[527] performed with great taste and execution. Stevenson's sublime anthem, 'Go forth to the mount,' was then sung." After a reading of the Declaration of Independence, "the following hymn was then sung by the whole choir, to the tune of 'Old Hundred'": first line, "Great God! beneath whose piercing eye." Following the oration, "the following Ode, written by Mr. Edwin Jocelyn, was sung with great effect": first line, "Awake, awake the song." Prior to the benediction, the "beautiful" anthem, 'Sing his praises,' was then performed. (*Salem Gazette*, 1, 4, and 8 July 1828, 2, 1, and 2, respectively.)

Southbridge: At "Rev'd Mr. Parks' Meeting House, two original odes" were sung in addition to a "highly applauded" oration ("Anniversary Celebrations," *Rhode-Island American and Providence Gazette*, 15 July 1828, 2).

New Hampshire

Epping: At 2 P.M. a procession marched to the meeting house "when the exercise commenced by singing an appropriate hymn, accompanied by excellent instrumental musick" (*New-Hampshire Patriot & State Gazette*, 21 July 1828, 1).

Goffstown: At the meeting house, "the Declaration of Independence was read, and an address delivered by Charles F. Gove, Esq. accompanied by some select pieces of music by the choir." Later a dinner was served and toasts were offered, "accompanied by the discharge of cannon and music from the band" (*New-Hampshire Patriot & State Gazette*, 21 July 1828, 2).

Plymouth: A celebration of Jacksonians assembled "at Woodbury's at 10 o'clock, A.M." and processed to the "chapel which is computed to hold more than five hundred was filled to over-flowing." The exercises begun with a "Hymn, music, Old Hundred." After the oration another "Hymn, musick, 'Harvest'" was sung ("Jacksonian Celebration of the 4th July 1828, at Plymouth, N.H.," *New Hampshire Patriot & State Gazette*, 14 July 1828, 1).

Portsmouth: The "Democratic Republicans friendly to the election of Gen. Andrew Jackson" met at the Universalian Meeting House where the exercises included "appropriate music by a volunteer choir" and instrumental music by a band. The choir sang an anthem titled "O Give Thanks Upon the Lord" ("Anniversary of American Independence at Portsmouth," *New-Hampshire Patriot & State Gazette*, 30 June 1828, 3, and 14 July 1828, 2). See also **Publications** above.

York County: "Invited guests, strangers, subscribers to the dinner, and citizens generally, formed a procession at noon, and proceeded under an escort to the Rev. Mr. Dow's Meeting-House." The exercises there included: "Voluntary-Prayer by the Rev. Mr. Dow-Hymn written for the occasion — Reading of the Declaration of Independence by Mr. Henry Simpson, Jr.— oration by Dr. J.S. Putnam-Ode." The newspaper reported that "the performances of the choir were highly satisfactory and pleasing" ("Celebration at York," *Portsmouth Journal and Rockingham Gazette*, 12 July 1828, 2).

Pennsylvania

Allentown: The Allentown Band[528] performed this day and is the earliest recorded report of this band active in this town.

Jackson: A band played from "a stage erected for the purpose" at a dinner celebration. The following music was performed: Tune, Hail Columbia — Washington's March — Yankee Doodle — Hail to the Chief— Let the Brazen Trumpet Sound — President's March — Blue Beard — Gov. Shulze's March[529] — Jackson's March — La Fayette's March — Liberty Mine — Pennsylvania March — Pennsylvania Quick Step — Life Let Us Cherish — Hail to the Morning — Jefferson's March — Grand March — Soldier's Return — The Battle of N. Orleans — Hurrah, Hurrah — Auld Lang Syne — Bruce's Address — Blue Ey'd Mary ("Jackson Celebration of the 4th of July," *Lancaster Journal*, 11 July 1828, 2).

Rhode Island

Bristol: Regarding the ceremony held in the church, a newspaper reported: "the music in the church is highly spoken of" ("Anniversary Celebrations," *Rhode-Island American and Providence Gazette*, 8 July 1828, 2).

Pawtucket: "There was an unusually spirited celebration of the Fourth by the citizens of that Village, Valley and Central Falls.... At the meeting house, which was thronged," following the reading of the Declaration, was "the singing by the Mozart Society of an original Ode by Albert G. Greene, Esq."[530] ("Anniversary Celebrations," *Rhode-Island American and Providence Gazette*, 8 July 1828, 2).

Providence: After a parade to the Universalist Chapel, "the performances at the Chapel were generally received with lively approbation by a numerous audience.... After the performances at the Chapel, during which two original odes were sung with excellent effect, the procession returned to the Bridge."[531] Included was a "Voluntary on the organ, by Mr. Shaw" (*Providence Patriot & Columbia Phenix*, 4 July 1828, 2; *Rhode Island American and Providence Gazette*, 8 July 1828, 2); at the Providence Museum, "on the evening anniversary of our national independence, the Museum will be fitted up in the best style for the reception of visitors, and during the day and evening the whole will be enlivened by a band of good music. In addition to other novelties, a distinguished musician has been engaged for the occasion to play on the Scotch bag-pipe, which will be an additional attraction to lovers of musical variety" ("Providence Mu-

seum," *Providence Patriot & Columbian Phenix*, 2 July 1828, 3); at the Providence Theatre, "this evening, July 4, will be performed Mrs. Inchbald's celebrated, in 3 acts, *Love and Honor or The Midnight Hour*.

General, Mr. Faulkner.
Nicholas, J.M. Brown.
Julia, Mrs. Young.
After the Comedy, a Double Hornpipe, by Mr. Chipp, and Mrs. Spooner. Comic Song, 'St. Patrick was a Gentleman' by Mr. Faulkner.
Recitations by Mrs. Young.
Comic Song, 'John Hobbs,' Mr. J.M. Brown.
The entertainments to conclude, for the last time, with the 2d act of the celebrated romantic Opera of *Der Freyschutz*.
Caspar, Mr. Archer.

Other Characters, see hand bills. Box Office open at the Theatre, on days of performance, from 3 o'-clock until the close of the performance when places and tickets may be had.

Boxes 75 cents, Pit 37 ½, Gallery 25 cents. Performance to commence at quarter before 8 o'clock [*Rhode-Island American and Providence Gazette*, 4 July 1828, 3].

Westerly: In Pawcatuck Village, at the "Union Meeting House, where a numerous audience were gratified by appropriate music, a prayer by the Rev. Mr. Swan, the reading of the Declaration of Independence by Mr. Rouse Babcock, Jr., and an oration by Mr. Samuel Hassard" were given. "In the evening the village band of music, assisted by vocal amateurs, gave a concert, which was numerously attended and afforded great satisfaction" ("Anniversary Celebrations," *Rhode-Island American and Providence Gazette*, 15 July 1828, 2).

South Carolina

Charleston: Sung or played at a celebration of the "Charleston Riflemen": America, Commerce and Freedom — Barney Leave the Girls Alone — Ere Around the Hugh Oak — Hail Columbia — Hail Liberty — Hearts of Oak — Is There a Heart that Never Loved[532] — Jackson's Morning Brush[533] — Let Patriot Pride — Marseilles Hymn — Solemn Dirge — South Carolina Hymn — The Vicar of Bray (*Charleston Courier*, 7 July 1828, 2); in Charleston at a celebration of the "Irish Volunteers": Dirge — Erin Go Bragh — Hail Columbia — Hail to the Chief— Jackson's Morning Brush — Life Let Us Cherish — Marseilles Hymn — Oh! 'Tis Love, 'Tis Love — President's March — Star-Spangled Banner — Yankee Doodle (*Charleston Courier*, 7 July 1828, 2).

Virginia

Mount Vernon: The U.S. Marine Band played Pleyel's Hymn at the tomb of George Washington with citizens from Washington in attendance (*National Intelligencer*, 8 July 1828, 3).

1829

Publications

"The following Ode, written for the occasion, was sung at the celebration of our national independence at Worcester": first line, "While joyous hearts exulting swell." The last line indicates the name of the tune used: "Our country's Auld Lang Syne" ("Poet's Corner," *Pittsfield Sun*, 23 July 1829, 4).

The following odes were sung in Portsmouth: first line: "We owe to no scepter'd power"; first line: "We who dwell in freedom's land"; "When the oppressor's arm is broken," tune "Dismission" (*Portsmouth Journal and Rockingham Gazette*, 11 July 1829, 2).

"Hymn sung at Hartford, July 4, 1829."[534] First line: "Awake! O Afric! desolate, forlorn."

"Hymn sung in the public meeting in Hartford, Connecticut, on the 4th of July, to aid the American Colonization Society." By Lydia H. Sigourney. First line: "When injured Afric's captive Claim."[535]

"Hymns for the anniversary of the Hartford Sunday Schools, Saturday, July 4, 1829." Includes three poems of hymns with tune name designated, and doxology. One hymn poem by Lydia Sigourney, first line: "There seems a voice of murmur's praise." Broadside.

"Military Song for the Fourth. Tune —'Auld Lang Syne.'" From the *Albany Argus*. First line: "Is there a heart forgets the day" (*Pittsfield Sun*, 2 July 1829, 3).

"The Nation's Birth Day. Air —'Scots Wha Ha." First line: "Arise! Columbia's sons, arise!" Note: "We would recommend to those who are disposed to celebrate this day, the following ode from the *New England Palladium*" (*Providence Patriot & Columbian Phenix*, 4 July 1829, 2; *Village Register and Norfolk County Advertiser*, 16 July 1829, 1).

"Ode, composed by the Rev. S.M. Phelps,[536] for the celebration of the fifty-third anniversary of American Independence, at Ridgfield, Conn." First line: "All hail to the day that gave Freedom its birth." Broadside. Ridgefield, CT, [1829]. Copy in Center for Popular Music, Middle Tennessee State University.

"Ode for the Fourth of July. By N.P. Willis, sung in Boston. Air —'I See Them on Their Wending Way.'" First line: "Our country's iron age is gone" (*Providence Patriot & Columbian Phenix*, 8 July 1829, 1; "Poetry," *Vermont Gazette*, 11 August 1829, 4).

"Odes, to be Sung at the Celebration of American Independence in Springfield, July 4, 1829." Ode (first line: "To thee, almighty king above"); Ode: (first line: "All hail the day, when freemen dear." Broadside, [Springfield, NH, 1829].

"With Thy Pure Dews and Rains,"[537] words by John Pierpont, and music by Lowell Mason. Boston: Mason Bros., 1829. This was sung at the Park Street Church in Boston.

Performances

Connecticut

Hartford: "The late anniversary of our national Independence was celebrated in an interesting manner by the Sunday Schools in this city.... The Centre Church was opened for their reception, and at ten o'clock nearly all the schools in the city, with their teachers, together with the schools from West Hartford, Wethersfield and Newington, were assembled for religious exercises. A Hymn written for the occasion by one of the teachers was first sung; Prayers were next offered by the Rev. Mr. Hawes; another Hymn, also written for the occasion, was then sung; after which an appropriate address was delivered by the Rev. Mr. Brace, of Newington. The exercises were concluded by singing another Hymn." Close to 1500 persons attended this event. ("Fourth of July," *Connecticut Courant*, 7 July 1829, 3). See **Publications** above.

Norwich: Members of the Norwich Lyceum and Mechanics' Institute marched to the town hall, where the exercises were held. "The music under the direction of Mr. Phelps, was admirably fine, far superior, we think, to that of any former occasion" (*Norwich Courier*, 8 July 1829, 3).

District of Columbia

"At one o'clock the President [Andrew Jackson] received the visits of his fellow citizens in the oval apartment of the Presidential mansion.... The fine military band attached to the Marine Corps attended in the outer hall, and gratified the company during the day by the performance of many national and other inspiring airs" ("Fourth of July," from the *Washington Telegraph* and published in *Farmer's Cabinet*, 18 July 1829, 2; *National Intelligencer*, 4 and 7 July 1829, 3 and 3, respectively); President Jackson along with the Marine Band were supposed to attend a cornerstone laying ceremony for lock of the C & O Canal but the event was canceled due to severe rain (*National Intelligencer*, 7 July 1829, 3; "Fourth of July, 1829," *Richmond Enquirer*, 7 July 1829, 2; *Pittsfield Sun*, 16 July 1829, 2).

Maine

Alfred: A band of music, under the direction of Moses Witham of Sanford, performed at the exercises held at the meeting house. Other musicians of the band included George Chadbourn, Robert Tripp, of Sanford, and James Garey of Alfred. The band also played tunes in front of the Adams' Hotel as a procession marched by. A dispute arose when William B. Holmes, chairman of the committee of arrangements, asked the band to play the "Rogues' March" as Republicans approached the hotel. The musicians refused but after several orders from Holmes they complied. The affair created a scandal that was printed in various newspapers ("Mr. Holmes and the Rogue's March" and "Mr. Holmes and His March," *Eastern*

Argus Semi-Weekly, 31 July and 18 August 1829, 2 and 2, respectively).

Maryland

Baltimore:

At five o'clock, on the morning of the fourth, agreeably to previous arrangement, the company was formed in Holliday St. and thence marched on board the steamboat *Independence*, Captain Robinson, for the purpose of celebrating the anniversary of the enfranchisement of their country. On leaving the wharf, the band attached to the corps, under the command of Captain Walter, struck up "Auld Lang Syne," the company then being on the upper deck, presenting to the numerous spectators an imposing and gratifying spectacle.

At 10 o'clock the company with the invited guests and passengers were assembled on deck, for the purpose of hearing read the Declaration of Independence. Mr. Edward J. Mosher appeared upon the stand, whilst the band played "Hail Columbia," and after having made some pertinent remarks, relative to the cause which led to its adoption, proceeded to read the Declaration in a distinct and audible voice; on the conclusion of which the band struck up "Washington's March." The company were then dismissed, and enjoyed themselves in various amusements until about 2 o'clock, when they sat down to a sumptuous and splendid dinner.

According to the newspaper report, a song "composed by a member, was sung on the occasion": first line, "Come join in mirth and glee." In addition, toasts were drank with the following tunes performed: Tune, Freedom's Jubilee — President's March — Yankee Doodle — Washington's March — Marion's March[538] — Carroll's March — Hail Columbia — Funeral Dirge — Lafayette's March — Home! Sweet Home! ("Celebration of the Fourth of July by the Marion Corps," *Baltimore Patriot*, 6 July 1829, 2).

Massachusetts

Boston: At the municipal celebration at the Old South Church, "in the course of the exercises, were sung three excellent Odes, appropriate to the occasion, and written, one, by Mr. N.P. Willis,[539] another by Mr. Wm. Hayden, and a third by Mr. Stephen Bates. They were sung with great effect by the choir" (see **Publications** above). A Colonization Society event held at the Palladium on Broomfield Street, "the following hymn sung on this occasion, speaks for itself; it was composed for the occasion, by Mr. [G.V.B.] Forbes; and for harmony of numbers and chasteness of sentiment, it is rarely surpassed": first line, "On mount, and tower, and fortress height" (*Columbian Sentinel*, 4 and 8 July 1829, 4 and 2, respectively; "At Boston," *Farmers' Cabinet*, 11 July 1829, 3); at a celebration of the Sunday Schools of the Baptist societies at Federal Street Meeting House, "the meeting was introduced by singing the following hymn — sung by the children": first line, "Our Father,

from thy throne above." After a reading from the Scriptures, the following hymn was sung by the congregation: first line, "Oh, sweet is Freedom's lovely ray." After an address, "the following hymn was sung by the children": first line, "Our Father, on this joyful day" ("Religious Celebration 4th July," *Farmers' Cabinet*, 18 July 1829, 1).

Hanson: Choirs made up of singers from Congregational, Methodist, and Universal societies spent the afternoon in singing (*An Address Delivered at Hanson, Mass. On the Fourth of July, 1829*. By Gad Hitchcock (Higham, [MA]: Farmer and Brown, 1829). Copy in Massachusetts Historical Society.

Salem: The "Order of Exercises" at the Tabernacle Church was:

  I. Anthem.
  II. Prayer.
  III. Reading of the Scriptures.
  IV. Hymn.
  V. Prayer.
  VI. Hymn.
  VII. An Address by the Rev. Professor Worcester.
  VIII. Collection in behalf of the American Colonization Society.
  IX. Anthem.
  XI. Doxology.
  XII. Benediction.

Both hymns were noted as originally composed: first lines, "Come, lift to God a rapt'rous song" and "Lo! in His temple we appear" (*Salem Gazette*, 3 and 7 July 1829, 3 and 2, respectively).

North Carolina

Salem: Moravians performed Haydn's oratorio *The Creation* with a "full corps of instrumental and vocal musicians of Salem" in the Church there "to the pleasure of the congregation."[540]

Pennsylvania

Lancaster: Friends of Andrew Jackson dined at Mr. Wien's, after the exercises at the Court House. Musical selections performed included: Music, Hail Columbia — Music, Washington's March — Music, Hail to the Chief — Long Life and Success to the Farmer — Governor's March[541] — Music, The Soldier's Return — Jefferson's March — Music, Auld Lang Syne — Dead March in Saul[542] — Yankee Doodle — The Star-Spangled Banner — Oh! 'Tis a Wonderful Alteration — Granule — Liberty Tree — Go to the Devil and Shake Yourselves — Home, Sweet Home — The Rogues March — The Vicar of Bray — Love's Young Dream ("The Fourth of July," *Lancaster Journal*, 10 July 1829, 2).

Rhode Island

Newport: After a procession from the "Parade" through city streets to the Meeting House, the exercises included prayers, reading of the Declaration and an oration. "The music will be under the direction of Messrs. B. Marsh, Jun, Wm. R. Atkinson and T.

Stacey, Jun." ("Fifty-third Anniversary of Independence," *Newport Mercury*, 4 July 1829, 2).

Providence: At the Providence Theatre, the play *Castle Spectre* was presented and included the "comic song of the beautiful boy" sung by Mr. Phillips. Also performed was "the new musical drama of the *Invicibles*, including the song "Fall Not in Love" (*Providence Patriot & Columbian Phenix*, 4 July 1829, 3).

South Carolina

Charleston: "The various patriotic associations, the purpose of whose institution is to honor the occasion, assembled at their usual places of meeting, and walked in procession, accompanied with bands of music, and attended by their respective orators, to the churches appropriated to receive them" ("Celebration of National Independence," *Richmond Enquirer*, 24 July 1829, 1).

Tennessee

Maryville: A hickory tree, "70 feet in height"was raised to the sound of a band of music "which slowly approached, and having taken their stand in front, were occasionally interrupted by the roar of the cannon." A procession to the church followed, where "an appropriate hymn was then sung, accompanied by the band of music." (*Knoxville Register* as reprinted in *Salem Gazette*, 1 September 1829, 2.)

Virginia

Petersburg: At the town's exercises held at the Theatre, there was "music from the band, and a patriotic song, 'Hail to the Morn,' sung with much force." At the "sumptuous dinner, prepared by Messrs. Blick and Rawlings" that followed, there was also "music from the band": Marseilles Hymn — Scots Wha Ha — Washington's March — Hail Columbia — Tyrolese Air — Ere Around the Huge Oak — Auld Lang Syne — Jefferson's March — Jackson's March — Star-Spangled Banner[543]— Minute Gun at Sea[544]— Pillar of Glory — Oh Say Not Woman's Heart is Bought[545] ("53rd Anniversary," *Richmond Enquirer*, 10 July 1829, 2).

1830

Publications

"The following–arranged from an Ode by William Hayden, Jr. was sung at the celebration in this town, July 5th, 1830. Tune 'Eaton.'" First line: "Again the glorious day dawns on" ("Poetry," *Berkshire Journal*, 15 July 1830, 1).

"The following Hymn, composed for the occasion by Park Benjamin, Esq.[546] was sung at the celebration of the 54th anniversary of American Independence, in this city [Norwich, CT]." First line: "No cloud sailed through the bright, blue sky" ("Poetry," *Norwich Courier*, 7 July 1830, 4).

"'Freedom's Jubilee.' An Anti-Slavery Song." New-

Britain, CT. Broadside. Copy in Connecticut Historical Society.

"'Hymn for Fourth of July.' By the Rev. J.D. Knowles." First line: "Hail, day of Freedom! let the beam" (*Westfield Register*, 21 July 1830, 4; "Poet's Corner," *Pittsfield Sun*, 22 July 1830, 4).

"Ode for the Fourth of July. Air – 'Hail to the Chief.'" First line: "Hallow'd the day from the eastward advancing" (*Portsmouth Journal and Rockingham Gazette*, 3 July 1830, 2).

Performances

Connecticut

Springfield: At the "festival in commemoration of our Independence ... near the village ... about 300 Gentlemen and Ladies" heard "a fine band of music [that] sent up its joyous notes to heaven, mingled with the rustling of the leaves as the evening breeze reveled among them" ("Springfield," *Connecticut Courant*, 13 July 1830, 3).

District of Columbia

At a dinner celebration held at Williamson's Hotel, music accompanying toasts included: America, Commerce and Freedom — Come Haste to the Wedding — Hail Columbia — Jackson's March — Lake Champlain — March (3) — Pleyel's Hymn — President's March — Roslin Castle — Star-Spangled Banner — Yankee Doodle (*National Intelligencer*, 12 July 1830, 2).

Maine

Portland: A Republican procession ended at the Baptist Meeting House where "a spirited choir of Music, whose performances were excellent, added to the animation of the scene." Following, 568 persons joined in a dinner at the Bower, after which toasts were drank accompanied by the following pieces: Air, Hail Columbia — Hail to the Chief Who in Triumph Advances, &c[547] — Jefferson's March — Yankee Doodle — Speed the Plough — Columbia Land of Liberty — Jefferson and Liberty — Perry's Victory — Scots wha hae wi' Wallace Bled — O, Here No Fetters Cramp the Mind[548] — Jackson's March — O, Dear, What Can the Matter Be — Funeral Dirge — Here's a Health to All Good Lasses ("Splendid Celebration!" *Eastern Argus Semi-Weekly*, 9 and 13 July 1830, 2, and 1, respectively).

Maryland

Baltimore: At 5 A.M. on July 5, "the company was formed in Holliday Street, and under the command of Capt. Wm. C. Cook, marched thence on board the steam boat *Philadelphia*" whose destination was Chestertown. "On leaving the wharf, the Band, under the command of Capt. Roundtree, struck up several appropriate airs. At 11 o'clock, the company, with the invited guests, were assembled on the deck for the purpose of hearing read the Declaration of Independence. The band played 'Hail Columbia.'" After the

Declaration was read, "the band struck up 'Washington's March.'" After visiting Chestertown, the group returned to the vessel "and at 2 o'clock sat down to a splendid and sumptuous dinner" followed by toasts and the following music: Hail Liberty — President's March — Yankey [sic] Doodle — Washington's March — Jefferson's March — Carrollton's March — Hail Columbia — All Hail to the Brave and Free — Funeral Dirge — Star-Spangled Banner — Lafayette's March — Auld Lang Syne — Home, Sweet Home ("Celebration of the Fourth of July by the Marion Corps," *Baltimore Patriot*, 8 July 1830, 2); at White Hall Gardens, a "series of entertainments" attended by "a full and sufficient orchestra," included "a grand dramatic olio: *The Happy Days of Robin Roughhead* and *Sylvester Daggerwood*, with the comic song "Melos Cos Maotis, or, Four and Twenty Fiddlers All in a Row," followed by "Jerry go Nimble, or, Honey and Mustard," by Mr. Durang. The production ended with the comic ballet the *Cobbler's Frolic, or the Devil among the Tailors* (*Baltimore Patriot*, 3 July 1830, 3).

Massachusetts

Dorchester: At the morning service, psalm 90 "from the version used by the Puritan settlers" was sung "as by them, line by line being read." First line: "Lord, thou hast been our sure defence." In the afternoon, three psalms 44 ("C.M., from the version of Tate & Brady, introduced into use here on the first Lord's day in July, 1762") 145 ("C.M., from Dr. Watt's version, introduced on the first Lord's day in July, 1793"), and 90 ("L.M., from the Collection of Psalms and Hymns by Dr. Belknap,[549] introduced on Thanksgiving-day, November 6th, 1801") were sung. "The day, being that on which the Lord's Supper was celebrated, the following Hymn was sung after the Communion": first line, "Give us, O Lord, the living bread" (*Memorials of the First Church in Dorchester, from Its Settlement in New England, to the End of the Seconde Century, En tivo Discouses, Delivered July 4, 1830*. By the Pastor, Thaddeus Mason Harris. Boston: W. L. Lewis, 1830).

Salem: At the Tabernacle Church in the afternoon, exercises included the singing of an "original hymn by the Rev. [James] Flint, of this town." First line: "Freemen, we our charter'd rights." Also, "the following original hymn, which also made a part of the services, was written for the occasion by Mr. J.F. Worcester,[550] of this town": first line, "Ah, from whence these notes of sadness" ("Independence," *Salem Gazette*, 6 July 1830, 2).

New Hampshire

Atkinson: "A very large and respectable number (about 500) of the citizens of Atkinson and its vicinity assembled at the Academy" and proceeded, "accompanied with a band of Musick from Plaistow," to the meeting house. "The exercises were attended with appropriate music under the superintendance of Mr. B.F. Carter." When the services ended, the group "marched back to the Academy, accompanied with music and the discharge of Artillery" ("Celebration of Independence at Atkinson," *New Hampshire Patriot and State Gazette*, 26 July 1830, 3).

Deerfield: The Deerfield Temperance Society met on July 5 at the Congregational Meeting House, with more than 1000 persons assembled there. The day began with a parade, "escorted by a band of excellent musick," from the "school room" to the meeting house. After an address, "the attention of the audience was then diverted by the ingenious performance of several pieces of musick" ("A New Mode of Celebration," *New-Hampshire Patriot and State Gazette*, 26 July 1830, 3).

New Boston: At the meeting house, "several pieces of appropriate Music were performed by the Choir, and a select piece by Mr. Milton Carter, much to the satisfaction of the assembly." Following at the town's "common," a dinner was served and toasts were drank, "accompanied by the ... cheers of a fine band of music" ("American Independence," *Farmers' Cabinet*, 10 July 1830, 3; "American Independence," *New Hampshire Patriot and State Gazette*, 19 July 1830, 2).

New York

Ithaca: The following program took place at the Methodist Chapel:

1. Prayer
2. Musick
3. Declaration of Independence by J.N. Perkins, esq.
4. Musick
5. Oration by B.G. Ferris, esq.
6. Prayer
7. Musick
8. Benediction

("National Anniversary," *Ithaca Journal and General Advertiser*, 30 June 1830, 3); "The day was ushered in by a salute of thirteen guns, the ringing of bells, and the playing of the national tune by the Ithaca Band"; at the Clinton House, dinner and toasts took place and the following tunes were performed: Tune, Yankee Doodle — Hail Columbia — Hail to the Chief ("Anniversary Celebration" and "At the Clinton House," *Ithaca Journal and General Adver*tiser, 7 July 1830, 2).

Libertyville: A parade included "an excellent band of musick" and "lady singers." At a grove near town, songs were sung and music by the band: Tune, Yankee Doodle — American March — Genesee March — New Constitution — Delanas Grand March[551] — Bennington's Assembly — Hail Columbia — Honey Moon — La Fayette's March — Jefferson and Liberty — York Fugelier [sic][552] — Freedom's March ("Anniversary Celebrations," *Ithaca Journal and General Advertiser*, 14 July 1830, 2).

West Point: The celebration took place on July 3. "At 11 o'clock the cadets marched from their encampment to the Chapel, preceded by their excellent band,

and displaying their banners." Following a reading of the Declaration, "the Choir next sang the Marseilles Hymn" (*National Intelligencer*, 12 July 1830, 2; *Rhode Island American, Statesman and Providence Gazette*, 13 July 1830, 1).

North Carolina

Tarborough: These three songs were noted in a Virginia newspaper as sung on Independence Day with selected toasts: Song, Hail Columbia — Song, Bruce's Address — Song, America, Commerce and Freedom ("Toasts Drank at Tarborough, N.C.," *Richmond Enquirer*, 16 July 1830, 2).

Pennsylvania

Philadelphia: Democratic citizens gathered for the exercises held at the Masonic Hall and heard the following pieces of music: Auld Lang Syne — Dirge — President's March — Roslin Castle — Grand March — Star-Spangled Banner — America, Commerce and Freedom — Over the Hills and Far Away — Dead March ("At the Masonic Hall," *Richmond Enquirer*, 16 July 1830, 2).

Rhode Island

Bristol: The Bristol Temperance Society met at the Congregational Meeting House for services which included a prayer, reading of the Declaration of Independence, and an address to the Temperance Society by John Howe. "The services were interspersed and enlivened by the singing of several anthems, which were performed in a very superior manner, by the choir under the direction of Col. Bourn" ("Celebrations of the Fourth," *Rhode Island American, Statesman and Providence Gazette*, 13 July 1830, 4).

Newport: The day included a parade through city streets to Trinity Church where the exercises featured music "under the direction of Mr. Wm. R. Atkinson" ("Anniversary of Independence," *Newport Mercury*, 3 July 1830, 2).

Providence: A parade took place to the First Baptist Meeting House where there was an "overflowing audience." "The performances were relieved at proper intervals by the singing of three odes. The manly and powerful voice of Mr. Coburn,[553] who sang solos, gave to this part of the services unusual attraction. Two of the odes were original, the first (first line: "Shout for the day which gave birth to a nation!") by Mr. A.C. Ainsworth, and the last a happy parody upon the 'Pilgrim Fathers' (first line: "Old England's flag wav'd high"), by Mr. S.M. Fowler" (*Rhode-Island American, Statesman and Providence Gazette*, 7 July 1830, 2).

Warren: At the exercises held at the First Baptist Meeting House, "the singing, under the direction of Capt. John Harte, was chaste and appropriate" ("Celebrations of the Fourth," *Rhode Island American, Statesman and Providence Gazette*, 13 July 1830, 4).

Virginia

Hallsboro: Celebrated on July 5. "The company began to assemble about half past ten, and by twelve,

the younger part were 'tripping it on the light fantastic toe,' to the sound of excellent music procured from Richmond." At dinner, "through the politeness of the commanding officer at Bellons arsenal, the military music was procured from that post, and played during dinner appropriate and patriotic tunes": Music, Hail Columbia — Music, Death March, Logan Water — Music, Death March in Saul — Music, Death March, Roslin's Castle — Music, Yankee Doodle — Music, America, Commerce, and Freedom — The Girl I Left Behind Me — Music, The Star-Spangled Banner — Music, Marseilles Hymn — Music, Soldier Sleep Thy Warfare O'er — Music, Believe Me, If All those Endearing Young Charms[554] (*Richmond Enquirer*, 16 July 1830, 1).

Lynchburg: Invited guests and militia numbering "about 130 or 140" heard the following two pieces that accompanied toasts: Jackson's March — March to the Battle Field ("Toasts Selected," *Richmond Enquirer*, 16 July 1830, 2).

1831

Among the many musical works sung and published across America this Fourth of July, the highlight was the premiere of Samuel F. Smith's "America,"[555] performed in Boston at the Congregation Church on Park Street by a children's choir led by renowned music educator Lowell Mason.

Publications

"Anthem to the Fourth of July." First line: "Oh God, in the midst of thy temple we stand." "From the *Charleston Courier*" (The Orchestra), *New-Hampshire Sentinel*, 22 July 1831, 4).

"The following Ode was written by Edwin Jocelyn, Esq. and sung at the late anniversary celebration of American Independence, at Salem, Mass. Ode — Tune — Marseilles Hymn." First line: "Wake, freemen, the song of glory" (*Rhode-Island Republican*, 16 August 1831, 4).

"Ode for the Fourth of July." First line: "Hark! Hark! from the mountains, a merry song" (*Genius of Universal Emancipation* [August 1831]: 63).

"Ode for the Fourth of July. By Richard Emmons." First line: "Let deaf'ning cannon peal to heaven" (*Workingman's Advocate*, 2 July 1831).

"Odes for the Fourth of July, 1831, at Hanover [NJ?]." Broadside, Hanover, 1831. Ode (first line: "Conven'd once more to celebrate")/Ode (first line: "O God, Supreme o'er earth and skies")/Ode (first line: "Hail, natal day, that gav'st our Nation birth"). Copy in Brown University.

"Odes Written for the Celebration of the Fifty-Fifth Anniversary of American Independence, in Warwick, Orange Co.," by Benjamin Burt.[556] Three untitled songs: Tune — Star of the East (first line: "All

"America" ("My Country, 'tis of thee),"" words by Samuel Francis Smith, to the tune "God Save the King," was first performed on July 4, 1831, by a children's chorus at the Park Street Church in Boston. Noted music educator Lowell Mason led the performance. "America" quickly became an important piece in the musical repertoire of the Sabbath school movement at that time, as well as a national patriotic icon having numerous performances on the Fourth. Shown is a print edition of "America," cited as a "National Hymn," in Lowell Mason's *Carmina Sacra: or Boston Collection of Church Music* (Boston: Wilkins, Carter & Co., 1844 (author's collection).

hail! ye sons of our blest independence"); Tune— Bruce's Address (first line: "Hail ye sons of liberty"); Tune—Columbia (first line: "Columbia! within thee a standard is found"). Broadside, [Goshen, NY?, 1831).

"Original ode. Written for the young men's celebration of American independence in Taunton—1831." First line: "God of universal nature." Broadside, [Taunton, MA, 1831]. Copy in Brown University.

"Song for the Fourth of July."[557] First line: "The Trumpet of liberty sounds thro' the world" (*Workingman's Advocate*, 25 June 1831; "Poetry," *Norwich Courier*, 29 June 1831, 4; *Atkinson's Saturday Evening Post*, 2 July 1831; *Vermont Gazette*, 5 July 1831, 4; *Liberator*, 9 July 1831[558]).

"The subjoined patriotic and beautiful Ode, written by William G. Simms, Esq., editor of the *Charleston City Gazette*, was sung with great effect at Charleston (S.C.), on the occasion of the celebration of the recent National Anniversary, by the 'Union and States' Rights Party,' previous to the oration by Col. Drayton. Air—'Bruce's Address.'" First line: "Hail, our country's natal morn" (*Connecticut Mirror*, 30 July 1831, 1; *Eastern Argus Semi-Weekly*, 29 July 1831, 1).

Performances

Connecticut

Hartford: A parade of military companies included "five or six excellent and full bands of music, whose superior performances added not a little to the spirit-stirring interest of the scene." After the exercises at the South Church, the procession reformed and marched to the City Hall, "where a dinner had been prepared by Mr. Bennett, of the Franklin House." Following the dinner, "toasts were then drunk, accompanied, at intervals, by the performances of an excellent band of music, and the firing of cannon" ("Hartford Celebration," *Connecticut Mirror*, 9 July 1831, 2).

District of Columbia

The U.S. Marine Band[559] performed the "Star-Spangled Banner" in the Rotunda of the Capitol immediately prior to an oration presented by Francis Scott Key[560] (*Globe*, 6 July 1831, 2); Gaetano Carusi and family hold a dinner for "Heads of Departments" and "foreign Diplomatic Corps"in their Washington assembly rooms for the participants of the ceremony that was held in the U.S. Capitol that day: Auld Lang

Syne — Come Haste to the Wedding — Franklin's March — Hail Columbia — Hail to the Chief — Jackson's March — Jefferson's March — Marseilles Hymn — The Meeting of the Waters[561] — Roslin Castle — Star-Spangled Banner — Washington's March (*National Intelligencer*, 4 and 9 July 1831, 3 and 3, respectively; *Globe*, 7 July 1831, 2).

Maine

Portland: A procession "under the escort of the Truckmen in Uniform, who kindly volunteered and the Mechanic Blues, commanded by Lieut. Stoddard" marched through city streets to the Union Meeting House on Casco Street. "An overture was here performed by the Portland Band and a voluntary upon the Organ, accompanied by the choir" ("Celebration of Independence," *Eastern Argus Semi Weekly*, 8 July 1831, 2).

Maryland

Chestertown: The Chester Republican Blues military company "marched to the wharf to meet the Marion Corps of Baltimore" which arrived in the steamboat *Maryland*. The Marions' band performed "inspiring" music from the deck and marched with "animating notes" to the Fountain Inn for refreshment. Later at the Protestant Church, "after the conclusion of each of the exercises, the Band animated the audience by the sweet strains of sacred or sprightly music" ("Fourth of July Celebration," *Baltimore Patriot*, 15 July 1831, 2).

Frederick: The day began with "some patriotic tunes from a band of intinerating musicians" (*Frederick-Town Herald*, 9 July 1831, 3).

Rockville: In the Protestant Episcopal Church, the exercises included the singing of "an ode composed for the occasion" ("Fourth of July," *Maryland Journal and True American*, 6 July 1831, 2).

Massachusetts

Boston: At the Sunday School celebration at the Park Street Church, "several original hymns were beautifully sung by the Juvenile Choir under the direction of Mr. Lowell Mason." Samuel F. Smith's "America"[562] is fifth on the "Order of Exercises" and was premiered that day ("Celebrations," *Boston Recorder*, 6 July 1831, 107; Broadside).

Marblehead: Citizens escorted by militia paraded to the Rev. Bartlett's meeting house, where after an oration by Nathaniel P. Knapp,[563] an Ode written by Knapp was presented: first line, "All hail! again, the day of glory!" ("Fourth of July," *Salem Gazette*, 8 July 1831, 4).

New Bedford: The "Young Men" of Bedford organized a procession at the town hall that included Washington Artillery and New Bedford Light Infantry, "accompanied by the Bridgewater Band of Martial Music to the First Congregational Church." George W. Warren composed an Ode which "was sung in a truly masterly style and with the happiest ef-

fect" ("Celebration of Independence," *New Bedford Mercury*, 8 July 1831, 2).

Quincy: "The following Psalm, written for the occasion by the Hon. J.Q. Adams,[564] was sung at the celebration in Quincy, July 4th, 1831." First line: "Sing to the Lord, a song of Praise" [Adams wrote in his diary, "my own version of the 149th Psalm"]; "The Pilgrim Fathers"[565] (first line: "The Breaking waves dashed high"). Sung by Col. Newhall, with the chorus "Glory to God in the highest, peace on earth, and good will towards men"; anthem, "Lord Byron's Hebrew melody, 'Go forth to the Mount, bring the Olive-branch Home'"; a song, "Trumpet of Liberty" (Website: *An American Time Capsule: Three Centuries of Broadsides and Other Printed Ephemera*.) Adams cites "Mrs. Hemans"[566] as the author of the song (*Newport Mercury*, 16 July 1831, 1; "Poetry for the Fourth of July," *Niles' Register*, 16 July 1831, 345–46; *Norwich Courier*, 20 July 1831, 4; *New Hampshire Patriot and State Gazette*, 1 August 1831, 4).

Salem: The exercises at the North Church:

    I. Voluntary on the Organ.
    II. Anthem. [First line: "O God! from the house where thou dwellest, we raise"]
    III. Prayer by the Rev. Lemuel Willis.
    IV. Hymn. [First line: "Begin the high celestial strain"]
    V. Oration by the Hon. Stephen C. Phillips.
    VI. Ode — Written by Edwin Jocelyn, Esq. Tune — 'Marseilles Hymn.' [First line: "Wake, Freemen, wake the song of glory"]
    VII. Prayer by the Rev. John P. Cleaveland.
    VIII. Anthem. [First line: "Lift your voices!"]
    IX. Benediction.

(*Salem Gazette*, 1 and 5 July 1831, 3 and 2, respectively; *An Oration, Delivered at the Request of the Young Men of Salem, July 4, 1831*. By S.C. Phillips. Salem: Printed by Warwick Palfray, Jun., 1831; "American Independence: Order of Exercises at the North Church, July 4, 1831." Broadside. Salem, MA: Foote and Brown, 1831. Copy in Brown University.

New Hampshire

Effingham: After a procession the celebration took place at "the new and elegant meeting house, where the exercises were introduced by singing an ode composed by Mr. E.C. Mason." Following an oration, "at the close of which a psalm, adapted to the occasion, was sung by the choir of singers, and the exercises were closed by benediction from the chaplain. The procession then moved with martial music to the bower, where an excellent dinner was furnished by Capt. Towle" ("Celebration at North Effingham," *New-Hampshire Patriot and State Gazette*, 25 July 1831, 2).

Newport: A parade from the Newport Hotel to the meeting house included "a superb band of music, which was collected and prepared for the occasion by Major David Harris." A dinner followed with toasts "interspersed with appropriate patriotic songs" and "accompanied by music by the band, and the discharge of artillery" ("Celebration at Newport," from the *New Hampshire Spectator* as printed in *New Hampshire Patriot and State Gazette*, 18 July 1831, 2).

New York

Ithaca: The Ithaca Youths' Temperance Society met at the Baptist Meeting House at 11 A.M. The exercises included singing several works (*Ithaca Journal and General Advertiser*, 29 June 1831, 3).

New York: At a celebration that included members of the Common Council, associations and guests, numbering about 204 persons and performed following toasts: Bruce's Address — Come Haste to the Wedding — Grand Canal March — Hail Columbia — Hail to the Chief— Home, Sweet Home — Marseillois Hymn — Oh Breathe Not His Name — La Parisienne — President's March — Star-Spangled Banner — Washington's March — Yankee Doodle (*Globe*, 9 July 1831, 3).

North Carolina

Salem: Moravian bandmaster Johann Heinrich Leinbach leads the Salem Light Infantry Band in its first parade there.[567]

Ohio

Zanesville: Performed by the Zanesville Band at a friends of Andrew Jackson dinner celebration at the "new Market House," before 500 persons: American National March — Come Haste to the Wedding — Euterpian Air — Grand Canal March — Hail Columbia — Hail to the Chief— Hurrah for the Bonnets of Blue — Jefferson's March — Life Let Us Cherish — March in Memory of Washington — Miss Musgrave's March — Swiss Guards March — Yankee Doodle (*Globe*, 16 July 1831, 3).

Pennsylvania

Pittsburgh: On Stewards Island, on the Allegheny River, opposite Pittsburgh for friends of "the National Administration" by a German Band and played following a toast: Hail Columbia — Jackson's March — The Last Rose of Summer — Little Wot Ye Wha's Coming — Yankee Doodle (*Globe*, 14 July 1831, 3).

Philadelphia: At a Fourth of July dinner, "Hon. John Sergeant" introduced a toast to Henry Clay which followed by a rendition of "Hail to the Chief" ("The 4th of July Dinner at Philadelphia," *Baltimore Patriot*, 8 July 1831, 2).

Rhode Island

Newport: The celebration included a parade and exercises at the Second Baptist Meeting House. "The music on the occasion was under the direction of Col. Benj. Marsh, and gave much satisfaction to a numerous audience" (*Rhode-Island Republican*, 12 July 1831, 3).

Providence: At the First Baptist Meeting House, citizens, members of the military, various dignitaries, including the Governor, heard selected pieces of music, including an ode, "under the direction of Mr. Marcus Coburn" ("National Festival," *Rhode Island American and Gazette*, 1 July 1831, 2).

South Carolina

Charleston: At a celebration of the "Union Party," accompanied the toasts: America, Commerce and Freedom — As a Beam O'er the Face of the Waters — Black Joke[568] — The Breeze Was Hush'd — Carry One — The Day is Departed — Governor's March — Hail Columbia — Home, Sweet Home — Jefferson's March — Keen Blows the Blast — The Last Rose of Summer — The Legacy — Let Every Pagan Muse Begone — The Light-House — Meeting of the Waters — President's March — Set from Ocean Rising — Solemn Dirge — Solemn Dirge — Tis All But a Dream — Yankee Doodle (*Globe*, 15 July 1831, 3); "About 4 o'clock in the afternoon, a dinner party of 1400 persons assembled at the 'Union Bower,' to partake of the good things of the occasion." Toasts were accompanied by the following pieces of music: Ye Sons of Columbia who Bravely Have Fought — The President's March — Let Every Pagan Muse Begone — Home, Sweet Home — Meeting of the Waters — 'Tis All but a Dream — Carry One — The Light House — Ye Mortals Whom Fancy and Troubles Perplex — America, Commerce and Freedom — The Day is Departed — Black Joke ("Fourth of July in Charleston," *Rhode-Island Republican*, 19 July 1831, 2); at the First Presbyterian Church, a four-voice choir sang: Ode ("Hail, our country's natal morn") to the tune "Scots wha hae wi' Wallace bled" — Ode[569] ("We will gather in pride to the glorious rite"), to the tune of "Star-Spangled Banner," and accompanied on organ by Jacob Eckhard[570] and a "Second Original Ode, sung by the Choir in like manner as the first (air — Scots wha hae we' Wallace bled; [first line]: 'Hail, our country's natal morn!") (*Charleston Courier*, 6 July 1831, 2; "Union and States Rights Celebration," *National Intelligencer* 14 July 1831, 2; *Globe*, 15 July 1831, 3; "Poetry for the Fourth of July," *Niles' Register*, 16 July 1831, 345; *Eastern Argus*, 2 August 1831, 1). See also **Publications** above.

Virginia

Mathews: A celebration held at the Mathews Court House and performed for the Volunteer Corps of Light Infantry: Auld Lang Syne — Come Haste to the Wedding — Hail Columbia — Jackson's March — Marsellois Hymn — Washington's March — Yankee Doodle (*Globe*, 12 July 1831, 3).

1832

Publications

"Celebration of Independence at Hingham, July 4, 1832." Includes Hymn by the Rev. Dr. Willard. First line: "Let freeborn empires offer prayer." Broadside. [Hingham, MA, 1832]. Copy in Brown University.

Grand Chorus for the Fourth of July. "Just received at J M Ives's [book store] ("New Piano Music," *Salem Gazette*, 29 June 1832, 4).

"An Ode for the 4th July 1832." Music composed by George Webb. For solo voices, chorus (SATB), and piano. Manuscript copy in New York Public Library.

"Ode for the Fourth of July.[571] Written for the New-England Anti-Slavery Society." By "J.E." Tune, "Auld Lang Syne." First line: "Shall Afric's children be forgot."

"Ode for the Fourth of July.[572] Written for the New-England Anti-Slavery Society." By "J.E." Tune, "Scots Wha Hae."

"Ode written for the 4th of July, 1832." First line: "Fearful and dark the clouds that hung" ("Poetry," *New-Hampshire Patriot and State Gazette*, 9 July 1832, 4).

Performances

Maine

Gorham: In the parade to the "Meeting House of the first Parish" were two military companies of infantry with "a Band of Music." At the meeting house, "with the other services, a number of pieces of music were performed by the choir, accompanied by the Organ and Band" ("Celebration at Gorham," *Eastern Argus*, 24 July 1832, 4).

Portland: Democratic Republicans gathered at Union Hall and marched, led by the Portland Band, to the "Church of the first Baptist Society.... The services were enlivened by music from a select choir, with taste, effect and excellence" ("Republican Celebration," *Eastern Argus*, 6 July 1832, 2).

York's Corner: Citizens of York's Corner, in Standish, Hollis, and Buxton met at the Methodist Church, in which after an address and prayer, "the hymn beginning with 'Before Jehovah's Awful Throne' was then sung" ("Celebration at York's Corner, in Standish," *Eastern Argus Semi-Weekly*, 3 August 1832, 3).

Massachusetts

Hingham: "It may not be amiss to notice, as something rare, that besides other novelties produced on the occasion, an Ode sung, written by the Rev. Mr. Pierpont of Boston" (*Salem Gazette*, 13 July 1832, 2). See **Publications** above.

Ipswich: After a parade, the exercises at the Rev. Kimball's Meeting House included a "voluntary by the band"; an anthem "Strike the Cymbal"; anthem "Great is the Lord." A newspaper reported that those in the parade "were accompanied by an excellent martial band, from Salem, whose beautiful tones echoed sweetly over 'the land of hills and streams,' and gave a striking brilliancy to the whole scene. The music at the church was under the direction of Mr. Josiah Caldwell, and the several anthems were performed

with much spirit and effect" (*Salem Gazette*, 6 July 1832, 2).

Methuen: After military parades, a flag presentation, and procession to the Baptist Meeting House, "religious services" included a reading of the Declaration of Independence, and an oration. "The performances by the band and choir of singers were highly acceptable and gratifying to a crowded audience ("Celebration of the 4th in Methen [sic]," *Essex Gazette*, 14 July 1832, 3).

Salem: "Religious celebration of American Independence, at the Tabernacle Church, July 4, 1832. Order of Exercises":

    I. Voluntary on the organ.
    II. Invocation, and reading select Scriptures, by the Rev. Brown Emerson.
    III. Anthem.
    IV. Prayer, by the Rev. Rufus Babcock.
    V. Hymn.
    VI. Address, by the Rev. Charles G. Porter, of Gloucester.
    VII. Collection in aid of the American Colonization Society.
    VIII. Anthem.
    IX. Prayer by the Rev. Wm. Williams.
    X. Doxology.
    XI. Benediction.

[*Salem Gazette*, 3 July 1832, 2].

Ohio

Darby Creek: "Ode for the Fourth of July, 1832" by Otway Curry "sung at the celebration at Darby-Creek, O." First line: "God of the high and boundless heaven!" (*Cincinnati Mirror, and Western Gazette of Literature, Science, and the Arts*, 21 July 1832, 175).

Rhode Island

Greenville: "The fifth-sixth [sic] anniversary of American Independence, will be celebrated at the house of Mr. Harvey Perry in Greenville. A procession will be formed, attended by a band of music, at Mr. Perry's at 11 o'clock, A.M. and move to the Meeting-house, where an oration will be pronounced by the Rev. Mr. Pickering of Providence, and other appropriate exercises at the meeting house..." (*Rhode Island American and Gazette*, 29 June 1832, 1).

Newport: The committee of arrangements for the exercises at the meeting house named Col. B. Marsh, Jr. as director of the music ("Anniversary of Independence," *Rhode-Island Republican*, 3 July 1832, 2).

Virginia

Powhatan: After the ceremony at the Court House, members of the military and citizens "sat down to a splendid dinner, furnished by Mr. Bellow." Music was provided as the toasts were drunk: Tune, Yankee Doodle — Tune Jackson's March — Washington's March — Jefferson and Liberty — Tyrolese Song of Liberty — Marseillois Hymn — Hail Columbia — Yankee Doodle — Star-Spangled Banner — The Campbells are Coming — Tune, Earl Moira — Tune, The

American Star[573]— Tune — Haste to the Wedding ("Fourth of July Celebrations," *Richmond Enquirer*, 13 July 1832, 4).

Richmond: An assemblage of military and citizens gathered at the Theatre and heard "Hail Columbia" and "Yankee Doodle" and other martial music performed during the exercises. Following that the group went to Howard's Grove where after a collation and dinner, the toasts included the following music: Washington's March — Tune, Home Sweet Home — Yankee Doodle — Marseillois Hymn — Auld Robin Gray[574]— Governor's March — Jefferson's March — The Glasses Sparkle on the Board[575]— Oh! say Not Woman's Heart is Bought ("Fourth of July Celebration," *Richmond Enquirer*, 10 July 1832, 3).

1833

Publications

"Anthem for the Fourth of July, 1833." First line: "On this auspicious day" (*National Intelligencer*, 4 July 1833, 3).

"The following hymn, composed for the occasion, was sung as a part of the services, to the tune of Old Hundred": first line, "Let grateful nations join to raise" (*An Oration Delivered before the Gloucester [Massachusetts] Mechanic Association, on the Fourth of July, 1833*. By Robert Rantoul, Jr. Published by request. Salem: Printed by Foote & Chisholm, 1833).

"Odes to be Sung at the Celebration of the Fourth of July, 1833, in the Third Presbyterian Church." Broadside, [Newark, NJ: Newark Young Men's Society, 1833]. Ode (First line: "Raise-raise the shout victorious"/Ode (First line: "Oer mountain, hill, and dale"). Copy in Brown University.

"The Triumph of Union," to the tune "The Star-Spangled Banner" (*Globe*, 6 July 1833, 2).

Performances

Georgia

Macon: Republicans of Macon celebrated with erecting "a splendid pole of great height," a procession from Washington Hall to the Baptist Church where the exercises were held. Later a public barbecue was attended by the assemblage at the warehouse of Mr. Goddards where toasts were presented with the following music: Tune, U.S. March — Hail Columbia — Presidents March — Yankee Doodle — Star-Spangled Banner — Auld Lang Syne — Washington's March — Ye Sons of Freedom Awake — The Trumpet Sounds — Governor's March — Dead March — Go to the Devil and Shake Yourself— O love, 'Tis Love — Star-Spangled Banner — Van Burens Grand March[576]— The Retreat — Fidelity, or Genius of Liberty — Aloft Columbia's Banner Waves — Stand Out of the Way Little Boys — Pleyels Hymn — Hail Columbia — Pillar of

Glory — Roslin Castle — America is Free — My Own Fire Side — Silent Honor — Thimble's Scolding Wife Lay Dead — Dirge — New York March ("Celebration of the 4th of July at Macon," *Georgia Telegraph*, 10 July 1833, 3).

Massachusetts

Boston: The exercises[577] at the Old South Church included:

    I. Voluntary on the organ, by G. J. Webb.
    II. Ode. [first line: "Come up, and praise Him, all the throngs"].
    III. Prayer, by the Rev. Mr. Fairchild.
    IV. Reading of the Scriptures, by the Rev. Mr. Barrett.
    V. Original Ode. Tune, Benecento [first line: "Many a year has rolled away"].
    VI. Oration, by Edward C. Prescott, Esq
    VII. Hymn. Tune, "Old Hundred" [first line: "Great God! beneath whose piercing eye"]
    VIII. Benediction
["Order of Services at the Celebration of American Independence, in the Old South Church, July 4, 1833." Broadside. Website, *An American Time Capsule*].

New York

Poughkeepsie: "At 11 o'clock the steamboats *Providence*, of Newburgh and the *Norfolk*, of New Windosr, arrived both crowded with passengers, among whom were a great number of ladies, and each boat with a band of music on board." At the service held at the Presbyterian Church, military units and citizens from these towns enjoyed "excellent" music by the choir. "A hymn and two odes appropriate to the occasion were sung to the good old tones of Old Hundred, Hail Columbia, and Bruce's Address. The Newburgh band also played Hail Columbia in fine style." Later the group enjoyed a dinner on the hill at the back of Mr. Jarvis' Hotel. Toasts were accompanied by music from the bands (*Independence*, 10 July 1833, 2).

South Carolina

Charleston: A number of military units and members of the Washington Society "with their invited guests" marched "with banners flying and spirit-stirring music" from the market to the 2nd Presbyterian Church. "At the commencement and close of the ceremonies in the church, were sung by a tuneful choir, the favorite anthems of the Union Party, composed by Wm. G. Simms, Esq. and the Rev. Mr. [Samuel Foster] Gilman, which so beautifully blend the spirit of poetry with the spirit of patriotism." The Washington Society dined at Hauschildt's on Charleston Neck at three o'clock P.M. A local newspaper reported that "a band of music was in attendance, and a spirit of social and patriotic hilarity animated the company." The following tunes were performed: Hail Columbia — Washington's March — The Legacy — The Meeting of the Waters — The Star-Spangled Banner — Dear Native Home — Jefferson's March — Hail to the

Chief— The Light House — Welcome to the Feast—
The Last Rose of Summer — Old Virginia Never
Tire — Go to the Devil and Shake Yourself— God
Save the United States — Union and Liberty; at the
dinner held by the Revolution Society and '76 Asso-
ciation, the following works were performed: Tune,
Hail Liberty — Star-Spangled Banner — Dear Native
Land — The Minstrel Boy — Governor's March —
Sound the Loud Timbrel — Remember the Glories of
Brian the Brave — Dirge — Hail to the Chief— Amer-
ica, Commerce, and Freedom — South Carolina
Hymn — Scots wha hae — Is There a Heart That
Never Loved; "A large number of the Volunteers dined
together at the City Hall" where toasts were drank
and the following works performed: Nullification
March — Tyrolese Air — Hail Columbia — Washing-
ton's March — Go to the Devil and Shake Yourself—
Home, Sweet Home — Hail to the Chief ("Fourth of
July," *Charleston Courier*, 19 July 1833, 4; "Fourth of
July," *Richmond Enquirer*, 19 July 1833, 4).

Virginia

Leesburg: "The Volunteer Company of Light Infantry, commanded by Capt. W.C. Selden, accompanied by the band, and attended by many citizens, proceeded to the Methodist Episcopal Church, about 12
o'clock, where the ceremonies were commenced by
the Rev. Mr. Hargrave, of the Presbyterian Church"
(*Richmond Enquirer*, 23 July 1833, 2).

Norfolk: After a large parade of military units and
a flag ceremony, there were exercises at the Presbyterian Church where "the prayer was followed by the 21st
Psalm, sung in admirable taste by the choir." An anthem followed a reading of the Declaration of Independence (*Richmond Enquirer*, 12 July 1833, 4).

Oakley (Charlotte County): "At 1 o'clock the
company sat down to a good and plentiful dinner,
well prepared by James Lawson." Toasts were accom-
panied by the following music: Hail Columbia —
Tune, Washington's March — Tune, Star-Spangled
Banner — Tune, Bruce's Address — Tune, Lafayette's
March — Tune, Auld Lang Syne — Tune, Jefferson's
March — Tune, Madison's March — Tune, Rousseau's
Dream — Tune, Home, Sweet Home — Tune, Jack-
son's March — Tune, Yankee Doodle — Tune, Come,
Haste to the Wedding (*Richmond Enquirer*, 30 July
1833, 3).

Petersburg: In the evening of July 4, five military
companies, three of which were from Richmond,
marched to Bath Spring "where a dinner had been
prepared for the occasion." Toasts were drank to the
sound of artillery and "accompanied by the grand
and sweet music of the Richmond Bands, which
are an honor to their city and an ornament to their
companies": Hail Columbia — Scots, wha hae[578] —
Washington's March — Jefferson's March — Auld Lang
Syne — Pillar of Glory — Jolly Fellows, Fill Your
Glasses — Jackson's March — Minute Gun at Sea[579] —
Ere around the huge oak — Tyrolese Air — Marseilles
Hymn — Oh Say Not Woman's Love is Bought

("The Anniversary," *Richmond Enquirer*, 16 July 1833,
1).

Richmond: "Our Volunteer Companies having accepted the invitation of their brethren of Petersburg,
our own celebration was stript [sic] of much of the
'pomp and circumstance' of military exhibition." At
the First Presbyterian Church, the various Sabbath
schools gathered to hear several addresses and "hymns
suitable to the occasion were sung by an excellent
Choir." At the dinner held at Buchanan's Spring,
"from 70 to 80 citizens and guests" heard the toasts
presented "interspersed with animating cheers and
some fine songs" ("Fourth of July," *Richmond Enquirer*, 9 July 1833, 3).

Scottville: At the Washington Tavern, the men celebrated with toasts accompanied by the following
music: Tune, Yankee Doodle — Tune, Hail Columbia — Washington's March — Tune, Jefferson and Liberty — Madison's March — Monroe's March — Marseillois Hymn — Tune, What signifies the life o' man,
if 'twere not for the lasses o (*Richmond Enquirer*, 16
July 1833, 2).

Winchester: A parade included the military, mechanics, citizens, officers of the railroad company, and
a band of music. The parade had floats, including a car
of printers at work with a printing press all "drawn by
four white hourses." During the parade, "the press
was busily employed in striking off an ode, written
by A.W. Settle, Esq. of Farquier County, of which
about one thousand copies were worked off, and scat-
tered through the crowd during the procession." Later,
services were held at the Lutheran Church. "The
choir, led by Peter Hardt and Wm H. Grove, poured
forth rich music" ("Domestic," *Richmond Enquirer*,
12 July 1833, 2).

1834

Publications

"Air, Adams, and Liberty. Ode, 4th July, 1834."[580]
Sung at a Whig celebration in Boston. Broadside, in
*An American Time Capsule: Three Centuries of Broad-
sides and Other Printed Ephemera* (Library of Congress
Website). For solo voice, chorus, and organ. Copy in
Newbury Library, Chicago.

"The following lines are written preparatory for the
59th anniversary of American Independence. Air —
'The Star-Spangled Banner.'" First line: "Republicans
hark! Hear the cannon's deep sound." Piece signed
"Y.B." ("Poetry for the N.H. Patriot," *New Hampshire
Patriot and State Gazette*, 14 July 1834, 4).

"Ode for a Jackson Celebration, July 4th 1834."
Sung to the tune "Hail to the Chief." First line:
"Ninety-nine cheers for the hot-headed hero!" (*Frederick-Town Herald*, 16 August 1834, 2, as a reprint
from the *Boston Mercantile Journal*).

"Ode for Fourth of July."[581] First line: "Again the

glorious morn returns" (*Farmer's Gazette*, 4 July 1834, 2).

"Ode, written for the Whig celebration, in Worcester, July 4th, 1834." By Charles Thurber. First line: "Where golden Phoebus shed his rays." Broadside, [Worcester, MA, 1834]. Copy in the American Antiquarian Society.

"Original Hymn[582] sung [twice, to different tunes] on the 4th of July, at the Chatham Street Chapel [New York City?]." By "John G. Whittier. Tune, "Old Hundred and Wells." First line: "Oh, Thou, whose presence went before."

"Original ode composed for the celebration of the 58th anniversary of American independence, by the Trades' Union of Boston and vicinity. Of which, several thousand copies were printed and distributed by the Printers Association as the procession marched through the streets." First line: "Hark! Hark! with a lengthened, exultant paean" ("Poetry," *Lancaster Journal*, 8 August 1834, 4); broadside, [Boston, 1834] is printed "By D.J.N." Copy in Brown University.

"Original ode, sung at the Whig celebration in this town [Portsmouth], 4th inst. Tune Adams and Liberty."[583] First line: "Come strike the bold paean, let the organ's soft note" (*Portsmouth Journal of Literature & Politics*, 8 July 1834, 1).

"Song. Written by C. Stark, Jr. and sung by Maj. J.E. Estabrook. Tune—Star-Spangled Banner. 'The American Star.'" First line: "All hail to the star, that so brightly is beaming" (*New-Hampshire Patriot*, 14 July 1834, 1).

"Song, written by John W. Moore, and sung by Maj. J.E. Estabrook,[584] at the Democratic celebration in Concord, July 4, 1834. Tune—'Knight Errant.'" First line: "Most glorious day—most happy hour" ("Poetry," *New Hampshire Patriot and State Gazette*, 21 July 1834, 4).

Songs for the Whig Celebration: July 4, 1834 (Boston: J. H. Eastburn, 1834). Includes "Ode, for the celebration of the 4th July, 1834," at Boston, by Grenville Mellen; "Ode," by I.[saac] McLellan: first line, "Praise to the warlike whigs of old," to the "Air—Auld Lang Syne"; "The Lyre and Sword" (first line: "The Freeman's glittering sword be blest") by George Lunt.[585] A newspaper reported that "several hymns, odes, and songs were produced for this celebration. We have room only for the following, Ode by Grenville Mellen": first line, "I see them on their winding way"; "Song": first line, "Come listen my friends, while to preface a toast" (*Salem Gazette*, 8 July 1834, 1); another report cited "the following Ode, written by William Hayden, Esz. For the Whig Celebration, we copy from the Boston Atlas": "The Constitution": first line, "The Constitution! Let it stand" (*Salem Gazette*, 8 July 1834, 2).

"Whig Celebration. 4th July. 1834. Order of exercises." No place of publication indicated. First lines: "Arise ye people clap your hands"; "When stern oppression's iron rod"; "My country! 'tis of thee"; "Clime!

beneath whose genial sun." Copy in New York Historical Society.

Performances

Maine

Gardiner: The Gardiner Union Temperance Society celebrated with a parade and exercises at the church. A band participated in the procession and a "hymn, L.M."[586] was sung during the services: first line, "Salvation doth to God belong" ("Fourth of July," *Christian Intelligencer and Eastern Chronicle*, 4 July 1834).

Maryland

Annapolis: The Theta Delta Phi Association of St. John's College celebrated in the State House. The Baltimore City Guards Band performed several "national airs" (*Baltimore Patriot*, 7 July 1834, 2).

Massachusetts

Barre: A procession formed at Hathaway's Hotel began with music and marched to "the Rev. Mr. Thompson's Meeting House" where the exercises began with a "Voluntary by Mr. Mandell,"[587] and included a Hymn and Ode, the latter's first line: "When stern oppression's iron rod" ("Fourth of July" and "Celebration of the Fourth of July at Barre," *Farmer's Gazette*, 4 and 11 July 1834, 2 and 2 respectively).

Boston: A Sabbath School Union celebration at the Baptist Church on Federal Street included two original hymns "sung by a choir of children under the direction of Mr. Lowell Mason.... At the close of the exercises, the 117th psalm was sung by the whole congregation to the tune of Old Hundred" ("Fourth of July," *Liberator*, 12 July 1834, 112). See **Publications** above.

Salem: There were two celebrations that day. At the "religious exercises at the South Church, commencing at 10 o'clock, A.M.," among the exercises was "excellent Music, by a select Choir." These three hymns and a doxology were sung: first lines: "Hark the song of jubilee"; "My country! 'tis of thee"; "Great God of nations, now to thee"; "From all that dwell below the skies." At the North Church, an "apprentices' celebration" took place. "Amongst the musical performances, was the singing of an Original Ode, composed for the occasion by Miss M.C. Ruce[588]—a very creditable production. After the services at the Church, the Escort, the Committee, the Marshals, and the Choir, partook of a bountiful Collation at the Town Hall." Present at the latter affair were over 200 apprentices of the Youthful Mechanics of Salem. First line for the ode: "Ye sons of America, weep o'er the dead" ("Apprentices' Celebration" and "Fourth of July," *Salem Gazette*, 4 and 8 July 1834, 2 and 1, respectively).

New Hampshire

Concord: At the Baptist Meeting House, in the ceremony there "several anthems were performed by the

Mozart Society, led by H.E. Moore"[589] ("Democratic Republican Celebration at Concord," *New-Hampshire Patriot*, 14 July 1834, 1).

New Ipswich: "A procession was formed preceded by a band of musick" and marched to the "new Meeting House "where prayers were offered by the Rev. Mr. Bates, a spirited oration was delivered by Mr. Silas Foster, singing of the first order by a choir of volunteers." At the dinner, toasts were drank "accompanied by musick and firing of canon" ("Celebration at New-Ipswich," *Farmers' Cabinet*, 11 July 1834, 2).

Portsmouth: Public school procession beginning at the Methodist Episcopal Meeting-House in State Street to the North Meeting House where the following exercises were held:

March by Band.
Voluntary.
Prayer.
Hymn.
Declaration of Independence.
Ode — "Hark! The Song of Jubilee."
Address.
Ode — "My Country 'Tis of Thee."
Benediction.

("Fourth of July School Celebration," *Portsmouth Journal of Literature & Politics*, 4 July 1834, 2.); a "Whig Celebration" in Portsmouth included a procession and at the North Church, it was noted that "the highly satisfactory performance of the musical choir at the church was more interesting from the fact, that ladies and gentlemen from the choirs of almost every society in town had voluntarily united in the interesting services of this occasion" ("Whig Celebration of Independence," *Portsmouth Journal of Literature & Politics*, 8 July 1834, 2). See **Publications** above.

North Carolina

Charlotte: The Salem Light Infantry Band, led by Johann Heinrich Leinbach, performed tunes for officials and citizens.[590]

Pennsylvania

Adamstown: A stage eight feet high was erected in a grove "for the use of the 'Adamstown Band of music' consisting of twenty four members [who] did infinite honor to themselves and to the day." A procession to the spring was preceded by the Band. Toasts included the following music: Hail Columbia — Capt. Warner's March — Garryown for Glory — Auld Lang Syne — Yankee Doodle — Washington's March — Roslin Castle — Adeste Fidel. — Scot's wha hae — Washing Day[591] — Oh Let Us In This Ae Night ("Fourth of July," *Lancaster Journal*, 18 July 1834, 1).

Rhode Island

Newport: The music for the parade and exercises at the Second Baptist Meeting House were "under the direction" of Mr. Benjamin Marsh, Jr. ("Anniversary of Independence," *Rhode-Island Republican*, 2 July 1834, 2).

Virginia

Cartersville: "A brilliant assemblage of ladies and gentlemen from Cumberland and the adjacent counties, were conducted into a ballroom, prepared for the purpose, at Thomas McCoy's Tavern, enlivened by the finest performers on the violin that the State affords" ("Celebration at Cartersville," *Richmond Enquirer*, 11 July 1834, 3).

Columbia: Performed at Mrs. Lee's Tavern following a toast: Auld Lang Syne — Hail Columbia — Hail to the Chief — Home! Sweet Home — The Star-Spangled Banner — Washington's March — Yankee Doodle (*Richmond Enquirer*, 15 July 1834, 3).

Nottoway: The day began with an "animated parade," in which the Nottoway Cadets "marched to the field, to the tune of 'Hail Columbia! happy land!'" At the grove, the musicians played "Yankee Doodle." Later the dinner was concluded with toasts and the following music: Tune, Hail Columbia — Tune, Washington's March — Star-Spangled Banner — Jackson's March — Tune, Gilderoy — The Campbells Are Coming — Tune, Yankee Doodle — O Say Not Woman's Love is Bought ("Nottoway Celebration at Jennings' Ordinary," *Richmond Enquirer*, 18 July 1834, 1).

Petersburg: At Poplar Springs, a dinner was available for the militia and citizens, and the mayor of Petersburg, George Harrison, presided. Toasts were accompanied by the following music: Washington's March — Scots Wha Hae — Ere around the Huge Oak — Jefferson and Liberty — Roslin Castle — Jackson's March — Pillar of Glory — Tweed Side[592] — The Campbell's Are Coming — Tyrolese Air — Marseilles Hymn — Oh! Say No Woman's Love is Bought (*Richmond Enquirer*, 11 July 1834, 2).

Richmond: At a dinner celebration held by the Volunteers of Richmond, music was supplied after the toasts "by the fine band at the R.L.I. Blues": Hail Columbia — Auld Lang Syne — Marseilles Hymn ("Fourth of July Celebration," *Richmond Enquirer*, 11 July 1834, 2).

1835

Publications

"The following Hymn, composed for the occasion, by the Rev. W.P. Lunt, was sung by the Choir": first line, "O Thou! to whom our fathers pour'd." (*An Oration Delivered before the Citizens of the Town of Quincy, on the Fourth of July, 1835, the Fifty-Ninth Anniversary of the Independence of the United States of America*. By Solomon Lincoln. Hingham: Jedidiah Farmer, 1835, 31).

"Hymn, written for, and sung at the commemoration of American independence in Geneva, July 4,

1835. Tune — Hark, the song of Jubilee." First line: "Hark! the hymn of liberty" (*The Zodiac; a Monthly Periodical, Devoted to Science, Literature, and the Art* ... (September 1835): 1, 3).

"National ode, written for the Fourth of July celebration at Southbridge, Mass ... 1835." First line: "Awake, arise, ye sons of liberty." Broadside, [Southbridge, Mass., 1835]. Copy in Brown University.

"Ode by Willis Gaylord Clark.[593] Celebration of the Athenian Society of Bristol College [Bristol, Pennsylvania]. July 4, 1835. Air — 'Star-Spangled Banner.'" First line: "Hail, hail to the day, when with Memory's wand." Library of Congress, *An American Time Capsule: Three Centuries of Broadsides and Other Printed Ephemera.*

"Original Hymn sung at Salem, July 4, 1835." First line: "Who are the Free? The Sons of God."[594]

"Original Hymn sung by the children of the Belknap St. Sabbath School, July 4, 1835, while celebrating the national jubilee." First line: "Soon shall the trump of freedom."[595]

"Original Ode. Written to be sung on the fiftyninth anniversary of American Independence, by Mrs. S.R.A. Barnes." First line: "The glad green earth beneath our feet" ("Poetry," *New Hampshire Patriot and State Gazette*, 20 July 1835, 4).

"Ode to Independence. Supposed to be sung at the celebration by the Ladies." Signed "M." First line: "Come from thy temple, Fame" (from the *Troy Budget* as printed in "Miscellaneous," *Pittsfield Sun*, 23 July 1835, 1).

"A Patriotic Song. Written for the celebration of independence at Londonderry [NH], by the Yankee Bard." First line: "The Federal clan has now began" (*New Hampshire Patriot and State Gazette*, 20 July 1835, 4).

"Select Hymn sung at the first annual meeting of the Old Colony, Plymouth County Anti-Slavery Society, July 4, 1835."[596] First line: "Soon Afric's long enslaved sons."

Sons of Columbia: a national song written for the Fourth of July, and set to music by Theodore Ascherfeld. Broadside, Philadelphia: A.. Auner, [1835?]. First line: "Rejoice, ye sons of Columbia!" "The music to the above with a spirited march, is for sale at G. Andre & Co's music store, 1104 Chestnut Street." Copy in Duke University Library.

Performances

Alabama

Montgomery: "On board the steamer *Little Rock*, which arrived on Sunday from Mobile," the Fourth was celebrated with an oration and an Ode composed by John Howard Payne[597] "and spoken by himself." First line: "When erst our sires their sails unfurl'd" (*Richmond Enquirer*, 24 July 1835, 4; "Poetry," *Salem Gazette*, 31 July 1835, 1).

Delaware

Wilmington: The Washington Band accompanied a parade of manufacturers and mechanics from Brandywine into the city. At City Hall, they were joined by Johnson's Band "and an elegant well disciplined company from Philadelphia ("Celebration of the Fourth of July," *Delaware Gazette and American Watchman*, 7 July 1835, 2).

Massachusetts

Beverly: At the Union celebration held at "the Rev. Mr. Abbott's Meeting House ... the services were interspersed with suitable music — anthems, hymns, and a spirited original ode, by Mr. Flagg,[598] of Beverly" ("Union Celebration of the Fourth of July, at Beverly" and "The Fourth of July," *Salem Gazette*, 3 and 7 July 1835, 3 and 2, respectively).

Boston: The celebration at the Old South Church included "musical services ... performed by the Boston Academy with much taste and effect" (*Farmers' Cabinet*, 17 July 1835, 2).

Lynn: Included a parade of military units with a band of music through the streets to the pavilion where the exercises began with an anthem. Two hymns were also sung, one "written by the Rev. Dr. [James?] Flint": first line: "In pleasant lands have fallen the lines." The ceremony also included an "ode written by Hon. Jonathan Shove,[599] the music composed by H.K. Oliver, Esq."[600] An anthem and benediction ended the service ("Whig Celebration at Lynn," *Salem Gazette*, 7 July 1835, 2).

New Bedford: A juvenile sabbath school celebration was scheduled to open with a "voluntary by the Juvenile Choir," followed by two hymns and a patriotic song. Luke P. Lincoln[601] was asked "to take charge of the music on the occasion, and that the music be juvenile" ("Sabbath School Celebration," *New Bedford Mercury*, 3 July 1835, 2).

Salem: At the Sabbath school celebration held at the South Meeting House the "order of exercises" were:

1. Voluntary and Hymn.
2. Invocation, and selections from Scripture
3. Hymn.
4. Prayer.
5. Hymn.
6. Address, by the Rev. Mr. Worcester.
7. Hymn.
8. Prayer.
9. Doxology.

"Exercises will commence at half past 8, A. M." ("Fourth of July," *Salem Gazette*, 3 July 1835, 3); at an anti-slavery celebration held at the Howard Street Church, the order of exercises were:

1. Voluntary.
2. Reading the Scriptures.
3. Prayer.
4. Hymn.

5. Address, by the Rev. Samuel J. May.
6. Collection for the Massachusetts Anti-Slavery Society.
7. Hymn, "Old Hundred."
8. Benediction.

"Exercises to commence at three o'clock, in the afternoon" ("Anti-Slavery Celebration," *Salem Gazette*, 3 July 1835, 3); at a political party held in a hall, two songs were sung: first line: "We've models worthy of all imitation"; "The Battle of Lexington"[602] (first line: "When the troops of Britain came") (*Salem Gazette*, 31 July 1835, 2). See also **Publications** above.

Missouri

St. Louis: An "ode, written for the occasion, by a lady of this city, was sung at the church by the choir, under the direction of Mr. Huntington." "Air—Star-Spangled Banner." First line: "Proud day for Columbia, we hail thee with song!"[603] ("The Fourth," *Daily Evening Herald*, 6 July 1835, 2); at Lucas's Grove, "about half a mile" from St. Louis, a Corps of Marions celebration had the following music interspersed with toasts: Hail Columbia—Jefferson's March—Washington's March—Hail to the Chief—President's March—Jefferson and Liberty—Star-Spangled Banner—Missouri Belle—Star-Spangled Banner—Hail Columbia—Yankee Doodle—Love's Young Dream and Auld Lang Syne (*Daily Evening Herald*, 7 July 1835, 1–2).

New Hampshire

Hancock: The Hillsborough Band and a choir at the meeting house—"The music selected for the occasion was well arranged and performed by the choir in a spirited and chaste manner" ("Celebration at Hancock," *New Hampshire Patriot and State Gazette*, 13 July 1835, 2).

New Chester: "The day was ushered in by the discharge of cannon and the ringing of bells. At eleven o'clock, the procession was formed under the direction of Col. John S. Bryant, as marshall [sic], assisted by four deputy marshals, and proceeded to the east meeting house, escorted by the Franklin Rifle Company, commanded by Capt. Jeremiah Green, where, after appropriate musick by the choir and prayer by Elder Martin, the following 'Ode,' composed for the occasion by G.W. Summer, Esq., was sung." First line: "Should independence be forgot." "The services closed with musick, and prayer by the Rev. J. Clement" ("Celebration at New-Chester," *New Hampshire Patriot and State Gazette*, 13 July 1835, 3).

Portsmouth: A procession assembled by the Young Men's Society for Mutual Improvement marched with an escort provided the Rockingham Guards to the "Universalists" Meeting House. The exercises included a "performance by the Juvenile Choir, under Mr. Gordon, [and] was not the least interesting part of the exercises. An hundred sweet voices, swelling the notes of joy on Freedom's Jubilee, partook in no small degree of a fairy illusion which poets are so prone to revel in"

(*Portsmouth Journal of Literature & Politics*, 11 July 1835, 2).

Whitefield: "The exercises at the Town House were interspersed with music both from the band and choir" ("Whitefield Celebration," *New Hampshire Patriot and State Gazette*, 20 July 1835, 3).

Rhode Island

Newport: At the Second Baptist Meeting House, "the music on the occasion, will be under the direction of Mr. W. Nutting"[604] ("Anniversary of Independence," *Newport Mercury*, 4 July 1835, 2).

Vermont

Burlington: Ode, by Willis Gaylord Clark, sung to the melody of "Star-Spangled Banner" at the Athenian Society celebration held at Bristol College. First line: "Hail, hail to the day." Broadside, "Ode by Willis Gaylord Clark," (Burlington: J. L. Powell, 1835); *American Time Capsule: Three Centuries of Broadsides and Other Printed Ephemera*

Virginia

Cumberland: The exercises included "the sound of the finest band of music that could be procured—the two Scotts, from Charlottesville, whose fame on the violin it would be superfluous to sound; Mr. Vaughan's celebrated performer, George; and Blind Bill, unequalled on the octave flute." At the dinner, "patriotic songs were occasionally interspersed, at the call of the company, which gave life and animation to the scene" (*Richmond Enquirer*, 14 July 1835, 1).

Petersburg: At the dinner prepared by "Mr. Nathaniel Blick, the Proprietor of the Poplar Spring House" at Poplar Lawn, the following music works accompanied the toasts: Tune, Hail Columbia—Washington's March—Marseilles Hymn—Jefferson's March—Lafayette's March—Ere Around the Huge Oak—Ca Ira—The Campbells Are Coming—Yankee Doodle—President's March—Star-Spangled Banner—The Pillar of Glory—Here's a Health ("Petersburg Celebration," *Richmond Enquirer*, 10 July 1835, 2).

Round Hill: Citizens of this town as well as Southampton, assembled near Boykin's Mill for a dinner with toasts "interspersed with appropriate music, and accompanied by a discharge of cannon": Hail Columbia—President's March—Yankee Doodle—Washington's March—Dirge—Home, Sweet Home—Hail Columbia—The Campbells Are Coming—Wife, Children and Friends ("Celebration at Round Hill," *Richmond Enquirer*, 31 July 1835, 3).

1836

Publications

"Columbia's Birth-day, Again We Behold."[605] Ode

for 4th July, 1836; written by H.F. Gould,[606] music by Lowell Mason. Boston: Shepley & Wright, 1836.

"The following original ode for independence, was sung on the 4th, during the services at the Old South Church, Boston, with excellent effect: Ode for Independence." First line: "Columbia's birthday again we behold" (*Farmer's Cabinet*, 15 July 1836, 4).

"Hymn for the Fourth of July. By N.P. Willis." First line: "Joy to the pleasant land we love" ("Poetry," *Youth's Companion*, 1 July 1836, 28).

Jackson's Grand March. By S. Knaebel. Boston: Parker & Ditson, 1836. Performed at the Boston Democratic Celebration by the Boston Brass Band. Copy in Johns Hopkins University.

"From the *Songs of the Free*. 'Fourth of July.'[607] Mary Ann Collier." First line: "Heard ye the mighty rushing?" ("Poetry," *Essex Gazette*, 2 July 1836, 1; *Haverhill Gazette*, 2 July 1836, 2).

"Song for the Fourth of July. Air — 'The Star-Spangled Banner.'" First line: "To the sages who spoke — to the heroes who bled" (*Atkinson's Casket*, no. 10 [October 1836]:503).

Performances

Connecticut

Berlin: A procession "escorted by an excellent band of music" from the Universalist Church to the Presbyterian Church at 10 A.M. was followed by a ceremony. "The singing at the church was of the first order — appropriate pieces were selected and well performed. A constant discharge of artillery was kept up while the procession was moving from one church to the other. After the services at the church, the procession was again formed, and — escorted by the band — proceeded to a beautiful grove, where about seven hundred persons partook of an entertainment" ("Fourth of July Celebration at Berlin," *Connecticut Courant*, 18 July 1836, 3).

Salisbury: "The anniversary of American independence was celebrated in Salisbury, by the Juvenile Temperance Society, under the direction of a committee of gentlemen appointed for that purpose.... At noon, a procession was formed and proceeded to the Congregational Church":

1. A Juvenile Choir of Singers, consisting of about one hundred children, under fifteen, and several of them not more than four or five years of age.
2. Members of the Juvenile Temperance society, and other children who were present.
3. President of the day, Clergy, Vice Presidents, and Committees for the day.
4. Parents and other citizens.

"Having entered the Church, the audience attended with great delight, to the following order of exercises":

1. Music, Voluntary, tune Old Hundred.
2. Reading of the Declaration of Independence, by Roger Averill, Esq.

3. Singing — Anniversary of Independence — "We come with joy and gladness," &c.
4. Prayer by the Rev. Mr. Lathrop.
5. Singing — Freedom's Star[608] — "When rolling orbs from chaos sprung."
6. Oration by the Rev. Mr. Merrick, Principal of the Methodist Episcopal Seminary, Amenia, N.Y.
7. Singing — God Save America — "My country, 'tis of thee, sweet land of liberty," and a Adieu to Dissipation — "O thou source of ills unnumbered."
8. Address to the children, by the Rev. Mr. Lathrop.
9. Singing, in succession, the following, viz.: "Daughter of Temperance, arise from thy mourning"; The Star-Spangled Banner, "O say, can you see by the dawn's early light"; The Jubilee, a parody on Bruce's Address; "Fourth of July Ode" [first line: "This is the day on which our sires"] for a Juvenile Temperance Society, by Mrs. Sigourney,[609] written for the occasion.

Later, "in a delightful and finely shaded grove," as the youth ate fruits and pastries,

the scene was occasionally enlivened by music from the youthful choir. To this choir, under the instruction and direction of Mr. Abel O. Root, the audience were indebted for a large share of the pleasure which was felt in every heart, and lighted up with the smile of joy, every countenance. This experiment of teaching children to sing, and connecting it with such an occasion, has been entirely successful, proving the practicability of teaching quite young children the art of singing, and also its important practical utility in promoting the cause of Temperance among the youth of our country. ["Celebration of the Fourth of July, at Salisbury, Conn.: Temperance and Independence," *Connecticut Courant*, 11 July 1836, 3].

South Glastenbury: In this "Factory Village ... engaged in the cotton manufacture," a procession "formed in front of their house of worship," was led by a music ensemble that marched to South Glastenbury

and through its principle [sic] streets, with perfect regularity and discipline; having their instrumental music, except at proper intervals, when the singers performed some select pieces that were suitable for the occasion. The appearance of this procession was well calculated to soften the heard; but at the same time, animate the feelings with an unusual degree of American freedom. They then marched back to the bower, by the Factory village, that had been formed for the occasion.

They took their seats "and when all were settled, an appropriate prayer was made, which was followed by singing the 'Ode on Science.' Then was read the Declaration of Independence, by Mr. W. Norton, Jun., which was followed by the singing of 'Hail Columbia.'" After the address, "another piece was sung, that had been selected for closing the expressions of joy and gratitude on the occasion, the refreshments were handed round, which consisted of cake, lemonade, wine, and water" (*Connecticut Courant*, 18 July 1836, 3).

Massachusetts

Boston: In the Charles Street Baptist Meeting House, the schools belonging to the Boston Baptist Sabbath School Union had "religious exercises" that included the singing of two hymns. The first line of the second hymn: "When our fathers long ago" ("Celebration Fourth of July for the Sabbath School Children," *Farmer's Cabinet*, 15 July 1836, 4). See **Publications** above.

Palmer: No less than 1500 persons participated in the celebration that included a procession with a female choir of singers, composed of about 30 young ladies dressed in uniform white, with blue sashes, their heads wear of flowers" (*Pittsfield Sun*, 28 July 1836, 2).

Pittsfield: A parade from the "coffee house of Mr. Field" to the Congregational Meeting House was "escorted by the Berkshire Band of music." The exercises were begun with music from the band, "under the direction of Mr. R. Osborn of Lenox," and "was executed in a creditable and satisfactory manner." Three pieces were performed during the ceremony ("Independence" and "Democratic Nominations," *Pittsfield Sun*, 30 June and 7 July 1836, 3 and 2, respectively).

Roxbury: At Mr. Putnam's meeting house the following works were performed: "Hymn" (first line: "Wake! the song of Jubilee"); "Original hymn" (first line: "Swell forth the organ's pealing notes!"); "Original ode, The Sons of the Pilgrims" (first line: "The watery waste they trod"), by Henry F. Harrington.[610] (Broadside, "Celebration of Independence, at Roxbury: Order of Exercises...." Boston: Marden & Co., 1836.)

Mississippi

Natchez: Performed at a dinner held at "Mr. West's Mansion House": Auld Lang Syne — Come Haste to the Wedding — The Fencibles March — Hail Columbia — Lafayette's March — Marseiles Hymn — Old Grimes is Dead[611] — Rail Road March — Scots Wha' Hae — Sprigg of Shillalah — The Square and Compass — The Star-Spangled Banner — Yankee Doodle (*Mississippi Free Trader*, 1 and 8 July 1836, 1–2 and 2, respectively).

New Hampshire

Amherst: An assemblage of the "Sabbath School Union, comprising the Sabbath schools of Amherst, Milford, and Mont Vernon" at the meeting house began with a "prayer by the Rev. Mr. Carpenter of Milford, and singing by the choir." The end of the services was signaled "by singing and an appropriate

concluding prayer" ("Fourth of July," *Farmers' Cabinet*, 8 July 1836, 3).

Rindge:

> At 11 o'clock, not withstanding the day was intensely wet, the choir of singers, consisting of about 30 ladies dressed in white, with a corresponding number of gentlemen, assembled at the Methodist Chapel, and were escorted thence to the Congregational Meeting House by Rindge Light Infantry, accompanied by a band of music. A prayer was then offered by the Rev. Mr. Burnham, and several pieces of music were performed by the choir [directed by S.B. and J.C. Sherwin and A. Cutler]; after which, an address, suited to the occasion, was delivered by the Rev. Mr. Morgan, followed by an Ode (composed for the occasion by Mr. B. Deane) sung by the choir.

First line: "Hail! Liberty! Celestial Maid!" "Several other pieces of music closed the exercises at the Meeting House" ("Fourth of July at Rindge," *New-Hampshire Sentinel*, 11 August 1836, 3).

1837

Publications

"Exercises at the Meeting-House." "Temperance Hymn."/ First line: "Now let us strike the cheerful strain." "'The Life-Boat: A Cold Water Song,' written for the Temperance Union Celebration, at Concord, Fourth of July, 1837 by George Kent, Esq."/ First line: "Where through the torn garb the wild tempest was streaming." "'An Original Hymn' by Prof. T.D.P. Stone"[612]/ First line: "Our fathers' pledge yet stands unbroken." Broadside, [Concord, NH], 1837. Copy in Center for Popular Music, Middle Tennessee State University.

"Hymn for the Fourth of July. Air, Duke-Street." First line: "God of this people! Thou whose breath." ["Utica, July 1, 1837. E.H.C."]. ("Poetry," *Evangelical Magazine and Gospel Advocate*, 7 July 1837, 216).

"Hymn sung at the annual meeting of the Plymouth County Anti-Slavery Society, on the 4th of July."[613] By George Russell. Tune, ["America?"]. First line: "Sons of the noble sires!'

"Ode for the Fourth of July. Written by James Aiken, Esq. and sung at a celebration in Centre County, Pennsylvania. Original." First line: "When Grim oppression's iron hand" (*Baltimore Monument: A Weekly Journal ...* 8 July 1837, 317).

"Ode. Written for July 4, 1837." First line: "String well the harp! ye chosen free" (*Farmer's Cabinet*, 30 June 1837, 3).

"Order of exercises at the celebration of the sixty first anniversary of American Independence."[614] Includes National Ode (first line: "Ye sons of Columbia who bravely have fought") by R.T. Paine; Hymn, 194 Belknap (first line: "O'er mountain tops, the mount of

God"). Broadside, Newburyport [MA], 1837. Copy in Brown University.

"Original Ode for the Fourth of July." First line: "Hail, hail Independence! all hail to the Fourth!" (*Ladies' Companion, a Monthly Magazine* [July 1837]:124).

"Whig Patriotic Song." July 4, 1837 to the air "Star-Spangled Banner." First line: "Midst the turmoil of party and anarchy's strife" (*Poulson's American Daily Advertiser*, 4 July 1837, 2).

Performances

Connecticut

New Haven: "Folsom," "Hamburg," "Yarmouth" were sung between addresses at the Sabbath School celebration. Broadside. "Order of exercises." Copy in New York Historical Society.

Massachusetts

Boston: The Boston Baptist Sabbath School Union celebrated at the meeting house on Baldwin Place. "The singing, performed by a juvenile choir, selected from the schools, under the superintendence of Mr. Charles D. Gould, assisted by Mr. Bruce, organist, was uncommonly excellent." Members of the Boston Sunday School Union of 18 churches celebrated at the Odeon.

> The music was performed by a juvenile choir, numbering nearly one hundred and fifty children, who sat back of the speakers, and facing the audience. Four hymns, appropriate to the celebration, were sung with the most perfect precision of time, and with the sweetest melody which youthful voices well trained could accomplish. Much credit is due these young performers, and to those who arranged and superintended the music. A young lad, by the name of Copeland, about twelve years of age, sung a patriotic hymn, commencing "Before all lands in east or west," in a most charming manner. ["Sunday School Celebrations of the Fourth of July," *Zion's Herald*, 12 July 1837, 110].

Quincy: "The children, about five hundred in number, and in a neat, uniform dress, under their several teachers, marched in procession to the first church, escorted by a fine band of music, and attended by the clergymen of the several religious societies, the school committee, municipal authorities, and citizens." A hymn "written for the occasion by the Rev. William P. Lunt" was sung at the church. First line: "When, driven by oppression's rod" ("Celebration of the Fourth of July, at Quincy," *Christian Register and Boston Observer*, 15 July 1837).

Mississippi

Jackson: Performed at "Spring Grove near the upper Steamboat Landing, on Pearl River, to a beautiful bower, formed by Nature's hand" by a band of musicians: Hail Columbia — Yankee Doodle ("Cele-bration of American Independence," *Mississippian*, 7 July 1837, 3).

New Hampshire

Fitzwilliam: A procession led by the Fitzwilliam Band gathered in front of the village school house at 11 A.M. Included in the parade were "female singers of both choirs." The group marched to the North Meeting House where the following program took place:

1. Anthem by the Choir.
2. Hymn.
3. Prayer by the Rev. Mr. Sabin.
4. Hymn.
5. Oration by A.A. Parker, Esq.
6. Voluntary by the Band.
7. Hymn.
8. Prayer by the Rev. Mr. Farmer.
9. Hymn.
10. Benediction.
11. Voluntary by the Band.

As reported in a local newspaper, "The Fitzwilliam Band, recently organized by some of our spirited young men, appeared in uniform, and by their skilful manner of performing our national airs, added much to the pleasures of the celebration." At the dinner held on the common, Mr. Shirley, a Revolutionary War soldier, "gave a patriotic song" and the band performed "spirit-stirring national airs" ("Celebration at Fitzwilliam," *New-Hampshire Sentinel*, 13 July 1837, 2).

Milford: The Sabbath schools of Milford, Mont Vernon and Amherst met at the Congregational Meeting House "in great numbers." The exercises included "well performed singing of the appropriate hymns by the choir, rendered the occasion highly interesting, and we trust profitable to all who attended" ("Fourth of July," *Farmers' Cabinet*, 7 July 1837, 3).

Rhode Island

Newport: The exercises held at the meeting house included music "under the direction of Messrs. Thos. Stacy, Jr. and Edward Landers" ("Anniversary of American Independence," *Newport Mercury*, 1 July 1837, 2).

Virginia

Petersburg: A procession through city streets to the theater included a band. After the exercises at the theater, a dinner was provided by Mr. Nathaniel Blick. Toasts were presented accompanied by the following music: Hail Columbia — Scots Wha Hae — Washington's March — Jefferson's March — Marseilles Hymn — Ere Round the Huge Oak — Tyrolese Air of Liberty — Should Auld Acquaintance be Forgot — President's March — Pillar of Light — Yankee Doodle — Haydn's Andante[615] — Here'a a Health, &c ("Fourth of July," *Richmond Enquirer*, 14 July 1837, 1).

Richmond: At a dinner for the Richmond Light Infantry Blues, the toasts presented included the following musical works: Tune, Hail Columbia — Washington's March — Scot's Wha Hae — Auld Lang Syne — Star-Spangled Banner — Marseilles Hymn — Dead March — Dirge — Texian March[616] — Hail to the Chief — Yankee Doodle — Old Virginia Never Tire — Here's Health to All Good Lasses ("Fourth of July Celebrations," *Richmond Enquirer*, 11 July 1837, 3).

Williamsburg: At William and Mary College, The Norfolk Light Artillery Blues and Williamsburg Guards, and "visitors, faculty and students" heard a number of addresses and later

> the ceremonies at the church, commenced with music from the organ, and prayer by the Rev. Mr. Parks of Norfolk.... One of the most striking as well as novel incidents of the day at Church, was an anthem to the tune "God save the King," by the organ and choir. It had upon some a very thrilling effect — Such sounds, I am sure, had not been hard there for more than half a century. Last year, it was said, that the keys were touched by the "pious and delicate fingers of one of Spottsylvania's beauteous daughters" — on the present occasion, they were acted upon by the more skilful hands of Mrs. Johnson, as organist, an accomplished English lady, who has for some time past, conducted with success, a female seminary in Williamsburg.[617] ["Fourth of July in Williamsburg," *Richmond Enquirer*, 11 July 1837, 3].

1838

Publications

"The following Odes were sung at the Celebration in this town on the 4th inst: 'Hail Columbia.'" First line: "Hail Columbia! Happy land!"[618]; "America." First line: "My Country! 'Tis of Thee"; "Marseilles Hymn." First line: "Ye Sons of Freedom, wake to glory" ("Poetry," *Rhode Island Republican*, 11 July 1838, 4).

"Hail Columbia," "Hymn," and "Ode" sung at "a juvenile temperance celebration." Litchfield, Connecticut. Broadside. Copy in Connecticut Historical Society.

"Hymn sung at East Bradford, on the 4th of July."[619] By M.P. Atwood. First line: "Bright dawns a nation's jubilee."

"Hymn sung at the anti-slavery celebration in Charlestown on the 4th of July."[620] By F. Howe. First line: "Now joyous hail the genial light."

"Hymns To Be Sung at the Sabbath School Celebration, on the 4th of July, 1838, at Lewisburg, Pa." Broadside. Includes text of five hymns. Copy in Bucknell University.

"Independence Celebration. A Juvenile Temperance Celebration will be Holden at Litchfield [Connecticut] on the 4th of July, 1838 ... Order of Exercises." Broadside. Includes text of three songs: Hail Columbia, Hymn, and Ode. Copy in Connecticut Historical Society.

"Lines sung at a meeting of the Westford Anti-Slavery Society on the 4th of July."[621] By Claudius Bradford. First line: "Behold, behold, how earth and sky."

"Ode for the Fourth of July. By Otway Curry." First line: "God of the high and boundless heaven!" (*Hesperian; or, Western Monthly Magazine* [July 1838]:244).

"Original Hymn sung at Marlboro' Chapel, July 4, 1838."[622] By P.H. Sweetser. First line: "Who fought their country to redeem."

Performances

Massachusetts

Barre: A town procession, and exercises in the church were praised. "Credit is due to the Fitchburg Brass Band for the rich music with which the day was enlivened" ("The Fourth in Barre," *Barre Weekly Gazette*, 6 July 1838, 2).

Lenox: Republicans and others representing "23 of the towns in Berkshire" processed to the Congregational Church where the music "under the direction of that deservedly popular teacher of psalmody, Mr. M.S. Wilson,[623] was of a very superior order, and reflected much credit upon the performers" ("The Fourth," *Pittsfield Sun*, 12 July 1838, 2).

Lowell: Nearly 3000 school children marched "two in two" with "the usual noisy accompaniment of martial music" to a grove where the exercises were held. They sang "Come, Holy Spirit, Heavenly Dove," to the tune "St. Martins," and "an appropriate original hymn, in Old Hundred, closed the exercises" ("Sabbath School Celebrations," *Farmer's Cabinet*, 13 July 1838, 2).

New Bedford: The revelry of the Fourth was somewhat diminished because the orator "did not arrive at all" and "the failure of the Boston Brass Band to make their appearance, which they probably would have done had they received a sufficient inducement and seasonable invitation.... Quite a number of the Truckmen we understand went out of town on the occasion, mounted on their horses and preceded by a band of music, intending thus the same day to feast their eyes with the beauties of the adjacent country, their ears with the 'sweet sounds' of martial music" (*New Bedford Mercury*, 6 July 1838, 2).

Salem: "Duett and Chorus" (Handel) and "National Hymn (Haydn)" performed "by a select choir, under the direction of Mr. Monds,[624] who will preside at the organ" at the Baptist Church (*Gloucester Democrat*, 3 July 1838, 2).

Worcester: A temperance celebration began with a parade "accompanied with excellent music by the brass band at Worcester" to the Central church. After an address and prayer, "an original hymn was then sung by choirs ... a large choir of singers, with a fine organ, well played by our friend Zeuner,[625] of Boston, added much to the intent of the occasion" ("Temperance Festivals," *Farmer's Cabinet*, 13 July 1838, 2).

New Hampshire

Portsmouth: The Whigs of Portsmouth held a dinner at Jefferson Hall that included spontaneous toasts. "These were interspersed with agreeable songs, one of which, to the tune of 'Yankee Doodle,' was sung by Major Larkin with inconceivable humour and effect; it was handed down, the Major said, from the days of the Revolution, with an injunction that it should never be printed nor sung except 'on great occasion'" ("Fourth of July," *Portsmouth Journal of Literature & Politics*, 7 July 1838, 2).

New Jersey

Elizabethtown: "As Israel's People in Despair," "Hail to the Day When the Bold Declaration," and "The Star-Spangled Banner" were sung "in the church." Broadside. (*Fourth of July Celebration at Elizabeth-town. 1838. Order of Exercises in the Church.* Elizabethtown, N.J., 1838.) Copy in Brown University.

New York

New York: At the Hamilton Literary and Theological Institution exercises, included: an "original hymn," to the tune "America" (first line: "Break forth, ye hills, in song") by Benj. F. Taylor and sung by the choir; an "original ode," to the tune "Parma" (first line: "Loud swell the Pean to the skies"), by Wm. Carey Richards and sung by the choir; "select music, 'Happy the land,'[626] &c," sung by the choir (broadside, "Order of Exercises on the Sixty — Second Anniversary of American Independence, Wednesday, July 4, 1838," *An American Time Capsule: Three Centuries of Broadsides and Other Printed Ephemera*).

Sing Sing: A procession of military companies and mechanics' trades was preceded by the Sing Sing Military Band. After marching to the Presbyterian Church, the exercises included a reading of the Declaration of Independence and an oration, after which "Mr. Robert George Paige[627] ascended the rostrum, and sang the following Ode, which some unknown author had the kindness to write for the occasion. Tune — 'Hurrah for the Bonnets of Blue.'" First line: "Here's a cheer for the land of our birth!"

> At the close of the song, we are sorry to say, a portion of sealing [sic] in the right wing of the Church gave way, and, falling upon the people below, for a moment created considerable alarm. It being ascertained that no material injury was done, the audience became composed, and listened to a national air from the Band, and the parting benediction.

At Circus Hill where the dinner was served, the band played airs ("Fourth of July," *Hudson River Chronicle*, 10 July 1838, 2).

Rhode Island

Newport: The exercises were scheduled at the meeting house where "the music on the occasion will be under the direction of Messrs. Edward Landers, Wm.

Coggeshall, and John E. Goff" ("Anniversary of American Independence," *Newport Mercury*, 30 June 1838, 3; *Rhode Island Republican*, 3 July 1838, 2).

Providence: At a dinner celebration, "several temperance songs were sung" (*Farmer's Cabinet*, 13 July 1838, 2).

1839

Publications

"Hymn for the Fourth of July. Air — The Marseilles Hymn."[628] ["Dear Brother Garrison: If the following extempore effusion be worthy a place in the *Liberator*, it is at your service. Wm. J. Snelling."] First line: "Heirs of the brave, who live in story."

"Hymns sung at the Reading Sunday school celebration, July 4, 1839 [Redding, CT]." Broadside, 1839.

"Hymns to be sung at the Sabbath school celebration, Millbury, July 4, 1839." Includes: Three hymns./ Fourth of July. Tune — Auld lang syne; first lines: "To thee, the little children's friend, their hymn to day shall rise." / Tune — Bruce's address; first lines: "Come, ye children, and adore Him, Lord of all, He reigns above." / Parting hymn. Tune — Old hundred; first line: "Come, Christian brethren, ere we part." Broadside, Worcester, MA: Spooner & Howland, 1839.

"Jonathan's Independence. Tune — Yankee Doodle." First line: "Says Jonathan, says he, to-day." "Pencil annotation reads: Sung in Faneuil Hall, July 4, 1839." Songsheet, copy in Rare Book and Special Collections Division, Library of Congress ("America Singing: Nineteenth Century Song Sheets," *American Memory* website.

"Metrical Diversions — No. XIII. By Wilson Flagg. A Song for the Fourth of July. Written for an anniversary in 1837." First line: "Hark! how the echoes of freedom delighted" (*Boston Weekly Magazine*, 29 June 1839, 339).

"National Temperance Ode, sung at the dinner, July 4, 1839, in Faneuil Hall. By Isaac P. Shepard. Air — America." First line: "Ye sons of freedom's clime." Songsheet. Copy in Rare Book and special Collections division, Library of Congress ("America Singing: Nineteenth Century Song Sheets," *American Memory* website).

"Ode for the Fourth of July. By Miss H.F. Gould. Air and chorus: "I see them on their winding way." First line: "Columbia's natal day all hail!" (*Rhode-Island Republican* (Newport), 17 July 1839, 4).

"Ode sung at the celebration of the 63d anniversary of our national independence, by the ladies and gentlemen of East Bridgewater, July 4th, 1839." First line: "All welcome here each cheerful friend." Tune, "Auld Lang Syne." Broadside, [East Bridgewater, Mass., 1839]. Copy in Brown University.

"Odes to be Sung at Newark, July 4th, 1839, at the Young Men's Celebration." Includes: Anthem: first line, "The glorious song of liberty"; Ode, first line: "Soldier — dost thou hear the song"; Ode, first line: "Columbia, if, still the patriot fires"; Ode, first line, "Strike the cymbal, roll the tymbal." Broadside. [Newark, MJ], 1839. Copy in Brown University.

"Odes to be Sung at the Juvenile Patriotic Festival, July 4, 1839." For 1–2 unacc. voices. Includes "Invitation to Praise"; "Jubilee Hymn"; "Anniversary of Independence"; "Before All Lands in East or West"; "Freedom's Home"; "Auld Lang Syne at School"; "Land of the West"/music by L. Mason; "Huzzah! The Constitution!/music by S[ylvanus] B[illings] Pond[629]; "Happy Independence Day"; "Hail Columbia"; "Ode"/by Mrs. L.H. Sigourney, to be sung at the Juvenile Celebration on the 4th of July; "Praise for National Prosperity and Liberty": tune, "Old Hundred." [United States]: H. Ludwig, printer, 74 Vesey-St., [1839]. Copy in Brown University.

"Original Ode" (tune, "Herald") sung by a choir at the Hamilton Literary and Theological Institution celebration in New York. First line: "Lo! the day, the East adorning." *American Time Capsule: Three Centuries of Broadsides and Other Printed Ephemera.*

"Patriotic Ode. The following Ode was written by a gentleman of Hubbardston, in this state [MA], for the occasion of the celebration of the Fourth, and communicated to the *Messenger*": first line, "Rejoice, ye sons of Columbia rejoice!" (*Barre Gazette*, 26 July 1839, 2).

Performances

District of Columbia

At Georgetown, "The Star-Spangled Banner" was sung by members and guests of the Philodemic Society at a dinner held at Georgetown College (*National Intelligencer*, 8 July 1839, 3); members of the Washington Musical Association celebrate the Fourth at the residence of Enoch Tucker, about 3 ½ miles from Washington (*National Intelligencer*, 8 July 1839, 3).

Maryland

Piney Point: Performed by the U.S. Marine Band: Hail Columbia — Here We Meet Too Soon to Part — Home, Sweet Home — Jefferson's March — Lafayette's March — President's March — A Rose Tree in Full Bearing — Star-Spangled Banner — Van Buren's March — Washington's March — Yankee Doodle (*National Intelligencer*, 11 July 1839, 3).

Massachusetts

Barre: "At half past five — time having been allowed for the return of our citizens from neighboring celebrations — a procession was formed at Wheelock's, under the conduct of efficient marshals, and marched to the accompanying music of the Brass Band, to the town hall. About two hundred of both sexes were there" and heard speeches and "Mr. Perry [who] sang

appropriate songs with his best effect.... As night closed around a goodly portion of the company adjourned to the upper hall, where the festivities closed with 'much dancynge to ryghte [sic] merrie musicke,' and temperate indulgence in ices and cooling draughts that care had provided" ("Celebration in Barre," *Barre Gazette*, 12 July 1839, 2).

Boston: At a temperance dinner at Faneuil Hall, "several original odes and other pieces of music were performed at intervals between the speeches. Mr. Colburn sang in his very best style, and the services of the glee club which had volunteered its aid, added much to the enjoyment of the day" ("Fourth of July," *Farmer's Cabinet*, 12 July 1839, 3); other musical ensembles active that day included a Brigade Band in the municipal parade, and a brass band in the parade of the Mechanic Apprentices ("Fourth of July in Boston, *New Bedford Mercury*, 12 July 1839, 1). See **Publications** above.

Hardwick: "Order of Exercises for the Celebration of the Declaration of Independence at Hardwick":

Music, by the Band.
Prayer.
Hymn.
Reading of the Declaration of Independence.
Hymn.
Oration, by Pliny Merrick, Esq.
Anthem.

The services took place at the "old Meeting House" (*Barre Gazette*, 28 June 1839, 2).

Mattapoisett: A Sabbath school celebration at the church was "interspersed with vocal and instrumental music" (*New Bedford Mercury*, 4 July 1839, 2).

Reading: At South Parish, a celebration by five Sabbath schools at the Meeting House. "The services began with singing the hymn, 'Joy to the pleasant land we love,' &c. Then a prayer was offered by Mr. Picket of the place, which was followed by the hymn, 'Welcome, teachers, now we meet you,' &c. Mr. Orcutt, of North Reading, then gave an appropriate address to the scholars, and offered a prayer. Then the hymn, 'Yes, dear children, well we love you,' &c. was sung." The exercises closed "with a doxology, and benediction" ("Celebration of the Fourth of July, 1839, at South Parish, Reading," *Boston Recorder*, 19 July 1839).

Taunton: At the celebration of Whigs, "the services at the church were closed by a Chorus from the Mozart Society"; "the following original hymns, the first from the classic pen of the Rev. Mr. Pierpont, were sung by a full choir, whose performances contributed much to the interest of the occasion. Ode — By the Rev. Mr. Pierpont": first line, "Day of glory! welcome day!"[630] and "Hymn": first line, "What thanks, O God, to thee are due" ("The Fourth of July," *New Bedford Mercury*, 12 July 1839, 1–2).

Templeton: "Order of Exercises for the Celebration of the Declaration of Independence at Templeton, July 4, 1839":

Music, by the Military Band.
Hymn.
Prayer.
Hymn.
Reading of the Declaration of Independence.
Original Ode.
Oration, by Joseph Mason, Esq.
Festival Anthem.
Benediction.
[*Barre Gazette*, 28 June 1839, 2].

New Hampshire

Acworth: A procession to the grove included the Acworth Band of Music; later at the dinner a toast was offered to "The Acworth Band of Music — Their generosity honors them as men, and their skill as musicians" ("4th of July at Acworth," *New Hampshire Patriot and State Gazette*, 15 July 1839, 2).

Alstead: Citizens met at the Paper Mill Village and marched, "escorted by the Alstead Artillery and the Walpole Band to the Meeting House, where the following appropriate services were performed":

1. Voluntary by the Band.
2. Hymn by Alstead Singing Society.
3. Prayer by the Rev. Mr. Adams.
4. Prefatory remarks and reading of Declaration by the Rev. J.V. Wilson.
5. Voluntary by the Band.
6. Hymn by the Choir.
7. Address by the Hon. Joseph Healy, of Washington.
8. The 'Pilgrim Fathers,' from the *Odeon*, was performed with spirit and power by the Choir.
["Celebration of the 4th of July, at Alstead," *New-Hampshire Sentinel*, 17 July 1839, 1].

Hanover: At Dartmouth College affair at the church, a "National Celebration," with a "band of music," "voluntary by the band," "ode by W.A. Giles," "Ode by J. Barrett — tune — Old Hundred." Dartmouth dinner at the "Assembly Rooms," includes a "national song by Pushee of Lebanon," "chorus — Marseilles Hymn," and "final chorus Auld Lang Syne" ("National Celebration at Dartmouth College on the 4th of July," *New Hampshire Patriot and State Gazette*, 24 June 1839, 3).

Loudon Ridge: After a procession from the meeting house through city streets and back, exercises were presented, including a reading of the Declaration of Independence, followed by "a piece selected for the occasion [and] sung by the choir." After the oration by Maj. G.T. Barker, "the choir sung a piece composed by Capt. J.K. Cate for the occasion" titled "Independence — July 4, 1839" (first line: "The day was dark while tyrants drear"). ("Celebration at Loudon Ridge," *New Hampshire Patriot and State Gazette*, 22 July 1839, 2).

Scropperstown: A mock celebration described by Jedediah Jumper; the services at the Meeting House attended by the Bungtown Fusileers and others. "At the commencement of the services the following patriot

Ode was sung." First line: "Columbia's natal day all hail!" ("Celebration of Independence at Scropperstown, N.H.," *Essex Gazette*, 19 July 1839, 2).

New York

New York: "Hail Columbia" was performed by a band as President Van Buren stepped onto a "canopied barge," and while the Marines "presented arms." When the President left the barge, the band played the "Star-Spangled Banner" (*New York Herald*, 8 July 1839, 2).

Peekskill: "The exercises in the Church," with military unites and citizens "was filled to overflowing" and the exercises included

1st Ode by the Choir.
2d Prayer by the Rev. Mr. Cooly.
3d National Hymn by the Choir.
4th Declaration of Independence, by Mr. Yerks.
5th Hail Columbia, by the Choir.
6th Oration by Mr. Thomas Nelson.
7th The Star-Spangled Banner, by the Choir.
8th Benediction by the Rev. Mr. Youngs.

Later at the dinner held at the Franklin Hotel, the toasts were "accompanied with appropriate music" ("Celebration at Peekskill — Fourth of July," *Hudson River Chronicle*, 16 July 1839, 2).

Rhode Island

Newport: The music for the exercises held at the meeting house was "under the direction of Mr. Edward Landers" (*Newport Mercury*, 29 June 1839, 2).

Virginia

Paris: Performed by a band at a dinner celebration in a grove: Auld Lang Syne — Bannockburn — Hail Columbia — Home — Jefferson's March — Madison's March — Marseilles Hymn — Meet Me by Moonlight Alone[631] — President's March — Star-Spangled Banner — U.S. Marine March — Washington's March — Yankee Doodle (*Alexandria Gazette*, 9 July 1839, 2).

1840

Publications

"The Banner of the Free. An Ode for July 4th, 1840 written by a Young Lady of Albany for the Young Men's Association. Composed by U.C. Hill." New York: Firth & Hall, [1840]. First line: "The bright flag of America." Soprano, chorus, and piano. "Music for the Nation: American Sheet Music," *American Memory*, Library of Congress.

"For the Fourth of July. Tune — 'Infancy.'" First line: "Come, genius of our happy land"; "Freemen of Columbia. By Henry Stanley, Esq. Tune — 'Ye Gentlemen of England.'" First line: "Ye freemen of Columbia"[632]; "The Fourth of July. Tune — 'Anacreon in Heaven.'" First line: "O'er the forest — crown'd hills, the rich valleys and streams"; "Yankee Chronology.[633] Written for the 4th of July, 1812 — The last verse was added on opening the Theatre." First line: "I need not now tell what it was drove our sires"; "Ode for the Fourth of July—1812." First line: "Wake once more to toil and glory"; "The Day to Freedom. Tune—'Gramachree.'" First line: "The day to freedom dear returns" (William McCarty, *The New National Song Book, Containing Songs, Odes, and Other Poems, on National Subjects. Compiled from Various Sources* [NY: Leavitt and Allen, 184–?]).

"The following was written for the occasion and sung at the celebration of the Fourth, in the Mount Pleasant Academy grove. Ode, by J.M. Knowlton.[634] Tune—"Hail to the Chief Who in Triumph Advances." First line: "Hail to the day when Columbia awaking" (*Hudson River Chronicle*, 14 July 1840, 1).

"Fourth of July Ode,"[635] by Alfred D. Street. "Air— 'The Star-Spangled Banner.'" First line: "Oh what is that sound swelling loudly on high" (*Tippecanoe Song Book: A Collection of Log Cabin and Patriotic Melodies* [Philadelphia: Marshal, Williams, and Butler, 1840]).

"Great God of Nations." Sung to the tune "Old Hundred" at the Colchester, Connecticut, Sunday School celebration. Broadside. Copy in the Connecticut Historical Society.

"Hymns, to be sung at the Juvenile Temperance Celebration at Colebrook, July 4, 1840." Includes these first lines of text: "Sons and daughters of the pilgrims"; "Happy the land, where lives and reigns"; "Now let us strike the cheerful strain." Broadside, [Colebrook, NH], 1840.

"Ode, for the Fourth of July. By Henry Hirst." First line: "Land of my fathers, of the free" (*Saturday Evening Post*, 4 July 1840).

"Ode to Liberty, by the Boston bard." First line: "When Freedom 'neath the battle storm"[636] ("Poetry," *Farmer's Cabinet*, 10 July 1840, 1).

"'Ode.' Tune—Auld Lang Syne." First line: "With cheerful hearts, we sons of toil." Broadside, [1840–1880?]. Copy in Center for Popular Music, Middle Tennessee State University.

"Order of Exercises at the Sabbath School Celebration in Sachem's Wood [New Haven, CT], July 4th, 1840." Includes Ode (first line: "See yonder on his burning way"), written for the occasion by J.S. Babcock; Ode (first line: "Now fling our eagle banner out—Hurrah!"), written for the occasion by Daniel March. Includes music. [New Haven]: W. Storer, Jun., 1840. Copy in Brown University.

"Order of Exercises, 4th of July, 1840." Hymn: first line, "O thou, whose arm of power surrounds"; original ode: first line, "Where'er our standard floats today" by Michael W. Beck;[637] Ode: first line, "My country! 'tis of thee." Broadside, 1840. Copy in Brown University.

"Original Ode for the Fourth of July. By W.H. Hayward." First line: "Hark! Hark! The shout of revelry" (*Liberator*, 3 July 1840, 107).

"Patriotic Hymn for the Fourth of July." First line:

"God of the free! Accept the strain" (*Examiner and Hesperian* [1840]:82).

"The Star of Freedom. An Ode for July Fourth 1840 written by Miss Martha H. Mitchell. At the request of the 'Young Men's Association of Albany' to Whom the Music is Respectfully Dedicated by Charles S. Hutet." New York: Firth & Hall, [1840]. First line: "The star of freedom sank." Duet, chorus and piano. "Music for the Nation: American Sheet Music," *American Memory*, Library of Congress.

Performances

Connecticut

Colchester: "Hail Columbia!," "National Hymn," and "New England" sung at the Colchester Sunday School celebration. Broadside. Copy in the Connecticut Historical Society.

Norwich: "Feed My Lambs." Sung to the tune "Shirland," at the "American Independence Sabbath School Celebration." Broadside. Copy in Connecticut Historical Society.

Massachusetts

Bridgewater: "At an early hour the delegations from the various towns came in with their banners, flags, log cabins, bands of music and military companies, under escort of the cavalcade of horsemen" ("Fourth of July at Bridgewater," *New Bedford Mercury*, 17 July 1840, 1).

Haverhill: The town's celebration was described as "very quiet," although "in the evening we had some good music from the Bradford Band" ("Fourth of July," *Haverhill Gazette*, 11 July 1840, 2).

Pittsfield: The Mechanics celebration began at the Berkshire Hotel when a parade was formed led by the Berkshire Brass Band "under the direction of their talented leader, Mr. Perry,[638] who also added much to the enjoyment of the occasion by their exercises in the church and at the dinner table and during the evening. The procession moved down South to Factory Street, and from thence to the Congregational Church. The exercises in the church were commenced with music by the Choir, under the direction of Col. Barr,[639] and it is great praise to say, that rarely, if ever, has it been surpassed on any anniversary occasion." The Band played a piece after the oration and also performed music during the presentation of toasts back at the hotel ("Independence" and "Mechanics Celebration of the 4th of July," *Pittsfield Sun*, 25 June and 9 July 1840, 3 and 2, respectively).

Quincy: A Revolutionary War soldier joins a parade sounding the drum which "for a long time [he] used in the war" (*Baltimore Sun*, 15 July 1840, 2).

New Hampshire

Center Harbor: At a grove, exercises took place, including an address by Joel Eastman, of Conway. "After Mr. E. concluded, songs were sung by Mr. Charles D. Hoar, Mr. Thomas Neal, and Mr. Folsom from Meredith." Following the singing was an address by Col. C.W. Cutter, after which "Harrison songs were again loudly demanded and the singers above named, reappeared with 'Harrison Melodies'[640] in their hands, and the 'woods rang again with the songs of the free'" ("Fourth of July at Centre-Harbour," *Portsmouth Journal of Literature and Politics*, 18 July 1840, 2).

Epping: At a dinner celebration in a tent at Major Smith's, "the music of the Band, and the many excellent Whig songs, sung at the dinner, not a little contributed." There followed "a musical concert, and fireworks in the evening" ("Whig Celebration at Epping," *Portsmouth Journal of Literature and Politics*, 18 July 1840, 1).

New York

Poughkeepsie: A group of Whigs from Albany celebrated with an excursion on the steamboat *Diamond* that included a band of music and all

> proceeded gaily down the River saluting the different landings and villages, and arrived off Poughkeepsie about 3 in the morning. The trip was one of delight, and almost unbroken melody. As the inspiring strains of music from the band ceased from time to time, the voice of song would awake throughout the night, to supply their place. Every popular, and especially every national air, seemed to invoke some new and beautiful tribute to the services and virtues of Gen. Harrison. Over forty different songs were sung during the evening, from the Whig minstrelsy of the day, the words of which seemed perfectly familiar to nearly every person on board the boat.

The excursion was followed by a procession through city streets of Poughkeepsie ("Poughkeepsie Celebration of the Fourth of July," *Hudson River Chronicle*, 14 July 1840, 2).

Rhode Island

Newport: A large procession marched from the Custom House to Zion Church where the "order of exercises" began with a "Voluntary on the organ by Mr. George Taylor" followed by an Ode by Mr. William M. Rodman." The services also included two additional "original odes." The choir sat in the gallery ("Fourth of July: Order of Arrangements," *Newport Mercury*, 4 July 1840, 2).

South Carolina

Charleston: At a meeting of the Washington Society at Boyd's Hotel, the following works performed with the toasts: A Beam of Tranquility Smiled in the West[641]— By the Hope within Us Springing — Come Rest in this Bosom — Come Send Round the Wine — Dirge — Governor's March — Hail Columbia — Home Sweet Home — Now Let the Warrior Plume His Steed — Oh! Tis Love, tis Love — Star-Spangled Banner — Strike the Bold Anthem — Tis Good to be Merry and Wise (*Charleston Courier*, 8 July 1840, 2);

"Hail Our Country's Natal Morn" and "Huzza, Here's Columbia Forever" (solo and chorus) performed by an orchestra, directed by E. Fenelon, at the "Old Medical College." The event was billed as "a sacred and national concert" and sponsored by "Messrs. Speissegger and Reeves" (*Charleston Courier*, 4 and 7 July 1840, 3 and 2, respectively).

1841

Publications

"Independence Day."[642] By Wm. Lloyd Garrison. To the tune, "Auld Lang Syne." First line: "The bells are ringing merrily."

"Odes to be Sung at Newark, on the Celebration of American Independence, July 5th, 1841." Anthem: first line, "Go forth to the Mount, bring the olive branch home"[643]; Ode, Washington's Address at the Battle of Princeton; Ode, The Battle of Trenton; Ode: first line, "Hail to the day, when the bold declaration." Broadside. [Newark, NJ, 1841]. Copy in Brown University.

Performances

Massachusetts

Charlemont: The celebration occurred on July 5 with a parade, exercises, and dinner. There was "good music under the direction of Mr. Parker, [which] served to enliven the time" ("The Deomocracy of Franklin 'Wide Awake,'" *Pittsfield Sun*, 15 July 1841, 3).

East Bradford: "About 10 [P.M.], the Bradford Band having returned from Haverhill, struck up a serenade in the yard" at the Academy Hall, "after which they came in and partook of the festivities of the occasion, and greatly enlivened the remainder of the evening with their excellent music.... Several pieces of music were sung." Another report stated "a young lady of the company" had written an Ode which "was sung at the 'Soiree'" on July 5 to the tune "Bonny Doon" (first line: "Say, heard ye not that mighty voice") ("Fourth of July at East Bradford," *Haverhill Gazette*, 10 July 1841, 2, and 17 July 1841, 2).

Haverhill: The parade of the "teachers and scholars of the several public schools in this village, the high school and seminary in Bradford, the officers and members of the W.T.A. Society, the Reverend Clergy, and all others" included a music component. The exercises held on "the grounds in the rear of the Summer Street Church," included the following program:

1. Reading of the Declaration of Independence of the Haverhill W.T.A. Society.
2. Singing.
3. Prayer, by the Rev. Mr. Plummer.
4. Collation.
5. Toasts, drunk in cold water, with music, speeches, &c.

6. Close with the following Ode, to be sung in chorus, by the whole assembly. Tune — "From Greenland's Icy Mountain." [First line]: "A beacon has been lighted."

"The following original Hymn, and other appropriate pieces, will also be performed. 'Temperance Hymn.' By the Rev. T.P. Abell.[644] Tune — 'Scots wha hae, &c.'" First line: "Men, who've felt the Rum — King's bane" (*Haverhill Gazette*, 3 July 1841, 2); a temperance meeting included temperance societies and several schools that marched to the Summer Street Chapel, with more than 1200 persons participating. Part of the entertainment was the Bradford Band, "whose music was very enlivenling," and the Haverhill Band, "it being the first public appearance of the latter." Following the dinner, "several songs were sung, among them an original one by Mr. R.S. Duncan" ("The Anniversary," *Haverhill Gazette*, 10 July 1841, 2).

Sheffield: "The procession will be formed at E.S. Callender's Hotel, at 11 o'clock, by the Sheffield Brass Band, under the direction of Wm. B. Saxton and Col. J. Wilcox, Marshals." At the church, the exercises included these musical works, "March to the Battle Field," "Minstrel's Return from the War,"[645] and "Grand Union March" ("Fourth of July Celebration in Sheffield," *Pittsfield Sun*, 1 July 1841, 3).

Missouri

St. Louis: "Hymn of Thanksgiving" sung in the Cathedral at St. Louis University (*Daily Missouri Republican*, 3 July 1841).[646]

New Hampshire

Amherst: Salem Brass Band at the pavilion on the Common (*Farmers' Cabinet*, 2 July 1841, 3).

Fitzwilliam: "On the 3d instant, the anniversary of our National Independence was commemorated in this place by appropriate religious exercises for the promotion of the cause of Sabbath schools." At the Town Meeting House, a ten o'clock service included voluntaries by the choir and the hymn "My country 'tis of Thee" ("S.S. Celebration at Fitzwilliam," *New Hampshire Sentinel*, 14 July 1841, 3).

Lebanon: A "social celebration" given by members of the Lebanon Ladies Social Society included a picnic and music from the Lebanon Band which played three pieces of during the exercises. A dinner followed which when ended, "on leaving the table the band (Mr. Bond in attendance), performed several pieces to the admiration of the company and an occasional ode from the choir, and songs from Capt. Pushee added a zest to the exercises generally." Toasts were "accompanied with music and the discharge of cannon" (*New Hampshire Patriot and State Gazette*, 9 July 1841, 2).

Milford: The celebration occurred on July 5. The Sabbath School Union celebration representing several towns met. The exercises included "appropriate music by the choir ... an original hymn was sung by the children under the direction of Mr. Joshua Hutchinson,[647]

with a happy effect" ("Independence," *Farmers' Cabinet*, 9 July 1841, 3).

Portsmouth: Members of the Washington Total Abstinence Society from Portsmouth and neighboring towns marched through the town's streets to "the rear of the late residence of Nath'l Adams, Esq., where the services of the day were performed.... The services were commenced by singing the following ode, in Auld-lang-syne": first line: "Can we forget the gloomy time." Another ode by "Mr. T.P. Moses was sung": first line: "All hail, all hail, ye soldiers bold." At the address by Samuel E. Cones, "the following ode, to the tune of Old Hundred, was sung by the vast auditory": first line "Hail temp'rance, fair celestial ray!" ("National Independence," *Portsmouth Journal of Literature and Politics*, 10 July 1841, 2).

New York

Whitlockville: At the Literary Association celebration held at the Methodist Church, "a national hymn by the choir ... 'Hail Columbia' by the band," and various other musical pieces ("Whitlockville Celebration," *Hudson River Chronicle*, 13 July 1841, 3).

Yonkers: A procession "formed at the Yonkers Hotel" to parade to the Episcopal Church. The procession included a band, which played "Hail Columbia" at the exercises after the reading of the Declaration of Independence and other unnamed music. ("Celebration of the 65th Anniversary of American Independence at Yonkers," *Hudson-River Chronicle*, 29 June 1841, 3).

1842

Publications

The Cold Water Army Song Book, for the Use of Juvenile Schools and Adult Homes: Adapted in Part to Temperance Meetings, and Fourth of July Celebrations. By S [imeon] B [utler] Marsh. Amsterdam, NY: S. B. Marsh, Printer, 1842.

"For Freedom, Honor, and Native Land"[648] (anthem), "For Thee, My Native Land, for Thee" (anthem), and "God Bless Our Native Land" (anthem) performed (*Order of Exercises at the Celebration of the Sixty-Sixth Anniversary of American Independence.* Boston: J. H. Eastburn, 1842; *Three Patriotic Songs, Suitable for the Public Celebration of American Independence, on the 4th of July.*[649] By Lowell Mason. Boston: Tappan & Dennet, 1842).

"Ode for the Temperance Celebration, Dedham, July 4, 1842." By Ellis Worthington. Tune — "America." First line: "Hail! Day of Glory, Hail!" Broadside. Dedham, MA, 1842. Copy in Brown University.

"Song — for the 4th of July" to the "Tune — 'Auld Lang Syne'" First line: "Leave vain regrets for errors past" (*Alexander Gazette*, 7 July 1842, 1).

"Temperance Ode for the Fourth of July, 1842. Tune — 'Yankee Doodle.' By the Rev. E.F. Hatfield and dedicated to the Washingtonians throughout the United States." First line: "We come, we come, in grateful bands." (*New York Evangelist*, 26 May 1842, 84.)

"We're Free. A Fourth of July Song. By H.S. Washburn." First line: "We're free! we're free! how glorious still' (*Christian Reflector*, 29 June 1842, 2).

Performances

Massachusetts

Great Barrington: The temperance exercises were "held at the 'Grove,' where the hymn and the voice 'My country, 'tis of thee!' sounded most charmingly (*Berkshire County Whig*, 14 July 1842, 1).

New Braintree: "At half past ten o'clock the Cold Water Army, of boys and girls, with buoyant hearts and cheeks blooming in health and beauty, unfurled their banners and took up their line of march, preceded by the Greenwich Band, for the meeting house, the lower part of which was already filled with ladies and gentlemen anxiously waiting for the commencement of the exercises. After the Band had discoursed some excellent music, Col. Mixter, the president of the day, offered a few appropriate introductory remarks...." Following an address by Charles Eames "came several well sung songs from the Cold Water Army stationed in the galleries." At the dinner held "under a spacious bower erected for the occasion, ... Mr. Hamilton of Worcester enlivened the assembly [of 400 persons] with several cold water songs" (*Barre Gazette*, 8 July 1842, 2).

Stockbridge: After a procession from the academy to the meeting house, "America" was "sung by a numerous choir, in deep-toned thrilling harmony." Following a reading of the Declaration of Independence, the 150th psalm was sung. The Pittsfield Brass Band closed the exercises with "an appropriate air." "After a recess of some two hours, and a most refreshing shower after the repast was over, the auditory again assembled for the afternoon's exercises — when it was greeted by the choir 'in full chorus with triumph and glee,' chaunting an Ode of the Rev. Mr. Mandell. In symphony with the address was sung the Ode of Mr. Palmer: "Then left not the wine cup/For dark in the depths of its fountains below/Lurk the spirits that lure to the vortex of woe!" ("Celebration of the 4th of July at Stockbridge," *Berkshire County Whig*, 7 July 1842, 2).

Waltham: The exercises included: "Original ode" (first line: "Have ye heard of our triumph, that far o'er the nation"), by Miss Tilden; "Original ode" (first line: "List, we are coming with banner and song"), by Miss Tilden. (Broadside. "Order of Exercises at the Temperance Celebration at Waltham, July 4, 1842." Waltham, MA: J. Hastings, [1842]).

West Cambridge: At the Congregational Meeting House, "Come, Ye Children, Learn to Sing," "This

Day to Greet, with Joy We Meet," and "Shall E'er Cold Water be Forgot" (by John Pierpont) were sung ("Order of Exercises at the Congregational Meeting House." Broadside. Boston?, 1842).

Westfield: At the Congregational Church, a "distinguished quartet" and singing by a choir, as well as a procession that included the Westfield Brass Band."[650]

New Hampshire

Merrimack: The "temperance societies of Merrimack, Bedford and Litchfield" marched, escorted by "an excellent band of music," to Read's Ferry, and there embarked in five large boats, containing from two to three hundred each, and sailed down the Merrimack river to a beautiful grove on an island.... Animating music echoed from boat to boat." On the island, there was "singing by the choir" and music by the band ("Celebration at Merrimack," *Farmers' Cabinet*, 15 July 1842, 3).

New Boston: A procession of over 1000 persons that included Sabbath schools and "friends of temperance" marched, preceded by a band of music, to the Presbyterian Meeting House. The exercises included "appropriate music, performed by the choir" ("Fourth of July Celebrations," *Farmers' Cabinet*, 15 July 1842, 3).

New York

Brooklyn: At the Military Garden, a concert by a band at 5 pm included "overtures, solos and marches." An 8 pm event was billed as "a grand military concert, consisting of several popular and favorite pieces of music, by the much admired and celebrated New York Brass Band." An orchestra presented a "promenade musicale in the Grand Saloon," the program including

1. Grand Overture to Amiklie
2. Napoleon's Imperial March (Donizetti)
3. Quick Step — Norma (Bellini)
4. Waltz — Nassau Guards (Grafulla)
5. Song — The Soldier's Tear (Bishop)
6. Quick Step — 6th Comp. Nat. Guards (Grafulla)
7. La Gitrana (Spanish)

[*Brooklyn Daily Eagle*, 2 July 1842, 2].

Sing Sing: After a military review, various companies and trade associations marched, preceded by the Sing Sing Brass Band,[651] to the Mt. Pleasant Female Seminary where the exercises were held (*Hudson River Chronicle*, 28 June and 12 July 1842, 3 and 3, respectively); "Musicians of the 15th Brigade" perform ("Sixty-Sixth Anniversary of American Independence," *Hudson River Chronicle*, 14 June 1842, 3).

Whitlockville: The Whitlockville Literary Association gathered in a grove belonging to Anthony M. Merritt. "The music engaged for the occasion, marching in front of a procession of upwards of one hundred interesting youth." After a reading of the Declaration and an oration, "a national hymn, original, prepared for the occasion, which reflected much credit to its author, was then sung by the Sunday School, under the direction of Mr. William Horton." In addition,

> several pieces were then sung by the Sunday School choir in the most sweet and lovely manner, which were greatly admired as reflecting much to their accomplished and gentlemanly teacher. The whole concluded with a variety of excellent sentiments, which were received amid the loud cheers of the audience, and the rich swelling notes of the instrumental music, which throughout, in a most admirable manner, contributed greatly to enliven the scene. ["Whitlockville Celebration of the Fourth of July," *Hudson River Chronicle*, 26 July 1842, 2].

Pennsylvania

Potter: The Earleystown and Mount Pleasant sunday schools marched to the Presbyterian church where the exercises began with "singing and prayer." After addresses in English and German,

> an anthem was sung, by the choir, which was present [sic] on the occasion, after which the Declaration of Independence was read by Dr. Wm. J. Wilson, and another anthem was sung. After this appropriate and well performed anthem was concluded, the schools were dismissed and returned to their respective homes.

> I cannot refrain from saying a few words in reference to the choir which was present on the occasion (generally termed the "Bank Singing School") of which Mr. Platt is the precentor. It met the approbation of all present. If such music emanates from the heart, and from the understanding, it cannot fail to "Swell with heavenly hope the pensive mind." I am informed that Mr. Platt is a scientific teacher of music, and should he continue his labors a while longer in this neighborhood, vocal music will undoubtedly be much improved through his instrumentality. ["Sunday School Celebration on the Fourth of July, in Potter Township, Centre Co, Pa," *Weekly Messenger*, 20 July 1842, 1422].

1843

Publications

"Fourth of July Ode"[652] (first line: "With patriotic glee"); "Fourth of July Washingtonian Song" ("first line: "A glorious day is breaking." By John Pierpont. Printed in *Cold Water Melodies, and Washingtonian Songster* (1843).

"Great temperance festival. Hymns for the temperance jubilee at the (late) Tremont Theatre, July 4, 1843." Includes: Four songs./ My country 'tis of thee [i.e., America, by Samuel Francis Smith]; first lines: My country 'tis of thee sweet land of liberty./ Song for Independent Day, Tune — Yankee doodle. Written

for the temperance jubilee ... by George Russell; first lines: To-day is Independent-Day, why should not we be merry?/ Yankee's Fourth of July song, "Composed for the occasion, by Charles W. Denison ... Tune — The fine old English gentleman;" first line: When lovely Freedom took her flight/ National temperance jubilee hymn, "By William B. Tappan. To be sung by M. Colburn, Esq.;" first line: What boots it that yon green hill-side/ "Notice. There will be music by the band, commencing at 7 o'clock. — Songs ... by Messrs. Colburn and Birds. Addresses by distinguished friends of temperance. — Refreshments for sale at all hours of the day. ... Admittance 12 1–2 cents. Children half price." Broadside, [Boston]: Tuttle & Dennett, 1843.

Hartley Wood's Anniversary Book of Vocal and Instrumental Music, Practical and Theoretical, for the Fourth of July, Temperance and Anti-Slavery Occasions.[653] Principally composed by Lowell Mason, I. B. Woodbury, and H.W. Day. Boston: The Musical Visitor Office, #8 Court Square, 1843.

"Hurrah for the Clay" (Philadelphia: J.C. Osbourn, 1843). Sung at the Whig Festival. Regarding Henry Clay. Copy in Johns Hopkins University.

"Music for the Fourth of July." By H.W. Day. Includes "Temperance Star." By Lowell Mason. First line: "Rise and shine through every nation." Includes another song, "The Nation Rousing." First line: "Hark! a voice from heaven proclaiming"[654] (*Boston Musical Visitor*, 7 June 1843, 134).

"Ode, for the celebration of the Fourth of July, by the Repeal Association of Philadelphia. Adapted to the Music of the Marseillaise Hymn. Miss Anne C. Lynch."[655] [Philadelphia?: 1843?]. First line: "A Nation's birth-day breaks in glory!" Broadside. Copy in Brown University.

"Ode for the Fourth of July" by John Pierpont. First line: "Who are the brave, if they were not." In *Cold Water Melodies, and Washingtonian Songster* (1843).

"Patriotic Poem" (11 stanzas to be sung to the tune "Nashville"). "Written for the Washingtonian and Sabbath School celebration of independence" in Andover, Connecticut. Broadside. Connecticut Historical Society

"A Song for the Fourth of July. Dedicated to John A. Collins." [Signed "Emily." "From the *National Anti-Slavery Standard*."] First line: "The Fourth! the Fourth! the glorious Fourth." (*Liberator*, 7 July 1843, 108.)

Performances

District of Columbia

At the cornerstone laying ceremony for the Temperance Hall, an ode was sung after the opening invocation and the "Apollo Association ... sung a national anthem. The services were closed by the singing of an ode, written and set to music by J.H. Hewitt,[656] Esq. — for its melody it was considered decidedly one of the best of the author's compositions" (*National Intelligencer*, 3, 6, and 10 July 1843, 3, 3, 3, respectively;

Baltimore Sun, 7 July 1843, 4); in Georgetown in the early morning, "the band at the College could be heard in the distance resounding the national anthem." At the Bridge Street Church, Sunday school teachers and students met. One of the "youth marched up the centre isle with the American flag in hand and the band struck up the soul-stirring air of 'Hail Columbia.' It was a moment that I am sure lead [sic] every one present to exclaim with pride, 'I am — I am, an American citizen.'" Those at the church then assembled at "the spacious park of Brook Mackall, Esq. in the very center of the lovely and attractive heights of Georgetown ... to the number of not less than 3000. Addresses were intervened by the singing of hymns" (*Baltimore Sun*, 7 July 1843, 4).

Massachusetts

Athol: A procession included a band which played "Yankee Doodle." At the Unitarian Church, the exercises included music by a "choir under Messrs Cleaveland and Hapgood [which] received united praise for the manner in which it performed the different parts assigned to it in the services" (*Barre Gazette*, 14 July 1843, 2).

Boston: At Faneuil Hall, "An Ode, by a select choir of pupils of the public schools, under the direction of L. Mason, Esq." was performed: first line, "To the good cause!" In addition, an "Ode, written by Mrs. L.H. Sigourney" was presented: first line, "Clime! beneath whose genial sun." Following an oration and prayer, a "Hymn" (first line: "God bless our native land"), by Lowell Mason, was sung. Mason's choir consisted of 57 boys and 73 girls. Broadside. ("Order of Performances at the Sixty-Seventh Anniversary of American Independence, by the City of Boston at Faneuil Hall, 1843").[657] Website, *American Time Capsule*; "Fourth of July in Boston," *Farmer's Cabinet*, 14 July 1843, 2.

Pittsfield: At the celebration of the Washington Total Abstinence Society, a procession to the Congregational Church was "escorted by the Berkshire Brass Band." The exercises included "music by the Cold Water Army, under the direction of Mr. W.T. Merriman." Another newspaper reported that "the exercises in the church were closed with music by the pupils of the Young Ladies Institute, who acquitted themselves with much credit" ("National Independence," *Berkshire County Whig*, 29 June 1843, 3; "The Fourth," *Pittsfield Sun*, 6 July 1843, 1).

New Hampshire

Concord: In the East Village,

the exercises of the day were commenced by the choir, under Mr. Page as leader, assisted by various amateurs and professors of music and the Concord Brass Band[658] under the direction of Mr. Drew, and it is needless to say that this part of the exercises was performed in admirable style. After an excellent and very appropriate prayer by the Rev. Mr. Cummings, and the reading of the Declaration of

Independence, the following Hymn, prepared for the occasion, was sung by the choir: [first line] "The circling sun his annual round."

Following the exercises the band accompanied the assemblage to "a beautiful grove at a short distance east from the meeting house, where the taste and hospitality of the ladies was most appropriately displayed" ("Celebration of the 4th at Concord East Village," *New-Hampshire Patriot and State Gazette*, 20 July 1843, 1).

Nashua: The day's attraction were a "boat ride" and the Sabbath School event. "In the evening many of our citizens passed an hour or two in attending the concert given by those charming singers, the Hutchinson Family, at the Town Hall" ("Fourth of July at Nashua," *Farmers' Cabinet*, 14 July 1843, 2).

New York

Sing Sing: At the grove, "Singing, 'Old Hundred,' to words composed for the occasion" — "Song — 'Hail Columbia'" — "Song — 'Star-Spangled Banner.'" "The choir consisted principally of a few young ladies and gentlemen of the vicinity ... and their efforts certainly increased the enjoyments of the day." Later, "under an arbour in front of the Hotel," the assemblage dined and toasted accompanied by the following music: Yankee Doodle — Washington's Grand March — Haymakers — Hail Columbia — Jefferson and Liberty — President's March — March — Cadet's Quick Step — Gen. Greene's March — Erie Canal March — Jefferson's March — Rory O'Moore ("Celebration of the 4th July, at North Salem," *Hudson River Chronicle*, 18 July 1843, 2).

Pennsylvania

Lititz: "Come Joyful Hallelujaha," composed by Peter Wolle, was performed at the first Fourth of July celebration in this town. The concert occurred in the evening and the orchestra was conducted by Wolle.[659]

Rhode Island

Kingston: At the Congregational Church, three odes and an anthem were performed: ode 1 (first line "Hail ever glorious day!"); ode 2 ("To Thee O God, in lofty strains"); ode 3 ("We sing our fathers' deeds of fame"); anthem ("O praise ye the Lord! prepare your glad voice"). Broadside, "Order of Exercises for the Celebration of the Sixty-Seventh Anniversary of American Independence, at the Congregational Church in the Village of Kingston, R.I. July 4th 1843." Copy in Brown University.

Virginia

Richmond: "Hail Columbia"and "Washington's March" performed by the Band of the Washington Riflemen at a celebration of the "military companies of Richmond," at the Second Baptist Church ("The Fourth at Richmond," *National Intelligencer*, 11 July 1843, 3).

1844

Publications

Glee for the Fourth of July. From *Glees for the Million.* Music arranged from S.S. Webbe. Words by O.W. Withington. First line: "From hearts uplifted." For quartet (SATB) or chorus. *American Journal of Music and Music Visitor* (1844–46), 25 November 1844, 24.

"Hymns: Sabbath School Celebration, Newark. July 4, 1844." Broadside, 1844.

Native American Grand March.[660] Extracted by Permission of the Author from Dr. Wm Geib's Fantasie of the American National Air. Published in Honor of the Native American Association for the Fourth of July 1844. Philadelphia: Osbourn's American Music Saloon, n.d.

"Odes to be sung at the Young Men's Celebration at Newark, N.J. July 4th, 1844." Contains: "Ode." First line: "For conscience and for liberty"; "Song. My Own Native Land" [by W.B. Bradbury][661]; "Ode." First line: "Remember the hour, ye sons of the brave." Broadside, Newark: Daily and Sentinel Office, 1844. Copy in Brown University.

"Order of Exercises at the Sabbath School Celebration, in Byfield, July 4th, 1844." Contains six original hymns: "Our God, we consecrate to Thee"; "Lo! Beneath the Bending Sky" (Daniel P. Noyes); "Glorious Day of Liberty" (William Dummer Northend); "To God Let All Our Songs Be Given" (Thomas Buchanan Read); "Ancients to Their Secret Bowers" (Sarah D. Peabody); "We Come from Pleasant Homes Away." Broadside, Byfield, MA, 1844. Copy in Brown University.

"Order of Exercises at the Sabbath School Celebration of Independence: in the South Church, July 4, 1844, at 7 ½ o'clock, A.M." Includes: "Song" (first line: "Awake ye awake"); "Ode" (first line: "Lift up, lift up the standard") by the Rev. J. Pierpont; "Song" (first line: "Before all lands in east or west"). Broadside, Boston, 1844. Copy in Brown University.

"Order of Exercises at the Temperance Convention on Boar's Head, Hampton Beach, July 4th, 1844." "Cold Water Pledge"; Song for the Fourth, by Mrs. H.C. Knight; Ode, by L. Simes: first line, "By the glow of hope excited"; Ode, by J.G. Adams: first line: "Up! To the winds of heaven"; Song: "Come hither all ye yankee boys, need be no learned scholar"; Song of the Redeemed, by J. Pierpont. Broadside. New Hampshire: Samuel Fabyan, Jr., 1844.

Songs, for the Boston City Celebration of American Independence, July 4th, 1844[662] (Boston: A. J. Wright's Steam Power Press, 1844). Two selections include "My Native Land" and "Anglican chant of seven measures duration, ten stanzas of text."

Performances

Massachusetts

Boston: Among the various celebrations in Boston was the "Truckmen" procession that was "accompanied by a band of music." Another celebration that included music was the "city celebration" that began at City Hall and marched to the Temple where the services "consisted of music, by a choir selected from among the pupils of the public schools.... The juvenile choir was composed of about two hundred masters and misses, who have received instruction from Mr. L. Mason. Their performance was one of the most agreeable incidents of the day." Later at the dinner held at Faneuil Hall, toasts were "followed by music from the band, and the company were entertained with several performances by a glee club." Another celebration was that of the Sabbath schools of the Boston Baptist Sabbath School Union at the Tremont Temple. "A choir of children, under the direction of Mr. H.W. Day, performed admirably, and imparted much interest to the occasion" ("Anniversary of Independence," *Farmers' Cabinet*, 11 July 1844, 2). See **Publications** above.

Rutland: The Westminster Band and a choir provided music at a gathering at a grove outside of town. Citizens from Holden, Hubbardston, and Paxton were also there to celebrate ("Temperance Celebration at Rutland," *Barre Gazette*, 12 July 1844, 3).

New Hampshire

Amherst: "In this place, the Sabbath Schools of Milford, Amherst and Mont Vernon, were assembled to participate in the festivities of the jubilee." A procession to a bower

> marched in due order, escorted by the 'Milford Washingtonian Band,' who kindly volunteered their services for the occasion, and it is due to them to say that they greatly heightened the interest of the occasion by their music, & to commend them for the stand they have taken in banding themselves in behalf of and sounding aloud the true Washingtonian principles — for which we learn they were presented on that day with a very handsome banner, inscribed with their name, by the ladies of Milford, and which they bore with them in the procession.

At the bower, "the audience being seated the exercises were commenced by singing a hymn of praise.... These exercises were interspersed with singing and prayer." After refreshments were served, the event ended with the singing of a hymn ("The Fourth," *Farmers' Cabinet*, 11 July 1844, 2).

Peterborough: Included in the procession were the Peterboro' Guards, with the Citizens' Band and 600 children from various schools in the area. At the Unitarian Meeting House, the exercises began with "music from the choir and Citizens' Band." Additional music was performed after both the prayer and oration. A dinner was held at Wilson's Grove. "The toasts and responses were interspersed very much to the gratification of the company, by songs from the glee club, and music from the Citizens' Band. About 3 o'-clock, after having sung the tune of 'Old Hundred,' the multitude dispersed with hearts beating with gratitude for the blessings of freedom, of liberty and independence" (*New-Hampshire Patriot and State Gazette*, 25 July 1844, 1).

New York

Flatbush, Brooklyn: The Brooklyn Brass Band "which played several new pieces, and among them one adapted from 'Our way across the mountains' etc. earned for themselves new laurels." The band also played the "Star-Spangled Banner" ("The Celebration," *Brooklyn Daily Eagle*, 5 July 1844, 2).

Rhode Island

Newport: A procession to the Congregational Meeting House included the Croyden Brass Band (*New-Hampshire Patriot and State Gazette*, 18 July 1844, 2).

Providence: "At Providence, the municipal celebration was held at the First Baptist Church." The exercises included the singing of an Ode "written by Wm. J. Pabodie,[663] Esq." (*Farmers' Cabinet*, 11 July 1844, 2).

Virginia

Mount Vernon: The U.S. Marine Band was on the steamboat *Sydney* returning from an excursion to Aquia Creek when the boat broke down trapping the band and all the passengers on board in front of Mount Vernon for the night. Meanwhile the band provided music for dancing which went on for several hours (*National Intrelligencer*, 8 July 1844, 3).

1845

Publications

"Anniversary of the Sabbath School Union: East Avaon, July 4th, 1845." Hymn 1 (first line: "God bless our native land"); Hymn II (first line: "We come, we come, with loud acclaim" [G.W. Bethune])[664]; Hymn III (first line: "O'er wild and stormy seas); Hymn IV (first line: "Let the songs of praise and gladness"). Broadside, East Avone {NY}: Press of Burleigh & Goodrich, 1845.

"'Fourth of July.' Words by Mrs. Sigourney. Music by G.W.C."[665] First line: "We have a goodly clime" (*The Liberty Minstrel*. Ed. George W. Clark. NY: Leavitt and Alden, 1844; *The Harp of Freedom*. Compiled George W. Clark (NY: Miller, Orton & Mulligan, 1856).

"Hail to the Morn. A song for the fourth of July." First line: "Hail to the morn, when the day-spring

arising." [Signed "W.G.K."] (*Cincinnati Weekly Herald and Philanthropist*, 9 July 1845).

"Hymn for the Fourth of July." First line: "The merry peal of freedom's bells" (*American Journal of Music and Musical Visitor*, 1 July 1845, 94).

"Songs, Prepared for the City Celebration of 4th July, 1845"[666] by L. Mason. Boston: Printed by A.B. Kidder, 1845. Includes: Ode, "Thrice hail, happy day"/ Ode, "When stern oppression's iron rod"/ Hymn, "God bless our native land." Copy in Salem State College Library.

Performances

Massachusetts

Boston: Flagg's Brass Band performed on the Common (*National Intelligencer*, 10 July 1845, 3).

Lanesborough: From a notice in a local newspaper: "Concert — On Friday, July 4th, at 5 o'clock, P.M. there will be a Concert at the Congregational Church in Lanesborough, by the Glee Club, under the direction of Mr. Crossett, their instructor. The music will be composed of selections from the Vocalist,[667] consisting of Glees, &c. Admittance 12 ½ cents, to defray expenses" (*Pittsfield Sun*, 3 July 1845, 3).

New York

Brooklyn: At the Brooklyn Garden, the Brooklyn Brass Band "will play, during the evening, some of their choicest airs" ("Fourth of July," *Brooklyn Daily Eagle*, 1 July 1845, 2).

1846

Publications

"Glee for the Fourth of July," "music arranged from S. Webbe, the words composed expressly for this work, by O.W. Withington, Esq."[668] First line: "From hearts uplifted." For four-voice "Quartette or chorus." (*American Journal of Music and Musical Visitor*, 31 March 1846, 4, 20). Music and lyrics.

"Hymns, for the rural anti-slavery celebration, at Dedham, July 4, 1846." Includes: "National anti-slavery hymn,[669] 4th July, 1846, written for the occasion by Thomas Wentworth Higginson; Hymn, first line: "Hark! Hark! it is the trumpet-call"[670] by Maria W. Chapman; "Children of the Glorious Dead; Hymn, first line: "Hear ye not the voice of anguish"; "Come all who claim the freeman's name"; "Spirit of freedom, wake!" Broadside. 1846.

"'Palos-Alto and Resaca.' By W.G. Simms. A New Song for the 4th of July, 1846." First line: "Now while our cups are flowing" ("Poetry," *Pittsfield Sun*, 25 June 1846, 1; *Baltimore Sun*, 9 July 1846, 1).

"Sunday School Celebration, at the First Presbyterian Church: July 4th, 1846." Includes: "Independence" (first line: "We come with hearts of gladness");

"Anniversary song" (first line: "O welcome, welcome, festal day"); "National Blessings" (first line: "Swell the anthem, raise the song"); "American Independence" (first line: "Sovereign of all the worlds above"); "America" (first line: "My country! 'tis of thee"). Broadside. [Columbus, Ohio?], 1846. Copy in Brown University.

Performances

Connecticut

New London: The procession was assembled in front of the City Hotel and led off with a music ensemble. At the church, the "order of exercises" included

1. Music by the Choir.
2. Prayer.
3. Reading Declaration of Independence, by H. Willey, Esq.
4. Singing by the Choir.
5. Oration by the Rev. T.J. Greenwood.
6. Singing by the Choir.
7. Benediction.

("Order of Exercises for July 4th 1846," *Morning News*, 3 July 1846, 2); "The Juvenile Singing Class of 120 masters and misses" gave a concert on July 2 in the 2nd Congregational Church whose proceeds went to provide a picnic for the class on Independence Day. Among the works sung was "Song for 4th July" ("Juvenile Concert," *Morning News*, 2 July 1846, 3).

Maryland

Baltimore: "Day of Freedom," by the Rev. J.N. McJilton,[671] set to music by J.M. Deems,[672] and "composed for the occasion" was performed at the public school celebration at the high school building (*Baltimore Sun*, 6 July 1846, 2).

Massachusetts

Barre: "Our village was early thronged with people, and betimes fine music gladdened the ear.... A band of music came in from Colebrook, followed by a huge omnibus drawn by eight horses and literally crammed and covered with people. On the steps was lashed a swivel, which sent forth music that would have done credit to a larger gun.... At 11 o'clock a procession was formed at Morel's Hotel and preceded by the Hubbardston Band, marched to the Universalist Church, where the Declaration of Independence was read by Gardner Ruggles, Esq. of Hardwick." At the dinner at Morel's Hall, "about two hundred gentlemen" enjoyed "much pleasure" from the "performances of the Hubbardston Band, under the lead of Mr. D.L. Johnson, than which there is no band in this region can discourse more acceptable music." Another was that of the Temperance procession which "marched through the village to the excellent music of the Baldwinville Band." The group celebrated at the town hall and consisted of 665 men, women, and children, "music

included." According to the *Barre Patriot*, "the afternoon was enlivened by appropriate songs from a choir of singers, and music by the band, both of which were of high order, and called forth the hearty applause of the multitude of listeners" ("The Fourth in Barre," *Barre Gazette*, 10 July 1846, 2; *Barre Patriot*, 10 July 1846, 2).

New Hampshire

Marlborough: A temperance celebration held at the hotel included a reading of a "Temperance Declaration of Independence" and oration. "The two choirs of singers and the band, by their skillful and appropriate performances, increased essentially the variety and pleasure of the entertainment" ("Celebration at Marlborough," *New-Hampshire Sentinel*, 5 August 1846, 1).

New York

Brooklyn: In the procession to Fort Greene and at the exercises there is the Brooklyn Brass Band, W. Granger, leader; also at the exercises two odes were performed: "Ode" by the Rev. T.B. Thayer for 4th July Celebration in Brooklyn" (first line: "Long ages had rolled by") and "Ode by Walter Whitman to be Sung on Fort Greene, 4th of July, 1846, tune 'Star-Spangled Banner'" (first line: "O, God of Columbia! O, shield of the Free!"); on July 6, the postponed fireworks takes place accompanied by the Navy Yard Band which played "some of their most admired overtures, airs and marches" ("Fireworks in Fort Greene," *Brooklyn Daily Eagle*, 2 and 6 July 1846, 2 and 2, respectively).

Sing Sing: The town's parade included a "band of music," various companies and societies, and later that evening the band provided background music to the fireworks A separate celebration of the Order of Rechabites took place and included a parade, as well a ceremony with four pieces of music ("Fourth of July," *Hudson River Chronicle*, 30 June 1846, 3).

Virginia

Alexandria: The U.S. Marine Band performed at the St. John's parsonage benefit celebration at Mount Welby near Berry's Farm, opposite of Alexandria (*National Intelligencer*, 3 July 1846, 4).

1847

Publications

"'Fourth of July Ode.' The *Albany Argus* publishes several songs, all by young ladies of that city, sung upon the late anniversary. We select the shortest." First line: "No more alone in glory" (*Pittsfield Sun*, 15 July 1847, 1).

"Freedom's Hymn, for the Fourth of July." First line: "The patriot sires in glory sleep" ("Poetry," *Boston Recorder*, 22 July 1847, 116).

"Ode for the Fourth of July, 1847." By William Cullen Bryant. First line: "Forth from the willows, where the wind" (*American Whig Review* 6/1 (July 1847): 55–59).

"Songs, for the Boston City Celebration of American Independence, July Fourth, 1847."[673] Copyright, June 4, 1847.

Performances

Connecticut

New Haven: A "Floral Procession" with 2,000 boys and girls, dressed in white, and their Sunday school teachers marched on behalf of the orphan school. The children sang an ode, "Fourth of July," written by Mrs. Sigourney; first line: "Wild was the battle strife." The youth also sang another work titled "Children's Song"; first line: "We bring no pearls of ocean" (*Pittsfield Sun*, 15 July 1847, 2).

Massachusetts

Boston: At the Boston museum, there were

Fourth of July four splendid performances.... On Monday, July 5th, 1847, will be presented (first time) the great myuthological, musical and dramatic Chinese spectacle entitled *The Dragon's Flight! Or The Pearl Diver.* Written for the museum, by S.S. Steele; original music by T. Comer[674]; the piece directed by W.H. Smith. The performances will commence with the excellent vaudeville, *Crimson Crimes: or — Deeds of Dreadful Note!*

Broadside, [Boston]: Hooton's Press, Haskins' Building, opposite head of Hanover Street, [1847]; a civic celebration occurred at the Tremont Temple where "several patriotic songs were here sung by about 300 young ladies, with a very pleasing effect" ("Fourth of July in Boston," *Farmers' Cabinet*, 15 July 1847, 2).

Dalton: After a procession from the "Hotel of G.W. Branch" to the Congregational Church, the following was the "Order of Exercises":

1. Prayer, by the Rev. Timothy Benedict.
2. Fourth of July Ode, by the Choir.
3. Reading of the Declaration of Independence, by F. Weston.
4. Oration, by the Rev. O. M. Sears.
5. Music by the Choir.
["Celebration at Dalton," *Pittsfield Sun*, 8 July 1847, 2].

Pittsfield: At the dedication ceremony on July 5 for the "new Chapel at the Young Ladies' Institute to the purpose of female education, ... the exercises commenced with singing the following National Ode. The music was composed by Col. Barr, a teacher in the Institute, and, as were all the pieces performed, was ably executed under his direction:" first line, "Come with a cheerful step and true." "No. 3 in the order of exercises was the following Solo and Chorus:" solo, first line: "But who shall see the glorious day." After

an address by Julius Rockwell, "the following original Ode, written for the occasion, was sung:" first line, "Lift up your voice in song." The ceremony closed "with the following Recitative and Chorus:" recitative, "Father, thy word is past, man shall find grace; air, "I for his sake will leave" ("Young Ladies' Institute," *Pittsfield Sun*, 8 July 1847, 2).

New Hampshire

Winchester: A procession of over 500 "scholars in the common schools of the town, and one or two schools from Hinsdale," ended at the town church. The services "were interspersed with appropriate music by the choir, by the Winchester Band,[675] and by the scholars" ("Fourth of July," *New Hampshire Sentinel*, 8 July 1847, 2).

Ohio

Cincinnati: At the College building, "the proceedings of the day were commenced with 'Hail Columbia,' sung in very good style by an amateur association." After a prayer, "an appropriate ode was then sung, set to the excellent tune" of "Old Hundred" and later "My country 'tis of thee" was also sung ("Fourth of July at Cincinnati, Ohio," *Anglo American, a Journal of Literature, News Politics, the Drama ...* 24 July 1847, 9, 14).

South Carolina

Charleston: Performed at a dinner celebration of The Fourth of July Association held at the Pavilion Hotel: All's Well — Buena Vista March — Gen. Worth's Quick-Step — Governor's March — Hail Columbia — Hail to the Chief — Ocean Wave Quick-step — Palmetto March — President's March — Rough and Ready Quick Step — Star-Spangled Banner — Washington's March (*Charleston Courier*, 9 July 1847, 2).

Chester: Performed by the Cedar Shoals Band and/or the Chesterville Band at a "barbecue" held at the town's Court House on the occasion of celebrating Independence Day and raising funds for a railroad from Columbia to Charlotte: Chester Volunteers Quick Step — Col. Butler's March — Gen. Taylor's March — Governor's March — Hail Columbia — Hail to the Chief — Lovely Woman — Old North State — Old South State — President's March — Rail Road Quick Step[676] — Soldier's Return — Yankee Doodle (*Charleston Courier*, 16 July 1847, 2).

1848

Publications

"Anti-slavery hymns and songs, for the convention at Abington [MA], July 4, 1848." Includes: "Spirit of freemen, wake!" (tune: America) — "Progress of the cause" (tune: Zion) — "Land of my sleeping fathers" (tune: Missionary hymn) — "Children of the glorious

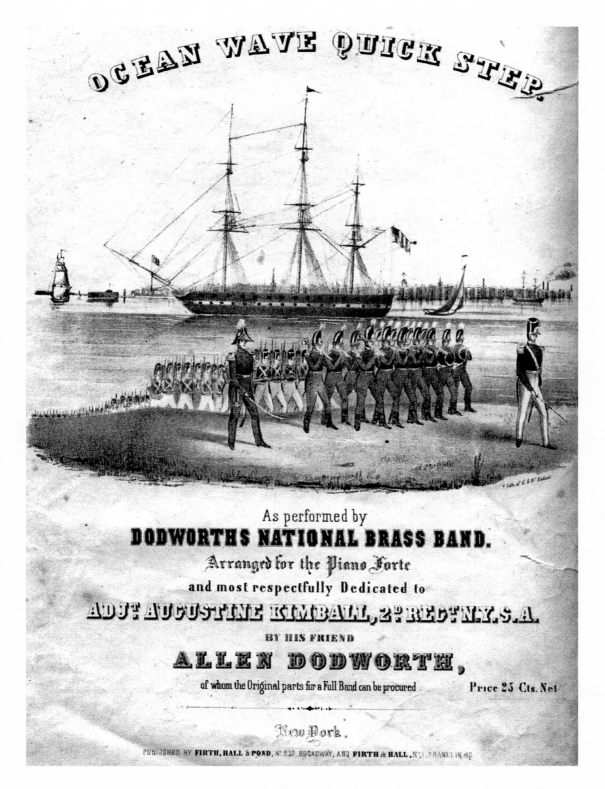

Ocean Wave Quick Step (New York: Firth, Hall & Pond, 1843), as arranged for the piano by Allen Dodworth and played at a celebration of The Fourth of July Association in Charleston, South Carolina, on July 4, 1847 (author's collection).

dead" (tune: Scots wha hae) — "We're coming, we're coming" (tune: Kinloch of Kinloch) — "Come all who claim the freeman's name" (tune: Away the bowl) — "Right on" (tune: Lenox). Broadside, [Abington, 1848].

"Fourth of July. An ode, by James Olcott, M.D., intended for the Fourth of July, 1848." First line: "The day has come! Our ears salute the sound" (*Mechanic's Advocate*, 18 December 1847, 11).

"Fourth of July Ode. By James R. Lowell." First line: "Our fathers fought for liberty" (*Christian Inquirer*, 1 July 1848, 150).

Music Arranged for the City Celebration of the Fourth of July, 1848. By B.F. Baker.[677] Boston: Printed by A.B. Kidder, [1848]. Boston: A.B. Kidder, [1848]. "To Music": first line, "Full and harmonious, let the joyous chorus"; "The Day, the Glorious Day Returns!": first line, "The day, the glorious day, returns!"; "For Fourth of July": first line, "Hark! those mingled sounds proclaim our jubilee"; "Boston": first line, "From all that dwell below the skies." "Music for the Nation: American Sheet Music," *American Memory*, Library of Congress.

"An Ode for the Fourth. From the Journal of Commerce." First line: "Ring, merry bells, from out your airy towers!" (*Liberator*, 14 July 1848, 112).

Performances

New York

Brooklyn: William Cutter's ode was sung by a choir and other music provided by Granger's and Tassies' Brass bands ("Celebration of the Fourth of July," *Brooklyn Daily Eagle*, 5 July 1848, 3).

Henrietta: Anti-slavery songs were sung at the Presbyterian Church, following a speech on human rights (*North Star*, 7 July 1848, 2).

New York: The Institution for the Blind Band played at Washington Square and Dodworth's Brass Band played tunes as bodies of soldiers recently fallen on the battlefields of Mexico are escorted through the city (*Weekly Herald*, 8 July 1848, 15).

1849

Publications

Hymn by Henry S. Washburn, esq. Tune — Old Hundred. (First line: "We gather from a thousand homes"). Broadside 124 (Leicester, Mass.?): State Library of Massachusetts. Sung at Leicester [Mass.?], July 4, 1849.

"Hymns and songs, for the anti-slavery celebration of the Declaration of Independence, at Abington, July 4, 1849." Includes: "Invocation. Hear'st thou, O God, those chains" [First line] by J. Pierpont. — "Original ode. The stripes and stars are waving free" [First line] by [?] ton. — "Hymn. Men! whose boast it is that ye"

[First line] by J.R. Lowell. — "Hymn. Montgomery. Ages, ages have departed" [First line]. — "Song. Friends of Freedom! ye who stand" [First line] by J.R. Lowell. — "Right on!" — "Come all who claim the freeman's name" [by J.H. Wilder]. Broadside, 1849.

"'The Leicester Boys and Girls.' By Hon. C. Thurber. (Sung at the Celebration in Leicester, Me., July 4, 1849)." First Line: "With buoyant hearts and merry feet." ("Poetry," *Barre Patriot*, 27 July 1849, 1.); "Song for the table, at Leicester's Gathering, July 4th, 1849. Tune — "Auld Lang Syne." First line: "With buoyant hearts and merry feet." Broadside. N.p., 1849. Copy in Brown University.

"Ode written by Mrs. Balmanno for the Fourth of July, 1849 [New York?]." First line: "Rise, to sing the deeds of glory." Library of Congress, *An American Time Capsule: Three Centuries of Broadsides and Other Printed Ephemera.*

"The Pillar of Glory." A song with score. *M'Makin's Model American Courier*, 4 July 1849.

"Song for the Fourth of July." First line: "The trumpet of liberty sounds through the world" (*North Star*, 20 July 1849).

Performances

District of Columbia

At the White House, children of the E Street Baptist Church visited President Zachary Taylor and sang two hymns: "Auspicious morning hail!" and "Loud raise the peal of gladness" ("Sabbath School Visit to the President," *National Intelligencer* 6 July 1849, 1).

Massachusetts

Boston: The Roxbury [brass] Band was "engaged to play for a fire company, to escort them to Boston common [sic] for a collation."[678]

Pittsfield: A procession was escorted by the North Adams Brass Band. At the Congregational Meeting House, a choir, directed by Col. A[sa] Barr provided music and Miss H.M. Dunham,[679] at the organ, "executed with the good taste and accuracy which have acquired for her a deserved reputation as an organist" ("Fourth of July," *Pittsfield Sun*, 4 and 12 July 1849, 2 and 2, respectively).

Minnesota

Saint Paul: The city's first Fourth of July celebration included a parade of 500 persons "headed by a military band from Fort Snelling." The event included a ceremony, fireworks, and a "grand ball."[680]

Vermont

Windham: A "Common School Celebration" made up of children from all the schools sat at a table some 200 feet in length. "The exercises of the day were frequently interspersed by anthems, songs, and glees by the choir. I did not anticipate such a treat on the hills of Windham. The singing was in good taste and admired by all present, especially the strangers" ("Fourth of July at Windham," *Semi-Weekly Eagle*, 16 July 1849, 1).

1850

Publications

"Firemen's Ode, delivered on the Fourth of July, 1850. By Wm. H. Coyle; dedicated to the firemen of Detroit." (Detroit: Dunklee, Wales, 1850).

"Hymns and songs, for the anti-slavery celebration of the Declaration of Independence, at Abington, July 4, 1850." Includes: "American hypocrisy," by W.L. Garrison.—"Slavery is falling," by E. Davis.—"We cannot falter," by J.G. Whittier.—"To the traitor," by A.P. Morris.—"Come all who claim the freeman's name" by J.H. Wilder. Broadside, [Abington, MA?].

"Song for July 4, 1850. Tune—'Auld lang syne.'" First line: "The sons of freedom gather now." Broadside, [Worcester, MA]: H.J. Howland, [1850]. Copy in American Antiquarian Society.

Performances

District of Columbia

Garcia's Band performed at Monument Place, in front of the White House (*Republic*, 4 July 1850, 3).

Massachusetts

Boston: "Children's Hymn for Independence," written by the Rev. John Pierpont, to the tune of "Old Hundred," is premiered (*Boston Courier*, 6 July 1850, 1).

Great Barrington: At the exercises, "an oration is to be delivered, and an original Patriotic Ode is to be procured and sung in the Church." The Ode (first line: "With joy we celebrate") was written by Samuel B. Sumner (*Pittsfield Sun*, 20 June and 11 July 1850, 2 and 2, respectively).

Pittsfield: In the parade, the Pittsfield Brass Band, and at the Congregational Church, "a Voluntary on the Organ, by Mr. Groenevelt, one of the Teachers at the Young Ladies Institute, who executed with great skill and much credit to himself; of Music by the Choir, under the direction of Col. Barr, distinguished in the musical service." The following were the "order of exercises at the church":

Voluntary on the Organ.
Prayer by the Rev. Bradley Miner.
Music.
Reading of the Declaration, by Robert W. Adam, Esq.
Music.
Oration, by N.S. Dodge, Esq.
Music.
Benediction by the Rev. Dr. Chapman.
["Independence" and "Independence Day in

Pittsfield," *Pittsfield Sun*, 4 and 11 July 1850, 3 and 2, respectively].

New York

Cohoes: At Dickey's Grove, the town exercises included an "Anniversary Hymn" and a hymn, "The Golden Rule," by the schools.[681]

Newburgh: At the dedication of the "'Old Hasbrouck House,' known as Washington's Head Quarters," while Gen. Winfield Scott raised a flag, an Ode (first line: "Freemen, pause, this ground is holy"), written by Mrs. J.J. Mondell, of Newburgh, was sung (*Literary World*, 13 July 1850, 36).

Sing Sing: A procession formed on State Street: "the Cold Spring Band of Putnam County preceded the procession, discoursing soul-stirring music." Another band marching included the Kemble Guard Brass Band of Cold Spring, William Brevet, leader. At a grove on Hunter Street, the exercises opened with "Hail Columbia" by the band. There followed a dinner at the Empire hotel with the toasts and the following pieces of music: tune, Save the Union — tune, Old Virginia — Tune, Dirge — Tune, Hail to the Chief — Tune, Yankee Doodle — Governor's March — Star-Spangled Banner — March, by the Band — Tune, The Campbells are Coming — Tune, Bold Soldier Boy — Tune, Perry's Victory — Tune, Harvest Home — Tune, Julian Polka ("Fourth of July," *Hudson River Chronicle*, 9 July 1850, 2).

1851

This year marked the 75th anniversary of the signing of the Declaration of Independence.

Publications

"Faithful, until the Master Calls," "Our Freedom, God's Gift,"written for the occasion, "My Country ['tis of thee], and "A Song of National Thanksgiving" (Raynortown, NY, now Freeport.) Broadside, 1851. Copy in New York Historical Society.

"Order of Services at the Tremont Temple before the City Council of Boston, on the Anniversary of American Independence, July 4, 1851." Includes: national song (First line: "Hear ye the song! Hear ye the song!); Hail Happy Day (first line: "Hail! hail! happy day!"); Hymn (first line: "God bless our native land"). Broadside. Boston: J. H. Eastburn, 1851. Copy in Brown University.

"Song." Composed by William J. Hamersley and sung at Centre Church. Broadside. Copy in Connecticut Historical Society.

"Song for the Fourth of July." First line: "Come, let us meet this pleasant day." ["The following song was sung, over and over again, to the tune of 'There is na luck about the house.' It was written for the occasion. It was afterwards sung in Hartford to the tune of 'Auld Lang Syne'"] (*Robert Merry's Museum*, 1 July 1851, 30).

Performances

District of Columbia

The U.S. Marine Band performed at the laying of the "cornerstone of the new Capitol edifice" (*National Intelligencer*, 7 July 1851, 2).

Illinois

Cleveland: The city presented an entertainment including performances of "The Star-Spangled Banner" and "Hail Columbia."[682]

Massachusetts

Lanesboro: A parade was "animated by excellent music by the Cheshire Brass Band" and they marched to a grove. During the exercises, "the song of the Lanesboro Glee Club broke upon the ear like the morning song of the uncaged bird" ("Pic-nic and Celebration at Lanesboro," *Pittsfield Sun*, 7 August 1851, 2).

Pittsfield: Martial Band and Pittsfield Brass Band in procession and "discoursed most excellent music." At the Baptist Church, "Voluntary on the organ — anthem — music by the choir," and "band will play during the [fireworks] exhibition" ("Fourth of July, 1851," *Pittsfield Sun*, 26 June, 3 and 10 July 1851, 3, 2 and 2, respectively).

New York

New York: Governor's March — Fence to the Souls of the Heroes — Hail Columbia — [Home] Sweet Home — Huzza, Here's Columbia Forever — Land of Washington — Let the Toast Be, Dear Woman — Liberty Forever — Our Flag is There — President's March — Rest Spirits Rest — Star-Spangled Banner — Union March — Yankee Doodle performed by Dodworth's[683] Band at the Tammany Hall celebration (*New York Herald*, 6 July 1851, 1); "Hail to the Chief," "Home, Sweet Home," and "Star-Spangled Banner" sung or played on board the American steamship *Baltic* at sea returning from Liverpool, England (*New York Herald*, 6 July 1851, 2).

Utah

Salt Lake City: Capt. Pitt's Nauvoo Brass Band performed at the "liberty pole" at the lake. On the following day, July 5, at 10 A.M., "a number were assembled around the band carriage, to hear the admirable singing of John Kay and Jacob Hutchinson, together with the music of bagpipes, etc., and the almost endless variety of tunes which were played by the band." The following music accompanied the toasts that were given: America — Comin through the Rye — Yankee Doodle — Washington's Grand March — Come Buy a Broom — Again, Shall the Children of Judah Sing — Come Holy Spirit — Jockey to the Fair — The Rose Tree — Sound the Loud Timbrel — Hark Listen to the Trumpeters — Hail to the Chief[584] ("The Celebration of the Fourth of July," *Deseret News*, 12 July 1851, 3. See also, "The Celebration

of the Twenty-Fourth of July 1851, in G.S.L. City," *Deseret News*, 19 August 1851, 9).

Vermont

Brattleboro: The Brattleboro Brass Band, in procession and at exercises in grove "in rear of Main streets" ("Declaration of Independence," *Semi-Weekly Eagle*, 30 June 1851, 2).

France

Paris: "Some Americans, dining together on the 4th of July at Paris, employed a band of music, which, after playing several times the Marsellaise Hymn, were ordered by the police not to repeat it. The Americans were determined not to give it up so, but stood under the broad folds of their flag, and shouted out the Revolutionary Hymn in full chorus. The large crowd standing around looked decidedly astonished" (*Pittsfield Sun*, 28 August 1851, 1).

1852

Publications

"Hymns, sung in the 1st Presbyterian Church by the sons of Temperance of Pottsville, July 4, 1852." First lines: "Intemperance, like a raging flood"; "The temp'rance trumpet blow." Broadside, [Pottsville, PA?], 1852.

"Songs, prepared for the Boston city celebration of American Independence, July fourth, 1852 (Boston: A.B. Kidder [1852?]. By George W. Pratt. Copy in Brown University.

Performances

District of Columbia

"God bless our native land" sung by a choir at the Union Chapel (*Baltimore Sun*, 5 July 1852, 4).

Maryland

Baltimore: "Hail Columbia performed by the Blues Band, under the direction of "Prof. Holland," at a city celebration held at the State Exhibition Grounds on North Charles Street extended (*Baltimore Sun*, 7 July 1852, 1).

Massachusetts

Dana: A celebration of over one thousand persons assembled for a ceremony and dinner. "The New Salem Band of music, than which there are few better in this section, rendered their musical services, and under a military escort the procession, graced by a large number of ladies, in uniform and appropriate dress, moved to the tables where the usual entertainments at such celebrations were had" ("Celebration in Dana," *Barre Gazette*, 9 July 1852, 3).

Pittsfield: Springfield Brass Band in a procession

that was "large and imposing, and surpassed any thing of the kind ever witnessed in Pittsfield." The band also provided music at Burbank's Hall where the exercises were held. Four pieces of music were performed. "The Springfield Brass Band performed during the fireworks display that evening" ("Independence!" and "The Fourth," *Pittsfield Sun*, 1 and 8 July 1852, 3 and 2, respectively).

Worcester: On July 5, the New England Band participated in a parade with residents and a military escort to a "spacious tent." After a dinner, toasts were offered. "After the delivery of the sixth toast, 'Henry Clay,' which was received in silence, the band played a dirge." Later, "at about 8 o'clock a band stationed on the common played familiar airs, until a large crowd had collected." A parade followed and over 2000 persons led by a band marched about town ("Whig Celebration at Worcester," *Barre Gazette*, 9 July 1852, 2).

New York

New York: Adkins Brass Band played "Hail Columbia," "Star-Spangled Banner," and "Yankee Doodle" in accompaniment to fireworks there ("The Fireworks," *New York Times*, 7 July 1852, 2); at the Tammany Society celebration on July 5, the following music accompanied the toasts presented: Hail Columbia — President's March — Governor's March — Yankee Doodle — St. Tammany's March — The Goddess of Liberty — The Red, White and Blue — Our Native Land — Jackson's March — General Cass' March — Hail to the Chief — Star-Spangled Banner — Let the Toast Be Dear Woman (broadside, "Tammany Society; Or, Columbian Order Celebration of the 76th Anniversary of National Independence, at Tammany Hall, Monday, July 5th, 1852," in "Hargrett Library Historical Broadsides," *Digital Library of Georgia*, University of Georgia Libraries) http://fax.libs.uga.edu/bro.

Pennsylvania

Pottsville: "Anniversary Hymn" sung at "Lawton's Hill, about one mile from town" by the members of the two German and English Lutheran schools (*Miner's Journal, and Pottsville General Advertiser*, 10 July 1852, 2). See **Publications** above.

Utah

Salt Lake City: Includes articles on the Fourth in Salt Lake City, including "Ode for the Fourth of July" by Miss E.R. Snow, "Independence Oration " by Thomas Bullock. Includes personal names and that the "Star-Spangled Banner" was performed by a band. ("Celebration of the Anniversary of the Fourth of July in Great Salt Lake City," *Millennial Star* [October 1852]).

1853

Publications

"Celebration of the Griffin Sunday Schools! Fourth July, 1853." Includes: "Bricher's Chant" (first line: "Lord, we come before thee now"); "God Bless Our Native Land" (first line: "God bless our native land"); "National Song" (first line: "Hail! our nation's birthday morning!"); "Sabbath School Hymn" (first line: "Father! Now the day is passing"). Broadside, in "Hargrett Library Historical Broadsides," *Digital Library of Georgia*, University of Georgia Libraries http://fax.libs.uga.edu/bro.

"Fourth of July, a New National Song" (Philadelphia: Lee & Walker, 1853). First line: "Today, today, on only heart is beating thro' the land." Written by "Miss Leslie," and "adapted to a popular military air." This work was "sung at the anniversary dinner of the Cincinnati Society of Philadelphia, July 4th 1853," and was probably a premiere performance.

"'Fourth of July' Chorus. An Easy Glee for Singing Classes & Choirs." *New York Musical World*, 25 June 1853 (6/8): 119–20.

Fourth of July Hymns and Songs Written for the Sabbath School of the M.E. Church in Sacramento. By Ernest George Barber. [Sacramento, CA]: Printed at the Daily Union Office, 1853.

"'Fourth of July.' Temperance Chant." By Frank Ford. *New York Musical World*, 2 July 1853 (6/9): [135].

"Ode for the Fourth of July." First line: "Another year has passed away"[685] (*Liberator*, 18 November 1853, 184).

"Ode — July Fourth, 1853. By Albert Pike." First line: "When shall the nations all be free" (*Spirit of the Times*, 6 August 1853, 291).

Performances

Connecticut

Norwalk: The Bridgeport Cornet Band performed ("The Day at Norwalk," *New York Times*, 6 July 1853, 2).

Kentucky

Carrollton: At a temperance celebration the children sang an opening hymn: first line, "God bless our native land." (*Kentucky Family Mirror*, 2 July 1853).[686]

Massachusetts

Boston: The order of services at the Old South Church:

    I. Voluntary by the [Boston] Brass Band.
    II. Chant.
    III. Prayer by the Rev. Joseph Cummings.
    IV. Song — "The Union." First line: "A song for our banner, the watchword recall."

V. Reading of the Declaration of Independence, by A.O. Allen, Esq.

VI. Hymn — "National Gratitude." First line: "Let every heart rejoice and sing."[687]

VII. Oration, by Timothy Bigelow, Esq.

VIII. Anthem — "Mighty Jehovah." First line: "Mighty Jehovah! accept our praises."

IX. Benediction.

"The music was performed by a choir selected from the public schools, under the direction of L.H. Southard, Esq."[688] *An Oration Delivered before the Municipal Authorities of the City of Boston, July 4, 1853.* By Timothy Bigelow. (Boston, 1853), 79–80.

Lowell: "The most interesting feature of the day was the parade of the 'Antiques and Horribles,' which took place early in the morning, and thousands of people from the neighboring towns and cities were present to witness this most interesting and comical procession." Among the groups in the parade were "the Warren Light Guard, Capt. Pearey, with a full band; the Spindletown Flying artillery, Capt. Davis, with 30 men mounted, accompanied with a band; the Middlesex Rangers, with band and banner; Ayer's New City Fencibles, with a band.... There was also in the procession the Calathumpian Band, with all

sorts of instruments, some manufactured of tin, sheet iron, &c. They numbered about 15, and performed their part well." The City Procession consisted of some military units "preceded by the Lowell Brass Band" ("Celebration at Lowell," *Farmer's Cabinet*, 14 July 1853, 2).

Pittsfield: "Music by the American Brass Band, of Springfield, and several bands of martial music" and at the Baptist Church, "music by the choir of the Society, under the direction of Mr. W.A. Hungerford" ("Independence" and "The Fourth," *Pittsfield Sun*, 30 June and 7 July 1853, 3 and 2, respectively).

New Hampshire

Milford: "The procession will be formed at ten o'clock, under the escort of the Milford Brass Band, the Fire Engine Company, and a cavalcade composed of the young men of that town.... The Hutchinson Family are positively engaged to be present. On any occasion, they are unrivalled, but on the Fourth they will be aided by an unwonted inspiration amid the friends and scenes of their early years.... the Hutchinsons will give a concert of their best and most popular songs at four P.M., in the Congregational Church (Milford). Tickets 25 cts, ladies and children 12 ½ cts." ("Free

"Let Every Heart Rejoice and Sing — National Anthem," from the collection *The Anthem Dulcimer* (New York: F.J. Huntington & Co., 1856) by I.B. Woodbury. This anthem was written "for Independence, Thanksgiving, or other National festivals" and likely had its first performance on July 4, 1853, at the Old South Church in Boston (author's collection).

Democratic Celebration at Milford," *Farmer's Cabinet*, 30 June 1853, 3).

Portsmouth: After a full day of parades, ceremonies and general revelry, in the evening there was a "'promenade concert' at the tent, by the fine bands present, which was very generally attended." The procession that day included the East Boston Brass Band, Bond's Boston Cornet Band, New-York Band of Music, and Saco Brass Band. ("The Fourth at Portsmouth," *Farmer's Cabinet*, 14 July 1853, 2; *The Reception of the Sons of Portsmouth Resident Abroad, July 4th, 1853, by the City Authorities and the Citizens of Portsmouth; A Record of the Proceedings, Decorations, Speeches, Sentiments, Names of Visitors, &c.* Portsmouth: C. W. Brewster & Son, 1853).

New York

New York: Departing from 23rd Street and East River, Dodworths Band for a "Grand Cotillion Excursion" aboard the steamer *General Scott* (*New York Times*, 4 July 1853, 5); in New York, the New York Brass Band performed at Barnum's American Museum (*New York Times*, 4 July 1853, 5); in New York, Wood's Minstrels in two performances at 444 Broadway (*New York Times*, 4 July 1853, 5; on board the ship *Hermann* as it sailed towards New York Harbor from Bremen and Southhampton, Americans and foreigners (about 170 passengers) sang the "Star-Spangled Banner" and "Hail Columbia." An ode written for the occasion by Stahl Freicht, "the well known lawyer" of New York City, was sung. A German national song was sung by Dr. Murich of Russia (*New York Herald*, 7 and 8 July 1853, 3 and 2, respectively); Shelton's Band provided music for the Tammany celebration. After an oration, "the banquet room being opened, the company marched in regular order, to the tune of Yankee Doodle, to their places at the well-furnished table" ("Annual Celebration of the Tammany Society or Columbian Order," *New York Times*, 6 July 1853, 5).

Tarrytown: Dodworth's Band and Van Cortlandt's Independent Brass Band perform at a ceremony and parade on the occasion of laying the "foundation of a monument to the memory of Paulding, Williams and Van Wart, the captors of Major Andre" (*New York Times*, 6 July 1853, 2).

Rhode Island

Providence: At the First Baptist Church, "the following was the order of exercises":

Voluntary on the Organ.
Introductory anthem — By the Juvenile Choir. Words by Geo. P. Morris. [First line: "Freedom spreads her downy wings."]
Prayer — By the Rev. J.C. Stockbridge
Music — By the American Brass Band[689]
Reading of the Declaration of independence. By William M. Rodman, Esq.
Music — By West's Cornet Band
Song — By the Juvenile Choir. Words by Mrs. L.H.

Sigourney. [First line: "Clime! beneath whose genial sun."]
Oration, by Thomas Durfee, Esq.
Music — By the American Brass Band
Song — By the Juvenile Choir. "The Flag of Our Union."[690] Words by Geo. P. Morris, Esq. ["First line: "A song for our banner? The watchword recall."]
Benediction — By the Rev. J.C. Stockbridge.

("Fourth of July in Providence," *New York Daily Tribune*, 6 July 1853, 6; *An Oration Delivered before the Municipal Authorities and Citizens of Providence, on the Seventy-Seventh Anniversary of American Independence, July 4, 1853*. By Thomas Durfee. Providence: Knowles, Anthony & Co., 1853).

Vermont

Burlington: On the anniversary of the founding of Burlington College, William Dempster, "the noted vocalist," sang the "Star-Spangled Banner" and the crowd there "joined vociferously in the chorus" ("Burlington College," *New York Times*, 6 July 1853, 2).

Washington

Olympia: At the Methodist Chapel, "thronged with people, ... 'America,' the 'Star-Spangled Banner,' and 'Hail Columbia' were sung by the choir" ("Proceedings on the Fourth," *The Columbian*, 9 July 1853, 2).

Wisconsin

Hartford: The first Fourth of July celebration took place in Hartford in this year and those assembled sang the "Star-Spangled Banner" and "My Country 'Tis of Thee" ("The First Fourth of July," *Hartford Press*, 12 March 1907).

1854

Publications

"'Hymn' sung at the celebration of the Fourth of July, in Salem, 1854." By Jones Very (1813–1880).[691] First line: "Hail, love of country! noble flame." In *The Complete Poems* (1993).

"Hymns and songs for the anti-slavery celebration of the Declaration of Independence at Framingham, July 4, 1854." Includes: Fourth of July 1854 (written for the celebration at Framingham). Tune, "Lenox" — Original hymn / by Miss Caroline Bacon. Tune, "Greenville" — Independence Day / by Wm. Lloyd Garrison. Tune, "Auld Lang Syne" — Hymn / by the Rev. John Pierpont. Tune, "America" — Freedom's banner / by the Rev. R.C. Waterston — Let all be free! / by James II. [sic] Wilder. Tune, "Away the bowl." Broadside, Boston: Prentiss & Sawyer, 1854.

"Music, for the City Celebration the Fourth of July, 1854" by B[enjamin] F[ranklin] Baker & A.N. Johnson. (Boston: Printed by A.B. Kidder, [1854].

The Stars & Stripes Forever: Brilliant Variations on the Star Spangled Banner (1854) by Charles Grobe, performed by the author at an Independence Day concert on July 3, 2008, in Clarksburg, Maryland. This was one of numerous renditions of the national anthem that were popular in the nineteenth century. Grobe's use of the phrase "The Stars and Stripes Forever" predates John Philip Sousa's popular march of the same title by forty years (author's collection).

"Ode for the Fourth of July." First line: "Ye sons of Columbia! oh, hail the bright day" (*Liberator*, 14 July 1854, 112).

Performances

Massachusetts

New Bedford: A parade to City Hall included the Newton Brass Band (*Pittsfield Sun*, 13 July 1854, 2).

Newburyport: "Order of Exercises at the Pleasant Street Church":

1. Voluntary on the Organ.
2. Chorus — "Praise the Lord, ye Nations all" — from Mozart's 12th Mass.
3. Reading of the scriptures and Invocation, by the Rev. D.M. Reed.
4. "Song of Welcome," by Hon. George Lunt, music by M.D. Randall. [first line: Welcome! a thousand times welcome home!"]
5. Reading Declaration of Independence, by Hiram B. Haskell.
6. Ode, by Jacob Haskell, music "Star-Spangled Banner." [first line: "All hail to the past — to the dark trying hour."]
7. Oration, by the Rev. George D. Wildes.
8. Chorus, "Hallelujah," from the Oratorio of the Messiah.
9. Benediction, by Daniel Dana, D.C.

"The music will be performed by a select choir, under the direction of M.D. Randall, Esq. Organists, Messrs J.W. Cheney and R.P. Morse."

The music which filled the house with strains now sweet and melodious — now bold and starling, that moved all hearts — that excited the best and noblest feelings of our natures, was performed by a select choir of fifty musicians of the highest musical talent of the city, under the direction of M.D. Randall, Esq., whose long experience in this department places him at the head of the catalogue of teachers in his profession. The Voluntary on the organ by Mr. R.P. Morss [sic], of this city, was played in the most exquisite manner. He commenced with the national song, "Hail Columbia," with the full organ, followed by the full strain of "Should Old Acquaintance be forgot," and closed with "Home, Sweet Home," upon the swell organ, so soft and sweet that the almost breathless silence of the audience became necessary to hear it. The final chorus of the Messiah, by Handel, was sung with wonderful effect; its lofty and sublime strains, sustained by so many flexible, yet full voices, were truly inspiring, particularly in the passage, "King of Kings and Lord of Lords." The other chorus, from Mozart's 12th Mass, "Praise the Lord the nations all," was no less grand in its performance than the one alluded to above. The "Song of Welcome," by Hon. George Lunt, is one of his best productions, and will speak for itself in thrilling tones. The music for this hymn was composed by M.D. Randall, and was listened to with delight,

and is another of the many gems of his compositions. The patriotic Ode, by Jacob Haskell, Esq., is replete with meaning, and its performance by the choir to the old tune of "The Star-Spangled Banner," seemed to carry the minds of the audience back to days long since passed, when its strains were as familiar to all as household words. The tenor solo in this piece was sung by Mr. George W. Hale, who possesses in the fullest extent all the elements which make a public singer. The organ accompaniments to the choir were performed by Mr. J.W. Cheney, in a style far surpassing any of his former efforts. His masterly touch upon this grand and powerful instrument in the sublime strains of Handel and Mozart, were truly inspiring.

(*A Report of the Proceedings on the Occasion of the Reception of the Sons of Newburyport Resident Abroad, July 4th, 1854, by the City Authorities and the Citizens of Newburyport.* Compiled and reported by Joseph H. Bragdon. Newburyport: Moses H. Sargent, 1854, 11, 35–36).

North Adams: In the procession, Hodge's Brass Band, North Adams Sax Horn Band, and at the exercises on Church Hill, "Voluntary by Sax Horn Band," and "music by the Choir — 'America'" ("Independence," *Pittsfield Sun*, 29 June 1854, 3).

New Hampshire

East Jeffrey: At the dedication of a new school house a "dedicatory hymn, by Mrs. E.K. Bailey and celebration hymn by the Rev. J.E.B. Jewett" were presented. [A.H. Bennett, *An Address Delivered at the Dedication of the New School House in East Jaffrey, N.H., July 4, 1854* (Peterborough, Transcript Press, E.H. Cheney, printer, 1854)].

New York

New York: At the Tammany Society celebration, "The American Boy," "Governor's March," "Hail Columbia," "Jackson's March" and "Washington's March" were performed by Shelton's Brass Band ("Independence Day," *New York Times*, 5 July 1854, 1); at a pyrotechnic display in one of the parks, Manahan's Band performed "Hail Columbia" and the Germania Band and orchestra of the Italian Opera performed at the Crystal Palace (*New York Times*, 4 and 5 July 1854, 5 and 1, respectively).

1855

Publications

"Liberty or Death. A Song for the Fourth of July. By Frank Easy." First line: "From the captive in his dungeon" (*Happy Home and Parlor Magazine*, 1 July 1855, 60).

"Municipal Celebration of the Seventy-Ninth Anniversary of American Independence, Wednesday, July 4, 1855." Includes Ode to Liberty: first line, "Hail, to thee, Liberty!"; National Ode, The Bright Flag of America: first line, "The bright flag of America." Broadside, Providence, RI: A.C. Greene, 1855. Copy in Brown University.

"Ode for the Fourth of July. By Colonel Eidolon." First line: "Again has come the glorious day." *United States Democratic Review* 36/1 (July 1855): 43–45.

Performances

Illinois

Chicago: "Two German song and music societies" assembled at Dearborn Park (*Daily Press*, 6 July 1855, 3).

Kansas

Council City (now Burlingame): This town held its first independence celebration in a grove with 75 persons present and included singing an original song titled "Land of Priceless Liberty" by Mrs. J.M. Winchell.[692]

Leavenworth: A Sabbath school celebration included a parade to a grove where an original song titled "We Will Join the Celebration" by J.I. Moore was sung.[693]

Massachusetts

Abington: At a Know Nothing Anti-Slavery Celebration, "addresses were interspersed with music by the Abington Brass Band" ("In Abington," *Boston Daily Journal*, 5 July 1855, 2).

Dorchester: "Old Dorchester Has Fame to Wear," performed in a large tent by "a select choir accompanied by the Band" to the air "God Save the Queen." The work was cited as "an original hymn" (*Boston Daily Journal*, 5 July 1855, 1; *New York Times*, 6 July 1855, 3).

Pittsfield: A parade included various military and fire companies. The "Firemens' Band" was one of the first to march. Another group included the Phoenix and Undine Companies, "escorted by the Pontoosuc Fire Company, to their Engine House, and the Hope Company of Gt. Barrington, accompanied by the Mahawie [cornet] Band....The fine appearance of the men and the excellent Bands which accompanied them, were greatly admired, and added much to the interest of the display." "The Music during the exercises in the Park was furnished by Hodge's [cornet] Band of North Adams and the Mahawie Band of Great Barrington." See **Publications** (1795), for reference to a Hymn text that was presented at this celebration but was acknowledged as having been performed fifty years prior. Another report noted that the North Adams Sax Horn Band performed in the parade ("Independence!" and "The Celebration of the Fourth," *Pittsfield Sun*, 5 and 12 July 1855, 3 and 2, respectively).

New Hampshire

Amherst: "The class of young ladies under the instruction of Miss L. H. Johnson, of Nashua, with their teacher, propose a free vocal and instrumental entertainment in the evening, which we are sure will call forth a full house, and prove none the less gratifying because sustained by home talent. Further particulars next week. P.S. Cannot our citizens treat the ladies, in return, with a sprinkling of fireworks, at the close of their concert? What say, gentlemen?" "The citizens of this place will enjoy a musical treat in the evening at the concert to be given by the class of Miss L.H. Johnson, as also those of Milford, at the concert of that prince of pianists and good fellows, E.T. Baldwin. The Ladies Levee at Mt. Vernon with musical 'fixins' by a part of our Brass Band, will afford a good time. Everybody should turn out" ("The Glorious Fourth," *Farmers' Cabinet*, 21 June and 5 July 1855, 2 and 2, respectively).

New Jersey

Newton: Flockton's Jersey City Brass Band performed ("The Fourth in Jersey," *New York Times*, 4 July 1855, 4).

New York

New York: Shelton's Band played "magnificent airs" from the balcony at the Tammany celebration. "An ode, written for the occasion by F.R. Hulbert, Esq., was then sung by Messrs. [Richard B.] Connolly, Taylor. G.B. Hall, and Abert Wallace, assisted by the audience." During the toasts, Shelton's Band played "We Are All a Band Brothers" and "Clear the Husky Raccoons Down" ("The Day at Tammany," *New York Times*, 5 July 1855, 1); at Niblo's Garden, after the first act of the "military opera," *Daughter of the Regiment*, "The National anthem, Hail Columbia!" was sung by the whole company, "solo parts by Miss Louisa Pyne and Mr. W. Harrison" (*New York Times*, 4 July 1855, 5).

Pennsylvania

Connellsville: This town was awoke on the Fourth "by sweet strains of music from the Connellsville Band" A newspaper reported that "the members of our band play their pieces well; their practice has been limited, yet they are learning rapidly. They have the material in the Band to make excellent musicians, and need but practice to bring them out" (*Connellsville Enterprise*, 6 July 1855, 2).

Virginia

Norfolk: On the steamer *Louisiana* off the coast near Norfolk, over 1000 persons enjoyed patriotic music performed by Barrett's "celebrated Brass Band of the city of Baltimore" (*Daily Southern Argus*, 6 July 1855, 2).

Washington

Olympia: At the farm of Mr. Isaac Wood, citizens of Thurston County heard a band perform music after the toasts that were presented: Yankee Doodle — President's March — Hail Columbia — The Marseilles

Hymn — The Star-Spangled Banner — Columbia, the Gem of the Ocean[694] — Home, Sweet Home ("Fourth of July, 1855," *Pioneer and Democrat*, 13 July 1855, 3).

1856

Publications

Five songs on a broadside having the heading "July 4th, 1856. For Fremont and Freedom!" ([New Haven]: J.H. Benham, [1856]) include: "Sparkling and Bright" (first line: "Hark! to the cry, which loud and high"); "Rally! The Marseillaise" (first line: "Behold! the furious storm is rolling"); "What We Shall Do. Rosin the Bow" (first line: "Gather ye! Men of New England!"); "Fremont on the Course. Camptown Races" (first line: "Who is the people's candidate? Fremont! Fremont!!"); "Finale. Auld Lang Syne" (first line: "The voice of freedom loudly calls").

"Written for July 4th, 1856 by T. Atwood. Tune 'America.'" First line: "Great God, to thee we raise." Broadside, 1856. Copy in Center for Popular Music, Middle Tennessee State University.

Performances

Massachusetts

Boston: At Tremont Temple, "O Sing Unto the Lord a New Song." By a "choir of children selected from the public schools," directed by Charles Butler. "The singers looked and sung admirably, showing the thorough training to which they had been subjected." Sung also was "O Firmly Stand, My Native Land" and "Hail Columbia" ("The Fourth," *Boston Evening Transcript*, 5 July 1856, 2).

Great Barrington: Music provided by the Mahaiwe Cornet Band and at Lee, MA, at the festival given by the Ladies of the Baptist Society, "the 'Old Folks Choir,' conducted by M.S. Wilson, will furnish a specimen of the music of olden time" ("The Fourth," *Pittsfield Sun*, 3 July 1856, 2.)

Pittsfield: The Springfield Brass Band marched in a parade to City Hall (*Pittsfield Sun*, 3 July 1856, 3).

New Hampshire

Keene: At a "Fremont[695] meeting" a parade to a grove on the "Perry Estate" included "3500 to 4000 people in the procession walking four abreast, the Keene Brass Band discoursing excellent music." Music during the exercises included a piece "'Freemont and Victory,' to the tune of Marseilles Hymn, was sung by a vocalist, all the company joining in the chorus with enthusiastic effect" ("Fourth of July in Keene, N.H.," *Farmers' Cabinet*, 10 July 1856, 3).

Manchester: At the ceremony for laying the cornerstone of the House of Reformation, the Lowell Cornet Band provided the music ("Fourth of July in Manchester" and "The Fourth in Manchester," *Farmers' Cabinet*," 3 and 10 July 1856, 3 and 3, respectively).

New York

New York: "Patrick Henry's Call" and "Pilgrims at Plymouth" (first line: "When the Pilgrim *Mayflower* sailed") performed by the choir of the M.E. Church (43rd Street, near Eight Avenue) (*New York Times*, 5 July 1856, 1).

1857

Publications

Concord Fourth of July "Ode" by Ralph Waldo Emerson. First line: "O tenderly the haughty Day." Sung in the town hall in Concord, NH. "Fourth of July breakfast and floral exhibition at the Town Hall, Concord, for the benefit of Sleepy Hollow Cemetary." Broadside. (*Liberator*, 17 July 1857, 116; *Every Saturday: A Journal of Choice Reading*, 29 June 1867, 818; *North American Review* 135/308 (July 1882): 24). Copies of broadsides in Harvard University, University of Florida, and University of Virginia.

"Dead Rabbits' Fight with the Bowery Boys/ New York July 4th 1857. Written at Hoboken, by Saugerties Bard. Air-'Jordan.'" First line: "They had a dreadful fight, upon last Saturday night." Broadside. "Music for the Nation: American Sheet Music," *American Memory*, Library of Congress.

Fourth of July: March.[696] By F.W. Smith. Boston: Oliver Ditson, 1857. For piano. Copy in University of Alabama.

"Ode for Fourth July, 1857. By Ralph Waldo Emerson." First line: "O, tenderly the haughty day" (*Liberator*, 17 July 1857, 116; *Ohio Farmer*, 18 July 1857, 115; *Christian Inquirer*, 25 July 1857, 1, and 4 September 1858, 4).

"Ode for July Fourth, 1857. By James Franklin Fitts." First line: "Raise we a strain to-day" (*Flag of Our Union*, 13 June 1857, 191).

"Songs & Hymns to be Sung by the Children of the Union Sabbath School, Plymouth, at Their Anniversary, July 4th, 1857." Includes five numbered songs and hymns. 4 pp. Copy: am. antiq. soc.

Performances

California

Sacramento: A procession included "bands of music" and at the Forrest Theatre, where the exercises were held, there were patriotic songs by the San Francisco Minstrels (*Weekly Bulletin*, 11 July 1857, 3).

Stockton: At the Stockton Theatre, the exercises included the performance of "several pieces of national music" by a choir (*Weekly Bulletin*, 11 July 1857, 3).

Connecticut

Nauvoo Island: "Mormon Creed" sung by Charles R. Savage, director of the band and "leader of the choir" at the celebration of the Mormons. The piece was cited as "a sort of medley, half secular, half religious." Words are printed. Also, "Brother Hall from Utah" sung the "Star-Spangled Banner" (*New York Times,* 6 July 1857, 3).

Iowa

Davenport: The Smokey Hill Brass Band at the exercises held at Churchill's Grove "about four miles from town" ("Celebration at Churchill's Grove," *Daily Iowa State Democrat,* 4 July 1857, 1).

Kansas

Clinton: The Lawrence Cornet Band provided music as they escorted a parade of "ox teams, covered carriages, and horses, from the store to the adjoining grove." About 1500 persons were present.[697]

Wilmington: At a grove, exercises were held with music provided by the Wilmington Quartette Club and the Germania Glee Club of Havana City.[698]

Pennsylvania

Philadelphia: At Parkinson's Gardens:

Grand gala day and night! Fourth of July, 1857: Music! Illumination!! Pyrotechny! And aeronautics!! On the occasion of the ever-glorious anniversary of the nation's birthday, the gardens will be illuminated in an unusually brilliant and magnificent manner. A careful and scientific gentleman has been engaged to furnish during the evening a succession of brilliant but harmless pyrotechny. The orchestra, will perform a splendid programme of national, operatic and popular music, interspersed with pyrotechnic displays of unusual splendor. Doors open at 6 ½ o'clock. Programme to commence at 8 o'clock. In the afternoon Mons. Eugene Godard will make a grand ascension! With several gentlemen of this city in his monster balloon. Inflation to commence at 2 o'clock. Ascension at 5 o'clock. Evening programme of pyrotechny. Admittance to each exhibition, 50 cents. Children, half price. Every care, for the safety and comfort of ladies and children, will be taken, as usual.

Broadside, [Philadelphia]: Alex C. Bryson, printer, 23 N. sixth St., [1857].

Texas

Palestine: At a barbecue and fish fry, the Palestine Brass Band "on their return from a musical engagement at Centerville upon a Houston occasion was there, and added greatly to the enjoyment of the occasion, by the magnificent and soul stirring music which they discoursed" (*Trinity Advocate,* 8 July 1857, 2).

Utah

Salt Lake City: A parade and festivities were highlighted by three bands: Nauvoo Brass Band, Ballo's Band, and a "martial band" ("Fourth of July Celebration in Great Salt Lake City," *Deseret News,* 8 July 1857, 5).

Wisconsin

Milwaukee: "Star-Spangled Banner" sung by Robert B. Lynch at a public gathering (*Milwaukee Daily Sentinel,* 4 July 1857, 2).

1858

"The Birth-Day of Freedom. A Song for the Fourth of July, 1858. Tune—Star-Spangled Banner. By Richard Wright." First line: "Glorious Birth-day of Freedom! thy advent we hail!" [Dated] June 28, 1858 (*Alexandria Gazette,* 5 July 1858, 2).

"The Declaration of Independence, Signed July 4th, 1776: a Song, Designed for the Public Schools and Academies." To be sung to the tune: "Twenty Years Ago." First line: "To memorize the names of those." Broadside. Pittsburgh: Hunt & Miner, 1858. Copy in Brown University.

"Independence Day. Sung by Mrs. Barney Williams and Mrs. Florence, in all the principle Theatres." First line: "Squeak the fife and beat the drum."[699] Broadsides. New York: H. De Marsan, ca. 1858; Philadelphia: J.H. Johnson, ca.1858.

"Patriotic Odes, to be Sung at the Independence Celebration at La Porte, California." First line: "Hail our country's natal morn." Broadside. [La Porte, CA]: Mountain Messenger Book, Card and Job Print. Office, [1858]. Includes 4 songs. Copy in Brown University.

"Stand by the Flag,"[700] words by John N. Wilder, recited in Albany, NY, and later sung in December 1863 by Capt. William F. Hartz in Chattanooga, TN, to the tune "Cheer, Boys, Cheer." (first line: "Stand by the flag! Its stars, like meteors gleaming"). (Marshal H. Bright, "Stand by the Flag," *Los Angeles Times,* 24 October 1896, 9).

"Virtue, Liberty, Peace, and Our Country Forever: A National Song, written for the Pittsfield celebration, July 4th, 1858. By Richard Wright, Washington, D.C." First line: "In sweet social friendship, we this day are meeting" (*Pittsfield Sun,* 8 July 1858, 3).

Performances

Connecticut

Bridgeport: The celebration occurred on Monday, July 5. "The military and fire department will parade ... The military have engaged Tompkins' Brass Band of Waterbury, and the Fire Department have engaged the Second Regiment Band of Union City" (*Pittsfield Sun,* 24 June 1858, 2).

District of Columbia

Georgetown: Sung by a group of children at a Union Sabbath School celebration at Jewett's Grove near Georgetown: Independence Day — My Country 'Tis of Thee — Star-Spangled Banner (accompanied by Wither's Band)—The Sunday School Army (*Washington Evening Star*, 6 July 1858, 2).

Massachusetts

Boston: An "al fresco concert" took place on the Common by "four principal bands[701] of the city." The works performed were "from the music of America, France, England, Italy, Turkey, and Russia." The "Light Artillery" fired salutes during the playing of "Hail Columbia" in order "to heighten the effect of America's national air." ("Massachusetts," *New York Times*, 6 July 1858, 2); "an original Ode by B.P. Shillaber will be sung" at the Young Men's Democratic Club ("The Fourth," *Pittsfield Sun*, 1 July 1858, 2).

Pittsfield: Hodge's Cornet Band, Pellett's Brass Band[702] (both of North Adams), and a band of martial music marched in a parade. The exercises at the park included four pieces of music by the bands (*Pittsfield Sun*, 1 and 8 July 1858, 2 and 2, respectively).

New York

East Greenbush ("landolders [sic] of Rensselaer County): Johnny Cook's Band of Albany "will discourse elegant music" ("The Fourth," *Pittsfield Sun*, 1 July 1858, 2).

Middletown: This town celebrated the Fourth on July 3 and a parade of 1,500 included military units and the Newburgh Brass Band which "discoursed most excellent music," as well as the Middletown Brass Band (*Banner of Liberty*, 7 July 1858, [6]).

New York: "Hail Columbia" and an Ode ("Lo! our fathers from the skies") performed at the Tammany Society meeting ("The Celebration in Tammany," *New York Times*, 6 July 1858, 1); Ode "prepared expressly for the occasion" and "peppered all over with points of exclamation," sung to the tune of "Hail Columbia," accompanied by a band, at the Tammany celebration in New York ("The Fourth in Tammany," *Brooklyn Daily Eagle*, 6 July 1858, 5); at the various parts in the city, no less than 10 bands performed, including Adkin's Band, Robertson's Band, Excelsior Band, Casse's Band, Connell's Band, Wannemaker's Band, Shield's Band, Shelton's Band, Monnaham's Band, Blind Band (*New York Times*, 5 July 1858, 3).

South Carolina

Graniteville: "America" and "O Come Let Us Sing" sung by the "factory girls" at a ceremony held at the "School House." First line: "Our land with mercies crowned" (*Charleston Courier*, 8 July 1858, 1).

Virginia

Charlottesville: At Monticello, a "vast assemblage" of persons was present and heard a band perform a funeral dirge in the chamber where Thomas Jefferson died. "Hilarity and merriment immediately ceased, and as the solemn music fell upon the ear the tear gushing from the eye, and the uncovered and bended heads of the listeners, told that they felt they were paying a tribute to the memory of a great man, and that

this chamber was truly a hallowed spot." The band also "played an appropriate air" in front of the tomb ("Celebration at Monticello," *Alexandria Gazette*, 8 July 1858, 3).

Warrenton: The United Sabbath School Societies celebrated, with the Leesburg Brass Band providing music at sunrise. Later that morning at a grove, the exercises included speeches and a reading of the Declaration of Independence. "The band discoursed sweet music throughout the day, and the children sang a number of appropriate pieces, which added much to the interest of the occasion (*Alexandria Gazette*, 7 July 1858, 3).

1859

Publications

"An Appeal to American Freemen, Fourth of July, 1859."[703] By "Justitia." Tune, "America." First line: "Sons of the boasted free."

"Fourth of July Ode. Air—'Star-Spangled Banner.'" By E. G. Barber. First line: "Bright, bright, be the heavens that smile on this morn." Broadside. [New Haven, Conn., 1859]. Copy in Brown University.

"Song: Concord, July 4th, 1859." By F[ranklin] B[enjamin] Sanborn. "Air, Auld Lang Syne." [Concord, Mass.?, 1859?]. Copy in Houghton Library, Harvard University.

"Sung by children at Milford for a July 4 celebration."[704] First lines: "From the pine of the North to the Southern savannah"; "That freedom the fathers from heaven receiving."

Performances

Colorado

Denver: "The city's first public concert [was] given on July 4, 1859.[705] Settlers from Omaha had brought the instruments of a brass band and knew how to use them." Works performed included "The Star-Spangled Banner," "Yankee Doodle," and "Hail Columbia" ("Denver's First Concert," *Rocky Mountain News*, 8 August 1999).

Connecticut

Bridgeport: At "a finely shaded part at East Bridgeport," workers of the Wheeler & Wilson Sewing Machine Company celebrated. The Wheeler & Wilson Brass Band provided music for the exercises ("The Fourth at Bridgeport," *New York Observer and Chronicle*, 14 July 1859).

Woodbury: On the occasion of the centennial celebration held on July 4–5, the exercises "were opened by the choir's singing to the air of 'Bruce's Address'" and an "Ode of Invocation" by William Cothren (first line: "Spirit of our sainted dead"). The exercises also included a "Song" by Cothren sung to the tune "Auld Lang Syne" (first line: "Should early ages be forgot").

On the second day an assemblage met at Bethel Rock at 8 A.M. and the music consisted of singing one verse of the hymn "Be Thou, O God, exalted high"(air, Old Hundred) and another hymn "Once more, my soul, the rising day." After some brief address, a verse from the 90th Psalm was sung and the ending of the meeting with "Lord, dismiss us with thy blessing." At 10 am a service began with a reading of the "Centennial Hymn" (first line: "Here, then, beneath the greenwood shade" and "supposed to be sung on the spot where the Pilgrim settlers held their first Sabbath worship") by the Rev. William Thompson Bacon. Included also was another "Ode" by Cothren sung to the air "Sweet Home" (first line: "Thrice welcome the day which now brings to the mind") and an "Ode" by Mrs. Ann S. Stephens sung to the tune "America" (first line: "All hail our brothers, friends!"). The New Milford Brass Band performed in the procession and Lydia Sigourney contributed a poem titled "Return to Woodbury." (*Second Centennial Celebration of the Exploration of Ancient Woodbury, and the Reception of the First Indian Deed, Held at Woodbury, Conn., July 4 and 5, 1859*. Edited by William Cothren. Woodbury: Published by the General Committee, 1859; "The Fourth," *Pittsfield Sun*, 21 July 1859, 1).

District of Columbia

The U.S. Marine Band performed at Philharmonic Hall (*States*, 30 June 1859).

Massachusetts

Athol: The Athol Brass Band provided music at a consecration ceremony for a cemetery and monument. A hymn titled "The Nameless Grave" was sung: first line, "Walk gently o'er that nameless grave" (*The Home of the Ancient Dead Restored. An Address Delivered at Athol, Mass., July 4, 1859*. By the Rev. John F. Norton. Athol: Rufus Putnam, 1858).

Boston: The city procession gathered at City Hall and included the Boston Brass Band[706] and Gilmore's Band.[707] The group marched to the Music Hall. "As the procession entered the hall a voluntary was played by the Boston Brigade Band. A choir of about one hundred children, under the direction of Mr. Charles Butler, then chanted the 'Venite Exultemus Domino'" (first line: "O come, let us sing unto the Lord"). After a prayer, the following original ode was sung by the choir of children": first line, "Jubilate! Jubilate!" "The Declaration of Independence was read by Mr. George H. Cumings, in a very effective manner." A national ode, the words by Mr. William Winter, and the music by Mr. B.A. Burditt, was then sung as follows: "Honor to Washington" (first line: "Honor to Washington, our nation's pride!"). After the oration by George Sumner, "the Doxology was sung." (*An Oration Delivered before the Municipal Authorities of the City of Boston, July 4, 1859*, by George Sumner. Boston: George C. Rand and Avery, 1859); on the Common, a "grand military concert" was presented and several national anthems were played (*New York Times*, 7 July 1859, 2).

Maplewood: The Maplewood Young Ladies' Institute hosted the celebration which included performances of *Pastoral Scene*, derived from John Milton's *Arcades*, and *Cantata of Liberty*, written by a teacher, Miss Z.A. Clark. The story is about the Goddess of Liberty who "invoked the nations of the past, who, seven in number, represented by as many pupils of the school" and each being introduced and accompanied by characteristic music of that nation. For America, "Yankee Doodle" and "Hail Columbia" were sung or played. The production ended with the singing of "The Star-Spangled Banner" by the entire cast ("The Celebration at Maplewood," *Pittsfield Sun*, 7 July 1859, 2).

Pittsfield: At the "public park," Pellett's Cornet Band of North Adams "supplied most excellent Music during the day, and in the evening at the Fire Works" ("Celebration at Pittsfield" and "Local Intelligence: The Fourth," *Pittsfield Sun*, 30 June and 7 July 1859, 3 and 2, respectively).

New York

Brooklyn: At City Hall, "music by Dodworth's Band" at the exercises and again at the "exhibition of fireworks in the evening" ("The National Anniversary," *Brooklyn Daily Eagle*, 2 July 1859, 2); at Fort Greene a "new liberty pole on Washington Park" took place and "H. Capt. DeBevoise of the 14th Regt., with their music [Navy Yard Band], will play the appropriate national airs." The pieces included "Hail Columbia," Star-Spangled Banner," and "Yankee Doodle" ("The National Anniversary," *Brooklyn Daily Eagle*, 2 July 1859, 2; *New York Times*, 6 July 1859, 2).

Williamsburgh: Turl's Band performed at fireworks celebration ("In Williamsburgh," *Brooklyn Daily Eagle*, 5 July 1859, 2).

Pennsylvania

Philadelphia: On the grounds of Pennsylvania College, the College Glee Club sang "patriotic odes and choice selections of music." The group sang "Hail Columbia," "Star-Spangled Banner," "that famous old College song 'Gaudeamus Igitur,'" "I See Them Still the Patriot Band," and "The Mariners" ("The Fourth at Pennsylvania College," *Republican Compiler*, 11 July 1859, 2).

1860

Publications

"Freedom's Battle-Song written for and sung at the Framingham A.S. Celebration, July 4."[708] By R. Thayer. Tune, "Auld Lang Syne." First line: "A Band of freemen we go forth."

"Hymns and Songs for the Anti-Slavery Celebration of the Declaration of Independence, at Framingham, July 4, 1860." Includes: Freedom's Battle Song by R. Thayer — Freedom's Summons — Hymn to Freedom — Hymns and prayer — Appeal to Massachusetts. Broadside. Boston: Prentiss and Deland, 1860. Copy in Brown University.

"Written for the celebration of July 4 at North Elba, and read by the Secretary, as it was not possible to arrange music for it at the time."[709] By "Mr. Sanborn." First line: "Eternal hills! that rise around."

Performances

Massachusetts

Boston: "At eight o'clock, a grand concert was given upon the Common, by a band composed of the Brigade, Boston Brass, Germania, and Gilmore's bands, all under the direction of Mr. B.A. Burditt. A programme of ten pieces of music was performed, including 'Hail Columbia' and the 'Star-Spangled Banner,' to heighten the effect of which the guns of the Light Artillery were introduced. The Concert concluded with 'Old Hundred'; the immense concourse of people, who had been listening with gratification to the previous pieces, joining in a grand and powerful chorus." The services at Music Hall included both vocal and instrumental music and "began with a voluntary by the Germania Band, after which the following chant was sung by the juvenile choir [150 boys and girls], under the direction of Mr. Charles Butler": first line, "O sing unto the Lord a new song." After a prayer, an "original ode, written by A. Wallace Thaxter," was sung: first line, "Raise the paean! swell the chorus." After a reading of the Declaration of Independence by Samuel H. Randall, an "original ode was then sung": first line, "Native Land! Our warm heart's adoration." Following an oration by Edward Everett, the choir sung the Doxology, "the audience rising and joining in singing the last verse": first line, "From all that dwell below the skies" (*Oration Delivered before the City Authorities of Boston, on the Fourth of July, 1860*, by Edward Everett. Boston: Geo. C. Rand & Avery, [1860]).

New Hampshire

Hillsboro: At 9 A.M. the Sabbath schools of Hillsboro and adjacent towns marched, "preceded by the Manchester Band," to the grove. Participating also was the Henniker Brass Band and the Concord Cornet Band. The proceedings included "singing from the [Hillsboro] glee club, under the direction of Prof. Barton" ("Fourth of July Celebration at Hillsboro," *Farmers' Cabinet*, 11 July 1860, 2).

New York

New York: Nyer's Twelfth Regiment Band[710] performed on the steamer *Hendrick Hudson* on an excursion "to Newbugh, Westpoint, and Coldspring," leaving from the 12th Street pier ("Excursions," *New York Times*, 3 July 1860, 6); Rohn's "New York Band" at the City Hall in Brooklyn, New York, at evening fireworks event ("The Fourth in Brooklyn," *Brooklyn Daily Eagle*, 5 July 1860, 2); at Niblo's Garden, "a new

national and patriotic overture," composed by John Cooke, is premiered (*New York Times*, 4 July 1860, 7).

Rhode Island

Seekonk: The "Order of Exercises" included a "National Ode by the Choir" and an "original Hymn written for the occasion" (first line: "What voices from the silent past") by the Rev. William M. Thayer, of Franklin, Mass.

> Spirited and tasteful music was set to these hymns by Dea. D.B. Fitts, formerly of Seekonk, but now organist at the Congregational Church in Holliston, Mass., who also wrote an original piece of music for the original hymn on this occasion; and the singing was beautifully executed by a choir of twenty-five well trained voices (Dea. Fitts presiding at the organ) the whole being under the direction of Daniel Perrin, Esq., of Seekonk, a gentleman who exhibited ample qualifications for the task he was called to sustain.

After a dinner prepared for the occasion, an Ode "originally written by William J. Pabodie of Providence for another purpose" was sung to the tune "Old Hundred": first line, "From dwellings by the stormy deep" (*Rehoboth in the Past. An Historical Oration Delivered on the Fourth of July, 1860. By Sylvanus Chace Newman*. Pawtucket: Robert Sherman, 1860).

Texas

Millican: "At the site selected for the Depot of the Houston & Texas Central Railroad" in Brazos County, eighty miles from Houston, a procession was formed headed by a band of music which played "several national airs" ("The Fourth at Millican's," *Weekly Telegraph*, 10 July 1860).

1861

Publications

Another 4th of July: The Wedding-Day is Coming. Song and March[711] (Evansville, Ind.: Herman Fluegel, 1861), by Herman Fluegel, for piano, guitar, and voice. First line: "Oh my dear your eyes look red was it weeping made them red?" Copy in Johns Hopkins University.

The Declaration of Independence of the United States of North America, July 4, 1776, Arranged and Adapted for Vocal and Instrumental Music, as the Great National Chant and Dedicated to the World. Baltimore: John E. Wilson, 1861. Copy in Johns Hopkins University.

"The Flag of Our Union — July 4th 1861." By J.M. Dunbar. First line: "Our country's bright flag greets the morning's first ray." No imprint data. Copy in Center for Popular Music, Middle Tennessee State University.

"Fourth of July Song. Air: Star-Spangled Banner."

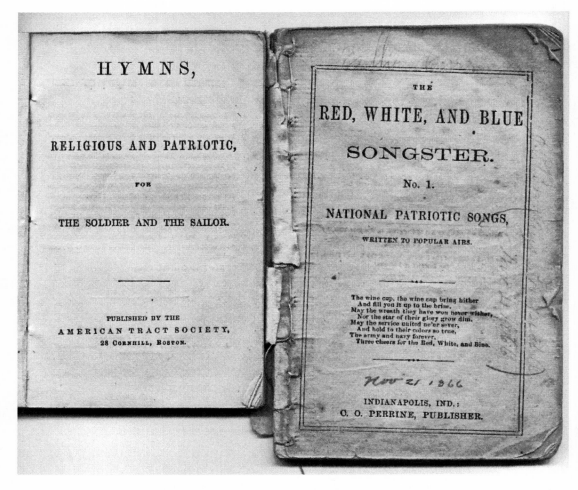

Examples of two Civil War Union songsters that troops carried into battle. Each contains typical popular Fourth of July song texts, such as "The Sword of Bunker Hill," "The Star-Spangled Banner,"
"Columbia, the Gem of the Ocean," and "My Country 'tis of thee." *Hymns, Religious and Patriotic,
for the Soldier and the Sailor* (Boston: American Tract Society, 1861), with music, and *The Red, White,
and Blue Songster* (Indianapolis: C.O. Perrine, 1861) (author's collection).

By M.J. Million. First line: "We hail, once again, the
glad day that gave." Broadside. New York: H. De
Marsan, [1861–63]. Copies in Center for Popular
Music, Middle Tennessee State University and New
York Historical Society.

"Fourth of July song: Gotten Up Expressly for
Those Who Have an Appreciative Mind." Broadside,
[between 1861 and 1865]. Copy in Wake Forest University.

"Hail! Glorious Banner of Our Land." By Charles
Warren. "Respectfully inscribed to Major General
George B. McClellan, by Mrs. Mary Farrell Moore,
Cincinnati, Ohio, July 4th, 1861." For voice and
piano. Philadelphia: Lee & Walker, 1861.

"Hymns and songs for the anti-slavery celebration
of the Declaration of Independence at Framingham,

July 4, 1861." Includes: "Secession" [First line: "They
threaten now to take their leave"] / by M. Trafton.—
"Liberty for all" [First line: "O shame! that e'en within
the shade"] / by A. Caldwell. Broadside, Boston: Prentiss & Deland, 1861.

*Hymns, Religious and Patriotic for the Soldier and
the Sailor.* Boston: American Tract Society, 1861. Includes lyrics for "My country 'Tis of thee," "The Star-
Spangled Banner," "Hail, Columbia," "Red, White,
and Blue," and "The Flag of Our Union."

"July 4th, 1861." [n.p.: Cooke & Danielson, Evening
Press Office], 1861. Copy in Brown University.

"An Ode for the Union" (first line: "No shorn republic name to me!) (*National Intelligencer*, 4 July
1861, 2).

"Patriotic Songs!: These songs of freedom will be

sung on the Mall, July 4th, 1861, by a large choir, commencing at 6 ½ o'clock. Hail Columbia (J. Hopkinson); Marseilles Hymn; Star-Spangled Banner (F.S. Key); American Hymn (Miss H.F. Gould); America (the Rev. S.F. Smith); Army Hymn[712] (O.W. Holmes). Copy in New York Historical Society.

The Red, White, and Blue Songster. No. 1, National Patriotic Songs, Written to Popular Airs. Indianapolis: C.O. Perrine, 1861. Includes: "Red, White, and Blue," "Hail Columbia," "Star-Spangled Banner," "Columbia! Arise to Glory!" (first line: "Columbia! Columbia! to glory arise!"), "Yankee Doodle," "Our Flag is There," "The Marseilles Hymn" (first line: "Ye sons of Freedom, awake to glory!"), "Hull's Victory," "The American Star" (first line: "Come, strike the bold anthem, the war-dogs are howling"), "The Clime Beneath Whose Genial Sun," "The Sword of Bunker Hill" (first line: "He lay upon his dying bed"), "America," "Our Native Land," "Viva L'America."

"The Standard of the Free: National Song and Chorus. Dedicated to Col Lefferts,[713] and officers and men of the gallant New-York Seventh Regiment. Sung with Great Applause at the Tammany Celebration, 4th July 1861. Words and music by John Mahon." First line: "Fling out that banner, the standard of the free." Broadside. [New York: H. De Marsan, 1861?]. Copy in New York Historical Society.

Performances

Maine

Portland: The Portland Band performed and some "original odes" were sung by a choir (*Daily Evening Traveller*, 5 July 1861, 2).

Massachusetts

Boston: "Star-Spangled Banner" was sung with new words by "Dr. Holmes"[714] at the Music Hall (*Daily Evening Traveller*, 5 July 1861, 2; *North American and United States Gazette*, 5 July 1861, 2); at the Academy of Music: T.W. Parson's ode, "Land of Columbia," is premiered by a children's choir of 300; the Germania Band performed; a song, "Stand by the Stars and Stripes," arranged to the "Pirate Chorus" from Enchantress was sung (*Daily Evening Traveller*, 5 July 1861, 2).

South Danvers: "Massachusetts Volunteers" sung by the children of the town at the public square and "Star-Spangled Banner" was sung by the audience and accompanied by the band (*South Danvers Wizard*, 3 July 1861, 2).

Michigan

Detroit: "Star-Spangled Banner" sung at a dinner held at "Simpson's" by H. J. Buckley (*Detroit Free Press*, 6 July 1861, 1).

New Hampshire

Lebanon: The exercises "on the stand" included "singing by a choir under the direction of Mr. J.M.

Perkins, who, during the day, furnished excellent music." (D. H. Allen, *July Fourth, 1761: An Historical Discourse in Commemoration of the One Hundredth Anniversary of the Charter of Lebanon, N.H., Delivered July Fourth, 1861*, 90).

New York

Brooklyn: Christy's Minstrels at the Brooklyn Athenaeum in New York: "everything new, original and unique. Burlesque operas, patriotic songs and choruses, artistic dancing, &c. Admission 25 cents"; at the Brooklyn Garden, "a grand extra concert, performed by twenty of the best musicians ... to commence at 3 o'clock P.M. Admission five cents. Ladies free" (*Brooklyn Daily Eagle*, 3 and 5 July 1861, 3 and 2 respectively).

New York: *Prize National Overture*, performed by "a grand orchestra under the direction of Mr. John Cooke" [715] (*New York Leader*, 29 June 1861, 8); "Standard of the Free," written by John Mahon was sung by the Tammany Glee Club at the Tammany celebration (*New York Times*, 6 July 1861, 2); Hirschman's Orchestra performed at Jones' Wood and the Seventh Regiment Band[716] and a choir from the Institution for the Blind performed at the Academy of Music. The choir and audience sang the "Army Hymn" to the tune "Old Hundred," words by Oliver Wendell Holmes (*New York Times*, 4 July 1861, 3). See **Publications** above.

Rhode Island

Providence: Order of exercises at the city celebration:

1. Music by Shepard's Cornet Band
2. Singing by a select choir from the High School and grammar schools under the direction of Seth Sumner, Esq., teacher of vocal music: "God bless our native land" (first line)
3. Prayer, by the Rev. A.H. Clapp, Pastor of the Beneficent Congregational Church
4. Reading of the Declaration of Independence, by N.W. DeMunn, Principal of the Benefit Street Grammar School
5. Singing, by the select choir: "Firmly Stand, My Native Land" (first line: "Firmly stand, firmly stand")
6. Oration, by the Rev. Dr. Samuel L. Caldwell, Pastor of the First Baptist Church
7. Singing, by the select choir: "Star-Spangled Banner!"
8. Benediction, by the Rev. A.H. Clapp

(*Oration Delivered before the Municipal Authorities and Citizens of Providence, on the Eighty-Fifth Anniversary of American Independence, July 4, 1861.* By Samuel L. Caldwell. Providence: Knowles, Anthony & Co., 1861.)

1862

Publications

"Ode by the Rev. T.J. Greenwood. Air — Star-Spangled Banner." First line: "We come not to-day, as we oft-time have come" (*Farmers' Cabinet*, 10 July 1862, 1).

"Original Hymn written for and sung at a July 4 celebration at Framingham."[717] By Caroline A. Mason. Tune, "Old Hundred." First line: "Our fathers worshipped Thee, O God."

"Our National Visitation,[718] written for and sung at the anti-slavery celebration at Framingham, (Mass.) July 4th, 1862." By W.L.G. [William Lloyd Garrison]. Tune: "John Brown Song." First line: "For the sighing of the needy, to deliver the oppressed."

"Pro Patria: a National Song for the Fourth of July, 1862." First line: "Our country's glorious birth." By Pilgrim John. Brooklyn, N.Y.: D.S. Holmes, 1862. Copy in Filson Historical Society.

"Song for the Fourth of July, 1862." By Eliza R. Snow. Broadside. [Salt Lake City?, 1862?]. Copy in Yale University Library.

"Song Written for the 4th, of July, 1862." Air: "Auld Lang Syne." First line: "Beside the flowing river's tide." Dedicated to President Lincoln. Broadside. Copy in Brown University.

Performances

Massachusetts

Amherst: An entertainment in the town hall was organized by the ladies of Amherst and consisted of "tableaux, vocal and instrumental music." Admission to the evening performance was 15 cents ("Independence Festival," *Farmers' Cabinet*, 3 July 1862, 3).

Boston: At 8 A.M. on the Common, a "grand union concert" was presented by all the military bands in the city ("The Fourth of July," *Boston Daily Courier*, 5 July 1862, 2); at Faneuil Hall, "Washington's March" was performed by a band (*Boston Daily Courier*, 5 July 1862, 2); "Star-Spangled Banner," with words by W.T. Adams, and "Union" sung by "a choir of pupils selected from the high and grammar schools, under the direction of Charles Butler (*City of Boston: Eighty-Sixth Anniversary of American Independence, July 4, 1862.* [Boston]: J.E. Farwell & Co., [1862]); "Old Glory" cited as an "original ode" and sung by "the young school misses, under the direction of Mr. Charles Butler," at the Academy of Music (*Boston Daily Courier*, 5 July 1862, 2).

Newton: "America" sung by church choirs and others at the celebration there. First line: "My country! 'Tis of thee"; "The Dear Old Flag": first line, "See the flag! The dear old flag"; "The Flag of Our Union": first line, "A song for our banner! The watchword recall"; "Marching Along"[719]: first line, "The Children are gathering from near and from far"; "Marseilles Hymn": first line, "Ye sons of freedom, wake to glory"; "Old Hundred": first line, "From all that dwell below the skies"; "Our Flag is There"[720]: first line, "Our flag is there! Our flag is there!"; "Song of the Contrabands": first line, "Oh praise an' thanks! De Lord he come"; "Battle Hymn": first line, "Mine eyes have seen the glory of the coming of the Lord"[721]; "Star-Spangled Banner"; "Viva l'America"[722]: first line, "Noble Republic! Happiest of lands." Broadside. (*Grand National Union Concert ... by the Sabbath and Public Schools of Newton and the Surrounding Towns.* Newton, Mass., 1862).

North Salem: A raising of a flag-staff 135 feet high on July 3 took place and on July 4 the Salem Brass Band provided music near the adjacent platform and Miss Mary E. Todd's ode (first line: "Sons of freedom, raise the banner!) was read by the mayor. (*Celebration at North Bridge, Salem, July 4th, 1862.* Oration by Dr. George B. Loring. Boston: J. E. Farwell, [1862]; "Celebration in Salem, *Boston Daily Courier*, 5 July 1862, 1).

New Hampshire

Amherst: "At 10 o'clock, the children, teachers, and friends of Sabbath Schools assembled at the Congregational Church" where the exercises included "singing by the choir and children." Afterwards "a procession was then formed, and under escort of Lawrence Engine Company, No. 2, and the New Boston Brass Band, marched around and saluted the 'dear old flag,' with rousing cheers. The procession then moved to the Atherton grove, where ample tables had been spread and furnished, and a stand for speaking erected. Here the 'Star-Spangled Banner' was sung by the children, under the direction of Mr. H.E. Abbott.... The exercises were closed with a song by the children." That evening, "the ladies gave an entertainment at the town hall' and the affair included music by the band. "The singing of the Marseilles Hymn and Old New England, by the quartette, consisting of Messrs. Mack and Sawtelle, Mrs. H.E. Abbott and Miss Lucy David, was in good taste and well received" ("The Fourth in Amherst," *Farmers' Cabinet*, 10 July 1862, 2).

New York

Brooklyn: At Fort Greene, while 20,000 persons watched fireworks, "a band of music was present and played patriotic and operatic airs at intervals" ("How the Day Was Observed," *Brooklyn Daily Eagle*, 5 July 1862, 2).

New York: At the Cooper Union Debating Society meeting, "Meeting of the Waters" sung by "Miss G. Hartshorne" who "received due appreciation" and "Star-Spangled Banner" sung by J.A. Adams who "received of course with the most vociferous applause" ("Cooper Institute," *New York Times*, 6 July 1862, 2); at Nixon's Cremorne Gardens, Mme. Strakosch sang "The Flag of Our Union" and Carlotta Patti sang "The Star-Spangled Banner," the latter "assisted by all the Italian artists" (*New York Times*, 4 July 1862, 7); at Niblos's Garden, Miss Caroline Richings appeared as Pauline in the musical drama *National Guard* (*New York Times*, 4 July 1862, 3).

Ohio

Cincinatti: At Shires' National Theater a "grand Fourth & Fifth of July celebration" included the Mammoth Minstrel Band and Rainford's Empire Minstrels. On Friday, July 4, an afternoon presentation included a "patriotic drama" titled *Fourth of July in the Morning*, followed by a "national dance," by Miss Rosa Hill (*Cincinatti Daily Gazette*, 4 July 1862, 4).

Virginia

James River: General George B. McClellan encouraged his bands to play national airs for the Army of the Potomac camped adjacent to the river banks (*Evening Star*, 9 July 1862, 2).

Wyoming

Fort Bridger: Near the fort, in a military camp, the morning began with "the firing of muskets and revolvers" and "elivening strains of our National airs, Hail Columbia, Star-Spangled Banner, Yankee Doodle, etc., performed with excellent spirit by our two brass buglers, Charles Evans and Josiah Eardley" ("The Celebration of the Fourth of July Near Fort Bridger, by Capt. Lot Smith's Command," *Deseret News*, 23 July 1862, 8).

1863

Publications

"Three Times Three, a Song for the Fourth of July" was introduced by G.H. Williams (*Daily Ohio State Journal*, 4 July 1863, 1).

Performances

Indiana

Cambridge City: From six to eight thousand persons enjoyed a celebration that included music by the Milton Band, Hagerstown

Band, and Richmond Band ("The 4th in Cambridge City," *Cincinnati Daily Gazette*, 6 July 1863, 4).

Kentucky

Lexington: Saxton's "celebrated band" provided music for a celebration and charitable event for poor children given by the St. John's Educational Society (*New York Freeman's Journal & Catholic Register*, 18 July 1863, 5).

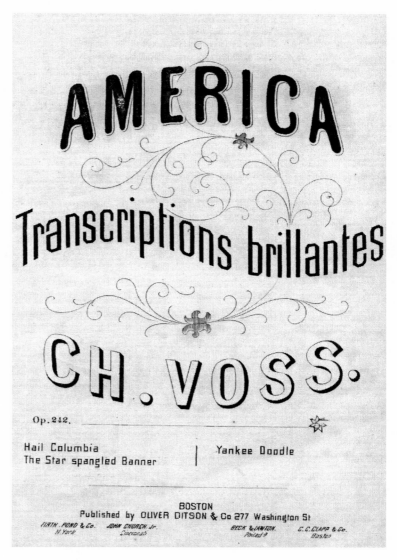

Cover of *America. Transcriptions Brillantes: No. 2, Yankee Doodle* (Boston: Oliver Ditson, 1860s) by Charles Voss. This work was performed by the author at an Independence Day concert in Clarksburg, Maryland, on July 3, 2008. The tune "Yankee Doodle" was performed annually on the Fourth of July in numerous cities and towns across the country during the eighteenth and nineteenth centuries (author's collection).

New Hampshire

New Boston: On the occasion of the centennial anniversary of this town, a procession, music, and speeches took place. At 9 A.M. the New Boston Cornet Band led a parade to the Presbyterian Meeting House, where a platform had been erected in front for the ceremony. An original hymn, by Mrs. S.T. Wason[723] "was sung by a large choir in which were several aged people (Mrs. Hannah Farley[724] being seventy-eight years old), under the direction of Jesse Beard,[725] a veteran school-teacher and singing-master, now seventy-four years old, assisted by Mr. A.P. Brigham." The hymn was titled "Centennial" (first line: "Our fathers' God, to thee"). Another hymn also by Wason was sung by the choir: "Our Century Plant" (first line: "Our century plant is in blossom to-day").

After music by the band, some 500 persons were seated for dinner and heard the following two songs: "Air, 'Auld Lang Syne.'" First line: "We come from northern snow-draped homes"; "Welcome of the Fathers." First line: "Hear ye not the soft, low whispers."

After dinner, the group reassembled in the church where the following additional two pieces written by Wason were sung: "Our Early Friends." First line: "Our childhood's friends have met once more"; "Our Fathers" (hymn). First line: "Our fathers' God, who dwell'st on high" (Elliott C. Cogswell, *History of New Boston, New Hampshire* [Boston: Geo. C. Rand & Avery S. Cornhill, 1864], 12–19; "Centennial at New Boston" and "Poetry," *Farmer's Cabinet*, 9 and 16 July 1863, 2 and 4, respectively).

New Jersey

Franklinville: "Professors Adams and Urion, will perform some of their best national airs" at an event that included an artillery salute, ice cream and other refreshments, speeches, and a "grand cotillion party in the evening." Broadside (titled "Fourth of July Celebration in Sharp's Grove, Franklinville, Gloucester County, N.J.") [Philadelphia]: Familton & Rogers, printers, [1863].

Pennsylvania

Warren: The German Brass Band provided music at Johnson's Hall (*Warren Mail*, 11 July 1863).

native land! our native land!"; Sound the Trumpet: first line, "Sound the trump-prepare for battle"; The Flag of Our Union: first line, "A song for our banner! the watchword recall." [Providence, RI]: A. Crawford, Greene, Steam Printer, 1864.

Performances

California

Sacramento: "America" cited as a hymn sung by the Philharmonic Society at the Pavilion. An overture was performed by the Sacramento Brass Band (*Sacramento Daily Union*, 6 July 1864, 3).

Illinois

Chicago: Sharpley's Minstrels gave a performance at Metropolitan Hall "to an excellent audience" (*Chicago Tribune*, 6 July 1864, 4).

New York

Buffalo: A "grand steamboat excursion" included music provided by the Union Cornet Band and a Quadrille Band, along with refreshments (*Buffalo Morning Express*, 4 July 1864, 2).

New York: At the Tammany Society celebration, "Prof. Colburn" conducted 24 pupils of the Twentieth Ward public schools in the song "The Voice of '76." Written for the occasion by Charles F. Olney, a pianist (*New York Daily News*, 6 July 1864, 2); George F. Bristow composed a *Rondo* to be played on the steeple bells at Trinity Church (Heintze, *The Fourth of July Encyclopedia*, 24).

Pennsylvania

Gettysburg: A year after the deadliest single battle of the Civil War, a gathering of four to five thousand persons included a ceremony with music by the Chambersburg Brass Band ("Gettysburg," *Philadelphia Inquirer*, 5 July 1864, 8).

Tennessee

Nashville: Buildings were gaily decorated and a parade of only military units included "three fine brass bands whose lively music seemed to put wings to the soldier's feet" ("Grand Celebration" and "The Celebration," *Nashville Daily Times*, 4 and 6 July 1864, 3 and 2, respectively).

1864

Publications

"Balloon 'Star-Spangled Banner.'" Signed H.F.D." Boston: J.E. Farwell & Co., 1864. Composed to honor the "aeronaut" Samuel A. King. First line: "Like the bird of our banner I soar on high."

"Municipal Celebration of the Eighty-Eighth Anniversary of American Independence, Monday, July 4th, 1864." Includes National Hymn: first line, "Our

1865

Publications

"Bright Republic: a Song and Chorus, Written for the National Jubilee, July 4th, 1865." By the Rev. J[oel] F[oote] Bingham; music by William Krauskopf. [Buffalo?, 1865]. Words only. Copies in University of Georgia, College of William & Mary, and other repositories.

"General Meade, the Hero of Gettysburg. Air —

Hail to the Chief who in Triumph Advances." July 4th, 1865. First line: "Hail to the chiefain who comes in his glory." Songsheet, copy in Rare Book and Special Collections Division, Library of Congress ("America Singing: Nineteenth Century Song Sheets," *American Memory* website).

"Hymn for the Fourth of July, 1865." First line: "Great God of Battles, unto Thee" (*Harper's Weekly*, 8 July 1865).

"Ode for July 4th, 1865. Air—'The Star-Spangled Banner.'" By Alfred Billings Street. First line: "The day, the bright day glows again in their skies." Broadside, [Monticello, NY,] 1865. Copy in New York Historical Society.

"We have just received from Horace Waters publisher, 481 Broadway, New York, two spirited and soul stirring pieces of music, appropriate for Fourth of July, and all patriotic occasions. The music of both is by the popular composer, Mrs. E.A. Parkhurst.[726] The first is 'The Peace Jubilee,'[727] a national song with chorus. The second a national anthem "Glory to God in the Highest"[728] (*Farmers' Cabinet*, 29 June 1865, 3).

Performances

District of Columbia

At the celebration by the National Lincoln Monument Association, music was provided by the Union Cornet Band.[729]

Massachusetts

Boston: Musical entertainment for the children of the public schools was provided at Music Hall and the Boston Theatre. At the Music Hall, "three National Organ Concerts were given by Mr. G.E. Whiting and Mrs. L.S. Frohock." James R. Elliott sang "Columbia, the Gem of the Ocean" with the audience joining in the chorus. The children sang a verse of "The Star-Spangled Banner" under the direction of Carl Zerrahn, "Chorus of Pilgrims," from *I Lombardi*, and an "original hymn" by Mrs. Julia Ward Howe[730] to the tune of "Old Hundredth Psalm": first line, "Our Fathers built the house of God." At Boston Theatre there were bands of music for dancing and promenading. One band played "Hail to the Chief" as Boston Mayor Frederic W. Lincoln, Jr. entered. A procession earlier that day included a band from Gallop's Island, Gilmore's Band with a Drum Corps, and Bond's Cornet Band[731] (*Peace under Liberty. Oration Delivered before the City Authorities of Boston, on the Fourth of July, 1865*, by J.M. Manning. Boston: J.E. Farwell, 1865.)

New Jersey

Trenton: "Battle Cry of Freedom,"[732] "Our Country's Birthday," "Star-Spangled Banner," and "Welcome, Heroes, Home" sung by a glee club, directed by Professor Harding, at a grandstand on the grounds of Mr. Perdicaris ("The Fourth of July in Trenton," *Daily State Gazette*, 7 July 1865, 3).

New York

New York: "The military display consisted of twenty-five regiments of infantry, cavalry and artillery, accompanied by thirteen bands, and was received with the greatest enthusiasm. Along the line of march the returned veterans had a perfect ovation" ("Fourth of July at New York," *Chicago Tribune*, 6 July 1865, O2); George F. Bristow wrote a work titled *Grand National Fantasia*, "in honor of our great victories" that was performed on the steeple bells of Trinity Church. The piece included arrangements of these tunes: "Vive l'America," "Bound Soldier Boy," "Old Folks at Home," "Coming through the Rye," "Hail Columbia," and "The Campbells Are Coming" (Heintze, *The Fourth of July Encyclopedia*, 24).

Saratoga Springs: William Ross Wallace's "national Song," "Washington's Red, White and Blue" was premiered (*New York Times*, 9 July 1865, 3).

Pennsylvania

Gettysburg: "French's Hymn," composed by B.B. French was sung by the Baltimore Musical Association at the cornerstone laying ceremony for the National Soldiers Monument. This work had previously been sung on November 19, 1863, at the consecration ceremony for the National Gettysburg Cemetary event in which Lincoln gave his "Gettysburg Address." Also sung by the Baltimore Musical Association was "This Battlefield," composed by Gen. W.H. Hayward, of Baltimore: first line, "This battle-field-our nation's glory." Martial music was supplied by the band of the Ninth Veteran Reserve Corps ("Gettysburgh," *New York Times*, 6 July 1865, 2 and 8).

Lititz: At the grove, "the Union League Band of Lancaster was present and discoursed excellent music" ("Fourth of July Excursions to Ephrata and Lititz," *Columbia Spy*, 8 July 1865, 3).

1866

Publications

"Anti-slavery hymns sung at Harmony Grove, Framingham, Mass., July 4, 1866." Includes: Onward to the work [First line: O, Father, from above] / by G.W. Stacy.— Fling out the anti-slavery flag [First line].— The happy day is dawning [First line]. Broadside, [Framingham, 1866].

Bald Mountain Schottish. By M.W.C. For piano. Troy, NY: Chas. W. Harris, [1866]. On p. 1: "To the pic-nic party, July 4th, 1866."

"Hymn for the Fourth of July. Tune, 'Old Hundred.'" First line: "To Thee, O God, all praise belongs" (*Littell's Living Age*, 21 July 1866, 144).

Performances

Illinois

Salem: "Sherman's March to the Sea" sung by a glee club of "young ladies and gentlemen" following a speech given by Gen. William T. Sherman (*Weekly Missouri Democrat*, 10 July 1866, 1).

New York

Flushing: A group of soldiers' orphans sang "Marching On" and "Peace to the Brave" at the laying of the cornerstone of the soldiers monument there ("The Glorious Fourth" *New York Times*, 5 July 1866, 8).

New York: Geo. Christy's Minstrels at 4 West 24th Street; "Hoffman's Full Band" at Lowe's Amphitheatre; "Theo Thomas'Garden Concerts," two concerts at Terrace Garden, 3rd Ave between 58th and 59th Streets (*New York Times*, 3 July 1866, 7).

Utica: A procession included the Utica Brass Band that also provided music for the exercises held at Chancellor Square (*Utica Daily Observer*, 5 July 1866, 1, 3).

Pennsylvania

Philadelphia: The Handel and Haydn Society sang "Old Hundred" for General George G. Meade and 10,000 war veterans (*New York Times*, 5 July 1866, 8).

Washington

Walla Walla: At the town ceremony held at the Council Grove, there was "singing by the choir" ("Fourth of July Celebration," *Walla Walla Statesman*, 7 July 1866, 2).

1867

Performances

District of Columbia

The U.S. Marine Band led a parade of temperance organizations (*Evening Star*, 5 July 1867, 1).

Maryland

Laurel: The Naval Academy Band, Peter Schoff, leader, provided music for the celebration of Independent Order of Rechahites (*Evening Star*, 5 July 1867, 1).

New York

Brooklyn: Myer's Brass Band "discoursed enliving and patriotic airs" during the fireworks display ("Fireworks," *Brooklyn Daily Eagle*, 5 July 1867, 2).

New York: Grafulla's Band performed at the laying of the cornerstone for the new Tammany Hall building on 14th Street ("General City News," *New York Times*, 26 June 1867, 5; *New York Citizen*, 29 June 1867, 8); in Central Park, Dodworth's Band pre-

sented a "National Medley" of tunes (*New York Times*, 4 July 1867, 5); in Harlem at Mount Morris Square, 15,000 persons heard music by Robertson's Brass Band and students from public schools sang "America" ("The Day in Harlem," *New York Times*, 5 July 1867, 1, 8).

Ohio

Cincinnati: At Fiedler's Loewen Garden, a concert at 2 P.M. was given by Wiegand's String and Silver Cornet Band; at the National Theater, a "Great National Jubilee" included the play *Wife with Four Husbands*, "after which the national anthem, 'The Star-Spangled Banner,' in character of the Goddess of Liberty, introducing the Grand Patriot Tableau of Washington Crossing the Delaware. To be followed by [a] Patriotic Song, introducing the Apothrosis of Lincoln, descriptive of the reception of this patriot martyr by Washington in the Temple of Liberty" (*Cincinnati Commercial*, 4 July 1867, 8).

Pennsylvania

Philadelphia: Hassler's "Full Military Band" provided music for the opening of the "new" Ledger Building ("Fourth of July at the New Ledger Building, Philadelphia," *Columbia Spy*, 13 July 1867).

1868

Performances

California

San Francisco: The California Minstrels performed twice at Platt's Music Hall (*San Francisco Dramatic Chronicle*, 3 July 1868, 2).

New Jersey

Newark: "Bright Sword of Liberty" and "Our Native Land" sung by the Orpheus Society at the First Baptist Church celebration ("Newark," *New York Times*, 5 July 1868, 8).

New York

Brooklyn: At Fort Greene, McCann's Band[733] of the 56th Regiment "played appropriate music during the intervals between the pieces [fireworks]" ("Independence Day," *Brooklyn Daily Eagle*, 6 July 1868, 2).

New York: At Trinity Church, James E. Ayliffe rang the following tunes using the bells in the church steeple:

Ringing the chimes of eight bells
"Hail Columbia"
"Yankee Doodle"
"Blue Bells of Scotland"
Airs from "Child of the Regiment"
"Red, White and Blue"
"Evening Bells"
"On the Field of Glory"

"The Soldier's Return"
"Columbia, the Gem of the Ocean"
"Spanish Melody"
"The Eclipse Polka"
Scotch Melody from *Guy Mannering*
"The Chimes Quadrile"
"Yankee Doodle"

(Heintze, *The Fourth of July Encyclopedia*, 24); at Lyric Hall, Blind Tom gave an evening concert and at Central Park Garden, Theodore Thomas and his orchestra gave two concerts on the Fourth. The afternoon concert featured Mrs. Jenny Kempton, "the distinguished and favorite contralto" and Mr. R. Henning, violoncellist. The program included works by Rossini, Strauss, Goltermann, Bellini, Meyerbeer, Offenbach, and Gounod. American works included "Central Park Garden," a march by Thomas and a "patriotic song" titled "Columbia, the Gem of the Ocean" as composed by [David T.] Shaw. (*New York Times*, 4 July 1868, 7).

New Mexico

Santa Fe: A parade included a military and citizen's band both alternately performing on their way to the State House. At the pagoda there the exercises also included music. A newspaper reported that "the bands generously lent their assistance on the occasion without compensation, for which they are entitled to the thanks of all who joined in the celebration" ("The Fourth of July," *Santa Fe Weekly Gazette*, 11 July 1868, 2).

1869

Publications

"That Banner of Stars: Fourth of July Ode," by J.C. Meininger. Lyrics by A. Fulkerson. Cincinnati: John Church & Co., 1869.

Performances

Massachusetts

Hingham: On the occasion of the dedication of the public library building on July 5, a town procession included the South Hingham Cornet Band and Hingham Brass Band. The "order of exercises" included:

I. Singing by a select choir. "Gloria" from Mozart's Twelfth Mass.
II. Presentation of the Deed of the Land and Building.
III. Original Song, to be sung by the pupils of the Derby Academy and public schools. First line: "Children, here, we meet together."
IV. Dedicatory Prayer, by the Rev. Calvin Lincoln.
V. Original Hymn (composed for the occasion), tune—"America." First line: "Thou great creative Cause!"

VI. Oration, by Hon. Thomas Russell, of Boston.
VII. Original Song, by the scholars. First line: "Hail our Nation's proudest day!"

"To be followed by the 'Star-Spangled Banner,' and other patriotic selections, by the choir" (*Dedication of the Hingham Public Library, July 5th, 1869*, by the Hon. Thomas Russell, with an Appendix. Hingham: Published by the Trustees of the Library, 1871).

Quincy: The celebration took place on Monday, July 5, with a procession that included the Quincy Brass Band and the following exercises at the church:

1. Voluntary on the organ.
2. Chorus, "Star-Spangled Banner."
3. Prayer, by the Rev. J.D. Wells.
4. Reading of the Declaration of Independence, by Henry Lunt.
5. Keller's American Hymn.[734]
6. Address, by Charles Francis Adams, Jr.
7. National anthem, "America."

"The choruses were sung by a choir of about fifty persons, and were finely rendered." In the evening the Quincy Brass Band performed "an excellent selection of popular and patriotic music, from sunset until the close of the [fireworks] display" (*The Double Anniversary: '76 and '63. A Fourth of July Address Delivered at Quincy, Mass. By Charles F. Adams, Jr. Boston: W. M. Parsons Lunt, 1869*).

New York

New York: At Carroll Park, the O'Reilly Band provided music before the fireworks display ("At Carroll Park," *Brooklyn Daily Eagle*, 6 July 1869, 2).

Pennsylvania

Philadelphia: "America," "Hail Columbia," "Star-Spangled Banner" and "Washington" were sung at the ceremony of dedication for a monument to George Washington (*The Age*, 5 July 1869, 1; *New York Times*, 5 July 1869, 1).

1870

Publications

"Liberty's Spirit, Come Home: Commended for Fourth of July Celebrations." By Robert Sinnickson. Salem, NJ: the author, 1870.

"The Land We Love," a "Chorus for the Fourth of July," by Theodore F. Seward.[735] Lyrics by George W. Birdseye. In William B. Bradbury, *The Victory: A New Collection of Sacred and Secular Music* (New York: Biglow & Main, 1870).

Performances

Connecticut

Woodstock: Gilmore's Band performed for a visit by President Grant ("Ovation to the President," *New*

"The Land We Love," a "Chorus for the Fourth of July," by Theodore F. Seward, of Orange, New Jersey, with words by George W. Birdseye, in William B. Bradbury, *The Victory: A New Collection of Sacred and Secular Music* (New York: Biglow & Main, 1870) (author's collection).

York Herald Tribune, 5 July 1870, 10); print musical program in *N.Y. Herald*, 4 July 1870, 10.

Colorado

Greeley: The Denver Band played Hail Columbia — Yankee Doodle — Columbia, the Gem of the Ocean — and a glee club sang "America" ("The Fourth at Greeley," *Rocky Mountain News*, 6 July 1870, 4).

Connecticut

New Haven: "Das ist der Tag des Hern (This is the Lord's Day)" sung by a group of German singing societies under the direction of "Prof. Wehner" at the City Hall (*Hartford Daily Courant*, 6 July 1870, 2).

Missouri

St. Charles: The first performance of the St. Charles Brass Band, Joseph Decker, bandleader, took place when the band marched in a parade on the Fourth (*The St. Charles Municipal Band, Inc.* website http://www.stc-muny-band.com/index.htm).

New Jersey

Newark: A parade included the Jefferson Brass Band and Sunderhaft's Band ("The Day in New-Jersey," *New York Times*, 5 July 1870, 1).

New York

Brooklyn: At Lofferts' Park, McCann's Band provided "excellent music," with "dancing till late in the evening" ("Fourth of July," *Brooklyn Daily Eagle*, 5 July 1870, 2).

New York: At the Tammany Hall celebration, "A Song, 'The Standard of Freedom'" was sung by William H. Davis ("The Celebration at Tammany Hall," *New York Times*, 5 July 1870, 1); in Central Park, Grafulla's Band performed the "National Overture" and the "Red, White, and Blue," as well as other works (*New York Times*, 4 July 1870, 1).

Randall's Island: "Fling Out the Starry Banner Wide," "Happy Hearts," "Let Us Seek the Sweet Bowers," "Unfurl the Glorious Banner,"[736] "Where Has Lula Gone?"[737] and "'Tis Well We Should be Gay" sung by 400 children ("The Day at Randall's Island," *New York Times*, 5 July 1870, 1).

Ohio

Cincinnati: Manning's Minstrels gave two performaces at Wood's Theater (*Cincinnati Commercial*, 4 July 1870, 8).

1871

Publications

"A Fourth of July Song. The following song, written for the occasion, is included in the programme for the Fourth of July celebration in New York. 'The Flag of Welcome.'" First line: "Her broad flag, her grand flag, Columbia uplifts" (*Cleveland Morning Herald*, 4 July 1871).

Performances

Massachusetts

Leicester: The exercises held in the grove began at 10 A.M. with music by the Worcester National Band followed the audience, "led by a well-trained choir of thirty singers," singing an "Invocation" to the tune of Old Hundred: first line, "Great God, to thee we raise our prayer." Additional music included: an original hymn, "written for the occasion by the Rev. A.C. Denison, of Middlefield, Conn., a former pastor of the First Congregational Church" of Leicester and sung by the choir: first line, "From far and near to-day we come"; "Yankee Doodle" and "Auld Lang Syne" played by the band. In the evening the band gave a concert on the town's common (*Celebration of the One Hundred and Fiftieth Anniversary of the Organization of the Town of Leicester, July 4, 1871.* Cambridge: Press of John Wilson and Son, 1871).

New Hampshire

New Boston: Over 1800 persons attended the celebration with music furnished by the New Boston Band (*Farmer's Cabinet*, 12 July 1871, 2).

New York

Brooklyn: Mayer's 47th Regiment Band at Capitoline Grounds (*Brooklyn Daily Eagle*, 3 July 1871, 1).

New York: Mr. Fisk's Erie Band marched in their "conspicuous 'lobster Back'" uniforms in the military parade that included between 7,000–8,000 men (*New York Times*, 5 July 1871, 1); Dan Bryant's Minstrels at the Park Theatre (*Brooklyn Daily Eagle*, 3 July 1871, 1).

Pennsylvania

Lititz: "The Citizens Band of York discoursed music at intervals throughout the afternoon and evening" ("The Glorious Fourth," *Columbia Spy*, 8 July 1871, 3).

Utah

Salt Lake City: The brass band of the 13th U.S. Infantry and Corinne Brass Band performed (*Salt Lake Tribune*, 4 July 1871, 2).

Tintic: The Provo Brass Band performed in the procession and public concert. The newspaper reported, "sentimental and comic songs, trios, duets, glees, etc, by Messers. Bee, Cannel, Davis, Robbins and others, under the direction of Prof. S.R. Bee" ("Fourth of July in Tintic," *Salt Lake Tribune*, 10 July 1871, 2).

1872

Performances

Colorado

Denver: Denver Brass Bands, played "airs most appropriate to the 'natal'" ("The Fourth in Denver," *Rocky Mountain News*, 6 July 1872, 4).

New Hampshire

Nashua: The day included music by the Calithumpian Band, a band concert, and "band concert and fireworks in the evening" (*Farmers' Cabinet*, 3 July 1872, 2).

New York

Brooklyn: At Prospect Park, the Twenty Third Regiment Band performed before "a large assemblage." The report including the following program of music:

Part I
1. Grand March. "Gemma di Fergy."[738] Donizetti
2. Ballad. "Kathleen Mavourneen." Crouch[739]
3. Overture. "Guy Mannoring." Bishop
4. Valse. "Les Gardes de Reine."[740] Godfrey
5. Galop. "Sleigh Ride." Folko
6. March. "Popular Airs." Conterno

Part Second
7. Overture. "Don Juan." Mozart
8. Song. "Scenes that are Brightest"[741] (Maritana). Wallace
9. Waltz. "Promotionea." Strauss
10. Selections. "La Grande Duchessa." Offenbach
11. Polka. "Education." Carolla
12. March. "Scotch Melodies." Conterno
["The Music in the Park," *Brooklyn Daily Eagle*, 5 July 1872, 2].

New York: At City Hall, the Eleventh Regiment Band provided music for those assembled there ("The Display of Fireworks at the City Hall and Elsewhere," *New York Times*, 5 July 1872, 1); at St. Ann's Church, J.M. Loretz, Jr., church musical director, performed "Fantasia-national airs" on the organ (*New York Times*, 4 July 1872, 5); Grafulla's Band on the steamer *Sleepy Hollow* on an excursion up the Hudson River (*Brooklyn Daily Eagle*, 3 July 1872, 1).

Utah

Salt Lake City: At a celebration held at the Liberal Institute, the Utah National Party Band performed *Faust's March, John Brown's Quickstep*, and other works (*Salt Lake Tribune*, 13 July 1872, 5).

1873

Publications

Fourth of July March (Philadelphia: Lee & Walker, 1873), for piano, by Frank Green.

Fourth of July March (Philadelphia: Lee & Walker, 1873), for violin and piano, by Septimus Winner.

Performances

Colorado

Golden: Golden Cornet Band "assembled in front of Jefferson Hall, played several pieces" ("At Golden," *Rocky Mountain News*, 6 July 1873, 4).

Massachusetts

Amherst: A "Union Picnic" at Babboosuck Lake attended by residents from neighboring towns included music by the Wilton Cornet Band. "The gentlemanly bearing and deportment of this band are worthy of high commendation. The proficiency they have made in music promises them a cordial reception wherever they shall be invited. At 6 P.M. the sun smiled upon us as we listened to the singing of 'America' by the Milford delegation accompanied by the band. A pastor of the M.E. Church in behalf of the large company that had enjoyed their music, and then the Milford friends were escorted home by the band to the tune, 'Red, White and Blue'" ("The Fourth in Amherst," *Farmer's Cabinet*, 9 July 1873, 2).

New Hampshire

Temple: The Milford Cornet Band provided escort services on the Fourth at the dedication of the Soldiers Monument. The band had just received "their new fine-toned instruments" consisting of "a full set (German silver) from the manufacturer, Hall & Quinby, Boston" ("Milford Matters," *Farmers' Cabinet*, 9 July 1873, 2).

New York

Brooklyn: Celebration of the residents of the 18th and 21st wards on Willoughby Avenue, near Broadway "which adjoins the Gethsemane Baptist Church.... the exercises began by the audience singing the national hymn, 'My Country 'Tis of Thee,' a band of half a dozen pieces, stationed in one of the front seats, playing the music." Also performed was the "'Star-Spangled Banner,' sung with stirring effect by Miss Lizzie Case, the audience joining in the chorus." Following a speech, "'God bless our native Land!' [with complete text printed] was next sung by the audience....The meeting was closed by the audience singing the doxology and the firing of another salute by the Carlisle Battery" (*Brooklyn Daily Eagle*, 5 July 1873, 3); at the Brooklyn Orphan Asylum celebration, "the day wound up with a delightful soiree musicale at the residence of Mr. Stone, where Mrs. Stone approved herself a model hostess, and where a skilled party of amateurs, including Mr. Spier and Mrs. Borneman, contributed to the pleasures of the occasion. Haydn's Joy [*sic*, ne Toy] Symphony was a feature of the concert, and was greeted with much laughter and applause ("At the Brooklyn Orphan Asylum," *Brooklyn Daily Eagle*, 5 July 1873, 3); the Constitution Club met on Bridge Street and Ald. Clancy, Honest John Pyburn and John Guilfoyle sang the "Star-Spangled Banner," and Prof. L.L. Parr sang the "Flag of Our Union" ("Constitution Club Celebration," *Brooklyn Daily Eagle*, 5 July 1873, 4); Conterno's Orchestra performed at the Brooklyn Rink and the music program is printed in the newspaper (*Brooklyn Daily Eagle*, 3 and 5 July 1873, 1 and 4, respectively).

New York: Harvey Dodworth's Band performed at City Hall (*New York Evening Mail*, 3 July 1873, 4).

Utah

Salt Lake City: "A grand concert by Madam Anna Bishop's troupe, at the Tabernacle, in the presence of 6000 persons" ("Elsewhere," *Chicago Daily Tribune*, 5 July 1873, 8; *New York Times*, 6 July 1873, 1).

Vermont

Burlington: At the unveiling of a statue in honor of Ethan Allen, a parade included the Sherman Cornet Band, of Winooski and the St. Mary's Cornet Band, of Burlington. The "inauguration service" began with an opening prayer. "The hymn 'God and Our Country,' composed by Oliver Wendell Holmes, was next sung by a choir of twenty male voices, furnished by the St. Albans Glee Club and the Harmonic Society of Burlington, to music specially composed for the occasion by S.C. Moore of Burlington" (*Exercises Attending the Unveiling and Presentation of a Statue of Gen. Ethan Allen at Burlington, Vermont, July 4th, 1873, including an Oration by Hon. L. E. Chittenden.* Burlington: Free Press Print., 1874, 10–11).

1874

Publications

"Fourth of July in Alabama."[742] By Joshua Simpson. Tune, "America." First line: "O, thou unwelcome day."

Fourth of July March, arr. for Violin and Piano by Sep. Winner. Violin and piano. Series: *The New Set of First Class Duets for the Violin and Piano* by Sep. winner. Philadelphia: Lee & Walker, [1874]. "Music for the Nation: American Sheet Music," *American Memory*, Library of Congress.

"'Huzza! 'Tis the Fourth of July!' Written and composed by T. Waldron Shear." San Francisco, 1874. First line: "Awake tis the loud signal gun." Voice and piano. "Music for the Nation: American Sheet Music," *American Memory*, Library of Congress.

Performances

Colorado

Denver: At the pavilion, "Keller's 'Hymn of Peace' was quite effectively sung by the Handel & Haydn Society," and also "Star-Spangled Banner" and "My Country, 'Tis of Thee."; "Music by the Mannerchor Society" ("The Fourth in Denver," *Rocky Mountain News*, 5 July 1874, 4).

Illinois

Quincy: "The first known band concert in the square was played by the Louis Kuehn Band on July 4, 1874, and the program included the *Washington Park March* by Kuehn" (Carl A.Landrum, *Historical Sketches of Quincy Illinois: The First 100 Years* [Quincy: Royal Printing Co., (n.d.)]; Quincy's Washington Park website, http://www.adamscohistory.org/washingtonpark.html.

Massachusetts

Boston: From 8–10 A.M. on the Common, Hall's First Regimental Band, Edimonds,' O'Connor's and the Metropolitan Bands, all totaling 80 instruments, conducted by Arthur Hall ("Boston Correspondence," *Westfield Republican*, 8 July 1874, 2).

Weymouth: On the 250th anniversary of the establishment of this town, the exercises included "excellent music by Stetson's Weymouth Band (including the performance of the 'General Bates Quickstep,'" composed by Mr. W.F. Burrell, of Weymouth), and by Bowles' South Abington Band." A hymn "composed for the occasion, with the accompanying music,[743] by John J. Loud, Esq., of Weymouth," was performed: first line, "Our fathers bequeath'd this fair heritage to us." (*Proceedings on the Two Hundred and Fiftieth Anniversary of the Permanent Settlement of Weymouth, with an Historical Address* by Charles Francis Adams, Jr. July 4th, 1874. Boston: Wright & Potter, 1874.)

New Hampshire

Milford: "At 9 o'clock a grand procession was formed on Union Square" and was led by the Milford Cornet Band. Also participating was the New Boston Band ("Milford Matters," *Farmers' Cabinet*, 8 July 1874, 2).

New York

Brooklyn: At the Constitution Club House, the Union Quartet Club sang "The Star-Spangled Banner" and "Nobly the Flag Floats O'er Us To-Day." The group was led by C. Wesley Sprague and John B. Tuttle accompanied at the piano ("At the Constitution Club," *Brooklyn Daily Eagle*, 6 July 1874, 2).

New York: Hall's Boston Brass, String and Reed Band and Orchestra performed on the steamer *Providence* for an excursion into New York Bay and the Atlantic Ocean, from Pier No. 28, North River (*New York Times*, 4 July 1874, 7); Continental Band provided promenade and dance music on board the steamer *William Cook* on its way to West Point and other cities, from 24th street pier (*Brooklyn Daily Eagle*, 3 July 1874, 1); Palmer's Brass and String Bands played tunes on the steamer *Thomas Cornell* leaving New York for West Point and other destinations (*New York Times*, 4 July 1874, 7); on the steamboat *Thomas Powell*, Schilling's Long Branch Orchestra and Cotillion Band performed as the vessel traveled to Newburgh, West Point, and other destinations (*Brooklyn Daily Eagle*, 3 July 1874, 1); at the Tammany celebration, the Tammany Glee Club sang the "Star-Spangled Banner" (*New York Times*, 5 July 1874, 1).

Pennsylvania

Philadelphia: On the occasion of the cornerstone ceremony of the "Public Buildings" on Penn Square, "the music was furnished by McClurg's Liberty Cornet Band of Philadelphia, Benjamin K. McClurg, leader" (*Proceedings at the Laying of the Corner Stone of the New Public Buildings on Penn Square, in the City of Philadelphia*. July 4, 1874; with a description of the buildings, the statistics and progress of the work, and a summary of legislative and municipal action relating to the undertaking; with a brief history of events pertaining thereto. Printed for the Commissioners. Philadelphia: 1874.)

1875

Performances

Colorado

Denver: "The 4th of July will be celebrated on the 3d at Loomis's Central Park, by which time the large pavilion for dancing now being constructed, will be ready for use. Gilman's band has been engaged for afternoon and evening. Admission to the grounds, free" ("Fourth of July at Central Park," *Denver Daily Times*, 17 June 1875, 4).

New Hampshire

Milford: The Fourth was celebrated on July 5. An early report noted: "The Nashua Cornet Band[744] will furnish music and give an open-air concert on Union Square in the evening." At 8 A.M. the Milford Band gave a concert. At 10 A.M. there was a parade which included the Nashua and Greenville bands ("Matters at Milford," *Farmers' Cabinet*, 23 June and 7 July 1875, 2 and 2, respectively).

New York

Brooklyn: Connor's Band[745] at the Printer's Association celebration at Oriental Grove via the barges *Chicago* and *Sarah Smith* (*Brooklyn Daily Eagle*, 3 July 1875, 1); at Prospect Park, the Twenty-Third Regiment Brass Band, L. Conterno, director:

Part I.
Grand March. *Fest*, Rietzel
Ballad, "Dreaming of Thee," J[ohn] R[ogers]
Thomas
Overture, *Il Barbiere di Seviglia*, Rossini
Waltz, "Les Gardes de la Reine," D. Godfrey
Solo for Cornet, *The Globe Polka* (William Griffin,
Cornet), Godfrey
Fantasie, *Railroad*, G [iovanni E.]. Conterno
Part II.
Overture, *Festival* (introducing "My Country 'Tis
of Thee"), Weber
Prayer, "Sweet Spirit Hear My Prayer," [William
Vincent] Wallace
Solo for Xylophon (William Former, xylophon), For-
mer
March, *Irish Melodies*, Arranged by Louis Conterno
Galop, *Sleigh Ride*, Folke
National Airs
["Independence Day," *New York Times*, 3 July
1875, 2].

New York: At Morningside Park, the Union Home
Cornet Band, "composed of youths" of St. John's
College ("Independence Day," *New York Times*, 3
July 1875, 2); on the steamer *Bristol*, originating
from New York, Hall's Boston Brass and String
Band provided celebration music on board during a
trip up the Hudson River (*New York Times*, 4 July
1875, 11); at Gilmore's Concert Garden, a corps of fife
and drums and Gilmore's Band performed national
airs, followed by Jules Levy,[746] cornetist, who performed the "American Polka" (*New York Times*, 5 July
1875, 7).

Ohio

Springfield: A parade was led by Hawkin's Band
(*Cincinnati Daily Gazette*, 6 July 1875, 1).

Pennsylvania

Philadelphia: At eleven o'clock, A.M. there were ceremonies at the site of the Columbus Monument by
the Christopher Columbus Monument Association.
Nunzio Finelli, President:

Music — Italian National Air, "Stella Confidente."
Introductory address, by Chev. Alonzo M. Vitl,
Vice-Consul of Italy at Philadelphia.
Music — *Il Trovatore*.
Oration, by John A. Clark, Esq., of Philadelphia,
on "The True Relations of Christopher Colum-
bus to the Discovery of America."
Music — *Lucretia Borgia*.
Address, by Chev. G.F. Secchi de Casali, of New
York.
Music — *Ernani*.
Closing remarks, by the Rev. A. Isoleri, Pastor of
the Italian Church, St. Mary Magdalen de Pazzi,
Philadelphia.
"Music by the Italian Bersaglieri Band. Prof. Fed-
erigo Nafoniello, Leader."

"Twelve o'clock Noon. Ceremonies of breaking
ground for the Agricultural Hall. His excellency, John
F. Hartranft, Governor of Pennsylvania, Presiding."

Anthem, by the Centennial Orchestra.
Prayer, by the Rev. William Newton, Rector of the
P.E. Church of the Nativity.
Reading the Declaration of Independence, by Prof.
Amasa McCoy, of Chicago.
Music — *Souvenirs of Boston*.
Breaking of Ground.
Opening Address, by His Excellency, John F. Har-
tranft.
Music — *The Greeting to the Stranger*.
Address, by Frederick M. Watts, Commissioner of
Agriculture.
Music — "National Airs."

"Orchestra: Mr. Simon Hassler, Director"; at Fairmount Park, at the cornerstone for the Humboldt
Monument, attended by 1500 men of various German singing societies, "a choir of singers composed of
over 100 male voices, under the leadership of Professor Kuenzel" sang "The German Maennergesang" by
Franz Abt and "The Watch on the Rhine," music by
Carl Wilhelm. Later at "the Hills" mansion, the audience sang "The Star-Spangled Banner" (*Celebration of
the Ninety-Ninth Anniversary of American Independence in Fairmount Park, Philadelphia, July 5th, 1875*.
Published by order of the Centennial Board of Fi-
nance. Philadelphia: King & Baird, printers, 1875, 11.)

1876

The nation celebrated the 100th anniversary of the
signing of the Declaration of Independence with numerous speeches, parades, 100-gun artillery salutes,
and musical performances. Philadelphia was chosen as
the city that hosted the official Centennial Exhibition
which attracted millions of visitors to Fairmount Park.
The exhibition opened to the public on May 10, 1876,
with President Ulysses Grant and Mrs. Grant sitting
with 4,000 dignitaries on a grandstand erected in front
of Memorial Hall, and all overlooking a crowd of tens
of thousands. An orchestra under the direction of
renowned conductor Theodore Thomas accompanied
a chorus of 1000 voices singing John Greenleaf Whittier's "Centennial Hymn," composed especially for
the May 10 event, but later performed in numerous locations on July 4. Other hymns composed for the
opening ceremonies included "Welcome to All Nations," by Oliver Wendell Holmes, and "Our National
Banner," by Dexter Smith (1839–1909). Also performed was *Centennial Inauguration March* by
Richard Wagner and "Centennial Cantata" by Dudley Buck and lyrics by Sidney Lanier. Eight-hundred
singers performed Handel's "Hallelujah Chorus" that
day.

As in Philadelphia, other cities staged their concerts in the grandest manner. Hundreds of vocalists

and instrumentalists presented "monster concerts," and multiple bands marched in parades to the delight of thousands of spectators crammed along city streets. In New York, a Centennial Union Choir of 600 voices sang at a midnight ceremony on July 3. In Worcester, Massachusetts, 1200 students presented a choral concert and five bands were mustered for the city's morning parade. In Port Richmond, New York, 500 children sang Matthias Keller's "American Hymn," one of the most popular pieces performed on the Centennial Fourth. In Boston, perhaps numerically symbolic of the Centennial, a choir of 100 sang the "Star-Spangled Banner" at a temperance meeting. It was also a day for the publication and premiere of numerous new works written especially for the Centennial by composers such as John Knowles Paine, David Coye, Theodore Moelling, B.P. Shallaber, Emil Dietzsch, George Phinney, Julius Edward Meyer, George F. Bristow, and Antônio Carlos Gomes.

These centennial musical events helped to provide a catalyst for the healing and bonding of the nation following the Civil War. Ethnic and minority musical groups fostered hope and expressions of aspirations as the nation looked towards the future. America's German-American communities proudly presented large and memorable concerts in towns in West Virginia, New York, New Jersey, Montana, Nebraska, and Illinois, while an Italian Band provided music in St. Paul, Minnesota, and an African-American band performed with gusto in Quincy, Massachusetts.

Publications

"'The Centennial Hymn.' By John G. Whittier." Music by John Knowles Paine. First line: "Our fathers' God! from out whose hand."[747] Broadside, [1876]. Copy in Center for Popular Music, Middle Tennessee State University.

Centennial National Songs and Anthems; or A Song Book for the Fourth of July, 1876. [n.p.], 1876. Copy in the Library of Congress.

"Centennial Song." By David Coye. To be sung to the tune: "Billy O'Rouke." First line: "It's a hundred years, July the 4th, since Uncle Sam became a nation." Broadside. Unadilla, [NY]: D. Coye, 1876. Copy in Brown University.

Centennial Songster: A Collection of Patriotic Songs for July 4, 1876. Lebanon, PA: Wm. M. Breslin, 1876. Copy in Brown University.

"A Hundred Years Ago To-day: (1776. July 4th, 1876): a soprano or tenor solo, with chorus; written and composed in honor of the Centennial." First line same as title. By Theodore Moelling. Words by R.H. Chittenden. New York: W.A. Pond, [1876]. Copy in the Library of Congress.

"Independence Hymn." By B.P. Shallaber. First line: "Come to the altar of the free" ("Poetry," *Farmer's Cabinet*, 4 July 1876, 1).

"Welcome to All Nations. Written for the 4th of July Centennial Celebration at Philadelphia by Oliver Wendell Holmes, to the Music of Keller's American Hymn."[748] Boston: Oliver Ditson & Co.; New York: Chas. H. Ditson & Co.; Chicago: Lyon & Healy, [1876]. Copies in Harvard University and University of Virginia.

Performances

California

San Francisco: The Silver Cornet Band performed at the official "literary exercises" there (*San Francisco Chronicle*, 6 July 1876, 1).

Colorado

Boulder: The Boulder Glee Club sang "Whittiers Centennial Hymn" and "Star-Spangled Banner" at the grove ("The Fourth in Boulder," *Boulder County News*, 7 July 1876, 2).

Sunset Crossing (Little Colorado, A.T.). The following program began at 9 A.M.:

"Star-Spangled Banner" by the Sunset Band
Opening prayer by James Welsh
Oration by Gen'l Lot Smith
Music "Hail Columbia" by the Band
Reading the Declaration of Independence by
    Daniel Davis
Song "Rally Round the Flag" by Wm. Hayes
Music "Sunset Quickstep" by the Band
Recitation "Liberty" by Alfred M. Derrick.
Historical Address by Jas. T. Woods
Music "Herdsman's Echo" by Woods and Band
Song "This New Land of Ours" by Mrs. Jas. T.
    Woods.
Recitation "Revolutionary Alarm" by Israel Call.
Song "The Flag of the Free"[749] by Daniel Davis
Song "Off to Arizona" (original) by H. Hobbs
Music "Way Up" by Woods and Band
Duet "The Orphan" by Mrs. Barlow and Mrs. Call
Recitation "Shamus O'Brien"[750] by Wm. Hayes
Song "Arizona Mission" (original) by Peter Wood
Song "Larboard Watch"[751] by A.M. Derrick, W.B.
    Hardy, H. Brewer
Song "Thou Hast Learned to Love Another"[752] by
    Mrs. Handon Rich
Song "All Hail, My Sabbath-School Mates" by
    Miss Annie Woods
Music "Yankee Doodle" by the Band
Benediction by Chaplain Welsh

"The singing of little Annie Woods is well worthy of mention; in fact, I may say all acquitted themselves splendidly, especially in the moonlight dance on the plaza, where the light fantastic toe seemed to have received new life for this special occasion" (Daniel Davis, "Celebration on Little Colorado," *Arizona Weekly Miner*, 21 July 1876, 1).

Denver: "Hail Columbia" and "Hymn of America" sung by the audience and "Centennial Hymn" sung by the Handel and Haydn Societies at a ceremony held at Denver Park ("The Fourth," *Daily Rocky Mountain News*, 6 July 1876, 1, 4).

Pueblo: A choir, led by William Bradford, sang "Whittier's Centennial Hymn," at Centennial Park ("Centennial 4th," *Colorado Chieftain*, 6 July 1876, 4).

Connecticut

Hartford: "Bright Sword of Liberty" sung by C.F. Adam and "Star-Spangled Banner" sung by Mr. T. J. Sullivan at the Opera House (*Hartford Daily Courant*, 4 July 1876, 2).

Litchfield: "Order of Exercises at the "Centennial Celebration" at the Congregational Church:

1. Voluntary, organ and cornet.
2. Reading of Centennial Proclamation, Hon. O.S. Seymour, President of the Day.
3. Prayer, the Rev. Allen McLean.
4. Singing, choir and congregation, Hymn, "America."
5. Reading of Declaration of Independence, Hon. Truman Smith.
6. Singing, choir and congregation, Selection from Whittier's *Centennial Hymn*. [first line]: "Our fathers' God! from out whose hand."
7. Historical Address, Hon. George C. Woodruff.
8. Singing, by the choir, Keller's American Hymn.
9. Benediction.
10. Voluntary, organ and cornet, national airs.

The choir was "exceedingly fine and well-instructed." The cornet and organ were played by Eugene W. Meafoy and Miss Ella Gibbud, respectively (*Litchfield Centennial Celebration, July 4th, A.D. 1876*. Historical Address by George C. Woodruff. Hartford: Press of the Case, Lockwood & Brainard Company, 1876).

Mystic: "[A] goodly company gathered in Central Hall at ten and a-half o'clock to listen to the services there, which were as follows: Singing by S.[abbath] S.[chool] children, Miss Estella Tribble presiding at the organ. The 'Star-Spangled Banner' was beautifully sung by Miss Nettie Greenman." Also sung were "America" and "Doxology" (*Mystic Press*, 6 July 1876).

New Hartford: Clara Louisa Kellogg sing the "Star-Spangled Banner" at the dedication of the new town hall ("Observances in Other Parts of the State," *Hartford Courant*, 6 July 1876, 1).

District of Columbia

"Whittier's Centennial Hymn" was performed by a choir at a ceremony held in the First Congregational Church (*Washington Evening Star*, 5 July 1876, 4).

Illinois

Chicago: "Hymn to Liberty" composed for the Chicago Turngemeinde by Emil Dietzsch and performed at Wright's Grove "by all the German singing societies of Chicago" advertised as the "Grand National Jubilee Chorus" ("The Germans," *Chicago Tribune*, 5 July 1876, 3).

Joliet: Members of the Chicago Musical College

performed at Werner Hall and William Lewis, a professor at the college, performed a violin solo at the State Penitentiary (*Chicago Tribune*, 5 July 1876, 7).

Meacham: "America" and "In That Far Off One Hundred Years Ago" sung by the M.E. Choir at Meacham's Grove, Dupage County ("Meacham," *Chicago Tribune*, 6 July 1876, 8).

Quincy: Participating in the parade and laying of the cornerstone of "the new Court House" were Grosch's Band, Gem City Band, Bardolph Cornet Band, "the colored band of Quincy," and the Concordia Singing Society of Quincy. In Washington Park that afternoon, the ceremonies there included music by the Bardolph Band (*Quincy Daily Herald*, 6 July 1876, 3).

Wilmette: "Star-Spangled Banner" was sung by J.D. Ludlam ("Suburban: Wilmette," *Chicago Tribune*, 5 July 1876, 3).

Maryland

Baltimore: "God Save Our Native Land"[753] and "Old Hundred" sung by an "excellent choir" at St. Peter's Episcopal Church (*Baltimore Bee*, 5 July 1876, 3).

Cumberland: "Centennial Hymn" and "Star-Spangled Banner" sung by a choir of fifty, directed by Joseph P. Wiesel, at the town's grandstand (*Cumberland Alleganian Times*, 6 July 1876, 1, 4).

Massachusetts

Amherst: The Amherst Cornet Band and Amherst Quintette Club (chorus) provided music for the parade and the exercises held "at the Grove." According to a local newspaper: "Several choruses were given by the singers under the leadership of the Rev. Mr. Bartlett; and the songs, 'Triumphantly the morning dawned' by Mrs. Hattie Walker, 'Little Maid of Arcandee' by Mrs. Susie Eaton, and 'Revolutionary Tea' by Miss Abbie Bosworth, were all admirably rendered and well received." The ceremony closed "by all joining in 'America'" (*Historical Address Delivered at the Centennial Celebration, in Amherst, Mass., July 4, 1876*. By M. F. Dickinson, Jr. Amherst, Mass.: McCloud & Williams, 1878, v, viii; "The Fourth at Amherst," *Farmers Cabinet*, 11 July 1876, 2).

Bolton: At the Meeting House of First Congregational Church, the Hudson Brass Band provided "suitable music" to begin. An "American Hymn" was sung by a select choir: and the "Star-Spangled Banner" was sung by public school children. Later "fireworks and a concert on the Common closed this highly-successful celebration of the birthday of the town and the nation" (*Address Delivered in the First Parish Church in Bolton, July 4th, 1876, at the Centennial Celebration of the Anniversary of American Independence; and Also in Observance of the 138th Anniversary of the Incorporation of the Town*. By Richard S. Edes. Clinton: Printed by W. J. Coulter, 1877).

Boston: The "Star-Spangled Banner" and "Te Deum," were sung by a choir of 100 at a temperance society celebration in St. Anne's Church ("Other Places," *Boston Evening Transcript*, 5 July 1876, 6).

Bradford: The town assembled "at the Common in front of the Meeting House" and at 1 P.M. marched, proceeded by the Groveland Brass Band, to the grounds of Bradford Academy, where the exercises included singing "the national air, 'Hail Columbia,' by a select choir under the lead of Prof. H.E. Holt, with chorus by the assembly" (*Celebration of the One Hundredth Anniversary of the Declaration of Independence of the United States of America, Held at Bradford, Mass., July 4th, 1876*. Haverhill: Gazette Book and Job Printing Office, 1877).

Brookline: "America" and "American Hymn," composed by Matthias Keller and sung by 150 children at the town hall. "Mr. Whitney" sang the "Star-Spangled Banner" (*Boston Evening Transcript*, 5 July 1876, 3).

Canton: The Canton Brass Band, Walter Ames, leader, "furnished music for exercises of the morning and evening." The program for the exercises held at First Congregational Parish:

1. Organ Voluntary, Miss Clara B. Lopez.
2. Reading from the Scriptures, the Rev. John W. Savage.
3. Prayer, the Rev. William H. Savary.
4. Chorus, *Centennial Hymn*,[754] J.K. Paine.
5. Introductory Address, Thomas E. Grover, Esq.
6. Chorus, "To Thee, O Country!" Julius Eichberg.[755]
7. Reading of the Declaration of Independence, Miss J. Annie Bense.
8. Chorus, *American Hymn*, Keller.
9. Historical Address, Hon. Charles Endicott.
10. Chorus, "The Star-Spangled Banner."
11. Addresses by citizens.
12. Hymn, "America." [First line: "My country, 'tis of thee"].
13. Benediction, the Rev. Clifton Fletcher.

(*July 4, 1876. Centennial Celebration, at Canton, Mass. Historical Address*, by Hon Charles Endicott. Boston: William Bense, 1876).

Hingham: "American Hymn," composed by Matthias Keller and sung by school children at the Agricultural Hall (*Boston Evening Transcript*, 5 July 1876, 6).

Lancaster: The following Ode, by Mrs. Julia A. Fletcher Carney was delivered at the town's celebration: first line, "One hundred years ago, our sires" (*Address, Delivered July 4, 1876, 1876, at Lancaster, Massachusetts, by Request of the Citizens*. By John D. Washburn. Copy in the University of Missouri.

Leicester: At the city celebration, the children of the public schools sang "My Country, 'tis of thee," a band played the "Star-Spangled Banner," "Home, Sweet Home," and "Hail to the Chief," a choir sang "The Flag Without a Stain,"[756] "The Marseilles Hymn," and "Yankee Doodle" to the words "Father and I went down to camp" (*Celebration of the Centennial Anniversary of American Independence, at*

Leicester; July 4th, 1876. Worcester: Charles Hamilton, 1876).

Melrose: Text of "America" and "Star-Spangled Banner" published in "Order of Exercises," *Centennial Celebration of the Town of Melrose, Mass., July 4th 1876* ([Boston]: Babb & Stephens, printers, Boston [1876]).

Newton: "The exercises of the occasion were opened by the Newton City Band playing the several American national airs, after which the audience arose, and joined with the choir in singing, to the tune of 'Old Hundred,' the accompanying verses": first line, "O God! beneath thy guiding hand." Other musical works performed included "My country, 'tis of thee" and two verses of Whittier's "Centennial Hymn" sung by the choir: first line, "Our fathers' God! from out whose hand"; hymn (first line: "God ever glorious! Sovereign of nations!") sung by the audience; "The Battle-Cry of Freedom" sung by Miss Cora G. Plimpton; "Long Live America" sung by Miss Patrick (*The Centennial Celebrations of the City of Newton, on the Seventeenth of June and the Fourth of July, by and Under the Direction of the City of Newton*. Newton: Published by Order of the City Council, 1876).

Springfield: "America," "Centennial Hymn," "Star-Spangled Banner," and "To Thee, O Country" sung at the First Baptist Church by a choir directed by Amos Whiting ("Springfield," *Springfield Daily Republican*, 4 July 1876, 6).

Waltham: Events included music from a band of music at Rumford hall throughout the day, performance of three hymns during the exercises in the tent on the Common, included "The Star-Spangled Banner"; "Columbia, the Gem of the Ocean"; Whittier's "Centennial Hymn"; "America." Military music was provided by the Waltham Band and "orchestral music" by Hull's Quadrille Band. A "Children's Concert" at 6 P.M. in the tent included "several hundred children from the public schools under the leadership of Mr. L.B. Marshall" and an "original Hymn, composed for this occasion by Mr. Geo. Phinney": "Waltham Centennial Fourth of July Hymn" (first line: "A Hundred years have come and gone"). (*Historical Address Delivered before the Citizens of Waltham, July 4, 1876*, by Josiah Rutter. Waltham: Waltham Free Press Office, 1877).

Weston: Music for the procession, exercises (held at the town hall) and fireworks was provided by the Weston Cornet Band. The ensemble performed a "Russian Hymn" at the exercises (*Oration Delivered before the Inhabitants of Weston, at the Town Hall, July 4, 1876*. By Charles H. Fiske. Weston, 1876).

Worcester: In the early morning a concert by 1200 pupils of the public schools took place in a tent.

The girls generally dressed in white, and the boys in their holiday attire, each carrying a neat national flag. They were arranged on tiers of seats in regular elevation from the conductor's stand in front. On the right of the conductor was an organ and piano,

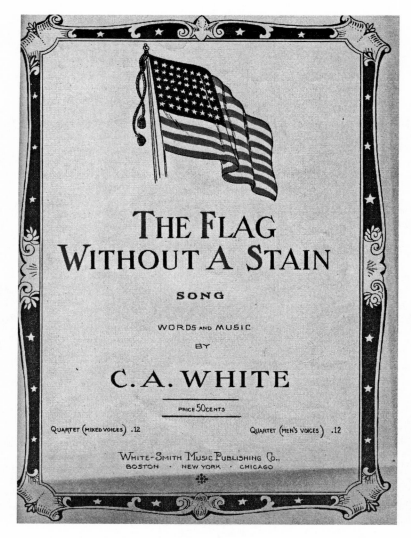

"The Flag without A Stain," by Boston composer and publisher Charles Albert White, was a popular song written for the centennial celebration in 1876 and sung numerous times in subsequent years on the Fourth of July. The chorus section has the phrase "Sweet land of liberty," borrowed from Samuel Francis Smith's "My Country, 'Tis of Thee." This edition, for voice and piano, was published by White-Smith in 1914 (author's collection).

and on the left the four Worcester bands for accompaniments. Mr. C.P. Morrison presided at the organ, and Mr. G.W. Sumner[757] at the piano, with Mr. E.S. Nason[758] for conductor.

The bands included the Worcester Brass Band, Worcester National Band, Worcester French Band, and Worcester Irish Band. The concert program included the following works;

1. America. Full chorus of 1200 voices, bands, organ and piano.

2. Our Native Land. Scholars of the eighth and ninth grades, organ and piano

3. Independence Day. Song, by the boys, chorus by all the voices, bands, &c., and tableau with flags.

4. Mount Vernon Bells[759]— To the memory of Washington. Song, by twenty-eight young ladies from the eighth and ninth grades.

5. The Red, White and Blue. Song, by boys, chorus by all, with bands, &c.

6. Keller's American Hymn. Full chorus, bands, organ and piano.

7. Flag of the Free. Song, by boys, with full chorus.

8. New England.

9. Star-Spangled Banner. Full chorus, bands, organ, piano, and tableau with flags.

Also that morning, a procession included the French Band, P.H.A. Baribeault, leader, 21 pieces; Johnson's Drum Corps, 13 pieces; Father Mathew Temperance Band, J.B. Waters, leader, 23 pieces; Worcester National Band, A. W. Ingraham, leader, 20 pieces; Swedish Brass Band, in a carriage, 15 pieces, C. Ekbled, leader. On a "Scandinavian Car," a number of well known figures were represented, including Ole Bull, "the celebrated musician personated by Nils Peterson" (*Celebration by the Inhabitants of Worcester, Mass., of the Centennial Anniversary of the Declaration of Independence. July 4, 1876. To which are Added Historical and Chronological Notes.* Worcester: Printed by order of the City Council, 1876).

Minnesota

St. Paul: A parade included the St. Paul City Band, Great Western Band, Crusader's Band, Wagner's Band, and Italian Band. The exercises at Rice Park included music by the Great Western Band, "My Country, 'Tis of Thee," "Star-Spangled Banner" and "Freedom's Land-A Centennial Hymn" (first line: "Age upon age has rolled away") sung by a chorus of male voices. "Programme: City of St. Paul, Fourth of July [1876]," Chilson Collection, Library, University of South Dakota.

Missouri

Rolla (Missouri?): "Whittiers Centennial Hymn" was "set to music of Mr. Viah's own composition" and "sung by all present" ("The Fourth at Rolla," *Phelps County New Era*, 8 July 1876, 3).

Montana

Helena: "America" and "Star-Spangled Banner" sung by the Gesang Verein and *Centennial March* by Wagner performed by the Silver Cornet Band at the Court House Square ("1876," *Helena Daily Herald*, 5 July 1876, 3).

Nebraska

Omaha: "The Flag Without a Stain" (cited as "a new song, also expressly ordered") and "Red, White and Blue" performed at Saunders' Grove. Sung by the Arions. ("Close of the Century," *Omaha Republican*, 6 July 1876, 4).

Nevada

Virginia City: "Speed Our Republic" performed at the Chollar-Postosi Mining Company grounds by a Centennial chorus of 40 voices, R.H. Lindsay, director ("Our Hundredth Birthday," *Daily Territorial Enterprise*, 6 July 1876, 3).

New Hampshire

Dover: The Dover Cornet Band, W.D. Taylor, leader, and the National Cornet Band participated in the parade from Franklin Square to the Park (*One Hundredth Anniversary of the National Independence, July 4, 1876; Its Celebration by the City of Dover, N.H., the Public Proceedings, and Oration*. By the Rev. Alonzo H. Quint, D.D. Dover, N.H.: Morning Star Steam Job Printing House, 1876).

Mont Vernon: "The exercises were held in Institute Hall, in the forenoon, the order being: singing of an original Ode written for the occasion by W.H. Conant[760]; address by the President, Dea. Geo. E. Dean; prayer by the Rev. W.H. Woodwell; singing of a Hymn; reading of the Declaration of Independence by Prof. G.W. Todd, who by interesting comments made the exercise very impressive; singing, 'Viva l' America'; oration by the Rev. W.H. Woodwell, which was an excellent production, and well appreciated and enjoyed.... The exercises at the hall closed with 'America'" ("Celebration at Mont Vernon," *Farmers' Cabinet*, 11 July 1876, 2).

New Jersey

Jersey City: "Hail Columbia" and "My Country, 'Tis of Thee" sung by Mme. Salvotti and a chorus at Kepler Hall. C.H. Benson sang the "Star-Spangled Banner" ("All around New York," *New York Times*, 5 July 1876, 10).

Newark: The New Jersey German Centennial Sangerbund gave a concert (*New York Times*, 4 July 1876, 5).

Trenton: A parade included two drum corps and Winkler's Band (*New York Times*, 5 July 1876, 10).

New York

New York: "Hail Columbia," "Marching through Georgia,"[761] "Red, White, and Blue," and "Star-Spangled Banner" sung by the employees of the Post Office "on the basement floor" ("Patriotic Post Office Clerks," *New York Times*, 5 July 1876, 12); at Fort Green, "Hail Columbia" performed by a band and "Hail Atlantis," cited as "Lechner's Hymn," sung by the Centennial Union Choir (600 voices), Carl Traeger, director, at a midnight ceremony on July 3. "Hymn" (first line: "A hundred years ago today") performed and "written for the occasion" by H.R.H. Chittenden and "set to music by Professor Julius Edward Meyer."[762] "Music arranged in quartet form for first and second tenors and first and second basses." ("Old Hundred," *Brooklyn Daily Eagle*, 5 July 1876, 1); "The Heavens are Telling"[763] performed during the late evening of July 3 by a chorus of German singers, directed by "Mr. Traeger" and with piano accompaniment, at Union Square. The work was barely heard due to the immense crowds. Another report cites a performance of "Waken, voice of the land's devotion"[764] (first line), lyrics by Bayard Taylor[765] and set to music by "Professor Knoeller of Guben, Germany" ("Centennial Songs," *Daily Territorial Enterprise* [Virginia City, Nevada], 4 July 1876, 3; "Scenes at Union Square," *New York Times*, 5 July 1876, 12); "Star-Spangled Banner" and "Sword of Bunker Hill"[766] sung by the St. James Glee Club at a celebration of the John M. Dowley Association at No. 184 East Broadway ("Celebration Notes," *New York Times*, 5 July 1876, 7); "Star-Spangled Banner," Handel's Hallelujah chorus, and other works were sung by German choral societies, accompanied by an orchestra, at the New York Centennial Saenger Verbund (19 societies) under the direction of Reinhold Schmeiz at the Jones' Woods Colosseum ("Centennial Saenger Verbund," *New York Times*, 5 July 1876, 7; see also *New York Times*, 4 July 1876, 2); at the Academy of Music, William Cullen Bryant's Centennial Ode (first line, "Through storm and calm the years have led"), performed with accompaniment "by Professor H. Mosenthal, of the Mendelssohn Glee Club" ("Centennial Songs for the Fourth," *New York Evangelist*, 29 June 1876, 3; *New York Times*, 5 July 1876, 1); at St. Stephen's Church, a choral concert was led by H.B. Danforth, organist ("Services at St. Stephen's Church," *New York Times*, 5 July 1876, 7).

Port Richmond, Staten Island: "American Hymn" (Keller), "Hail Columbia," and Star-Spangled Banner" sung by "500 children from the public schools" in the park "on Heberton Street, in front of the School-House." The singing was led by Mr. W.L. Sexton and the instrument music by Mr. Jas. Whitford.

(*New York Times*, 5 July 1876, 10; *An Account of the Centennial Celebration of the 4th of July, 1876, by the Citizens of the Town of Northfield, Richmond County, New York, Including the Oration by Hon. Geo. Wm. Curtis, and Historical Sketch by John J. Clute, Esq.* New York: Charles Vogt, Steam Printer, 114 Fulton Street, 1876).

Sinclairville: "Hail Our Country's Natal Morn" was sung, with the solo by Mrs. L.M. Lincoln; chorus by the Glee Club (*Celebration of the One Hundredth Anniversary of American Independence at Sinclairville, N.Y., July 4, 1876, in the Sixty-Eighth Year of Settlement of the Town of Charlotte.* Sinclairville: E. L. Husted, 1876).

Westfield: "Centennial Hymn," by Whittier, sung by a Glee Club at the Park (*Westfield Republican*, 5 July 1876, 3).

Yorkville: "Hail Columbia" performed by Wallace's Band at the Seventh District Court House ("Celebration at Yorkville," *New York Times*, 5 July 1876, 7).

Pennsylvania

Montrose: The town held a Centennial celebration that included a parade and cornerstone laying ceremony[767] for a monument dedicated to the soldiers that fought in the Civil War. On the evening of July 3 the Telford Guards marched and the Susquehanna Band played "stirring music" at midnight. There was also a "Centennial Hop" held on the street in front of the Engine House, with music provided by the Rough & Ready Orchestra. A parade on July 4 began at noon and included the Elk Lake Band, Brooklyn Band, Tunkhannock Band, Montrose Drum Corps, and Rough & Ready Band. At the exercises which followed, "the opening Hymn, to the tune of Old Hundred, was very effectively rendered by a large chorus of trained voices led by Mr. Chas. S. Foster." The chorus, accompanied by an organ, also sang the "Centennial Hymn," "America," "Hail Columbia," "Star-Spangled Banner," and "Auld Lang Syne," the latter concluding the exercises. The cornerstone ceremony followed with speeches and appropriate music by the Brooklyn Band, and the singing of "Ship of State" by a vocal quartet (*The Republican*, 10 July 1876, 2–3; *Montrose Democrat*, 12 July 1876, 6).

Philadelphia: "The Great Republic,"[768] cited as a "Grand Overture," by George F. Bristow of New York, and performed by an orchestra of 250 musicians, conducted by Patrick Gilmore at Independence Square. The band also accompanied the singing of "Hymn of Welcome to All Nations" (first line: "Bright on the banners of lily and rose") and the *Grand Triumphal March*, lyrics by Dexter Smith, music by Sir Julius Benedict and "Hymn for the First Centennial of the American Independence"[769] composed by Bazilian composer Antônio Carlos Gomes (*Farmer's Cabinet*, 4 July 1876, 2; "City of the Declaration," *New York Times*, 5 July 1876, 3; "The Fourth," *Helena Daily Herald*, 11 July 1876, 1; "Home and Foreign Gossip," *Harper's Weekly*, 15 July 1876).

Rhode Island

Providence: The order of exercises at the First Baptist Meeting House included: music by Herrick's Brigade Band; "singing by the choir under the direction of B.K. Glezen, 'O come hither and behold the works of the Lord,'" "The Star-Spangled Banner," and "Whittier's Centennial Hymn" (*The Progress of Providence. A Centennial Address to the Citizens of Providence, R. I. By Hon. Samuel Greene Arnold.* Providence: OProvidence Press C., 1876).

Vermont

Windsor: A parade included a drum corps and the Windsor Cornet Band (18 members). At the exercises, the band played "Hail Columbia" and band members who are indivudally named, led by Henry W. Stocker, sang "The National Hymn." (*The Centennial at Windsor, Vermont, July 4, 1876.* Windsor: The Journal Company, 1876).

West Virginia

Wheeling: "An das Vaterland" sung by the Beethoven Society and Concordia and "Deutscher Mainer Tesigesang" sung by the Maennerchor; "Liederfreiheit" sung by the Beethoven Society; "Gruss" (Vercino) sung by Germania. "Hail Columbia" was sung by the five societies, directed by William Kryter ("The Eve!" *Wheeling Daily Register*, 4 July 1876, 4).

Germany

Berlin: Silas Pratt[770] conducted his own work, *Centennial Overture*, on July 4.

1877

Publications

"Ode: July 4th, 1877" by Charles H. Denison. To the air "America." First line: "Come wake the joyous lay." Broadside, 1877. Copy in Brown University.

Performances

Colorado

Greenhorn: At the hall near the Harrington school house, "Prof. Tom Austin's well-known string band" furnished music for a dance that included fifty couples ("Greenhorn Items," *Colorado Weekly Chieftain*, 19 July 1877, 1).

District of Columbia

"Star-Spangled Banner" sung by Robert Ball, with the audience joining in the chorus, at a meeting of the Oldest Inhabitants Association of Washington at City Hall ("The Day We Celebrate," *Evening Star*, 5 July 1877, 4).

Soldiers Monument on the Public Square in Montrose, Pennsylvania. The cornerstone was laid on July 4, 1876, and dedicated on July 4, 1877, "in memory of the Citizen Soldiers of Susquehanna County, who gave their lives for the preservation of the Union in the war of 1861–5." Music was provided for these events by the Brooklyn Cornet Band, Rough and Ready Band, the 44th Regiment Band of Bing-hamton, and Mud Lake Drum Corps. At the cornerstone ceremony, a vocal quartet sang a work titled "Ship of State" (courtesy Hilary Caws-Elwitt and the Susquehanna County Historical Society & Free Library Association).

Independence Hall in Philadelphia, where the assembly house of the Pennsylvania government was located and the Second Continental Congress (1775–76), under which the Declaration of Independence was debated and signed, and the Constitutional Convention of 1787. Some of the milestone performances that took place on Independence Square included the 1876 Centennial when an orchestra of 250 musicians (Patrick Gilmore, conductor) performed *The Great Republic*, composed by George F. Bristow, and the 1976 Bicentennial when bands performed throughout the day and noted singer Marian Anderson read passages from the Declaration as "America the Beautiful" was played on an organ (author's photograph).

Indiana

Indianapolis: The "formal opening" of the Court House takes place and the ceremony included prayers, speeches, and the performance of two "national hymns" by the Choral Union ("Indiana," *Chicago Daily Tribune*, 5 July 1877, 7).

Maryland

Baltimore: Garrett Park was dedicated on this day and a band played "The Star-Spangled Banner," and other musical selections were sung by the West End Glee Club ("Dedication of Garrett Park," *Baltimore Bee*, 5 July 1877, 4).

New Hampshire

Peterboro: In a parade were "six bands of music and several drum corps" and "the concert by the six bands of music was an interesting musical feature" ("The Peterboro Celebration," *Farmers' Cabinet*, 10 July 1877, 2).

New York

Brooklyn: At Ridgewood Park, near Brooklyn, "A patriotic cornet solo by Albert Smith of Baehr's Band" ("At Ridgewood Park," *Brooklyn Daily Eagle*, 5 July 1877, 4); on the "palace steamer" *Long Branch*, from Fulton Ferry, Brooklyn, to Newburgh, Iona Island, West Point and other destinations, "Bauland's grand military brass band will play select airs during the entire trip" (*Brooklyn Daily Eagle*, 3 July 1877, 1); on the new steamer *Columbia* from Jewell's Wharf in Brooklyn to Rockway Beach, "Conterno's Twenty Third Regiment Band, the Columbia Glee Club, and Professor Soltan, the cornet soloist, will discourse sweet music on the trip" ("Far Rockaway," *Brooklyn Daily*

Eagle, 3 July 1877, 4); at Tompkins Park, "the Navy Yard Band consisting of a drummer and fifer, furnished the instrumental music" and the audience sang "America" and the "Star-Spangled Banner" ("At Tompkins Park," *Brooklyn Daily Eagle*, 5 July 1877, 1).

New York: "The Girl I Left Behind Me" and "Yankee Doodle" were performed for the Corps of Veterans, with about 24 members, by "two drums and a fife ... furnished by Major Bush, commanding officer of Governor's Island," as the group marched out of Sturtevant House following a dinner there (*New York Times*, 5 July 1877, 8).

Pennsylvania

Montrose: At a dedication of a soldiers' monument,[771] the ceremonies began with a parade, with music provided by the Brooklyn Cornet Band, Capt. E.N. Barney, director; Mud Lake Drum Corp, drum major Snow; 44th Regiment Band of Binghamton; the ensembles "elicited the highest praise and won admiration on account of their perfection in the musical art." The band had marched in the town's parade earlier that day ("The Fourth of July," *The Republican*, 16 July 1877, 1 and 4).

Rush: At Butterfield Springs, Susquehanna County, the exercises were held in the afternoon with the Elk Lake Band providing the music ("Butterfield Springs," *The Republican*, 16 July 1877, 4).

Warren[772]: The following bands marched in the parade: Youngsville Band; Citizens Band of Warren; Kane Marching Band; Frewsburg Band. At the park, the exercises included: the Warren Musical Association singing "Hail to Thee, Liberty" and "America"; the Warren Band performing "Columbia"; Frewsburg Band playing "Yankee Doodle." The ceremony closed with the music "Dixie" (*Warren Mail*, 10 July 1877).

Virginia

Arlington: At the White House Pavilion adjacent to the Potomac River: "Blest Be the Tie That Binds" sung by members of the Congregational Church and Assembly Church of Washington, D.C. ("The Day We Celebrate," *Washington Evening Star*, 5 July 1877, 4).

1878

Performances

Colorado

Colorado Springs: A parade that began at noon included the Colorado City Band, a brass band, and the Colorado Springs Band ("Our Glorious Fourth, *Colorado Springs Gazette*, 6 July 1878, 6).

Georgetown: A parade was led by the Silver Queen Cornet Band. "Arriving at the public ground, the representatives of the States, the speakers and the band, occupied the platform erected for the purpose. After

the cornet band had played 'Hail Columbia'—which was rendered very creditably by the boys—the Rev. O.L. Fisher opened the exercises with prayer, after which the little girls sang 'America.'" The girls sang another song after a reading of the Declaration of Independence (*Colorado Miner*, 6 July 1878, 3).

Golden: A parade was led by the Golden Band, "which dispensed some excellent martial music *en route*" ("The Fourth in Golden," *Colorado Transcript*, 10 July 1878, 3).

Green Lake: Citizens from Leavenworth enjoyed the day at the lake. "At 10 o'clock the Brownville band arrived and commenced to entertain the crowd by appropriate selections." At the bandstand, after a reading of the Declaration of Independence, "the band played the soul-stirring 'Star-Spangled Banner.'" After the exercises, "the dancing commenced, and during the evening thirty-seven couples whirled in mazy circles to the dictating strains of the band" ("A Gala Day at Green Lake," *Colorado Miner*, 6 July 1878, 2).

New York

Sea Cliff, Long Island: The day "was ushered in with a grand national salute at sunrise." At 10 a.m. a brass band performed "national airs." The day's events included a reading of the Declaration and an oration by C.H. Fowler. Philip Phillips,[773] "the widely-known 'Singing Pilgrim,'" sang "several patriotic airs" at the Metropolitan Tabernacle. ("Fourth of July at Sea Cliff," *New York Times*, 17 June 1878, 8).

Wisconsin

Geneva Lake: The Hebron Martial Band, The Harvard Glee Club, and Chemung Quadrille Band performed at the celebration held at Kaye's Park (Program, 1878. Wisconsin Historical Society).

1879

Performances

Colorado

Denver: The day's events included a parade of three divisions, the second led by Gilman's Band. The third "was headed by an unnamed band—probably the Colorado Springs Cornet Band."[774]

District of Columbia

Pistorio's Orchestra provided music at the Caledonian Club celebration held at Beyer's Seventh Street Park (*Washington Post*, 4 July 1879, 4).

Missouri

Liberty: The Liberty Cornet Band performed in Long's Pasture ("The Picnic at Liberty July 4th," *Liberty Weekly Tribune*, 11 July 1879, 2).

New Hampshire

Milford: "There was a large number out on the evening of the Fourth to enjoy the open-air band concert. The selections from 'Pinafore' were received with such prolonged applause that they were repeated" ("Matters at Milford," *Farmers' Cabinet*, 8 July 1879, 2).

New York

Chateaugay: The Chateaugay Brass Band led a parade starting from St. Patrick's Roman Catholic Church ("Chateaugay," *Franklin Gazette*, 20 June 1879, 3).

Coney Island: Jules Levy, cornetist, played before 20,000 persons at Manhattan Beach; the Red Hussar Band[775] performed at West Breighton Hotel and Gilmore's Band performed "Millard's March" and "Viva l'Amerique" ("July 4," *Brooklyn Daily Eagle*, 5 July 1879, 2).

Ogdensburg: Four bands were scheduled to perform: Montreal Band (27 pieces); St. Albans Brigade Band (24 pieces); Ogdensburg City Band (20 Pieces), La Fayette Band (19 pieces). "They are all handsomely uniformed, and give an aggregate of 90 musicians" (*Franklin Gazette*, 20 June 1879, 3).

Pennsylvania

Harrisburg: A "grand fireman's parade" included 24 bands and 1 drum corps ("Celebrations in Other Places," *New York Times*, 5 July 1879, 3).

England

London: At Westminster Palace Hotel, the band of the Coldstream Guards played American patriotic tunes (*New York Times*, 5 July 1879, 3).

1880

Publications

"American Girl Fourth of July! Song." By Col. Waldron Shear. Arranged by H. M. Bosworth. First line: "Again over Columbia's domain." For voice, chorus (SATB) and piano. San Francisco, 1880.

Performances

Colorado

Fort Collins: The Fort Collins Cornet Band[776] participated in a town parade and provided music at Vecelius' Grove where the exercises were held. The Collins Glee Club also performed that day ("The Coming Celebration," *Fort Collins Courier*, 1 July 1880, 3).

District of Columbia

Georgetown: "Prof. Hoskins" Band played "national airs, with other choice selections" at a celebration of the Hancock and English Club of Georgetown, near

Goddard's Hall, the "Headquarters of the Club" ("Political Jubilation," *Washington Post*, 6 July 1880, 1).

New York

Brooklyn: At Tompkins Park, performances included: the Fort Hamilton Band; a "vocal quartet from Dr. Jeffery's Church under the lead of Mr. Burns, and Mr. Muir, a skillful cornetist"; a Glee Club singing "The Star-Spangled Banner," and led by Mr. Muir, and "the whole assemblage joining in the chorus with thrilling effect"; and Mr. Richards who "sang the 'Red, White and Blue' in spirit style" ("Speeches," *Brooklyn Daily Eagle*, 6 July 1880, 2); at the Tammany Society meeting, "Star-Spangled Banner" was "sung by the members of the society and audience" and the Tammany Glee Club sang Charles Morton's rendition of a song titled "A Knot of Blue and Gray" ("The Day Elsewhere," *Washington Post*, 6 July 1880, 1; *New York Times*, 6 July 1880, 8).

Coney Island: On the porch of the Manhattan Beach Hotel, three members of "Gilmore's Band" played selections of "sacred music" and 300 ladies and gentlemen sang "America," "Come, Thou Almighty King," and "Old Hundred" directed by Patrick Gilmore, and accompanied by "Mr. Levy," a cornetist ("A Hot Day by the Sea," *New York Times*, 5 July 1880, 8); at West Brighton, Coney Island, L. Conterno and his orchestra of forty instrumentalists, including Adam Seifert and Sig. Camello Cioone (?), clarinetists performed. At the Hotel Ocean Pavilion, the Tyrolean Singers, directed by Hans Lachner performed selections ("Coney Island," *Brooklyn Daily Eagle*, 3 July 1880, 2).

Pennsylvania

Philadelphia: "Hail Columbia" sung at the Centennial Building "by the full chorus of church choirs and amateur societies, under the direction of Professor A.R. Taylor." Miss Anna L. Fuller sang the "Star-Spangled Banner"; "Yankee Doodle" was played on a fife and drum at the Centennial Building as a group formed a tableau of "the Spirit of '76" ("At the Centennial," *Philadelphia Inquirer*, 6 July 1880, 1–2).

West Virginia

Moundsville: A picnic and celebration was held "in the grove near the Taylor's Ridge M.E. Church and Calvary M.E. Sunday Schools." A large platform was erected "which was occupied by two organs, a select choir and those who addressed the audience.... Miss Martin and Miss Lutes presided at the organs while R.H. McFarland performed the duties of musical director." Music included "Glory to God in the Highest," "Beautiful Flag," and "America." "After dinner the people were called together and the exercises commenced with music by the choir," included "Beulah Land" and "Doxology" ("Picnic and Celebration on Taylor's Ridge Last Saturday," *Moundsville Commercial*, 9 July 1880, 3).

1881

Publications

"Veteran Guard Cadets." By Dave Braham; lyrics by Ed Harrigan. First line: "Shout, you darkies, shout, it's Independence Day." NY: William A. Pond and Co., 1881. Copy in Center for Popular Music, Middle Tennessee State University.

Performances

Colorado

Fort Collins: The Collins Brass Band performed tunes on the morning of the Fourth in a parade. "We have never heard them play so well.... [The band] has improved of late under the quiet but effective leadership of Andy Hottel. It will soon be one of the best bands in the state." That evening at the Opera House, music for a dance was provided by Fisk's Band of Greeley, "the leading violin of which is a thorough musician" ("Independence Day in Fort Collins," *Fort Collins Courier*, 7 July 1881, 2).

Massachusetts

Boston: At the Boston Theatre, a vocal quartet from the First Church sang an "Ode," "composed by the distinguished orator of the day [George Washington Warren], and sung fifty years ago,[777] on the celebration of the Anniversary of American Independence, July 4th, 1831, at New Bedford." First line: "Survey the wide-spread land" (*Oration Delivered before the City Council and Citizens of Boston, in the Boston Theatre ... July 4, 1881 by George Washington Warren* (Boston: City Council, 1881), 9–11); on the Common, "a concert of popular and patriotic music was given in the morning" (7:30 A.M.) by four military bands, "numbering one hundred musicians." The ensembles included: Cadet Band, Metropolitan Band, Brown's Band, and Carter's Band. The program:

March, "Our Flag." Reeves.
Theme, "Star-Spangled Banner." J. Thomas Baldwin, conductor
Overture, "Pique Dame." Suppé
J. Thomas Baldwin, conductor
Concert waltz, "Metropolitan," E.A. Blanchard
Arthur Hall, conductor.
Potpourri, "Rechaufe 1880." Carter
T.M. Carter, conductor
Russian Fantasie. Performed by H.C. Brown
H.C. Brown, conductor
Gems from "Olivete." Audran[778]
Thomas W. Henry, conductor
National airs of America
Hail Columbia; Gilmore's "Columbia; Yankee Doodle"
J. Thomas Baldwin, conductor

("Independence Day," *Boston Evening Transcript*, 5 July 1881, 3; "Boston," *Church's Musical Visitor*, (Au-

gust 1881): 10–11); at Jamaica Pond, a regatta held there included a concert by Reever's American Band of Providence; at the Boston Theatre, with the mayor in attendance, the Cadet Band played an overture and Julius Eichberg's *To Thee, O Country, Great and Free*. "An ode written by the orator [George Washington Warren] of the day for the celebration half a century ago was sung by the quartette of the First Church"; at Tremont Temple, a concert included "songs, trios, readings, violin and cornet solos, humorous and descriptive songs and quartettes"; the Boston Juvenile Opera Company performed *Chimes of Normandy*[779] at Monument Hall in Charlestown; the Park Quartette gave concerts at Parker Memorial Hall; the Germania Band performed at the Turnverein celebration at Forest Garden ("Independence Day," *Boston Evening Transcript*, 5 July 1881, 3).

Missouri

Liberty: The Plattsburg Brass Band "furnished excellent and soul-inspiring music" at Reed's Mineral Springs, near Liberty, Missouri (*Liberty Tribune* (Missouri), 8 July 1881, 2).

St. Charles: The St. Charles Brass Band was scheduled to march in the city parade ("Picnic and Parade," *St. Charles Journal*, 24 June 1881).

New Hampshire

North Conway: The first Fourth of July in this town was held on Mt. Washington and included fireworks on the mountain along with the singing of patriotic songs (*Boston Evening Transcript*, 5 July 1881, 3).

New York

Brooklyn: On the palace steamer *Long Branch*, from the Brooklyn Bridge Dock, to Newburgh, West Point, and other sites on the Hudson River, "music furnished by Lent's Band,[780] under the direction of Professor Lent, assisted by the great Australian cornet virtuoso, T.V. Short" (*Brooklyn Daily Eagle*, 3 July 1881, 3).

Coney Island: At Manhattan Beach Hotel, "there were three concerts by Gilmore's Band–one at eleven o'clock in the morning, the second at half past three in the afternoon, and the third and last at eight o'-clock in the evening. The music partook mostly of a national character, and suited well the tastes of the patriotic individuals who listened to it. Gilmore's National Anthem, 'Columbia,' was not forgotten. It was rendered with a rare degree of skill, and was followed by 'The Star-Spangled Banner,' and another of Gilmore's compositions entitled 'Our Country.' Signor Le Fevre gave satisfaction with his saxophone solos, and Mr. Walter Emerson, who is the cornetist at Manhattan Beach this season, played well enough to please"; at the Brighton Hotel, the following music program was provided: Part I — March, "Olivette" (arranged by Conterno) — Overture, "Semiramide" (Rossini) — Musical Molange, "This and That" (arranged by Boettger; introducing "Scotch Lassie Jean," etc.) — Cornet Solo. Levy — Part II — Overture,

"Marsaniello" (Auber) — Galop, "Rick Rack" (Clara Tompkins) ("The Seaside," *Brooklyn Daily Eagle*, 5 July 1881, 2).

New York: At the Tammany Hall celebration, the Tammany Glee Club, directed by "ex–Assistant Alderman George J. Kraus," sang "Columbia," "Flag of the Free," "Praise of the Soldier," "Knot of Blue and Grey," "Army and Navy," "Pleasure Fly Swiftly," "Star-Spangled Banner," and "Columbia's Lamentation," the latter in memory of Garfield who had been shot. ("Symphony from Tammany," *New York Times*, 5 July 1881, 8).

1882

Publications

"Independence: a Song for the Fourth of July (1882), words and music by J. Henry Dwyer. First line: "Come! wake! arouse! up Freemen all." For vocal quartet. "Music for the Nation: American Sheet Music," *American Memory*, Library of Congress.

"The Glorious Fourth of July" (1882), by E.D. Beddall. First line: "Hurrah! For the morning of gladness is here." For 4-part mixed chorus and piano. "Music for the Nation: American Sheet Music," *American Memory*, Library of Congress.

Performances

California

Los Angeles: The Los Angeles City Band performed "Hail Columbia" and "Yankee Doodle" at the "literary exercises" ("The Thirty-Eights" and "Fourth of July," *Los Angeles Times*, 1 and 6 July 1882, O3 and O2, respectively).

Connecticut

Hartford: "Star-Spangled Banner" and "Watch on the Rhine"[781] were sung by "a large chorus of children and adults" at the First Regiment Armory (*New York Times*, 5 July 1882, 1).

Georgia

Atlanta: "The band of the Atlanta Musical Union will play a series of concerts at different points of the city on the fourth of July, as follows: at 6 o'clock A.M. at the union depot; at 10 o'clock A.M. at the union depot; at 5 o'clock P.M. at city hall park. The following is the programme for the city hall park concert:

No. 1. Quickstep — *The Glorious Fourth*
No. 2. *Serenade*, by Leightner
No. 3. Selection — *Olivette*, Audran
No. 4. *Andante and Waltz* by Holton
No. 5. Allegro — *The Talisman*, Leighton
No. 6. Aria — O, Take Me to Thy Heart [Again], [M.W.]Balfe
No. 7. Galop — *Trumpeter*, Faust.

At 8 o'clock P.M. the band will serenade through the city.

["The First Music" and "A Serenade Last Night," *Atlanta Constitution*, 2 and 4 July 1882, 9 and 5, respectively].

Idaho

Silver City: The Silver City Quadrille Band was scheduled to provide music for a ball on the evening of the Fourth at Masonic Hall, "for the benefit of the band." Tickets were 2 dollars. ("Fourth of July Ball!" *Idaho Avalanche*, 1 July 1882).

Missouri

St. Charles: "Before 9 o'clock the sound of the drum aroused such as were not aware of it before to a consciousness of the fact that there was a procession on hand, and soon afterwards the Fourth Ward Hose and Hook and Ladder Company with the Eintracht Society made its appearance, all marching in true military style to the music of the St. Charles Band" ("The Fourth of July," *St. Charles Journal*, 5 July 1882).

New York

Brooklyn: On Lynch Street, Eastern District: Lent's Band of Fort Hamilton "played a number of patriotic airs" ("Eastern District Celebration," *Brooklyn Daily Eagle*, 5 July 1882, 2); "Prospect Park: Potpourri, 'National airs' — Selection, 'Olivetti,' Audran — Galop, 'Love's Greeting,' Michaelis — Romance, 'Oft in My Slumbers,' Thomas — Waltz, 'Les Direnes,' Wildtenfel — Medley, 'How Delightful,' Catlin — Overture, 'Devotion to Art,' Gumbert — Potpourri, 'Huguenots,' Meyerbeer — Gavotte, 'Forget Me Not,' Giese — Selection, 'Billee Taylor,' Solomon — Hibernia, 'The Irish Patrol,' [Charles] Puerner — Overture, 'American Centennial,' Wiegand ("The Exodus," *Brooklyn Daily Eagle*, 3 July 1882, 4).

Coney Island, Brighton Beach: At Brighton Hotel, Conterno's Orchestra[782] performed "the Blue and the Gray" and "plantation songs," with Jules Levy, cornetist ("Brighton Beach," *Brooklyn Daily Eagle*, 5 July 1882, 2); "On the Fourth of July Mr. Joseph Bolten distributed for the Brighton Beach Hotel 10,000 musical programmes, notwithstanding the condition of the weather" ("Coney Island Notes," *Brooklyn Daily Eagle*, 6 July 1882, 2).

Buffalo: On the occasion of the city's semi-centennial celebration of its founding and the cornerstone-laying ceremony for a Soldiers' and Sailors' monument on the Fourth, the day "opened with a praise service at St. Paul's Episcopal Church.... A regimental band, orchestra, organ, a Presbyterian chorus, and the leader of the First Church choir, were added to the regular musical staff of the church. The pieces selected were patriotic, and the music, vocal and instrumental, was really superb." There was also a very large military and civic parade that included "two Indian bands — one from Tonawanda and one from Cattaraugus. The appearance of the Indians as well as their playing was most creditable; the latter was decidedly in advance of some of the white bands (Edward Bristol,

"Buffalo's Semi-Centennial," *New York Evangelist*, 13 July 1882).

New York: "Mr. Ball sang a patriotic song entitled 'The American Boy'" at a celebration held by the National Labor Association of Eleventh Assembly District at their headquarters, no. 511 1/2 Bedford Avenue ("National Labor Association," *Brooklyn Daily Eagle*, 5 July 1882, 2).

Southold, Long Island: The Southold Cornet Band played tunes on the church lawn and Lawrence Horton sang "New Jerusalem." D.P. Horton, director of the music was "seated at a fine toned melodeon on the pulpit platform. A choir of twenty-four, including 'Uncle Johnny Payn,' well known in Brooklyn, sang in the gallery, and they were accompanied on the organ by Miss May Horton. In accordance with the proclamation the Cornet Band were in the southeast corner of the gallery and started the programme by a vigorous rendering of 'Hail Columbia,' after which the choir sang 'The Pilgrims' Planting.'" ("Southold," *Brooklyn Daily Eagle*, 6 July 1882, 2).

Long Beach: Schreiner's Orchestra performed the following program before a crowd of 8,000.

"Hail Columbia"
Friedensmarch, from *Rienzi* (Wagner)
Overture, *Egmont* (Beethoven)
Waltz, *New Vienna* (Strauss)
March and Chorus, from "Flute Magique" (Mozart)
Polka, "Godenkblatt" (Leitermayor)
Overture, *Oberon* (Weber)
Quadrille, "American Songs" ([Anthony J.?] Stasny)
Scene and Cavatine, from *Macbeth* (Verdi)
Potpourri, "Ye Olden Times" (Beyer)
Galop, "Die wilde Tagd" (Michaelis)
["Long Beach," *Brooklyn Daily Eagle*, 5 July 1882, 2].

England

London: "Star-Spangled Banner" was sung by Miss Agnes B. Huntington at Westminster Palace Hotel for Americans and other guests ("General Foreign News: The Fourth Abroad," *Washington Post*, 5 July 1882, 1).

1883

Performances

District of Columbia

The "entire United States Marine Band" gave "daily concert between heats" at the Ivy City Race Course, July 3–6, sponsored by the Washington Driving Club (*Washington Post*, 4 July 1883, 4).

Maine

Bangor: The Bangor Band (24 pieces) and 62nd Fusiliers Band (21 pieces) performed in the city parade[783] (*Bangor Daily Commercial*, 5 July 1883, 1).

New York

Brooklyn: "Ladies Aid Society of the James M.E. Church, corner of Reid avenue and Monroe street, held an old time Fourth of July celebration.... Miss Ida Place and Mr. L.W. Partridge, the church organist, gave a piano duet in excellent style, after which the Declaration of Independence was read.... The church choir won hearty applause by singing Keller's American Hymn" (*Brooklyn Daily Eagle*, 5 July 1883, 1).

Malone: A procession was led by the Huntingdon Band ("The Day We Celebrate," *Franklin Gazette*, 6 July 1883, 3).

Ogdensburg: The City Band and Montreal Band provided music, the latter band "always delighted thousands with its exquisite, enlivening, and soul awakening music. Also the Governor General's Foot Guard Band of Ottawa. This is one of the best bands on the continent and this is the first time they have been allowed to leave the Dominion" (*Ogdensburg Advance*, 21 June 1883, 3).

Potsdam: "The St. Albans and Norwood Bands furnished the music together with martial music by the Floodwood Brigade" (*Ogdensburg Advance*, 21 June 1883, 3).

North Dakota

Fargo: A parade of local hook and ladder companies and Fargo commercial company floats were led by the city band. The exercises at the pavilion in the park included the singing of the "Star-Spangled Banner" by a choral society. That evening a dance was held and "the dancing platform was filled with lovers of the waltz and quadrille, who whirled and pirouetled before a large concourse of spectators to the enlivening music of Powell's Orchestra; this amusement was kept up until midnight" ("Independence," *Daily Argus*, 5 July 1883, 3–4).

Texas

Houston: The following concert was presented at the Fair Grounds by an unnamed orchestra:

March "Grenadier" (H.B. Dodworth)
Favorite Overture (Minker)
"Sturm and Stille" Gallop (Faust)
Aria from the opera *Lucrezia Borgia* (Donizetti)
March, "Bride of the Ball" (F.J. Keller)
Lieder-Potpourri (Ostertag)
"Come Where My Love Lies Dreaming" (E. Bollingson)
"Reverie," Andante and Allegro (F.J. Keller)
["The Fourth of July Volksfest," *Houston Daily Post*, 4 July 1883, 3].

Utah

Ogden: Ogden Brass Band, Capt. John A. Boyle, leader, in parade and exercises ("The Fourth!" *Ogden Daily Herald*, 5 July 1883, 1).

1884

Publications

"A Fourth of July Song." First line: "Johnnie Wilson celebrated" (*Milwaukee Sentinel*, 6 July 1884, 6).

Performances

New Hampshire

Littleton: The Saranac Cornet Band, Major A.H. Bowman, leader, followed by the Eureka Drum Corps led a procession to the grove where the exercises were held. Also in the parade was the Littleton Brigade Band, D.F. Chase, leader. The two bands and a Glee Club, led by Frank R. Brackett provided music for the ceremony (*Exercises at the Centennial Celebration of the Incorporation of the Town of Littleton, July 4th, 1884*. Published by the town, 1887. Concord, N.H.: N. H. Democratic Press Company).

New York

Hermon: The exercises took place in the Methodist Episcopal Church and included music by a glee club and band. "The music was furnished by Mrs. E.G. Seymour, Mrs. A.A. Matteson, Miss Mattie Derby, and Messrs. Gale, Derby, and Dresser. To say the least, it was excellent" (*Ogdensburg Advance*, 10 July 1884, 3).

Morristown: "At 9 o'clock [A.M.] the Farmersville Band of 18 pieces arrived and serenaded the president and trustees of the village." Following was a parade led by the band. That also provided music for the exercises held in the grove (*Ogdensburg Advance*, 10 July 1884, 3).

New York: "Columbia, We Love Thee" and "Star-Spangled Banner" sung by the Union Glee Club at the Tammany celebration ("Tammany's Great Day," *New York Times*, 5 July 1884, 3).

Ogdensburg: Four bands paraded in different sections of the town: Montreal Band, Gouverneur Band, Ogdensburg Band, and Madrid Band. At the Opera House where every seat was filled, "the exercises opened with a selection by the Montreal Band," that sat on the stage together with the City Band. The latter played "Hail Columbia" ("The Fourth of July Celebration," *Ogdensburg Advance*, 10 July 1884, 3).

1885

Performances

California

Los Angeles: "Flag of Our Heroes,"[784] "Our Country," and "Star-Spangled Banner" sung by a "double quartette" at the grand stand ("Independence Day," *Los Angeles Times*, 5 July 1885, 6).

Sacramento: Miss Lida Clinch sang the "Star-Span-

gled Banner" in the Assembly Room of the Capitol Building (*Sacramento Daily Record-Union*, 6 July 1885, 2).

Illinois

Blommington: A monument in honor of the popular vocalist Marie Litta was unveiled before a large audience. Litta was born Marie Eugenia Von Elsner in Bloomington in 1850 and died "in the zenith of her fame" in 1883. Music for the event "was furnished by the best trained voices. A number of duets and solos, favorites of the dead prima donna, were sung." The monument is 19 feet high, made of "fine Barre (Vt.) granite." Inscribed in the upper portion of the base is a book with musical notes "representing simple music sung by her, and on the other leaf is more difficult classical music, emblematic of her success" ("Marie Litta's Monument," *New York Times*, 7 July 1885, 3).

New York

New York: "Old Uncle Joe" sung by Wilson Macdonald at the celebration of the Veterans of 1812, at the Military Hall in the Bowery (*New York Times*, 5 July 1885, 5).

Pennsylvania

Philadelphia: "My Country, 'Tis of Thee" and "The Star-Spangled Banner" sung by the Veterans of the War of 1812 celebration held at the "Old Court House" ("Military Gatherings," *Philadelphia Inquirer*, 6 July 1885, 2).

Washington

Centralia: The Winlock Brass Band played music from a grandstand with Governor Watson C. Squire in attendance. The Exercises took place at a grove where the music included "Red, White and Blue," "The Home on the Deep," both sung by a choir, and "America" played by the band. Other songs sung included "Let the Hills and Vales Resound" and "Yankee Doodle" (*Chehalis Nugget*, 11 July 1895, as reported in "Research Success Story: The 1885 Winlock Band," *Washington State Library* website, accessed September 6, 2008, <http://wastatelib.wordpress.com/>).

1886

Performances

California

Los Angeles: On July 4, Mrs. Mamie Perry Davis sang the "Star-Spangled Banner" and on July 5 the Eagle Corps Band played "patriotic airs" from the head of First Street as fireworks there were set off ("The Fourth," *Los Angeles Times*, 6 July 1886, O4).

San Pedro: "Our Boys' brass band" was in charge of "the management of a literary entertainment and ball in the evening" of the Fourth ("San Pedro," *Los Angeles Times*, 26 June 1886, O2).

Colorado

White Pine: The White Band with Howard Pierce, leader, provided music for a dance at Bassler Hall, with "a speaker's stand and open air pavilion in front." Music was available from 3 P.M. to midnight ("4th o' July," *White Pine Cone*, 4 June 1886, 4).

Windsor: "The 110th anniversary was celebrated at Windsor entirely by home talent, the Windsor Cornet Band — a six months old organization — taking the lead." The members of the band provided the fireworks for the evening's display ("Windsor," *Fort Collins Courier*, 8 July 1886, 1).

District of Columbia

"At the "commemoration of our national independence" held at the "M.E. Church, Massachusetts Avenue, between Ninth and Tenth Streets, northwest," with Senator Warner Miller of New York presiding, "the music under the direction of the McKendree Church Choir, Miss Katie Wilson, leader," was "assisted by some of the best talent of our city" and "a solo, 'Our Native Land' by Mrs. H.H. Mills; 'The Star-Spangled Banner,' and 'The Lord of Hosts, Thou God of Nations,' by the Mckendree Choir, and 'America' and other appropriate selections by the congregation" ("The Nation's Birthday," *Washington Post*, 3 July 1886, 2).

Massachusetts

Boston: The Cadet Band performed at the Boston Theatre ("The Day in Boston," *Washington Post*, 6 July 1886, 1).

Minnesota

Chaska and Minneopolis: The Harmonia Singing Society performed. In Minneapolis at Germania Park, the West Minneapolis Turnverein celebrated and "the Frohsinns sang a few patriotic songs ... and a brass band from St. Paul discoursed music until 8 o'clock in the evening" ("The Fourth in Minneapolis," *Daily Pioneer Press*, 5 July 1886, 6).

New York

Malone: On July 5 "a grand procession" included the Fort Covington, Ogdensburg, St. Alban's and other bands; an earlier report noted six brass bands, including the Ogdensburg, Plattsburgh, Huntingdon, St. Albans, Fort Covington, "and our own 27th Separate Company Band" (*Franklin Gazette*, 18 and 25 June 1886, 3 and 3, respectively).

New York: At Tammany Hall, a band played "Carry Me Back to Old Virginia" and "Yankee Doodle" ("In a Patriotic Manner," *Washington Post*, 6 July 1886, 1; see also, "Tammany's Patriotic Day, *New York Times*, 6 July 1886, 8).

Port Jervis: "Star-Spangled Banner" played by the Erie Cornet Band at a ceremony for the unveiling of a soldiers monument. As the monument was unveiled, "Brennan's Band, of Wappinger's Falls, struck up

'Rally Round the flag'" (*New York Times*, 6 July 1886, 3).

1887

Performances

California

Los Angeles: *Skipped by the Light of the Moon*, a musical play "with new music," presented by Louis Harrison "and his talented company of comedians" at the "Grand Opera House" in Los Angeles ("Amusements," *Los Angeles Times*, 28 June 1887, 4); The Seventh Infantry Band accompanied the fireworks with the following program:

March, Dude's Selection, Joseph Claudin
Overture, Zethus, Pette
Medley Waltz, I'll Await My Love, H. Prindeville
Overture, Belle of the Village, P. Bouillon
Potpourri, Black Brigade, Bever
Schottische, My Black-Eyed Mae, J.O. Cassey
Medley Overture, Sitting on the Golden Fence,[785]
    H. Prindeville.
["The Fourth," *Los Angeles Times*, 3 July 1887, 1].

Colorado

Denver: Two bands provided music: Denver Central Band (African-American) and another unnamed band.[786]

Telluride: The Telluride Band performed on Independence Day in 1887, three of whose members included Charles F. Painter, O.C. Thomas, and Max Hippler. (Based on a photograph reported in "Picture Brings Back Memories, July 4, 1887," *Daily Journal*, 3 July 1922, 1).

Illinois

Quincy: The parade included Gauweiler's Band, Central Drum Corps, Gem City Band, and the Democratic Drum Corp., arranged in pairs ("Our Glorious Fourth," *Quincy Daily Whig*, 29 June 1887, 3).

Indiana

Indianpolis: On July 5 the Music Teachers National. Association (MTNA) featured its concert whose Independence Day program that consisted entirely of American works by composers Arthur Foote, F.Q. Dulcken, Frank V. Van der Stucken, Henry Holden Huss, John Knowles Paine, Otto Singer and Dudley Buck whose composition *Festival Overture, "The Star-Spangled Banner"* was a premiere.[787] The morning session featured the singing of Miss Hattie J. Clapper of New York. "In the afternoon recital songs, with descriptive comments and piano music, were given. The evening was devoted to American compositions." There was a chorus of 400 voices. "Arthur Foote's 'In the Mountains'[788] was remarkably well received, and the third part of Dulcken's 'Mein

Sotenelle'[789] caused prolonged applause and continuous calls for the author. The soloists were Mrs. Emma Thurston Whitehead, of Brooklyn; Miss Hattie J. Clapper, of New York; William Courtney, of New York, and L.G. Gottschalk, of Chicago. William H. Sherwood, of New York, was the pianist." The event took place in Tomlinson Hall ("Hundreds of Musicians," *New York Times*, 6 July 1887, 2).

Maryland

Baltimore: At Patterson Park, the Francis Scott Key Memorial Association met "and a choir under Professor Harry Sanders" sang "a number of patriotic airs" ("Ready for the Fourth," *Baltimore Morning Herald*, 4 July 1887, 1).

New York

New York: At Morningside Park, at a sham battle by the Veteran Zouaves, a section of the drum corps played "the 'Rogues' March'" ("Zouaves in a Sham Battle," *New York Times*, 5 July 1887, 5).

Saranac Lake: The Elizabethtown Band performed and was cited as "one of the finest bands in the State, and has been secured by the management at an enormous price" ("The Fourth of July at Saranac Lake," *Elizabethtown Post and Gazette*, 30 June 1887, 2).

Saratoga Springs: The New York Mainzer Carnaval Verein and Liedertaefel provided music ("At Saratoga Springs," *Brooklyn Daily Eagle*, 3 July 1887, 5).

Pennsylvania

Columbia: A parade included the Maytown Band, Mountville Band, Prospect Band, Columbia Band, Wrightsville Band, and Sprenkle's Drum and Fife Corp. The program of exercises held in the park, included the Columbia Maennerchor singing "The Red, White and Blue," "Star-Spangled Banner," and "Hail Columbia." A band played "national airs" ("Columbia in Her Glory," *Columbia Spy*, 9 July 1887, 3).

1888

Performances

California

Chico: Girard Leon's Monster Circus performed with music provided by a "brass band of twelve pieces" (*Chico Daily Enterprise*, 3 July 1888, 1).

Los Angeles: The city parade included the Continental Drum Corps, Eagle Corps Band, Veteran Drum Corps, Tyroleers' Band of Anaheim, City Band, and Meine Band. The Seventh Infantry Band provided music on the grandstand where the exercises were held. After an introduction by the band, Louise Manfred "sang two verses of the 'Star-Spangled Ban-

ner,' the band accompanied her. She bowed and returned to her seat; but the crowd wanted more of the best feature of the programme, and signified it by a vigorous clapping of hands and calls for more. The little lady responded and gave a third verse, which was warmly applauded" ("The Fourth," *Los Angeles Times*, 5 July 1888, 2).

San Francisco: The dedication of the first monument to Francis Scott Key in the West is unveiled and music is provided by the Second Regiment Band (*San Francisco Chronicle*, 5 July 1888, 8).

Illinois

Chicago: Arthur Foote's Suite No. 1 in E, op. 12[790] had its Chicago premiere by the Thomas Orchestra, Theodore Thomas, conductor, at the Exposition Building on July 4 at the meeting of the Music Teachers National Association (July 3–5); Edward MacDowell's Concerto No. 1 for Piano in A, Op. 15 has its Chicago premiere (Teresa Carreno, piano) ("Thomas' Concert," *Daily Inter-Ocean*, 5 July 1888, 4).[791]

Massachusetts

Amesbury: On the occasion of the unveiling of the Bartlett[792] Monument, two bands gave an evening concert:

Chandler's Band
Overture, *Morning, Noon and Night*, [Franz von] Suppé
Gitana Waltz, [Ernest] Bucalossi
On the Plantation, Puerna
Cheerfulness (cornet duet), [Ferdinand] Gumbert
Patrol Comique, [Thomas] Hindley
Clarinet solo (selected), Philip E. Robinson, clarinet
Ten Minutes with the Minstrels, Beron
Infernal Galop, Béla Kéla
Hunting Scene, [P.] Bucalossi
American Overture, Catlin

Newburyport Cadet Band
Preliminary March
Overture, "American," Catlin
Concert Waltz, "Nantasket," Fahrbach
Reverie, "The Wayside Chapel," Wilson
Concert Schottische, Missud[793]
March, "General Banks," Rollinson
Overture, "Belle of the Village," Bouillon
Mariana, "Chillian Dance"[794]
Concert Waltz, "American Student,"[795] Missud
Presto

(*Presentation of the Bartlett Statue to the State of Massachusetts* by Jacob R. Huntington, Esq. Unveiled at Amesbury, Mass., July 4th, 1888. Newburyport: News Publishing Co., [1888], 42).

Winchester: The 17-piece Winchester Band performed in this town.[796]

New York

Coney Island: At Brighton Beach, Anton Seidl[797] provided music and at Manhattan Beach ("Herr Seidl will forsake Wagner and furnish patriotic music to a large extent"). Seidl performed Wagner's *Centennial March*, and "Gillmore will fire cannons and beat big drums to the tune of the national anthem"; "at West Brighton the boy cornetist and the Acme Quartet will entertain the people who look at Niagara Falls in the Sea Beach Palace" ("A Fiery Fourth" and "Fire and Fun," *Brooklyn Daily Eagle*, 3 and 5 July 1888, 4 and 2, respectively); "Manhattan Beach" performed by P.S. Gilmore's Band on July 3 (*New York Times*, 4 July 1888, 5).

New York: "Anthem of Liberty" performed at a ceremony of letter carriers associations at the Academy of Music. The piece is cited: "by Mrs. Agatha Munier, assisted by the Concordia Chorus." Also, "Hail Columbia, Happy Land" performed by a band after the introduction of Congressman S.S. Cox ("The Carriers' Parade," *New York Times*, 5 July 1888, 8).

Utah

Ogden City: At Lester Park, Utah, Miss Flora Purdy sang "The Flag of Our Union" and Miss Mollie Phelan sang the "Star-Spangled Banner," accompanied on the organ by "Prof. Navoni" ("The Fourth," *Ogden Standard Examiner*, 5 July 1888, 1).

Wisconsin

Chippewa Falls: A "Female Brass Band" consisting of "sixteen young ladies" performed music at a race course (*Saint Paul and Minneapolis Pioneer Press*, 5 July 1888, 3).

1889

Performances

California

Los Angeles: Musicians are prevented from working on the Fourth due to a ban by the Musicians Union because the Citizens' Fourth of July Committee reduced the fee from $8 to $6 per man. But because most of the musicians affected were in the military regimental bands they faced mutiny charges for not showing up to perform. This situation reoccurred in 1897 ("Fourth of July," *Los Angeles Times*, 26 June 1889, 5; "Charged with Mutiny" and "Two Lessons for Strikers," *New York Times*, 7 and 8 July 1889, 3 and 4, respectively; "Thrifty Patriots" and "Non-Union Bands," *Los Angeles Times*, 27 June and 30 June 1897, 24 and 12, respectively); "America" and "Star-Spangled Banner" sung by a chorus of 200 children and the audience at the Pavilion ("The Exercises," *Los Angeles Times*, 5 July 1889, 2).

Colorado

White Pine: The North Star Cornet Band "will furnish excellent music during the day and evening" at "a large pavilion ... erected on Main Street" ("The Fourth," *White Pine Cone*, 5 July 1889, 4).

District of Columbia

J.R. Slater played piano solos at the celebration at the Literary Society of the Young Men's Christian Association on New York Avenue ("Appropriate Fourth of July Orations," *Washington Post*, 5 July 1889, 2).

Illinois

Chicago: Edvard Grieg's overture *In Autumn*, op. 11 (1865) had its Chicago premiere in the Exposition Building, on July 5, by the Chicago Orchestra, Theodore Thomas, conductor.[798]

Maryland

Bay Ridge: Jules Levy, the cornetist, performed on the same program with the Naval Academy Band, Charles A. Zimmermann, leader ("Old Fashioned Fourth of July Celebration at Bay Ridge," *Washington Post*, 3 July 1889, 8).

Missouri

Rolla: A parade was led by the Rolla Silver Cornet Band ("Grand Fourth of July Celebration," *Rolla New Era*, 15 June 1889, 3).

New York

Brooklyn: At the opening reception of the Twenty-Sixth Ward Republican Club "on Pennsylvania Avenue, near Atlantic," Professor A. Salmond began the celebration with a song. "Professor A. Stagg sang a medley of national airs, in which all joined. William Macdonald played Scotch airs on the flute. That part of the entertainment concluded with a violin solo by Professor Stagg" ("It's First Public Reception," *Brooklyn Daily Eagle*, 5 July 1889, 1).

New York: The 69th Regimental Band played music at the Empire City Colloseum sporting event in Jones's Woods on 69th street ("Not a Very Noisy Fourth," *New York Times*, 5 July 1889, 8); the "Star-Spangled Banner" was sung by celebrants at the Harlem Democratic Club event, the Benevolent Order of Veteran Firemen affair, held at Mount Morris Hall, and the Anti-Poverty Society meeting, held at the Cooper Institute; "America" was also sung at the Harlem Democratic Club affair ("Not a Very Noisy Fourth," *New York Times*, 5 July 1889, 8); the Hamilton Republican Club celebrated with singing by the Knickerbocker Glee Club ("Displays of Patriotism," *New York Times*, 4 July 1889, 2).

Ohio

Columbus: The Maennerchor sang and the Fourteenth Regiment Band played tunes at the dedication of a monument to the German poet Schiller (*Daily Ohio State Journal*, 5 July 1889, 5).

Millersburg: A band contest took place and the Walnut Creek Band captured first place (*Daily Ohio State Journal*, 5 July 1889, 1).

Pennsylvania

Cornwall: The Perseverance Band and Trinity Col-

lege Glee Club furnished music for the town's celebration (*Philadelphia Inquirer*, 5 July 1889, 3).

Reading: "The Harmonie-Maennerchor, Reading's
strongest musical organization, celebrated their anniversary in their hall on North Sixth Street (Ibid., 2)

Tioga: The Athletic Band gave a concert at 6 P.M.
(Ibid., 3).

1890

Publications

Thayer & Gustin's 4th of July Grand March. Composed and arranged by Thos. H. Kane. Bay City,
Mich.: Thayer & Gustin, [1890?]. For piano. "Written expressly for the grand celebration at Bay City,
July 4th 1890." Copy in Library of Congress.

*War Songs and National Melodies: Comprising the
Words To All the Principal War Songs and National
Melodies Now in Use. Especially Appropriate for G.A.R.
Gatherings, Fourth of July Celebrations, etc.* Cincinnati,
Ohio: A. Squire, [189–?]. Copy in South Dakota State
University.

Performances

California

Downey: "Three Cheers for the Red, White and
Blue" performed by the Norwalk Brass Band, "Hail
Columbia" by the Vocal Club, and "Praise God from
Whom all Blessings flow" ("Old Hundred") by the
Downey Double Quartette at a celebration held at a
grove near the town. Also, Miss Josie Welden sang
"The Star-Spangled Banner" (*Los Angeles Times*, 5 July
1890, 3).

Long Beach: "America" sung by the audience and
"Star-Spangled Banner" sung by Miss Osborne at
a celebration there (*Los Angeles Times*, 5 July 1890, 3).

Los Angeles: A large parade included the Anaheim
Band, Walter Crowther, drum major; Monrovia Band
of 24 instrumentalists; the Pomona Band, W.A. Lewis,
drum major and 16 pieces ("The Glorious Fourth,"
Los Angeles Times, 5 July 1890, 2); a Fourth of July
service on July 6 at the Universalist Church included
"Prof. Kyle" who sang the "Star-Spangled Banner"
and the Harmonia Quartette that "rendered several
patriotic songs" ("Brevities," *Los Angeles Times*, 7 July
1890, 7); at the Vienna Buffet at the corner of Main
and Requena Streets, a "grand patriotic programme"
featuring "Miss Randall, the whistling Patti," Franz
Reihofer's Tyrolean Quartette, and the Hungarian
Trio, with R. Andres, solo violinist and leader (*Los
Angeles Times*, 3 July 1890, 1).

Pasadena: "The Red, White and Blue" sung at the
Tabernacle by the Polymnia Quartette (*Los Angeles
Times*, 5 July 1890, 7).

Colorado

Leadville: A parade included "the G.A.R. Drum
Corps in their brilliant uniforms 17 strong and under
the leadership of Leonard Worcester, Jr" and "the
Leadville Band, 12 pieces, the baton being wielded by
Mr. Fen. G. Barker" ("Leadville's Day," *Evening
Chronicle*, 5 July 1890, 2).

Illinois

Auburn: A procession from the Public Square to
Union Park included the Auburn Brass and Reed
Band and a choir of 100 youth. The exercises at the
Park included music by the band; "Doxology, "Praise
God from Whom all blessings flow" (choir); song,
"Red, White and Blue" (choir); song, "Marching
through Georgia" (choir); song, "Yankee Doodle"
(choir).[799]

New York

New York: "My Country, 'Tis of Thee" performed
by a brass band at the Fleetwood Track Clubhouse
("On the Nation's Birthday," *New York Times*, 5 July
1890, 2); national airs were performed by the Hungarian Band and Casino orchestra on the Casino roof
garden where reportedly it was "a desirable place from
which to view the fireworks in this and neighboring
cities" ("Theatrical Gossip," *New York Times*, 3 July
1890, 8); Gabe Case sang "We'll Hunt the Buffalo" at
the Fleetwood Track Clubhouse ("On the Nation's
Birthday," *New York Times*, 5 July 1890, 2).

Tennessee

Chatanooga: Brass bands played "national airs,"
including "Dixie," and "Bonny Blue Flag" in a parade
of Confederate veterans, with 50,000 spectators present ("The Fourth at Chatanooga," *New York Times*, 5
July 1890, 2; "Confederate Veterans' Fourth," *Washington Post*, 5 July 1890, 1).

Germany

Berlin: "Hail Columbia," "Die Wacht am Rhein,"
and "Heil Dir im Seigerkranz" performed for a group
of Americans by the Second Regiment of Guards Band
at the Kaiserhof Hotel ("Fourth of July Concert at
Berlin," *Washington Post*, 5 July 1890, 1).

1891

Publications

"Origin of Fireworks. A Song for the Fourth of
July." [By "H.M. Greenleaf."] First line: "Away, far
off in China" (*Youth's Companion*, 2 July 1891, 378).

Performances

California

Los Angeles: At Hazard's Pavilion, Mrs. W.T. Barnett sang "The Red, White and Blue" and Albert

Hawthorne sang the "Star-Spangled Banner" ("At the Pavilion," *Los Angeles Times*, 5 July 1891, 2).

Colorado

Pueblo: The formal opening of Pueblo's Mineral Palace with Gov. John L. Routt and his staff in attendance included music by the Seventh Regiment Band ("Mineral Palace Open," *Boulder Daily Camera*, 5 July 1891, 1).

Georgia

Buford: The Buford Brass Band performed "sweet music" at an evening ceremony in which members of the Alliance Farmer spoke ("Booming Cannon, Big Alliance Guns," *Atlanta Constitution*, 5 July 1891, 21).

Maryland

Glen Echo: At this Chautauqua site, the amphitheater held ceremonies that included "patriotic music by the band and solos on the organ by Prof. Baker; then following the exercises there was a concert by all the local talent. Mr. C.B. Hanford recited the 'Star-Spangled Banner,' which literally brought down the house, and although the rule of no encores was strickly observed in every other selection, the audience couldn't be stilled until he recited again this time giving them the oration of Mark Anthony over Caesar's body"; another newspaper reported that the Roberts' Band, Chautauqua Chorus, an organist, and others performed the following concert at 4 P.M.:

Overture, "Barber of Seville" Rossini
Chorus, "The American Union" Widdows
Organ solo, "The March of the Priests" Mendelssohn
From *Athalie* by Prof. Woodruff
Recitation, "Star-Spangled Banner" Mr. C.B. Hanford
Chorus, "Our Country" Sanders
Soprano solo, "Staccata Polka" Mulder, sung by Miss C. Gertrude Smith
Selection, "Macbeth" Verdi, Rogers' Band
Chorus, "To Thee, O Country" Eichberg
Tenor solo, "Stand Firm for the Right"[800] Danks, sung by Prof. Mark C. Baker
Chorus, "The Land of Lauds" Sanders
Overture, "American" Catlin
Hymn, "America" performed by Rogers' Band, organ, piano, choir, audience.
["G.A.R. Day at Glen Echo," *Washington Post*, 4 July 1891, 2; "Glen Echo Chautauqua," *Washington Evening Star*, 6 July 1891, 2].

Indian Head: At Marshal Hall Amusement Park, the National Guard Band advertised the following holiday program:

Waltz, "Independence Day" Schroeder
Lancers, "America" Wiegand
Polka, "Yankee Doodle" Tobani
Quadrille, "My Maryland" Boettcher
Schottische, "Auld Lang Syne" Moses
Lancers, "The Boys of '76" Weingarten
York, "Star-Spangled Banner" Ross
Waltz, "Fleeting Days" Bailey
Quadrille, "Hail, Columbia" Phile
Polka, "Gwine Back to Dixie" Foster
Lancers, "Red, White and Blue" Wiegand
Schottische, "Stars and Stripes" Ross
Quadrille, "Centennial" Boettcher
York, "By-Gone Days" Strauss
Lancers, "A Hundred Years Ago" Lutz
Waltz, "Home, Sweet Home" [John Howard] Payne
[*Washington Post*, 3 July 1891, 6].

Minnesota

Ely: This town held its first Fourth of July celebration that included artillery salutes, parades, and speeches. At 4 A.M., a cornet band marched through the streets playing patriotic airs. Later, a calithumpian band of 16 pieces played a march "in the wildest disorder." The Ely Cornet Band provided music for a dance that night.[801]

Missouri

Newburg: The Rolla Cornet Band performed in this town ("Fourth of July Celebration," *Rolla New Era*, 4 July 1891, 3).

New Jersey

Newark: At Caledonian Park, *American Fantasy*, composed by Max Spicker, was performed by an orchestra of 200 instruments conducted by Frank Van der Stucken at a celebration of "The Grand Saengerfest of the Northeastern Saengerbund" (147 societies); "Freedom of Nations," a work by Carl Attenhofer, performed by a chorus led by singer William Bartels (*New York Times*, 4 and 5 July 1891, 2 and 2, respectively); a concert was given by the "united singers of Newark" to an audience of eighteen German singing societies representing five cities and Governor Leon Abbett gave a welcoming address. "The noteworthy numbers on the musical programme were the aria of 'Elizabeth' from *Tannhauser* [Wagner], sung by Ida Klein Euler, and [Robert] Schumann's 'Wanderlied,' sung by William Bartels of this city." One report noted that 5,000 Saengerbunders, assisted by an orchestra of 200 pieces, conducted by Johannes Werschinger, sang the "Star-Spangled Banner" ("The National Saengerfest," *Brooklyn Daily Eagle*, 5 July 1891, 1; "Patriotism and Music," *New York Times*, 5 July 1891, 2).

Ocean Grove: At the Auditorium, there was music by a monster choir and "patriotic songs were sung while the audience assembled" ("Asbury Park," *New York Times*, 5 July 1891, 13).

New York

New York: Bayne's Band played patriotic music at the Tammany Hall event and the Tammany Glee Club sang "Where Would I Be!" ("The Fourth at Tammany Hall" and "Tammany's Fourth of July," *New York Times*, 4 and 5 July 1891, 8 and 9, respectively); Cappa's Seventh Regiment Band performed in Central Park and Connor's Eighth Regiment Band at Paradise Park ("Coming Events," *New York Times*, 4 July 1891, 5); at a cornerstone ceremony for a new schoolhouse at St. Paul's Parish, the Rev. Alfred Young's hymn "What Is the Land We Love So Well?" was premiered (*New York Times*, 5 July 1891, 9).

Pennsylvania

Pittsburgh: At Schenley Park, a march titled *Schenley Park*, by B. Weis, was premiered by the Great Western Band (*Pittsburgh Dispatch*, 5 July 1891, 1).

Tennessee

Chatanooga: A parade "nearly two miles long" included "two hundred gorgeous floats and five brass bands" ("Booming Cannon, Big Alliance Guns," *Atlanta Constitution*, 5 July 1891, 21).

1892

Performances

Colorado

Breckenridge: A parade started from Fireman's Hall and "the American Drum Corp furnished music for the march" ("Glorious Fourth," *Summit County Journal*, 9 July 1892, 5).

Maryland

Frederick: The Frederick City Orchestra performed for the B&O Railroad Co. at the Relay House ("The Glorious Fourth," *Frederick Daily News*, 5 July 1892, 3).

Glen Echo: Emile E. Mori directed a musical program with musicians Signor Vitale, violinist; Mark C. Baker, tenor; Eva Augusta Vescilius, soprano Louise V. Sheldon, contralto; and John P. Lawrence, organist ("Celebration at Glen Echo," *Washington Post*, 3 and 4 July 1892, 3 and 5, respectively).

Baltimore: "Columbia," "Doxology," "Hail Columbia," "Red, White and Blue," and "Star-Spangled Banner" performed by a choir under the direction of Charles F. Vodery at a celebration of the Francis Scott Key Monument Association at Patterson Park ("Fun on the Fourth," *Baltimore Morning Herald*, 4 July 1892, 1).

Minnesota

Winona: At the ceremony for the dedication of the New High Bridge, music was provided by Fakler's Band, which played "two selections" as the crowd gathered. After a brief prayer, the band played "Columbia, the Gem of the Ocean" ("Royally Remembered," *Winona Daily Republican*, 5 July 1892, 3).

New York

Brooklyn: A "Watch Night of Liberty" event on Sunday evening, July 3, at Greene Avenue Baptist Church hosted by "a detachment of Knights Templar and Sons of Veterans" included "stirring music of Yerkes' Band" Also, "W.A. Norton, the precentor of the church, sang the solo of 'Columbia, the Gem of the Ocean,' the congregation joining with great fervor in the chorus....Then Miss Annie L. Walker, soprano, sang 'The Star-Spangled Banner' as if inspired and in response to a rapturous recall gave 'Home, Sweet Home' with a tenderness that brought tears to the eyes of many veterans.... At 11:59 the organ began the familiar strains of 'America' and promptly at 12, amid the booming of cannon crackers and the volleys of lesser caliber, all joined in singing 'My Country 'Tis of Thee, Sweet Land of Liberty.' The scene was deeply impressive and a memorable lesson in patriotism, especially to the large number of young people present." In the course of the evening, "Professor Norton" also sang the "Battle Hymn of the Republic" ("Liberty Watch Night," *Brooklyn Daily Eagle*, 5 July 1892, 12).

New York: At the Tammany Society meeting, Bayne's Band performed the tune "We'll Hunt the Buffalo" and the Tammany Glee Club sang "Our Glorious Union Forever" ("Tammany Tocsin Sounded," *New York Times*, 5 July 1892, 1).

Oregon

Portland: A Fourth of July "opening concert" on July 2 was given by the Marine Band, Ernest Fleck, director, "in the Plaza":

Overture, "Zampa" (Hérold)
Czardas, "Last Love" (John J. Braham)
Waltz, "Morgenblatter" (Johann Strauss)
"Polish Dance" (Scharwenka)
Grand descriptive fantasia, "A Hunting Scene" (Bucalossi)
Grand selection from the opera, "Cavaleria Rusticana" (P. Mascagni)
Danza Mexicann, Rosas 'y Abrojas (Roses and Thorns) (By Ridengue)
Trip to Coney Island (Theodore Tobani)
"Home Sweet Home"
Paraphrase, "Loreley" (J.R. Claus)
The American Patrol (Meacham)
[*Morning Oregonian*, 2 July 1892, 6].

Texas

Brenham: "Star-Spangled Banner" was sung by hundreds of persons at Fireman's Park ("The Glorious Fourth," *Houston Daily Post*, 5 July 1892, 1).

Utah

Provo City: A military band led the town's procession. At the Tabernacle, the following program was presented:

Music by the band.
Prayer by the chaplain.
Song by the choir.
Reading of Declaration of Independence by Lars E. Eggertsen.
Yankee Doodle by Drum Corps.

Oration by the orator of the Day, D.C. Houtz,
   Esq.
Song, "Star-Spangled Banner," by Herbert S. Pyne,
   the audience joining in chorus.
Short address.
Song, "Sword of Bunker Hill" by John R. Twelyes.
Short address.
Music.
Prayer by the chaplain.
["Fourth of July Programme" and "Fourth of July,"
Daily Enquirer, 25 June and 5 July 1892, 4 and 4,
respectively].

1893

This was the year that Katharine Lee Bates was
inspired to write "America the Beautiful," as a result
of her trip west to Chicago and eventually Pike's Peak,
Colorado. On July 4 she was in Kansas and wrote in
her diary "Fertile prairies" and "a better American for
such a Fourth." On July 22 she was at the summit
of Pike's Peak and noted "Most glorious scenery I ever
beheld." She began writing "America" which was first
published on July 4, 1895, in the weekly church publication *The Congregationalist*.[802] Her song was to become a national anthem in both spirit and sentiment.

Another highlight of the Fourth was the day's events
held at the World's Columbian Exposition in Chicago.
The fair opened on May 1, 1893, and closed on October 30 of that year. The Fourth of July was one of
the best attended days and crowds numbering over
100,000 got to hear various musical performances by
several bands and choirs.[803] One of the highlights was
the joint meeting of significant musical organizations,
including Music Teachers National Association,
Women's Musical Congress, College of American Musicians, and Illinois Music Teachers' Association.[804]

Performances

California

Redondo: "Services were held in the Chautanqua
building" in the morning. "There were national airs by
a male quartette, and music by Arend's Orchestra"
("At Redondo," *Los Angeles Times*, 5 July 1893, 4).

San Bernardino: The day's events began with a parade that included the Ninth Infantry Regiment Band,
T.R. Gable's Brass Band of Needles, "supplied with
most beautiful instruments," San Bernardino Band,
"without uniforms." The exercises at the pavilion
"opened with a musical selection by the band." Later
"The Star-Spangled Banner" was sung by Margaret
McGee, "each stanza being greeted with applause."
After an oration, Miss Tidy Buford sang "'I Dreamt'
(Schirer) accompanied by Prof. Steinbrunner on the
piano and Prof. Erbe on the piano." That evening "an
open-air concert was given, in which the visiting
bands participated, rendering the following selections":

March, "The Governor's Guard" (O'Hara)
Polka, "Bright Eyes" (Rollinson)
Q.S., "I.O.A." (Southwell)
Waltz, "Papa, Sweet Mamma and Me" (Prendiville)
March, "Twenty-fifth Battallon" (Monteil)
Polonaise, "Royal Decree" (Swift)
March, "The Big Four" (Southwell)
March, "Corcoran Cadets" (Sousa)
["At San Bernardino," *Los Angeles Times*, 5 July
   1893, 4].

Santa Ana: A parade included music by the Santa
Ana Brass Band and a drum corps. The exercises were
held in the park where a "chorus of voices sang 'Columbia, the Gem of the Ocean.'" The "Star-Spangled
Banner" was sung "by hundreds of voices" followed
by more selections by the band ("At Santa Ana," *Los
Angeles Times*, 5 July 1893, 4).

Santa Monica: An afternoon parade included music
by the Santa Monica and Soldiers' Home Band. Exercises at the bandstand included singing patriotic
songs ("At Santa Monica," *Los Angeles Times*, 5 July
1893, 4).

Colorado

Creede: This town celebrated its first Fourth of July
celebration and music was provided by a brass band
from Del Norte ("Fourth of July at Creede," *Creede
Candle*, 7 July 1893, 1).

Louisville: "A delightful orchestra under the excellent management of Fred L. McIlmoyle of the People's Theater of Denver furnished the music of the
day. The orchestra is a first class club and the sweet
stream which they caused to flow all afternoon added
much to the occasion" ("In Louisville," *Boulder Daily
Camera*, 6 July 1893, 1).

Illinois

Chicago: A procession from City Hall to Washington Park and the World's Fair Grounds that included
Mayor Carter H. Harrison and city officials, was led
by the band of the Second Regiment.

Musical Director Pratt will have a stand at the
front center of the platform, where he will be in
sight of the great chorus of 2,000 singers, who are
to be grouped in the galleries of the Terminal Station, Machinery Hall, and Mines and Mining
Building. The musical selections are all well known .
patriotic melodies and it is expected that the people will generally join in the singing. During the
singing of the 'Doxology' the land battery will
thunder a salute and will be answered by the guns
on the [steamer] *Michigan*.

At noon will come the climax of the day's glory.
While the crowds are singing the "Star-Spangled
Banner," the original Paul Jones flag and the banner
of the League of Human Freedom will be thrown
to the breeze while the guns will thunder and whis-
tles and bells will add to the patriotic uproar.
The program in detail is as follows:

Prayer. The Rev. John Henry Barrows, D.D.
Opening address. Adlai E. Stevenson.
Song. "Columbia, the Gem of the Ocean."
Address. Carter H. Harrison, Mayor of Chicago.
Address. Hampton L. Carson of Philadelphia
Salute of the flags.
Song. "Star-Spangled Banner."
Oration and reading of the Declaration of Independence. J.S. Norton of Chicago.
Song. "My Country, 'Tis of Thee.
Doxology.

("Nation's Natal Day," *Chicago Daily Tribune,* 4 July 1893, 1; *New York Times,* 5 July 1893, 5); the overture *Witchis,* op. 10 by Margaret Ruthven Lang (1867–1972) was premiered at the Exposition Hall by the Chicago Orchestra, Theodore Thomas, conductor.[805]

At 6 P.M. a "grand chorus" directed by S.G. Pratt, assisted by J.H. Howenstein, Warren C. Coffin, H. L. Perkins, and F. M. Hicks performed:

Prayer—Von Weber, united bands.
"The Old Folks at Home," chorus and populace.
Medley of national airs by the bands.
"Nearer, My God, to Thee," chorus and populace.
"Sweet Spirit, Hear My Prayer,"[806] bands.
"Love and Liberty."
"Home, Sweet Home."
Grand March by united bands.

At 7 P.M. "on the grand basin," the Dudley Buck Glee Club of Pueblo, Colorado, a 20-voices choir directed by C.S. Cornell performed:

"Comrades in Arms," Adam.[807]
"To Thee, O Country," Eichberg.
"Serenade, baritone obligato," Nevin, sung by Mr. Cornell.
"On the Sea," Buck.[808]
"On the March," Becker.
"Vintage Song," Mendelssohn.

("Will Join in a Patriotic Chorus," *Chicago Daily Tribune,* 3 July 1893, 1.); the *New York Times* reported that Silas G. Pratt conducted three bands—Second Regiment Band, Pullman Band, and the Chicago Band—at the "terminal building":

He stood on the stairway a few feet above the heads of the musicians with a programme of the music in one hand and a book in the other, using both as batons to bring out the volume of patriotic melody to its fullest extent and in the most harmonious unison. They played the Doxology, "The Red, White, and Blue," "The Star-Spangled Banner," and "America" while the multitude applauded after each selection. ["Patriotism in the Very Air," *New York Times,* 5 July 1893, 5].

Maryland

Frederick: The Independent Drum Corps "paraded the streets playing martial airs"; at All Saints Episcopal Church, Miss Campbell, organist, played "Hail Columbia" for an assemblage of the D.A.R. The group

also sang "God Bless Our Native Land," "Happy Time," Sparkling and Bright," and "The Star-Spangled Banner." Miss Lucy Schroeder, piano, accompanied a choir singing "America" ("A Quiet Day," *Frederick Daily News,* 5 July 1893, 3).

Missouri

Victor: Music was provided by the Victor Cornet Band ("Fourth of July Celebration," *Rolla New Era,* 17 June 1893, 3).

New York

Coney Island: At Brighton Beach, the Royal Hungarian Band provided music ("Day of Patriotism and Noise," *New York Times,* 4 July 1893, 9); Sousa's Band performed at Manhattan Beach and included "Lottie Collins' latest song, 'Marguerite'" (*Brooklyn Daily Eagle,* 3 July 1893, 2 and 4).

New York: The celebration of the Tammany Society at their Hall on East Fourteenth Street included the Tammany Glee Club that sang "The Land of the Free" and "Huzza! Columbia Forever." Bayne's Sixty Ninth Regiment Band provided instrumental music; at Paradise Park, Conterno's military band gave a concert at 8 P.M.:

"The Star-Spangled Banner"
Overture, *National Airs,* Wiegand
Waltz, *Santiago,* A. Corbin
Selection, *Wang,* [Woolson] Morse
Patrol, *American,* Meacham
Hunting Scene (Descriptive), Sucalossi
Overture, *College Songs,* Moses
Gavotte, *Enthusiasm,* Bernstein
Selection, *Italian Airs,* Conterno
Ethiopian Dance, Lowenberg
March, *The Bow Wow,*[809] [L.O.] DeWitt
"Hail Columbia";

At Tompkins Square Park, the Fourth Regiment Band performed ("Day of Patriotism and Noise," *New York Times,* 4 July 1893, 9).

North Carolina

Greensboro: At the Guilford battle ground, the Lexington Silver Cornet Band (16 pieces) provided music for the dedication ceremonies for the monument to Governor Thomas M. Holt.[810]

Pennsylvania

Philadelphia: At Independence Square, "This Is the Day of Our Lord" was sung by the German singing societies, conducted by A.C. Hartinman ("On Hallowed Ground," *Philadelphia Inquirer,* 5 July 1893, 1).

Utah

Logan: Watt S. Lamoreaux sang "Oh Promise Me" and music by the Thatcher Opera House Band at Johnson's Grove ("The Fourth of July," *Utah Journal,* 8 July 1893).

Provo: In the opera house, John R. Twelyes sang "Sword of Bunker Hill" and Herbert S. Pyne sang the

All Saints Episcopal Church in Frederick, Maryland. The parish was founded in 1742 and the present church built in 1855. On Independence Day in 1893, the Daughters of the American Revolution celebrated here with singing "The Star-Spangled Banner," "God Bless Our Native Land," and other patriotic songs, to the accompaniment of a piano and organ (author's photograph).

"Star-Spangled Banner." A choir sang "Hail Columbia" and "America" while Olson's Band played national airs ("Fourth of July," *Daily Enquirer*, 5 July 1893, 1).

1894

Performances

Connecticut

Woodstock: "Flag Song" by Harriet Prescott Spofford was sung by a chorus to the tune "Yankee Doodle" at Roseland Park (*Chicago Times*, 5 July 1894, 8; *New York Times*, 5 July 1894, 8).

District of Columbia

"America," "Red, White and Blue," and "Star-Spangled Banner" were sung by the Mount Pleasant Choral Society at a celebration at Ingleside Manor, just west of Mount Pleasant; "Marching through

Georgia" played by the Mount Pleasant Drum and Bugle Corps. (*Washington Evening Star*, 3–4 July 1894, 8 and 2, respectively); the U.S. Marine Band led a parade from the Arlington Hotel to the Washington Monument ("Observances in Washington," *New York Times*, 5 July 1894, 8).

Maryland

Baltimore: The Francis Scott Key Association Choir, directed by George W. Gibson, accompanied by Miss Alice Russell, organist, sang "Yankee Doodle," "The Red, White and Blue," and "Star-Spangled Banner" at Patterson Park for association members ("Down with Disloyalty," *Baltimore Morning Herald*, 5 July 1894, 6).

Massachusetts

Ashby: At the dedication of the Fitch Memorial, the Ashby united choirs sang "the Star-Spangled Banner" and "America." (*John Fitch. An Address with Appendix* by Hon. Ezra S. Stearns. Fitchburg, [MA]: Sentinel Printing Company, 1895).

Patterson Park in Baltimore was a popular location for performances in the 1880s and 1890s by the Francis Scott Key Association. Shown is the park's Observation Tower, designed by Charles H. Latrobe, and completed in 1892. This was the likely site in the park for the performance on July 3, 1894, of national airs by the Key Association Choir, conducted by George W. Gibson, accompanied by Miss Alice Russell, organist (author's photograph).

Boston: The Germania Band played music at the municipal event held in the Boston Theatre ("Celebrations in General," *Washington Post*, 5 July 1894, 7).

Missouri

St. Louis: At the dedication of St. Joseph's Catholic Orphan Asylum at Grand Avenue and Delore Street, the "Star-Spangled Banner" was sung by 1,500 Sunday school children ("Celebrations in General," *Washington Post*, 5 July 1894, 7).

New Jersey

Asbury Park: At the celebration of the Ocean Grove Camp Association, "a choir of 200 trained voices" sang "My Country 'tis of Thee" and Miss Sadie Marsh of Newark sang the "Star-Spangled Banner" ("Celebrations in General," *Washington Post*, 5 July 1894, 7).

New York

Brooklyn: At the 30th Ward, a band concert and "singing by a chorus of 500 school children and instru-mental music by the full regimental band of the First Artillery, U.S.A., as part of the morning exercises; "a concert will be given at the Flatbush insane asylum at 2 o'clock, with professional artists" ("Plans for the Fourth," *Brooklyn Daily Eagle*, 3 July 1894, 2).

Coney Island: At Brighton Beach, Edward Reményi,[811] violinist, "will play American and Hungarian airs at the Seidl Concerts"; Louise Natlie and Conrad Behrens, vocalists with the Sousa Band[812] at Manhattan Beach. The Sousa band played: America — The Blending of the Blue and Gray — A Calvary Charge — A Day in Camp — Dixie — The Great Republic[813] — The Liberty Bell[814] — Maryland, My Maryland — My Old Kentucky Home — Sheridan's Ride — The Songs Our Soldiers Sang in '63 [possibly a medley] — Star-Spangled Banner — Tone Pictures of the North and South[815] (*Brooklyn Daily Eagle*, 3 July 1894, 3; "Coney Island's Big Crowd," *New York Times*, 5 July 1894, 9).

Huntington: At the unveiling of a memorial shaft in honor of Nathan Hale in this Long Island town, a

Cover sheet of *The Liberty Bell March* (Cincinnati: John Church Company, 1893) by John Philip Sousa as arranged for piano by the composer. This march has had numerous performances on the Fourth of July beginning with the Sousa Band at Manhattan Beach on Coney Island on July 4, 1894 and 1895, and others in later years by the U.S. Marine Band (author's collection).

Bridge's Celebration," *New York Times*, 5 July 1894, 8).

Ohio

Cleveland: At a dedication ceremony for a soldiers monument, with Governor William McKinley presiding, "a chorus of 5,000 school children sang patriotic songs" ("Celebrations in General," *Washington Post*, 5 July 1894, 7).

Utah

Park City: The Park City Brass Band led a fund drive to mount a Fourth of July celebration and so that music could be included in the exercises ("The Fourth of July," *Park Mining Record*, 30 June 1894, 3).

Washington

Snohomish: At the Cathcart Opera House, a chorus of eight voices sang a newly composed patriot hymn by W.T. Elwell, "set to the air" of Wagner's *Lohengrin* (*Seattle Post–Intelligencer*, 4 July 1894, 8).

1895

Performances

California

Los Angeles: At Hazard's Pavilion, the Blanchard-Fitzgerald Band performed "Hail Columbia" and "Star-Spangled Banner," and Mrs. Celia Fisher sang the "Star-Spangled Banner" ("Now Celebrate" and "Patriotic Exercises," *Los Angeles Times*, 3 and 5 July 1895, 3 and 8, respectively).

Redondo: The Royal Hawaiian Band and Jules Levy, "the greatest living cornettist" performed ("City Briefs," *Los Angeles Times*, 2 July 1895, and 12 and 3 July 1895, 10).

Santa Barbara: The program prepared by the "Fourth of July Committee" included the following music: Grand overture, "America, Our Nation," Santa Barbara Military Band; "Professional March," band; grand medley of war songs, band; "Ye Olden Times," Santa Barbara City Band ("Programme for the Fourth," *Los Angeles Times*, 4 July 1895, 13).

local band performed "Hail Columbia" ("In Memory of Nathan Hale," *New York Times*, 5 July 1894, 4).

New York: The Tammany Hall Quartet sang "Columbia," "My Country, 'Tis of Thee," and "Star-Spangled Banner" at the "Tammany organization of the Ninth Assembly District," held at Abingdon Square (*New York Times*, 1 July 1894, 9); at Fort Prince Henry, near North Marble Hill "at the north end of Manhattan Island," a flag-raising ceremony at the ruins of the fort included "a procession of children, headed by the drum corps of Grammar School No. 66" and the Old Guard Band that "played 'The Star-Spangled Banner' and other national airs" ("King's

The Coulterville Brass Band, July 4, 1895, in Coulterville, California (courtesy of Northern Mariposa County History Center, Coulterville, California).

Illinois

Chicago: "The Cook County Cabinet of the National Union celebrated the Fourth of July yesterday morning in Central Music Hall with patriotic music and oratory.... The exercises opened with an organ voluntary by Louis Falk, and the first two bars of 'The Star-Spangled Banner' were vigorous.... After the Apollo Quartet had sung 'The Battle Hymn of the Republic,' which was warmly applauded and encored, Mr. Kavanagh read the Declaration of Independence. The quartet then sung 'Vive L'Amerique,' which was encored" ("Long May It Wave," *Chicago Tribune*, 5 July 1895, 10).

Maryland

Baltimore: Hail Columbia — Maryland, My Maryland — My Country 'Tis of Thee — The Star-Spangled Banner sung by "hundreds" of persons at Druid Hill Park. With orchestra, directed by Harry S. Emrich and organist Mrs. Charles H. Hael (*Baltimore Morning Herald*, 5 July 1895, 5).

Frostburg: "Gem of the Ocean," "Maryland, My Maryland," and "Star-Spangled Banner" sung by a choir at St. Michael's Church ("4th at Frostburg," *Cumberland Evening Times*, 5 July 1895, 1).

Hagerstown: "Strains of national airs" were played by the First Hose Fife, Drum and Bugle Corps on the roof of the First Hose Company's building to announce the start of Independence Day. Then "the exercises began with music by the Boonsboro Band. The parade included these ensembles, as well as the Keedysville Band and the Drum Corps of Chambersburg (*Baltimore Morning Herald*, 5 July 1895, 7).

Missouri

Lecoma: The Lake Spring Brass Band performed ("Program," *Rolla New Era*, 29 June 1895, 1).

New Jersey

Rahway: The Rahway Cornet Band marched alone in the pouring rain even though the city parade was canceled because the band wanted to be paid for their services. The Union County roadsters informed the band members that they would not be paid unless the band marched

over the route of the parade and to play as often as though the parade was taking place, and, on arriving at the roadsters' grounds, to go through the entire advertised concert. It was pouring rain at the time, but the band started. They passed through the principal streets, playing march music and followed by a few hardy urchins who did not appear to mind the rain. On arriving at the grounds, the members of the band were wet and bedraggled, but took their places in the bandstand and started in. The first two numbers of the programme were gone through, when five members of the band declared they could stand it no longer and would have to go home. There was a committee of roadsters on hand to check off the numbers on the programme as they were played, so that the work would not be shirked. The desertion of the five members threw the rest of the band into a position where they were worse off than ever, for the contract called for eighteen pieces, and, as nineteen had turned out, but fourteen remained on the stand. This settled matters, and the leader ordered his men home. Members of the band say they will commence a lawsuit against the roadsters to recover $54 for the work done. ["Musicians and Wheelmen at Odds," *New York Times*, 5 July 1895, 1].

New York

Brooklyn: Nolan's Band at Jackson Hall, near Myrtle, at the Andrew Jackson Democratic Club of the Seventh Ward event (*Brooklyn Daily Eagle*, 3 July 1895, 14); Ulmer Park, "Professor McGarry's Orchestra at the Brooklyn Letter Carriers celebration (*Brooklyn Daily Eagle*, 3 July 1895, 4); at the Logan Club event at their club house, Logan Quartet sang: Star-Spangled Banner — Columbia — America ("Plans for the Glorious Fourth," *Brooklyn Daily Eagle*, 3 July 1895, 2)

Coney Island: At Manhattan Beach, Sousa's band gave two concerts, with Conrad Behrens, bass, and Marie Barnard, soprano, as soloists. Afternoon: Overture, *Jubal — Grand Fantasia* (Weber) — *My Old Kentucky Home* (Dalby) — Excerpts from *Lohengrin* (Wagner) — bass solo, Patria; My Native Land (Mattei)[816] — Second *Hungarian Rhaps*ody (Liszt) — symphonic poem, *The Chariot Race* (Sousa) — *Paraphrase on Dixie* (Mollenhauer — soprano solo, Enchantress Waltz (Arditi)[817] — intermezzo, *Springtime* (Thome) — march, *The Liberty Bell* (Sousa) — humoresque, *The Band Came B*ack (Sousa) — The Star-Spangled Banner

Evening: Overture, *The Jolly Students* (Suppé) — night scene, *Tristan and Isolde* (Wagner) — fantasia, Songs of Other Days (Foster) — bass solo, Leporello aria from *Don Giovanni* (Mozart) — scenes historical, *Sheridan's Ride* (Sousa) — *Pasquinade* (Gottschalk) — soprano solo, Venzano Valse (Venzano) — humoresque, *The Band Came Back* (Sousa) — The Star-Spangled Banner ("Music for the Fourth," *Brooklyn Daily Eagle*, 3 July 1895, 10; see also, *Brooklyn Daily Eagle*, 5 July 1895, 4).

Freeport: The Freeport Cornet Band performed at the residence of James K. Meade ("The Fourth on Long Island," *Brooklyn Daily Eagle*, 3 July 1895, 7).

Hicksville: The Hicksville Brass Band performed in the town parade ("Programme at Hicksville," *Brooklyn Daily Eagle*, 3 July 1895, 7).

Point of Woods: At a Chautauqua event, a newspaper noted a "concert by Professor Koerner's Patchogue Brass Band. Miss Ina M. Lawson, concert soprano, of Brooklyn, and Mrs. Wilmot M. Smith, wife of the county judge are the soloists. They will sing patriotic airs" ("The Fourth on Long Island," *Brooklyn Daily Eagle*, 3 July 1895, 7).

1896

Publications

"A Fourth of July Love Song." First line: "Far from the picnic's hum and buzz" (*Milwaukee Sentinel*, 6 July 1896, 6).

Performances

California

Los Angeles: Bands that performed included: Seventh Regiment Band on the balcony of the Nadeau Hotel; Los Angeles Military Band on the balcony of the Hollenbeck Hotel; Pasadena City Band at Westlake Park in the evening; Orange City Band (twenty instruments) at Central Park with performances of "The Illinois Battleship," "Seminole March," a medley, "Mixed Drinks," a cornet solo, "Warrior's Dream" and various other tunes ("Band Concerts," *Los Angeles Times*, 5 July 1896, 10).

Ventura: The city parade included the Ventura City Band, Veteran's Fife and Drum Corps, directed by Sam Kutz, Santa Barbara Military Band, and Ojai Band. The "Star-Spangled Banner" was sung by a "grand chorus of 200 voices"; "Red, White, and Blue," Miss Eileen Sanborn and chorus; "Battle Hymn of the Republic" and "America," chorus. ("Ventura County," *Los Angeles Times*, 5 July 1896, 15.)

Illinois

Chicago: Two monster concerts took place in the Coliseum building for raising funds to erect a bronze statue of the American composer George F. Root to be placed in a city park. The afternoon concert included a choir of 1200 children, led by William L. Tomlins and Frederick W. Root, son of the composer. The evening concert included a chorus of 1200 men and women, including members of the Apollo Club and Mendelssohn Club. A military band of 100 instruments and the Second Regiment Drum, Fife and Bugle Corps accompanied the chorus.[818] Soloists included Genevra Johnstone Bishop, J.M. Hubbard, J.G. Lombard, and John R. Ortengren ("Composer Root," *Los Angeles Times*, 3 July 1896, 2; "Honor to Composer Root," *Washington Post*, 3 July 1896, 7).

Missouri

St. Charles: A town celebration at the Fair Grounds was preceded by a morning parade led by the St. Charles Cornet Band ("A Grand Success," *St. Charles Monitor*, 6 July 1896).

New Hampshire

East Jaffrey: At the dedication of Clay Library, a celebration concert at 11 A.M. by the East Jaffrey Cornet Band was well received. At 2 P.M. 800 persons filled the tent on the common and the opening of the program was announced by Greissinger's Orchestra, "a well-known organization of the musicians of Jaffrey." At the conclusion of the exercises, "America" was sung by the audience (*Dedication of the Clay Library Building at East Jaffrey, New Hampshire, Saturday, July 4, 1896.* Concord, NH: Republican Press Association, 1896).

New York

Brooklyn: The cornerstone laying ceremony for the Bay Ridge Library was held and exercises included the singing of the "Star-Spangled Banner" and "America" by "the scholars of the Bay Ridge Public School" who joined with "the audience in the chorus" and a band ("News from the Suburbs" and "Bay Ridge Free Library," *Brooklyn Daily Eagle*, 3 and 5 July 1896, 3 and 24, respectively); on Decatur Street, Habernicht's Military Band performed "The Red, White and Blue" and "the Star-Spangled Banner" ("Decatur Street Patriots," *New York Times*, 5 July 1896, 8); at Prospect Park, a bronze statue of Gen. G.K. Warren was unveiled "near the plaza entrance" and music provided in the park was courtesy of the Twenty-Third Regiment Band:

"America"
March: *Colonel Langdon*, Alfred D. Fohs
Overture: *Jubilee*,[819] Von Weber (Introducing "My Country, 'Tis of Thee")
American Patrol, Meacham
Tarantelle, Alfred D. Fohs
Bass Trumpet Solo: *Variations on "Tramp! Tramp! The Boys are Marching"* (by Mr. J.G. Frank)
Overture: *Merry Wives of Windsor*, Nicolai
Tenor solo: "Let Me Like a Soldier Fall," Wallace[820] (By Mr. Walter H. McIlroy, solo tenor of the Cathedral of the Incarnation, Garden City, L.I.)
Concert Waltz: *Our Boys*, Alfred D. Fohs
Polonaise Militaire, opus 40, no. 1, Chopin
Finale: *The Union*, Harvey B. Dodworth

("No Fireworks at Fort Greene," *Brooklyn Daily Eagle*, 3 July 1896, 7); at Washington Park, Conterno's Band furnished this program:

"Star-Spangled Banner"
March: *Gettysburg*, Louis Conterno (Dedicated to Colonel H.W. Michell)
Overture: National airs, Wiegand
Waltz de Concert: *La Serenata*, Yaxone
Selection: *Erminie*, Jakobowski[821]
Patrol: *Salvation Army*, Holst
Selection: *College Songs*, Moses
Bolero: *Invisible*, Arditi[822]
Gems for the opera *Martha*, Flotow
Fantasia: *Recollections of the South*, Beyer

March: "Songs of the Day," arranged by Louis Conterno
"Hail Columbia"

("No Fireworks at Fort Greene," *Brooklyn Daily Eagle*, 3 July 1896, 7); at Winthrop Park, Halle's Concert Band provided this program:

March: *Old Glory*, R.L. Halle (to the Defender Syndicate)
Overture: *Light Cavalry*, Suppé
A Musical Tour Through Europe, Conradi (introducing the European national airs)
Waltz: *Moonlight on the Hudson*, Tobani
Recollections of the War, E. Beyer
Priests' war march from *Athalie*, Mendelssohn
Cornet solo, selected, R.L. Halle
Patrol: *America*, Meacham
"Shamrocks": *Potpourri of Irish Airs*, R.L. Halle
Medley: *A Jolly Night*, F. Beyer
Finale: "Hail Columbia"

("No Fireworks at Fort Greene," *Brooklyn Daily Eagle*, 3 July 1896, 7); at Tompkins Park, L. Borjes' Forty-Seventh Regiment Band performed these works:

Salutation: "The Star-Spangled Banner"
March: *American Republic*, Thiele[823]
Overture: *Cosmopolitan*, Prendiville
Waltz: *World's Fair, 1893*, Herman
Cornet solo: "Inflammatus," from *Stabat Mater*, Rossini, Mr. A. Schwarzkopf
National medley: *Scenes of the War*, Beyer
Overture: *American*, White
Caprice: *On the Mississippi*, Christy
Comique: *Rastus on Parade*, Kerry Mills[824]
Patrol: *Yankee Doodle*, Meacham
Potpourri: *Songs of Olden Days*, Rollinson
March Patriotic: *Cuban War*, Otto Langey
Finale: *Our Flag is There*

("No Fireworks at Fort Greene," *Brooklyn Daily Eagle*, 3 July 1896, 7); at the Lyceum in the Eastern District of Brooklyn, the Socialist Labor Party and various trade unions assembled for speeches with instrumental music under the leadership of Stephen J. Mummery, bandmaster. Members of the International Maennerchor sang the "Marsellaise" and other songs, including a socialist parody of "My country 'tis of thee": first line, "My country said to be" ("Socialist Labor Parade," *Brooklyn Daily Eagle*, 5 July 1896, 24).

Coney Island: At the Brighton Beach Hotel, the Seidl Orchestra and Seidl Society Chorus included two concerts: Afternoon: Sacred march — "Prophet" (Meyerbeer — Overture, "William Tell" (Rossini — Wedding chorus from "Lohengrin" (Wagner), Seidl Society Chorus — Fantasia, "Cavalleria Rusticana" (Mascagni) — Largo (Handel), violin solo, Henry Schmitt — Second polonaise (Liszt) "Jerusalem" from *Galia* (Gounod, Seidl Society Chorus) — "Bal Costume" (Rubinstein), (a) Toreador et Andalouse (b) L'enolle du Soir (c) Les Tambours Royal — "America," national anthem, Seidl Society Chorus. Evening: Prelude — Aragonaise and the Toreadors from "Carmen" (Bizet) — Spanish dances from "Le Cid" (Massenet): (a) Castillane (b) Aragonaise (c) Navarraise — Overture, "Tannhauser" Wagner — Bridal chorus (Cowen), Seidl Society Chorus — Traumerei (Schumann) — Intermezzo from "Cavaleria Rusticana" (Mascagni) — "Invitation to the Dance" (Weber), orchestration by Weingartner — "The Lost Chord" (Sullivan), orchestration by Reitzel — Wedding chorus from "Lohengrin" (Wagner), Seidl Society Chorus — "First Rhapsody" (Liszt) — "America," national anthem, Seidl Society Chorus ("The Day on the Beach," *Brooklyn Daily Eagle*, 5 July 1896, 11).

Mamaroneck: At the town's ceremonies, "singing was by the village school children, under the direction of Miss W.S. Palmetier" ("Flags, Fireworks, and Speeches," *New York Times*, 5 July 1896, 9).

Oyster Bay, Long Island: On the occasion of the dedication of a new liberty pole, an audience of 2,000 sang "America," "The Star-Spangled Banner," and "Columbia, the Gem of the Ocean."

Choirs from the following churches led the singing: Methodist Church, Miss Annie Cheshire, organist; Baptist Church, Miss Wright, organist; Presbyterian Church, William L. Swan, organist, and St. Dominick's Church. The Oyster Bay Band, N.H. Disbrow, leader, and the Oyster Bay Amateur Band led by Samuel Underhill also added to the musical part of the exercises.

One of the bands played "Hail Columbia" ("New Liberty Pole," *Brooklyn Daily Eagle*, 5 July 1896, 24).

Saratoga: At the Daughters and Sons of the American Revolution celebration at Convention Hall: "Music, 'Hail to the Chief'"; "'Star-Spangled Banner,' [recited] by Miss Sarah M. Weeks of St. Albans, Vt. and sung by the audience, led by Miss Lillie Berg of New York City"; "music, 'Hail Columbia'"; "music, 'Home and Country,' sung by the audience, led by the Daughters of the American Revolution from Connecticut"; "music, 'Red, White and Blue'"; "music, 'Libertas et Patria,' sung by the audience, led by the Sons of the American Revolution from Illinois"; "The exercises were closed by all joining in singing 'My Country 'Tis of Thee'" ("Enjoy the Day in Saratoga," *Brooklyn Daily Eagle*, 5 July 1896, 11; *New York Herald*, 5 July 1896, 2, 12; *New York Times*, 5 July 1896, 17).

Utah

Manti: At the tabernacle, a children's chorus sang "Land of Washington," "Star-Spangled Banner," and "When Johnny Comes Marching Home Again"; Stephen Vorhees sang "Sword of Bunker Hill, and the audience sang "America" (Fourth of July Programme," *Manti Messenger*, 3 July 1896, 1).

'Ogden: A parade included the Ogden Business Men's Band, Charles Hiser, director — Horribles and Calithumpian Band from Fort Douglas, W.L.P. Marks Peyton, director — "combined drum corps," directed by A.T. Corey and L.B. Treseder. Morning Program:

Prof. Squire Coop, musical director; Charles Riser, band director. Hail Columbia, full chorus — selection, Ogden B.M. Band — medley of national airs, Ogden Choral Union — Red, White and Blue, full chorus — Oh, Ships of State, Sail On, Sail On, Mrs. Kate Bridewell-Anderson and chorus refrain — Glorious Song of Freedom, full chorus — Star-Spangled Banner, band and full chorus ("July 4 — Glorious Time Assured — July 4," *The Standard*, 4 July 1896, 1).

Provo: At the tabernacle, "the children of the district schools sang "Star-Spangled Banner" and "Hail Columbia." Mrs. R.R. Irvine, Jr., sang "Fair Land of Poland"[825] and Prof. W.E. Gillman played a clarinet solo ("Fourth of July Program," *Daily Enquirer*, 3 July 1896, 4).

Wisconsin

Thorp: A march to the grove was led by the Stanley City Band. The exercises included music by the band, and "America" and "Native Isle" sung by the Woodman Glee Club. The ceremony closed with a song by the Skandia Quartette ("Grand Fourth of July," *Thorp Courier*, 25 June 1896).

1897

Performances

California

Los Angeles: At the hall of the Friday Morning Club on the evening of July 3, "a quartette consisting of Misses Edna Foy, Beatrice Kohler, Vella Knox, and Sarah Simonds played Schubert's 'March Militaire' which was enthusiastically received" and "Largo" by Haydn. The song "Red, White and Blue" was sung by Capt. J.A. Osgood and the audience sang "America." ("Fifty Years Ago," *Los Angeles Times*, 4 July 1897, 12); at Fort Moore (also known as Fort Hill), a ceremony in commemoration of the first Fourth celebration in Los Angeles in 1847 took place and included "patriotic music, and the singing of old Spanish songs"[826]; at the "musical and literary exercises" held in the morning on July 5 at the Simpson Tabernacle, Mrs. Jessie Padgham Conant sang the "Star-Spangled Banner"; at the evening exercises at the Tabernacle, an orchestra performed and Mrs. Minnie Hance Owens sang a solo. Prof. C.S. Cornell, baritone, sang "The Grenadiers" followed by the Amphion Quartette who sang "The Flag Without a Stain." Miss Mary L. O'Donoughe served as accompanist ("Programme," *Los Angeles Times*, 4 July 1897, 19).

Illinois

Evanston: On Monday, July 5, a parade at 10 A.M. included the Evanston Military Band, that marched from City Hall to the university. The Program included:

"Recollection of the War." Beyer. Performed by the Evanston Military Band.

Music, Children's chorus of 1,000 voices under J.H. MacGregor.

Music, under the direction of W.F. Hynes. Männerchor of Evanston Musical Club

Music, "American Overture." Catlin. Band

Song, "America." Chorus, Männerchor, band, and audience.

("City's Three Days of Celebration," *Chicago Tribune*, 4 July 1897, 1).

New York

Brooklyn: At the Church of St. Agnes (Hoyt and Sackett Streets), a "grand celebration" will include music for a mass. "Professor Alexander McGuirk, the organist of the church, has been working hard to eclipse all former services in this edifice and has arranged the following programme":

"March of the Priests," Mendelssohn
"Ecce Sacerdes," Riga
"Kyrie," Haydn, no. 2
Gloria; Rossini
Offertory
"Tues Caderdos," Sterns, adapted by Alexander McGuirk
Credo, Rossini
Sanctus, Gounod
Agnes Dei, Haydn, no. 2
"March et Cortege," Gounod
Te Deum.

At the vesper service, at 7:30 P.M.:

March, Tannhauser, Wagner
Domini Dixit,[827] Mercadante
Confitebor, Beatus and Laudate Pueri, Le Jeal
Laudate Dominum, Giorza
"Tues Sacerdos," Sterns
Magnificat,[828] Emmerrig
O Sulutaris, Pecher
Tantum Ergo, Millard[829]
"Coronation March," Meyherbeer [sic].

"The soloists will be Miss Anna F. Murray, soprano, of the Hartford, Conn., Cathedral; Miss Marie L. Clary, alto; A.P. McGuirk and P.E. Arencibia, tenors, and John C. Dempsey, basso. A chorus of fifty voices and an orchestra of fifteen pieces will assist in the rendering of the mass. The organist will be Charles J. Stupp" ("Father Duffy's Jubilee," *Brooklyn Daily Eagle*, 3 July 1897, 16).

Coney Island: Sousa's Manhattan Beach concerts features performances of his march *The Stars and Stripes Forever*[830] and the premiere of *Fanfare Militaire* [op.40] by Joseph Ascher ("Summer Amusements," *Brooklyn Daily Eagle*, 3 July 1897, 7).

Elizabethtown: At Hand Park on July 5, the Westpoint Military Band performed during the day and the Westport Orchestra (8 instrumentalists) "for dancing in the evening" (*Elizabethtown Post*, 24 June 1897, 1).

Schroon River: At Root's Hotel on July 5, the Moriah Center Brass Band was scheduled to perform (*Ticonderoga Sentinel*, 17 June 1897).

Williamsburg: H.T. Humpstone sang the "New National Hymn" written by Thomas Wentworth Higginson, at the New England Congregational Church, South Ninth Street (*New York Times*, 5 July 1897, 3).

Pennsylvania

Philadelphia: "Die Ehre Gottes" (Beethoven) sung by the "united German singing societies" at Independence Square ("A Glorious Holiday It Was Indeed," *Philadelphia Inquirer*, 6 July 1897, 1).

Utah

Ogden: At Lester Park, the Ogden City Brass Band provided music for the dance held there ("The Fourth of July Holiday," *Ogden Standard Examiner*, 6 July 1897, 5).

1898

The Trans-Mississippi and International Exposition held in Omaha, Nebraska, was a significant event in 1898 that introduced a wide array of musical performers and ensembles to residents in this western city. The fair ran from June 1 through November 1, and highlighted the development of the territories west of the Mississippi River to the Pacific Coast. Over 2.5 million people viewed over 4000 exhibits. The featured musical ensembles for opening day were the U.S. Marine Band and Theodore Thomas Orchestra. The Fourth of July events included four concerts throughout the day with three performances by the Fourth Regiment Band on the Grand Plaza and Government Building and the Theodore Thomas Orchestra in the Auditorium.

Performances

Alabama

Mobile: This city celebrated the Fourth, the first time in 38 years that included fireworks, "a tremendous parade" and "bands of music." At the exercises held in Blenville Square, the audience sang "America" and "The Star-Spangled Banner" ("Mobile's Demonstration," *Los Angeles Times*, 5 July 1898, B4).

California

Santa Barbara: At Burton Mound, the Santa Barbara Concert Band performed "Columbia" and "America"; Alice Todd-Delmar sang "The Red, White and Blue"; a double male quartette sang "The Flag Without a Stain" and "The Star-Spangled Banner"; at the Plaza del Mar, "a patriotic open-air concert by the Santa

30111 PIANO SOLO Pd Add	.50	35233 TREBLE VOICES (TWO PART)	.12
30112 PIANO DUET	.75+	35234 SCHOOL CHORUS (S.A.B.)	.10
30113 PIANO, SIX HANDS	1.00	35260 MIXED VOICES	.10
30114 SONG FOR MEDIUM VOICE	.60	35428 MEN'S VOICES (Arr. Tidmarsh)	.15
30552 PIANO SOLO (SIMPLIFIED)	.50	30883 Bb CORNET (or CLARINET) SOLO	
30862 TWO PIANOS, FOUR HANDS		WITH PIANO ACCOMP. (Arr. Page)	.65
(Arr. Zadora)	1.00	30886 MARIMBA AND PIANO	
35119 MEN'S VOICES	.12	(Arr. Edwards)	.75
35232 UNISON SCHOOL CHORUS	.10	34002 BAND (STANDARD) .75 (SYMPHONIC) 1.50	
		34011 ORCHESTRA	1.15

THE JOHN CHURCH COMPANY
THEODORE PRESSER CO., DISTRIBUTORS
BRYN MAWR, PENNSYLVANIA

C   120–30111   .50

"The Stars and Stripes Forever" by John Philip Sousa ranks among the most popular pieces performed on the Fourth of July during the twentieth century to the present. The work was composed in 1896 and published in the following year. Shown is the cover page for the 1897 piano solo version printed by The John Church Company (author's collection).

Barbara Concert Band ("Santa Barbara County," *Los Angeles Times*, 5 July 1898, A11).

Colorado

Durango: The program for the day included a concert at 4:30 P.M. by the Smelter City Band ("Durango Will Celebrate," *Durango Wage Earner*, 30 June 1898, 3).

District of Columbia

At the E Street Baptist Church [by 1902 renamed Temple Baptist Church], Miss Mattie Wade sang the "Star-Spangled Banner" (*Evening Star*, 4 July 1898, 12).

Georgia

Atlanta: "Oratory and music will unite to give soulful expression to the memories which the day evokes" at the Columbia Theater. "Music for the occasion will be furnished by the Fifth Infantry Band [of Fort McPherson] .... This is the time for Atlanta to exhibit outwardly the patriotism which feeds her blood and to show to the world that she fully understands how the Fourth of July ought to be observed" ("Atlanta to Celebrate," *Atlanta Constitution*, 3 July 1898, 16).

Macon: With Governor William Y. Atkinson in attendance, a flag ceremony at Central City Park, included "a chorus of 500 school children" singing "The Star-Spangled Banner," and a regimental band performing martial music "and the children joining in the choruses" ("Atkinson Will Review Ray's Men," *Atlanta Constitution*, 4 July 1898, 6).

Maryland

Baltimore: "Star-Spangled Banner" sung by a "chorus of 500 voices" ("Picnics in the Park," *Baltimore Morning Herald*, 5 July 1898, 4).

Emmittsburg: At a flag-raising ceremony, "America," "Columbia, the Gem of the Ocean," and "Star-Spangled Banner" were sung (*Baltimore Morning Herald*, 6 July 1898, 8).

Mississippi

Vicksburg: This city celebrated the Fourth the first time in 36 years and the revelry included brass bands that played "national airs" ("Vicksburg Celebrates," *Los Angeles Times*, 5 July 1898, B4).

Nebraska

Omaha: The Independence Day concerts for The Trans-Mississippi International Exposition included the following programs:

11 A.M. Fourth Regiment Band and Exposition Chorus-Grand Plaza
3 P.M. Fourth Regiment Band in the Government Building
  March, "Bartholdi" Giovanni E. Conterno
  Overture, "America" Theo. Moses[831]
  Fantasie, "Auld Lang Syne" Dalbey
  Waltz, "Jolly Fellows" Robert Vollstedt
  Medley Overture, "A Good Thing" Beyer
  Characteristic, "The Goblin's Frolic" O'Neill
  Grand Selection, "The Beggar Student" Milloecker
  "Star-Spangled Banner" Key
7 P.M. Fourth Regiment Band on the Grand Plaza
  March, "Commander-In-Chief" Horst
  Overture, "From the Sunny South"[832] Isenman
  Waltz, "Haunting Eyes" Theo Tobani
  "Hungarian Fantasie" Herman
  Medley, "Crème de la Crème" Laurendeau
  Galop de Concert, "Infernal" Béla Kéler[833]
  "Tone Pictures from North and South" Bendix
  "America" Key
8:15 P.M. Theodore Thomas Orchestra-Auditorium

(Grace Carey, *Music at the Fair! The Trans-Mississippi and International Exposition. An Interactive Website* (2006), 28). <http://digitalcommons.unl.edu/cgi/viewcontent.cgi?article=1003&context=musicstudent>

New York

Brooklyn: At Prospect Park, the Forty-Seventh Regiment Band, led by Louis Borjes, performed the following program:

Star-Spangled Banner
March, "American Republic," Henry H. Thiele
Overture, "America," ten national airs, M.C. Meyrelles
Selection, "Grand Medley of War songs," E. Beyer
Cornet solo, "Grand American Fantasia," performed by William Jaeger
Fantasia, "Soldier's Life," Béla Kéler
Selection, "Tone Pictures of the North and South," Bendix
Waltz, "Columbian Exposition," Herman
Descriptive fantasia, "Way Down South," L.P. Laurendeau
"American Patrol," Meacham
March, "The Stars and Stripes Forever," Sousa.
["Fun For All To-Morrow," *Brooklyn Daily Eagle*, 3 July 1898, 12].

Coney Island: At Manhattan beach, Victor Herbert's band played patriotic airs throughout the day ("To Celebrate the Fourth," *New York Times*, 3 July 1898, 7).

New York: The Educational Alliance celebrated in their auditorium at East Broadway and Jefferson Street with "a musical and literary programme, consisting of patriotic airs" and "cornet solos by Thomas Clark" ("Educational Alliance to Celebrate," *New York Times*, 3 July 1898, 7); at Corlear's Hook Park, John Link's military band performed: a march titled "Under the Double Eagle," by Wagner and an overture, "Fantasia on American National Airs," by Theodore Moses Tobani. A work for cornet titled "Young America," with variations, composed by Jules Levy, was performed by W.S. Mygrant[834] (*Brooklyn Daily Eagle*, 3 July 1898, 12).

Pennsylvania

Pittsburgh: The dramatic overture *Melpomene* by George Whitefield Chadwick (1854–1931) had its Pittsburgh premiere at the Exposition Auditorium for a meeting of the National Congress of Musicians. The Thomas Orchestra, with Chadwick conducting, performed the work.[835]

Washington

Seattle: A Canadian military band marched in a parade performing "The Red, White and Blue" and other American tunes ("Stockton's Eagle Screams," *Los Angeles Times*, 5 July 1898, B4).

England

London: "Star-Spangled Banner" sung by Zipporah Montieth at the Congregational Church near Stepney Green ("Hearty British Feeling," *Los Angeles Times*, 5 July 1898, B4).

1899

Performances

California

Rodondo Beach: The Seventh Regiment Band performed (*Los Angeles Times*, 4 July 1899, 1).

Connecticut

Durham: On the evening of July 3 in the Congregational Church, the following music was performed:

Bi-Centennial Hymn — "God, we own thy gracious hand." Roster of Durham Men in the Wars, Mr. E.N. Brainerd
Hymn 760 — "Love divine, all love excelling."
Bi-Centennial Ode, Mr. Wedworth Wadsworth
Solo, Miss Susanne Mathewson
Hymn 1284 — "Who are these in bright array?"
Solo, Miss Susanne Mathewson
Hymn 164 — Quartette — "Softly now the light of day."
The Doxology.

On July 4 in Durham, at 10 A.M., music was provided by the National Band of Wallingford. The Bi-Centennial exercises on the Green included music by the band; Singing — "My Country, 'Tis of Thee"; "Mine eyes have seen the glory of the coming of the Lord." Later that evening, the fireworks were accompanied with music by the band. (1699. *Programme. Bi-Centennial*. Town of Durham, Connecticut: 1899).

District of Columbia

"America," "Independence" (a march), "Red, White and Blue," and "Star-Spangled Banner" were performed by the U.S. Marine Band at a meeting of patriotic societies held at the Columbia Theater ("Will Observe the Fourth" and "No Exercises at Monument," *Washington Post*, 1 and 3 July 1899, 2 and 7, respectively).

New York

Coney Island: At Bergen Beach, Rosati's Naval Reserve Band in the Palm Garden ("Bergen Beach," *Brooklyn Daily Eagle*, 5 July 1899, 8); at Manhattan Beach, Sousa's band gave two concerts on July 5:

Afternoon at 4
Overture, *A Summernight's Dream* (Suppé)
Grand scenes from *Cavalleria Rusticana* (Mascagni)
Excerpts from *The Bride Elect* (Sousa)
Prelude to *Lohengrin* (Wanger)
Gems from *The Jolly Musketeer* (Edwards)[836]
Valse, *Ernestine* (Chambers)
March, *Carillon de Noel* (new, Smith)
The Charlatan (Sousa)
Concert gallop, *The Sleigh Ride* (Jullien)
Evening at 7
Overture, *Sunlight and Shade* (Parker)
Ballet Suite, *The Nut Cracker* (Tchaikovsky)
Scenes from *Il Trovatore* (Verdi)
Valse, *Jolly Fellows* (Volstedt)
March, *Hands Across the Sea* (new, Sousa)

Brighton Beach: Anton Seidl directed a "grand chorus of selected soloists from the boy choirs of New York and Brooklyn" at the Music Hall (*Brooklyn Daily Eagle*, 3 and 5 July 1899, 4 and 8, respectively).

Long Island: At the hotel in Long Beach, the musical program presented by Gustave L. Kroll's Orchestra included: Grand national march, Foster; overture, "America," Tobani; fantaise, "The Old Kentucky Home," Langey; potpourri, scene from North and South, Bendix; patrol, comic, Asher; selection, college airs, Moses; overture, "American Empire," Langey; "Star-Spangled Banner" ("The Day at Long Beach," *Brooklyn Daily Eagle*, 5 July 1899, 8); at Greenport, the Greenport Cornet Band marched in the parade (*Brooklyn Daily Eagle*, 5 July 1899, 8).

New York: The Thirteenth Regiment Band performed the following program at Prospect Park:

March, *My Maryland* (W.S. Mygrant)[837]
Overture, *Grand American* (Bendix). Combing the national melodies of the North and South.
Selection, *The Circus Girl* (Caryll)[838]

Concert waltz, *American Citizen* (Witmakr)
Fantasia on "Dixie" (Langey). Variations for piccolo, clarinet and cornet, by Messrs. Rodriguez Belluci and S.O. Mygrant, respectively.
Grand fantasia, descriptive, *A Day in Camp* (Dodworth)
Indian War Dance (Bellstedt)
The Moorish Pageant, characteristic (Laurendeau)
Cornet solos, *When Dewey Comes Sailing Home* (Mills).[839] Written expressly for the *New York Sunday World*.
Tramp, Tramp, Tramp, with variations (Rollinson). Played by W.S. Mygrant.
Patrol, *American* (Meacham)
Excerpt, *Echoes of Arabic Song*, new, first time (Shon Kair). (a) "Warrior's Song" (b) "Sword Combat" (c) "Dance of the Brides" (d) "Sword Combat" (e) "Camel Song"; finale, "Grand Sword Combat."
["Nation's 123D Celebration," *Brooklyn Daily Eagle*, 3 July 1899, 16];

McCormick's Band[840] provided the following musical program at Fort Greene Park:

Salutation, Hail Columbia
March, *Hands Across the Sea* (Sousa)
Overture, *Festival* (Bach)
Intermezzo, *Dance of the Shadows* (Newman)
Fantasia on American Airs (Thomas E. King)
Selection, *Music Hall "Favorites"* (Seitz)
Selection from opera *Wang* (Morse)[841]
Melodies of the North and South (Bendix)
Selection from *The Runaway Girl* (Moncton)[842]
Negro oddity, *Hannah's Promenade* (Ellis)[843]
Medley, *The Winner* (Mackie)
["Nation's 123D Celebration," *Brooklyn Daily Eagle*, 3 July 1899, 16];

At Kings Park, Jamaica, the Forty-Seventh Regiment Band presented this program:

March, *Dewey's Return* (W. Keller)
Overture, *America* (Theo. Moses)
Waltz, *Alliance Musicale* (Gung'l)
Selection from opera *Faust* (Gounod)
American Patrol (Meacham)
Grand American Fantasia (Bendix)
Song, "The Palms" (Gabriel Fauré)
Southern pastimes, *Darkies Jubilee* (J.M. Turner)[844]
Frolics of the Sylphs (Voelker)
Southern Hospitality, descriptive (A. Pryor)
March, *American Republic* (H. Thiele)
Finale, *America*
["Nation's 123D Celebration," *Brooklyn Daily Eagle*, 3 July 1899, 16].

Utah

Ogden: The exercises at Lester Park included music by the Ogden City Band, vocal selections, including "America" and "Star-Spangled Banner," by a quartet, directed by Mrs. B.M. Short ("Fourth of July Program," *Ogden Standard Examiner*, 4 July 1899, 6).

Virginia

Falls Church: The Fort Myer Band and a choir provided patriotic music, the event sponsored by several committees, headed by town Mayor G.W. Hawxhurst ("Fourth at Falls Church," *Washington Post*, 2 July 1899, 13).

Philippines

Manila: Several hundred "children of Filipinos, Spaniards and Chinese" sang "America" at a large celebration there (*New York Times*, 5 July 1899, 5).

1900

A highlight of this year was the Glyndon Park celebration in Baltimore when Edwin Higgins delivered an address upon "the Life and Times of Francis Scott Key." Higgins mentioned the Baltimorean James Lick who built the Key Monument in Golden Gate Park in San Francisco. "Lick honored Key and his song because they helped to make his own achievements and benefactions possible."[845]

Performances

Colorado

Basalt: At the town's grove, a group of school children sang and there was "music all day by the Calathumpian Band." Hugh McCabe sang a "vocal solo" ("We Will Celebrate," *Basalt Journal*, 30 June 1900, 3).

Castle Rock: "In the morning there was music and good music, too, by the Castle Rock band.... The 10:30 train brought five members of the Cook Drum Corps, and music of fife and drum called the patriotic citizens together for the speeches at the Grand Army Campfire.... In the evening there was a dance at Woltzen's hall, and that, too, was a complete success, 66 numbers being sold. The music for this event was furnished by the Parker orchestra" ("'Twas a Glorious Day," *Castle Rock Journal*, 6 July 1900, 1).

Silverton: A parade was "headed by the San Juan Brass Band." Music for "a grand ball" that evening was provided by the Silverton Brass Band ("At Silverton," *Durango Democrat*, 5 July 1900, 3).

District of Columbia

The U.S. Marine Band was scheduled to perform at an event held in the Columbia Theater, sponsored by the Sons of the American Revolution. Mr. J.D. McFall was scheduled to sing "as a solo, the patriotic song 'The Sword of Bunker Hill'" ("Services by Society of the S.A.R.," *Washington Post*, 4 July 1900, 10); another article has an event by the Society of the Sons of the Revolution taking place at the Church of the Ascension with music provided by the Marine Band. To be sung was "A Hymn for the Fourth of July" and the "Star-Spangled Banner" by a choir accompanied by the band. The band also performed "The Lost Chord" and "Hail Columbia" ("Sons of the Revolution to Cel-

ebrate" and "Independence Day Service," *Washington Post*, 4–5 July 1900, 10 and 10 respectively).

Georgia

Atlanta: The Atlanta Fire Department Drum Corps, John Peel, drum major, marched in the city parade (*Atlanta Constitution*, 5 July 1900, 7).

Maryland

Baltimore: At Glyndon Park, music was provided by the Glyndon Cornet Band at the Temperance Camp Association event (*Baltimore Morning Herald*, 5 July 1900, 10).

Missouri

Kansas City: At the opening day of the Democratic National Convention, described as "an innovation in a National Convention," Mattie Fultoni (Miss Mattie Edyle Bowen of Fulton, NY) who took her stage name from the home of her birth, sang the "Star-Spangled Banner," "Maryland," and "America," accompanied by a brass band, to wild cheers from the audience (*New York Times*, 5 July 1900, 1).

New York

New York: A band at the Tammany Society meeting played "The Wearing of the Green" and "Rally Round the Flag, Boys." The ceremony ended with the singing of "The Star-Spangled Banner" ("Bryan Greets the Tammany Society," *New York Times*, 5 July 1900, 7).

France

Paris: John Philip Sousa provided music for the unveiling of monuments of George Washington and Marquis de Lafayette. On July 3, the band performed the European premiere of *The Stars and Stripes Forever* for the unveiling of an equestrian bronze statue of Washington. The band performed the U.S. and French national anthems. At a ceremony unveiling a statue of Lafayette on the following day with French president Émile Loubet in attendance, Sousa's band "played a new and specially composed march—*Hail to the Spirit of Liberty*." The band again played American and French national anthems, as well as *The Stars and Stripes Forever* ("Statue in Paris of Washington" and "Lafayette Statue Unveiled in Paris," *New York Times*, 4 and 5 July 1900, 10 and 7, respectively; Heintze, *The Fourth of July Encyclopedia*, 162–63 and 306–07).

1901

Publications

The Fourth of July Parade; or, Celebrating the Fourth. "Three act musical farce comedy, by Charles Melville Poor; libretto by C.A. Reade. 1901. Copy in Library of Congress.

Left: A statue of the French general Marquis de Lafayette, who fought in the American Continental Army during the Revolutionary War. On July 4, 1900, at the site for the statue, John Philip Sousa and his band presented the first European performance of his march "Hail to the Spirit of Liberty." The statue was recently moved from its location near the Louvre to its present site near the river Seine (photograph by Terry Heintze). *Right:* The Statue of George Washington on the Place d'Iena in Paris, France, where John Philip Sousa and his band performed "The Stars and Stripes Forever" for the unveiling of the monument on July 3, 1900 (photograph by George Arnold).

Our Glorious Banner; a Fourth of July Patriotic March by Lieut. Wm. H. Santelmann[846] of the U.S. Marine Band. [Chicago]: Hearst's Chicago American, 1901. For piano. Copy in the University of Alabama. The work was also published in the "Music Supplement," *New York Journal and Advertiser*, 30 June 1901.

Performances

Alaska

Nome: At Barrack Square, Edwin Engelstad sang the "Star-Spangled Banner" (*Nome News*, 6 July 1901, 1).

California

Los Angeles: Lillian Scanion sang the "Star-Spangled Banner" and the first verse of "The Blue and the Gray," the latter by popular demand from the audience (*Los Angeles Times*, 5 July 1901, 10).

Pomona: The patriotic exercises held at the corner of Third and Thomas streets, included music by the Pomona Band (25 instruments); "America" sung by the audience; music by a male quartet ("Pomona: Events of the Fourth," *Los Angeles Times*, 29 June 1901, 15).

San Diego: 300 voices sang patriotic songs at the public square ("At San Diego," *Los Angeles Times*, 5 July 1901, 11).

San Francisco: Concerts took place at Union Square, Washngton Square, and Columbia Square from 2–5 P.M. ("Concerts for the Multitude," *San Francisco Call*, 5 July 1901).

Santa Cruz: At the "Literary exercises" held on the Lower Plaza, Miss Kate Bauer was the singer and "during the day band concerts were given" ("Santa Cruz Programme," *Los Angeles Times*, 5 July 1901, 11).

OUR GLORIOUS BANNER
MARCH.

WM. H. SANTLEMANN.

Copyright 1901 by Sol Bloom. Foreign Copyright Secured.

The opening page of "Our Glorious Banner" (1901), a "Fourth of July patriotic march" by Lieutenant William H. Santelmann (the correct spelling), and shown in its arrangement for piano. Santelmann joined the Marine Band in 1887 and served as its director from 1898 to 1927. From 1903 to 1935, Santelmann's march was performed on the Fourth of July by the U.S. Marine Band on several occasions (courtesy "The President's Own" United States Marine Band, Washington, D.C.).

District of Columbia

U.S. Marine Band had several engagements that day. The band was scheduled to provide music for a meeting of the Sons of the American Revolution and "all patriotic organizations" at 10 A.M. in the Columbia Theater; elements of the band were to furnish music for a dance held at the Soldiers, Sailors and Marines' Club, 317 C Street in Northwest, in order to help raise funds to equip a gymnasium there. The event included an athletic meet; that evening at 6 P.M. on the White House grounds the band performed the following program:

> March, "True to the Flag."
>   von Blon[847]
> Overture, "Semiramide."
>   Rossini
> Selection, "The Ameer."
>   Herbert
> Saxophone solo, "American
>   Favorite," Moermans
> Musician, Jean B.H. Moermans
> Fragments from
>   "Mefistofele." Boito
> Waltz, "On the Beautiful
>   Blue Danube." Strauss.
> Grand March,
>   "Huldigung." Wagner.
> "Hail Columbia." Phile

("Army and Navy to Cross Bats," "White House Concert Programme" and "Patriotic Meeting July 4," *Washington Post*, 28–29 June and 2 July 1901, 8, 11, and 2, respectively).

New Jersey

Ocean Grove: In the Auditorium, "Prof. Morgan[848] and his choir and orchestra rendered patriotic hymns and songs" before an audience of 10,000. "When 'The Star-Spangled Banner' was sung the vast assemblage arose, and the 'Cambric' salute was given" ("Ocean Grove's Celebration," *New York Times*, 5 July 1901, 14).

New York

Coney Island: At the Manhattan Beach Theatre, the musical comedy *The Circus Girl* ("For Summer Amusement," *New York Times*, 30 June 1901, 10).

Colorado

Colorado City: George H. Crampton of Denver sang "a newly written patriotic song, 'The Land of the Free,'" by H.H. Godfrey (*Colorado Springs Gazette*, 4 July 1901, 7).

Iron Springs: Two "grand concerts" that included American music were given by the Iron Springs Orchestra (*Colorado Springs Gazette*, 4 July 1901, 3).

Telluride: "The band gave an open air concert about noon and another between 4 and 6 o'clock in the afternoon" ("Telluride's Fourth of July," *Daily Journal*, 5 July 1901, 1).

New York: At the Tammany Society meeting, scheduled were "national airs by Bayne's Sixty-Ninth Regiment Band," "patriotic songs" by the Tammany Glee Club, and the "Star-Spangled Banner," to be sung by the audience ("Tammany's Fourth of July," *Brooklyn Daily Eagle*, 30 June 1901, 35).

Utah

Castledale: At the Academy, Miss Hannah Larsen sang "The Star-Spangled Banner" and Mrs. Amelia Cluff sang "Loved and Saved"; a male quartette sang "Flag Without a Stain" and "My Country" ("The Glorious Fourth," *Emery County Progress*, 6 July 1901, 1).

Denmark

Copenhagen: "A reception, given on board the United States training ship *Hartford*, was attended by the Danish authorities and a number of American tourists. The bands on several Danish warships, when passing the *Hartford*, played "The Star-Spangled Banner," and the *Hartford's* band replied by playing the Danish national anthem." The *Hartford* band played at Tivoli Garden for those participating in the celebration there (*New York Observer and Chronicle*, 11 July 1901, 79, 28).

1902

Performances

California

Corona: Choruses sing patriotic songs, "also solos by Mmes. M.F. Patterson and F. Geith" ("Corona," *Los Angeles Times*, 6 July 1902, 8).

Los Angeles: Seventh Regiment Band played "patriotic airs" at Hazard's Pavilion ("Patriotism High at Hazard's Pavilion," *Los Angeles Times*, 5 July 1902, 10).

Ventura: The Whittier Band played patriotic selections at the Plaza and Miss Addie N. Meek of Los Angeles played "a cornet solo." ("Big Day for Everyone at Ventura Fair," *Los Angeles Times*, 5 July 1902, 14).

Yountville: At the Veterans' Home of California, the ceremony included the "Star-Spangled Banner" sung by Miss Millie Flynn, soprano of Trinity Church in San Francisco, and "Columbia, the Gem of the Ocean," sung by Miss Miriam Coney of San Francisco. Both sang duets of music by Stephen Foster, including "My Old Kentucky Home" and other ballads. "The singers were accompanied by Miss Mamie Warren and the home orchestra, under the leadership of Professor Fiedler. The exercises in Social Hall closed with the singing of 'America' in which the veterans joined" ("At the Veterans' Home," *San Francisco Call*, 5 July 1902, 7).

Colorado

Alma: "The Fairplay Band will supply music for

the day and the orchestra for the ball" ("Everybody!" *Fairplay Flume*, 20 June 1902, 2).

Breckenridge: The Woodmen Brass Band from Leadville led a parade "which traversed the principal streets of the town, dispersing patriotic music" ("A Cool Fourth," *Summit County Journal*, 5 July 1902, 5).

District of Columbia

The program for the celebration of the "Association of Oldest Inhabitants of Washington" held at John H. Small's house included the following music: "Star-Spangled Banner," Mrs. Adelaide Lynham Humphrey; "medley of national airs, Prof. I.A. Heald (late leader of the American Brass Band of San Francisco)," a selection sung by the Foundry Quartet (Mrs. Joseph Chun, soprano, Mrs. Adelaide Lynham Humphrey, contralto; Mr. Dana C. Holland, basso; Mr. Howard Butterworth, tenor; Mr. W.E. Cohen director). Other musicians that performed included: Louise B. Curtis, Mrs. E.D. Tracy, accompanist; piano solo, Miss Anna Schrader; vocal solo, Miss Helen Lackey; violin solo, Prof. William F. Huntress; solo, Mr. J.H. Cathell. At the conclusion, all sang "Auld Lang Syne." ("Birthday of Nation," *Washington Post*, 4 July 1902, 9.); on the Georgetown University grounds, the Newsboys' Band performed in the evening (*Ibid.*)

Georgia

Marietta: At the Chautauqua event, an afternoon concert by a band, orchestra and glee club ("Marietta Books Tillman," *Atlanta Constitution*, 2 July 1902, 4).

Maryland

Chevy Chase: A section of the U.S. Marine Band provided music at this small recreational setting just north of Washington, D.C. (*Washington Post*, 3 July 1902, 11).

Glen Echo: *At Freedom's Gate*, by Emile E. Mori,[849] and cited as "the great American Opera" was premiered with a cast of 16, a chorus of 32, and "full orchestra." The performance included "new scenery and original costumes." There were two performances that day. A newspaper reported that "the opera is of the romantic type, and deals with the stirring incidents of the war which Cuba raged so long and so bravely for independence." The production was scheduled to run until July 12 but was canceled prematurely due to the difficulty of patrons to access Glen Echo (*Washington Post*, 29 June, 3–5 July 1902, 30, 11, 7 and 7, respectively).

New York

Brooklyn: At Gerken's Ridgewood Grove, the Mozart Maennerchor held its annual picnic and the United Singing Societies, Robert Kramer, conducting, sang "Tag des Herrn," "Nach der Heimath," Studenten Nachtgesang," and "Daheim, Daheim." ("Big Outings Yesterday of Various Local Organizations,

The entrance to Glen Echo Park, Maryland, just outside Washington, D.C. The park was originally a Chautauqua site for the literary and music arts in the 1890s and early twentieth century. It was here that the opera *At Freedom's Gate* by local Washington composer Emile Mori was premiered on July 4, 1902. Advertised as the "great American Opera," the work was performed only a few times and was later forgotten. The park is administered by the National Park Service (author's photograph).

with Feasting and Music," *Brooklyn Daily Eagle*, 5 July 1902, 7); between Nostrand and Brooklyn Avenues, the citizens of Sterling Place had a block party with music provided by the Brooklyn Letter Carriers' Band. The band also performed during the fireworks display ("A Unique Celebration," *Brooklyn Daily Eagle*, 5 July 1902, 7).

Jamaica, Long Island: At Kings Park, Louis Borjes' Forty-Seventh Regiment Band performed these works:

Salutation, "The Star-Spangled Banner"
March, "When the Boys Are Marching By" (Blon)
Overture, "Raymond" (Thomas)[850]
Concert waltz, "Helmet of Navarre" (Charles R. Hirst)
Selection, popular airs (Von Tilzer)
Baritone solo, "A Little Boy in Blue" (Theodore F. Morse), with William Murray [vocalist]
Overture, "Morning, Noon and Night [in Vienna]" (Franz von Suppé)
Cornet solo (F. Glinz)
Fantasie, "Way Down South" (Laurendeau)

"Patrol of the Gnomes" (Richard Eilenberg)
Triumphale "Soldiers Return" (Lange)
Finale, "America"
["The Fourth on the Island," *Brooklyn Daily Eagle*, 3 July 1902, 8].

Ohio

Put-In-Bay: The Music Teachers National Association met for the final day on July 4 for its annual national meeting. In the morning, "at 10 o'clock the closing concert of the convention presented Ray Finel of Boston in a programme of songs. Mrs. M.D. Bentley of Detroit gave the opening numbers, and Miss Pauline Woltmann [contralto] of Boston, pressed into service on short notice, delighted the delegates with a group of songs by Brahms" ("Convention of Musicians, *New York Times*, 5 July 1902, 12).

Pennsylvania

Pittsburgh: Six hundred members of the United German Societies of Allegheny sing the "Star-Spangled Banner" for President Roosevelt in Schenley Park and a band played "Hail to the Chief" (*New York Times*, 5 July 1902, 1).

Utah

Castle Dale: The Dry Climate Band, directed by John Evans, provided music at the Social Hall and Mrs. Hector Evans sang "The Star-Spangled Banner" ("The Fourth at Castle Dale," *Emery County Progress*, 5 July 1902, 1).

Glenwood: The Glenwood Military Band was scheduled to perform at Glenwood Park ("Fourth of July Program," *Ogden Standard Examiner*, 3 July 1902, 5).

1903

In 1903 the American Medical Association (AMA) in Chicago began to methodically record injuries and deaths caused from the widespread use of Independence Day fireworks, toy cannons, and other explosives. The casualty results submitted to the AMA by medical personnel across the country numbered in the thousands and seemed to be an accurate indicator of just how extensive this problem had been for many years. The AMA recommended new legislation be adopted to ban the sale of fireworks to the general public. Gradually a reform movement commonly referred to as "safe and sane celebrations" emerged as other associations took up the cause. A principal goal was to find find new ways in which national pride and patriotism could be expressed. Organizations such as the Department of Child Hygiene of the Russell Sage Foundation worked with municipal authorities to find alternative activities such as musical and sporting events, daylight public fireworks staged by city officials, historic pageants, and expanded parades in which thousands of children and adults could take part.[851] By 1909–11 the movement had gained considerable momentum. Safe and sane celebrations were provided in many major cities and towns across the country. Washington and Cleveland had their first safe and sane celebrations in 1909, followed by Boston a year later. Music was an important component of these celebrations. In 1911, for example, Chicago "celebrated its second sane Fourth of July" with a "patriotic pageant, three miles in length" and "band concerts in the public parks." In Kansas City, "morning, afternoon, and evening concerts by thirteen bands in parks and squares in all quarters of the city were given by the municipality." Citizens of Cleveland "heard a concert by a band of 200 in the public square in the morning" and in Denver, "'My country, 'tis of thee,' was sung or hummed by more than 100,000 persons."[852]

A significant musician in the safe and sane movement was noted American composer Arthur Farwell who was appointed supervisor of municipal concerts in New York City in 1910–12 and who published a seminal article, "Music for the Fourth of July,"[853] in

which he called for an increased use of full orchestras for musical performances on the Fourth. He believed large orchestras were "immeasurably superior" than bands for providing patriotic concerts. "Its published literature is immensely broader and is up-to-date. It is much better adapted for accompanying voices than the band, and especially for accompanying part singing by chorus, for which the band is practically unavailable." Farwell's creative insight that orchestral concerts would "prove itself thoroughly satisfacutry for use out-of doors, requiring only a simply constructed sound screen or "shell" of wood to give its best effect" correctly forecasted the future of Fourth of July musical concerts that were given in outdoor amphitheaters across the nation. Farwell, leading the way with his musical composition *Hymn to Liberty*, premiered on July 4, 1911, in New York, " urged other composers far and wide to write musical compositions that would represent the best of "America's glory and freedom."

> This music should be obtained in one of two ways: either by the annual appointment, by the committee, of a composer (local, if possible) known to be capable of undertaking the task assigned him; or by instituting a competition, open, when practicable, only to local composers. The receiving or winning of this commission or award should be held as a great honor, and the successful one would be honored in some fitting manner during the celebration. The same is equally true of poets or authors participating.[854]

Farwell's ideas for engaging local composers to write works for the Fourth of July using their best "creative powers" in order to add to the national patriotic spirit of the events was no better exemplified that the Continental Harmony millennium-year project, a community-based music commissioning program beginning in 2000 by the American Composers Forum in partnership with the National Endowment for the Arts (NEA). Continental Harmony sponsored composer residencies in all 50 states and many composers chose to have their music, representing a wide range of symphonic, chamber, opera, choral, and ethnic genres, performed as part of Independence Day events.[855]

Performances

Alabama

Eufaula: This town celebrated "the old-fashioned way" and included "a programme of music, consisting of a fine brass band and one hundred voices" As "The Daughters of the Confederacy ... have the cornerstone of the proposed confederate monument laid on that day" ("In the Old-Fashioned Way," *Atlanta Constitution*, 4 June 1903, 7).

California

Santa Monica: A number of musical groups provide music for the town's gala celebration, including

Soldiers' Home Band, Seventh Regiment Band, Ontario Band, Garr Brothers Orchestra, Y.M.C.A. Fife and Drum Corps, and Imperial Male Quartette ("Santa Monica Will Celebrate the Fourth," *Los Angeles Times*, 28 June 1903, C1).

Colorado

Castle Rock: Fees paid to the Palmer Lake Band $25 and hotel expense for band $7.85 for their Independence Day performance sponsored by the Odd Fellows ("The Glorious Fourth," *Castle Rock Journal*, 10 July 1903, 5).

Mancos: The Mancos Band performed in the procession and at the grandstand "in the grove by the riverside," the "band and choir alternately rendered patriotic music" ("Our Celebration," *Mancos Times*, 10 July 1903, 1).

District of Columbia

A morning parade along Pennsylvania Avenue included: U.S. Marine Band, "the band from the cruiser *Topeka*, the Engineers' Band, the Second Cavalry Band and the whole corps of field musicians of the District combined" ("Marching Troops Win Applause of the City," *Washington Times*, 5 July 1903, 3); on the White House grounds, with Admiral Dewey in attendance, the U.S. Marine Band, dressed in white, performed the "Merseilaise" "as a mark of respect to the French ambassador, M. Jusserand," and E.D. Tracy directed children of the city's public schools in singing "My Own United States."[856] An adult choir, numbering 75 to 80 persons, sang the "Anvil Chorus" and the audience called for an encore. The audience sang "My Country 'Tis of Thee" and "The Star-Spangled Banner" ("The Fourth at the Capital," *New York Times*, 3 July 1903, 8; "The Official Programme," *Washington Post*, 4 July 1903, 12; "Greatest Fourth in District Annals," *Washington Times*, 5 July 1903, 4); a concert by the Marine Band at the White House included the following program:

> March, "Battleship Oregon" (Fulton)
> Overture, "Jubilee"[*Jubel Overture*] (Weber)
> Medley, *Sounds from the Sunny South* (Emil Isenman)
> Waltz, "Stories from Vienna Woods" (Strauss)
> March, *Our Glorious Banner* (Santelmann)
> March, *Thomas Jefferson*[857] (Santelmann)
> Descriptive, "A Comical Contest" (Godfrey)
> Patriotic Hymn, "Hail Columbia" (Fyles)

("Program Records," U.S. Marine Band Library); at the Christian District Endeavor Union at the Calvary Baptist Church, Mr. Percy S. Foster sang "The Battle Hymn of the Republic" and Miss Elizabeth Wahley[858] sang the "Star-Spangled Banner" ("The Endeavorers Celebrate," *Washington Post*, 4 July 1903, 12).

Georgia

Atlanta: The exercises were sponsored by the Joseph Habersham Chapter, Daughters of the American Revolution, in the hall of the house of representatives in the State capitol. "The chorus of high school girls, under the leadership of Professor B.C. Davis, sang 'America,' their voices filling the hall." The group also sang "The Star-Spangled Banner" ("Fourth Celebrated by Patriotic D.A.R.," *Atlanta Constitution*, 5 July 1903, A3).

Kentucky

Breathitt County (near Perry): On the grounds of Witherspoon College, the program included "organ music and Gospel hymns." The "recitations by the children" were "interspersed with patriotic music and hymns under the management of the Rev. Mr. Murdoch and his wife" ("The Fourth of July in the Kentucky Cumberlands," *Christian Observer*, 15 July 1903).

Maryland

Chevy Chase Lake: A section of the U.S. Marine Band gave a concert, 7:30–9 P.M., at this small recreational setting north of Washington ("Excursions," *Washington Post*, 2 July 1903, 14).

Glen Echo: "Patriotic airs by Haley's Band" at this recreational setting ("Excursions," *Washington Post*, 2 July 1903, 14).

Washington Grove: Following an address by Col. George A. Pearre, music was "sung by the Grove chorus choir of fifty voices, under the leadership of P[ercy] S. Foster, of Washington, D.C." ("The Fourth at Washington Grove," *Washington Post*, 24 June 1903, 4.)

Pennsylvania

Gettysburg: The Gettysburg G.A.R. Band performed "The Old North State," "Dixie," "Maryland, My Maryland," "My Country 'Tis of Thee," and "The Star-Spangled Banner" for Civil War Union and Confederate veterans ("Old Foes Met at Gettysburg," *Atlanta Constitution*, 4 July 1903, 5).

Utah

Manti: At the Tabernacle, a "Young Men's Brass Band" performed; "The Sword of Bunker Hill" sung by L.A. Lauber; "National Air" by Crawford-Stringham Orchestra and "Serenade" sung by Eloise Vorhees; a "mixed quartette" (Eloise Vorhees, Mrs. H.G. Bradford, L.A. Lauber, Nephi Bessey) performed (Fourth of July Celebration," *Manti Messenger*, 3 July 1903, 1).

1904

Performances

California

Los Angeles: At Westlake Park, the Woodmen of the World Band; at Central Park, Pacific Railway Band; at Eastlake Park, Deeble Band and Moore's Fi-

Original manuscript (first page) for piano solo arrangement of "Thomas Jefferson March" (1903) for band by William H. Santelmann, leader of the U.S. Marine Band, 1898–1927. This march was composed in honor of the Thomas Jefferson Memorial Association for its meeting at the Hotel Barton in Washington on April 13, 1903. The march received its first Fourth of July performance that year by the Marine Band at the White House (courtesy "The President's Own" United States Marine Band, Washington, D.C.).

singing two songs; an octet of vocalists singing patriotic songs ("Atlanta Chapter Celebrates," *Atlanta Constitution*, 5 July 1904, 8).

Maryland

Chevy Chase Lake: A section of the U.S. Marine Band[859] provided popular music at this recreational setting in an early evening concert ("Excursions," *Washington Post*, 30 June 1904, 11).

Missouri

St. Louis: The Universal Exposition of 1904 that celebrated the anniversary of the acquisition of Louisiana Territory had a parade that day with participants including the 26th U.S. Infantry Band and the Government School Indian Band. At Festival Hall, a full assemblage of persons, heard "selections on the grand organ by Charles Galloway," the official organist for the event. Ellery's Band performed at the State building of Missouri. At the Iowa State building, a morning organ recital by Mason Slade of Des Moines and "Professor Peck, of St. Louis," who led the audience in singing patriotic songs, were highlights. An afternoon organ recital was presented by H. Dyer Jackson of Quincy, Illinois. California and Illinois combined their exercises and "a notable event was the singing of 'My Own United States' by Mrs. E.B. Willis of California." David R. Francis, *The Universal Exposition of 1904* (St. Louis: Louisiana Purchase Exposition Company, 1913), 224–25.

New Jersey

Atlantic City: The Ladies' Symphony Orchestra performed at the Hotel Rudolf ("At Atlantic City," *Washington Post*, 3 July 1904, E6).

Virginia

Leesburg: Charles B. Hanford, "the actor," sang "The Star-Spangled Banner" and other songs (*Washington Post*, 5 July 1904, 5).

delia Band; at Echo Park, "South Park and Holenbeck Park Bands will be provided by Prof. Rykert" ("Plans for Fourth," *Los Angeles Times*, 30 June 1904, A6).

Ocean Park: Crown City Band of Pasadena ("Ocean Park," *Los Angeles Times*, 24 June 1904, A9).

Georgia

Atlanta: The Atlanta Chapter of the Daughters of the American Revolution celebrated at the Craigle house with a musical concert that included Ryals Connor playing a selection by Beethoven; Thomas Weaver singing "The Two Grenadiers" by Schumann and "Red, Red Rose" by Chadwick; Mrs. W.S. Conway

1905

Publications

"Hurrah for the Fourth of July." A Song for Every Home in U.S.A. March song. Words & Music by Arnt A. Aadne. Brooklyn, NY: Arnt A. Aadne, 1905. Piano and voice. First line: "The Best thriving nation in all the creation is truly said to be ours."

Performances

California

Hemet: Elsinore Band performed ("Hemet," *Los Angeles Times*, 4 July 1905, II8).

Oakland: A parade and exercises at the Macdonough Theater, included a male chorus of 16 persons, directed by Clement P. Rowlands, that sang "Stand by the Flag" and "Proudly as the Eagle" (by Louis Spohr). "America" was sung by the audience, led by Rowlands. Julian Edwards sang "My Own United States" ("Will Celebrate Nation's Birth," *San Francisco Call*, 4 July 1905, 4).

Ocean Park: At the exercises held at the Pier Avenue bandstand, Miss Bertha Amet sang the "Star-Spangled Banner" and a children's chorus sang patriotic songs ("Throngs Gather at New Baths," *Los Angeles Times*, 5 July 1905, III1).

San Mateo: The "literary exercises" included "a chorus of children" and an orchestra. Songs sung included "Columbia, the Gem of the Ocean" by the children and "The Star-Spangled Banner" by Miss E.W. Smith and children ("Hurrah for the Fourth," *San Francisco Call*, 5 July 1905, 3).

Vallejo: Surrounding towns celebrated in this city with a large parade having four bands and the Eagles Drum Corp. At the exercises "at a stand erected in front of the library building," Miss Carlin sang the "Star-Spangled Banner" and "the big assembly concluded the exercises by singing 'America'" ("Lively Day in Vallejo," *San Francisco Call*, 5 July 1905, 3).

Venice: Held its first Fourth of July celebration. The program included performances by Arend's Venice Band "of forty-two pieces, a patriotic chorus of 400 children [that sang "Hail Columbia,"] and solos by Mme. Genevra Johnstone Bishop, Sidney Lloyd Wrightson, [who sang "A Thousand Years, My Own Columbia"], and A.E. Walper,"[860] and "the grand Venice pipe organ" was a "feature of the day" ("Venice's First Fourth of July" "Throng Storms Fair Venice," and *Los Angeles Times*, 3 and 5 July 1905).

Yountville: "Mrs. Snyder Johnson, the gifted singer, touched the hearts of the old veterans with her magnificent rendering of the 'Star-Spangled Banner' and 'My Old Kentucky Home.' The sweet singing of Miss Peyton McAllister was well received" ("Men Who Followed the Flag Celebrate the Fourth," *San Francisco Call*, 5 July 1905, 3).

Colorado

Breckenridge: The Breckenridge Cornet Band provided music for the day ("Two Glorious Days," *Summit County Journal*, 8 July 1905, 5).

Golden: "There will be music in plenty, the Golden band playing for the Sunday school association at the park, while the military band from Fort Logan has been engaged by the firemen.... Before dinner there will be singing of national airs by the assembled crowd...." That evening Gray's orchestra was invited to perform music for a "grand ball" ("Big Celebration on the Fourth," *Colorado Transcript*, 22 June 1905, 1).

District of Columbia

At the Capitol, the U.S. Marine Band played a medley of Stephen Foster songs arranged by W. Paris Chambers (Berenice Thompson, "Music and Musicians," *Washington Post*, 8 July 1905, C5); at a celebration of the Daughters and Sons of the American Revolution celebration at the Memorial Continental Hall, "25 pieces of the U.S. Marine Band" played a number of works including *Washington's Inaugural March* "which has been discovered by Leader Santelmann, and was played for the first time in many years at the recent commencement exercises of George Washington University." Walter F. Smith led the band. In addition, the "Salute to the Flag" was sung by the children of the American Revolution descendants. George A. Prevost led the singing of the patriotic songs ("D.A.R. Patriotic Exercises," "Patriotic Orders to Join," and "D.A.R. Honor Flag," *Washington Post*, 30 June, 2 and 5 July 1905, 11, 9 and 2, respectively).

Maryland

Chevy Chase Lake: A section of the U.S. Marine Band gave an evening concert (*Washington Post*, 2 July 1905, T11).

New Jersey

Asbury Park: The Ocean Grove Festival Orchestra performed at the annual convention of the National Education Association and "concerts afternoon and evening by Arthur Pryor's Band ... Prof. Tali Esen Morgan will direct a big musical event with soloists of national renown" ("Fourth of July at Asbury Park," *Washington Post*, 17 June 1905, A8; *New York Times*, 5 July 1905, 4).

Utah

Huntington: Miss Luella Guymon sang the "Star-Spangled Banner" "in good style," and a quartet (C.R. Johnson, James Johnson, William Green, Jr., J.F. Wakefield, Jr., and Ellis Johnson) sang "My America" ("A Rousing Old Time at Huntington," *Emery County Progress*, 8 July 1905, 1).

Manti: At the Tabernacle, "America" was sung — violin solo by Eva Crawford — "The BYU Orchestra will be in attendance and will furnish some choice selections" ("The Fourth of July," *Manti Messenger*, 29 June 1905, 1).

Virginia

Falls Church: At a grandstand on the lawn of the Falls Church Inn, a choral society led by "Mrs. Dudley," and accompanied on piano by Miss Alice Noble, sang "The Miller's Wooing" and "America" ("Falls Church Celebration," *Washington Evening Star*, 5 July 1905, 12).

1906

Performances

Colorado

Craig: The Hayden Brass Band gave a concert ("The Fourth at Craig," *Yampa Leader*, 30 June 1906, 1).

District of Columbia

At the Oldest Inhabitants Association celebration at the country home of Crosby S. Noyes, Alton Farm, Mrs. Thomas C. Noyes (nee Dorothy Byrde Rogers) sang the "Star-Spangled Banner" and "Annie Laurie." The G.A.R. Glee Club sang "To the Old Country" and an orchestra played patriotic airs. All of the participants sang "Auld Lang Syne" ("Guests of Mr. Noyes," *Washington Post*, 5 July 1906, 7); the U.S. Marine Band ("entire membership," Santelmann conducting) performed a medley of Stephen Foster songs arranged by W. Paris Chambers at the U.S. Capitol. "One of the largest crowds ever assembled in Washington on a similar occasion enjoyed and applauded the patriotic strains and every number on the programme was enthusiastically encored. One of the best features of the concert was a grand potpourri of American melodies, arranged in a superb style for military band by W. Paris Chambers. This selection contains a great many of the old songs dear to all Americans, such as 'Suwanee River,' 'Dixie,' 'Old Black Joe,' 'Nellie Gray,' 'Old Kentucky Home,' 'Nellie Bly,' and 'Massa's in the Cold, Cold Ground.' Each one of the Stephen Foster gems was applauded in its turn, and when the grand finale came there was a burst of enthusiasm such as rarely has been witnessed at a band concert in Washington" (Berenice Thompson, "Music and Musicians," *Washington Post*, 8 July 1906, C5); the complete program of the U.S. Marine Band at the Capitol:

March, *The Stars and Stripes Forever* (Sousa)
Overture, "Jubilee" [*Jubel Overture*] (Weber)
Grand Fantasia, "Reminiscences of the South" (Chamoers/Rollinson)
Solo for cornet, "Columbia"[861] (Rollinson), Mus. Llewellyn
Waltz, *The Debutante Waltz* (Santelmann)
Humoresque, "A Comical Contest" (Godfrey)

Descriptive Galop, "A Trip on the Limited Express" (Downing)
"Star-Spangled Banner" (Key)
["Program Records," U.S. Marine Band Library].

Maryland

Chevy Chase Lake: A section of the U.S. Marine Band provides music in this recreational setting just outside D.C. (*Washington Post*, 3 July 1906, 4).

New Jersey

Newark: The final day of the 21st national song festival of the Northeastern Saengerbund of America, Carl Lenz, bund president, with 100,000 persons attending took place, and the Gesangverein Concordia of Wilkes-Barre, Pennsylvinia, won the top prize. Other groups that competed included: Junger Maennerchor of Philadelphia; Frank Schubert Maennerchor and the Kreutzer Quartet Club of New York; Arions and Germanias of Newark ("Song Festival Ends," *Washington Post*, 5 July 1906, 3).

New York

New York: At a celebration of Russian refugee children at the Educational Alliance on the evening of July 3, after a reading of the Declaration of Independence, the children sang "Our Own United States" and "America." A reporter noted that "although the words had been printed for them on their programmes, they were in English, and they floundered badly in the tune" ("Little Russans Here Celebrate the Fourth," *New York Times*, 4 July 1906, 7).

Oyster Bay: In a pouring rain President Theodore Roosevelt gave an Independence Day speech and a county band played "Hail to the Chief." Then everyone present including school children in the village, sang "The Star-Spangled Banner" ("President Spoke on in Drenching Rain," *New York Times*, 5 July 1906, 1–2).

Utah

Lehi: In the city pavilion, music included instrumental tunes by the Lehi Silver Band; male quartette (Samuel Jackson, Walter Woofinder, Roy Davis, and William Larson) singing "Flag Without a Stain"; solo by Dulcie Webb; quartette (Trysa Child, Sadie Davis, Isaac Fox, and Joseph Kirkham, singing "Star-Spangled Banner"; piano solo by Arevia Davis; duet by Sadie Davis and Birdie Stoddart; music by the Garland Silver Band ("Lehi Has Made Preparations for Big Celebration," *Salt Lake Herald*, 3 July 1906, 10).

Washington

Squalitchew Lake: This site in Pierce County is where Naval officer and explorer Charles Wilkes and his men gave the first Fourth of July celebration west of the Missouri River in 1841. This 1906 commememorative ceremony, and the unveiling of a monument to permanently mark the site, included the singing of "America" and the "Star-Spangled Banner," led by Dudley Eshelman, of Tacoma, Washington.[862]

1907

Performances

Alaska

Juneau: Thlinget Brass Band and drum (16 pieces) performed that day. Photograph, Alaska State Library, Historical Collection, in *Alaska's Digital Archives*.

Arizona

Flagstaff: The United States Indian School Band performed in this town.[863]

California

Los Angeles: At Central Park, the Majestic Band, Joseph Watson, leader, performed the following:

"Star-Spangled Banner."
March, "Victorious America" (The President). Tobani.
"Grand International Fantasia" (patriotic airs of two continents). T.H. Rollinson.
March, "War and Peace." Nick Brown.
"Hearts and Flowers."
Overture, "Poet and Peasant." Franz von Suppé.
"Sleeping Beauty Lullaby." Theo M. Tobani.
March, "The Peacemaker"[864] (America, Japan, Russia). Harry Alford
Solo, "The Star-Spangled Banner." Miss Isabelle Isgrig, dramatic soprano

At Eastlake Park, Moore's Fidelia Band, gave this concert:

March
"Grand American Fantasia" (national and patriotic airs). Herbert.
Waltz, "Philippino." Arr. by Greissinger.
"Sounds from England" (selection on English melodies). Tobani.
Polonaise, "Court Festival." Treukler.
Overture, "Jubel." Offenbach.
"American Patrol." Meacham.
Medley, "German Airs." Moses.
"Spanish Dance." Espinoza.
"The Stars and Stripes Forever" Sousa.

At Westlake Park, Rykett's Military Band presented this concert:

March, "Red, White and Blue." Arr. by Ripley.
Waltzes, "Queen of Hearts." Goetz.
Overture, "Belle of the Village." Bouillon.
Schottische, "Song and Dance." Casey.
Overture, "Fraternal." M.M. Snyder.
"Honey of the Southern Belles." Childs.
March, "Stars and Stripes Forever" Sousa.
Hymn, "The Marseilles." Beyer.
Medley, "Sweet Old Songs." Dalbey.
Selection, "Southern Plantation Songs." Arr. By Conterno.
Overture, "Happy Minstrels." Laurendeau.
"Star-Spangled Banner." Arr. by Ripley.

At South Park, the following "patriotic selections by Rykert's Military Band" No. 2:

March, "St. Louis Cadets." Laurendeau.
"Hail Columbia." Ripley.
"She Was Bred in Old Kentucky." Boettger.
Two-step, "Cheer Up, Mary."[865] Paley.
"Rally 'Round the Flag.'" Ripley.
"My Little Coney Isle,"[866] [and] "Down on the Farm."[867] Von Tilzer.
Medley waltz, "Mollie and the Baby." W.H. Mackie.
"On a Moonlight Winter's Night."[868] Powell.
"Introducing Carolina Diana." Durand.
"When the Flowers Bloom in Spring-time."[869] Evans.
"Star-Spangled Banner." Beyer.

At Hollenbeck Park, the Soldiers' Home Military Band gave a concert ("Speeches to Take Fireworks' Place," *Los Angeles Herald*, 3 July 1907, 8).

Colorado

Creede: "The Cow Boy Band of Creede has been engaged to furnish music throughout the occasion and will upon the arrival of the train in the morning assist in receiving our guests, and render a band concert while they are being assigned their quarters and getting located" ("Creede's Fourth of July Celebration," *Creede Candle*, 29 June 1907, 1).

Maryland

Chevy Chase Lake: A section of the U.S. Marine Band provided music for recreationers visiting this site (*Washington Post*, 4 July 1907, 4).

Minnesota

Deluth: "Flaaten's Third Regiment Military Band will play the following program of martial music on the Fourth":

March —"American Bugler." Frenling.
Overture —"America [Forever!]." Tobani
Comic —"Humoresque." [E.C.?] Wheeler
Southern Plantation Medley. Conterno
Intermezzo "Cherry." Alberth
Intermission
Two Step —"The Free Lance." Sousa
Patrol —"Blue and the Gray." Dalhey
"College Overture." Moses
Characteristic march —"Paddy Whack." Lampe[870]
Evening
March —"Stars and Stripes Forever" Sousa
Overture —"America." Tobani
Selection —"When Johnny Comes Marching Home." Edwards
American Fantasia —"Gems of Stephen Foster." Tobani
Remembrance from "Army Chaplain." Millrocker
Two Step —"With Trumpet and Drum." Waldon
Intermezzo "Iola." Johnson[871]
Cornet Solo —"Good Night Beloved, Good Night." Fay[872]

Mr. Chas. Helmer [cornet]
Gallop — "Always Welcome." Lumby
["Big Crowd is Anticipated," *Deluth News Tribune*, 3 July 1907].

New York

New York: Alexander Szalay and his Tzigane Orchestra gave a concert of "popular and patriotic selections" at the Harlem Casino (*New York Times*, 5 July 1907, 7).

Utah

Price: At 10 A.M. at the town hall, the exercises included the following music:
"America" by the congregation
Music — Price Band
Song, "Yankee Doodle Boy," Philip Flack
Double Quartette, "The Homesick Yankee"[873]—
Vera Fausett, Maud Wilson, Vesta Robb, Alice and Jesse Fouits, Ella Empey, Effie Purgess.
Solo, "The Sword of Bunker Hill" — L.A. Lauber.
Piano Duet — Mrs. J.A. Crockett and Gladys Nelms
Vocal Trio — Grace Fausett, Elizabeth Crockett and Ivan Mathis
Vocal Duet, "Sweet Summer," Ada Shiner and Ella Empey
Music by the band
("Fourth of July at Price," *Eastern Utah Advocate*, 11 July 1907).

Virginia

Norfolk: A Jamestown Exposition sponsored by the Thomas Jefferson Memorial Association of the United States with Woodrow Wilson, guest speaker, was scheduled to occur on July 4 and to include a "reunion of the descendents of the signers of the Declaration of Independence." The program included a parade of "army and naval forces" with a rendition of "America" to be played "by all bands in concert, to be followed by 'salute to the colors.' ... The band [unnamed] will play 'The Thomas Jefferson March,' inscribed to the Memorial Association by Lieut. William Santelmann, leader of the United States Marine Band." Also, "The Star-Spangled Banner" was to be "sung as a solo and chorus, the solo by a lineal descendent of one of the signers." The formal ceremony "opened with the singing of "America" by a chorus of several hundred school children, and music by the Mexican National Band, now visiting the exposition." The children also sang "Columbia" and "other patriotic songs." There were evening band concerts also scheduled ("Sons of Signers to Unite" and "Jail for Trust Heads," *Washington Post*, 20 May and 5 July 1907, 14 and 4, respectively).

1908

Publications

"On Independence Day Give Three Cheers for the Fourth of July." By Tom Kelley; lyrics by Earle C. Jones. First line: "Hark! Awake! Ye freemen rally." For voice and piano. NY: Jos. W. Stern & Co., 1908.

Performances

California

Berkeley: At the Greek Theatre on the campus of the University of California, the Third U.S. Artillery Band, Armand Putz, bandmaster, performed the following program:

March, "Coronation" from "The Prophet." Meyerbeer
Overture, "Hungarian Lustspiel." Béla Kéla[874]
Cornet solo, "Fantasia Columbia." Rollinson.[875] ([performed by] chief trumpeter Gaudet)
Medley of southern plantation songs. Conterno
Descriptive military fantasia, "The Ambuscade." Laurendeau
[Intermission] "Mr. L.A. Larsen sang "My Own United States, with full band accompaniment."
Excerpts from "The Bohemian Girl." Balfe
Patrol, "The Blue and the Gray." Dalby
"Chorus of the Romans" (from "Herodiade"). Massenet
Selection of popular songs. Stearns.
"Reminiscence of 1863." Calvin
Finale, "The Star-Spangled Banner." Key
["Military Program at Greek Theater," *San Francisco Call*, 4 July 1908, 8].

San Francisco: At Golden Gate Park Stadium, 10,000 school children were invited to sing, under the direction of Miss Estelle Carpenter, "musical director of the school department." Songs included: America — Star-Spangled Banner — Columbia the Gem of the Ocean — My Own United States — San Francisco Forever ("Call Children to Sing on July 4," *San Francisco Call*, 1 July 1908, 8).

District of Columbia

At the opening of the new Municipal Building with the Vice President in attendance both the Marine and National Guards Bands provided music. In addition there was "a male chorus of about 250 trained voices from the Washington Saengerbund and the Arion Singing Society, the Young Men's Christian Association, the Musurgia Club, and various choirs. At 9:30 A.M. the Marine Band performed the following:

March. *Our Glorious Banner*. W.H. Santelmann.
Overture. *Jubilee*. Von Weber
March. *Pride of the Nation*. E.H. Droop[876]
American Patrol. Meacham.
"The Star-Spangled Banner." Francis Scott Key

As the "Star-Spangled Banner" was performed the flag was raised to a 21-gun salute and "two ariel bombs containing large silk flags" were set off. After an hour of speeches, "the audience joined with the Band and chorus in singing the first verse of 'America.'" At the reception in the Municipal Building the National Guard Band performed the following:

March. *Old Faithful.* Holzman.[877]
Overture. *Light Cavalry.* Suppé.
Duo for flute and horn. *Serenade.* Titi.
Medley of National Airs.
Spring song. *Aubade.* Lacombe[878]
Selection. *The Red Mill.* Herbert.
Overture. *William Tell.* Rossini.
Ballet music. *Nalla.* Delibes.
Fantasia. *Hungarian.* Tobani.
Waltz. *Blue Danube.* Strauss.
Pilgrims' chorus from *Tannhauser.* Wagner.
American Patrol. Meacham.

("Plans for Festivities: Program for Opening of Municipal Building" and "Ready for Festivities," *Washington Post*, 25 June and 4 July 1908, 2 and 2, respectively); a concert at the White House by the Marine Band, William H. Santelmann, leader, included:

March, "The Stars and Stripes Forever" (Sousa)
Overture, "America" (Santelmann)

Music de ballet "Coppelia" (Delibes)
Waltz, "In the Vienna Woods" (Strauss)
Grand patriotic fantasia, "Remembrances of the Plantation" (Chambers)
"Grand Military Tattoo" (Rogan)
Patrol, "Blue and the Grey" (Dalbey)
"The Star-Spangled Banner"
["Program Records," U.S. Marine Band Library].

Florida

Fort Pierce: The Fort Pierce Band performed and was considered "one of the best to be found in our city" (*Fort Pierce News*, 10 July 1908).

Maryland

Chevy Chase Lake: A section of the U.S. Marine Band provided music for those enjoying a day of relaxation at this setting just outside D.C. (*Washington Post*, 4 July 1908, 10).

Minnesota

St. Peter: This town held a grand three-day event (July 2–4) which included four concerts provided by the First Regiment Band and Redman Band of the Ottawa tribe on July 4. Both bands marched in the morning parade that day ("Big Celebration Now in Full Blast," *St. Peter Free Press*, 4 July 1908 and 11 July 1908; *St. Peter Herald*, 10 July 1908, 1).

The Redman Band of the Ottawa tribe, St. Peter, Minnesota, July 2–4, 1908. The band, dressed in their full regalia, gave a concert on July 3 likely in the bandstand shown on the right and marched on July 4 in the morning parade. A local newspaper reported "the Redman Band made a fine showing during the celebration" (courtesy of the Nicollet County Historical Society, St. Peter, Minnesota).

New York

New York: Bandmasters for bands assigned for public performance in the city parks were not in agreement with the mayor's proclamation that only patriotic airs be played on the Fourth ("Bandmasters Protest," *New York Times*, 4 July 1908, 12).

Utah

St. George: At the tabernacle, the "Battle Hymn of the Republic" and "My Own United States" was sung by a choir; "The Star-Spangled Banner was sung by Mrs. C.M. Clark and "The Sword of Bunker Hill" was sung by W. Lenzi MCallister, piano teacher; a quartette sang "The Flag Without a Stain" ("Independence Day," *Washington County News*, 2 July 1908, 1).

1909

Performances

Colorado

Breckenridge: The Breckenridge Brass Band provides music for the event ("Breckenridge Celebrates the Natal Day in Becoming Style," *Summit County Journal*, 10 July 1909, 1).

District of Columbia

On Sunday, July 4, an "open air patriotic service" was held "on the Cathedral Close." Music was sung by "a vest choir led by detachment of the United States Marine Band," which performed just prior to the service (*Washington Post*, 3 July 1909, 4); at the civic celebration[879] held at Seventh Street and Louisiana Avenue, "a large chorus composed of public school children under the direction of Miss Sallie Mason, a 'Hymn to the Fatherland' and 'Our Flag,'" as well as the Marine Band were musical highlights of the event ("Safe and Sane Day in Capital Proves Success of Idea," *Washington Times*, 5 July 1909, 1–2). On Monday the official celebration took place, sponsored by the Board of Trade and Chamber of Commerce, and held at the Stephenson statue. The program included the following music:

"Voices of Our Nation." Smith
"Melodies of Stephen Foster."
"Stars and Stripes Forever" Sousa. U.S. Marine
    Band, W.H. Santelmann, leader
"The Star-Spangled Banner." Mrs. T.C. Noyes
"Hymn to the Fatherland." Haller. Chorus of
    pupils of the public schools.
"Out on the Breeze." Root
"Our Flag." Chorus of pupils of the public schools.
"Our Starry Banner." Santelmann. U.S. Marine
    Band

At the Ellipse that afternoon, the brigade band of the District National Guard, led by Donald B. McLeod,

gave a concert ("Safe and Sane Day," *Washington Post*, 5 July 1909, 1–2).

Georgia

Homer: "Homer celebrates the annual reunion of Confederate Veterans and the Fourth of July at Home July 3, 1909, with Gen. Clement A. Evans as principal speaker. Other speeches and recitations will be delivered by prominent citizens, and the music of the day will be made by an excellent brass band from the city of Commerce" (*Atlanta Constitution*, 30 June 1909, 6).

New York

New York: Nahan Franko's Orchestra played *The Stars and Stripes Forever*, in Central Park (*New York Times*, 5 July 1909, 3).

Denmark

Copenhagen: At the National Exposition, a cantata, *The Fourth of July*, by Ivar Kirkegaard of Racine, WI, music by Carl Busch of Kansas City, was premiered on the occasion of the Aarhus National Bronze Exposition.[880] The work was written for baritone solo and mixed chorus (*New York Times*, 5 July 1909, 2).

1910

The National Education Association met in Boston over the Fourth of July holiday. On July 5, Charles I. Rice, "director of music in the Worcester schools and president of the music department of the NEA" gave an address titled "Boston, the Cradle of Public School Music," at the New England Conservatory of Music. Other addresses given there included one by Mary L. Regal on music in the high school in Springfield, Massachusetts, and another by Mrs. Constance Barlow-Smith of the University of Illinois "on the educational value of folk songs."[881]

Performances

California

Sutter Creek: Bowers Orchestra played for a "grand ball" and Joseph Quirolo sang Sousa's "Stars and Stripes Forever" (*Amador Ledger*, 1 July 1910, 4).

Colorado

Creede: The Del Norte Band which was offered $100 was invited to perform in the town's morning parade ("Celebration!" and "Fourth of July Program," *Creede Candle*, 25 June and 2 July 1910, 1 and 4, respectively).

Maryland

Chevy Chase Lake: "Full section of U.S. Marine Band at dancing pavilion" (*Washington Post*, 4 July 1910, 10).

Massachusetts

Boston: The Society of the Cincinnati met at Young's Hotel. "An interesting feature was the rendering of 'Adams and Liberty,' 'The Sword of Bunker Hill,' and other songs, by Lester M. Bartlett, tenor, who gave an interesting talk about the songs of long ago" ("Society of the Cincinnati Dines," *Boston Evening Transcript*, 5 July 1910, 16).

New York

New York: *Girl of the Golden West*,[882] "by Corse Payton's stock company at the Academy of Music, beginning with the Fourth of July matinee." Cast included Minna Phillips, as the girl, and Joseph W. Girard, as Jack Rance.

Coney Island: At Brighton Beach Music Hall, "a musical comedy sketch called the Leading Lady, played by a company of fifteen," the Five Musical Avolos "will appear as instrumentalists"; Julia Frary, singing comedienne ("Amusements of the Summertime," *New York Times*, 3 July 1910, X8).

Utah

Centreville: The "Star-Spangled Banner" was sung by Julian E. Young ("Fourth of July in Centreville," *Davis County Clipper*, 1 July 1910).

Park City: The exercises were held at the bandstand and began at 7:30 P.M. and included the following music:

Instrumental Selection, "Southern Melodies." Park City Military Band.
Music, "Star-Spangled Banner." Choir.
Selection, "Good Old Days." Park City Military Band.
Quartette, Miss Martha Smith, Vlera Padfield, Mr. Padfield and Wm. J. Lewis.
Music, "Stars and Stripes Forever" Park City Military Band.
"America." Everybody join in.
[*Park Record*, 2 July 1910, 1].

Price: Patriotic services at the town hall included music by the Price Brass Band; "The Dream of the U.S.A." sung by Lora Harmon; vocal solo by Gwilym Jones; "The Sword of Bunker Hill" sung by L.A. Lauber; instrumental music by Levi N. Harmon, Jr. ("Program for Fourth of July Celebration," *Eastern Utah Advocate*, 30 June 1910).

Virginia

Alexandria: A "safe and sane" celebration was held at George Washington Park, "under the auspices of the Civic Improvement League." A section of the U.S. Marine Band gave a concert at 5 P.M. ("To Have a Quiet Fourth," *Washington Post*, 2 July 1910, 2).

Washington

Irondale: The celebration included residents from Seattle, Everett, and other towns. Music was provided by the Sixth Artillery Band from Fort Worden. A newspaper reported that "a dancing pavilion has been built and dancing will be indulged in by all who like that amusement" ("Eagle to Scream at Irondale," *Port Townsend Daily Leader*, 3 July 1910, 1).

1911

Performances

Colorado

Golden: The Georgetown Band "will be down on the morning train and will take part in the parade from the C&S depot." The Central City Band was also invited to perform in Golden ("All Ready for Big Time on July Fourth" and "Golden's Sane Fourth a Successful Celebration," *Colorado Transcript*, 29 June and 6 July 1911, 1 and 1, respectively).

Gypsum: The day's program included music by the Red Cliff Band[883] ("Fourth of July at Gypsum," *Eagle County Blade*, 23 June 1911, 1).

District of Columbia

U.S. Marine Band at Municipal Building event; Fifteenth Cavalry Band from Fort Myer at the Ellipse; Second Infantry Band, District of Columbia National Guard, at the municipal swimming pools; U.S. Engineer Band at Potomac Park ("Ready for Fourth," *Washington Post*, 3 July 1911, 1).

Maryland

Chevy Chase Lake: U.S. Marine Band (*Washington Post*, 3 July 1911, 11).

Frederick: On Market Street, the City Band of Martinsburg, WV, and Charles Town Band, of Charles Town, WV, gave a concert ("4th Most Brilliant," *Frederick Evening Post*, 5 July 1911, 3).

New York

New York: New York provided music in more than "500 centres," with 10,000 singers and musicians, "including many military bands, orchestras, choirs, and singing societies." Also, "about 125 organized German choruses have volunteered, the largest being at the City Hall, where the choir will number 350 singers.... A feature will be the singing of a new national anthem called the *Hymn to Liberty*, written and composed by Arthur Farwell."[884] In Central Park, the Volpe Orchestra[885] played classical music; Streta's Military Band and the Police Band performed at City Hall Park and Giacomo Quintano's "new setting" of "America" was sung; at Borough Hall, Brooklyn, Shannon's Band and Thiele's Band at Washington Square; Johnston's Military Band at Abingdon Park; Fanciulli's[886] Band at Bryant Park ("Music for the Fourth" and "Safe and Sane the Nation Over," *New York Times*, 3 and 5 July 1911, 3 and 4, respectively).

At Washington Square Park, at the site of the Garibaldi statue, a celebration "planned for Italians,

French, and Americans," the New York Banks Glee Club, led by H.R. Humphries, provided music, as well as an unnamed band ("Celebrate in Three Tongues," *New York Times*, 5 July 1911, 5); at the Tammany celebration, the Sixty-Ninth Regiment Band and a glee club quartet ("Tammany Plans Big Show," *New York Times*, 3 July 1911, 3); at the Century Theatre on July 3–4, orchestra concerts under the direction of Elliott Schenck were "devoted chiefly to national, patriotic, and war music," and included the 1812 Overture,[887] "Kaiser Marsch" (Wagner); "Light Calvary Overture" (Suppé); "American Fantasie" (Herbert) and the "Indian Overture" to the *The Arrow Maker* (Schenck) ("Summer Night Concerts," *New York Times*, 2 July 1911, X5).

1912

Publications

A new American hymn, "America Befriend," words by Henry Van Dyke, music by William Pierson Miller, is printed in *New York Times*, 5 July 1912, 5.

Performances

District of Columbia

U.S. Marine Band at the Pan-American Union Building for a "safe and sane" celebration; National Guard Band at the Ellipse; U.S. Engineer Band at the municipal swimming pools ("Spirit of '76 Afire," *Washington Post*, 5 July 1912, 2).

Maryland

Chevy Chase Lake: Members of the U.S. Marine Band provided music for recreationers (*Washington Post*, 3 July 1912, 11).

New York

Brooklyn: A carnival in Prospect Park sponsored by the Knights of Columbus, included "patriotic songs sung by the Knights under the direction of Prof. James Truns"; at Homewood, music included "several patriotic medleys" by Duffy's Military Band ("Big Day in Brooklyn," *New York Times*, 5 July 1912, 20).

New York: The city launched a "song festival" in support of a "safe and sane" holiday. Continuous song from 9 A.M. to 11 P.M. throughout the five boroughs of the city was planned. The initiative under the directorship of Sumner Gerard, was "extended to soloists, quartets, glee clubs, and school children." At City Hall, "For Thee, America"[888] by Alexander Maloof was sung by 500 school children directed by Frank Rix ("Singing for Sane Fourth," *New York Times*, 18 June, and 5 July 1912, 11, and 20, respectively; "Music Notes," *New York Times*, 4 July 1912, 7).

Utah

Park City: The Park City Military Band, J.C. Whitta, leader, paraded and presented an open-air concert that included a choir led by Mrs. Ethel Lewis. The program:

"Star-Spangled Banner." Choir
"Reminiscences of the South." Mixed Quartette
"For Country, God and Liberty." West Family Cornet solo. James F. Watson.
"Alice, Where Art Thou"
"Columbia, the Gem of the Ocean." Choir
"Medley Selection." Band
"America." Choir
Finale. Band

Following, there was a "Grand Ball" in Rasband's Hall with Miss Ruth Stromness, organist, providing the music ("The Real Fourth of July Spirit," *Park Record*, 6 July 1912, 1).

England

London: At Dorchester House, U.S. Ambassador Whitelaw Reid held an Independence Day reception for 2000 guests who heard two orchestras play national airs ("Reids Held Big Reception," *Washington Post*, 5 July 1912, 1)

Switzerland

Lucerne: At the Kursaal, Louis Lombard "who directs an orchestra of his own at Trevano Castle in Switzerland" gave a concert of American music. The program included *The Culprit Fay* (Henry Hadley); "Praeludium" from opus 63 (Arthur Foote); suite from the opera *Errisinola* (Louis Lombard); and a suite (Edward MacDowell) ("Music Notes," *New York Times*, 4 July 1912, 7).

1913

Performances

California

Los Angeles: At Exposition Park, the Whittier State School Band, Moore's Military Band, Los Angeles Veterans' Fife and Drum Corps provided music and Miss Grace Jones sang the "Star-Spangled Banner" ("Plans Complete for the Fourth," *Los Angeles Times*, 27 June 1913, I15).

Maryland

Chevy Chase Lake: U.S. Marine Band in the afternoon ("Excursions," *Washington Post*, 3 July 1913, 7).

Pennsylvania

Gettysburg: A veterans celebration began at 5 A.M. when the Fifth U.S. Regiment Band marched through the East Side streets performing a medley, including "America," "Yankee Doodle," "Marching through

Georgia," "Dixie," "The Star-Spangled Banner," and other tunes. As President Wilson arrived there to give an address, a band played "Hail to the Chief" (J.A. Watrous, "Veterans Cheer Patriotic Airs," *Los Angeles Times*, 5 July 1913, 12; "Gettysburg Cold to Wilson's Speech," *New York Times*, 5 July 1913, 1).

Pittsburgh: The International Welsh Eistedfodd celebrated the Fourth at the "great hall of the Pittsburgh Exposition with a competition for male voices consisting of 15 choirs, including 1,200 men ("Awards at Song Festival," *New York Times*, 5 July 1913, 9).

New York

New York: At City Hall Park, the Fife and Drum Corps of the Sons of the Revolution, dressed in Continental uniforms, marched (*New York Times*, 5 July 1913, 14).

Utah

Heber: A band, directed by A.W. Palmer performed tunes, Miss Anna Duke sang "Flag Without a Stain," and Jowett Fortie sang "The Sword of Bunker Hill" ("Fourth of July," *Wasatch Wave*, 4 July 1913, 5).

Price: A concert by the Price Brass Band was scheduled at 9 A.M. on Main Street. "The Sword of Bunker Hill" was sung by L.A. Lauber; a cornet solo by Fred Woods; a selection titled "Girl and Kaiser" by the Griffith Orchestra ("Fourth of July Program at Price," *Eastern Utah Advocate*, 26 June 1913, 1).

1914

During the war years, many new songs were composed on behalf of the war effort and to serve as an inspiration for those enlisting in the armed forces. There were newly harmonized renditions of "America" and "Star-Spangled Banner." An excellent article which mentions numerous works in this genre is "Songwriters Doing Their Bit in War," *New York Times*, 29 July 1917.

Performances

Colorado

Breckenridge: "Music by the Breckenridge Brass Band all through the day" ("The Eagle Screams in Old Breckenridge," *Blue Valley Times*, 4 July 1914, 1).

Leadville: A parade included a brass band (16 pieces) led by John M. Kerns. The band also played in the evening "for the open-air dancing on Harrison Avenue" ("A Glorious Fourth Is Promised," *Carbondale Chronicle*, 29 June 1914, 5).

Telluride: The Telluride Concert Band gave a performance in the evening ("Saturday, July Fourth," *Daily Journal*, 30 June 1914, 1).

District of Columbia

U.S. Marine Band at the Zoo; U.S. Engineers Band on the Mall performed music during intermissions of patriotic films being shown ("All Happy on Fourth," *Washington Post*, 5 July 1914, 6); Marine Band performs the following program at the White House:

> March, "The Liberty Bell" (Sousa)
> Overture "America" (Tobani)
> "Offenbachiana" (arr. Godfrey)
> *Our Glorious Banner* (Santelmann)
> "A Village Festival"[889] (Le Thiere)
> "Spring Jubilee in the Alps (Gungl)
> "Gems of Steven Foster" (Tobani)
> March, "Stars and Stripes Forever" (Sousa)
> ["Program Records," U.S. Marine Band Library].

Maryland

Chevy Chase Lake: A section of the U.S. Marine Band provided music (*Washington Post*, 3 July 1914, 5).

New York

New York: At City Hall, 5,000 persons sang "Yankee Doodle" and "My Old Kentucky Home," accompanied by a 50-piece military band conducted by Ernest E. Mouland (*New York Times*, 5 July 1914, 3); at Grant's Tomb, a celebration of tribute to the general was held and the exercises included "selections by the band" and patriotic songs by a quartet, the audience joining in the choruses ("Brilliant at Grant's Tomb," *New York Times*, 5 July 1914, 3).

Utah

Park City: "Concert in Band Stand." Selection, Park City Independent Band — Star-Spangled Banner, choir — trombone solo, William Stephens — Tenting To Night, solo and chorus, Mrs. W.J. Lewis and Charles T. Prisk, assisted by the choir — cornet duet, Bert and W.J. Bircumshaw — Battle Hymn of the Republic, choir — selection, Park City Independent Band — America, choir, everybody joining. Chorister, Mrs. W.J. Lewis and organist, Mrs. J.C. Whitta ("Park City Celebrates," *The Park Record*, 4 July 1914, 1).

Saint George: A celebration ·at the tabernacle included a choir singing "Columbia, the Gem of the Ocean"; a selection by the orchestra; "The Sword of Bunker Hill," sung by Chester Snow; a violin solo by Prof. Rygg; and "America" sung by the choir ("Program for 4th of July," *Washington County News*, 2 July 1914, 1).

1915

July 4 was designated "Americanization Day" by the editors of *Immigrants in American Review* magazine, with assistance by Frederic C. Howe, commissioner of immigration at Ellis Island, to foster a better understanding of the diversity of the races in the United States. A National Americanization Day Committee urged cities across the country to offer Independence Day "citizenship receptions" and other programs that included "appropriate exercises in honor of our nat-uralized fellow-citizens and declarants." "Americaniza-tion Day" became the theme for many Independence Day celebrations.[890] A number of celebrations in-cluded music representative of other countries.

Publications

The Birth of a Nation. Words by Thomas S. Allen. Music by Joseph M. Daly. Boston: Daly, 1915. First line: "'Twas in the year of seventy six."

Performances

California

Los Angeles: At Point Firmin "under the auspices of Angel Gate Council" of the Knights of Columbus, the exercises included the singing of the national an-them by Miss Helen Darling. A band concert was pro-vided at 10 A.M. ("Knights of Columbus," *Los Ange-les Times*, 5 July 1915, I16); "An interesting patriotic service was held last evening [July 4] at the first Methodist Church. The auditorium was profusely decorated with the flags of various nations, and the choir and congregation, accompanied by the great organ and the church orchestra of twenty-five pieces, sang the war and peace songs of different lands, in-cluding 'Rule Britannia,' 'Mother Machree,' 'Die Wacht am Rhein,' 'The Marseillaise,' 'Italia Beloved,' and the 'Star-Spangled Banner.'" At the First Con-gregation Church, accompanying a sermon on "the Old Liberty Bell," was a tenor solo by G. Haydn Jones and "a violin solo by Wallace Grieves of Illinois" ("How Republics Rise and Fall," *Los Angeles Times*, 5 July 1915, I13); at Exposition Park, a "band concert by city and county band of forty-eight pieces" and music by the G.A.R. Fife and Drum Corps were pre-sented. "Mrs. Noble will sing a patriotic song" and "Miss Eileen Sanborn and chorus consisting of Daughters of Veterans, will sing 'The Old Flag Shall Never Touch the Ground.'" The audience sang "America" led by Mme. L.E. Curtis Shaffer; The New England Society of Southern California met at Sycamore Grove where Frank Geiger sang "The Sword of Bunker Hill" ("Hills to Echo Eagle Scream," *Los Angeles Times*, 5 July 1915, I12).

Pasadena: The "presentation of the new bandstand to the city" took place and "Germond's concert band of forty pieces played patriotic selections throughout the afternoon" (*Los Angeles Times*, 5 July 1915, I16).

Riverside: At the Business center, the Cantadores Club "of sixty male voices" was scheduled to present "a full hour's programme" at 8:30 P.M. ("Riverside Plans," *Los Angeles Times*, 5 July 1915, I16).

District of Columbia

The celebration took place on July 5. The Fifth Cavalry Band provided music for the parade beginning at the Peace Monument. The U.S. Marine Band pro-vided music at the fireworks event on the Washington

Monument grounds ("Fetes Fill Gala Day," *Washing-ton Post*, 5 July 1915, 4).

Illinois

Chicago: At Gaelic Park, at a flag raising ceremony, "'The Star-Spangled Banner' will be sung by a chorus of 100 children, under direction of Profs. John E. Mc-Namara and Daniel J. Ryan, and thirty-two couples, representing counties of Ireland, will dance around the flag pole" (*Chicago Daily Tribune*, 4 July 1915, 3).

Missouri

Kansas City: "Americanization Day" was celebrated and 220 new citizens sang "America" and other pa-triotic songs (*New York Times*, 5 July 1915, 14).

New York

New York: At a Woman Suffrage Party demonstra-tion and march through city streets, Miss May Peter-son, "an American flag draped about her, sang 'The Star-Spangled Banner'" and "a military band of twenty pieces played" ("Women Ask Votes at Liberty's Feet," *New York Times*, 6 July 1915, 9); at the Lewisohn Sta-dium of the College of the City of New York, in an event billed as "American Day," the Rev. O.W. Peter-son's composition titled "God Save the President" was premiered by the audience ("City Waves Flag and Cheers Wilson," *New York Times*, 6 July 1915, 18).

1916

Performances

District of Columbia

U.S. Marine Band (58 pieces) performed at a "Sons of the Revolution open air service" at Washington Monument at 9:30 A.M. and later at fireworks event in the evening. "Program Records," U.S. Marine Band Library.

Georgia

Atlanta: Seven band and five drum corps in the city parade included the following groups: Eagles' Drum Corp, led by R.E. Lawshe; a Greek Society band and participants singing "Oh, say, can you see" in Greek; D.N. Baldwin's Alabama State Band (61 pieces, from Lawrenceville); Shriners' Drum Corp of Yaarub Tem-ple ("Parade Notes and Sidelights," *Atlanta Constitu-tion*, 5 July 1916, 8).

Macon: A large military parade occurred in which "the regimental band played patriotic airs" in honor of governor of Georgia Nathaniel E. Harris ("Georgia Troopers Given Big Ovation in Macon Parade," *At-lanta Constitution*, 5 July 1916, 9).

Kansas

Topeka: A concert by Jackson's Twenty-Third Reg-iment Band and Marshall's Band[891] were highlights of the city's celebration ("Topeka to Celebrate Sane

The Peace Monument, with the U.S. Capitol in the background, constructed in 1877 and 1878 in commemoration of naval personnel who lost their lives during the Civil War. The site has been a popular gathering place in downtown Washington, D.C., for the start of parades. On July 5, 1915, the Fifth Cavalry Band provided music for a parade that began here. One of the earliest musical performances in the U.S. Capitol was that given by the U.S. Marine Band in the Hall of the House of Representatives on July 4, 1812 (author's photograph).

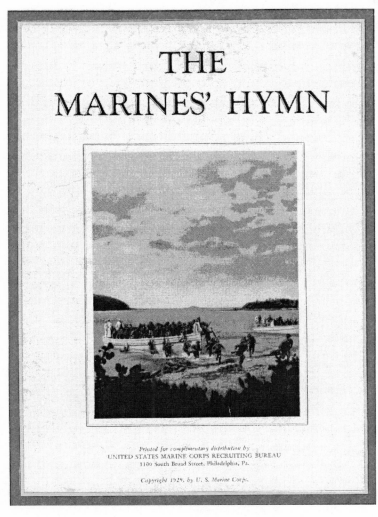

THE MARINES' HYMN

Printed for complimentary distribution by
UNITED STATES MARINE CORPS RECRUITING BUREAU
1100 South Broad Street, Philadelphia, Pa.

Copyright 1929, by U. S. Marine Corps.

"The Marines' Hymn" (cover sheet), the oldest song of the American military services. The source for the hymn is believed to be a galop that was added in 1867 to the opera *Geneviéve de Brabant* written by the French composer Jacques Offenbach in 1859. An arrangement by A. Tregina was first printed in 1918 by the U.S. Marine Corps Publicity Bureau in New York. This 1929 version was printed by the U.S. Marine Corps Recruiting Bureau in Philadelphia. One of the band's earliest Independence Day performances of the hymn occurred on July 3, 1916, at the Marine Barracks in Washington, D.C. (author's collection).

Fourth with Quiet in Place of an Uproar," *Topeka Daily Capital*, 4 July 1916, 1).

Maryland

Chevy Chase Lake: The Meyer Davis Orchestra (*Washington Post*, 2 July 1916, MT2).

New York

New York: At a Labor Forum celebration at Union Square, Edwin Markham's song "New America" is

premiered and "sung by the labor singing societies" (*New York Times*, 5 July 1916, 12); at the Lewisohn Stadium of the College of the City of New York, Johanna Gadski appeared as Columbia in the pageant *The Spirit of Preparedness* "aroused the audience to a high pitch of enthusiasm by her singing of 'The Star-Spangled Banner.'" Other music was furnished by the Halevy Chorus, Serbian Chorus, "assisted by a double band." An Independence Day ceremony held in the morning in the "Great Hall" of the college included a musical program directed by Henry T. Fleck[892] ("15,000 Gather in Stadium," *New York Times*, 5 July 1916, 12).

Virginia

Great Falls Park: American Ladies Orchestra, "patriotic concert" and "music for dancing on the great pavilion" located just outside Washington, D.C. ("Great Falls Park," *Washington Post*, 4 July 1916, 2 and 7).

1917

Publications

Fourth of July. Melody Pictures for Four Hands.. By Paul Bliss. Cincinatti: Willis Music Company, 1917. Includes 9 sections: Time to Get Up; Fire-Crackers; Going into Town; Flag Waving; The Parade; The Balloon Ascension; The Merry-Go-Round; Fire-Works; Night-Song. Some of the sections are set to lyrics.

Performances

Alaska

Anchorage: The Moose Band performed in a parade. Photograph, Anchorage Museum of History & Art, Library and Archives, in *Alaska's Digital Archives*, http://vilda.alaska.edu/index.php.

California

Los Angeles: At Hollenbeck Park, "community singing was enjoyed, the large audience taking up the refrains of 'America,' 'Columbia, the Gem of the Ocean,' 'Dixie,' and 'The Star-Spangled Banner'"; at Westlake Park, "music by the jazz band, both instrumental and vocal, was one of the features"; at Echo Park, the Southern Pacific Band provided the music ("Spectators Sing Patriotic Airs," *Los Angeles Times*, 5 July 1917, II6).

District of Columbia

"Washington's first celebration of Independence Day by pageantry and song in a government-owned theater took place" at the Sylvan Theater "when *The Call of the Allies* was presented before 15,000 spectators." The pageant was written by Alice Pike Barney (Mrs. Christian Hammick) in honor of the military and featured the allegorical figures, Joy, Peace, Liberty, and Freedom. "As each character appeared," the U.S. Marine Band played the national anthem of its representative country. Before the pageant, a chorus, led by William Stansfield, sang patriotic songs, and singers Miss Edna Thomas, contralto, Miss Annie Brett Summey, soprano, Louis Thompson, tenor, contributed a number of solos ("Solemn 4th for City," *Washington Post*, 4 July 1917, 1; "Give 'Call of the Allies' at the Sylvan Theater," *Washington Evening Star*, 5 July 1917, 12); "An open-air concert will be held in front of the Cosmos theater from 10 to 12 in the morning. A band and quartet will render national airs" ("Solemn 4th for City," *Washington Post*, 4 July 1917, 1); in the evening at Memorial Continental Hall, employees of the Interior Department presented a play titled *The Continental Congress*. Music by a section of the U.S. Marine Band was provided at this event ("Spirit of '76 Rules D.A.R. Hall Drama," *Washington Post*, 5 July 1917, 5).

New York

Brooklyn: At the stadium of the College of the City of New York, Miss Margaret George sang "The Marseillaise" before a crowd of 50,000 ("Be Loyal Here as Men Battle Abroad," *Chicago Daily Tribune*, 5 July 1917, 5).

France

Paris: American and French military bands performed as French citizens celebrate the Fourth and General Pershing receives American flags from French President Poincare (*New York Times*, 5 July 1917, 1).

1918

Publications

"Fighting for Freedom": Independence Day Pageant. By Thomas Wood Stevens; music by Ernest R.

Kroeger. St. Louis, Britt Printing and Publishing Co., 1918. Copy in New York State Library and Library of Congress.

Performances

District of Columbia

At Petworth, a concert by the Naval Gun Factory Band[893] (*Washington Post*, 5 July 1918, 12); on the steps of the Capitol, several hundred vocalists sang the "Hallelujah Chorus" (Handel) (*Evening Star*, 5 July 1918); at a celebration of the two organizations, Sons of the Revolution and the Sons of the American Revolution, "as in past years the Marine Band will play patriotic music" ("Complete Elaborate Plans for 'American' July 4th," *Washington Post*, 23 June 1918, 9).

Illinois

Urbana: At the University of Illinois a celebration in the auditorium,[894] Miss Edna A. Treat performed a processional march on the organ. The audience sang the following: "By Thy Rivers"[895]; Doxology; "Star-Spangled Banner"; "America"; hymn, "For All the Saints Who from Their Labors Rest"; "On, Forever, Illinois!,"[896] written by Mr. Langdon ("All Are Set for Big Celebration," *Urbana Daily Courier*, 3 July 1918, 1–2).

New York

Lake George: Louise Homer of the Metropolitan Opera Company sang "The Star-Spangled Banner" at a celebration there (*New York Times*, 5 July 1918, 9).

New York: At the Lewisohn Stadium, music was provided for the event there by the naval band from the USS *Recruit* ("U.S. Marines Thrill Throng in Stadium," *New York Times*, 5 July 1918, 11).

Utah

Richfield: Exercises at the Opera House included music by a local band; David Reese, tenor, who sang "The Star-Spangled Banner" and "The Marseillaise"; Mrs. R.G. Clark who sang "When the Boys Come Home"; Naomi Heppler and a chorus of girls who sang "Old Glory"; J.W. West, violin solo; band and audience, "America" ("Fourth of July," *Richfield Reaper*, 29 June 1918, 4).

England

London: At Westminster Abbey, the "Battle Hymn of the Republic" was sung and "The Star-Spangled Banner" played (*New York Times*, 5 July 1918, 7).

1919

The victory celebrations marking the end of World War I were the highlights of this year.

Performances

District of Columbia

At the "Offering of Peace" parade and pageant held on the Capitol steps, a chorus of several thousand, accompanied by the U.S. Marine Band, sang patriotic songs. "One great event of the day will be the massing of all bands [15 in number] under the baton of Lieut. William H. Santelmann of the Marine Band, when the parade reaches the Capitol. This great musical organization will play 'The Star-Spangled Banner' while it is sung by 15,000 [ie., 1500] voices," made up of "approximately 100 vocal units." Some of the bands included Engineers Band, Salvation Army Band of New York City, Boy Scout Band, and various military bands. "In the list of songs that follow will be three thrilling choruses: 'Land of Hope and Glory,' by Elgar; 'The Home Road,' by Carter, and 'Sweet Bells of Peace,'[897] by Roma. Arrangements for the songs have been in the hands of Peter W. Dykema of the War Camp Community Service and chairman of the music committee." Other performances of the Marine Band included the Washington Monument at 10 A.M., Elipse at 5:30 P.M., and the parade at 7:00 P.M. ("Rush Pageant Plans," *Washington Post*, 27 June 1919, 4); additional works performed by the Marine Band in the pageant included "Columbia, the Gem of the Ocean," "The Stars and Stripes Forever," and excerpts of works by Delibes, Tchaikovsky, and others ("Program Records," U.S. Marine Band Library).

Idaho

Pocatello: Two concerts in celebration of returning troops were given by the Gate City Band and a military parade included the Municipal Band (*Pocatello Tribune*, 3 July 1919, 2).[898]

New York

New York: As part of the "Victory Pageant" held in the city, the "Stadium of the College of the City of New York," Rosa Ponselle of the Metropolitan Opera Company sang "America" and the People's Liberty Chorus, L. Camilieri,[899] conductor, sang "Ring Out, Sweet Bells of Peace" (*New York Times*, 4 July and 5 1919, 5 and 9, respectively); at the Tammany Hall celebration, 69th Regiment Band and the Tammany Glee Club provided music ("Wigwam to Hear Woman," *New York Times*, 30 June 1919, 12).

Paris

A joint Franco-American celebration[900] included a parade with "a wild west band" and a performance of Gounod's *Faust*, with Marshal Ferdinand Foch and General John J. Pershing as honored guests" ("Great Fourth of July in French Capital," *Atlanta Constitution*, 5 July 1919, 4).

1920

Performances

District of Columbia

At the Ellipse at 4 P.M., a celebration of the Washington Federation of Churches and Boy Scouts and Community Service included a "community songfest of patriotic airs," arranged by Prof. Wengerd, song director of Community Service, and "the Boy Scouts Band, led by James L. Kidwell," provided a concert; at the Walter Reed Army Hospital, the Department of the Interior Band and a "chorus singing by a choir of nurses and aids" occurred in the evening ("D.C. to Fete Liberty," *Washington Post*, 4 July 1920, 3).

New York

Elizabethtown: "A tablet embedded in a huge bolder" memorializing Elizabethtown soldiers was unveiled to the sound of the Keeseville Band. An eight-piece orchestra provided music for a dance in the evening ("Elizabethtown Firemen Will Celebrate the Fourth," *Ticonderoga Sentinel*, 17 June 1920, 1).

Mineville: The day's events included music by the Mineville Band and dancing on the pavilion in the park, with music by Wiley's Orchestra. The day ended with an evening band concert ("The Fourth at Mineville," *Ticonderoga Sentinel*, 17 June 1920, 1).

New York: At Columbia University, on July 5, Goldman's Band performed works by American composers Francis Hopkinson, Edward MacDowell, Carl Busch (premiere, *A Chant from the Great Plains*), and others[901] (*New York Times*, 6 July 1920, 17).

Willsboro: Nypen Club Band performed in a parade (July 5), followed by dancing in the evening at the Grange Hall, music "by a twelve-piece orchestra from the Nypen Club Band" ("Fourth of July Celebration at Willsboro," *Ticonderoga Sentinel*, 17 June 1920, 1).

Utah

Vernal: A parade included the Vernal Brass Band which also provided music for the exercises at the Tabernacle. The Oriel Quartet sang "America," "The Americans Come,"[902] and "Washington." The congregation sang the "Star-Spangled Banner," led by Ashley Bartlett ("Fourth of July in Vernal Proves a Grand Success," *Vernal Express*, 9 July 1920, 1).

Virginia

Great Falls Park: A July 4 picnic included music by the Great Falls Ladies' Orchestra ("D.C. to Fete Liberty," *Washington Post*, 4 July 1920, 3).

Germany

Coblenz: "Two United States infantry bands played 'The Star-Spangled Banner' and the men under the command of Gen. [Henry T.] Allen, of the American army of occupation, stood at attention here today. Mary Pickford and Douglas Fairbanks sang the national anthem as thousands of German citizens watched with heads uncovered.... When the last note of the great hymn was sounded Fairbanks leaped high into the air and waving his arms above his head shouted for three cheers for America" ("The Fourth, Mary, 'Doug!'" *Washington Post*, 18 July 1920, 49).

1921

Publications

"A Song for the Fourth. By Harrison Long." First line: "What can I do, America" (*Youth's Companion*, 2 June 1921, 346.)

Performances

District of Columbia

"The Marine Band, under the direction of Capt. Santelmann, will give a band concert at 8 o'clock. A group of classic dancers will be seen. One of the features will be dramatized patriotic songs under the direction of Charles S. Wengerd, assisted by the entire community chorus. As a climax to the program, 'The Star-Spangled Banner' will be sung by the audience, accompanied by the Marine band, when the stadium [of Central High School] will be lighted with red lights" ("Patriotic Display at Central July 4," *Washington Post*, 29 June 1921, 7).

New York

New York: A large Irish parade sponsored by the American Association for the Recognition of the Irish Republic took place and British music and jazz was prohibited in a parade of 50 bands totaling 922 musicians. Performed were "How Dry I Am" and "Hail, Hail, the Gang's All Here" (*New York Times*, 5 July 1921, 1, 3); at the Tammany celebration the Tammany Glee Club sang and Ward's Band performed ("Tammany Observes Day with Oratory," *New York Times*, 5 July 1921, 2).

Utah

Beaver: The city band directed by Prof. Frisby "of Salt Lake City" gave a concert at Stake Square. At the opera house the music included: a song by the Murdock Academy Quartet (Charles Murdock, Milo Baker, Frank Smith and Kent Morgan); "The Sword of Bunker Hill," sung by Raymond Williams, with Miss Irene Tolton, pianist; a selection on the saxophone by Prof. Frisby, "accompanied on the piano by his wife"; "Star-Spangled Banner," sung by Mr. Rigby "of Salt Lake City, and the audience." The day ended with a "splendid musical concert, given by Raymond Williams at the opera house. Mr. Williams has a splendid voice and it was nothing but a pleasure to sit and listen to his singing. He was assisted by Mr. George Woodhouse on the cornet, who gave two very pleasing selections, and Miss Bonnie Anderson, who

sang very sweetly her closing number 'Humoresque.' It was wonderful. Miss Irene Tolton accompanied on the piano throughout the evening. Everyone who heard Miss Tolton play, knows how much it added to the performance of the evening. The rest of the night was spent in dancing" (4th of July Celebration," *Beaver Press*, 8 July 1921, 1).

Box Elder: The "Patriotic Services" included music by a brass band, a "Quartet" by the Harmony Male Chorus, a selection by the Tabernacle Choir, and the singing of "America" by the congregation, accompanied by the band ("The Fourth of July Programme," *Box Elder News*, 1 July 1921, 1).

France

Paris: Members of the Harvard Glee Club sang at the Trocadero as part of July Fourth celebrations there (*New York Times*, 5 July 1921, 2).

Germany

Berlin: Americans in Berlin celebrated and Germans reciprocated with orchestras eagerly playing American tunes. "The crowded restaurant of the Adlon was the scene of a rousing patriotic demonstration when the orchestra played an all–American medley, including the 'Swanee River' and 'Dixie' and climaxing it with the 'Star-Spangled Banner' ("Americans in Berlin Celebrate the Day," *New York Times*, 5 July 1921, 17).

1922

Performances

Colorado

Gypsum: "The brass band from Glenwood Springs, which is to furnish the music for the entire day, will open up at 9 o'clock Tuesday morning with a good, old fashioned band concert that will last untill 10 o'clock." Red Smith was director of the band and his orchestra, made up of members of the band, provided music for a dance later that evening in the high school auditorium ("A Big Fourth of July Celebration Is Promised Eagle County by Gypsum," *Eagle Valley Enterprise*, 30 June 1922, 5).

Telluride: The Gunnison Band (25 pieces) of the State Normal School was invited to perform. They gave three concerts, one at 9 A.M., one at 12:45 P.M., and another at 6:30 P.M. The concerts took place on a newly constructed bandstand located "on Colorado Avenue in front of the old Metropole Theatre." Newspapers reported that the band "played excellently" and "is the best known band on the west slope and recently won several prizes in open competition in Denver." It was also reported that "an orchestra [7 pieces] from the band members played at both the American Legion and the Firemen's dances," July 3–4, respectively. "Miss Fields, the only lady member of the band played the piano in the orchestra and also played a slide trombone in the band. Many favorable comments were heard on her playing" (*Daily Journal*, 1, 3 and 6 July, 1, 2, 3–4, respectively).

1923

A key musical event of this year was the formal dedication of the Rowan home in Bardstown, Kentucky, where Stephen Foster wrote "My Old Kentucky Home." "The chamber of commerce of Pittsburg had prepared a bronze plate recording the fact that Foster had written the song at Federal Hill and also had entrusted to its delegation a full length oil portrait of the composer, copied from an original which hangs in the Foster memorial at Pittsburg, to be placed above the mantel in the parlor of the house." The U.S. Army Band from Camp Knox performed in the Bardstown parade that day.[903]

Performances

Colorado

Ignacio: This town celebrated July 3–4 and the Pagosa Springs Jazz Band provided the music ("Celebration to be Worth While," *Weekly Ignacio Chieftan*, 29 June 1923, 1).

Telluride: The Telluride Municipal Band gave a performance at 12:45 P.M. and another at 6:30 P.M. ("Official Program," *Daily Journal*, 30 June 1923, 1).

Georgia

Atlanta: "The Elks' band and the city band will furnish music for" the procession and gathering at Piedmont Park and march to the Peace Monument. Some of the works performed included "America the Beautiful," "Dixie" (Elks' Band), and "Star-Spangled Banner" ("Heroes of Three Wars Will March in Parade Today," *Atlanta Constitution*, 4 July 1923, 1).

Massachusetts

Lenox: In the city parade, "there were seventy floats led by the Lenox Band and the East Lee Drum Corps" ("Pageant in Lenox Depicts Progress," *New York Times*, 5 July 1923, 15).

Utah

Richfield: The exercises occurred at the courthouse. Included was a band and "Mrs. Leslie Poulson was in splendid voice and gave a fine rendition of the 'Star-Spangled Banner,' the band playing a nicely balanced accompaniment." A girls chorus led by Mrs. Callaway "never appeared to better advantage than in its rendition of 'Stars and Stripes Forever' Sousa's wonderful march in a vocal setting, and here again the band appeared to advantage in its accompaniment" ("Nation's Birthday Observed Locally," *Richfield Reaper*, 12 July 1923, 1, 4).

Saint George: A Dixie brass band played patriotic airs in the morning. At the Stake Tabernacle, a patriotic pageant was presented in three episodes, the *Spirit of 1776, 1861, and 1917*. Music included "The Sword of Bunker Hill," sung by George Miller; a girls chorus that sang "There's a Long, Long Trail"[904]; violin duet by Earl J. Bleak and Vera Seegmiller playing "Massa Dear"; a Boy Scouts Brass Quartet played *Stars and Stripes Forever*; audience sang "Star-Spangled Banner" ("Independence Day Loyally Observed," *Washington County News*, 5 July 1923, 1).

Netherlands

A "novel celebration took place in the Hague at the American Legation when thirty Frisian girls in national costumes from the Province of Zealand sang "The Star-Spangled Banner" and "Hail Columbia" in the Dutch language ("American Songs in Dutch" and "Dutch Help Celebrate," *New York Times*, 3 and 5 July 1923, 3 and 17, respectively).

1924

Performances

California

Oceanside: The city's Municipal Band and Escondido Merchants' Association Band performed in a parade ("Celebrate Natal Day, *Los Angeles Times*, 5 July 1924, 6).

Georgia

Dawson: The Dawson Concert Band provided music for the town's celebration ("Dawson Lays Plans to Celebrate July 4," *Atlanta Constitution*, 29 June 1924, 8).

New York

Brooklyn: At the Lewisohn Stadium, the Philharmonic Orchestra (105 players), Willem van Hoogstraten, conductor. The July 4 program consisted of "The Star-Spangled Banner"; *A Negro Rhapsody* (Rubin Goldmark), a Stadium premiere; "Love Song" and "Village Festival" from *Indian Suite* (MacDowell); *American Fantasie* (Victor Herbert); Symphony No. 4 (Tchaikovsky) ("The Stadium Series Begins July 3," *New York Times*, 29 June 1924, X5).

New York: The Bureau for American Ideals presented an outdoor pageant titled *Our Own United States*, led by Irish baritone Thomas Hannon, at Columbus Circle (*New York Times*, 5 July 1924, 13); Thomas E. Ward's Park Concert Band performed on a float in the center of the lake in Central Park, at 8 P.M.:

Program
Salutation "Star-Spangled Banner"
March, *Stars and Stripes Forever*, Sousa
Overture, *William Tell*, Rossini

American Patrol, Meacham
Selection, *Faust*, Gounod
Solo, Emily Hallock, Soprano, and Herman Neuman, pianist
American Fantasia, *The North and South*, Bendix Part II
Overture, *Orpheus*, Offenbach
Medley 1863, Calvin
Group of Songs: Emily Hallock, soprano, Herman Neuman, pianist
Selection, *Princess Pat*, Herbert

("Smith May Attend Wigwam Exercises," *New York Times*, 4 July 1924, 24); The Sixty-Ninth Regiment Band and the Tammany Quartet provide music at the 135th annual Fourth of July celebration of the Tammany Society (*Ibid.*).

Utah

Brigham City: At the Court House grounds, the Brigham City Municipal Band provided music and Ed Lee sang "The Flag Without a Stain" ("Brigham City Celebrates July Fourth," *Box Elder News*, 8 July 1924).

1925

National Defense Day was the principal theme for Independence Day this year. Appropriate exercises helped to test the nation's readiness in case of war, to bring attention to the need for national defense, and to determine how quickly volunteers could be mustered for war duties. Activities were scheduled for towns and cities across the country. Twenty-nine radio stations from around the country were 'hooked up' for broadcast simultaneously.[905] Patriotic songs and martial music were some of the day's highlights.

Performances

District of Columbia

Defense Day activities were to include "a concert by the Marine Band, patriotic addresses and a display of fireworks at the Central High School stadium" ("Citizen Defenders to Enroll July 4 Without Marching," *Washington Post*, 13 June 1925, 18).

Georgia

Quitman: Thousands of persons heard the Moultrie Band as they "led the big Defense Day parade." That afternoon following the town lunch, "the Old Time Fiddlers' Convention started and dancing began in the [newly dedicated tobacco] warehouse" ("Quitman Scene of Celebration," *Atlanta Constitution*, 5 July 1925, 11).

New York

New York: In Central Park Hugo Riesenfeld gave a concert in memory of Elkan Naumburg, who donated the bandstand there. Compositions performed

included: "The Star-Spangled Banner"; war march from *Athalie* (Mendelssohn); C Major Symphony (Schubert); overture to *Freischütz*; *Polonaise in D* (Chopin); First Rhapsodie (Liszt); selections from *Lohengrin* (Wagner) and *Inflammatus* (Rossini), Cappo di Ferro, cornet ("Concert in Memory of Elkan Naumburg," *New York Times*, 5 July 1925, 21).

Pennsylvania

Philadelphia: On the occasion of National Defense Day, a chorus of school children sang songs at a gathering of 4,500 persons.[906]

Utah

Richfield: At the Opera House, the Third Ward Orchestra, M.C. Christensen, director and "Vocal offerings" by Mrs. Vern Blomquist and Clifford Pearl. Also, a girls chorus, accompanied by Anna Callaway and Miss Lenna Thurber, performed ("July Fourth Celebration Here Great Success," *Richfield Reaper*, 9 July 1925, 1).

1926

The principal event this year was the Sesquicentennial International Exposition,[907] held in Philadelphia, although many other cities celebrated the 150th anniversary of the signing of the Declaration of Independence as well. Over 30 countries participated in the exposition which was presided over by President Calvin Coolidge. In Washington, 25,000 persons assembled at the Capitol where they heard the United States Marine and Army bands and a pageant titled *The Story of America* written by Marie Moore Forrest and presented by 35 "leading patriotic and civic organizations,' with a cast of 1000. The work's three episodes depicted the "foundation," "progress," and "strength and hope of America."[908] In Valley Forge, Pennsylvania, the "Star-Spangled Banner" peace chime was dedicated.[909] John Philip Sousa composed his *Sesquincentennial Exposition March* with a dedication to Philadelphia mayor W. Freeland Kendrick. At Schenley Park in Pittsburgh, the 100th anniversary of Stephen Foster's birth was celebrated while in New York other concerts in his honor took place.

Broadcasts

Over KHJ, Roberts' Golden State Band, Harold William Roberts, leader, performed *Stars and Stripes Forever*, Sousa, and *Grand Naval Potpourri*, in honor the Pacific Fleet. The quartet Orpheus Four performed "songs of the wars of 1776, 1812, 1845, 1863, 1898, and 1914," including "Columbia, the Gem of the Ocean" ("KHJ Presents Musical Cycle," *Los Angeles Times*, 5 July 1926, A9).

Over KDKA (Pittsburgh), the Pittsburgh Symphony Orchestra and a chorus performed a Stephen Foster 100th anniversary program in Schenley Park

("Pittsburgh Honors Foster," *New York Times*, 6 July 1926, 23; "Long Range Radio Entertainment" and "Pittsburgh Celebrates Composer's Centennial," *Washington Evening Star*, 5 July 1926, 19 and 20, respectively).

Over WJZ, a performance of *1620 Overture*[910] by Mayhew Lake that "describes in music the landing of the Pilgrims at Plymouth, gives a sample of the 'jazz' of 1620 and also depicts a battle with the Indians and concludes with a musical portrayal of the 'First Thanksgiving'" and patriotic selections by the U.S. Sixteenth Infantry Army Band (*New York Times*, 4 July 1926, XX13).

Performances

District of Columbia

The Washington Federation of Colored Church Choirs (including 500 men and women), led by Virginia Williams, sang patriotic songs and a spiritual on the Capitol steps (*Washington Evening Star*, 6 July 1926, 5); at the new Sylvan Theater on the Mall, the U.S. Navy Band presented an evening musical performance prior to the fireworks display (*Washington Evening Star*, 5 July 1926, 1); at the Church of the Epiphany, the Imperial Quartet provided music for the celebration of the Association of Oldest Inhabitants of D.C. ("Pioneer Citizens Mark Anniversary," *Evening Star*, 5 July 1926, 2); at an event sponsored by the Daughters of the American Revolution, the U.S. Marine Band performed with D. C. mezzo-contralto Mrs. Flora McGill Keefer (Helen Fetter, "Music," *Washington Sunday Star*, 4 July 1926, 12); the U.S. Marine Band and U.S. Army Band provided background music for a pageant titled *The Story of America* (*Ibid.*); at the East front of the Capitol, the U.S. Marine Band and U.S. Army Band, led by 2nd Leader Taylor Branson and Capt. William J. Stannard, respectively, performed these works: *Stars and Stripes Forever* (Sousa); *Jubel Overture* (Weber); *Semper Fidelis* (Sousa); *American Fantasie* (Victor Herbert); *American Patrol* (Meacham); *National Emblem* (Bagley). ("Program Records," U.S. Marine Band Library).

Georgia

Atlanta: At the city auditorium with Mayor Walter A. Sims and several hundred persons attending, Charles A. Sheldon, Jr., "city organist," presented "a program of patriotic music" (Loy Warwick, Jr., "City Observes Fourth Today as Holiday," *Atlanta Constitution*, 5 July 1926, 1–2).

The Sylvan Theater, located adjacent to the Washington Monument in Washington, D.C., has the distinction as the first outdoor theater supported by the federal government. The idea for a theater on the Mall was introduced by Alice Pike Barney, a wealthy patron of the arts and herself an artist. The first Independence Day event at the Sylvan occurred on July 4, 1917, when a chorus, soloists, and the U.S. Marine Band provided music for a pageant, written by Barney, titled *The Call of the Allies*, that was presented before 15,000 spectators. In subsequent years numerous musical performances took place there on the Fourth of July. On July 5, 1926, the new official U.S. Navy Band, Lt. Charles Benter, leader, presented its first Independence Day concert preceding the evening fireworks (author's photograph).

Massachusetts

Pittsfield: The South Mountain String Quartet[911] gave an all–American program (works by G.W. Chadwick, David Stanley Smith, and Rubin Goldmark) at Mrs. Frederick S. Coolidge's Temple of Music, with 500 persons attending ("Play in Temple of Music," *New York Times*, 5 July 1926, 6).

New Jersey

Newark: At Asbury Park, an Independence Day program included Pryor's Band,[912] Monterey Society Orchestra, and Ben Bernie's Orchestra. The event was broadcast over radio station WOR ("Long Range Radio Entertainment," *Washington Evening Star*, 5 July 1926, 19).

New York

Gouverneur: Music was scheduled throughout the day with "the 35-piece Troop 3 Fife and Drum Corps, the 20-piece Philadelphia Band and the 25-piece Gouverneur Citizens' Band" ("Gouverneur's Biggest Fourth of July Celebration to Be Held Monday, July 5," *Gouverneur Free Press*, 30 June 1926, 1).

New York: At Central Park, the Goldman Band, Edwin Franko Goldman, conductor, presented the following program, broadcast over radio stationsW-JAR and WTAG:

All American Program
March, *The Stars and Stripes Forever*, Sousa
Overture, *Herod*,[913] Hadley
A Chinese Episode,[914] Kelley
Entr' acte, *Mlle. Modiste*, Herbert
Woodland Sketches, MacDowell
Zouaves' Drill, Mana-Zucca[915]
On the Go, Goldman[916]
A Soldier's Dream, Rogers[917] (Waino Kauppi, cornetist)
Bandanna Sketches, White[918]
American Fantasie, Herbert

("Philharmonic Stadium Concerts July 7," *New York Times*, 27 June 1926, X5 and 4 July 1926, XX13); at the Park Avenue Baptist Church, Percival Price, organist, gave a concert on the 53-bell Rockefeller Memorial Carillon (*New York Times*, 5 July 1926, 3); the celebration at the Tammany Society was "accompanied by a symphonic orchestra and a chorus singing ballads and other music of the period" (*New York Times*, 4 July 1926, XX13); vocalist Crystal Waters, assisted by Harold Milligan, author of a biography of Stephen Foster, presented a recital of songs by Foster at the headquarters of the National Music League and a Foster centennial concert was presented by the Hotel Majestic String Ensemble, directed by Theodore Fishberg.[919]

Schuylerville: Adam Albright directed 1,000 school children in singing patriotic songs as the town presented a reenactment of its colonial history (*New York Times*, 6 July 1926, 5).

Pennsylvania

Philadelphia: On July 5, trumpeters in the uniform of Revolutionary War soldiers played tunes for President Coolidge at Christ Church as he read the names of seven signers of the Declaration of Independence on a bronze replica of a tablet that was unveiled there (*New York Times*, 6 July 1926, 12); a grand Chorus of the States led by Henry K. Hadley featured representative choral organizations across the country in a performance (Helen Fetter, "Music," *Washington Sunday Star*, 4 July 1926, 12).

Utah

Fillmore: The music for the morning program included

Orchestra Selections.
Community Singing, Mrs. Dean C. Evans, director.
Dancing, two appropriate selections directed by Mrs. Lucy Huntsman
Mixed Quartette, "Flag Without a Stain," by Mrs. Horace Day, Byron Ray, Mr. and Mrs. George Huntsman.
Vocal Solo by Mrs. Horace Day.
Accordion solo, Claude Warner.
Male quartette, "The Stars and Stripes Forever," by Claude Warner, George Huntsman, Charles Ray and Byron Ray; directed by Mrs. D.C. Evans.
["Morning Program July 4th," Millard County Progress, 2 July 1926, 1].

Parowan: The assembly included singing "The Star-Spangled Banner" and "America"; "The Sword of Bunker-Hill," sung by Rex C. Ward; "America the Beautiful," by a double mixed quartet; "The Stars and Stripes Forever," by a ladies chorus ("Nation's Birthday Observed," *Parowan Times*, 7 July 1926, 1).

Virginia

Clarendon: In this town, located just outside the District of Columbia, the musical performers at a celebration arranged by the Arlington County School Federation included the U.S. Calvary Band of Fort Myer, Miss Phyllis Ransdell who sang "I Salute Thee, Old Glory,"[920] and Mrs. B.D. Shreve who sang "Lest We Forget"[921] ("America Eternal, Speaker Declares," *Evening Star*, 5 July 1926, 2).

1927

Broadcasts

The Goldman Band,"playing on the Mall at Central Park," was broadcast over WEAF, WLIT, WWJ, and WSAL. The program included: *The Stars and Stripes Forever*, Sousa; overture, *Herod*, Hadley; excerpts, *Woodland Sketches*, MacDowell; excerpts, *The Fortune Teller*, Victor Herbert; *Bandanna Sketches*, White; "Thy Beaming Eye" and "A Birthday," Mac-

Christ Church, a national historic landmark in Philadelphia, whose congregation was founded in 1695. Its current building dates to 1744, and in addition to other historic performances there, on July 5, 1926, Sesquicentennial trumpeters in the uniform of Revolutionary War soldiers played tunes for President Calvin Coolidge as he read the names of seven signers of the Declaration of Independence on a bronze replica of a tablet that was unveiled there (author's photograph).

Dowell, Olive Marshall, soprano; *The Lady Picking Mulberries*, Kelly; *Sunapee*, Goldman; *American Fantasie*, Victor Herbert ("Coming Events on the Air," *New York Times*, 3 July 1927, X16).

In Hawaii, the South Sea Islanders performed *The Stars and Stripes Forever*, "Old Black Joe," "Tomi, Tomi," and "Don't Say Aloha When I Go," over WEAF, WTIC, WLIT, WWJ, and WSAI ("Coming Events on the Air," *New York Times*, 3 July 1927, X16).

Performances

District of Columbia

The U.S. Marine Band,[922] Taylor Branson, leader and Arthur S. Witcomb, second leader, presented the following concert at the Sylvan Theater at 7:30 P.M.:

March "Hail to the Spirit of Liberty." Sousa
Jubel Overture, op. 59. Carl Maria von Weber
American Patrol. Meacham
Morceau characteristic "Panamericana." Herbert

American Fantasie Herbert
March *The Liberty Bell* Sousa

The program continued with singing "America," audience led by William E. Braithwaite
Reading of the Declaration of Independence by Charles F. Carusi,[923] president of the Board of Education

Addresses by Isaac Gans and Col. William B. Ladue
Massing of the flags with music by the Marine Band
"Oath of Allegiance to the Flag," led by Judge Mary O'Toole
"America the Beautiful," by the audience. First line: "O beautiful for spacious skies."
"March of the States," with Boy and Girl Scouts of America
"The Star-Spangled Banner," by the audience.
Note: During the singing of the national anthem the audience is asked to face the Washington

Monument, where the flag will be displayed. A plane from the naval air station will circle the Monument as the formal program closes. Fireworks.

("Program Records," U.S. Marine Band Library; "Program of Independence Day Celebration at Sylvan Theater," *Washington Post*, 4 July 1927, 2; *Washington Evening Star*, 5 July 1927, 2; "Citizens to Gather at Sylvan Theater in Honor of Fourth," *Washington Post*, 4 July 1927, 1).

Maryland

Frederick: At the dedication ceremony of the restored Barbara Fritchie House and Museum, the First Regiment Band performed appropriated tunes ("Barbara Fritchie's Home Is Dedicated," *Baltimore Sun*, 5 July 1927, 4; "Barbara Fritchie Home Dedicated," *Washington Evening Star*, 5 July 1927, 12).

New York

New York: At the annual Tammany celebration a band played "The Sidewalks of New York" ("New York Enjoys Dignified Fourth," *New York Times*, 5 July 1927, 5).

South Dakota

Rapid City: A cowboy band from Terry, Montana, performed for President Calvin Coolidge (*New York Times*, 5 July 1927, 1).

1928

Publications

"August, Where Were You on the Fourth of July?" First line: "There's a trav'ling salesman living in our house." For voice and piano. New York: Longacre Music Co., 1928. Copy in Indiana University Library.

Performances

California

Monrovia: "A program of patriotic music furnished by the Arcadia Municipal Band" ("Patriotic Music Heard at Monrovia," *Los Angeles Times*, 5 July 1928, 12).

District of Columbia

On the Washington Mall, "a sham attack on the Capital by a squadron of army airplanes" takes place, while at 7:30 P.M. at the Sylvan Theater there, the U.S. Marine Band presented a concert.... Following the concert, choral groups and the entire audience of thousands joined in the singing of 'America' led by Percy S. Foster." The audience also sang "The Star-Spangled Banner" ("Mimic Air Battle Gives Capital Real Thrill for July 4," *Washington Post*, 5 July 1928, 1); The U.S. Marine Band, Capt. Taylor Branson,

leader, gave a concert at 7:30 P.M. at the Sylvan Theater, adjacent to the Washington Monument. Works included *The Liberty Bell* (Sousa), *National Emblem* (Bagley), *Stars and Stripes Forever* (Sousa), *Hail to the Spirit of Liberty* (Sousa), *Jubel Overture* (Weber), *American Patrol* (Meacham). ("Program Records," U.S. Marine Band Library).

Washington

Everett: A pageant titled *The Spirit of the Snohomish*, sponsored by the Pioneer Association, was presented with one of the characters being George Bane, bandmaster of the Tulalip Indian School, and "great grandson of Sitting Bull." "A feather of the pageant will be the singing by Andrew Joe of an old Skagit war song" ("Great Grandson of Sitting Bull Will Be in Big Pageant," *Everett Daily Herald*, 25 June 1928).

1929

Broadcasts

Pageant of the Years, a drama in four acts, including patriotic songs such as "Columbia," "Dixie," "Over There," and "Madelon,"[924] broadcast over ABC, on July 4 (Ralph L. Power, "Radio Hurrahs Will be Heard," *Los Angeles Times*, 4 July 1929, A6).

Performances

District of Columbia

The U.S. Marine Band performed patriotic music at the Sylvan Theater and Herman Fakler conducted the audience in singing "The Star-Spangled Banner"; works performed by the band included *Hail to the Spirit of Liberty* (Sousa); *American Patrol* (Meacham); *The Liberty Bell* (Sousa); "National Songs" (Herbert; *National Emblem* (Bagley); ("Program Records," U.S. Marine Band Library); at Wesley Heights Mrs. Ethel H. Gawler led an audience in "The Star-Spangled Banner"; at the Oldest Inhabitants of the District of Columbia event, "The Americans Come"[925] was sung by the Oodlothian Quartet and the ceremony ends with the group singing "Auld Lang Syne"; at Petworth the Sycamore Orchestra gave a concert at 6:30 P.M. and included a trombone solo by L.Z. Phillips "of the Washington College of Music and vocal solos by Sergt. David Martin [Marine Corps] and Miss Thelma Mills Rector" (Capital Celebrates Today," *Washington Post*, 4 July 1929, 3).

Maryland

Takoma Park: A morning parade was led by the U.S. Army Band, an afternoon band concert by the Review and Herald Band, D. Robert Edwards, conductor, and the exercises held at the Takoma Park Presbyterian Church included the singing of the "Star-Spangled Banner" by Mrs. E. Clyde Shade (Capital Celebrates Today," *Washington Post*, 4 July 1929, 3).

Massachusetts

Boston: Arthur Fiedler conducted the first Fourth of July Esplanade concert in Boston, including Sousa's *The Stars and Stripes Forever*, Herbert's *American Fantasie*, Nicolai's *Merry Wives of Windsor*, Romberg's *New Moon*, among other works (Program, Boston Symphony Orchestra Archives)

Pennsylvania

Philadelphia: A concert by the Philadelphia Police Band performed with a chorus of 500 voices at Independence Hall and the music was broadcast over radio station WABC ("Radio Offers Independence Hall Program," *Washington Post*, 4 July 1929, 7).

Antarctic

Explorer Robert Byrd at camp Little America heard patriotic music, including Sousa's *Stars and Stripes Forever*, performed by the Westinghouse Band and broadcast over station KDKA. "National airs of several countries followed" ("July 4 Greetings Broadcast to Byrd," *New York Times*, 7 July 1929, 15).

Czechoslovakia

Prague: "A military orchestra played the national anthem" for members of the American Legation amidst a large gathering of citizens ("Czechs Celebrate Independence Day," *New York Times*, 5 July 1929, 7).

Ireland

Dublin: "A military band furnished music" at a garden party given by U.S. Minister Frederick A. Sterling ("Irish at Independence Party," *New York Times*, 5 July 1929, 7).

1930

Broadcasts

In Washington, D.C., over CBS, the U.S. Marine Band, Capt. Taylor Branson, leader, provides a morning concert at the Marine Band Auditorium consisting of *Marines' Hymn*; *Hail to the Spirit of Liberty* (Sousa); *American Patrol* (Meacham); *The American Army* (Lasilli); Overture *John and Sam* (Ansell); *The Liberty Bell* (Sousa); *Allegiance* (Shutt); *Anchors Aweigh* (Zimmerman); *Spirit of Independence*[926] (Abe Holzmann); *United States Field Artillery* (Sousa); *Semper Fidelis* (Sousa). ("Program Records," U.S. Marine Band Library).

Performances

California

Huntington Beach: The Huntington Beach Municipal Band presented a morning concert (*Los Angeles Times*, 5 July 1930, A6).

Moonridge Bowl, Bear Valley, near San Bernardino, California: *Never-the-less Old Glory*, "a spectacular historical drama," containing five new songs composed by Fannie C. Dillon, with collaborating lyricist Margaret E. Talmadge, and Sigurd Fredericksen, orchestra director. The work "tells the story of the first Fourth of July celebration in the valley in the '60's, thrown into confusion with the discovery of gold" ("Songs Written for Historical Drama," *Los Angeles Times*, 20 June 1930, 8. Photo of Dillon in Georgetown University Library).

District of Columbia

Taylor Branson conducted the U.S. Marine Band on the Monument Grounds at 7:30 P.M. (*Washington Post*, 5 July 1930, 1).

Maryland

Takoma Park: Members of the U.S. Army Band performed at the exercises held on the grounds of Takoma Park Trinity Episcopal Church. There were solos by Miss Dorothy Skinner and C. Wilfred Smith ("Takoma Park Fete is Holiday Feature," *Washington Post*, 5 July 1930, 14).

Utah

Park City: The event included the Park City Band, Byron Jones, leader, with soloists Bert Bircumshaw, baritone, and Phil Anderson. The program:

Popular — "Stein Song." [E.A.] Fenstad
Valse — "Tesoro Mio."[927] Becucci.
Selection — "American Patrol." Mecham
March — "National Emblem." Bagley
Serenade — "A Night in June." King, Bert Bircumshaw and band
Vocal — "Out of the Dusk to You." [Dorothy] Lee; Phil Anderson, [vocalist?]
March — "Little Giant." [H.] Moon
Selection — "Best Loved Southern Melodies." [Al] Hayes
Overture — "American Federation." Skagg
"Star-Spangled Banner." Key
["Evening of the Fourth," *Park Record*, 4 July 1930, 1].

1931

Reknown pianist Ignace Paderewski presented a memorial statue, designed by Gutzon Borglum, of President Wilson to the Polish people (*New York Times*, 5 July 1931, 1). Through a Congressional resolution on March 3, 1931, "The Star-Spangled Banner" became the official national anthem.

Broadcasts

Japanese music played by native Japanese Shochiku Band is relayed to American audiences at 8 am EST over WJZ radio network while the Americans respond with a ten-minute concert broadcast from San Francisco to the Orient; "Independence Day" depicted in music with narrative by Edgar White Burrill, together with a reproduction of the tolling of Liberty Bell" was broadcast in the evening over WEAF; "a concert of Stephen Foster melodies celebrating the 105th anniversary of the composer's birth" was broadcast over WEAF ("Patriotism to Ride on All Radio Waves," *New York Times*, 4 July 1931, 3); a medley of Foster melodies performed by a group of soloists and orchestra was broadcast over WEAF, New York ("A Glorious Fourth on the Air," *New York Times*, 28 June 1931, 29).

Performances

District of Columbia

The U.S. Marine Band provided music prior to the fireworks celebration on the Mall and Mrs. Gertrude Lyons led the audience in singing "America" and "America the Beautiful" (*Washington Post*, 5 July 1931, M3).

California

Los Angeles: At Sycamore Grove, a concert by the Playground Boys Band and at Westlake Park, music was provided by the Sixtieth Infantry Band "and in the evening by Roberts' Golden State Band, with Ernie Owen's Orchestra playing for a community dance." "Nine band concerts were presented throughout the city during the day: at the Greek Theater in Griffith Park, Hollenbeck Park, South Park, Point Fermin Park, Lincoln Park, Westlake Park, Reseda Park, Banning Park and Sycamore Grove" ("Holiday Crowd Fetes Fourth," *Los Angeles Times*, 5 July 1931, A2).

Maryland

Takoma Park: The U.S. Army Band led a parade through town streets (*Washington Post*, 5 July 1931, M1).

1932

Broadcasts

Columbia Broadcasting System over KHJ, American Legion concert of martial music[928] with an address by the Rev. Father Edmund Walsh, of Georgetown University; KFI presented a "Parade of States" program featuring Pennsylvania and "symphonic arrangments of music of 1776; a tribute to Stephen Foster in his own melodies and Elizabeth Lennox sang Nevin's 'Little Boy Blue'" ("Patriotic Programs Broadcast: Fourth of July Music on Radio," *Los Angeles Times*, 4 July 1932, 10); the U.S. Navy Band was scheduled to perform and Cyrena Van Gordon, Metropolitan Opera contralto, "will sing a group of patriotic selections" over WEAF at 3:30 P.M.; over WABC, at 9 P.M., the U.S. Marine Band at the Washington Monument

("The Microphone Will Present," *New York Times*, 3 July 1932, XX5).

Performances

District of Columbia

The massing of the colors with music by the U.S. Marine Band took place at the Sylvan Theater. Mrs. Gertrude Lyons conducted the entire audience in singing patriotic songs. "America" was sung by Eva Whitford Lovette and Mathilde W. Kolb. The audience sang "Star-Spangled Banner," accompanied by the band (*Washington Post*, 4–5 July 1931, 1 and 2, respectively; "Program Records," U.S. Marine Band Library).

New York

New York: Kaltenborn Symphony Orchestra, Franz Kaltenborn, conductor, at Central Park Mall at 8:30 P.M.

Program
"The Star-Spangled Banner"
American Fantasie, Herbert
Overture to *William Tell*, Rossini
Excerpts from *The Flying Dutchman*, Wagner
Orgies of the Spirits, Il'imskii, A.
Symphony No. 1 in C Minor, Brahms
Overture to *Orpheus*, Offenbach
Selection for *Hansel and Gretel*, Humperdinck
Waltz, *Southern Roses*, Strauss
Whispering Flowers, Franz von Blon
March Slav, Tchaikovsky
"America"

("Concert Programs of the Week," *New York Times*, 3 July 1932, X4); in the Bronx at St. Ann's Protestant Episcopal Church, "Mrs. Roberta Keene Tubman, a descendant of William Hooper, a signer of the Declaration of Independence, sang 'The Star-Spangled Banner'" at the unveiling of a monument erected in honor of Gouverneur Morris, framer of the Constitution, diplomat, and businessman ("Monument to Gouverneur Morris Unveiled at Church Where He and Brother Are Buried," *New York Times*, 5 July 1932, 3).

Utah

Park City: At the Egyptian Theater, Drum and Bugle Corps, Park City High School Band — vocal solo, "Flag Without a Stain" — clarinet and saxophone duet, Dasil and Lowell Smith — "Star-Spangled Banner," community singing, and a rendering of Sousa's *Stars and Stripes Forever* by the band ("Fourth of July to be Celebrated," *Park Record*, 1 July 1932, 1).

1933

Broadcasts

Over WNYC, "Naumberg concert in Central Park," Franz Kaltenborn, conductor; WJZ: New York

Philharmonic-Symphony, Willem van Hoogstraten, conductor, at Lewisohn Stadium, 9 P.M.; WEAF: "Dedication of Morristown National Historical Park, with American Legion Band; WJZ: R.O.T.C. independence day program, with U.S. Marine Band ("Today on the Radio, *New York Times*, 4 July 1933, 19).

Performances

District of Columbia

The evening's festivities at the Washington Monument began with a concert by the U.S. Marine Band at 8 P.M. Works included *Spirit of Independence* (Abe Holzmann); overture, "Songs of the American soldier"; cornet solo, *Home on the Range: Texas Cowboy Song* (David W. Guion), performed by Winfred Kemp; *American Patrol* (Meacham); fantasie, *Voice of Our Nation* (Santelmann); *Hail to the Spirit of Liberty* (Sousa); "Star-Spangled Banner" ("Monument July 4 to Be Site of Rites," *Washington Post*, 25 June 1933, 2; "Program Records," U.S. Marine Band Library); A Pan-American Union concert in joint tribute to the 122nd anniversary of the independence of Venezuela and the 157th anniversary of the American Declaration of Independence was given on July 5, with the U.S. Army Band, William J. Stannard, conductor, and Leopoldo Gutierrez, Chilean baritone (*Washington Post*, 6 July 1933, 3).

Kentucky

Bardstown: At My Old Kentucky Home State Park, 3,000 voices sang "My Old Kentucky Home" and other melodies by Stephen Collins Foster as a tribute to the composer (*Washington Post*, 5 July 1933, 5).

Maryland

Takoma Park: The U.S. Army Band marched in the town's parade ("Bombs Burst in Salute as Fourth Ends," *Washington Post*, 5 July 1933, 1).

New York

New York: New York Philharmonic-Symphony Orchestra, Willem Van Hoogstraten,[929] conductor, performed in the Lewisohn Stadium:

"The Star-Spangled Banner"
Grand Festival March, Wagner
Negro Rhapsody, Rubin Goldmark
Indian Suite (two movements), Edward MacDowell
Stars and Stripes Forever, Sousa
New World Symphony, Antonin Dvořák.
["Stadium Concert Varied," *New York Times*, 4 July 1933, 16].

Brazil

Rio de Janeiro: The Brazilian Marine Bugle Corps sounds reveille in front of the U.S. Embassy in honor of the Fourth (*New York Times*, 5 July 1933, 6).

1934

Performances

District of Columbia

The U.S. Army Band gave a concert at the Sylvan Theater on the Mall ("Sylvan Theater Fetes Extended," *Washington Post*, 1 July 1934, A3).

Illinois

Chicago: At the World's Fair, the Detroit Symphony performed works by Sousa, Herbert, Grainger, Kreisler, and others at Ford Gardens and the Chicago Symphony Orchestra presented a free concert with works by American composers in the Swift Bridge Amphitheater. "At 4:15 P.M. the Chicago Symphony will broadcast a patriotic program to Japan, which will be answered fifteen minutes later by the American ambassador to Tokio [sic] and a Japanese prince." Throughout the day, Army, Navy, and Marine Corps Bands provided martial music. That evening the Mundy Jubilee Singers presented a program in the Court of States; other musical events included the Jubilee C.M.E. Choir in the Hall of Religion; concerts by Army, Navy and Marine bands in Hall of States (Earl Mullin, "Fair to Observe 4th with Varied Program Today," *Chicago Daily Tribune*, 4 July 1934, 9).

New York

New York: At Lewisohn Stadium, Robert Russell Bennett's *Concerto Grosso for Small Dance Band and Symphony Orchestra*[930] and Deems Taylor's *Circus Day*[931] had their New York premieres and each composer conducted his own work. José Iturbi, guest conductor, led the orchestra in other American works ("Activities of Musicians," *New York Times*, 1 and 5 July 1934, X4 and 20, respectively).

Russia

Moscow: At the first Fourth of July celebration held in this country, at Ambassador William C. Bullitt's residence, a Russian orchestra played dance music and "The Star-Spangled Banner," whose score the Russian musicians wrote out by hand based on a phonograph disc recording of the song that had jazzy variations. "At intervals, Americans standing at attention were startled by interpolations of a saxophone crooning and an occasional bewildering 'Hey nonny nonny and hotcha cha'" ("American Mark Fourth in Russa," *New York Times*, 5 July 1934, 8).

1935

Broadcasts

A "Stephen Foster Birthday Memorial Concert" was broadcast from Greenfield Village, Michigan, over

WABC, New York ("Today on the Radio," *New York Times*, 4 July 1935, 28); Stephen Foster is honored over WOL, under John Tasker Howard's direction, and at Central Park Mall, a concert by the Naumburg Orchestra, Jaffrey Harris, conductor, is also carried over WOL ("On the Air Today," *Washington Post*, 4 July 1935, 18); over WMAQ-NBC, the U.S. Marine Band accompanied "an anti-crime independence day program with Patrick J. Hurley, former secretary of war, as speaker." Sponsored by the United States Flag Association (Larry Walters, "News of the Radio Stations," *Chicago Tribune*, 4 July 1935, 18).

Publications

"Fourth of July." A suite for piano, by Eastwood Lane (1879–1951). New York: Robbins Music, 1935. Includes: "Parade"—"Minuet for Betty Schuyler"—"Swing Your Partner"—"Quadrille"—"Waltz on the Village Green."

Performances

District of Columbia

The U.S. Marine Band presented an evening concert at the Washington Monument grounds. Works performed included *Our Glorious Banner* (Santelmann); *Jubel Overture* (Weber); *The Liberty Bell* (Sousa); *American Fantasie* (Herbert); *The Stars and Stripes Forever* (Sousa); "Fantasie on National Songs" (compiled and arranged by Santelmann); *American Patrol* (Meacham); *Hail to the Spirit of Liberty* (Sousa); "Star-Spangled Banner" ("Patriotic Groups to Parade July 4," *Washington Post*, 23 June 1935, 14; "Program Records," U.S. Marine Band Library).

Illinois

Chicago: The Chicago Symphony Orchestra, Eric DeLamarter, conductor, performed the following works at Grant Park on July 4: *In Bohemia* (Henry Hadley); *Irish Rhapsody* (Victor Herbert); *Hill Billy* (Saunders); *Moments Musical* (Franz Schubert); *The Irish Washer Woman* (Leo Sowerby); *March on American Airs* (Frank V. Van der Stucken); *Capriccio Espagnol* (Rimsky-Korsakoff); 1812 Overture (Tchaikovsky) "with appropriate gunfire by shot guns, machine guns, and light artillery" (Edward Moore, "Launch Free Music Series Tomorrow" and "Great Throng Hears Concert at Grant Park," *Chicago Daily Tribune*, 30 June and 4 July 1935, D13 and 11, respectively).

Utah

Moeb: Scheduled was a band parade and concert, directed by V.P. Walker and LaDue Williams ("Legion Will Sponsor Fourth of July Celebration at Moeb," *Times Independent*, 27 June 1935, 1).

1936

Performances

District of Columbia

The U.S. Marine Band, Capt. Taylor Branson, leader, and the Fort Stevens Drum and Bugle Corps of the American Legion provides music (*Stars and Stripes Forever*, "Hail Columbia," "Star-Spangled Banner") for the massing of the colors at the evening ceremony held at the Washington Monument. A concert by the band included the following works:

Hail to the Spirit of Liberty. Sousa.
Song of the Marching Men. [Henry Kimball] Hadley.
American Patrol. Meacham.
March, *My Own United States*. [Julian] Edwards
Selection, *From the Days of George Washington*. Arr. Schmidt.
March, *The Spirit of Independence*. Abe Holzmann.
["Gala Fireworks Display to End July 4th Fete," *Washington Post*, 28 June 1936, M8; "Program Records," U.S. Marine Band Library].

Illinois

Chicago: At the "Sky roofed theater on the lakefront," the Max Bendix Band, "a concert band, capable of giving a good account of itself evening music drawn from the orchestral repertoire," performed, with Rosalinda Morini, who sang the polonaise from *Mignon* and the song "Voices of the Spring" ("Thousands Hear Bendix Band in Holiday Concert," *Chicago Daily Tribune*, 5 July 1936, 11).

Maryland

Glen Echo: Dave McWilliams' 12-piece swing band provided music in the Spanish Ballroom (Nelson B. Bell, "About the Showshops," *Washington Post*, 3 July 1936, X18).

New York

New York: On the Mall in Central Park, Pasquale Acito conducted the Manhattan Concert Band of the Works Progress Administration's Federal Music Project in a program of "patriotic airs, and Miss Lily Wolman, soprano, sang several war-time selections" ("Band Concert on Mall," *New York Times*, 5 July 1936, N6).

1937

Performances

District of Columbia

On July 4, the Marine Band, Capt. Taylor Branson, leader, had this "preliminary" concert program at the "Grand National Convocation" of the Boy Scouts Jamboree:

Hands Across the Sea (Sousa)
"My Own United States" (Edwards)
The Liberty Bell (Sousa)
Hail to the Spirit of Liberty (Sousa)
America Victorious (Bagley)
Boy Scouts of America March (Sousa)
American Patrol (Meacham)
The Rosary (Ethelbert W. Nevin)
Song, "On to Washington" (Corbett)
American Fantasie (Herbert)
Grand march, *Hail America* (Georg Drumm)
Lift Up Your Hearts (Elgar)
"Largo" (Handel)
Finlandia (Sibelius)
[excerpt from] *Judas Maccabaeus* (Handel)

The convocation program followed with the Fort Stevens Drum and Bugle Corps and Marine Band. The ceremony included the *Stars and Stripes Forever* (Sousa); "My Country, 'tis of thee"; "America the Beautiful"; "God of our Fathers, known of old" (Rudyard Kipling), sung by Lanny Ross; "Hail, Hail, Scouting Spirit," led by Oscar Kirkham; "Star-Spangled Banner," with Marine Band accompaniment ("Program Records," and "Grand National Convocation at the Washington Monument" program, U.S. Marine Band Library)

On July 5, the U.S. Marine Band's concert at the Ellipse, 7 p.m., as printed in the newspaper:

March, *The Liberty Bell*, Sousa
Fantasia, *American*, Herbert
March, *America Victorious*, Bagley
Selection, "Frim's Favorites," Grofé
March, *Hail to the Spirit of Liberty*, Sousa
Song of the Marching Men, Hadley
American Patrol, F.W. Meacham
Song, "My Own United States," Edwards
Grand March, *Hail America*, Drumm
"The Star-Spangled Banner."

Another report had the band playing "Dixie," "Yankee Doodle," and Sousa's *Stars and Stripes Forever* ("Band Concert" and "50,000 Watch Greatest Show on D.C. Fourth," *Washington Post*, 4 and 6 July 1937, 7 and 1, 6, respectively).

Illinois

Chicago: Sir Ernest MacMillan, Canadian conductor, led the Chicago Symphony Orchestra in two concerts at Ravinia Park:
Afternoon

"Star-Spangled Banner"
Cockaigne (In London Town), Concert Overture, op. 40 (Elgar)
Symphony No. 8 in F Major, Op. 93 (Beethoven)
Concerto in A Minor, Op. 16, for piano and orchestra (Grieg; José Iturbi, piano)
Three Poems for Orchestra on Traditional Aramaic Themes (a premiere; Harl McDonald)
Negro Heaven: Symphonette (a premiere; Otto Cesana)

Evening
Symphony No. 4 in E Minor, Op. 98 (Brahms)
American Fantasie (Herbert)
Concerto No. 1 in E-flat (Liszt; José Iturbi, piano)
1812 Overture (Tchaikovsky)
[Edward Barry, "Ravinia Wins Acclaim with Holiday Music," *Chicago Tribune*, 5 July 1937, 19, 21].

New York

Mount Marion: President Roosevelt attended a Ladies Aid Society fair held at the Pattekill Dutch Reformed Church on July 5, gave a speech, and heard "The Star-Spangled Banner" sung by Miss Cecile Jacobson, accompanied by the Ernest Williams Band ("Roosevelt Affirms Nation's Soundness," *New York Times*, 6 July 1937, 7).

1938

Broadcasts

Over KECA in Los Angeles, the American opera *Gettysburg* composed by Arthur Robinson and Morris Hutchins Ruger from the El Capitan Theatre, with Emery Darcy, baritone, as the voice of Abraham Lincoln. The work was produced under the auspices of the Works Progress Administration Federal Music Project.[932]

Performances

District of Columbia

U.S. Marine Band on the Washington Monument grounds at 7:15 P.M.:

March, *The Liberty Bell*, Sousa
American Fantasie, Herbert
Overture, *Jubilee*, Weber
March, *Hail to the Spirit of Liberty*, Sousa
American Patrol, Meacham
Selection, "Friml's Favorites," Friml
Song of the Marching Men, Hadley
March, *The Stars and Stripes Forever*, Sousa
"The Star-Spangled Banner."

A slightly different order and selection of works are recorded in Marine Band records. Following the concert was a "procession of flags" ceremony with music provided by the band, with the Fort Stevens Drum and Bugle Corps ("Band Concerts," *Washington Post*, 4 July 1938, 2; "Program Records," U.S. Marine Band Library).

Maryland

Glen Echo: The Howard Becker Orchestra[933] provided dance music in the park's Spanish Garden Ballroom ("Glen Echo Park Ready to Serve Holiday Crowds," *Washington Post*, 3 July 1938, TT3).

New York

Lake Placid: At the Olympic Arena, the Canadian Dominion Day Weekend (July 1–4) is celebrated in tandem with the Fourth of July. On that day the "Governor General's Band of Ottawa, Canada" presented two concerts (*Ticonderoga Sentinel*, 30 June 1938, 3).

New York: At Lewisohn Stadium, a concert included these works: "The Star-Spangled Banner"; "The Stars and Stripes Forever"; Overture, "In Bohemia" (Hadley); "The Pleasure Dome of Kubla Khan" (Griffes); "American Fantasie" (Victor Herbert); symphony, "From the New World" (Dvořák) ("Programs of the Week," *New York Times*, 3 July 1938, 102).

Germany

Orb: The overture to "1776" by composer Charles Flick-Steger, has its first performance. "A dominant note in the opus is Liberty Bell's ring, scaled at C" ("Liberty's Note," *Washington Post*, 1 June 1938, X8).

1939

The highlight of this year's Fourth were the two world's fairs held in New York and San Francisco. The principal theme of the ceremonies held "in the Court of Peace of New York's World Fair and at the Golden Gate Exposition in San Francisco was 'American Declaration of Tolerance and Equality.'" An opening excerpt of the declaration explains the theme:

> This has ever been a free country. It was founded by men and women who fled from persecution and oppression; it was founded upon religious liberty and human equality. The signers of the Declaration of Independence built their hopes for America on these principles. Succeeding generations have cherished them. They are the most precisiou heritage of the American people

Songs composed specifically for the occasion included "We Sing America" by Harold J. Rome and "On Freedom's Shore" by Gilbert Patten, "author of the Frank Merriwell stories."[934] A composer of considerable merit was Robert Russell Bennett who wrote *The Spirit of George Washington*,[935] a 15-minute piece for band, to accompany the New York "Lagoon of Nations" water fountain display on July 4. The effect consisted of a pool 400 feet wide and 800 feet long, with synchronized water, light, and sound, and a 150-foot-high burst of water.

Performances

District of Columbia

The U.S. Marine Band gave an evening concert on the Monument grounds. Works performed included:

The Liberty Bell (Sousa)
The Voice of Our Nation (Santelmann)
American Fantasie (Herbert)
American Patrol (Meachan)
Song of the Marching Men (Hadley)
Hail America (Drumm)
Jubel Overture (Weber)
Stars and Stripes Forever (Sousa)

Following the concert was a "Progression of Flags" ceremony which included the Fort Stevens Drum and Bugle Corps ("Rain Threats Peril Fourth Program Here," *Washington Post*, 2 July 1939, 1 and 5; "Program Records," U.S. Marine Band Library).

New York

New York: At the World's Fair, the six water fountains and fireworks situated in the Lagoon of Nations that "tell the story of 'The Spirit of George Washington,'" was synchronized to music composed by Robert Russell Bennett.[936] The work was performed "by the Trytons, the Fair's official forty-four–piece symphonic band," directed by Joseph Littau; the Hebrew Tabernacle Choir, Artur Holde, director, was scheduled to perform at the Temple of Religion at the World's Fair. "The soloists will be cantor Richard Cohn, baritone; Erni Stern-Feitler, soprano, and Bashka Shasberger, alto. Ernest White will give his customary organ recitals"; also participating in the Fair were the Hall Johnson Negro Choir and Myra Manning soprano, Chicago Opera Company; Ferde Grofé's orchestral work *Ode to Freedom*, "inspired by the text rather than the music of 'The Battle Hymn of the Republic,'" was scheduled to be conducted by the composer "on the July 4 program of his New World Ensemble at the Ford Exposition at the New York World's Fair" ("Notes Here and Afield," "Hebrew Choir to Sing," and "'Spirit of George Washington' to be Portrayed in Giant Fireworks" *New York Times*, 2 and 4 July 1939, X6 and 3, respectively); the Naumburg concert on the mall in Central Park, directed by Philip James, had the following program:

Overture, "Rienzi" Wagner.
Symphony No. 8. Beethoven.
Violin concerto. Mendelssohn, with Carroll Glenn, violinist
Tone poem, "Vitava" [from *Má Vlast*). Smetana.
Overture, "In Olden Style."[937] James.
Tuba solo, "Song without Words." Composed and performed by Fritz Geib, tuba.
Swedish Rhapsody. [Hugo] Alfvén.
Tambourin Chinois. Fritz Kreisler/arr. Erno Rapée.
American Fantasie. Herbert.
["Microphone Presents," *New York Times*, 2 July 1939, X8].

England

London: The *Fourth of July*, a play written as a radio broadcast, by Alistair Cooke, with music arranged and conducted by Josef Honti, was broadcast ("Broadcasting: The Fourth of July," *London Times*, 4 July 1939, 26).

1940

Broadcasts

Over WJSY (Washington, D.C.), "Charles Lemisch played the Army antitank gun under the baton of Eugene Ormandy with the Philadelphia Orchestra. It was the conductor's idea to play Tchaikovsky's 1812 Overture in Robin Hood Dell exactly as the Russian had scored it — with cannon. Musician Lemisch was chosen as guest artist and he tells about it on *Strange As It Seems*" ("Today's Radio Highlights," *Washington Post*, 4 July 1940, 22).

Over WGN (Chicago), the W-G-N Orchestra, Henry Weber, director, provided music for the premiere of a play *Man with a Country*, written by Frederick Hazlitt Brennan, for a new radio program series titled *Chicago Tonight* (Larry Wolters, "New W-G-N Show to Make Bow in July 4 Premiere," *Chicago Daily Tribune*, 3 July 1940, 7).

Over NBC, a live broadcast titled "The Dream Hour"[938] with music by the Marine Band from the auditorium of the Marine Barracks in Washington, D.C., included these works:

The Marines' Hymn
Grand, March, "The Pilgrim" (Lake)
"1776" (Zamecnik)
March, *The Spirit of Independence* (Abe Holzmann)
American Fantasie (Herbert)
Trombone solo, "The Volunteer" (Simons), performed by Robert Isele
Grand march, "Hail America" (Drumm)
American Patrol (Meacham)
The Stars and Stripes Forever (Sousa)
"American the Beautiful"
"The Star-Spangled Banner"
["Program Records," U.S. Marine Band Library].

Performances

District of Columbia

The U.S. Marine Band, Henry Weber, second leader, conducting, gave a concert at 7:15 P.M. on the Monument grounds. Works performed included:

Grand March "United States of America" (Henckels)
American Fantasie (Herbert)
The Liberty Bell (Sousa)
American Patrol (Meacham)
Hail to the Spirit of Liberty (Sousa)
Suite, "From the Days of George Washington" (arr. Schmidt)
March, *Spirit of Independence* (Abe Holzmann)
The Stars and Stripes Forever (Sousa)

A flag raising ceremony included the Fort Stevens Drum and Bugle Corps ("Program Records," U.S. Marine Band Library; "Ickes to Make July 4 Speech at Monument," *Washington Post*, 30 June 1940, 16).

Illinois

Chicago: At Grant Park in the afternoon, the American Legion Band, Col. Armin F. Hand, conductor, provided music. In the evening A.F. Thaviu's Band performed. The soloists were Henry Thompson, tenor, and Edward B. Straight, drummer. In the evening concert, Thompson sang a duet with Teresa Ferrio, soprano. Another evening soloist was Paul Mallory, tenor. "The printed programs of the two concerts were made up largely of standard music, with a generous number of excerpts from opera and operetta" (Edward Barry, "Record Crowds Hear Concerts in Grant Park," *Chicago Tribune*, 5 July 1940, 15).

Massachusetts

Boston: The Esplanade concert featured Arthur Fiedler conducting the Boston Pops in a performance of *The Stars and Stripes Forever* (Sousa); Scherzo from the "New World" Symphony (Dvořák); *Minuet for Strings* (Bolzoni), Nutcracker Suite (Tchaikovsky), Second Hungarian Rhapsody (Liszt), Prize Song from *The Mastersingers of Nuremberg* (Wagner), *Pop Goes the Weasel* (Lucien Cailliet); *American Fantasie* (Herbert) (Program, Boston Symphony Orchestra Archives).

New York

Brooklyn: At Lewisohn Stadium, William Schuman's secular cantata, *This Is Our Time*, is premiered by the People's Philharmonic Choral Society, Max Helfman, conductor, and the Philharmonic-Symphony Orchestra, Alexander Smallens, conductor (*New York Times*, 5 July 1940, 10).

New York: At the World's Fair, Alma Dormagen sang "My Own United States" at the Court of Peace at 10:45 A.M.; Horace M. Hollister gave an organ recital in the Temple of Religion at 1 P.M.; the World's Fair Band presented a "patriotic concert" at 2 P.M.; the "American Jubilee" pageant with "300 actors, dancers and singers and 'America' sung by special chorus," in the Court of Peace at 2:30 P.M.; "National Open Championship of Fife, Drum and Bugle Corps, Court of Peace, at 5:30 P.M.; World's Fair Official Band, at American Common Bandshell, at 6:15 P.M.; "symphony of water, color, flame and music" at the Lagoon of Nations ("The Fair Today, *New York Times*, 4 July 1940, 13).

Uruguay

Montevideo: Arturo Toscanini had the NBC Orchestra play the "Star-Spangled Banner" at a rehearsal on the 4th for the farewell concert at the Soder Theatre marking the end of the orchestra's South American tour.[939] ("Toscanini Provided Surprise on Fourth," *New York Times*, 5 July 1940, 10).

1941

Broadcasts

Over NBC, the Marine Band, Capt. William Santelmann, leader, performed a half-hour concert at 9 P.M. from the Marine Barracks in Washington, D.C. Music included: the "Marines's Hymn"; "Our Fighting Men"; "General Holcomb March"[940] (premiere) (Balfoort); "National Defense" (premiere, Rudolph Hall); "The United States Marines" ("Program Records," U.S. Marine Band Library).

Publications

The Star-Spangled Banner, hymn national américain.[941] Mixed choeur ad libitum et orchestra. Composed by Igor Stravinsky, Los Angeles, 4 July 1941. New York: Mercury Music Corporation, s.d. Manuscript in Library of Congress.

Performances

District of Columbia

The U.S. Marine Band gave a concert on the Washington Monument grounds at 7 P.M. A flag raising ceremony included "The Stars and Stripes Forever" ("D.C. Program for July 4 Takes Form," *Washington Post*, 29 June 1941, 14; "Program Records," U.S. Marine Band Library); at Loew's Capitol Theater, a stage revue titled *Three Cheers*, which featured a new song, "Wave that Flag, America" by Howard Acton and Phelps Adams of the National Press Club was presented. The Ben Yost Singers also performed ("Red-White and- Blue Revue," *Washington Post*, 4 July 1941, 5).

New York

New York: "On the lower East Side," at the Temple of Americanism at 196 East Broadway, at a celebration representing the diversity of the East Side population, the ceremony began with the singing of "The Star-Spangled Banner" and closed with "God Bless America"[942] ("Solemn Hush Here Is Holiday Climax," *New York Times*, 5 July 1941, 1).

Utah

Kanab: In Ward Hall: national anthem, congregation — song by Shirlynn Judd, Mary Lou and Avin Chamberlain — accordion solo, Reuve Chamberlain — song, Shirley and Marleah Rust — song by Ramona Church — song by Buddy Heaton and Euzell Tietjen —"God Bless America" sung by congregation ("Preparations Complete for Gala Fourth of July Celebration in Kanab," *Kane County Standard*, 3 July 1941, 1).

1942

This was the first Fourth of July following the attack on Pearl Harbor and the nation was entrenched in a war to preserve its liberties and freedom. The War Department was as concerned with preserving and fostering unity at home and sought no better way than through the performance of patriotic music. Its efforts resulted in a comprehensive list[943] of patriotic music recommended for performance by orchestras, bands, vocal ensembles, and others. This list identifies much of the patriotic music likely performed on the Fourth of July from the late nineteenth century through the war years. As Americans listened attentively to news broadcast via radio regarding progress of the war, Fourth of July musical radio programs helped to foster hope and spirit as the war progressed.

Broadcasts

Over WRC and other NBC affiliates, the United States Treasury presented "Homage to Gershwin," with Bing Crosby, Dinah Shore, and the Paul Whiteman Orchestra; over WMAL, an American Legion program included Eleanor MacKinlay, singing the "Star-Spangled Banner"; over WOL, "'What So Proudly We Hail,' written, produced and acted entirely by soldiers of Camp Upton, Long Island," included music by the Bob Stanley Orchestra; over WOL, a program titled "Faith of a Fighting Nation" included music sung by the Metropolitan Opera soprano, Grace Moore ("The Post Radio Highlights," *Washington Post*, 4 July 1942, 24); "over W-G-N and the coast-to-coast Mutual Broadcasting system," the show titled "America Loves a Melody" featured medleys in tribute to George M. Cohan and Stephen Foster with vocalists Marion Claire and Attilio Baggiore and the W-G-N Symphony Orchestra and Chorus, Henry Weber, conductor ("Spirit of Fourth to Reign Tonight on Melody Hour," *Chicago Daily Tribune*, 4 July 1942, 12).

Publications

Water Music for Fourth of July Evening. By George Antheil; for string orchestra.[944] (1942–43). Manuscript. Holograph in New York Public Library; microfilm, Library of Congress.

Performances

District of Columbia

Aaron Copland's *Lincoln Portrait* ("completed mid–April 1942"), with Carl Sandburg, narrator, and André Kostelanetz, conductor, had its Washington premiere "on a barge in the Potomac with the Lincoln Memorial in the background."[945] (Aaron Copland and Vivian Perlis, "Looking Back with Aaron Copland," *New York Times*, 9 September 1984, SM82, 96).

New York

Brooklyn: At Lewisohn Stadium, 5,500 persons heard the New York Philharmonic-Symphony Orchestra, Alexander Smallens, conductor, perform these works: *In Bohemia* (Henry Hadley); Piano Concerto No. 2 (Edward MacDowell) Jacques Abrams, piano; *Billy the Kid* (Aaron Copland); Symphony, "From the New World" (Antonin Dvořák). ("American Works Heard at Stadium," *New York Times*, 5 July 1942, 28).

1943

Performances

District of Columbia

The premiere of William Schuman's *Prayer 1943* was given at the Watergate Concert, with the National Symphony performing, Leon Barzin, conductor (*Washington Post*, 5 July 1943, 1B); the U.S. Marine Band provided music for the ceremony at the Sylvan Theater, at the Washington Monument. Some of the works included "National Emblem" (Bagley); "Triumphal March" (Dudley Buck); "American Patrol" (Meacham); "Revolutionary Fantasy" (Ernest S. Williams); Overture, "John and Sam" (Ansell); "The Stars and Stripes Forever" (Sousa). After the pledge of allegiance to the flag, William R. Schmucker led the audience in singing of "America" and "America the Beautiful." The program closed with the singing of "The Star-Spangled Banner" ("Plans Ready for July 4th Celebration," *Washington Post*, 2 July 1943, B8; "Program Records," U.S. Marine Band Library).

Maryland

Baltimore: A band played "Yankee Doodle" as the liberty ship *George M. Cohan* was launched in honor of the late songwriter-showman of the same name who was supposedly born on July 3, 1878. Also, Eddie Cantor sang a selection of Cohan's songs (*Washington Evening Star*, 5 July 1943, A2).

New York

New York: At the Lewisohn Stadium on July 4, Morton Gould conducted the Philharmonic Symphony Orchestra for the second time, the first on the day previous. Works included *Newsreel*, William Schuman; *Billy the Kid*, Copland, *Ode to Truth*, Roy Harris; *American Symphonette*, no. 2, Gould; "St. Louis Blues," arr. Gould; "Smoke Gets in Your Eyes," Kern; "Stardust," Carmichael; marching songs of the United Nations ("Stadium Concerts," *New York Herald Tribune*, 4 July 1943, 2VI; "Gould Conducts at the Stadium" and "American Music Heard at Stadium," *New York Times*, 4 and 5 July 1943, 23 and 10, respectively).

North Africa

A celebration "attended by French and British officers" and presided over by Gen. Dwight D. Eisenhower, at allied headquarters included "a red-fezzed Spahi band" that played *The Stars and Stripes Forever* "and a United States band followed with 'Over There.'" According to another report, a French military band played "The Star-Spangled Banner" ("British to Salute Fourth," *New York Times*, 4 July 1943, 15; "Fourth Celebrated in Africa with Eisenhower Presiding," *Washington Post*, 5 July 1943, B1.)

Russia

Moscow: Russian artists presented an all–American concert program at Philharmonic Hall and Capt. Edward V. Rickenbacker was there (*Evening Star*, 5 July 1943, A5).

1944

Performances

California

Los Angeles: At the Hollywood Bowl, Bing Crosby hosted a "military music spectacle," on behalf of the Fifth War Loan drive, that included various military bands, and solos by Crosby, Ginny Simms, Ella Mae Morse, and James Melton. Other instrumental music included "excerpts from Rachmaninoff's Second Piano Concerto by Lt. Eddie Dunstedter, musical director of the orchestra." The event was sponsored through the sale of war bonds in exchange for tickets to the event ("'Times' Spectacle to Draw 20,000," *Los Angeles Times*, 4 July 1944, A1).

District of Columbia

The U.S. Marine Band, Capt. William F. Santelmann, conductor, gave a concert at the Washington Monument, 7:30 P.M., as part of the city's first "Cavalcade of Freedom" event. Beginning at 8:45 P.M., the Army Air Force Band was led by Paul Whiteman, with a cavalcade of Hollywood stars that followed ("D.C. to Have Spectacular July 4 Show," *Washington Post*, 30 June 1944, 4; "Program Records," U.S. Marine Band Library).

Illinois

Chicago: Capt. L.E. Watters, chief of the athletics and recreation branch of the 6th army service command organized a special concert that included Bagley's "National Emblem" march, Sousa's *Stars and Stripes Forever*, and works by Weber, Liszt, Wagner, and Victor Herbert at the Grant Park Bandshell. The orchestra consisted of "members of the 344th army service forces band of Fort Sheridan and musicians from the 740th military police battalion of Camp Skokie" and was conducted by Staff Sgt. Hubert Finlay, bandmaster of the 740th Military Police Band, and Sgt. Carmen Del Giudice (Albert Goldberg, "30,000 Enjoy Army Bands in Park Concert," *Chicago Daily Tribune*, 5 July 1944, 17); on July 1, at the Chicago Theater of the Air at Grant Park, "a 4th of July pageant" titled *Minstrels of the Masses*, "commemorating the birthdays of Stephen C. Foster and George M. Cohan were scheduled, with radio broadcast over W-G-N, WGNB, and Mutual." Musicians included the W-G-N Orchestra, Henry Weber, conductor, with vocal soloists Bruce Foote, Ruth Slater, Attilio Baggiore, and Earle Wilkie. ("Theater of Air in Grant Park Next Saturday," *Chicago Daily Tribune*, 25 June 1944, NW2).

1945

Performances

District of Columbia

A "Cavalcade of Freedom" event on the Washington Monument grounds, included an Army, Air Corps, and Marine Service Band and a number of Hollywood stars, including Roddy McDowell, Dinah Shore, Dennis Morgan, Lucille Ball, and others ("Program Records," U.S. Marine Band Library).

Illinois

Chicago: At the American Legion's 11th annual celebration held at Soldiers' Field, the Board of Trade Post Band, directed by Armin F. Hand, "played throughout the evening" (*Chicago Tribune*, 5 July 1945, 6).

1946

Performances

District of Columbia

At 12 noon, the Marine Band presented this concert program at the Marine Barracks:

"The Marines' Hymn"
March, "Hail to the Spirit of Liberty" (Sousa)
Cornet solo "Carnival of Venice"[946] (Staigers)
Selections from "Porgy and Bess" (Gershwin)
March, "Americans We"[947] (Fillmore)
Hymn, "Oh God, Our Help in Ages Past"[948] (Croft)
"The Star-Spangled Banner"

At the "Calvalcade of Freedom" celebration at the Washington Monument, three services bands (U.S. Navy Band, Army Air Corps Band, and U.S. Marine Band) performed and a 300-voice production of Earl Robinson's "Ballad for Americans"[949] was presented. The flag raising ceremony included the American and Philippine flags, with Philippine music. Stars appear-

ing at the Calvalcade included The Ross Sisters,[950] Joan Brooks,[951] Joe Dosh,[952] and Lucy Monroe[953] who sang "The Star-Spangled Banner" (*Washington Post*, 5 July 1946, 1; "Program Records," U.S. Marine Band Library).

Illinois

Chicago: At the Ravinia Festival, the Chicago Symphony Orchestra, George Szell, conductor, with Leon Fleisher, pianist (*Chicago Tribune*, 4 July 1946, 18).

Russia

Moscow: George Antheil's Symphony No. 4[954] was featured on a Fourth of July program by the Moscow Philharmonic Orchestra ("In the World of Music," *New York Times*, 29 September 1946, 69).

1947

Performances

District of Columbia

On the evening of July 3 at the Watergate, the National Symphony Orchestra, Richard Bales, conductor, performed a number of works by American composers including "Dance Overture" (Burrill Phillips), "Dedication" from *Through the Looking Glass* (Deems Taylor), "Suite" from *The Incredible Flutist* (Walter Piston), *Semper Fidelis* and *Stars and Stripes Forever* (John Philip Sousa) (Alice Eversman, "Work of American Composers Heard in Water Gate Concert," *Evening Star*, 4 July 1947, B10; *Washington Post*, 3 July 1947, 15).

1948

This year's significant event was the three-day centennial celebration of the Washington Monument, July 3–5. The occasion marked the commemoration of the cornerstone laying ceremony held in 1848 and presided over then by President James K. Polk. For this celebration, President Truman presented a speech that was "broadcast over all network stations at 2 P.M."

Publications

"Fourth of July" from *Holiday Music* by Morton Gould (New York: Chappel & Co., 1948).

Performances

Connecticut

Westport: The Little Symphony, John Burnett, conductor, provided music for a pageant, written by Julie Haggeman, that tells the story of George Washington's visit to this town in 1775 "when on his way from Philadelphia to Boston to take command of the patriot army." This was one of ten episodes of Westport's involvement in Revolutionary War history depicted. "Tylor Long, concert artist, sang 'A Toast to George Washington,' a song composed by Francis Hopkinson'" ("Westport Relives Washington's Visit," *New York Times*, 5 July 1948, 5).

District of Columbia

A grand parade on July 3 starting the 3-day event commemorating the centennial anniversary of the Washington Monument included 12 bands, one of which mentioned was the Metropolitan Police Boys Club Band. Other groups that performed on July 4–5, included the National Symphony Orchestra and the U.S. Navy Band and Marine Band, the latter two providing music for the color guard ceremony, as well as Lynn Allison[955] who sang the "Star-Spangled Banner" (*Washington Post*, 3 July 1948, 1, 9; "Program Records," U.S. Marine Band Library); on July 4, at the Watergate, the National Symphony Orchestra, Howard Mitchell, conductor, with guest soprano Dorothy Maynor, presented this program:

"A Mighty Fortress Is Our God" (Bach-Damrosch)
"Song to the Moon," from *Rusalka* (Dvořák)
"Pace, Pace, Mio Dio," from *La Forza del Destino* (Verdi)
Dorothy Maynor, soprano
"Legend," from Second Indian Suite (MacDowell)
American Salute (Gould)
Dirge (Mary Howe)
Money Musk (Leo Sowerby)
"As I Ride" (Rathaus)
"Sweet Music" (Rathaus)
"I Hear an Army" Barber
"Ecstasy" (Rummel)
Dorothy Maynor, soprano
Grand Canyon Suite (Grofé)
["Watergate Program," *Washington Post*, 4 July 1948, M2].

Illinois

Chicago: The Grant Park Symphony Orchestra, Nicolai Malko, conductor, performed a concert featuring mostly American compositions: *American Jubilee Overture* by Joseph Wagner; *Grand Canyon Suite* by Ferde Grofé; *American Patrol* by Meacham; *Stars and Stripes Forever* by Sousa; and other works by Rossini and Khachaturian (Seymour Raven, "U.S. Composers on Grant Park Program Tonight," *Chicago Tribune*, 4 July 1948, F5).

Maryland

Frederick: At Staley Park, the North End Civic Association Band, S. Fenton Harris, director, gave a concert and John Insley "led in singing patriotic airs and there were audience requests for marches and operatic selections" ("600 Attend NECA Events," *The News*, 6 July 1948, 1).

1949

Performances

District of Columbia

A concert by the U.S. Navy and Marine Bands at 7:30 P.M. at the Monument grounds, followed by a 'progression of the colors' ceremony, including the audience singing "America the Beautiful," led by Ben Mitchell Morris, tenor and "chief musician" of the Navy Band., who also sang "This Is My Country"[956] (*Washington Post*, 4 July 1949, 1; "Program Records," U.S. Marine Band Library).

Maryland

Hyattsville: The following bands marched in a parade from the University of Maryland to Magruder Park: United States Air Force Band; 356th Army Band from Fort Belvoir; Greenbelt Community Band; Prince George's County School Band (*Washington Post*, 4 July 1949, 1).

Massachusetts

Boston: The Esplanade concert featured Arthur Fiedler conducting the Boston Pops in a performance of *The Stars and Stripes Forever* (Sousa), "The Star-Spangled Banner," and other works by Offenbach, Khachaturian, Alexandre Luigini, Richard Strauss, Mendelssohn, and Tchaikovsky (Program, Boston Symphony Orchestra Archives).

1950

Performances

District of Columbia

The National Symphony Orchestra, Howard Mitchell, conductor, performed the 1812 Overture[957] on July 6 at the Watergate after a postponement due to rain. On the Monument grounds, a brief concert by U.S. service bands (Navy, Marines, and Army) followed by vocal works by the Sesquicentennial Chorus. A patriotic production titled "The Spirit of Independence Day" followed that included the Army, Navy, Marine, and Air Force Bands, Sam Jack Kaufman and orchestra,[958] Singing Patriots, and Sesquicentennial Chorus (Paul Hume, "Tschaikowsky Wanted Cannon, Watergate Gets Four," *Washington Post*, 6 July 1950, A1; "Program Records," U.S. Marine Band Library).

Illinois

Chicago: Eugene Ormandy and the Chicago Symphony Orchestra presented a mostly Wagner program in Ravinia Park's "expensively handsome new pavilion" (Claudia Cassidy, "On the Aisle: Brilliant Wagner with Firecracker Assistance Observes Ravinia 4th," *Chicago Tribune*, 5 July 1950, A1).

The U.S. Marine Band conducted by Major William F. Santelmann on the grounds of the Washington Monument, July 4, 1950. Together with other services bands, the Marine Band provided music for the "Massing of the Colors" ceremony (courtesy "The President's Own" United States Marine Band, Washington, D.C.).

Massachusetts

Boston: Arthur Fiedler and the Boston Pops performed *The Stars and Stripes Forever*, 1812 Overture (Tchaikovsky), *Invitation to the Dance* (Weber), *Salute to Our Fighting Forces* (Bodge), "The Star-Spangled Banner," *Rhapsody in Blue*, with Leo Litwin, pianist, selections from *Annie Get Your Gun*, and *Sleigh Ride* and *Classical Juke Box* by Leroy Anderson (Program, Boston Symphony Orchestra Archives).

1951

Performances

District of Columbia

A brief evening concert by the Marine Band, Major William F. Santelmann, leader, followed by the U.S. Navy School of Music Band, MUC James H. Moon, director. The "massing of the colors" followed accom-

panied by the Bolling Field Air Force Drum and Bugle Corps and Marine Band. Following was a program that included: a choir of 175 voices "in red, white and blue robes" that sang the "Hallelujah" chorus and "Battle Hymn of the Republic"; vocalist Vic Damone; a performance of *Ballad for Americans*, with vocalist Lee Fairfax[959] and a cast of 50; Billy Williams Quartette; a scene from *Faith of Our Fathers*[960]; "God Bless America," sung by the entire company after an address by President Harry Truman ("Truman Talk to Highlight July 4 Here," *Washington Post*, 4 July 1951, 1; "Program Records," U.S. Marine Band Library).

Illinois

Chicago: In Grant Park, the Grant Park Symphony Orchestra, Nicolai Malko, conductor, with Barbara Gibson,[961] soprano. The following program was presented:

Symphony No. 9 in E Minor. Dvořák
Excerpts from *Romeo & Juliet*. Gounod
"Caro Nome," from *Rigoletto*. Verdi.

NATIONAL CAPITAL
INDEPENDENCE DAY
Celebration

1776   1951

Symbol of Independence
JULY 4, 1951
WASHINGTON MONUMENT GROUNDS
WASHINGTON, D. C.

COMMEMORATING THE 175TH
ANNIVERSARY OF THE SIGNING OF
THE DECLARATION OF INDEPENDENCE

★ *Now* FREEDOM NEEDS YOU ★

Program for the 175th Fourth of July "National Capital" celebration held at the Washington, D.C., Monument Grounds with President Harry Truman, speaker, on July 4, 1951. Music was provided by the United States Marine Band, Major William F. Santelmann, director, United States Navy School of Music Band, MUC James H. Moon, director, and popular singers Vic Damone and Lee Fairfax (program provided by the U.S. Marine Band Library).

Three Dance Episodes from *Rodeo*. Copland
Arias & Polonaise from *Mignon*. Ambroise Thomas
"Una voce poco fa," from *Barber of Seville*. Rossini.
Selections from *Oklahoma*. Rodgers-Bennett
["Grant Park Programs," *Chicago Tribune*, 1 July
    1951, E8].

1952

Broadcasts

Illinois

Chicago:

A second composition by Mr. and Mrs. Philip Maxwell, of 5510 Sheridan Rd., will be heard on the Cities Service Band of America, conducted by Paul Lavalle at 8:30 P.M. tomorrow night on WMAQ. It will be "The American Way," a patriotic number dedicated to the pioneers of America. In march tempo, the Green and White quartet of the program will salute Washington, Lincoln, Jefferson, Clay, Nathan Hale, and Betsy Ross. The other Maxwell song heard on the nationwide radio show was "Let's Sing to Victory." Other numbers to be featured on the broadcast which pays tribute to the Fourth of July will be Holzmann's "The Spirit of Independence," "The Liberty Bell March" by Sousa; "The Ballyhoo March" by [Paul] Lavalle, and medleys of Cohan and service songs. Maxwell is director of the annual Chicagoland Music Festival, sponsored by Chicago Tribune Charities, Inc.

("Cities Service Band Will Play Maxwell Piece," *Chicago Daily Tribune*, 29 June 1952, SW12); at Grant Park, the Grant Park Symphony Orchestra, Nicolai Malko, conductor, performed "The Star-Spangled Banner"; "America the Beautiful"; *American Salute* (Gould); *American Patrol* (Meacham); and other works ("Tonight's Program at Grant Park," *Chicago Daily Tribune*, 4 July 1952, A3).

New York

New York: Radio station WQXR programs music by American composers all day (*New York Times*, 4 July 1952, L15).

Performances

District of Columbia

"A new patriotic anthem, 'Lead, My America,'" by Harold M. Dudley of Bethesda, MD, "founder and director of the Washington Pilgrimage of religious leaders," and lyrics by Badger Clark, "poet laureate of South Dakota," was premiered on the Washington Monument grounds. The song was sung by Marine PFC. Charles W. Oliver, baritone, with accompaniment by the Marine Band. Senator Francis Case of South Dakota introduced the performance ("Patriotic Anthem to be Introduced Here on July 4th," *Washington Post*, 21 June 1952, 9); on the monument grounds, "A Salute to Independence Day" program began at 8 P.M. with a musical fanfare by trumpeters and a "special announcement lyric" by the U.S. Army Glee Club. Bands performing included: U.S. Army Band, Captain Hugh Curry, leader; U.S. Marine Band, William

F. Santelmann, leader; U.S. Navy Band, Lt. Commander Charles Brendler, leader; U.S. Air Force Band, Col. George Howard, leader. All four bands played the "Star-Spangled Banner" in unison; U.S. Army Band Chorus sang a "Song of Freedom"; Ben Mitchell Morris sang "For You Alone" and "This Is My Country"; the Air Force Band performed "Triumph of Old Glory," "America Sings with George M. Cohan," and "God Bless America"; popular singer Eddie Fisher sang songs ("Program Records," U.S. Marine Band Library).

Virgin Islands

Charlotte Amalie: At the exercises after a parade, Mrs. Audry Vanterpool Harrison "gave a splendid rendition of 'America.'" There were patriotic songs by the Bel Aire Choir and the "Star-Spangled Banner" by the Community Band ("Thousands Join in 4th of July Celebration Here," *Daily News*, 5 July 1952).

1953

Publications

The 4th of July; words & music by Albert, Joseph and Thomas Gindhart. Philadelphia: Myers Music, 1953.

Performances

California

Pasadena: 50,000 spectators viewed the 27th annual Independence Day show in the Rose Bowl with patriotic songs sung by the Pasadena Boys Choir (*Los Angeles Times*, 5 July 1953, 2A).

District of Columbia

Four service bands performed on the Monument grounds in a program similar to that of 1952, except that a trumpet sextette performed "Hungarian Rhapsody" and "13 Street Rag." Ben Mitchell Morris sang "I Love Life," "This Is My Country," and "Mardi Gras" from *Mississippi Suite*. The U.S. Army Chorus, four military bands, and soloist Ben Mitchell Morris performed "America the Beautiful" ("Program Records," U.S. Marine Band Library).

Illinois

Chicago: At the Ravinia Festival, the Chicago Symphony Orchestra, Eugene Ormandy, conductor, with Rudolf Serkin, pianist (*Chicago Tribune*, 4 July 1953, 13).

1954

Performances

District of Columbia

On Sunday, July 4, at an evening concert at the Watergate, the Marine Band presented this program:

Commando March (Samuel Barber)
Overture, *In Springtime* (Carl Goldmark)
Encore, march, *Flag of Victory*
Perpetual Motion (Moto Perpetuo, Nicolò Paginini), performed by the entire clarinet section
"Prologie" to the opera *Pagliacci* (Leoncavallo)
March, *Staunch and True* (Carl Teike)
Encore, march, *From Tropic to Tropic* (Russell Alexander)
Tubby the Tuba (George Kleinsinger), Angelo Saverino, tuba and Dale Harpham, narration
Rhapsodic Dance, *Bamboula* (Samuel Coleridge-Taylor)
Encore, march "True to the Flag"
Irish Rhapsody (Victor Herbert)
The Marines' Hymn
The Star-Spangled Banner

On July 5, at the "Massing of the Colors" ceremony with Bryson Rash, master of ceremonies, the Marine Band provides music; Air Force MSgt John Osiecki performs "Andalucia" and "Green Light" on the accordian; Ben Mitchell Morris of the U.S. Navy Band sings "Stout Hearted Men" and "This Is My Country"; trombone and harp solos; Justin Lawrie Singers sing "Serenade" from *The Student Prince* and "Battle Hymn of the Republic" ("Program Records," U.S. Marine Band Library).

Maryland

Frederick: A U.S. Marine "drum and bugle unit as well as a drill team" performed at Municipal Airport; in Baker Park, the Browningsville Band provided music ("Huge Crowds at Air Fair, Motor Races," *The News*, 6 July 1954, 9).

Glen Echo: Jimmy Dean[962] and His Texas Wildcats provided music for Independence Day revelry (*Washington Post*, 4 July 1954, 6).

1955

Performances

New York

New York: At Lewisohn Stadium, The Stadium Symphony Orchestra, André Kostelanetz, conductor, premiered Ferde Grofé's *Hudson River Suite*, and performed *Circus: Overture* (Ernst Toch); *Western Symphony* (Hershy Kay); and works by Debussy and

The U.S. Marine Band conducted by Lt. Col. William F. Santelmann on the grounds of the Washington Monument, Monday, July 5, 1954. The band performed John Philip Sousa's "The Stars and Stripes Forever" and other patriotic music (courtesy "The President's Own" United States Marine Band, Washington, D.C.).

Prokofiev. Vocalist Roberta Peters was the principal soloist in singing various Italian arias ("Music: 'Pop' Concert," *New York Times*, 5 July 1955, 35); the Naumburg Orchestra, Tibor Serly, conductor, gave a concert in Central Park with the following selections: *The Merry Wives of Windsor* overture (Nicolai); *Night on Bald Mountain* (Mussorgsky); *Les Preludes* (Liszt); Symphony No. 9 in E Minor (Dvořák); *Stars and Stripes Forever* (Sousa). The principal soloist was Sy Shaffer, trombone, who performed selections from Haydn and Schumann and his own composition *Lullaby* ("Park Concert Is Heard," *New York Times*, 5 July 1955, 35).

Port Washington: At Manhasset Bay, 50,000 spectators heard the New York State Naval Militia Band perform in concert in honor of the day ("4th Greeted Here by 48-Gun Salute," *New York Times*, 5 July 1955, 1).

1956

Performances

California

Los Angeles: The Los Angeles Breakfast Club celebrated the Fourth of July and the Hollywood Bowl, with speeches, and The Roger Wagner Chorale performing "Oh Dear, What Can the Matter Be?"; "I Whistle a Happy Tune"; and "Dry Bones" ("Breakfast Club Salutes Nation's Fete and Bowl," *Los Angeles Times*, 5 July 1956, 28).

Massachusetts

Lenox: The 17th annual Berkshire Festival opened on Independence Day with a performance "by the Kroll String Quartet in the Theatre-Concert Hall at Tanglewood" in works by Mozart, Prokofiev, and Beethoven ("Berkshire Fete Begins," *New York Times*, 5 July 1956, 19).

Top: The "Spanish Ball Room" at Glen Echo Park, Maryland, was a popular Fourth of July venue for dancing in the 1930s and concerts in the 1950s by such headliners as Jimmy Dean and his Texas Wildcats. The ballroom opened in 1933 and is now under the care of the National Park Service (author's photograph). *Above:* The U.S. Marine Drum and Bugle Corps performing at Independence Day ceremonies at the U.S. Marine Corps War Memorial (Iwo Jima Memorial) in Arlington, Virginia, July 4, 1955 (courtesy "The President's Own" United States Marine Band, Washington, D.C.).

New Jersey

Plainfield: "A fifty-piece high school band from Plainfield, Vermont, performed tunes at a dedication ceremony for a memorial to Julian A. Scott, recipient of a Civil War Congressional Medal of Honor, and who was originally from Vermont but settled in New Jersey "until his death on July 4, 1901, when 55 years old" ("Boy War Hero Honored," *New York Times*, 5 July 1956, 14).

New York

Ellenville: "The Empire State Music Festival began its second season of outdoor concerts" on July 4. Carlos Chávez directed the Symphony of the Air in Symphony No. 5 by Shostakovich, *Three-Cornered Hat* by Manuel de Falla, and *Pavane pour une infante défunte* by Maurice Ravel (John Briggs, "Music: Ellenville Fete," *New York Times*, 5 July 1956, 19).

New York: "Although the Naumburg Symphony Orchestra bravely started its concert last night [July 4] at the Central Park Mall, rain forced an end" at intermission. "Up to that point Julius Grossman had conducted a Mozart overture and the first movement of Beethoven's 'Eroica' Symphony, and Robert Notkoff had been violin soloist in the Vieuxtemps Fifth Concerto" ("Rain Halts Concert on Mall," *New York Times*, 5 July 1956, 19); the concert at Lewisohn Stadium was canceled due to rain but took place on 5 July. The Kings Point Glee Club sang two excerpts from *Testament of Freedom* by Randall Thompson. Raymond Massey was narrator in *Lincoln Portrait* by Aaron Copland, and Howard Mitchell conducted the orchestra in Symphony No. 2 by Paul Creston and *Adagio for Strings* by Samuel Barber. Richard Dyer-Bennet performed solo guitar in "folk songs of many lands" ("Stadium Concert Off," *New York Times*, 5 July 1956, 18).

1957

Performances

California

Los Angeles: A number of bands were provided by the Los Angeles Bureau of Music and the American Federation of Musicians, Local 47: "Louis Palange conducted the 32-piece Community Band" at Hansen Dam Park; "Echo Park audiences heard the 32-piece band, under the direction of Herb Wilkings"; "Jose Cordova Cantu conducted the 28-piece Mexican Tipica Orchestra in a concert at Cheviot Hills Playground"; at South Park, "the 28-piece Metropolitan Band, Percy McDavid conducting," presented a concert (*Los Angeles Times*, 5 July 1957, 17).

Pasadena: At the Rose Bowl, "screen star Dennis Morgan is to lead the expected audience of 60,000 persons in singing the national anthem during a patriotic interlude between the circus performance and the hour-long fireworks display" ("Duel Spectacle to Be Presented at Rose Bowl," *Los Angeles Times*, 30 June 1955, 25).

District of Columbia

At 7A.M., the U.S. Marine Band presented music at the National Archives, and was the first televised (WRC–TV, NBC affiliate) performance by the band there. Music included *Semper Fidelis* (Sousa); Hail Columbia; Columbia, the Gem of the Ocean; America the Beautiful. A concert on the Monument grounds that evening, included broadway tunes, Sousa marches, *March of the Steelmen* (Charles Belsterling), and other favorite patriotic music ("Program Records," U.S. Marine Band Library; "Highlights on TV Today," *Washington Post*, 4 July 1957, B17).

Earl Robinson's *Ballad for Americans*,[963] to be sung by the University of Maryland Chorus, Fague Springman, director, with the U.S. Marine Band, Maj. Albert Schoepper, on the Fourth at the Washington Monument grounds was suddenly canceled due to accusations that the composer "had taken the Fifth Amendment in a House Un-American Activities Subcommittee hearing" and by implication was considered by some as a Communist. But Schoepper "said the *Ballad* was not performed because the orchestration was late in arriving and was not suited to the band." Springman "said a rehearsal of the work had been canceled on Tuesday and he was told about the composer taking the Fifth." ("'July 4' Fete Skips Ballad on America," *Washington Post*, 6 July 1957, B1; see also *Washington Post*, 5 July 1957, C1); Navy Sea Chanters, Chief Julius Whitinger, director, at the Washington Mall prior to the fireworks and during ceremony (*Washington Post*, 3 July 1957, A10).

1958

Performances

California

Huntington Beach: 23 Bands participated in the parade and at the Open Air Beach Amphitheater, the 72nd Army Band from Fort MacArthur played patriotic music (*Los Angeles Times*, 5 July 1958, B1).

District of Columbia

The U.S. Marine Band provided the music for the formal dedication of Theodore Roosevelt Island to the president "in the Potomac River just north of Memorial Bridge." In attendance and officially dedicating the island was Maryland Governor Theodore Roosevelt McKeldin. The program began with a concert by the Marine Band, Lt. Col. Albert F. Schoepper, conducting. The program included:

Yankee Doodle (arr. Gould)
The Liberty Bell (Sousa)
Tulsa (Don Gillis)

American Overture for Band (Joseph Wilcox Jenkins)
American Salute (Gould)
Hail America (Georg Drumm)
America the Beautiful
American Patrol (Meacham)
Spirit of Independence (Abe Holzmann)
A Soldier's Dream (Walter B. Rogers)
A Trumpeter's Lullaby (Leroy Anderson)

The ceremony also included "This Is My Country," sung by William D. Jones, and the band performed "Chester" from *New England Triptych*[964] by William Schuman; at an "Evening Parade" ceremony at the Marine Barracks, the U.S. Marine Drum and Bugle Corps, C.G. Stergiou, drum major, performed; the United States Army Band performed at the Watergate (Harry Gabbett, "Thunderstorms May Mar Area Holiday Celebrations," *Washington Post*, 4 July 1958, B1; "Program Records," U.S. Marine Band Library).

Belgium

Brussels: The Philadelphia Orchestra, Eugene Ormandy, conductor, and Isaac Stern, violinist, celebrated the Fourth with a mostly American music program: *Chant of 1942*, Paul Creston; *Violin Concerto*, Samuel Barber; *An American in Paris*, Gershwin; Symphony No. 1, Brahms; *The Stars and Stripes Forever*, Sousa (Howard Taubman, "Philadelphians Mark Fourth with U.S. Music in Brussels," *New York Times*, 5 July 1958, 13).

1959

Performances

Maryland

Baltimore: At Fort McHenry, the Marine Band, Lt. Col. Albert Schoepper, leader, performed patriotic music on the occasion of Alaska's entry in the United States and the official hoisting of the new 49-star flag. At exactly 12 midnight on July 3, the Marine Band played the "Star-Spangled Banner" as the flag was raised (*Chicago Daily Tribune*, 4 July 1959, 3; "Program Records," U.S. Marine Band Library).

1960

Performances

Connecticut

Woodbury: *Woodbury Fanfare*, by Leroy Anderson, and "completed in 1959 for the Woodbury, Connecticut, 1959 Tercentenary celebration," was premiered on July 4 by the Governor's Footguard Band as "an introduction to a 'Pageant of Ancient Woodbury.'" http://www.pbs.org/sleighride/Biography/Bio.htm

Program cover for the first official raising of the 49-star flag of the United States admitting Alaska to the union by Secretary of the Interior Fred A. Seaton on July 4, 1959, at Fort McHenry, Baltimore. The music was provided by the United States Marine Band, Lieutenant Colonel Albert Schoepper, director (program provided by the United States Marine Band Library).

Maryland

Baltimore: At Fort McHenry, the Marine Band, Lt.Col. Albert Schoepper, leader, provides a concert at 10:45 P.M., July 3, on the occasion of the official flag raising of the 50-star flag for Hawaii's entry in the United States. As the flag reached the top of the pole, Camille Elias of the National Park Service sang the opening stanza of "The Star-Spangled Banner,"

First Raising

Of The

50-Star Flag

July 4, 1960

HAWAII

FORT McHENRY NATIONAL MONUMENT AND HISTORIC SHRINE
BALTIMORE 30, MARYLAND

UNITED STATES DEPARTMENT OF THE INTERIOR
NATIONAL PARK SERVICE

Program cover for the first official raising of the 50-star flag of the United States admitting Hawaii to the union by Secretary of the Interior Fred A. Seaton on July 4, 1960, at Fort McHenry, Baltimore. The music was provided by the United States Marine Band, Lt. Col. Albert Schoepper, director, and Capt. James King, assistant director (program provided by the United States Marine Band Library).

accompanied by the band ("Program Records," U.S. Marine Band Library).

Pennsylvania

Philadelphia: "Amid the roll of drums and the blare of a bugle the nation's fifty-star flag was raised at Independence Hall today by a Marine Corps color guard in colonial uniforms.... Music for the Fourth of July salute to Hawaii was provided by the Broomall String Band, its members wearing costumes with a Hawaiian motif; the singing of the state song of Hawaii and the National Anthem by Charles L.K. Davis, Metropolitan Opera star and a native of Hawaii, and by the Philadelphia police and fireman band" (William G. Weart, "Fifty-Star Flag Flies for Fourth," *New York Times*, 5 July 1960, 1, 24).

1961

Performances

Michigan

Ann Arbor: Robert Ashley, *The Fourth of July*, at Cohen's Space Theatre, University of Michigan (See Bernard Waldrop," ONCE: Festival of New Music; Complex to Excellent," *Michigan Daily*, 28 February 1961).[965]

New York

New York: At the stadium, The Lewisohn Stadium Orchestra performed works by American composers Paul Creston and William Schuman ("Music: Elman at Stadium," *New York Times*, 5 July 1961, 28).

England

The American Wind Symphony Orchestra gave its first British concert performing from a barge on the Thames River and one of the works was Aaron Copland's *Fanfare for the Common Man* (*New York Times*, 5 July 1961, 30).

1962

Broadcasts

The U.S. Marine Band, Lt.Col. Albert Schoepper, leader, broadcast the following pieces on Radio station WBAL in Baltimore:

The Liberty Bell (Sousa)
Bugler's Holiday (Leroy Anderson)
American Overture for Band (Joseph Wilcox Jenkins)
"Chester," from *New England Triptych* (Schuman)
American Salute (Gould)
"This Is My Country," sung by William Jones, baritone
"Pledge of Allegiance to the Flag" (Irving Caesar, arr. Donald Hunsberger), sung by William Jones
Stars and Stripes Forever (Sousa)
"America the Beautiful"
Gate City March: Atlanta (Alfred F. Weldon)
"Yankee Doodle" (arr, Morton Gould)
["Program Records," U.S. Marine Band Library].

Performances

Massachusetts

Boston: At the Esplanade, Arthur Fiedler conducted the Boston Pops Orchestra in performances of *The Stars and Stripes Forever* (Sousa), *Indian War Dance* (Charles Sanford Skilton), *American Patrol* (Meacham), and other works (Program, Boston Symphony Orchestra Archives).

1963

Performances

Massachusetts

Boston: Arthur Fiedler conducted the Esplanade Orchestra in the following works: *The Stars and Stripes Forever* (Sousa); *Irish Suite* (Leroy Anderson); excerpt from *West Side Story* (Bernstein); "America"; "The Star-Spangled Banner"; *Battle Hymn of the Republic* (Steffe-Gould); *American Salute* (Gilmore-Gould); *Rhapsody in Blue* for piano and orchestra (Gershwin), Leo Litwin, piano; *Pops Round-Up* (arr. Hayman); *Salute to the Armed Forces* (arr. Bodge). Program, Boston Symphony Orchestra Archives.

1964

Publications

Fourth of July Parade; piano solo, by Ethel Tench Rogers. Westbury, NY: Pro Art6 Publications, 1964.

Performances

District of Columbia

The U.S. Marine Band, second leader Capt. Dale Harpham, performed Morton Gould's "Fourth of July" from *Holiday Music* on the grounds of the Wash-

ington Monument ("Music Performance Record," catalog 1100-R, U.S. Marine Band Library).

Massachusetts

Boston: Harry Ellis Dickson conducts the Esplanade Orchestra in the following works: Symphony No. 9, in E Minor, Op. 95 (Dvořák); "The Star-Spangled Banner"; *Rhapsody in Blue* (Gershwin), with Leo Litwin, piano; *Bostonia Suite* (Keith Brown; arr. Jacobus Langendoen). Program, Boston Symphony Orchestra Archives.

1965

Performances

District of Columbia

At the Watergate, the U.S. Marine Band presented the following program:

The Star-Spangled Banner
The Liberty Bell (Sousa)
Overture to *Semiramide* (Rossini)
Encore, Yankee Doodle (arr. Gould)
Bride of the Waves (Herbert L. Clarke)[966], Jeffrey Price, euphonium soloist
"Mardi Gras" from *Mississippi Suite* (Grofé)
Selection from *The Fortune Teller* (Victor Herbert)
Encore, *Golden Friendships* (Henry Fillmore)
Concertino (Weber), with Karl Longmire, clarinet soloist
"Waltz" from *Tales from the Vienna Woods* (Strauss)
Encore, *Gate City March: Atlanta* (Alfred F. Weldon)
"Caprice Brillant," from *Jota Aragonesa* (Glinka)
Pineapple Poll: Suite from the Ballet (Arthur Sullivan)
The Marines' Hymn
["Program Records," U.S. Marine Band Library].

Illinois

Chicago: The 5th Army Band led a parade "sponsored by the South Deering Improvement Association" ("Parades to Greet Fourth," *Chicago Tribune*, 4 July 1965, S3).

Massachusetts

Boston: Harry Ellis Dickson conducted the Esplanade Orchestra in the following works: Symphony No. 5, in C minor, Op. 67 (Beethoven); The Star-Spangled Banner; *Lincoln Portrait* (Copland); *The Grand Canyon Suite*, excerpts (Grofé); *The Stars and Stripes Forever* (Sousa). Program, Boston Symphony Orchestra Archives.

1966

Performances

District of Columbia

Duke Ellington, Ella Fitzgerald, and the Jimmy Jones Trio performed at the Carter Barron Amphitheatre (Harry MacArthur, "Ella and the Duke Make Fine Music," *Evening Star*, 5 July 1966, A18).

1967

Performances

California

Los Angeles: The Los Angeles Philharmonic Orchestra and Eugen Jochum in "his bowl debut" as conductor, with piano soloist Van Cliburn, at the Hollywood Bowl ("Baskets, Bowl to Team Up for the Holiday," *Los Angeles Times*, 4 July 1967, E1).

Illinois

Crystal Lake: The Great Lakes Naval Band performed at Veteran Acres Park (*Chicago Tribune*, 5 July 1966, A14).

Massachusetts

Boston: At the Esplanade, Arthur Fiedler and the Boston Pops Orchestra perform *Semper Fidelis* (Sousa); Symphony "From the New World" (Dvořák); The Star-Spangled Banner; *Rhapsody in Blue* (Gershwin), Leo Litwin, soloist; *Bostonia Suite* (Keith Brown) (Program, Boston Symphony Orchestra Archives).

1968

Performances

District of Columbia

The U.S. Marine Band provides music for the evening "parade of the colors" at the Washington Monument. Music included Rolling Thunder, Stars and Stripes Forever!, National Emblem March; To the Colors, Brassman's Holiday (Al Hirt), and Star-Spangled Banner ("Program Records," U.S. Marine Band Library).

New York

Brooklyn: In Prospect Park, Goldman Band, Richard Franko Goldman, conducting ("Entertainment Events, *New York Times*, 4 July 1968, 15).

New York: Jazz in the Garden with the Max Kaminsky Dixieland Band, at the Museum of Modern Art; Naumburg Symphony, Boyd Neel, conducting, with Charles Castleman, violinist, in Central Park (Ibid.)

1969

Performances

District of Columbia

The U.S. Marine Band, 1stLT, Jack Kline, conductor, presented the following program at the Marine Barracks:

Song, "God Bless America"
Selection, *American Salute* (Gould)
Medley, America the Beautiful and Battle Hymn of the Republic
March, Ye Boston Tea Party (Pryor)
Paro Doble, Bravada (Curzon)
Selection, by Richard Rodgers
The Liberty Bell (Sousa)

The Marine Drum and Bugle Corps, Warrant Officer Gary L. Losey ("Program Records," U.S. Marine Band Library).

Florida

Key Biscayne: Forty members of the U.S. Marine Band performed "Hail to the Chief" and other patriotic music in a parade reviewed by President Nixon and then returned to the Capitol for a performance there (*New York Times*, 5 July 1969, 1; *Washington Post*, 5 July 1969, A1).

Massachusetts

Boston: At the Esplanade, Arthur Fiedler and the Boston Pops Orchestra performed *Strike Up the Band* (Gershwin); Symphony "From the New World" (Dvořák); The Star-Spangled Banner; *Rhapsody in Blue* (Gershwin), Leo Litwin, soloist; selections from *South Pacific* (Rodgers) (Program, Boston Symphony Orchestra Archives).

1970

The highlight of this year was Honor America Day held on the steps of the Lincoln Memorial in Washington. The program's theme was best summarized in the program notes provided to the program participants: "A National Memorial Service will honor America on her 194th Birthday, serving as the keynote for this day of celebration in the Nation's Capitol. The United States Army Band, a massed church choir of 500 voices, The Centurymen Choir of Fort Worth, Texas, representatives of all faiths, musical soloists, and the Reverend Billy Graham will participate."

Performances

District of Columbia

"Honor America Day" memorial service on the steps of the Lincoln Memorial began with a concert by the U.S. Army Band, Chief Warrant Officer Frederic W. Boots, associate bandmaster, and The Centurymen[967] of the Southern Baptist Convention, Buryl Red, director, that included in this order:

> March Adoration (Ralph H. Woods), band
> Prelude and Fugue in G minor (J.S. Bach), band
> March National Spirit (Silas E. Hummel), band
> Fugue in E flat Major (J.S. Bach), band
> "Oh, God, Our Help in Ages Past" (arr. Buryl Red), sung by choir
> "Joyful, Joyful We Adore Thee" (arr. Buryl Red), sung by choir
> *Freedoms Foundation March* (Col. Samuel R. Loboda), band and choir
> *Up and Get Us Gone* (William Reynolds and Buryl Red), band and choir
> *Once to Every Man and Nation* (David Stanley York), band and choir
> *Ode to Freedom* (Ferde Grofé). Band
> *The Testament of Freedom* (Randall Thompson), band and choir

The "Star-Spangled Banner" was then sung by Pat Boone, accompanied by the Army Band and Herald Trumpets, Col Samuel R. Loboda, leader; "America the Beautiful," The Centurymen and band; Kate Smith sang "God Bless America," accompanied by the band; *The Stars and Stripes Forever* by band, "with special lyrics expressly for Honor America Day, written by Tom Adair, and adapted by John Scott Trotter, titled "Here Comes the Flag," sung by The Centurymen. After the program ended, the following bands provided music on the stage for the remainder of the afternoon: U.S. Marine Band; U.S. Naval Academy Band, U.S. Navy Band, U.S. Air Force Band. An evening ceremony began at 6:30 P.M. and included *Fanfare for the Common Man* (Copland), "Salute to America" (George M. Cohan), "Star-Spangled Banner," "Service Men on Parade" (a medley of the songs of the five services), "This Is My Country," and *Stars and Stripes Forever* performed by the Navy Band and Sea Chanters (18 male voices), Donald W. Stauffer, leader. Also on the program were U.S. Army Herald Trumpets, Les Brown Band, The Centurymen, The Pennsylvanians (30–40 female voices), The Young Americans (18 male and 18 female voices), with choirs directed by Fred Waring and the show's special guest Bob Hope ("Program Records," U.S. Marine Band Library; *Washington Post*, 5 July 1970, A1).

1971

Performances

District of Columbia

"A rock band will perform in place of the U.S. Air Force Band at the Washington Monument evening program." A concert presented by the Marine Band,

Col. Albert Schoepper, leader, at the Watergate included this program:

> March, *Wellington* (Wilhelm Zehle)
> Overture, *The King of Lahore* (Jules Massenet)
> Trumpet solo, *Hungarian Melodies*[968] (Vincent Bach)
> Encore, *Post Horn Galop* (Herman Koenig), with Terrance Detwiler, soloist
> *American Salute: Based on When Johnny Comes Marching Home* (Morton Gould)
> Encore, *The Footlifter* (Henry Fillmore)
> Clarinet solo, *Concerto for Clarinet* (Burnet Tuthill)
> Encore, *Arabesques* (Paul Jeanjean), with Darrell Hoard, soloist
> Overture, "Chester" [from *New England Triptych*] (William Schuman)

The Independence Day Reception
July 4, 1970

"Those who led America's Revolution spoke to their time, and to all time; . . . they captured an ideal and gave it life."

—Excerpt from President Nixon's statement appointing members of the American Revolution Bicentennial Committee

The Program cover for White House Reception on July 4, 1970, with President Richard Nixon presiding. Guests heard a concert by the White House Orchestra of the U.S. Marine Corps Band followed by the viewing of fireworks from the South Balcony. The guests then danced to the music of the Camaros (program provided by the United States Marine Band Library).

The Lincoln Memorial in Washington, D.C., the site for Honor America Day, held on the steps July 4, 1970. The musical performances that day were milestones in the history of the Fourth of July and included military service bands, the Centurymen Choir of Fort Worth, Texas, and popular singers Pat Boone ("The Star-Spangled Banner") and Kate Smith ("God Bless America)." Other performers included the Les Brown Band, Fred Waring and The Pennsylvanians, The Young Americans, and Bob Hope (author's photograph).

Encore, *The Gladiator* (Sousa)
Baritone solo, *Old American Song*s (Aaron Copland), with Michael Ryan, soloist
Selection, *George M!* (George M. Cohan)
"Polovetzian Dances" from *Prince Igor* (Borodin)
Marines' Hymn (with vocal)
Michael Ryan, concert moderator

("Nixon Opens Bicentennial," *Columbia Missourian*, 4 July 1971, 1; "Program Records," U.S. Marine Band Library); on July 5, the cast of the musical *Hair* was scheduled to present a performance at the P Street Beach in Georgetown (*Evening Star*, 4 July 1971, D10).

Illinois

Chicago: At Grant Park, the Grant Park Symphony Orchestra, Carmen Dragon, conductor, in music by American composers. Participating was George Goodman, bass-baritone ("Chicago Entertainment Calendar," *Chicago Tribune*, 4 July 1971, E3).

New York

New York: The cast of *1776*, a musical based on the Declaration of Independence, gave a public reading in costume of the document in Times Square (*Los Angeles Times*, 5 July 1971, 7).

1972

Publications

Symphonie de chamber: pour le 4 Juillet (*Chamber Symphony: for the 4th of July*). By Eugene Kurtz. Paris: Jobert, 1972. For celesta, percussion (2 players), piano, 2 violins, 2 violas, and 2 violoncellos.

Performances

District of Columbia

The biggest rock concert in six years in this city occurred with the Rolling Stones event at Robert F. Kennedy Stadium (*Washington Post*, 5 July 1972, A1).

Massachusetts

Boston: Boston Esplanade Orchestra, Harry Ellis Dickson, conducting, presented the following program at the Hatch Memorial Shell:

Overture to Egmont (Beethoven)
Symphony No. 5 in C Minor, Op. 67 (Beethoven)
"The Star-Spangled Banner"
Violin Concerto (Kabalevsky)
Medley of Burt Bacharach tunes (arr. Knight)
[Program, Boston Symphony Orchestra Archives].

Oklahoma

Oklahoma City: "The Stars and Stripes Show" hosted by Ed McMahon, and featuring Bob Hope, Anita Bryant, Nancy Wilson, and Kenny Rogers and the First Edition, took place on the Oklahoma State Fairgrounds. The event was broadcast over NBC–TV. (*Chicago Tribune*, 4 July 1972, 16).

1973

Performances

California

Los Angeles: At the Hollywood Bowl, David Zinman conducted the Los Angeles Philharmonic. The program included *Young Person's Guide to the Orchestra* (narration by Ralph Story), Britten; *The Stars and Stripes Forever*, Sousa; *Bolero*, Ravel; two *Hungarian Dances*, Brahms; *Roman Carnival*, Berlioz; *Façade*, Walton; *Tubby the Tuba*, Kleinsinger. Prior to the concert, the Sandefjord Girls Choir of Norway sang a number of songs (Robert Riley, "A Fine Fourth at the Bowl," *Los Angeles Times*, 6 July 1973, C17).

District of Columbia

U.S. Marine Band concert, Capt. William Rusinak, conductor, on the Capitol steps included these works:

> *The Liberty Bell* (Sousa)
> Overture to *Candide* (Bernstein)
> *La Virgen de la Macarena* (Rafael Méendez, arr. Charles Koff), trumpet solo
> *A Manx Rhapsody* (Haydn Wood)
> "The Genius of Victor Herbert" (Nestico)
> *A Jubilant Overture* (Alfred Reed)
> *Slavische Tänze* (Dvořák)
> "Vision Fugitive" [from the opera *Hérodiade*] (Jules Massenet)
> *Third Suite [for band]* (Robert Jager)
> *Ride of the Valkyries* (Wagner)
> ["Program Records," U.S. Marine Band Library].

Massachusetts

Boston: At the Esplanade concert, Harry Ellis Dickson conducted the Boston Symphony's Esplanade Orchestra in the following program: *American Salute* (When Johnny Comes Marching Home) (Gould); *The Stars and Stripes Forever* (Sousa); and Violin Concerto no. 22 (Giovanni Viotti), with Nicholas Danielson, violin; works by Mozart, Haydn, and Tchaikovsky (Program, Boston Symphony Orchestra Archives).

Texas

Dripping Springs: The first Willie Nelson Fourth of July picnic[969] takes place on this day with musicians Waylon Jennings, Charlie Rich, Kris Kristofferson, Tom T. Hall, Billy Joe Shaver, Sammi Smith, Greezy Wheels, and John Prine (Patrick Carr, "It's So

'Progressive' in Texas," *New York Times*, 22 July 1973, 97; Heintze, *The Fourth of July Encyclopedia*, 203).

Virginia

Vienna: The U.S. Air Force Band, Col. Arnald Gabriel, leader, at Wolf Trap Farm Park, Filene Center (*Washington Post*, 1 July 1973, F4).

1974

This was the year that Arthur Fiedler and David Mugar, executive producer and founder of Boston's Fourth of July, with the assistance of Bob Carey, the concert's emcee, and Nancy Randall, the event's producer, initiated the first Boston Pops performance of the 1812 Overture with live artillery fire (six 105mm Howitzers provided by the Fifth Battalion, Fifth Field Artillery of the 187th Infantry Brigade), church bells[970] (The Church of the Advent) Tchaikovsky had written into the score, and fireworks provided by Rockingham Fireworks in Seabrook, New Hampshire. Not long after, numerous orchestras were performing the work in the same manner.[971] Today most orchestras' Fourth of July repertoire includes the 1812 Overture.

Broadcasts

Over NBC TV, the "Stars and Stripes Show," with Bob Hope, Dionne Warwick and Tennessee Ernie Ford as headliners in the "sixth annual salute to the Fourth of July." Musical groups included Les Brown and his band, the Westchester Wranglerettes, and the Texas Boys' Choir ("TV Highlights," *Washington Post*, 4 July 1974, E8).

Performances

California

Los Angeles: At the Hollywood Bowl, the Los Angeles Philharmonic, Isaiah Jackson, conductor, performed Overture to "Ruslan and Ludmilla" (Glinka); "The Sorcerer's Apprentice" (Dukas); "Introduction and Rondo Capriccioso" (Saint-Saëns), with Lilit Gampel, violinist; *Variations on 'America'* (Charles Ives/orchestrated by William Schuman); "The Stars and Stripes Forever." The Paul Revere Junior High School Concert Choir sang four songs by Gershwin (Robert Riley, "Fourth of July Fare at Bowl," *Los Angeles Times*, 6 July 1974, A8).

Maryland

Fort Washington: The National Symphony Orchestra, Murry Sidlin, conductor presented this program:

> Overture to *Candide* (Bernstein)
> American Salute (Gould)
> *Variations on 'America'* (Charles Ives/arr. William Schuman)

An American in Paris (Gershwin)
"Four Dance Episodes" from *Rodeo* (Copland)
Royal Fireworks Music (Handel)
Stars and Stripes Forever (Sousa)
[*Washington Post*, 30 June 1974, F5].

Massachusetts

Boston: The first Boston Pops performance of Tchaikovsky's 1812 Overture with live cannons, and fireworks, through the initiative of Arthur Fiedler and David Mugar, and others. Also coordinated with the performance was the ringing of a steeple-bell at The Church of the Advent (Boston Symphony Orchestra Archives).

Missouri

Columbia: The Missouri Band performed in Cosmopolitan Park ("Symphony to Give Summer Concerts," *Columbia Missourian*, 28 June 1974, 5).

Kansas City: Kenny Rogers and the First Edition ("Superstars and Stripes Night," *Columbia Missourian*, 4 July 1974, 2).

1975

Performances

District of Columbia

At the Kennedy Center, the National Symphony Orchestra, Mstislav Rostropovich, conductor, performed *Scheherazade* (Rimsky-Korsakov), Symphony No. 5 (Prokofiev), and *Stars and Stripes Forever* (Sousa) (*Washington Post*, 5 July 1975, B1, B4).

Maryland

Callaway: On a nearby farm, a Summer Music Festival featured these performers: Gil Scott-Heron, soul musician; Brian Jackson and the Midnight Band; Stanley Turrentine, saxophone; Mandrill, funk band (*Washington Post*, 29 June 1975, 93).

Virginia

Staunton: The Statler Brothers presented their 6th annual "Happy Birthday U.S.A." celebration on July 3–4 at Gypsy Hill Park. A community vesper service on July 3 included these musical compositions: "Fanfare with Alleluia" (Philip Young), "God of Our Fathers" (George Warren), "My Country 'Tis of Thee," "Battle Hymn of the Republic," "America" (Bates). The July 4 event included the Statler Brothers, with guests Johnny Russell and Charlie McCoy ("Staunton's Sixth Annual Happy Birthday U.S.A." program, author's collection).

1976

This year marked the 200th anniversary of the founding of the nation with over 5000 colorful events staged across the country.[972] The planning for the Bicentennial began in July 1966 through authorization of a Congressional resolution by President Lyndon Baines Johnson. Philadelphia was elected as the official city that would host the national celebration. Music played an important part in many celebrations. In preparation for the event, the Music Educators National Conference (MENC) Bicentennial Commission, with the aid of several affiliated musical associations, issued a series of lists of choral, band, orchestra, opera, and piano works recommended for programming concerts and other performances.[973] Another MENC list focused on music and materials especially for elementary schools.[974] New recordings were issued to honor the Bicentennial, including the landmark 100-LP Record Anthology of Music, Inc. issued by New World and funded by a Rockefeller Foundation grant, presented free or at cost to thousands of cultural and educational organizations. Public readings of the Declaration of Independence took place across the country. In New York, composer Leonard Bernstein, read the Declaration at Battery Park and praised "its precision of rhetoric, subtle adherence to facts and barely contained rage."[975]

Noteworthy performances on July 4 included renowned vocalist Marian Anderson who read passages from the Declaration of Independence in Philadelphia; the premiere of Alan Hovhaness' new work *Ode to Freedom* at the Wolf Trap Farm Park, Filene Center, in Vienna, Virginia; and on July 5, the premiere of the new musical, *Forge of Freedom*, in Washington, D.C at Ford's Theater. Other works premiered during the Bicentennial year included *Echoes from an Invisible World*, by Leslie Bassett, commissioned by the Philadelphia Orchestra; *1600 Pennsylvania Avenue*, produced in Washington and on Broadway, by Leonard Bernstein; "A Mirror on Which to Dwell: Six Poems by Elizabeth Bishop," a vocal work, by Elliott Carter, and commissioned by Speculum Musicae; *The Bicentennial March* by Ervin Litkei; *Final Alice*, for orchestra, by David Del Tredici, commissioned by the National Education Association; *Mirage* for orchestra by Jacob Druckman; *Bicentennial Symphony* for chorus and orchestra, by Roy Harris, commissioned by the California State, Los Angeles Foundation for the Bicentennial; *Be Glad Then America*, a pageant for solo and choral voices by John La Montaine; *Es war einmal*, a work for mixed-media, by Robert Moran; *Bicentennial Fanfare*, an orchestral work by Walter Piston.

Performances

California

Los Angeles: At the Hollywood Bowl, the concert began with "a ceremonial march by the fife and drum corps of the Los Angeles Unified School District," followed by the Los Angeles Philharmonic and conductor Zubin Mehta in "his first appearance at these Fourth concerts." Sherrill Milnes sang "America the Beautiful," "Shenandoah" and a "setting of Lincoln's Gettysburg Address by William Stearns Walker." The *Ballad for Americans* (Earl Robinson) was performed by an Interdenominational Choir, with Brock Peters, bass-baritone. The choir also sang "Use Me, Lord, Use Me," "Joy Is on the Way" and "I Believe in Liberty." Orchestral works included *Variations on 'America'* (Ives/arr. William Schuman); Overture to *Candide* (Bernstein); *An American in Paris* (Gershwin), and three Sousa marches: *Washington Post, El Capitan,* and *The Stars and Stripes Forever* (Robert Riley, "Bicentennial Concert at Bowl," *Los Angeles Times,* 6 July 1976, G10).

District of Columbia

At Ford's Theater, the musical *Forge of Freedom,*[976] written by John Allen; music by Shelly Markham, was premiered on July 5 (*Washington Post,* 5 July 1976, B9); country music singer Johnny Cash[977] was grand marshal of the D.C. parade on Saturday and master of ceremonies at the Sylvan Theater. He and his group the Tennessee Three performed, as well as the Grambling State University Marching Band, U.S. Army Band, and the Morman Tabernacle Choir (Lawrence Meyer, "America Joyfully Toasts Birth of a Nation," *Washington Post,* 5 July 1976, A1, A14).

Louisiana

New Orleans: Dixieland musicians performed in historic Jackson Square to honor both the Bicentennial and the birth of Louis Armstrong (*Washington Post,* 5 July 1976, A14).

Massachusetts

Boston: Arthur Fiedler conducted the Boston Pops at the Esplanade in the following works: *Jubilee Overture* (Carl Maria von Weber); Concerto No. 1 in B-flat Minor, Op. 23 (Tchaikovsky), with Shigeo Neriki, piano; The Star-Spangled Banner; Patriotic Singalong (arr. Hayman); *1812, Ouverture Solennelle* (Tchaikovsky). Program, Boston Symphony Orchestra Archives.

The Main entrance to Ford's Theater, Washington, D.C. On July 5, 1976, the musical *Forge of Freedom,* by John Allen and Shelly Markham, was premiered here. Photograph by the author.

New York

New York: At Central Park, the New York Philharmonic, Leonard Bernstein, conductor, "gave a free, all–American Bicentennial concert." The program included "Symphonic Dances" from *West Side Story*, *Rhapsody in Blue* (Gershwin), *American Festival Overture* (William Schuman), *Lincoln Portrait* (Copland), *An American in Paris* (Gershwin), and *Stars and Stripes Forever* (Sousa) (John Rockwell, "Music: Philharmonic Plays to 50,000," *New York Times*, 5 July 1976, 6); at Battery Park, the American Symphony, Morton Gould, conductor, presented a program of "light American pop-concert music" (Peter G. Davis, "Concert: American Symphony in Rousing Holiday Fare," *New York Times*, 5 July 1976, 8).

Pennsylvania

Philadelphia: At Independence Hall, with President Gerald Ford presiding, singer Marian Anderson read passages from the Declaration of Independence, while an organist played "America the Beautiful." An interfaith service in the morning included 10,000 persons who sang "God of Our Fathers." "At 10:30 A.M., on a platform draped with red, white and blue bunting in the shadow of George Washington's statue and Independence Hall's simple brick façade, the Armed Forces Bicentennial Chorus sang "The Star-Spangled Banner" (Margot Hornblower, "A Pride-Filled Day for Philadelphia, Where It All Began," *Washington Post*, 5 July 1976, A16).

Rhode Island

Providence: The United States Army Field Band,[978] Maj. Samuel J. Fricano, commander, performed this program at Roger Williams Park:

George Washington Bicentennial
American Salute (Gould)
Lola Flores
Dramatic Essay
Deep Purple
Pas Redouble
Impossible Dream
A Salute to Show Biz'
Stars and Stripes Forever
Encore: God Bless America
[Program, 4 July 1976, U.S. Army Field Band, courtesy of SFC Sarah Anderson, Library].

Virginia

Williamsburg: "A fife and drum corps played an 18th century musical air for each of the original states," each followed by an artillery blast. For Virginia, the tune was "The World Turned Upside Down" (Thomas Grubisich, "'Volleys of Joy' Fired in Williamsburg," *Washington Post*, 5 July 1976, A20).

Vienna: At Wolf Trap at the Filene Center on July 3, a concert by the National Symphony Orchestra, André Kostelanetz, conductor, began at 10:30 P.M. Works performed included: *Ode to Freedom* (world premiere "specifically for Wolf Trap's Bicentennial cel-

ebration") for violin and orchestra, by Alan Hovhaness, with Yehudi Menuhin, violinist; *Night of the Tropics* (L.M. Gottschalk), arranged by Howard Shanet; *The White Knight* by Deems Taylor: *New England Triptych* by William Schuman; a medley of music from *Showboat*. At midnight Kostelanetz and Menuhin led the audience in singing "The Star-Spangled Banner." "Then, while the orchestra played *The Stars and Stripes Forever*, a screen at the back of the stage, behind the orchestra's trumpets and trombones, erupted into electronically projected fireworks while a string of outsized red, white, and blue lights strung across the front of the stage blazed." (Paul Hume, "Musical Midnight Excitement," *Washington Post*, 5 July 1976, B7).

1977

Broadcasts

Over CBS, "They Said It with Music: Yankee Doodle to Ragtime," a two-hour "salute to America and the American songwriter" featured Jean Stapleton, Bernadette Peters, Tony Randall, Jason Robards, and Flip Wilson. "The special was conceived and created by Goddard Lieberson." The songs illustrated the nation's heritage: "workers, wars, black history, romance, suffragettes" ("CBS Tunes Up for July 4 Musical," *Los Angeles Times*, 3 July 1977, N3).

Performances

California

Los Angeles: At the Hollywood Bowl, Sidney Harth conducted the Los Angeles Philharmonic in works by Morton Gould, Grofé, Mussorgsky, Ginastera, Copland and Sousa. Assisting was Sesame Street's Big Bird ("Fireworks Picnic Concert Set," *Los Angeles Times*, 20 June 1977, E12; Robert Riley, "Saved by the Bird at the Bowl, *Los Angeles Times*, 6 July 1977, H13).

Massachusetts

Boston: Arthur Fiedler conducted the Boston Pops at the Hatch Memorial Shell in the following works: *Washington Post March*[979] (Sousa); Suite from *The Water Music* (Handel-Harty); *Voices of Spring*, Waltzes (Strauss); Overture to *Orpheus in Hades* (Offenbach); The Star-Spangled Banner; Pops Hoe-Down (arr. Hayman); America Sings (arr. Bodge); *1812, Ouverture Solennelle* (Tchaikovsky). Program, Boston Symphony Orchestra Archives.

Missouri

Columbia: The following musical groups performed: Missouri Symphony Society Youth Band; Oak Tower Kazoo Band; Columbia Civic Band. "Frank and Diane Hennessy of Crosroads Music" gave an organ concert ("Get Ready for Fun on the Fourth," *Columbia Missourian*, 3 July 1977, 1).

New York

New York: The U.S. Navy band is on board the aircraft carrier USS *Forrestal* providing music for the bicentennial events.[980]

Saratoga Springs: U.S. Army Field Band, Maj. Samuel J. Fricano, commander, performed this program at the Hall of Springs:

Purple Carnival (Herold Alford)
Italian Girl in Algiers (Rossini)
Clarinet Favorites
Thunder and Lightning Polka (Johann Strauss)
'Largo al Factotum' from *The Barber of Seville* (Rossini)
Skip to My Lou
Dance of the Hours
A Salute to Show Biz'
Washington Grays (Grafulla)
Zorba the Greek (Mikis Theodorakis)
America the Beautiful
Stars and Stripes Forever (Sousa)
[Program, 4 July 1977, U.S. Army Field Band].

Virginia

Arlington: The U.S. Marine Band, Capt. John Bourgeois, conductor, presented a patriotic program at the Iwo Jima Memorial at 7 P.M. ("Program Records," U.S. Marine Band Library).

1978

Broadcasts

"'Sing America Sing': a musical celebration of America written by Oscar Brand who performed with a cast headed by John Raitt." KCET (PBS) Los Angeles, CA. ("Tuesday's TV Programs," *Los Angeles Times*, 4 July 1978, H11).

Performances

District of Columbia

The U.S. Marine Band provided music for a ceremony at the National Archives ("Program Records," U.S. Marine Band Library).

Illinois

Wheaton: The following bands provided music in the town's parade: The Medinah Brass Band; the 60-member Arabesque Oriental Band; the 30-member Scotland Highlands Band, "with kilts and bagpies"; 46-member Navy Band of Great Lakes; Glenhard North High School Band; and 50-member Wheaton Municipal Band ("Medinah Unit to Lead Wheaton's Parade," *Chicago Tribune*, 29 June 1978, W4).

Massachusetts

Boston: Arthur Fiedler and the Boston Pops Esplanade Orchestra performed the following program:

American Salute, When Johnny Comes Marching Home (Gould); First movement (Allegro con brio) from Symphony No. 5 in C Minor, Op. 67 (Beethoven); *By the Beautifuil Blue Danube*, waltzes (Strauss); Stephen Foster Medley (arr. Knight); The Star-Spangled Banner; Patriotic Sing-along (arr. Hayman); *1812, Ouverture Solennelle* (Tchaikovsky). (Program, Boston Symphony Orchestra Archives).

Needham: The U.S. Army Field Band, Maj. Samuel J. Fricano, commander, presented this concert at Needham High School:

His Honor
Fanfare for the Common Man (Copland)
Prince Igor (3 & 4) (Alexander Borodin)
Feels So Good
Espani Cani
A Tribute to Nat "King" Cole
The Sorcerer's Apprentice (Paul Dukas)
Begin the Beguine
Italian Street Song
Veve L'Amour
Dixie
Little David
Home on the Range
Battle Hymn of the Republic
Robinson's Grand Entree (Karl King)
Drum Act
From Sea to Shining Sea
Stars and Stripes Forever
God Bless America
[Program, 4 July 1978, U.S. Army Field Band].

Virginia

Staunton: The Statler Brothers presented their "Happy Birthday U.S.A." celebration on July 3–4 that included a parade and gospel concerts on July 3 with Crestman Quartet, The Stewards, and Tru-Tones Quartet. The July 4 program included the Statler Brothers and guest Johnny Rodriguez ("Happy Birthday U.S.A." program, author's collection)

1979

Performances

District of Columbia

On the Capitol steps at 10:30 A.M., the U.S. Army Band provided music for an "Honor America Day" event with various religious leaders participating; On the West Lawn of the Capitol in the evening, the National Symphony Orchestra, Mstislav Rostropovich, conductor, with Festival Chorus, performed: *Egmont Overture* (Beethoven); *Finlandia* (Sibelius); *Husitska Overture* (Dvořák); *Fourth of July* (Charles Ives); *The Testament of Freedom* (Thompson); *The Stars and Stripes Forever* (Sousa) ("Music File" *Washington Post*, 29 June 1979, 16; Paul Hume, "A Very Musical Fourth," *Washington Post*, 1 July 1979, K4); U.S. Marine Band, Alive Singers, and McCullough Kings Harmony Band at Washington Monument grounds preceding the fireworks (Joseph Contreras, "Varied Activities, Sunny Day Forecast for Fourth of July," *Washington Post*, 2 July 1979, C1–C2).

New York

Hyde Park: The U.S. Army Field Band, Col. William E. Clark, commander, performed this program at the Vanderbilt Estate:

Block M March (Jerry H. Bilik)
American Overture for Band (Joseph Wilcox Jenkins)
Soliloquy from *Carousel*
Sea Portrait
Through the Air
Memorable themes from the screen
A Salute to Show Biz'
Stars and Stripes Forever
[Program, 4 July 1979, U.S. Army Field Band].

Virginia

Vienna: At Wolf Trap Farm Park, the U.S. Air Force Band performed works by Schuman, Sousa, Clarke, Creston, Gould, Goldman, and Dragon ("Music File," *Washington Post*, 29 June 1979, 16).

1980

Performances

District of Columbia

The Beach Boys gave a free concert on the Mall (*Washington Post*, 5 July 1980, 1); at the Jefferson Memorial, pianist Marden Abadi played selections by Chopin before a large crowd and Sarah Caldwell was guest conductor of the National Symphony Orchestra in works by Charles Ives and Elliott Carter (*Washington Post*, 5 July 1980, A8, B1–B2); an "evening parade" concert, Lt Col John R. Bourgeois, Leader, in Sousa Hall at the Marine Barracks by the Marine Band included this program:

The Liberty Bell (Sousa)
"America the Beautiful" (Samuel A. Ward)
American Patrol (F.W. Meacham)
"God of Our Fathers" (George William Warren)
George M! (arr. William Jolly)
"God Bless America" (Irving Berlin)
The Stars and Stripes Forever (Sousa)
["Program Records," U.S. Marine Band Library].

Maryland

Oxon Hill: The Prince George's County Symphony Orchestra at Fort Washington Park ("This Week," *Washington Post*, 3 July 1980, VA14).

Massachusetts

Boston: John Williams conducted his first Boston Esplanade Fourth of July concert as resident conductor of the Boston Pops (Program, Boston Symphony Orchestra Archives).

Old Sturbridge Village: A reenactment of a "typical New England town celebration of American Independence in 1840" took place, including a parade with the Sturbridge Martial Band and "members of the militia group" (Suzanne Donner, "Notes Celebrating the Fourth of July," *New York Times*, 22 June 1980, sec. 10, 3).

New York

East Meadow: The U.S. Army Field Band, William E. Clark, commander, performed this program at Eisenhower Park:

El Capitan (Sousa)
American Overture for Band (Joseph Wilcox Jenkins)
Reaching Out to You
Light Cavalry Overture (Franz von Suppé)
A toast to "pops"
Pm with the Show
National Emblem (Bagley)
America the Beautiful
1812 Overture
Stars and Stripes Forever (Sousa)
[Program, 4 July 1980, U.S. Army Field Band].

New York: At the Metropolitan Opera House, the American Ballet Theater began its program with the orchestra conducted by a Briton, John Lanchbery, performing "The Star-Spangled Banner" and "the audience gustily singing along" (Anna Kisselgoff, "Ballet: 'Improvisations' at Tudor Celebration," *New York Times*, 6 July 1980, 26).

Tarrytown: On the grounds of Lyndhurst, "the former Jay Gould estate," the 10th anniversary of "Summer of Music on the Hudson" that annually takes place on Independence Day weekend continued. The County Symphony, Stephen Simon, performed on July 5, *Souvenirs* (Samuel Barber); *Series for a Festival* (Jacob Stern), commissioned for this event; *Rhapsody in Blue* (Gershwin), with Vera Appleton, piano; *Grand Canyon Suite* (Grofé); *Stars and Stripes Forever* (Sousa). Also performing was the Germantown Ancient Fife and Drum Corps (Allen Hughes, "'Music on Hudson' Series Opens," *New York Times*, 4 July 1980, C3.)

South Dakota

Mount Rushmore: At the fiftieth anniversary of the unveiling of the monument, the ceremony included music performed by the Strategic Air Command Band from Offutt Air Force Base in Omaha.[981]

Virginia

Staunton: The Statler Brothers gave their 11th annual free concert in this town where they were born (*Washington Post*, 5 July 1980, C1).

Vienna: At the Wolf Trap Farm Park, the U.S. Air Force Band, narrated by Johnny Holliday (*Washington Post*, 4 July 1980, C10).

1981

Performances

District of Columbia

At the White House on the South Lawn, a number of down-home groups from Connecticut performed, including A Touch of Class (12 woman vocalists); Eastonaires (barber-shop quartet); Bourbon Street Seven (Dixieland band); Soundsmen (barber-shop quartet); Easton Banjo Society. Jane Foster of *A Touch of Class* sang "God Bless America" (Ruth Robinson, "State Musicians at White House," *New York Times*, 28 June 1981, 8, sec. 11); at the White House staff picnic celebration, the U.S. Marine Band, Maj. Charles P. Erwin, conducting, presented this program:

> *The Liberty Bell* (Sousa)
> *The Music Man*
> "This Is My Country"
> Gershwin Medley
> Change of Pace
> Stephen Foster Medley
> *Americans We* (Henry Fillmore)
> Mary Poppins
> Sound of Music
> "God Bless America"
> Four Score and Seven
> *American Pageant* (Thomas Knox)
> *The Stars and Stripes Forever*
> *Armed Forces Medley*
> *Semper Fidelis*
> *Hail to the Spirit of Liberty*
> "The Yankee Doodle Boy"

("Program Records," U.S. Marine Band Library); the Beach Boys performed on the Mall; Pearl Bailey sang "The Star-Spangled Banner" "Battle Hymn of the Republic," and "God Bless America" with the National Symphony Orchestra, Mstislav Rostropovich, conducting, on the West Lawn of the Capitol. Orchestral works performed included: "Jubilee" overture from *Symphonic Sketches* (George Whitefield Chadwick); *Adagio for Strings* (Barber); *The Incredible Flutist* (Piston); *Feu d'artifice [Fireworks]* (Stravinsky); *Semper Fidelis* and *The Stars and Stripes Forever* (Sousa) ("A Safe and Sane (but Glorious!) Fourth," *Washington Post*, 3 July 1981, W3, and 5 July 1981, A11, B5; Paul Hume, "Concert at the Capitol," *Washington Post*, 6 July 1981, C13); an organ concert featuring "American music and other suprises" by Douglas Major at Washington National Cathedral, at 11 A.M. included these works: *Arioso for Organ* (Leo Sowerby); *Concert Variations on the Star-Spangled Banner*[982] (Dudley Buck); "The Stars and Stripes Forever" (arr. Douglas Major); *Adagio for Strings* (Samuel Barber, arr. William Strickland); *Graceful Ghost Ra*g (William Bolcom)' "Round of the Princess" from *Firebird* (Stravinsky); "My country, 'tis of thee" (singalong); *Fanfare for Organ* (Ronald Arnatt) ("This

Week," *Washington Post*, 2 July 1981, MD7; Paul Hume, "Douglas Major," *Washington Post*, 6 July 1981, C13).

Massachusetts

Boston: John Williams and the Boston Pops Esplanade Orchestra performed the following program: *Semper Fidelis* (Sousa); Overture to *Candide* (Bernstein); Three Dance Episodes from *Rodeo* (Copland); George M. Cohan Medley (Cohan-Bodge); "The Star-Spangled Banner"; *Superman* March (Williams); "Pops on Broadway" (arr. Burns); *1812, Ouverture Solennelle* (Tchaikovsky). Program, Boston Symphony Orchestra Archives.

Lenox: At Tanglewood, Leonard Bernstein's *Halil*, a work for flute and orchestra, had its American premiere here, performed by the Boston Symphony Orchestra (BSO), with flute soloist Doriot Anthony Dwyer, first flutist of the BSO. "The 15-minute piece is dedicated to the memory of an Israeli flutist with the Israel Philharmonic who was killed in the 1973 war" ("Fourth of July Premiere for Bernstein Flute Work," *New York Times*, 28 June 1981).

Pennsylvania

Pittsburgh: First performance of the Pittsburgh Symphony Orchestra at Point State Park (Druckenbrod, Andrew, and Timothy McNulty, "PSO Dropped from July 4 Celebration," *Pittsburgh Post-Gazette*, 28 April 2006, B1).

1982

Performances

District of Columbia

Fourth of July March[983], a work for band by composer-in-residence Andreas Makris, with the National Symphony Orchestra was premiered at the first annual "Capitol Fourth" concert held on the West Lawn of the Capitol. Other works played included the overture to *The School for Scandal* (Barber); *Promenade* (Gershwin); selections from *Romeo and Juliet* (Prokofiev). Robert Merrill sang "Largo al Factotum" from *Il Barbiere di Siviglia* (Rossini), "I Got Plenty of Nothin'" (Gershwin), and "The Star-Spangled Banner" (Joseph McLellan, "Let the Cannons Roar, Strike Up the Band!" and "The NSO Amid the Rockets' Red Glare," *Washington Post*, 4 and 5 July 1982, A1, H9 and D3, respectively); Douglas Major, organist, in a concert of American music at the National Cathedral ("This Week," *Washington Post*, 30 June 1982, C8).

Illinois

Palatine: The Palatine Concert Band (established in the 1870s), Barbara Buehlman, leader, presented this concert at Palatine Community Park:

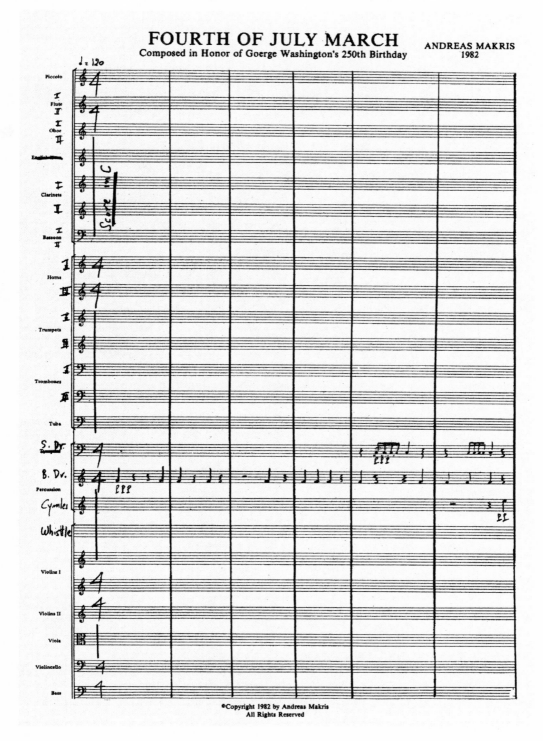

Manuscript page of the *Fourth of July March* composed by Andreas Makris and premiered by the National Symphony Orchestra at the Capitol Fourth celebration on July 4, 1982, in Washington, D.C. (with permission by Piotr Gajewski, Andreas Makris Endowment at the National Philharmonic).

"America the Beautiful" (arr. Carmen Dragon)
Broadway Show-Stoppers Overture (arr. Warren Barker)
Irish Tune from County Derry (Percy Grainger)
Beguine for Band (Glenn Osser)
Dixieland Front and Center (arr. John Warrington)
Phantom Regiment (Leroy Anderson)
Sandpaper Ballet (Leroy Anderson)
Selections from *The Music Man* (Meredith Willson)
1812, Ouverture Solennelle (Tchaikovsky)
The Stars and Stripes Forever (Sousa)

Palatine Concert Band website, http://www.palconband.org/.

Massachusetts

Boston: Works performed by the Boston Pops, John Williams, conductor, at the Esplanade, included: *Jubilee 350 Fanfare*[984] (Williams); selections from *The Planets* (Holst); Flying Theme from *E.T.* (Williams); "The Star-Spangled Banner"; *Strike Up the Band* (Gershwin); Patriotic Sing-along (arr. Hayman); *1812, Ouverture Solennelle* (Tchaikovsky) (Program, Boston Symphony Orchestra Archives).

Tanglewood: Lena Horne "opened her national tour" here on the Fourth (Barbara Saltzman, "Lena Horne: Spirit of 65 Lives On," *Los Angeles Times*, 3 July 1982, E4).

New York

Chautaugua: The U.S. Army Field Band, Col. William E. Clark, commander, performed this program at the amphitheatre:

Hands Across the Sea (Sousa)
American Overture for Band (Joseph Wilcox Jenkins)
Kenny
Third Organ Symphony
Nightingale Polka (tambourine)
TV Themes
Those glorious MGM musicals
The Conqueror
A Dixieland tribute
Battle Hymn of the Republic
Stars and Stripes Forever
God Bless America (encore)
[Program, 4 July 1982, U.S. Army Field Band].

1983

The major news of this Fourth of July year focused on Secretary of the Interior James Watt who on April 6 prohibited all "rock bands" from performing on the Washington Mall, fearing such bands would "attract the wrong element." The Beach Boys concert scheduled for July 4 was canceled, amidst an uproar from many who believed the group to be a rock icon and an "American institution." Afterall, "it was the Beach Boys who originated the Fourth of July pop concerts on the Mall in 1980," quoted a local newspaper.[985]

Statements were issued by the Beach Boys and Vice President George Bush, who said "They're my friends and I like their music." The Beach Boys were replaced by singer Wayne Newton and the U.S. Army Blues Band. Undaunted, the famed rock group presented a free Independence Day concert that year in Atlantic City, attracting thousands. The next year they were back on the Mall as headliners for a star-studded performance.

Performances

District of Columbia

At the Capitol Fourth celebration, the National Symphony Orchestra, Mstislav Rostropovich, conductor, with Leontyne Price and Willie Stargill, narrator. Works included *Leonore Overture* (Beethoven); "Summertime" from *Porgy and Bess* (Gershwin); "Vissi d'Arte," from *Tosca* (Puccini); America's Youth in Concert Chorus at a 7 A.M. flag raising ceremony at the U.S. Capitol reflecting pool ("This Week," *Washington Post*, 29 June 1983, VA14).

Maryland

College Park: At Byrd Stadium, University of Maryland, the U.S. Marine Band, Col. John R. Bourgeois, leader, presented the following evening concert:

The Chimes of Liberty March (Edwin Franko Goldman)
"Chester" from *New England Triptych* (William Schuman)
Columbian Fantasy, cornet solo (Walter B. Rogers, with Fredric Erdman, soloist)
Second Regiment Connecticut National Guard March (David W. Reeves)
Selections from *The Music Man* (Meredith Willson, arr. Philip J. Lang), featuring the Marin-aires Barbershop Quartet
Selections by the U.S. Marine Band Dixieland Combo
1812 Ouverture Solennelle (Tchaikovsky)
The Stars and Strips Forever! (Sousa)
["Program Records," U.S. Marine Band Library].

Massachusetts

Boston: John Williams conducted the Boston Pops in the following program: *Midway March, Esplanade Overture*, and excerpts from *Return of the Jedi* (Williams); The Star-Spangled Banner; *The Thunderer March* (Sousa); Patriotic Sing-along (arr. Hayman); *1812 Ouverture Solennelle* (Tchaikovsky). Program, Boston Symphony Orchestra Archives.

New Jersey

East Rutherford: Willie Nelson's Fourth of July Picnic takes place on July 3 in the Giants Stadium in the Meadowlands. Included in this 10-hour marathon were country music artists Merle Haggard, Waylon Jennings, Linda Ronstadt, Emmylou Harris, and the

Stray Cats (Stephen Holden, "Willie Nelson Festival Rolls Into Meadowlands," *New York Times*, 1 July 1983, C6).

Virginia

McLean: New Mode Blue Grass Band at McLean Community Center ("This Week," *Washington Post*, 29 June 1983, VA14).

Sterling Park: Rock group of the U.S. Navy Band at Northern Virginia Community College ("This Week," *Washington Post*, 29 June 1983, VA14).

Vienna: U.S. Air Force Band and Singing Sergeants at the Filene Center at Wolf Trap Farm Park ("This Week," *Washington Post*, 29 June 1983, VA14).

West Virginia

Wheeling: The U.S. Army Field Band and Soldiers' Chorus, Col. William E. Clark, commander and conductor, and Capt. Gary F. Lamb, director of chorus, presented the following program:

Patriotic Prologue (arr. David Wolpe)
Sabre and Spurs (Sousa)
American Salute (Morton Gould/ trans. Philip Lang)
Selections from *South Pacific* (Rodgers/ arr. Sp6 Robert Lichtenberger), performed by SFC Cheryl A. Pietsch and SFC James K. Woodel
Savannah River Holiday (Ron Nelson)
Solo de Concours (Andre Messager/arr. Jack Snavely) performed by Sp6 Gary S. Spaulding, clarinet
007 (arr. SFC Ken McCoy)
His Honor (Henry Fillmore/ed. Frederick Fennell)
"Wild about Harry" (arr. SFC Ken McCoy), performed by S6 Daniel L. Nevius, trumpet
Armed Forces Medley (arr. Ken Whitcomb and Sp6 Robert Lichtenberger)
Stars and Stripes Forever (Sousa)
[Program, 4 July 1983, U.S. Army Field Band and Soldiers' Chorus].

1984

In Washington, D.C., a ribbon cutting-ceremony for a bandstand that was originally built in 1878 and stood "on the grounds of the Illinois Central Hospital for the Insane in Jacksonville, Illinois" and recently moved and re-assembled on the Mall adjacent to the Museum of American History occurred in the evening of the Fourth. Music was provided by a brass band, its members in period uniforms.[986]

Performances

Illinois

Chicago: Composer Gunther Schuller addressed an audience on the Grant Park Mall for a Fourth of July concert about indigenous American music. (1 sound tape reel; originally broadcast on Public Radio, July 4, 1984). Copy in Michigan State University.

Massachusetts

Boston: John Williams conducted the Boston Pops in the following program: *Hands Across the Sea* (Sousa); *Academic Festival Overture*, op. 80 (Brahms); *Trumpeter's Lullaby* (Leroy Anderson), with Bruce Hall, trumpet; *Irish Suite* (Anderson); The Star-Spangled Banner; selections from *West Side Story* (Bernstein-Mason); Patriotic Sing-along (arr. Hayman); *1812 Ouverture Solennelle* (Tchaikovsky). Program, Boston Symphony Orchestra Archives.

1985

Performances

Delaware

Georgetown: The U.S. Army Field Band and Soldiers' Chorus, Col. William E. Clark, commander and conductor, and Maj. Frank G. Dubuy, director of chorus, presented this program:

Patriotic Prologue (arr. David Wolpe)
The Gridiron Club (Sousa)
Olympic Fanfare and Theme (John Williams/arr. Jim Curnow)
Something Original (SGM Lance Sweigart/arr. MSG Ken McCoy), performed by SGM Sweigart
Euryanthe Overture (C.M. von Weber/arr. V.F. Safranek)
All Those Endearing Young Charms (Simone Mantia/arr. Harold Bracsh), performed by S6 Donald Burleson, euphonium
Entertainment Tonight (arr. MSG Ken McCoy, Sp6 Eric Richards and Keith Laurent)
My Fair Lady (Alan Jay Lerner & Frederick Loewe/arr. MSG Ken McCoy, sung by the Soldiers' Chorus)
The Southerner (Russell Alexander/arr. G.C. Bainum)
1812 Overture (arr. Mayhew Lake)
Stars and Stripes Forever, encore (Sousa)
[Program, 4 July 1985, U.S. Army Field Band and Soldiers' Chorus].

District of Columbia

"Sea to Shining Sea Concert" on the Mall with Beach Boys, Jimmy Page, the Four Tops, Oak Ridge Boys, Bellamy Brothers, and others; National Symphony, Leonard Bernstein, conductor, with excerpts from *West Side Story* and "'Songfest,' a 13-song salute to American poetry," at West Lawn of the U.S. Capitol; at the Decatur House Museum, the Takoma Brass Quintette played music of Joplin and Sousa; outside the National Air and Space Museum, the U.S. Air Force Symphony Orchestra and singer/composer Paul Williams performed ("District of Columbia Neighborhood Report," *Washington Post*, 4 July 1985, DC5); The U.S. Air Force Band, Singing Sergeants, and Airmen of Note at Smithsonian Air and Space Museum ("This Week," *Washington Post*, 4 July 1985, VAE6).

Massachusetts

Boston: John Williams conducted the Boston Pops in the following program: *Olympic Fanfare and Theme* (Williams); *Cowboys Overture* (Williams); "Simple Song," from *Mass* (Bernstein); The Magic of Walt Disney (arr. Ferguson); "The Star-Spangled Banner"; "This Land Is Your Land" (Guthrie-Reisman); Patriotic Sing-Along (arr. Hayman); 1812, *Ouverture Solennelle* (Tchaikovsky). Program, Boston Symphony Orchestra Archives.

New York

Jones Beach: Leonard Bernstein and the National Symphony performed the conductor's *Songfest* "which he wrote for the Bicentennial," Symphonic Dances from *West Side Story*, and Sousa's *The Stars and Stripes Forever* (Bernard Holland, "Music: Bernstein at Jones Beach," *New York Times*, 9 July 1985, C13).

Virginia

Fairfax: *The City of Fairfax March* by Virginia Wayland, "the winning composition in a competition funded by the Commission on the arts" was premiered by the City of Fairfax Band,[987] with guest conductor, James Kessler, the march's arranger, at Fairfax High School Stalnaker Stadium ("Bicentennial Fanfare," *City and Art Scene* 10/1 (January 2005–July 2005): iv).

Vienna: At Wolf Trap, Filene Center, the Marine Band, Col. John R. Bourgeois, leader, presented this program:

Hail to the Spirit of Liberty (Sousa)
"Chester" [from *New England Triptych* by William Schuman]
Encore, The Liberty Bell (Sousa)
Saratoga Quickstep, Battle Hymn, Dixie[988] (Morton Gould)
The Volunteers March (Sousa)
Encore, Born Free
Esprit de Corps (Robert Jager)
Old American Songs
American Pageant[989] (Thomas Knox) (stand-by)
South Rampart Street Parade (Ray Bauduc)
The High School Cadets (Sousa)
Stephen Foster Medley (stand-by)
God of Our Fathers (stand-by)
Marching Along (Sousa)
Soliloquy from Carousel
Largo from New World Symphony (Dvořák)
Second Symphony (Charles Ives)
Stars and Stripes Forever (Sousa)
God Bless America (Irving Berlin)
Armed Forces Medley (stand-by)
["Program Records," U.S. Marine Band Library].

1986

Performances

Connecticut

Willimantic: Annual tradition of the boombox parade began this year and was created due to funding cuts that previously supported a high school marching band. Participants typically carried boombox radios with popular music blasting at full volume (Tim Clark, "Traveler's Journal: Favorite Fourths (People's Choice — Willimantic, CT, Boom Box Parade Where Paraders Supply their Own Music by Carrying Radios Tuned to WILI, Local Station," *Yankee* 54 [July 1990]: 26+; Philip Morgan, "America's Day: The Fourth of July Mixes History, Patriotism, Offbeat Parades and Musical Inspiration," *Tampa Tribune*, 4 July 1997 [Baylife], 1; "A Radio Active Parade," *Washington Post*, 5 July 2000, C1, C9).

District of Columbia

Smithsonian National Air and Space Museum: U.S. Air Force Concert Band, Singing Sergeants with Tom Wopat and Katharine Buffaloe, and Airmen of Note with Toni Tennille; at the Sylvan Theater: U.S. Air Force Dixieland Band and Singing Sergeants; U.S. Army Blues Jazz Ensemble; Army Chorale; U.S. Air Force Tops in Blue; at the Old Post Office Pavilion: Shoreline Youth Symphony; American Christian Youth Chorale; White Rock United Methodist Youth Choir; Blue Rose Trio; Hill Murray High School Band, and other groups ("This Week," *Washington Post*, 3 July 1986, VAC8).

Maryland

Baltimore: International Brass Quintet Festival with Baltimore Choral Arts Society at Wyman Park Dell ("Music," *Washington Post*, 4 July 1986, WK18).

Massachusetts

Boston: A "Go Fourth on the Fifth!" program took place on July 5 by the Boston Pops esplanade Orchestra, with John Williams, conductor. Works performed included:

Liberty Fanfare (John Williams)
Selection, *Kiss Me Kate*
"Come fly With Me — (A Tribute to Frank Sinatra), selected songs
Carnival of Venice (arr. T. Stevens)
Star-Spangled Banner
"I Love a Parade" from the Cotton Club (Arlen, arr. Hayman)
"Patrioc Sing-along"
1812 Overture (Tchaikovsky)
[Program, Boston Symphony Orchestra Archives].

New York

New York: The U.S. Marine Band provided background music on the USS *Iowa* on the morning of

"The President's Own" United States Marine Band with President Ronald Reagan (upper deck) on the USS *Iowa* in New York Harbor, celebrating Liberty Weekend, the centennial celebration of the Statue of Liberty, the morning of July 4, 1986 (courtesy "The President's Own" United States Marine Band, Washington, D.C.).

July 4, to accompany the tall ships parade, with President Ronald Reagan presiding, at the Liberty Centennial Celebration Weekend. That evening the band was on board the aircraft carrier USS *John F. Kennedy* providing music for President Reagan, including "Hail to the Chief," and pieces to accompany the fireworks. The following four works by composer Joe Raposo were written especially for the 1986 New York fireworks and were performed by the Marine Band: *Call to Liberty Fanfare*; *Parade of Nations*; *Strike Up the Band* (medley), and *America Is* ("the official song of the Statue of Liberty-Ellis Island Foundation, Inc."),[990] with lyrics by Hal David. Following the fireworks, as President Reagan left the ship, the band played *Invincible Eagle* by John Philip Sousa ("Program Records," U.S. Marine Band Library); John Williams and members of the Boston Pops Orchestra performed the following works at Liberty State Park on July 4: *Liberty Fanfare*[991] (Williams) — "America, the Dream Goes On" (sung by John Denver) — *Candide Overture* (Bernstein) — "Bess, You Is My Woman Now," sung by Clamma Dale and Simon Estes of the Metropolitan Opera — *Lincoln Portrait* (Copland), with narration by James Whitmore — Sousa marches (Joseph McLellan, "At Liberty Park, the Pops' Sere-

nade," *Washington Post*, 5 July 1986, D1, D4); The U.S. Navy Band, Sea Chanters, and Commodores performed on July 3 at Liberty State Park for the "Operation Sail" event.[992]

At Highland Park on July 3, the U.S. Army Field Band and Soldiers' Chorus, presented this program:

> The Liberty Bell (Sousa)
> New World Symphony (Dvořák)
> Dance of the Southern Lights (Eric Roberts)
> Indiana Jones (John Williams)
> Oklahoma
> Tenth Regiment March (Robert Browne Hall)
> Glenn Miller medley
> Stars and Stripes Forever (Sousa)

(Program, 3 July 1986, U.S. Army Field Band and Soldiers' Chorus); at Liberty Park, on July 4, the U.S. Army Field Band and Soldiers' Chorus, presented this program:

> Star-Spangled Banner
> American Soldier
> National Emblem (Bagley)
> Hands Across the Sea (Sousa)
> Army Goes Rolling Along

Ruffles and Flourishes
Hail to the Chief
[Program, 4 July 1986, U.S. Army Field Band and
Soldiers' Chorus].

Virginia

Fairfax: Polish American String Band and the City
of Fairfax Band ("This Week," *Washington Post*, 3 July
1986, VAC8).

Vienna: U.S. Marine Band at the Filene Center of
Wolf Trap Farm Park presented this program:

Hail to the Spirit of Liberty (Sousa)
American Pageant (Knox)
The Southern Cross (Herbert L. Clarke), with Jim
    Klages, cornet soloist
Danza Alegre (James F. Burke), with Jim Klages,
    cornet soloist
The Liberty Bell (Sousa)
Man of La Mancha (Fantasy), with Michael Ryan,
    baritone soloist (Bulla)
Dixieland Combo
Music of George Hamilton Green (Bulla): Valse
    Brilliant and Charleston Rag, with John R.
    Beck, xylophone soloist
Semper Fidelis (Sousa)
Rodgers and Hammerstein Songbook (arr. Knox),
    with Michael Ryan, baritone soloist
The Stars and Stripes Forever (Sousa)
God Bless America (Berlin)
Armed Forces Medley (Knox)

("Program Records," U.S. Marine Band Library); Vi-
enna Community Band at the Vienna Community
Center; James Brothers Country Band ("This Week,"
Washington Post, 3 July 1986, VAC8).

1987

Performances

District of Columbia

At the Sylvan Theater, a "We the People Concert"
presented by the U.S. Navy Band, Sea Chanters, and
the Commodores jazz ensemble, with vocalist Ethel
Ennis; on the West Lawn of the Capitol, National
Symphony Orchestra, James Conlan, conductor, with
Roberta Flack and Marvin Hamlisch; at the National
Air and Space Museum, the Airmen of Note, U.S. Air
Force Concert Band and the Singing Sergeants (*Wash-
ington Post*, 2 July 1987, DC6).

Louisiana

Baton Rouge: The Baton Rouge Symphony, James
Paul, conductor, presented its Independence Day con-
cert on the deck of the Louisiana Arts and Science
Center (*The Advocate*, 28 June 1987).

Massachusetts

Boston: John Williams and the Boston Pops Esplanade Orchestra performed the following program:

"A Salute to John Philip Sousa" (arr. Williams);
"Shaker Hymn" from *Appalachian Spring* (Copland);
The Songs of Stephen Foster (arr. Knight); *Bugler's
Holiday* (Anderson); *The Spirit of '76*, with Johnny
Cash (arr. Walker); The Star-Spangled Banner; Se-
lections from *The Wizard of Oz* (Arlen-Stevens); Pa-
triotic Sing-along (arr. Hayman); *1812 Ouverture
Solennelle* (Tchaikovsky); "We're Lookin' Good!"[993]
(Williams). Program, Boston Symphony Orchestra
Archives.

Virginia

Vienna: At Wolf Trap Farm Park, the U.S. Marine
Band presented the following program:

The Invincible Eagle (Sousa)
"Chester" from *New England Triptych* (William
    Schuman)
The Carnival of Venice (Herbert L. Clarke)
A Morton Gould Suite (Saratoga Quick Step;
    Dixie; Battle Hymn of the Republic; American
    Salute)
Second Symphony (Ives)
"Soliloquy" from *Carousel*
"You'll Never Walk Alone"
Looking Upward suite (Sousa)
The High School Cadets (Sousa)
Dixieland Combo
South Rampart Street Parade (Ray Bauduc)
Marching Along (Sousa)
The Music Man
American Pageant
The Stars and Stripes Forever
Armed Forces Medley '72
["Program Records," U.S. Marine Band Library].

1988

Performances

District of Columbia

On the West Lawn of the Capitol, a star-studded
tribute to Irving Berlin took place including E.G.
Marshall, Tony Bennett, and Sherrill Milnes of the
Metropolitan Opera, with the National Symphony
Orchestra; at the Sylvan Theater, "Up with People
Show," U.S. Navy Country Current and Commodores
Jazz Ensemble, U.S. Navy Band and Sea Chanters,
with guest vocalist Shirley Jones; 9th annual D.C. Free
Jazz Festival at Freedom Plaza (Karina Porcelli,
"Weekend's Best," *Washington Post*, 1 July 1988, WE3);
a "White House Old-Fashioned Fourth of July" was
presented at the White House by President and Mrs.
Reagan, with the following musical groups perform-
ing: The United States Marine Band and Marine Dix-
ieland Band; "The Sugarfoot" Cloggers, "The Arlington Soundworks" Barbershop Quartet; The U.S.
Marine Dixieland Band. ("Program Records," U.S.
Marine Band Library).

THE PRESIDENT
AND
MRS. REAGAN

Welcome You to

A WHITE HOUSE
OLD-FASHIONED FOURTH OF JULY

Program

THE UNITED STATES MARINE BAND • "THE SUGARFOOT" CLOGGERS
"THE ARLINGTON SOUNDWORKS" *Barbershop Quartet*
THE MARINE DIXIELAND BAND • THE UNITED STATES MARINE BAND

Special Thanks to:
THE WONDER COMPANY PERFORMERS   THE NATIONAL PARK SERVICE CHARACTERS
Joe Jeff Goldblatt - Executive Director   AND PET-A-FARM
Jim Ryan - Director of Talent   ABRACADABRA MAGICIAN
                                               JIM SHEA · *Clown*

Program, for a "White House Old-Fashioned Fourth of July," July 4, 1988, hosted by President and Mrs. Ronald Reagan. The musical groups performed a variety of marches, Dixieland, and works for barbershop quartet, including the "Ronald Reagan March," played by the U.S. Marine Band (program provided by the United States Marine Band Library).

Massachusetts

Boston: At the Esplanade, the Boston Pops, John Williams, conductor, performed Williams' *The Olympic Spirit*, which had been written for the 1988 Summer Olympic Games, as well as the 1812 Overture and music by Irving Berlin, Jule Styne, and Andrew Lloyd Webber (Program, Boston Symphony Orchestra Archives).

New York

Eisenhower Park: The United States Army Field Band, Col. William E. Clark, commander and conductor, and Soldiers' Chorus, Capt. Robert A. Mc-

Cormick, director, presented this program:

> Patriotic Prologue (arr. David Wolpe and Keith Laurent)
> Armed Forces Medley (arr. Ken Whitcomb, SFC Robert Lichtenberger and Keith Laurent)
> The Rifle Regiment (Sousa)
> American Salute (Morton Gould/trans. Philip J. Lang)
> Irving Berlin: A Vaudeville Tribute (Berlin/trans SSG Eric Richards), with MS Steven L. Marvin and SFC Robert P. Barnett, soloists
> A.T.V. Fantasy (arr. Skip Norcott)
> The Constitution: A Living Document (compiled and arranged by SFC Beth Hough), with Soldiers' Chorus [Program, 4 July 1988, U.S. Army Field Band and Soldiers' Chorus].

Ohio

Cincinnati: The Percussion Group premiered *Percussion and String Octet* (1983–85) by composer William DeFotis (1953–2003) ("William DeFotis Papers," Archives, University of Illinois at Urbana-Champaign).

1989

Broadcasts

A newly discovered piece for piano by Stephen Foster was premiered over National Public Radio by Mark Graf, pianist of the Pittsburgh Opera ("Public Radio to Play Long-Lost Foster Tune," *New York Times*, 4 July 1989, 23).

Performances

Arizona

Tucson: A city parade included Beavers Concert Band (75 pieces) and an evening concert was given by the Arizona Symphonic Winds (45 pieces), Laszlow Veres, conductor, at the Tucson Community Center ("Fireworks, Parade Set for Holiday," *Arizona Daily Star*, 4 July 1989, B1).

District of Columbia

On the South Balcony of the White House, the following program by the Marine Band:

"America the Beautiful"
American Pageant (Thomas Knox)
American Patrol (Meacham)
Annie (Charles Strouse)
The Beau Ideal March (Sousa)
Can-Can
El Capitan (Sousa)
From Tropic to Tropic (Russell Alexander)
Girl I Left Behind Me (Leroy Anderson)
Jack Tar (Sousa)
Man of La Mancha (Mitch Leigh)
The Music Man (Meredith Willson)
New Colonial (Robert Browne Hall)
Second Regiment Connecticut National Guard March.
Semper Fidelis (Sousa)
Sound of Music (Richard Rodgers)
The Stars and Stripes Forever (Sousa)
Stephen Foster Medley
The Thunderer March (Sousa)
"This Is My Country" (Al Jacobs)
Thunder and Blazes
The Washington Post (Sousa)
Combo, MGySgt Wundrow
["Program Records," U.S. Marine Band Library].

Massachusetts

Boston: Harry Ellis Dickson conducted the Boston Pops Esplanade Orchestra in performances of *The Washington Post March* (Sousa), *American Salute* (Gould), *Bostonia Suite* (Brown), "Music of the Night," from *The Phantom of the Opera* (Lloyd Webber), selections from *West Side Story* (Bernstein), and the 1812 Overture (Program, Boston Symphony Orchestra Archives).

New York

Buffalo: The Grateful Dead performed at Rich Stadium "in the midst of a tour that was arguably the peak of the band's latter-era career." The nearly 3-hour Independence Day show is preserved in its entirety and includes a host of classics, including "Deal," "Ship of Fools," "Bertha," and an apropos encore performance of "U.S. Blues." The concert is available on the group's album titled "Truckin' Up to Buffalo" (Barry A. Jeckell, "DVDs Celebrate 40 Years of Grateful Dead Music," *Chicago Sun–Times*, 8 July 2005).

Pennsylvania

Carlisle: The United States Army Field Band presented this program on July 4:

The Gallant Seventh
American Celebration Overture (Pascuzzi)
Selections from Showboat

El Camino Real
A Salute to Show Biz'
The Klaxon
Hooray for Hollywood
Armed Forces Medley
The Stars and Stripes Forever
God Bless the U.S.A. or Saints (encore)
[Program, 4 July 1989, U.S. Army Field Band and Soldiers' Chorus].

Virginia

Vienna: At Wolf Trap Farm Park at the Filene Center, the Marine Band presented the following program:

Girl Crazy (Gershwin)
Ragtime Nightingale (Joseph F. Lamb)
John Henry
Washington Post (Sousa)
Slaughter on Tenth Avenue (Richard Rodgers)
Three Quotations (Sousa)
Blue and Gray Quadrille
The Stars and Stripes Forever (Sousa)
Rhythm and Blues, Mgy Sgt Williams
Combo, MgySgt Wundrow
["Program Records," U.S. Marine Band Library].

1990

Performances

District of Columbia

Well-known actor E.G. Marshall hosted the Capitol Fourth concert with the National Symphony Orchestra, Mstislav Rostropovich, conductor, with Beverly Sills. Simon Estes, and Henry Mancini; at the Sylvan Theater, Crystal Gale, the 150-member singing and dancing group "Up with People"; U.S. Navy Band, Sea Chanters, Commodores, and Country Current (Eugene Sloan, "Tops in Holiday Viewing," *U.S.A. Today*, 3 July 1990, 3D; Larry Fox, "Going Back and Forth on the Fourth," *Washington Post*, 29 June 1990, 3).

Massachusetts

Boston: Conductor John Williams' *Celebrate Discovery* and the Cynthia Mann/Barry Weil work *Celebrate America* are premiered[994] at the Boston Pops Esplanade Concert. Other works performed included

Cowboys Overture (Williams)
America, the Dream Goes On (Williams), with Byron Motley, soloist and members of the Newton Choral Society, Back Bay Chorale, and Harvard Summer Chorus
Theme from *Born on the Fourth of July* (Williams)
"This Land Is Your Land" (Guthrie)
1812 Overture (Tchaikovsky)
[Program, Boston Symphony Orchestra Archives].

Michigan

Grand Rapids: The U.S. Army Field Band presented this program:

Patriotic Prologue (arr. David Wolpe, Keith Laurent, and SGM Ken McCoy)
The Black Horse Troop (Sousa)
American Pageant (Thomas Knox)
Panis Angelicus (César Franck)
Funiculi, Funicula (Luigi Denza/arr. SSG Eric Richards)
Overture to William Tell (Gioacchino Rossini/arr. J. Sommer)
South Pacific (Rodgers and Hammerstein/arr. SGM Ken McCoy)
The Chimes of Liberty (Edwin Franco Goldman)
Ike's Favorites (arr. SGM Ken McCoy), including "Beer Barrel Polka," "As Time Goes By," "One Dozen Roses," "I'll Be Seeing You," and "Alexander's Ragtime Band"
God Bless the U.S.A. (Lee Greenwood/arr. SGM Ken McCoy)
The Stars and Stripes Forever (Sousa)
[Program, 4 July 1990, U.S. Army Field Band and Soldiers' Chorus].

Virginia

Vienna: U.S. Marine Band at Wolf Trap Farm Park with this program:

Star-Spangled Banner
George Washington Bicentennial (Sousa)
Overture to *Candide* (Bernstein)
The Southerner (encore, Russell Alexander)
Rainbow Ripples (George Hamilton Green)
Xylophonia (encore, Joe Green))
The Music Man (Meredith Willson)
The House I Live In (That's America To Me) (Earl Robinson)
"Pride of a People" (vocal)
Semper Fidelis (Sousa)
Dixieland Band (30–40 minute program)
Liberty Fanfare (John Williams)
Esprit de Corps (Robert Jager)
Rodgers & Hammerstein Songbook (vocal)
American Pageant (Thomas Knox)
The Stars and Stripes Forever (Sousa)
Armed Forces Medley '72 (Sousa, arr. Thomas Knox)
[Larry Fox, "Going Back and Forth on the Fourth," *Washington Post*, 29 June 1990, 3; Program Records" U.S. Marine Band Library].

1991

Andrew Fox was one of a number of composers who won the Music Teachers National Association Distinguished Composer of the Year Award for his work *Three Pieces for the Fourth of July*, scored for brass quintet ensemble.[995]

Performances

California

Los Angeles: The Hollywood Bowl Orchestra, John Mauceri, conductor, presented its debut concerts[996] on July 2–4 with an American program (John Henken, "Music Review," *Los Angeles Times*, 4 July 1991, 1).

District of Columbia

The U.S. Marine Band and Dixieland Band presented the following "Serenade' on the South Lawn of the White House prior to the evening fireworks:

Rifle Regiment March (Sousa)
King Cotton March (Sousa)
The Bride Elect (Sousa)
The Beau Ideal March (Sousa)
Dixieland Band set
El Capitan (Sousa)
Hands Across the Sea (Sousa)
Washington Grays (Grafulla)
Dixieland Band set
Annie (Charles Strouse)
American Patrol (Meacham)
Minstrel Boy
Irish Tune from County Derry (Percy Grainger)
American Salute (Morton Gould)
Dixland Band set
Stephen Foster Medley
The Music Man, selections
Mary Poppins
The Black Horse Troop (Sousa)
Jack Tar March (Sousa)
Semper Fidelis
American Pageant (Thomax Knox)
The Stars and Stripes Forever
Armed Forces Medley (arr. Knox)
["Program Records" U.S. Marine Band Library].

Michigan

Grand Rapids: The U.S. Army Field Band, Col. Jack H. Grogan, Jr., commander and conductor, and Soldiers' Chorus, Maj. Finley R. Hamilton, director, presented this program:

Patriotic Prologue (arr. David Wolpe, Keith Laurent, and SGM Ken McCoy)
The Diplomat March (Sousa)
Cowboys Overture (John Williams/arr. Bill Holcombe)
Country Legends, various composers (arr. SFC Eric Richards), sung by SS Jeffrey S. Woods
An American in Paris (Gershwin (trans. and arr. John Krance)
Scenes from World War II, various composers (arr. Keith Laurent and SFC Beth Hough)
The Chimes of Liberty March (Edwin Franko Goldman)
Big Band Salute, various composers (arr. SGM Ken McCoy)
Armed Forces Medley (arr. Ken Whitcomb, Keith Laurent, and SFC Robert Lichtenberger)

The Stars and Stripes Forever (Sousa)
[Program, 4 July 1991, U.S. Army Field Band and
    Soldiers' Chorus].

Virginia

Vienna: The U.S. Marine Band with Dixieland
Combo presented the following program at the Wolf
Trap Farm Park:

[National] Anthem
Hail to the Spirit of Liberty
Chester
Sea Songs
American Salute (Morton Gould)
Battle Hymn of the Republic (arr. Wilhousky)
Marching Song of Democracy (Percy Grainger)
The High School Cadets (Sousa)
South Rampart Street Parade (Ray Bauduc)
Dixieland Band Set
Bless My Naughty Sweetie
New Orleans
Dixie 1-Step
Squeeze Me
When the Saints Go Marching In
Semper Fidelis
The Music Man Panorama
American Pageant (Thomas Knox)
The Stars and Stripes Forever
Armed Forces Medley (arr. Knox)
"God Bless America" (arr. Knox, "sing-along")
["Program Records" U.S. Marine Band Library].

1992

Performances

District of Columbia

A concert at the White House by the U.S. Marine
Band included these works:

Overture to *Candide* (Bernstein)
La Reine de la Mer (Sousa)
Creole Belles (J.B. Lampe)
Stephen Foster Medley
American Overture for Band (Joseph Wilcox Jenk-
    ins)
Girl I Left Behind Me (Leroy Anderson)
"Irish Washerwoman"
"Rakes of Mallow"
"Tribute to Irving Berlin"
["Program Records," U.S. Marine Band Library].

Massachusetts

Boston: John Williams conducted the Boston Pops
Esplanade Orchestra in the following works: The
Star-Spangled Banner; *Liberty Fanfare* (John
Williams); March from *The Love for Three Oranges*
(Prokofiev); *Greeting Prelude* (Stravinsky); "Parade of
the Charioteers," from *Ben Hur* (Rosza); Brünnhilde's
Battle Cry, from *Die Walkure* (Wagner); "Give Me
Your Tired, Your Poor," from *Miss Liberty* (Berlin),

with Jane Eaglen, soloist; "Hooray for Hollywood"
(Whiting-Williams); Tara's Theme from *Gone with
the Wind* (Steiner-Morley); March from *Robin Hood*
(Korngold); Creation of the Female Monster, from
The Bride of Frankenstein (Waxman); Throne Room
and Finale, from *Star Wars* (Williams); The Star-
Spangled Banner; "Guadalcanal March," from *Vic-
tory at Sea* (Rodgers); "They All Laughed," from *Shall
We Dance* (Gershwin); "Love Walked In" and "Love
Is Here to Stay," from *The Goldwyn Follies* (Gersh-
win), with Jennifer Holliday, soloist; Begin the
Beguine (Porter-May); Sing, Sing, Sing (Prima/Good-
man-Hyman); 1812 Overture (Tchaikovsky). Program, Boston Symphony Orchestra Archives.

New York

East Meadow: The U.S. Army Field Band, Col.
Jack H. Grogan, commander and conductor, and Soldiers' Chorus, Maj. Michael D. Pyatt, director, presented the following program:

Patriotic Prologue
The Globe and Eagle (Sousa)
Festive Overture (Dmitri Shostakovich)
Songs of the Emerald Isle (arr. SFC Eric Richards),
    sung by MS Robert P. Barnett, tenor
Hooray for Hollywood (arr. SFC Eric Richards)
Scenes from World War II (arr. Keith Laurent and
    SFC Beth Hough)
The Screamer March (Frederick Alton Jewell)
Dixieland Tribute (arr. SGM Ken McCoy), with
    SS Michael L. Johnston, trumpet
Armed Forces Medley
The Stars and Stripes Forever (Sousa)
[Program, 4 July 1992, U.S. Army Field Band and
    Soldiers' Chorus].

Virginia

Vienna: The U.S. Marine Band, Col. John R.
Bourgeois, leader, presented this program at Wolf
Trap Farm Park at 1 P.M.:

"Grand Walkaround" from *Cakewalk: Suite from
    the Ballet* (Hershy Kay)
"Chester" from *New England Triptych* (William
    Schuman)
Cornet solo, *Hungarian Melodies* (Vincent Bach),
    Frederick Marcellus, soloist
"Andante teneramente, con semplicita" (second
    movement) from Symphony No. 1 in E Minor,
    Op. 21 (Howard Hanson)
Golden Jubilee March, encore (Sousa)
Euphonium solo, *Auld Lang Syne Fantasia* (Simone
    Mantia, arr. Taylor Branson), Michael Colburn,
    soloist
Selections from *The Wiz* (Charles Small, arr.
    Robert Lowden)
The New York Hippodrome: March (Sousa)
Intermission (Marine Band Dixieland Band)
"Clarinet Marmalade"
"Royal Garden Blues"
"That's a Plenty"
"Tin Roof Blues"

"Leinlandberg Joys"
"Fanfare" from *Festive Music, for Orchestra* (Morton Gould)
"Jubilee" from *Symphonic Sketches* (George Whitefield Chadwick)
Ragtime Dance (Scott Joplin)
"*Oklahoma*-An American Portrait" (Rodgers and Hammerstein II), with Michael Ryan, baritone
"America the Beautiful"
The Stars and Stripes Forever (Sousa)
["Program Records," U.S. Marine Band Library].

1993

Performances

Massachusetts

Boston: At the Esplanade Concert, "A Musical Tour of the United States," with Ossie Davis, narrator and Maureen McGovern, vocalist, was presented. Included are Broadway and motion picture tunes, including the theme from *Jurassic Park* (Williams) with the Tanglewood Festival Chorus and Boston Pops, and excerpts from the *Magnificent Seven* (Elmer Bernstein), *Superman* (Williams), *On the Town* (Leonard Bernstein), and *Oklahoma* (Rodgers). "America the Beautiful" was "performed in honor of the 100th anniversary of Katharine Lee Bates's poem" (Program, Boston Symphony Orchestra Archives).

Michigan

Grand Rapids: The U.S. Army Field Band, Col. Jack H. Grogan, commander and conductor, and Soldiers' Chorus, Maj. Michael D. Pyatt, director, presented the following program:

Patriotic Prologue
The Liberty Bell (Sousa)
Orpheus in the Underworld (Jacques Offenbach)/arr. M.L. Lake and H.R. Kent)
Love that Latin (arr. SFC Eric Richards), with SFC Eileen F. Lyle, alto and SFC Thomas S. Puwalski, woodwinds
A Walt Disney Songbook (arr. SFC Eric Richards)
Fantasy and Variations on an American Air (Wilhelm Popp/arr. C.M. Schultz)
Scenes from World War II (arr. Keith Laurent and SFC Beth Hough)
The Melody Shop March (Karl Lawrence King)
In a Miller Mood (arr. SGM Ken McCoy)
Armed Forces Medley
The Stars and Stripes Forever (Sousa)
[Program, 4 July 1993, U.S. Army Field Band and Soldiers' Chorus].

Virginia

Vienna: The U.S. Marine Band performed this program at Wolf Trap Farm Park:

Strike Up the Band (Gershwin)
The Girl I Left Behind Me (Leroy Anderson)
America the Beautiful

Cole Porter Symphonic Portrait (arr. Wayne Robinson)
Washington Post March (Sousa)
Variations on a Theme from "Norma" [for cornet] (Jean-Baptiste Arban), with John Abbracciamento, cornet soloist
Galop from Geneviève de Brabant (Jacques Offenbach/arr John R. Bourgeois)
Fandango (Frank Perkins/arr. Floyd E. Werle)
Combination March (Scott Joplin/arr. Gunther Schuller)
Fiddler on the Roof (Jerry Bock)
The House I Live In (That's America To Me) (Earl Robinson), Mike Ryan, soloist
The Stars and Stripes Forever (Sousa)
["Program Records," U.S. Marine Band Library].

1994

Performances

District of Columbia

On the White House south balcony, the U.S. Marine Band, Capt. Dennis R. Burian, conductor, U.S. Marine Dixieland Band, and chorus cast of *Miss Saigon*, presented the following program:

The New Colonial March (Robert Browne Hall)
Chicago Tribune March (William Paris Chambers)
American Overture for Band (Joseph W. Jenkins)
"Fidgety Feet," Dixieland Band
"Basin Street Blues," Dixieland Band
"This Is My Country" (Al Jacobs)
"America the Beautiful"
Pentagon Fanfare (Thomas Knox)
"God, Bless America" (Irving Berlin) sung by cast chorus of *Miss Saigon*
Selections from *Les Misérables* (arr. Warren Barker)
"That's a Plenty," Dixieland Band
"Muskrat Ramble," Dixieland Band
Golden Jubilee March (Sousa)
Selections from *My Fair Lady*[997] (Frederick Loewe)
"Black and Blue," Dixieland Band
"Indiana," Dixieland Band
The Liberty Bell (Sousa)
Creole Belles (J. Bodewalt Lampe/arr. Keith Brion)
"Royal Garden Blues,"[998] Dixieland Band
The Stars and Stripes Forever (Sousa)
["Program Records," U.S. Marine Band Library].

Massachusetts

Boston: Marvin Hamlisch conducted the Esplanade Orchestra, with guests Reginald Jackson, Bowzer and the Stingrays, Anita Baker, Harolyn Blackwell, Stephen Lehew, and members of the Dorchester Youth Collaborative (Program, Boston Symphony Orchestra Archives).

Michigan

Grand Rapids: The U.S. Army Field Band, Col. Jack H. Grogan, commander and conductor, and Soldiers' Chorus, Lt.Col. Michael D. Pyatt, director, presented the following program:

Patriotic Prologue
Hands Across the Sea (Sousa)
Light Cavalry Overture (Franz von Suppé)
A Tribute to Nat and Natalie (arr. SFC Loran McClung), with SS Martha L. Canipe, soprano, and SS Victor C. Cenales, baritone
Barnum and Bailey's Favorite (Karl Lawrence King/arr. Glenn Cliffe Bainum)
American Drummer (various composers/arr. SFC Doug Webber)
And the Winner Is (various composers/arr. SFC Beth Hough), with the Soldiers' Chorus
Armed Forces Medley (various composers)
God Bless America (arr. Keith Laurent)
The Stars and Stripes Forever (Sousa)
[Program, 4 July 1994, U.S. Army Field Band and Soldiers' Chorus].

New Jersey

Westfield: *Westfield Bicentennial Celebration*, a work by Jerry Nowak and commissioned by the Westfield Community Band, Elias J. Zareva, conductor, was performed at Tamaques Park on the Fourth. *Westfield Community Band* Website, http://westfieldcommunity band.com

New York

New York: At Woodlawn Cemetery, the Bronx Arts Ensemble mounted its annual Independence Day tribute to George M. Cohan, including the songs "over There" and "Yankee Doodle Dandy." Soloists included Cathy Gale and Tony Sotos, accompanied by the B.A.E. Jazz and Dixieland Band (Robert Sherman, "Music: Americana Gains Prominent Spot on Holiday Programs," *New York Times*, 3 July 1994).

Purchase: World premiere of the musical *Over the Rainbow*, "based on lyrics of E.Y. Harburg," was presented by the Phoenix Theater Company at Purchase College on July 3 (Robert Sherman, "Music: Americana Gains Prominent Spot on Holiday Programs," *New York Times*, 3 July 1994).

1995

Publications

July Fourth Celebration 95: Patriotic Medley. By Oliver W. Wells. [Atlanta?: Wells Music, 1995]. Copy in the Library of Congress.

Performances

California

San Francisco: The Treasure Island Navy Band (12th Naval District Band), directed by Lieutenant Manual Constancio, Jr., gave its final performance in Alameda and Oakland. "The band is one of the first

to be broken up as part of base closures in the Bay area" ("Bay Area Report — San Francisco," *San Francisco Call*, 4 July 1995).

Colorado

Boulder: The Colorado Music Festival's Wind and Brass Ensemble provided music on Independence Day at Chautauqua Park ("Fourth of July Events," *Daily Camera*, 4 July 1995).

District of Columbia

At the Capitol Fourth celebration on the West Lawn of the U.S. Capitol, the 100th birthdays of Oscar Hammerstein and Boston Pops conductor Arthur Fiedler are celebrated in music by the National Symphony Orchestra, Erich Kunzel, conductor; at the White House Balcony, the U.S. Marine Band, Capt. Dennis R. Burian, conductor, and Dixieland Band presented the following program:

The Gridiron Club (Sousa)
The Chimes of Liberty March (Edwin Franko Goldman)
American Overture for Band (Joseph Wilcox Jenkins)
Combination March (Scott Joplin)
American Salute (Morton Gould)
U.S. Marine Dixieland Band
"God Bless America" (Berlin)
Hello Dolly (Jerry Herman)
Fandango (Frank Perkins)
Overture to *Candide* (Bernstein)
U.S. Marine Dixieland Band
"America the Beautiful"
Man of La Mancha (Mitch Leigh)
U.S. Marine Dixieland Band
The Sinfonians, Symphonic March (Clifton Williams)
Funny Girl (Jule Styne)
Onward-Upward March (Edwin Franko Goldman)
U.S. Marine Dixieland Band
The Stars and Stripes Forever[999] (Sousa)
["Program Records," U.S. Marine Band Library].

Massachusetts

Boston: As newly appointed conductor of the Boston Pops, Keith Lockhart gave his first Fourth of July concert at the Esplanade, with special guests, The Pointer Sisters, Mel Tormé, and the Air Force Band of Liberty, in works that commemorate the 50th anniversary of the end of World War II. Performed were *The Washington Post March* (Sousa), tunes that saluted the Andrews Sisters and Glenn Miller, and the theme from *Schindler's List* (Williams). A sing-along included "I'm a Yankee Doodle Dandy," "This Land is Your Land," You're a Grand Old Flag," and "Battle Hymn of the Republic." The concert ended with the 1812 Overture (Program, Boston Symphony Orchestra Archives).

Michigan

Grand rapids: The U.S. Army field Band and Soldiers' Chorus presented this program:

Patriotic Prologue
The Black Horse Troop (Sousa)
Jolly Robbers (Suppé)
An American Romance
Trumpet Legends
Xylophone Ragtime
Hollywood to Broadway
Armed Forces Salute
Stars and Stripes Forever (Sousa)
[Program, 4 July 1995, U.S. Army Field Band and
 Soldiers' Chorus].

1996

Performances

Colorado

Denver: The Denver Concert Band performed at
Four Mile Historic Park ("Fourth Bashes around the
State," *Denver Post*, 4 July 1996, E-01).

Englewood: The Colorado Symphony Orchestra,
Newton Wayland, conductor, with Kathleen Knight
and the Blue Knights Drum and Bugle Corps at Fiddler's Green Amphitheatre ("Fourth Bashes around
the State," *Denver Post*, 4 July 1996, E-01).

Thornton: The Longmont Symphony Orchestra
performed followed by a fireworks display with synchronized music ("Fourth Bashes around the State,"
Denver Post, 4 July 1996, E-01).

District of Columbia

On the West Lawn of the Capitol, the National
Symphony Orchestra premiered a long-forgotten anthem, *O Land of Mine, America*, by George Gershwin, with D.C. soprano Harolyn Blackwell and The
Choral Arts Society. Other performers included
Robert Goulet, Peabo Bryson, K.T. Oslin, and Ben
E. King from the Drifters (*Washington Post*, 5 July
1996, F2); The U.S. Marine Band presented a concert of patriotic pieces at the White House, including:

El Capitan (Sousa)
Hands Across the Sea (Sousa)
[Combo]
Glory of the Yankee Navy (Sousa)
Superman (Williams)
[Combo]
King Cotton March (Sousa)
America the Beautiful (arr. Carmen Dragon)
Walt Disney Band Showcase (Floyd Werle)
[Combo]
Other works

("Program Records," U.S. Marine Band Library); the
75-piece Watsonville Band from California, Gonzalo
Viales, conductor, performed during the evening at
the White House by invitation of President Clinton
(Website, Watsonville Band's Washington D. C. Tour,
July 4th, 1996, 29 June 2000; "Members Make Musical 4th at White House," *Teaching Music* 4/2 (October 1996): 29).

Illinois

Chicago: At the 19th annual 3rd of July celebration, the Grant Park Symphony, Michael Morgan,
conductor, with the U.S. Army Chorus, provided
music for the fireworks display ("Fireworks to Follow
Concert on July 3," *Chicago Sun–Times*, 28 June 1996,
Weekend, 2).

Massachusetts

Boston: Boston Pops Esplanade Orchestra, Keith
Lockhart, conductor, at the Hatch Shell, with Bebe
Neuwirth, "A Tony Award-winner for her role in *Sweet
Charity* and 'All That Jazz' from the show *Chicago*."
Other performers included "The Furman Singers," a
chorus from Furman University and vocalists George
Wesley, Jr., Jean Louisa Kelly, Sandy Duncan, Don
Correia, and Guy Stroman. The theme from this cel-
ebration, "A Salute to the American Musical," fea-
tured selections from *Victor/Victoria* (Mancini),
Chicago (Kander), *Oh, Kay!* (Gershwin), *The Lion
King* (Elton John) and *The Music Man* (Willson)
(Ellen Pfeifer, "Classical Music Review," *Boston Her-
ald*, 5 July 1996, S17; program, Boston Symphony Orchestra Archives).

Michigan

Detroit: The Detroit Symphony Orchestra and the
U.S. Army Field Band and Soldiers' Chorus per-
formed in tandem (Program, 4 July 1996, U.S. Army
Field Band and Soldiers' Chorus).

New Jersey

Ocean Grove: The Ridgewood Concert Band performed the following program:

"Star-Spangled Banner"
Overture to *Nabucco* (Verdi)
Suite in E Flat for Military Band (Gustav Holst)
Alleluia Laudamus Te (Alfred Reed)
Ye Banks and Braes O'Bonnie Doon (Percy Grainger)
Napoli (Herman Bellstedt), John Palatucci, eupho-
   nium
Variants on a Moravian Chorale (James Barnes)
Crown Imperial (William Walton)
Organ selection, "The Squirrel" (Powell Weaver)
Symphony marches: "The Raiders March," "The
   Imperial March," "Olympic Fanfare" (John
   Williams, arr. By John Higgins)
Polka and Fugue from *Schwanda the Bagpiper*
   (Jaromir Weinberger)
The Stars and Stripes Forever (Sousa)

(Carl Christian Wilhjelm, Jr., "A Case Study of the
Ridgewood Concert Band: A New Jersey Community Band Dedicated to Life-Long Learning" (D.Ed.
dissertation, Columbia University, 1998), 130.

New York

Buffalo: Buffalo Philharmonic Orchestra, Michael
Krajewski, conductor, performed "Take Me Out to
the Ball Game," *Olympic Fanfare and Theme*, theme
from *Chariots of Fire*, *Strike up the Band*, and other

favorites, at North AmeriCare Park (Herman Trotter, "Philharmonic Fireworks," *Buffalo News*, 5 July 1996, 23G).

North Dakota

Bismarck: The Bismarck-Mandan Symphony Orchestra, Thomas Wellin, conductor, at the Capitol, with the El Zagal Plainsmen, singing cowboy songs. Works performed by the orchestra included *Fanfare for the Common Man* (Copland); *American Salute* (Morton Gould); selections from *Porgy and Bess* (Gershwin); *Chicken Reel* (Leroy Anderson); *Armed Forces Salute* (Lowden); "Hoe-Down," from *Rodeo* (Copland); 1812 Overture; *Washington Post March* and *The Stars and Stripes Forever* (Sousa) (Jeff Olson, "July Fourth Concert a Musical Gift to Community," *Bismarck Tribune*, 29 June 1996, 10A).

Rhode Island

Bristol: Rick's Music World's All-Scholastic March Band of 171 members, Doug Kelley, director, marched in the city parade ("Towne Talk: Getting in Musical Step for a Bristol Fourth," *Providence Journal*, 1 July 1996).

Texas

Corpus Christi: The Corpus Christi Symphony Orchestra, Hywel Jones, conductor, was scheduled to perform the 1812 Overture on the deck of the USS *Lexington*, with the Navy firing artillery (*Corpus Christi Caller-Times*, 20 June 1996).

Dallas: The Dallas Wind Symphony presented "A Sousa Spectacular":

Civil War Fife and Drum Medley, David T. Kehler, conductor
On Parade (Sousa)
Esprit de Corps (Robert Jager)
Melody Shop (Karl L. King)
Star Spangled Spectacular (George M. Cohan)
The Official West Point March (Philip Egner)
Rushmore (Alfred Reed)
Midnight Fire Alarm (arr. John Krance)
Washington Grays (Claudio S. Grafulla)
Yankee Doodle: Fantasie Humoresque (David Wallis Reeves; ed. Keith Brion)
New Colonial (R.B. Hall)
Light Cavalry Overture (Franz von Suppé/arr. Henry Fillmore)
Barnum and Bailey's Favorite (Karl L. King)
The Freelance (march) (Sousa; ed. Frederick Fennell)
Trumpeter's Lullaby (Leroy Anderson), with Tim Andersen, trumpet
Armed Forces Salute (arr. Bob Lowden)
"America the Beautiful" (arr. Carmen Dragon)
[Program and *Dallas Wind Symphony* website, accessed February 13, 2008, <http://www.dws.org/>].

Virginia

Vienna: At Wolf Trap Farm Park, the U.S. Marine Band, Maj. Timothy W. Foley, conductor, and Dixieland Band presented the following program:

Band
The Cowboys Overture (John Williams)
Amazing Grace (Frank Ticheli)
Tribute to Rudy Weidoeft (arr. Gunther Schuller), with Ron Hockett, saxophone soloist
Carousel Waltz (Rodgers/Bennett)
Yankee Doodle Fantasie Humoresque (David Wallis Reeves/Brion)
Encore, *The Teddy Bear's Picnic* (John Bratton/Frank Saddler)
Encore, *Semper Fidelis* (Sousa)
Dixieland set:
"Honky Tonk Town"
"I Can't Say"
"Since My Best Gal"
"Bourbon Street Parade"
Band
Belle of the Ball Waltz (Leroy Anderson)
"Hoe-Down" from *Rodeo* (Aaron Copland)
Showboat Review (Kern/Bulla), with Michael Ryan, baritone
"America the Beautiful"
Encore, *The Stars and Stripes Forever* (Sousa)
Encore, "God Bless America" (Berlin/Knox)
Encore, *Armed Forces Medley* (arr. Knox)
["Program Records," U.S. Marine Band Library].

1997

Performances

District of Columbia

At the White House, the U.S. Marine Band presented this program [listed in alphabetical order]:

American Overture for Band (Joseph Wilcox Jenkins)
American Salute (Morton Gould)
Beguine for Band
Combination March (Scott Joplin)
English Folk Song Suite (Ralph Vaughan Williams)
Fandango (Frank Perkins)
Florentiner March (Julius Fucik)
Folk Song Suite
Inglesina: "The Little English Girl" (D. Delle Cese)
Man of La Mancha (Mitch Leigh)
Les Misérables
The Music Man (Meredith Willson)
Rakes of Mallow (Leroy Anderson)
La Reine de la Mer (Sousa)
West Side Story (Bernstein)
Selected marches

("Program Records," U.S. Marine Band Library); the Staple Singers performed at the "American Roots" concert on the Mall (Geoffrey Himes, "Staple Singers' American Roots," *Washington Post*, 4 July 1997, N14).

Georgia

Atlanta: The Atlanta Symphony with conductor Jere Flint performed excerpts from *Dances with Wolves* (John Barry), *Grand Canyon Suite* (Grofé), *1812 Overture* (Tchaikovsky), and a selection of Sousa marches at Chastain Park Amphitheater (Amy Frazier, "Four for the Fourth," *Atlanta Constitution*, 4 July 1997, O1E.); the Allman Brothers Band performed at the Grand Prix Stadium stage at the Georgia International Horse Park ("Gwinnett's Neighbors," *Atlanta Constitution*, 4 July 1997, O23).

Louisiana

Kenner: at Laketown, the New Orleans Concert Band, Milton Bush, director, and Nighthawk, Heart & Soul, and the U.S. Navy Band (Christine Bordelon, "Kenner July 4 Fest Moves to Lakefront," *Times-Picayune*, 26 June, 1997, D1).

Massachusetts

Boston: Keith Lockhart and the Boston Pops Esplanade Orchestra hosted this performance and included the U.S. Army Field Band and Soldiers' Chorus; Tara Holland, Miss America 1997; Roberta Flack and Lance Sweigart, soloists. Among the works performed were *National Emblem March* (Bagley), *American Patrol* (Meacham), "God Bless the U.S.A." (Lee Greenwood) sung by Sgt. Maj. Lance Sweigart, baritone, and 1812 Overture. Roberta Flack sang "Killing Me Softly," "It Might Be You," "Where Is the Love," and song in tribute to Elvis Presley (Program, Boston Symphony Orchestra Archives (Program, 4 July 1997, U.S. Army Field Band and Soldiers' Chorus).

New York

New York: At Battery Park, Frank Sinatra, Jr., directed "a 55-piece orchestra playing Gershwin tunes" (*Daily News*, 5 July 1997, 5).

Texas

Houston: At the Miller Outdoor Theater in Hermann Park, the Houston Symphony performed Tchaikovsky's 1812 Overture and William Grant Still's *Afro-American Symphony*, among other works (*Houston Chronicle*, 4 July 1997, 8).

1998

The Las Vegas Philharmonic marked the highlight of this year as the second major symphony orchestra to have made its performing debut on Independence Day. The concert occurred, in part, due to the cancellation of the summer concerts by the Nevada Symphony Orchestra.[1000] See Las Vegas below.

Publications

Boy Who Stole the Fourth of July. Music and lyrics by

Pat Zawadsky. Schulenburg, TX: I.E. Clark Publications, 1998. Copy in the Library of Congress.

Performances

District of Columbia

The U.S. Marine Band, Lt.Col Timothy W. Foley, conductor, presents this concert at the White House:

America the Beautiful (Carmen Dragon)
American Pageant '95
Cowboys Overture (Williams/Curnow)
Looney Tunes Overture (Bill Holcombe)
Oliver! (Bart/Leyden)
Superman Suite for Concert Band (Williams/Lowden)
The Teddy Bear's Picnic (John Bratton/Grank Saddler)
Walt Disney Band Showcase (Floyd Werle)
Wizard of Oz Fantasy (Harburg/Arlen/Yoder)
Wonderful World of Disney (John Edmondson)
["Program Records," U.S. Marine Band Library].

Hawaii

Kaneohe: At Dewey Square, the Marine Forces Pacific Band performed the 1812 Overture ("Do It," *Honolula Star Bulletin* website, 2 July 1998, http://Starbulletin.com.

Illinois

Evanston: The Palatine Concert Band, Ronald H. Polancich, guest conductor, performed the following concert:

Olympic Fanfare and Theme (John Williams/James Curnow)
The Blue and the Gray (Clare Grundman)
Sailing Songs (Elliot del Borgo)
March "Grandioso" (Roland Seitz/Alfred Reed)
Hollywood (Warren Barker)
Amazing Grace (Frank Ticheli)
Washington Post March (Sousa)
Kentucky 1800 (Clare Grundman)
Irving Berlin showstoppers (arr. John Higgins)
The Chimes of Liberty (Edwin Franco Goldman)
Star Spangled Spectacular (George M. Cohan/J. Cacavas)
The Wizard of Oz (Harold Arlen/James Barnes)
Armed Forces Salute (arr. Bob Lowden)
America the Beautiful (Samuel Ward/Carmen Dragon)
The Stars and Stripes Forever (Sousa)

Palatine Concert Band website, http://www.palconband.org/; *Evanston Fourth of July Association* website, http://www.evanston4th.org/.

Massachusetts

Boston: Melissa Manchester, Buckwheat Zydeco, and Marin Mazzie, Tony Award nominee, for the musical *Ragtime* with the Boston Pops at the Esplanade for salutes to George Gershwin and Frank Sinatra (*Boston Globe*, 28 June 1998, Television Week, 4).

Michigan

Dearborn: At Greenfield Village, the Detroit Symphony Orchestra and the U.S. Army Field Band and Soldiers' Chorus provided music for the fireworks celebration (Program, 4 July 1998, U.S. Army Field Band and Soldiers' Chorus).

Minnesota

Deluth: Musicians and dancers representing Russia, Sweden, Japan, and Canada sing folksongs accompanied by fiddle music and wooden spoons at Fourth Fest, Bayfront Festival Park.[1001]

Missouri

St. Louis: St. Louis Symphony at Faust County Park with works by Aaron Copland, George Gershwin, and Leonard Bernstein, ending with Sousa's *Stars and Strips Forever*, at the Soldier's Memorial, the Lewis & Clark Drum & Fife Corps (from St. Charles) and the St. Louis Letter Carriers Band performed (*St. Louis Post-Dispatch*, 3 July 1998, A1).

Nevada

Las Vegas: The Las Vegas Philharmonic, Harold Weller, director, made its debut as a major city orchestra at the Hills Park Fourth of July festivities. Mayor Jan Jones was master of ceremonies and the event was billed as "A Star-Spangled Fourth of July Spectacular." The program included the following works:

Star-Spangled Banner
William Tell Overture (Rossini)
Pops Hoedown (Richard Hayman)
Music from *E.T.* (John Williams), Richard McGee, conductor
America the Beautiful (arr. Carmen Dragon)
Salute to the Armed Services (arr. Richard Hayman)
Selections from *Hook* (John Williams)
Disney's *The Lion King Orchestral Suite* (Elton John), Richard McGee, conductor
"Somewhere Over the Rainbow" and "New York New York Medley," Woody Norvell, conductor, with Beth Nicastro, vocalist

The Las Vegas Philharmonic with Harold Weller, founding director and conductor, in the orchestra's debut performance on July 4, 1998, at the Hills Park Summerlin amphitheater in Las Vegas, Nevada. Las Vegas Mayor Jan Jones was master of ceremonies for this "Star-Spangled Fourth of July Spectacular" (Photograph by Audrey Dempsey, Infinity Photo and courtesy Las Vegas Philharmonic).

1812 Overture (Tchaikovsky)
National Emblem March

(Julia Osborne, "Philharmonic Celebrates First Birthday at Fourth of July Event," *Las Vegas Review-Journal*, 7 July 1999; program, Las Vegas Philharmonic).

New York

Chautauqua: The Chautauqua Symphony Orchestra, Uriel Segal, director, presented these works at the amphitheater: *Dance Overture* (Paul Creston); *Rhapsody in Blue* (Gershwin), with Arkady Figlin, pianist; *Tap Dance Concerto* (Morton Gould); 1812 Overture (Herman Trotter, "Noteworthy Music Coming to America," *Buffalo News*, 2 July 1998, 5G).

Rhode Island

Bristol: The Old Guard Fife & Drum Corps of Washington, D.C., marched in the city parade (Manny Correira, "Military Music Set for Holiday Weekend," *Providence Journal*, 3 July 1998).

1999

Performances

Alabama

Jasper: The Jasper Men's Chorale, and other groups, performed prior to the fireworks show at the old airport (Justin Hart, "Large Crowd Expected for Fireworks Show," *Daily Mountain Eagle*, 3 July 1999).

California

San Francisco: The San Francisco Lesbian and Gay Freedom Band, Dixieland Dykes, and other groups performed at Yerba Buena Gardens; at the "San Francisco Chronicle Fourth of July Waterfront Festival," the U.S. Air Force Band, Zydeco Flames, Sy Klopps Blues Band, and "the navy band from Ecuador's tall ship Guayas," and other groups; San Francisco Opera Orchestra and Chorus performed excerpts from Wagner and popular tunes as well, at Sigmund Stern Grove; at South Bay, a "world premiere excerpts from *The George Washington Bicentennial Opera*," at the Burgess Theater ("Fourth of July; Celebrations of Independence," *San Francisco Chronicle*, 27 June 1999, 36).

District of Columbia

At the White House, the Marine Band performed this program:

Rifle Regiment March (Sousa)
The Music Man [selection]
The Bride-Elect March (Sousa)
The Beau Ideal March (Sousa)
Les Misérables [selection]
Thunder and Blazes[1002]
West Side Story [selection]
Hail to the Spirit of Liberty
Golden Jubilee March (Sousa)

Fandango
"America the Beautiful"
The Stars and Stripes Forever
["Program Records," U.S. Marine Band Library].

Massachusetts

Boston: Conductors Keith Lockhart and Seiji Ozawa led the Boston Pops, with singer Trisha Yearwood, at the Esplanade. Both conductors wore "white Red Sox jerseys" and together with Carl Yastrzemski, the trio sang "Take Me Out to the Ballgame" (Yvonne Abraham and James Bandler, "In Boston, Celebrating a Yankee Doodle Day," *Boston Globe*, 5 July 1999, B1).

Michigan

Dearborn: The seventh annual "Salute to America" celebration took place at Greenfield Village with the Detroit Symphony Orchestra, William Eddins, conductor, and the U.S. Army Field Band and Soldiers' Chorus, Col. Finley Hamilton and Capt. Otis French, conductors. The program included:

The Star-Spangled Banner
Overture to *Gypsy* (Styne)
Washington Post March (Sousa)
Polovtsian Dances from Prince Igor (Borodin)
Overture to *Candide* (Bernstein)
Yankee Doodle (Gould)
Armed Forces Salute
Hoe-Down from *Rodeo* (Copland)
Variations on 'America' (Ives)
Lennon and McCartney Songbook (arr. Richards)
1812 Overture (Tchaikovsky)
Stars and Stripes Forever (Sousa)
[Program, 4 July 1999, U.S. Army Field Band and
    Soldiers' Chorus].

Missouri

St. Louis: Temptations at Fair St. Louis with a medley, including "The Way You Do the Things You Do," "Ain't Too Proud to Beg," and other hits (John Burnes, "High-Energy Temptations Bring Motown Hits to Arch," *St. Louis Post-Dispatch*, 6 July 1999, B2).

Pennsylvania

Pittsburgh: Pittsburgh Symphony Orchestra at Point State Park (*Pittsburgh Post-Gazette*, 4 July 1999, G2).

Virginia

Richmond: The Richmond Concert Band, Mark W. Poland, director, presented this evening concert at Dogwood Dell:

Capitol Square March[1003] (Warren Barker)
Stat Spangled Banner
The Chimes of Liberty (Goldman)
Tales of a Traveler (Sousa/arr. R. Mark Rogers)
Symphony on Themes of John Philip Sousa, Mvt.
    II-Thunderer (Ira Hearshen)
Summertime (Gershwin/arr. Calvin Custer)
Hitsville, U.S.A. (arr. John Wasson)

You Can Call Me Al (Paul Simon/arr. Joy Dawson)
6th Cavalry March (John Perkins)
The National Game March (Sousa/arr. Harold Gore)
Bavarian Polka (low brass)
Variations on a Kitchen Sink (Don Gillis)
Disney at the Movies (arr. John Higgins)
America the Beautiful (Ward/arr. Carmen Dragon)
This Land Is Your Land
Armed Forces Salute
1812 Overture[1004]
The Stars and Stripes Forever (Sousa)
[Concert program, Richmond Concert Band].

Wyoming

Jackson Hole: The Jackson Hole Community Band's concert on the Fourth included: Star-Spangled Banner — The Liberty Bell (Sousa) — Bugler's Holiday (Anderson) — The Fourth of July (John Cacavas) — Dixieland Jamboree (arr. J. Warrington) — Armed Forces Salute (arr. B. Lowden) — Them Basses (G.H. Huffine) — Themes Like Old Times II (arr. W. Barker) — The Stripper (D. Rose, arr. B. Lowden) — National Emblem March (E.E. Bagley) — Seventy-Six Trombones (M. Willson, arr. L. Anderson) — Patriotic Sing-along, with Bev Kemper Wanner, vocalist (arr. J.D. Ployhar) — This Land is Your Land (W. Guthrie, arr. B. Moffit) — America the Beautiful — The Stars and Stripes Forever March (Sousa). *Jackson Hole Community Band: Programs* Website <http://www.JHCB.org/Programs.htm>

2000

This year, Continental Harmony, a community-based music commissioning program was established as part of a millennial year project, with many musical works subsequently premiered on the Fourth of July. Sponsored by the American Composers Forum, in partnership with the National Endowment for the Arts (NEA), composer residences were created in all 50 states. Musical compositions were written in a diverse range of genres, including symphonic, chamber, opera, choral, and ethnic. A complete roster of compositions under the auspices of the Continental Harmony, including biographies of the composers, is found at the organization's website.[1005]

Performances

Arizona

Sedona: At the Grand Canyon Music Festival, *Guardians of the Canyon*, a Continental Harmony funded composition for four flutes, by Brent Michael Davids was premiered. This Native American composition included performers Claire Hoffman and the Havasupai Dancers.[1006] (*Continental Harmony* http://www.continentalharmony.com)

California

Arcadia: The California Symphony performed at the Arboretum of Los Angeles County, and the program included Copland's *Lincoln Portrait*, with Annette Bening, narrator (Web site, *Los Angeles Dailynews.com*)

Pasadena: The Pasadena Pops Orchestra, conducted by Rachael Worby, presented a "We the People" program (Web site, *Los Angeles Dailynews.com*)

San Francisco: At a Fourth of July picnic celebration, *Freedom Dreams* by Jennifer Higdon was premiered by the San Francisco Lesbian/Gay Freedom Band at the Yerba Buena Center for the Arts (*Continental Harmony* http://www.continentalharmony.com)

Colorado

Breckenridge: The National Repertory Orchestra premiered *Nature's Universal Throne* by David Heckendorn (*Continental Harmony* http://www.continentalharmony.com)

Delaware

Wilmington: The Delaware Symphony premiered the work *Delaware Rhapsody* by Robert Macht as a Continental Harmony project[1007] (*Continental Harmony* http://www.continentalharmony.com)

District of Columbia

At the Capitol Fourth concert that honored the 100th anniversary of Aaron Copland's birth, the National Symphony Orchestra, led by Leonard Slatkin, performed Copland's *Fanfare for the Common Man* and "Hoe-Down" from *Rodeo*, Tchaikovsky's 1812 Overture, and Ray Charles sang "America the Beautiful"; the U.S. Army 3rd Infantry "Old Guard" Fife and Drum Corps performed in front of the National Archives (Mary Cadden, "Celebrations Borne On the 4th of July," *U.S.A. Today*, 16 June 2000, 14.D; *Washington Post*, 5 July 2000, A1, C1); the U.S. Marine Band gave this evening concert at the White House:

Washington Grays (Grafulla)
Florentiner March
Selections from *The Music Man*
(combo)
Second Regiment Connecticut National Guard March (David Wallis Reeves)
Man of La Mancha
American Salute (Gould)
(combo)
The Liberty Bell[1008]
The Black Horse Troop March (Sousa)
West Side Story
(combo)
March of the Woman Mariner
"God Bless America"
The Stars and Stripes Forever
["Program Records," U.S. Marine Band Library].

Indiana

Carmel: On July 3–4, as part of Carmel's millennial celebration, the Carmel Symphony Orchestra and Indianapolis Symphony Orchestra (ISO) premiered *Liberty for All*,[1009] written by composer James A. Beckel, Jr., "the principal trombonist with the Indianapolis Symphony Orchestra since 1969." The performances occurred at "ISO's Conner Prairie outdoor venue and at Carmel's annual July Fourth festivities" (*Continental Harmony* http://www.continentalharmony.com)

Kentucky

Scottsville: In the renovated Tabernacle, the Adams County Chorus ("combined singing groups from throughout the region") premiered *Three songs: The Song of the Redeemed, We're Singing Heaven's Song, Heaven's Jubilee* by H. Depp Britt, Jr. (*Continental Harmony* http://www.continentalharmony.com)

Maryland

Baltimore: The Baltimore Symphony presented a "Star-Spangled Spectacular" at Oregon Ridge Park (*Baltimore Sun*, 4 July 2000, 5F).

Takoma Park: Liz Lerman Dance Exchange premiered *Improvisation*, a work by composer Lisa DeSpain (*Continental Harmony* http://www.continentalharmony.com)

Massachusetts

Boston: The Boston Pops Orchestra, Keith Lockhart, conducting, performed the 1812 Overture at the Esplanade (*Baltimore Sun*, 4 July 2000, 5F).

Fitchburg: *Raging River, Rolling Stone: Overture and March for Band and Orchestra*, by Barbara White of Princeton, New Jersey, was premiered at the celebration there by the Thayer Symphony Orchestra, Toshimasa Francis Wada, conductor; and Fitchburg State College Band and Fitchburg High School Band, Paul Morey, conductor (George Barnes, "Music Noisily Premieres," *Telegram & Gazette*, 5 July 2000, B1; *Continental Harmony* http://www.continentalharmony.com)

Missouri

St. Joseph: The St. Joseph Symphony, St. Joseph Community Chorus, Frank D. Thomas, director, and the St. Joseph Show Chorus of Sweet Adelines International premiered *I Am St. Joseph*,[1010] composed by John Bisharat, at Riverfront Park (*Continental Harmony* http://www.continentalharmony.com)

St. Louis: The Equinox Chamber Players premiered *Bushy Wushy Rag* by composer Phillip Kent Bimstein as part of St. Louis millennial celebration held at Fair Saint Louis before an audience of 100,000 (*Continental Harmony* http://www.continentalharmony.com; Sarah Bryan Miller, "Composer's St. Louis Work Takes Him Out to the Ball Game," *St. Louis Post-Dispatch*, 1 February 2000; Paul A. Harris, "The Voice of the City," *St. Louis Magazine*, February 2000).

Nevada

Las Vegas: The Las Vegas Philharmonic, Harold Weller, music director, with Richard McGee, associate conductor, presented this "Star-Spangled Fourth of July Spectacular" at Hills Park:

The Star-Spangled Banner, with Lynette Boggs McDonald, vocalist
National Emblem March (Bagley)
Music from *The Big Country* (Jerome Moross)
Hollywood Blockbusters (James Horner)
100th Birth Anniversary Tribute to Aaron Copland: *Variations on a Shaker Melody* and "Hoedown" from *Rodeo*
Songs sung by Bob Anderson
Sing-along medley
Armed Forces Salute (arr. Richard Hayman)
Olympic Fanfare & Theme (John Williams)
Rhapsody in Blue (Gershwin), with John Kane, pianist
The Liberty Bell March (Sousa)
Rushmore for narrator and orchestra (Alfred Reed), with Senator Richard Bryan, narrator and Councilperson Lynette Boggs McDonald, vocalist
1812 Overture (Tchaikovsky)
Stars and Stripes Forever (Sousa)
[Program, 2000, Las Vegas Philharmonic].

New Hampshire

Hanover: At Dartmouth College, the New Bedford Symphony Orchestra performed the 1812 Overture with accompanying musket fire and fireworks ("Fourth of July Festivities," *Providence Journal*, 2 July 2000).

New York

Chautauqua: The Chautauqua Symphony Orchestra, Keith Brion, conductor, performed works by Sousa, Strauss, and Dvořák and popular American tunes. Additional musicians included Charles Berginc, trumpet, Virginia Croskery, soprano, Chautauqua Children's Chorale, Fair City Singers from Scotland, Young People's Chorus of New York City and Da-Ton Middle High School Choir of Taiwan (Riley Graebner, "Apple Pie: Chautauqua Symphony Does It Up Big for July 4th," *Buffalo News*, 30 June 2000, 2G).

New York: Aboard the USS *John F. Kennedy*, President Clinton and other viewing the tall ships parade, Heather Headley, headliner from Broadway's *Aida* sang "the Star-Spangled Banner" (Marty Rosen, "Saluting Diversity," *Daily News*, 5 July 2000, 5).

Ohio

Carrollton: *Suite: Carroll County*, by Mona Lyn Reese, is premiered "by a community chorus, children's choir, and chamber wind ensemble" (*Continental Harmony* http://www.continentalharmony.com)

Cincinnati: Rosemary Clooney and Doc Severinsen join the Cincinnati Pops Orchestra for its musical celebration (*Baltimore Sun*, 4 July 2000, 5F); The U.S. Army Field Band & Soldiers' Chorus presented this program:

George Washington Bicentennial
American Salute
Divas from the Sixties
Summertime
America the Beautirul
Celebrate
Yankee Doodle Cohan songbook
Ol' Man River
Proud Mary
12th Street Rag
Fanfare for the Common Man
The House I Live In
Louis Armstrong Tribute
Olympic Fanfare
Casey at the Bat
Strike up the Band
Our Love Is Here to Stay
Ode to Doc
Armed Forces Medley
This is a Great Country
God Bless America
Finale
[Program, 4 July 2000, U.S. Army Field Band].

Cleveland: Conductor Jahja Ling and the Cleveland Orchestra and Chorus participated in the 11th annual Independence Day concert on Public Square, with a performance of *Liberty Fanfare*, composed by John Williams (John Petkovic, "As American as Apple Pie and a Russian Anthem," *Plain Dealer*, 3 July 2000, 1E).

Pennsylvania

Gettysburg: The Adams County Bicentennial Band premiered *South Mountain Echoes* by composer Robert Maggio (*Continental Harmony* http://www.continentalharmony.com)

Rhode Island

Newport: The Northeast Chamber Ensemble's woodwind quintet and the Community Baptist Church Gospel Choir premiered *Testimonials*, a work written by composer Stephen Newby and performed at Washington Square (*Continental Harmony* http://www.continentalharmony.com)

South Dakota

Sioux Falls: The Sioux Falls Master Singers and Sioux Falls Municipal Band, Christopher Hill, director, premiered *Spiritscapes: A South Dakota Cantata* by Bruce Craig Roter (*Continental Harmony* http://www.continentalharmony.com) and Bruce Craig Roter website http://www.bruceroter.com/bio.html.

Texas

Austin: Willie Nelson's picnic is held at Southpark Meadows and included forty acts with headliners Rodney Hayden and Doc Mason.[1011]

Virginia

Richmond: The Richmond Concert Band, Mark W. Poland, director, presented the following evening concert at Dogwood Dell:

Capitol Square March (Warren Barker)
Star-Spangled Banner
Sabre and Spurs (Sousa/arr. Keith Brion/Loras Schissel)
Russian Christmas Music (Alfred Reed)
As Time Goes By (Herman Hupfeld/arr. Warren Barker)
S'Wonderful (George and Ira Gershwin/arr. Warren Barker)
A Salute to Spike Jones (arr. Calvin Custer)
The Homefront, musical memories from World War II (arr. James Christensen)
Candle in the Wind (Elton John/arr. Jay Bocook)
You Can Call Me Al (Paul Simon/arr. Jay Dawson)
76 Trombones (Meredith Willson/arr. Paul Jennings)
Cable at Night (arr. Paul Jennings)
Hooked on TV Reruns (arr. Jack Bullock)
Let There Be Peace on Earth (Sy Miller and Jill Jackson)
Armed Forces Salute
Patriotic Sing-along
1812 Overture (Tchaikovsky/arr. Mayhew L. Lake)
The Stars and Stripes Forever (Sousa)
[Concert program, Richmond Concert Band].

Wintergreen: On July 3, as part of a millennial celebration combined with the Fourth of July, the Richmond Symphony premiered *From Time to Time*, a work by composer Anthony Iannaccone. The event was hosted by Wintergreen Performing Arts (*Continental Harmony* http://www.continentalharmony.com)

Wisconsin

Osceola: The ArtBarn Community Choir and area high school choirs premiered *River Spirit* by composer Craig Thomas Naylor in the ArtBarn, "a magnificent 100-year-old dairy barn that has been renovated, almost entirely by community volunteers, into a theatre auditorium and art gallery" (*Continental Harmony* http://www.continentalharmony.com)

2001

Performances

Alabama

Fairhope: The Baldwin Pops, Joe Riemer, music director, gave a performace. Featured also was vocalist Rebecca Stevens, the Eastern Shore Choral Society and the Mobile Community Chorus ("Baldwin Pops to Present Free Fourth of July Concert," *Mobile Register*, 28 June 2001).

California

Santa Ana: The Pacific Symphony Orchestra (PSO), conducted by Jack Everly, premiered *John Brown's Body for Narrator and Orchestra*, composed by Kevin Puts. The work was commissioned by the PSO. "G. Randolph Johnson, former board chairman of the orchestra, spearheaded the commission and acted as narrator on the evening of the premiere." http://www.kevinputs.com/John.html

Santa Fe: The Pacific Coast Concert Band and Singers gave a concert following the city's 20th annual parade (*San Diego Union-Tribune*, 4 July 2001, NC-4).

Delaware

Dover: The 287th Army Band of the Delaware National Guard gave a concert ("2001 Summer Concert Schedule," *DNG News* website)

District of Columbia

NASA members of the space station crew sent out a message celebrating the birth of America during the Capitol Fourth concert and images from space were displayed on a gigantic screen as the National Symphony Orchestra performed "2001: A Space Odyssey"; performers included Luther Vandross and the Pointer Sisters ("NASA Puts America's Independence Day Celebration Out of this World," News Release, National Auronautics and Space Administration, 2 July 2001; *Baltimore Sun*, 4 July 2001, 8G); at the National Cathedral, an organ recital of American music, including works by Sousa and Copland's *Fanfare for the Common Man*, was presented by Douglas Major, cathedral organist and choirmaster (Peggy Carlson, "Find Your Place to Celebrate the Fourth of July," *Fredericksburg.com* Website, 28 June 2001).

Maine

Dresden: An Independence Day music festival on the Pownalborough Court House grounds featured the 2nd Hampshire Regiment Serenade Band in period costumes playing music from the Civil War era (Mechele Cooper, "Independence Day Parades, Events Abound throughout Augusta Area," *Kennebec Journal/Morning Sentinel Online*, 3 July 2001).

Massachusetts

Fitchburg: The Thayer Symphony Orchestra, Toshimasa Francis Wada, conductor, performed *Raging River, Rolling Stone* by Barbara White (Barbara White website, acessted August 27, 2008, http://www.princeton.edu/~bwhite/perform.htm#2001).

Michigan

Dearborn: At Greenfield Village, the Detroit Symphony Orchestra, Leslie B. Dunner, conductor, and the U.S. Army Field Band & Soldiers' Chorus, Col. Finley Hamilton, commander and conductor, gave concerts of patriot music (Program, 4 July 2001, U.S. Army Field Band).

New York

New York: "Macy's Fourth of July fireworks spectacular show" featureed Bon Jovi, Jessica Simpson and the cast of the musical *42nd Street* (Sarah Kickler Kelber, "An Indoor Guide to a Fabulous Fourth," *Baltimore Sun*, 4 July 2001, 8G).

Pennsylvania

Pittsburgh: At Point State Park, the Pittsburgh Symphony Orchestra performed the 1812 Overture and Sousa's *Stars and Stripes Forever* (*Pittsburgh Post-Gazette*, 27 June 2001, E1)

Texas

Dallas: The Dallas Wind Symphony performed this concert at the Morton H. Meyerson Symphony Center:

> The Gallant Seventh (Sousa)
> Orpheus in the Underworld (Jacques Offenbach)
> "O Mio Babbino Caro" from Gianni Schicchi
>   (Puccini), performed by Teresa Gomez, soprano
> Italian Street Song (Victor Herbert), encore
> The Gliding Girl — Tango (Sousa)
> El Capitan (Sousa), encore
> *American Salute* (Morton Gould)
> The Carnival of Venice (arr. Del Staigers), performed by David Lovrien, saxophone
> The Last Rose of Summer (Thomas Moore, arr. David Lovrien), encore
> Old-Fashioned Sing-along (arr. John Gibson)
> National Emblem March (E.E. Bagley)
> Shenandoah (Frank Ticheli)
> The Walking Frog, Two-Step (Karl King), encore
> Armed Forces Salute (arr. Bob Lowden), Major
>   Timothy J. Holtan, U.S. Army, guest conductor
> America the Beautiful (arr. Carmen Dragon),
>   Major Holtan, conductor
> The Stars and Stripes Forever (Sousa), encore
> [*Dallas Wind Symphony* website, accessed February 13, 2008, http://www.dws.org/].

Virginia

Orkney Springs: 12th annual Red, White and Blue Festival, featuring Seldom Scene, Blue Highway, and New Dominion Bluegrass, at Shrine Mont Hotel. Poster, Virginia House (formerly known as the Orkney Springs Hotel).

Richmond: The Richmond Concert Band, Mark W. Poland, director, presented this evening concert at Dogwood Dell:

> Themes from Thus Spake Zarathustra (Richard Strauss/arr. Dick Thomas)
> Star-Spangled Banner
> Capitol Square March (Warren Barker)
> The Light Eternal (James Swearingen)
> Let It Shine (arr. James L. Hosay)
> The Beatles: Echoes of an Era (Lennon & McCartney/arr. John Higgins)
> Time to Say Goodbye (Francesco Sartori/arr. Jerry Brubaker)

Smokey Joe's Café (arr. Johnnie Vinson)
Over the Rainbow (Harold Arlen/arr. Warren
 Barker)
Someone to Watch Over Me (Gershwin/arr. War-
 ren Barker)
Pop and Rock Legends: Chicago (arr. John Was-
 son)
Broadway in the 90's (arr. John Higgins)
Armed Forces Salute
Patriotic Sing-along
1812 Overture
The Stars and Stripes Forever (Sousa)
[Concert program, Richmond Concert Band].

Wisconsin

La Crosse: At the Riverfest event in Riverside Park,
the Johnny Holm Band provided music (Geri Parlin,
"Riverfest Offers Fun for Almost Anyone," *LaCross
Tribune.com* website, accessed 12 March 2008.

Jordan

Oman: Red, Hot & Blue performed on a USO tour
(*St. Louis Post-Dispatch*, 4 July 2001, [*St. Charles
County Post*],1).

2002

A highlight of this year includes conductor Keith
Lockhart's broadcast of the Boston Pops Independence
Day performance being nominated for an Emmy
Award for Outstanding Classical Music/Dance Pro-
gram.

Performances

Alabama

Gadsden: *Tribute for Orchestra* by James Grant was
premiered by the Etowah Youth Symphony Orchestra, Michael Gagliardo, conductor. The work, written
in memory of September 11, 2001, "reflects upon the acts
of valor that surfaced in its wake; and acknowledges the
resilience and preservation of human spirit" <http://.
jamesgrantmusic.com/orchestral/_tribute.htm>

California

Los Angeles: At the Hollywood Bowl, the Los Angeles Philharmonic Orchestra, John Williams, conductor, with James Taylor, singer and narrator, presented this program:

Liberty Fanfare (Williams)
Battle Hymn of the Republic (Steffe)
"Arlington" from JFK (Williams)
Summon the Heroes (Williams)
Waltz from *Carousel* (Rodgers)
Lincoln Portrait (Copland)
"It's a Grand Night for Singing" from *State Fair*
 (Rodgers)
Song selections (James Taylor)
The Washington Post (Sousa)

Semper Fidelis (Sousa)
The Stars and Stripes Forever (Sousa)
Main title from *Star Wars* (Williams)
"Raiders March" from *Raiders of the Lost Ark*
 (Williams)
[*John Williams Web Pages* website, accessed Sep-
 tember 5, 2008, www.johnwilliams.org].

Delaware

Bethany Beach: The 287th Army Band of the
Delaware National Guard gave a concert ("2002 Summer Concert Schedule," *DNG News* website)

District of Columbia

The U.S. Marine Band with a combo performed
the following program at the White House:

Americans We March (Henry Fillmore)
Overture to *Candide* (Bernstein)
King Cotton March (Sousa)
Second Prelude (Gershwin)
The Liberty Bell (Sousa)
[combo]
National Emblem (Bagley)
The Music Man (Willson)
Washington Post March (Sousa)
[combo]
The Chimes of Liberty March (Goldman)
West Side Story (Bernstein)
"This Is My Country" (Al Jacobs)
[combo]
Belle of the Ball Waltz (Anderson)
Syncopated Clock (Anderson)
The Girl I Left Behind Me (Anderson)
[combo]
Semper Fidelis (Sousa)
Washington Grays (Grafulla)
The Black Horse Troop March (Sousa)
His Honor March (Henry Fillmore)
Barnum and Bailey's Favorite (Karl. L. King)
[combo]
"God Bless America"
"America the Beautiful" (Hunsberger)
The Stars and Stripes Forever (Sousa)
["Program Records," U.S. Marine Band Library].

Kentucky

Nicholasville: A reenactment ceremony of the 1794
celebration by Col. William Price and forty Revolutionary soldiers, one of the earliest Fourth of July celebrations southwest of the Alleghenies, took place at
the site of Col Price's farm, five miles west of the town.
Members of the Jessamine County Historical and Ge-
nealogical Society were dressed in costume, as a bagpiper played "Amazing Grace" at a wreath-laying ceremony ("1700's Jessamine Independence Gathering
Re-Enacted," *Lexington Herald-Leader*, 5 July 2002,
B1-B2).[1012]

Nevada

Las Vegas: The Las Vegas Philharmonic, Harold
Weller, director, and Richard McGee, associate con-

ductor, presented "A Star Spangled Fourth of July Spectacular":

Star-Spangled Banner, with Lynette Boggs Mc-
    Donald, vocalist
Selections from *Hook* (John Williams)
Overture to *Candide* (Bernstein)
Selections from *West Side Story* (Bernstein)
Who Will Stand, featuring Clint Holmes and Bill
    Fayne
Variations on a Shaker Melody (Copland)
Armed Forces Salute
American Salute (Morton Gould)
Pops Hoedown (Richard Hayman)
Selections from *Porgy & Bess* (Gershwin)
The Liberty Bell March (Sousa)
America the Beautiful (arr. Carmen Dragon)
1812 Overture (Tchaikovsky)
[Program 2002, Las Vegas Philharmonic].

New York

Cazenovia: The Mario DeSantis Orchestra performed at Lakeland Park ("July Fourth Celebrations,"
Post-Standard [Syracuse], 4 July 2002).

Rochester: At Manhattan Square Park, the
Rochester Philharmonic Orchestra, Michael Butter-
man, conductor, presented an evening concert (*Democrat and Chronicle*, 4 July 2002, 5B).

North Dakota

Bismarck: Bruce Craig Roter's *TR: A "Bully" Portrait* received its North Dakota premiere, with a performance by the Bismarck-Mandan Symphony Orchestra, Tom Wellin, conductor, on the grounds of
the North Dakota State Capitol building. The work
was narrated by Metropolitan Opera bass-baritone
LeRoy Lehr. Bruce Craig roter website, http://www.
bruceroter.com/bio.html.

Ohio

Cincinnati: The United States Army Field Band &
Soldiers' Chorus presented this program:

His Honor (Henry Fillmore)
Candide (Bernstein)
Porgy and Bess
Pineapple Poll
El Capitan (Sousa)
This is a Great Country
Big Band Sounds
Hymn to the Fallen (John Williams)
Hands Across the Sea (Sousa)
Hoe-Down
Star Spangled Spectacular
Uncle Sammy March (Abe Holzmann)
Salute to the Army
76 Trombones
Yankee Doodle
Where Were You
Let Freedom Ring
Americana Medley
[Program, 4 July 2002, U.S. Army Field Band and
    Soldiers' Chorus].

Oregon

Portland: At the Chamber Music Northwest summer festival, *Singing in the Dark* for jazz alto saxophone and string quartet by David Schiff was premiered by Marty Ehrlich, saxophone, and the Miami
String Quartet. "The music was shaped by the events
of September 11, 2001, although not in any specifically
programmatic way" (information courtesy of David
Schiff, e-mail, 2 October 2008).

Virginia

Richmond: The Richmond Concert Band, Mark
W. Poland, director, presented this evening concert at
Dogwood Dell:

America the Beautiful (Ward/arr. Carmen Dragon),
    with Lou Dean —"Why I Love Her"
Star-Spangled Banner
Capitol Square March (Warren Barker)
Symphony on Themes of John Philip Sousa, Mvt.
    II (Ira Hearshen)
New York: 1927 (Warren Barker)
The Invincible Eagle (Sousa)
Hollywood Milestones (arr. John Higgins)
Amazing Grace (arr. John Edmondson)
God Bless the U.S.A. (Lee Greenwood/arr. Roger
    Holmes), with Karl Heilman, vocalist
On the Mall (Edwin Franko Goldman), with the
    Richmond Concert Band Singers
Let There Be Peace on Earth (Sy Miller & Jull
    Jackson), with the Richmond Concert Band
    Singers
Battle Hymn (arr. James Neilson), with the Rich-
    mond Concert Band Singers
America the Beautiful (Ward/arr. Wyrtzen), with
    Karl Heilman, vocalist, and the Richmond Con-
    cert Band Singers
Armed Forces Salute, with the Richmond Concert
    Band Singers
Patriotic Sing-along, with the Richmond Concert
    Band Singers
1812 Overture
The Stars and Stripes Forever
[Concert program, Richmond Concert Band].

Wisconsin

Madison: At Elver Park, the 17th annual Fourth of
July celebration featured the Madison Municipal Band
(Brian Williamson, "July 4th Events Set for Area,"
Capital Times, 2 July 2002).

2003

Performances

California

Los Altos: Ye Olde Towne Band performed the following program at Shoup Park:

Block M March (Jerry H. Bilik)
The King and I (Richard Rodgers)

76 Trombones (Meredith Willson)
The Homefront: Musical Memories from World
    War Ii (arr.James Christensen)
American Patrol (F.W. Meacham)
Star Spangled Spectacular: the Music of George M.
    Cohen (arr. Cacavas)
Themes Like Old Times (arr. Warren Barker)
This Is My Country (Don Raye and Al Jacobs)
Star-Spangled Banner
America the Beautiful
God Bless American (Irving Berlin)
[*Ye Olde Towne Band* website, accessed September
    5, 2008, http://www.windband.org/oldtowne/].

Mountain View: At the Shoreline Amphitheatre,
the San Francisco Symphony with guest conductor
Edwin Outwater performed "selections from Grofé's
Grand Canyon Suite, Copland's *Rodeo*, and Gershwin's
Cuban Overture" ("Fire and Music for the Fourth,"
Mountain View Voice Online Edition, 4 July 2003).

Delaware

Dover: At Legislative Mall, an evening concert that
included the 1812 Overture was presented by the
Delaware National Guard Band (Jenny Kania, "Have
a Blast in Dover, Delaware, this Fourth of July,"
Delaware State News, 3 July 2003).

District of Columbia

At the Capitol Fourth event, Dolly Parton, the
Chieftains, and Earl Scruggs performed and a tribute
to music composed by John Williams was played by
the National Symphony Orchestra; at Georgetown,
the U.S. Marine Brass Quintet and the Wildcat Regiment Band, Bruno Pino, Jr., director, provided music
at a C&O Canal reenactment barge trip commemorating the 175th anniversary of President John Quincy
Adams' canal ground-breaking ceremony of 1828
(*Northwest Current*, 16 July 2003, 10); the Marine
Band presented this program on the South Lawn of the
White House:

El Capitan (Sousa)
Strike Up the Band
Solid Men to the Front
Star-Spangled Salute
The Entertainer
Adoration March
Concord
American Folk Rhapsody No. 3
The Fairest of the Fair (Sousa)
Cinderella Waltz
Fandango
The Gridiron Club (Sousa)
Selections from *The Music Man*
Highlights from *Ragtime*
Corcoran Cadets
Selections from *The Sound of Music*
Washington Post
The Stars and Stripes Forever
Marines' Hymn

("Program Records," U.S. Marine Band Library); U.S.
Air Force Concert Band and Singing Sergeants at
Smithsonian National Air and Space Museum, 6 P.M.
("Concert Schedule," *United States Air Force Band*
website, <http://www.usafband.af.mil>.)

Hawaii

Honolulu: The Honolulu Community Concert
Band, Thomas Hesch, director, performed on July 4
at the Battleship Missouri Memorial, at Ford Island in
Pearl Harbor (*Honolulu Community Concert Band*
website, accessed August 1, 2008, http://members.aol.
com/hccbl/missouri2.html).

New York

Brockport: The Excelsior Cornet Band presented
this concert[1013] at the Morgan-Manning House:

"Star-Spangled Banner"
Battle Cry of Freedom/Kingdom Coming Quick-
    step (George F. Root/Henry C. Work, arr 1st
    Brigade Band, Brodhead, Wisconsin)
Dixie/Bonnie Blue Flag (Daniel D. Emmett/Harry
    Macarthy, arr. 26th North Carolina Regiment
    Band)
I'm Going Home to Dixie (Daniel D. Emmett)
Hero's Quickstep (Henry Schmitt)
Manual of Arms Polka (Claudio Grafulla)
Tenting Tonight on the Old Camp Ground/taps
    (Walter Kittredge/Daniel Butterfield)
Cheer Boys Cheer! (Henry Russell)
When John Gets Home from the War (Patrick
    Gilmore)
Damen Souvenir Polka (Johann Strauss)
Washington Grays (Claudio Grafulla)
Battle Hymn quickstep (Julia Ward Howe)
Skyrockets! (Claudio Grafulla)

New York: At the Macy's Fireworks Spectacular,
Kelly Clarkson, "American Idol" winner, Sheryl Crow
and John Mellencamp performed.

Rochester: The U.S. Army Field Band & Soldiers'
    Chorus presented this program:
Patriotic Prologue (various composers)
Garry Owen (traditional/arr. James Fulton)
Variations on a Korean Folk Song (John Barnes
    Chance), with SS Samuel Chung, baritone
The Mamas and the Papas (arr. MSG Eric Richards
    and SFC Laura Dause), with SM Joel Dulyea,
    MS William Gabbard, SFC Laura Dause, and SS
    Samantha Hammer, vocalists
Casey at the Bat (Steven Reineke)
Bride of the Waves (Herbert Clarke), with SS Al-
    berto Torres, euphonium
Yankee Doodle (Morton Gould)
A Billy Joel Songbook (arr. MSG Eric Richards),
    featuring the Soldiers' Chorus
From Maine to Oregon (Sousa)
Benny and Lionel (arr. SGM J. Loran McClung),
    with SFC Julia Mahan, clarinet, and SFC
    Thomas Enokian, xylophone

The Excelsior Cornet Band of Brockport, N.Y., following a performance on July 4, 2003, at the historic Morgan-Manning House in Brockport. Formed in 2001, and at the time of this publication is the only authentic Civil War brass band in New York State, performing Civil War era music on original Civil War era brass instruments from the collection of bandleader Jeffrey Stockham on the Fourth of July. Their uniforms authentically represent those of a typical early-war New York state militia band. The Excelsior Cornet Band presents concerts, educational programs, and living history portrayals for a variety of organizations and municipalities across the state (photograph by Victoria Stockham, courtesy Jeffrey R. Stockham).

Armed Forces Salute (arr. Ken Whitcomb and Robert Lichtenberger)
The Stars and Stripes Forever (Sousa)
[Program, 4 July 2003, U.S. Army Field Band and Soldiers' Chorus].

Pennsylvania

Lancaster: At Long's Park, with Governor Edward G. Rendell in attendance, the Lancaster Symphony Orchestra performed the 1812 Overture ("Patriotism and Pride," *Lancaster New Era*, 7 July 2003).

Philadelphia: The National Constitution Center officially opened on July 4 and the Philly Pops, Peter Nero, conductor, provided an opening-day concert ("The Philadelphia Orchestra Association and Peter Nero and the Philly Pops Consolidate Administrative Operations," *The Philadelphia Orchestra website*, access

July 26, 2008, http://www.philorch.org/news_200 50824.html?cur_month=2008–06.

South Carolina

Georgetown: The Indigo Choral Society performed on the lawn of the Kaminski House Museum and premiered a piece composed for the society titled *Tidelands of Georgetown* by James Clemons. (Clayton Stairs, "Independence Day Festivities Bring Out Red, White and Blue," *The Times*, 2 July 2003; *Continental Harmony* http://www.continentalharmony.com)

South Dakota

Aberdeen: The Aberdeen Community Municipal Band premiered *Prairie River Reflections* by Dan Rager that was written in honor of the 100th year anniversary of the National Wildlife Refuge System with the

The National Constitution Center, Philadelphia, which opened on July 4, 2003, with U.S. Supreme Court Justice Sandra Day O'Connor and Philadelphia Mayor John Street presiding. The Philly Pops conducted by Peter Nero provided the music for the event (author's photograph).

event hosted by Sand Lake National Wildlife Refuge (*Continental Harmony* http://www.continentalharmony.com)

Tennessee

Nashville: At Riverfront Park, the Nashville Symphony Orchestra, Fisk Jubilee Singers, Lee Ann Womack, and Al Green performed (*The Tennessean*, 27 June 2003).

Texas

Dallas: The Dallas Wind Symphony, with Kevin Sedatole, guest conductor, gave the following concert at the Meyerson Symphony Center:

Washington Post March (Sousa)
Grand March from Aida (Verdi), arr. Seredy)
Fairest of the Fair (Sousa)
The Girl I Left Behind Me (Leroy Anderson)
Napoli (Herman Bellstedt), Wiff Rudd, trumpet soloist
Flirtations, Trio for Three Cornets (Herbert L. Clarke)
Pride of the Wolverines (Sousa)
"Fourth of July" from Holiday Music (Morton Gould)
American We (Henry Fillmore, edition by Fennell)
Second Prelude (Gershwin)

Galop from Genevieve Brabant (Offenbach, arr. Bourgeois)
Colonel Bogey (Kenneth J. Alford, edition by Fennell)
God of Our Fathers
The Glory of the Yankee Navy (Sousa), encore
Armed Forces Salute (arr. Bob Lowden)
America the Beautiful (arr. Carmen Dragon)
[*Dallas Wind Symphony* website, accessed February 13, 2008, http://www.dws.org/].

Spicewood: In Two River Canyon Amphitheatre near Austin, Willie Nelson held his 30th anniversary Fourth of July family Picnic Weekend concert which was broadcast for the first time over XM Satellite Radio (NASDAQ: XMSR). Performers included The Grateful Dead, Merle Haggard, Leon Russell, Ray Price and Billy Bob Thornton ("SM to Air First Ever National Radio Broadcast of Willie Nelson's July 4th Picnic Concert," *XM Satellite Radio Press Release*, 29 June 2003).

Virginia

Arlington: U.S. Air Force Silver Wings at Netherlands Carillon, 7 P.M. ("Concert Schedule," *United States Air Force Band* website, <http://www.usafband. af.mil>.)

Orkney Springs: Bishop's annual "Red, White, and

Blue Grass" event, featured Vassar Clements, Jackass Flats, and Steep Canyon Raiders, at the Shrine Mont conference Center. Poster, Virginia House (formerly known as the Orkney Springs Hotel).

Richmond: The Richmond Concert Band, Mark W. Poland, director, presented this evening concert at Dogwood Dell:

America the Beautiful (Ward/arr. Carmen Dragon)
Star-Spangled Banner
Capitol Square March (Warren Barker)
Main Street Celebration (Steven Reineke)
Each Time You Tell Their Story (Samuel R. Hazo)
Royal Fireworks (Handel/arr. Frank Erickson)
Billboard March (John N. Klohr/arr. Frederick Fennell)
Three Tenors (arr. James Christensen)
Cute (Neal Hefti/arr. Sweeney)
76 Trombones (Meredith Willson/arr. Leroy Anderson)
Music of the Beatles (arr. Michael Sweeney)
Mamma Mia! (arr. Roy Phillippe)
Governor's March (Leroy Anderson)
Queen in Concert (arr. Jay Bocook)
Themes Like Old Times III (Warren Barker)
Liberty (John Drymon), with Karl Heilman, vocalist
God Bless the U.S.A. (Lee Greenwood/arr. Roger Holmes), with Karl Heilman, vocalist
Armed Forces Salute
Patrio Sing-along
1812 Overture
The Stars and Stripes Forever (Sousa)
[Concert program, Richmond Concert Band].

West Virginia

Charleston: The Air Force Ceremonial Brass Band with country artist Patty Loveless performed at the Haddad Riverfront Park (Brad McElhinny, "Same Time Next Year," *Charleston Daily Mail*, 5 July 2003, P1A).

2004

Performances

Alabama

Selma: The third annual "City of Selma" celebration had performances scheduled by the Alabama National Guard Armory Band and a community choir at Memorial Stadium (John Gullion, "Selma's Fourth Honors 'God and Country,'" *Selma Times-Journal*, 20 June 2004).

California

Hollywood: John Mauceri leads the Hollywood Bowl Orchestra in a tribute to American music (*Los Angeles Times*, 4 July 2004, B4).

Vallejo: The Vallejo Symphony Orchestra, with David Ramadanoff, conductor, performed at the waterfront ("Independence Day Guide," *San Francisco Chronicle*, 3 July 2004).

Delaware

Dover: The Milford Community Band performed on the Green and the Dover Air Force Band Chorus sang in the evening at Legislative Mall (*DNREC News* 34/176, 16 June 2004. Website: www.dnrec.state.de. us.

District of Columbia

Capitol Fourth concert featured a 150th birthday salute to composer John Philip Sousa and a commemoration to music legend Ray Charles by Cicely Tyson. Performers included Vince Gill, Amy Grant, Robin Gibb, Clay Aiken, and Yolanda Adams (Website, Capitol Fourth, www.pbs.org/capitolfourth/concert. html); U.S. Air Force Concert Band and Singing Sergeants at the Smithsonian National Air and Space Museum, 6 P.M. ("Concert Schedule," *United States Air Force Band* website, <http://www.usafband.af. mil>.); Marine Band, Col. Timothy W. Foley, leader, presented a concert on the south lawn of the White House, prior to the fireworks; MSgt Robert Boguslaw, played piano in the Grand Foyer of the White House during the reception; at the U.S. Marine Corps War Memorial, Free Country with MGySgt Wilson performed ("Program Records," U.S. Marine Band Library).

Hawaii

Waialua: The Hawaii National Guard Band (40 pieces), Warrant Officer Curtis Hiyane, bandmaster, presents a concert at the bandstand ("Isles Light Off Celebrations," *Star Bulletin* website, 2 July 2004, http://Starbulletin.com; *Honolulu Advertiser*, 1 July 2004).

Idaho

Twin Falls: The Twin Falls Municipal Band and College of Southern Idaho Band premiered *Magic Valley*, composed by Anthony Scott Watson. The event was hosted by the Magic Valley Arts Council (*Continental Harmony* http://www.continentalharmony. com)

Illinois

Chicago: At Highland Park, the costumed River Valley Colonial Fife & Drum Corp performed in a parade there (*Chicago Tribune*, 5 July 2004, section 2, 1).

Louisiana

New Orleans: The New Orleans Concert Band with the U.S. Navy Band, with conductors Frank Mannino and Lt. J.G.R.J. Warren present this program:

Star-Spangled Banner with vocalist
Star Spangled Spectacular
Golden Age of Broadway

God Bless the U.S.A., with vocalist
Duty, Honor, Country with narrator
A Chorus Line
Armed Forces Salute
Washington Grays
Ray Charles
America the Beautiful
Broadway Show Stoppers
'S Wonderful, with vocalist
Someone to Watch Ove Me with vocalist
Westside Story
Them Basses
Cole Porter on Broadway
Stars and Stripes Forever
[New Orleans Concert Band website, accessed August 27, 2008, http://neworleansconcertband. org/].

Maryland

Largo: U.S. Air Force Airmen of Note at Six Flags America ("Concert Schedule," *United States Air Force Band* website, <http://www.usafband.af.mil>).

Massachusetts

Boston: At the Hatch Shell, the Boston Pops Esplanade Orchestra, Keith Lockhart, conductor, and the Tanglewood Festival Chorus, with Tracy Silva, winner of the "Por-Search 2004 talent search" (*Boston Globe*, 5 July 2004, B3).

Michigan

Muskegon: The U.S. Army Field Band and Soldiers' Chorus presented a concert (Program, 4 July 2004, U.S. Army Field Band and Soldiers' Chorus).

New York

Morristown: The Northern New York Parade Music Judges Association adjudicated the bands in the town's Independence Day parade. The Gouverneur High School Marching Band, directed by Kathleen Moses, won first prize. Other bands included the Ogdensburg Free Academy Band and the Edwards-Knox Marching Cougars Band (Dick Sterling, "GHs Marching Band 1st at Morristown," *Gouverneur Tribune-Press*, 8 July 2004, 1).

Texas

Dallas: The Dallas Wind Symphony, with Col. Arnald D. Gabriel, guest conductor, gave the following concert at the Meyerson Symphony Center:

Emblem of Unity March (J.J. Richards)
God of Our Fathers (Claude T. Smith)
The Chimes of Liberty March (Edwin Franko Goldman)
Bugler's Holiday (Leroy Anderson)
Irving Berlin: A Symphonic Portrait (Berlin, arr. Hawley Ades)
The Volunteer (Walter Rogers), with Brian Bowman, euphonium

Carnival of Venice (Herbert L. Clarke), with Brian Bowman, euphonium
Salute to the Armed Forces (arr. Robert Cray)
Porgy and Bess (Gershwin, arr. Bennett)
Hymn to the Fallen (John Williams, arr. Paul Lavender)
1812 Overture (Tchaikovsky), with members of the Greater Dallas Youth Orchestra Wind Symphony
[*Dallas Wind Symphony* website, accessed February 13, 2008, http://www.dws.org/].

Fort Worth: At the historic stockyards, Willie Nelson's 31st annual Fourth of July Picnic occurred (Web site, *Official Texas Music*, www.williespicnic.com).

Virginia

Orkney Springs: At Shrine Mont Conference Center, the Bishop's 15th Annual Bluegrass Festival, Sunday, on July 4, featuring Tony Rice Unit, King Wilkie, and Jackass Flats. Poster, Virginia House (formerly known as the Orkney Springs Hotel).

Richmond: The Richmond Concert Band, Mark W. Poland, director, presented this evening concert at Dogwood Dell:

Capitol Square March (Warren Barker)
Star-Spangled Banner
The Battle Pavane (arr. Bob Margolis)
Fantasy on "When Johnny Comes Marching Home" (Robert Starer), with Kathy Kreutzer, piccolo
Let the Earth Hear His Voice[1014] (Rob Blankenship)
In the Mood (Joe Garland)
Bugler's Holiday (Leroy Anderson), with Ron Tucker, Tom McCarty, and Randy Abernathy, buglers
The Girl from Ipanema (Antonio Carlos Jobim/arr. Ted Ricketts)
George M. Cohan Medley, with Garet Chester, vocalist
Tijuana Brass in Concert (arr. Ted Ricketts)
Beach Boys Forever (arr. Jerry Brubaker)
Shrek Dance Party (arr. Paul Murtha)
SpongeBob SquarePants (arr. Jay Bocook)
The Mask of Zorro (arr. John Moss)
O Brother, Where Art Thou? (arr. Michael Brown)
The Land Is Your Land (Woody Guthrie/arr. George Kenny)
Armed Forces Salute
Patriotic Sing-along (arr. James Ployhar/arr. Warren Barker)
1812 Overture
The Stars and Stripes Forever
[Concert program, Richmond Concert Band].

West Virginia

Charleston: U.S. Air Force Ceremonial Brass, 7 P.M. ("Concert Schedule," *United States Air Force Band* website, <http://www.usafband.af.mil>; Mike Andrick, "City Gala a Booming Success," *Charleston Daily Mail*, 5 July 2004, P1A).

2005

Performances

California

Burbank: At the Starlight Bowl, the Tex Beneke Orchestra, the Modernaires, Chordettes, and the Coasters (Max Baumgarten and Rebecca Epstein, "Fourth of July Fireworks," *Los Angeles City Beat* (30 June 2005).

Oakland: After 17 years as conductor of the Oakland Municipal Band, Dwight LaRue Hall presents his final concert of the band on the Fourth at Lakeshore Park. The band was formed in 1911 (Tony C. Yang, "Oakland Municipal Band Passes the Baton," *Oakland Tribune*, 5 July 2005).

Pasadena: At the Rose Bowl event, "The Great American," a song by composer Nolan Gasser, was performed by the Pasadena Pops and tenor Dennis McNeil (*The Classical Archives*, http://www.classical archives.com/artists/gasser.html.

Rohnert Park: The Santa Rosa Symphony, with guest conductor Jeff Tyzik, presented a concert on the grounds of Sonoma State University. The program included *American Fanfare* by composer James Stephenson. (James Stephenson website, http://www.stephen sonmusic.com and *Sonoma State University Newsroom*, 15 June 2005, http://www.sonoma.edu/pubs/news release/archives/2005_06.html.

San Francisco: San Francisco Symphony with Edwin Outwater, conductor, with Gilles Apap, violin, and members of Melody of China. Works by Shostakovich, Gabriela Lena Frank, Gang Situ, and Ravel ("Go Boom. Fun, Music and Fireworks in Unlimited Supply on Fourth of July," *San Francisco Chronicle*, 3 July 2005).

District of Columbia

At the Capitol Fourth event, popular singer Gloria Estefan, winner of the 2005 National Artistic Achievement Award (*Washington Post*, 5 July 2005, C1-C2); U.S. Air Force Concert Band and Singing Sergeants at Smithsonian National Air and Space Museum, 6 P.M. ("Concert Schedule," *United States Air Force Band* website, <http://www.usafband.af.mil>; the U.S. Marine Band at the White House in the following program:

> *Hail to the Spirit of Liberty* (Sousa)
> Overture to *Candide* (Bernstein)
> *Porgy & Bess* (Gershwin)
> *76 Trombones* (Willson)
> "Pride of a People" (Stephen Bulla), with Kevin Bennear, soloist
> *Stephen Foster Medley* (arr. Sammy Nestico)
> *The Stars and Stripes Forever* (Sousa).
> Free Country of the U.S. Marine Band performed this set on the White House South Lawn:
> "With Me" (Lonestar)
> "I Try to Think about Elvis" (Patty Loveless)

"No Place I'd Rather Be" (Alan Prather)
"I Feel Lucky" (Mary Chapin Carpenter)
"An American Child" (Phil Vassar)
"American Soldier" (Toby Keith)
"Bless the Broken Road" (Rascal Flatts)
"Live Like You Were Dyin'" (Tim McGraw)
"I'm Already There" (Lonestar)
"Sold" (John Michael Montgomery)
"Devil Went Down to Georgia" (Charlie Daniels)
"19 Somethin'" (Mark Will)
"An American Pledge" (Peter Wilson)
"Only in America" (Brooks & Dunn)
"God Bless the U.S.A." (Lee Greenwood)
["Program Records," U.S. Marine Band Library].

Illinois

New Lenox: On the occasion of the dedication of the new Performing Arts Pavilion in the commons area, the Illinois Philharmonic Orchestra, Carmon DeLeone, director, performed this Fourth of July concert that included a performance of James A. Beckel, Jr., *Liberty for All*, with Jeff Mattsey, narrator (*Herald News*, 29 June 2005).

Indiana

South Bend: The South Bend (Indiana) Symphony Pops, directed by Tsung Yeh, performed music honoring French, German and Polish immigrants on July 2 (Andrew S. Hughes, "Orchestra Celebrates Immigrants," *South Bend Tribune*, 4 July 2005, B6).

Massachusetts

Boston: On the Esplanade, Boston Pops, with Nashville country music artist Gretchen Wilson, and Big & Rich (John Rich and Big Kenny) (2005 Media Release)

Quincy: The Plymouth Philharmonic Orchestra was scheduled to perform "patriotic music, Broadway tunes, Sousa marches, and the 1812 Overture accompanied by cannons fired by the National Guard" (Jody Feinberg, "Get Up and Go," *Patriot Led*ger, 2 July 2005).

Nebraska

Grand Island: The Stuhr Museum hosted an "1890s Fourth of July" that included a concert by the Railroad Town Silver Cornet Band (*Lincoln Journal Star*, 3 July 2005).

Nevada

Las Vegas: The Las Vegas Philharmonic presented a concert, featuring the premiere of *Las Vegas Rhapsody*,[1015] composed by Richard McGee, associate conductor of the Philharmonic, and narrated live by Las Vegas mayor Oscar Goodman. The concert included patriotic tunes, and in acknowledgement of its seventh annual Independence Day concert, had music from *The Magnificent Seven*. The event also featured "a tribute to Howard Hughes using two large screens to show slide show highlights from Hughes' life, accompanied by music from *The Boy That Could Fly*."

The program also featured "a centennial march by local composer Bernard Baskin" ("Going Fourth: McGee's 'Rhapsody' Highlights Annual LV Phil Concert," *Las Vegas Sun*, 30 June 2005).

New Jersey

South Orange/Maplewood: A "coalition of local performers" premiered *An American Dale* by composer Janet Albright on July 3, "an annual interfaith community gathering on the evening of independence day to celebrate the vision of our founding fathers for a nation of people free from segregation." The event was hosted by South Orange/Maplewood Coalition on race and "community partners for this project include Opera for the Young, Maplewood Community Bands, Youth Orchestras of Essex County, Stirling Chamber Orchestra, Voices in Harmony, South Orange/Maplewood School District Fine Arts Department along with district music teachers and school bands, orchestras and choirs and Maplewood/South Orange Adult School, and SO-MAcom (South Orange/Maplewood community cable station). (*Continental Harmony* http://www.continentalharmony.com)

Pennsylvania

Erie: The U.S. Army Jazz Ambassadors, CWO, Kevin Laird, director, presented this program:

Flight of the Foo Birds (Neal Hefti)
It Never Entered My Mind (Richard Rodgers & Lorenz Hart/arr. Tom Matta), with SFC Christopher Buckholz, trombone
Harlem Airshaft (Duke Ellington)
Next Chapter (SGM Eugene Thorne)
The Song is You (Jerome Kern & Oscar Hammerstein II/arr. Gerald Wilson), with SFC Marva Lewis, vocalist
Candy (Mack David/arr. Gary McCourry)
Our Love is Here to Stay (George & Ira Gershwin/arr. Ken McCoy)
Critic's Choice (Oliver Nelson)
One Note Samba (Antonio Carlos Jobim/arr. SGM Eugene Thome)
Going to Chicago (Count Basie & Andrew Rushing/arr. Quincy Jones), with SFC Marva Lewis, vocalist
A Visit to New Orleans
Armed Forces Salute (various composers/arr. MSG Vince Norman)
God Bless the U.S.A. (Lee Greenwood/arr. SGM Eugene Thorne)
[Program, 4 July 2005, Jazz Ambassadors, U.S. Army Field Band and Soldiers' Chorus].

Lancaster: The Lancaster Symphony Orchestra, Stephen Gunzenhauser, conductor, performed on July 3 in Longs Park and included "a Ray Charles medley" and the 1812 Overture ("Fun for the Fourth," [Lancaster] *Sunday News*, 3 July 2005, H2).

Philadelphia: Patti LaBelle, Sir Elton John, and Peter Nero with the Philly Pops[1016] at the Philadelphia Freedom Concert at the Benjamin Franklin Parkway. That day Philadelphia Mayor John F. Street presented Sir Elton John with the Philadelphia City of Brotherly Love Award for his efforts to improve the lives of those living with HIV/AIDS (*Philadelphia Inquirer*, 5 July 2005, 1).

Texas

Dallas: The Dallas Wind Symphony, with Col. Arnald D. Gabriel, guest conductor, gave the following concert at the Meyerson Symphony Center:

Fanfare, colonial fife & drum medley (arr. David Lovrien)
American Salute (Morton Gould)
Eagle Squadron March (Kenneth J. Alford)
Glenn Miller in concert (arr. Wayne Scott)
The March from "1941" (John Williams, arr. Lavender)
MacArthur/Patton Suite (Jerry Goldsmith, arr. Davis)
The Last Full Measure of Devotion (arr. Frasier/trans. Davis), Jacob Villarreal, tenor
Victory at Sea (Richard Rodgers, arr. R.R. Bennett)
Washington Grays (Claudio Grafulla)
Variations on 'America' (Charles Ives)
Four Cohan Songs (George M. Cohan, arr. Villanueva), audience sing-along
Battle Hymn of the Republic (William Steffe, arr. Wilhousky)
Salute to the Armed Forces (arr. Robert Cray)
America the Beautiful (aff. Carmen Dragon
(*Dallas Wind Symphony* website, accessed February 13, 2008, http://www.dws.org/)

Virginia

Chantilly: U.S. Air Force Airmen of Note at the Smithsonian National Air and Space Museum ("Concert Schedule," *United States Air Force Band* website, <http://www.usafband.af.mil>.)

Mount Vernon: The Concert Band of America, "an 80-member company of retired musicians from each of the U.S. armed services bands," marked its 12th year performing at the home of George Washington on Independence Day ("First President's Home Celebrates American Independence," 9 June 2005, on Mount Vernon website, http://www.mountvernon.org/pressroom/index.cfm/fuseaction/view/pid/794/.

Richmond: The Richmond Concert Band, Mark W. Poland, director, presented this evening concert at Dogwood Dell:

Capitol Square March (Warren Barker)
Star-Spangled Banner
American Exultant (Henry Fillmore/arr. Andrew Glover)
We Shall Lift Lamps of Courage (Gary Fagan)
Sweet Land of Liberty (James Sochinski)
West Wing (W.G. Snuffy Walden/arr. Roy Phillippe)
What's Up at the Symphony? (arr. Jerry Brubaker)
Harry's Wondrous World (John Williams/arr. Jerry Brubaker)

The Genius of Ray Charles (arr. Michael Brown)
Light the Fire Within (David Foster &Linda
   Thompson/arr. Paul Lavender)
Liberty (an Anthem for a Free World) (John Dry-
   mon & Michael Gerardi)
Midway March (John Williams/arr. James
   Curnow)
Elvis (themes from Thus Spake Zarathustra
   (Strauss/arr. Dick Thomas) and "A Tribute to
   Elvis (arr. James Christensen), with Ron Sim-
   mons, Elvis portrayer
Armed Forces Salute
Patriotic Sing-along (arr. James Ployhar and War-
   ren Barker)
1812 Overture
The Stars and Stripes Forever (Sousa)
[Concert program, Richmond Concert Band].

2006

Performances

California

Redlands: On June 30, at the Redlands Bowl, the
Redlands Fourth of July Band celebrated its 25th anniversary with a concert and fireworks. Founder and
conductor of the band Curtiss B. Allen, Sr. was
dressed in his "traditional red coat" (*Redlands Daily
Facts*, 6 July 2006).

San Diego: The San Diego Symphony Summer
Pops, Matthew Garbutt, conductor, presented "An
American Salute" concert at the Embarcadero Marina
Park South and included favorites by Aaron Copland,
Richard Rodgers, and John Philip Sousa. Accompa-
nying the production were the voices of the La Jolla
Symphony Chorus. "A giant flag appeared on stage
during George M. Cohan's "You're a Grand Old Flag."
(Valerie Scher, "'An American Salute' Kicks Off 10-
Week Summer Pops Schedule," *SignOnSanDiego.com*
by the *Union-Tribune*, 3 July 2006).

Colorado

Colorado Springs: The U.S. Army Field Band and
Soldiers' Chorus presented a concert (Program, 4 July
2006, U.S. Army Field Band and Soldiers' Chorus).

District of Columbia

U.S. Air Force Airmen of Note at Smithsonian Na-
tional Air and Space Museum, 6 P.M.; U.S. Air Force
Concert Band and Singing Sergeants at the Jefferson
Memorial, 4:30 P.M. ("Concert Schedule," *United States
Air Force Band* website, http://www.usafband.af.mil>;
Marine Band, Col. Michael J. Colburn, leader, pro-
vides a concert on the south lawn of the White House
("Program Records," U.S. Marine Band Library).

Florida

Coral Gables: Greater Miami Symphonic Band
(*Miami Herald*, 4 July 2006. 2B).
Miami: Carlos Olivia y Los Sobrinos de Juez (Ibid).

Illinois

Elmwood Park: The Jazz Ambassadors, Chief Warrant Officer Kevin Laird, director, of the U.S. Army
Field Band presented the following program:

Whirlybird (Neal Hefti)
Waltz for Debby (Bill Evans/arr. SGM Eugene
   Thorne), with SFC Andrew Layton, saxophone
Big Jim Blues (Mary Lou Williams)
On the Sly (SGM Darryl Brenzel)
Exactly Like You (Dorothy Fields and Jimmy
   McHugh/arr. MSG Vince Norman), with SFC
   Marva Lewis, vocalist.
This Bitter Earth (Clyde Lovern Otis/arr. SGM
   Eugene Thorne)
What a Little Moonlight Can Do (Harry
   Woods/trans. MSG Vince Norman)
Nasty Magnus (Quincy Jones)
Here There and Everywhere (John Lennon, Paul
   McCartney/arr. SGM Eugene Thorne)
Taking a Chance on Love (Vernon Duke, Ted Fet-
   ter, and John Latouche/arr. Jim Perry), with
   SFC Marva Lewis, vocalist
Dixie Medley
Armed Forces Salute
God Bless America (Irving Berlin/arr. Jim Roberts)
[Program, 4 July 2006, Jazz Ambassadors, U.S.
   Army Field Band and Soldiers' Chorus].

South Holland: The South Holland Municipal
Band, Darrell A. Dalton, conductor, presented this
program:

Pride of the Fleet (James L. Hosay)
Star-Spangled Banner (arr. Bill Moffit)
South Holland Band (Jack Wonnell)
The Liberty Bell (Sousa)
Armed Forces Salute (arr. Bob Lowden)
American Salute (Morton Gould/arr. Phillip J.
   Lang)
Freedom's Promise (James Hosay)
A Copland Tribute (arr. Clare Grundman)
America the Beautiful (arr. Carmen Dragon)
Thine Alabaster Cities Gleam (Jerry Brubaker)
1812 Overture (Tchaikovsky)
The Stars and Stripes Forever (Sousa)
[*Village of South Holland* website, http://www.
   southholland.org/Events/fourth.phtml].

Maryland

Annapolis: The Naval Academy Band, Brian O.
Walden, leader, performed at Susan C. Campbell
Park.

Baltimore: The Baltimore Symphony Orchestra at
Oregon Ridge Park ("Spectacular Ways to Celebrate
the Fourth of July," *BaltimoreSun.com*, 4 July 2006).

Takoma Park: On the occasion of the town's
117th Independence Day celebration, featured were:
Takoma Zone Band , the Takoma Park Concert Band,
with Alec Garrin and David Goette, soloists; MacMillan of Montgomery Pipe Band; DC Motors; Mecca
Temple #10 Drum and Bugle Corps; Morning Few;
D.C. Pan Jammers; Image Band; Trinidad and To-

bago Steel Band ("Fourth of July Approaches," *Takoma Park Newsletter*, July 2006).

Massachusetts

Bedford: The Yankee Notions Band gave a concert at the town common ("Locals Towns Plan for Fourth of July Fun Today," *Lowellsun.com*, 4 July 2006).

Boston: Aerosmith performed with the Boston Pops at the Esplanade and "American Idol" contestant Ayla Brown sang the "Star-Spangled Banner" ("Rains Fail to Dampen a Spirited Fourth," *Boston Globe*, 5 July 2006, B3).

Lowell: The University of Massachusetts Lowell Orchestra performed at the Sampas Pavilion on Pawtucket Boulevard ("Locals Towns Plan for Fourth of July Fun Today," *Lowellsun.com*, 4 July 2006).

Tanglewood: LeAnn Rimes, country music star and winner of the Grammys in 1997 for "Best Female County Singer and Best Country Song" had her first appearance here (Jeffrey Borak, *Berkshire Eagle*, 7 April 2006).

Minnesota

Ashland: The Ashland City Band performed at Memorial Park ("Fourth of July Celebrations," *DuluthNewsTribune.com*, 4 July 2006).

Nevada

Las Vegas: The Las Vegas Philharmonic, Harold Weller, music director, with Richard McGee, associate conductor, presented a "Star Spangled Spectacular" at Hills Park. The program included:

The Stars Spangled Banner, with Tod Fitzpatrick, vocalist
"Gallop" from the William Tell Overture (Rossini)
Pops Hoedown (Richard Hayman)
Music from the film score *The Patriot* (John Williams)
American Salute (Morton Gould)
Salute to the Armed Forces
"Habanera" from *Carmen* (Bizet), with Juline Gilmore, mezzo-soprano
"Some Enchanted Evening," from *South Pacific* (Rodgers & Hammerstein), with Tod Fitzpatrick, baritone
"So in Love" from *Kiss Me Kate* (Cole Porter), with Juline Gilmore and Tod Fitzpatrick
"Raider's March" from *Raiders of the Lost Ark* (John Williams)
"Coming to America" (Neil Diamond/arr. Vincent Falcone)
"Luck Be a Lady" (Frank Loesser/arr. Billy May), with Bill Acosta, vocalist and Vincent Falcone, conductor
1812 Overture (Tchaikovsky)
"America the Beautiful"
A Sousa Medley: Washington Post March, Semper Fidelis, and Stars and Stripes Forever
[Program, 2006, Las Vegas Philharmonic].

New York

Lake Placid: Music included The Standards, The Fetish and the Lake Placid Sinfonietta ("Fourth of July Events Schedule," *Press Republican*, 4 July 2006).

Syracuse: At the Empire Expo Center on the New

The St. Charles Municipal Band, Nancy Garza, conductor, in concert, July 4, 2006, Frontier Park, St. Charles, Missouri. The heritage of this band dates to a July 4, 1870, performance in a parade. During the 1880s and after, the band marched in local Independence Day parades (courtesy Earl R. Kreder).

York State Fairgrounds, the Syracuse Symphony Orchestra, Daniel Hege, director performed a concert and the Syracuse University Brass Ensemble added to the revelry ("4th of July Fireworks," *All News*, 4 July 2006, *News 10 Now* website (accessed 5 July 2006).

Ohio

Akron: The Akron Symphony Orchestra and ETC Show Choir performed in the evening ("Fourth of July Holiday Events," *Akron Beacon Journal*, 3 July 2006).

Oklahoma

Enid: At Meadowlake Park, residents enjoyed the "14th year the fireworks were set to music and the Enid Symphony Orchestra again provided selections for the display," including excerpts from the musical *Grease* and selections from *La Cage Aux Follies*, 1812 Overture (Tchaikovsky) and *Stars and Stripes Forever* (Cass Rains, "Enid Celebrates Fourth of July with Fireworks, A Hometown Celebration," *EnidNews.Com*, 5 July 2006).

Pennsylvania

Johnstown: The Johnstown Symphony Orchestra performed polkas and other works at the Johnstown Festival Park (Kecia Bal, "Fourth of July Fireworks, Picnics Go On Despite Weather," online *Tribune-Democrat*, 5 July 2006).

Pittsburgh: For the first time in twenty-five years, the Pittsburgh Symphony Orchestra did not perform at Point State Park and is replaced with the River City Brass Band (Andres Druckenbrod and Timothy McNulty, "PSO Dropped from July 4 Celebration," *Pittsburgh Post-Gazette*, 28 April 2006, B1; Nate Guidry, "A Touch of Brass," *Pittsburgh Post-Gazette*, 2 July 2006, E5).

Tennessee

Nashville: The Nashville Symphony provided background music as the fireworks were set off at Riverfront Park (Leon Alligood, "Patriots Party Like It's Fourth of July," *Tennessean.com*, 5 July 2006).

Pigeon Forge: At the Pigeon Forge Patriot Festival, Don Edwards, balladeer; Gillette Brothers; Oak Ridge Boys; Blue Mother Tupelo; Pigeon Forge Community Chorus ("Ramblin' Man: Dispatches from the Leisure Side," *Knoxnews.com*, 29 June 2006).

Texas

Austin: Austin Symphony, Peter Bay, director, at Zilker Park ("Fourth of July Fireworks Light Up Zilker Park," *News8Austin.com*, 5 July 2006).

Dallas: The Dallas Wind Symphony, Mike Holbrook, guest conductor, presented this program twice on July 4 at the Meyerson Symphony Center:

Civil War Medley (DWS Fife & Drum Corps, arr. David Lovrien)
On Parade (Sousa)
Esprit de Corps (Robert Jager)

The Melody Shop (Karl King)
Star-Spangled Salute (George M. Cohan)
The Official West Point March (Philip Egner)
Rushmore (Alfred Reed)
Hail to the Spirit of Liberty (Sousa), encore
Midnight Fire Alarm! (John Krance)
Washington Grays (Claudio Grafulla)
Yankee Doodle Fantasy Humoresque (D.W. Reeves)
New Colonial March (Robert Browne Hall)
Light Cavalry Overture (Suppé, arr. By Henry Fillmore)
The Freelance (march) (Sousa)
Barnum and Bailey's Favorite (Karl L. King)
*A Trumpeter's Lull*aby (Leroy Anderson), with Tim Andersen, trumpet
Armed Forces Salute (arr. Bob Lowden)
"America the Beautiful" (arr. Carmen Dragon)
The Stars and Stripes Forever (Sousa), encore
[*Dallas Wind Symphony* website, accessed February 13, 2008, http://www.dws.org/].

Virginia

Mount Vernon: Performing were the Fifes and Drums of Prince William IIII and the Concert Band of America (Mount Vernon website, press release, 16 June 2006, http://www.mountvernon.org/pressroom/index.cfm/fuseaction/view/pid/980/.

Richmond: The Richmond Concert Band, Mark W. Poland, director, presented this evening concert at Dogwood Dell:

Capitol Square March (Warren Barker)
Star-Spangled Banner
Patton's 6th Calvary March (John Gray Perkins)
Abduction from the Seraglio (Mozart)
Main Street Celebration (Steven Reineke)
On Angel Wings (Ed Huckeby)
Arrival of the Queen of Sheba (Handel/arr. Ted Ricketts)
Somewhere (Bernstein/arr. Jay Bocook)
Superman (John Williams/arr. Bob Lowden)
Sinatra in Concert (Jerry Nowak)
A Klezmer Karnival (Philip Sparke)
Vaudeville Spectacular (Paul Jennings)
Thunder (David Robidoux/arr. John Moss)
Selections from 1776 (Sherman Edwards/arr. Frank Erickson
Let Freedom Ring (Kay Seamayer/arr. Raul Prado)
Home of the Brave (Rob Blankenship)
Patriotic Sing-along (arr. James Ployhar and Warren Barker)
1812 Overture
The Stars and Stripes Forever (Sousa)
[Concert program, Richmond Concert Band].

2007

Broadcasts

The U.S. Ceremonial Brass of the Air Force broadcast "Today Show" over NBC television from Rocke-

Members of the Dallas Wind Symphony, led by David T. Kehler, performing a fife and drum Civil War medley by David Lovrien in the lobby of the Morton H. Meyerson Symphony Center, in Dallas, Texas, before the symphony's concert on July 4, 2006. Kehler has served as associate conductor of the Dallas Wind Symphony since 2001, conducts the full ensemble at various civic and community events and is also conductor of the Wind Symphony of the Greater Dallas Youth Orchestras, Inc. Jerry Junkin is artistic director of the DWS, which is noted for beginning every concert with "The Star-Spangled Banner" (courtesy Dallas Wind Symphony).

feller Plaza, New York City, 7–10 A.M. ("Concert Schedule," *United States Air Force Band* website, <http://www.usafband.af.mil>.)

Performances

Alabama

Fairhope: The Baldwin Pops Band concert was held in Henry George Park, with patriotic music performed during the fireworks ("Fourth of July Events," *Mobile Register*, 20 June 2007, Z2).

California

Alameda: Music by Livewire, Tall Shadows, Starboard Watch, and Tempest at the USS *Hornet* Museum (*San Francisco Chronicle*, 3 July 2007, A10).

San Francisco: Max Perkoff Jazz Ensemble, Marcus Shelby Jazz Quartet, Latoya London, and other groups at the Aquiatic Park Stage; at Pier 39 Stage, Tainted Love and Big Bang Beat; at the Golden Gate Park, the Golden Gate Park Band (*San Francisco Chronicle*, 3 July 2007, A10).

Irvine: The Pacific Symphony presented a "Good Vibrations: a Fourth of July Celebration" with Papa Doo Run Run, a popular surf band. Program:

Suite from *Victory at Sea* (Rodgers)
Love theme from *Splash* (Lee Holdridge)
"Under the Sea" from Disney's *The Little Mermaid* (Alan Menken/Howard Ashman)
Theme from *Jaws* (John Williams)
Hornpipe from *Down to the Sea in Ships* (Alfred Newman)
Selections from *Pirates of the Caribbean* (Klaus Badelt)
Selected Beach Boys hits, including "Love," "California Girls" and "Surfin' U.S.A."
Military tribute (marches of the armed forces)
[concert program, *Pacific Symphony* website, http://www.pacificsymphony.org/show_details.php?shid=129].

Mountain View: The San Francisco Symphony, Randall Craig Fleischer, conductor (*San Francisco Chronicle*, 3 July 2007, A10).

District of Columbia

The U.S. Air Force Singing Sergeants and Concert Band at the Air Force Memorial (Sharon Schultz, *The Capital*, 29 June 2007, 17); U.S. Air Force Airmen of Note at the Smithsonian National Air and Space Museum, 6 P.M. ("Concert Schedule," *United States Air Force Band* website, http://www.usafband.af.mil>; at the Capitol Fourth concert, National Symphony Orchestra, Erich Kunzel, conductor, with Little Richard, Hayden Panettiere, Dierks Bentley, Yolanda Adams, Elliott Yamin of "American Idol," and Bebe Neuwirth ("A Guide to Festivities," *Washington Post*, 4 July 2007, B4); at Anderson House, David and Ginger Hildebrand performed the following music at a gathering of the Society of the Cincinnati:

> A Toast (Francis Hopkinson) — President's March (Philip Phile) — Sweet Richard (George Bush manuscript, 1779–89) — Liberty song, and two parodies (John Dickinson, 1768, to the tune "Hearts of Oak") — White Cockade (Johannes T. Schley manuscript, ca. 1770) — Irishman's Epistle to the Officers, 1775, and troops at Boston, to the tune "Lilliburlero" — A New Song to the old tune of "Black Joke" — Medley: If the Heart of a Man/ Since Laws were Made/Over the Hills and Far Away (from *The Beggar's Opera*, 1728) — Liberty-Tree, a New Song, to the tune "The Gods of the Greeks" — The Drum (anon., George Bush manuscript, 1779–89) — Mother Country: A song (words, attributed to Benjamin Franklin, 1779; tune: song XXII in *The Convivial Songster*, 1782) — Fancy Minuet/Jefferson & Liberty/ March to Boston (Pierre Duport manuscript, ca. 1787–1826/ *The Village Fifer*, 1800/ Joseph Cabot manuscript, 1784 — The Dance, a Ballad to the tune of "Yankey Doodle" (*Pennsylvania Packet*, 27 November 1781).

(Program, "An Eighteenth-Century Musical Celebration of American Independence, 2 July 2007, courtesy of David and Ginger Hildebrand.); The U.S. Marine Band at the White House presented this music:

> *Washington Post March*
> A Patriotic Overture (Hearshen)
> *Chicago* (Kander/Bulla)
> *Americans We March* (Fillmore)
> *The Incredibles* (Michael Giacchino)
> *76 Trombones* (Willson)
> *Semper Fidelis*
> *The Stars and Stripes Forever*
> ["Program Records," U.S. Marine Band Library].

Maine

Bangor: The Bangor Band in Bass Park ("Fourth of July Events," *Bangor Daily News*, 2 July 2007, B2).

Bath: The Bath Municipal Band at Library Park (*Portland Press Herald*, 30 June 2007, B3).

Betje: Portland Brass Quintet at the Middle Intervale Meeting House (*Portland Press Herald*, 30 June 2007, B3).

Brunswick: The Bowdoin International Music Festival featured classical pianist Frank Glazer at Crooker Theatre, at Brunswick High School (*Portland Press Herald*, 30 June 2007, B3).

Maryland

Annapolis: The Annapolis Symphony Orchestra, José-Louis Nove, conductor, at Anne Arundel Community College's Siegert Stadium, performed Tchaikovsky's 1812 Overture and Sousa's *Stars and Stripes Forever*; the Naval Academy Concert Band at City Dock (Sharon Schultz, *The Capital*, 29 June 2007, 17); at the William Paca House, the All Children's Chorus of Annapolis sang "The Star-Spangled Banner" and the audience sang "America" and "America the Beautiful" as immigrants took the oath of allegiance (Sara Neufeld, "A Journey Complete for 51 New Americans," *Baltimore Sun*, 5 July 2007, 1B-2B).

Baltimore: Jazz musician David Bach at the Inner Harbor Amphitheatre, along with Almost Recess, an a cappella band (Sharon Schultz, *The Capital*, 29 June 2007, 17).

Shady Side: The Bay Winds Concert Band gave a concert at Captain Salem Avery House Museum (Sharon Schultz, *The Capital*, 29 June 2007, 17).

Dundalk: Calvert Hall Marching Band at the Dundalk Heritage 4th Parade (Brent Jones, "Independence on Parade," *Baltimore Sun*, 5 July 2007, 1B).

Massachusetts

Boston: At the Esplanade, Keith Lockhart conducted the Boston Pops, with guest host Craig Ferguson, and guest singer John Mellencamp, who sang his patriotic hit "Our Country."

Fitchburg: The Thayer Symphony Orchestra continued its 17-year tradition of Independence Day concerts at the Bernardian Bowl (Alexander Perloe, "Thayer Symphony Orchestra Scaling Down Fourth of July Concert," *Sentinel & Enterprise*, 31 May 2007).

Nebraska

Fort Atkinson: Near Fort Calhoun, reenactors presented the following musical selections that were originally performed at the fort on July 4, 1824, the Sixth Army Regiment band: Hail Columbia — Yankee Doodle — Patriotic Diggers — Soldier's Joy — Hearts of Oak. The presentation ended with singing the "Star-Spangled Banner" by the audience ("Independence Day Celebration" program, 2007, Fort Atkinson, Council Bluff).

Nevada

Reno: Reno Jazz Orchestra performed as part of the "Food for the Soul" music series (LaRae Pfeffen and Genny Howe, "Find a Flurry of Fourth Fun Here," *Sacramento Bee*, 2 July 2007).

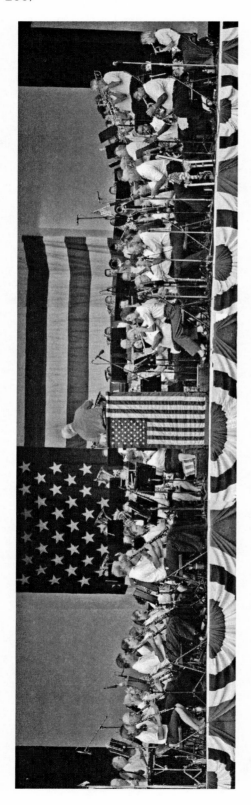

New York

New Paltz: The Excelsior Cornet Band performed at the Mohonk Mountain House (*Excelsior Cornet Band* website, accessed February 15, 2008, < http://www.excelsiorcornetband.com/>

New York: Macy's celebration featured Martina McBride, Joss Stone and Jordin Sparks, "American Idol" winner ("U.S. Celebrates Its Birthday," *Baltimore Sun*, 5 July 2007, 3A).

North Carolina

Wilmington: Minute Men of the 440th N.C. Army National Guard Band and the UNC-Wilmington Wind Symphony at Riverfront Park (*News & Observer*, 24 June 2007, H4).

Ohio

Cincinnati: The United States Army Field Band & Soldiers' Chorus presented the following program:

Call of the Champions (John Williams)
Foshay Tower Washington Memorial (Sousa)
Overture from *Zampa* (L.J.F. Herold/arr. V.F. Safranek)
A Tribute to Johnny and June (arr. MSG Vincent Norman), with MS Jeffrey Woods and SFC Laura Dause, soloists
Malagueña (Ernesto Lecuona/arr. Jerry Ascione), featuring The U.S. Army Field Band Trombone Quartet
Battle Hymn of the Republic (William Steffe/arr. Peter wilhousky)
America the Beautiful (arr. SGM J. Loran Mc-Clung), with MS Janet Hjelmgren, soprano, and SM Virginia Turner, trumpet
[Program, 4 July 2007, U.S. Army Field Band and Soldiers' Chorus].

Pennsylvania

Philadelphia: "Sweet Sounds of Liberty Concert" with Hall & Oates and the Philadelphia Boys Choir, at the Benjamin Franklin Parkway (PR Newswire Association, 14 June 2007; "Rain Fears Fail to Dampen Fun," *Philadelphia Inquirer*, 5 July 2007, B5).

Texas

College Station: Texas Unlimited Band and Brazos Valley Symphony Orchestra provide music at the

The Richmond Concert Band, July 4, 2006. The band, conducted by Mark W. Poland, has performed on the Fourth at the Dogwood Dell amphitheater in Byrd Park, Richmond, Virginia, since 1972. Each year the band presents an authentic performance of Tchaikovsky's 1812 Overture with cannon fire, courtesy of the Virginia National Guard, live carillon bells, performed by Lawrence Robinson on the carillon in the World War I memorial bell tower that is adjacent to the amphitheater, and fireworks (photograph by Christopher and Cecelia Jaquez).

July 4th At The National Archives

PATRIOTISM
SACRIFICE
FREEDOM

231st Anniversary of the Declaration of Independence
Wednesday, July 4, 2007, 10 A.M.

Greetings from Archivist of the United States Allen Weinstein

Presentation of Colors

"National Anthem," led by Duane Moody

Performance of 3rd Infantry "Old Guard" Fife and Drum Corps

Reading of the Declaration of Independence

Special guests: Honored veterans from World War II, Thomas Jefferson,
John Adams, Benjamin Franklin, Ned Hector

Film Presentation, *The War*

Remarks by Ken Burns

Closing Remarks by Allen Weinstein

"God Bless America" Patriotic Video Presentation

Left: The program for the National Archives celebration of 2007 in Washington, D.C. The 3rd Infantry "Old Guard" Fife and Drum Corps performs Revolutionary War–era tunes at this event. The ceremony also includes a public reading of the Declaration of Independence and the singing of "The Star-Spangled Banner" (author's collection). *Below:* The William Paca House in Annapolis, Maryland, built 1763–1765, is a site for naturalization ceremonies and musical performances. Paca was a signer of the Declaration of Independence. On July 4, 2007 and 2008, the All Children's Chorus of Annapolis sang "The Star-Spangled Banner" and the audience sang "America" and "America the Beautiful" as immigrants took the oath of allegiance (author's photograph).

events held at the George Bush Presidential Library and Museum ("Fourth of July Events," *The Eagle* (Bryan, Texas), 1 July 2007).

Dallas: The Dallas Wind Symphony, with Lt. Col. Thomas H. Palmatier, guest conductor, gave the following concert at the Meyerson Symphony Center:

Fanfare: Plano Fanfare (David Lovrien)
Star-Spangled Banner
The Gallant Seventh (Sousa)
American Overture for Band (Joseph Wilcox Jenkins)
West Side Story (Bernstein, arr. Duthoit)
The Klaxon (Henry Fillmore)
Grand Night for Singing (arr. Palmatier)
Broadway Showcase (arr. Palmatier)
American Salute (Morton Gould)
Liberty Fanfare (John Williams, arr. Curnow)
An American in Paris (Gershwin), arr. Krance)
The Washington Post March (Sousa)
Amazing Grace
Land that I love (arr. Palmatier)
Armed Services Medley (arr. Taylor)
Variations on a Shaker Melody (Aaron Copland)
The Stars and Stripes Forever (Sousa)

(*Dallas Wind Symphony* website, accessed February 13, 2008, http://www.dws.org/); at the Chapel of the Cross, "A Musical Fourth" concert by Carl Fischer, organist, a choir of 24, and soloists performed the following program:

Star-Spangled Banner
"Texas Our Texas" (William J. Marsh/Gladys Yoakum Wright)
United We Stand (a premiere, composed by Noël Goemanne), with soloist Bill Simpson
El Capitan (Sousa)
"Give Me Your Tired, Your Poor" (Berlin)
"America, the Beautiful"
"Darling, Darling, Dallas (Schotta/Singer), with Rick Harding soloist
"Methinks I See a Heavenly Host" (Billings)
"Eternal Father" (John Dykes)
Stars and Stripes Forever (Sousa)
"Offertory: Partita on Simple Gifts" (Goemanne)
Symphony of Praise (Goemanne)
"My country, 'tis of thee"
"I Hate Music!" (Bernstein), with Jessica Anderson, soloist
"This Land is Your Land" (Traditional/Woody Guthrie)
Battle Hymn of the Republic (Steffe/Howe)
"You're a Grand Old Flag" (Cohan)
"God Bless America" (Berlin)
[Program, July 4, 2007, *Chapel of the Cross*, accessed August 20, 2008, http://www.musical fourth.com/files/musicalfourth2005.pdf].

Houston: *Stars and Stripes Fanfare* by James Stephenson, commissioned by the Houston Symphony, was performed by the orchestra, Michael Krajewski, conductor (James Stephenson website, http://www.stephensonmusic.com.

Utah

Salt lake City: The following program by the Utah Symphony Orchestra was presented at the Deer Valley Outdoor Amphitheater on the Fourth:

Smith/Key, *Star-Spangled Banner*
Sibelius, *Finlandia*, op. 26
Williams, *Liberty Fanfare*
Sousa, The Liberty Bell
Sousa, *Semper Fidelis*
Gould, *American Salute*
Vieuxtemps, *Yankee Doodle Fantasie*
Anderson, *Fiddle Faddle*
Debussy, *Clair de Lune*
Williams, *Star Wars: Suite for Orchestra*
Sousa, *Washington Post March*
Lowden, *Armed Forces Medley*
Sousa, *Stars and Stripes Forever*
Sousa, *Thunderer March*
"Deer Valley Music Festival Press Room," 25 June 2007 <http://www.deervalleymusicfestival.org/press.php?rid=9>

Vermont

Brownsville: Vermont Symphony Orchestra at Ascutney Mountain Resort, performed Tchaikovsky's 1812 Overture ("Fourth of July Events, Visit-vermont.com/event (June 2007).

Jefferson: 40th Army Band performed on the Village Green in the evening ("Fourth of July Events, Visit-Vermont.com/event (June 2007).

Killington: Bourbon Street Grass performed ("Fourth of July Events," *Visit New E*ngland Website, 16 June 2007).

Virginia

Norfolk: The U.S. Navy Atlantic Fleet Band at Town Point Park (*Virginia-Pilot*, 1 July 2007).

Richmond: At Dogwood Dell, the Richmond Concert Band performed the 1812 Overture and patriotic tunes, accompanying the fireworks (*Richmond Times-Dispatch*, 5 July 2007, B5).

Virginia Beach: The Revolution presented a Beatles tribute performance at 17th Street Park; Symphonicity and the Virginia Beach Chorale at 20th Street Stage; a "Bruce in the U.S.A." Springsteen tribute at 31st Street Neptune's Park (*Virginia-Pilot*, 1 July 2007).

Washington

George: Willie Nelson's "Fourth of July Picnic" takes place at the amphitheater, with Son Volt, Old 97's, Drive by Truckers, and Amos Lee.

Spokane: At Riverfront Park, Java Kola (Jimi Hendrix tribute band) and Nobody Famous (Jimmy Buffet tribute band) (*Spokesman Review*, 28 June 2007, V1).

West Virginia

Martinsburg: 249th Army Band of the West Virginia Army National Guard provided music for President Bush's ceremony ("President Bush Celebrates Independence Day with West Virginia Air National Guard" <www.whitehouse.gov/news/releases/2007/07/20070704.html>

2008

A musical highlight on this year's Fourth of July occurred at Lenox, Massachusetts, when an audience of thousands joined with singer James Taylor for his 60th birthday celebration (his actual birthdate is March 12), with Taylor and Carole King performing. In 2002 Taylor had released his song "On the Fourth of July" on his album *October Road*.

Arizona

Flagstaff: At the Pine Mountain Amphitheater at Fort Tuthill County Park, the Flagstaff Symphony Orchestra, with James Kirk, vocalist, performed music "representing America's favorite pastime, baseball." Selections included *Damn Yankees Overture*, "Center Field," sung by James Kirk, "Casey at the Bat," "Take Me Out to the Ball Game," and selections from *Field of Dreams* and *The Natural*. The second half of the program featured music representing the planetary system, including *The Planets* (Gustav Holst), *Star Wars Suite* (Williams), and accompanied by "the laser and light choreography of Creative Laser Media" (*Pine Mountain Amphitheater* website, accessed July 20, 2008, http://pinemountain.inticketing.com/evinfo.php?eventid=25874).

California

Camarillo: In its 23rd year, the Camarillo Community Band, with guest conductor John Stava, performed patriotic favorites at the local high school (Christy Fenner, "Camarillo Community Band Ready to Jam Again," *VenturaCountyStar.Com* website, 29 June 2008, accessed July 12, 2008).

Irvine: The Pacific Symphony, Richard Kaufman, conductor, with guest Don McLean and the Southern California Children's Chorus, Lori Loftus, director, presented "American Pie with Don McLean: A 4th of July Celebration," at the Verizon Wireless Amphitheater. The program included:

National Emblem (Bagley)
George M. Cohan Overture (Cohan)
Central Park Rag (Roger Fratena)
Cloudburst from *Grand Canyon Suite* (Grofé)
Belle of the Ball/Chicken Reel/Buglers' Holiday (Anderson)
Seventy-Six Trombones from *The Music Man*
Military Tribute
America the Beautiful
[concert program, *Pacific Symphony* website, http://www.pacificsymphony.org/pdfs/programNotes/PS_SummerProg1.pdf].

Santa Barbara: The Santa Barbara Symphony, with guest conductor Diane Wittry, presented a pops con-

cert at the Courthouse Sunken Gardens. Featured as well were vocalist Jason Catron and the Santa Barbara Choral Society, Jo Anne Wasserman, director. Works performed included "God Bless the U.S.A.," *Liberty Fanfare* (Williams), and *Fanfare for the Common Man* (Copland) (Santa Barbara Symphony website, accessed August 3, 2008, http://www.thesymphony.org/newsite2008/archive.html.

Yountville: At the Lincoln Theater, the Festival del Sole presented a free Independence Day concert that featured the premiere of *American Festivals*, composed by Nolan Gasser on poetry by poet Robert Trent Jones, Jr. and narrated by noted actor Craig T. Nelson, as well as *Festival Overture, "The Star-Spangled Banner"* (Dudley Buck) and *Rhapsody in Blue* (Gershwin, with Conrad Tao, pianist). The ensemble performing was the Napa Valley Symphony and Chorus, Asher Raboy, conductor, with soloists Jill Grove, mezzo-soprano, and Eric Owens, baritone (Sue Gilmore, "Strike Up the Symphony to Celebrate the Fourth," *Contra Costa Times*, 27 June 2008; "Press Release," *Festival del Sole* website, accessed July 22, 2008, <http://www.festivaldelsole.com/napavalley/press.html>).

Colorado

Breckenridge: The National Repertory Orchestra, Carl Topilow, music director, presented these concerts on July 4: at Breckenridge Riverwalk Center in the evening, and earlier in the day at the Dillon (Colorado) Amphitheater and at Evergreen Lake Music Festival (*National Repertory Orchestra* website, accessed August 27, 2008, http://nromusic.com/index.cfm?PID=636&ID=4630,16701,0).

Connecticut

Mystic: At Mystic Seaport, the Museum of America and the Sea, an "1876 Independence Day Celebration" reenactment took place in which a six-member singing society (Denise Canella, soprano; Rebecca Bayreuther Donohue, alto; Geoff Kaufman, tenor; Richard Franklin Donohue, tenor and ensemble leader, David Littlefield, baritone, William Steinmayer, bass) sang the doxology ("Praise God from Whom all blessings flow"), "America," and the "Star-Spangled Banner," as originally performed in 1876. "America" was sung as a sing-along, with "lyric sheets printed on the original presses in the museum." In addition, the Mystic Silver Cornet Band performed in the parade that preceded the patriotic exercises and later provided a concert from the bandstand (information courtesy of Rebecca Bayreuther Donohue). See also, Mystic, Connecticut in 1876.

Norfolk: At the Yale Summer School of Music, on the occasion of the Norfolk Chamber Music Festival on July 4, the following were performed by Martin Beaver, violin; Clive Greensmith, cello; Ole Akahoshi cello; Boris Berman, piano:

July 4 Fanfare (composed for the Fourth by Kim Scharnberg)

Duo for Violin and Cello (Zoltán Kodály)
Cello Sonata in D Minor (Dmitri Shostakovich)
Piano Trio No. 2 (Dmitri Shostakovich)
[*New York Times*, 4 July 2008, B19].

District of Columbia

At the Capitol Fourth celebration on the West Lawn of the Capitol, the National Symphony Orchestra, Erich Kunzel, conductor provided music, with "American Idol" winner Taylor Hicks, Huey Lewis and the News, Hayley Westenra, Jerry Lee Lewis, Broadway star Brian Stokes Mitchell, soprano Harolyn Blackwell, as well as the U.S. Army Herald Trumpets, United States Marine Drum and Bugle Corps, and The Choral Arts Society of Washington, Norman Scribner, director. (*Capitol Fourth* website, accessed July 14, 2008, http://www.pbs.org/capitol-fourth/concert.html); at the National Archives, Robert Cantrell led the audience in "The Star-Spangled Banner," and the Fife and Drum Corps of the U.S. 3rd Infantry, the Old Guard, played Revolutionary War era tunes (Program, National Archives, from the author's collection); a performance by salsa performer Tito Puente, Jr. at Woodrow Wilson Plaza (*Washington Post*, 4 July 2008, C11); at the base of the Washington Monument, various Air Force ensembles, including Max Impact, the Air Force Strings, the Concert Band and Singing Sergeants, and Silver Wings at the National Air and Space Museum (the United States Air Force Band website, accessed July 17, 2008, http://www.usafband.af.mil/news/story.asp?id=123097532); at an Independence Day concert at the Washington National Cathedral presented by Scott Dettra and Christopher Jacobson, the program included the follow works:

Fanfare for the Common Man (Copland)
The Star-Spangled Banner, sing-along
Concert Variations on "The Star-Spangled Banner," op. 23 (Dudley Buck)
Adagio for Strings (Samuel Barber)
Amazing Grace (William Bolcom)
America the Beautiful, sing-along
Soliloquy (David Conte)
Double Fugue on "God Save the Queen" (John Knowles Paine)
The Music Quiz: Name that Disney Tune
The Stars and Stripes Forever (John Philip Sousa)
[Concert program, courtesy of Scott Dettra and Christopher Jacobson].

The United States Army Old Guard Fife and Drum Corps (3rd Infantry), MSG Russell Smith, drum major, performing at the National Archives in Washington, D.C., on July 4, 2008. This fife and drum corps, stationed at Fort Myer, Virginia, was founded on February 23, 1960 (author's photograph).

Illinois

New Lenox: The Joliet American Legion Band and Lincolnway Area Community Chorale provided the music for the town's Independence Day event (Ashley Mefford, "New Lenox Set to Celebrate the 4th with Fun," *New Lenox Patriot*, 26 June 2008).

Indiana

Terre Haute: At a flag folding ceremony "by members of the Honor Guard from the 181st Intelligence Wing of the Indiana Air National Guard" in Fairbanks Park, the Terre Haute Community Band performed "The Star-Spangled Banner," "Stars and Stripes Forever," and "You're a Grand Old Flag." Included in the ceremony also was a "moving narration of 'America the Beautiful' by James Chesterson, retired Command Chief Master Sergeant" ("Terre Haute Community Band to Perform during Fourth of July Celebration," *TribStar.Com* website, 26 June 2008, accessed July 12, 2008, http://www.tribstar.com/features/local_story_178175201.html).

Iowa

Le Mars: The Le Mars Municipal Band, Jerry Bertrand, conductor, with featured soloist Rick Lacy, bassoonist, performed these works at Foster Park:

Washington Post (Sousa)
The Spirit of '76 (Clare Grundman)
The Blue and the Gray (Grundman)
A medley of music by George M. Cohan
Selections from The Music Man (Willson)
National Emblem (Bagley)
Lest We Forget (James Swearingen)
Stars and Stripes Forever (Sousa)
[Beverly Van Buskirk, "Municipal Band Presents Traditional July 4th Concert," *Le Mars Daily Sentinel*, 2 July 2008].

Maine

Portland: The American Wind Symphony Orchestra, Robert Boudreau, conductor, performed in the evening at Portland Yacht Services on the Eastern Prom (*portlandmaine.com*, accessed July 12, 2008); on July 3, the Portland Symphony Orchestra, Robert Moody, conductor, with Jenn Raithel Newman, soprano, presented this "Independence Pops" concert at Fort Williams Park:

America, the Dream Goes On (Williams)
Music from The Patriot (Williams)
Irving Berlin: A Symphonic Portrait (arr. Ades)
Songs We Knew during World War II (arr. Munford)
American Salute (Gould)
Armed Forces Salute (Lowden)
1812 Overture
[Portland Symphony Orchestra website, accessed July 19, 2008, http://www.portlandsymphony.com/Event-97.html].

Maryland

Annapolis: At the William Paca House, as 50 immigrants took the oath of citizenship, the All Children's Chorus of Annapolis sang "The Star-Spangled Banner" and "America the Beautiful"; the U.S. Naval Academy Band's Electric Brigade performed at Susan Campbell Park (*Baltimore Sun*, 3 and 5 July 2008, 9T and B1, B3, respectively).

Baltimore: At the Inner Harbor, the U.S. Naval Academy's Ceremonial Band performed an evening concert (*Baltimore Sun*, 3 July 2008, 9T).

Clarksburg: James Heintze,[1017] pianist, performed this concert of American patriotic music on July 3: *Rail Road March, for the Fourth of July* (Christopher Meineke, 1828); *The Stars & Stripes Forever: Brilliant Variations on the Star-Spangled Banner* (Charles Grobe, 1854); *America: Transcriptions Brillantes, No. 2, Yankee Doodle* (Charles Voss, 1860s); *America Forever! March* (E.T. Paull, 1898); *Salute the Flag: Military March & Two-Step* (George H. Holcombe, 1910); *The Stars and Stripes Forever* (Sousa, 1896). Concert Program, 3 July 2008.

Cumberland: The Potomac Concert Band performed *Semper Fidelis* (Sousa), *George Washington Bicentennial, El Capitan, Stars and Stripes Forever*, "God Bless America," and other works at Constitution Park (Potomac Concert Band website, access July 12, 2008, http://www.potomacconcertband.org/.

Greenbelt: The Greenbelt Concert Band, G. Thomas Cherrix, conductor, performed at Albert S. Buddy Attick Lake Park:

The Star-Spangled Banner, sung by Linda Koch, soprano
National Emblem March (E.E. Bagley)
Emissary Fanfare, from Otello, Act III (Verdi/arr. Ross Hastings)
Disney Razzamatazz (arr. James Christensen)
A Tribute to Harold Arlen, Jim Moore, assistant conductor (arr. James Kessler)
1776, The American War of Independence: A Patriotic Overture (J.S. Zamecnik)
Over the Rainbow, Linda Koch, soprano (Harold Arlen/arr. Warren Barker)
Sing for America, Linda Koch, soprano (arr. James Ployhar)
The Blue and the Gray (arr. Clare Grundman)
[Program, courtesy of G. Thomas Cherrix; *Washington Post*, 4 July 2008, B3].

Sharpsburg: On July 5, at Antietam National Battlefield, the Maryland Symphony Orchestra, Elizabeth Schulze, director, presented its 23rd annual "Salute to Independence." Featured works performed included *Ghosts of Antietam* by Joseph McIntyre and *Soul's Journey* by Rob Hovermale. Other works included *The Liberty Bell* and *Stars and Stripes Forever* (Sousa), 1812 Overture (Tchaikovsky), *Armed Forces Salute* (Robert Lowden), *Waltz in Swing Time* (Jerome Kern), and *Yankee Doodle Variations* (Morton Gould) (Maryland Symphony Orchestra website, accessed

July 12, 2008, http://www.marylandsymphony.org/
press/06_13_08.shtml).

St. Mary's City: At St. Mary's College of Maryland, jazz vocalist Hilary Kole sang works by George
Gershwin, Jerome Kern, and Cole Porter. In addition, the Chesapeake Orchestra, Jeffrey Silberschlag,
conductor, performed various marches, ragtime
music, and the 1812 Overture (*Southern Maryland Online*, accessed July 12, 2008, http://somd.com/news/
headlines/2008/7885.shtml.

Towson: The Monumental City Ancient Fife and
Drum Choir performed in the town's parade (*Baltimore Sun*, 5 July 2008, B1, B3).

Massachusetts

Boston: At the 27th annual Harborfest celebration,
on July 5, the Middlesex County Volunteer Fifes and
Drums performed in the Old City Hall Courtyard
(Press release, "Drums in the Night," 4 July 2008);
Rascal Flatts performed with the Boston Pops, Keith

Lockhart, conductor, at the city's "fireworks spectacular."

Milford: At Plains Park, the Claflin Hill Summer
Winds, Paul Surapine, director, with members of New
World Chorale and The Charles River Chorale per-
formed popular music on July 3 (Denise Taylor,
"Fourth of July Celebrations," *Boston Globe*, 29 June
2008, West, Reg 6).

Michigan

Dearborn: The Detroit Symphony Orchestra presented a patriotic concert at Greenfield Village (*Detroit
Symphony Orchestra* website, accessed August 8, 2008,
http://www.detroitsymphony.com/main.taf?erube_fh
=dso&dso.submit.viewHomepage=1.

Nebraska

Fort Atkinson: Near Fort Calhoun, reenactors presented the following musical selections based on the
repertoire of the Sixth Army Regiment band in the

Reenactors performing musical selections on July 4, 2008, at Fort Atkinson, Nebraska, based on the
repertoire of the Sixth Army Regiment band under the command of Col. Henry Leavenworth that performed there on July 4, 1824 (courtesy John Slader, superintendent of Fort Atkinson State Historical
Park).

early 1800s and music presented at the fort on July 4, 1824: Soldier's Joy — Hail Columbia — Yankee Doodle — Auld Lang Syne — The Liberty Tree — Hearts of Oak — Hail Liberty — The American Star (information courtesy of John Slader, Superintendant, Fort Atkinson State Historical Park, 2008).

Nevada

Las Vegas: The Las Vegas Philharmonic, David Itkin, music director and conductor, with Richard McGee, associate conductor, and Brent Barrett, vocalist, celebrated its 10th anniversary Fourth of July concert at the Hills Park Amphitheater. The program included:

The Star-Spangled Banner
Summon the Heroes (John Williams/Calvin Custer)
George M. Cohan Medley (arr. David Itkin)
Salute to Ol' Blue Eyes (arr. Joan Moss)
Something's Coming (Leonard Bernstein), with Brent Barrett
"All I Care About Is Love" (John Kander/Fred Ebb), with Brent Barrett
Celebrate (David Itkin)
Variations on a Shaker Melody (Copland)
American Salute (Morton Gould)
"They Call the Wind Mariah" (arr. Christopher Denny), with Brent Barrett
"Here's to the Heroes" (John Barry), with Brent Barrett
National Emblem March (E.E. Bagley)
Pirates of the Caribbean (Klaus Badelt)
Armed Forces Salute (arr. Richard Hayman)
1812 Overture (Tchaikovsky)
Battle Hymn of the Republic (arr. Peter Wilhousky)
Fireworks Medley: Washington Post, Semper Fidelis, and The Stars and Stripes Forever (Sousa)

(Program, Las Vegas Philharmonic; John Katsilometes, "At LV Phil Event, Hearts Go Boom," *Las Vegas Sun*, 4 July 2008); "The Philharmonic Celebrates 10th Anniversary Star Spangled Spectacular with New Surprises," Press Release, *Philharmonic* website, accessed July 19, 2008, http://www.lasvegasphilharmonic.com/press/releases.php).

New Mexico

Socorro: On the campus of New Mexico Institute of Mining and Technology, the Socorro Community Band, Eileen Comstock, director, provided patriotic music (Fourth of July Extravaganza," NMT Website, http://www.nmt.edu/mainpage/pas/fourth.html).

New York

New York: "Macy's 4th of July Fireworks Spectacular" featured Natasha Bedingfield, Kenny Chesney, Jordin Sparks, Gavin DeGraw, and Katharine McPhee singing "Save the Last Dance for Me" (*Baltimore Sun*, 4 July 2008, 8C); the New York Philharmonic presented its first Fourth of July concert on Governors

Island on July 5 with works by Rossini, Copland, Rimsky-Korsakov, as well as Tchaikovsky's 1812 Overture ("Press Release, *Governors Island* website, accessed July 27, 2008, http://www.govisland.com/Press_Room/04-09-08philharmonic.asp).

Ohio

Cleveland: An evening concert at Public Square on July 2 by the Cleveland Orchestra, Giancarlo Guerrero, guest conductor, was titled "A Star Spangled Spectacular" and featured Indra Thomas, soprano. The concert included a tribute to Leroy Anderson celebrating the composer's 100th birthday and a recognition of Cuyahoga County's 200th birthday. On July 3–4, at Blossom Music Center, the Blossom Festival Band, Loras John Schissel, conductor, performed patriotic works, including the 1812 Overture (Blossom website, accessed July 12, 2008, http://www.clevelandorchestra.com/html/Performance/ViewBy-Month.asp).

Delaware: The Central Ohio Symphony, Jaime Morales-Matos, director, presented its 22nd annual July Fourth concert, including a performance of the 1812 Overture, on the campus of Ohio Wesleyan University (*Central Ohio Symphony* website, accessed July 18, 2008, http://www.centralohiosymphony.org/july4concert.php).

Pennsylvania

Lancaster: On July 6 at Long's Park Amphitheater, the 257th Army Band performed the 1812 Overture with a "17-cannon explosion" and fireworks (*Philadelphia Inquirer*, 4 July 2008, W2).

Philadelphia: At the Sunoco Welcome America! celebration, the Waterfront Concert & Festival featured Boys II Men as headliners ("July 4 Staples," *Philadelphia Inquirer*, 4 July 2008, W30).

Pittsburgh: The United States Army Field Band and Soldiers' Chorus presented the following program:

Patriotic Prologue (various composers)
Summon the Heroes (John Williams/arr. Paul Lavender)
Ruslan and Lyudmila (Mikhail Glinka/trans. Mark Hindsley)
A Stephen Foster Songbook (arr. Robert Lichtenbergert), with SM Robert Barnett, tenor
Other works
[Program, 4 July 2008, U.S. Army Field Band and Soldiers' Chorus].

South Carolina

Simpsonville: The Greenville Symphony Orchestra, with Edvard Tchivzhel, conductor, presented a Fourth of July concert at the Heritage Park Amphitheater (Greenville Symphony Orchestra website, accessed August 15, 2008, http://www.greenvillesymphony.org/concerts/view_event.aspx?event_id=48).

Tennessee

Knoxville: The Knoxville Symphony Orchestra, Lucas Richman, conductor, performed *The Stars and*

Stripes Forever, 1812 Overture, and other works at the World's Fair Park (*Knoxville Symphony Orchestra* website, accessed July 19, 2008, http://www.knoxvillesymphony.com/kso.asp?id=46&evt=1046).

Texas

Austin: The Austin Symphony Orchestra, Peter Bay, director, performed the 1812 Overture and Sousa's Stars and Stripes Forever at Auditorium Shores (Mark Lisheron, "Each Austin Fourth Has Had Its Own Flair," *Austin American Statesman*, 4 July 2008, B01).

Dallas: Dallas Wind Symphony, Major Jim Keene of the U.S. Army Band, conductor, performed the following program at Myerson Symphony Center:

> Fanfare to Awaken a Sleeping Giant (David Lovrien of Plano, Texas)
> Summon the Heroes (John Williams)
> The Thunderer (Sousa)
> Salute to American Jazz (Sammy Nestico)
> Yankee Doodle (Morton Gould)
> America the Beautiful
> Armed Forces Medley (arr. Bob Lowden)
> The Stars and Stripes Forever (Sousa)
> [*Dallas Wind Symphony* website, accessed July 14, 2008, http://www.dws.org/content/view/16/116/#jul].

Houston: Willie Nelson's Fourth of July picnic took place at the Sam Houston Race Park with special guests Merle Haggard, Pat Green, Ray Price, Los Lonely Boys, and other performers; the Houston Symphony with Michael Krajewski, pops conductor, and Kaitlyn Lusk, vocalist, performed a "Star Spangled Salute." Works included "God Bless America," *Stars and Stripes Forever*, and the 1812 Overture ("Press Release," 14 May 2008, *Houston Symphony* website, accessed August 8, 2008, http://www.houstonsymphony.org/about/press/detail.aspx?id=163).

Southlake: The Southlake Community Band, David Stone, director, and Choir and Southlake Swing Band, Paul Elder, director, performed on July 3 at Southlake Town Square (*Keller Citizen*, 27 June 2008).

Waco: The Waco Community Band, Brian Harris, director, played Sousa marches and other patriotic music on the Brazos (Carl Hoover, *Waco Tribune-Herald*, 3 July 2008).

Utah

Provo: At the Stadium of Fire, Miley Cyrus, star of *Hannah Montana*, the Disney channel show, premiered songs from her new album *Breakout* that was scheduled for release on July 22 (David Burger, *Salt Lake Tribune*, 4 July 2008).

Virginia

Alexandria: At St. Paul's Episcopal Church, Douglas A. Beck, organist, performed the 2nd annual "Organ Fireworks" concert which included these works:

> Star-Spangled Banner
> Theme and Variations on The Star-Spangled Banner (John Knowles Paine)
> The Battle of Trenton (James Hewitt)
> Yankee Doodle (Tori Garcia, recorder)

Poster for the nineteenth annual Bishop's Bluegrass Festival at Orkney Springs, Virginia, July 4, 2008. Each year the event features traditional bluegrass bands from Southwest Virginia and nearby areas with performances presented under the auspices of the Episcopal Diocese of Virginia (author's collection).

Camptown Mozart (by John David Peterson, and based on music by Mozart and Stephen Foster)

The Entertainer (Scott Joplin)

My Country, 'Tis of Thee

Variations on 'America' (Charles Ives)

1812 Overture (Tchaikovsky)

Stars and Stripes Forever (assisted by Jennifer Broetzmann, organ)

[Concert Program, courtesy of Douglas Beck].

Arlington: The Airmen of Note at the Air Force Memorial presented patriotic music.

Fairfax: The City of Fairfax Band, Robert Pouliot, director, performed *Liberty Fanfare* and other works at Fairfax High School (information courtesy of Donald Hester).

Orkney Springs: The 19th annual "Bishop's Bluegrass Festival" featured Valerie Smith and Liberty Pike, No Speed Limit, and The Harwell Grice Band (Poster of event, author's collection).

Richmond: The Richmond Concert Band, Mark W. Poland, director, with Lou Dean, master of ceremonies and narrator, presented this program at Dogwood Dell:

Pictures at an Exhibition (Modest Mussorgsky/arr. Jim Prime)

Star-Spangled Banner

Capitol Square March (Warren Barker)

Each Time You Tell Their Story (Samuel R. Hazo)

Old Glory Triumphant (Charles E. Duble/arr. Andrew Glover)

Robin Hood "Prince of Thieves" (Michael Kamen/arr. Erick Debs)

Someone to Watch Over Me, with Nicole Wakefield, vocalist (Gershwin/arr. Warren Barker)

'S Wonderful, with Nicole Wakefield, vocalist (Gershwin/ arr. Warren Barker)

Immer Kleiner, with Rebecca Gill and Rob Blankenship, clarinets (Adolf Schreiner/arr. George S. Howard)

Jersey Boys (arr. Michael Brown)

Mamma Mia (arr. Roy Phillippe)

Alpha & Omega (Paul Yoder)

Raiders of the Lost Ark Medley (John Williams/arr. Jack Bullock)

In the Mood (Joe Garland)

Back in the Good Old Days, with Ron Simmons, vocalist (arr. John Higgins)

Lawrence Robinson playing the World War I Memorial Carillon in Byrd Park in Richmond, Virginia, on July 4, 2008. The carillon was built by John Taylor Bell Founders of England and has 53 bells. Each year on the Fourth, Robinson performs a concert of solo works, as well as Tchaikovsky's 1812 Overture with the Richmond Concert Band (author's photograph).

America ... the Dream Goes On, with Ron Simmons, vocalist) (John Williams/arr. J. Higgins & P. Lavender)

God Bless the U.S.A., with Ron Simmons, vocalist (Lee Greenwood/arr. Roger Holmes)

Patriotic Sing-along, with Nicole Wakefield & Ron Simmons, vocalists (arr. James Ployhar and Warren Barker)

Home of the Brave (arr. Rob Blankenship)

1812 Overture, with Lawrence Robinson, carillon (arr. Rob Blankenship)

The Stars and Stripes Forever (Sousa/arr. Brion/Schissel)

Virginia Beach: At the 20th Street Stage, Symphonicity, David S. Kunkel, conductor, and Virginia Beach Chorale, Lou Sawyer, director (*Beach Street U.S.A.* website, "Press Release,"accessed July 22, 2008, <http://www.beachstreetusa.com/press-release>.

West Virginia

Charleston: The West Virginia Symphony Orchestra, Grant Cooper, conductor, presented a concert at Haddad Riverfront Park, with Ryan Hardiman as featured soloist. "Mayor Danny Jones provided narration for 'God Bless America'" (*West Virginia Symphony Orchestra* website, accessed July 12, 2008, http://www.wvsymphony.org/).

Morgantown: The Morgantown Municipal Band, C.B. Wilson, leader, performed works by Sousa, Gershwin, Rimsky-Korsakov, and others at Hazel Ruby McQuain Park (Matt Armstrong, "Morgantown Municipal Band Performs Friday, *The Daily Athenaeum*, 2 July 2008).

Afghanistan

Kabul: The 101st Woodwind Quartet performed at the U.S. Embassy on July 3 with 1600 persons in attendance and on July 4 at the International Security Assistance Force's Fourth of July BBQ held at Destille Gardens (SSG Nicole Flory, "101st Woodwind Quartet Celebrates the 4th at ISAF and the U.S. Embassy in Kabul, Afghanistan,"in "U.S. Army Band News," U.S. Army Bands website, accessed July 16, 2008, http://bands.army.mil/news/default.asp?NewsID=371.

Iraq

Baghdad: At a re-enlistment ceremony for 1,215 "soldiers, Marines, sailors, and airmen," with General David Petreaus administering the oath, the 4th Infantry Division Band performed a medly of Sousa marches accompanied by cheers from the service men and women (Mike Tharp, "Re-enlisting En Masse," in "U.S. Army Band News," *U.S. Army Bands* website, accessed July 16, 2008, http://bands.army.mil/news/default.asp?NewsID=373.

England

London: *Thinking*, a mixed chamber sextet for clarinet, bassoon, trumpet, violin, cello, and piano by James Stephenson, was premiered on July 4 at the Victoria and Albert Museum in South Kensington by the Salmagundi Ensemble (Information courtesey of James Stephenson).

Notes

1. *Independent Chronicle & Boston Patriot*, 6 July 1822, 2.

2. "1776: Songs Sung in the Revolutionary War," *Los Angeles Times*, 2 July 1893, 22.

3. Richard Crawford, *America's Musical Life* (New York: W.W. Norton, 2001), 272.

4. Numerous musical societies were established and incorporated through legislation in the early nineteenth century demonstrating the popularity of musical performances in small-town America. In New Hampshire, for example, some of the societies formed with years incorporated noted, include: Londonderry Musical Society (1808); Chester Musical Society (1819); Alton Harmony Society (1821); Portsmouth Handel Society (1823); Baptist Musical Society in Sandbornton (1823); Wentworth Musical Society (1824); Haverhill Musick Society (1825); Hillsborough Instrumental Band (1825); Rochester Musical Society (1825); Cheshire Sacred Musical Society (1826); Candia Music Society (1827); Portsmouth Sacred Music Society (1839). *Farmers' Cabinet*, 7 July 1821, 3, 14 June 1823, 2, and 27 December 1808, 3; *Concord Observer*, 5 July 1819, 3; *New-Hampshire Patriot & State Gazette*, 29 November 1824, 1, 27 June 1825, 1, and 19 June 1826, 2; *Portsmouth Journal of Literature & Politics*, 16 June 1827, 2, and 15 June 1839, 3.

5. For example, as written in the *Vermont Gazette*, 5 August 1828, 3: "Previous to the day, public notice is given of a meeting of the citizens to prepare for the approaching anniversary. They assemble, appoint a committee to make the necessary arrangements, and the same or another committee to collect the feelings of the people upon the great principles of liberty and upon passing events, and condense them into sentiments or toasts."

6. For example, the editor of the Hartford, Connecticut, newspaper *American Mercury*, 25 July 1805, 3, printed: "It gives us pleasure to behold the unbounded rejoicings of our countrymen, in almost every part of the union, on the return of the glorious anniversary of American Independence. Our papers from the North; from the South, the East, and the West, abound with the proceedings of our citizens on this auspicious day."

7. A description of the artillery used at a celebration in Trenton, New Jersey, on July 4, 1812, captures the essence of these occasions: "The field-piece belonging to the old artillery company was brought out on the occasion under the direction of Captain Yard, and the management of some of our old revolutionary soldiers. It was surmounted with an arch handsomely decorated, inscribed with the motto, 'for our country.' Its deeptoned thunder shook the town, as it answered to patriotic toasts of the Cincinnati." "Fourth of July," *Alexandria Daily Gazette*, 15 July 1812, 2.

8. Description and ode printed in *Kentucke Gazette*, 5 July 1788, as reported in Robert Pettus Hay, "Freedom's Jubilee: One Hundred Years of the Fourth of July, 1776–1876" (Ph.D. dissertation, University of Kentucky, 1967), 49–50.

9. *Tennessee Gazette*, 9 July 1800, as reported in Hay, "Freedom's Jubilee: One Hundred Years of the Fourth of July, 1776–1876," 51–52.

10. James R. Heintze, *The Fourth of July Encyclopedia* (Jefferson, NC: McFarland, 2007), 194–95.

11. J. Peter Burkholder, "The Organist in Ives," *Journal of the American Musicological Society* 55/2 (Summer 2002): 265.

12. Charles Ives, *Memos*. John Kirkpatrick, ed. (New York: W.W. Norton, 1972), 104n.

13. "The Fair Today," and "Hyde Park Library is Given to Public," *New York Times*, 4 and 5 July 1940, 13 and 1, 15, respectively.

14. The Beach Boys (Brian, Carl, and Dennis Wilson, with Mike Love and Al Jardine) gave their first Independence Day concert in Leningrad in 1978, and their first Fourth of July concert on the Mall in Washington in 1980. On July 4, 1986, the group performed in Manor, Texas, as part of Willie Nelson's Farm Aid II concert and on July 4, 2000, they were in Houston, Texas, in that city's "Power of Freedom" event. On July 4, 2001, "An All-Star Tribute to Brian Wilson," was broadcast on television. James R. Heintze, *The Fourth of July Encyclopedia*, 32–33.

15. Guest performers at these concerts included, for example, Johnny Rodriguez, Reba McEntire, Tammy Wynette, Conway Twitty, Jerry Reed, Barbara Mandrell, Johnny Cash, Charley Pride, Charlie McCoy, and Johnny Russell. Harold Reid and Don Reid, *The Statler Brothers: Random Memories* (Nashville, TN: Yell, 2007), 70–73; *The Statler Brothers: A Souvenir Book* (Staunton, VA: Charles F. McClung, ca.1980). A DVD of one of their Independence Day concerts is available under the title *Happy Birthday, USA: a 4th of July Celebration* (Nashville: Jim Owens Entertainment, 2005).

16. Including Ossining, New York (1971); Battery Park in New York (1973); Philadelphia (1974); on the steps of the Capitol, Washington, D.C. (1976); Milwaukee (1978); Chicago (1980); Holmdel, New Jersey, on July 5 (1982); Fort Myers, Florida (1989); Horseheads, New York (1990); Norfolk, Virginia (1992); World Trade Center in New York, with Gary U.S. Bonds (1993); Duluth, Minnesota (1996); Boston (2000); Dublin, Ohio (2002); Chicago (2003); Atlanta (2004); Akron, Ohio (2005). Information courtesy of Don McLean by telephone conversation with the author, September 22, 2008. See also, *New York Times*, 4 July 1982 and 4 July 1993, NJ16 and H31, respectively.

17. The light show was premiered on July 3 and was "hosted by Nellis Air Force Base's Honor Guard" and included "a live performance of the National Anthem." McLean's album "became the anthem for a generation and is still one of the most well-known songs in American musical history." The work was "inspired partly by the deaths of Buddy Holly, Richie Valens, and J.P. Richardson (The Big Bopper) in a plane crash in 1959." "Freemont Street Experience Hosts a 'American Pie 4th of July' Weekend," Reuters newswire, 26 June 2008, accessed August 30, 2008, http://www.reuters.com/article/pressRelease/idUS19236 7+26-Jun-008+PRN20080626.

18. According to Karen Mueller Coombs, "On July 4, 1941, Woody and three other members of the Almanac Singers — Peter

Seeger, Lee Hayes, and Millard Lampell—opened the tour in Philadelphia, Pennsylvania" and spent "that summer in union halls across the country." *Woody Guthrie: America's Folksinger* (Minneapolis: Carolrhoda, 2002), 73.

19. Schenck was born in Paris and made his debut as a composer and conductor on November 24, 1894, at Carnegie Hall in New York. He later was chorusmaster of the Metropolitan Opera House, and "appeared as conductor of the Damrosch and Savage Grand Opera Companies." *New York Times*, 25 November 1894 and 6 March 1939, 3 and 15, respectively.

20. Edward Moore, "Launch Free Music Series Tomorrow" and "Great Throng Hears Concert at Grant Park," *Chicago Daily Tribune*, 30 June and 4 July 1935, D13 and 11, respectively.

21. The report mentioned that this "was perhaps the loudest performance in Ravinia's history." A description of the bells was not provided, but may have simply been tubular bells (chimes) in the percussion section of the orchestra. Edward Barry, "Mitropoulos at Ravinia Park Provides Critic with a Theory," *Chicago Daily Tribune*, 6 July 1942, 17.

22. The program was scheduled for July 4, but postponed to July 6 due to rain.

23. According to the *Chicago Daily Tribune*, "Mitchell wanted the artillery set up on a barge behind the orchestra, which will perform on a floating stage at the Watergate stadium on the Potomac river, but the army rejected the idea, suggesting that concussion might sink not only the barge but the orchestra." "Army Contributes Four Cannon for '1812' Overture," *Chicago Daily Tribune*, 2 July 1950, G2.

24. Information courtesy of Pam Picard, producer, Boston 4 Celebrations Foundation, Inc., by telephone conversation with the author, October 1, 2008. According to Dianne S.P. Cermak, public relations officer, North American Guild of Change Ringers, the bells have been rung every year since the Bicentennial and are "rung live by the local guild of change ringers. The eight bells in the ring at the Advent are conveniently cast in the same key [E flat] as the '1812' and are rung in 'rounds,' that is a repeated descending scale, for this performance." Dianne Cermak to James Heintze, e-mail, 2 October 2008.

25. For a historic recording of the 1812 Overture produced in 1958 in which the Minneapolis Symphony Orchestra, Antal Dorati, conductor, utilized a bronze cannon, originally manufactured in Douay, France, in 1775, courtesy of the Museum of the U.S. Military Academy at West Point, New York, and a recording of the 74 bells of the Laura Spelman Rockefeller Memorial Carillon played by Kamiel Lefévere at the Riverside Church in New York, see Mercury SR 90054 (LP, 1958); Mercury 434360-2 (CD, 1995).

26. July 4, 2002 was a day of remembrance. In spite of terrorist threats and amidst heightened security across most major cities in the country, Americans celebrated with a greater sense of unity and patriotism. In Washington, D.C., with extra police on duty and sensors in place for monitoring radioactivity, headliners Aretha Franklin, Chuck Berry, and Lee Ann Womack performed with the National Symphony Orchestra on the West Lawn of the Capitol. In Boston attendees at the concert at the Hatch Shell on the Esplanade were videotaped, and some 10,000 persons passed through screening checkpoints. Heintze, *The Fourth of July Encyclopedia*, 322–23.

27. Hymn no. 4 in *An Abridgement of Dr. Watts's Psalms and Hymns, with Some Alterations* (Birmingham, 1785?), 150–51.

28. Gordon was "pastor of the third Church in Roxbury."

29. According to the *Pennsylvania Evening Post*, 31 December 1776, and reported in Simon V. Anderson, "American Music during the War for Independence, 1775–1783" (Ph.D. dissertation, University of Michigan, 1965), 87, the band consisted of 25 drummers and 9 musicians.

30. The band was possibly Thomas Proctor's Band of the 4th Regiment of Artillery of the Continental Army, according to Raoul F. Camus, *Military Music of the American Revolution* (Chapel Hill: University of North Carolina Press, 1976), 138. The occasion is mentioned in Anderson, "American Music during the War for Independence, 1775–1783," 73.

31. Ellery, a signer of the Declaration of Independence, pre-

sented an ode to the Society of Cincinnati in Newport, Rhode Island, on July 4, 1801.

32. "Diary of the Hon. William Ellery of Rhode Island," *Pennsylvania Magazine of History and Biography* 11 (1888):477. Quoted also in Camus, *Military Music of the American Revolution*, 138, and Jane E. Ellsworth, "The Clarinet in Early America, 1758–1820" (D.M.A. dissertation, Ohio State University, 2004), 15. For a comprehensive study of music in this establishment, see Sterling E. Murray "Music and Dance in Philadelphia's City Tavern, 1773–1790," in *American Musical Life in Context and Practice to 1865*. Ed. James R. Heintze (New York: Garland, 1994), 3–47.

33. Reported in Oscar Sonneck, *Early Concert-Life in America, 1731–1800* (Wiesbaden: M. Sändig, 1969), 287.

34. Listed in Gillian B. Anderson, *Freedom's Voice in Poetry and Song* (Wilmington, DE: Scholarly Resources, 1977), 236.

35. Listed in Anderson, *Freedom's Voice in Poetry and Song*, 285.

36. William Billings' published "Independence" in his collection *The Singing Master's Assistant or Key to Practical Music* (1778). See *Complete Works of William Billings*. Hans Nathan, ed. 4 vols. (New Haven: American Musicological Society, 1977–90) II:244–55.

37. From minutes of the Salem elders' meeting of 2 July 1783, as written by Friedrich Peter, a principal musician in the congregation, and reported in Marilyn Gombosi, *A Day of Solemn Thanksgiving: Moravian Music for the Fourth of July, 1783, in Salem, North Carolina* (Chapel Hill: University of North Carolina Press, 1977), 18. Gombosi provides extensive information on this event and the Moravians, as well as a musical score "based on manuscript parts contained in the Salem Congregation music and preserved in the archives of The Moravian Music Foundation in Winston-Salem, North Carolina."

38. The "solemn dirge" was played "for the space of 13 minutes" and the artillery fired "13 minute guns."

39. Reprinted in "From Dr. Ladd's Poems," *The Investigator*, 29 October 1812, 3.

40. The lyrics for this song first appeared in 1783 in Philadelphia in a piece written on the occasion of the birthday of George Washington. *Independent Gazetteer*, 4 March 1783, 4. The lyrics are printed under the title "Liberty Tree" in *The Universal Songster and Museum of Mirth* (Boston: Charles Gaylord, 1835).

41. Listed in Oscar Sonneck, *A Bibliography of Early Secular American Music, 18th Century* (New York: Da Capo, 1964), 311.

42. Printed in Laura Rigal, "'Raising the Roof': Authors, Spectators and Artisans in the Grand Federal Procession of 1788," *Theatre Journal* 48/3 (1996): 253–77. Important sources for the procession include: "Grand Federal Procession," *Pennsylvania Gazette*, 9 July 1788; Benjamin Rush, "Observations on the Grand Federal Procession By a Gentleman in This City," *American Museum, or Repository of Ancient and Modern Fugitive Pieces* (July 1788): 75–76.

43. Richard C. Spicer, "Popular Song for Public Celebration in Federal Portsmouth, New Hampshire," *Popular Music and Society* 25/1-2 (Spring-Summer 2001): 1–99, discusses the derivation of this tune, composed by Thomas Paine, and based on "the death of young General James Wolfe at Quebec in 1759." A facsimile of the "first American imprint in the *Pennsylvania Magazine* (March 1775)" is in Spicer, 34.

44. Vera Brodsky Lawrence, *Music for Patriots, Politicians, and Presidents* (New York: Macmillan, 1975), 109.

45. Facsimile in Lawrence, *Music for Patriots, Politicians, and Presidents*, 109.

46. Cited in Sonneck, *A Bibliography of Early Secular American Music, 18th Century*, 309 and Danny O. Crew, *Presidential Sheet Music: An Illustrated Catalogue of Published Music Associated with the American Presidency and Those Who Sought the Office* (Jefferson, NC: McFarland, 2001), 231–32. Reprinted in *American Musical Miscellany* (1798) and Spicer, "Popular Song for Public Celebration," 38; Lawrence Bennett, ed., *Two Patriotic Odes: for Men's Voices* (New York: Broude Bros., 1976).

47. The "thirteen young ladies" represented the thirteen original colonies and the eleven dressed in white represented the eleven states that had ratified the Constitution.

48. For more information on the Fourth and other celebrations in Portsmouth, see Spicer, "Popular Song for Public Celebration," 1–99.

49. Horatio Garnet advertised his services in Portsmouth, New Hampshire, on June 23, 1788, as a teacher of violin, bassviol, hautboy, clarionet, flute, and guitar. Garnet studied music in Europe and his "lodgings" in Portsmouth were at Mr. Samuel Place's house. According to Spicer, "Popular Song for Public Celebration," 7, Garnet lived in Portsmouth for a few years, but also resided for a time in other New England towns. *New-Hampshire Spy*, 8 July 1788, 88.

50. The anthem may have been one of the following two solo anthems that Blagrove sang a few days later (July 14) at a "sacred music" concert held at College Hall in Philadelphia: "O Lord! whose mercies numberless" (G.F. Handel?) and "Acquaint Thyself with God." *Federal Gazette and Philadelphia Evening Post*, 14 July 1790, 3.

51. "American Independence," *New-York Journal & Patriotic Register*, 2 July 1791, 207.

52. Different lyrics than the poem with the same first line performed on July 4, 1798. See 1798, Portsmouth, New Hampshire.

53. A stanza of this ode was reprinted in *The Berkshire Reporter* (Pittsfield, Massachusetts), 6 July 1811, 3.

54. Spicer, "Popular Song for Public Celebration," discusses the origin of this English tune, how it was frequently associated with George Washington, and subsequently given "new American titles transferring royal associations from one side of the Atlantic to country and president on the other." Some of these pieces with altered titles performed on the Fourth include: "God Save Columbia's Sons," "God Save Great Washington," "God Save America," "God Save the United States," "God Save the Commonwealth," "God Save the Queen," "God Save Our Native Land," and "God Save the President."

55. Bangs was invited to present an Independence Day oration in Worcester, Massachusetts, in 1800. *Columbian Centinel*, 24 May 1800, 3. He was a representative for his county in the state legislature and later an associate justice of the Court of Common Pleas. He was married to Hannah Bangs who died on September 9, 1806. Bangs died in late June 1818 at the age of 62. *Massachusetts Spy, or Worcester Gazette*, 10 September 1806, 3; "Died," *Boston Daily Advertiser*, 4 July 1818, 2.

56. Mellen, son of John Mellen, "a respectable clergyman" in Massachusetts, wanted to pursue interests in literature at Harvard University but then turned to law, receiving his degree in 1784. In 1792 he married Eliza Hovey, daughter of Dr. Ivory Hovey. Mellen, a master mason, was elected junior grand warden of the grand lodge of New Hampshire in 1808. In July of that year a humorous protest song titled "The Embargo!" (facsimile of printed song in Lawrence, 185) which Mellen composed was sung at Dover, New Hampshire. See 1808, **Publications**. Mellen died on July 31, 1809, at the age of 52. *Eastern Herald*, 30 January 1792, 3; *Portland Gazette and Maine Advertizer*, 18 July 1808, 3; *New-Hampshire Gazette*, 1 August 1809, 3; *Portland Gazette*, 7 August 1809, 2; "Biographical Sketch," *Newburyport Herald*, 11 August 1808, 4; *Portsmouth Oracle*, 19 August, 1809, 4.

57. The new Tannenberg organ had just been installed and completed in late summer 1790. The organist was John Christopher Moller and the choir director was David Ott. See Edward C. Wolf, "Music in Old Zion, Philadelphia, 1750–1850," *The Musical Quarterly* 58/4 (October 1972): 622–52.

58. In 1792 Richards and Oliver Wellinton Lane advertised a proposal for publishing a *New Universal Hymn Book*, containing "psalms, hymns and spiritual songs, interspersed with original American compositions." *General Advertiser*, 8 June 1792, 1.

59. Likely *A Discourse Intended to Commemorate the Discovery of America by Christopher Columbus* (Boston: Printed at the Apollo Press by Belknap and Hall, 1792) by Jeremy Belknap (1744–1798).

60. Likely Nathaniel F. Fosdick, collector of the port of Portland and Falmouth, as cited in *Jenks' Portland Gazette*, 24 February 1800, 4.

61. Lyrics printed in *The Nightingale; or Rural Songster* (Dedham [MA]: Printed by H. Mann, 1800) and *The American Patriotic Song-Book, a Collection of Political, Descriptive, and Humourous Songs of National Character, and the Production of American Poets Only* (Philadelphia: John Bioren, 1816). Music printed in *The American Patriotic Song-Book, a Collection of Political, Descriptive, and Humourous Songs of National Character, and the Production of American Poets Only. Interspersed with a Number Set to Music* (Philadelphia: W. M'Culloch, 1813).

62. As reported in Oscar Sonneck, *Early Opera in America* (New York: B. Blom, 1963), 164.

63. By William Selby.

64. Prolific poet whose real name was Robert Merry. Born in London in 1755, Merry studied at Christ's College in Cambridge. He went to Florence, Italy, and "was elected a member of the celebrated academy Della Crusca, the name of which academy he used as a signature to many poems." "Biography: Della Crusca," *Federal Orrery*, 6 November 1794, 21.

65. Also published as a broadside [Philadelphia: Printed by John McCulloch? 1794?]. Listed in Priscilla S. Heard, *American Music 1698–1800: An Annotated Bibliography* (Waco, TX: Markham Press Fund, 1975), 54. Printed in *The Nightingale; or Rural Songster* (Dedham [MA]: Printed by H. Mann, 1800).

66. "Timothy Dwight, D.C. of Grienfield [sic], Connecticut." With text of song, in *New Jersey Journal*, 30 July 1788, 4, and reprinted for the Fourth in 1807. *True Republican*, 1 July 1807, 4. According to Richard J. Wolfe, *Secular Music in America: A Bibliography*. 3 vols. (New York: New York Public Library, 1964), I:261 (hereafter Wolfe), Dwight wrote and set the text to music in 1777 "while he was serving as chaplain to General Parsons brigade of Connecticut Volunteers." The lyrics are printed in *The Federal Songster Being a Collection of the Most Celebrated Patriotic Songs, Hitherto Published, with a Variety of Others, Sentimental and Convivial* (New-London: James Springer, 1800). The lyrics were reprinted under the title "Columbia" in Rufus W. Griswold, *The Poets and Poetry of America*. 16th ed. (Philadelphia: Parry and McMillan, 1856), 54.

67. Reported also in Sonneck, *Early Concert-Life in America*, 294.

68. First performed in 1793. See **Publications** (1793). Listed in Sonneck, *A Bibliography of Early Secular American Music, 18th Century*, 309.

69. Listed in Sonneck, *A Bibliography of Early Secular American Music, 18th Century*, 176.

70. "La Marseillaise" was composed by French royalist Claude-Joseph Rouget de l'Isle in 1792 and it was designated as the French National Anthem in July 1795. The tune was extremely popular in America and was often sung and performed in honor of Marquis de Lafayette who served admirably in the Revolutionary War. The tune was quoted in Tchaikovsky's 1812 Overture, a popular orchestral work performed across the United States on the Fourth beginning in the early part of the 20th century. Robert Frédéric: 'Claude-Joseph Rouget de l'Isle,' *Grove Music Online* ed. L. Mary (accessed 4 December 2007), <http://www.grovemusic.com.proxyau.wrlc.org>.

71. Printed in *The Nightingale; or Rural Songster* (Dedham [MA]: Printed by H. Mann, 1800).

72. "When freedom's sons, at Heav'n's command" published under the title "Old Seventy-Six" and sung to the tune "Yankee Doodle" as published in *The American Patriotic Song-Book, a Collection of Political, Descriptive, and Humourous Songs of National Character, and the Production of American Poets Only. Interspersed with a Number Set to Music* (Philadelphia: W. M'Culloch, 1813) and *The American Patriotic Song-Book, a Collection of Political, Descriptive, and Humourous Songs of National Character, and the Production of American Poets Only* (Philadelphia: John Bioren, 1816).

73. Boullay, a violinist and composer, was from Port au Prince. During the 1790s, he gave concerts in Philadelphia and Boston. See, for example, *Dunlap's American Daily Advertiser*, 31 August 1792, 2.

74. In 1796 Joseph Herrick advertised his "Evening School, for the purpose of teaching psalmody" in Portland. *Eastern Her-*

ald and Gazette of Maine, 12 October 1796, 3. Herrick died on April 20, 1807, in Milford, NH, when he attempted to cross a raging river in a boat and drowned. *Farmers' Cabinet*, 21 April 1807, 3.

75. Daniel George, publisher of the *Eastern Herald*. George died in 1804 at the age of 45. *Newburyport Herald*, 14 February 1804, 3.

76. Likely "Gen. Wayne's March," honoring Major General Anthony Wayne (1746–1796), who was born in Waynesborough, Pennsylvania, and served admirably in the Revolutionary War. Music printed in Samuel Holyoke's *The Instrumental Assistant* (1800). Listed in Sonneck, *A Bibliography of Early Secular American Music, 18th Century*, 210. *General Wayne's New March* for piano, published by B. Carr's musical repositories, 1794–97, is listed in Wolfe III:1008. See additional information on Wayne and a monument dedicated to him in *Gleaner and Luzerne Advertiser*, 5 July 1811, 2, and *Rhode-Island American*, 18 June 1811, 1.

77. Reported in Sonneck, *Early Opera in America*, 192.

78. Philip Morin Freneau (1752–1832) was friends with Adams, Franklin, Jefferson, Madison, and Monroe. During the years 1786–1809 he published three collections of his own poetry. Rufus W. Griswold in a biographical sketch of Freneau thought he "was the most distinguished poet of our revolutionary time." *The Poets and Poetry of America*, 31. A full biography of the poet by Richard C. Vitzthum is in the online database, *Dictionary of Literary Biography, vol. 37: American Writers of the Early Republic* (Detroit, MI: Gale Group, 1985), 163–81.

79. George James Warner.

80. As reported in Charles H. Kaufman, "Music in New Jersey, 1655–1860: A Study of Musical Activity and Musicians in New Jersey from Its First Settlement to the Civil War" (Ph.D. dissertation, New York University, 1974), 282–83.

81. Popular title for lyrics originally titled "Sweet Lillies of the Valley," with first line: "O'er barren hills and flow'ry dales." The poem describe how "Little Sally" continued to love her beau who went off to war and later returned. See *Hartford Gazette*, 10 March 1794, 4.

82. James Hewitt was a celebrated violinist, music teacher, conductor, and music publisher in New York and Boston.

83. "Here in Cool Grot and Mossy Cell" composed by Garret Wesley, 1st Earl of Mornington (1735–1781).

84. For information on this music publisher, see Paul R. Osterhout, "Andrew Wright: Northampton Music Printer," *American Music* 1/4 (Winter 1983): 5–26.

85. Listed in Sonneck, *A Bibliography of Early Secular American Music, 18th Century*, 310. Facsimile in Louis C. Elson, *History of American Music* (Boston, 1904), 145–46. This is a different ode from the one that has the same words for the first line written by Mr. Stoddard and printed in 1792. See **Publications**, 1792.

86. Listed in Oscar Sonneck, *A Bibliography of Early Secular American Music, 18th Century*, 310.

87. Printed in *The Universal Songster and Museum of Mirth* (Boston: Charles Gaylord, 1835).

88. Advertised as to be published on July 4, 1798, and including "A Song for the 4th of July, tune 'Hail Columbia,' and many others that have never before appeared in print." *Federal Gazette & Baltimore Daily Advertiser*, 3 July 1798, 1. Listed in Sonneck, *A Bibliography of Early Secular American Music, 18th Century*, 327, and Irving Lowens, *A Bibliography of Songsters Printed in American before 1821* (Worcester, MA: American Antiquarian Society, 1976), 57.

89. Published as a "favorite patriotic song" in New York by G. Gilfert, ca. 1798. Sonneck, *A Bibliography of Early Secular American Music*, 175.

90. Robert Treat Paine, Jr. (1773–1811), poet, lawyer, orator, and son of Robert Treat Paine, signer of the Declaration of Independence. Heintze, *The Fourth of July Encyclopedia*, 213–14. Paine's ode "Adams and Liberty" was frequently referred to in primary sources examined by its first line of text, "Ye sons of Columbia, who bravely have fought." One of the first printings of the song with this text was in *Federal Gazette & Baltimore Daily*

Advertiser, 3 July 1798, 2. The tune designated was "Anacreon in Heaven." The poem is printed in Griswold, *The Poets and Poetry of America*, 76.

According to Spicer, "Popular Song for Public Celebration," 44, "In 1801, Thomas Paine legally renamed himself Robert Treat Paine, Jr., after an eldest brother who died of yellow fever in 1798."

91. Printed with music in *American Musical Miscellany* (1798), 103–05. First line: "When first the Sun o'er Ocean glow'd."

92. *American Musical Miscellany*, 211–18; printed in *The Nightingale; or Rural Songster* (Dedham [MA]: Printed by H. Mann, 1800). First line: "Ye sons of Columbia, who bravely have fought." Facsimile of sheet music published by Thomas and Andrews in Boston (1798), cited as such in *Columbian Centinel*, 6 June 1798, 4, with modern print edition in Lawrence, 148–49, and W. Thomas Marrocco and Harold Gleason, *Music in America: An Anthology from the Landing of the Pilgrims to the Close of the Civil War, 1620–1865* (New York: Norton, 1964), 289–90. The song was set to the tune "To Anacreon in Heaven" and was an immediate success. The song was sung again on July 23 at Boston's Hay Market Theatre by Mr. Hodgkinson, with the audience joining in the chorus. "Theatrical," *Columbian Centinel*, 25 July 1798, 3.

93. Rea was a countertenor who gave numerous concerts in Boston.

94. Samuel Holyoke (1762–1820) was a singing master and tune book compiler who wrote over 700 works. He founded the Essex Musical Association in 1797. Richard Crawford and Nym Cooke: 'Holyoke, Samuel,' *Grove Music Online* ed. L. Mary (accessed 8 May 2008), http://www.grovemusic.com.proxyau.wrlc.org.

95. This tune, known also as "Hail, Columbia" as a vocal rendition, was composed by Philip Phile in 1789 for George Washington's inauguration. The lyrics were written by Joseph Hopkinson. For an example of an instrumental version "from a manuscript book of songs (1825) compiled by Portsmouth saddler Nathaniel March," see Spicer, "Popular Song for Public Celebration," 49.

96. Listed also in Sonneck, *Early Concert-Life in America*, 216.

97. This section of musical works performed reprinted in Sonneck, *Early Concert-Life in America*, 213.

98. Concert listed in Sonneck, *Early Concert-Life in America*, 213.

99. Thomas Green Fessenden. This ode was reprinted several years later in "Poetry," *New-England Palladium* 9 November 1804, 4.

100. In his obituary of his death in Vermont, Thomas H. Atwell was described as "an able performer in church music." *Essex Register*, 12 March 1814, 3. He was also compiler of *The New-York Collection of Sacred Harmony ...* (Lansingburg: Abner Reed, 1795) and *The New York & Vermont Collection of Sacred Harmony ...* (Albany: Buckley, 1804). The latter was available for sale in Albany at Henry Spencer's shop (*Albany Centinel*, 11 September 1804, 4) and some years later at H. & E. Phinney's Bookstore in Cooperstown, New York (*Otsego Herald*, 14 September 1815, 4).

101. Royall Tyler (1757–1826). For further information and a critique of Tyler's Fourth of July Ode, see *Harper's New Monthly Magazine* 80/479 (April 1890): 786.

102. For more on Jonathan Mitchell Sewall (1748–1808), lawyer and fervent poet who published a selection of his pieces in *Miscellaneous Poems* (Portsmouth, NH: Treadwell, 1801), see Spicer, "Popular Song for Public Celebration," 17–19. According to Sonneck, *A Bibliography of Early Secular American Music, 18th Century*, 310, a broadside, with "engraved music for three-part chorus" with accompanying text, names the Rev. Chauncy Lee as the composer.

103. Todd was president of the First Medical Society in Vermont and was described as "a distinguished practitioner of physic [sic] in the State of Vermont." He died in 1806 at the age of 46. *Rutland Herald*, 15 June 1795, 4; *Connecticut Herald*, 23 December 1806, 3.

104. Probably "Alknomook, the Death Song of the Cherokee Indians," from Tammany (1794) composed by James Hewitt. Modern reprint of music in Marrocco, *Music in America*, 213. Based on a poem of a similar title that dates to at least 1785. *New-Haven Gazette*, 18 August 1785, 3. For a compact disc recording, see *Music of the Federal Era* (New York: New World Records, 1994).

105. Either Peter Albrecht van Hagen, Sr., or his son who shared the same name. The Hagen family had emigrated from the Netherlands to Charleston in 1774 and by 1789 were in New York, active as musicians and teachers. Barton Cantrell and H. Earle Johnson: 'Hagen, P.A., Jr.,' *Grove Music Online* ed. L. Mary (accessed 18 April 2008), http://www.grovemusic.com. proxyau.wrlc.org.

106. This first song title appears on a broadside (1799) together with a second song, in five stanzas "Heav'n and the fates this day decreed" to the tune "President's March." Reprinted in *Early American Imprints*, first series, no. 36462. Apparently both songs were sung "in all parties" that day, including that held at Piscataqua Bridge Tavern, a popular place with "a beautiful hall and "a delightful summer-room, under the arc to the bridge, where large parties may amuse themselves in fishing, dancing, singing." "Improvements at the Piscataqua Bridge Tavern," *United States Oracle*, 25 July 1801, 3.

107. Listed in Sonneck, *A Bibliography of Early Secular American Music, 18th Century*, 433.

108. Alexander Thomas was a postmaster in Walpole, New Hampshire, but was dismissed from his position in 1802 because he had Federalist leanings. By 1804, he was operating a book store there and also served as one of the editors of *Farmer's Weekly Museum*. Thomas died on July 2, 1809, in Saratoga Springs, New York. *Boston Gazette*, 19 April 1802, 2; *Farmer's Weekly Museum*, 14 January 1804, 3; *New-York Weekly Museum*, 22 July 1809, 3.

109. White was author of *Orlando: Or, Parental Perfection*, a tragedy that was performed at the Theatre on Federal Street in Boston and *Poor Lodger*, a comedy, also performed in Boston. Respectively, *Massachusetts Spy*, 2 August 1797, 4, and *New Hampshire Patriot*, 25 December 1810, 3. He was also active on the Fourth of July as an orator in Worcester (1804), Petersham (1805), and Boston (1809). White died in Worcester on May 2, 1818. *National Aegis*, 4 July 1804 and 3 July 1805, 3 and 1, respectively; *Essex Register*, 12 July 1809, 3; *American Advocate and Kennebec Advertiser*, 16 May 1818, 3.

110. Possibly the song "Lady Washington's Lamentation," described as a "celebrated new song" by Francis Adancourt in his newly published song collection *The Merry Medly, or Pocket Companion* (1804). *Farmers' Register*, 22 May 1804, 4. The lyrics (first line: "When Columbia's brave sons call'd my hero to lead 'em") were published and to be sung to the tune "Bellifarius" in *Federal Gazette & Baltimore Daily Advertiser*, 12 January 1801, 3.

111. The first line of this text was slightly altered to "When Holland gag'd and fetter'd sprawls" in the stanzas published in "The Rivulet," *Mirror*, 8 July 1799, 4.

112. Jonathan M. Sewall was toasted at the celebration: "J.M. Sewall, Esq.— the American Pollo and the poet of the day."

113. Lyrics published under the title "Rise Columbia!" in *The Patriotic Vocalist, or Fourth of July Pocket Companion. A Selection of Approved Songs, on National Subjects, for the Use of Public Assemblies, Celebrating the Anniversaries of American Independence, and Washington's Birth Day* (Salem: Cushing & Appleton, July, 1812).

114. Composed by Justin Morgan and "first published in Asahel Benham, *Federal Harmony* (New Haven, 1790)." *The Core Repertory of Early American Psalmody*, xlv–xlvi. Another modern reprint of music in Marrocco, *Music in America*, 151–53.

115. "To Anacreon in Heaven," a popular song that dates to circa 1771 and connected to the Anacreontic Society of London, the tune composed by the English composer John Stafford Smith. The melody was used as a setting for numerous newly composed texts in America such as, for example, "Adams and Liberty" by Robert Treat Paine in 1798, and later "The Star-Spangled Banner," by Francis Scott Key in 1814. Modern reprint

of "To Anacreon in Heaven" in Marrocco, *Music in America*, 287–88.

116. Victor Pelissier, composer and horn player who was residing in New York in 1793 and was an instrumentalist in the Old American Company. Wolfe II:672. Production listed in Sonneck, *Early Opera in America*, 96.

117. *Universal Gazette*, 10 July 1800, 3.

118. The "President's March" performed was likely based on the version of the tune published in Holyoke's collection *The Instrumental Assistant* (Exeter, New Hampshire, 1800).

119. The band was established by an act of Congress that was signed by President Adams on 11 July 1798. For an article on the 160th anniversary of the band, see "Marine Band Takes Note of Birthday," *Washington Post*, 3 July 1958, A11. William Farr was leader of the band from 1799 to 1804.

120. *The First Forty Years of Washington Society in the Family Letters of Margaret Bayard Smith*. Ed. Gaillard Hunt (New York: Frederick Ungar, 1965), 397–98.

121. Uri K. Hill (1780–1844), teacher, tunebook compiler, who resided in Northampton, Massachusetts, 1800 to 1825, then Boston where he served as organist of the Brattle Street Church, and finally in New York, by late 1810, where he taught vocal music, violin and other instruments. Wolfe I:384–85.

122. "Bill Bobstay" cited as "a new song" in January 1793, with verses printed: first line, "Tight lads have I sail'd with, but none e'er sp sightly." *Massachusetts Mercury*, 10 January 1793, 4.

123. Facsimile of title page in Lawrence, 171. Listed in Wolfe I:373. "Advertised by Hewitt in the *New York Daily Advertiser* 30 September 1801 as 'just published.'"

124. "Jefferson & Liberty," a song set to the air of "Jefferson's March" with words by Michael Fortune, was published just prior to the Fourth in 1801. See *Kline's Carlisle Weekly Gazette*, 24 June 1801, 4; Wolfe I:448. In the following year a poem published shortly before the Fourth and under the title "Jefferson & Liberty" had this set of first-line text: "The gloomy night before us flies." *Weekly Wanderer*, 3 July 1802, 4. According to Clyde S. Shive, Jr., Alexander Wilson (1766–1813), "a poet and ornithologist who came to Philadelphia from England in the mid–1790s," was the author of "Jefferson and Liberty." See Shive, "*National Martial Music and Songs*, a Musical First," *American Music* 9/1 (Spring 1991): 92–101.

125. Facsimile of music in Lawrence, 170. Modern reprint of music in Marrocco, *Music in America*, 283–85. See also, *First Forty Years of Washington Society*, 30. The lyrics of "Hail Columbia!" were published in the following additional newspapers around the time of the Fourth of July that year: *Federal Gazette & Baltimore Daily Advertiser*, 8 July 1801, 2; *Philadelphia Gazette*, 9 July 1801, 3; *Poulson's American Daily Advertiser*, 10 July 1801, 2.

126. Captain Thomas Tingey, first commandant of the Washington Navy Yard, who was noted for his excellent voice. Elise K. Kirk, *Musical Highlights from the White House* (Malabar, Florida: Krieger, 1992), 13–14.

127. For a history of the band see Kenneth William Carpenter, "A History of the United States Marine Band" (Ph.D. dissertation, University of Iowa, 1970).

128. As reported by Richard Crawford in *The Core Repertory of Early American Psalmody*, xxxi.

129. Facsimile of B. Carr's (New York and Baltimore) print edition in Lawrence, 83.

130. "America, Commerce, and Freedom" was written by the Philadelphia composer Alexander Reinagle (1756–1809) for his ballet pantomime *The Sailor's Landlady* (1794). Listed in Sonneck, *A Bibliography of Early Secular American Music, 18th Century*, 15.

131. First performed March 4, 1801, at the "Grand Processional at Philadelphia." Facsimile of edition printed by the Philadelphia publisher G. Willig, in Lawrence, 168. There were several tunes under this title published, one composed by James Hewitt, another by Alexander Reinagle. See Wolfe I:376 and 448 and II:730.

132. "Ou peut on etre meiux qu' au sein de sa famille" published as "a favorite French song, arranged for the military bands

and for the piano fortes by H.N. Gilles" (Baltimore, Geo. Willig, 1825?), as listed in Wolfe I:313.

133. Music originally composed for piano by John J. Hawkins of Philadelphia. Published edition (1801) listed in Wolfe I:350.

134. An example of "Yankee Doodle" arranged in three parts "suitable for a small militia band" from a music book dated 1799 is in Carolyn Bryant, *And the Band Played On, 1776–1976* (Washington, D.C.: Smithsonian Institution, 1975), 9.

135. "Rise, Cynthia, Rise" was advertised for sale in 1793 by Benjamin Carr in Philadelphia. The song was frequently sung as a duet. *Dunlap's American Daily Advertiser*, 13 December 1793, 1.

136. Listed in Wolfe II:647. See also, *Magazine of History with Notes and Queries* 2:1 (July 1905): 33.

137. The last two lines of this song refers to the year 1801: "Thy peaceful victories that grace the glorious eighteen hundred one" and probably is a reprint of the same song printed in *Bee*, 12 August 1801. See **Publications**, 1801.

138. Probably William Felton (1715–1769). See Wolfe I:275.

139. Possibly by Stephen Jenks (1772–1856) as published in the *Musical Harmonist* (New Haven, CT: A. Doolittle, 1800). For additional information, see MLA *Notes* 36/2 (December 1979): 342.

140. Probably the tune having the same title composed by Benjamin Carr and published in *The Musical Journal for the Piano Forte* (Baltimore, 1800–01). Wolfe I:161.

141. See "The Lass of Richmond-Hill," cited as "a new Vauxhall song." First line: "On Richmond Hill lives a lass." "Poetry," *Norfolk and Portsmouth Gazette*, 23 September 1789, 3. The story regarding the lyrics revolves around a young wealthy lady that lived in the vicinity of Richmond, Virginia, who took her own life because her desire to marry her loving beau who was not wealthy was not fulfilled due to her father's intervention. "The Lass of Richmond Hill," *Eastern Argus*, 16 May 1826, 1.

142. The Trojan Band consisted of 80 students including a corp of infantry and another of artillery, with a musical component. "The Trojan Band," *Salem Gazette*, 18 June 1802, 3.

143. A note by the editor of this newspaper dodged any partiality to different political perspectives as represented in the songs performed that day: "We lay some claims to impartiality ourselves today — we publish both Federal and Democratic Songs, and surely neither party can complain that the poison is not accompanied with its antidote."

144. First line same as title as published in *The Nightingale* (Portsmouth: printed for William and Daniel Treadwell, 1804), 239–40. Listed in Wolfe II:641.

145. Commemorates Nathaniel Greene (1742–1786) of Rhode Island, a Continental general who served admirably throughout the Revolutionary War, and who gained distinction in several successful campaigns.

146. A popular tune frequently played at funerals and on the Fourth of July after toasts offered to the memory of George Washington. According to Raoul Camus, "the music and text of the song were printed in the *Boston Magazine* in November 1783." Tune is reprinted in Camus, *Military Music of the American Revolution*, 116–17.

147. A dramatic patriotic production with a similar title, *Federal Oath, Death or Liberty*, described as "a patriotic effusion in two parts," written by Anthony Pasquin, was performed at the Hay Market Theatre in Boston on July 23, 1798. *Russell's Gazette*, 19 July 1798, 3. On June, 2, 1800, a "character piece" titled "July 4th, 1776," with "America" played by Mrs. Rowson and the Goddess of Liberty played by Mrs. Durang, was presented at the "Old Theatre" on South Street in Philadelphia. *Philadelphia Gazette*, 2 June 1800, 3.

148. Note that accompanied the ode: "Mr. Bartois: a number of genuine republicans intend to celebrate the Fourth of July under the broad spreading oaks of Allegany — for which purpose the enclosed song (composed for the occasion) will be sung. Please to give it a place in your *Hornet*, so that the friends of Jefferson may be informed that this little place contains a great many big republicans. Cumberland, (Allegany). June 24,

1803." Actually the ode was not "composed for the occasion," but rather had been previously sung at a celebration in Newark, NJ, in 1794. See **Publications**, 1794

149. Newspapers cite a Jacob Fisher in Kennebunk as a merchant and justice.

150. Reported in Oscar Sonneck, *Report on The Star-Spangled Banner, Hail Columbia, America Yankee Doodle* (Washington, D.C.: Library of Congress, 1909; reprint, New York: Dover, 1972), 25.

151. George K. Jackson (1745–1822) was "organist, music teacher, music publisher, and composer, born at Oxford, England." He came to America in 1796, first opened a music school in Newark, New Jersey, and later lived in various cities along the Eastern Seaboard. Wolfe I:440.

152. Reported in Sonneck, *Report on The Star-Spangled Banner*, 25.

153. Possibly the song "The Health of Our Sachem," with the first line: "Well met, fellow freemen! Let's cheerfully greet" ("Poetry," *Vermont Gazette*, 1 July 1805, 4).

154. Full text with the "Yankee Doodle let us sing" chorus printed in "Miscellaneous Repository," *New-Hampshire Gazette*, 16 August 1803, 4.

155. In this issue of the *National Intelligencer*, the editor clearly distinguished between the U.S. Marine Band and a "Neapolitan" band, the latter likely made up of mostly Italian musicians. These musicians were possibly those attached to the Corps of Artillerists based at the Washington Arsenal. Warren P. Howe names the musicians that are written on a muster roll: Francis Masi, Luis Masi, Vincent Masi, Serafino Masi, Phylip Maurizi, Michael Marisse, Joseph Sardo, and Charles White. Warren P. Howe, "Early American Military Music," *American Music* 17/1 (Spring 1999): 105.

156. Accompanied the toast: "The Fair Daughters of Columbia — without their sensibility, their love and society, liberty and even life itself would be but dreary things."

157. A 1780 rendition of the tune is printed in Lawrence, 86. The toast accompanying the performance of this tune: "The Vice President [Aaron Burr] of the United States —'O! fling away ambition, by that sin fell the Angels.'" As reported by Anderson, "American Music during the War for Independence, 1775–1783," 38–39, from an article published in 1923 in the *Journal of the Society of Army Historical Research* (2/7), the tune was used for "drumming out any person who has behaved disorderly, etc., in a camp or garrison." The tune was performed on the Fourth a number of times to highlight those who were socially and politically disfavored.

158. To the toast: "The wisdom that suggested, and the policy which directed the purchase of Louisiana. Millions for purchase, not a cent for conquest. 3 time 3."

159. Warren P. Howe compares two manuscript editions in "Drum Books" for this Revolutionary War–era tune. Howe, "Early American Military Music," 96, 103–04.

160. "Son of the Reverend Doctor M'Knight."

161. According to J. Bunker Clark, George K. Jackson (1745–1822) "was one of the best educated musical figures in Boston in the early 19th century." He was born in Oxford, received a doctorate from St. Andrews University in 1791 and came to the United States where he pursued his musical interests, first in New York in 1806 and then by 1812 in Boston. He was organist in Boston's King's Chapel, Trinity Church, and St. Paul's Church. *New-York Evening Post*, 31 May 1806, 2; J. Bunker Clark, *The Dawning of American Keyboard Music* (Westport, CT: Greenwood Press, 1988), 296. See also, H. Earle Johnson, "George K. Jackson, Doctor of Music (1745–1825)," *Musical Quarterly* 29/1 (January 1943): 113–21. Modern reprint of Dr. Jackson's music for Mrs. Jackson's ode is in Marrocco, *Music in America*, 228–31.

162. Music in *Music in America*, 228–231. Listed in Wolfe I:444–45.

163. Victor Pelissier. For an article on this play, see Richard Moody, "The Glory of Columbia: Her Yeomanry!" in *Dramas from the American Theatre, 1762–1909*, ed. Richard Moody (Cleveland, OH: World, 1966), 87–93.

164. Sonneck has the words and music composed by the singer Mrs. Mary Ann Pownall and the music first published in New York in 1794. *A Bibliography of Early Secular American Music, 18th Century*, 216.

165. A theatrical song popular in Philadelphia, New York, and Boston, with performances spanning 1799 to 1825.

166. Composed by John Stafford Smith (1750–1836). The printed sheet music (New York: Printed & sold at J. Hewitt's musical repository, [1803]) also describes this work as "a new patriotic song": first line, "Well met fellow freemen let's cheerfully greet"; tune, "To Anacreon in heaven." Listed in Wolfe II:820.

167. Possibly the same work listed in Wolfe II:729 under the title "How blest the life a sailor leads" to the tune "America, Commerce, and Freedom," the music attributed to Alexander Reinagle (manuscript, ca. 1808).

168. Probably a parody on "Ye sons of Mars attend," music and text published in Anderson, *Freedom's Voice in Poetry and Song*, 822–23.

169. Possibly the tune of this popular song of the same title printed in the collection *The Songster's Museum* (Northampton, MA: Andrew Wright, 1803), 95–97. Listed in Wolfe II:831.

170. Mrs. Jones, an "excellent Actress" from Boston had "stampt her fame, both as a singer and performer," and had performed, for example, in Salem on July 4, 1797, and June 17, 1801. *Salem Gazette*, 4 July 1797, 3; *Salem Impartial Register*, 15 June 1801, 3.

171. Wentworth also presented an oration and in the year before had attended the ceremony in Portsmouth. *The Gazette*, 13 July 1803; 2; *Political Observatory*, 30 June 1804, 3.

172. "Song, composed by Mr. [Joseph] Story, and sung at the close of the performances in the meeting house" in Salem, Massachusetts. Printed in Joseph Story, *An Oration, Pronounced at Salem, on the Fourth Day of July, 1804, in Commemoration of Our National Independence* (Salem: William Carlton, 1804).

173. Spicer, "Popular Song for Public Celebration," 53–54, identifies him as Samuel Larkin (1773–1849), a musician and compiler of the following song collections: *Columbian Songster and Freemason's Pocket Companion* (1798); *Social Companion, and Songster's Pocket Book* (1799); and *The Nightingale* (1804). In addition to the information that Spicer provides, he points readers to James Kences, *George Washington: A Biography in Social Dance* (Sandy Hook, CT: Hendrickson, 1998) for additional details.

174. The poet must have been Jonathan Mitchell Sewall in that he was toasted that afternoon at Washington Hall by Mr. Garland: "The poet of the day, J.M. Sewall, Esq.— the legitimate offspring of Homer and Milton." *Portsmouth Oracle*, 7 July 1804, 3.

175. "Song for the Fourth of July, 1804." First line: "Come, let us banish ev'ry care." "The Wreath," *The Balance, and Columbian Repository*, 3 July 1804, 216.

176. "New Yankee Doodle for the Fourth of July, 1804." First line: "The tune of seventy-six let's sing."

177. Accompanied a toast to Alexander Hamilton. Coincidentally, it was reported that Hamilton had sung this song that day at a meeting of the Society of the Cincinnati in New York, with Aaron Burr present. A few day later, on July 11, the two gentlemen fought a duel in which Hamilton was shot. For additional information, see "Burr-Hamilton Duel," in Heintze, *The Fourth of July Encyclopedia*, 42.

178. "A Genuine Song to the genuine tune — Black Sloven." First line: "All ye genuine dupes of the genuine breed." "The Wreath," *The Balance, and Columbian Repository*, 17 April 1804, 128. One of the early instances of the song "Black Sloven" performed was at Vaux-Hall Garden in New York on June 30, 1769. *New-York Journal*, 29 June 1769, 3. Through the years the tune was set to various newly composed lyrics. See for example, *New-Haven Gazette*, 15 February 1787, 399, and *Political Observatory*, 26 May 1804, 4.

179. A song titled "Banks of Kentucke" and sung to the tune "The Banks of the Dee" was published in a number of newspapers in 1786, including, for example, the *New Jersey Journal*, 17 May 1786, 4.

180. According to *the Republican Watch-Tower*, 7 July 1804, 2, "The Odes which follow were designed to be sung in the church, but owing to the absence of vocal and instrumental performers, this part of the ceremony was dispensed with."

181. William Pirsson was active from 1797 to 1812 and in 1818 and 1819 in New York as a teacher, conductor, composer and music engraver. He composed a set of *Twelve Anthems* (1801–05) which were sold at "Mr. Hewit's Musical Repository" in New York City. *American Sacred Music Imprints*, 490–91; Wolfe II:689.

182. Tune was used by the military in the Revolutionary War. One example titled "The Roags March," for fife, was copied by Henry Blake in his diary and the image is printed in Howe, "Early American Military Music," 88.

183. As reported in John A. Cuthbert, "Rayner Taylor and Anglo-American Musical Life" (Ph.D. dissertation, West Virginia University, 1980), 344. Raynor [Rayner] Taylor (1747–1825), composer, singer, and organist, born in London, came to America in 1792. He was active as a musician in Baltimore, Annapolis, and Philadelphia. Anne Dhu McLucas: 'Taylor, Raynor [Rayner],' *Grove Music Online* ed. L. Mary (accessed 30 December 2007), http://www.grovemusic.com.proxyau.wrlc.org.

184. Psalm 100 [old] was one of the most popular tunes sung on the Fourth during the nineteenth century and supports the evidence proffered by Richard Crawford that the tune received the most printings (226 times) considerably passing other popular tunes of that time. For the Fourth it was common for new texts to be set to the tune. *The Core Repertory of Early American Psalmody*, li–lii.

185. "The Spinning Wheel" printed with tune in *American Musical Miscellany* (1798), 61–64. First line: "To ease his heart, and own his flame."

186. *Ibid.*, 66–68. First line: "Oh think on my fate once I freedom enjoy'd." Sonneck lists this work as from the *Purse, or Benevolent Tar*, by William Reeve and first published as sheet music in Philadelphia at Carr's Musical Repository, [1794]. Sonneck, *A Bibliography of Early Secular American Music, 18th Century*, 153. An edition published in New York between 1799 and 1803 is listed in Wolfe III:1015.

187. This song was sung at a gathering on July 4, 1821, in Washington. *Washington Gazette*, 5 July 1821, 2. The toast for this 1804 performance: "Modern philosophy, which teaches, that the happiness of the many, ought not to be sacrificed to the ambition of the few — May its disciples encrease 'till it becomes universal — 6 guns."

188. Sumner was recorder for the Massachusetts Society of the Cincinnati.

189. Gleason presented an "American Independence" oration on July 5, 1819, in Charlestown, Massachusetts. He was a teacher and gave public lectures on geography and other subjects. *Independent Chronicle*, 9 September 1816, 2; *Franklin Monitor*, 11 September 1819, 2.

190. Nathaniel Hill Wright who began publishing the *Columbian Patriot* in late 1813 and also was publisher of the *Independent Whig* of Newburyport. He married Miss Mary Hudson in Boston in 1809 and died in 1824 at the age of 37. He wrote various poems including the collections *Monody, on the Death of Brigadier General Zebulon Montgomery Pike; and Other Poems* (1814) and *The Fall of Palmyra and Other Poems* (1817). *Farmer's Museum*, 27 November 1809, 3; *Connecticut Gazette*, 7 August 1811, 3; *Dedham Gazette*, 10 September 1813, 3; *Columbian Patriot*, 6 July 1814, 3; *Independent Chronicle and Boston Patriot*, 15 May 1824, 3.

191. To the toast: "The Constitution of Connecticut (so called) — Used as a looking-glass by the knavith gambler to cheat those on the other side of the table."

192. Probably Gen. James Wilkinson who, according to Warren P. Howe, "organized a band in 1798" that subsequently "played for the inauguration of Thomas Jefferson in 1801" and who "appreciated music's military value due to their experience in the Revolution." Howe, "Early American Military Music," 104.

193. Possibly "Truxton's Victory or Brave Yankee Boys." First line: "Come all you Yankee sailors with swords and pikes advance." Facsimile reprint of Boston edition printed by Nathaniel Coverly, Jun., in Lawrence, 153. An advertisement noting the publication of this song, in *Massachusetts Mercury*, 29 March 1799, 3, cites it as "a naval patriotic song written by Mrs. Rowson." In early 1799, Commodore Thomas Truxtun (or Truxton, 1755–1822) commanding the USS *Constellation*, captured the French frigate, *Insurgente*. The toast for this 1805 performance: "The American Navy — The only security for our *Fleeting* Property."

194. Selden was a justice of the peace of Bennington County who also dabbled in various literary pursuits. It was noted in his obituary that as an attorney he had "judicial talents and [his] decisions commanded respect." His "prose and poetry were of the fugitive class, but had a chasteness, ease, delicacy and finish of style, sentiment and moral, which few equal.... He did not write with facility, yet his poems, though few and occasional, will some of them long survive, because of their perspicuity, aptitude, sentiment, and moral tendency." Selden died on September 7, 1825. *Vermont Gazette*, 24 December 1804, 3, and 13 September 1825, 3.

195. Listed in Sonneck, *A Bibliography of Early Secular American Music, 18th Century*, 339. Premiered in New York on December 2, 1785. Facsimile edition in the series *Recent Researches in American Music* (Madison, WI: A–R Editions, 1978), vol. 6.

196. The event took place in Faneuil Hall and ex–President John Adams was there.

197. Ellison delivered a "discourse" on July 4, 1808, in Camden. *Carolina Gazette*, 12 August 1808, 1.

198. According to the *National Intelligencer*, this song was "originally sung at an entertainment given by George W. Erving, esq. in London, to celebrate the anniversary of the installation of Thomas Jefferson as President of the United States of America, the 4th March 1803."

199. In March 1806, Blyth advertised the opening of his school in Salem for the instruction of "young ladies." *Salem Register*, 31 March 1806, 4.

200. Lyrics printed in *The Universal Songster and Museum of Mirth* (Boston: Charles Gaylord, 1835).

201. Prentiss was editor of no less than five newspapers at different times in various cities along the Eastern Seaboard. A poem of his was read at the Fourth of July celebration in 1813 in Brookfield, Massachusetts. Prentiss died in 1820. *Massachusetts Spy*, 14 July 1813, 3; *The American*, 3 November 1820, 3.

202. Jezaniah Sumner (1754–1836) "is the author of the well-known and still popular anthem, 'Ode on Science,' both words and music, which he wrote in 1798, on the occasion of the first exhibition of the Bristol Academy, Taunton." *The Stoughton Musical Society's Centennial Collection of Sacred Music* (1878), 162–63, 304 (with music).

203. To the toast: "The Clergy, let them remember their kingdom is not of this world."

204. In 1802 this tune was cited as "a favorite song in fashionable circles." First line: "Why are we fond of toil and care." *Democratic Republican; and Commercial Daily Advertiser*, 29 July 1802, 3.

205. Sung also in Washington, D.C. the same day. See footnote 198.

206. Titled "Chester," the sprightly tune for this text was composed by William Billings and first published in his collection *The New-England Psalm-Singer* (Boston 1770) and set to a text by Isaac Watts. The setting of "Chester" with the "Let tyrants" text first appeared in Billings's collection *The Singing Master's Assistant* (1778). Richard Crawford cites this tune as "probably the most famous early American musical composition today." It was published 56 times during the period studied and received great acclaim throughout the Eastern Seaboard. *The Core Repertory of Early American Psalmody*, ed. Richard Crawford (Madison, WI: A–R Editions, 1984), xxx–xxxi. A facsimile of "Chester" is found in Lawrence, 81. Music printed in Marrocco, *Music in America*, 112. In the twentieth century, William Schuman used the tune in his popular work *New England Trip-*

tych, which also had numerous performances on the Fourth of July.

207. A toast was offered to "The Cadet Band — May they continue to exert their talents, for the accommodation and gratification of this company, as has hitherto merited our highest applause."

208. *Connecticut Herald*, 7 July 1807, 3.

209. *American Mercury*, 6 August 1807, 1.

210. Reprinted in 1810, with the first line: "Ye sons of Columbia! oh, hail the great day," and again in 1814 under the title "American Freedom." *New-York Weekly Museum*, 30 June 1810, 4; *Essex Register*, 6 July 1814, 1.

211. The same work that was published in the *Centinel of Freedom* in 1798. See **Publications**, 1798.

212. The newspaper reported that attending were members of the Society of the Cincinnati and "a large number of the inhabitants of Elizabeth" and that "patriotic songs" were sung.

213. An earlier performance of this work took place at a celebration held in Bennington, Vermont, on the occasion of the "national jubilee" on May 12, 1804, "for the glorious acquisition of Louisiana." *Political Observatory*, 26 May 1804, 4.

214. The text of a song with this identical first line, "composed by a gentlemen of this town" (Salem, Massachusetts) was published in the *Salem Gazette* and reprinted in *Gazette of the United States*, 30 July 1798, 2.

215. Lyrics printed in *The Universal Songster and Museum of Mirth* (Boston: Charles Gaylord, 1835).

216. Possibly Daniel L. Peck compiler of *The Musical Medley: Containing the Necessary Rules of Psalmody in a Very Concise and Explicit Manner; Together with a Number of Set Pieces , and a Great Variety of Psalm Tunes Adapted to All the Different Metres Usually Sung in Churches* (Dedham, MA: H. Mann, 1808). The collection was advertised as appropriate for "singing schools and musical societies" and was available, for example, at Bronson, Walter, & Co. in New Haven, Connecticut. *Connecticut Herald*, 9 May 1809, 1.

217. Accompanied this toast: "The clergy — We consider them while devoted to the duties of their profession, as the pillars of morality and religion."

218. One of the more popular pieces of music performed on the Fourth, "Ere around the Huge Oak," a song from the opera *The Farmer*, was composed by William Shield (1748–1829) and first printed ca. 1802–03. See Wolfe II:798. Lyrics printed in *The Universal Songster and Museum of Mirth* (Boston: Charles Gaylord, 1835).

219. Probably Robert R. Kendall. See Freeport, 1826.

220. To the toast: "The Clergy — As the principles of our religion are unchangeable — may their doctrines never be contaminated by the breath of popular faction."

221. Possibly the Watertown composer Samuel Babcock who published a musical repository titled *The Middlesex Harmony* (1795). Babcock died on November 23, 1813, at French Mills. *New-England Palladium*, 14 December 1813, 2.

222. Facsimile of one instrumental version of the song from "John Greenwood's Book" in Lawrence, 179.

223. *New York Commercial Advertiser*, 5 July 1811, 3.

224. An article published in the *New Hampshire Patriot and State Gazette*, 13 January 1840, 1, describes the origin of Mellen's song, composed at the time of the embargo and given that title. "During that time, when the fears of all the working classes were appealed to with starvation staring them in the face, Mr. Mellen's song ... was circulated throughout the State before an election; it had a fine run for a few weeks — it was even introduced into parties of ladies to be 'said or sung' as a matter of mortification to any straggling democrat who chanced at that time to be let into 'good society.'"

225. Facsimile in Lawrence, 185.

226. This work, cited as "a national song," was awarded the prize medal offered by the Philadelphia Militia Military Association for a contest of 22 poems and 6 musical compositions. *Aurora General Advertiser*, six April, 27 and 30 June, and 4 July 1808, as reported in Cuthbert, "Rayner Taylor and Anglo-American Music Life," 344–45. In 1813 "the following patriotic lines

... from the pen of a senator" in the "western district" of New York, written and set to the tune "Exile of Erin" had this first line: "While Europe's proud kings, o'er creation, are ranging." "Poetry," *Albany Argus*, 13 August 1813, 2.

227. For more on this collection and its contents, see Clyde S. Shive, Jr., "*National Martial Music and Songs*, a Musical First": 92–101.

228. As listed in Wolfe I:327 and II:831, the piece (music and text, first line: "Guardian angels now protect me") was published in the *Songster's Museum* (Northampton, MA: Andrew Wright, 1803).

229. Probably the song composed by William Shield and published in New York by J. Hewitt's Musical Repository & Library in 1807. On title page: "sung with great applause by Mr. Darley." Wolfe II:800.

230. *Pittsfield Sun* cited this as Psalm 74.

231. To the toast: "The Federal Babel in Massachusetts — a monument of confusion, bread at the beginning, terminating in a Gore, or the tip end of a Cobb."

232. Samuel Parker was debenture clerk in the Custom House at Boston. He died in 1831 at the age of 54. "Deaths," *Salem Gazette*, 17 June 1831, 3.

233. Moses L. Neal was "Register of Deeds for the County of Strafford." His "Song" (first line: "Shall New-Hampshire's sons forget"; tune, "Scots wha ha") was published on Independence Day in 1825. He died in Dover in late fall 1829, at the age of 63. He was cited as "an accomplished gentleman, a fine scholar." "Poetry," *New-Hampshire Patriot & State Gazette*, 4 July 1825, 4; *New-Hampshire Gazette*, 30 November and 8 December 1829, 3 and 3, respectively.

234. Spicer names the source for this tune: Joseph Herrick's *Instrumental Preceptor* (1807).

235. In 1843 an individual sent a note to the *New Hampshire Patriot* recalling a "popular song of twenty years since" having this title and submitted the verses for publication: first line, "When the black letter'd list to the gods was presented" (*New Hampshire Patriot and State Gazette*, 16 November 1843, 4). The verses were reportedly composed by "Mr. Spencer, son to the Duke of Marborough" ("Poetry," *Haverhill Museum*, 17 September 1805, 4).

236. Allen composed an ode that had been presented at a meeting of the Providence Association of Mechanics and Manufacturers in 1800 and another at a gathering of the Female Charitable Society of Providence in 1802. Allen, referred to as "a writer of considerable talents, both in prose and verse," had spent the last 12 years of his life in Baltimore as editor of the *Federal Republican*, *Morning Chronicle*, and *The American*. He died in 1826 at the age of 65. *Philadelphia Gazette*, 7 June 1800, 3; *Providence Phoenix*, 21 September 1802, 4; *Baltimore Patriot*, 21 August 1826, 2; *Boston Commercial Gazette*, 24 August 1826, 2.

237. Wolfe II:565.

238. Listed in Wolfe I:182 as "a favorite Italian air by Cimarosa."

239. Hodges was appointed postmaster in Taunton in fall 1810. *Old Colony Gazette*, 21 December 1810, 2.

240. Mr. Stebbins also sang an "Original Ode" in Boston at the Triennial Festival of the Massachusetts Charitable Mechanick Association in December. *Rhode-Island American, and General Advertiser*, 29 December 1809, 3.

241. According to Wolfe I:377, James Hewitt advertised this work in the *New York Evening Post* (12 September 1809) as a "new song just published."

242. Another poem by Price titled "Christmas Hymn" was published in the *Albany Register* (26 December 1809) and reprinted in *Weekly Wanderer* (Randolph, Vermont), 23 February 1810, 4.

243. The lyrics for this song title with first line "Ma chere amie, my charming fair" were printed in *Antihipnotic Songster Containing Original and Select Songs Patriotic, Sentimental, Anacreontic, Comic & Masonic* (Philadelphia: T. Town and S. Merritt, 1818).

244. In 1809 two marches having this title were in print: one by Philip Mauro and the other by Alexander Reinagle, pub-

lished B. Carr's Music Store (Baltimore) and G. Willig (Philadelphia), respectively. See Wolfe II:549 and 730.

245. *Castle Spectre* was a drama originally produced in London and introduced to American audiences in New York at the theater there on June 1, 1798. *Commercial Advertiser*, 31 May 1798, 3.

246. "Plymouth Ode" was composed in 1793 for the anniversary of the landing of the Pilgrims at Plymouth in 1620. *Courier of New Hampshire*, 4 January 1800, 2.

247. Wolfe I:334–35, lists a song with this title ("The New Hail Columbia, or the Birth Place of Liberty") as advertised in 1817 by James Hewitt as "new in publication" and available at his Musical Repository in New York. The first performance of the work may have been that given by Mr. Incledon in New York in 1817. The work is unlocated. See *New York Evening Post*, 22 November 1817.

248. Likely the celebrated actor, originally from the Drury Lane Theatre in London, who performed with the Boston Theatre and at Mechanic Hall in New York. *New-York Herald*, 4 July 1807, 1; *Democrat*, 28 January 1809, 3; *New-York Commercial Advertiser*, 6 June 1809, 2.

249. To the toast: "The liberty of the press; the terror of despots and political jugglers — 1 gun — 9 cheers."

250. Lyrics printed in *The Universal Songster and Museum of Mirth* (Boston: Charles Gaylord, 1835).

251. Noted on the earliest edition of the sheet music (Philadelphia: B. Carr's Musical Repository, 1797): "sung by Mr. Darley, Junr. at the Vauxhall Gardens, Philadelphia and in the Patriot." Sonneck, *A Bibliography of Early Secular American Music, 18th Century*, 175. A song having the same title and first line of text is in *The Baltimore Musical Miscellany, or Columbian Songster* (Baltimore: Sower & Cole, 1804), 49–50. See Wolfe I:335.

252. First line: "James Madison, my Joe-Jem, now tell us what you mean." Verses printed in *Vermont Courier*, 27 May 1809, 4. Another newspaper also printed the text and had this note about the song: "It is a very pretty parody of the popular and well known song of 'John Anderson My Joe, John.' The word Joe, in the Scottish dialect is sweetheart." "Poetry," *Salem Gazette*, 27 June 1809, 4. The toast that preceding the song was: "James Madison, President of the United States — while he shall desert the interests of a party, and pursue a true national policy, he will merit our approbation."

253. Listed in Wolfe I:145, as published in *Boston Musical Miscellany* (1815) 2:34–36, and to be sung to the tune of "Ye Gentlemen of England." Advertised for sale in 1813 at D. Longworth on Park [Avenue], New York. *National Advocate*, 9 January 1813, 1.

254. The editor of the *Independent American* (Georgetown), 15 August 1810, 3, published a response to a critique of the poem in the *Freeman's Journal*. He disagreed with the latter newspaper's editor who characterized certain passages in Paine's work as simply evoking "mystery and paradox."

255. Printed in James J. Wilson, *A National Song-Book, being a Collection of Patriotic, Martial, and Naval Songs and Odes, Principally of American Composition* (Trenton: James J. Wilson, 1813), 43, as reported in Sonneck, *Report on The Star-Spangled Banner*, 26.

256. Edward D. Bangs (1790–1838) was Massachusetts secretary of state and son of Edward Bangs. Bangs presented an oration in Worcester on July 4, 1819. He died in 1838. *Massachusetts Spy, or Worcester Gazette*, 7 July 1819, 3; *New Bedford Mercury*, 5 April 1838, 2.

257. Printed under the title "Freedom" in James J. Wilson, *A National Song-Book, being a Collection of Patriotic, Martial, and Naval Songs and Odes, Principally of American Composition* (Trenton: James J. Wilson, 1813), 70, as reported in Sonneck, *Report on The Star-Spangled Banner*, 26. Lyrics printed in William McCarty, *The New National Song Book, Containing Songs, Odes, and Other Poems, on National subjects. Compiled from Various Sources* (New York: Leavitt and Allen, 184–?).

258. A song titled "Retaliation" is printed in *The Nightingale* (Portsmouth, 1804), 255–57, as reported in Wolfe II:733.

259. Performed at the National Theatre in Washington on

July 4, 1809, under the title *Independence of Columbia*. See 1809, District of Columbia.

260. As reported in Linda Davenport, *Divine Song on the Northeast Frontier: Maine's Sacred Tunebooks, 1800–1830* (Lanham, MD: Scarecrow, 1996), 34.

261. This popular Irish tune had one of its earliest printings in *The Gift of Apollo* (New York, 1802?), no. [2], p. 16. Listed in Wolfe I:317; tune printed in Kate Van Winkle Keller, *Dance and Its Music in America, 1528–1789* (Hillsdale, NY: Pendragon, 2007), 456. The tune was typically cited in the newspapers examined as "Go to the Devil and Shake Yourself."

262. Cole compiled two collections of music: *A Collection of Psalm Tunes and Anthems* (1803) and *David's Harp* (1813).

263. The author of this "hymn" borrowed the first line and other portions of the lyrics from William Billings song "Chester."

264. This song was previously sung at a meeting of the Hibernian Provident Society in 1810 at an anniversary event of the society. "Hibernian Provident Society," *Public Advertiser*, 20 March 1810, 3.

265. To the toast: "Simon Synder governor of Pennsylvania. The Patriot, the Statesman and the friend of man. 3 guns."

266. A comic song sung in various theaters, one of the earliest in the City Theatre, Charleston, South Carolina, in 1796. *Columbian Herald*, 11 April 1796, 3.

267. Accompanied the toast: "The Sons of Tammany — may the virtues of patriotism, sincerity and hospitality, united with an inextinguishable love of liberty, ever remain their 'savage' characteristics."

268. Accompanied the toast: "The memory of Stephen Hopkins whose signature has pledged us to support the glorious declaration of Independence."

269. Accompanied the toast: "May we cherish the remembrance of those times, when private virtue was the road to public honour."

270. Accompanied a toast to Timothy Pickering.

271. According to information published on the sheet music (Baltimore: J. Carr's; New York: J. Hewitt's, 1797), an earlier performance of this song by Mr. Darley occurred in Philadelphia at Vauxhall Gardens.

272. Story had given orations in Salem on July 4, 1804, and July 4, 1808, at the new South Meeting House. *The Repertory*, 29 June 1804, 3, and *Essex Register*, 2 July 1808, 3. His ode was popular and had several Independence Day performances and reprintings.

273. Reprinted with a slightly varied first line ("Welcome! welcome the day, when, assembled as one") in William McCarty, *The New National Song Book, Containing Songs, Odes, and Other Poems, on National subjects. Compiled from Various Sources* (New York: Leavitt and Allen, 184–?).

274. Peter Bryant (1767–1820) was father of the noted poet William Cullen Bryant. Peter was born at West Bridgewater, Massachusetts, studied medicine, and lived most of his life at Cummington, Massachusetts, where he died. *Historical Magazine and Notes and Queries Concerning the Antiquities* [June 1873]: 334. For more information on Peter Bryant and his poetry, see Donald M. Murray, "Dr. Peter Bryant: Preceptor in Poetry to William Cullen Bryant," *New England Quarterly* 33/4 (December 1960): 513–22.

275. Brazer was editor of the *National Aegis* in Worcester, Massachusetts, and later assistant editor of the *Baltimore Patriot*. He was born in Worcester and "as a poet he had some claims to celebrity." On July 4, 1811, Brazer gave an oration in Charleton, Massachusetts, and he advertised a print edition of his presentation in his newspaper. Brazer died in Baltimore on February 24, 1823 at the age of 38 or 40 (according to various accounts). *National Aegis*, 24 July 1811, 1; *Baltimore Patriot*, 28 February 1823, 2; *Essex Register*, 6 March 1823, 3; *New Hampshire Sentinel*, 22 March 1823, 3.

276. Wolfe I:27.

277. This popular song was sung by Mr. McFarland at the Washington Theatre on June 16, 1817, and at the Alexandria Theatre on June 19, 1817. *National Intelligencer*, 16 June 1817, 3;

Alexandria Herald, 18 June 1817, 3. The lyrics were published under song title "Arouse! Arouse! Columbia's Sons Arouse!" in *Antihipnotic Songster* (1818). Lyrics also printed in William McCarty, *The New National Song Book, Containing Songs, Odes, and Other Poems, on National Subjects. Compiled from Various Sources* (New York: Leavitt and Allen, 184–?).

278. McFarland was popular in theatrical circles as a singer of patriotic songs; for example, "Arouse, Arouse, Columbia's Sons Arouse" (July 4, 1812), New York City, and "Let Patriotic Pride Our Patriot Triumph Awake" and "Columbia, Land of Liberty" (1817), Alexandria, Virginia. *Columbian*, 3 July 1812, 3; *Alexandria Gazette*, 19 June 1817, 3. McFarland was also cited as a singer of "The Star Spangled Banner" aside the lyrics printed in *Antihipnotic Songster* (1818).

279. Graupner's publication of this work was "corrected" by Paine prior to being issued. *Columbian Centinel*, 3 August 1811, 3. Paine's work continued to be sung after the Fourth of July. For example, at the Providence Theatre (Rhode Island) on September 3, 1811, the song was sung after the first play of the evening was presented. *Rhode-Island American*, 3 September 1811, 3.

280. Sargent was a Boston poet. He married Mary Binney of Philadelphia in May 1816, who died on February 2, 1824. *Franklin Herald*, 14 May 1816, 3; *Rhode-Island American*, 10 February 1824, 3. Sargent later became involved in the temperance movement and gave addresses on that behalf.

281. Woodworth was born in 1785 in Scituate, Massachusetts, and had a considerable reputation as a poet. He wrote a number of Independence Day odes; one of the earliest likely written in Scituate was his "Ode, sung at the celebration of Independence by the Society of Juvenile Patriots" (first line: "When from our shores Bellona's car"). In 1809 Woodworth had moved to New York City where he wrote a set of three Odes for the Fourth: (first lines: "The Genius of Freedom, escap'd from the flood"; "When the fiend of fell discord has delug'd in gore"; "Come crowd around the festive board"). Another noteworthy patriotic ode he wrote and published in 1827 was "Freedom's Star" (first line: "Hail, star of freedom, hail"). *Vermont Gazette*, 17 July 1827, 1. His collections include *The Poems, Odes, Songs, and Other Metrical Effusions, of Samuel Woodworth* (1818), *Melodies, Duets, Trios, Songs, and Ballads, Pastoral, Amatory, Sentimental, Patriotic, Religious, and Miscellaneous* (1830), and *The Poetical Works of Samuel Woodworth* (1861), 2 vols. edited by Woodworth's son.

282. Reins was a member of the Society. In 1829 he was elected secretary. *Baltimore Patriot*, 2 July 1829, 2.

283. Reprinted in *American Advocate and Kennebec Advertiser*, 24 May 1817, 4.

284. An "Ode, by J. Story" listed in the contents for a songster titled *The Star Spangled Banner: Being a Collection of the Best Naval, Martial, Patriotic Songs, &c* as advertised for sale at the Watchman Printing Office and Bookstore in Wilmington, Delaware, in 1816. *American Watchman*, 15 May 1816, 2.

285. Possibly a tune from the "grand melo drama" *Tekeli; Or, the Siege of Montgate*, performed in Boston in 1810–11. *Boston Gazette*, 18 October 1810, 3.

286. The *Mercantile Advertiser* (New York), 11 June 1800, 2, advertised a new song to be published, "The Death of Crazy Jane." The song was an immediate success, likely first sung in New York, and subsequently in theaters and other locations across New England and elsewhere. According to a note in the *New-York Evening Post*, 29 December 1801, 2, "numerous imitations" of the song were subsequently published. Some of these included: "Sequel to Crazy Jane," "Crazy Paul," "Crazy George," "Crazy Jane's Epitaph," and "Junr. Crazy Jane." One rendition of the song, likely the original, was published in "The Muses," *Farmer's Weekly Museum*, 8 December 1801, 4: first line, "Why, fair maid, in every feature." See Wolfe for various published editions.

287. To the toast: "Timothy Pickering — Five such men would have saved Sodom."

288. Accompanied the toast: "General Madison's Orders: Fire! but first see that nobody's in the way."

289. To the toast: "Old Salem — again *bewitched*: May those who exercise the *black art* soon boil in their own cauldron."

290. To the toast: "Salem Light Infantry Company — The supporters of good principles, and defenders of their country."

291. Sung to the following toast: "Alexander Hamilton — 'We will cherish thy memory; we will embalm thy fame' — (drank standing)."

292. Sung to the following toast: "Fisher Ames — 'Thy country wept, when, on her natal day, Heaven claimed its own and beckoned thee away.'" Ames, a member of Congress, died on July 4, 1808.

293. Accompanied the toast: "The illustrious traitors, Pickering, Burr, and Otis; and their popgun army of Boston who are to resist the general government. Let a hemp harvest reward the three first, and may their Lilliputian tribe of echo's be wafter to mother Britain by the first fair breeze in a fleet of cock-boats."

294. Handy was grand secretary of the Rhode Island Grand Lodge of Free and Accepted Masons. On April 30, 1811, he and fellow musician Levi Tower received thanks from the Lodge for music they provided that day at an assemblage of members that was held at the First Baptist Church in Newport. *Providence Gazette*, 16 October 1802, 1; *Rhode-Island Republican*, 1 May 1811, 3.

295. An early publication of this march was in *A Favourite Selection of Music* (Dedham, 1806), 4, as listed in Wolfe I:293.

296. Possibly "Gen. Bates' Quick March," printed in 1807 and listed in Wolfe II:790.

297. Wolfe II:675.

298. Wolfe II:675.

299. Thomas, Jr. (1771–1837), son of the Rev. Thomas Fessenden, was editor of the *New England Farmer* and in 1817 the *Vermont Intelligencer*. He had spent time in England where he "acquired uncommon eminence as a poet." He was considered "a man of excellent principles, and author of several useful publications well known to the public." *Political Observatory*, 14 July 1804, 2; *Newburyport Herald*, 7 March 1817, 1; *Connecticut Courant*, 18 November 1837, 3.

300. Foster, attached to the 3rd Regiment, U.S. Artillery, wrote a poem titled "The Dying Soldier." *The Patrol*, 16 February 1815, 4.

301. Wolfe I:386.

302. Printed and attributed to E.D. Bangs in William McCarty, *The New National Song Book, Containing Songs, Odes, and Other Poems, on National subjects. Compiled from Various Sources* (New York: Leavitt and Allen, 184–?).

303. "Old Johnny" refers to England and how "We'll clear the land of all his rogues." The tune used for this ditty was likely "Yankee Doodle."

304. Listed in Lowens, *A Bibliography of Songsters Printed in America before 1821*, 129.

305. Performed following this toast: "The Navy — No 'Leopard' shall hereafter leave a spot on its honor." Refers to the shelling of the USS *Chesapeake* by the English frigate *Leopard* in June 1807, resulting in several American sailors killed and their ship suffering severe damage.

306. Accompanied the toast: "Our impressed seamen — the thunder of the American cannon shall rive their prisons, and restore them to freedom and their native land."

307. Peter Dolliver was also a pianist who performed occasionally at Bowen's Columbian Museum in Boston from 1797 to 1803, and in 1824. In Salem in 1809 he led a concert at St. Peter's Church and in 1824 played the apollino at the Boston Museum. *Massachusetts Mercury*, 14 November 1797, 2; *The Gazetteer*, 6 July 1803, 4; *Salem Gazette*, 22 December 1809, 3; *Boston Patriot*, 26 May 1824, 3.

308. Len Travers, *Celebrating the Fourth: Independence Day and the Rites of Nationalism in the Early Republic* (Amherst: University of Massachusetts Press, 1997), 195–96.

309. An 1813 print edition (words and music) of "Hail Columbia" was published in *The American Patriotic Songbook* (Philadelphia: W. M'Culloch, 1813). Facsimile in Lawrence, 170.

310. According to George Thornton Edwards, *Music and Musicians of Maine* (Portland, ME: Southworth Press, 1928), as reported in Gordon W. Bowie, "R.B. Hall and the Community Bands of Maine" (Ph.D. dissertation, University of Maine, 1993), 52, this was the first instance of a band performing in Maine.

311. To the toast: "The Enemies of our Government — Who Judas like, betray their country, may they meet the fate of spies, and traitors, or make their exit."

312. To the toast: "By the Orator — Our Union — May those who would dissolve it, speedily find an asylum in the 'world's last hope.'"

313. The reporter is referring to the band either playing out of tune or incorrect notes unintentionally creating a dissonant sound. William Billings' composition titled "Jargon" was a unique work purposely composed to create clashing and jarring sounds, perhaps for the amusement of his listeners.

314. On July 4, 2008, an "1813 Independence Day Celebration" included reenactors, an 18-gun salute, toasts, and fife and drum music. *Fort Meigs State Memorial Park website*, accessed August 1, 2008, http://www.fortmeigs.org/.

315. A melody and bass rendition of "God Save America" is in *The American Patriotic Song Book* (Philadelphia: W. M'Culloch, 1813), 39–40. First line: "God save America, free from tyrannic sway." To the tune "God Save the King." See Wolfe I:317.

316. Listed in Lowens, *A Bibliography of Songsters Printed in America before 1821*, 158.

317. Knight (1789–1835) "was a clergyman of the Protestant Episcopal Church and a poet of some distinction." His collections include *Broken Harp* (Philadelphia: J. Conrad, 1815) and a two-volume set, *Poems* (Boston: Wells and Lilly, 1821). About "The Birth-Day of Freedom," the editor of the *Port Folio*, thought the work had "great merit" but that "with all the ballad excellence which it possesses, it wants, we think, certain qualities essential to a permanent national song — such a one as time must render more and more popular, and ultimately incorporate with the sentiments of the people." "National Song," *Port Folio* (July 1814), 129.

318. Note in *Otsego Herald*: "The following patriotic song is from the pen of Captain Josiah Dunham, late editor of the celebrated Vermont *Washingtonian*. The sentiments it breathes are such as must inspire every American, on a day, and at a time when local jealousies, foreign partialities and party spirit, should yield to a genuine glow of liberty and love of country."

319. Place of publication and residency of authors of odes in Worcester identified in *Dexter's Yale Graduates*, vol. 6, p. 481.

320. Probably the tune of the song composed by Alexander Reinagle, words by C. Harford, ca. 1804. Wolfe II:731.

321. Song (from the opera *The Mountaineers*), composed by Samuel Arnold (1740–1802) and published in Philadelphia in 1807. Wolfe I:27.

322. Alternate title "Sandy's Ghost" published in the *Baltimore Musical Miscellany* (1805) and other publications listed in Wolfe II:732.

323. Published under the title "The Topsails Shiver in the Wind" in the *Baltimore Musical Miscellany* (1804). Wolfe I:17.

324. Francesco Masi and his brother Vincent, a dancing master, sailed on board the USS *Washington* to Annapolis in May 1816. Other passengers included the Carusi family, an Italian-born musical family who participated in Fourth of July celebrations. All of these musicians eventually lived in Washington, D.C. James R. Heintze, "'Tyranny and Despotic Violence': An Incident Aboard the U.S.S. *Washington*," *Maryland Historical Magazine* 94/1 (Spring 1999): 37–38.

325. Governor Elbridge Gerry of Massachusetts, 1810–12.

326. Derived from the song "The Birthday of Freedom," composed by F. Yaniewicz, ca.1804 and reissued likely in the following year under the title "The Battle of Derne," referring to "General Eaton's march across the desert to capture the town of Derna in 1805, during the American war with the pirates of Tripoli." Wolfe I:447–48.

327. Governor Caleb Strong of Massachusetts, 1800–07 and 1812–16. *Governor Strong's March* (Boston: G. Graupner, 1813) and *Governor Strong's New March*, composed and published

(New York, 1813?) by James Hewitt, is listed in Wolfe I:320–21 and 375, respectively.

328. Several earlier arrangements of this work, composed by Michael Kelly, are listed in Wolfe.

329. Editions were published in Northampton, Baltimore, Philadelphia, and New York under the titles "There's Nae Luck about the House" and "Nae Luck about the House." Wolfe II:905.

330. To the toast: "The Administration of the United States — May they find some other way to keep up their popularity, if they must continue in office, besides ruining the resources and reputation of our country. 3 groans."

331. To the toast "The Commander in Chief of the Militia of New Jersey."

332. Possibly "The American Patriot's Prayer" by Thomas Paine, "written in the year 1775." First line: "Parent of all omnipotent." *Democrat*, 22 August 1804, 2.

333. In the *New-York Herald*, the author describes how the ode was written by him in 1798 when he was a boy and the words were "suggested by a consideration of the relative situation of the U.S. and France" at that time.

334. Susanna Haswell who "acquired a considerable reputation ... for her literary attainments." Haswell came to this country as a young girl and was provided an excellent education. She married William Rowson in the 1780s and began publishing novels and other literary works. In the early 1790s, Susanna "was engaged in the Philadelphia theatrical company." She wrote the libretto for an opera titled *The Volunteers* (1795), "a farce after the whiskey insurrection in Pennsylvania, and a work titled the *Female Patriot*. "Mrs. Rowson came to Boston in 1796, and was engaged for that year at the Federal Street Theatre.... Odes, for Masonic purposes, hymns for charitable associations, & songs for patriotic festivals came from her pen too numerous to mention singly; and each of them did credit to her poetical powers." Susanna Rowson died in Boston on March 2, 1824. "Female Literature," *Eastern Argus*, 23 March 1824, 1. For more information on Haswell, see Maureen J. Ladd, "The Feminine Perspective: Six Early American Women Writers" (Ph.D. dissertation, University of Delaware, 1982).

335. Reprinted a year later in *Shamrock*, 3 August 1816, 360.

336. This is the first identified work published for the Fourth of July to borrow lyrics from Francis Scott Key's "Star Spangled Banner." The author, signed "Leander," used the phrase "O'er the land of the free and the home of the brave."

337. Listed in the contents for a songster titled *The Star Spangled Banner: Being a Collection of the Best Naval, Martial, Patriotic Songs, &c* as advertised for sale at the Watchman Printing Office and Bookstore in Wilmington, Delaware, in 1816. *American Watchman*, 15 May 1816, 2.

338. Jeremiah Fellowes (1791–1865).

339. This song was first published anonymously under the title "The Defence of Fort McHenry." See, for example, *The War*, 6 September 1814, 54; *Baltimore American*, 17 September 1814; and *Baltimore Patriot*, 20 September 1814, 2. The editor of the latter newspaper noted with keen foresight: "The following beautiful and animating effusion, which is destined long to outlast the occasion, and outlive the impulse, which produced it." First line: "O! say can you see, by the dawn's early light." Facsimiles of "Defence" and the first publication of Key's poem with the printed tune is in William Lichtenwanger, "Richard S. Hill and the Unsettled Text of the Star Spangled Banner," in *Richard S. Hill: Tributes from Friends* (Detroit 1987), 70, 140, 142–43. The use of the words "star spangled banner" derives from the phrase "by the light of the star-spangled flag of our nation" in a song composed by "a gentlemen from Georgetown" and "prepared for the occasion about an hour before dinner" that was held in honor of Capt. Stephen Decatur, Jr., and Charles Stewart at McLaughlin's Tavern in Georgetown on December 6, 1805. Lyrics in the song that was accompanied in the performance by two clarinets "and the company joining in the chorus," bear other similarities to the "Star-Spangled Banner" leading one to conclude that the "gentleman from Georgetown" was Key. First line: "When the warrior returns from the battle afar,"

set to the tune "Anacreon." *American Citizen*, 21 December 1805, 2. See also the article, "Star Spangled Banner," in Heintze, *The Fourth of July Encyclopedia*, 269–71; Francis Scott Key, *Poems* (New York: Robert Carter & Brothers, 1857).

340. To the toast, "Massachusetts — she has shown by melancholy example, how degraded a brave people may appear, when guided, by weak and infatuated rulers."

341. To the toast, "The Hartford Convention — a demon who has whet the sword of civil war, and has only laid it aside until there is less danger, of himself becoming the victim." Refers to the convention in Hartford whereby New England's opposition to the War of 1812 resulted in discussion of secession from the United States.

342. Probably Capt. John Coolidge who sang on the Fourth in Worcester in 1820. A newspaper reported Capt. John Coolidge of Worcester as the second son of Nathaniel Coolidge and John's death at the age of 25 in Worcester in January 1824. *Independent Chronicle and Boston Patriot*, 24 January 1824, 1.

343. The Londonderry Musical Society was "incorporated" in 1808. *Farmers' Cabinet*, 27 December 1808, 3.

344. At a dinner that followed, "the following toast was given by the Washington Benevolent Society of Londonderry, to the band of music from Haverhill, who volunteered their services — The gentlemen from Haverhill — the harmony of their Society has been equal to the harmony of their music."

345. Pritchard was a veteran actor and considered "a favorite of the New York audience." He performed in a number of patriotic productions, such as *Glory of Columbia, or What We Have Done We Can Do* (January 1816), *She Would Be a Soldier, or the Battle of Chippewa* (July 1819) and *Tars from Tripoli, or The Heroes of Columbia* (July 1819). *New-York Courier*, 8 January 1816, 3; *New-York Daily Advertiser*, 5 July 1819, 2; *New-York Evening Post*, 7 May 1821, 2.

346. Similar tune titles appear in various newspaper in 1814–15: "Far Off at Sea" to be sung to the lyrics titled "The Patriotic Diggers" in *True American*, 7 September 1814, 4, and *Columbian Patriot*, 12 October 1814, 4; "Great Way Off at Sea, or, Love and Whisky" in *The Columbian*, 12 April 1815, 3.

347. See Peter Wolfe's diary in Vincent A. Cannino, "Celebrating the Fourth in Salem" (M.A. thesis, University of North Carolina at Greensboro, 1998), 49.

348. To the toast: "The Vermont and New York militia on the ever memorable 11th September, 1814 — The goddess of liberty descended, dropped on their brows the wreaths of victory, and stamped on their actions the seal of omnipotence. 'Whom God delights to honor we will praise.'"

349. According to newspaper reports, "Hotham's Victory" (first line: "Come, all ye noble host"), "celebrates the ironical satire, the capture of the President frigate, by Admiral Hotham's British squadron." *New Jersey Journal*, 11 July 1815, 4; *National Aegis*, 12 July 1815, 4; *Pittsfield Sun*, 13 July 1815, 1.

350. Song published in "Weekly Song-Book," seven books (Philadelphia" H.C. Lewis, 1818), book 7. Advertised with songs listed in *Ladys and Gentlemans Weekly Museum and Philadelphia Reporter* (1818): 32.

351. This song with lyrics, and author cited as J.N. Barker, is printed in *Antihipnotic Songster* (1818).

352. Accompanied the toast: "The President — He holds the pen of a ready writer, and ably fills the chair of state."

353. To the toast: "The battles of Plattsburgh and Put-in-Bay — The waves of the Lakes too boisterous for 'Rule Britannia.'"

354. For information on this band and the Carusi family of musicians, see James R. Heintze, "Gaetano Carusi: From Sicily to the Halls of Congress," in *American Musical Life in Context and Practice to 1865*, 75–131.

355. Aaron Ball advertised services for his singing school in Elizabethtown in 1787. *New Jersey Journal*, 14 February 1787, 4.

356. Daniel D. Tompkins (1774–1825) was governor of New York, 1807–17, and served as vice president under James Monroe. Tompkins was an active participant in Fourth of July events. *Governor Tompkin's March*, composed and published (New York, 1807–1810) by James Hewitt, is listed in Wolfe I:375. *Governor*

Tompkin's Grand March, composed by T. Cooke and published in New York (1817–1818) is listed in Wolfe I:211.

357. Likely "Hull's Victory or, Huzza for the Constitution." First line, for verses from an 1812 edition: "Ye true sons of freedom, give ear to my song." *An American Time Capsule: Three Centuries of Broadsides and Other Printed Ephemera*, Library of Congress. The song refers to the defeat of the HMS *Guerriere* by the USS *Constitution*, commanded by Isaac Hull, on August 19, 1812. See *The Columbian Naval Songster* (New York: Edward Gillespy, 1813) that includes "50 original songs" of naval victories of Hull and 4 other naval commanders. The work advertised as just published in *National Advocate*, 29 May 1813, 4.

358. To the toast "Animosity and party spirit — may they subside, and the two great political parties be united in one. 6 cheers."

359. Richard Wolfe II:890, proposes that, based on a listing in the Richmond city directory of 1856, Sally Sully was a "professor music" in that city and was probably the same "Miss S. Sully" as noted in the sheet music.

360. His father, Edward Bangs, was present and heard his son's ode sung.

361. Peter Gilles, Sr., published *President Monroe's March* (for piano and an accompaniment for flute or violin) likely in New York, ca. March 1817. A tune with that title also published in *Riley's Flute Melodies* in 1818. *New-York Daily Advertiser*, 6 February 1818, 3. Gilles was a music teacher, composer, and instrumentalist (oboe and English horn) in New York. Wolfe I:315. There were a number of other marches composed in honor of Monroe. Facsimile pages of examples of P.K. Moran, Stephen Cristiani, and an "amateur" are in Lawrence, 224–25.

362. Music composed by Victor Pelissier and first published in Baltimore, Carr's music store, ca. 1807, as listed in Wolfe II:674.

363. An Irish tune composed by James Hook (1746–1827). Several editions in Wolfe.

364. For information on musicians at West Point at that time, see Howe, "Early American Military Music," 105–10. According to Howe, the band had at least 18 players. The academy was formally opened on July 4, 1802. The U.S. Military Academy Band was first organized by Richard Willis, "prominent musician, composer and inventor of the E-flat keyed bugle." Heintze, *The Fourth of July Encyclopedia*, 311–12.

365. A song having this title was composed by James Hewitt and published in 1800 (New York, J. Hewitt's Musical Repository). Listed in Heard, *American Music 1698–1800: An Annotated Bibliography*, 99. Various editions and music are discussed in Charles Hamm, *Yesterdays: Popular Song in America* (New York: W.W. Norton, 1979), 32–34.

366. Toast: "The honourable John Marshal, Chief Justice of the United States — the compass of legal and political science."

367. Toast: "The constitution of the United States — Its energies have been tested: happily adapted to peace or war."

368. To the toast: "South America — Success to her struggles for independence. 2 guns." For information on this tune that had become officially associated with the president of the United States, see Elise K. Kirk, "'Hail to the Chief': The Origins and Legacies of an American Ceremonial Tune," *American Music* 15/2 (Summer 1997): 123–36; Heintze, *The Fourth of July Encyclopedia*, 131–32. An early printing of its text "Hail to the Chief who in triumph advances" (first line) was printed in *Antihipnotic Songster* (1818).

369. Storer was asked to recite a poem at the celebration of Federal Republicans of Portland on July 4, 1816. *Portland Gazette and Maine Advertiser*, 25 June 1816, 2.

370. Also printed in *Antihipnotic Songster* (1818), with the tune designated "Hail to the Chief" as sung by "Mr. M'Farland [McFarland].

371. In this year (1818), the lyrics of "Life let us cherish, while yet the taper glows" (first line) were published in *Antihipnotic Songster* (1818).

372. Likely the same work sung at the New York's Typographical Society meeting on the Fourth in 1811. See Publications, 1811. Another song with the same title, "The Art of Print-ing," written by Joseph Kite, was sung to the tune "Hail to the Chief" at an anniversary celebration of the Typographical Association at Philadelphia in 1818. First line: "Chaunt we that act which all others advances." *Baltimore Patriot & Mercantile Advertiser*, 14 November 1818, 2.

373. To the toast: "Benjamin Franklin — The professor and patron of our art — Who, from a small capital, acquired a capital reputation, and became one of the most conspicuous characters in the headline of American worthies."

374. This regiment army band commanded by Col. Henry Atkinson was considered one of the finest and popular ensembles at that time. They performed in a variety of entertainments including a steamboat excursion in 1817 and for President James Monroe when he visited Plattsburgh in July of that year. The regiment itself consisted of some 600 men. By May 1819 the regiment and band had left Plattsburgh, reassigned to a "Missouri Expedition" with a final destination of "Yellow Stone," now Wyoming. By 1820 they wound up at the site of what is now Fort Atkinson State Historical Park, north of Omaha, Nebraska. *Plattsburgh Republican*, 19 July 1817, 2 and 20 March 1819, 3; "The President," *Essex Register*, 6 August 1817, 3; *Vermont Gazette*, 15 June 1819, 2. For additional tunes in the band's repertoire, see *Plattsburgh Republican*, 20 March 1819, 3. See also, Fort Atkinson (1824) and reenactment ceremonies in 2007 and 2008.

375. Possibly *Carolan's Concerto* (published 1808–09), an Irish tune, listed in Wolfe I:150. Here the tune accompanied the toast: "Peace — May its olive wave over every free country and every enslaved one fight till they are free."

376. Composed by Charles P.F. O'Hara and printed in his collection *The Gentleman's Musical Repository* (1813). See Wolfe II:650. Here the tune accompanied the toast: "The State of New-York — The largest and strongest link in the chain of our union."

377. A song titled "Decatur's Return," to the tune "Anacreon in Heaven," and having the identical first line is published in *American Beacon and Commercial Diary*, 5 April 1816, 2.

378. "Paddy Carey" with first line, "Twas at the town of nate Clogheen," in *Antihipnotic Songster* (1818), *The Universal Songster and Museum of Mirth* (Boston: Charles Gaylord, 1835), and *The American Vocalist, Containing the Best Collection of the Most Popular Sentimental, Patriotic, Comic, Irish, and Other Songs* (New York: Huestis & Cozans, 1853).

379. Scott C. Martin, *Killing Time: Leisure and Culture in Southwestern Pennsylvania, 1800–1850* (Pittsburgh: University of Pittsburgh Press, 1995), 82–83.

380. To the toast "The Governor of South Carolina — Regardless of unmerited censure, he pursues the dictates of justice and impartiality."

381. Accompanied the toast "Old Iron Sides — she remains at once a model of architecture, and a monument of naval glory."

382. Holland, a resident of Charleston, South Carolina, "was a young man of uncommon talents — the author of several controversial publications of merit — a writer of talent and interest — at one time editor of *Charleston Times*, and author of several poetical pieces, among which was the prize ode, called 'The Pillar of Glory.'" Holland died in 1824 at the age of 35. *Salem Gazette*, 28 September 1824, 3. "The Pillar of Glory" first published in *Port Folio* ser 4, v. 2/5 (Nov. 1813), *Dedham Gazette*, 17 December 1813, 4, and in sheet music format: Philadelphia: G. E. Blake, [1813?]; New York: J. Appel, [1813]. *Secular Music in America, 1801–1825*, I:263–64, 309.

383. First line: "Hail, hail to the heroes whose triumphs have brighten'd." Holland "was awarded a medal of the value of one hundred dollars" for this work. The music was composed by Charles Gilfert. *Olio*, 20 November 1813, 354; *Dedham Gazette*, 17 December 1813, 4; listed in Wolfe I:309. Advertised for sale by Inskeep & Bradford of New York in their periodical *Port Folio* 5/2 (November 1813). *New-York Herald*, 13 November 1813, 4. The lyrics were also published in *Antihipnotic Songster* (1818).

384. John M'Creery was referred to as the "bard" of Petersburg. In 1810, he was elected principal of the Petersburg Acad-

emy. In 1822, he wrote "a beautiful Ode" in celebration of the "Third Virginiad," held at Jamestown on May 24 that year. He died in 1825. *Virginia. Shamrock or Hibernian Chronicle*, 15 December 1810, 3; *Watch-Tower*, 10 June 1822, 1; *New-Hampshire Patriot & State Gazette*, 8 July 1822, 4; "Deaths," *Rhode Island American*, 2 September 1825, 1.

385. This tune is titled "Bruce's Address" but was frequently referred to by its first line "Scots wha hae wi' Wallace bled."

386. According to information published in *Washington Society: An Historical View* (Boston, 1823), the author was Francis Mores Adlington (1789–1884).

387. Dana was a native of Amherst, New Hampshire, who entered the army in 1814. He was attached to the 1st Regiment, U.S. Artillery, and at the time of his death at Ft. McHenry on February 4, 1833, he had achieved the rank of Captain. *New-Hampshire Gazette*, 19 February 1833, 3.

388. Fort Constitution is located near New Castle, New Hampshire, and construction was completed in 1808. The event took place in 1818, according to newspaper reports.

389. William Billings published "Jargon" in his collection *The Singing Master's Assistant* (1778). For modern reprints, see *Complete Works of William Billings* II:263, and Marrocco, *Music in America*, 113.

390. Sonneck, *A Bibliography of Early Secular American Music, 18th Century*, 456–57, lists pieces with this title published in Philadelphia, Boston, and New York, 1793, ca. 1795 and 1799.

391. Listed in Wolfe I:146 as written by L.M. Sargent, published in 1812, and originally "sung at the dinner given to the officers of the United States Frigate *Constitution* after the victory over the British Frigate *Guerrier*." A reprinting of the music from the "Boston magazine *Polyanthos* (1812)" is in Spicer, "Popular Song for Public Celebration," 69.

392. To the toast: "The American Fair — Their smiles and approbation, the soldiers best and richest reward. 9 cheers." An advertisement for a concert in New York in November 1809 attributes the music to J. Willson and lyrics by Thomas Moore. *Evening Post*, 16 November 1809, 2. The lyrics were also published in *Green Mountain Farmer*, 1 October 1810, 4, and *Northern Post*, 31 August 1815, 4.

393. Accompanied this toast: "The River Mississippi — An emblem of the great republic, of which it will become the centre; its rapidity her march to power and intelligence; as it throws its waters into the great gulph, so will that republic give into the vast ocean of future times the purest waves of national feeling and virtue that ever laved the rainbow lined column of history."

394. Pratt also maintained a local grocery store in Providence and was a member of the Psallonian Society, a musical association that had given concerts in Providence as early as 1811. *Rhode-Island American, and General Advertiser*, 9 January 1821, 3.

395. Cited in Crew, *Presidential Sheet Music*, 287.

396. The Reverend Tappan's talents were exhibited in a number of collections, including *New-England and Other Poems* (1819). He "devoted a large portion of his life to the cause of sabbath schools" in the New England area. *Columbian Centinel*, 25 September 1819, 4; *Farmers' Cabinet*, 20 September 1849, 2. Tappan wrote a poem on the occasion "for the fiftieth anniversary celebration of American independence at Trenton" (first line: "When thy own Israel, God of love!" "Poetry," *Portsmouth Journal of Literature and Politics*, 5 August 1826, 4.

397. Possible date based on the Franklin Square location of the firm through advertisements in local newspapers at that time.

398. Advertised as just published and for sale in New York in number 9 of *Riley's Flute Melodies* (*New York Daily Advertiser*, 13 August 1818, 3).

399. Composed by O. Shaw and published in Thomas Moore's *Sacred Melodies. Boston Gazette*, 3 April 1817, 3. Full text (first line: "This world is all a fleeting show") in "Poetry," *The Reporter*, 25 August 1818, 4.

400. To the toasts: "The surviving patriots of the Revolution — [drank standing]."

401. Probably the piece of the same title written by Samuel

Woodworth, published in New York on July 2, 1818, by E. Riley, and subsequently a favorite song sung on the Fourth by several popular singers. It was composed to the tune, "Bruce's Address to His Army." First line: Freedom's jubilee again." *New-York Columbian*, 6 July 1818, 3. "Freedom's Jubilee" was advertised for sale by Mack & Morgan's Book Store in Ithaca, NY. *Ithaca Journal*, 23 July 1823, 3.

402. An edition published in "Weekly Song-Book," seven books (Philadelphia) H.C. Lewis, 1818, book 1, and in *The Universal Songster and Museum of Mirth* (Boston: Charles Gaylord, 1835). Advertised in *Ladys and Gentlemans Weekly Museum and Philadelphia Reporter* (1818): 32.

403. *Raising the Wind: A Farce in Two Acts* by James Kenney (1780–1849).

404. "Giles Scroggins Ghost: A Favorite Comic Song" (Philadelphia: G.E. Blake, 1806) by William Reeve (1757–1815).

405. The ode was printed in *The Universal Songster and Museum of Mirth* (Boston: Charles Gaylord, 1835) and to be sung to the tune "Scots wha hae," and also printed under the title "Ode for the Fourth of July" in Griswold, in *The Poets and Poetry of America*, 104.

406. To the toast: "The State of Maine — a copartnership dissolved by mutual consent. In winding up the concern, we regret to see the appalling item, 'war expences one million' — bad debt."

407. Newhall was a music teacher and popular singer in the Boston area. On October 7, 1824, he sang at Faneuil Hall for a "Triennial" celebration of Boston and on January 2, 1825, he directed a sacred music concert at Ware's Church in that city. In 1830, he advertised the startup of a singing school in Keene, New Hampshire. *Essex Register*, 11 October 1824, 2; *Boston Commercial Gazette*, 30 December 1824, 2; *New-Hampshire Sentinel*, 26 November 1830, 1.

408. Probably John Brooks (1752–1825), governor of Massachusetts (1816–23).

409. Commander of the Worcester Light Infantry.

410. To the toast: "The heroes and sages of the Revolution — Their patient suffering, and their glorious triumphs, never to be forgotten while a free descendant remains to celebrate their deeds."

411. To the toast: "John Adams — His country his polar star. 3 cheers."

412. Florant Meline (1790–1827), clarinetist and teacher of wind instruments, was cited as a member of the Baltimore Harmonic Society in 1809. He taught and performed at various times in New York and Philadelphia. Ellsworth, "The Clarinet in Early America, 1758–1820," 48, 269–71.

413. Probably "The Hunter's Horn: A New Sporting Cavatina" (Philadelphia: G.E. Blake, 1819?) by Thomas Philipps (1774–1841).

414. In June 1817, advertised as "a new song" available from E. Riley, 23 Chatham Street, in New York.

415. Job Plimpton (1784–1864), music teacher, composer, and organ builder who lived in New York City, ca. 1806 to mid-1820 and later in Brookline, Massachusetts. The apollino which he invented was exhibited at the Columbian Museum in Boston in 1820. Plimpton was a "pupil of Dr. G.K. Jackson" and frequently performed with his wife and daughter, both vocalists. His principal publication for his compositions was *The Universal Repository of Music*, copyright in 1808 (manuscript, New York Public Library); no printed copy has ever been located. Wolfe II:700–03. For a detailed description of the apollino and more information on Plimpton, see *American Beacon and Norfolk & Portsmouth Daily Advertiser*, 16 November 1819, 2.

416. In *The Universal Repository of Music*.

417. One identified instance of this song may have carried over from the year 1775 when a "Pennsylvania March" was printed in *Pennsylvania Packet*, 23 August 1775. See "The Pennsylvania March" in Anderson, *Freedom's Voice in Poetry and Song*, 105, 636–37. Rayner Taylor also wrote a piece having this title (Philadelphia: Engrav'd by John Aitken and sold at his musical repository, ca [1807]) as listed in Wolfe II:901.

418. To the toast: "Baron Steuben, the disciplinarian of the

revolution — Our militia were enlightened by his instructions, and inspired by his example."

419. A "Capt. Minor" and "Col. Minor" were cited as participants in the celebration.

420. Accompanied this toast: "The Alexandria Band — A Band of Musicians, a Band of Brothers, a Band of Gentlemen."

421. To the toast: "The Congress of the U. States — The last session proves to the world that our union is too strong to be severed by faction or intrigue."

422. Arthur Keene was a highly acclaimed vocalist who performed at a number of theaters in various cities. A reporter noted: "We think we have not heard a sweeter voice than Mr. Keene possesses." Two years prior, on July 4, 1818, at the Pavilion Theatre in New York City, Keene sung a patriotic song, words by Samuel Woodworth. That song was probably "Freedom's Jubilee," copyrighted on 30 June 1818, and from the title page, "written by Samuel Woodworth," and "sung by Mr. Keene with great applause" (New York: E. Riley, 1818). "The Pavilion Theatre," *New-York Columbian*, 7 July 1818, 2; Wolfe I:284. In the following year Keene was at the Boston Theatre singing. Again a local reporter noted: "The sweetness of his tones we have never heard surpassed" (*New-England Galaxy & Masonic Magazine*, 2 April 1819, 98).

423. Tune composed ca. 1813 by Jacob Eckhard, organist of St. Michaels Church, Charleston, South Carolina. Wolfe I:263.

424. Cited as an "Irish melody" and print copies available in 1811. *New-York Commercial Advertiser*, 25 July 1811, 4.

425. Text with title listed in the contents for a songster titled *The Star Spangled Banner: Being a Collection of the Best Naval, Martial, Patriotic Songs, &c* as advertised for sale at the Watchman Printing Office and Bookstore in Wilmington, DE in 1816. *American Watchman*, 15 May 1816, 2.

426. Listed in Wolfe I:445.

427. This is a revised version of the ode with the first line, "Say, should we search the globe around" that was sung in Elizabethtown, NH on July 4, 1807, and published in the *New Jersey Journal*. See Publications, 1807.

428. The editor decided to reprint this a week later because the song "was inaccurately printed in last Friday's paper." *Washington Gazette*, 9 July 1821, 2. The song was reprinted in 1827 under the title "Roll of the Brave." See **Publications**, 1827.

429. A note in the newspaper, *Washington Gazette*, 6 July 1821, 2: "an original and charming air, by Mr. Joseph Wood, the celebrated portrait painter of this city — an artist of the very first order of talents."

430. To the toast: "May our future representative assemblies, actuated by the most lively feelings of gratitude, estimate in an honorable manner, the services of our remaining Revolutionary Heroes — Liberal pensions to the time-honor'd veterans. 9 cheers."

431. To the toast: "The Fair Sex of Columbia — Their charms and refinements command our attention; their smiles and embraces over pay for all our labors and toil. May they never want an admirer to adore, or an arm to protect them. 3 cheers."

432. Published edition, Boston: J. Hewitt's Musical Repository & Library, 1812–13. Wolfe I:286–87.

433. Toast to Governor John Brooks, 1816–23: "The governor of the Commonwealth of Massachusetts. 6 cheers."

434. From the dramatic production *Forty Thieves*, Act I, scene 7. See *New-York Commercial Advertiser*, 18 March 1809, 2.

435. S.P. Taylor "from New York" and organist to the Handel and Haydn Society of Boston, advertised his services in Dedham as a teacher of piano, organ, and singing. *Dedham Gazette*, 5 March 1819, 4.

436. First Religious Society.

437. The organist was likely Edward Little White (d.1851), a teacher and music dealer. Barbara Owen, "Edward Little White, Professor of Music," in *American Musical Life in Context and Practice to 1865*, 133–47.

438. Mr. T. Cooper was a popular organist. Some of his concerts included one at the Salem Female Charitable Society in Au-

gust 1816, another at an Evangelical Missionary Society meeting in May 1818, and yet another with the Handel Society of Salem in November 1818. *Salem Gazette*, 2 August 1816, 3, and 19 May 1818, 3, and 3 November 1818, 3.

439. Known also as Miriam's Song, the verses were written by Thomas Moore, the music by British composer Charles Avison (1710–1770. First line: "Sound the loud timbrel, o'er Egypt's sea." Music scores were available in print editions in Philadelphia and New York in 1817.

440. This popular song was sung by a number of female vocalists: Mrs. Ferguson at a concert held at "Vauxhall, Washington Garden" in Boston, August 27, 1816; Mrs. Hewson at Vauxhall Gardens, New York, July 10, 1817; Mrs. J. West in the Park Theater at the circus, New York, in October 1820. Regarding the latter performance, a newspaper commented that she "will accompany herself on the piano forte, a feat never attempted by any other person." *New-England Palladium & Commercial Advertiser*, 27 August 1816, 3; *New-York Columbian*, 9 July 1817, 3; *National Advocate*, 28 October 1820, 3.

441. See Harry R. Stevens, "The Haydn Society of Cincinnati, 1819–1824," *Ohio History* 52: 95–116.

442. Probably the song with the same title by William Dunlap and introduced as "a new song" in New York City in December 1812. *The Columbian*, 9 December 1812, 2.

443. As reprinted in Oral Sumner Coad and Edwin Mims, Jr., *The American Stage* (New Haven, Connecticut: Yale University Press, 1929), 68.

444. This obituary of Peabody was published in *Farmers' Cabinet*, 13 July 1848, 3: "In Burlington, Vt., after the illness of a week, the Rev. O.W.B. Peabody, aged 48, formerly of Exeter. He was twin brother of the Rev. W.B.O. Peabody, of Springfield, Mass. The deceased was an accomplished scholar, as well as of a most amiable and exemplary character."

445. Listed in Wolfe I:403.

446. "Wreaths to the Chieftain" had earlier been used as the tune for a "Song, a new Patriotic Ode, written by L.M. Sergeant, esq. of Boston," with Mr. McFarland performing the work in New York, on July 10, 1817. "Grand Concert at Vauxhall Gardens," *New-York Columbian*, 9 July 1817, 3.

447. Brewer was clerk of the House of Delegates of the Legislature of the State of Maryland. "State Legislatures," *Richmond Enquirer*, 11 December 1821, 3.

448. "Fourth of July Odes. We are informed that only one of the Odes sung at the Faneuil-Hall celebration was written by the gentleman alluded to in our last; the second being from the pen of Mr. N.H. Wright, whose muse has often animated the votaries of Independence." The other Ode was "from the pen of one of our best gifted and most classic poets." *American Federalist Columbian Centinel*, 10 July 1822, 2.

449. Arthur Clifton's original name was Philip Antony Corri (1946–1825). He arrived in Baltimore in 1817 having lived for a time in London. Clark, *Dawning of American Keyboard Music*, 167. "Huzza! Here's Columbia Forever!" (published title, Philadelphia: G.E. Blake; first line: "Triumphant victorious Columbia be") was first performed in Baltimore by Mr. Incledon on December 4, 1817. *Baltimore Patriot*, 4 December 1817, 3; *Secular Music in America, 1801–1825*, I:195. According to *The Times* (Hartford, Connecticut), 20 January 1818, 3, Incledon hailed from the Theatre Royal, Covent Garden, London.

450. George Geib (1782–1842?) "arrived from England" and was active in New York as an organist, pianist, and "professor of music," beginning in 1810. *Evening Post*, 27 October 1810, 3; Clark, *Dawning of American Keyboard Music*, 131. Geib's version of "God Save America" ("published & sold by the author at his piano forte & music store, No. 208 Broadway") was scored for four voices with piano accompaniment and was likely its premiere performance. "God Save America" (first line: "God Save America from ev'ry foe") as listed in Wolfe I:290.

451. See Stevens, "The Haydn Society of Cincinnati, 1819–1824": 95–116.

452. Alderman Barker participated in a parade in honor of the return of Lafayette to Philadelphia in 1824. Barker wrote an ode for the occasion that was printed during the parade on "a

large car, containing a body of printers" at work. "Arrival at Philadelphia," *New-Hampshire Patriot & State Gazette*, 11 October 1824, 2.

453. Venerando Pulizzi, leader of the band (1816, 1818–27), and his father Felice were among a group of 14 musicians enlisted for the Marine Band brought over from Italy in 1805. Heintze, "Gaetano Carusi: From Sicily to the Halls of Congress," 79.

454. This song was available for purchase in a guitar arrangement from J. Coles, no. 125, Market Street, Baltimore. "New Music," *Baltimore Patriot*, 12 April 1822, 3.

455. Brigadier General R. K. Heath.

456. Brigadier General Joseph Sterrett.

457. To the toast: "Our Navy — The splendor of its actions has brightened our national character, may its glory never be tarnished. 6 cheers."

458. Governor William Eustis of Massachusetts, 1823–25.

459. A "Song" with this text published in *The World*, 25 July 1808, 4, and a "patriotic song" titled "Columbia, Land of Liberty" with this first-line text and written by "Mr. Barker, of Philadelphia" was published in *The Shamrock, or Hibernian Chronicle*, 15 June 1811, 4, and *Independent Chronicle*, 24 June 1811, 4. Also published with the note, "Ode, sung at the Republican celebration of independence in Boston [1823]" in "Miscellany," *Providence Patriot*, 26 July 1823, 1.

460. Anthony Philip Heinrich (1781–1861), a German-Bohemian by birth, this remarkable composer helped introduce music of European classical composers to America. Heinrich composed across a gamut of musical forms, from piano pieces to large orchestra works.

461. "The Day — A period, when the light of liberty dawned on the shades of despotism, guiding wanderers to a home of freedom."

462. Waters was an attorney of the Court of Common Pleas. *Salem Gazette*, 21 December 1821, 3.

463. For more on this celebration and the society, see Richard I. Kegerreis, "The Handel Society of Dartmouth," *American Music* 4/2 (Summer 1986): 177–93.

464. Kegerreis notes that "Intercession" is a "simple cantata" printed in *The Boston Handel and Haydn Society Collection of Sacred Music* (1821).

465. M'Creery's Ode (first line: "Oh! that I could, with genius strong") was recited at Petersburg on July 4, 1820. *National Intelligencer*, 13 July 1820, 4.

466. Moore was a printer and bookseller in Concord, New Hampshire.

467. Maryland Gov. Samuel Stevens, Jr., 1822–26.

468. According to the *Providence Patriot*, 26 June 1819, 3, the song is from Thomas Moore's *Irish Melodies*. A performance of this song, sung by Mrs. French with O. Shaw accompanying on piano, was to take place in Providence, Rhode Island, on June 28, 1819.

469. Wolfe I:333, lists a work for piano titled *Governor Eustis's March,* composed by Peter A. von Hagen, Jr. (1779/81– 1837) and published as sheet music in Boston by S. Wetherbee (1824?). William Eustis was governor of Massachusetts from 1823 until his death in 1825.

470. Gottlieb Graupner (1767–1836), oboist, was born in Hanover and performed in Haydn's orchestras in 1791–92. He emigrated to the United States, first appearing in Charleston in 1795 and by 1797 in Boston, where he led the Philharmonic Society (1809–24) and helped establish the Handel and Haydn Society in 1815. He composed *Governor Brooks' Grand March* for flute and piano that was performed on the Fourth in Newburyport (1821) and Salem (1821 and 1823). Douglass A. Lee: "Graupner, Gottlieb," *Grove Music Online* ed. L. Mary (accessed 4 December 2007), http://www.grovemusic.com.proxyau.wrlc. org.

471. Oliver Shaw (1779–1848) was an organist, publisher, and compiler of tunebooks. By 1805 he was active in Dedham, Massachusetts, as a keyboard teacher. He compiled his first collection, *The Columbian Sacred Harmonist*, in 1808. He moved to Providence, Rhode Island, in 1807 where he quickly became

a significant figure in the musical life of that city. Bruce Degen, "Shaw, Oliver," *Grove Music Online* ed. L. Mary (accessed 4 December 2007), http://www.grovemusic.com.proxyau.wrlc. org.

472. Jocelyn was secretary of the Salem Debating Society in 1824 and secretary of the Musical Society of Salem in the following year. *Salem Gazette*, 17 December 1824, 3, and 1 July 1825, 3.

473. Lyrics (first line: "Johnny Bull beware") and sung to the tune "Far Off at Sea" printed in *Essex Register*, 3 September 1814, 4. A note describes that "the patriotic zeal manifested by every description of the citizens of New York in assisting to throw up works for the defence of the city, has produced the following song."

474. Text of song (first line: "How glorious the death for our country to die") in Jackson, *Early Songs of Uncle Sam*, 101–02.

475. A tune having this title published in Riley's *Flute Melodies*. *New-York Daily Advertiser*, 6 February 1818, 3.

476. Possibly the song "La Fayette's Welcome: a New Patriotic Song written by W.B. Tappan. Adapted to a celebrated air by F. Fest" (Philadelphia: G. E. Blake, 1824). The song was advertised in Baltimore as available at J. Robinson, Circulating Library. *Baltimore Patriot*, 14 October 1824, 4.

477. To this toast: "The Judiciary — Its independence and integrity, present a barrier, insurmountable alike to Tyranny and Licentiousness. 3 cheers."

478. To the toast: "The Governor [Joseph C. Yates] of the State of New-York — A beacon to warn his successors that bad counsel may corrupt the most upright intentions. 3 cheers."

479. Possibly *The Grand Canal March*, "composed and most respectfully inscribed to his excellency, DeWitt Clinton by C. Gilfert" (New York: Dubois & Stodart, 1824). Listed in Wolfe I:307.

480. Accompanied this toast: "Our next President — The man who most unites with an unsullied reputation, the principles of a Republican, the talents of a statesman, and an ardent attachment to the land of his birth."

481. Another instance of the text of "Ode on Science" published around the Fourth in 1824 is in *Ithaca Journal*, 7 July 1824, 4.

482. John B. Derby was an attorney in Dedham. In 1830, he was in Boston at the Fourth of July celebration of the Washington Benevolent Society. *Pittsfield Sun*, 15 July 1830, 2.

483. For additional information on Mann and his activities as a manufacturer of paper, see Richard J. Wolfe, *The Role of the Mann Family of Dedham, Massachusetts, in the Marbling of Paper in Nineteenth-Century America and in the Printing of Music, the Making of Cards and Other Booktrade Activities* (Chestnut Hill, MA: Perspectives on Printing and Publishing, 1980).

484. The Salem Musical Society met at "Mr. Pratt's Room" on July 5, 1825. *Salem Gazette*, 1 July 1825, 3. By September 1825 the Musical Society had been renamed the Mozart Association. *Salem Gazette*, 6 September 1825, 3.

485. Jacob Kimball, Jr. (1761–1826).

486. J.H. Rollo and his family had been giving vocal concerts in Ithaca as early as 1822. Their repertoire included works by Handel, Mozart, and Haydn. *American Journal*, 2 October 1822, 3.

487. Marsh advertised his singing school "for the instruction of sacred music" located "at Mr. Tower's Academy" in Newport in 1831–32. *Rhode-Island Republican*, 3 January 1832, 4.

488. An accompanied article describes how this song by Robert T. Paine "was sung by millions of freemen, and a spirit started from every wave to protect the honor of our flag in every clime."

489. She was likely Mrs. L.H. Sigourney.

490. Woodworth wrote no less than five odes for Independence Day celebrations of the Typographical Society are printed in Woodworth, *The Poems, Odes, Songs, and Other Metrical Effusions* (1818).

491. See Calvin Elliker, "Early Imprints in the Thomas A. Edison Collection of American Sheet Music: Addenda to Sonneck-Upton and to Wolfe," *Notes* 57/3 (March 2001): 555–73.

492. Mrs. K.A. Ware's *The Bower of Taste* was advertised for sale in Portland, Maine, by S. Colman in 1829. *Eastern Argus Semi-Weekly*, 1 September 1829, 3.

493. Percival, a poet with a number of pieces to his credit, was living in Boston in 1825. *Boston Commercial Gazette*, 21 April 1825, 2.

494. Caleb Cushing (1800–1879) had an extensive career as a statesman, serving in the Massachusetts Senate in 1826, among other state congressional tenures. He served in the U.S. Congress from 1835 to 1843.

495. This poem was read again on July 4, 1858, at a meeting of the Association of the Surviving Soldiers of the War of 1812, in Washington, D.C.

496. A popular work by Vincenzo Pucitta (1778–1861) with numerous publications and performances in America. Full first line of text: "Strike the cymbal, roll the tymbal, let the trump of triumph sound."

497. Kendall was a member of the Freeport Lodge of Masons. *Eastern Argus Semi-Weekly*, 14 December 1827, 3.

498. Often referred to as simply "Mrs. A.M. Wells of Boston," she was one of four poets to receive prizes "offered by the editor of the *New-York Mirror*." "The prize awarded to this lady was $20, for the second best poem." A few months following, Mrs. Wells was also awarded a prize for an address she gave for the opening of the new Nashville Theatre. *Boston Commercial Gazette*, 27 February and 13 November 1826, 2 and 2, respectively.

499. Governor of Georgia George M. Troup, 1823–27.

500. G.W. Adams was the eldest son of John Quincy Adams who was also in attendance. John Q. Adams, *Memoirs of John Quincy Adams*. 12 vols. (Philadelphia: J.B. Lippincott, 1874–77; reprint, N.Y.: Books for Libraries Press, 1969) 8:376.

501. An article in the *Essex Register* (Salem), 6 March 1826, 2, mentions the "Mozart Association ... as lately formed in this town." Edwin Jocelyn served as secretary of the association.

502. Lyrics from Handel's *Judas Maccabaeus* (1747), act 1.

503. Lyrics to the poem titled "Go Forth to the Mount" by Thomas Moore. *The Poetical Works of Thomas Moore Including His Melodies, Ballads, Etc.* (Paris: A. and W. Galignani, 1829), 339.

504. Composed in honor of Marquis de Lafayette who fought in the Revolutionary War and returned to the United States in August 1824 a national hero. He traveled throughout this country and was honored in each locale. Several marches were composed as a tribute to him. J. Bunker Clark, "American Musical Tributes of 1824–25 to Lafayette: A Report and Inventory," *Fontes Artis Musicae* 26/1 (1979):17–35.

505. E. Briggs, Jr. operated a "grave stone manufactory" in Keene. "Village Register," *New Hampshire Sentinel*, 12 June 1827, 2.

506. Papanti performed in concert with a number of reputable musicians. With James Hewitt accompanying, he played *Variations on the Horn* at the Boston Concert Hall on February 15, 1825. On April 26 of that year, he performed at Boston's Boylston Hall. On the program was the premiere performance of Anthony Philip Heinrich's *The Columbiad*, "composed for a full orchestra." *Boston Commercial Gazette*, 14 February 1825, 3, and 25 April 1825, 3. See also *Portsmouth Journal of Literature & Politics*, 8 July 1826, 3.

507. Elliot was appointed vice president of the Portsmouth Handel Society in August 1826. *Portsmouth Journal of Literature & Politics*, 5 August 1826, 3.

508. Philip Henry Smith, *General History of Duchess County from 1609 to 1876, Inclusive* (Paling, NY: the author, 1877), 208.

509. Lt. George W. Patten, U.S. Army, wrote the following poems: "Song of the Wrecker" (1837), "Stanzas for Music" (1838), and "Bride's Departure" (1848) published respectively in the following New England newspapers: *Newport Mercury*, 4 March 1837, 4, and 8 September 1838, 4, and *Semi-Weekly Eagle*, 17 July 1848, 4. For a biographical sketch of Patten, see Griswold, *The Poets and Poetry of America*, 407.

510. The parade included "an old drummer thumping upon the unelastic head of the very instrument with which he had often roused the soldier of 76 to the onset, but with which we believe, he never beat a retreat before an enemy."

511. Greene, an attorney in Providence, Rhode Island, member of the Rhode Island Historical Society and later Rhode Island attorney general, was "favorably known as a talented and agreeable writer." He was also a prolific orator on the Fourth. Some of his addresses include: Providence, July 4, 1823; speaking before the "inhabitants of Centreville and Coventry," July 4, 1825; Universalist Chapel, Providence, July 4, 1827. Greene died at the age of 71 in Providence, January 1863. "Mr. Greene's Oration," *Rhode-Island American*, 15 July 1823, 3; *Rhode-Island American*, 1 July 1825, 2; *Providence Patriot & Columbian Phenix*, 4 July 1827, 2; *New Bedford Mercury*, 14 June 1833, 2; "Decease of Prominent Men," *Farmers' Cabinet*, 15 January 1863, 2.

512. To the toast: "Andrew Jackson, the Star of the West — May he quickly come to his meridian to gladden the almost benighted land of his fathers."

513. *Genius*, new series, 8 September 1827, 80, as reported and with lyrics printed in Vicki L. Eaklor, *American Antislavery Songs: A Collection and Analysis* (New York: Greenwood, 1988), 98.

514. *Genius*, new series, 1 December 1827, 176, as reported and with lyrics printed in Eaklor, *American Antislavery Songs*, 98–99.

515. Printed in *The Universal Songster and Museum of Mirth* (Boston: Charles Gaylord, 1835).

516. Reported in Davenport, 293n42.

517. Words of this "celebrated and beautiful song" by John Howard Payne, who wrote "several dramatic pieces and poems of merit, and many miscellaneous literary productions. He was originally appointed consul at Tunis by Mr. Tyler, was superseded by Mr. Polk, and reappointed by Mr. Fillmore in 1851." *Semi-Weekly Eagle*, 7 June 1852, 2.

518. Governor Enoch Lincoln of Maine, 1827–29.

519. Attached to the First Baltimore Light Brigade and commanded by Capt. John F. Hoss.

520. Probably the hymn titled "Thanksgiving" having the same first line. Printed in *A Collection of Psalms and Hymns for Christian Worship* (Boston: Carter, Hendee & Co., 1835).

521. 6th toast: "The surviving officers and soldiers of the army of independence — Congress can refuse compensation for their unpaid services, but cannot avert from them the gratitude of future times and the admiration of the world."

522. Three years later, Atkinson was appointed member of the committee of arrangements for the 1830 Independence Day celebration in Newport. *Newport Mercury*, 5 June 1830, 2. In fall 1834 Atkinson advertised a singing school "for the instruction of sacred vocal music" held at the 4th Baptist Church in Newport. *Newport Mercury*, 8 November 1834, 3.

523. Composed by Arthur Clifton. The work is reprinted in Arthur Clifton, *Complete Piano Music*. Ed. Nathan Buckner. 4 vols. (Philadelphia: Kallisti, 1997).

524. A "patriotic Song" having this identical first line of text was published in *Newburyport Herald*, 8 June 1798, 158.

525. A song heralding the impending election of Andrew Jackson.

526. A letter to the *Norwich Courier*, 2 July 1828, 3, states that the Chelsea Band performed "on all public days without pay, and the reason given, is that the public have subscribed liberally towards purchasing instruments of music for the band," but that the ensemble is still in debt.

527. It was printed in a local newspaper in 1806 that a correspondent who had witnessed "surprising musical performances of Miss Mallet" (age 7) reported her father, a music teacher in Boston, had arranged for a public "exhibition of her skill" in Salem. On June 16, 1809, Mr. Mallet, bass viol player, Miss Mallet, pianist and vocalist, and her two older brothers, F. Mallet, violinist, and W. Mallet, pianist, presented a concert in Burlington, Vermont. The Mallet family gave numerous concerts, some in tandem with such noted musicians as Gottlieb Graupner and James Hewitt. Mr. Mallet was likely Francis Mallet who died in 1834 at the age of 84 in Boston and who had come to America "in company with Lafayette" and fought in the

Revolutionary War and later became a member of the orchestra of the Federal Street Theatre in Boston and also a dealer in musical instruments. *Salem Gazette*, 20 June 1806, 3; *Vermont Centinel*, 16 June 1809, 3; *Salem Gazette*, 15 August 1834, 3; *Farmer's Gazette*, 29 August 1834, 3.

528. This band is cited as the longest performing civic band in America. Ronald Demkee, "Upbeat: America's Oldest Civilian Concert Band Marks 175th Anniversary," *International Musician* 101/1 (January 2003): 21.

529. John Andrew Shulze (1774–1852), governor of Pennsylvania, 1823–29.

530. Greene (1802–1868) delivered orations in Providence, Rhode Island, on July 4, 1823 (published, Providence: John Miller, 1823), and on July 4, 1827 (published, Providence: Smith & Parmenter, 1827).

531. Forty-four Revolutionary War soldiers attended this event among whom were Charles Freeman Cumberland, age 64, "a drummer in the Revolutionary War, having with him a drum, carried by him at that time," and Benjamin Peck, "of Providence, formerly of Connecticut, [age] 59. Mr. Peck was the youngest of those present. He enlisted as a drummer at the age of ten years in 1780, and served to the end of the war. He draws a pension, having established his claims, to the satisfaction of the war department."

532. From the opera *The Devil's Bridge* by the English singer/composer John Braham (1774–1856) and premiered at Druary Lane Theatre on October 10, 1812. The song was sung in Boston and Baltimore. *Boston Gazette*, 2 April 1818, 3; *Albany Argus*, 29 September 1818, 3; *Baltimore Patriot & Mercantile Advertiser*, 31 October 1818, 3. The verses are printed in "Poetry," *American Watchman*, 24 October 1818, 4. The tune is printed in *Riley's Flute Melodies. New-York Daily Advertiser*, 6 February 1818, 3.

533. Traditional Irish jig.

534. *Genius*, new series, 6 November 1829, 68, as reported and with lyrics printed in Eaklor, *American Antislavery Songs*, 19.

535. *Genius*, new series, 9 October 1829, 36, as reported and with lyrics printed in Eaklor, *American Antislavery Songs*, 5.

536. The Rev. Samuel Merrick Phelps (1770–1841).

537. *Genius*, new series, 2 September 1829, 3, with introduction by "W.L.G." [Garrison], as reported and with lyrics printed in Eaklor, *American Antislavery Songs*, 18.

538. Possibly the tune of the *March of the Marion Corps*. The Corps was "attached to the First Battalion, Maryland Riflemen"and the work (published, Baltimore: John Cole, 1824) was composed by Baltimore composer Frederick Damish. Wolfe I:230.

539. Willis (d. 1867) had considerable talent as a poet, winning a Gold Medal at Yale College for one of his student works. He later served as an editor for the *New York Mirror*. Willis worked together with the noted song writer George P. Morris in the editing of *Home Journal*. *Farmer's Cabinet*, 7 April 1827, 3; 14 July 1864, 2; 7 February 1867, 2.

540. Cannino, "Celebrating the Fourth in Salem," 52.

541. Toast: "The Hon. George Wolf. A stirring Republican; an able and experienced statesman; a firm and efficient friend of the hero of New Orleans: his majority on the second Tuesday of October next, will not be less than fifty thousand."

542. Toast: "The late Mrs. Jackson. Her virtues cannot be forgotten, nor can her traducers be forgiven."

543. Accompanied the toast: "The cause of civil and religious liberty — The Declaration of Independence, and the Bill of Religious Freedom, have become the manuals of monarchs. 4 guns."

544. Accompanied the toast: "The Army and Navy –'At once our Spear and Shield.' 3 guns." "Minute Gun at Sea" was likely the tune for the duet of that title by W.P. King and published in 1814 by John Paff "at his music store" in New York. *The Columbian*, 6 May 1814, 4. The duet was sung on July 5, 1814 by Miss Dellinger and Mr. Entwisle at a benefit concert held at the theatre in New York. *Evening Post*, 5 July 1814, 3.

545. Correct title as first line is "Oh! Say not woman's love is bought." The lyrics are from a character ("Dinah Primrose")

song in the comedy, *The Young Quaker, or The Fair American*, performed by the Old American Company and as a separate song in concerts in a number of cities, 1796–1834.

546. "Mr. Benjamin is favorably known as a young gentleman of talents. His literary attainments have secured him an enviable reputation at an early age, and give promise of an enduring fame." *Norwich Courier*, 10 October 1832, 2.

547. To the toast, "The President of the United States — Great in all that is good — and good in all that is great."

548. To the toast, "Free Schools — The nurseries of Democracy."

549. Jeremy Belknap's *Sacred Poetry; Consisting of Psalms and Hymns Adapted to Christian Devotion in Public and Private. Selected from the Best Authors, with Variations and Additions* (Boston: Belknap, 1795), and subsequent editions.

550. Worcester advertised his services in 1833 as a school teacher of various languages. *Salem Gazette*, 3 September 1833, 3.

551. The toast for this piece: "The Judiciary of the United States and of this State — Justice through their influence sits strong and unshaken as a castle upon a rock."

552. This tune and the one following were not performed because the cannon being used to accompany the toasts exploded, injuring several persons and bringing the affair to an abrupt end.

553. A newspaper report in 1831 has Marcus Coburn performing in concert with the Providence Band on June 22, 1831. *Rhode-Island Republican*, 21 June 1831, 2.

554. From Moore's *Irish Melodies*. This song was sung some years prior by Mrs. French in concert with O. Shaw accompanying on the piano, in Providence, Rhode Island, on June 28, 1819. *Providence Patriot*, 26 June 1819, 3.

555. First line: "My country, 'tis of thee." For an article on the various lyrics set to this famous tune, some on the Fourth of July, see Robert James Branham, "'Of Thee I Sing': Contesting America," *American Quarterly* 48/4 (1996): 623–52.

556. Benjamin Burt (1790–1873).

557. See *Memoirs of John Quincy Adams* 8:376.

558. As reported and printed with lyrics in Eaklor, *American Antislavery Songs*, 100–01.

559. Joseph Cuvillier, leader.

560. Key's poem, "Hymn for the Fourth of July, 1832" (first line: "Before the Lord we bow") is printed in *Poems* (1857).

561. Listed in the contents for a songster titled *The Star Spangled Banner: Being a collection of the best Naval, Martial, Patriotic songs, &c* as advertised for sale at the Watchman Printing Office and Bookstore in Wilmington, Delaware, in 1816. *American Watchman*, 15 May 1816, 3.

562. According to an article in *The Portsmouth & Great-Falls Journal of Literature & Politics*, 15 July 1837, 2, this "national patriotic song ... is sung with great patriotic fervor at all the Fourth of July celebrations in our churches. What must be the surprise of an Englishman who heard the singing of this ode to find that we had stolen the English national air of God Save the King, and arranged it to a song dedicated to America the 'sweet land of liberty.'" Smith also wrote a "Hymn for the Fourth of July" (first line: "Land of the freemen and home of the brave!") published in *Poems of Home and Country* (1895).

563. Knapp was an attorney practicing in Marblehead. *Salem Gazette*, 24 May 1831, 1.

564. John Quincy Adams (1767–1848) also presented an oration that day. See *Diary of John Quincy Adams* (Harvard University Press, 1981) and *Memoirs of John Quincy Adams* 8:376. For more information on Adams and the Fourth of July, see Heintze, *The Fourth of July Encyclopedia*, 8–10. The Old Hundred tune is ideal for the set of Adams' verses. Adams relates to us in his diary that the dinner that followed the ceremony had some 120 persons in attendance that toasts were alternated "with symphonies and songs."

565. Printed in *The Universal Songster and Museum of Mirth* (Boston: Charles Gaylord, 1835).

566. In 1820 Mrs. Hemans had been described as a rising poet. "Her poetry is full of glorious shapes instinct with spirit.

She has little of sad retrospection, little of the 'pale cast of thought,' and nothing of metaphysical subtlety." Her poetry "is replete with grace and beauty." "Female Literature," *Lancaster Journal*, 21 July 1820, 2.

567. See Leinbach's diary in Cannino, 57.

568. An example of "Black Joke" is found in the John Seely Manuscript (in private hands and compiled 1810–1820s) as reported in the compact disc *Sackett's Harbor: Nineteenth-Century Dance Music from Western New York State* (Sampler Records, 1988).

569. Possibly the "Union Ode" composed by the Rev. Samuel Foster Gilman (1791–1858), whose text was reprinted 33 years later in "A South Carolina Ode for the Fourth of July," *Harper's Weekly*, 9 July 1864.

570. For an article on Eckhard, see George W. Williams, "Jacob Eckhard and His Choirmaster's Book," *Journal of the American Musicological Society* 7/1 (Spring 1954): 41–47. Eckhard is listed in the Charleston city directory: Abraham Motte, *Directory and Stranger's Guide for the Year 1816* (Charleston, 1816).

571. *Liberator*, 30 June 1832, 103, as reported and with lyrics printed in Eaklor, *American Antislavery Songs*, 102–03.

572. *Liberator*, 30 June 1832, 103, as reported and with lyrics printed in Eaklor, *American Antislavery Songs*, 103–04.

573. Possibly the same work written by the Petersburg, Virginia, composer John M'Creery. First line: "Come, strike the bold anthem, the wardogs are howling." Words in *The World*, 25 July 1808, 4; *A Selection from the Ancient Music of Ireland* (Petersburg, VA: Yancy & Burton, 1824), 59–60; *The Red, White, and Blue Songster: No. 1, National Patriotic Songs Written to Popular Airs* (Indianapolis: C.O. Perrine, 1861).

574. Cited as a "favorite Scotch song" purportedly composed by James Hook (1746–1827) and sung at the Charleston, South Carolina, theater on February 16, 1796. *City Gazette and Daily Advertiser*, 15 February 1796, 3. Lyrics published in *The Universal Songster and Museum of Mirth* (Boston: Charles Gaylord, 1835).

575. A popular song, text by J. Stevenson, sung in a number of venues, including Boston at the Exchange Coffee-House by Mr. McFarland in 1811, and in New York at Tammany Hall by Mr. Duffy in 1813. *Columbian Centinel*, 31 July 1811, 3; *Columbian*, 16 March 1813, 2. Full text printed in *Shamrock, or Hibernian Chronicle*, 18 April 1812, 4, and in *The Universal Songster and Museum of Mirth* (Boston: Charles Gaylord, 1835).

576. Possibly *President Van Buren's Grand March*, Composed & Arranged for the Piano Forte by Samuel Carusi (Washington, D.C.: Author's Music Store). Copy in the Office of the Curator, The White House.

577. The numbering of the order of exercises is as printed on the broadside.

578. The Scottish traditional tune "Bruce's Address to His Army," i.e., Robert Bruce at the Battle of Bannockburn in 1314, is frequently referred to by its first line: "Scots, wha ha'e wi' Wallace bled." The poem was written by Robert Burns and was printed as such, e.g., in *The Balance, and Columbian Repository*, 17 July 1804, 232. The tune was advertised as published, e.g., in *Riley's Flute Melodies. New York Daily Advertiser*, 1 December 1817, 3.

579. Accompanied the toast: "The Army and Navy: Their genius and valor guard, their virtues adorn, the Republic. 3 guns."

580. Cited in Crew, *Presidential Sheet Music*, 423.

581. This is the same ode as that sung in Salem on July 4, 1823.

582. *Genius*, fourth series, July 1834, 104–05; *Liberator*, 12 July 1834, 110; *Reporter*, July 1834, 112, as reported and printed with lyrics in Eaklor, *American Antislavery Songs*, 105–06.

583. Music reprinted in Spicer, "Popular Song for Public Celebration," 45. Copy of song in Johns Hopkins University.

584. Possibly the J.E. Estabrook, owner of Estabook's Dry-Goods Store in Concord, New Hampshire. *New-Hampshire Patriot and State Gazette*, 23 September 1833, 3.

585. George Lunt (1803–1885) presented an oration in Newburyport, Massachusetts, on July 4, 1833. *An Oration Delivered in Newburyport, on the Fifty-Seventh Anniversary of American Independence* (Newburyport: J.G. Tilton & B.E. Hale, 1833); *Salem Gazette*, 23 July 1833, 3. Lunt was an attorney who practiced in Boston. In 1849 he was appointed U.S. Attorney for Massachusetts by President Zachary Taylor. Lunt published several collections of his own poetry, one of which included *Lyric Poems, Sonnets, and Miscellanies* (1854). "The Lyre and Sword" is printed in Griswold, *The Poets and Poetry of America*, 365. See also *Oak Hill Cemetery in Newburyport, from its Establishment and Consecration to 1878* (Newburyport, MA: William H. Huse, 1878) for original hymns without music by Lunt.

586. "L.M." refers to "long meter," a metric pattern, readily identifiable to singers at that time.

587. Mandell was an instructor in the Barre High School. *Farmer's Gazette*, 21 November 1834, 2.

588. Newspapers have variant spellings of her name.

589. Henry E. Moore advertised the publication of the *Grafton Journal* in Plymouth in October 1824. He married Susan D. Farnum in 1825. Moore, as secretary of the Concord Mechanics Association, assisted in arrangements for the group's Independence Day celebration in 1832. He published the *New-Hampshire Collection of Church Music* in fall of 1832 and wrote a song for a "Typographical Festival" in December of 1833. According to Robert W. John, Moore organized the first music educators convention in September 1829, "with the cooperation of the New Hampshire Central Musical Society of Goffstown." Moore died in East Cambridge on October 23, 1841. *New Hampshire Sentinel*, 15 October 1824, 3, and 21 November 1833, 4; *Eastern Argus*, 11 November 1825, 2; *New Hampshire Patriot*, 2 July 1832, 3; 2 December 1833, 2; and 28 October 1841, 3; Robert W. John, "Origins of the First Music Educators Convention," *Journal of Research in Music Education* 13/4 (Winter 1965), 207.

590. See Leinbach's diary in Cannino, 59.

591. Published in Philadelphia by A. Fiot, 1834? Facsimile in *19th Century American Sheet Music Digitization Project* (University of North Carolina), website http://www.lib.unc.edu/music/eam/index.html.

592. Tune printed in No. 8 of Riley's *Flute Melodies*, as reported in *New-York Daily Advertiser*, 6 February 1818, 3.

593. Clark achieved some distinction for his literary talents as a contributor to various magazines. He wrote a number of poems and assumed the editorship of the *Philadelphia Daily Gazette* in February 1831. One remarkable poem of his was a hymn written for the American Sunday School Union and first sung at a society meeting in May 1832. He died in June 1841 at the age of 32. *Connecticut Mirror*, 26 February 1831, 3; *Rhode-Island American and Gazette*, 29 May 1832, 4; *Farmer's Cabinet*, 18 June 1841, 3.

594. *Liberator*, 11 July 1835, 112, as reported and with lyrics printed in Eaklor, *American Antislavery Songs*, 23–24.

595. Liberator, 18 July 1835, 116, as reported and with lyrics printed in Eaklor, *American Antislavery Songs*, 24.

596. *Liberator*, 11 July 1835, 110, as reported and with lyrics printed in Eaklor, *American Antislavery Songs*, 22. A lithograph print of this song is in the Library of Congress and cataloged under the lithographer Otto Knirsch.

597. American actor, author, and composer, John Howard Payne (1791–1852) "made his first appearance on the American stage at the Park Theatre, New York, on July 26, 1809" and later wrote the lyrics for the celebrated song "Home Sweet Home." Wolfe II:670–71.

598. Isaac Flagg operated a private school in Beverly where music lessons were provided and in 1830 he was referred to in advertisements as secretary of the Beverly Marine Insurance Company. *Salem Gazette*, 31 March 1829, 4, and 13 July 1830, 3.

599. Jonathan Shove, of Danvers, was a senator for Essex County, State of Massachusetts.

600. Henry Kemble Oliver (1800–1885) was headmaster of the Salem Classical School during the 1830s. He was also co-compiler with S.P. Tuckerman and S.A. Bancroft of *The National Lyre: A New Collection of Sacred Music* (Boston: Wilkins, Carter,

and Co., 1848) and he issued his own compilation *Oliver's Collection of Hymn & Psalm Tunes, Sentences, Anthems & Chants* (Boston: Oliver Ditson, 1860).

601. Lincoln operated the New Bedford Musical Academy where he offered instruction in vocal and instrumental music. *New Bedford Mercury*, 13 March 1835, 3. By August 1836, Lincoln was conducting the music at North Congregational Church in Boston and advertising his services as a private instructor in vocal music in Hartford, Connecticut. On February 28, 1837, he directed a "concert of sacred music" at the church, with performances of works by "Handel, Haydn, Mozart, Pergolesi, Rossini, &c." *Connecticut Courant*, 22 August 1836, 3, and 25 February 1837, 3.

602. "By this time, loud cries of 'Bribed by the Bank,' 'Nick Biddle's gold,' &c., caused such a disturbance that the song was broken off in the middle, and as the bottles were mostly empty, the company broke up in confusion."

603. Ode reprinted in *The Western Examiner*, 9 July 1835, 206, with this note: "The following Ode ... was chaunted with thrilling effect at the late celebration of the Fourth of July by the Franklin Society of this city. It claims for its author, a Lady of well known literary acquirements — one whose name, if permitted to accompany the effusions of her pen, would add luster to the already bright fame of American female writers."

604. In October 1835 Nutting advertised a school for "instruction in singing" to be held at the Moravian Meeting House and "taught upon the Pestilozzian system." In March 1836, he intended to move to New Bedford and advertised a farewell "juvenile concert at Zion Church," to take place on April 15. *Newport Mercury*, 10 October 1835, 3; 12 March 1836, 3; and 9 April 1836, 3.

605. Bound also with *Collection of Anthems and Hymns*. Boston, n.p., 1836. Copy in the Newberry Library, Chicago. Listed in Carol A. Pemberton, *Lowell Mason: A Bio-Bibliography* (Westport, CT: Greenwood, 1988), 58.

606. Miss Hannah Flagg Gould (1789–1865) was considered a "highly gifted writer." She composed an "Ode to Liberty," sung on April 29, 1835, at Lyceum Hall in Salem, Massachusetts. Some of her earlier poems were published in the collection *Poems* (Boston, 1832). Another patriotic poem, "Columbia's Birth-Day: An Ode for the Fourth of July" (first line: "We hail Columbia's natal day"), was published in her collection *Poems* (1839). This is a different poem from the one having the identical first line published in 1811 in Rhode Island. See Publications, 1811. *Eastern Argus*, 1 May 1832, 2; "Grand Musical Melange," *Salem Gazette*, 28 April 1835, 3. See also, *Oak Hill Cemetery in Newburyport, from its Establishment and Consecration to 1878* (Newburyport, MA: William H. Huse, 1878) for original hymns without music by Gould.

607. Printed with lyrics in Eaklor, *American Antislavery Songs*, 112–13.

608. In 1812, "Freedom's Star" was cited as a new song by John M'Creery of Petersburg, Virginia. *Shamrock, or Hibernian Chronicle*, 16 May 1812, 3–4. Full text of this song, to the tune, "Hermit of Killarney," is printed on page 4 and in *New Jersey Journal*, 25 January 1814, 4, and William McCarty, *The New National Song Book, Containing Songs, Odes, and Other Poems, on National Subjects. Compiled from Various Sources* (NY: Leavitt and Allen, 184–?).

609. Lydia Huntley Sigourney (1791–1865) was a respected and prolific poet who, born in Norwich, Connecticut, was frequently asked to write verses for special occasions. She published considerable prose, including "biographies, histories, and advice manuals," as well as several collections of poems including *Poems* (1827) and *Zinzendorff, and Other Poems* (1835), and a posthumous autobiography, *Letters of Life* (1866). Nina Baym, "Lydia Sigourney," *American National Biography*. 24 vols. (New York: Oxford University Press, 1999) 19: 926–28. For more on Sigourney and the Fourth of July, see Heintze, *The Fourth of July Encyclopedia*, 258–59.

610. Harrington was principal of the Walpole Academy. *New-Hampshire Sentinel*, 5 December 1838, 1.

611. Song based on the life of Ephraim Grimes of Hubbard-

ston, Massachusetts, who was known for his "mischievous tricks" and general mischief. A description in "Old Grimes is Dead," *Barre Gazette*, 9 February 1844, 2.

612. Stone was principal of the Concord Literary and Teachers Seminary, a "high school" opened in fall 1834, where English, the classics, and chemistry were taught. In 1835 he held an exhibition that demonstrated examples of "original composition and declamation with vocal music," among other topics. *New-Hampshire Patriot*, 24 November 1834, 3, and 16 November 1835, 2.

613. *Liberator*, 4 August 1837, 128, as reported and with lyrics printed in Eaklor, *American Antislavery Songs*, 115–16.

614. John Quincy Adams refers to this as "Adams and Liberty" sung at the meeting house. *Memoirs of John Quincy Adams* 9:358.

615. Probably based on Haydn's second movement of Symphony No. 94 ("The Surprise"), as indicated by its popularity in America at that time. See Wolfe I:351–52, for various printed arrangements.

616. To the toast: "Texas: May the star of political and religious liberty which has appeared in the firmament of our sister republic, illumine all Mexico."

617. Written as a letter to the newspaper from a visitor from Yorktown, Virginia. Another similar letter, written in 1835 about the Fourth of July that year in Williamsburg, also mentions music played on the organ in the church. *Richmond Enquirer*, 10 July 1835, 3.

618. An article in this newspaper discusses how "Hail Columbia" came to be written.

619. *Liberator*, 20 July 1838, 116, as reported and with lyrics printed in Eaklor, *American Antislavery Songs*, 119–20.

620. *Liberator*, 20 July 1838, 116, as reported and with lyrics printed in Eaklor, *American Antislavery Songs*, 120–21.

621. *Liberator*, 20 July 1838, 116, as reported and with lyrics printed in Eaklor, *American Antislavery Songs*, 118–19.

622. *Liberator*, 13 July 1838, 110, as reported and with lyrics printed in Eaklor, *American Antislavery Songs*, 117–18.

623. In April 1837 Wilson had led the Singing Society of the Methodist Episcopal Church in Pittsfield, Massachusetts, in "a concert of sacred music" on 6 April 1837. In 1840 he was elected Town Clerk of Lenox and in 1858 the Governor of New York had appointed him Commissioner of that state. *Pittsfield Sun*, 6 April 1837, 3; 5 March 1840, 3; and 17 June 1858, 2, respectively.

624. In 1834, Mr. and Mrs. Monds operated a private school in Salem where piano instruction was taught. *Salem Gazette*, 26 December 1834, 4.

625. Charles Zeuner (1795–1857) was a composer and organist at St. Paul's Church in Boston. He published a collection of church music and composed the music for a patriotic piece titled "The American Banner," words by Thomas Power, in December 1834. *Connecticut Courant*, 27 December 1831, 4; *Salem Gazette*, 6 January 1835, 4. .

626. Possibly "Happy the Land, A Pastoral Glee" by Thomas Hastings, published in *The Harmonist: A Collection of Tunes from the Most Approved Authors* (New York: T. Mason & G. Lane, 1839).

627. Paige was the author of *Hymns and Canticles of the Church* (New York, 1844) and arranged a number of songs, including "I Hear Thee Speak of a Better Land" (music by Mrs. Hemans, 1836) and "They Have Given Thee to Another" (music by Henry R. Bishop, 1830s).

628. *Liberator*, 5 July 1839, 107, as reported and with lyrics printed in Eaklor, *American Antislavery Songs*, 125–26.

629. Pond (1792–1870) was the compiler of several tune books, including, for example, *Union Melodies: Designed as a Companion for the 'Union Hymns' of the American Sunday School* (New York: Firth & Hall, 1838) and *The United States Psalmody* (New York: Firth & Hall, 1841).

630. First introduced by Pierpont in Boston on Independence Day in 1820.

631. Titled "Meet Me by Moonlight," by J.A. Wade, the song was advertised for sale at Elias Hook's store in Salem in

1828 and a guitar arrangement at G. M'Dowell & Son in Baltimore, in 1829. *Salem Gazette*, 26 December 1828, 3; *Baltimore Patriot*, 13 November 1829, 3.

632. Stanley's lyrics for this song were published in the Norwich, New York, newspaper *The Telegraph*, 29 March 1814, 1.

633. This song by William Dunlap was advertised for sale by D. Longworth in New York City in January 1813. The song had a successful run with performances in New York, Boston, Providence, Rhode Island, and Charleston, South Carolina. *The Columbian*, 11 January 1813, 4.

634. Knowlton was an attorney practicing in Sing Sing. He was also a frequent contributor of articles to the *Hudson River Chronicle*. His poem "Beauty" was printed in 1848 by Swain & Platt, Sing Sing, New York. *Hudson River Chronicle*, 4 November 1845, 2, and 15 August 1848, 2.

635. Lyrics in *Abraham Lincoln Historical Digitization Project*, University of Chicago: <http://lincoln.lib.niu.edu>.

636. A slight variation of R.S. Coffin's ode with first line "When Freedom midst the battle storm" published in 1827. See Publications, 1827.

637. This was perhaps the same Michael W. Beck, publisher of the *Maine Democrat*, ca. 1837–41, who married Sarah A.H. Gordon in Saco in 1841. At the time of his death, at age 27, on March 9, 1843, he was cited as "a practical printer." *Portsmouth Journal of Literature & Politics*, 13 February 1841, 3; *New-Hampshire Patriot and State Gazette*, 23 March 1843, 3.

638. "Mr. D. Perry," a clarinetist who had spent time in Worcester, was described as "a very superior professor of instrumental music." Another musician with that last name active in Worcester was "Emery Perry, professor of music" and was listed as a co-owner of "Perry & Andrews' Piano Forte and Music room, no 7 Harrington Corner, Worcester," in *Barre Gazette*, 11 February 1853, 3. The band's repertoire consisted of "marches, quick steps, waltzes, songs, and duets." *Pittsfield Sun*, 26 December 1839, 3, and 2 January and 14 May 1840, 3 and 3, respectively.

639. Asa Barr was a reputable choral conductor, highly regarded for his performances in Pittsfield, but also in towns, such as New Braintree where he presented a concert in October 1846, and South Adams, where in May 1856 he directed a concert of sacred music at the Congregational Church. On December 30, 1856, Barr conducted a performance of Haydn's *Creation* at West Hall in Pittsfield. Col. Barr also operated a music store in Pittsfield, was president of the Harmonic Society there and directed the chorus at the Pittsfield Young Ladies Institute. *Barre Patriot*, 30 October 1846, 2; *Pittsfield Sun*, 2 March 1854, 8; May 1856, 2; 14 September 1854, 2; 25 December 1856, 3.

640. Refers to William Henry Harrison. "Harrison Melody No. 1" to the tune "The King and the Countryman" was published in *New-Hampshire Sentinel*, 22 April 1840, 4.

641. Possibly a song set to the popular poem with identical first line by Thomas Moore. See *Green-Mountain Farmer*, 1 October 1810, 4.

642. Liberator, 18 June 1841, 99; *Standard*, 1 July 1841, 16, as reported and with lyrics printed in Eaklor, *American Antislavery Songs*, 130–31.

643. Words by Thomas Moore.

644. Abell was pastor of the Universalist Society church in Haverhill. *Haverhill Gazette*, 17 April 1841, 2.

645. Lyrics in *The Universal Songster and Museum of Mirth* (Boston: Charles Gaylord, 1835).

646. Reported in Howard Hastings Martin, "Orations on the Anniversary of American Independence, 1777–1876" (Ph.D. dissertation, Northwestern University, 1955), 57.

647. Hutchinson, a singer, operated a "wool carding and cloth dressing" business in Milford. By 1850 he was head of a school and gained an excellent reputation as a vocalist in concerts he gave in Milford, Keene, New Hampshire, Amherst, Massachusetts, and other New England towns. *Farmers' Cabinet*, 26 December 1850, 2, and 20 April 1854, 3.

648. This first line title has lyrics and music printed in *The Harp of Freedom*. Compiled by George W. Clark (New York: Miller, Orton & Mulligan, 1856).

649. Listed in Pemberton, 70.

650. Cited in Anne Marie Hickey, "The Celebration of the Fourth of July in Westfield, 1826–1853," *Historical Journal of Massachusetts* 9/2 (1981): 41–42.

651. A newspaper commented in 1843: "The Sing Sing Brass Band is one of the best companies of the kind that we have ever seen. It is composed of highly respectable and enterprising gentlemen, mostly young men, and is truly an ornament to the place." *Hudson-River Chronicle*, 7 February 1843, 3.

652. This temperance poem is printed in Paul D. Sanders, *Lyrics and Borrowed Tunes of the American Temperance Movement* (Columbia: University of Missouri Press, 2006), 10–11.

653. Listed in Pemberton, 71.

654. Reported (with lyrics) in Eaklor, *American Antislavery Songs*, 232–33, as printed in the *Liberator*, 28 May 1836, 88, and various other publications, and sung in 1836 at an "annual meeting of the Vermont Anti-Slavery Society."

655. Anne C. Lynch Botta (1815–1891) wrote an "Ode for the Fourth of July" (first line: "A glorious vision burst") published in her collection *Poems* (1853).

656. John Hill Hewitt (1801–1890), noted composer of Civil War songs including his best known "All Quiet on the Potomac To-Night" (1863) published the patriotic song "Our Native Land: A National Song" (Baltimore: Geo. Willig Jr., 1833).

657. John Quincy Adams refers to this occasion in *Memoirs of John Quincy Adams* 11:389.

658. The band was formed ca.1841, "under the scientific tuition of Mr. Bond, who is known to be *au fait* in music, its members have made very rapid progress." By 1845, the band was under the direction of a "Mr. Drew." *New-Hampshire Patriot and State Gazette*, 7 May 1841, 2, and 19 June 1845, 3.

659. R. Ronald Reedy, *Celebration in Lititz, Pennsylvania: The 175th Anniversary History of Independence Day Observances with a Narrative of the Lititz Springs Park, 1818–1992* (Lititz, PA: Anniversary Celebration General Committee, 1992), 3–4.

660. Cited in Heintze, *The Fourth of July Encyclopedia*, 200.

661. William Batchelder Bradbury (1816–1868).

662. Listed in Pemberton, 73.

663. In 1839 Pabodie was a justice of the peace in Providence. "The General Assembly," *Newport Mercury*, 11 May 1839, 2.

664. George W. Bethune (1805–1862).

665. Lyrics in *Abraham Lincoln Historical Digitization Project*, University of Chicago: http://lincoln.lib.niu.edu, and Eaklor, *American Antislavery Songs*, 114–15.

666. Listed in Pemberton, 74.

667. As advertised: "The Vocalist — consisting of short and easy glees, arranged for soprano, alto, tenor and bass voices by L. Mason and G.J. Webb — a very popular work." *New Hampshire Sentinel*, 18 November 1846, 4.

668. Withington wrote the verses for a collection titled *Evening Melodies*, music by Edward L. White. *New-Bedford Mercury*, 19 June 1840, 3.

669. First line: "The Land our fathers left to us," *Liberator*, 17 July 1846, 116, as reported and with lyrics printed in Eaklor, *American Antislavery Songs*, 73.

670. Under the title "Freemen, Awake!" as reported and with lyrics printed in Eaklor, *American Antislavery Songs*, 134–35.

671. McJilton was a member of the Baltimore Union Lyceum. *Baltimore Patriot*, 8 October 1834, 3.

672. James Monroe Deems (1818–1901), Baltimore composer who played the cornet, clarinet and French horn. Deems taught at the University of Virginia (1849–58). Richard Jackson, "An American Muse Learns to Walk: The First American-Music Group," in *American Musical Life in Context and Practice to 1865*, 301–02.

673. According to Pemberton, 77, "it is not known whether the work was actually published, and if so, by whom and when."

674. T. Comer was a reputable musician and composer who taught music in the Boston Grammar Schools. He helped organize the annual New Hampshire and Vermont Music Teachers' Conventions held in various towns during the 1840s. He compiled *A Collection of New Church Music* (1841) and co-

edited with J.B. Woodward *The Choral*, among other numerous publications. *Pittsfield Sun*, 24 March, 1842, 4; *New-Hampshire Patriot and State Gazette*, 15 August 1844, 4; *Morning News* (New London, CT), 19 October 1847, 3.

675. A newspaper article reported in 1839 that "the celebrated clarinet player," J.R. Kendall was director of the Winchester Band at that time. *New Hampshire Sentinel*, 10 July 1839, 3.

676. Accompanied a toast to the Charlotte and South Carolina Railroad.

677. Benjamin Franklin Baker (1811–1889) co-compiled, with William Oscar Perkins, *The Atlantic Glee Book* (Boston: Russell & Tolman, 1861).

678. "Rhodolph Hall Letters," 21 June 1849, as reported in Robert E. Eliason, "Rhodolph Hall: Nineteenth-Century Keyed Bugle, Cornet, and Clarinet Soloist," *Journal of the American Musical Instrument Society* 29 (2003): 25.

679. In 1846, after an organ was purchased in Boston for the church, Helen Dunham "became the organist, and although having little or no previous acquaintance with the instrument, building upon her skill as a pianist, she soon became an accomplished performer, especially admired for the grace of her voluntaries, and her excellent judgment in accompanying either the choir, or solo-vocalists. Her salary was one hundred dollars per annum." In 1847 Dunham advertised her services as a teacher of piano and for "instructions in thorough bass." J.E.A. Smith, *The History of Pittsfield, Massachusetts* (Springfield: C.W. Bryan, 1876), 421; *Pittsfield Sun*, 17 June 1847, 3.

680. J. Fletcher Williams, *A History of the City of Saint Paul, and the County of Ramsey, Minnesota* (Saint Paul: Minnesota Historical Society, 1876), 227.

681. Arthur H. Masten, *The History of Cohoes, New York, from Its Earliest Settlement to the Present Time* (Albany: J. Munsell, 1877), 109–10.

682. As reported in Lonn Taylor, Kathleen M. Kendrick, and Jeffrey L. Brodie, *The Star-Spangled Banner: The Making of an American Icon* (Washington, D.C.: Smithsonian Institution, 2008), 47.

683. Harvey B. Dodworth, band master, was born in Sheffield, England. "As the director of the Seventh Regiment Band he rapidly brought this organization to the front, and contributed largely toward giving it its highest rank. It was, however, through his connection with the Thirteenth Regiment Band of this city that he was know to Brooklynites." "Professor Dodworth Dying," *Brooklyn Daily Eagle*, 14 January 1891, 6.

684. To the toast: "The territory of Utah. Rocky mountains, sandy plains; truth and labor have their gains."

685. By James Monroe Whitfield (1822–1871) and titled "Ode for the Fourth of July" in his *"America and Other Poems* (Buffalo: James S. Leavitt, 1853), 74–75.

686. Reported in Hay, "Freedom's Jubilee: One Hundred Years of the Fourth of July, 1776–1876," 142.

687. Text with vocal music printed in I.B. Woodbury, *The Anthem Dulcimer* (NY: F.J. Huntington & Co., 1856).

688. Lucien H. Southard (1827–1881) was music supervisor in the Boston school system and an organist in Hartford in 1860–61. After serving in the Civil War he became director of the Peabody Conservatory in Baltimore from 1868–71. *Grove's Dictionary of Music and Musicians: American Supplement* (New York Macmillan Co., 1928), 27.

689. This band was formed in Providence in 1837 and was led by Joseph C. Greene from 1837 to 1866. Robert E. Eliason, "Bugles Beyond Compare: The Presentation E-flat Keyed Bugle in Mid-Nineteenth-Century America," *Journal of the American Musical Instrument Society* 31 (2006): 100.

690. Music by William Vincent Wallace and published 1851 by William Hall & Son, New York City. Facsimile of title page in Lawrence, 339. Listed in Board of Music Trade of the United States of America, *Complete Catalogue of Sheet Music and Musical Works, 1870*; reprint, New York: Da Capo, 1973, 37. Published in the Sabbath singing book: *Bradbury's Golden Chain of Sabbath School Melodies* (New York: Ivison, Phinney & Co., 1861) by William Bradbury who advertised the work in "Music

for the Fourth of July," *New York Evangelist*, 20 June 1861, and in the pocket songster *Hymns, Religious and Patriotic for the Soldier and the Sailor* (Boston: American Tract Society, 1861). Also published with music under the title "The Flag of Our Union For Ever!" (first line: "A Song for our banner, the watchword recall"), "and harmonized by G.W.C." in *The Harp of Freedom*, compiled by George W. Clark (New York: Miller, Orton & Mulligan, 1856).

691. A brief biographical sketch and several of his poems are in Griswold, *The Poets and Poetry of America*, 437–39.

692. Cora Dolbee, "The Fourth of July in Early Kansas 1854–1857," *Kansas Historical Quarterly* 10/1 (February 1941): 47.

693. *The Kansas Territorial Register*, 7 July 1855, as reported in Dolbee, "The Fourth of July in Early Kansas 1854–1857": 47.

694. First published in Philadelphia in 1843 under the title "Columbia the Land of the Brave" with music composed by David T. Shaw and words by the actor Thomas A. Becket. The lyrics include the phrase "the red, white, and blue" and frequently the tune was identified by those words as an alternate title. An edition published in the following year in Philadelphia bears the title "Columbia the Gem of the Ocean." In 1861 the lyrics were published under the title "Red, White, and Blue" in *Hymns, Religious and Patriotic, for the Soldier and the Sailor* (Boston: American Tract Society, 1861) and the first song in the collection *The Red, White, and Blue Songster: No. 1, National Patriotic Songs Written to Popular Airs* (Indianapolis: C.O. Perrine, 1861).

695. John Charles Fremont (1813–1890) ran for the presidency in 1856.

696. Listed in Board of Music Trade of the United States of America, *Complete Catalogue of Sheet Music and Musical Works, 1870*, 519.

697. *Lawrence Republican*, 2 and 9 July 1857, as reported in Dolbee, "The Fourth of July in Early Kansas 1854–1857": 69.

698. *Kansas Tribune*, 4 July 1857 and *The Kansas News* [Emporia], 18 July 1857, as reported by Dolbee, "The Fourth of July in Early Kansas 1854–1857": 73.

699. An ode with this opening line was composed by Royal Tyler and first introduced on the Fourth of July in 1801. The poem is reprinted in *Landmark Anthologies: Specimens of American Poetry* (1829), *The Verse of Royall Tyler* (1968); Heintze, *The Fourth of July Encyclopedia*, 287.

700. The music printed in *Los Angeles Times*, 4 July 1897, 12.

701. One of the bands was the Boston Brass Band, led by D.C. Hall, with Rhodolph Hall, second leader and soloist. In a letter written by Rhodolph on July 28, 1858, he spoke highly of the "monster concert," and noted the four bands included 72 musicians, "all brass played well. Hail Columbia with Lt. Artillery accompaniment. The 6 canon came in just right." Reported in Eliason, "Rhodolph Hall: Nineteenth-Century Keyed Bugle, Cornet, and Clarinet Soloist."

702. Led by H.C. Pellett of North Adams who in 1858 taught 10 instrumentalists of the Hancock Brass Band. *Pittsfield Sun*, 7 October 1858, 2.

703. *Liberator*, 1 July 1859, 104, as reported and with lyrics printed in Eaklor, *American Antislavery Songs*, 225–26.

704. These untitled songs in *Liberator*, 8 July 1859, 107, as reported and with lyrics printed in Eaklor, *American Antislavery Songs*, 226.

705. The event was originally described in *Rocky Mountain News*, 9 July 1859, as reported in Henry Miles, *Orpheus in the Wilderness: A History of Music in Denver, 1860–1925* (Denver: Colorado Historical Society, 2006), 111. The band was the Council Bluffs Band.

706. For more information on the Boston Brass Band during the 1850s, see Eliason, "Rhodolph Hall: Nineteenth-Century Keyed Bugle, Cornet, and Clarinet Soloist."

707. Led by Patrick Sarsfield Gilmore (1829–1892). Born near Dublin, Ireland, he reportedly had a propensity for music at an early age. Gilmore played the cornet and by fifteen years of age had written some marches and polkas for bands. He was in Boston in 1858 starting his band that was considered by some

at that time "the leading musical organization of the kind in the country." His group frequently toured the country, was enlisted during the Civil War, and was later known for its participation in monster concerts. In 1873 he had moved to New York and became the bandmaster of the 65-member Twenty-Second Regiment Band. His fame and contributions to musical development in the country continued to grow until his death. "A Noted Bandmaster Gone," *New York Times*, 25 September 1892, 1. For additional information on Gilmore, see Jere T. Humphreys, "Strike up the Band! The Legacy of Patrick S. Gilmore," *Music Educators Journal* 74/2 (October 1987): 22–26, and Frank J. Cipolla, "Patrick S. Gilmore: The Boston Years," *American Music* 6/3 (Autumn 1988): 281–92. An image of Gilmore's band in 1885 is in Bryant, *And the Band Played On, 1776–1976*, 28.

708. *Liberator*, 13 July 1860, 112, as reported and with lyrics printed in Eaklor, *American Antislavery Songs*, 483–84.

709. *Liberator*, 27 July 1860, 118, as reported and with lyrics printed in Eaklor, *American Antislavery Songs*, 484.

710. Listed as Neyer's Band, George Neyer, leader in *The American Musical Directory 1861* (New York: T. Hutchinson; reprint, New York: Da Capo, 1980), 86.

711. Cited in Heintze, *The Fourth of July Encyclopedia*, 103.

712. For information on variant printings and other performances of this work, see Thomas Franklin Currier, *A Bibliography of Oliver Wendell Holmes* (New York: Russell & Russell, 1971), 93–97.

713. Marshall Lefferts (1821–1876).

714. Oliver Wendell Holmes composed a third verse to this song. Information from a four-page program printed in Currier, *A Bibliography of Oliver Wendell Holmes*, 104, states "the singing will be performed by a choir of pupils selected from the grammar schools under the direction of Charles Butler. Mr. H.M. Dow will preside at the organ."

715. A "J. Cooke" listed as the leader of the Albany Brass Band in *The American Musical Directory 1861*, 85.

716. Claudio S. Grafulla (1810–1880) was the group's bandmaster, 1860–1880. The ensemble was popularly referred to as "Grafulla's Band" in the sources examined.

717. *Liberator*, 11 July 1862, 112, as reported and with lyrics printed in Eaklor, *American Antislavery Songs*, 497–98.

718. *Liberator*, 11 July 1862, 112, as reported and with lyrics printed in Eaklor, *American Antislavery Songs*, 90–91.

719. Published in *The Golden Chain* by William Bradbury.

720. Lyrics published in *The Red, White, and Blue Songster: No. 1, National Patriotic Songs Written to Popular Airs* (Indianapolis: C.O. Perrine, 1861).

721. Words by Julia Ward Howe (1819–1910). This was the first recorded performance of "The Battle Hymn of the Republic." The lyrics were first published in the *Atlantic Monthly* (February 1862) and quickly became the unofficial Civil War hymn of the Union Army. Heintze, *The Fourth of July Encyclopedia*, 144.

722. "Viva L'America" (Boston: O. Ditson & Co., 1859), subtitled "Home of the Free," by H. Millard. Lyrics published in *The Red, White, and Blue Songster: No. 1, National Patriotic Songs Written to Popular Airs* (Indianapolis: C.O. Perrine, 1861).

723. S. Theresa Wason, an amateur poet, wrote several other pieces: "Memories" and "Praised God for Victories Achieved" in *Farmers' Cabinet*, 15 November 1861, 1 and 20 April 1865, 1, respectively, and another, a hymn sung to the tune of "Auld Lang Syne," at the golden wedding anniversary of her parents, Capt. and Mrs. John Lamson in *Farmer's Cabinet*, 24 February 1870, 2.

724. Died on March 13, 1876, in New Boston at the age of 91. "The Old Folks," *Farmers' Cabinet*, 30 January 1877, 2.

725. Years prior, Major Jesse Beard had been a participant in the 1830 Independence Day celebration in New Boston. He presented the following toast at the dinner: "The ladies of New-Boston — Beauty their uniform, virtue their shield, may we yield to no arms but theirs." He died in 1879 at the age of 90 in New Boston. His obituary stated: "During his life Mr. Beard had taught sixty-seven terms of school, been superintending school committee for twenty-one years, and had taught eighty-seven

singing-schools." *New-Hampshire Patriot*, 19 July 1830, 2; "Deaths," *Farmers' Cabinet*, 11 November 1879, 3.

726. Susan McFarland Parkhurst (1836–1918) was a prolific composer of popular songs on a variety of topics.

727. Words by Mrs. M.A. Kidder. First line: "'Tis the peace jubilee, sing Hosanna!"

728. Words by A.J.A. Duganne. For 4-part chorus (SATB) and piano.

729. Heintze, *The Fourth of July Encyclopedia*, 199.

730. Howe recited poetry at a Woodstock, Connecticut, celebration on July 4, 1893. *New York Times*, 5 July 1893, 9. Her "Hymn for the Fourth of July" (first line: "Our fathers built the house of God"), was printed in *At Sunset* (1910).

731. Of Boston, and led by Alonzo Bond who had advertised in 1837 in Concord his "Music School" where he gave "private lessons on any instruments," as well as offered his services as a music arranger for military bands. In 1844 he was leader of the Manchester Brass Band. *New-Hampshire Patriot and State Gazette*, 2 October 1837, 3, and 13 June 1844, 2.

732. Composed in 1862 by George F. Root (1825–1895).

733. James McCann led this popular orchestra which had a national reputation for its excellence. For example, he was engaged to perform with 16 of his top instrumentalists in Cincinnati, to join John Robinson's Mammoth Circus for a nationwide tour. "Personal," *Brooklyn Daily Eagle*, 29 March 1871, 4.

734. Matthias Keller (1813–1875). Printed: Boston: Oliver Ditson & Co., 1866. First line: "Speed our republic O Father on high." According to Hezekiah Butterworth in *The Story of the Hymns* (New York: American Tract Society, 1875), 262, the piece was first sung in New York and became "a favorite of bands in Boston" and "by an adopted custom is the first piece played on the Common by bands on Independence Days."

735. Seward (1835–1902) was born in Florida, New York, and was a cousin of Secretary of State William H. Seward. In 1870 he presented a paper at the National Musical Congress held in New York. "He devoted many years to the study and teaching of music and the editing of musical journals." A principal collection he compiled was *The Temple Choir* (New York: Mason Brothers, 1867). *New York Times*, 1 September 1870 and 19 December 1897, 1 and 7, respectively.

736. Music by Henry Kleber (b. 1818), lyrics by Edward J. Allen. Score published: New York: Firth, Pond & Co., 1861. First line: "Unfurl the glorious banner, let it sway upon the breeze."

737. Composed by Stephen Foster. Published: New York: Firth, Pond, 1858.

738. *Gemma de Vergy: an Opera in Four Acts* (1848), by Gaetano Donizetti (1797–1848).

739. F. Nicholls Crouch.

740. *Les Gardes de la Reine Valse* (1865) by Daniel E. Godfrey.

741. From the opera *Maritana* (1861) by William Vincent Wallace (1812–1865).

742. *The Emancipation Car* (1874), as reported and with lyrics printed in Eaklor, *American Antislavery Songs*, 209–10.

743. Includes the score.

744. For a number of year, the band was led by E.T. Baldwin, pianist, composer, music teacher and dealer in keyboard instruments.

745. George A. Connors and his band of 15 musicians were assigned to the 14th Regiment during the Civil War, after which the group performed together for the next 30 years, gaining considerable popularity in the New York area. A note in a local newspaper reported that "their repertoire is extensive, their command perfect." *Brooklyn Daily Eagle*, 3 July 1867, 2.

746. For an article on this celebrated cornet player, see "Brighton's Crowd," *Brooklyn Daily Eagle*, 3 July 1882, 3.

747. First line printed as "Our fathers! God! From out whose hand" in *The Complete Poetical Works of John Greenleaf Whittier* (New York: Houghton Mifflin, 1894), 234. "Centennial Hymn" was premiered by the Grand Centennial Chorus and Theodore Thomas Orchestra at the opening concert of the "Centennial Inauguration Ceremonies" in Philadelphia. Facsimile of program

reprinted in Ezra Schabas, *Theodore Thomas: America's Conductor and Builder of Orchestras, 1835–1905* (Urbana: University of Illinois Press, 1989). "Centennial Hymn" was advertised as available in sheet music, octavo, and an arrangement for orchestra (*Quincy Daily Herald*, Illinois, 4 July 1876). Whittier also wrote a patriotic poem titled "Our Country" that was read at Woodstock, Connecticut, on July 4, 1883.

748. An "octavo form for societies" at ten cents a copy was advertised in the *Quincy Daily Herald* (Illinois), 4 July 1876. The program for the Philadelphia International Exhibition in which Holmes' hymn is listed, as well as citations for newspapers that published additional information on his piece is in Currier, *A Bibliography of Oliver Wendell Holmes*, 157, 417.

749. "The Flag of the Free: National Ode" (1861) by H. Millard.

750. Probably from "Shamus O'Brien: Answer to Nora O'Neal: a Beautiful Song and Chorus (1870) by Will. S. Hayes.

751. Probably the duet composed by T. Williams.

752. Possibly the song published in 1849 by Charles Slade.

753. According *to Farmers' Cabinet*, 1 February 1861, 2, a song having this title was composed by J.W. Turner.

754. Op. 27 for chorus and orchestra. Original manuscript in the Boston Public Library. Facsimile of first page of printed music in Lawrence, 467.

755. Eichberg (1824–1893), an accomplished German violinist and composer who emigrated to New York in 1857, and later worked in Boston where he directed concerts at the Boston Museum and helped establish the Boston Conservatory of Music. F.H. Jenks and John Moran: "Eichberg, Julius," *Grove Music Online* ed. L. Mary (accessed 4 December 2007), http://www.grovemusic.com.proxyau.wrlc.org.

756. By Charles Albert White, this song was subtitled "Centennial Hymn," and published in *White's Male Quartette Book* (Boston: White, Smith & Co., 1884), 131–33.

757. G. William Sumner.

758. Edward S. Nason.

759. By Stephen Foster.

760. For many years, William H. Conant served as secretary of the Appleton Academy in Mont Vernon. *Farmers' Cabinet*, 30 January 1868, 3.

761. Words and music by Henry Clay Work. Printed: Chicago: Root & Cady, 1865. Facsimile of title page in Lawrence, 423. Modern reprint of music in Marrocco, *Music in America*, 304–06.

762. According to Richard Jackson, Julius Meyer (1822–1899) "came to the United States from Germany in 1852, and became known as a vocal teacher in Brooklyn." Jackson, "An American Music Learns to Walk: The First American-Music Group," in *American Musical Life in Context and Practice to 1865*, 315.

763. Likely the chorus "The heavens are telling the glory of God" in Haydn's oratorio *The Creation*.

764. One example of this song published under the title "National Song," with the "music composed and respectfully dedicated to Gen. John A. Dix by John P. Morgan." Oakland, CA: J. E. White, 1876. First line: "Waken, waken, waken voice of the land's devotion." Lyrics also printed in "Centennial Songs for the Fourth," *New York Evangelist*, 29 June 1876, 3. The work was performed at midnight on July 3.

765. Taylor (1825–1878) publicly recited his "National Ode" (first line: "Sun of the stately day") from memory at Independence Square in Philadelphia on July 4. On the same day, in Washington, D.C., his poem "Centennial Bells" was read by John Tweedale at the First Congregational Church. Heintze, *The Fourth of July Encyclopedia*, 279.

766. Music by Bernard Covert (b. 1820), with lyrics by William Ross Wallace (1819–1881). Printed: Boston: G. P. Reed & Co., 1855). First line: "He lay upon his dying bed."

767. For the dedication ceremony exactly a year later, see Performances 1877.

768. Full title: *The Great Republic: An Ode to the American Union* (New York: Biglow & Main, 1880).

769. The hymn was set to the music "American Hymn" com-

posed by Matthias Keller (Edith L. Markham, "Poetry Written for the Opening Exercises and the Fourth of July Celebration at the 1876 Centennial Exhibition in Philadelphia" [M.A. thesis, Univeresity of North Carolina, 1950]).

770. Pratt (1846–1916) was an American composer who lived in Chicago and New York. He had studied music in Germany. Robert Stevenson, "Pratt, Silas G (amaliel)," *Grove Music Online* ed. L. Mary (accessed 18 April 2008), http://www.grovemusic.com.proxyau.wrlc.org.

771. A re-dedication of the monument took place on May 7, 2006, with a booklet published for the occasion.

772. For descriptions of Fourth of July celebrations and music on the Fourth of July in Warren, see David Allen Crossett, "One-Night Stand: A History of Live and Recorded Entertainments in Warren, Pennsylvania, from 1795 to the Present" (Ph.D. dissertation, New York University, 1983).

773. Philip Phillips (1834–1895) was also a composer of hymn tunes and was known for his singing of evangelical tunes. His book *Song Pilgrimage Around and Throughout the World* (New York, 1882) provides his reflections of his worldwide tours.

774. Miles, *Orpheus in the Wilderness*, 118.

775. Band included 30 instrumentalists and was conducted by K. Scheriner. *Brooklyn Daily Eagle*, 4 September 1879, 1.

776. This popular 10-piece band was active in the 1880s and changed membership several times. For lists of members and the instruments they played, see *Fort Collins Courier*, 26 June 1884, 2 December 1886, and 11 April 1889.

777. See New Bedford, Massachusetts, celebration of 1831.

778. Edmond Audran (1840–1901), *Les noces d'Olivette*.

779. *Les Cloches de Corneville* (Paris: L. Bathlot, 1877), opera-comique by Robert Planquette.

780. Band included 24 instrumentalists. *Brooklyn Daily Eagle*, 23 July 1875, 4.

781. "Die Wacht am Rhein" by Carl Wilhelm (1815–1873).

782. It was noted in a local newspaper that Conterno had 5000 pieces of music stored in the pavilion where he performed. "Coney Island," *Brooklyn Daily Eagle*, 7 July 1882, 3.

783. Reported in Bowie, "R.B. Hall and the Community Bands of Maine," 109.

784. Possibly the song "Union and Liberty: Solo and Chorus" (Toledo, OH: Louis Doebele, 1863) by Charles G. Degenhard; words by Oliver Wendell Holmes. First line: "Flag of the heroes who left us their glory."

785. Possibly "Sitting on the Golden Fence: Plantation Song" (Boston: Oliver Ditson & Co., 1884) by A. Wiggins.

786. Miles, *Orpheus in the Wilderness*, 122.

787. Heintze, *The Fourth of July Encyclopedia*, 194–95; H. Earle Johnson, *First Performances in America to 1900: Works with Orchestra* (Detroit: Information Coordinators, 1979), 100. MTNA was organized in 1876 in Delaware, Ohio, by Theodore Presser and a group of teachers. Other Fourth of July concerts sponsored by the association included: Chicago, in the Exposition Building (1888); Philadelphia, in the Academy of Music (1889); Detroit (1890); Saratoga Springs, New York (1894).

788. For orchestra and likely an Indianapolis premiere.

789. Possibly *Messe solennelle: à quatre voix, soli et choeurs avec accompagnement d'orgue ou d'orchestre*, op. 145, by Ferd Dulcken.

790. Listed in Johnson, *First Performances in America to 1900*, 137.

791. As cited by E. Douglas Bomberger (p. 19) who reported that W. S. B. Matthews, "a Chicago writer and music teacher, [who was there] noted that there was no reserved seating, and the acoustics were such that those sitting in the back of the building could not understand the words of the choral pieces" and that other reports indicated that the instruments had to compete with fireworks being set off outside the building. Bomberger, "*A Tidal Wave of Encouragement": American Composers' Concerts in the Gilden Age* (Westport, CT: Praeger, 2002), 18–19, 21; Heintze, *The Fourth of July Encyclopedia*, 195; Johnson, *First Performances in America to 1900*, 109, 225.

792. Josiah Bartlett, signer of the Declaration of Independence.

793. Jean M. Missud was a Salem, Massachusetts, composer and bandmaster who led the Salem Cadet Band during those years. "Jean M. Mussud Papers," Peabody Essex Museum, Salem, Massachusetts.

794. Probably *Mañana Chilian Dance* by Jean M. Missud.

795. Correct title is *American Student's Waltz*.

796. Ellen Knight, "Music in Winchester, Massachusetts: A Community Portrait, 1830–1925," *American Music* 11/3 (Autumn 1993): 271.

797. Seidl's orchestra included 70 instrumentalists. A description of the works performed for this concert is in "Coney Island Music," *New York Times*, 4 July 1888, 5. It was noted that "those who want to hear the lighter orchestral compositions of the best writers, interspersed with vocal and choral numbers, can go to Mr. Seidl's concerts, and those who are fond of the martial bare of trumpets and clang of cymbals can sit under the ministrations of Mr. Gilmore." The reporter noted that Gilmore had "an uncommonly good band, and he arranges his programmes with a view to pleasing all tastes."

798. Johnson, *First Performances in America to 1900*, 207.

799. Program, reproduced in Margaret Hindle Hazen and Robert M. Hazen, *The Music Men: An Illustrated History of Brass Bands in America, 1800–1920* (Washington, D.C.: Smithsonian Institution Press, 1987), 122.

800. "Stand Firm for the Right: Patriotic Song and Chorus" (New York: Charles W. Harris, 1872), by H.P. Danks (1834–1903).

801. As reported in Dorothy D. Perry, "Fourth of July in Ely, 1891," *Minnesota History* 40/2 (Summer 1966): 60–61.

802. The poem was set to music by Samuel Augustus Ward, organist at Grace Episcopal Church in Newark, New Jersey, to the melody of the hymn "Materna" that had been published in 1888. Lynn Sherr, *America the Beautiful: The Stirring True Story Behind Our Nation's Favorite Song* (New York: BBS Public Affairs, 2001).

803. For a discussion of some of the musical works performed at the fair, see Anne E. Feldman, "Being Heard: Women Composers and Patrons at the 1893 World's Columbian Exposition," *Notes*, Second Series, 47/1 (September 1990): 7–20.

804. "The Music Congress Assembles," *New York Times*, 4 July 1893, 8.

805. Johnson, *First Performances in America to 1900*, 207.

806. Probably the song with the same title from the opera *Lurline* (1860) by William Vincent Wallace (1812–1865).

807. Adolphe Adam (1803–1856).

808. Dudley Buck (1839–1909), *On the Sea* (New York: G. Schirmer, 1908).

809. Probably "Daddy Won't Buy Me a Bow-Wow, Schottische" (1893).

810. *A Memorial Volume of the Guilford Battle Ground Company* (Greensboro, NC: Reece & Elam, 1893), 28–29.

811. Hungarian violinist who in 1853 toured in Germany with Johannes Brahms and came to America in 1878. In 1886 he performed in Japan, China, and South Africa.

812. As reported in a local newspaper: "The best of the band concerts are those given by Sousa and his well drilled forces in the cool pavilion at Manhattan beach. His programmes are well arranged and contain music that is not only good but popular.... Mr. Sousa's marches are good. They are whistled and played all over the land.... Mr. Sousa adds to the popularity of his programmes by the introduction of singers." "The Sousa Concerts," *Brooklyn Daily Eagle*, 5 July 1894, 7. For more on Sousa and his concerts, see Paul Edmund Bierley, *The Incredible Band of John Philip Sousa* (Urbana: University of Illinois Press, 2006).

813. Possibly *The Great Republic, Ode to the American Union* (1880) by George Frederick Bristow.

814. Likely the first Fourth of July performance of *The Liberty Bell March*.

815. *Grand American Fantasia: Tone Pictures of the North and South* was composed by Theo Bendix in 1892 and published Boston: Oliver Ditson, 1899.

816. See Tito Mattei (1841–1914), *Patria (My Native Land)*. New York: G. Schirmer, 1881.

817. Luigi Arditi (1822–1903).

818. Children's bands often performed on the Fourth in Illinois. See, for example, a list of works performed by the band of the Illinois Asylum for Feeble Minded Children on July 4, 1896, reported in Phillip M. Hash, "Development of School Bands in Illinois: 1863–1930" (Ed.D. dissertation, University of Illinois at Urbana-Champaign, 2006), 294–95.

819. *Jubel Overture*, op. 59.

820. William Vincent Wallace (1812–1865), "Yes! Let Me Like a Soldier Fall," from the composer's *Maritana*, a theatrical work introduced in New York in 1848.

821. Edward Jakobowski (b.1858), *Erminie: Comic Opera* (Boston: White, Smith & Co., 1896).

822. Luigi Arditi (1822–1903), "Leggero Invisible."

823. Henry H. Thiele (1855–1899), *American Republic March*.

824. Kerry Mills (1869–1948), *Rastus on Parade: Two Step March* (1895).

825. Probably "The Fair Land of Poland," from the opera of *The Bohemian Girl* by M.W. Balfe (1808–1870).

826. Heintze, *The Fourth of July Encyclopedia*, 104–05.

827. *Dixit Dominus* by the Italian composer Saverio Mercadante (1795–1870).

828. Probably "Emmerig's Grand Magnificat" (Baltimore: W.C. Peters, 1858).

829. H. Millard (1830–1895). Score published: Boston: McLaughlin & Reilly Co., 1923.

830. Premiered on May 14, 1897, in Philadelphia. *Philadelphia Public Ledger*, 15 May 1897, as reported in Paul E. Bierley, *The Works of John Philip Sousa* (Columbus, OH: Integrity Press, 1984), 84.

831. Theodore Moses Tobani (1855–1933), American composer born in Germany who arranged a number of national airs.

832. *Sounds from the Sunny South Overture* by Emil Isenman.

833. Béla Kéler (1820–1882), Hungarian composer who wrote 13 galops and other instrumental works.

834. Mygrant was a composer, cornetist, and leader of the Thirteenth Regiment Band. In 1901 he also led the Twenty-Sixth Ward Young Men's Christian Association Military Band (30 members). His family was musical. His son Percy also played the cornet and his daughter S. Louise played the piano. *Brooklyn Daily Eagle*, 4 June 1901 and 2 August 1902, 6 and 6, respectively.

835. Johnson, *First Performances in America to 1900*, 108.

836. Comic opera by Julien Edwards (1855–1910).

837. *My Maryland: March & Two Step* (New York: Leo Feist, 1906), by W.S. Mygrant.

838. Ivan Caryll (1861–1921).

839. Kerry Mills (1869–1948).

840. This popular band performed at the Gravesend Bay Yacht Club of New York on July 4, 1897. "Triple Holiday Joys," *New York Times*, 3 July 1897, 5.

841. *Song Words of Wang: Operatic Burletta in Two Acts* (New York: T.B. Harms, 1891) by Woolson Morse (1858–1897).

842. A musical play, music by Lionel Monckton (1861–1924).

843. *Hannah's Promenade: Characteristic March and Two-Step Dance* (New York: Willis Woodward & Co., 1897) by Jacob Henry Ellis.

844. John M. Turner.

845. *Baltimore Morning Herald*, 5 July 1900, 10.

846. William H. Santelmann was leader of the Marine Band, 1898–1927.

847. Franz von Blon (1861–1945).

848. Tali Esen Morgan (1858–1941) was a well known choral conductor and teacher who had a penchant for "monster" concerts having choirs of 300 or more vocalists. He was conductor of the West End Choral Union of 300 voices and one of his concerts at the Ocean Grove Auditorium had 400 voices, assisted by Damrosch's orchestra. Morgan held his post as official conductor at the Auditorium for 17 years. He died in Asbury Park. "Notes of Musical Doings," *New York Times*, 28 October 1900, 22; "Asbury Park's Season," *New York Times*, 16 June 1901, 7; "Ocean Grove's Celebration," *New York Times*, 5 July 1901, 14; "Tali Esen Morgan, Choral Conductor," *New York Times*, 2 July 1941, 21.

849. Mori was a composer, teacher, and conductor of the Germania Maennerchor in Washington, D.C., beginning in the 1880s. He composed another opera *Telemach* (1893) which was premiered in Washington's Metzerott Hall in 1895. *Washington Post*, 21 January 1884, 1, and 14 April 1895, 18.

850. *Raymond, ou, Le secret de la reine: opéra comique en 3 actes* (1851) by Ambroise Thomas.

851. Diana Karter Appelbaum, *The Glorious Fourth: An American Holiday, an American History* (New York: Facts On File, 1989), 132–48.

852. "Fourth Quiet Also in Other Cities," *New York Times*, 5 July 1911, 6.

853. In William Chauncy Langdon, *The Celebration of the Fourth of July by Means of Pageantry* (Division of Recreation, Russell Sage Foundation, 1912), 42–55.

854. Ibid, 49.

855. For additional information, see Heintze, *The Fourth of July Encyclopedia*, 69–70.

856. "My Own United States: a Song from the Patriotic Opera 'When Johnny Comes Marching Home'" (New York: M. Witmark & Sons, 1909) by Julian Edwards (1855–1910).

857. The *Thomas Jefferson March* was performed on April 13, 1903, by the U.S. Marine Band with Lieutenant Santelmann, conducting, at a meeting of the Thomas Jefferson Memorial Association at the Hotel Barton in Washington, D.C. "Debt to Jefferson," *Washington Post*, 14 April 1903, 1. Evidently, an earlier performance by the Marine Band took place. According to Admiral of the Navy George Dewey in a "complimentary letter [he wrote to Santelmann prior to April 10] upon the most recent musical composition of the popular leader of the Marine Band," he wrote, "I have heard it played by your band, and enjoy it thoroughly." "Praise by Admiral Dewey," *Washington Post*, 10 April 1903, 12.

858. Wahley was a vocalist of some note, having performed with the U.S. Marine Band and as a member of Washington's Lyric Quartet.

859. As of July 1904, the membership of the full band was 69. For an article describing the band, the pay for its members, and how the band compares to other D.C. ensembles, see "Music for the Parks," *Washington Post*, 30 June 1904, 9.

860. Possibly the violinist Alfred E. Walper.

861. *Columbia: Fantasia Polka* (1893), solo for cornet, op. 345, by T.H. Rollinson.

862. *Commemorative Celebration at Sequalitchew Lake, Pierce County, Washington, July 5th, 1906* (Tacoma, WA: Vaughan and Morrill, 1906). In Tacoma, band concerts were presented on July 3 and 5 to help mark the commemoration of the first Fourth in the Pacific Northwest (p. 51). For additional information, see Heintze, *The Fourth of July Encyclopedia*, 315–16.

863. B.M. Bakkegard, "Music in Arizona before 1912," *Journal of Research in Music Education* 8/2 (Autumn 1960): 74.

864. *The Peacemaker: Characteristic March, Introducing Russian & Japanese Battle Songs* (Chicago: W. Rossiter, 1895) by Harry L. Alford.

865. Music of this song by Herman Paley (b. 1879) and James Kendis (1883–1946). Score published: New York: Cooper Kendis & Paley Music Pub. Co., 1906.

866. Score (NY: Harry Von Tilzer Music Pub. Co., 1903) for this song by Harry Von Tilzer (1872–1946).

867. Score (NY: Harry Von Tilzer Music Pub. Co., 1902) by Harry Von Tilzer.

868. Score (Chicago: Victor Kremer Co., 1902) by W.C. Powell.

869. The music for this medley overture is by Harry Von Tilzer; score arranged by Everett J. Evans.

870. *Paddy Whack: Characteristic March and Two-Step* (Detroit: Jerome H. Remick & Col., 1907) by J. Bodewalt Lampe (1869–1921).

871. *Iola: Intermezzo* (New York: Jerome H. Remick & Co., 1906) by Charles L. Johnson (1876–1950).

872. "Good-Night Beloved, Good-Night: A Serenade" (New York: M. Witmark & Sons, 1890), lyrics by Jack Everett Fay; music by James B. Oliver.

873. "The Homesick Yankee, or You're Thinking of Home Sweet Home" from *The Rich Mr. Hoggenheimer* (Cincinnati: John Church, 1906) by Kenneth S. Clark.

874. *Hungarian Lustspiel: Overture*, op. 108 (New York: C. Fischer, 1896) by Béla Kéler (1820–1882).

875. *Columbia: Fantasia Polka, Solo for Cornet*, op. 345 (Boston: O. Ditson, 1893), by T.H. Rollinson (1844–1928).

876. Edward H. Droop was a local pianist, accompanist, and later proprietor with his father of E.F. Droop and Sons, musical instrument firm in Washington. In 1930 he participated on a committee for the newly formed National Symphony Orchestra for its inaugural concert that took place on January 31 that year. *Washington Post*, 3 November 1895, 9, and 31 January 1930, 9.

877. Abe Holzmann (1874–1939).

878. *Aubade printanière*, op. 37 (Paris: Heugel, 1890) by Paul Lacombe (1837–1927).

879. This was Washington's first "safe and sane" celebration for which legislation was passed in November 1908 forbidding "the sale, storage or delivery, and the use except in public celebrations of fireworks" in the city. To replace the "old fashioned" style of noisy revelry, the official events included public "daylight fireworks" and an expanded musical program. It was reported that "never was there a more cheerful or good-tempered crowd." Henry B.F. Macfarland, "Washington's Safe and Sane Fourth," *The American City* 2/5 (May 1910), 212–13.

880. Additional information on the exposition and Busch's composition is in Donald R. Lowe, "Sir Carl Busch: His Life and Work as a Teacher, Conductor, and Composer" (D.M.A. dissertation, University of Missouri–Kansas City, 1972), 37, 209.

881. "Music in Boston," *Boston Evening Transcript*, 5 July 1910, 2.

882. Opera in three acts by Giacomo Puccini.

883. For an article on the band and lists of members in 1881 and 1887, see "Entertainments of '80s at Red Cliff," *Eagle Valley Enterprise*, 1 July 1921, 8.

884. Manuscript copy in Arthur Farwell Collection, Sibley Music Library, University of Rochester. Score listed in *A Guide to the Music of Arthur Farwell and to the Microfilm Collection of His Work* (New York: published by his children, 1972). For more information on Farwell, see Evelyn Davis Culbertson, "Arthur Farwell's Early Efforts on Behalf of American Music, 1889–1921," *American Music* 5/2 (Summer 1987): 156–75.

885. Led by Arnold Volpe, who, born in Russia, came to America in 1898. In 1902, he formed the Young Men's Symphony Orchestra.

886. Francesco Fanciulli, composer-conductor, was born in Italy and came to America in 1876. His skills and prowess as a musician resulted in his appointment as director of the U.S. Marine Band from 1892–1897. For more information on Fanciulli, see the website *"The President's Own": United States Marine Band.*

887. Perhaps the first identified performance of Tchaikovsky's popular work on the Fourth of July.

888. Premiered in New York on May 28, 1912, at the Settlement House, 53 East Third Street "by the pupils of the Music School Settlement" and "four orchestras under the leadership of David Mannes will assist." "Music Notes," *New York Times*, 28 May 1912, 11.

889. *Village Life in the Olden Time* (1894) by Charles Le Thiere and arranged by George Wiegand.

890. "Make the Fourth of July, 1915, 'Americanization Day,'" *American City* 12 (June 1915): 492–93; "Clark Asks Loyalty of New Americans" and "New Citizens Celebrate," *New York Times*, 5 July 1915, 4.

891. John Bromell Marshall founded the band in 1884. For more information, see Larry Laneer, "Marshall's Band of Topeka: A Study of the Golden Age of Bands in Kansas" (M.A. thesis, University of Kansas, 1978).

892. Fleck was a professor of music at Hunter College and had presented a series of 63 concerts that were sponsored by the Board of Education. *The New International Year Book: A Com-*

pendium of the World's Progress for the Year 1914. Ed. Frank Moore Colby (New York: Dodd, Mead, 1915), 478.

893. Organized in 1904 at the Washington Navy Yard and later changed the name to Washington Navy Yard Band. Jimmie Wayne Dyers, "A History of the United States Navy Band, Washington, D.C. (1918–1988)" (Ed.D. dissertation, University of Houston, 1988), 16–17.

894. See William Chauncy Langdon, *Abraham Lincoln Today: A War-Time Tribute* (University of Illinois, 1918).

895. Likely the song "By Thy Rivers Gently Flowing" (1901) by Walter Howe Jones.

896. Lyrics by W.C. Langdon; music by J. Lawrence Erb.

897. "Ring Out! Sweet Bells of Peace" (1918) by Caro Roma (1866–1937) and published Chicago: M. Witmark & Sons, 1918.

898. As reported in Mary DuPree, "Early Bands in an Idaho Railroad Town: Pocatello, 1887–1930," in *Vistas of American Music: Essays and Compositions in Honor of William K. Kearns* (Warren, MI: Harmonie Park, 1999), 258.

899. Lorenzo Camiliere (d. 1956) was a Greek composer-conductor who emigrated to America in 1905. For additional information, see George Leotsakos, "Camiliere, Lorenzo," *Grove Music Online* ed. L. Mary (accessed 4 December 2007), <http://www.grovemusic.com.proxyau.wrlc.org>.

900. See also, Heintze, *The Fourth of July Encyclopedia*, 220.

901. According to sources cited by Donald R. Lowe, "Sir Carl Busch: His Life and Work as a Teacher, Conductor, and Composer," 245–46, the concert had 18,000 attendees and Busch's piece soon after became one of the composer's "most frequently played compositions."

902. "The Americans Come!: an Episode in France in the Year 1918," by Fay Foster.

903. "Honor Writer of 'Old Kentucky Home,'" *Atlanta Constitution*, 5 July 1923, 4; photo of band on postcard printed by Standard Printing Company of Louisville, KY.

904. Possibly the song with that title by Zo Elliott and published: New York: M. Witmark & Sons, 1915.

905. "Big Radio Program for Defense Day," *New York Times*, 24 June 1925, 31.

906. Heintze, *The Fourth of July Encyclopedia*, 198.

907. For an article on musical events held during the exposition, see Herbert J. Tily, "Music and Musical Organizations," in Erastus L. Austin, *The Sesqui-Centennial International Exposition* (Philadelphia: Current, 1929; reprint, New York: Arno, 1976), 210–27.

908. "District Unites Tomorrow to Observe Independence Day," *Washington Evening Star*, 4 July 1926, 8; "District Ready for Gala Independence Day Fete," *Washington Post*, 4 July 1926, 1.

909. *New York Times*, 5 July 1926, 5.

910. Published: New York: Feature Music, 1924.

911. The quartet was founded in 1923 by Mrs. Coolidge. Members included Willem Willeke, cello and leader; Conrad Held, viola; William Kroll and Karl Kraeuter, violins.

912. Arthur Pryor's Band was very popular and by 1916 had teamed up with Sousa's band to issue a recording titled "American Patriotic Airs" (no. 16137) by the Victor Recording Co. Advertisement in *Washington Post*, 21 June 1916, 2. In 1911, Victor Recording Co. had issued Pryor's *Arms of America March* in time for the Fourth of July. "Music Appropriate to the Glorious 4th," *Atlanta Constitution*, 2 July 1911, A14.

913. *Herod Overture*, op. 31 (1901) by Henry Kimball Hadley.

914. *The Lady Picking Mulberries: A Chinese Episode* (1888) by Edgar Stillman Kelley.

915. *The Zouaves' Drill: Characteristic Composition for the Piano*, [op. 68] (J. Church; Philadelphia: T. Presser, distributors, 1920) by Mana Zucca (1885–1981).

916. A march by Edwin Franko Goldman (1878–1956).

917. *A Soldier's Dream: Fantasy* (New York: Carl Fischer, 1936) by Walter B. Rogers (1865–1939).

918. *Bandanna Sketches: Four Negro Spirituals*, op. 12, for violin and piano (New York: C. Fischer, 1918) by Clarence Cameron White (1880–1960).

919. Heintze, *The Fourth of July Encyclopedia*, 106.

920. Published in *The Flambeau: A Book of Songs for Schools,*

Institutes, Academies, Etc. (Winona Lake, IN: Rodeheaver Hall-Mack, 1931).

921. Published in *Parks' Sacred Three-Part Choruses and Trios for Mixed Voices* (S.A.B.) (York, NE: J.A. Parks, 1927).

922. Included 62 instrumentalists.

923. Grandson of Nathaniel Carusi, the latter who performed with his father Gaetano at a celebration in Annapolis on July 4, 1816. Heintze, *The Fourth of July Encyclopedia*, 102.

924. A World War I French song.

925. "The Americans Come!" By Fay Foster, words by Elizabeth A. Wilbur. Published: New York: J. Fischer, 1918.

926. Full title: *Spirit of Independence: Military March and Two-Step* (New York: Jerome H. Remick, 1912).

927. *Tesoro Mia! [My Sweetheart] Valzer* by Ernesto Becucci.

928. Another newspaper reports that it was the U.S. Army Band that provided the music. Robert D. Heinl, "Radio Dail Flashes," *Washington Post*, 4 July 1932, 8.

929. Hoogstraten directed the New York Philharmonic Orchestra during the 1924–25 seasons. He conducted the Stadium concerts from 1922–25, and became resident conductor of the Portland Symphonic Orchestra in Oregon in November 1925. "Philharmonic Stadium Concerts July 7," *New York Times*, 27 June 1926, X5.

930. Subtitled "Sketches from an American Theatre," the work is in "five short movements."

931. Subtitled "Eight Pictures from Memory," the piece was originally written for Paul Whiteman.

932. In addition a "special concert version" took place this same day live in Griffith Park at the Greek Theater in Los Angeles, with Gastone Usigli, conducting the orchestra. Kenneth J. Bindas, *All of This Music Belongs to the Nation: the WPA's Federal Music Project and American Society* (Knoxville: University of Tennessee Press, 1995), 54; "Opera Tonight," *Los Angeles Times*, 4 July 1938, A7–A8.

933. A popular orchestra with 20 pieces that was organized on July 3, 1934, with ten members. Orchestra director Becker was born in Altoona, Pa., in 1916 and also sang with the ensemble.

934. "Tolerance Pledge Offered to Nation," *New York Times*, 4 July 1939, 2. The New York World's Fair ran from April to October in 1939 and 1940 and closed on October 27, 1940. The San Francisco International Exposition, referred to also as the Golden Gate Exposition, was held on Treasure Island and ran from February to October 1939 and May to September 1940.

935. Bennett wrote the following additional short compositions to accompany the display on other days: *Call to the Nations, Fountain Lake Fanfare, Postlude, The Hunt, Story of Three Flowers, Garden of Eden, The World and the Cathedral*, and *From Clay to Steel*. Roy Benton Hawkins, "The Life and Work of Robert Russell Bennett" (Ph.D. dissertation, Texas Tech University, 1989), 84.

936. The music and spectacle was described in this way by a reporter for the *New York Times*: "A martial burst of music fills the air for thirty seconds.... Then the music quickens in tempo and blue-green sprays, in tangled, misty patterns, supplant the white: the 'gathering of forces.' Then — and the murmur of approval from the crowd changes to a gasp — a tremendous, surging white jet, 150 feet in height, shoots up from the center of the lagoon to dominate the entire scene: this forceful, roaring stream is Washington. Then the music becomes more ominous, and the fountain colors change to red; the spray traces fitful, erratic patterns, fireworks soar overhead, and smoke and flame add a restless, disturbed note to the scene." *New York Times*, 4 July 1939, 3.

937. *Overture in Olden Style on French Noëls* (1931) by Philip James.

938. This program was created for "shut-ins" and was aired from 1931 to 1954. Musical numbers were often selected from listener requests.

939. For more information, see Donald C. Meyer, "Toscanini and the Good Neighbor Policy: The NBC Symphony Orchestra's 1940 South American Tour," *American Music* 18/3 (Autumn 2000): 233–56.

940. Balfoort wrote this work for Major General Thomas Holcomb, Marine Corps commandant.

941. In January 1944, Stravinsky conducted the Boston Symphony Orchestra in a premiere of this work. In an interview with the composer, reported by the *New York Times*, Stravinsky "went back to music of Puritan times to obtain his choral-like treatment of the anthem." Stravinsky said, "I gave it the character of a real church hymn, not that of a soldier's marching song or a club song, as it was originally. I tried to express the religious feelings of the people of America." "Revise's Nation's Anthem," *New York Times*, 13 January 1944, 16. On July 4, 1998, Stravinsky's arrangement was broadcast over radio WNYC-FM. "Radio Highlights," *New York Times*, 4 July 1998, B15.

942. It was popular singer Kate Smith (1907–1986) who first introduced Irving Berlin's "God Bless America" on an Armistice Day broadcast, November 11, 1938. The song was an immediate hit. She also sang it at the opening day ceremonies of the New York World's Fair on May 5, 1940. Berlin had composed the song in 1918 "as a finale to the successful comedy *Yip, Yip Yaphank*," but it was never used. *New York Times*, 5 May and 11 July 1940, 46 and 21, respectively. Opal Craven, soprano, with the Continentals Quartet and an orchestra directed by Leo Kempin, sang the song on a 1939 Fourth of July broadcast over radio station WEAF in New York. "Microphone Presents," *New York Times*, 2 July 1939, X8.

943. A brochure released by Radio Branch, Bureau of Public Relations, War Department, and reprinted in "Music in the National Effort," *Music Educators Journal* 28/4 (February 1942): 25–28, 31.

944. Listed in Linda Whitesitt, *The Life and Music of George Antheil, 1950–1959* (Ann Arbor, MI: UMI Research Press, 1981), item 176.

945. Lincoln Portrait is "a 13-minute work for speaker and full orchestra, divided roughly into three sections." It was believed at first the performance was "a flop" because there was no applause from the audience but it was quickly realized that was because the audience was deeply moved. The concert was repeated in Washington on July 15.

946. *Carnival of Venice: Fantasia Brillante* (NY: C. Fischer, 1928) by Del Staigers.

947. *Americans We: March* (Cincinnati, OH: Fillmore Bros. Co., 1929) by Henry Fillmore.

948. Based on the hymn tune "St. Anne" by William Croft (1678–1727).

949. Based on a poem by John Latouche. In 1940, the work was cited as the "most performed work in concert repertoires of this season." The song was first introduced under the title "Ballad for Uncle Sam" in the Broadway production of *Sing for Your Supper*, but went mostly unnoticed. Paul Robeson, vocalist, revived the song under its new title for a radio program. A newspaper noted "it has become almost an unofficial national anthem and a best seller." "Song Is Ended but Sales Linger On," *Washington Post*, 14 July 1940, A4. For the Fourth of July production, Charles Dana Beaschler, director of music at the New York Avenue Presbyterian Church, conducted, and Fague Springman, of Lorton, Virginia, who had sung with the Westminster Choir and had several radio engagements, was soloist. For a photograph and information about Springman, see *Washington Post*, 19 June 1939, 5.

950. The Ross Sisters were among a number of headliners in the 1944 MGM movie *Broadway Rhythm* (songs by Johnny Mercer and Harold Arlen).

951. Brooks was a popular radio singer during the 1940s. On July 4, 1942, she broadcast sang over WMAL in Washington, D.C. In February 1948 she hosted a new program titled *Hospitality House* over CBS. *Washington Post*, 4 July 1942, 24, and 1 February 1948, L4.

952. A Washingtonian and former FBI clerk whose singing talents led him to New York appearances. Nelson B. Bell, "Capital Adds Two More to Its Footlight Galaxy," *Washington Post*, 23 June 1946, S6.

953. Lucy Monroe was referred to in 1941 as the "Star-Spangled Soprano," and who "more often than any other living person" sang the national anthem. For a photograph of Monroe, see "Soprano to Sing for Service Men," *Washington Post*, 20 June 1941, 19.

954. Antheil's symphony was composed in 1942 and was also broadcast on the Fourth in 1946 in Zurich over a radio program by the German conductor Hermann Scherchen.

955. A popular singer in revues and other stage productions at Loew's Capitol Theater in Washington.

956. Music composed in 1940 by Al Jacobs with lyrics by Don Raye.

957. During the rehearsal, Mitchell stood too close to a Howitzer cannon that was being fired and he wound up with black soot on his face.

958. Kaufman was conductor of the Capitol Theatre Orchestra.

959. Stage name for Fague Springman, a talented singer who appeared on a radio show titled *The Telephone Hour*, and who had a Carnegie Hall debut in April 1949. Sonia Stein, "Springman Wants to 'Show' Horace," *Washington Post*, 15 May 1949, L1.

960. *Faith of Our Fathers*, by Paul Green, was billed as a new show consisting of "Star-Spangled pageantry," with an orchestra, chorus and cast of 150 that was concurrently playing at the Carter Barron Amphitheatre in Washington, D.C.

961. Gibson was ill on July 4 and was replaced with the Eva Jessye Choir. *Chicago Daily Tribune*, 4 July 1951, B2.

962. Jimmy Dean was a frequent performer at Glen Echo's Spanish Ballroom. His road to stardom was begun in the Washington area and notably at this park. He was also a "star of the Connie B. Gay 'Town and Country Time' on local radio station WARL and television station WMAL" and "one of the most popular bands in the Washington area" (Paul Herron, "On the Town," *Washington Post*, 27 April 1955, 54).

963. *Ballad for Americans* was sung at the Republican National Convention at Philadelphia in 1940 to the sound of "cheers" by the delegates. "Sidelights of the Week," *New York Times*, 30 June 1940, 54.

964. *New England Triptych: 3 Pieces for Orchestra after William Billings* (1956).

965. See program notes on the recording released by New World Records 80567 (2003).

966. For information on this composer, see James Thomas Madeja, "The Life and Work of Herbert L. Clarke (1867–1945)" (Ed.D. dissertation, University of Illinois at Urbana-Champaign, 1988).

967. The Centurymen "is comprised of 100 men, two from each state in the union, flown to Washington, D.C. expressly to appear on this Honor America Day program."

968. *Magyar Dallamok: Fantasie Brillante for Cornet Solo*.

969. Willie Nelson gained a reputation, in part, as "country music renegade" for featuring non-mainstream country music artists at these annual Independence Day events, most of which were held in Texas, drawing thousands of music lovers. Some of the other Fourth of July picnics included those in Gonzales (1976), Dallas (1978), Austin (1981, 1984, 2000), East Rutherford, New Jersey (1983), Luckenbach (1995, 1998–99), Spicewood (2003), Fort Worth (2004), George, Washington (2007), (Houston (2008). For more information on Willie Nelson and the Fourth, see Heintze, *The Fourth of July Encyclopedia*, 203, and Joe Nick Patoski, *Willie Nelson: An Epic Life* (New York: Little, Brown, 2008).

970. Geoffrey Davies was ringing master at The Church of the Advent for this 1974 event. The church's eight bells were rung "in full circle changes" by eight persons, each individual responsible for one bell. Radio contact between Davies and the orchestra assured that the bells would be "cued in with the score." The success of that first concert "led to the restoration of the Advent bells in 1976 by the Whitechapel Bell Foundry of London, who had originally installed them in 1900." Arthur Fiedler "wrote a note of thanks on a concert program that hangs in the Advent ringing room to this day." Geoffrey Davies to James Heintze, e-mail, 12–13 October 2008.

971. "Boston's 4th of July," a 25th anniversary book (Boston: Boston 4 Celebrations, 1998), 14–18, courtesy of Pam Picard,

producer, Boston 4 Celebrations; Carey Goldberg, "A Revolution in Fourth of July Concerts Also Started in Boston," *New York Times*, 4 July 1998, A7.

972. *Comprehensive Calendar of Bicentennial Events* (Washington, D.C.: American Revolution Bicentennial Administration, 1975).

973. The series was published under the general title "Selective List of American Music for the Bicentennial Celebration" with designations for choral, band, orchestra, opera and piano works respectively, in *Music Educators Journal* 61/8 (April 1975):54–61; 61/9 (May 1975): 48–52; 62/2 (October 1975): 66–72; 62/6 (February 1976): 55–63; 62/8 (April 1976): 87–89, 98–101, 103–04.

974. Ibid., 62/4 (December 1975): 64–71.

975. Fred Ferretti, "Ethnic Diversity Adds Spice to the Holiday," *New York Times*, 5 July 1976, 1, 22.

976. The story is part of a triology with this segment focusing on Valley Forge in 1778. The musical had only a small run of performances. For a review, see Don Shirley, "And Now on to 1778," *Washington Post*, 13 July 1976, B9.

977. Johnny Cash died in 2003. His recording of "American V: A Hundred Highways" was released posthumously on July 4, 2006, and includes "the last song Cash ever wrote." "Johnny Cash's 'American V: A Hundred Highways' to Be Released on the Fourth of July," *Business Wire*, 1 May 2006.

978. Known as "The Musical Ambassadors of the Army," the band was formed in March 1946 and has appeared in all fifty states and over thirty countries. The four performing groups of the band are Concert Band, Soldiers' Chorus, Jazz Ambassadors, and Volunteers. The band is based at Fort George G. Meade in Maryland. *The United States Army Field Band* website, http://www.army.mil/FIELDBAND/. For additional information on this band, see Josh Mitchell, "Army's Musical Ambassadors," *Baltimore Sun*, 4 July 2008, B1, B4.

979. For the story behind the composing of this work of which the last page of the manuscript is dated "July 3, 1889" and which resides in the Library of Congress, see Paul Hume, "Library Given Manuscript," *Washington Post*, 28 May 1953, 1.

980. Dyers, "A History of the United States Navy Band, Washington, D.C. (1918–1988)," 429.

981. Heintze, *The Fourth of July Encyclopedia*, 191.

982. Modern edition in Dudley Buck, "Selected Organ Works," in *Recent Researches in American Music*, 63. Ed. N. Lee Orr (Middleton, WI: A–R Editions, 2008): 95–106.

983. Full title: "Composed in honor of George Washington's 250th birthday." Published Silver Spring, MD: Mediterranean, 1982.

984. "Dedicated to the City of Boston."

985. Phil McCombs and Richard Harrington, "Watt Sets Off Uproar With Music Ban," Washington Post, 7 April 1983, A1. For a descriptive narrative of all Beach Boys Fourth of July performances, see Heintze, *Fourth of July Encyclopedia*, 32–33.

986. Michael Kernan, "Bandstand of History," *Washington Post*, 4 July 1984, C7.

987. Information on this composition and performances is in Thomas H. Hill, *The City of Fairfax Band, the First 25 Years: Fact and Opinion* (Fairfax, VA: City of Fairfax Band Association, 2001). For information on this 70-member band and its conductor Thomas H. Hill, see Barbara H. Blechman, "Fairfax Band's Reputation Grows," *Washington Post*, 20 June 1985, VAA1.

988. From *American Ballads: Setting of Familiar Tunes*, for orchestra which was commissioned by the Queens Symphony Orchestra for the Bicentennial.

989. Composed by a former chief arranger for the Marine Band, the piece was "written for and premiered at the inaugural ceremony for President Richard Nixon, January 20, 1973." Thanks to MGySgt Michael Ressler, for this information.

990. Published, New York: Jonico Music & Casa David, 1985.

991. Premiered on June 4, 1986, by the Boston Pops, and commissioned by the Statue of Liberty-Ellis Island Foundation, Inc. A CD recording titled "Liberty for All" is available by the U.S. Coast Guard Band.

992. Dyers, 372.

993. "Composed for the Special Olympics in celebration of the 1987 International Summer Games."

994. Both works "Written for the 500th anniversary of the 1492 discovery voyages."

995. "MTNA Recognizes Commissioned Composers through the Years," *American Music Teacher* 51/1 (August-September 2001): 38–55.

996. Reestablished as the Hollywood Bowl Orchestra in 1991, it was originally founded in 1945 as the Hollywood Bowl Symphony Orchestra under its director Leopold Stokowski.

997. As the band began playing, "President Clinton makes a surprise appearance and shakes the lawn guests' hands."

998. "Dixieland Band is cut off as President Clinton steps up to the balcony microphone to address the crowd. After a short speech, he turns to greet the band and then exits while greeting the saxophone section." The Dixieland Band resumes playing.

999. "Fireworks on the Mall began during the piccolo chorus."

1000. "Perfect Harmony: Philharmonic Conductor Harold Weller Enthusiastic about Holiday Concert," *Las Vegas Sun*, 3 July 2001.

1001. Ray Privett, "Independence: An Intercultural Experience in North America," *The Drama Review* 44/2 (2000): 101–06.

1002. *Einzug der Gladiatoren (Entrance of the Gladiators)* by Julius Fucik, and known also under the title *Thunder and Blazes*. The work was published in 1903.

1003. "Commissioned by the Richmond Concert Band in celebration of their 25th anniversary" in 1996.

1004. Accompanied by "cannon-fire by the 2nd Battalion, 111th Field Artillery, U.S. Army National Guard" and live bells performed on the carillon by Lawrence Robinson in the World War I memorial adjacent to the amphitheater in Byrd Park.

1005. http://www.continentalharmony.com. For an article on Continental Harmony and a list of premieres in 2000–2001, see Patricia A. Shifferd, "Continental Harmony: A Community-Based Celebration of the American Millennial Year," in James R. Heintze and Michael Saffle, *Reflections on American Music: The Twentieth Century and the New Millennium* (Hillsdale, NY: Pendragon Press, 2000), 328–50.

1006. Shifferd, "Continental Harmony," 346.

1007. Shifferd, "Continental Harmony," 346.

1008. President and First Lady Clinton spoke to the guests following this piece.

1009. For a recording by the U.S. Coast Guard Band available for listening online, see "Media" on *The United States Coast Guard Band* website.

1010. Compact disc: *I Am St. Joseph* (Los Angeles: Din Music, 2001).

1011. Dan Willging, "Concerts: Willie Nelson's Fourth of July Picnic," *Dirty Linen* 90 (October-November 2000): 30.

1012. As reported in Heintze, *The Fourth of July Encyclopedia*, 228–29.

1013. Concert reported to me by Jeffrey Stockham, cornet player and bandleader, Excelsior Cornet Band, February 8, 2008. The Morgan-Manning House is the home of the Western Monroe Historical Society.

1014. "Commissioned by the Richmond Concert Band in celebration of Mark W. Poland's Silver Jubilee in 2003."

1015. "The eight-minute instrumental narrative is one of three commissioned works written to celebrate the Los Angeles Centennial and the only one to tell the city's history."

1016. The Philly Pops has provided Fourth of July concerts to Philadelphia audiences since 1981.

1017. For additional information on James Heintze and the Fourth of July, see Marc Fisher, "The History and Hazards of the Fourth," *Washington Post*, 4 July 2004, C1, C8; Nafeesa Syeed, "All Things Fourth," *Frederick News-Post*, 4 July 2008, A2 and printed also under these titles: "A Historian in Love with All Things Fourth," *Baltimore Sun*, 4 July 2008, 8B, "Independent Studies," *Philadelphia Inquirer*, 4 July 2008, A6, and "Meet Mr. Fourth of July," *Houston Chronicle*, 4 July 2008.

Bibliography

Adams, John Quincy. *Diary of John Quincy Adams.* 2 vols. Ed. Robert J. Taylor, et al. Cambridge, MA: Belknap, 1981.

_____. *Memoirs of John Quincy Adams.* 12 vols. Philadelphia: J.B. Lippincott, 1874–77; reprint, N.Y.: Books for Libraries, 1969.

All American Patriotic Songbook. 2nd edition. U.S.A.: Creative Concepts, 1996.

The American Musical Directory 1861. New York: T. Hutchinson, 1861; reprint, New York: Da Capo, 1980.

American National Biography. Ed. John A. Garraty and Mark C. Carnes. 24 vols. New York: Oxford University Press, 1999.

American Patriotic Songs: Yankee Doodle to The Conquered Banner with Emphasis on The Star-Spangled Banner. An Exhibition Held at The Lily Library, Indiana University, Bloomington, July-September 1968. Foreword by David A. Randall.

Anderson, Gillian B. *Freedom's Voice in Poetry and Song.* Wilmington, DE: Scholarly Resources, 1977.

Anderson, Simon V. "American Music during the War for Independence, 1775–1783." Ph.D. dissertation, University of Michigan, 1965.

Appelbaum, Diana Karter. *The Glorious Fourth: An American Holiday, an American History.* New York: Facts On File, 1989.

Bakkegard, B.M. "Music in Arizona before 1912." *Journal of Research in Music Education* 8/2 (Autumn 1960): 67–74.

Bentley, William. *The Diary of William Bentley ...* 4 vols. Salem, MA: Essex Institute, 1905–14; reprint 1962.

Bierley, Paul Edmund. *The Incredible Band of John Philip Sousa.* Urbana: University of Illinois Press, 2006.

_____. *The Works of John Philip Sousa.* Columbus, OH: Integrity, 1984.

Billings, William. *Complete Works of William Billings.* Hans Nathan, ed. 4 vols. New Haven, CT: American Musicological Society, 1977–90.

Bindas, Kenneth J. *All of This Music Belongs to the Nation: The WPA's Federal Music Project and American Society.* Knoxville: University of Tennessee Press, 1995.

Board of Music Trade of the United States of America. *Complete Catalogue of Sheet Music and Musical Works, 1870.* New Intro. Dena J. Epstein. New York: Da Capo, 1973.

Bomberger, E. Douglas. "*A Tidal Wave of Encouragement*": American Composers' Concerts in the Gilded Age. Westport, CT: Praeger, 2002.

Bowie, Gordon W. "R.B. Hall and the Community Bands of Maine." Ph.D. dissertation, University of Maine, 1993.

Branham, Robert James. "'Of Thee I Sing': Contesting America." *American Quarterly* 48/4 (1996): 623–52.

Britton, Allen P., and Irving Lowens. *American Sacred Music Imprints, 1698–1810: A Bibliography.* Worcester, MA: American Antiquarian Society, 1990.

Bryant, Carolyn. *And the Band Played On, 1776–1976.* Washington, D.C.: Smithsonian Institution, 1975.

Burg, David F. *Chicago's White City of 1893.* Lexington: University Press of Kentucky 1976.

Burkholder, J. Peter. "The Organist in Ives." *Journal of the American Musicological Society* 55/2 (Summer 2002): 255–310.

Calkin, Homer L. "Music during the Centennial of American Independence." *Pennsylvania Magazine of History and Biography* 100/3 (July 1976): 374.

Camus, Raoul F. *Military Music of the American Revolution.* Chapel Hill: University of North Carolina Press, 1976.

Cannino, Vincent A. "Celebrating the Fourth in Salem." M.A. thesis, University of North Carolina at Greensboro, 1998.

Carpenter, Kenneth William. "A History of the United States Marine Band." Ph.D. dissertation, University of Iowa, 1970.

Cipolla, Frank J. "Patrick S. Gilmore: The Boston Years." *American Music* 6/3 (Autumn 1988): 281–92.

Clark, J. Bunker. *The Dawning of American Keyboard Music.* Westport, CT: Greenwood, 1988.

Clifton, Arthur. *Complete Piano Music.* Ed. Nathan Buckner. 4 vols. Philadelphia: Kallisti, 1997.

Coad, Oral Sumner, and Edwin Mims, Jr. *The American Stage*. New Haven, CT: Yale University Press, 1929.

Comprehensive Calendar of Bicentennial Events. Washington, D.C.: American Revolution Bicentennial Administration, 1975.

Coombs, Karen Mueller. *Woody Guthrie: America's Folksinger*. Minneapolis, MN: Carolrhoda, 2002.

The Core Repertory of Early American Psalmody. Ed. Richard Crawford. Madison, WI: A–R Editions, 1984.

Crawford, Richard. *America's Musical Life*. New York: W.W. Norton, 2001.

Crew, Danny O. *Presidential Sheet Music: An Illustrated Catalogue of Published Music Associated with the American Presidency and Those Who Sought the Office*. Jefferson, NC: McFarland, 2001.

Crossett, David Allen. "One-Night Stand: A History of Live and Recorded Entertainments in Warren, Pennsylvania, from 1795 to the Present." Ph.D. dissertation, New York University, 1983.

Culbertson, Evelyn Davis. "Arthur Farwell's Early Efforts on Behalf of American Music, 1889–1921." *American Music* 5/2 (Summer 1987): 156–75.

Currier, Thomas Franklin. *A Bibliography of Oliver Wendell Holmes*. New York: Russell & Russell, 1971.

Cuthbert, John A. "Rayner Taylor and Anglo-American Musical Life." Ph.D. dissertation, West Virginia University, 1980.

Davenport, Linda. *Divine Song on the Northeast Frontier: Maine's Sacred Tunebooks, 1800–1830*. Lanham, MD: Scarecrow, 1996.

Demkee, Ronald. "Upbeat: America's Oldest Civilian Concert Band Marks 175th Anniversary." *International Musician* 101/1 (January 2003): 21.

Dolbee, Cora. "The Fourth of July in Early Kansas 1854–1857." *Kansas Historical Quarterly* 10/1 (February 1941): 34–78.

DuPree, Mary. "Early Bands in an Idaho Railroad Town: Pocatello, 1887–1930," in *Vistas of American Music: Essays and Compositions in Honor of William K. Kearns*, ed. Susan L. Porter and John Graziano. Warren, MI: Harmonie Park, 1999.

Dyers, Jimmie Wayne. "A History of the United States Navy Band, Washington, D.C. (1918–1988)." Ed.D. dissertation, University of Houston, 1988.

Eaklor, Vicki L. *American Antislavery Songs: A Collection and Analysis*. New York: Greenwood, 1988.

Eliason, Robert E. "Bugles Beyond Compare: The Presentation E-flat Keyed Bugle in Mid-Nineteenth-Century America." *Journal of the American Musical Instrument Society* 31 (2005): 67–132.

_____. "Rhodolph Hall: Nineteenth-Century Keyed Bugle, Cornet, and Clarinet Soloist." *Journal of the American Musical Instrument Society* 29 (2003): 5–71.

Elliker, Calvin. "Early Imprints in the Thomas A. Edison Collection of American Sheet Music: Addenda to Sonneck-Upton and to Wolfe." *Notes* 57/3 (March 2001): 555–73.

Ellsworth, Jane E. "The Clarinet in Early America, 1758–1820." D.M.A. dissertation, Ohio State University, 2004.

Feldman, Anne E. "Being Heard: Women Composers and Patrons at the 1893 World's Columbian Exposition." *Notes*, Second Series, 47/1 (September 1990): 7–20.

Fuld, James J., and Mary Wallace Davidson. *18th-Century American Secular Music Manuscripts: An Inventory*. Philadelphia: Music Library Association, 1980.

Gerson, Robert A. *Music in Philadelphia*. Westport, CT: Greenwood, 1940.

Gombosi, Marilyn. *A Day of Solemn Thanksgiving: Moravian Music for the Fourth of July, 1783, in Salem, North Carolina*. Chapel Hill: University of North Carolina Press, 1977.

A Guide to the Music of Arthur Farwell and to the Microfilm Collection of His Work. New York: published by his children, 1972.

Hamm. Charles. *Yesterdays: Popular Song in America*. New York: W.W. Norton, 1979.

Hash, Phillip M. "Development of School Bands in Illinois: 1863–1930." Ed.D. dissertation, University of Illinois at Urbana-Champaign, 2006.

Hay, Robert Pettus. "Freedom's Jubilee: One Hundred Years of the Fourth of July, 1776–1876." Ph.D. dissertation, University of Kentucky, 1967.

Hazen, Margaret Hindle, and Robert M. Hazen. *The Music Men: An Illustrated History of Brass Bands in America, 1800–1920*. Washington, D.C.: Smithsonian Institution, 1987.

Heard, Priscilla S. *American Music 1698–1800: An Annotated Bibliography*. Waco, TX: Markham Press Fund, 1975.

Heintze, James R., ed. *American Musical Life in Context and Practice to 1865*. New York: Garland, 1994.

_____. *The Fourth of July Encyclopedia*. Jefferson, NC: McFarland, 2007.

_____. "'Tyranny and Despotic Violence': An Incident Aboard the U.S.S. *Washington*." *Maryland Historical Magazine* 94/1 (Spring 1999): 37–38.

_____ and Michael Saffle, eds. *Reflections on American Music: The Twentieth Century and the New Millennium*. Hillsdale, NY: Pendragon, 2000.

Hickey, Anne Marie. "The Celebration of the Fourth of July in Westfield, 1826–1853." *Historical Journal of Massachusetts* 9/2 (1981): 41–46.

Hill, Thomas H. *The City of Fairfax Band, the First 25 Years: Fact and Opinion*. Fairfax, VA: City of Fairfax Band Association, 2001.

Howe, Warren P. "Early American Military Music." *American Music* 17/1 (Spring 1999): 87–116.

Huxford, John C. "John Knowles Paine: His Life and Works." Ph.D. dissertation, Florida State University, 1968.

Jackson, George Stuyvesant. *Early Songs of Uncle Sam*.

Intro. Kenneth B. Murdock. Boston: Bruce Humphries, 1933.

Jackson, Richard. *U.S. Bicentennial Music I*. Brooklyn, NY: Institute for Studies in American Music, Brooklyn College, CUNY, 1977.

Johnson, H. Earle. *First Performances in America to 1900: Works with Orchestra*. Detroit, MI: Information Coordinators, 1979.

_____. "George K. Jackson, Doctor of Music (1745–1825)." *Musical Quarterly* 29/1 (January 1943): 113–21.

Kaufman, Charles H. "Music in New Jersey, 1655–1860: A Study of Musical Activity and Musicians in New Jersey from Its First Settlement to the Civil War." Ph.D. dissertation, New York University, 1974.

Kegerreis, Richard I. "The Handel Society of Dartmouth." *American Music* 4/2 (Summer 1986): 177–93.

Keller, Kate Van Winkle. *Dance and Its Music in America, 1528–1789*. Hillsdale, NY: Pendragon, 2007.

Kirk, Elise K. *Music at the White House: A History of the American Spirit*. Urbana: University of Illinois Press, 1986.

_____. *Musical Highlights from the White House*. Malabar, FL: Krieger, 1992.

Knight, Ellen. "Music in Winchester, Massachusetts: A Community Portrait, 1830–1925." *American Music* 11/3 (Autumn 1993): 263–82.

Kreitner, Kenneth. *Discoursing Sweet Music: Town Bands and Community Life in Turn-of-the-Century Pennsylvania*. Urbana: University of Illinois Press, 1990.

Krohn, Ernst C. *Missouri Music*. New York: Da Capo, 1971.

Ladd, Maureen J. "The Feminine Perspective: Six Early American Women Writers." Ph.D. dissertation, University of Delaware, 1982.

Laneer, Larry. "Marshall's Band of Topeka: A Study of the Golden Age of Bands in Kansas." M.A. thesis, University of Kansas, 1978.

Langdon, William Chauncy. *The Celebration of the Fourth of July by Means of Pageantry*. With an article and notes on the music by Arthur Farwell. New York: Russell Sage Foundation, 1912.

Lawrence, Vera Brodsky. *Music for Patriots, Politicians, and Presidents*. New York: Macmillan, 1975.

Lichtenwanger, William. "The Music of 'the Star-Spangled Banner': From Ludgate Hill to Capitol Hill." *Quarterly Journal of the Library of Congress* 34 (1979):136–70.

_____. "Richard S. Hill and the Unsettle Text of the Star Spangled Banner." *Richard S. Hill: Tributes from Friends*. Detroit, 1987, 71–184.

"Louis Moreau Gottschalk's Visit to Vermont in 1862." *Vermont History* 39/2 (1971): 125–27.

Lowens, Irving. *A Bibliography of Songsters Printed in America before 1821*. Worcester, MA: American Antiquarian Society, 1976.

Madeja, James Thomas. "The Life and Work of Herbert L. Clarke (1867–1945)." Ed.D. dissertation, University of Illinois at Urbana-Champaign, 1988.

Markham, Edith L. "Poetry Written for the Opening Exercises and the Fourth of July Celebration at the 1876 Centennial Exhibition in Philadelphia." M.A. thesis, University of North Carolina, 1950.

Martin, Howard Hastings. "Orations on the Anniversary of American Independence, 1777–1876." Ph.D. dissertation, Northwestern University, 1955.

Martin, Scott C. *Killing Time: Leisure and Culture in Southwestern Pennsylvania, 1800–1850*. Pittsburgh: University of Pittsburgh Press, 1995.

McKay, David. "William Selby, Musical Émigré in Colonial Boston." *Musical Quarterly* 57/4 (October 1971): 609–27.

Meyer, Donald C. "Toscanini and the Good Neighbor Policy: The NBC Symphony Orchestra's 1940 South American Tour." *American Music* 18/3 (Autumn 2000): 233–56.

Miles, Henry. *Orpheus in the Wilderness: A History of Music in Denver, 1860–1925*. Denver: Colorado Historical Society, 2006.

"MTNA Recognizes Commissioned Composers through the Years." *American Music Teacher* 51/1 (August-September 2001): 38–55.

Murray, Donald M. "Dr. Peter Bryant: Preceptor in Poetry to William Cullen Bryant." *New England Quarterly* 33/4 (December 1960): 513–22.

Murray, Sterling E. "A Checklist of Funeral Dirges in Honor of General Washington." *Notes* 36/2 (December 1979): 326–44.

_____. "Weeping and Mourning: Funeral Dirges in Honor of General Washington." *Journal of the American Musicological Society* 31/2 (Summer 1978): 282–308.

Music in America: An Anthology from the Landing of the Pilgrims to the Close of the Civil War, 1620–1865. Ed. Thomas Marrocco and Harold Gleason. New York: W. W. Norton, 1964.

"Music in the National Effort." *Music Educators Journal* 28/4 (February 1942): 25–28, 31.

"My Country, 'Tis of Thee." *Zion's Herald*, 23 June 1909.

Osterhout, Paul R. "Andrew Wright: Northampton Music Printer." *American Music* 1/4 (Winter 1983): 5–26.

Patoski, Joe Nick. *Willie Nelson: An Epic Life*. New York: Little, Brown, 2008.

Pemberton, Carol A. *Lowell Mason: A Bio-Bibliography*. Westport, CT: Greenwood, 1988.

Perry, Dorothy D. "Fourth of July in Ely, 1891," *Minnesota History* 40/2 (Summer 1966): 60–61.

Peter, Johann Friedrich. *Psalm of Joy of the Congregation in Salem for the Peace Celebration July 4, 1783*. New York: Boosey & Hawkes, 1975.

Pichierri, Louis. *Music in New Hampshire 1623–1899*. New York: Columbia University Press, 1960.

Privett, Ray. "Independence: An Intercultural Experience in North America." *The Drama Review* 44/2 (2000): 101–06.

Reedy, R. Ronald. *Celebration in Lititz, Pennsylvania: The 175th Anniversary History of Independence Day Observances with a Narrative of the Lititz Springs Park, 1818–1992.* Lititz, PA: Anniversary Celebration General Committee, 1992.

Reid, Harold and Don Reid. *The Statler Brothers: Random Memories.* Nashville, TN: Yell, 2007.

Sanders, Paul. *Lyrics and Borrowed Tunes of the American Temperance Movement.* Columbia: University of Missouri Press, 2006.

Saylor, Nicole. "Patriotic Measures: Today Was Made for Music, from the Traditional 'God Bless America' to Modern 'Fight the Power.'" *Wisconsin State Journal,* 4 July 2001, A1.

Sherr, Lynn. *America the Beautiful: The Stirring True Story Behind Our Nation's Favorite Song.* New York: BBS Public Affairs, 2001.

Shive, Clyde S. "*National Martial Music and Songs,* a Musical First." *American Music* 9/1 (Spring 1991): 92–101.

Smith, Margaret Bayard. *The First Forty Years of Washington Society in the Family Letters of Margaret Bayard Smith.* Ed. Gaillard Hunt. New York: Frederick Ungar, 1965.

Sonneck, Oscar. *A Bibliography of Early Secular American Music, 18th Century.* New York: Da Capo, 1964.

_____. *Early Concert-Life in America, 1731–1800.* Wiesbaden: M. Sändig, 1969.

_____. *Early Opera in America.* New York: B. Blom, 1963.

_____. *Report on The Star-Spangled Banner, Hail Columbia, America, Yankee Doodle.* Washington, D.C.: Library of Congress, 1909; reprint, New York: Dover, 1972.

Spicer, Richard C. "Popular Song for Public Celebration in Federal Portsmouth, New Hampshire." *Popular Music and Society* 25/1-2 (Spring-Summer 2001): 1–99.

The Stoughton Musical Society's Centennial Collection of Sacred Music Consisting of Selections from the Earliest American Authors, as Originally Written, Together with a Few Selections from European and Modern Composers. Boston: Oliver Ditson, 1878; reprint, with a new introduction by Roger L. Hall, New York: DaCapo, 1980.

Taylor, Lonn, Kathleen M. Kendrick and Jeffrey L. Brodie. *The Star-Spangled Banner: The Making of an American Icon.* Washington, D.C.: Smithsonian Institution, 2008.

Travers, Len. *Celebrating the Fourth: Independence Day and the Rites of Nationalism in the Early Republic.* Amherst: University of Massachusetts Press, 1997.

"What was Hamilton's 'Favorite Song.'" *William and Mary Quarterly,* 3rd ser 12/2 (April 1955): 298–307.

Whitesitt, Linda. *The Life and Music of George Antheil, 1950–1959.* Ann Arbor, MI: UMI Research Press, 1981.

Willging, Dan. "Concerts: Willie Nelson's Fourth of July Picnic." *Dirty Linen* 90 (October-November 2000): 30.

Williams, George W. "Jacob Eckhard and His Choirmaster's Book." *Journal of the American Musicological Society* 7/1 (Spring 1954): 41–47.

Wolf, Edwin. *American Song Sheets.* Philadelphia: Library Company of Philadelphia, 1963.

Wolfe, Richard J. *The Role of the Mann Family of Dedham, Massachusetts, in the Marbling of Paper in Nineteenth-Century America and in the Printing of Music, the Making of Cards and Other Booktrade Activities.* Chestnut Hill, MA: Perspectives on Printing and Publishing, 1980.

_____. *Secular Music in America 1801–1825: A Bibliography.* 3 vols. New York: New York Public Library, 1964.

First Line Index

General Index